EQ

EQ

Encyclopaedia of the Qurʾān

INDEX VOLUME

Jane Dammen McAuliffe, *General Editor*

Brill, Leiden–Boston

2006

Koninklijke Brill NV incorporates the imprints Brill,
Hotei Publishing, IDC Publishers, Martinus Nijhoff Publishers and VSP.

ISBN 90 04 14764 0 ISBN 978 90 04 14764 5

Printed in The Netherlands on acid-free paper.

CONTENTS

Preface vii

Author List 1

Article List 16

Index of Proper Names 36

Index of Arabic Words and Phrases 229

Index of Qurʾān Citations 417

PREFACE

In my Preface to the first volume of the *Encyclopaedia of the Qurʾān*, I promised that the final volume would include "a very thorough indexing of both English words and transliterated Arabic terminology." With the publication of this volume, I am pleased to deliver on that promise. As initially conceived, I expected this index to form part of the fifth volume of the *EQ*. When the effort of indexing got underway in earnest, however, two recognitions quickly asserted themselves: (1) to serve readers well, the *EQ* would require multiple indices and (2) the size and scope of these combined indices would demand an additional volume. So it was decided to add a sixth volume to the *EQ* and to complete the print publication of this reference work with a tool that could significantly enhance its utility, particularly for scholars.

This concluding volume of the *EQ* offers five separate indices: (1) a roster of contributing scholars and their academic affiliations, (2) a comprehensive list of all articles, (3) a registry of the proper names of people, places, religious and social groupings, etc., (4) a lexicon of transliterated Arabic words and phrases, and (5) an inventory of the qurʾānic verses and sūras that are cited in the five volumes of the *EQ*.

The first three of these indices require little additional explanation. The *Author List* furnishes an alphabetically ordered record of all those scholars who have contributed to the *EQ*. It also notes the article (or articles) that each author has written as well as his or her institutional affiliation. The *Article List*, which is divided by volume, provides both the name of the author and the inclusive pagination of each article. Blind entries have not been included in this list.

The *Index of Proper Names* gathers the references to persons, places, languages, clans, tribes, religions, rulers and dynasties as these are found in the *EQ*. Ordinarily, this index captures terms that were consistently capitalized in the *EQ*. The death dates of individuals, frequently in both *hijrī* and *mīlādī* forms, have been supplied when these could be drawn from *EQ* articles or from commonly available reference sources. In some cases, information that amplifies what is found in the *EQ* has been added where this could be helpful to the researcher. Recognizing the name variation that occurs in both primary and secondary sources, an effort has been made to direct readers to the version of a name that most regularly identifies a noted figure from the formative or classical period of Islam. Honorifics, such as Imām, Shaykh,

Saint, King, have been placed before the individual's name but do not affect the alphabetization of the name itself. Occasionally, Arabic transliteration for technical terms has been provided and placed in square brackets after the term. In those instances where a proper name designates an *EQ* entry, the page and column number are given in bold. Finally, nominal and adjectival forms have frequently been consolidated. For instance, the listing "Ṣūfī(s)" will include volume, page and column indicators that refer to the ascetical-mystical trend in Islam, as well as to individuals associated with that trend.

The fourth of these indices, the *Index of Arabic Words and Phrases*, may require a bit more explanation. In the Preface to the first volume of the *EQ* I described the critical decision that the associate editors and I took during our first editorial meeting as we gathered to discuss the development of the *EQ*. In order to make this reference work useful to scholars beyond the fields of Islamic and qurʾānic studies, to assure its accessibility to readers who have no background in Arabic, we decided to organize the *EQ* under English-language lemmata and to supply the translation of key qurʾānic words and phrases wherever possible. While a few exceptions were permitted to this policy, it provided the primary guidance for authors as they drafted their articles. We felt, moreover, that this decision need not compromise the scholarly integrity of the *EQ*. Since the authors who contributed to these five volumes are among the finest international scholars of the Qurʾān, their entries draw upon the depth of their research concentrations and the range of their many publications, making frequent use of Arabic terms and phrases, as well as occasional reference to the vocabulary of other languages. Work in the field of qurʾānic studies normally proceeds on the basis of Arabic sources and of secondary literature that is keyed to those sources. Consequently, the associate editors and I felt that it would be important, especially for our scholarly colleagues, to produce an index for the *EQ* that collected all its important Arabic words and phrases in their transliterated forms.

In this *Index of Arabic Words and Phrases*, the individual listings are alphabetized as in a modern Arabic-English dictionary, i.e. by the Arabic triliteral root. Doubled root letters also follow this alphabetical order so, for example, *ḥ-q-q* appears after *ḥ-q-b* rather than at the beginning of *ḥ-q-*.... Within each triliteral listing, verbal forms, in their usual dictionary order, precede nominal ones. Verbs are catalogued in the third, masculine singular *māḍī* while nominal forms are represented as found in the *EQ*. Thus plural, collective and feminine forms sometimes follow the masculine singular or are sometimes listed separately, depending on their *EQ* occurrences. The purpose of this index, as exemplified in the choices that guided its production, was not the creation of a comprehensive qurʾānic dictionary but of a focused research tool that would offer scholars access to the Arabic vocabulary found in *EQ* articles.

Phrases have been included selectively but have not been extensively cross listed. Deciding the entry under which to place a phrase is necessarily a subjective judgment so users are urged to look for phrases under more than one of their constituent elements. As is the case with the listing of single words, in the alphabetization of phrases, the singular form of the term under which the phrase is listed precedes its plural forms. Within each of these groupings, phrases in which the entry term is the first word are listed before those in which it is a subsequent term. Multiple phrases appear in *English* alphabetical order as based on the first letter of the first word that is not the entry word. The definite article and parenthetical terms are ignored in this ordering. Again with this index, page and column numbers are given in bold in the few instances where an Arabic term (e.g. ḥadīth, sūra) is the title of an entry.

The *Index of Qurʾān Citations*, the last of these five indices, attempts to collect all significant *EQ* references to the qurʾānic text whether these are given by sūra name or by numeric citation of sūra and verse. Citations have been arranged by sūra order, beginning with the first sūra, al-Fātiḥa, and ending with the last, al-Nās. In cases where a sūra has been known by more than one title, that found in the standard Cairo edition has been used. Within each sūra, *EQ* references to the entire sūra are placed first and are arranged by volume number. References to individual verses within each sūra follow these. Clusters of verses are incorporated after the individual listing of the first number in the cluster, with the order running from short to long clusters. In addition to inclusive page numbers and column indications, all these listings note the title of the entry itself. This should give the interested researcher a cursory overview of the range of topics for which a given Qurʾān citation may be adduced. *EQ* mentions of those verses that have acquired special names, such as the "Throne Verse" or the "Light Verse," can be found in the *Index of Proper Names* when such verses were identified by name, rather than sūra and verse number.

I hope that this final volume of the *EQ* will help its readers derive maximum benefit from the five volumes that preceded it. I hope that it will assist them in opening new avenues of insightful investigation and of productive research within the field of qurʾānic studies and well beyond. Finally, I hope that it will allow those who revere the Qurʾān as a life-guiding sacred text and those who approach it as a cultural achievement of immense importance to deepen their understanding and appreciation of this singularly significant scripture.

As I pen these final words for a project that has occupied my mind and tapped my energy for the last thirteen years, I cannot resist the temptation to thank again those colleagues whose contribution of time and effort has sustained me and has made the *EQ* possible. Particular thanks are due both Foke Deahl and Clare Wilde for their painstaking work in the compilation and proofreading of these indices. Theirs was an arduous task and one requiring extraordinary patience and dedication. The editorial team at Brill, despite numerous personnel changes over the years, has consistently supported the *EQ* at every stage of its development. The associate editors, Claude Gilliot, William Graham, Wadad Kadi and Andrew Rippin, suggested potential entries and authors, saw every article and contributed countless comments, citations and bibliographic suggestions. The assistant editors, Monique Bernards and John Nawas, carefully reformatted every submission for editorial consistency, and drew attention to matters requiring further clarification. My editorial assistant Clare Wilde and her predecessors and helpmates, Eerik Dickinson, Paul Heck, David Mehall and Bethany Zaborowski, have been a constant source of support at every point in the editorial process. The Advisory Board, Nasr Hamid Abu-Zayd, Mohammed Arkoun, Gerhard Böwering, Gerald Hawting, Frederik Leemhuis, Angelika Neuwirth and Uri Rubin, wrote major articles for the *EQ* and, in several instances, responded to my pleas for help when a promised piece by a commissioned author was not forthcoming. Finally, these six volumes could never have been published without the willing collaboration of all the friends and colleagues who so graciously agreed to share their expertise by writing for the *EQ*. To this host of generous souls, I offer my most sincere thanks. May the enduring value of the *Encyclopaedia of the Qurʾān* be a tribute to each one of them.

Jane Dammen McAuliffe
Georgetown University

AUTHOR LIST

A

Khaled M. Abou El Fadl, University of California at Los Angeles
- Jibt (iii)
- Rebellion (iv)
- Retaliation (iv)

Binyamin Abrahamov, Bar-Ilan University
- Signs (v)
- World (v)

Ibrahim M. Abu-Rabiʿ, Hartford Seminary
- Ezra (ii)

Nadia Abu-Zahra, University of Oxford
- Adultery and Fornication (i)

Nasr Hamid Abu Zayd, University of Leiden
- Arrogance (i)
- Everyday Life, Qurʾān In (ii)
- Illness and Health (ii)
- Intention (ii)
- Oppression (iii)

Charles J. Adams, McGill University
- Joy and Misery (iii)
- Maturity (iii)

Camilla P. Adang, Tel Aviv University
- Belief and Unbelief (i)
- Hypocrites and Hypocrisy (ii)
- Torah (v)

Asma Afsaruddin, University of Notre Dame
- Garden (ii)
- Reciters of the Qurʾān (iv)

M. Shahab Ahmed, Harvard University
- Satanic Verses (iv)

Michael W. Albin, Library of Congress, Washington, DC
- Printing of the Qurʾān (iv)

Scott C. Alexander, Catholic Theological Union, Chicago
- Fear (ii)
- Trust and Patience (v)

Ilai Alon, Tel Aviv University
- Noon (iii)

Mohammad Ali Amir-Moezzi, École Pratique des Hautes Études, Paris
- Dissimulation (i)
- Heresy (ii)

Ludwig Ammann, Freiburg im Breisgau
- Laughter (iii)
- Mockery (iii)

Mohammed Arkoun, Sorbonne University
- Contemporary Critical Practices and the Qurʾān (i)
- Islam (ii)
- Violence (v)

TALAL ASAD, The Graduate Center, CUNY
Kinship (III)

ALI S.A. ASANI, Harvard University
ʿAlī b. Abī Ṭālib (I)
Family of the Prophet (II)
South Asian Literatures and the Qurʾān (V)

B

MARGOT BADRAN, Northwestern University
Feminism and the Qurʾān (II)
Gender (II)
Sister (V)

AḤMAD MUBĀRAK AL-BAGHDĀDĪ (trans. Brannon M. Wheeler), Kuwait University
Consultation (I)

JULIAN BALDICK, University of London
Asceticism (I)

MOHAMMED A. BAMYEH, Macalester College
Patriarchy (IV)

MEIR M. BAR-ASHER, Hebrew University, Jerusalem
Hidden and the Hidden (II)
Shīʿism and the Qurʾān (IV)

SHAHZAD BASHIR, Carleton College
Anger (I)
Consolation (I)
Eternity (II)

MICHAEL L. BATES, The American Numismatic Society, New York
Numismatics (III)

THOMAS BAUER, University of Münster
ʿIfrīt (II)
Insanity (II)

DANIEL BEAUMONT, University of Rochester
Lie (III)
Simile (V)

DORIS BEHRENS-ABOUSEIF, University of London
Cups and Vessels (I)
Instruments (II)

JAMES A. BELLAMY, University of Michigan
Textual Criticism of the Qurʾān (V)

HERBERT BERG, University of North Carolina at Wilmington
African Americans (I)
Computers and the Qurʾān (I)
Polysemy in the Qurʾān (IV)

SHEILA BLAIR, Boston College
Ornamentation and Illumination (III)
Writing and Writing Materials (V)

KHALID YAHYA BLANKINSHIP, Temple University, Philadelphia
Court (I)
News (III)
Obedience (III)

JONATHAN M. BLOOM, Boston College
Mosque (III)
Ornamentation and Illumination (III)

HARTMUT BOBZIN, University of Erlangen
Pre-1800 Preoccupations of Qurʾānic Studies (IV)
Translations of the Qurʾān (V)

MICHAEL BONNER, University of Michigan
Byzantines (I)
Poverty and the Poor (IV)
Wealth (V)

MAURICE BORRMANS, Pontificio Istituto di Studi Arabi e d'Islamistica, Rome
Disobedience (I)
Pride (IV)
Resurrection (IV)
Salvation (IV)

ISSA J. BOULLATA, McGill University
Literary Structures of the Qurʾān (III)
Parody of the Qurʾān (IV)

DONNA LEE BOWEN, Brigham Young University
Birth (I)
Birth Control (I)
Infanticide (II)

Gerhard Böwering, Yale University
Chronology and the Qurʾān (i)
Covenant (i)
God and his Attributes (ii)
Prayer (iv)
Time (v)

Paolo Luigi Branca, Catholic University, Milan
Weeping (v)

William M. Brinner, University of California, Berkeley
Ararat (i)
Election (ii)
Hārūt and Mārūt (ii)
Jūdī (iii)
Noah (iii)
People of the Heights (iv)
Ṭuwā (v)

Jonathan E. Brockopp, Pennsylvania State University
Captives (i)
Concubines (i)
Justice and Injustice (iii)
Prisoners (iv)
Servants (iv)
Slaves and Slavery (v)

Angelika Brodersen, University of Gottingen
Reflection and Deliberation (iv)
Remembrance (iv)

Patrice C. Brodeur, Connecticut College
Religion (iv)

Christopher George Buck, Michigan State University, East Lansing
Bahāʾīs (i)

Ronald Paul Buckley, University of Manchester
Markets (iii)

David B. Burrell, University of Notre Dame
Truth (v)

John Burton, University of St. Andrews
Abrogation (i)
Collection of the Qurʾān (i)

Heribert Busse, Christian-Albrecths University of Kiel
Cain and Abel (i)
Dhū l-Kifl (i)
Jerusalem (iii)
Jonah (iii)
Lot (iii)
Nimrod (iii)

Amila Buturovic, York University, Canada
Evening (ii)
Vision (v)
Wish and Desire (v)

C

Simonetta Calderini, University of Surrey Roehampton
Lord (iii)

Juan Eduardo Campo, University of California, Santa Barbara
Burial (i)
Cave (i)
Furniture and Furnishings (ii)
House, Domestic and Divine (ii)

Jacqueline Chabbi, University of Paris
Jinn (iii)
Mecca (iii)
Whisper (v)

Masudul Alam Choudhury, Sultan Qaboos University, Oman
Usury (v)

Paul M. Cobb, University of Notre Dame
Hūd (ii)
Iram (ii)

Frederick S. Colby, Miami University, Oxford, OH
Symbolic Imagery (v)

Michael Cook, Princeton University
Virtues and Vices, Commanding and Forbidding (v)

Patricia Crone, Institute for Advanced Study, Princeton
War (v)

Stefania Cunial, Ca' Foscari University, Venice
Spiritual Beings (v)

D

Stephan Dähne, Orient-Institut der Deutschen Morgenländischen Gesellschaft, Beirut
Weights and Measures (v)

Maria Massi Dakake, George Mason University
Ṣiffīn, Battle of (v)

Ahmad Salim Dallal, Georgetown University
Calendar (i)
Day and Night (i)
Science and the Qurʾān (iv)

William R. Darrow, Williams College, Williamstown, MA
Magians (iii)

François de Blois, University of London
Sabians (iv)

Jean-Louis Déclais, Centre Diocésain, Oran
Names of the Prophet (iii)

Natana J. DeLong-Bas, Boston College
Wahhabism and the Qurʾān (v)

Frederick Mathewson Denny, University of Colorado, Boulder
Boast (i)
Circumcision (i)
Community and Society in the Qurʾān (i)
Corruption (i)
Ears (ii)
Eyes (ii)
Face (ii)
Feet (ii)
Hand(s) (ii)

François Déroche, École Pratique des Hautes Études, Paris
Manuscripts of the Qurʾān (iii)

Eerik Dickinson, Washington, DC
Difficult Passages (i)

Nelly van Doorn-Harder, Valparaiso University
Teaching and Preaching the Qurʾān (v)

E

Abul Fadl Mohsin Ebrahim, University of Durban Westville
Biology as the Creation and Stages of Life (i)

Dale F. Eickelman, Dartmouth College
Social Sciences and the Qurʾān (v)

Herbert Eisenstein, University of Vienna
Animal Life (i)
Coral (i)
Hides and Fleece (ii)
Hunting and Fishing (ii)
Spider (v)

Salwa M.S. El-Awa, University of Birmingham
Zaqqūm (v)
Zealotry (v)

Nadia Maria El-Cheikh, American University of Beirut
Byzantines (i)
Immunity (ii)
Iraq (ii)

Jamal J. Elias, Amherst College
Face of God (ii)
Lamp (iii)
Light (iii)
Throne of God (v)

Amira El-Zein, Tufts University
Water of Paradise (v)

Yoram Erder, Tel Aviv University
Idrīs (ii)

F

Moḥammad Fadel, Augusta, GA
Chastisement and Punishment (i)
Murder (iii)

Toufic Fahd, University of Strasbourg
Consecration of Animals (i)
Divination (i)
Foretelling in the Qurʾān (ii)

Rizwi Faizer, Independent Scholar
Expeditions and Battles (ii)

Majid Fakhry, Georgetown University
Philosophy and the Qurʾān (iv)

Muhammad al-Faruque, Stanford University
Emigrants and Helpers (ii)
Emigration (ii)

R. Michael Feener, The University of California, Riverside
Southeast Asian Qurʾānic Literature (v)

Reuven Firestone, Hebrew Union College, Los Angeles
Abraham (i)
Abyssinia (i)
Āzar (i)
Enemies (ii)
Ethiopia (ii)
Fighting (ii)
Isaac (ii)
Ishmael (ii)
Midian (iii)
Pharaoh (iv)
Sacrifice (iv)
Ṣafā and Marwa (iv)
Shekhinah (iv)
Thamūd (v)
Tubbaʿ (v)

Kais M. Firro, University of Haifa
Druzes (i)

Ersilia Francesca, Università degli Studi di Napoli "L'Orientale"
Khārijīs (iii)
Slaughter (v)

Yohanan Friedmann, Hebrew University, Jerusalem
Aḥmadiyya (i)
Dissension (i)
Tolerance and Coercion (v)

Dmitry V. Frolov, Moscow University
Decision (i)
Freedom and Predestination (ii)
Path or Way (iv)
Stone (v)
Stoning (v)

Bruce Fudge
Dog (i)

G

Anna M. Gade, Oberlin College
Recitation of the Qurʾān (iv)

Patrick D. Gaffney, University of Notre Dame
Friday Prayer (ii)
Load or Burden (iii)

Geert Jan H. van Gelder, University of Oxford
Hearing and Deafness (ii)

Avner Giladi, University of Haifa
Children (i)
Family (ii)
Fosterage (ii)
Guardianship (ii)
Lactation (iii)
Orphans (iii)
Parents (iv)
Wet-Nursing (v)

Claude Gilliot, University of Aix-en-Provence
Exegesis of the Qurʾān: Classical and Medieval (ii)

Informants (II)
Language and Style of the Qurʾān (III)
Mosque of the Dissension (III)
Narratives (III)
Traditional Disciplines of Qurʾānic Studies (V)

JOSEPH GINAT, University of Haifa
Vengeance (V)

HUGH PHILIP GODDARD, University of Nottingham
Baptism (I)

SHALOM L. GOLDMAN, Emory University
Joseph (III)

VALÉRIE GONZALEZ, Dartmouth College
Sheba (IV)
Silk (V)

MATTHEW S. GORDON, Miami University, Oxford, OH
Journey (III)
Troops (V)
Victory (V)

OLEG GRABAR, Princeton University, Institute for Advanced Studies
Art and Architecture and the Qurʾān (I)

WILLIAM A. GRAHAM, Harvard University
Basmala (I)
Fātiḥa (II)
Orality (III)
Scripture and the Qurʾān (IV)

FRANK GRIFFEL, Yale University
Moderation (III)

SIDNEY H. GRIFFITH, The Catholic University of America
Christians and Christianity (I)
Church (I)
Gospel (II)
Holy Spirit (II)
Monasticism and Monks (III)

DENIS GRIL, University of Aix-en-Provence
Love and Affection (III)
Miracles (III)

BEATRICE GRUENDLER, Yale University
Arabic Script (I)
Sheets (IV)

SEBASTIAN GÜNTHER, University of Toronto
Bloodshed (I)
Clients and Clientage (I)
Day, Times of (I)
Illiteracy (II)
Literacy (III)
Teaching (V)
Ummī (V)

LI GUO, University of Notre Dame
Gift-Giving (II)

ROSALIND WARD GWYNNE, University of Tennessee
Beauty (I)
Hell and Hellfire (II)
Impotence (II)
Youth and Old Age (V)

H

SHAHLA HAERI, Boston University
Temporary Marriage (V)

WAEL B. HALLAQ, McGill University
Apostasy (I)
Contracts and Alliances (I)
Forbidden (II)
Innovation (II)
Law and the Qurʾān (III)

TIMOTHY P. HARRISON, University of Toronto
Ḥijr (II)

ISAAC HASSON, Hebrew University, Jerusalem
David (I)
Egypt (II)
Last Judgment (III)
Left Hand and Right Hand (III)

GERALD R. HAWTING, University of London
Atonement (I)
Calf of Gold (I)
Idolatry and Idolaters (II)
Idols and Images (II)

Kaʿba (III)
Oaths (III)
Parties and Factions (IV)
Pilgrimage (IV)
Pre-Islamic Arabia and the Qurʾān (IV)
Tradition and Custom (V)
Worship (V)

PETER HEATH, American University of Beirut
Metaphor (III)

PAUL L. HECK, Georgetown University
Politics and the Qurʾān (IV)
Poll Tax (IV)
Scrolls (IV)
Taxation (V)
Vow (V)

MARGARETHA T. HEEMSKERK, Radboud University, Nijmegen
Speech (V)
Suffering (V)

MARCIA HERMANSEN, Loyola University, Chicago
Talent (V)
Womb (V)

CHARLES HIRSCHKIND, University of Wisconsin
Media and the Qurʾān (III)

VALERIE J. HOFFMAN, University of Illinois
Festivals and Commemorative Days (II)
Hospitality and Courtesy (II)
Intercession (II)

THOMAS EMIL HOMERIN, University of Rochester
Conceit (I)
Drowning (I)
Soul (V)

ROBERT HOYLAND, University of Oxford
Epigraphy (II)

SHIU-SIAN ANGEL HSU, Santa Ana, CA
Modesty (III)

QAMAR-UL HUDA, United States Institute of Peace
Anatomy (I)

ALICE C. HUNSBERGER, Asia Society, New York
Marvels (III)

JOHN O. HUNWICK, Northwestern University, Evanston IL
African Literature (I)

J

SHERMAN A. JACKSON, University of Michigan
Cheating (I)
Debt (I)
Property (IV)

JOHANNES J.G. JANSEN, University of Leiden
Hostages (II)

ROBERT KEVIN JAQUES, Indiana University
Visiting (V)

MAHER JARRAR, American University of Beirut
Heaven and Sky (II)
Houris (II)

HERBJØRN JENSSEN, University of Oslo
Arabic Language (I)

ANTHONY HEARLE JOHNS, Australian National University
Air and Wind (I)
Benjamin (I)
Fall of Man (II)
Hāmān (II)
Hot and Cold (II)
Job (III)
Water (V)

NOLA J. JOHNSON, University of Toronto
Aqṣā Mosque (I)

DAVID JOHNSTON, Yale University
Virtue (V)

Alan Jones, University of Oxford
Orality and Writing in Arabia (iii)
Poetry and Poets (iv)

G.H.A. Juynboll, Leiden
Ḥadīth and the Qurʾān (ii)
Sunna (v)

K

Wadad (al-Qāḍī) Kadi, University of Chicago
Authority (i)
Caliph (i)
Literature and the Qurʾān (iii)

Shigeru Kamada, University of Tokyo
Secrets (iv)

Nico J.G. Kaptein, University of Leiden
Seasons (iv)

Ahmet T. Karamustafa, Washington University, St. Louis
Darkness (i)
Fate (ii)
Strangers and Foreigners (v)
Suicide (v)

Enes Karic, Sarajevo University
Gambling (ii)
Intoxicants (ii)

Marion Holmes Katz, Mount Holyoke College, South Hadley, MA
Cleanliness and Ablution (i)
Menstruation (iii)
Nudity (iii)

Philip F. Kennedy, New York University
Samuel (iv)

Navid Kermani, Wissenschaftskolleg zu Berlin
Intellect (ii)

Linda L. Kern, St. John's College, Annapolis, MD
Companions of the Prophet (i)

Tarif Khalidi, American University of Beirut
Arabs (i)

Ruqayya Khan, University of California, Santa Barbara
Envy (ii)
Error (ii)

Bustami Mohamed Khir, University of Birmingham
Sovereignty (v)

Raif Georges Khoury, University of Heidelberg
al-ʿArim (i)
ʿArafāt (i)
Babylon (i)
Camel (i)

Richard Kimber, University of St. Andrews
Blood Money (i)
Boundaries and Precepts (i)
Qibla (iv)

Leah Kinberg, Tel Aviv University
Ambiguous (i)
Apparition (i)
Dreams and Sleep (i)
Insolence and Obstinacy (ii)
Paradise (iv)
Piety (iv)

Meir-Jacob Kister, Hebrew University, Jerusalem
Musaylima (iii)

Ernst Axel Knauf, University of Bern
Nomads (iii)

Alexander D. Knysh, University of Michigan
Courage (i)
Months (iii)
Possession and Possessions (iv)
Power and Impotence (iv)
Ṣūfism and the Qurʾān (v)

KATHRYN KUENY, Fordham University
Laudation (III)
Portents (IV)
Wine (V)

S. KUGLE, University of Leiden
Vision and Blindness (V)

PAUL KUNITZSCH, University of Munich
Planets and Stars (IV)
Sun (V)

L

ARZINA R. LALANI, Institute of Ismaili Studies, London
Judgment (III)
Shīʿa (IV)

ELLA LANDAU-TASSERON, Hebrew University, Jerusalem
Jihād (III)
Tribes and Clans (V)

PIERRE LARCHER, University of Aix-en-Provence
Language, Concept of (III)
Language and Style of the Qurʾān (III)

JACOB LASSNER, Northwestern University
Bilqīs (I)

FREDERIK LEEMHUIS, University of Groningen
Apocalypse (I)
Codices of the Qurʾān (I)
Ḥamza b. ʿAbd al-Muṭṭalib (II)
ʿIlliyyūn (II)
Readings of the Qurʾān (IV)

KEITH LEWINSTEIN, Smith College
Commandments (I)
Gog and Magog (II)

FRANKLIN LEWIS, Emory University
Persian Literature and the Qurʾān (IV)

JEAN-YVES L'HÔPITAL, University of Rennes II
Prayer Formulas (IV)

JAMES E. LINDSAY, Colorado State University
Goliath (II)

SHARI LOWIN, Stonehill College, Easton, PA
Plagues (IV)
Revision and Alteration (IV)

JOSEPH LOWRY, University of Pennsylvania
Lawful and Unlawful (III)
Ritual Purity (IV)
Theft (V)

M

DANIEL A. MADIGAN, Pontifical Gregorian University, Rome
Book (I)
Criterion (I)
Preserved Tablet (IV)
Revelation and Inspiration (IV)

FEDWA MALTI-DOUGLAS, Indiana University
Avarice (I)

GABRIEL MANDEL KHĀN, Milan, Italy
Magic (III)

ROXANNE D. MARCOTTE, The University of Queensland, Australia
Night of Power (III)

MANUELA MARÍN, University of Madrid
Odors and Smells (III)

LOUISE MARLOW, Wellesley College
Friends and Friendship (II)
Kings and Rulers (III)
Scholar (IV)

DAVID MARSHALL, Cambridge Theological Federation
Punishment Stories (IV)
Transitoriness (V)
Zechariah (V)

Richard C. Martin, Emory University
Anthropomorphism (I)
Createdness of the Qurʾān (I)
Inimitability (II)

Ulrich Marzolph, Enzyklopädie des Märchens, Göttingen
Humor (II)

Keith Massey, Jessup, MD
Mysterious Letters (III)

Ingrid Mattson, Hartford Seminary
Ḥunayn (II)
Manual Labor (III)
Work (V)

Jane Dammen McAuliffe, Georgetown University
Abraha (I)
Bible (I)
Debate and Disputation (I)
Fāṭima (II)
Heart (II)
Religious Pluralism and the Qurʾān (IV)

Sheila McDonough, Concordia University, Montreal
Abstinence (I)
Hope (II)

Christopher Melchert, University of Oxford
Maintenance and Upkeep (III)
Reciters of the Qurʾān (IV)

Josef W. Meri, Ahl al-Bayt Institute for Islamic Thought
Ritual and the Qurʾān (IV)

Barbara D. Metcalf, University of California, Davis
Deobandis (I)

Mustansir Mir, Youngstown State University
Ashes (I)
Bread (I)
Dialogues (I)
Glorification of God (II)
Glory (II)
Grace (II)
Literature and the Qurʾān (III)
Names of the Qurʾān (III)
Polytheism and Atheism (IV)
Theophany (V)
Unity of the Text of the Qurʾān (V)

Ebrahim Moosa, Duke University
Loyalty (III)

Robert G. Morrison, Whitman College
Year (V)

Roy P. Mottahedeh, Harvard University
Brother and Brotherhood (I)

Harald Motzki, Radboud University, Nijmegen
Bridewealth (I)
Chastity (I)
Marriage and Divorce (III)
Muṣḥaf (III)
Nāmūs (III)
Waiting Period (V)

N

Tilman Nagel, University of Göttingen
Theology and the Qurʾān (V)

Azim Nanji, The Institute of Ismaili Studies, London
Almsgiving (I)

John A. Nawas, Catholic University, Leuven
Badr (I)
Days of God (I)
Inquisition (II)
People of the Thicket (IV)
Trial (V)

Ian Richard Netton, University of Leeds
Life (III)
Nature as Signs (III)

Angelika Neuwirth, Free University, Berlin
Cosmology (I)
Exhortations (II)

Form and Structure of the Qurʾān (II)
Geography (II)
Myths and Legends in the Qurʾān (III)
Ramaḍān (IV)
Rhetoric and the Qurʾān (IV)
Spatial Relations (V)
Sūra(s) (V)
Verse(s) (V)

GORDON DARNELL NEWBY, Emory University
Ark (I)
Baal (I)
Deferral (I)
Forgery (II)
Generations (II)

O

KATHLEEN MALONE O'CONNOR, University of South Florida
Amulets (I)
Popular and Talismanic Uses of the Qurʾān (IV)

SOLANGE ORY, University of Aix-Marseille
Calligraphy (I)

P

IRMELI PERHO, The Royal Library, Copenhagen
Medicine and the Qurʾān (III)

RUDOLPH PETERS, University of Amsterdam
Booty (I)

DANIEL CARL PETERSON, Brigham Young University
Creation (I)
Forgiveness (II)
Good News (II)
Mercy (III)

UTE PIETRUSCHKA, Philipps University, Marburg
Bedouin (I)
Tents and Tent Pegs (V)

Venetia Porter, The British Museum
Epigraphy (II)

DAVID STEPHAN POWERS, Cornell University
Inheritance (II)

R

NASSER RABBAT, Massachusetts Institute of Technology
City (I)

MATTHIAS RADSCHEIT, Bonn, Germany
Provocation (IV)
Responsibility (IV)
Springs and Fountains (V)
Table (V)
Witnessing and Testifying (V)
Word of God (V)

BERND R. RADTKE, University of Utrecht
Saint (IV)
Wisdom (V)

WIM RAVEN, University of Frankfurt
Martyrs (III)
Reward and Punishment (IV)
Sīra and the Qurʾān (V)

A. KEVIN REINHART, Dartmouth College
Contamination (I)
Ethics and the Qurʾān (II)

G. JOHN RENARD, St. Louis University
Adoration (I)
Alexander (I)
Deliverance (I)
Despair (I)
Khaḍir/Khiḍr (III)

BASSEL A. REYAHI, Toronto, Canada
Sirius (V)

GABRIEL SAID REYNOLDS, University of Notre Dame
ʿUthmān (V)

EFIM A. REZVAN, Russian Academy of Sciences, St. Petersburg
Orthography (III)

ANDREW RIPPIN, University of Victoria
Aaron (I)
Abū Bakr (I)
Abū Lahab (I)
Anointing (I)
Colors (I)
Devil (I)
Foreign Vocabulary (II)
Ḥudaybiya (II)
Iblīs (II)
Isaiah (II)
Jacob (III)
John the Baptist (III)
Numbers and Enumeration (III)
Occasions of Revelation (III)
Sabbath (IV)
Seeing and Hearing (IV)
Tools for the Scholarly Study of the Qurʾān (V)
Trade and Commerce (V)
Witness to Faith (V)

CHRISTIAN JULIEN ROBIN, Centre National de la Recherche Scientifique, Aix-en-Provence
South Arabia, Religions in Pre-Islamic (V)
[al-]Ukhdūd (V)
Yemen (V)

CHASE F. ROBINSON, University of Oxford
Conquest (I)
Warner (V)

NEAL S. ROBINSON, University of Wales
Antichrist (I)
Clay (I)
Crucifixion (I)
Jesus (III)

RUTH RODED, Hebrew University, Jerusalem
Women and the Qurʾān (V)

† FRANZ ROSENTHAL, Yale University
History and the Qurʾān (II)

EVERETT K. ROWSON, New York University
Gossip (II)
Homosexuality (II)

URI RUBIN, Tel Aviv University
Caravan (I)
Children of Israel (I)
Ḥafṣa (II)
Ḥanīf (II)
Ilāf (II)
Israel (II)
Jews and Judaism (III)
Muḥammad (III)
Oft-Repeated (III)
Prophets and Prophethood (IV)
Quraysh (IV)
Races (IV)
Remnant (IV)
Repentance and Penance (IV)
Sacred Precincts (IV)
Vehicles (V)

S

ABDULAZIZ SACHEDINA, University of Virginia
Abortion (I)

ABDULLAH SAEED, University of Melbourne
Economics (II)

DANIEL J. SAHAS, University of Waterloo
Iconoclasm (II)

SAID S. SAID, University of Durham
Measurement (III)

LAMIN SANNEH, Yale University
Gratitude and Ingratitude (II)

USHA SANYAL, Charlotte, NC
Barēlwīs (I)

ZEKI SARITOPRAK, John Carroll University
Rod (IV)
Sand (IV)

ROBERT SCHICK, Henry Martyn Institute of Islamic Studies, Hyderabad
Archaeology and the Qurʾān (I)
Place of Abraham (IV)
Protection (IV)

ARIE SCHIPPERS, University of Amsterdam
Psalms (IV)

Sabine Schmidtke, Free University, Berlin
Creeds (i)
Destiny (i)
Muʿtazila (iii)
Pairs and Pairing (iv)

Irene Schneider, Martin Luther University, Halle-Wittenberg
Illegitimacy (ii)

Cornelia Schöck, University of Freiburg im Breisgau
Adam and Eve (i)
Moses (iii)

Marco Schöller, University of Köln
Medina (iii)
Naḍīr (Banū al-) (iii)
Opposition to Muḥammad (iii)
Post-Enlightenment Academic Study of the Qurʾān (iv)
Qaynuqāʿ (Banū) (iv)
Qurayẓa (Banū al-) (iv)

Hannelore Schönig, Martin Luther University, Halle-Wittenberg
Camphor (i)
Gold (ii)

Michael B. Schub, Hartford, CN
Uncertainty (v)

Stuart D. Sears, American University in Cairo
Money (iii)

Michael A. Sells, University of Chicago
Ascension (i)
Memory (iii)
Spirit (v)

Irfan Shahīd, Georgetown University
Najrān (iii)
People of the Elephant (iv)
Ships (iv)
Sinai (v)
Syria (v)

Moshe Sharon, Hebrew University, Jerusalem
People of the Book (iv)
People of the House (iv)

William E. Shepard, University of Canterbury, New Zealand
Age of Ignorance (i)
Ignorance (ii)

Mona Siddiqui, University of Glasgow
Flogging (ii)
Veil (v)
Widow (v)

Kemal Silay, Indiana University
Turkish Literature and the Qurʾān (v)

Jane I. Smith, Hartford Seminary
Eschatology (ii)
Faith (ii)

Priscilla P. Soucek, New York University
Material Culture and the Qurʾān (iii)
Solomon (v)

Denise A. Spellberg, University of Texas, Austin
ʿĀʾisha bint Abī Bakr (i)

Paul Stenhouse, Sacred Heart Monastery, Kensington, NSW
Samaritans (iv)

Devin J. Stewart, Emory University
Blasphemy (i)
Blessing (i)
Curse (i)
Farewell Pilgrimage (ii)
Pit (iv)
Rhymed Prose (iv)
Sex and Sexuality (iv)
Smell (v)
Soothsayer (v)
Teeth (v)

Barbara Freyer Stowasser, Georgetown University
Khadīja (iii)
Mary (iii)
Wives of the Prophet (v)

MARK N. SWANSON, Luther Seminary, St. Paul, MN
Proof (IV)

T

LIYAKAT TAKIM, University of Denver
Samson (IV)
Saul (IV)

RAFAEL TALMON, University of Haifa
Dialects (I)
Grammar and the Qurʾān (II)

DAVID THOMAS, University of Birmingham
Apologetics (I)
Conversion (I)
Trinity (V)

HEIDI TOELLE, Sorbonne University
Earth (II)
Fire (II)
Smoke (V)

SHAWKAT M. TOORAWA, Cornell University
Clothing (I)
Trips and Voyages (V)

JAMES A. TORONTO, Brigham Young University
Astray (I)

ROBERTO TOTTOLI, Università degli Studi di Napoli "L'Orientale"
ʿĀd (I)
Bowing and Prostration (I)
Elijah (II)
Elisha (II)
Ezekiel (II)
ʿImrān (II)
Korah (III)
Men of the Cave (III)
People of the Ditch (IV)
Raqīm (IV)
Rass (IV)
Ṣāliḥ (IV)
Shuʿayb (IV)
Sleep (V)

GÉRARD TROUPEAU, École Pratique des Hautes Études, Paris
Metals and Minerals (III)

V

DANIEL MARTIN VARISCO, Hofstra University
Moon (III)
Numerology (III)

NARGIS VIRANI, Washington University
Ranks and Orders (IV)

W

JACQUES WAARDENBURG, University of Lausanne
Death and the Dead (I)

KEES WAGTENDONK, University of Amsterdam
Fasting (II)
Vigil (V)

DAVID WAINES, Lancaster University
Agriculture and Vegetation (I)
Carrion (I)
Date Palm (I)
Famine (II)
Food and Drink (II)
Grasses (II)
Honey (II)
Milk (III)
Sustenance (V)
Tree(s) (V)
Weather (V)

PAUL E. WALKER, University of Chicago
Impeccability (II)
Knowledge and Learning (III)

EARL H. WAUGH, University of Alberta
Artery and Vein (I)
Blood and Blood Clot (I)

Flying (II)
Peace (IV)

Gisela Webb, Seton Hall University
Angel (I)
Gabriel (II)
Michael (III)

Bernard G. Weiss, University of Utah
Prohibited Degrees (IV)

Alford T. Welch, Michigan State University, East Lansing
Afternoon (I)

Brannon M. Wheeler, University of Washington
Breaking Trusts and Contracts (I)
Consultation (I) [trans.]
Evil Deeds (II)
Good and Evil (II)
Good Deeds (II)
Pledge (IV)

Lutz Wiederhold, Martin Luther University Halle-Wittenberg
Morning (III)
Profane and Sacred (IV)
Suspicion (V)

Rotraud Wielandt, University of Bamberg
Exegesis of the Qurʾān: Early Modern and Contemporary (II)

Clare E. Wilde, The Catholic University of America
Praise (IV)
Religious Pluralism and the Qurʾān (IV)

Timothy Winter, University of Cambridge
Failure (II)
Honor (II)

Robert Wisnovsky, Harvard University
Heavenly Book (II)

Y

Imtiyaz Yusuf, Assumption University, Bangkok, Thailand
Imām (II)

Z

A.H. Mathias Zahniser, Asbury Theological Seminary
Apostle (I)
Indifference (II)
Invitation (II)
Luqmān (III)
Messenger (III)
Parable (IV)

Mohsen Zakeri, University of Frankfurt am Main
Arbitration (I)

Mona M. Zaki, Princeton University
Barrier (I)
Barzakh (I)

Muhammad Qasim Zaman, Brown University
Oppressed on Earth, The (III)
Sin, Major and Minor (V)

Kate P. Zebiri, University of London
Polemic and Polemical Language (IV)

ARTICLE LIST

VOLUME ONE

A – D

Articles *Page numbers*

A

Aaron (Andrew Rippin) 1-2
Abortion (Abdulaziz Sachedina) 2-4
Abraha (Jane Dammen McAuliffe) 4-5
Abraham (Reuven Firestone) 5-11
Abrogation (John Burton) 11-19
Abstinence (Sheila McDonough) 19-20
Abū Bakr (Andrew Rippin) 20
Abū Lahab (Andrew Rippin) 20
Abyssinia (Reuven Firestone) 20-21
ʿĀd (Roberto Tottoli) 21-22
Adam and Eve (Cornelia Schöck) 22-26
Adoration (John Renard) 26-28
Adultery and Fornication (Nadia Abu-Zahra) 28-30
African Americans (Herbert Berg) 30-32
African Literature (John O. Hunwick) 32-35
Afternoon (Alford T. Welch) 35-36
Age of Ignorance (William E. Shepard) 37-40
Agriculture and Vegetation (David Waines) 40-50
Aḥmadiyya (Yohanan Friedmann) 50-51
Air and Wind (Anthony H. Johns) 51-55
ʿĀʾisha bint Abī Bakr (Denise A. Spellberg) 55-60
Al-ʿArim (R.G. Khoury) 60-61
Alexander (John Renard) 61-62
ʿAlī b. Abī Ṭālib (Ali S. Asani) 62-63
Almsgiving (Azim Nanji) 64-70
Ambiguous (Leah Kinberg) 70-77

Amulets (Kathleen Malone O'Connor) 77-79
Anatomy (Qamar-ul Huda) 79-84
Angel (Gisela Webb) 84-92
Anger (Shahzad Bashir) 92-93
Animal Life (Herbert Eisenstein) 93-102
Anointing (Andrew Rippin) 102-103
Anthropomorphism (Richard C. Martin) 103-107
Antichrist (Neal Robinson) 107-111
Apocalypse (Frederik Leemhuis) 111-114
Apologetics (David Thomas) 115-119
Apostasy (Wael Hallaq) 119-122
Apostle (A.H. Mathias Zahniser) 123-124
Apparition (Leah Kinberg) 124-125
Aqṣā Mosque (N.J. Johnson) 125-127
Arabic Language (Herbjørn Jenssen) 127-135
Arabic Script (Beatrice Gruendler) 135-144
Arabs (Tarif Khalidi) 144-145
ʿArafāt (R.G. Khoury) 145-146
Ararat (William M. Brinner) 146-147
Arbitration (Mohsen Zakeri) 147-148
Archaeology and the Qurʾān (Robert Schick) 148-157
Ark (Gordon D. Newby) 157-158
Arrogance (Nasr Abu Zayd) 158-161
Art and Architecture and the Qurʾān (Oleg Grabar) 161-175
Artery and Vein (Earle H. Waugh) 175-176
Ascension (Michael Sells) 176-181
Asceticism (Julian Baldick) 181-184
Ashes (Mustansir Mir) 184-185
Astray (James A. Toronto) 185-186
Atonement (Gerald R. Hawting) 186-188
Authority (Wadad Kadi [al-Qāḍī]) 188-190
Avarice (Fedwa Malti-Douglas) 191-192
Āzar (Reuven Firestone) 192-193

B

Baal (Gordon Darnell Newby) 194
Babylon (R.G. Khoury) 195-196
Badr (John Nawas) 196-197
Bahāʾīs (Christopher George Buck) 197-199
Baptism (Hugh Goddard) 200-201
Barēlwīs (Usha Sanyal) 201-203
Barrier (Mona M. Zaki) 203-204
Barzakh (Mona M. Zaki) 204-207
Basmala (William A. Graham) 207-212
Beauty (Rosalind Ward Gwynne) 212-214
Bedouin (Ute Pietruschka) 214-218
Belief and Unbelief (Camilla Adang) 218-226
Benjamin (A.H. Johns) 226-228
Bible (Jane Dammen McAuliffe) 228

Bilqīs (Jacob Lassner) 228-229
Biology as the Creation and Stages of Life (Abul Fadl Mohsin Ebrahim) 229-232
Birth (Donna Lee Bowen) 233-234
Birth Control (Donna Lee Bowen) 234-235
Blasphemy (Devin J. Stewart) 235-236
Blessing (Devin J. Stewart) 236-237
Blood and Blood Clot (E.H. Waugh) 237-238
Blood Money (Richard Kimber) 239-240
Bloodshed (Sebastian Günther) 240-241
Boast (Frederick Mathewson Denny) 241-242
Book (Daniel Madigan) 242-251
Booty (Rudolph Peters) 251-252
Boundaries and Precepts (Richard Kimber) 252-254
Bowing and Prostration (Roberto Tottoli) 254-255
Bread (Mustansir Mir) 255-256
Breaking Trusts and Contracts (Brannon M. Wheeler) 256-258
Bridewealth (Harald Motzki) 258-259
Brother and Brotherhood (Roy P. Mottahedeh) 259-263
Burial (Juan Eduardo Campo) 263-265
Byzantines (Michael Bonner and Nadia Maria El-Cheikh) 265-269

C

Cain and Abel (Heribert Busse) 270-272
Calendar (A. Dallal) 272-273
Calf of Gold (Gerald R. Hawting) 273-276
Caliph (Wadad Kadi) 276-278
Calligraphy (Solange Ory) 278-286
Camel (R.G. Khoury) 286-287
Camphor (Hanne Schönig) 287-288
Captives (Jonathan E. Brockopp) 289-290
Caravan (Uri Rubin) 290-291
Carrion (David Waines) 291-292
Cave (Juan Eduardo Campo) 292-294
Chastisement and Punishment (Moḥammad Hossam Fadel) 294-298
Chastity (Harald Motzki) 298-300
Cheating (Sherman A. Jackson) 300-301
Children (Avner Giladi) 301-303
Children of Israel (Uri Rubin) 303-307
Christians and Christianity (Sidney H. Griffith) 307-316
Chronology and the Qur'ān (Gerhard Böwering) 316-335
Church (Sidney H. Griffith) 335-336
Circumcision (Frederick Mathewson Denny) 336-338
City (Nasser Rabbat) 338-339
Clay (Neal Robinson) 339-341
Cleanliness and Ablution (Marion Holmes Katz) 341-344
Clients and Clientage (Sebastian Günther) 344-346
Clothing (Shawkat M. Toorawa) 346-347
Codices of the Qur'ān (Frederik Leemhuis) 347-351
Collection of the Qur'ān (John Burton) 351-361

Colors (Andrew Rippin) 361-365
Commandments (Keith Lewinstein) 365-367
Community and Society in the Qurʾān (Frederick Mathewson Denny) 367-386
Companions of the Prophet (Linda L. Kern) 386-390
Computers and the Qurʾān (Herbert Berg) 391-395
Conceit (Th. Emil Homerin) 395-396
Concubines (Jonathan E. Brockopp) 396-397
Conquest (Chase F. Robinson) 397-401
Consecration of Animals (T. Fahd) 401-405
Consolation (Shahzad Bashir) 405-406
Consultation (Aḥmad Mubārak al-Baghdādī [trans. Brannon M. Wheeler]) 406-410
Contamination (A. Kevin Reinhart) 410-412
Contemporary Critical Practices and the Qurʾān (M. Arkoun) 412-431
Contracts and Alliances (Wael B. Hallaq) 431-435
Conversion (David Thomas) 435-438
Coral (Herbert Eisenstein) 438-439
Corruption (Frederick Mathewson Denny) 439-440
Cosmology (Angelika Neuwirth) 440-458
Courage (Alexander D. Knysh) 458-462
Court (Khalid Yahya Blankinship) 462-464
Covenant (Gerhard Böwering) 464-467
Createdness of the Qurʾān (Richard C. Martin) 467-472
Creation (Daniel Carl Peterson) 472-480
Creeds (Sabine Schmidtke) 480-486
Criterion (Daniel Madigan) 486-487
Crucifixion (Neal Robinson) 487-489
Cups and Vessels (Doris Behrens-Abouseif) 489-491
Curse (Devin J. Stewart) 491-492

D

Darkness (Ahmet T. Karamustafa) 493-494
Date Palm (David Waines) 494-495
David (Isaac Hasson) 495-497
Day and Night (A. Dallal) 497-498
Day, Times of (Sebastian Günther) 499-504
Days of God (John A. Nawas) 505
Death and the Dead (Jacques Waardenburg) 505-511
Debate and Disputation (Jane Dammen McAuliffe) 511-514
Debt (Sherman A. Jackson) 514-515
Decision (Dmitry V. Frolov) 515-517
Deferral (Gordon Darnell Newby) 517-518
Deliverance (John Renard) 518-519
Deobandis (Barbara D. Metcalf) 519-521
Despair (John Renard) 521-522
Destiny (Sabine Schmidtke) 522-524
Devil (Andrew Rippin) 524-527
Dhū l-Kifl (Heribert Busse) 527-529
Dialects (Rafael Talmon) 529-531
Dialogues (Mustansir Mir) 531-535

VOLUME TWO

E – I

Articles *Page numbers*

E

Ears (Frederick Mathewson Denny) 1-2
Earth (Heidi Toelle) 2-5
Economics (Abdullah Saeed) 5-10
Egypt (Isaac Hasson) 10-11
Election (William M. Brinner) 11-12
Elijah (Roberto Tottoli) 12-13
Elisha (Roberto Tottoli) 14
Emigrants and Helpers (Muhammad al-Faruque) 14-18
Emigration (Muhammad al-Faruque) 18-23
Enemies (Reuven Firestone) 23-24
Envy (Ruqayya Khan) 24-25
Epigraphy (Robert Hoyland with contributions from Venetia Porter [Coins; Seals and amulets]) 25-43
Error (Ruqayya Khan) 43-44
Eschatology (Jane I. Smith) 44-54
Eternity (Shahzad Bashir) 54-55
Ethics and the Qurʾān (A. Kevin Reinhart) 55-79
Ethiopia (Reuven Firestone) 79
Evening (Amila Buturovic) 79-80
Everyday Life, Qurʾān In (Nasr Hamid Abu Zayd) 80-98
Evil Deeds (Brannon M. Wheeler) 98-99
Exegesis of the Qurʾān: Classical and Medieval (Claude Gilliot) 99-124
Exegesis of the Qurʾān: Early Modern and Contemporary (Rotraud Wielandt) 124-142
Exhortations (Angelika Neuwirth) 142-143
Expeditions and Battles (Rizwi Faizer) 143-153
Eyes (Frederick Mathewson Denny) 153-154
Ezekiel (Roberto Tottoli) 154-155
Ezra (Ibrahim M. Abu-Rabiʿ) 155-157

F

Face (Frederick Mathewson Denny) 158-159
Face of God (Jamal Elias) 159-161
Failure (Timothy Winter) 161-162
Faith (Jane I. Smith) 162-172
Fall of Man (Anthony Hearle Johns) 172-173
Family (Avner Giladi) 173-176
Family of the Prophet (Ali S.A. Asani) 176-177
Famine (David Waines) 177-178
Farewell Pilgrimage (Devin J. Stewart) 178-180
Fasting (Kees Wagtendonk) 180-185
Fate (Ahmet T. Karamustafa) 185-188

Fātiḥa (William A. Graham) 188-192
Fāṭima (Jane Dammen McAuliffe) 192-194
Fear (Scott C. Alexander) 194-198
Feet (Frederick Mathewson Denny) 198-199
Feminism and the Qurʾān (Margot Badran) 199-203
Festivals and Commemorative Days (Valerie J. Hoffman) 203-208
Fighting (Reuven Firestone) 208-210
Fire (Heidi Toelle) 210-214
Flogging (Mona Siddiqui) 214-215
Flying (Earle H. Waugh) 215-216
Food and Drink (David Waines) 216-223
Forbidden (Wael B. Hallaq) 223-226
Foreign Vocabulary (Andrew Rippin) 226-237
Foretelling in the Qurʾān (T. Fahd) 237-242
Forgery (Gordon Darnell Newby) 242-244
Forgiveness (Daniel C. Peterson) 244-245
Form and Structure of the Qurʾān (Angelika Neuwirth) 245-266
Fosterage (Avner Giladi) 266-267
Freedom and Predestination (Dmitry V. Frolov) 267-271
Friday Prayer (Patrick D. Gaffney) 271-272
Friends and Friendship (Louise Marlow) 273-275
Furniture and Furnishings (Juan Eduardo Campo) 275-277

G

Gabriel (Gisela Webb) 278-280
Gambling (Enes Karic) 280-282
Garden (Asma Afsaruddin) 282-287
Gender (Margot Badran) 288-292
Generations (Gordon Darnell Newby) 292-293
Geography (Angelika Neuwirth) 293-313
Gift-Giving (Li Guo) 313-314
Glorification of God (Mustansir Mir) 314-315
Glory (Mustansir Mir) 315-316
God and his Attributes (Gerhard Böwering) 316-331
Gog and Magog (Keith Lewinstein) 331-333
Gold (Hannelore Schönig) 333-334
Goliath (James E. Lindsay) 334-335
Good and Evil (Brannon M. Wheeler) 335-339
Good Deeds (Brannon M. Wheeler) 339-340
Good News (Daniel C. Peterson) 340-342
Gospel (Sidney H. Griffith) 342-343
Gossip (Everett K. Rowson) 343-344
Grace (Mustansir Mir) 344-345
Grammar and the Qurʾān (Rafael Talmon) 345-369
Grasses (David Waines) 369-370
Gratitude and Ingratitude (Lamin Sanneh) 370-373
Guardianship (Avner Giladi) 373-375

H

Ḥadīth and the Qurʾān (G.H.A. Juynboll) 376-397
Ḥafṣa (Uri Rubin) 397-398
Hāmān (Anthony Hearle Johns) 399-400
Ḥamza b. ʿAbd al-Muṭṭalib (Frederik Leemhuis) 400-401
Hand(s) (Frederick Mathewson Denny) 401-402
Ḥanīf (Uri Rubin) 402-404
Hārūt and Mārūt (William M. Brinner) 404-405
Hearing and Deafness (Geert Jan H. van Gelder) 405-406
Heart (Jane Dammen McAuliffe) 406-410
Heaven and Sky (Maher Jarrar) 410-412
Heavenly Book (Robert Wisnovsky) 412-414
Hell and Hellfire (Rosalind W. Gwynne) 414-420
Heresy (Mohammad Ali Amir-Moezzi) 420-423
Hidden and the Hidden (Meir M. Bar-Asher) 423-426
Hides and Fleece (Herbert Eisenstein) 426-427
Ḥijr (Timothy P. Harrison) 427-428
History and the Qurʾān (Franz Rosenthal) 428-442
Holy Spirit (Sidney H. Griffith) 442-444
Homosexuality (Everett K. Rowson) 444-445
Honey (David Waines) 445-447
Honor (Timothy Winter) 447-448
Hope (Sheila McDonough) 448-449
Hospitality and Courtesy (Valerie J. Hoffman) 449-454
Hostages (Johannes J.G. Jansen) 454-455
Hot and Cold (Anthony Hearle Johns) 455-456
Houris (Maher Jarrar) 456-458
House, Domestic and Divine (Juan Eduardo Campo) 458-462
Hūd (Paul M. Cobb) 462-464
Ḥudaybiya (Andrew Rippin) 464
Humor (Ulrich Marzolph) 464-465
Ḥunayn (Ingrid Mattson) 465-466
Hunting and Fishing (Herbert Eisenstein) 466-468
Hypocrites and Hypocrisy (Camilla P. Adang) 468-472

I

Iblīs (Andrew Rippin) 473
Iconoclasm (Daniel J. Sahas) 473-475
Idolatry and Idolaters (Gerald R. Hawting) 475-480
Idols and Images (Gerald R. Hawting) 481-484
Idrīs (Yoram Erder) 484-486
ʿIfrīt (Thomas Bauer) 486-487
Ignorance (William E. Shepard) 487-489
Īlāf (Uri Rubin) 489-491
Illegitimacy (Irene Schneider) 491-492
Illiteracy (Sebastian Günther) 492-500
ʿIlliyyūn (Frederik Leemhuis) 500-501
Illness and Health (Nasr Hamid Abu Zayd) 501-502

Imām (Imtiyaz Yusuf) 502-504
Immunity (Nadia Maria El-Cheikh) 504-505
Impeccability (Paul E. Walker) 505-507
Impotence (Rosalind W. Gwynne) 507-508
ʿImrān (Roberto Tottoli) 509
Indifference (A.H. Mathias Zahniser) 509-510
Infanticide (Donna Lee Bowen) 511-512
Informants (Claude Gilliot) 512-518
Inheritance (David Stephan Powers) 518-526
Inimitability (Richard G. Martin) 526-536
Innovation (Wael B. Hallaq) 536-537
Inquisition (John A. Nawas) 537-539
Insanity (Thomas Bauer) 539-541
Insolence and Obstinacy (Leah Kinberg) 541-543
Instruments (Doris Behrens-Abouseif) 543-547
Intellect (Navid Kermani) 547-549
Intention (Nasr Hamid Abu Zayd) 549-551
Intercession (Valerie J. Hoffman) 551-555
Intoxicants (Enes Karic) 555-557
Invitation (A.H. Mathias Zahniser) 557-558
Iram (Paul M. Cobb) 559
Iraq (Nadia Maria El-Cheikh) 559-561
Isaac (Reuven Firestone) 561-562
Isaiah (Andrew Rippin) 562-563
Ishmael (Reuven Firestone) 563-565
Islam (M. Arkoun) 565-571
Israel (Uri Rubin) 571-572

VOLUME THREE

J – O

Articles *Page numbers*

J

Jacob (Andrew Rippin) 1-2
Jerusalem (Heribert Busse) 2-7
Jesus (Neal Robinson) 7-21
Jews and Judaism (Uri Rubin) 21-34
Jibt (Khaled M. Abou El Fadl) 34-35
Jihād (Ella Landau-Tasseron) 35-43
Jinn (Jacqueline Chabbi) 43-50
Job (A.H. Johns) 50-51
John the Baptist (Andrew Rippin) 51-52
Jonah (Heribert Busse) 52-55
Joseph (S. Goldman) 55-57
Journey (Matthew S. Gordon) 57-59
Joy and Misery (Charles J. Adams) 59-64
Judgment (Arzina R. Lalani) 64-68
Jūdī (William M. Brinner) 68-69
Justice and Injustice (Jonathan E. Brockopp) 69-74

K

Kaʿba (Gerald R. Hawting) 75-80
Khadīja (Barbara Freyer Stowasser) 80-81
Khaḍir/Khiḍr (John Renard) 81-84
Khārijīs (Ersilia Francesca) 84-90
Kings and Rulers (Louise Marlow) 90-95
Kinship (Talal Asad) 95-100
Knowledge and Learning (Paul E. Walker) 100-104
Korah (Roberto Tottoli) 104-105

L

Lactation (Avner Giladi) 106-107
Lamp (Jamal J. Elias) 107-108
Language, Concept of (Pierre Larcher) 108-109
Language and Style of the Qurʾān (Claude Gilliot and Pierre Larcher) 109-135
Last Judgment (Isaac Hasson) 136-145
Laudation (Kathryn Kueny) 145-146
Laughter (Ludwig Ammann) 146-149
Law and the Qurʾān (Wael Hallaq) 149-172

Lawful and Unlawful (Joseph E. Lowry) 172-176
Left Hand and Right Hand (Isaac Hasson) 176-180
Lie (Daniel Beaumont) 180-181
Life (Ian Richard Netton) 182-185
Light (Jamal J. Elias) 186-188
Literacy (Sebastian Günther) 188-192
Literary Structures of the Qurʾān (Issa J. Boullata) 192-205
Literature and the Qurʾān (Wadad Kadi [al-Qāḍī] and Mustansir Mir) 205-227
Load or Burden (Patrick D. Gaffney) 227-229
Lord (Simonetta Calderini) 229-231
Lot (Heribert Busse) 231-233
Love and Affection (Denis Gril) 233-237
Loyalty (Ebrahim Moosa) 237-242
Luqmān (A.H.M. Zahniser) 242-243

M

Magians (William R. Darrow) 244-245
Magic (Gabriel Mandel Khān) 245-252
Maintenance and Upkeep (Christopher Melchert) 252
Manual Labor (Ingrid Mattson) 253-254
Manuscripts of the Qurʾān (François Déroche) 254-275
Markets (Ronald Paul Buckley) 275-276
Marriage and Divorce (Harald Motzki) 276-281
Martyrs (Wim Raven) 281-287
Marvels (Alice C. Hunsberger) 287-288
Mary (Barbara Freyer Stowasser) 288-296
Material Culture and the Qurʾān (Priscilla P. Soucek) 296-330
Maturity (Charles J. Adams) 330-332
Measurement (Said S. Said) 332-337
Mecca (J. Chabbi) 337-341
Media and the Qurʾān (Charles Hirschkind) 341-349
Medicine and the Qurʾān (Irmeli Perho) 349-367
Medina (Marco Schöller) 367-371
Memory (Michael A. Sells) 372-374
Men of the Cave (Roberto Tottoli) 374-375
Menstruation (Marion Holmes Katz) 375-377
Mercy (Daniel C. Peterson) 377-380
Messenger (A.H. Mathias Zahniser) 380-383
Metals and Minerals (Gérard Troupeau) 383-384
Metaphor (Peter Heath) 384-388
Michael (Gisela Webb) 388-389
Midian (Reuven Firestone) 389-391
Milk (David Waines) 391-392
Miracles (Denis Gril) 392-399
Mockery (Ludwig Ammann) 400-401
Moderation (Frank Griffel) 401-403

Modesty (Shiu-Sian Angel Hsu) 403-405
Monasticism and Monks (Sidney H. Griffith) 405-408
Money (Stuart D. Sears) 408-409
Months (Alexander Knysh) 409-414
Moon (Daniel Martin Varisco) 414-416
Morning (Lutz Wiederhold) 416-419
Moses (Cornelia Schöck) 419-426
Mosque (Jonathan M. Bloom) 426-438
Mosque of the Dissension (Claude Gilliot) 438-440
Muḥammad (Uri Rubin) 440-458
Murder (Mohammad Fadel) 458-460
Musaylima (M.J. Kister) 460-463
Muṣḥaf (Harald Motzki) 463-466
Muʿtazila (Sabine Schmidtke) 466-471
Mysterious Letters (Keith Massey) 471-477
Myths and Legends in the Qurʾān (Angelika Neuwirth) 477-497

N

Naḍīr (Banū al-) (Marco Schöller) 498-499
Najrān (Irfan A. Shahid) 500-501
Names of the Prophet (Jean-Louis Déclais) 501-505
Names of the Qurʾān (Mustansir Mir) 505-515
Nāmūs (Harald Motzki) 515-516
Narratives (Claude Gilliot) 516-528
Nature as Signs (Ian Richard Netton) 528-536
News (Khalid Yahya Blankinship) 536-537
Night of Power (Roxanne D. Marcotte) 537-539
Nimrod (Heribert Busse) 539-540
Noah (William M. Brinner) 540-543
Nomads (Ernst Axel Knauf) 543-545
Noon (Ilai Alon) 545-548
Nudity (Marion Holmes Katz) 548-549
Numbers and Enumeration (Andrew Rippin) 549-554
Numerology (Daniel Martin Varisco) 554-555
Numismatics (Michael L. Bates) 555-560

O

Oaths (G.R. Hawting) 561-566
Obedience (Khalid Yahya Blankinship) 566-569
Occasions of Revelation (Andrew Rippin) 569-573
Odors and Smells (Manuela Marín) 573-574
Oft-Repeated (Uri Rubin) 574-576
Opposition to Muḥammad (Marco Schöller) 576-580
Oppressed on Earth, The (Muhammad Qasim Zaman) 580-583
Oppression (N. Abu Zayd) 583-584
Orality (William A. Graham) 584-587

VOLUME FOUR

P – Sh

Articles *Page numbers*

P

Pairs and Pairing (Sabine Schmidtke) 1-9
Parable (A.H. Mathias Zahniser) 9-12
Paradise (Leah Kinberg) 12-20
Parents (Avner Giladi) 20-22
Parody of the Qurʾān (Issa J. Boullata) 22-24
Parties and Factions (Gerald R. Hawting) 24-27
Path or Way (Dmitry V. Frolov) 28-31
Patriarchy (Mohammed A. Bamyeh) 31-33
Peace (Earle H. Waugh) 33-35
People of the Book (M. Sharon) 36-43
People of the Ditch (Roberto Tottoli) 43-44
People of the Elephant (Irfan Shahīd) 44-46
People of the Heights (William M. Brinner) 46-48
People of the House (M. Sharon) 48-53
People of the Thicket (John Nawas) 53-55
Persian Literature and the Qurʾān (Franklin Lewis) 55-66
Pharaoh (Reuven Firestone) 66-68
Philosophy and the Qurʾān (Majid Fakhry) 68-90
Piety (Leah Kinberg) 90-91
Pilgrimage (Gerald Hawting) 91-100
Pit (Devin J. Stewart) 100-104
Place of Abraham (Robert Schick) 104-105
Plagues (Shari L. Lowin) 105-106
Planets and Stars (Paul Kunitzsch) 106-109
Pledge (Brannon M. Wheeler) 109-110
Poetry and Poets (Alan Jones) 110-114
Polemic and Polemical Language (Kate Zebiri) 114-125
Politics and the Qurʾān (Paul L. Heck) 125-151
Poll Tax (Paul L. Heck) 151-155
Polysemy in the Qurʾān (Herbert Berg) 155-158
Polytheism and Atheism (Mustansir Mir) 158-162
Popular and Talismanic Uses of the Qurʾān (Kathleen Malone O'Connor) 163-182
Portents (Kathryn Kueny) 182-184
Possession and Possessions (Alexander D. Knysh) 184-187
Post-Enlightenment Academic Study of the Qurʾān (Marco Schöller) 187-208
Poverty and the Poor (Michael Bonner) 208-210
Power and Impotence (Alexander D. Knysh) 210-213
Praise (Clare E. Wilde) 213-215
Prayer (Gerhard Böwering) 215-231
Prayer Formulas (Jean-Yves L'Hôpital) 231-235
Pre-1800 Preoccupations of Qurʾānic Studies (Hartmut Bobzin) 235-253

Pre-Islamic Arabia and the Qurʾān (Gerald R. Hawting) 253-261
Preserved Tablet (Daniel A. Madigan) 261-263
Pride (Maurice Borrmans) 263-264
Printing of the Qurʾān (Michael W. Albin) 264-276
Prisoners (Jonathan E. Brockopp) 276-278
Profane and Sacred (Lutz Wiederhold) 278-284
Prohibited Degrees (Bernard Weiss) 284-286
Proof (Mark N. Swanson) 286-287
Property (Sherman A. Jackson) 287-289
Prophets and Prophethood (Uri Rubin) 289-307
Protection (Robert Schick) 307-308
Provocation (Matthias Radscheit) 308-314
Psalms (Arie Schippers) 314-318
Punishment Stories (David Marshall) 318-322

Q

Qaynuqāʿ (Banū) (Marco Schöller) 323-325
Qibla (Richard Kimber) 325-328
Quraysh (Uri Rubin) 329-333
Qurayẓa (Banū al-) (Marco Schöller) 333-335

R

Races (Uri Rubin) 336-337
Ramaḍān (Angelika Neuwirth) 338-348
Ranks and Orders (Nargis Virani) 348-350
Raqīm (Roberto Tottoli) 351-352
Rass (Roberto Tottoli) 352-353
Readings of the Qurʾān (Frederik Leemhuis) 353-363
Rebellion (Khaled Abou El Fadl) 363-367
Recitation of the Qurʾān (Anna M. Gade) 367-385
Reciters of the Qurʾān (Christopher Melchert and Asma Afsaruddin) 386-393
Reflection and Deliberation (Angelika Brodersen) 393-394
Religion (Patrice C. Brodeur) 395-398
Religious Pluralism and the Qurʾān (Clare Wilde and Jane Dammen McAuliffe) 398-419
Remembrance (Angelika Brodersen) 419-424
Remnant (Uri Rubin) 425
Repentance and Penance (Uri Rubin) 426-430
Responsibility (Matthias Radscheit) 430-434
Resurrection (Maurice Borrmans) 434-435
Retaliation (Khaled Abou El Fadl) 436-437
Revelation and Inspiration (Daniel A. Madigan) 437-448
Revision and Alteration (Shari Lowin) 448-451
Reward and Punishment (Wim Raven) 451-461
Rhetoric and the Qurʾān (Angelika Neuwirth) 461-476
Rhymed Prose (Devin J. Stewart) 476-484
Ritual and the Qurʾān (Josef W. Meri) 484-498
Ritual Purity (Joseph E. Lowry) 498-508
Rod (Zeki Saritoprak) 508-509

S

Sabbath (Andrew Rippin) 510-511
Sabians (François de Blois) 511-513
Sacred Precincts (Uri Rubin) 513-516
Sacrifice (Reuven Firestone) 516-518
Ṣafā and Marwa (Reuven Firestone) 518-520
Saint (B. Radtke) 520-521
Ṣāliḥ (Roberto Tottoli) 521-522
Salvation (Maurice Borrmans) 522-524
Samaritans (Paul Stenhouse) 524-525
Samson (Liyakat Takim) 525-526
Samuel (Philip F. Kennedy) 526-530
Sand (Zeki Saritoprak) 530-531
Satanic Verses (Shahab Ahmed) 531-536
Saul (Liyakat Takim) 536-537
Scholar (Louise Marlow) 537-540
Science and the Qurʾān (Ahmad Dallal) 540-558
Scripture and the Qurʾān (William A. Graham) 558-569
Scrolls (Paul L. Heck) 569-571
Seasons (Nico J.G. Kaptein) 571-572
Secrets (Shigeru Kamada) 572-573
Seeing and Hearing (Andrew Rippin) 573-576
Servants (Jonathan E. Brockopp) 576-580
Sex and Sexuality (Devin J. Stewart) 580-585
Sheba (Valérie Gonzalez) 585-587
Sheets (Beatrice Gruendler) 587-589
Shekhinah (Reuven Firestone) 589-591
Shīʿa (Arzina R. Lalani) 591-592
Shīʿism and the Qurʾān (Meir M. Bar-Asher) 593-604
Ships (Irfan A. Shahīd) 604-605
Shuʿayb (Roberto Tottoli) 605-606

VOLUME FIVE

Si – Z

Articles *Page numbers*

S (continued)

Ṣiffīn, Battle of (Maria Massi Dakake) 1-2
Signs (Binyamin Abrahamov) 2-11
Silk (V. Gonzalez) 11-13
Simile (Daniel Beaumont) 13-18
Sin, Major and Minor (Muhammad Qasim Zaman) 19-28
Sinai (Irfan Shahīd) 28-29
Sīra and the Qurʾān (Wim Raven) 29-51
Sirius (Bassel A. Reyahi) 51-53
Sister (Margot Badran) 53-54
Slaughter (Ersilia Francesca) 54-56
Slaves and Slavery (Jonathan E. Brockopp) 56-60
Sleep (Roberto Tottoli) 60-62
Smell (Devin J. Stewart) 62-64
Smoke (Heidi Toelle) 64-65
Social Sciences and the Qurʾān (Dale F. Eickelman) 65-76
Solomon (Priscilla Soucek) 76-78
Soothsayer (Devin J. Stewart) 78-80
Soul (Th. Emil Homerin) 80-84
South Arabia, Religions in Pre-Islamic (Christian Julien Robin) 84-94
South Asian Literatures and the Qurʾān (Ali S. Asani) 94-98
Southeast Asian Qurʾānic Literature (R. Michael Feener) 98-102
Sovereignty (Bustami Khir) 102-104
Spatial Relations (Angelika Neuwirth) 104-108
Speech (Margaretha T. Heemskerk) 108-112
Spider (Herbert Eisenstein) 112-114
Spirit (Michael Sells) 114-117
Spiritual Beings (Stefania Cunial) 117-121
Springs and Fountains (Matthias Radscheit) 121-128
Stone (Dmitry V. Frolov) 128-129
Stoning (Dmitry V. Frolov) 129-130
Strangers and Foreigners (Ahmet T. Karamustafa) 131-132
Suffering (Margaretha T. Heemskerk) 132-136
Ṣūfism and the Qurʾān (Alexander D. Knysh) 137-159
Suicide (Ahmet T. Karamustafa) 159-162
Sun (Paul Kunitzsch) 162-163
Sunna (G.H.A. Juynboll) 163-166
Sūra(s) (Angelika Neuwirth) 166-177
Suspicion (Lutz Wiederhold) 177-178

Sustenance (David Waines) 178-180
Symbolic Imagery (Frederick S. Colby) 180-184
Syria (Irfan Shahīd) 184-187

T

Table (Matthias Radscheit) 188-191
Talent (Marcia Hermansen) 191-192
Taxation (Paul L. Heck) 192-200
Teaching (Sebastian Günther) 200-205
Teaching and Preaching the Qurʾān (Nelly van Doorn-Harder) 205-231
Teeth (Devin J. Stewart) 231-232
Temporary Marriage (Shahla Haeri) 232-234
Tents and Tent Pegs (Ute Pietruschka) 234-237
Textual Criticism of the Qurʾān (James A. Bellamy) 237-252
Thamūd (Reuven Firestone) 252-254
Theft (Joseph E. Lowry) 254-256
Theology and the Qurʾān (T. Nagel) 256-275
Theophany (Mustansir Mir) 275-276
Throne of God (Jamal J. Elias) 276-278
Time (G. Böwering) 278-290
Tolerance and Coercion (Yohanan Friedmann) 290-294
Tools for the Scholarly Study of the Qurʾān (Andrew Rippin) 294-300
Torah (Camilla P. Adang) 300-311
Trade and Commerce (Andrew Rippin) 311-316
Tradition and Custom (G.R. Hawting) 316-318
Traditional Disciplines of Qurʾānic Studies (Claude Gilliot) 318-339
Transitoriness (David Marshall) 339-340
Translations of the Qurʾān (Hartmut Bobzin) 340-358
Tree(s) (David Waines) 358-362
Trial (John Nawas) 362-363
Tribes and Clans (Ella Landau-Tasseron) 363-368
Trinity (David Thomas) 368-372
Trips and Voyages (Shawkat M. Toorawa) 372-376
Troops (Matthew S. Gordon) 376-378
Trust and Patience (Scott C. Alexander) 378-385
Truth (David B. Burrell) 385-389
Tubbaʿ (Reuven Firestone) 389-390
Turkish Literature and the Qurʾān (Kemal Silay) 390-395
Ṭuwā (William M. Brinner) 395-396

U

[al-]Ukhdūd (Christian Julien Robin) 397-398
Ummī (Sebastian Günther) 399-403
Uncertainty (Michael B. Schub) 403-405
Unity of the Text of the Qurʾān (Mustansir Mir) 405-406
Usury (Masudul Alam Choudhury) 406-408
ʿUthmān (Gabriel Said Reynolds) 408-410

V

Vehicles (Uri Rubin) 411-412
Veil (Mona Siddiqui) 412-416
Vengeance (Joseph Ginat) 416-419
Verse(s) (Angelika Neuwirth) 419-429
Victory (Matthew S. Gordon) 429-430
Vigil (K. Wagtendonk) 430-432
Violence (M. Arkoun) 432-433
Virtue (David Johnston) 433-436
Virtues and Vices, Commanding and Forbidding (Michael Cook) 436-443
Vision (Amila Buturovic) 443-445
Vision and Blindness (S. Kugle) 445-448
Visiting (R. Kevin Jaques) 448-449
Vow (Paul L. Heck) 449-451

W

Wahhabism and the Qurʾān (Natana J. DeLong-Bas) 452-453
Waiting Period (Harald Motzki) 453-455
War (Patricia Crone) 455-459
Warner (Chase F. Robinson) 459-461
Water (Anthony H. Johns) 461-466
Water of Paradise (Amira El-Zein) 466-467
Wealth (Michael Bonner) 467-470
Weather (David Waines) 470-471
Weeping (Paolo Branca) 471-472
Weights and Measures (Stephan Dähne) 472-476
Wet-Nursing (Avner Giladi) 476-478
Whisper (Jacqueline Chabbi) 478-480
Widow (Mona Siddiqui) 480-481
Wine (Kathryn Kueny) 481-483
Wisdom (Bernd Radtke) 483-484
Wish and Desire (Amila Buturovic) 484-488
Witness to Faith (Andrew Rippin) 488-491
Witnessing and Testifying (Matthias Radscheit) 492-506
Wives of the Prophet (Barbara Freyer Stowasser) 506-521
Womb (Marcia Hermansen) 522-523
Women and the Qurʾān (Ruth Roded) 523-541
Word of God (Matthias Radscheit) 541-548
Work (Ingrid Mattson) 548-551
World (Binyamin Abrahamov) 551-554
Worship (G.R. Hawting) 555-557
Writing and Writing Materials (Sheila S. Blair) 558-559

Y

Year (Robert G. Morrison) 560-561
Yemen (Christian Julien Robin) 561-569
Youth and Old Age (R. Gwynne) 569-570

Z

INDEX OF PROPER NAMES[1]

A

Aaron [Hārūn] I **1a**, 1b, 2a, 159a, 245b, 260a, 260b, 261a, 261b, 274a, 275b, 276a, 304b, 486b, 518b, 532b, 534a, 536b, 537a; II 10a, 199a, 341b, 509a, 509b, 542a; III 29a, 50a, 105a, 112a, 113b, 186b, 229b, 421b, 422a, 423b, 444b, 498a, 518b, 519b, 521a, 522a, 525b, 540b, 567b; IV 20a, 34a, 67a, 223b, 224a, 291a, 294a, 319b, 425b, 438b, 483a, 536a, 536b, 577a, 590a; V 54a, 155b, 300b, 396a, 524b
ʿAbbād b. Sulaymān (d. 250/864) III 468b
[Shāh] ʿAbbās III 433b
al-ʿAbbās (uncle of the Prophet) II 20b, 21a, 554a; III 581b; IV 51a; V 44a
[Khedive] ʿAbbās I (r. 1848-54) IV 270b
ʿAbbās b. ʿAbd al-Muṭṭalib V 47a
ʿAbbās Shafīʿ IV 266b

[1] Due to their frequency of occurrence in the *EQ*, the following are only selectively indexed: God, Islam, Muḥammad, Muslim, Qurʾān.

ʿAbbāsid(s) I 125b, 126b; II 34b, 560a, 560b; III 86a, 301a, 301b, 310a, 321b, 423b, 430b, 557a, 558a, 594a; IV 50b, 51a, 142a, 143a, 333a, 364a, 364b, 524b, 598b; V 137a, 503b
Abbott, N. I 136a, 280a, 280b; III 256b, 298a
ʿAbd al-ʿĀṭī, H. IV 397b, 398a, 398b
ʿAbd al-ʿAzīz (Ottoman sultan) IV 273b
ʿAbd al-ʿAzīz b. ʿAbdallāh, ʿUmar (d. 66/685–6) II 29a, 29b; III 556a
ʿAbd al-ʿAzīz Ismāʿīl II 130b
ʿAbd al-Bāqī, M.F. II 377a, 377b; V 296a, 296b
ʿAbd al-Bāqī Ḥaddād III 324b
[Shaykh] ʿAbd al-Bāqī al-Jarī IV 271a
ʿAbd al-Basīṭ ʿAbd al-Ṣamad (Qurʾān reciter) III 345a; IV 381b, 392a
[Banū] ʿAbd al-Dār II 514b
ʿAbd al-Fattāḥ al-Qāḍī IV 272a
ʿAbd al-Ghaffār Sulaymān al-Bundārī II 377b
ʿAbd al-Ḥamīd (or Ḥumayd; d. 249/863) II 110b; V 319a
ʿAbd al-Ḥamīd II IV 267a
ʿAbd al-Ḥamīd b. Bādīs II 129a, 130b
ʿAbd al-Ḥamīd al-Kātib (d. 132/750) III 215a, 217a
ʿAbd al-Ḥaqq al-Islāmī V 305a
ʿAbd al-Ḥaqq Shīrāz Amānat Khān III 324a
ʿAbd al-Ḥayy IV 266a
ʿAbd al-Jabbār b. Aḥmad al-Asadābād al-Qāḍī al-Hamadhānī (d. 414–15/1025) I 117b, 118b, 267b, 470a, 470b, 484b; II 114b, 115b, 532a, 533a, 534a, 534b, 535a, 535b; III 396b, 468b, 469b, 470b, 471a; IV 123a; V 111b, 135b
ʿAbd al-Karīm b. ʿAjarrad (fl. second/eighth cent.) III 86b
ʿAbd al-Karīm al-Jīlī (d. ca. 832/1428) II 119b
ʿAbd al-Karīm al-Qushayrī see al-Qushayrī, Abū l-Qāsim ʿAbd al-Karīm b. Hawāzin (d. 465/1072)
ʿAbd al-Khāliq IV 266b
ʿAbd al-Laṭīf al-Baghdādī see al-Baghdādī, ʿAbd al-Laṭīf (d. 629/1231)
ʿAbd al-Malik see ʿAbd al-Malik b. Marwān, Umayyad caliph (r. 65/685–86/705)
ʿAbd al-Malik b. ʿAbd al-ʿAzīz b. Jurayj (d. 150/767) II 388a, 388b; IV 533a
ʿAbd al-Malik b. Ḥabīb see Ibn Ḥabīb, ʿAbd al-Malik (d. 238/853)

ʿAbd al-Malik b. Hishām see Ibn Hishām, ʿAbd al-Malik (d. 218/833)
ʿAbd al-Malik b. Jurayj see Ibn Jurayj, ʿAbd al-Malik (d. 150/767)
ʿAbd al-Malik b. Marwān (r. 65-86/685-705) I 125a, 126a, 126b, 131a, 139b, 156b, 169b, 279a; II 30a, 30b, 34a, 268a; III 142b, 258b, 298b, 299a, 299b, 429b, 465a, 556a, 559b; IV 73a, 386b; V 31b, 32a, 166b, 185b, 186a, 502b, 503a, 503b, 504a
ʿAbd al-Malik b. ʿUmayr (d. 136/754) II 395a
ʿAbd al-Malik Mujāhid IV 273b
ʿAbd Manāf I 290b; II 296b, 490a, 577b
ʿAbd Manāt IV 577b
ʿAbd al-Masīḥ al-Kindī see al-Kindī, ʿAbd al-Masīḥ
ʿAbd al-Muʾmin (Almohad ruler; d. 558/1163) I 174a; III 303b, 307b
Abd al-Muʾmin Ṣafī al-Dīn al-Urmawī (d. 693/1294) IV 381a
ʿAbd al-Muṭṭalib (grandfather of the Prophet) II 19b, 466a; III 119b; IV 45a, 51b, 329b; V 122b, 508b
[Shāh] ʿAbd al-Qādir (d. 1813) III 223b; V 341b
ʿAbd al-Qādir al-Jīlānī see al-Jīlānī, ʿAbd al-Qādir (d. 561/1166)
ʿAbd al-Qāhir al-Baghdādī see al-Baghdādī, ʿAbd al-Qāhir (d. 429/1037)
ʿAbd al-Qāhir al-Jurjānī see al-Jurjānī, ʿAbd al-Qāhir (d. 471/1078)
ʿAbd Rabbih III 523a
ʿAbd al-Raḥmān, ʿĀʾisha (Bint al-Shāṭiʾ) II 125b, 132b, 133b, 291b, 535b; V 521a, 537a, 537b
ʿAbd al-Raḥmān b.ʿAlī b. al-Jawzī see Ibn al-Jawzī, ʿAbd al-Raḥmān b. ʿAlī (d. 597/1200)
ʿAbd al-Raḥmān b. al-Aswad IV 96a
ʿAbd al-Raḥmān b. ʿAwf I 389a
ʿAbd al-Raḥmān al-Bisṭāmī III 316b
Abd al-Rahman Ibrahima (d. 1829) I 30a
ʿAbd al-Raḥmān Jāmī (d. 898-9/1492) III 223b
ʿAbd al-Raḥmān al-Rāzī V 336a
ʿAbd al-Raḥmān al-Saʿdī see al-Saʿdī, ʿAbd al-Raḥmān
ʿAbd al-Raḥmān al-Suddī see al-Suddī al-Kabīr, ʿAbd al-Raḥmān (d. 127-8/745-7)
ʿAbd al-Raḥmān b. Zayd b. Aslam (d. 182/798) II 407b
ʿAbd al-Raʾūf Singkeli V 98a, 98b
ʿAbd al-Rāziq IV 148b, 149a

ʿAbd al-Razzāq b. Hammām al-Ṣanʿānī (d. 211/827) i 399a, 528a; ii 107a, 377b, 389b, 390b, 400a, 408a; iii 283a;
ʿAbd al-Razzāq Kamāl al-Dīn al-Qāshānī see al-Qāshānī, ʿAbd al-Razzāq Kamāl al-Dīn (d. 730-1/1329-30)
ʿAbd al-Razzāq Nawfal ii 130b
ʿAbd al-Razzāq al-Sanhūrī i 434b
[Shaykh] ʿAbd al-Ṣabūr Shāhīn ii 136b
ʿAbd al-Salām Badayūnī v 342a
ʿAbd al-Salām Faraj see Faraj, ʿAbd al-Salām (d. 1982)
ʿAbd al-Ṣamad iii 345a; iv 381b
[Banū] ʿAbd al-Shams i 290b; ii 513b; iii 339b, 422a, 461a; iv 577b; v 508b
ʿAbd al-ʿUzzā b. ʿAbd al-Muṭṭalib see Abū Lahab
ʿAbd al-ʿUzzā b. Qatan i 110b; iv 577b
ʿAbd al-Wahhāb (vocalist) iv 381b
ʿAbd Yaghūth v 92a
ʿAbdallāh (father of the Prophet) ii 317a; iii 110b, 283a, 283b
ʿAbdallāh b. al-ʿAbbās see Ibn (al-)ʿAbbās, ʿAbdallāh (d. 68-9/686-7)
ʿAbdallāh b. ʿAbbās (d. 98/716-17) ii 17b, 18a, 183a
ʿAbdallāh b. ʿAbd al-Raḥmān al-Dārimī see al-Dārimī, ʿAbdallāh b. ʿAbd al-Raḥmān (d. 255/869)
ʿAbdallāh b. Aḥmad (d. 290/903) i 481b; ii 110b
ʿAbdallāh b. Aḥmad b. Dhakwān see Ibn Dhakwān, ʿAbdallāh b. Aḥmad (d. 242/857)
ʿAbdallāh b. ʿAlī iii 423b
ʿAbdallāh b. ʿĀmir (118/736) see Ibn ʿĀmir, ʿAbdallāh
ʿAbdallāh b. ʿAmr al-ʿĀṣ (d. 63/682) iv 570b, 588a; v 307b
ʿAbdallāh b. ʿAṭūs i 284b
ʿAbdallāh b. Bisṭam i 78a
ʿAbdallāh b. Ibāḍ see Ibn Ibāḍ, ʿAbdallāh
ʿAbdallāh b. Ismāʿīl al-Hāshimī ii 531a; iv 236a
ʿAbdallāh b. Jaʿfar iii 131b
ʿAbdallāh b. Kathīr al-Dārī see Ibn Kathīr al-Dārī, ʿAbdallāh (d. 120/738)
ʿAbdallāh b. Kullāb (d. 240/854) i 470b, 471a
ʿAbdallāh b. Masʿūd see Ibn Masʿūd
ʿAbdallāh b. Muʿāwiya (r. 129/746-7) iii 557a
ʿAbdallāh b. al-Mubārak see Ibn al-Mubārak, ʿAbdallāh (d. 181/797)
ʿAbdallāh b. al-Muqaffaʿ (d. 139/756) iv 73b
ʿAbdallāh b. Rawāḥa (d. 8/629) iii 215b
ʿAbdallāh b. Sabaʾ iii 33a
ʿAbdallāh b. Salām see Ibn Salām, ʿAbdallāh

ʿAbdallāh b. al-Shikhkhīr v 471b
ʿAbdallāh b. Thābit al-Tawwazī see al-Tawwazī, ʿAbdallāh b. Thābit (d. 308/920)
ʿAbdallāh b. ʿUbayd b. ʿUmayr iii 408b
ʿAbdallāh b. Ubayy see Ibn Ubayy b. Salūl, ʿAbdallāh
ʿAbdallāh b. ʿUmar see Ibn ʿUmar, ʿAbdallah (d. 73/693)
ʿAbdallāh b. Wahb see Ibn Wahb, ʿAbdallāh (d. 197/813)
ʿAbdallāh b. Yaḥyā b. Kunāsa (d. 207/822) iii 215a
ʿAbdallāh b. Yazīd al-Fazārī iii 87b
ʿAbdallāh b. Zayd ii 241a
ʿAbdallāh b. al-Zubayr see Ibn al-Zubayr, ʿAbdallāh
ʿAbdallāh Anṣārī iv 62a
ʿAbdallāh al-Anṣārī al-Harawī see al-Anṣārī al-Harawī, ʿAbdallāh (d. 481/1089)
ʿAbdallāh al-Hāshimī iv 71b
ʿAbdallāh M. Shaḥāta see Shaḥāta, ʿAbdallāh M.
ʿAbdallāh Ṣayrafī iii 598b
ʿAbdallāh al-Ṭāhir al-Muṭahhar (son of the Prophet and Khadīja) v 507b
ʿAbdallāh al-Ṭayyib see al-Ṭayyib, ʿAbdallāh
ʿAbdallāh Yūsuf ʿAlī see Yūsuf ʿAlī, ʿA. (1872-1953)
Abḍuʿum v 90b
ʿAbdu l-Bahāʾ i 198a, 199a
ʿAbduh, Muḥammad (Grand Muftī of Egypt; d. 1324/1905) i 29a, 29b, 471a; ii 126a, 127b, 128a, 128b, 129a, 129b, 286b, 535b; iii 291b, 293b, 294b, 348b; iv 148b, 149b, 535a, 555a; v 10a, 56a, 99a, 206a, 217b, 228a, 442b, 536b, 537a
ʿAbdul ʿAzeem al-Matʿani iv 493a
Abdul Hamid, S.M. iv 274a
Abdul Majeed Azzindani see Azzindani, Abdul Majeed
Abdul Majid Daryabadi v 343b
Abdullah Gymnastiar, K.H. see Gymnastiar, A.
Abdulrazak, F. iv 267a, 267b, 271b
Abel [Hābīl] i 10a, 26b, 98b, 260a, 264a, **270a**, 270b, 271a, 271b, 439b, 533b; ii 436a; iii 190a, 459a, 459b, 521b; v 416b
Abibahath (wife of Tubbaʿ) v 390b
ʿAbīd ii 301a
ʿAbīd b. al-Abraṣ v 81b
Abīkarib Asʿad v 563a, 564a, 565b, 566b, 567b, 568a

Abou El Fadl, Kh. III **35b**; IV **367a**, **437b**
Abraha I **4a**, 4b, 5a, 20b, 98b, 155a; II 148a, 162a; III 518a; IV 45a, 46a, 257b, 258a, 329a, 329b, 531a; V 374a, 565b, 566a, 566b
Abraham [Ibrāhīm] I **5b**, 6a, 6b, 7a, 7b, 8a, 8b, 9a, 9b, 10a, 14b, 20b, 38b, 40a, 62a, 66b, 97a, 98a, 146a, 156a, 162b, 163b, 166a, 179b, 192a, 192b, 193a, 222a, 236b, 237a, 245b, 287a, 295b, 310a, 310b, 317b, 325a, 326b, 328a, 330a, 330b, 331a, 337b, 371b, 373a, 377b, 379b, 380b, 423b, 438a, 464b, 465b, 511a, 513a, 513b, 519a, 521b, 532a, 533a, 533b, 534a, 536b, 546b, 547a, 547b, 548a; II 23b, 24a, 31b, 33a, 43b, 71a, 73a, 84b, 118a, 145b, 163b, 164a, 174a, 179a, 197a, 198a, 199b, 204b, 205a, 205b, 211b, 212a, 218b, 228a, 240b, 241b, 259b, 260a, 273b, 279a, 295b, 298a, 304b, 311b, 324a, 329a, 335a, 339a, 372b, 402a, 402b, 403a, 408a, 412b, 414b, 434a, 436a, 439a, 447b, 449b, 455b, 458b, 474b, 476b, 480a, 481a, 481b, 483a, 489a, 497b, 501b, 502b, 503b, 504a, 509a, 553a, 558a, 561a, 561b, 562a, 563b, 564a, 564b, 569a, 569b; III 1a, 1b, 2a, 4b, 13a, 17a, 27b, 28a, 30b, 31a, 34a, 38a, 50a, 53a, 76b, 77a, 78a, 78b, 79b, 90b, 92b, 93a, 95a, 99b, 118a, 148a, 148b, 189b, 190a, 210b, 212a, 212b, 217a, 219a, 223a, 224b, 231b, 239a, 242a, 287a, 289b, 339b, 340b, 341a, 381a, 381b, 383b, 388b, 389b, 393a, 396a, 398a, 401b, 415a, 425b, 427a, 427b, 441a, 444b, 445b, 446a, 453b, 479b, 486a, 486b, 494a, 494b, 495a, 519b, 520a, 520b, 521a, 521b, 522a, 525b, 529b,

530b, 536b, 539a, 539b, 540a, 540b, 543b, 561b, 592b; IV 21a, 31b, 32b, 33a, 34a, 37a, 40a, 49a, 49b, 52b, 54b, 78a, 92a, 96a, 96b, 98a, 104b, 108b, 116a, 159b, 160a, 161a, 178b, 195b, 211a, 223a, 223b, 225a, 226b, 227a, 229a, 255a, 287a, 290a, 291a, 291b, 292a, 292b, 294a, 295a, 296b, 297b, 298a, 299a, 299b, 302a, 302b, 303a, 304a, 306a, 316b, 319b, 325b, 327a, 327b, 329b, 337a, 337b, 339b, 401a, 402a, 403a, 405a, 407a, 408a, 408b, 410b, 413a, 421b, 429a, 429b, 438b, 445a, 473b, 485b, 488a, 505b, 513b, 514a, 514b, 516a, 517b, 519a, 523b, 559b, 561a, 569b, 577a, 577b, 591a, 591b, 592a, 604b; V 45b, 63b, 68b, 95b, 108a, 109a, 109b, 130a, 130b, 132a, 133b, 171a, 171b, 179a, 186a, 242a, 248b, 249a, 256b, 257b, 258a, 258b, 259a, 259b, 260a, 261b, 262a, 262b, 263a, 263b, 264b, 268b, 269a, 269b, 270b, 273a, 301a, 302a, 304a, 317a, 363a, 373b, 374b, 390a, 423b, 444a, 444b, 483a, 497b, 534b, 545a, 551b, 555b, 570b, 574b

People of — III 583a

Place/Station of [*maqām ibrāhīm*] — I 7b, 9a; II 295b, 458b; IV **104a**, 104b, 105a, 218a, 514a

Abrahamian, E. — III 582b

Abrahamov, B. — V **11a**, **554b**

Absalom — I 496a; IV 316a

Abū l-ʿAbbās al-Būnī — see al-Būnī, Abū l-ʿAbbās (d. 622/1225)

Abū l-ʿAbbās al-Ḥasan b. Saʿīd b. Jaʿfar al-Muṭawwiʿa al-Baṣrī (d. 371/981) — IV 360a, 360b

Abū l-ʿAbbās al-Mahdawī — V 332a

Abū ʿAbd al-Raḥmān al-Sulamī — see al-Sulamī, Abū ʿAbd al-Raḥmān (d. 412/1021)

Abū ʿAbdallāh Jābir b. Ḥayyān — III 250b

Abū ʿAbdallāh Muḥammad b. Yūsuf al-Sanūsī	see al-Sanūsī, Abū ʿAbdallāh Muḥammad b. Yūsuf
Abū ʿAbdallāh Muḥammad b. Zayd al-Wāsiṭī (d. 307/918-19)	II 533a
Abū ʿAbdallāh al-Qurṭubī	see al-Qurṭubī, Abū ʿAbdallāh Muḥammad b. Aḥmad (d. 671/1272)
Abū ʿAbdallāh al-Tamīmī	V 334b
Abū l-ʿAlāʾ al-Maʿarrī	see al-Maʿarrī, Abū l-ʿAlāʾ (d. 449/1057)
Abū l-ʿAlāʾ al-Mawdūdī	see al-Mawdūdī, Sayyid Abū l-ʿAlāʾ
Abū l-ʿAlāʾ al-Ṭabrisī	III 470b
Abū ʿAlī b. al-Ḥusayn al-Masʿūdī	see al-Masʿūdī, Abū ʿAlī b. al-Ḥusayn
Abū ʿAlī al-Fārisī	see al-Fārisī, Abū ʿAlī (d. 377/987)
Abū ʿAlī Ḥasan b. ʿAlī al-Baṣrī	see Japheth b. Eli
Abū ʿAlī b. Sīnā	see Ibn Sīnā (Avicenna; d. 428/1037)
Abū ʿAlī al-Jubbāʾī	see al-Jubbāʾī, Abū ʿAlī (d. 303/915)
Abū l-ʿĀliya al-Riyāḥī (Rufayʿ b. Mihrān; d. 93/711)	II 103a; IV 533a; V 440a
Abū ʿĀmir (opponent of Muḥammad)	III 438b, 439a
Abū ʿĀmir al-Faḍl b. Ismāʿīl al-Tamīmī al-Jurjānī (d. after 458/1066)	V 326a
Abū ʿAmr ʿAbdallāh b. Aḥmad b. Bishr b. Dhakwān	see Ibn Dhakwān, ʿAbdallāh b. Aḥmad (d. 242/857)
Abū ʿAmr al-Dānī	see al-Dānī, Abū ʿAmr (d. 444/1053)
Abū ʿAmr Ḥafṣ b. Sulaymān b. al-Mughīra (d. 180/796)	IV 359b
Abū ʿAmr Ḥafṣ b. ʿUmār b. ʿAbd al-ʿAzīz (d. ca. 246/291)	IV 359b
Abū ʿAmr al-Hudhalī	I 530a
Abū ʿAmr Muḥammad b. ʿAbd al-Raḥmān (d. 280/893 or 291/904)	IV 359b
Abū ʿAmr Zabbān b. al-ʿAlā (Baṣra, d. 154/770-1)	II 348b, 349b, 355a, 356b, 357a, 359a, 360b, 363b; III 120b, 124a, 605b, 606a; IV 356a, 356b, 357a, 357b, 359b, 360a, 360b, 361a 372a, 373a, 389a, 389b; V 239b
Abū l-Aswad al-Duʾalī or al-Dīlī (d. 69/688)	I 140b; III 259b, 605b
Abū l-ʿAtāhiya (d. 211/826)	IV 317b
Abū ʿAttāb ʿAbdallāh	III 530b
Abū ʿAwāna al-Waḍḍāḥ b. ʿAbdallāh (d. 175/791)	II 388a
Abū Ayyūb Sulaymān b. Ayyūb b. al-Ḥakam al-Baghdādī (d. 235/849)	IV 360a

Abū Bakr (r. 11-13/632-4) — i 18a, **20a** 57a, 67a, 121a, 121b, 189b, 209b, 267a, 278a, 293b, 332a, 332b, 333a, 355a, 355b, 358a, 358b, 359a, 360b, 387b, 388b, 389a, 398a, 405b, 408a, 462a, 518a, 540b; ii 12a, 20a, 147b, 148a, 183a, 205b, 214b, 282a, 382b, 383b, 384a, 384a, 384b, 396a, 398b, 514b, 530a, 555a; iii 85a, 152b, 153a; 179b, 456a, 457a, 462a, 462b, 464b, 465a, 605a; iv 22b, 63b, 97b, 125b, 134b, 240a, 339b, 387a, 599a; v 59a, 113b, 197a, 334a, 376a, 404b, 409a, 409b, 471b, 517a, 520a

Abū Bakr (Ṣandal) — iii 600b, 601b

Abū Bakr Aḥmad b. ʿAbdallāh al-Ghaznawī — i 282a

Abū Bakr Aḥmad b. ʿAlī al-Ikhshīdh — see Ibn Ikhshīdh (d. ca. 320/932)

Abū Bakr al-Anbārī (d. 328/940) — ii 109b

Abū Bakr al-Aṣamm — see al-Aṣamm, Abū Bakr (d. 200/817)

Abū Bakr ʿAtīq b. Muḥammad al-Sūrābādī (d. 494/1101) — v 325b

Abū Bakr b. Abī Shayba (d. 235/849) — ii 377b

Abū Bakr b. al-ʿArabī — see Ibn al-ʿArabī, Muḥammad b. ʿAbdallāh Abū Bakr (d. 543/1148)

Abū Bakr b. Mihrān (d. 381/991) — v 332a

Abū Bakr b. Mujāhid — see Ibn Mujāhid, Abū Bakr (d. 324/936)

Abū Bakr b. al-Mundhir — see Ibn al-Mundhir, Abū Bakr (d. 318/930)

Abū Bakr al-Bāqillānī — see al-Bāqillānī, Abū Bakr Muḥammad b. al-Ṭayyib (d. 403/1012-3)

Abu Bakr Gumi — i 33a

Abū Bakr al-Khallāl — see al-Khallāl, Abū Bakr (d. 311/922)

Abū Bakr Muḥammad b. Ibrāhīm b. al-Mundhir al-Mundhirī al-Nīshābūrī — see Ibn al-Mundhir al-Mundhirī al-Nīshābūrī, ʿAbū Bakr Muḥammad b. Ibrāhīm (d. 318/930)

Abū Bakr al-Rāzī — see al-Rāzī, Abū Bakr (d. 313/925)

Abū Bakr al-Shiblī — see al-Shiblī, Abū Bakr (d. 334/946)

Abū Bakr Shuʿba b. ʿAyyāsh b. Sālim (d. 193/809) — iv 359b, 390a

Abū Bakr al-Sijistānī — see al-Sijistānī, Ibn Abū Dāwūd (d. 316/929)
Abū Bakr al-Wāsiṭī (d. 320/932) — see al-Wāsiṭī, Abū Bakr (d. 320/932)
Abū l-Baqāʾ al-ʿUkbarī (d. 616/1219) — II 109b; V 333a
Abū l-Barakāt al-Nasafī (d. 710/1310) — I 484a; II 112b
Abū Bilāl Mirdās b. Udayya al-Tamīmī — III 86b
Abū l-Dardāʾ — III 352a
Abū Dāwūd Sulaymān b. al-Ashʿath al-Sijistānī (d. 275/889) — I 389a, 391b; II 22b, 270b, 334a, 377a, 387a, 389b; III 391b; IV 370a, 371a, 379a, 423a
Abū Dāwūd al-Ṭayālisī (d. 203-4/819-20) — II 377b
Abu Dhabi — I 155a
Abū Dharr al-Ghifārī (d. 32/653) — I 26a, 408a
Abū Dulaf — III 431a
Abū l-Faḍl Ḥubaysh (of Tiflis) — IV 58a
Abū l-Faḍl Jaʿfar b. Ḥarb al-Hamadhānī (d. 236/850) — II 420b
Abū l-Faḍl Rashīd al-Dīn Aḥmad al-Maybudī — see al-Maybudī, Abū l-Faḍl Rashīd al-Dīn Aḥmad (d. 530/1135)
Abū l-Faraj al-Iṣfahānī — see al-Iṣfahānī, Abū l-Faraj (d. 356/967)
Abū l-Faraj Muḥammad b. Aḥmad b. Ibrāhīm al-Shannabūdhī al-Baghdādī (d. 388/998) — IV 360b
Abū Fāris (Ḥafṣid sultan) — III 597b
Abū l-Fatḥ Nāṣir b. Ḥusayn al-Daylamī (d. 444/1052) — IV 602b
Abū l-Fatḥ al-Sāmirī b. Abī l-Ḥasan — IV 524b
Abū Fukayha Yasār — II 513a
Abū l-Futūḥ Ḥusayn b. ʿAlī Rāzī (d. 525/1131) — II 106b, 117b, 148b, 193b; III 93b, 470a; IV 58a, 539b, 602b
Abū Ḥafṣ ʿUmar b. Jamīʿ (eighth/fourteenth-ninth/fifteenth century) — I 485a
Abū Ḥafṣ ʿUmar Najm al-Dīn al-Nasafī (d. 537/1142) — I 483b, 484a; IV 59b
Abū Ḥafṣ ʿUmar al-Suhrawardī — see al-Suhrawardī, Abū Ḥafṣ ʿUmar (d. 632/1234)
Abū Hāla Hind b. al-Nabbāsh (of Tamīm) — V 507b
Abū Ḥāmid Aḥmad b. Muḥammad b. Isḥāq al-Najjār (d. 433/1041) — III 471a
Abū Ḥāmid al-Ghazālī — see al-Ghazālī, Abū Ḥāmid (d. 505/1111)
Abū Ḥamza — III 86a
Abū Ḥanīfa (d. 150/767) — I 17a, 210a, 354b, 482b; II 90a, 171b, 215a, 555a; III 67b, 232b, 331a, 467b, 468a; IV 58b, 431a; V 24a
Abū Ḥanīfa al-Dīnawārī — see al Dīnawārī, Abū Ḥanīfa

Abū l-Hārith ʿĪsā b. Wirdān al-Madanī	see Ibn Wardān al-Madanī, Abū l-Ḥārith (d. 160/777)
Abū l-Hārith al-Layth b. Khālid al-Baghdādī (d. 240/854)	IV 360a, 390a
Abū l-Ḥasan, H.	I 153a
Abū l-Ḥasan Aḥmad b. Muḥammad al-Bazzī (d. 240/845 or 250/864)	IV 359b
Abū l-Ḥasan ʿAlī al-Ashʿarī	see al-Ashʿarī, Abū l-Ḥasan ʿAlī
Abū l-Ḥasan ʿAlī b. Aḥmad al-Wāḥidī al-Nīsābūrī	see al-Wāḥidī, Abū l-Ḥasan ʿAlī b. Aḥmad al-Nīsābūrī (d. 468/1076)
Abū l-Ḥasan ʿAlī b. Ibrāhīm al-Qummī	see al-Qummī, Abū l-Ḥasan ʿAlī b. Ibrāhīm (d. 328/939)
Abū l-Ḥasan ʿAlī b. Muḥammad al-Baghdādī	see al-Khāzin (d. 740-1/1340-1)
Abū l-Ḥasan al-Ḥaysan b. Muḥammad (d. 467/1075)	II 112b
Abū l-Ḥasan Idrīs b. ʿAbd al-Karīm al-Ḥaddād al-Baghdādī (d. 295/908)	IV 360a
Abū l-Ḥasan al-Māwardī	see al-Māwardī, Abū l-Ḥasan (d. 450/1058)
Abū l-Ḥasan Muḥammad b. Aḥmad b. Ayyūb b. Shannabūdh	see Ibn Shannabūdh, Abū l-Ḥasan Muḥammad b. Aḥmad b. Ayyūb (d. 328/939)
Abū l-Ḥasan Muqātil b. Sulaymān al-Balkhī	see Muqātil b. Sulaymān al-Balkhī, Abū l-Ḥasan
Abū l-Ḥasan Rawḥ b. ʿAbd al-Muʾmin al-Baṣrī (d. 234/848)	IV 360a
Abū l-Ḥasan Saʿīd b. Masʿada Akhfash al-Awsaṭ	see Akhfash al-Awsaṭ, Abū l-Ḥasan Saʿīd b. Masʿada
Abū Ḥasan Ṭāhir b. ʿAbd al-Munʿim b. Ghalbūn	see Ibn Ghalbūn, Abū Ḥasan Ṭāhir b. ʿAbd al-Munʿim (d. 399/1008)
Abū Ḥasan al-Wāḥidī	see al-Wāḥidī, Abū l-Ḥasan ʿAlī b. Aḥmad al-Nīsābūrī (d. 468/1076)
Abū Hāshim b. al-Jubbāʾī	see al-Jubbāʾī, Abū Hāshim ʿAbd al-Salām (d. 321/933)
Abū Ḥātim al-Sijistānī	see al-Sijistānī, Abū Ḥātim (d. 255/869)
Abū Ḥayyān al-Andalusī /al-Gharnāṭī (d. 745/1344)	I 268a, 269a, 399a; II 109b, 189a; III 83b; IV 15a, 54a, 351a, 533b; V 330a, 332a, 333a
Abū Ḥayyān al-Tawḥīdī (d. 414/1023)	IV 130a
Abū Hilāl al-ʿAskarī	see al-ʿAskarī, Abū Hilāl (d. 1010)
Abū Hilāl al-Ṣābī (d. 384/994)	III 215b
Abū Ḥudhayfa (Mūsā b. Masʿūd al-Nahdī al-Baṣrī, d. 220/835)	II 105b; IV 134b
Abū l-Hudhayl (d. 227/841)	II 532a; III 466b, 469b; IV 74a, 303a

Abū Hurayra (d. ca. 57-8/677-8)	I 234b, 408a; II 102b, 160b; III 392a, 502a, 502b; IV 233a, 304b, 370b, 384a; V 21b, 134b, 161b, 471b
Abū l-Ḥusayn al-Baṣrī (d. 436/1044)	I 484b; III 467a, 469a
Abū l-Ḥusayn al-Khayyāṭ	see al-Khayyāṭ, Abū l-Ḥusayn (d. ca. 300/913)
Abū l-Ḥusayn al-Nūrī	see al-Nūrī, Abū l-Ḥusayn (d. 295/907)
Abū ʿĪsā Khallād b. Khālid al-Baghdādī	see Khallād b. Khālid al-Baghdādī, Abū ʿĪsā (d. 220/835)
Abū ʿĪsā al-Tirmidhī	see al-Tirmidhī, Abū ʿIsā
Abū ʿĪsā al-Warrāq (d. ca. 246/860)	I 115b, 117b; IV 123a; V 372a
Abū Isḥāq Ibrāhīm (of Nayshāpūr)	IV 61a
Abū Isḥāq Injū, Shīrāz Jamāl al-Dīn (r. 743-54/1343-53)	III 313b
Abū Isḥāq al- Isfarāʾīnī (d. 418/1027)	III 156b
Abū Isḥāq al-Naẓẓām	see al-Naẓẓām, Abū Isḥāq Ibrāhīm b. Sayyār (d. ca. 221/835)
Abū Isḥāq al-Thaʿlabī	see al-Thaʿlabī, Abū Isḥāq (d. 427/1035)
Abū ʿIṣma Nūn b. Abī Maryam (d. 173/789)	II 394a
Abū l-ʿIzz al-Wāsiṭī al-Qalānisī (d. 521/1127)	III 115a; V 332a
Abū Jaʿfar Aḥmad b. Faraḥ b. Jibrīl al-Baghdādī (d. 303/915)	IV 360a
Abū Jaʿfar al-Bāqir (d. 114/733)	I 550b
Abū Jaʿfar Muḥammad b. Jarīr al-Ṭabarī	see al-Ṭabarī, Abū Jaʿfar Muḥammad b. Jarīr (d. 310/923)
Abū Jaʿfar al-Naḥḥās	see al-Naḥḥās, Abū Jaʿfar Aḥmad b. Muḥammad (d. 338/950)
Abū Jaʿfar al-Ṭūsī	see al-Ṭūsī, Abū Jaʿfar (d. 459/1067)
Abū Jaʿfar Yazīd b. al-Qaʿqāʿ al-Makhzūmī (d. 130/747)	IV 358a, 358b, 360a, 389b
Abū Jahl	I 196a, 196b; II 400a; III 422a, 425a, 545b; IV 331b; V 59a, 359b
Abū l-Jārūd (d. after 140/757-8)	II 117a
Abū l-Kalām Āzād	see Āzād, [Mawlānā] Abū l-Kalam
Abū l-Khayr (of Seville)	I 48b
Abū l-Khayr Ṭashkubrīzādah (d. 968/1561)	V 329a
Abū Khuzayma	I 355a
Abū Lahab (ʿAbd al-ʿUzzāʾ b. ʿAbd al-Muṭṭalib, uncle of the Prophet)	I **20a**, 319b, 491b; II 19a, 176b, 401b, 418a, 439a; III 455b, 456a; IV 216b, 259a, 309a, 330a, 331b

Abū l-Layth Naṣr b. Muḥammad b. Aḥmad al-Samarqandī (d. 373-5/983-5)	I 114a; II 111b; IV 109b
Abū l-Maʿālī ʿUzayzī	III 506a
Abū Malik al-Quraẓī	IV 334b
Abū Manṣūr ʿAbd al-Qāhir al-Baghdādī	see al-Baghdādī, Abū Manṣūr ʿAbd al-Qāhir (d. 429/1037)
Abū Manṣūr al-Azharī (d. 370/980)	V 331b
Abū Manṣūr al-Māturīdī	see al-Māturīdī, Abū Manṣūr (d. 333/944)
Abū Maʿshar al-Sindī (d. 170/786)	IV 533a
Abū Maʿshar al-Ṭabarī (d. 478/1085)	V 332a
Abū Maydab (d. 594/1197)	V 153a
Abū Maysara al-Hamdānī (d. 63/682)	II 227b; III 117a
Abū Mijlaz Lāḥiq b. Ḥumayd (al-Sadūsī al-Baṣrī, d. 106/724)	II 103a; IV 133a
Abū Muʿāwiya Muḥammad b. Khāzim (d. 195/811)	II 395a
Abū Muḥammad Aḥmad b. Muḥammad b. ʿAlī	see al-ʿAṣmī (d. 450/1058)
Abū Muḥammad al-Barbahārī	see al-Barbahārī, Abū Muḥammad (d. 329/941)
Abū Muḥammad al-Ḥusayn al-Baghawī	see al-Baghawī, Abū Muḥammad al-Ḥusayn
Abū Muḥammad Makkī b. Abī Ṭālib al-Qurṭubī	see Makkī b. Abī Ṭālib al-Qaysī (d. 437/1045)
Abū Muḥammad Sulaymān b. Mahrān al-Aʿmash al-Kūfī	see al-Aʿmash al-Kūfī, Abū Muḥammad Sulaymān b. Mahrān (d. 148/765)
Abū Muḥammad Yaḥyā b. al-Mubārak b. al-Mughīra al-Baṣrī (d. 202/817)	IV 360a
Abū Muḥammad Yaʿqūb b. Isḥāq	see al-Ḥaḍramī, Abū Muḥammad Yaʿqūb b. Isḥāq (d. 205/821)
Abū Muqātil al-Samarqandī (d. 208/823)	I 482b
Abū Mūsā al-Ashʿarī	see al-Ashʿarī, Abū Mūsā (d. 42/662)
Abū Mūsā ʿĪsā b. Mīnā al-Zarqī (d. 220/835)	IV 359b
Abū Muslim (d. 137/755)	III 557a
Abū Muslim Muḥammad b. Baḥr al-Iṣfahānī (d. 332/934)	II 445a; III 470a
Abū Muṭīʾ al-Balkhī	see al-Balkhī, Abū Muṭīʾ (d. 199/814)
Abū Nadra	IV 350b
Abū l-Naṣr Aḥmad al-Darwājikī	see al-Darwājikī, Abū l-Naṣr Aḥmad (d. 549/1154)
Abū Naṣr b. Manṣūr Asadī (d. bef. 423/1041)	III 222a
Abū l-Naṣr Hāshim b. al-Qāsim (d. 205-7/820-2)	II 390a
Abū Naṣr al-Sarrāj (d. 378/988)	see al-Sarrāj, Abū Naṣr (d. 378/988)
Abū Nuʿaym	IV 386b, 387b

Abū Nuʿaym al-Iṣfahānī (d. 430/1038)	I 78a; II 387a; III 350b; V 31b, 466b
Abū Nuʿaym Shujāʿ b. Abī Naṣr al-Balkhī Baghdādī (d. 190/806)	IV 360a
Abū Nūḥ al-Anbārī	IV 236a
Abū Nūḥ Ṣāliḥ al-Dahhān	III 88b
Abū Nuwās (d. 198/810)	II 223a; IV 57a, 527b
Abū l-Qāsim al-Balkhī (al-Kaʿbī)	see al-Balkhī, Abū l-Qāsim (al-Kaʿbī; d. 319/931)
Abū l-Qāsim Isḥāq b. Muḥammad al-Ḥakīm al-Samarqandī	see al-Ḥakīm al-Samarqandī, Abū l-Qāsim Isḥāq b. Muḥammad (d. 342/953)
Abū l-Qāsim al-Junayd (d. 298/910)	V 141a
Abū l-Qāsim al-Khūʾī (d. 1992)	IV 492a
Abū l-Qāsim Maslama b. Aḥmad al-Majrīṭī (d. 398/1007)	III 250b
Abū l-Qāsim Muḥammad b. ʿAbdallāh al-Hāshimī al-Qurashī	III 30b
Abū l-Qāsim Muḥammad b. Juzayy al-Gharnāṭī (d. 741/1340)	IV 359a
Abū l-Qāsim al-Qushayrī	see al-Qushayrī, Abū l-Qāsim ʿAbd al-Karīm b. Hawāzin (d. 465/1072)
Abū l-Qāsim al-Rāfiʿī (d. 623/1226)	V 448b
Abū Qatāda	III 250a
Abu-Rabiʿ, I.	II **156b**
Abū l-Rabīʿ Sulaymān b. Muslim b. Jummāz al-Madanī (d. 170/786)	IV 360a
Abū l-Raddād	II 27b, 28a; III 303b
Abū Rashīd al-Nīsābūrī	II 534a, 534b
Abū Rayḥān al-Bīrūnī	see al-Bīrūnī, Abū l-Rayḥān (d. 443/1050)
Abū Righāl	IV 45a, 45b, 522a
Abū Saʿīd	I 267b; II 35a; III 559a
Abū Saʿīdi Abī Khayr (d. 440/1049)	IV 55b
Abū Saʿīd al-Kharrāz (d. 286/899)	I 522a; V 140b
Abū Saʿīd al-Khudrī (d. 74/693)	III 119b, 250a, 538b
Abū Salama b. ʿAbd al-Asad	III 178a; V 508a
Abū Ṣāliḥ (Companion)	IV 100b
Abū Ṣāliḥ Bādhām al-Kūfī (d. 120/738)	II 103a; IV 533a
Abū Ṣāliḥ Manṣūr b. Nūḥ (Sāmānid ruler; r. 349-63/961-74)	V 341a
Abū l-Sarāyā	III 558a
Abū Shāma al-Maqdisī (d. 665/1267)	V 327b
Abū al-Shaykh al-Anṣārī (d. 369/979)	III 288a
Abū Shuʿayb Ṣāliḥ b. Ziyād al-Riqqī	see al-Sūsī, Abū Shuʿayb Ṣāliḥ b. Ziyād (d. ca. 261/874)
Abū Sufyān	I 399a; III 422a, 498b

Abū Ṭāhir Fīrūzābādī	see Fīrūzābādī, Abū Ṭāhir
Abū Ṭāhir al-Silafī	see al-Silafī, Abū Ṭāhir (d. 576/1180)
Abū Ṭālib (uncle of the Prophet)	II 19a, 19b; II 514b, 553b; III 456a; IV 216b, 331a; V 185a
Abū Ṭālib al-Makkī	see al-Makkī, Abū Ṭālib
Abū Tammām (d. 231/845)	III 384b
Abū l-Ṭayyib Aḥmad b. al-Ḥusayn	see al-Mutanabbī (d. 354/965)
Abū l-Ṭayyib b. Ghalbūn (d. 389/999)	V 332a
Abū Thābit Muḥammad al-Daylamī	see al-Daylamī, Abū Thābit Muḥammad (d. 593/1197)
Abū ʿUbayd al-Bakrī	II 559b
Abū ʿUbayd al-Qāsim b. Sallām (d. 224/838)	I 320b, 321a; II 101a, 108a, 228b, 230a, 389a; III 123b; IV 157a; V 291b
Abū ʿUbayda b. al-Jarrāḥ (d. 18/639)	I 389a
Abū ʿUbayda Maʿmar b. al-Muthannā (d. 209/824-5)	I 530a; II 104a, 104b, 229b, 347b, 403a, 531b; III 87b, 606a; V 234b, 434b
Abū ʿUbayda Muslim b. Abī Karīma al-Tamīmī	III 88b
Abū ʿUmar Ḥafṣ b. ʿUmar al-Dūrī	see al-Dūrī, Abū ʿUmar Ḥafṣ b. ʿUmar (d. ca. 246/860-1)
Abū ʿUthmān al-Jāḥiẓ	see al-Jāḥiẓ, Abū ʿUthmān (d. 255/869)
Abū ʿUthmān al-Ṣābūnī (d. 449/1057)	II 112a
Abū l-Walīd al-Bājī al-Mālikī (d. 474/1081)	V 401b
Abū l-Walīd Hishām b. ʿAmmār al-Sulamī al-Dimashqī (d. 245/859)	IV 359b
Abū l-Walīd Marwān b. Janāḥ (d. 441/1050)	IV 12b
Abū Yaʿlā b. al-Farrāʾ	see Ibn al-Farrāʾ, Abū Yaʿlā (d. 458/1066)
Abū Yaʿqūb Isḥāq b. Ibrāhīm al-Warrāq al-Baghdādī (d. 286/899)	IV 360a
Abū Yaʿqūb b. Isḥāq al-Kindī	see al-Kindī, Abū Yūsuf Yaʿqūb b. Isḥāq (d. ca. 252/866)
Abū Yaʿqūb al-Sijistānī (fl. fourth/tenth century)	IV 490b
Abū Yaʿqūb Yūsuf II	III 307a
Abū l-Yaqẓān (r. 241-81/855-94)	III 88b
Abū Yazīd al-Bisṭāmī (d. 261/874)	I 88b; II 452a; V 148b
Abū Yūsuf (d. 182/798)	I 67b; IV 143b
Abū Yūsuf al-Kindī	V 371b
Abū Yūsuf al-Qazwīnī	see al-Qazwīnī, Abū Yūsuf (d. 488/1095)
Abū Zahra, M.	IV 124a
Abu-Zahra, N.	I **30a**
Abū Zayd, M.	II 128b, 129a; IV 266b

Abu Zayd, N. — I **161b**, 426a, 426b, 530b; II **97a**, 135b, 136a, 136b, 137a, 139b, 140b, **502a**, **551a**; III **584a**; IV 89b; V 69b
Abū Zayd al-Anṣarī (d. 214-15/830-1) — II 348b; III 606a; V 234b
Abū Zayd al-Balkhī (d. 322/934) — II 114b
Abyāna — III 432a
Abyssinia [al-Ḥabasha] — I 4b, **20a**, 20b, 21a, 320a, 323b; II 15b, 18b, 19a, 79a; III 8a, 32b, 35a; IV 257b, 329a, 406b, 410a, 410b, 411a, 532a, 533a; V 409a, 508a, 508b, 516b
Abyssinian(s) — I 4a, 21a, 98b, 223b, 293a, 296b; II 490a; III 8a, 45a, 46a; IV 329a; V 389b
Achaemenids — V 124b
Achan — V 193a
Acoluthus, Andreas (d. 1704) — IV 249b, 250a
Acts of the Apostles — I 275b, 310b
ʿĀd — I **21b**, 22a, 150b, 261b, 395b, 500b, 502a, 519b, 532a; II 212a, 259b, 305b, 399b, 438a, 462b, 463a, 541b, 543a, 559a; III 200b, 381a, 393a, 418a, 485b, 486a, 518b, 520b, 521b, 522a; IV 160a, 258a, 263b, 309a, 321a, 352a, 421a, 521b, 586b; V 52b, 107b, 164a, 171b, 253a, 280a, 389a, 460b
  People of — I 54b, 93a, 160b, 189a, 505a, 536b; II 293a, 338b, 455b, 459b, 462b, 510a, 541b, 542a, 559a; III 209a, 353a, 443a, 519a, 519b, 583a; IV 352b, 425a; V 15b, 252b, 261b, 317b, 318a, 471a
ʿĀd b. ʿŪṣ b. Aram b. Sām b. Nūḥ — V 390a
Adam [Ādam] — I 3a, 9b, **22b**, 23a, 23b, 24a, 24b, 25a, 25b, 26a, 38b, 52a, 84a, 86a, 86b, 135a, 146a, 160a, 189a, 190b, 205b, 230a, 230b, 231b, 233a, 233b, 240a, 240b, 255a, 258a, 264a, 270a, 270b, 271a, 277a, 277b, 278a, 312a, 313a, 317b, 340a, 346b, 395b, 436b, 446b, 447b, 448a, 449b, 451b, 452a, 453a, 454b, 455b,

456a, 457a, 463a, 465b, 474a, 476a, 476b, 477b, 496a, 508a, 525a, 525b, 526b, 532a, 532b, 536b, 537b; II 4a, 23b, 24a, 52b, 54a, 54b, 57a, 65a, 66a, 98b, 106a, 166b, 172b, 173b, 175a, 187a, 202a, 202b, 216b, 219b, 224a, 245a, 283a, 285a, 291a, 292a, 325a, 326b, 327b, 332a, 335b, 336a, 337a, 339b, 372b, 419a, 435b, 442b, 443b, 447b, 503a, 506b, 509a, 541b, 543a, 553a; III 13a, 15b, 44b, 45a, 45b, 69a, 78a, 92b, 102b, 103a, 118b, 119a, 184a, 211a, 217a, 254b, 289b, 293a, 293b, 295a, 295b, 393a, 441a, 484b, 485b, 486b, 489a, 490b, 491b, 503b, 519a, 519b, 520b, 521a, 521b, 532a, 536b, 540a, 541a, 541b, 543b, 548a, 548b, 563b; IV 9b, 13a, 47a, 71a, 95b, 130a, 162a, 195b, 220a, 223b, 263b, 291a, 291b, 302b, 303b, 304a, 305a, 337a, 429a, 475a, 508b, 517a, 569b, 580b, 581b, 584a; V 25a, 33a, 45b, 46a, 81b, 84a, 109a, 109b, 114a, 114b, 115b, 116a, 152b, 200a, 201b, 260a, 267b, 269b, 270a, 270b, 274b, 281b, 360a, 360b, 374b, 411a, 487a, 502a, 529b, 530a, 530b, 536a, 536b, 539a, 545b, 551b, 571a

Children/Sons of [*banū ādam*] I 378a; II 328b; V 3b
Adams, C. III **64a**, **332a**
ʿAdan III 138b
Ādan b. Iyās (d. 220-835) II 105a
Adang, C. I **226a**; II **472a**; V **309b**
ʿAddās II 513b, 514a, 515b, 516a, 517a
Aden II 559a
Adhriʿāt IV 324a
Adhruḥ V 2a, 185a
ʿAdī (son of Ḥātim and Māwiyya) V 233a, 508a
ʿAdī, Adiyy b. Zayd (d. ca. 600) I 136b; IV 111b
ʿĀdite(s) I 22a; II 463a, 463b, 559a
Adler, J. I 136b

Adrianople (Edirne)	I 197a
Aegedius of Viterbo (Egidio da Viterbo)	V 345a
Afarīdūn	III 542a
al-Afḍal al-ʿAbbās b. ʿAlī	I 47a
al-Afghānī, Jamāl al-Dīn (d. 1897)	IV 554b
Afghanistan	I 171b, 282a; II 15a, 267a, 313a; III 314b; IV 56b, 211b
al-Afghānistānī, M.	III 251a
Africa	I 32a, 286a; II 10a, 79b; III 265a, 306a, 326b, 327a; IV 275b, 361a; V 342a
East	III 327b, 328a, 432b, 435b; V 60a
Muslim	III 326b
North	I 264a, 286a, 334a, 414b, 554b; II 503b, 530b; III 296b, 300b, 304a, 306b, 308a, 309a, 315b, 317a, 327a, 435b, 559a, 607b; IV 240a, 249a, 360b, 361b, 389b
South	I 201a; III 582b, 584a; V 402a
sub-Saharan	III 297a, 308a
West	I 33b, 557a; III 327a, 432b, 435b; IV 170a, 360b
African(s)	I 30a
Muslim Africans	I 30a
African Americans	see Americans
Afrikaans (language)	I 136a
Afsaruddin, A.	II **287a**, IV **392b**
Aga Khan	II 503b
Agabus	III 521a
Age of Ignorance [*jāhiliyya*]	I 34b, **37a**; II 219b, 403a, 479a, 482a, 483a; III 72a, 73b, 78b, 97a, 97b, 120b, 121a, 401b, 448a, 501b; IV 51b, 96b, 109a, 146b, 590b; V 435b, 486a
Aggada	see Haggada
Aghlabids	III 558b
Agra	I 165a, 265a; III 323b
Ahab	I 194a
[King] Ahasuerus	II 399b
Aḥiqār	III 242b
Ahl al-ʿĀliya	I 529b, 530a
Ahl al-Ḥawrān	I 529b
Ahl al-Ḥijāz	I 529b, 530a
Ahl al-Yaman	I 529b
al-Aḥqāf	I 21b, 22a
Aḥmad	I 306a; III 445b; V 516b

Aḥmad, Ḥ.	II 130b
Aḥmad, M. Gh.	I 50a, 51a
Aḥmad ʿAbd al-Raḥmān al-Bannā al-Sāʿātī	II 377b
Aḥmad ʿAlī	I 340b
Aḥmad b. ʿAbd al-Jabbār al-ʿUṭāridī	see al-ʿUṭāridī, Aḥmad b. ʿAbd al-Jabbār (d. 272/886)
Aḥmad b. ʿAbdallāh b. Salām	V 306a
Aḥmad b. Abī ʿUmar al-Zāhid al-Andarābī	see al-Andarābī, Aḥmad b. Abī ʿUmar al-Zāhid (d. 470/1077)
Aḥmad b. Ḥanbal	see Ibn Ḥanbal, Aḥmad (d. 241/855)
Aḥmad b. Ḥamdān b. Shabīb al-Ḥarrānī	see al-Ḥarrānī, Aḥmad b. Ḥamdān b. Shabīb (d. 695/1295)
Aḥmad al-Ḥuṣarī	see al-Ḥuṣarī, A.
Aḥmad b. al-Ḥusayn b. Abī Hāshim	see Mānkdīm (d. 425/1034)
Aḥmad b. al-Ḥusayn al-Muʾayyad-bi-llāh (d. 411/1020)	IV 23a
Aḥmad b. Muḥammad al-Bazzī	see al-Bazzī, Aḥmad b. Muḥammad (d. ca. 250/864-5)
Aḥmad b. Muḥammad Hamadhānī	IV 603a
Aḥmad b. Muḥammad b. Ibrāhīm al-Thaʿlabī	see al-Thaʿlabī, Abū Isḥāq Aḥmad b. Muḥammad b. Ibrāhīm (d. 427/1035)
Aḥmad b. Muḥammad al-Khallāl al-Baṣrī (alive in 377/987)	III 471a
Aḥmad b. Muḥammad al-Sayyārī	IV 593b
Aḥmad b. Mūsā al-Riḍā	III 313b
Aḥmad b. Shuʿayb al-Nasāʾī	see al-Nasāʾī, Aḥmad b. Shuʿayb (d. 303/915)
Aḥmad (b.) al-Suhrawardī	III 311a, 601b
Aḥmad b. Yūsuf	see al-Samīn al-Ḥalabī (d. 756/1355)
[Shaykh] Aḥmad of Jām	IV 58a
Aḥmad Khān Nayrizī	III 319a
Aḥmad Maṭar	III 217b
Aḥmad al-Mawṣilī	III 312a
Aḥmad Muḥammad Shākir	II 377a
Aḥmad Qarāḥiṣārī	see Qarāḥiṣārī, Aḥmad (d. 963/1556)
Aḥmad Riḍa Khān Barēlwī	I 201a, 201b, 202a, 202b
Aḥmadiyya(s)	I **50a**, 50b, 51a, I 31a, 31b, 210a, 393b, 489a; III 139a; V 99a, 342b, 343b
Ahmed, S.	IV **535b**
Ahren, K.	IV 194b
Ahriya	see Uriah
Ahwāzī (d. 446/1055)	V 332a, 335b

ʿĀʾisha ʿAbd al-Raḥmān (Bint al-Shāṭiʾ) see ʿAbd al-Raḥmān, ʿĀʾisha (Bint al-Shāṭiʾ)
ʿĀʾisha bt. Abī Bakr (wife of the Prophet; d. 58/678-9) I 12a, 18b, 29a, **55b**, 56a, 56b, 57a, 57b, 58a, 58b, 59a, 59b, 60a, 121b, 122a, 293b, 342b, 348b, 353a, 353b, 357b, 358a, 369b, 389a; II 17b, 193a, 205b, 240b, 241a, 242a, 344a, 359b, 391a, 391b, 397b, 398a, 446b, 453b, 461a, 469b, 555a; III 81a, 81b, 250a, 250b, 290b, 291a, 448a, 493b, 494a, 538a, 538b, 573b; IV 70a, 93b, 134b, 494a, 495a, 518b, 598b; V 38a, 55b, 135a, 178a, 334a, 471b, 472a, 508a, 511a, 511b, 515b, 516a, 517a, 518a, 518b, 520a, 520b, 521a, 534a, 535a, 535b, 550a
Aiton (Savoy) IV 243a; V 341b
Monastery of V 345a
Ajārida II 505a; III 86b
al-ʿAjjāj (d. 97/715) V 560b
Ajnādayn V 185a
Akbar (r. 962-1014/1556-1605) I 165a; III 323a, 323b, 325b
Akber Khan IV 274b
al-Akhfash al-Awsaṭ, Abū l-Ḥasan Saʿīd b. Masʿada (d. 221/835) I 131a, 348a, 530b; II 109a, 347a, 355a; IV 354a, 355b
al-Akhṭāl (90/709) III 215b
Akhṭūb I 529a
Akkadian (language) II 235b; III 142a, 244a
Aksum V 568a
Aksūm (son of Abraha) V 566b
Aksumites V 562a
al-Aʿlā II 295a
ʿAlāʾ al-Dawla al-Simnānī see al-Simnānī ʿAlāʾ al-Dawla (d. 736/1336)
ʿAlāʾ al-Dīn al-Kaḥḥāl b. Ṭarkhān see al-Kaḥḥāl b. Ṭarkhān, ʿAlāʾ al-Dīn (d. 720/1320)
ʿAlāʾ al-Dīn mosque III 434b
ʿAlāʾ al-Dīn al-Samarqandī see al-Samarqandī, ʿAlāʾ al-Dīn (d. 539/1144)
ʿAlam al-Dīn al-Bulqīnī see al-Bulqīnī, ʿAlam al-Dīn
ʿAlam al-Dīn al-Sakhāwī see al-Sakhāwī, ʿAlam al-Dīn (d. 643/1246)
Alāmiqa V 93a
al-Albānī, Muḥammad Nāṣir al-Dīn (d. 1999) IV 535a

Albin, M.W.	IV **276a**
Alcmaeon	III 242b
Aleppo	I 138a, 169a, 171b, 172b; III 309b, 310a, 430a; IV 237a, 248b
Alessandro de Paganini	IV 244b
Alexander, S.	II **198a**; V **385a**
Alexander the Great [al-Iskandar]	I **61b**, 62a; II 332a, 332b, 333a, 437a; III 190a, 245a; IV 62b, 210b, 540b; V 37a, 122b, 236b, 375b; see also Possessor of the Two Horns
Alexandria	I 396b; II 10b, 527b, 559b; III 407b; IV 270b; V 37a, 346b
Alfonso de Spina (d. ca. 1491)	IV 243b
Algeria	I 127b; II 116b; III 86b; IV 275b, 349a, 360b; V 216b, 538b
ʿAlī (d. 151/768-9, brother of al-Ḥasan b. Ṣāliḥ b. Ḥayy [d. 199/814-5])	IV 387b
ʿAlī, ʿAbdallāh Yūsuf	see Yūsuf ʿAlī, ʿA. (1872-1953)
ʿAlī Akbar al-Ghaffārī	II 377b
ʿAlī b. ʿAbd al-Raḥmān	III 601b
ʿAlī b. Abī Ṭalḥa	II 103b
ʿAlī b. Abī Ṭālib (r. 35-40/656-61)	I 9b, 36a, 57a, 58a, 58b, **62b**, 63a, 67a, 68b, 122a, 155b, 211a, 219a, 261a, 272a, 333b, 347a, 348b, 350a, 355b, 388b, 389a, 390a, 462a, 518a, 539b, 540b, 550b; II 12b, 20b, 34b, 102b, 147a, 148a, 169b, 177a, 179a, 179b, 193a, 206a, 273a, 281a, 334a, 396a, 396b, 398a, 400a, 400b, 503b, 504a, 522b, 523a; III 65b, 66a, 81a, 84b, 85a, 85b, 88a, 153b, 178b, 255b, 276b, 304a, 309b, 322b, 364a, 370a, 429a, 538b, 558b, 559a, 571a, 598b, 600a, 605a, 605b; IV 9b, 26a, 44a, 50a, 52a, 52b, 60b, 61a, 63b, 72b, 73b, 134b, 135a, 135b, 136a, 137a, 139a, 150a, 178a, 365b, 386a, 387a, 496b, 592a, 592b, 596a, 596b; V 1a, 1b, 2a, 23b, 24a, 31b, 32b, 37b, 38b, 39a, 46b, 135a, 222b, 238b, 307a, 319a, 319b, 324a, 334a, 361b, 363b, 482b, 535b

ʿAlī b. Aḥmad iii 265a
ʿAlī b. Aḥmad al-Wāḥidī see al-Wāḥidī, Abū l-Ḥasan ʿAlī b. Aḥmad al-Nīsābūrī (d. 468/1075-6)
ʿAlī b. Ḥamza al-Kisāʾī see al-Kisāʾī, ʿAlī b. Ḥamza (d. 189/804-5)
ʿAlī b. Hilāl al-Sitrī see Ibn al-Bawwāb
ʿAlī b. Ibrāhīm al-Qummī see al-Qummī, Abū l-Ḥasan ʿAlī b. Ibrāhīm (d. 328/939)
ʿAlī b. ʿĪsā al-Rummānī see al-Rummānī, ʿAlī b. ʿĪsā (d. 384/994)
ʿAlī b. Karmak iii 414b
ʿAlī b. al-Madīnī (d. 264/849) v 331a
ʿAlī b. Muḥammad iii 558a, 601b
ʿAlī b. Muḥammad b. Muḥammad i 282a
ʿAlī b. Muḥammad b. al-Walīd see Ibn al-Walīd, ʿAlī b. Muḥammad (d. 612/1215)
ʿAlī b. Rabban al-Ṭabarī see al-Ṭabarī, ʿAlī b. Sahl Rabban
ʿAlī b. Rifāʿa iv 334b
ʿAlī b. Shādhān al-Rāzī al-Bayyiʿ v 559a
ʿAlī b. ʿUthmān al-Ūshī (d. 569/1173) i 483b; iv 450a
ʿAlī al-Harawī i 126b
ʿAlī Ḥusaynī al-Sistānī see al-Sistānī, ʿAlī Husaynī
ʿAlī Muḥammad (d. 1850) i 198b, 199a; iii 124b
[Imām] ʿAlī Riḍā Ardakānī iii 313b, 319a
ʿAlī Sharīʿatī (d. 1977) iii 286a, 582a
ʿAlī al-Warrāq i 284a
ʿAlī Zayn al-ʿĀbidīn ii 419b
ʿAlid(s) i 540a; ii 560b; iii 6a, 313b, 558a, 558b; v 503b, 504b
Aligar iv 266a
Aligarh Movement i 201a; iii 223b
al-ʿĀliya (of Yathrib) ii 20b
Aljamiado i 136a; v 341b
Allāh i 30b, 329a, 329b, 330a, 555a; ii 94a, 316a, 317a, 317b, 318a, 318b, 319b, 320a, 322b, 329b, 369b, 467b, 474b; iii 45b, 461a, 504b; iv 20b, 175a, 380a; v 88b, 248b, 539b
Allahabad iv 266a
ʿAllāl al-Fāsī ii 135b
Allāma al-Ḥillī (d. 726/1325) i 484b
Allāma Majlisī (d. 1110/1698) v 402a
Allard, M. v 297
Almaq v 93a

Almaqah	v 85b, 86a, 89b, 90a, 90b, 91a, 91b, 92b, 93a, 562b
dhū Hirrān	v 89b
al-ʿAlmawī (d. 981/1573)	iii 267a
Almeria	i 48b
Almohad(s) [al-Muwaḥḥidūn]	iii 307a, 307b, 559a; v 345a
Almohad Mosque	iii 597b
Almoravid(s)	ii 34b; iii 307a, 559a
Alon, I.	iii **547b**
ʿAlqama	iv 439a, 440b
Al Safi, A.	iv 177a
Alṭāf Ḥusayn Ḥālī (d. 1914)	iii 223b
al-Ālūsī, Maḥmūd b. ʿAbdallāh Shihāb al-Dīn (d. 1270/1854)	ii 120b, 130a; iii 507b; iv 531a; v 330a, 442b
Alyasaʿ	i 527b
Amājūr (ʿAbbāsid governor of Damascus)	i 279b; iii 261b, 594a; v 558b
Amalekites	ii 335a, 463b; iv 536b
Amānī	iv 62a
Amanus	v 184b
Amari, M.	iii 256b, 257a
ʿAmariyya Madrasa	iii 312b
al-Aʿmash al-Kūfī, Abū Muḥammad Sulaymān b. Mahrān (d. 148/765)	ii 386b, 387a, 391a, 395b; iv 54a, 360a, 389b
Amasiya	iii 320b
Ambros, A.	ii 303b, 352a, 360a; iv 199b; v 296a, 297a
Ameretat (Zoroastrian archangel)	ii 404a
America	i 30a, 31a, 385b, 424b; ii 31b; iii 584a; v 347a
North	i 264a, 385b; ii 567b; iv 176a; v 76a, 216a, 228b
American(s)	
African American(s)	i **30a**, 30b, 31a, 31b; v 206b
American Islamic College in Chicago	see Islam
American Muslim Mission	see Islam
Amieu, Jean (d. 1653)	iv 237a
al-Amīn (r. 193-8/809-13)	ii 560b; iii 557b
Amīn Aḥsan Iṣlāḥī	see Iṣlāḥī, Amīn Aḥsan (d. 1997)
Amīn al-Khūlī	see al-Khūlī, Amīn (d. 1967)
Amina Wadud-Muhsin	see Wadud-Muhsin, Amina
[Banū] ʿĀmīr	i 529b; ii 16b; iv 114a; v 79b, 366a, 507b
Amīr^um	v 86b
ʿĀmīr b. al-Ḥaḍramī al-Qurashī	ii 513a, 517a
ʿĀmīr b. Luwayy	ii 514b

ʿĀmīr b. Ṣaʿṣaʿa	V 508a, 508b
ʿĀmīr b. Sharāḥīl al-Shaʿbī	see al-Shaʿbī, ʿĀmīr b. Sharāḥīl (d. 103-10/721-8)
ʿĀmir b. al-Ṭufayl	IV 111b, 114a
Amir-Moezzi, M. Ali	I **542a**; II **422b**; IV 593b
al-Amīr al-Sayyid Jamal al-Dīn ʿAbdallāh al-Tanūkhī (d. 1417/1479)	I 556b, 557a
al-ʿĀmirī (d. 381/992)	IV 129b
ʿĀmiriyya	V 79b
Amittai	IV 303a
AMM	see Islam
ʿAmm	V 85b, 86a, 91b, 92b
Amman	I 151b, 155b; V 75b, 222b
Ammann, L.	III **149b, 401a**
ʿAmmār al-Baṣrī	V 8b
ʿAmmār b. Yāsir (governor of Kūfa; d. 37/657)	I 408b; II 391a; V 59a
Ammīʾanas	V 92a, 92b
Amos	II **562b**
ʿAmr (tribe)	II 16b
ʿAmr b. al-ʿĀṣ	II 102b; IV 328a; V 1b, 2a, 161a
Mosque of	see Cairo
ʿAmr b. Asad (uncle of Khadīja)	III 80b
ʿAmr b. ʿAwf	III 438b, 439a
ʿAmr b. Bar al-Jāḥiẓ (d. 255/865)	see al-Jāḥiẓ, ʿAmr b. Bar (d. 255/865)
ʿAmr b. Dīnā	III 89a
ʿAmr b. Harim	III 89a
ʿAmr Khālid (contemporary preacher)	V 224a, 224b
ʿAmr b. Kulthūm	II 487b, 488a; V 416b
ʿAmr b. Luḥayy	V 122a
[Banū] ʿAmr b. Qurayẓa	IV 334a, 334b
Amr b. ʿUbayd (d. 143-4/760-1)	II 105a, 114a; III 466b
ʿAmra bt. Yazīd	V 509a
Amram [ʿAmrām]	II 509a; III 540b; IV 291a; see also Imrān
ʿAmrān	V 89b
Amrullah, H.A.K.	V 99b
Amzūra (one name of Noah's wife)	III 541b
Anak	II 53b
ʿAnānī, M.	IV 272a
ʿAnaq	III 543a
Anas b. Malik (d. ca. 91/709)	I 209b, 235a, 355b, 356b, 544a; II 102b, 214b, 383b, 384a, 446a, 461a; III 120a, 391b; V 63b, 384a, 517a
Anatolia	I 169a, 265b; III 306b, 308b, 310b,

	311a, 432a, 434a, 434b; v 390b, 391a, 391b
Anatolius of Berytos	i 48b
al-Anbār	i 136a
Anbī	v 85b, 86b, 91b
Ancient Egyptian Arabic Order of Nobles of the Shrine	i 30b
Adang, C.	ii **472a**
Anawati, G.C.	iii 327a
Andalusia [al-Andalus]	i 46b, 47b, 48a, 283b; ii 39a, 119a, 223a, 471b, 472a; iii 240b, 371a; iv 317a, 359a, 360b
al-Andarābī, Aḥmad b. Abī ʿUmar al-Zāhid (d. 470/1077)	v 325a, 325b, 331b
Andrae, T.	i 181b, 417b; iii 144a; iv 47b, 399b
Ankara	i 285b
University, Faculty of Theology	v 211b
al-Anṣār	i 529b; see Medinan(s)
Ansar Pure Sufis	iv 176a; v 450b
al-Anṣārī al-Harawī, ʿAbdallāh (d. 481/1089)	iv 59b; v 148a, 148b
Anṣārī of Herat	see Anṣārī al-Harawī, ʿAbdallāh (d. 481/1089)
Ansarullah Community	iv 176a
al-Anṭākī, Dāʾūd (d. 1008/1599)	iii 364a, 364b, 365a
Antichrist [al-Masīḥ al-Dajjāl]	i 73b, 103a, **107b**, 108a, 109a, 109b, 110a, 110b, 111a, 114a, 488a; ii 47a; iii 17a, 19b, 20a, 138a
Antioch	iii 407b, 521a; iv 74a, 352b, 353a; v 185b, 186b
Antiochus	ii 146b; iv 44a
Antiochus IV	i 108b
Antiquity, Late	iii 309a
[Dhāt] Anwāt	v 87a
Antoun, Richard	v 219b, 222a
Apartheid	v 206b
Aphraates (Aphrahat)	i 477b
Aphrodito	i 126a, 126b
Apollo	v 122a
Apollonius	i 45b
Apostle	i **123**; ii 499a, 513a
Aqaba [ʿAqaba]	i 138a, 154b, 256b, 320a, 407a; ii 14b, 15a, 16b, 20a, 20b, 21a; iii 390a, 568a, 578b; v 31b, 44a, 190a, 255b
Gulf of	i 149b; iv 153b
ʿAqabat al-Ḥirāʾ	see Thawr, Mount

al-Aqmar Mosque — I 171b
ʿAqrabāʾ — II 530b
Battle of — II 384b; III 462b; V 79a
Aqṣā Mosque [al-Masjid al-Aqṣā] — I **125a**, 125b, 126a, 156a, 156b, 501b; III 2b; V 186a
Aqṣā I — I 126a, 126b
Aqṣā II — I 126a, 126b
Aqṣā III — I 126a, 126b
ʿAqūla — I 308a
Arab(s) [*al-ʿarab*] — I 6b, 10b, 21b, 37b, 38a, 38b, 40a, 40b, 97a, 110b, 129a, 129b, 132a, 132b, 134b, 135a, 137b, **144b**, 145a, 146b, 150a, 151b, 181b, 191a, 214a, 217a, 218b, 221a, 221b, 222a, 228b, 236a, 262b, 272b, 286a, 287b, 299b, 308a, 308b, 310a, 313b, 315a, 318a, 319a, 337a, 363b, 372b, 382a, 403a, 404b, 406b, 407a, 459a, 461a, 468a, 495a, 499a, 507b, 508a, 508b, 516a, 530a, 543b; II 78b, 100a, 100b, 108a, 108b, 127a, 127b, 128a, 130a, 132a, 134a, 136a, 147a, 150a, 169a, 174a, 209a, 213a, 227a, 229b, 230a, 230b, 231a, 232a, 233b, 235a, 238a, 239b, 298a, 299a, 317b, 318b, 346a, 386a, 403a, 403b, 411a, 426b, 470a, 475a, 479a, 480a, 485b, 492a, 494a, 494b, 495a, 496a, 497b, 498b, 499a, 513a, 527a, 528b, 532b, 534a, 545a; III 11a, 30a, 84b, 97a, 106b, 111a, 112b, 114a, 114b, 115a, 115b, 119a, 119b, 120a, 120b, 122a, 123a, 128a, 164b, 209a, 214a, 219b, 242a, 248a, 281a, 350a, 402b, 417b, 457a, 500a, 501a, 502b, 507a, 508b, 541a, 543a, 544a, 545a, 561b, 571b, 589a, 589b; IV 46a, 59a, 69b, 106b, 112a, 152a, 157b, 160a, 160b, 162a, 216b, 219b, 249a, 254a, 254b, 255a, 256a, 257a, 258b, 259a, 297b, 313a, 313b, 329a, 329b,

337b, 349a, 356a, 381a, 389b, 405b, 415a, 416b, 439b, 519b, 531a, 550a, 599b; v 11a, 29a, 33a, 35b, 67a, 87b, 88a, 88b, 92b, 246a, 248b, 259a, 279b, 280b, 305a, 318a, 321b, 340b, 364b, 365a, 365b, 399a, 435b, 436a, 476a, 486b, 561a

Christian — II 209a; III 462a, 500a; IV 416b; V 29a, 257a, 400a

Jewish — II 209a

pre-Islamic — I 127b, 130a, 234a, 329b, 336b, 337a, 401b; II 54b, 237b, 280b, 317a, 346b, 463b, 479b, 511a; III 96b, 185a, 246a, 410a, 411a, 411b, 413a; IV 91a, 218a, 255a, 256b, 259b, 260a, 430b, 491b, 504b; V 184b, 234b, 318a, 348a, 350b, 561a

Arabia — I 6a, 9b, 20b, 37a, 41a, 42a, 43a, 43b, 44a, 110b, 120b, 121a, 130b, 138a, 149a, 149b, 150a, 150b, 151a, 151b, 152a, 152b, 154a, 155a, 155b, 166a, 181b, 215b, 249b, 266a, 307b, 308a, 309a, 309b, 311b, 315b, 324a, 353b, 368a, 404a, 443b, 473a, 508b, 515a, 516a, 530b, 532a, 534b, 543a; II 19b, 26b, 45a, 79b, 156a, 165a, 170a, 174b, 209a, 224b, 239a, 272a, 294a, 296a, 305a, 310b, 317b, 318a, 374b, 426b, 427a, 429b, 432b, 437a, 438a, 439a, 467b, 479a, 480a, 483a, 492a, 516a, 523b, 529b, 566a; III 1a, 6a, 9a, 9b, 34a, 45b, 46a, 47a, 47b, 49b, 69a, 85b, 122a, 122b, 138b; III 188a, 200b, 207a, 238a, 241b, 248a, 275a, 275b, 339a, 380b, 405a, 405b, 410a, 411a, 413b, 428b, 429b, 432b, 455b, 483a, 483b, 508a, 510b, 511b, 550b, 564b, 578a, **587b**, 591a; IV 11b, 22b, 37a, 45b, 46a, 54b,

107b, 108a, 160a, 162b, 208b, 253b, 254a, 255b, 256a, 257a, 257b, 258a, 258b, 259a, 259b, 260a, 260b, 288b, 328a, 399a, 405a, 405b, 408b, 410b, 416b, 434b, 512a, 571a, 572a, 579a; v 29b, 33b, 52a, 66b, 67b, 68a, 86b, 87a, 88a, 88b, 130a, 180b, 232b, 235a, 236a, 245b, 268a, 286a, 292b, 298b, 314b, 365a, 365b, 420b, 431a, 477a, 481b, 549b, 550a, 550b, 558a

Central ii 429b, 437b; iii 79a; v 565b, 567b

Felix iv 585b

North iv 405b

pre-Islamic i 302a, 317a, 329b, 344a, 369b, 383a, 385b, 401a, 432a, 448b, 450b, 542b; ii 25, 345b, 478a, 511b, 523b, 525a; iii 44b, 76a, 128a, 196b, 245a, 246b, 415a, 500a, 587a, 589a; iv 188a, 209a, **253b**, 254a, 254b, 255a, 256b, 257a, 258a, 258b, 260a, 400a, 405b, 406a, 512b, 571b, 583b; v 78b, 84b, 162b, 180a, 449a

Provincia/Province of i 137b, 308a

South i 20b, 21a, 61b, 155a, 209a, 309a; ii 211a, 299a, 437b, 438a; iii 326b, 412b, 500b; iv 45b, 46a, 204a, 258b, 406b, 411a, 411b, 511a, 585b, 586b; v **84b**, 87a, 87b, 88a, 88b, 90a, 90b, 91b, 93a, 397b, 561b, 562b

Arabian(s) i 353b; iii 381a; v 85a, 88a, 89b

Arabic (language) i 33b, 45b, 46b, 48b, 77a, **127b**, 128a, 128b, 129a, 129b, 130a, 130b, 131a, 132a, 132b, 133a, 133b, 134a, 134b, **135a**, 136a, 138a, 138b, 139a, 139b, 145a, 158a, 164b, 170a, 173a, 188b, 311a, 315a, 315b, 316b, 317a, 317b, 318a, 319a, 521a, 524b, 529b; ii 10b, 37a, 88b, 89b, 90a,

93a, 97a, 131a, 226b, 227a, 227b, 228a, 228b, 229a, 229b, 230a, 230b, 234a, 234b, 235a, 235b, 243a, 282b, 285b, 287a, 288a, 288b, 291b, 292a, 292b, 320a, 342b, 343a, 346a, 347b, 350b, 352a, 366b, 405a, 406b, 431b, 434b, 441a, 458b, 481b, 484b, 498a, 513a, 513b, 515b, 516b, 532a, 537a; III 1a, 2a, 8b, 9a, 10b, 14b, 35a, 49a, 51b, 69b, 99a, 101a, 108a, 108b, 109a, 109b, 110a, 112a, 112b, 113b, 114a, 114b, 115a, 115b, 116a, 117b, 118a, 118b, 119a, 119b, 120a, 120b, 121b, 122a, 123a, 123b, 124a, 127a, 128a, 129a, 130b, 131b, 141b, 148b, 156b, 164b, 176a, 186b, 188a, 192b, 193b, 196b, 198a, 198b, 201a, 201b, 204a, 204b, 207b, 213b, 215b, 221b, 225b, 244b, 258b, 299a, 325a, 325b, 367b, 407b, 409a, 443a, 451a, 471b, 472a, 505b, 507a, 515b, 528b, 544b, 549a, 553a, 553b, 590a, 592a, 605a; IV 18b, 23a, 26a, 28b, 39a, 48a, 51b, 54a, 56b, 57a, 58a, 58b, 59a, 59b, 60a, 63b, 90a, 92a, 155b, 177a, 183a, 228b, 230b, 235b, 237a, 237b, 239a, 240a, 240b, 245b, 246a, 247a, 248b, 257b, 259a, 268a, 272a, 273a, 275a, 280b, 287b, 289a, 316a, 317a, 337b, 355a, 374a, 375b, 383a, 395a, 397a, 398a, 400a, 439a, 445b, 447a, 477a, 500a, 512a, 516b, 517a, 525b, 563b, 565b, 566a, 566b, 574b, 586a; V 3a, 54b, 72b, 74a, 81a, 94a, 98a, 98b, 106a, 112a, 117a, 131a, 148b, 152a, 167a, 189b, 207a, 208a, 209a, 210b, 211b, 213b, 216a, 218a, 220a, 222a, 225a, 226a, 228b, 241a, 241b,

286b, 296b, 306a, 306b, 308b, 321b, 323b, 324a, 333a, 335a, 340b, 341a, 343a, 345b, 346b, 349b, 391a, 391b, 393a, 419b, 432a, 449a, 537b, 538a, 539a, 540a, 540b, 555a
Classical (CA) I 128a, 128b, 129a, 130a, 130b, 131a, 133a, 134a; II 346b, 347a, 350a, 352a, 357a; III 122a, 123a, 129a, 408a, 408, 415a; IV 193b, 250b, 355b, 357a, 357b; V 57a, 188a, 218a, 224a, 299a
neo- II 346b
Old (OA) II 346b, 498a
pre-Islamic I 138b; II 346a, 351b; III 122a; V 314b, 439a
Qurashī IV 449b
South I 398b
Standard II 89b, 346a, 347a
Modern Standard (MSA) I 128a, 129b; II 346b; III 416b
Arabism IV 57a
Arabist(s) III 109a, 111b, 121b, 122b, 123a, 124a, 126b, 129b; IV 249a
ʿArafa II 205a, 297a, 297b, 298a; III 75b; IV 95b, 96a, 96b, 97b
Arafat, W.N. II 150b
ʿArafāt I 25b, **145b**, 146a, 363a, 547a; IV 95b, 96a, 96b, 259a, 330b, 515b; V 146a
Day of V 127a
Mount I 319b; III 69a; IV 98a
Aram II 559b
Aramaeans II 559a
Syriac-speaking III 405b
Aramaic (language) I 316b, 490a; II 231b, 234a, 342b, 361b, 404b, 485b, 513a, 544a; III 9a, 10a, 114a, 131a, 231a, 244a; IV 28b, 37a, 56b, 397a, 517a, 586a; V 3a, 105a, 551b, 564b
Imperial I 137b
Ararat I **146b**, 147a; III 68b, 541a
Mount III 68b
Arathat V 90b

Arbad b. Qays	IV 114a
Arberry, A.	I 36a, 200a, 399a; III 70a, 114b, 182a, 196a, 198a; IV 48a; V 354a
Arculf	I 125b, 156b; III 429a
Ardaf	I 306a
Arethas	see Ḥārith
Arghūn al-Kāmilī	III 601b
Arian(s)	II 515b
Arīb b. Saʿīd	I 47b
al-ʿArim	I **60b**, 151a; III 521a; IV 586a
Aristotelians	IV 83a
Aristotle	I 62a, 477b; III 183a; IV 68b, 73b, 75a, 75b, 76b, 83b, 548b; V 8b, 81a
Arizona	III 553b
Arjumand Bānū Begum	III 324a
Arkoun, M.	I **430a**, 471a; II 137a, 191a, **570b**; V 101b, 298a, 349b, **433b**
Armageddon	I 31a
Armenia	I 146b, 332b; III 68b
Armenian(s)	I 146b
Armenian (language)	III 244a
Arnaldez, R.	III 183a
Arnold, T.	V 348b
Arrivabene, A.	V 346a
Arslanhan Mosque	I 285b
Artemis	V 122a
Artuk, I.	III 299a
Arūtīn, Yaʿqūb (d. after 1738)	IV 248b
[Banū] Asad	I 121a, 529b; II 357a, 530a; III 80a; V 79a, 366a
Asad, M.	I 200a, 200b, 340a, 340b, 489a, 530b; III 241a; IV 54a; V 380a, 430a; see also Weiss, L.
Asad, Ṭ.	III **100a**
Asʿad Abū Karib (Qarib; Yemenite ruler)	IV 333b; V 389b
Asad b. Khuzayma	V 508a
Asadī-yi Ṭūsī	IV 61a, 63a
Āṣaf b. Barakhyā	III 395a, 396b
al-Aṣamm (Abū Bakr; d. 200/817)	II 114a, 337b; III 470a, 470b
Asani, A.	I **63b**; II **177a**; V **98a**
Asante	IV 170a, 177b
Asclepius	V 122a
Ash Shiddieqy	V 100b
al-Aʿshā, Maymūn b. Qays	II 447b; IV 111b, 112a

al-Ashʿarī, Abū l-Ḥasan ʿAlī (d. 324/935) I 105a, 105b, 106a, 106b, 107a, 436b, 437a, 468a, 471a, 484a; II 53a, 171b, 532b; III 87b; IV 74b, 75a, 77b, 85b, 86a, 459a, 460b, 477a; V 8b, 112a, 334b
al-Ashʿarī, Abū Mūsā (d. 42/662) I 333a, 333b, 348b, 353a, 356a, 357a, 528a; II 102b; III 502b, 503b; IV 369a; V 2a
Ashʿarī(s)/Ashʿarites I 469a, 483a; II 52b, 53a, 160b, 286a, 413a, 533b, 535a; III 73a, 352b, 353a, 385b, 470b; IV 77b, 79a, 80a, 81a, 81b, 85b, 86a, 89a, 433a, 433b; V 12b, 111b
Ashʿarism I 483a, 484a; II 421a; V 136a, 273b, 324b, 487b
Asher III 9b
Ashera V 86b
al-Ashmāwī, M.S. (b. 1932) IV 149a, 149b
[Mawlānā] Ashraf ʿAlī Thānawī I 520b
al-Ashraf ʿUmar (Rasūlid ruler) I 47a, 47b
ʿĀshūrāʾ I 38b, 518b; II 182a, 182b, 204a, 208a; III 54b, 412b, 538a, 541b; IV 227a, 305a, 341a, 342a, 413a; V 556b
Ashurbanibipal III 544a
Asia I 78b, 264a, 286a; III 297a, 306a, 306b, 314a, 315b, 316a, 317a, 346a, 432a, 432b; IV 269a, 275b, 382a; V 13a, 98b, 99b, 100a, 101a, 213a, 342a, 567b
  Central II 530b; III 247b, 248a, 312b, 313a, 313b, 317a, 432b, 433b; IV 267a, 269a, 271b; V 94a, 137a
  East III 314a, 315a, 319b, 325a
  South I 201a; III 314a, 319b; IV 172b; V 94a, 94b, 98b
ʿĀṣim b. Abī al-Najūd Bahdala (Kūfa; d. 127/745) I 334a; III 15a; IV 54a, 109b, 357a, 358a, 359b, 373a, 389a; V 238b
al-ʿAṣimī, Abū Muḥammad Aḥmad b. Muḥammad b. ʿAlī (d. 450/1058) II 102b, 112b; III 126a; V 325a
ʿAsīr II 294b; V 92a
Āsiya I 59a, 519a; II 193b; III 501a; V 375a, 532a, 532b, 534a

al-ʿAskarī, Abū Hilāl (d. 1010) IV 479b, 481b
al-ʿAskarī, [Imām] al-Ḥasan (d. 260/874) II 117a, 504a; IV 593b, 594b, 599b, 602a
Asmāʾ bt. al-Nuʿmān V 509a
al-Aṣmaʿī (d. 213/828) III 120b, 121a, 606a; V 232b
al-Assiouty, Sarwat Anis III 9b, 10a
Assmann, A. II 248b
Assmann, J. II 248b, 310a; IV 346a
Assyria III 143b
Assyrian(s) I 147a, 149b, 487b; IV 524a
Assyrian (language) IV 517a
Assyrian Church of the East I 209a
Astarte, Temple of III 249b
Asṭūs (of Men of the Cave) IV 351a
al-Aswad see Dhū l-Ḥimār ʿAbhala b. Kaʿb
al-Aswad al-ʿAnsī (d. 10/632) I 121a; II 530a; V 79a
al-Aswad b. Yaʿfūr III 588b
al-Aswād b. Zayd III 250a
Āsya (wife of Pharaoh) III 81a, 81b, 290b, 291a
ʿAṭaʾ b. Abī Rabāḥ (d. 114-15/732-3) IV 99a, 533a; V 55b, 255a, 417b
Atala Mosque III 434a
Atatürk, Kemal V 342b
ʿAthar V 85b, 86b, 87b, 91b, 93a
Athenians I 499b
Athirat V 86b
ʿAthtar dhū-Qabḍum V 92b
ʿĀtika II 241a
ʿAtīq b. ʿĀbid (of Makhzūm) V 507b
ʿAṭiyya al-Quraẓī IV 334b
ʿAṭiyya b. Saʿd al-ʿAwfī (d. 111/729) III 87b; IV 533a
Atlantic Ocean V 13a
ʿAṭṭār, Farīd al-Dīn (d. 627/1230) I 542a; III 222b
[St.] Augustine (d. 430) V 8b
Austin, J. III 97a
Austrian State National Library III 590a
Australia I 385b, 557a; IV 273b
Averroës see Ibn Rushd (d. 595/1198)
Avicenna see Ibn Sīnā (d. 428/1037)
ʿAwf b. Mālik III 502b
Awran V 87b
Awrangzīb III 324b
Awres II 116b
Aws I 389b, 407a, 409a, 409b; II 15a, 16a, 16b, 17a, 20a, 21b, 299a; II 29a, 30a, 369a, 369b, 438b; V 272b, 279b

Aws Allāh	ii 16b, 20a
Aws b. al-Ṣāmit	i 513a
Aws b. Thābit al-Anṣārī	ii 519a
Aws al-Manāt	ii 16b, 20a
Awsān	v 87b, 91b, 92b
ʿAwwam	i 152a; v 91a
al-Awzāʿī (d. 157/774)	i 481a; iv 323b
Axum	i 20b; ii 79b
Aydughdī b. ʿAbdallāh al-Badrī	iii 601b
al-Ayka	iv 425b, 605b, 606a
Ayla	i 154b; v 37a, 185a
Ayoub, M.M.	ii 435a; iv 383b; v 377a
Ayuba Suleiman Ibrahima Diallo	see Job ben Solomon (d. ca. 1773)
al-ʿAyyāshī, Muḥammad b. Masʿūd (d. ca. 320/932)	i 550b; ii 117a; iv 593b, 602a
Ayyūb	see Job
Ayyūb al-Anṣārī	iii 322b
Ayyūbids	ii 206b; iii 308b
Azamahxeri	see al-Zamakhsharī (d. 558/1144)
ʿAyzār	i 192a
al-ʿAyzāra	i 192a
Āzād, [Mawlānā] Abū l-Kalām	i 201a; ii 129a; iii 224a
Āzar	i 7a, 166b, **192a**, 521b; v 95b, 248b, 249a, 250a, 258a
Azāriqa	i 540a, 540b; ii 505a; iii 85b, 86b, 87b
ʿAzāzīl	v 96a
Azd	ii 16b
Azd ʿUmmān	i 529b, 530a
Azerbayjan	i 332b; iv 352b
Azeri (language)	i 136a
Azhar Fatāwa Committee	i 29b
al-Azhar Mosque, Cairo	iii 312a, 436b, 595b
al-Azhar Mosque, Kebayoran, Jakarta	v 100a
al-Azhar University, Cairo	i 186b; ii 90b, 128a, 128b, 131a, 133b, 134a; iii 230b; iv 270b, 272a, 272b, 273a; v 205b, 208b, 209b, 211a, 214a, 217a, 217b, 218a, 218b, 219a, 220a, 224a, 342b
College for Girls	v 227b
Department of Culture and Islamic Missions	v 218a
Faculty for Islamic Mission	v 218a
Qurʾān Review Section	iv 272b, 273a
al-Azharī (d. 905/1499)	i 217a, 217b; ii 500b, 501a
Azharī, M.	iv 267a, 271b

al-ʿAzīz — III 234b; IV 584b; V 392a, 529b, 530b, 531a, 531b, 532a
al-ʿAzīz (r. 365-86/976-96) — IV 525a
Azīz al-Azmeh — IV 475a
Aziza al-Hibri — see al-Hibri, Aziza
al-Azraqī (d. 222/837) — I 309b; IV 590b
al-Azraqī (d. 250/865) — V 565b
al-Azraqī, Ibrāhīm b. ʿAbd al-Raḥmān (d. after 890/1485) — I 78a; III 363b, 364a, 364b, 365a
Azzindani, Abdul Majeed — IV 554a, 555b, 556a, 556b

B

Baal [Baʿl] — I **194a**, II 13a, 13b
Baalam [Ibn Bāʿūra] — III 242a
Baalbaki, R. — II 228a, 233a
Baalbek — II 13a
Bāb — see Sayyid ʿAlī Muḥammad Shīrāzī
Bāb al-Futūḥ — II 84b
Bab al-Mandab Strait — I 20b
Bāb al-Raḥma — see Gate of Mercy
Bāb al-Wuzarāʾ — see Vizier's Gate
Bāb Zuwaylah — II 84b
Bābā Farīd (d. 665/1691) — III 225b
Babel — III 539a
  Tower of — I 340b; III 488b, 522a, 539b; V 236b
al-Bābī al-Ḥalabī — IV 266b, 271b
Bābism — I 197a; III 124b
Babylon [Bābil] — I **195a**, 195b, 155b; II 404a, 404b, 405a, 563a; III 249b; IV 165a, 524a; V 202b, 203a
Babylonia — IV 37a, 328a, 585b; V 162b, 176a
Babylonian(s) — I 108a, 499b; III 247a
Babylonian Tower — see Babel
al-Badʿ — I 149b
Badawi, Jamal — V 206a, 224b
Badawi, S. — I 133b
Badīʿ al-Zamān al-Hamadhānī (d. 398/1008) — IV 57b
Badr — I **196a**, 196b, 242a, 266b, 268a, 320a, 398a, 406a, 460b, 461a, 505b; II 147b, 148b, 149a, 183b,

184a, 241a, 299b, 400b, 508a; III 283a, 369b, 398a, 425a, 456a; IV 16a, 44b, 332b, 345b, 346a, 406a, 460b; V 37a, 43a, 379b, 430a, 465a, 491a, 508a

Battle of (2/624) I 124b, 196b, 248b, 267a, 325b, 328b, 389a, 409a, 409b, 462a, 487a, 500b, 505b, 550a, 550b; II 16b, 17a, 148b, 181b, 186b, 221b, 262b, 335a, 341b, 374a, 397b, 400a, 554b; III 33b, 183a, 438b, 496b, 579a, 581b, 603b; IV 219, 226b, 227a, 321b, 323b, 324a, 332a, 345a, 349a; V 5a, 42a, 42b, 65a, 107b, 140a, 175b, 194b, 279a, 284b, 292b, 359b, 377b, 409a, 490b

Badr al-Dīn al-Hūthī, Ḥusayn V 206b

Badr al-Dīn Simawī (d. 820/1420) V 158a

Badr al-Dīn al-Zarkashī see al-Zarkashī, Badr al-Dīn (d. 793-4/1391-2)

Badr Ḥunayn see Badr

Badran, M. II **203a**, **292b**; V **54b**

Badshahi Mosque III 434a

Bagh V 147a

al-Baghawī, Abū Muḥammad al-Ḥusayn V 147a, 147b

al-Baghawī, al-Ḥusayn b. al-Farrāʾ (d. 516/1122) II 112a; IV 533a; V 98b

Baghdad [Baghdād] I 105a, 197a, 197b, 279b, 436a, 469b, 471b, 542a; II 111a, 112b, 119b, 384a, 420b, 421a, 422a, 532b, 533a, 533b, 534a, 538b, 560a, 560b, 561a; III 131b, 301b, 311a, 312a, 415b, 430b, 467a, 468b, 606a; IV 59b; V 18a, 33b, 139a, 143b, 210b, 325b, 326a, 326b

ʿAbbāsid III 310b, 312b, 313a

al-Baghdādī, ʿAbd al-Laṭīf (d. 629/1231) III 351a

al-Baghdādī, Abū Bakr Aḥmad b. ʿAlī al-Khaṭīb (d. 463/1071) I 191b; IV 564a

al-Baghdādī, Abū Manṣūr ʿAbd al-Qāhir b. Ṭāhir (d. 429/1037) III 119a, 215a, 396b; IV 75a, 86a, 414a, 433b

al-Baghdādī, A.M. I **410a**

al-Baghdādī, Ḥāshim Muḥammad IV 273b

al-Baghdādī, M. Abū ʿAlī	II 493b, 495a
Baghshūr	V 147a
Bahāʾ al-Dawla	I 282a
Bahāʾ al-Dīn al-Muqtanā (d. after 434/1032)	I 554b, 556b
Baha Muhaiyadden	I 90a
[Shaykh] Bahāʾī	IV 64b
Bahāʾīs [*ahl al-bahāʾ*]	I **197a**, 393b
Universal House of Justice	I 199a
Bahasa Indonesia (language)	V 99b
Bahāshima	III 467a
Bahāʾullāh	I 197a, 197b, 198a, 198b, 199a
al-Bahbūdī, M.	II 378a
Baḥīrā	II 514b, 515a, 515b; III 405b; IV 410b; V 186a
Baḥithat al-Bādiya	see Malak Ḥinfī Nāṣif
Baḥr	I 314b
Bahrain [al-Baḥrayn]	I 121a, 127b; III 589a
Bahrām Gūr	III 221b
Bahrām Shāh	IV 56a
al-Baḥrānī, Hāshim b. Sulaymān (d. 1107/1696 or 1109/1697)	II 117b; IV 595a, 602b
Bahrul Ulum (publisher)	IV 275a
al-Bahshamiyya	I 484b; II 532b, 534a; III 467a, 471a
Bahtiar Effendy	V 218b
Bahupal	V 342a
al-Bājī	V 401b
Bakka	I 155a; III 77a, 97a; IV 327b, 514a
Bakker, D.	IV 197a
[Banū] Bakr	I 256b
Baʿl	see Baal
Balaam	I 228b, 545b; IV 445a
al-Balādhurī	I 400b; II 15b; V 409b
Balʿama	I 228b
Balʿamī (Persian trans. of al-Ṭabarī)	II 146b
Balata	III 57a
Balaw	V 91b, 92b
al-Balāwī, Bishr b. Abī Kubār al-Balawī (d. after 202/817)	III 215a, 217a, 221b
Baldick, J.	I **184a**
Balḥārith	I 530b; III 500a, 500b, 501a
Balḥārith b. Kaʿb (of Najrān; d. 10/632)	I 492b
Balkans	III 435b
Balkh (Afghanistan)	II 105b, 106b, 421b; III 432b; IV 51b

Balkhaʿ	v 92a, 92b
al-Balkhī, Abū Muṭīʿ (d. 199/814)	i 482b
al-Balkhī, Abū l-Qāsim (al-Kaʿbī; d. 319/931)	ii 114b; iii 131b, 466b, 469b, 470a, 470b; v 324b
Balochi/Baluchi (language)	v 94a, 342a
Balqāʾ	v 122a, 185a
Bamyeh, M.	iv **33b**; v 469b
Bandung	v 101b
Bangladesh	iv 273b; v 94a, 538b
Bankipore (India)	iv 601a
al-Bannā, Ḥasan (d. 1949)	iv 144a, 145a; v 103b, 225a, 228a, 228b
al-Bannāʾ al-Dimyāṭī	see al-Dimyāṭī (d. 1117/1705)
Banū	see under respective tribal eponyms
Banū-yi Iṣfahānī (d. 1403/1982)	v 159a
al-Bāqillānī, al-Qāḍī Abū Bakr Muḥammad b. al-Ṭayyib (d. 403/1013)	i 269b, 425b, 470b, 471a; ii 424b, 529a, 533b, 535a, 535b; iii 66b, 206a, 214b, 396b; iv 74b, 86a, 423b, 424a, 477a; v 8b, 14a, 79a, 112a, 136a, 309a, 325b, 334b
al-Bāqir, [Imām] Muḥammad (d. 113-14/731-2 or 119/737)	i 541a; ii 117a; iv 594a
Baqiyya b. al-Walīd (d. 197/813)	ii 394a
Bāqūm	iv 604b
Bar-Asher, M.	ii 117a, 117b, **426a**; iv **603a**
Bar Hebraeus (d. 1286)	iv 249a
Bar Kokhba	ii 298b
Barāqish	v 89a
al-Barbahārī, Abū Muḥammad (d. 329/941)	i 481b, 482a
Bareilly	iv 266a
Barēlwī(s)	i **201a**, 201b
Barhūt	ii 463b
Bāriq River	iii 285a
Barmakids	iv 51b
Barqūq al-Yalbughawī	iii 312a
Barṣalībī (d. 565/1170)	v 344a
Barth, J.	ii 358a; v 240a, 240b, 245a
Bartholomaeus Picenus de Monte Arduo	iv 242a, 245b
Baruch	ii 240b
Barzillay	iv 316a
Basel	iv 245b; v 344b
Council of (1431-49)	iv 242b
Bashshār b. Burd	v 14a
Bashir, S.	i **93b**, **406a**; ii **55a**; iii 97a

Basil al-Bayati (contemporary architect)	I 172b
Baṣra	I 127b, 210a, 271a, 332b, 333a, 333b, 357a; II 108a, 108b, 295a, 347b, 532b, 560a, 560b; III 85a, 85b, 86b, 87b, 88b, 429a, 467a, 555a, 605b; IV 277a, 355a, 373a, 388a; V 63a, 325b, 409b
al-Basyūnī, [Shaykh] ʿAbd al-Ḥalīm	IV 272b
Bates, M.	III **559b**
Bateson, M.	I 127b
Baṭḥa	II 295a
Bathsheba	I 496a, 496b; IV 315b, 316b, 317a
Bauer, H.	III 474a, 474b; IV 193b
Bauer, Th.	II **487a**, **541a**; IV 471a
Baumstark, A.	V 500a
Baʿūra	III 242a
Bausani, A.	V 354b
Bavarian Illuminati	I 30b
Bawa Muhaiyadeen	I 90a; IV 176a
Bāyazīd/Bāyezīd II (r. 886-918/1481-1512)	III 320a, 320b; IV 268a
Baybars I	III 434a
Baybars al-Jāshnikīr (r. 708-9/1309-10)	III 311b, 601b
al-Bayḍāwī, ʿAbdallāh b. ʿUmar (d. 685/1286)	I 33a, 36a, 45a, 53a, 268a; III 56a, 57a, 92a, 94a, 95a, 200b, 541b; IV 538a, 538b, 539a, 539b
al-Bayḍāwī, Nāṣir al-Dīn (d. 716/1316)	I 175b, 203b, 205a, 261a, 322a, 389b; II 113a, 116a, 116b, 138a, 150b, 151b, 195b, 196a, 272b, 278a, 356b, 500b; III 65b, 70a, 73a, 228a, 249b, 381a; IV 3a, 250b, 266b, 274b, 275a, 289b, 503b; V 98b, 131a, 157a, 160b, 296b, 341a, 346b, 348a, 353a, 359b, 380a, 382a, 414b, 510a
al-Bayḥāqī (d. 458/1066)	II 339a
Bayhasiyya	III 86b
Bayjūrī	V 499b
Baysān (today Bet Shean, Israel)	V 489b
Baysonghur	III 268a
al-Bazzī, Aḥmad b. Muḥammad (d. ca. 250/864-5)	IV 360a, 390a
Beaucamp, J.	I 155a
Beaumont, D.	III **181b**; V **18b**
Beck, E.	I 330b; II 352a; IV 189b
Beck, M.F.	IV 246b
Bedouin(s)	I 5b, 67a, 131b, **214a**, 214b, 215a,

215b, 216a, 216b, 217a, 217b, 287a, 375a; II 72b, 294a, 470a, 552b; III 483b; IV 18b, 34b, 54a, 107a, 189b, 259b, 465b, 503a; V 198b, 234b, 235a, 418b, 457b, 458a, 511a, 549a, 550b
Syrian IV 23a
Bedwell, William (d. 1632) IV 248b
Beer-Sheba [*biʾr sabaʿ*] I 9a; IV 54b
Beeston, A.F.L. III 390b; V 389b
Behrens-Abouseif, D. I **491a**; II **547a**
Beijing III 315a
Beirut II 200b
Bektashiyya (Ṣūfī order) I 30b; III 247b; IV 175a
Belial I 108b
Bell, R. I 36a, 112a, 200a, 248b, 270b, 322b, 323a, 325a, 325b, 331a, 340a, 417b, 506b; II 191a, 252a, 255a, 262a, 506a; III 110b, 457b, 474b, 522a, 538a; IV 101b, 188b, 191a, 191b, 192a, 193a, 399b, 449a; V 240a, 241a, 249b, 261b, 262a, 266a, 271a, 352b, 353a, 354a
Bellah, R. V 67b, 68a, 298a
Bellamy, J. III 474a; IV 101b, 102b, 193b, 195a, 196a, 351b; V **252a**
Ben ʿAshūr, M. I 427b
Ben Shemesh, A. V 350b
Ben Solomon, Job I 30a
Bench, People of the [*ahl al-ṣuffa*] I 389b
Bengal V 96b, 97a
Bengali (language) V 94a, 96a, 342a
Bengno de Muruiondo y Ugartondo V 351a
Benjamin [Binyamīn] I **226b**, 227a, 227b, 228a, 521b, 532b; III 94a; IV 308b, 529a, 536b; V 255b
Berber (language) I 136a
van Berchem, M. I 169a
Berg, H. I **31b**, **394b**; IV **158b**
Bergsträsser, G. I 322b, 334a, 350b, 361a, 417b; II 235a, 351b; IV 189a, 189b, 392b; V 239b, 297b
Berlin III 312a
Berlin, B. I 361b

[St.] Bernard of Clairvaux (d. 1153) III 503a; IV 239a
Bernardo de Rossi (d. 1831) IV 244b
Bernardo Pérez de Chinchón, B. IV 244b
Berque, J. III 110b; IV 449b; V 354b
Berti (northern Sudanese people) IV 176b, 177a
Beth Arshām I 309b
Bethelea V 258b
Bey Arifin V 100b
Bībī Khānum III 314a, 431b
Bible(s) I 7a, 98b, 116a, 118a, 149a, 149b, 195a, 226b, **228b**, 248b, 264a, 270a, 313b, 314b, 315b, 339b, 379b, 418b, 425a, 497a, 528a, 534b; II 10b, 11a, 13a, 50a, 131b, 156b, 240a, 435a, 436b, 437a, 444a, 458a, 485a, 561b, 563b, 564a; III 1b, 4a, 9b, 45b, 51a, 52a, 104a, 142b, 143a, 147b, 148a, 179b, 211b, 213b, 231b, 342a, 417b, 418b, 420a, 481b, 487a, 504a, 515b, 539a, 541a, 544a, 585a, 593b; IV 37b, 52a, 92a, 106a, 123b, 124a, 217a, 239a, 241b, 290b, 302a, 304a, 315b, 413a, 448b, 450b, 451a, 451b, 473b, 527b, 528b, 536a, 553a, 559a, 560a, 564b, 577b, 578a; V 35b, 41b, 43a, 48a, 48b, 82a, 86b, 104a, 106b, 114a, 128b, 129a, 130a, 130b, 193a, 248a, 248b, 259a, 276a, 299a, 306a, 340b, 354a, 381a, 433a, 574a; see also Testament
  Christian I 31a, 208a; III 407b
  Hebrew I 42b, 104a, 108a, 208a, 237b, 303a, 303b, 316a, 379b, 475a, 476a, 496a; II 146b, 222a, 235b, 268b, 435a, 436b, 564a, 566b; III 16b, 56a, 57a, 126b, 127a, 143a, 144a, 146b, 147a, 389b, 390a, 408b, 417b, 477b, 479b, 484b, 545a, 554b; IV 68b, 122b, 221b, 241b, 314a, 445a, 450b, 586a; V 7a, 48a, 66b, 129a, 176a, 245a, 300b, 309b, 416b, 427a, 531b

  Jewish ii 233b
  of Alcalá iv 249b
  of Antwerp iv 249b
  of London iv 249b
  of Paris iv 249b
Bibliander, Th. iv 236b, 242a, 245a, 245b, 248b, 249b, 265a; v 346a
Bibliotheca Vaticana v 345a
Bibliothèque Nationale de Paris i 283a
Biḥārī iii 265a
Bijlefeld, W.A. v 299a
Bilāl b. Rabāḥ (d. ca. 20/656; first muezzin) i 408b; ii 514b; iv 226a; v 58b, 59a
Bilqīs i 61a, **228b**; ii 291a, 558a; iii 92a; iv 586a; v 77b, 93a, 277a, 390a, 533a, 533b
Bint Abī Ṭālib see Umm Hāni
Bint al-Shāṭiʾ see ʿAbd al-Raḥmān, ʿĀ.
Binyamīn see Benjamin
al-Biqāʿī, Burhān al-Dīn Abū l-Ḥasan Ibrāhīm (d. 885/1480) ii 114b; iii 126b; v 330a, 405b
Biʾr Maʿūna i 16b, 321a
Birkeland, H. i 76a, 417b; ii 101b
al-Bīrūnī, Abū l-Rayḥān (d. 443/1050) ii 228a; iv 57b, 62b, 525a, 540a, 540b, 541a, 552b; v 306b, 309a
Bishr (son of Job) i 528b
Bishr [b. Abī Kubār] al-Balawī see al-Balawī, Bishr b. Abī Kubār (d. after 202/817)
Bishr b. al-Muʿtamir (d. ca. 210/825) ii 421b; iii 469a
Bisri Mustofa v 99a
al-Bisṭāmī, Abū Yazīd see Abū Yazīd al-Bisṭāmī (d. 261/874)
Bivar, A. i 33a
[King] Bīwarasb (al-Ḍaḥḥāk) iii 542a
Blachère, R. i 5a, 112a, 210b, 322b, 417b, 420b; ii 191a, 250a, 255a, 504b; iv 188b, 191a, 191b, 194a, 196a, 395b; v 236a, 240a, 240b, 247a, 252a, 297a, 297b, 298a, 352b, 353a, 398a
Black Shriners see Ancient Egyptian Arabic Order of Nobles of the Shrine
Blair, S. i 169a; iii 304b, **602b**; v **559a**
Blankinship, K. i **463b**; iii **537b**, **568b**
Blau, J. ii 362a, 364a
Bloch, A. ii 360b, 361a, 366b

Blois, F.C. de III 412a; IV **512b**
Bloom, J. III **437b**, **602b**; IV 265a
Bne Hinnom V 106a
Bobzin, H. IV **251a**; V **354b**
Bodleian Library IV 362a
Boethius (d. 524) V 8b
Bombay IV 265b, 266a
Bonanate, U. IV 195a
Bonelli, L. V 352b, 354b
Bonner, M. I **266a**; IV **209b**; V **470a**
Book I **242b**, 262a, 305a; II 246a
Mother of the I 468b
People(s) of the [*ahl al-kitāb, alladhāna ūtū al-kitāb*] I 10b, 93a, 118a, 120a, 182b, 207a, 219a, 222, 223a, 223b, 224a, 224b, 247a, 266b, 267a, 303a, 305a, 306a, 310a, 312a, 314a, 374a, 377a, 377b, 378b, 379a, 380b, 381a, 431b, 432b, 440b, 464b, 502b; II 25a, 26a, 63b, 65b; II 72b, 73a, 73b, 147b, 150a, 150b, 182a, 220a, 221a, 243b, 401b, 443a, 444a, 459b, 496b, 498b, 499a, 515b, 544b, 545b, 569b, 570a; III 15a, 17a, 19b, 21b, 22b, 23a, 24a, 24b, 25a, 25b, 26a, 26b, 27a, 27b, 28a, 28b, 30a, 31a, 32a, 32b, 33a, 34a, 35a, 40a, 41b, 141a, 236a, 238a, 240b, 244a, 245a, 277b, 372b, 381a, 402a, 443b, 445b, 449a, 450a, 456b, 484a, 508b, 513a, 563b, 564a, 567b, 592b; IV 26a, **36a**, 36b, 38a, 38a, 38b, 39b, 40b, 42a, 85a, 120a, 120b, 121a, 121b, 152b, 153a, 153b, 160b, 161a, 222b, 226b, 298a, 309a, 311a, 326b, 334b, 394b, 400a, 402b, 403a, 405a, 406b, 407a, 407b, 409a, 409b, 412a, 414b, 415a, 416a, 458b, 511b; V 7a, 56a, 56b, 173a, 291b, 292a, 301a, 301b, 303b, 304b, 370b, 417b, 418a, 431a, 437b, 456a, 458a, 458b, 459a, 496a

of God — IV 370b; V 320a, 320b
of Prayer — IV 230b
Bornu — I 33a
Borrmans, M. — I **538a**; IV **264b**, **435b**, **524a**
Bosra — I **138a**
Bostra [Būṣrā] — I 207b, 308a; II 514b; V 184b, 186a
Bosworth, C.E. — V 353a
Boullata, I. — III **204b**, 206a; IV **23b**
Bouman, J. — II 533a; IV 197a
Bourdieu, P. — I 413a
Bousquet, G. — II 523b; IV 488b, 491b; V 349b
Bowen, D.L. — I **233b**, **235a**; II **512a**
Bowen, J. — II 191b
Böwering, G. — I 91b, **335a**, **467a**; II **331b**; IV **230b**; V 141a, 142a, 151b, 170a, **290a**
Boyarin, D. — IV 404b
Boysen, F. — V 349a
Brahui (language) — V 342a
Braille — II 90a
Branca, P. — V **472b**
Bravmann, M. — I 417b; II 567b, 568b; IV 204a, 458a
Brethren of Purity — see Brotherhood of Purity [ikhwān al-ṣafāʾ]
Brill Publishers — IV 273 a
Brinner, W. — I **147a**, 367a; II **12b**, **405a**; III **69a**, **543b**; IV **48a**; V **396b**
Britain — I 201a; IV 273b; V 347a
British India — see India
British Museum — II 36a, 37a, 38a; III 312a
Brockelmann, C. — II 113b, 235a, 350b, 352b, 357b, 362a; V 326b
Brockopp, J. — I **290a**, **397a**; III **73b**; IV **277b**, **580a**; V **60a**
Brodersen, A. — IV **394b**, **424b**
Brodeur, P. — IV **398b**
Bronze Age, Late — I 149b
Broomfeld, G.W. — V 342a
Brotherhood of Purity [*ikhwān al-ṣafāʾ*] — I 263a, 488b; II 118a; III 555a; IV 381a
Brown, P. — IV 209b
Browne, E.G.A. — III 222a, 222b
Buʿāth — II 16b, 20a, 205b
Buchmann, Th. — see Bibliander

Bucaille, M. IV 553a
Buck, C. I **199a**
Buckley, R.P. III **276b**
Buczacki, J.M. V 350b
Buddha IV 561a
Buddhism I 169b, 180b, 316a, 418b; IV 407b; V 66a
Buhatia see Ibn ʿAṭiyya al-Andalusī (d. 546/1151)
Buhl, F. I 323a, 465a
al-Buḥturī (d. ca. 284/897) III 384b
Bujayr b. Zuhayr b. Abī Sulmā IV 114a
Bukhārā III 315b, 320b, 433b
al-Bukhārī, Abū ʿAbdallāh Muḥammad b. Ismāʿīl (d. 256/870) I 36a, 38b, 44a, 44b, 61a, 67a, 77b, 292a, 391b, 481b; II 110b, 222a, 222b, 270b, 272b, 377a, 400a, 446a, 446b, 502a; III 140b, 350b, 392a, 541b, 546a; IV 303a, 369a, 369b, 370a, 372b, 384a, 423b, 442a, 488b, 591a; V 35a, 179b, 278a, 330a, 330b, 360b, 401b, 415a, 466b, 471b
al-Bukhārī, Nūr al-Dīn al-Ṣābūnī (d. 580/1184) I 484a
Būlāq Press IV 269b, 271a
Bulgaria III 322b, 602a; V 76a
Bullhe Shāh (d. 1172/1758) III 225a; V 97a, 98a
al-Bulqīnī, ʿAlam al-Dīn V 328a
al-Bulqīnī, Jalāl al-Dīn ʿAbd al-Raḥmān (d. 824/1421) V 328a
al-Būnī, Abū l-ʿAbbās Shihāb al-Dīn (d. 622/1225) I 78a; II 38b; III 250b, 306a; V 329a
Burāq III 327a; IV 60b
Burhān al-Dīn Abū l-Ḥasan Ibrāhīm al-Biqāʿī see al-Biqāʿī, Burhān al-Dīn Abū l-Ḥasan Ibrāhīm (d. 885/1480)
Burhān al-Dīn Ibrāhīm b. Muḥammad al-Ḥalabī al-Dimashqī (d. 956/1549) III 288a
Burrell, D. V **388b**
Burton, J. I **19a**, 45b, 323a, 334b, 351a, **361a**, 417b, 530a; II 352a, 384b; III 465b; IV 199a, 201b, 202a, 203b, 326b, 327a
al-Buṣīrī III 321a
Būṣrā see Bostra
Busse, H. I **272a**, **529a**; II 146b; III **6b**, **55a**, **232b**, **540a**
Bust (Afghanistan) III 601b
Buturovic, A. II **80b**; IV **445a**; V **488a**

Byzantine(s) [*al-rūm*] I 110b, 144b, **265a**, 265b, 266a, 266b, 267a, 267b, 268a, 268b, 308a, 308b, 314b, 399b, 528b; II 147a, 147b, 282a, 296b, 438b, 490a; III 298b, 405b, 543b; IV 410a, 524b; V 40a, 80a, 456a, 504a; see also Roman(s)
Byzantinists II 475a
Byzantium I 265b, 267b, 269a, 308b; II 105b, 296a, 475a, 524a; III 91a, 436a, 573b; IV 242b, 329a, 413b; V 430b, 568a

C

Caetani, L. II 151b; V 48b
Cahen, C. I 424b
Cain [Qābīl] I 26b, 98b, 101a, 260a, 264a, **270a**, 270b, 271a, 271b, 439b, 533b; II 418a, 436a; III 190a, 459a, 459b, 521b, 542a, 542b; IV 428b; V 416b
  Children of II 484b
Cairo I 29b, 169a, 171b, 174a, 293b, 554a; II 31b, 84b, 137a, 200b, 204b, 207a, 484b, 553b; III 5b, 268a, 272b, 304a, 309a, 311b, 312b, 345b, 371a, 434a, 436b, 526b, 607b; IV 175b, 266b, 269a, 272a, 275b, 276a; V 60a, 75b, 213b, 218a, 224a, 228a, 342a, 346b
  ʿAmr b. al-Āṣ Mosque III 298a, 303b, 304a
  Congress on Arab Music (1932) IV 381b
  Ibn Ṭūlūn Mosque III 436b
  Ottoman II 461b
  University of II 133b, 135b; V 537b
Calcutta IV 265b
Calder, N. II 232b; IV 386a
Calderini, S. III **231b**
Caleb IV 577b
California V 101a
Caliph(s) see kh-l-f in Index of Transliterated Terms
Calverley, E.E. V 555b

Calza, C.V.	V 350b
Cambridge	IV 249a
Camel, Battle of the	IV 365b, 494a; V 1b, 515b, 521a
Campo, J.	I **265a**, **294a**, **276b**; II **462a**
Canaan [Kanʿān]	I 227a, 303b; III 223a, 541a; V 28a, 63a, 176a, 392b
Canaan, T.	IV 493a
Canaanite(s)	I 108a; IV 338b
Canada	V 215b
Canis Maioris	IV 109a
Carlyle, T.	III 195b; IV 190a
[Mt.] Carmel	I 199a
Carter, M.	I 131a, 131b
Carthage	II 511b
Carthaginians	I 487b
Casanova, P.	II 148a, 485a; III 141a; V 249b
Cassianus Bassus	I 45b
Catherine II (empress of Russia)	IV 250b, 251a, 265b; V 248a
Cave, Men/People of the [*aṣḥāb al-kahf*]	I 151a, 292b, 314b, 386b, 387a, 388a, 388b, 389b, 539a, 545b; II 11a, 12a, 20b, 80a, 101a, 102b, 198a; III 219a, 321b, **374a**, 375a, 396a, 396b; IV 351a; V 61b, 251a; see also Seven Sleepers
Celts	I 487b; V 52a
Chabbi, J.	I 421a, 422a, 423a, 423b; III **49b**, **341a**; V **480a**
Chalcedon, Council of (451)	IV 406b; V 566a
Chaldean(s)	I 195a; III 247a
Challenge Verse	see Verse
Chelhod, J.	III 231a; V 67a
Cheng Ho	III 315b
Chester Beatty Library	I 173b, 282a; III 265b, 318a
Chicago, University of	II 135a
Children of Adam	see Adam
Children of Cain	see Cain
Children of Israel	see Israel
Childs, B.	II 249a
China	I 287b, 288b; II 31b; III 267a, 271a, 306b, 314a, 315a, 315b, 325b, 326a, 432b, 435b, 472a; V 226a, 226b
Cultural Revolution	I 172b
Xian, Great Mosque of	III 315b
Yuan	III 315a, 315b

Yunnan — III 315a, 315b
Zushan — III 325b
Chinese (language) — III 316a, 326a; V 342a, 439a
[Shāh] Chirāgh — III 313b
Chittick, W. — V 388a
Choudhury, M.A. — V **408b**
Chouémi, M. — II 351b, 357a, 358a; IV 199b; V 297b
Chouraqui, A. — V 354a
Christ — I 11b, 73b, 102a, 116b, 312b, 313a, 314a, 404b; II 155b, 156a, 208a, 342b, 474a, 496a; III 13a, 585b; IV 41a, 241a, 564b; V 122b, 246b, 369a, 369b, 370b; see also Jesus
Last Supper — III 16b
True Cross of — I 265b
Christendom — III 503a; IV 122b
Christian Reineccius — see Reineccius, Christian
Christian(s) [*naṣāra*] — I 2a, 7b, 8a, 10b, 45a, 97a, 104a, 107b, 109a, 115a, 115b, 116a, 116b, 117a, 118a, 146b, 154a, 183b, 185b, 200a, 222b, 223a, 223b, 247a, 248b, 249a, 299a, 299b, 303a, 305b, **307b**, 308a, 309b, 310a, 310b, 311a, 311b, 312a, 312b, 313a, 313b, 314a, 314b, 315a, 315b, 325a, 335b, 336a, 340b, 372a, 372b, 373a, 374a, 377a, 377b, 378a, 378b, 380a, 380b, 382a, 389b, 415b, 429a, 429b, 432b, 443b, 464b, 466a, 466b, 478b, 538b; II 29a, 72a, 73a, 100a, 146b, 149b, 155b, 163b, 184b, 193a, 220a, 221a, 240a, 243a, 243b, 274a, 274b, 296a, 318b, 342a, 391b, 402b, 403a, 407b, 429b, 430a, 437b, 499a, 513a, 516a, 530b, 531a, 544b, 561b, 562a, 566a, 569b; III 7a, 9a, 9b, 11b, 12a, 12b, 13a, 13b, 19b, 21b, 22a, 24a, 24b, 26b, 27a, 27b, 28a, 32b, 33a, 33b, 53b, 138b, 141a, 151a, 151b, 155b, 181b, 189b, 190a, 233b, 236a, 238a, 238b,

239b, 244a, 244b, 282a, 301a, 303a, 341b, 377b, 406a, 407a, 407b, 429a, 429b, 445a, 446a, 449a, 453b, 462a, 494a, 500a, 502a, 508a, 518a, 521b, 536b, 556b, 559a, 571b, 572a, 576b, 578a, 579b, 588b, 592b, 593b; IV 17a, 36a, 36b, 37a, 37b, 38a, 38b, 39a, 39b, 40a, 41a, 42b, 43a, 44a, 71a, 80b, 88a, 91a, 114b, 115a, 116b, 118a, 118b, 119b, 120a, 120b, 121a, 121b, 122a, 122b, 129a, 133a, 133b, 152a, 153a, 153b, 159a, 160b, 217a, 226b, 235a, 235b, 236a, 241a, 255, 257b, 264a, 286b, 298a, 299b, 302a, 309a, 311a, 325a, 327b, 341a, 396b, 400a, 401a, 402a, 403a, 403b, 404a, 404b, 405a, 405b, 406a, 406b, 407a, 408a, 408b, 409a, 409b, 410a, 410b, 411a, 411b, 412a, 412b, 413a, 413b, 414a, 414b, 415a, 416b, 421b, 428a, 450b, 451a, 497a, 511b, 525a, 559b, 564b, 578a, 586a, 591b, 595a; V 3a, 29a, 33b, 35b, 41a, 56a, 56b, 121b, 186b, 190a, 224b, 231a, 231b, 246b, 249b, 250b, 259a, 292a, 301a, 304a, 304b, 316b, 370a, 370b, 371a, 371b, 389b, 409a, 417b, 423a, 431a, 474a, 534b, 565a, 567a

Abyssinian	III 16b
Arab(ian)	I 312b, 315a, 336a; II 234a; III 8b, 515b
Aramaic/Syriac-speaking	II 429a; III 10b; IV 37a
Catholics	IV 248b
Eastern	III 69a
Ethiopian	III 11b
Gnostic	III 20b
Iconoclast	II 475a
Jacobite(s)	I 313b, 314a; II 515b, 531a; IV 71b, 74a, 236a
Melkites	I 313b, 314a
Monophysite	IV 406b, 410a

Mozarabic IV 239a
Nestorian(s) I 309a, 313b, 314a; II 515b, 531a; III 8b, 15b; IV 74a, 406b; V 344b, 431a, 566a
Orthodox II 531a
Spanish II 472a; IV 18b
Syriac IV 226b
Syrian II 234a
Christianity I 7b, 11b, 12a, 13b, 20b, 21a, 30b, 46a, 85a, 103b, 113b, 116b, 154a, 155a, 164b, 169b, 170b, 181b, 200a, 222b, 223a, 302a, **307b**, 308b, 309a, 314a, 314b, 315a, 316a, 316b, 331a, 373a, 376a, 378a, 475a, 509a; II 164a, 228a, 246a, 248b, 263a, 266b, 296a, 309a, 342a, 403a, 437a, 496a, 561a, 566b, 567a; III 2b, 32b, 107a, 129b, 142a, 143a, 144a, 405a, 406a, 478b, 492b, 493b, 500a, 501a, 540a; IV 33a, 38b, 40a, 50b, 115a, 119b, 120a, 121b, 122a, 122b, 123a, 124a, 194b, 195a, 232a, 232b, 236a, 238b, 243a, 243b, 249a, 313a, 327b, 340a, 399a, 399b, 404a, 405b, 406a, 407b, 413a, 474a, 485a, 492b, 519b, 567a; V 47b, 48a, 66a, 81a, 107a, 167b, 175b, 176a, 185b, 186b, 243b, 315b, 320b, 340b, 423a, 431a, 542a, 566a, 568a
Eastern I 509a; V 241a
Monophysite IV 411b
Protestant III 348b
Christology I 170b
Church Fathers I 104a; II 404b; IV 281b
Chwolsohn, D. IV 512a
Cizre [Jazīrat Ibn ʿUmar] I 146b, 147a; III 69a
Claremont Main Road Mosque (South Africa) V 227a
Clement of Alexandria I 104a
Cloak, People of the [*ahl al-kisāʾ*] I 390a
Clodius, Johann Christian (d. 1745) IV 250b
Closed Official Corpus (of the Qurān) I 426b, 427b, 429a, 429b
Cluny V 344b
Clysma, Gulf of V 184b

Cobb, P. II **463b**, **559b**
Colby, F. V **184a**
Collyridians I 313b; V 370a
Commander of the Faithful see al-Mutawwakkil (r. 232-47/847-61)
Communists II 471b
Companion(s) (of the Prophet) [*aṣḥāb al-nabī; ṣaḥāba*] I 12a, 15b, 16b, 17a, 17b, 36a, 63a, 110a, 110b, 111a, 121b, 189b, 278b, 289b, 331b, 332b, 353b, 354a, 355a, 357b, 358a, 358b, 359a, 359b, 360b, **386b**, 388a, 389a, 390b, 538b, 539a; II 15a, 15b, 100b, 103a, 112a, 117b, 190b, 221b, 222b, 279a, 356a, 378a, 382b, 383a, 383b, 385a, 388a, 388b, 389a, 390b, 392a, 393a, 398a, 420a, 493a, 498a, 520b, 521b; III 98b, 112a, 117b, 118b, 119b, 120a, 142a, 154a, 156a, 169a, 177b, 178a, 194a, 214b, 221b, 226b, 254a, 377a, 398a, 406a, 428a, 464b, 465b, 569a; IV 69b, 99a, 100b, 101a, 139a, 149b, 174a, 241a, 255b, 324a, 326a, 326b, 334b, 340b, 359a, 369a, 371b, 387a, 388b, 389a, 410a, 412a, 430a, 430b, 442a, 509b, 563b, 588a, 593b; V 24a, 30a, 34b, 35a, 40a, 45a, 46a, 47a, 47b, 113b, 131b, 142b, 147a, 147b, 185b, 219b, 255a, 318b, 320b, 321b, 328b, 335b, 434b, 535b
See also Cave; Elephant; Thicket.
Conrad, L. IV 5a
Constantine (emperor) III 435a
Constantine V Copronymus (r. 741-75) II 474a
Constantine VI (Byzantine emperor) V 306a
Constantinople I 110b; II 527b; III 435a; IV 242b
Constantinus II (r. 337-610) V 563b
Cook, M. II 150a; IV 198b, 201b, 328a, 402a, 402b, 589a; V 48b, **443b**
Copenhagen V 216a
Copt(s) II 234a, 395a; III 83a; IV 604b
Coptic (language) I 313b; II 231b, 233b, 234a

Cordoba — I 174a; III 255b, 256a, 302b, 307a, 432a; V 305b
[Great] Mosque of — III 256a, 302b, 303a, 303b, 307b, 436a
Correll, C. — II 352a
Coromandel — III 316a
Corpus Toletanum — see Toledo
Council of Chalcedon — see Chalcedon
Council of Nicea (Second) — see Nicea
Council of Vienna — see Vienna
Covenant of ʿUmar — see ʿUmar b. al-Khaṭṭab
Cowen, J.S. — III 315b
Cragg, K. — I 200a, 445b; II 162a, 293b, 307a, 310b; IV 195a; V 315a, 502b
Creswell, K. — I 126b
Crimea — IV 265b
Crone, P. — I 43a, 291a; II 150a, 150b, 151b, 296a; III 97a, 201b; IV 328a, 402a, 402b, 589a; V 24a, 48b, 314b, **459a**
Crusaders — V 220b
Crusades — I 269a; II 30a; IV 240a, 417a
Crusenstolpe, J.F. — V 350b
Cudi Dağ — see Jūdī, Mount
Cunial, S. — V **121a**

D

Dacca — IV 274a
al-Ḍaḥḥāk (King Bīwarasb) — see Bīwarasb
al-Ḍaḥḥāk b. Muzāḥim (d. 105/723) — II 103a, 105b, 106a; III 17b, 117a; IV 15b, 533a
Dahlan, A. — V 228a
Dähne, S. — V **476b**
Dajjāl — see Antichrist
Dakake, M.M. — V **2b**
Dakhla Oasis — IV 361a
Dale, G. — V 342a
Dallal, A. — I **273b**, **498b**; IV **557b**
al-Dāmaghānī, al-Ḥusayn b. Muḥammad (d. 478/1085) — IV 156a; V 333a
Damascenes — IV 492b
Damascus — I 110b, 138a, 165b, 271a, 289b, 293b, 307b, 332b, 333a, 348a; II 11a, 5b; III 255b, 265b, 272b, 275b, 298a, 299a, 309a, 309b,

429b, 430a, 433a, 436a, 556a, 556b, 600a; IV 317a, 355a, 373a, 497a; V 58b, 185b, 186a, 186b, 220b, 328b, 409b, 499a, 558b
Covenant Scroll of II 485b
Great Mosque of I 165a; III 256a, 300a, 436b
pre-Islamic II 559b
Damhān V 86b
al-Damīrī (d. 808/1405) II 487a; V 113b
al-Dānī, Abū ʿAmr ʿUthmān b. Saʿīd (d. 444/1052-3) IV 358a, 374a; V 332b, 334b, 335b
Daniel I 195b; III 529b
Book of I 108b
Dante II 419b
Danz, Johann Andreas (d. 1727) IV 247a
Daqyāʾīl I 90b
Dār al-Khilāfa V 324b
Dār al-Makhṭūṭāt III 261a
Dār al-Salām Publishing House IV 273b
Dar al-ʿUlum College V 212b, 217b
al-Dārimī, ʿAbdallāh b. ʿAbd al-Raḥmān (d. 255/869) I 468a; II 377b; V 165a, 165b
Darb al-Ḥajj II 428a
Darb al-Ṣabī V 89a
Darb Zubaydah I 156a
Darrow, W. III **245b**
Darul Uloom Haqqania V 211b
Dārūm V 185a
al-Darwājikī, Abū l-Naṣr Aḥmad (d. 549/1154) V 148a, 148b
Darwaza, Muḥammad ʿIzza II 125a; IV 126b; V 443a
Darwin, Ch. I 23a; III 530b; V 10b, 351a
Dāʾūd al-Anṭākī see al-Anṭākī, Dāʾūd (d. 1008/1599)
Davenport, R. V 348b
[King] David [Dāwūd] I 61b, 99a, 102a, 149a, 165a, 192b, 211b, 245b, 254b, 277a, 277b, 305a, 317b, 352b, **495b**, 496a, 496b, 497a, 516b, 537b; II 30b, 145b, 198b, 309a, 315a, 334b, 335a, 337a, 344b, 345b, 372b, 394b, 403b, 412b, 436a; III 4a, 4b, 13a, 16a, 50a, 65a, 90b, 92a, 93b, 94a, 94b, 95a, 103a, 226a, 242a, 253b, 310a, 373a, 381b, 383a, 395a, 427a, 444b, 453a, 479b, 487a, 487b, 520a, 521a, 522a, 522b, 525b, 537a; IV 36b,

52a, 68b, 128a, 135b, 213b, 214b, 219b, 291a, 304a, 304b, 315a, 315b, 316a, 316b, 317a, 369a, 429b, 438b, 516b, 536b, 537a, 538a, 561a, 577a; V 31b, 41b, 76b, 77a, 77b; V 103a, 113b, 152a, 152b, 200a, 438b, 455b, 458a, 483a
Daʿwa Academy (Islamabad, Pakistan) V 218b
Dāwardān II 155a
[Wādī] al-Dawāsir II 295a
Dawood, N. I 200a; V 354a
Daws Dhū Thaʿlabān IV 44a
Dāwūd b. Abī Hind (d. 139-41/756-8) II 395b
Dāwūd b. Salm (d. ca. 132/750) I 511b
Day of Atonement I 253a, 276b; II 182a; III 54b, 55a, 496b, 538a; IV 227a, 340b; V 284b
Daya [al-]Rāzī see Najm al-Dīn Dāya al-Rāzī (d. 654/1256)
Ḍayfa Khātūn (d. 641/1243) III 310a
Daylam III 558b
al-Daylamī, Abū Thābit Muḥammad (d. 593/1197) V 141a, 151b, 152a
Dayr al-Jamājim V 505a
Dayr Samʿān III 405b
al-Dayrabī, Aḥmad (d. ca. 1151/1739) I 78a
Dead Sea I 149a; III 232b
Decalogue I 365a, 365b, 366a, 366b, 367a; II 71a; V 28a, 28b
Decius III 374b, 375a; IV 351a, 351b
Déclais, J.L. III **505a**
Dedan [Dedān] I 150b, 152b; II 427a
Delhi I 519b; III 314a, 314b
  Great Mosque of III 314b
DeLong-Bas, N. V **453a**
Dème, M. I 33a
Denia V 401b
Demetrios Kydones (d. ca. 1398) see Kydones, Demetrios (d. ca. 1398)
Denmark V 216a
Denny, F.M. I **242a**, **337b**, **372b**, **386a**, **440b**, II **2a**, **154b**, **159b**, 253b, **402a**; IV 372a, 383b, 392b
Deobandī(s) I 201a, **519b**, 520a, 520b; IV 275b
Déroche, F. I 136b, 282b, 283a, 283b; III **273a**, 298a

Derrida, J.	I 413a
al-Dhahabī, Shams al-Dīn Muḥammad b. Aḥmad) (d. 748/1348)	I 78a; II 114a, 441b; III 309a, 351a, 351b, 354a, 354b, 357a, 358a, 358b, 359a, 362a, 362b, 363a, 363b, 364b, 366b, 391b; IV 166a, 386a; V 19b, 20a, 20b, 143a
Dhara''amar Ayman	V 563a, 564a, 567b
Dhāt Badān^{un}	V 85b, 87a
Dhāt Ḥimyam	V 85b, 90a
Dhāt Kahl	I 153a
Dhāt Ṣanat^{um}	V 85b
Dhāt Ẓahrān	V 85b
Dhū Abhī	V 89b
Dhū al-Faqār	I 155b
Dhū al-Ḥijja	I 146a, 445a, 500b; II 83b, 179b, 182b, 298a; III 410b, 411a, 411b, 413b, 427b; IV 282b, 283a
Dhū al-Ḥimār ʿAbhala b. Kaʿb	I 544a
Dhū al-Kaʿbāt	V 87a
Dhū al-Kaffayn	V 87a
Dhū al-Khalaṣa	II 237b, 238b; V 87a
Dhū al-Kifl	I **527b**, 528a, 528b; II 14a, 155a, 564a; III 520a, 521a; V 246a, 246b, 249b, 575b
Dhū al-Labaʾ	V 87a
Dhū al-Majāz	II 298a; III 411a
Dhū al-Nūn	see Jonah
Dhū al-Nūn Abū l-Fayḍ al-Miṣrī (d. 246/861)	III 250b; V 140b
Dhū Nuwās	II 148a; III 521b; IV 44a, 257b, 258a
Dhū Qabḍ^{um}	V 86b, 87a
Dhū al-Qaʿda	II 179b, 298a; III 410b, 411a, 411b, 413b
Dhū al-Qarnayn	see Possessor of the Two Horns
Dhū (al-)Samāwī	V 86b, 88a, 89b
Dhū Tubbaʿ	V 390a
Dhū Ṭuwā	V 248a
al-4ibāʿ, [Shaykh] ʿAlī Muḥammad	IV 272b
Dickinson, E.	I **536a**
Diem, W.	I 141b; II 359a, 363b
Dieterici, F.H.	V 297a
Dilthey, W.	II 139b
al-Dimashqī, Qāsim b. Khalīl	III 469b
al-Dimashqī, Shams al-Dīn Muḥammad b. Abī Ṭālib (d. 727/1327)	I 539a; III 287b
al-Dimyāṭī (d. 1117/1705)	IV 389a; V 332a

al-Dīn al-Ṭaʿī, [Shaykh] Kamal iv 274a
al-Dīnawarī (fl. late fifth/eleventh cent.) iv 169b
al-Dīnawarī, Abū Ḥanīfa (d. 308/920) ii 104a; ii 211b
Dionysius Rijkel (Dionysius Carthusianus; d. 1471) iv 236b, 242b
Dioscorides i 46a, 47b
Ḍirār b. ʿAmr (d. 200/815) iii 469a; iv 73a, 431b, 460b
Ditch [Khandaq] i 320a, 398a; ii 17a, 148b, 149a
  Battle of the i 216a, 380a; ii 16b; iii 456b, 500b, 579a; iv 332b, 334a; v 43a, 377b
  People of the [*aṣḥāb al-ukhdūd*] i 154a; ii 211b; iii 521b, 522a; iv **43b**, 44a, 44b
Ḍiyāʾ al-Dīn b. al-Athīr see Ibn al-Athīr, Ḍiyāʾ al-Dīn (d. 637/1239)
Diyanet v 227a
Diyār Bakr iii 430a
Djibouti i 127b
Dodd, E. i 169b; iii 297b
Dols, M. ii 540b
Dome of the Rock [Qubbat al-Ṣakhra] i 126b, 139b, 156a, 156b, 170a, 170b, 285a; ii 219b, 325b, 329b; iii 2b, 258b, 299b, 300a, 429b, 430a, 556a; iv 282b, 361b; v 123a, 186a, 489b, 503a, 504a
Dominican(s) iv 240a, 240b
Dominicus Germanus de Silesia (d. 1670) iv 237a; v 345a
Donaldson, D. ii 71a
Dongsi Mosque iii 315a
Donner, F. i 370b, 371a, 378b, 379a; iii 97a, 480a
van Doorn-Harder, N. v **228b**
Doughty, C.M. ii 428a
Douglas, M. ii 222a
Dounaas v 565a; see also Yūsuf Asʾar Yathʾar
Dozy, R. iv 399b
Draz, M. iv 196b
Drāz, ʿA. iii 509b
Drew Ali, Noble i 30a, 30b
Druze(s) [*durzī*, pl. *durūz*] i **554a**, 555a, 557a; iii 390a; iv 597b, 598a
  Canon of i 554a, 554b, 555b, 556a, 556b, 557a
Dublin i 282a; iii 301b
Ḍulaʿ v 92b
Ḍumām b. al-Sāʾib iii 88b

Dūmat al-Jandal i 152b; iii 275b; v 2a, 86b
Dūmat al-Jawf i 152b
Dupont-Sommer, A. iii 45a
Durayd b. al-Ṣimma i 38a; iv 111b
al-Dūrī, Abū ʿUmar Ḥafṣ b. ʿUmar (d. ca. 246/860-1) iv 359b, 360a, 360b, 390a
Durkheim, E. iv 278a, 279a
Dusares iii 79b
Dutch (language) iv 238b; v 342b, 347a
Dworkin, R. ii 68b

E

Easter iv 338a, 339a, 346a, 347b
Ebrahim, A. i **232b**
Eden [ʿAdn] i 90a, 550a, 550b; ii 3b, 51a, 52b, 60a, 202a, 282b, 335b; iii 45a, 143a, 211a, 534a; iv 12a, 12b, 13b, 42b; v 62b, 106b, 124b, 547a
Edessa i 308a; iv 74a
Edirne iii 429b, 435a
EFA see Islam
Effendi, S. i 199a
Egypt [Miṣr] i 39b, 44a, 47a, 127b, 150a, 159a, 173b, 181b, 227a, 227b, 255a, 265b, 276a, 293a, 297a, 299b, 303b, 304b, 334a, 338b, 349b, 404a, 433b, 434b, 439a, 488a, 521b, 532b, 548b, 549b, 554b; ii **10a**, 10b, 11a, 26b, 28a, 34b, 38b, 40a, 79b, 81a, 88b, 89a, 90b, 105b, 124b, 184a, 200b, 206a, 206b, 207a, 208a, 213a, 213b, 309a, 399a, 437a, 452a, 452b, 461b, 527b, 554a, 555a; iii 5a, 5b, 56a, 56b, 57a, 60b, 93a, 143b, 183a, 208b, 223a, 299a, 300b, 301a, 303b, 304a, 306b, 308b, 309a, 310b, 311a, 311b, 326b, 328b, 348b, 394a, 405a, 421a, 422a, 423b, 428b, 429a, 488a, 495b, 496a, 520b, 556a, 557a, 562a, 590a; iv 66b, 67a, 68a, 105b, 143a, 149a, 204b, 224a, 268b, 269b, 272b,

	275b, 276b, 328a, 328b, 338b, 346a, 360b, 361a, 381b, 383a, 492b, 525a, 555a, 585b; V 28a, 60a, 63a, 75a, 83a, 96b, 104b, 107b, 133a, 214b, 217a, 217b, 218a, 255b, 260b, 346b, 375a, 392a, 392b, 409a, 465a, 508b, 537b, 538b, 549a
Civil Code	I 434b
Fāṭimid	IV 496b
Feminist Union	II 200b
Lower	I 137b; II 10b
Mamlūk	III 268a, 311a, 311b, 595b
Muftī of	I 29b; V 220a
National Library of	I 175a; IV 272b
Republic of	IV 212a
Upper	I 139b; II 10b; IV 175b
Egyptian(s)	I 21a, 98b, 133a, 274b, 276a, 297a, 499b, 519a; II 23b, 399a; III 211b, 420b; IV 106a; V 52a, 206a, 224a
Ehud	III 479b
Eichler, P.A.	II 540a
Eickelman, D.	V **76a**
Eisenstein, H.	I **101b**, **439a**; II **436b**, **467b**; V **113b**
Eklund, R.	I 207a; IV 197a
El-Awa, S.	V **572b**, **574a**
Elat	V 29a
El-Cheikh, N.	I **269b**; II 147a, **505b**, **561a**
El-Naggar, Z.	IV 541b
Elchasaites	IV 408a, 512a, 512b
Elephant	
People of the [*aṣḥāb al-fīl*]	I 4a, 20b, 100b, 101a; II 129b, 212b, 490b; IV **44b**, 45a, 45b, 46a
Year of the [*ʿam al-fīl*]	I 4b, 5a; II 148a; III 455b; IV 45a
Elephantine	see Knum
Eli	IV 528b
Eliade, M.	IV 278b, 488a
Elias, J.	II **161a**; III 50a, 51b, **108a**; III **187b**; V 158b, **278a**
Eliash	IV 450b
Elijah [Ilyās]	I 62a, 194a, 528b; II **12b**, 13a, 13b,

	14a, 240b, 332b, 340b, 364a, 484b, 558a; III 83a, 83b, 381a, 521a, 522a, 525b; IV 34a, 291b; V 41b, 575b
Elijah Muhammad (d. 1975)	I 31a, 31b
Elisha [al-Yasaʿ]	I 528b, 528b; II 13a, **14a**, 155a, 564a; III 50a, 520a, 522a, 525b; V 246b
Elizabeth	I 2a, 477a
Elmalılı	V 131a, 161a
El-Zein, A.	V 69b, **467a**
Emesa	V 186a
Emigrants	see Meccans
Empedocles	III 529a, 530b
Endress, G.	I 136a
Engels, F.	V 66a
England	I 30a; II 555a; V 66a
English (language)	I 52a; II 288b; III 129b, 416b; IV 395a; V 212b, 213b, 216a, 225a, 228b, 342b, 343b, 537b, 538b, 540b
Enlightenment	II 126a, 127b, 128b, 549a; IV 250b
Enoch ben Jared	II 484b, 485a, 485b, 486a; III 542a; IV 303b; V 41b, 249b
Ephesus	I 164b, 292b; II 37b; III 13b, 374a, 374b, 537a; V 251a
[St.] Ephrem/Ephraim the Syrian	II 110a, 456b; III 57a; V 125a
Epiphanius of Salamis	I 311a, 370a
Erder, Y.	II **486a**
Ernst, C.	V 152b, 153a
Erpenius, Thomas (d. 1624)	IV 235a, 246a, 246b, 248b; V 346a, 347b
Esack, Farid	V 206b
Esau	I 21a; III 2a
Esdras	II 485a; V 249a, 249b, 250a, 250b
Esra	V 249a
Eşrefoğlu (mosque at Beyşehir)	III 432a
van Ess, J.	I 372b, 417b, 418a, 421a, 421b; II 246a, 539a; IV 446b
Essenes	IV 226b
Esther	II 399b
Ethiopia [Bilād al-Ḥabash]	I 168b, 307b; II **79b**, 295a, 437b; III 405a, 578b; IV 604b; V 45a, 47b, 361b, 431a
Ethiopian(s)	II 232a; III 242a, 500a; IV 45b

Ethiopic (language) I 129b, 316b, 398b, 490a, 524b; II 231a, 231b, 544a; III 45b, 49a, 117b; IV 517a; V 106a, 188a, 189b
Eucharist III 16b, 521b; IV 347a, 517a, 564b; V 122b, 189a, 189b, 190b; see also Christ, Last Supper
[Pope] Eugene IV IV 242b
Eulogius of Cordoba (d. 859) IV 238b
Euphrates I 308b, 332b; II 295b, 559b; V 1a, 126b, 184b, 360a, 466b
Europe I 201a, 385b, 424b; II 287a, 567b; III 316a, 342a, 343a, 348b, 365a; IV 188a, 267b, 268a, 269a; V 73a, 99a, 216a, 225a, 241a, 344b
European(s) I 30b, 36b; III 343a; IV 554b
Eusebius of Caesarea I 192b, 310a, 310b
Euthymios Zigabenos IV 238a
[St.] Euthymius III 405a
Eve [Ḥawwā] I **22b**, 24b, 25a, 25b, 84a, 146a, 230a, 270a, 346b, 476a, 476b, 525a, 532a; II 65a, 172b, 173a, 173b, 175a, 202a, 202b, 224a, 292a, 332a, 335b; III 211a, 295b, 542a, 548a, 548b, 563b; IV 130a, 580b, 581b, 584a; V 260a, 530b, 538a, 539a, 539b, 571a
Ewald II 350b
Exodus I 274a, 275b, 332a; IV 346a
Ezekiel [Ḥizqīl b. Būzī/Būdhī/Būrī] II 13a, 14a, **154b**, 155a, 240b; III 143b; V 286a
ʿĒzer see Teraḥ
Ezra [ʿEzrā; ʿUzayr] II **155b**, 156a, 156b, 485a; III 5b, 26b, 396a; IV 38b, 39a, 120a, 153a, 160b, 412b, 451a; V 249a, 249b, 250a, 250b, 304b

F

Faculty for Islamic Mission see al-Azhar University, Cairo
Fadak II 148b, 150a, 151a; III 580a
Fadel, M. I **298a**; III **460b**
al-Faḍl b. al-Ḥasan al-Ṭabarsī (d. 548/1153) see al-Ṭabarsī, Abū ʿAlī al-Faḍl b. al-Ḥasan (d. 548/1153); III 469b

Fahd, T.	I 46b, **404b**, **545a**; II 237b, **242b**
Failaka (Kuwait)	I 155a
Faizer, R.	II **152a**
Family of the Prophet	see Prophet
Fakhr al-Dīn al-Rāzī	see al-Rāzī, Fakhr al-Dīn (d. 606/1210)
Fakhry, M.	IV **89b**
al-Fākihī (historian of Mecca)	IV 105a
Fanon, F.	III 582a
al-Fārābī, Abū Naṣr (d. 339/950)	IV 74b, 75a, 80b, 81a, 87a, 87b, 381a
Faraj, ʿAbd al-Salām (d. 1882)	IV 146a, 146b, 147a
al-Farazdaq (d. 110/728)	I 398b, 400a, 400b; II 349a; III 216b
Fard Muhammad, Wali (d. 1934)	I 31a, 31b
Farewell Pilgrimage	I 400a; II **178a**, 179a, 180a, 520b; IV 97b, 99a; V 44a, 515b, 561a
Farewell Speech	II 179b, 180a
Farghānā Valley	III 305a
Fariba Adelkhah	III 346b
Farīd al-Dīn ʿAṭṭār	see ʿAṭṭār, Farīd al-Dīn (d. 627/1230)
al-Fārisī, Abū ʿAlī (d. 377/987)	II 114b; III 471a; IV 109b; V 331b
al-Farrāʾ, Abū Zakariyyāʾ Yaḥyā b. Ziyād (d. 207/822)	I 266b, 348a, 349b, 350a, 529b, 530a, 530b; II 104a, 104b, 109a, 114b, 313b, 348a, 349a, 349b, 356b, 357a, 357b, 358b, 359a, 361a, 362a, 366b, 531b; III 115b, 123b, 124a, 175a, 606a; IV 7b, 13a, 54a, 354a, 354b, 355a, 355b; V 255a
Farrakhan, L.	I 31b
Fars	II 30a
Farther Mosque	see Aqṣā Mosque
Fārūq (Egyptian king; r. 1936-52)	IV 272b
al-Faruque, M.	II **18a**, **23a**
Fās	II 35a
Fatehpur Sikri	III 323b
Fāṭima (daughter of the Prophet and Khadīja)	I 59b, 60a, 62b, 347a, 357b, 390a; II 118a, 162a, 177a, 188b, **192b**, 193a, 193b, 206a, 503b, 504a; III 80b, 81a, 81b, 290b, 291a, 291b, 292b, 492b, 558b; IV 50a, 50b, 178a, 601b; V 135a, 223a, 507b, 532a, 533b, 534a, 534b

Fāṭima (nurse of al-Muʿizz b. Bādīs)	III 265a
Fāṭima bt. al-Ḍaḥḥāk b. Sufyān	V 509a
Fāṭimid(s)	I 126b; II 34b, 206a; III 216a, 301a, 437a, 558b
Fawwāz Aḥmad Zamarlī	II 377b
Fayrūz (vocalist)	IV 381b
Fazlur Rahman	see Rahman, Fazlur
Feast of Tabernacles	V 236a
Feener, R.M.	V **102a**
Felix (Roman governor)	I 310b
Ferguson, D.	I 133a, 133b
Fertile Crescent	I 130b, 433b; III 254b, 411b; V 314b
Fez	III 345b; V 75b
Fiḥl	V 185a
Fikret, T.	V 394b
Filiz Çağman	III 320b
Fīmiyyūn	III 406a
Finḥāṣ al-Yahūdī	IV 323a
al-Firdaws *madrasa* (Aleppo)	I 171b; III 310a
Firdawsī (d. 411/1020)	I 61b; III 221b, 317b; IV 62a
Firestone, R.	I **10b, 21a**, **193a**, 330b; II **24b**, **79b**, **209b**, **562a**, **564b**; III **391a**; IV **68a**, **518a**, **519b**, **591a**; V **254a**, **390b**
Firro, K.	I **557b**
First World War	see World War I
al-Fīrūzābādī, Abū Ṭāhir (d. 817/1415)	II 18a, 104a; III 12a; V 327b
al-Fīrūzābādī, Majd al-Dīn Muḥammad b. Yaʿqūb	I 102b; V 572a
Firūzkūh	see Jām
al-Firyābī	II 470b
Fischer, A.	I 334a; II 346b, 350a, 356a, 366a, 366b, 486b; IV 101a; V 352a
Flavius Josephus	see Josephus
Fleischer, F.	II 350b; III 122a; V 349a
Fleischer, H.	V 350a
Flügel, G.	I 169a; III 15b; IV 247b, 265a; V 295a, 350a
Fodiye, Asmāʾ bt. ʿUthmān	I 33b
Forskal, Peter (d. 1763)	V 360b
Forster, E.M	III 212a
Fraenkel, S.	V 297a
France	I 425a; V 346b
Francesca, E.	III **89a**; V **56b**
Franciscans	IV 240a
Franciscus of Romontin (d. ca. 1700)	IV 237a

Free University of Amsterdam v 216b
Freemasons ii 471b
French (language) v 538b, 540b
French Revolution iii 582b
Freud, S. v 538a
Friday i 36b; ii 271b, 272a; iv 226a
  Mosque i 271a
  Prayer [*al-ṣalāt min yawm al-jumʿa*] ii 90b, 94a, **271b**, 272b; iii 222a, 261b, 547a; iv 487a, 497a; v 71b, 224a, 227a
Friedl, E. i 57b, 58a
Friedmann, Y. i **51a, 539b**; v **294a**
Frolov, D. i **517a**; ii **271a**; iv **31a**; v **129b, 130b**
Froriep, Justus Friedrich (d. 1800) iv 250b
Frye, N. i 425b
Fuʾād I (king of Egypt) v 239a, 295a
Fück, J. iii 124a; iv 194a; v 348a
al-Fuḍayl b. ʿIyāḍ (d. 187-8/803) iv 379a; v 147a
Fudge, B. i **546a**
Fulani (language) i 136a
Fulfulde (language) i 33b
Furāt al-Kūfī see al-Kūfī, Furāt b. Furāt b. Ibrāhīm (d. 922)
Fusṭāṭ (Egypt) iii 303b, 304a, 429a, 432b
Futa (Senegal) i 30a
al-Fūtī, Aḥmād Mālik Ḥammād i 33b
Fūṭīs iv 10b

G

Gabriel [Jibrīl] i 9a, 55a, 84b, 87a, 87b, 88a, 88b, 89a, 90a, 91a, 113b, 146a, 178a, 220a, 229b, 249a, 274b, 293b, 317b, 343a, 359a, 360a, 545b; ii 66a, 86b, 87a, 168a, 227a, 241a, **278a**, 278b, 279a, 279b, 381a, 381b, 382a, 382b, 392a, 412b, 442b, 514a, 553a; iii 12a, 13a, 13b, 16a, 26a, 78b, 117a, 139b, 232b, 293b, 388b, 389a, 389b, 394b, 442a, 454b, 460b, 461a, 515a, 516a, 538a, 542b, 545b, 546a, 546b; iv 14a, 78a, 217a, 228a, 282b, 290a, 290b, 293a,

295b, 301b, 353a, 372b, 374a, 438a, 441b, 442a, 444a, 445a, 445b, 446b, 449a, 519b, 532a, 600a; v 39b, 41b, 63b, 80a, 81a, 109b, 115a, 115b, 116a, 117a, 118b, 201a, 261a, 278a, 361a, 361b, 466b, 473a, 517a
Gadamer, H. ii 139b
Gade, A.M. iv **384b**; v 209b
Gaffney, P. ii **272b**; iii **229a**; v 206a
Galen iii 349b, 351b
Galilee i 210b
  Sea of i 109a
Ganges v 96b
Garcia-Bravo, J. v 349b
Gate of Mercy [Bāb al-Raḥma] iii 5a
Gaudefroy-Demombynes, M. iii 144a; v 297b
Gayo (Indonesian people) i 77a
Gaza v 29a, 184b, 185a, 258b
  Strip ii 457b
Gdoura, W. iv 267b
Geber see Abū ʿAbdallāh Jābir b. Ḥayyān
Gedeon, G. v 345b
Geertz, C. i 64b
Gehenna v 547b
Geiger, A. ii 234b; iv 194b, 399b; v 350a
van Gelder, G. ii **406b**
Gentile(s) ii 498a, 499a
[St.] George [Jirjīs] iv 525b
Gerizim (mountain in Nablus) iv 524a
German (language) iv 238b; v 342b
Germany v 343b, 350a
Geyer, R. iv 193b
al-Ghadir Mosque i 172a
Ghālib (d. 1869) iii 224a, 224b
Ghana iii 327b; iv 170a
Ghanm b. ʿAwf iii 438b
Ghassān i 308a; iii 122a
Ghassānids i 308a, 308b, 309a; ii 296b; iii 300b; iv 111b
[Banū] Ghaṭafān i 121a; iv 25a
[Mt.] Ghawl ii 300b
Ghaylān al-Dimashqī iii 87b; iv 72b, 73a
al-Ghazālī, Abū Ḥāmid (d. 505/1111) i 49a, 85a, 90a, 90b, 118a, 159b, 198a, 354b, 436a, 463b, 484b;

	II 55a, 96b, 142b, 371a, 371b, 372b, 373a, 409b, 413b, 417b, 419a, 451a, 451b, 453a, 502a, 511b, 552b; III 72b, 137b, 175b, 176a, 250b, 269a, 288a, 352b, 353a, 387a, 387b, 402b, 502b, 503a, 546b, 586b, 587a, 607a; IV 57b, 75a, 77b, 78a, 78b, 80a, 81b, 83a, 84b, 86a, 370a, 370b, 371a, 371b, 379a, 384a, 388a, 442a, 487b, 494a, 494b, 542b, 543a, 549a, 579b; V 8b, 13a, 18a, 57b, 136a, 143b, 148b, 149a, 149b, 150a, 150b, 151a, 219b, 334b, 383b, 384a, 384b, 388a, 388b, 401a, 447b, 465b, 491b, 499b, 552b, 557a
Ghaziyya	I 38a
Ghaznavid(s)	II 41a, 421a
Palace	I 171b
Ghūrid	III 313a, 314a, 314b
Ghūṭa (of Damascus)	I 271a; III 5b
Gibb, H.	III 144a; IV 111b
Gideon	II 334b; IV 530a; V 43a
Gil, M.	II 485b
Giladi, A.	I **302b**; II **176a**, **267a**, **374b**; III **107b**, **604a**; IV **22a**; V **478a**
Gilgāl	V 248a
Gilgamesh	III 479b
Gilliot, C.	I 425a; II 109a, **121a**, **517b**; III **132a**, **439b**, **526b**; IV 199b; V **336b**
Gimaret, D.	I 514a; III 470b, 471a
Ginat, J.	V **419a**
Girish Chandra Sen	V 342a
Glaser, E.	I 148b
Glazemaker, Jan Hendrikz (d. 1682)	V 347a, 347b
Gluck, J.J.	IV 471a
God	passim
House of	I 338a
Throne of	III 370b; V **276b**, 466b
Goddard, H.	I **200b**
Goethe, J.	II 131b; III 111a; V 348b
Gog [Yajūj]	I 61b, 110b, 111a, 112b, 398b; II **331b**, 332a, 332b, 333a;

III 139a, 143a, 143b, 520a, 543a; IV 210b, 434b; V 375b
Goitein, S. II 183b, 191a; III 538a; IV 341a
Golden Gate III 5a
Goldenberg, G. II 352a, 361a, 363a, 367a
Goldman, S. III **57b**
Goldziher, I. I 11a, 37a, 417b; II 70a, 250b, 364a, 487b; III 402a; IV 197b, 400b, 589a; V 48a, 67a, 490b, 491a
Goliath [Jālūt] I 460b, 461a, 496a; II 145b, 198b, **334b**, 335a, 404a; III 9a, 521a; IV 211a, 316a, 536a, 536b, 537a; V 200b, 377a, 455b
Golius, Jacob (d. 1667) IV 246a
Gomorra II 299b; III 489b; IV 584b
Gonzalez, V. I 168a; IV **586b**; V **13a**
Goosens, E. III 474a
Gordon, M. III **59a**; V **378a**, **430b**
Gordon Memorial College I 34a
Gordyene I 147b; III 68b
Gospel(s) [*injīl*] I 118a, 123b, 228b, 245b, 310b, 312b, 314b, 418b, 425a, 488a, 516b; II 221a, 235b, **342a**, 342b, 343a, 434a, 494a, 499a, 513a, 516b, 536b; III 16a, 24b, 25b, 28a, 65a, 126b, 127a, 150b, 151a, 186b, 191a, 260a, 445a, 445b, 503a; IV 3b, 37b, 40a, 41a, 68b, 133a, 236a, 241a, 293b, 297b, 298a, 299a, 302a, 450b, 451a; V 41a, 116a, 152a, 152b, 176a, 189b, 200b, 231b, 270a, 300b, 301a, 304a, 305b, 307b, 399b, 433a, 437b, 483b, 533b
  Christian II 342a, 343a
  of John I 474a; III 14b; IV 339b
  People of the [ahl al-injīl] I 310b; II 342a; IV 402b
Göttingen University Library IV 251a
Grabar, O. I **174b**
Graham, W. I **211b**; II 81a, 84b, 88a, **192a**, 396a; III **587a**; IV 384a, 392b, **569a**
Grämlich, R. III 397a
Granada II 109b; III 559a; V 305b

Grand Shaykh of Mecca — see Mecca
Grande Bibliothèque de France — I 283a
Great Britain — I 149a
Great Occultation — see Occultation
Greece — I 62a; V 73a
Greek (language) — I 102a, 138a, 311a, 313b, 490a; II 231a, 231b, 234a, 342b, 513a, 515b, 544a; III 8b, 9b, 10a, 44b, 117b, 244a, 258b, 299a, 407b, 590a; IV 242a, 249a; V 188a, 246a, 306a, 306b
  Attic — III 122b
  Hellenistic — V 439a
Greek(s) — I 103b, 214b; II 240a, 511b; IV 71b, 439a, 440b; V 52a; see also Hellenism
Greek New Testament — see Testament
Greimas, A. — I 425a
Gressmann, H. — III 143b
Gribetz, A. — IV 99b
Griffel, F. — III **402b**
Griffith, S. — I **315b**, **336b**; II **343a**, **444a**; III **407b**; IV 405b
Gril, D. — III **237a**, **399a**
Grimme, H. — I 323a, 417b; IV 190b, 191a; V 398a
Grohmann, A. — I 138a; III 256a, 257a; III 258a, 298a
Gruendler, B. — I **142b**; III 590a; IV **589a**
von Grünebaum, G.E. — II 206b; IV 450a
Guillaume, A. — I 417b
Guillaume Postel — see Postel, Guillaume (d. 1581)
Guinea — IV 177b
Gujarat — III 326a
Gujarati (language) — V 342a
Gulgee — I 172b
Gumi, Abū Bakr — I 33a
Günther, S. — I **241a**, **346a**, **504b**; II **499b**; III **192a**; V **204b**, **402b**
Guo, L. — II **314a**
Gutenberg — IV 267a, 275b
Gwynne, R. — I **213b**; II **419b**, **508b**; III 470b; V **570b**
Gymnastiar, A. — V 206a, 224b

H

Ha-Amen ii 399b
al-Ḥabash, Muḥammad iv 130a
al-Ḥabash(a) see Abyssinia
Ḥabīb (carpenter in Antioch) iii 521a; iv 11a
Ḥabīb b. Khidma Abū Rāʾiṭa v 371b
Ḥabīb al-Raḥmān al-Aʿẓamī ii 377b
Ḥabrūn see Hebron
Ḥacī Özbek iii 434b
Hackspan, Theodor (d. 1659) iv 246b
Hadad (Aramaic god) v 86b
Ḥadaqān v 89b
Ḥadath v 87b
Haddad, Y.Y. i 89b; iii 529b; iv 395b
al-Hādī ilā l-Ḥaqq iii 558b
Ḥaḍramawt i 121a, 152a, 529b; ii 338b, 463b; iii 85b, 86a, 472a; iv 352b, 360b, 361a, 585b; v 86a, 87a, 89a, 90a, 91b, 92b, 93a, 562b, 563a
Ḥaḍramawt b. Qaḥṭān i 21a, 22a
al-Ḥaḍramī, Abū Muḥammad Yaʿqūb b. Isḥāq (d. 205/821) iv 358a, 359b, 360a, 389b; v 332a
Hadrian iv 524a
Haeri, S. v **234a**
Haeuptner, E. i 490a; ii 544a
Ḥāfiẓ (d. 791-2/1389-90) i 542a; ii 240a; iii 222b, 317b; iv 62b
Ḥāfiẓ Muḥammad Amīn Rushdī iv 273b
Ḥāfiẓ ʿUthmān Efendi (d. 1110/1698) iii 321a
Ḥafṣ (d. 190/805) i 334a
Ḥafṣ b. Sulaymān (also called Ḥufayṣ; d. 180/796) iv 373a, 390a, 392a; v 238b
Ḥafṣ al-Qūṭī iv 317a
Ḥafṣa [bt. ʿUmar b. al-Khaṭṭāb] i 332b, 333a; ii **397b**, 398a, 398b; iii 464b; iv 449a, 587b, 598b; v 409b, 508a, 517a, 517b, 518a, 520a, 535b, 550a
Hagar [Hajār] i 6b, 8b, 9a, 9b; ii 11a, 205a, 563b; iii 78a, 341a; iv 445a, 519a, 519b; v 127a, 463a
Haggada ii 485a; iii 419b
Hagia Sophia iii 435a
Haifa i 199a
University of v 296a
al-Ḥajar (oasis) iii 275a

Haji Abdul Malik Karim Amrullah — see Hamka
al-Ḥajj Aḥmad b. al-Ḥajj — IV 267a
Hajja(h) Maria Ulfah — III 345a; IV 382a
al-Ḥajjāj b. Yūsuf (d. 95/714) — I 348a; III 605a, 605b; IV 140b, 386b
al-Ḥakam (d. 366/976) — III 303a
al-Ḥakam b. Abī l-ʿĀs — see Ibn Abī l-ʿĀs, al-Ḥakam (governor of Fars and Khūzistān; r. 56-8/676-8)
al-Ḥākim — III 304a
  Mosque of — III 304a, 311b, 436b, 437a
al-Ḥakīm, Tawfīq — I 140b, 293a
al-Ḥākim bi-Amr Allāh (caliph; r. 386-411/996-1021) — I 554a, 555a, 555b
al-Ḥākim al-Jishumī (d. 494/1101) — II 115a; III 470a, 470b, 471a
al-Ḥākim al-Naysābūrī/Nīsābūrī — see al-Nīsābūrī, Abū l-Qāsim al-Ḥasan b. Muḥammad b. Ḥabīb (d. 404-6/1014-16)
al-Ḥakīm al-Samarqandī, Abū l-Qāsim Isḥāq b. Muḥammad (d. 342/953) — I 482b, 483a
al-Ḥakīm al-Tirmidhī — IV 520b; V 484a
al-Ḥakīm Ibn al-Hayṣam al-Nabī (d. 409/1019) — V 326a
Hāla (son of Khadīja bt. Khuwaylid and Abū Hāla Hind b. al-Nabbāsh of Tamīm) — V 507b
Haleem, A. — III 530b; IV 7b
al-Ḥalīmī (d. 403/1012) — V 20a, 20b
al-Ḥallāj (d. 309/922) — I 89a, 140b, 160a, 160b, 428a, 541b, 542a; II 286a, 409b; V 141b, 386b
Hallaq, W. — I **122b**, 226a, **434b**; II **226a**, **537b**; III **171a**
Ham [Ḥām b. Nūḥ] — I 21a; II 10b; III 541a, 543a
Ḥamā — V 185b
Hamadān — III 305a, 311a
al-Hamadhānī, al-Ḥasan b. Aḥmad (d. 319/932) — III 417a; IV 60a; V 561b
Hāmān — I 190a, 340b, 478a; II 338a, **399a**, 399b; III 104b, 423b, 518b, 520b; IV 67b, 68a
  People of — II 338a
Hamburg — IV 247a, 265a
[Shaykh] Ḥamd Allāh — III 320b
Ḥamd b. Muḥammad al-Khaṭṭābī (d. ca. 386/996) — see al-Khaṭṭābī, Ḥamd b. Muḥammad (d. ca. 386/996)
Hamdān — V 92a, 390a
al-Hamdānī (d. 334/945) — III 215a; III 380b
al-Hamdānī, al-Ḥasan b. Aḥmad (d. 360/971) — V 92a, 92b, 93a
Hamid, Abdul — IV 274b

Ḥamīd al-Dīn al-Farāhī (1863-1930)	IV 8; V 406a
Hamidullah, M.	V 343b
Hamilton, R.	I 126a, 126b
Hamka (Haji Abdul Malik Karim Amrullah)	V 99b, 100a
Ḥammād b. Salama (d. 167/783-4)	IV 386b, 387a
Ḥammām al-Shifā	V 127a
von Hammer-Purgstall, J.	III 110b
Ḥammūdah ʿAbd al-ʿĀṭī	see ʿAbd al-ʿĀṭī, Ḥammūdah
Hamori, A.	II 301a; IV 472b
Ḥamza b. ʿAbd al-Muṭṭalib (paternal uncle of the Prophet)	II 149a, **400a**, 400b; III 80b; IV 64b; V 42b, 59a
Ḥamza b. ʿAlī al-Zawzanī (d. after 411/1021)	I 554b
Ḥamza b. Ḥabīb al-Zayyāt (d. 156/773)	IV 357a, 358b, 359b, 360b, 373a, 389a
Ḥamza Fansūrī	III 225b
Ḥamza al-Kūfī	III 87b
Ḥanafī(s)	I 18b, 19a, 122b, 210a, 252b, 412a; II 171a, 171b; III 404b; IV 58b, 110a, 415a; V 482b, 495b, 498a, 498b
Ḥanafī, Ḥ.	II 139a, 139b
Ḥanbalī(s)	I 265a, 468b, 469a, 470b, 481a, 481b, 482a, 483a; II 506b; III 179a, 385b, 404a, 404b; IV 81a, 81b, 89a; V 111b, 112a, 415a
Ḥanīf (Arab tribe)	II 530a
[Banū] Ḥanīfa	I 121a; III 460b, 461a, 462a, 462b, 463a; V 67b
Ḥanīfism	II 569b
Hanna (mother of Samuel)	IV 527b
Ḥannā Maqār	IV 236b
Ḥanẓala b. Bayhas	III 86b
Ḥanẓala b. Ṣafwān	III 381; IV 353a
Ḥanẓala Usayyidī	IV 423a
Happel, E.W.	V 347b
Haram (in al-Jawf)	V 86b, 87a
Ḥaram al-Khalīl	III 57a
al-Ḥaram al-Sharīf	see Temple Mount
Haran [Ḥarrān]	I 8b, 138a; III 430a; IV 408a, 511b, 512a
al-Harawī al-Mawṣilī, ʿAlī	II 463b; V 186b
Harī Rūdh	III 313a
al-Ḥarīrī	II 361b
Ḥārith (Arethas)	I 308b; III 500b
Ḥārith b. ʿAmr	I 309b; III 381a
al-Ḥārith al-Aʿwar (d. 64/684)	II 522b

[Banū] Ḥārith b. Kaʿb	I 154a, 154b, 529b, 530b
al-Ḥārith b. Kalada (d. 13/634-5)	III 392a
al-Ḥārith b. Khuzayma	I 355b
al-Ḥārith b. Sinān	V 306b
al-Ḥārith b. Surayj	I 468a
[Banū] Ḥāritha	II 16b; V 379b
Ḥarra	I 539b
al-Ḥarrānī, Aḥmad b. Ḥamdān b. Shabīb (d. 695/1295)	I 482a
Ḥarrānians	IV 512b
Harrison, T.	II **428a**
Hartford Seminary (Connecticut)	V 217a, 306a
Hārūn	see Aaron
Hārūn b. Mūsā (d. 170/786)	V 333a
Hārūn al-Rashīd (d. 193/809)	I 67b, 156a; IV 525a; V 323a
Ḥarūrāʾ	III 84b
Ḥarūrīs	III 84b, 85a
Hārūt	I 195a; II **404a**, 404b, 405a; III 249b; IV 165a; V 118b, 202b
Harvard University Library	IV 265b
Ḥasan (son of ʿAlī, grandson of the Prophet; d. 49/669-70)	I 347a, 390a, 412a, 550b; II 177a, 193a, 450b, 451b; IV 50a, 60b, 596a
al-Ḥasan (eunich)	II 28a
Ḥasan (r. 757-64/1356-62)	II 31b
Ḥasan Aḥmad al-Ṭūkhī	IV 266b
[Imām] al-Ḥasan al-ʿAskarī	see al-ʿAskarī, [Imām] al-Ḥasan (d. 260/874)
al-Ḥasan b. Aḥmad al-Hamadhānī	see al-Hamadhānī, al-Ḥasan b. Aḥmad (d. 319/932)
al-Ḥasan b. Aḥmad al-Hamdānī	see al-Hamdānī, al-Ḥasan b. Aḥmad (d. 360/971)
al-Ḥasan b. Muḥammad al-Mālikī (d. 438/1046)	III 123a
al-Ḥasan b. Ṣāliḥ b. Ḥayy (d. 199/814-5)	IV 387b
Ḥasan al-Bannā (d. 1949)	see al-Bannā, Ḥ.
al-Ḥasan al-Baṣrī (d. 110/728)	I 23a, 23b, 89a; II 103a, 105a, 116b, 118b, 268a, 270b, 356b, 389b, 409b, 470b; III 4b, 89a, 154a, 378b; IV 54a, 360a, 386b, 389b; V 124b, 139a, 139b, 165b, 277b, 440b
Ḥasan Ḥelebi (d. 1002/1593)	III 320b
Ḥasan Ḥanafī	see Ḥanafī, Ḥ.
al-Ḥasan al-Nīsābūrī	I 461b
Ḥasan al-Sharaf	IV 266b
Hashemite Kingdom	see Jordan

[Banū] Hāshim — I 290b; IV 51a, 51b; V 185a
Hāshim b. Sulaymān al-Baḥrānī — see al-Baḥrānī, Hāshim b. Sulaymān (d. 1107/1696 or 1109/1697)
al-Ḥaskāfī (d. 1088/1677) — III 404b
Hassan, A. — V 99b
Hassan, R. — II 202a, 203a
Ḥassān b. Thābit (d. ca. 40/659) — I 398b, 400a; III 121a, 215b, 504b; IV 56a, 113b; V 43b
Ḥaśśān Yuhaʾmin — V 565b
Hasson, I. — I **497a**, II **11a**, III **144b**, **180a**
Ḥātim (of Ṭayy) — I 38a
Ḥātim b. al-Aṣamm — V 383a
Haurvatat (Zoroastrian archangel) — II 404a
Hausa — III 327b
Hausa (language) — I 33b, 136a
Hawary, M. — I 169a
Hawāzin — II 19b, 466a, 466b
Hawbas — V 85b, 86a, 87b
Hawdha — III 461b
al-Ḥawfī, Abū l-Ḥasan ʿAlī b. Ibrāhīm (d. 430/1039) — V 325b, 333a
Hawfiʾīl — V 87b
Ḥawl — V 91b
Ḥawrān — I 530b
Hawting, G. — I **188a**, **276b**, 421a; II **480a**, **483b**; III **79b**, **566a**; IV **27b**, **99b**, 200b, 204a, **260b**, 342a; V **318a**, **557b**
Ḥawwāʾ — see Eve
Ḥawwā, Saʿīd — II 138a
Ḥaydar-i Āmulī (d. after 787/1385) — V 159a
Ḥaydara — V 307a
Hayderabad — V 343b
Hayek, M. — IV 195b
al-Haytamī — V 20b
Ḥayyān al-Aʿraj — III 88b
Hazard, H.W. — III 559a
Heath, P. — III **388a**
Hebrew
Language [*ʿibrī*/ *ʿibrānī*] — I 102a, 316b; II 13b, 231a, 231b, 235b, 243a, 342b, 350b, 485b, 498a; III 1a, 2a, 9b, 10a, 45b, 49a, 114a, 118a, 131b, 148b, 244a; IV 28b, 37a, 39a, 92a, 239a, 289a, 517a; V 3a, 105a,

105b, 112a, 306a, 306b, 551b, 564b
People i 236a, 403a, 499b; iii 242a; v 382b
Rabbinical ii 234b; iv 314a
Hebron [Ḥabrūn] i 5b, 156a, 496b; iii 57a; v 185a, 186a, 259a
Heck, P. iv **150a**, **154b**, **571a**; v **199b**, **451a**
Heemskerk, M. v **112a**, **136b**
Hegra ii 427a; see also Ḥijr
Heidegger, M. ii 139b
Heights, People of the iv **46b**, 47b; v 244a
Hejaz see Ḥijāz
Heidelberg iv 249a
Hellenism i 46a; v 260a; see also Greek(s)
Hellenization iii 129b
Helpers [*anṣār*] see Medinans
Henniger, J. iv 195a
Henning, M. v 352a, 352a
Heraclius i 265b
Herat v 147a
Hermansen, M. v **192a**, **523a**
Hermes [Hīrmīs] (Trismegistus) ii 484b, 485a, 485b
Hermitage Museum, St Petersburg iii 319a
Hernandez Cata, J. v 349b
[King] Herod iii 52a
Herzfeld, E. i 169a
Hesiod i 104a; ii 240a
Heyne, C.G. iv 251a
Hezbollah see Ḥizbullāh
[King] Hezekiah iii 54a
al-Hibri, A. ii 203a; v 239b
Ḥijāz i 10a, 42a, 149b, 154b, 155b, 307b, 368a, 433b; ii 108a, 149b, 294b, 295a, 307b, 346b, 358a, 365a, 426b, 428a, 479a; iii 4a, 4b, 58b, 88b, 96b, 112a, 123a, 123b, 254a, 361a, 363a, 367b, 368a, 370a, 390a, 406a, 409a, 500a, 572b, 578a, 580a; iv 254a, 256b, 258b, 260a, 360b; v 66b, 90b, 263a, 333a
Codex iii 244a, 260a
Language i 530a; iii 112b

Ḥijr — I 150b, 152b; II 260a, 339a, **427a**, 427b, 438a; III 418a, 519b; IV 54a, 454a; V 253b, 254a
Hikmet, N. — V 394b
Hilāl — V 508a, 508b
Hillenbrand, R. — III 297b
al-Ḥillī, al-Muḥaqqiq (d. 676/1277) — IV 489a, 492a
Ḥilwān — III 328b
Ḥims — see Ḥums
Ḥimyar — I 152a, 214b, 296b; III 119a; IV 405b; V 91b, 93a, 389b, 390a
Ḥimyarīs/Ḥimyarites — I 309b; IV 586b; V 91a, 92a, 93a, 390a, 561b, 563a, 563b, 564a
  Christian — V 566b
Hinckelmann, Abraham — IV 247a, 247b, 248a, 250a, 265a
Hind — see Umm Salama bt. al-Mughīra
Hind (son of Khadīja bt. Khuwaylid and Abū Hāla Hind b. al-Nabbāsh of Tamīm) — V 507b
Hind (daughter of Khadīja bt. Khuwaylid and ʿAtīq b. ʿĀbid of Makhzūm) — V 507b
Hind bt. ʿUtba — II 400b
Hinduism — I 169b, 316a, 418b; III 247b
Hindus — II 479b; IV 409b, 417a
Hippocrates — III 242b, 349b, 351b
al-Ḥīra — I 121a, 136a, 278b, 308b, 309a; II 295a, 296b, 430a; III 275a, 405b, 518a, 589a; IV 111b, 407b, 431a
Ḥirāʾ — II 240b, 487b; V 403b
  Mount — I 182a; II 181a; IV 217b, 443b; V 41b, 284b
Hirschfeld, H. — I 322b; III 475a, 476a; IV 190b, 191a, 191b, 193b, 194b
Hirschkind, C. — III **348b**
Hishām (r. 105-25/724-43) — IV 73a, 588a
Hishām b. Abī ʿAbdallāh al-Dastuwāʾī — II 381b
Hishām b. ʿAmmār al-Sulamī (d. 245/859-60) — I 357a, 358a; IV 390a
Hishām b. al-Ḥakam (d. 179/795-6) — V 25b, 26a
Hishām b. al-Kalbī — see Ibn al-Kalbī, Hishām (d. 206/821)
Hishām b. ʿUrwa (d. 146/763) — II 382a, 387b, 391a
Hishām al-Fuwaṭī (d. ca. 229/844) — III 468b; V 8b
Ḥizbullāh — III 286a
Ḥizqīl b. Būzī/Būdhī/Būrī — see Ezekiel
Hodgson, M. — I 64b

Hoffmann, M.W. v 352a
Hoffman, V. ii **208a**, **453b**, **555a**
Holon (in Israel) iv 524a
Holws, C. i 127b
Holy Land i 260a, 308b; iii 489b, 496a
Holy Mountain see al-Jabal al-Muqaddas
Holy Spirit i 87a; ii 84a, 279a, **442b**, 443a, 443b; iii 12a, 13b, 16a, 16b; iv 292a, 295b; v 41a, 190a
Homer i 104a; ii 131b, 240a; iii 479b
Homerin, T. i **396a**, **554a**; v **84a**
[Mount] Horeb v 248a
Horovitz, J. i 398b; ii 155b, 308a, 308b, 498a; iii 480a, 489a, 493a, 522a; iv 106a, 194b, 321a, 351b; v 106b, 125a, 236b, 398a
Hottinger, Johann Heinrich (d. 1667) iv 249a, 249b
Hourani, G. ii 65a, 67a
House, People of the [*ahl al-bayt*] i 390a; ii **176b**; iii 236a; iv **48b**, 178a; v 324a
House of God see God
Housman, A.E. v 237b
Hoyland, R. ii **41a**; iv 328a, 405b; v 48b
Hoziq (of Bukhara) iv 62a
Hrbek, I. v 354b
Hsu, S.S.A. iii **404b**
Hubal ii 237b
Hubas v 93a
Ḥubbā iv 577b
Hubert, E. iv 245b
Hūd i 21b, 54b, 93a, 222a, 261b, 296b, 411b, 511a, 512b, 519a, 519b, 536b; ii 64a, 293a, 336a, 438a, **462a**, 462b, 463a, 463b, 488a, 510a, 541b, 558a, 559a; iii 118b, 200b, 212b, 232a, 380b, 381a, 381b, 393a, 479b, 519b, 520b, 525b, 540a, 540b, 567b; iv 130b, 258a, 263b, 319a, 523b, 586b; v 16a, 313b
People of ii 338a; iv 605b
Hūd b. Muḥakkam/Muḥkim al-Hawwārī (d. ca. 280/893 or 290/902-3) ii 116b
Huda, Q. i **84a**
al-Ḥudaybiya i 216a, 216b, 320a, 398a, 399a,

400a, 406a, 464a, 547a, 551a; II 147b, 148a, 149b, **464a**, 538a; III 4a, 4b, 340a, 456b, 568a, 568b, 579a; IV 16a, 17a, 95a, 332a, 332b, 456b; V 44b, 194a, 255b, 362a, 401b, 409a, 435a, 444b
Hudhaliyya V 79b
Ḥudhayfa I 332b, 353a, 357a; IV 47b
Ḥudhayfa b. al-Yamān I 538b; III 502b
Hudhayl I 529b, 530a; II 354b; III 544a; IV 439a; V 79b
Hugo Grotius (d. 1645) IV 243b
al-Hujwīrī (d. 465/1072) II 452a; IV 491a
Hūlāgū (Mongol chief) II 35a, 561a
Ḥulubān V 565b
Ḥumayd I 354a
Humphreys, R.S. I 375a
Ḥum IV 45a, 96b, 256b, 320b; V 185b
Ḥunayn I 337a, 398a, 400a, 405b, 461a, 500b; II 21b, 148b, 299b, 439a, **465b**; III 398a, 456a; V 430a
Battle of II 465b, 466a; III 579a; IV 457a; V 42a, 279a
Ḥunayn b. Isḥāq (d. 260/873) V 306a, 306b
Hunsberger, A. III **288a**
Hunwick, J. I **35a**
Hur I 276a
Hurgronje, C. see Snouck Hurgronje
Ḥurūfiyya III 247b; IV 175a
Husain, M. I 169a
al-Ḥuṣarī, A. IV 489b
al-Ḥuṣarī, M. Kh. IV 361a
[Shāh] Ḥusayn (d. 1002/1593) III 225b
Ḥusayn, Ṣaddām I 161b; III 584a
Ḥusayn, Ṭahā II 131a
Ḥusayn b. ʿAlī (grandson of the Prophet; d. 61/680) I 78a, 306a, 347a, 390a, 550b; II 147a, 177a, 193a, 204a, 208a, 553b; III 281a, 286a, 291a; IV 56b, 60b, 342a, 342b, 596a; V 135a, 223a
al-Ḥusayn b. Biṣṭām b. Shāpūr III 350b
al-Ḥusayn b. al-Farrāʾ al-Baghawī see al-Baghawī, Abū Muḥammad al-Farrāʾ (d. 516/1122)

al-Ḥusayn b. Manṣūr al-Ḥallāj — see al-Ḥallāj (d. 309/922)
Ḥusayn b. Muḥammad al-Najjār (d. middle of third/ninth century) — IV 85b
Ḥusayn Taqī Nūrī al-Ṭabarsī — see Nūrī al-Ṭabarsī, Ḥusayn Taqī (d. 1320/1902)
Hushaym b. Bashīr (d. 183/799) — II 387b, 388a
Hutcheson, F. — II 77b
Ḥuwayṭib b. ʿAbd al-ʿUzza — II 517a
Ḥuyayy b. Akhṭab — III 35a, 498b

I

IAIN — see Islam
Iathrippa — II 298b; see also Yathrib; Medina
Ibāḍī(s)/Ibāḍites — I 485a; II 116b; III 85b, 86a, 86b, 87a, 88a, 88b, 89a
Ibāḍism/Ibāḍiyya — II 503b; III 86b, 87b; V 23b
Iberian Peninsula — IV 238b
Iblīs — I 86b, 140a, 441a, 447a, 447b, 451b, 452a, 452b, 453a, 453b, 457a, 476a, 511a, 525a, 525b, 526a, 527a, 527b; II 166b, 325a, 336a, 419a, **473a**, 541b, 543a, 550a; III 44b, 45a, 45b, 490b, 491a, 519a, 519b, 520b, 521b, 529a, 532a, 543a; IV 220a, 263b, 336b; V 96a, 109a, 118b, 120a, 120b, 142b, 145a, 267b, 360a, 377b; see also Satan
Ibn ʿAbbād (Būyid vizier) — III 436b
Ibn (al-)ʿAbbās, ʿAbdallāh (d. 68-9/686-7) — I 45a, 88a, 89a, 121b, 122a, 208a, 257a, 321b, 322a, 340a, 348b, 349a, 354a, 360a, 367a, 389a, 410b, 412a, 454b, 455a, 455b, 488a, 535b; II 99a, 100b, 101b, 102b, 103a, 103b, 104a, 104b, 106a, 106b, 107a, 147b, 151b, 180a, 189b, 190a, 210b, 219a, 227a, 230b, 231b, 337a, 338a, 355a, 378a, 389a, 389b, 390a, 396b, 457a, 523a; III 5b, 14b, 17b, 67b, 89a, 103b, 118b, 119a, 120b, 148a, 175a, 179a, 380a, 391b, 392a, 412b, 438b, 459b, 538a, 548b, 552b, 581b;

iv 69a, 70a, 135b, 136a, 157b, 228a, 303b, 305a, 340b, 351a, 444a, 519a, 533a, 588a; v 19b, 21b, 63a, 63b, 64a, 118b, 202a, 249a, 255a, 277b, 321b, 329a, 333a, 441a, 472a, 551b
Ibn ʿAbd al-Kāfī v 331a
Ibn ʿAbd al-Munʿim al-Ḥimyarī ii 559b
Ibn ʿAbd Rabbihi (d. 328/940) ii 222b
Ibn ʿAbd al-Raḥīm al-Nihāwandī, Muḥammad v 319b
Ibn ʿAbd al-Wahhāb, Muḥammad (d. 1206/1791) i 39a, 482b; v 452a, 452b, 453a; see also Wahhābī(s)
Ibn Abī l-ʿĀs, al-Ḥakam (governor of Fars and Khūzistān; r. 56-8/676-8) ii 29a
Ibn Abī Dāwūd al-Sijistānī see al-Sijistānī, Ibn Abī Dāwūd (d. 316/929)
Ibn Abī l-Dunyā (d. 281/894) i 263a; v 552b
Ibn Abī Ḥātim al-Rāzī see al-Rāzi, Ibn Abī Ḥātim (d. 327/938-9)
Ibn Abī Isḥāq al-Ḥaḍramī (d. 117-18/735-6) ii 348a, 356b; iii 605b
Ibn Abī Jumhūr al-Aḥsāʾī (d. after 904/1499) i 484b
Ibn Abī Najīh (d. 131/749) ii 105a
Ibn Abī Sarḥ ii 514b
Ibn Abī Shayba (d. 235/849) ii 390b; iii 123b; iv 232a; v 35a, 330b
Ibn Abī Zamanīn (d. 399/1008) v 335a
Ibn Abī l-Zinād iii 131b
Ibn ʿĀbidīn (d. 1258/1842) iii 404b
Ibn Abīhi iii 11a
Ibn Ādam i 16b
Ibn ʿAjība (d. 1224/1809) ii 120b; v 158a
Ibn al-ʿAjūz see Ezekiel
Ibn ʿĀmir, ʿAbdallāh (d. 118/736) iii 15b; iv 357a, 359b, 360b, 373a, 389a, 389b
Ibn ʿAmr iv 109b
Ibn al-Anbārī (d. 328/940) v 324a
Ibn ʿAqīl ii 115b, 356b
Ibn al-Aʿrābī (d. ca. 231/846) ii 239b
Ibn al-ʿArabī, Muḥammad b. ʿAbdallāh Abū Bakr (d. 543/1148) ii 98a, 114a; iii 82b, 83b, 107a; iv 110a; iv 349b, 553b; v 319b, 324b, 334b
Ibn al-ʿArabī, Muḥyī al-Dīn (d. 638/1240) i 51a, 61b, 85a, 206b, 211a, 257a, 426a, 428a, 430a; ii 36a, 95b, 96a, 119a, 119b, 120b, 279b, 409b, 419a, 551a; iii 82b,

83b, 230b, 236b, 246a, 306a, 389a, 505a, 508a; IV 67b, 263a, 424a, 520b; V 151a, 153a, 153b, 154a, 154b, 155a, 155b, 156a, 156b, 157b, 158a, 159a, 191b, 275a, 277b, 382b, 383b, 388b, 465b, 467a, 484a

Ibn al-ʿArīf (d. 536/1141) V 153a

Ibn ʿArrāq, Muḥammad b. Aḥmad b. ʿAbd al-Raḥmān (d. 933/1526) V 328b, 329a

Ibn ʿAsākir, ʿAlī b. al-Ḥasan b. ʿAsākir (d. 571/1176) I 135a; IV 51b

Ibn al-Ashʿath (d. 82/701) IV 140b; V 505a

Ibn al-Ashraf, Kaʿb (d. 3/625) III 32a, 35a, 498b, 580a

Ibn ʿAskar (of Malagá; d. 636/1239) V 334a

Ibn ʿAṭaʾ, Aḥmad (d. 309/922) V 140b, 141a, 143a

Ibn Aʿtham al-Kūfī I 400b

Ibn al-Athīr, Ḍiyāʾ al-Dīn Abū l-Fatḥ Muḥammad b. Muḥammad (d. 637/1239) IV 477b, 479a, 480a

Ibn ʿAṭiyya al-Andalusī (d. 541/1147) II 112b; V 330a

Ibn al-ʿAwwām (d. 663/1265) I 48b

Ibn Bābawayh (d. 381/991) I 484b

Ibn al-Bādhish al-Gharnāṭī (d. 540/1145) V 332a

Ibn Balbān al-Fārisī (d. 729/1329) V 336a

Ibn al-Bannāʾ al-ʿAdadī al-Marrākushī (d. 721/1321) V 332b

Ibn Barrajān (d. 536/1142) II 119a; V 153a, 153b, 154a

Ibn Baṣṣāl (d. 499/1105) I 48b

Ibn Baṭṭa (d. ca. 365/975) III 306a

Ibn Baṭṭa al-ʿUkbarī (d. 387/997) I 482a

Ibn Baṭṭūṭa (d. 770/1377) III 59a; IV 492b

Ibn Bāʿūra see Balaam

Ibn al-Bawwāb (d. 413/1022) I 137a, 142a, 173b, 282a, 282b; III 264a, 301b, 302a, 595b, 596b, 597a, 597b, 600a, 601a; V 559b

Ibn Bisṭām al-Ṭuḥayrī, Abū Muḥammad Ḥāmid b. Aḥmad b. Jaʿfar IV 166a; V 325a

Ibn Budayl IV 138a

Ibn Dhakwān, ʿAbdallāh b. Aḥmad (d. 242/857) IV 359b, 390a

Ibn Dūmīt Makhlūf (d. ca. 1707) IV 237a

Ibn Durayd (d. 321/933) II 228a, 228b

Ibn Durustawayh I 141a

Ibn Faras al-Gharnāṭī (d. 599/1202) V 333b

Ibn Farḥūn (d. 799/1397) III 371a

Ibn Fāris (d. 395/1004) III 112a, 112b, 113a

Ibn al-Farrāʾ, Abū Yaʿlā (d. 458/1066) I 482a

Ibn al-Fujāʾa, Qaṭarī II 30a

Ibn Fūrak (d. 406/1015) I 514a; V 324b
Ibn Ghalbūn, Abū Ḥasan Ṭāhir b. ʿAbd al-Munʿim (d. 399/1008) IV 358a; V 332a
Ibn Ḥabīb, ʿAbd al-Malik (d. 238/852-3) II 222b, 446a; III 118a, 118b, 391b, 392a; IV 108a
Ibn Ḥabīb (d. 245/860) V 397b
Ibn Ḥabīb al-Nīsābūri see al-Nīsābūri, Ibn Ḥabīb (d. 406/1016)
Ibn Ḥajar al-ʿAsqalānī (d. 852/1449) II 231b; III 570b; IV 534b; V 20b, 330a, 330b
Ibn Ḥajar al-Haytamī (d. 974/1567) V 20a
Ibn al-Ḥajj (d. 737/1336) IV 487b, 491a
Ibn al-Ḥajjāj (of Seville) I 48b
Ibn Ḥanbal, Aḥmad (d. 241/855) I 105b, 106b, 107a, 389a, 463b, 468a, 468b, 469a, 469b, 470a, 471a, 481a, 481b; II 110b, 116b, 382b, 390a, 418b, 446a, 533a, 554a; III 254a, 467b, 502b, 543a; IV 72a, 73b, 81a, 89a, 262b, 351, 371a, 371b, 565a, 588a; V 18a, 165b, 361a, 417b
Ibn al-Ḥanbalī (d. 634/1236) I 514a
Ibn al-Ḥasan al-Shaybānī, Muḥammad V 323a
Ibn Ḥazm, ʿAlī b. Aḥmad b. Saʿīd al-Andalusī (d. 456/1064) I 118b, 160a, 205b, 225a, 514a; II 228a, 228b, 511b; III 289a; 502b; IV 77b, 123b, 317a, 414a, 451a, 587b; V 305a, 306a, 306b, 308b, 309a, 309b
Ibn Ḥibbān (d. 354/965) V 334b, 336a
Ibn Hishām, ʿAbd al-Malik (d. 218/833) I 21a, 401b, 531a; II 103b, 145a, 528b; III 29a, 455a, 541a; IV 323b, 586b; V 30a, 31b, 33b, 34a, 36b, 79b, 80a, 113b
Ibn Ibāḍ, ʿAbdallāh III 86b; IV 386b
Ibn Ikhshīdh, Abū Bakr Aḥmad (d. 326/938) II 533b, 534a; III 468b, 471a
Ibn ʿĪsā (d. 335/946) III 605a, 606a
Ibn Isḥāq, Muḥammad (d. 150/767) I 4a, 20b, 293a, 306a, 337a, 399b, 401b, 407a, 409a; II 15b, 104a, 105a, 145a, 148a, 149b, 150a, 338b, 388a, 392b, 478b, 516a, 528b, 530a; III 29a, 29b, 30a, 30b, 31a, 31b, 32a, 104b, 190b, 408b, 455a, 541a, 579b; IV 303b, 304a, 324a, 324b, 408b, 463b, 533a; V 30a, 31b, 33a,

	33b, 34a, 34b, 36a, 36b, 37a, 37b, 38a, 38b, 41a, 42a, 42b, 43a, 44a, 44b, 47b, 64a, 122b, 194a, 389b, 460a
Ibn Jammāz, Sulaymān b. Muslim (d. after 170/77-7)	IV 390a
Ibn Janāḥ	IV 13a
Ibn al-Jaṣṣās	II 465a
Ibn al-Jawzī, Abū l-Faraj ʿAbd al-Raḥmān b. ʿAlī (d. 597/1200)	I 71b, 78a, 203a, 206a, 522a, 528a; II 111b, 112b, 193a, 505a; III 287b, 358b; IV 156a, 166a; V 143a, 220a, 220b, 223a, 277b, 326b, 327a, 333a, 335b
Ibn al-Jazarī, Shams al-Dīn Abū l-Khayr Muḥammad b. Muḥammad (d. 833/1429)	IV 358b, 359a, 373a, 374a, 374b, 389b, 390a, 391a, 391b; V 332a
Ibn Jinnī, Abū l-Fatḥ ʿUthmān (d. 392/1002)	I 347b; II 356b; III 112b, 119b
Ibn Jubayr (d. 614/1217)	III 59a, 117b; V 127a
Ibn Jurayj, ʿAbd al-Malik (d. 150/767)	IV 96a, 533a; V 255a, 491a
Ibn Juzayy al-Kalbī al-Gharnāṭī (d. 741/1340)	V 327b, 330a
Ibn Kaʿb al-Quraẓī, Muḥammad (d. 118-20/736-8)	I 389b; II 516a; IV 334b, 533a
Ibn al-Kalbī, Hishām (d. 206/821)	I 154b; II 479a; IV 51b; V 90b, 92a, 92b, 93a, 122a, 389b
Ibn Karrām (d. 255/869)	V 325a
Ibn Kathīr al-Dārī, ʿAbdallāh (d. 120/738)	IV 357a, 359b, 360a, 360b, 372a, 373a, 389a, 391b
Ibn Kathīr, ʿImād al-Dīn Ismāʿīl b. ʿUmar (d. 774/1373)	I 44b, 45a, 114a, 203b, 204a, 206a, 257b, 337a, 366a, 367a, 439a, 461b, 522a; II 88b, 113a, 113b, 124a, 217b, 218a, 219a, 220a, 222b, 232b, 271a, 336b, 337a, 337b, 338a, 340a, 419a, 426b, 446a, 446b, 468b; III 83a, 138a, 177a, 378b, 381b, 410b; IV 109b, 349b, 350a, 397a, 533b, 539b; V 9a, 113b, 330a, 434b, 444b, 448b, 474b, 510a
Ibn Kaysān	see Abū Bakr al-Aṣamm (d. 200/816)
Ibn Khafāja (d. 533/1139)	IV 317b
Ibn Khafīf (d. 371/981)	V 141a
Ibn Khālawayh (d. 370/980)	V 331b, 335a
Ibn Khaldūn, ʿAbd al-Raḥmān (d. 784/1382)	I 69a, 195b; II 441b; III 250b, 251a, 362b, 429a, 552b, 586b; IV 271a IV 443a, 445b; V 103b, 179b
Ibn al-Khallāl	III 469b
Ibn Khurradādhbīb	II 333a
Ibn Kullāb (d. ca. 241/855)	IV 446a, 446b; V 112a

Ibn Luyūn (d. 750/1349) I 48b
Ibn Mājā, Muḥammad b. Yazīd (d. 273/886) II 191b, 377b, 446b; III 350b
Ibn Mammātī I 47a
Ibn Manẓūr (d. 711/1311) I 432b; III 130a, 141b; IV 36a, 51b; V 359a
Ibn al-Masarra al-Jabalī (d. 319/931) II 119a; V 153a
Ibn Mas'ūd, 'Abdallāh (d. 32/652-3) I 15a, 17a, 36a, 209b, 332b, 333a, 348a, 348b, 349a, 349b, 350a, 350b, 354a, 354b, 356a, 356b, 357a, 359a, 359b, 360a, 412a; II 102b, 247a, 329a, 393b, 522b; III 117a, 117b, 156b, 257b, 392a, 463a; IV 69a, 354b, 355a, 356a, 358a, 359a, 371a, 388b, 509b; V 46b, 64a, 64b, 238b, 318b, 321b, 409b
Ibn Mihrān V 332b
Ibn Miqsam, Muḥammad b. al-Ḥasan IV 357a, 388b
Ibn al-Mubārak, 'Abdallāh (d. 181/797) II 421b; V 139a, 139b
Ibn Muḥayṣin, Muḥammad b. 'Abd al-Raḥmān (d. 123/740) IV 359b, 360a, 389b, 391b
Ibn Mujāhid, Abū Bakr Aḥmad b. Mūsā (d. 324/936) I 334a; II 247b; III 301b, 606a, 606b; IV 354b, 355b, 356a, 356b, 357a, 357b, 358a, 358b, 359a, 360b, 373a, 374a, 388b, 389a, 391b; V 238b, 239b, 331b
Ibn al-Mundhir al-Mundhirī al-Nīshābūrī, Abū Bakr Muḥammad b. Ibrahīm (d. 318/930) II 110b; III 117b; IV 58a
Ibn al-Muqaffa' II 529b; IV 23a, 57b, 143a, 143b, 144a, 144b, 146a
Ibn Muqla (d. 328/940) I 137a, 173a, 282a; III 301b, 605a, 606a; IV 356a
Ibn Muslim, Muḥammad (d. 150/767) IV 599a
Ibn al-Nadīm, Muḥammad b. Isḥāq (d. ca. 385/995) I 136a, 136b, 173a, 280a; II 102b; III 250b, 256b, 262a, 467b, 469a, 469b; IV 512a
Ibn al-Nafīs (d. 687/1288) III 363a
Ibn al-Naqīb, Abū 'Abdallāh b. Sulaymān (d. 698/1298) IV 287a
Ibn Nāqiyā (d. 485/1092) V 14a, 14b
Ibn Nubāta al-Fāriqī (d. 374/984) III 219b; V 220b
Ibn al-Nu'mān (d. 413/1022) IV 594b
Ibn Qasī (d. 541/1151) V 153a
Ibn al-Qāsim (d. 191/806) V 417a
Ibn Qayyim al-Jawziyya (d. 751/1350) I 78a, 89a, 90a, 205b, 206a, 425b, 482b; II 446b, 447a, 498a; III

	309a, 351a, 351b, 353a, 353b, 354a, 354b, 355a, 356a, 357b, 358a, 359a, 359b, 360a, 361a, 361b, 362a, 362b, 363a, 364a, 364b, 365b, 366b; IV 123b, 166a, 174b; V 306a, 417a, 466b, 554a, 554b
Ibn al-Qifṭī (d. 646/1248)	V 483b
Ibn Qilāba	II 559a
Ibn Qudāma (d. 690/1291)	IV 430b
Ibn Qudāma, Muwaffaq al-Dīn (d. 620/1223)	I 482a; IV 77b
Ibn Qutayba, Abū Muḥammad ʿAbdallāh b. Muslim al-Dīnawarī (d. 276/889)	I 203b, 205b, 287a; II 108b, 222b, 228a, 231b, 343a, 397b, 398a, 531b; IV 156a, 169b, 355b, 564a; V 306a, 306b, 309a, 333b, 550b
Ibn Rajab (d. 795/1395)	V 319b, 336a
Ibn al-Rāwandī (d. ca. 298/910-11)	II 531a; IV 23b
Ibn Rushd (d. 520/1126)	V 305b
Ibn Rushd (Averroës; d. 595/1198)	I 475b; II 55a; III 386b, 387a; IV 75a, 75b, 76a, 76b, 77a, 79a, 79b, 80a, 81a, 81b, 82a, 82b, 83a, 88a, 89a, 89b; V 8b
Ibn Saʿd, Sahl	III 6a
Ibn Saʿd Muḥammad b. Saʿd (d. 230/845)	I 58b, 293b, 294a, 389a; II 15b, 16b, 19a, 397b; III 501b, 502b, 541a; IV 49b, 125b, 153a, 153b, 305a; V 34b, 35a, 45a, 46a, 47b, 199a, 254a, 402a, 514b, 519a
Ibn al-Sāʾib al-Kalbī, Muḥammad	see al-Kalbī, Muḥammad b. al-Sāʾib Abū-Naḍr al-Kalbī (d. 146/763)
Ibn Said, O.	I 30a
Ibn al-Ṣāʾigh al-Ḥanafī, Shams al-Dīn Muḥammad b. ʿAbd al-Raḥmān (d. 776/1375)	IV 103a, 482b, 483a
Ibn Salām, ʿAbdallāh	I 223b; III 32a, 32b; IV 236a, 323a, 539a; V 203b
Ibn Sallām	II 116b
Ibn al-Ṣayrafī (d. 542/1147)	III 216a
Ibn Ṣayyād (or Ibn Ṣāʿid)	I 110b, 111a
Ibn Sayyār al-Warrāq	II 223a
Ibn Shāh Rukh, B.	III 313b, 314a
Ibn Shāh Rukh, I.	III 313b
Ibn Shannabūdh, Abū l-Ḥasan Muḥammad b. Aḥmad b. Ayyūb (d. 328/939)	IV 356a, 356b, 357a, 360a, 388b, 389a

Ibn al-Shaykh (d. 926/1520) III 320b
Ibn Shihāb al-Zuhrī, Muḥammad (d. 124/742) II 108a, 381b, 383a; III 154b, 465a; IV 324b, 533a
Ibn Shuhayd (d. 393/1003) III 221a
Ibn Shurayḥ al-Ruʿaynī al-Ishbīlī (d. 476/1083) V 332a
Ibn Sīnā (Avicenna; d. 428/1037) I 85b, 88b; II 279a; III 182b, 349b; IV 57b, 74b, 75a, 79a, 80b, 81a, 83a, 87a, 87b, 88a, 88b, 169b, 381a
Ibn Sīrīn (d. 110/728) II 281a; IV 169b
Ibn Siwār al-Baghdādī (d. 496/1103) V 332a
Ibn al-Subkī (d. 771/1369) II 231b
Ibn al-Sunnī (d. 364/974) IV 232a
Ibn Sunqur al-Baghdādī, Muḥammad III 312a
Ibn Taghrībirdī IV 492b
Ibn al-Tammār (Iraqi poet) II 39b
Ibn Ṭāwūs (d. 664/1266) II 106a; III 471a
Ibn Taymiyya, Taqī al-Dīn Aḥmad b ʿAbd al-Ḥalīm (d. 728/1328) I 205b, 482b; II 111b, 113a, 554a, 554b; III 143b, 285b; IV 77b, 123b, 146b, 147a, 147b, 148a, 166b, 414b, 444b, 489b, 493b, 494b, 495a, 495b, 534a, 534b; V 25b, 143a, 219b, 316b, 554a
Ibn Ṭūlūn al-Dimashqī (d. 953/1546) III 363a
Ibn Ubayy b. Salūl, ʿAbdallāh I 409a; II 469a, 469b; IV 324a
Ibn ʿUmar, ʿAbdallāh (d. 73/693) I 53a, 265b, 266b, 267b, 268a, 412a; II 147a, 189b, 190a; III 538a; IV 52a, 96a; V 472a, 504b
Ibn ʿUqda (d. 333/947) IV 603a
Ibn Wāfid (d. 466/1074) I 48b
Ibn Wahb, ʿAbdallāh (d. 197/812-3) I 88a, 349b; II 104a, 107b, 108a; IV 354a
Ibn Wahb, Sulaymān II 28a, 29b
Ibn Waḥshiyya (fl. prob. fourth/tenth cent.) I 45b, 46a, 47a, 47b; II 37a; III 250b
Ibn al-Walīd, ʿAlī b. Muḥammad (d. 612/1215) IV 591b, 592a
Ibn al-Ward (d. 351/962) III 131b
Ibn Wardān al-Madanī, Abū l-Ḥārith (d. 160/777) IV 360a, 390a
Ibn Wathīq al-Ishbīlī (d. 654/1256) V 334b
Ibn Zabāla (d. ca. 200/815) III 368a
Ibn Zayd b. Aslam, ʿAbd al-Raḥmān (d. 182/798) II 407b, 411a, 456b, 457a; V 116a
Ibn al-Zubayr, ʿAbdallāh II 30a; 102b; III 189a; IV 136b
Ibrahim, M. V 469b
Ibrāhīm see Abraham
Ibrāhīm (of Ghazna) II 35a
Ibrāhīm (son of the Prophet and Mary the Copt) II 11a; V 472a, 508b, 518a

Ibrāhīm b. ʿAbd al-Raḥmān al-Azraqī see al-Azraqī, Ibrāhīm b. ʿAbd al-Raḥmān (d. after 890/1485)
Ibrāhīm b. ʿAbdallāh al-Kirmānī IV 169b
Ibrāhīm b. Adham (d. 160/777) V 147a
Ibrāhīm b. Dāʾūd (d. 576/1181) V 309b
Ibrāhīm b. Ḥusayn IV 271b
Ibrāhīm b. al-Nakhaʿī (d. 95/713) III 154a
Ibrāhīm b. Saʿd II 394a
Ibrāhīm b. ʿUmar al-Biqāʿī see al-Biqāʿī, Burhān al-Dīn Abū l-Ḥasan Ibrāhīm (d. 885/1480)
Ibrāhīm Dhawq (1790-1854) III 224a
Ibrāhīm al-Kūrānī (d. 1101/1690) III 371a
Ibrahim Niasse (modern Senegalese shaykh) see Niasse, [Shaykh] Ibrāhīm
Ibrāhīm Sulṭān b. Shāh Rūkh b. Tīmūr I 283b; III 313b
al-Ibshīhī II 487a
Idrāsīn see Idrīs
Idrīs I 38b, 527b; II 13a, 13b, 71a, **484a**, 484b, 485a, 485b, 486a; III 83a, 83b, 118a, 253b, 519b, 521a; IV 291b, 303b; V 41b, 246a, 246b, 249a, 249b, 250b
Idrīs b. ʿAbd al-Karīm al-Ḥaddād (d. ca. 292/905) IV 390a
al-Idrīsī, Abū ʿAbdallāh (d. 560/1166) IV 525a
Idrīsids III 558b
Ifrīqiyya I 283b, 284a; V 359b
ʿIfrīt II **486a**
Iḥsān al-Qūsī II 201a
IIQ see Islam
Ikhshīdhiyya II 534a
ʿIkrima (d. 105-7/723-5) II 103a, 147b, 193a, 389b; III 408b; IV 533a
ʿIkrima b. Abī Jahl IV 493b
Īl V 87b, 88b
Īl-Khān Ghazan III 311a
Iletmish (first Delhi sultan) III 314b
Īlkhāns/Īlkahānid(s) I 173b, 174a, 283a; III 559a, 600b; V 559a
Ilkiyā al-Harrāsī (d. 504/1110) II 114a; IV 110a
Illuminationism [*ishrāq*] I 85a
Ilyās/Ilyāsīn see Elijah
ʿImād al-Dīn Abū l-Fidāʾ b. Kathīr see Ibn Kathīr, ʿImād al-Dīn Abū l-Fidāʾ (d. 774/1373)
Imām(s) I 162a, 555a; II 117b, 207b, **502b**, 503b, 504a; III 20b, 68a; V 135a, 222b, 223a, 226a

Seven Imāms — I 546a
Twelfth Imām — III 304b
Twelve Imāms — III 433a
Imām al-Ḥaramayn — see al-Juwaynī, Imām al-Ḥaramayn ʿAbd al-Malik
Imāmī(s) — I 484b, 554b; III 470b; IV 450a, 450b; V 192b, 442b
ʿImrān — I 1b, 2a, 26a, 233b; II 176b, 439a, **509a**; III 289b, 293a, 486b, 519b; IV 291a, 337a; V 81b, 552a; see also Amram
ʿImrān b. Mātān/Māthān — I 2b; II 509b
ʿImrān b. Qāhith — II 509b
ʿImrān b. Yaṣhar — II 509b
Imruʾ al-Qays (d. ca. 540) — I 470b; II 529a; III 545a, 573b, 588b; V 14a
Incarnation — I 30b, 117b, 312a, 312b; IV 122a, 412b
India — I 25b, 30b, 39b, 48a, 168b, 169a, 171b, 202b, 265a, 271a; II 15a, 472a; III 223b, 265a, 267a, 269a, 271a, 272a, 309b, 314a, 316a, 317b, 325a, 326a, 328b, 343b, 365b, 432b, 542a; IV 265b, 266a, 269a, 274a, 275b, 409b, 411b, 416b, 540a, 555a; V 13a, 94a, 97a, 148b, 186a, 211b, 212a, 212b, 341b, 342a, 343b, 361b, 536b, 538b
British — II 15a
Congress Party — I 202b
Mughal — I 165a; III 223b; IV 18a
Non-Cooperation Movement — I 202b
al-Qurʾān Printers, Bombay — IV 274b
Indians — I 487b; IV 57b
Indo-European (languages) — III 416b
Indonesia — II 191b; III 267a, 309b, 316a, 326b, 343b, 435b; IV 273b, 377b, 382a, 382b, 383a, 383b; V 99a, 100a, 101b, 207a, 209a, 210a, 211b, 213a, 214a, 214b, 217a, 218b, 222a, 222b, 225b, 226a, 538b
Islamic State University Indonesia — V 209b
MUT (Majelis Ulama Indonesia) — V 214b

YKF (Indonesian women's group) v 223a
Indonesian(s) iv 275a, 382b; v 206a,
Indonesian (language) v 101a, 213a, 342a
Inquisition iv 142b
Institut Fondamentel d'Afrique Noire Cheikh Anta Diop i 33a
Institut Français d'Archéologie Orientale i 169a
Internet i 393a; ii 231a, 347b; iii 353b; iv 23b, 75b; v 223a, 225a
Iowa, University of v 101b
Iqbāl, Muḥammad (d. 1938) iii 224b, 225a; iv 317b, 555a; v 98a, 120b
Iram [Dhāt al-ʿImād] i 21b, 22a, 152a; ii 338b, 438a, 462b, **559a**, 559b; iii 518b; v 184b, 252b
Iran i 43b, 44a, 161b, 168b, 169a, 171b, 282a, 415a; ii 40a, 454b, 457b, 503b; iii 221b, 264a, 267a, 269a, 271a, 272a, 286a, 300b, 301b, 305a, 306b, 308b, 309a, 309b, 310b, 311a, 312b, 313a, 313b, 317a, 318b, 319a, 319b, 325a, 409a, 431a, 432a, 433a, 556a, 598a, 599b; iv 18a, 56b, 57a, 59a, 260b, 266b, 268b, 275b, 489b, 495b, 595a; v 76a, 137a, 148b, 159a, 209b, 215a, 215b, 225b, 226a, 232a, 232b, 233a, 233b, 234a, 325b, 354a, 415b
Constitution of the Islamic Republic of iv 145a
early Islamic iii 305a, 433b
Islamic Republic of i 161b; iv 60a, 144b; v 540b
Nashr-e Hadith-e Ahl al-Bayt Institute v 296b
Safavid iii 266a; iv 602b
pre-Safavid iv 58b
Shahs of iii 559b; iv 143a
Iran-Iraq War (1980-88) iii 582b
Iranian(s) i 146b; iii 49b; iv 57b
Iraq i 43b, 44a, 45b, 46a, 127b, 136a, 282a, 307b, 308a, 332b, 335b, 378a, 469b; ii 40b, 110a, 223a, 384b, 421a, 503b, **559b**, 560a, 560b, 561a; iii 68b, 85b, 86a, 179b, 286a, 302a, 302b, 308b, 310b, 312a, 428b, 429a, 430b,

431a, 432a, 501a, 542a, 557a; IV 44a, 134b, 180a, 273b, 328a, 349a, 389a, 407b, 408a, 512a; V 1a, 33a, 214b, 215a, 215b, 222b, 234a, 235a, 309a, 450a, 481b
ʿAbbāsid III 310a, 313b, 317b, 319b, 405a
Iraqi(s) I 353b
al-ʿIrāqī (d. 567/1171) III 570b
Irbil II 206a
Iron Age III 391a
Irving, T.B. V 343b
Irving, W. V 350b
ʿĪsā (b. Maryam) see Jesus
ʿĪsā b. Minā Qālūn see Qālūn, ʿĪsā b. Minā (d. ca. 220/835)
ʿĪsā Dhā Jābir (alias Yça Gidelli, Yça of Segovia) IV 243a; V 341b, 345a
ʿĪsā Muḥammad IV 176a
ʿĪsā al-Tanūkhī see al-Tanūkhī, ʿĪsā
Isaac [Isḥāq/Yiṣḥāq] I 6b, 7b, 8a, 10a, 10b, 26a, 245b, 330b, 513a; II 13b, 228a, 335a, 341a, 402a, 434a, **561a**, 561b, 562a, 563b, 564b, 571a; III 1a, 1b, 4b, 27b, 50a, 118a, 148a, 148b, 231b, 289a, 339b, 393b, 395b, 444b, 520a, 521a, 522a, 525b; IV 49a, 179a, 223b, 290a, 291a, 294a, 297b, 298b, 401a, 438b, 439b, 445a, 577b; V 186a, 259b, 305a, 364a, 444b, 534a, 545b
Isaac of Nineveh I 183b
Isāf IV 519a; V 90b, 90b
Isaiah [Shaʿyā] I 195a, 195b; II 240b, 312a, **562b**, 563a; V 245a, 245b, 246b, 308a
Iṣfahān I 171b; II 29a; III 264a, 264b, 319a, 433a, 433b, 436b
Great Mosque of III 305a
al-Iṣfahānī, Abū l-Faraj (d. 356/967) III 589b; IV 381a
Isfandiyār II 517a
al-Isfarāyinī, [al-Ustādh] Abū Isḥāq (d. 418/1027) I 484a
Isḥāq b. Ibrāhīm (fl. third/ninth century) I 514a
Isḥāq b. Rāhawayh (d. 298/853) V 334b
Isḥāq Ibrāhīm al-Warrāq see al-Warrāq, Isḥāq Ibrāhīm (d. 286/899-900)

Ishmael [Ismāʿīl]	I 6b, 7a, 7b, 8a, 8b, 9a, 9b, 10a, 10b, 40b, 163b, 245b, 325a, 330b, 403b; II 13b, 14a, 73a, 205a, 228a, 295b, 554b, 561a, 561b, 562a, **563b**, 564a, 564b; III 1a, 1b, 4b, 27b, 50a, 76b, 77a, 78a, 118b, 119a, 223a, 339b, 341a, 381a, 444b, 446a, 519b, 520a, 521a, 522a, 525b; IV 52b, 104b, 179a, 223b, 227a, 255a, 290a, 291b, 294a, 298b, 327a, 337b, 429a, 438b, 445a, 488a, 505b, 514b, 519a, 519b, 604b; V 45b, 127a, 246a, 246b, 249b, 305a, 364a, 423b, 463a
Ishmaelites	II 563b
Ishtar	V 52a
Isis	V 52a
Iskāf Banī Junayd	IV 328a
al-Iskāfī, Muḥammad b. ʿAbdallāh (d. 240/854)	III 352b
al-Iskandar	see Alexander the Great
al-Iskandarānī, Aḥmad	IV 272a
al-Iskandarānī, Muḥammad b. Aḥmad	II 130a
Iṣlāḥī, Amīn Aḥsan	II 316a; III 194b, 195a, 213a, 507b, 513b; IV 8b; V 406a
Islam	passim; see under the various eponymous law schools, as well as the various trends [Sunni; Shīʿī; Ṣūfī, etc.]
American Islamic College in Chicago	V 217a
American Muslim Mission	I 31b
AMM (Angkatan Muda Masjid dan Musholla, Youth groups for mosque and prayer house)	V 210a
EFA (Godsdienst Islam, Educatieve Faculteit Amsterdam)	V 216a
First World Conference on Muslim Education (Mecca 1977)	V 218b
Higher Council of Islamic Affairs [*majlis al-aʿlā lil-shuʾūn al-islāmiyya*]	V 228a
IAIN (Institut Agama Islam Negeri, State Institute for Higher Islamic Studies, Indonesia)	V 208b, 209b, 218b, 219a, 224b, 225b, 226b
IIQ (Institut Ilmu Al-Quran)	V 214a
International Islamic Colloquium in Lahore	II 135a
International Islamic University Islamabad (Pakistan)	V 209b, 218b

International Islamic University Kuala Lumpur (Malaysia)	v 209b, 218b
ISNA (Islamic Society of North America)	v 217a, 228b
IUE (Islamic University of Europe in Schiedam)	v 216b
IUR (Islamic University of Rotterdam)	v 216b
Law	i 11a, 148a, 396b, 434a, 434b; ii 454b, 511b; iii 71b, 73a, 88b, 98a, 176a, 201b, 252a, 307a, 331b, 336a, 376a, 562b; iv 146b, 223a, 224b, 277a, 289a, 378a, 392a, 402b, 417a, 499a, 500b, 502a, 504b, 506a, 507b, 575a, 584a; v 23a, 124b, 209b, 217b, 231b, 255a, 293a, 452b, 528a, 528b
MSA (Muslim Student Association)	v 228a
Muslim Brothers/Brotherhood [*jamʿiyyat al-ikhwān al-muslimīn*]	ii 138a; iii 285b, 286a; iv 144a, 145a; v 206a, 225a, 228b
Muslim College (London)	v 216b
Muslim World League [*rābiṭat al-ʿālam al-islāmī*]	v 228a
Nation of	i 31a, 31b, 393b, 568a; iii 182b, 183a, 185a, 188b, 225b, 226a, 236a, 238a, 240b, 241a, 370a, 370b, 463a
Organisation of the Islamic Conference	i 33a
Pax Islamica	iii 241b
PPIM	v 219a
Progressive Muslims Union (United States)	v 227a
PSW	v 219a
Psalms of	iv 232b
School of Islamic and Social Sciences (Viginia)	v 217a
TKA (Tamam Kanak-kanak Al Quran)	v 210a
TPA (Tamam Pendidikan Anak-anak)	v 210a
United Submitters International	iii 553b
World Community of al-Islam in the West	i 31b
World Conference of Mosques in Mecca	v 220a
World Mission	i 202b
Islamabad	i 172b
Islamdom	v 137a
Islamicist(s)	ii 403a, 496a; iii 129b, 130b, 150b, 231a; iv 383b; v 364a, 407a, 415b
Islamism	iv 146b
Islamist(s)	ii 131a; iii 285b; iv 143a

Ismāʿīl | i 527b; iv 227a
Ismāʿīl b. ʿAbd al-Raḥmān al-Suddī (d. 127-8/745) | ii 146b, 389b; iv 533a
Ismāʿīl b. Abī Khālid (d. 146/763) | ii 393b
Ismāʿīl b. Abī ʿUbayd Allāh Muʿāwiya b. ʿUbayd Allāh al-Ashʿarī (d. first half third/ninth cent.) | iii 112b
Ismāʿīl b. Aḥmad (r. 279-95/892-907) | i 483a
Ismāʿīl b. Hibat Allāh (d. 1184/1770) | iv 602a
Ismāʿīl b. Muḥammad al-Tamīmī | see al-Tamīmī, Ismāʿīl b. Muḥammad
Ismāʿīl b. Ḥammād al-Jawharī (d. ca. 392/1002) | iii 301b
Ismāʿīl Ḥaqqī al-Brūsawī (d. 1137/1725) | ii 120b, 281a; v 158a
Ismāʿīlī(s) | i 68b, 137b, 540b, 554b, 555a, 555b, 556a; ii 471a; iv 129b, 497a, 598a
  Sulaymānī | iv 602a
ISNA | see Islam
Israel [Isrāʾīl] | i 1b, 5b, 123a, 128a, 199a, 214a, 245b, 258b, 261a, 303b, 304a, 306a, 307a, 369b, 379b, 465b, 508b, 518b, 557a; ii 1a, 24a, 156b, 345a, 399a, 362b, **571a**, 571b, 572a; iii 1a, 1b, 2a, 11b, 23b, 25a, 143b, 240b, 286a, 390a, 422a; iv 129a, 132a, 146a, 223b, 291a, 314b, 341b, 413a, 417a, 526b, 527a, 530a; v 28a, 190a, 197a, 285b, 303a, 309b, 364a, 438b, 500b, 564b
  Children/Sons of [Banū Isrāʾīl] | i 79b, 98a, 102a, 149a, 188a, 194a, 240b, 245b, 270a, 275a, 275b, 276a, 297a, **303a**, 304a, 304b, 305a, 305b, 306a, 307a, 369a, 377b, 381a, 439b, 465a, 465b, 478a, 496a, 536b, 537a, 553b; ii 10a, 31a, 146a, 215b, 274a, 309a, 309b, 310b, 311a, 311b, 312a, 334b, 399a, 416a, 481a, 542b, 562b, 571a, 571b, 572a; iii 1b, 2a, 16a, 21b, 24a, 25a, 29b, 56a, 82a, 93b, 95a, 118a, 189b, 239a, 312b, 373b, 392a, 393b, 394a, 394b, 395b, 421b, 423a, 423b, 424b, 443b, 445b, 459a, 480a, 486a, 486b, 488a; iv 67a, 67b, 116b, 120b, 121a, 211a, 290b, 295b, 305a, 309a,

	343a, 403a, 403b, 405a, 406b, 412a, 425b, 428b, 430b, 513b, 516a, 523b, 527a, 529a, 539a, 577b, 595a; v 4b, 22b, 104b, 107b, 190a, 190b, 200b, 246b, 260b, 261a, 301a, 301b, 302a, 302b, 363a, 377a, 468a, 502a, 546b, 551b
Israelite(s)	i 99a, 149a, 157a, 158a, 188a, 194a, 222b, 236b, 254b, 260a, 270b, 273b, 274b, 275a, 302a, 303a, 303b, 304b, 305a, 305b, 306a, 306b, 307a, 365a, 528b, 532b, 534a; ii 11b, 13a, 145b, 146b, 154b, 155a, 182a, 185b, 198b, 199a, 204a, 212b, 213a, 217b, 309a, 316a, 337a, 338a, 344b, 345a, 399a, 399b, 431b, 432b, 433a, 434b, 481a, 497b, 563a; iii 5a, 16b, 54a, 94a, 94b, 208b, 210a, 290a, 390a, 495b; iv 67a, 105b, 106a, 131a, 132b, 137b, 302b, 304a, 316b, 338b, 340b, 421b, 428b, 436b, 488a, 517a, 524b, 527a, 529b, 536a, 536b, 590a; v 28a, 61b; v 111a, 160a, 188b, 193a, 200b, 246b, 248a, 260b, 261a, 276a, 302b, 303a, 304b, 305a, 307a, 309a, 375b, 455b, 502a
Israfel [Isrāfīl]	i 92a, 113b; ii 412b; iii 3b, 139b, 140a, 389b; iv 61a, 345b, 405a;
Isrāʾīlī (d. ca. 323/935)	ii 223a
al-Iṣṭakhrī	ii 427b; iv 525a
Istanbul	i 155b, 285b, 270a; iii 270a; 301b, 320b, 321a, 435a, 598a; iv 266a, 267a, 267b, 269a, 271b, 276a, 415b; v 342a, 346a, 346b
Italian (language)	iv 238b
Italy	iv 248b, 265a
Ittiḥādiyya	i 482b
IUE	see Islam
IUR	see Islam
Ivanov, W.	i 211a
[al-Qāḍī] ʿIyād al-Yaḥṣubī (d. 544/1149)	iii 501b, 503b, 504a; iv 533b

Izalazallāt v 87b
Iznīq see Nicea
ʿIzrāʾīl (angel of death) i 89b
Izutsu, T. i 37a, 344a, 375a; ii 60a, 61b, 63b, 70a, 194b, 196a, 487b, 565b; iv 197a, 202b, 440a, 447a, 463b; v 21b, 69a, 70a, 298b, 379a
ʿIzz al-Dīn Aybak al-Miṣrī i 125b
ʿIzz al-Dīn b. ʿAbd al-Salām al-Sulamī (d. 660/1262) v 220b
ʿIzz al-Dīn al-Dīrīnī (d. 697/1297) v 331a

J

Jabal al-Lawdh see al-Lawdh, Jabal
al-Jabal al-Muqaddas i 271a
Jabal Murrān see Murrān
Jabal Nawdh see Nawdh
Jabal Qāsyūn see Qāsyūn
Jabal al-Raḥma see Mount of Mercy
Jabal Ramm see Ramm
Jabal Says see Usays
Jabal Thawr see Thawr
Jabal Usays (Sēs) see Usays
Jābalqā i 22a
Jābarasā i 22a
al-Jaʿbarī (d. 732/1333) iii 570b
Jābir b. ʿAbdallāh iii 283a, 284b
Jābir b. Ḥayyān (fl. second/eighth century) i 541b; ii 102b; iv 170a
Jābir b. Zayd (d. ca 100/718-19) iii 88b, 89a
Jabr (slave of the Banū ʿAbd al-Dār) ii 514b, 517a
Jabr (slave of the Banū l-Ḥaḍramī) ii 513a
Jabriyya i 74a
Jackson, S. i **301a**, **515b**; iv **289b**
Jacob [Yaʿqūb] i 7b, 8a, 26a, 52a, 62a, 124a, 226b, 227a, 227b, 245b, 303b, 347a, 364a, 379b, 465a, 521b, 532b, 533a, 534a, 548b, 549a; ii 12a, 25a, 43b, 153b, 335a, 341a, 402a, 434a, 561a, 561b, 563b, 571a, 572a; iii **1a**, 1b, 2a, 27b, 50a, 50b, 56a, 56b, 118a, 148a, 223a, 234a, 234b, 290a, 444b, 479b, 520a, 522a, 525b, 562a; iv 32b, 37a, 49a, 223b, 290a, 291a, 292b, 294a, 297b, 298b,

304a, 316b, 352b, 401a, 438b, 439b, 445a; V 38a, 63a, 63b, 134a, 186a, 200b, 303a, 363a, 364a, 392a, 444b, 570b
Jacob of Edessa IV 328a, 328b
Jacob Golius see Golius, Jacob (d. 1667)
Jacob of Sarug (d. 521) II 332a
Jacobi, R. IV 471a
Jacobite(s) see Christian(s)
Jaʿd b. Dirham (d. 125/743) I 105a, 468a
Jadd b. Qays V 37a, 40a, 40b
Jaʿfar II 19a
Jaʿfar b. Abī Ṭālib (d. 8/629) II 240a; V 44a
Jaʿfar b. Ḥarb (d. 236/850) III 469a
Jaʿfar b. Manṣūr al-Yaman IV 602a
Jaʿfar b. Muḥammad II 450b
[Imām] Jaʿfar al-Ṣādiq (d. 148/765) I 27b, 68a, 211a, 470a, 541a, 546a; II 117a, 118b, 190a, 396b, 522a; III 178b, 302b, 467b, 575b; IV 171b, 593b, 602a; V 17a, 139a, 139b, 140a, 140b, 141a, 143a, 233a, 320b, 321a
Jaʿfar al-Sammāk III 88b
Jaʿfar al-Sijānī IV 489b
Jaʿfarī(s) I 225b
Jaʾafaru Ishaq (emir of Zaria) III 344b
al-Jāḥiẓ, Abū ʿUthmān al-Baṣrī (d. 255/868-9) I 118b, 191b, 287a; II 36b, 114b, 487a; III 115b, 468b; IV 59a, 71b, 123a, 313b; V 8b
al-Jāḥiẓ, ʿAmr b. Baḥr (d. 255/865) II 532b, 533a, 533b, 535a
[Shāh] Jāhān (r. 1037-68/1628-57) I 265a; III 323a, 324a, 324b
Jahm b. Ṣafwān (d. 128/745-6) I 105a, 468a, 468b, 469a; II 418b; III 467b; IV 73a, 85b, 86b; V 111a
Jahmiyya I 468b, 470a, 482b; III 468a
al-Jahshiyārī III 262a
Jakarta IV 275a, 382a, 382b; V 214b, 219a
Jakobson, R. III 127b, 528b
Jalāl al-Dīn ʿAbd al-Raḥmān al-Bulqīnī see al-Bulqīnī, Jalāl al-Dīn ʿAbd al-Raḥmān (d. 824/1421)
Jalāl al-Dīn al-Maḥallī see al-Maḥallī, Jalāl al Dīn (d. 864/1459)
Jalāl al-Dīn al-Rūmī see al-Rūmī, Mawlānā Jalāl al-Dīn (d. 672/1273)
Jalāl al-Dīn al-Suyūṭī see al-Suyūṭī, Jalāl al-Dīn (d. 911/1505)

Jalāl al-Dīn Yūsuf b. Muḥammad al-Surramarrī (d. 776/1374) III 363a
al-Jalālayn III 70a; IV 266b, 274b; V 57b
Jālūt see Goliath
Jām I 171b; III 313a
Jamāl al-Dīn al-Afghāni see al-Afghāni, Jamāl al-Dīn (d. 1897)
Jamāl al-Dīni Iṣfahānī (d. 588/1192) IV 56a
Jamāl al-Dīn Muḥammad b. Yaḥyā al-Waṭwāṭ see al-Waṭwāṭ, Jamāl al-Dīn Muḥammad b. Yaḥyā
Jamāl al-Dīn al-Qāsimī see al-Qāsimī, Muḥammad Jamāl al-Dīn
Jamāl al-Dīn Yūsuf al-Kindī (d. 256/870) III 302b
Jamāʿat-e/Jamāʿat-i Islāmī IV 145b; V 228a
James, D.L. III 310b
Jāmī (d. 898/1492) IV 62a, 64a, 64b
Janissary Corps V 60a
Jannes (Egyptian magician) I 276a
Jansen, J.J.G. II **455a**
Janssen, A. II 428a
Japan I 287b; III 472a
Japanese (language) V 342a
Japheth [Yāfith] II 331b; III 543a
Japheth b. Eli (Abū ʿAlī Ḥasan b. ʿAlī al-Baṣrī; fl. fourth/tenth century) IV 317a
Jaques, R.K. V **449a**
Jār Allāh al-Zamakhsharī see al-Zamakhsharī, Maḥmūd b. ʿUmar (d. 538/1144)
Jarīr I 531a
Jarīr b. Ḥazim (d. 175/791) II 386b
Jārūdites II 117a; IV 603a
Jarrar, M. II **412a**, **457b**
Jaspers, K. I 373b
al-Jaṣṣāṣ, Abū Bakr Aḥmad b. ʿAbdallāh (d. 370/981) I 28a; II 114a; IV 157a
Jassin, H.B. V 100b, 101a
Jaunpur III 314b, 434a
Java III 343b; V 213a, 213b, 223a
al-Jawālīqī, Abū Manṣūr Mawhūb b. Aḥmad (d. 539/1144) I 228b, 231a
al-Jawf V 86a, 86b, 88b, 90a, 90b
al-Jawharī (d. 398/1007) IV 13a
Jawharī, [Shaykh] Ṭanṭāwī II 130a; IV 555a, 555b
Jazīra III 310b, 462b
Jazīrat Ibn ʿUmar see Cizre
Jebel Naffūsa III 86b
Jeddah I 25b; II 464a

Jeffery, A. I 204b, 334a, 350b, 361a, 398b, 417b, 489b; II 233a, 235a, 236a, 543b; III 231a; IV 101b, 189a, 194b, 196a, 351b, 440a, 450a, 503b; V 249a, 249b, 295b, 297a, 299a
Jehenna V 554b
Jehoshaphat III 143b
Jehovah's Witnesses II 471b
Jehuda ha-Levi (d. 1141) V 309b
Jenssen, H. I **135a**
Jerba (island in Tunisia) III 86b
Jeremiah I 5b
Jericho III 5b; V 248a
Jerome IV 317a
Jerusalem I 8a, 8b, 10a, 12b, 14b, 88a, 108b, 109b, 114a, 125a, 126a, 126b, 169a, 170a, 177a, 195b, 196b, 268b, 269a, 284b, 320a, 328b, 378b, 496b, 497a; II 11a, 41a, 146a, 146b, 147a, 150a, 155b, 215b, 224b, 261a, 263b, 299b, 306b, 308b, 309a, 309b, 310a, 310b, 311a, 311b, 312a, 325b, 562b, 563a; III **2b**, 3a, 3b, 4a, 4b, 5a, 5b, 6a, 6b, 18b, 27b, 31a, 52a, 76a, 139a, 140a, 142a, 142b, 143a, 143b, 162b, 340a, 407b, 412b, 427a, 428a, 429a, 436a, 488b, 491a, 491b, 496a, 539b; IV 92a, 226b, 227a, 325b, 326a, 326b, 327b, 413a, 514a, 515b, 524a, 598a; V 77b, 104b, 105a, 106a, 107b, 108a, 122b, 127a, 172b, 184b, 185a, 185b, 186a, 222b, 334b, 376a, 423b, 455b, 556b
Jesuit(s) IV 248b
Jesus [ʿĪsā (b. Maryam)] of Nazareth I a, 30b, 38b, 51a, 52b, 56a, 59a, 66b, 97a, 98a, 102a, 102b, 103a, 108b, 109b, 110a, 110b, 111a, 114a, 116b, 117a, 118a, 118b, 123a, 123b, 124b, 156a, 160b, 161a, 162b, 163b, 164a, 167a, 183b, 222a, 223a, 233b, 237b, 245a, 265b, 271a, 298b, 303a,

305a, 308b, 309b, 310b, 312a, 312b, 313a, 317b, 318a, 328a, 340b, 379b, 380b, 389b, 403a, 464b, 471b, 475b, 476a, 488a, 488b, 492a, 507a, 516b, 537b; II 10a, 12b, 13b, 19a, 47a, 193b, 199b, 216a, 217a, 241a, 276a, 285a, 290b, 305b, 329b, 331b, 332b, 339a, 340b, 341a, 342a, 342b, 343a, 408b, 411b, 412b, 425a, 425b, 435b, 436b, 442b, 443a, 443b, 474b, 509a, 527b, 534a, 536b, 553a, 558a, 562b, 563a, 569a; III 4a, 5b, **7a**, 7b, 8a, 8b, 9a, 9b, 10a, 10b, 11a, 11b, 12a, 12b, 13a, 13b, 14a, 14b, 15a, 15b, 16a, 16b, 17a, 17b, 18a, 18b, 19a, 19b, 20a, 23b, 50a, 51b, 52a, 53a, 55a, 65a, 81a, 83a, 83b, 128b, 138a, 141a, 143a, 151a, 174b, 181a, 190a, 207a, 214a, 226a, 234a, 244b, 288b, 289a, 289b, 290b, 291a, 291b, 292a, 292b, 293a, 293b, 294a, 294b, 295a, 295b, 300a, 378a, 381a, 381b, 382a, 382b, 395b, 396a, 398a, 406b, 444a, 444b, 445a, 445b, 484b, 486b, 493b, 494a, 501b, 502a, 503a, 517b, 519b, 521a, 521b, 522a, 525b, 531a, 542b, 543a, 567b, 572a, 583a; IV 9b, 11a, 26b, 27b, 33a, 36b, 39b, 41a, 50b, 61b, 68b, 70a, 88b, 116a, 120a, 121a, 121b, 124a, 153a, 160b, 183a, 195b, 212b, 224a, 238a, 282b, 291a, 291b, 292a, 292b, 294a, 295b, 296a, 298a, 298b, 302a, 303a, 304b, 305a, 313a, 406b, 407a, 409b, 410b, 411a, 412b, 413a, 413b, 428a, 434b, 435b, 438b, 439a, 439b, 505a, 509b, 524a, 577a, 578a, 578b, 579a, 585a; V 28b, 33a, 41a, 41b, 45b, 46a, 48a, 68b, 81a, 81b, 95b, 109b, 110b,

114a, 114b, 115a, 115b, 116a, 117a, 127b, 133b, 152a, 168b, 188b, 189a, 189b, 190a, 190b, 197a, 200b, 250b, 251a, 300b, 303a, 361a, 369a, 369b, 370a, 370b, 387a, 430a, 438b, 445b, 483a, 489a, 533b, 545b, 547b, 570b, 573b, 575a; see also Christ

Jethro [Shuʿayb] III 234b, 540a; IV 606a; V 375b, 465a; see also Yathrā

Jew(s) [Yahūd] 7b, 8a, 10b, 11b, 12b, 45a, 83a, 93a, 97a, 97b, 98b, 100a, 103b, 104a, 107b, 108b, 110b, 111a, 115a, 117b, 124b, 146b, 148a, 149a, 200a, 222b, 223a, 223b, 224b, 236b, 240b, 241a, 245b, 248b, 270b, 295b, 296a, 299a, 299b, 303a, 305b, 306a, 310a, 310b, 311a, 311b, 312a, 312b, 314a, 325a, 330b, 337a, 342b, 366a, 372b, 373a, 374a, 377a, 377b, 378a, 378b, 380a, 380b, 382a, 405b, 409a, 409b, 429b, 432b, 440a, 443b, 466b, 468a, 475a, 488a, 488b, 537b, 538b; II 16b, 25a, 72a, 73a, 100a, 131b, 146b, 147a, 148b, 149b, 150a, 150b, 151a, 155b, 156b, 163b, 182a, 184a, 184b, 190b, 204a, 220a, 221a, 243a, 243b, 271b, 274a, 274b, 318b, 325a, 339a, 342b, 391b, 399b, 400b, 402b, 403a, 407b, 429b, 437b, 468b, 469b, 471b, 475a, 494b, 496b, 498b, 499a, 508a, 513a, 530b, 544b, 561b, 562a, 566a, 569b, 571b; III 8b, 9a, 12a, 17a, 18a, 18b, 19a, 19b, 20a, **21b**, 22a, 22b, 23b, 24a, 24b, 25a, 25b, 26a, 26b, 27a, 27b, 28b, 29a, 29b, 30a, 30b, 31a, 31b, 32a, 32b, 33a, 33b, 34a, 53b, 56a, 61b, 69a, 92b, 118b, 141a, 141b, 143a, 151a, 151b, 155b, 173a, 174a, 174b, 181a, 181b,

189b, 190a, 191a, 195a, 233b, 236a, 238a, 239b, 240a, 244a, 244b, 303a, 340a, 341a, 341b, 368b, 369a, 369b, 370a, 377a, 377b, 392a, 406a, 419b, 428a, 445a, 446a, 449a, 449b, 450a, 453b, 455b, 456a, 456b, 459b, 499b, 507a, 508a, 515a, 536b, 563b, 571b, 576b, 577a, 578a, 579a, 579b, 580a, 588b, 592b, 593b; IV 17a, 18b, 36a, 36b, 37a, 37b, 38a, 38b, 39a, 39b, 40a, 41b, 42a, 42b, 43a, 71a, 91a, 110a, 114b, 115a, 116b, 118b, 119b, 120a, 120b, 121a, 121b, 122a, 129a, 133a, 133b, 152a, 153a, 153b, 159a, 160b, 217a, 224b, 226b, 227a, 235a, 235b, 236a, 241a, 255a, 268a, 286b, 298a, 298b, 299b, 301a, 302a, 305a, 306a, 309a, 311a, 323a, 324a, 325a, 325b, 326a, 326b, 327b, 328a, 333b, 334a, 340a, 340b, 341a, 342a, 396b, 400a, 401a, 402a, 403a, 403b, 404b, 405a, 405b, 406a, 406b, 407a, 408a, 408b, 409a, 409b, 411b, 412a, 412b, 413a, 413b, 414b, 415a, 415b, 416b, 450b, 451a, 453b, 484b, 497a, 510a, 512b, 525a, 539a, 559b, 582b, 586a, 591b, 595a; V 3a, 15b, 16a, 33b, 35b, 41a, 44b, 56a, 107b, 160a, 175a, 202b, 222b, 231a, 231b, 236a, 249b, 250a, 259a, 260a, 272b, 280b, 291b, 292a, 301a, 303a, 303b, 304a, 304b, 305a, 305b, 306b, 308b, 309a, 344b, 389b, 400a, 409a, 417b, 423a, 469b, 474a, 500b, 561a, 564b, 567a, 575a

  Arabian — III 578a, 579a
  Arabic speaking — II 458a
  Mosaic — V 260a
Jibāl (Iranian Province) — V 156b
Jibrīl — see Gabriel

Jibt III 26b, **34a**
Jidda II 295a
al-Jīlānī, ʿAbd al-Qādir (d. 561/1166) IV 173b; V 384a, 384b
al-Jīlī (d. 561/1166) V 277b
Job [Ayyūb] I 245b, 528b; II 199a, 455b; III 50a, **50b**, 51a, 57a, 242a, 373a, 395b, 444b, 520a, 521a, 522a, 525b; IV 291a, 292b, 294a, 429b, 438b, 577a; V 134a, 363b, 380a, 380b, 381a, 381b, 465a
Job ben Solomon (born Ayuba Suleiman Ibrahima Diallo; d. ca. 1773) I 30a
Joenoes, M. V 99b
Johann Buxtorf IV see Lang, Johann Michael (Johann Buxtorf IV; d. 1732)
Johannes Andreas Maurus see Juan Andrés
Johannes Gabriel Terrolensis see Terrolensis, Johannes Gabriel
Johannes Oporinus IV 245b
Johannesburg V 227a
John see John the Baptist; Testament
John VI Kantakuzenos (r. 1347-54) IV 242a
John the Baptist [Yaḥyā b. Zakariyyā] I 2a, 109b, 165a, 537a; II 12b, 146b, 241a, 340b, 341a, 342b; III 10b, 14b, 17b, 50a, **51b**, 52a, 52b, 210b, 234a, 289a, 290a, 395b, 492a, 519b, 521a, 522a, 525b; IV 11a, 291b, 435b, 578a; V 186b, 545b, 570b, 574a, 574b, 575a
[St.] John of Damascus (d. 130/748) I 104a, 116a; II 463b; IV 71a, 74a, 122b, 237a, 237b, 238b, 409a, 409b; V 8b
John of Segovia (Juan de Segovia, d. 1458) IV 240b, 242b, 243a, 243b; V 341b, 344b, 345a
Johns, A.H. I **55a**, **228a**; II **173b**, **399b**, **456a**; III **51a**, 212b; V **466a**
Johnson, N. I **126b**
Johnston, D. V **436b**
Jomier, J. I 523b; IV 195a, 197a
Jonah/Jonas [Yūnus or Dhū l-Nūn, son of Mattā] I 93a, 93b, 95b, 99a, 195a, 245b, 494a; II 14a, 282a, 293a, 305a, 315a, 514a, 527b, 564a; III 50a, **52a**, 53a, 53b, 54a, 54b, 55a, 105a, 207b, 381a, 395b, 444b, 476b, 521a, 522a, 525b; IV 223b, 291b, 294a, 303a,

319b, 429a, 429b, 438b, 523b, 604a, 604b; v 361b, 373b
Jonathan ii 238a
Jones, A. ii 151b; iii 127b, 128a, **593a**; iv **114a**, 193b
Jones, D. v 347a
Jordan [al-Urdunn] i 43a, 127b, 150a, 151b, 153a, 153b, 154b, 155b, 158a, 557a; ii 39b; iii 3b, 10a, 390a; iv 536b; v 92a
Hashemite Kingdom of i 335b
Queen Alia International Airport i 155b
River i 335b; iii 52a; v 184b
Joseph [Yūsuf] i 19b 28a, 40b, 52a, 65a, 68a, 80b, 99a, 124a, 226b, 227a, 227b, 228a, 255b, 260a, 276a, 286b, 289b, 290a, 299b, 346b, 347a, 364a, 465a, 488a, 490b, 491a, 521b, 532a, 532b, 533a, 534a, 534b, 546b, 548b, 549a, 549b; ii 10a, 12a, 25a, 43b, 145b, 153b, 161b, 178a, 185b, 218a, 241b, 242a, 261a, 285a, 335b, 341a, 433a, 435b, 436a, 441a, 444b, 447a, 506b, 507a, 514b, 547a, 550a; iii 1a, 5b, 11a, 13a, 50a, **55a**, 55b, 56a, 56b, 57a, 58b, 60b, 92a, 99b, 203a; iii 181b, 208a, 209b, 210a, 211a, 211b, 212a, 217a, 219a, 222b, 223a, 224b, 229b, 230a, 234b, 290a, 331b, 336a, 408b, 415a, 441b, 479b, 491b, 492a, 494a, 517b, 522a, 525b, 528b, 536b, 552a, 553a, 554b, 573a; iv 33a, 44a, 50b, 60b, 62a, 67a, 108b, 179a, 217a, 276b, 277b, 288a, 291a, 291b, 292b, 304a, 308a, 308b, 316b, 401a, 452b, 537b, 538a, 577a, 580b, 584b, 585a; v 5b, 61b, 62a, 63a, 63b, 64b, 82b, 96a, 96b, 104b, 134a, 152b, 198a, 200b, 221a, 239b, 255b, 277a, 281b, 285b, 313a, 363a, 375a, 391b, 392a, 392b, 444a, 472a, 481b, 497b, 529b,

530b, 531a, 531b, 532a, 549a, 549b, 564b, 570b
Joseph Justus Scaliger see Scaliger, Joseph Justus (d. 1609)
Josephus I 228b; III 9b, 10a; IV 106b
Joshua (son of Nūn) [Yashūʿ b. Nūn] I 1b, 528b; III 8b, 9b, 82a, 426b; IV 528a, 577b; V 248a
Josiah III 52a
Juan Andrés (Johannes Andreas Maurus) IV 243b, 244a; V 341b
Juan Luis Vives (d. 1540) IV 243b
Juan de Segovia see John of Segovia (d. ca. 1458)
Jubayl (Saudi Arabia) I 155a
Jubayr b. Muṭʿim III 502a, 502b, 503b
al-Jubbāʾī, Abū ʿAlī (d. 303/915) II 14a; III 467a, 468b, 469a, 469b, 470a, 470b; IV 74a; V 324b
al-Jubbāʾī, Abū Hāshim ʿAbd al-Salām (d. 321/933) I 484b; II 532a, 534a; III 467a, 469b
Judaeans IV 524a
Judah [Yahūdhā] IV 304a; V 63a
Judaism I 7b, 11b, 12a, 14a, 46a, 85a, 103b, 113b, 116b, 164b, 200a, 222b, 274a, 276b, 292a, 302a, 314b, 316a, 316b, 373a, 376a, 475a; II 148a, 164a, 183b, 228a, 235a, 246a, 263a, 266b, 268b, 309a, 403a, 403b, 437a, 561a, 566b; III 2b, **21b**, 29a, 73b, 107a, 129b, 142a, 143a, 368b, 500a, 540a, 543b; IV 38b, 39b, 40a, 44a, 115a, 119b, 120a, 194b, 195a, 216a, 243b, 257b, 313a, 327b, 333b, 399a, 399b, 404a, 413a, 432a, 474a, 485a, 492b, 511b, 519b, 567a; V 21a, 66a, 167b, 175b, 176a, 241a, 243b, 260a, 300b, 305a, 309b, 315b, 320b, 350a, 389b, 390a, 423a, 542a, 543b, 546b, 562a, 564a, 564b, 565a, 566a, 567b, 568a
  Mosaic V 28a
  Samaritan IV 195a
  Second Temple III 144a
Judas Iscariot III 19a; V 190b
Judean Desert II 485b
Judhām (Arab tribe) I 308a
Jūdī III 69a
  Mount I 146b, 147a II 437a; III **68b**, 69a, 541a; IV 604a

Judith iii 479b
Juhaym ii 241a
Julian of Halikarnassos i 312a
[Shaykh] Junayd al-Baghdādī (d. 297-8/910) ii 161a; iv 273b; v 147a, 148b
Juqmuq (Mamlūk sultan) iv 494a
Jurhum v 90b
al-Jurjānī, ʿAbd al-Qāhir (d. 471/1078) i 425b; ii 535a, 535b; iii 125b, 201b, 206a, 385a; v 326a
Jurash i 154b; v 92a
Jurjir Mosque (Iṣfahān) iii 436b, 437a
Justin Martyr iii 9b, 10a
Justinian (emperor) iii 435a; v 29a
al-Juwaynī, Imām al-Ḥaramayn ʿAbd al-Malik (d. 478/1085) i 118b, 514a; iii 396b; iv 75a, 79a, 86a, 459b; v 112a, 136a
Juwayriyya v 508a, 518a
Juynboll, G. ii 381b, 384a, **396b**; v **166a**
[Imām] al-Juzūlī (d. 869/1465) iii 503a

K

Kaʿb al-Aḥbār (d. 32/652-3) iv 236a, 351a; v 127a, 307a, 307b, 308a, 390a
Kaʿb b. Asad b. Sulaym iv 334b
Kaʿb b. al-Ashraf see Ibn al-Ashraf, Kaʿb
[Banū] Kaʿb b. Qurayẓa iv 334a
Kaʿb b. Zuhayr (d. 26/645) iii 215b; iv 114a; v 43b
Kaʿba i 4b, 7a, 7b, 9b, 40b, 97b, 110a, 154a, 163b, 164b, 168b, 176b, 177a, 179b, 236b, 263b, 268b, 309b, 319b, 328b, 329a, 330b, 354a, 382a, 406b, 423b; ii 20a, 34a, 84b, 85a, 91a, 148a, 149b, 159a, 173b, 178b, 179a, 204b, 205a, 206b, 224a, 237b, 263a, 295a, 295b, 297a, 297b, 310a, 311a, 311b, 319a, 390b, 403a, 458b, 461b, 479a, 490a, 555a, 564a, 564b; iii 3a, 4a, 4b, **75a**, 75b, 76a, 76b, 77a, 77b, 78a, 78b, 79a, 159b, 179a, 337a, 338b, 339a, 340a, 340b, 370b, 446a, 552b, 589a; iv 45a, 46a, 49b, 52b, 53a, 92a, 92b, 93a, 97a, 98a, 104b, 105a, 175b, 216b, 218b, 219a, 226a, 226b, 227a, 255a, 256b, 259a, 282a,

326a, 326b, 327a, 328a, 328b, 329a, 329b, 330a, 337b, 409a, 423b, 491b, 493b, 502a, 502b, 503a, 505a, 505b, 514a, 514b, 515a, 518a, 518b, 519a, 529a, 604b; v 28b, 33b, 44a, 89a, 90b, 91a, 108a, 127a, 140b, 286a, 374a, 374b, 390a, 423b, 448a, 448b, 450b, 463b, 556b, 557a, 567b

al-Kaʿbī see al-Balkhī, Abū l-Qāsim (al-Kaʿbī)

Kābul v 476b

Kadi (al-Qāḍī), W. i **190b**, **278a**; iii **226b**

al-Kāfiyajī, Muḥammad b. Sulaymān (Hanafī of Bergama; d. 879/1474) v 328a

Kafr Manda iii 390a

al-Kaḥḥāl b. Ṭarkhān, ʿAlāʾ al-Dīn (d. 720/1320) iii 351a

Kāhilān v 88a

Kahle, P. iii 123a, 123b, 124a; iv 193b

Kākūyids iii 304b

Kalān mosque iii 433b

Kalb i 308a; v 86b

al-Kalbī, Muḥammad b. al-Sāʾib Abū Naḍr al-Kalbī (d. 146/763) i 528a; ii 100b, 103b, 104a, 106a, 106b, 107a, 109a, 112a, 114a, 116b, 148a, 150a, 150b, 313b, 347b, 515b, 516a; iii 175a; iv 533a; v 321b

Kaleb (Christian Aksumite king) v 565b

Kamada, S. iv **573a**

Kaminahū v 87a

Kampur iv 266a

Kanʿān (heathen king) i 528b

Kandil, L. v 296b

Kanembu i 33a

Emir of iii 344b

Kano (Nigeria) v 211b

Kaptein, N. ii 206a; iv **572a**

Karabacek i 136b

Karaite v 136a

Karamustafa, A. i **494a**; ii **186b**; v **132b**, **162a**

Karbalāʾ i 306b, 541a; ii 40b, 147a, 208a, 282a; iv 342a; v 215b, 225a

Battle of ii 400b

Karic, E. ii **282b**, **557b**

Kārimīs iv 494a

Karrāmī(s)/Karrāmite	I 106a; II 102b, 106b, 112b; V 325a
Karshūnī	I 136a
Kāshān	II 40a
al-Kāshānī, ʿAbd al-Razzāq	see al-Qāshānī, ʿAbd al-Razzāq Kamāl al-Dīn (pseudo. Ibn al-ʿArabī) (d. 730-1/1329-30)
Kāshānī, [Mullā] Muḥsin Fayḍ (d. 1091/1680)	I 550a; IV 595a, 602b
al-Kāshānī, Mawla Nūr al-Dīn Muḥammad b. Murtaḍa	IV 350a
al-Kāshī (d. 910/1505)	V 16b, 17a
Kashmiri (language)	I 136a
Kasimirski	IV 48a
Kasimov Khānate	III 319a
Kassis, H.E.	V 296a
Katsh, A.	IV 195a
Katz, M.H.	I **344a**; III **377b**, **549a**
Kawthar	II 283b, 284b, 395a; IV 61a
Kay, P.	I 361b
Kaysāniyya	I 540a
Kayyisa bt. al-Ḥārith	III 461a
Kazakhstan	V 226a
Kazan	III 607a; IV 251a, 265b; V 351b
Kazimirski, A. Biberstein	III 48b; V 349b, 350a
Kedah (Malaysia)	V 213a
Kedar	V 245b
Kedron Valley [Wādī Jahannam]	III 5a
Keijzer, S.	V 350a
Kelantan (Malaysia)	V 213a
Kemāl, N.	V 103b
Kennedy, Ph.	IV **530a**
Kerbala	see Karbalā
Kermani, N.	II **549b**; IV 204b, 442b, 461b, 470a, 471a
Kern, L.	I **390b**
Keshab Chandra Sen	V 342a
Keturah	III 389b
Khaddām Ḥusayn	IV 266a
Khadduri, M.	III 70a
Khadīja	III 515a, 516a; V 59a, 185a, 404a
Khadīja bt. Khuwaylid (the Prophet's first wife)	I 59b; II 19a, 192b, 193b, 400a, 513a, 514a, 515a, 517b; III **80a**, 80b, 81a, 81b, 290b, 291a; IV 217a, 408b, 410b, 442a; V 507b, 509a, 509b, 516b, 518a, 520a, 520b, 529b, 532a, 534a, 550a
al-Khaḍir/al-Khiḍr	I 61b, 62a, 204a, 534a; II 13a, 14a, 332b; III 5b, **81a**, 81b, 82a, 82b,

83a, 83b, 118b, 184b, 224b, 225a, 287a, 330b, 395a, 396a, 396b, 426a; IV 21a, 61b, 113b, 505a, 577a; V 136a, 200v, 375b, 381b, 382a, 464a
Khafājī (d. 1069/1659) IV 396b
Khairallah, S. I 169b; III 297b
Khalaf Abū Muḥammad al-Asadī al-Bazzār al-Baghdādī (d. 229/844) IV 359b
Khalaf Allāh, Muḥammad Aḥmad (d. 1997) I 426b; II 133b, 134a, 134b, 139b; III 526b; IV 149b, 150a
Khalaf b. Hishām al-Bazzār (d. 229/843-4) IV 358b, 389b, 390a, 391a
Khālid b. Sinān I 206b
Khālid b. al-Walīd (d. 21/642) I 121a; II 151a, 530b; III 179b, 462a, 462b; V 79a
Khālid al-Sabʿ al-ʿAlamī II 377b
Khālid al-Sinān al-ʿAbsī III 118b
Khalidi, T. I **145b**
Khalifa, R. I 394a; III 533b
Khalīfa ʿAbdullāhī (d. 1317/1899) III 328a
al-Khalīl (d. ca. 160/776) II 229a, 501a
al-Khalīl b. Aḥmad (d. 175/791) I 131a, 140b; II 104a, 347b, 348b, 349b, 361a, 364b; III 606a, 607a
al-Khalīlī (d. 447/1055) II 103b
Khalili Collection see Nasser D. Khalili Collection of Islamic Art
Khallād b. Khālid al-Baghdādī, Abū ʿĪsā (d. 220/835) IV 360a, 390a
al-Khallāl, Abū Bakr (d. 311/922) I 481b
Khan, G. I 136b, 141b
Khan, M.Z. I 488b
Khan, Q. IV 126a
Khan, R. II **25b**, **44a**
Khan, S.A. (d. 1898) I 201a; II 126a, 126b, 127a, 128a, 129a; III 223b; IV 275b, 554b
Khan-i Khānān III 323b
Khan al-Zabīb III 432b
Khanbaliq III 315a
al-Khandaq see Ditch
Kharīf V 87b
Khārija b. Zayd II 383b
Khārijī(s)/Khārijites I 73b, 74a, 221a, 462a, 517b, 518a, 540a; II 22b, 30a, 148a, 169b, 170a, 243b, 421b, 503b, 504a, 505a, 553b, 560a; III 33a, 72b, **84a**, 84b, 85a, 85b, 86a, 86b,

87a, 87b, 88a, 88b, 135a, 135b, 136a, 136b, 138a, 138b, 139a, 146b, 557a; IV 26a, 72b, 129b, 132b, 133a, 135b, 386a, 450b, 460b; V 2b, 23b, 103b, 192b, 503b, 504b
al-Kharkūshī (d. ca. 406/1015) IV 169b
Kharraqān III 305a
Khartoum I 34a
al-Khaṭīb al-Baghdādī (d. 463/1071) I 191b; IV 564a
al-Khaṭīb al-Iskāfī (d. 421/1030) V 333b
al-Khaṭīb al-Kāzarūnī (d. 940/1553) II 116b
al-Khaṭṭābī, Ḥamd b. Muḥammad (d. ca. 386/996) II 535a; V 409b
Khawārij see Khārijīs
Khawlān II 478b
Khawlān-Ṣaʿda V 92a
Khaybar I 154a, 270b, 320a, 398a, 399a, 399b; II 147a, 148b, 150a, 150b, 151a, 262b; III 30a, 456b, 498b, 499a, 577a, 580a; IV 341a; V 175b, 444b, 508b, 515b, 517a
Khaywān V 92a
al-Khayyāṭ, Abū l-Ḥusayn (d. ca. 300/913) II 532a
al-Khāzin (ʿAlī b. Muḥammad al-Baghdādī; d. 740-1/1340-1) V 98b, 147b, 401a
Khazraj I 389b, 407a, 409a, 409b; II 15a, 16a, 16b, 17a, 20a, 21b, 299b; III 29a, 30a, 369a, 369b, 438b; V 272b, 279b
al-Khiḍr see al-Khaḍir
Khilāfat Movement I 202b
Khir, B. V **104a**
Khirbat al-Mafjar I 155b
Khl[m] V 88a
Khomeini, [Ayatollah] Ruhollah I 27b, 161b; II 454b; III 582a, 582b; IV 143b, 144b, 145a; V 215b
Khoury, A.Th. IV 189b; V 298a, 353b
Khoury, R. I **61a**, 141b, **146b**, **195b**, **287b**
al-Khūlī, A. (d. 1967) II 130b, 131a, 131b, 132a, 132b, 133a, 133b, 134b, 136a, 140b; V 537b
Khumays b. Ḥudhāfa II 397b; V 508a
Khurāfā I 544a
Khurāsān I 106a, 110a, 110b, 518a; II 106a, 106b, 110b, 112b, 116a; III **86a**, 557b; IV 56a, 56b; V 324b

al-Khurayba i 152b
Khusraw II Parviz i 265b
Khuwaylid b. Asad (father of Khadīja) iii 80b
[Banū] Khuzāʿa i 257a; ii 16a, 151b, 297b; v 508a
Khuzayma b. Thābit i 355b
Khwārazm ii 115a
al-Khwārizmī iii 415b
Khwāya Mīr Dard (1721-85) iii 224a
[Banū] Kilāb v 199a, 509a
Kilwa i 155a
Kimber, R. i **239b**, **253b**; ii 525a, 525b; iv **328b**
[Banū] Kināna i 4b, 530b; ii 297b; iii 411b
Kinberg, L. i **76b**, **125a**, 529b, **553a**; ii 349a, 351b, 360a, **543b**; iv **19b**, **91a**
Kinda i 152b, 307b, 309a, 309b, 529b; v 509a
al-Kindī, ʿAbd al-Masīḥ b. Isḥāq ii 515b, 531b; iv 18b, 71b, 236a, 236b, 238b
al-Kindī, Abū Yūsuf Yaʿqūb b. Isḥāq (d. ca. 252/866) iv 71a, 71b, 72a, 74a, 74b, 76b, 79a, 82a, 83b, 87a, 236a, 381a
King, D. iv 328a
King, G. i 149a
King ʿAbd al-ʿAzīz mosque iii 432b
King Fahd Holy Koran Printing Complex iv 273a, 273b
King Faisal Mosque i 172b
King Fuʾād University (now University of Cairo) ii 133b; see also Cairo
King Saʿūd University i 153a
al-Kirmānī (d. ca. 500/1106) v 333b
Kirsten, Petrus (d. 1640) iv 246b
al-Kisāʾī, ʿAlī b. Ḥamza (d. 189/804-5) ii 349b, 361a, 363b; iii 53b, 542a, 543a; iv 357a, 358b, 360a, 373a, 389b, 528b; v 333b, 335a
al-Kisāʾī, Muḥammad b. ʿAbdallāh i 62a, 462b, 463a; iii 53b, 54b, 542b; v 390a
Kisāʾī of Marw iv 63b
Kish ii 110b
Kishk, [Shaykh] ʿAbd al-Ḥamīd (b. 1933) v 223b, 224a
Kisrā ii 40b
Kister, M.J. ii 150b, 568a; iii 368a, **463a**; v 502b
Kln[m] v 563a
Knauf, E.A. iii **545a**
Knights Templar i 125b
Knum (ram god of Elephantine) i 339b
Knysh, A. i **462a**; iii **414a**; iv **187a**, **212b**; v **159a**

Koffler, H. I 531a
Kohlberg, E. IV 450a, 450b, 593b
Kolmakov, A. V 348b
Komaruddin Hidayat V 218b
Konya III 308b, 434b
Kopf, L. II 235a, 250a
Korah [Qārūn] I 190a; II 338a, 338a, 338b, 399a, 399b, 436a; III 61a, **104a**, 104b, 105a, 394b, 423b, 518b, 520b; IV 68a
Koren, J. I 155a
Krackovskij, I. V 354b
Krishna V 96b
Kubrā, Najm al-Dīn (d. 617-18/1220-1) II 120a; V 153a, 158a, 158b
al-Kubrāwiyya II 120a
Küçük Kaynarca IV 250b
Kueny, K. III **146b**; IV **183b**; V **482b**
al-Kūfa I 127b, 154b, 156a, 308a, 332b, 333a, 348a, 360a; II 105b, 108a, 347b, 421b, 560a, 560b; III 84b, 85a, 85b, 88b, 370a, 429a, 463a, 501a, 542a, 558a, 605b; IV 72b, 154b, 355a, 373a, 388a; V 63a, 335a, 409b, 473a
Kūfan(s) II 354b; III 600a
al-Kūfī, Furāt b. Furāt b. Ibrāhīm (d. 309/922) II 117a; IV 602a
Kūfic (script) I 279b, 280b, 281a, 281b, 282b, 283b, 284a, 285a, 285b; IV 356b; V 558b
  Andalusian I 283b, 284a
  North African I 283b, 284a
Kugle, S. V **447b**
Kullābī(s) V 111b
Kulsiriswasd, D. V 101a
al-Kumayt b. Zayd (d. 126/173) I 511b
Kunitzsch, P. IV **109a**; V **163b**
Künstlinger, D. II 565b
Kurd(s) I 147a; III 68b
Kurdish (language) I 136a
Kurdistan III 68b
Kūthā I 8b
Kuwait National Museum I 127b, 155a, 309a, 318b
Kydones, Demetrios (d. ca. 1398) IV 242a, 242b, 245b
Kyrillos Lukaris V 345a

L

Laban I 379b
al-Labbān al-Miṣrī (d. 749/1349) V 329a
Labīb al-Saʿīd IV 381b
Labīd b. al-Aʿṣām I 468a; III 588a, 589a, 589b, 590a, 590b
Labīd b. Rabīʿa IV 111b, 114a
al-Lāh V 87a
Laḥayʿathat V 87b
Lahore III 434a; IV 266a, 274b
Lakemacher, Johann Gottfried (d. 1736) IV 250b
Lakhm I 308a; III 122a
Lakhmids I 278b, 308a, 309a; III 275a
Lāl Shāhbāz Qalandar V 95b
Lalani, A. III **68a**; IV **592b**
Lamech III 541a
Lammens, H. in5a; IV 190b, 399b; V 40a, 48b, 314a, 314b
Landau-Tasseron, E. III **42b**; V **368a**
Landberg, C. II 463b
Lane, E. I 40b, 200b, 291b, 389b; II 369b; III 71a; V 297a, 360b
Lane Poole, S. III 585a; V 351b
Lang, Johann Michael (Johann Buxtorf IV; d. 1732) IV 244b, 250a
Larcher, P. III **109b**, **132a**
Las Navas de Tolossa III 307a
Lashkar-i Bāzār I 171b
Lassner, J. I **229b**
al-Lāt I 37b, 95a, 194b, 208a, 330a, 337a; II 278a, 317b, 319a, 329b, 392a, 474a, 483b; V 87a, 88a, 122a, 261a, 362a
Late Antiquity see Antiquity
Latin (language) II 231b; III 179b; IV 18b, 28b, 236b, 238b, 249a, 265a, 275a; V 188a, 344b
Latrator Anubis V 52a
al-Lawdh, Jabal V 89a
Layaʿathat the Sabaean V 390b
Laylat al-Qadr see Night of Power
al-Laysaʿ see Elisha
[Banū] Layth V 509a
al-Layth b. al-Muẓaffar (d. ca. 200/815) II 104a
Lazarus-Yafeh, H. IV 451a
Le Strange, G. III 69a

Leah (Jacob's wife) IV 528a
Lebanon I 127b, 557a; II 200b, 454b, 503b; III 286a; IV 274b; V 234a
Lecker, M. III 368a
Leemhuis, F. I **114b**, **351a**; II **400b**, **501a**; IV 199b, **362b**; V 297b
Leiden IV 246a, 246b, 247a
University V 219a
Leipzig IV 248a, 250b; V 352a
Lejāʾ I 138a
Leo III (the Isaurian; r. 717-41) II 475a
Leontius (of Neapolis; fl. ca. 590-650) II 463b
Leuchter, H. IV 248b
Levant II 427a; III 306b, 308b, 309b
Levi I 276b
Levi-Strauss, C. III 97b, 121a
Leviticus I 276b
Lewinstein, K. I **367b**; II **333a**
Lewis, A. III 256b
Lewis, F. IV **65b**
L'Hôpital, J.-Y. IV **234a**
Libya I 127b; IV 349a, 360b; V 215a, 216b
Lidzbarski, M. II 565b
Light Verse see Verse
Liḥyān(s) I 152b
Lindsay, J. II **335a**
Lings, M. I 283a, 284a; II 150b
Linnaeus, Carolus (d. 1778) V 360b
Lions (modern community service organization) II 471b
Lohmann, T. III 538a
Lohnse, K.G. IV 274a
Løkkegaard, F. I 252a
London IV 249a, 250a, 265b; V 66a
Lope de Obregón IV 244b
Lord, A. II 254a
Lot [Lūṭ] I 6a, 59b, 149a, 222a, 236b, 261b, 296b, 319a, 340a, 405a, 500b, 513a, 518b, 519a, 532a, 533b; II 14a, 63a, 64a, 145b, 174a, 212b, 259b, 260a, 293a, 309a, 418a, 436a, 439a, 444b, 462b, 483a, 488a, 503a; III 50a, 62a, 118b, 212b, 219a, **231b**, 232a, 232b, 381a, 381b, 393b, 449a, 485b, 486a, 519a, 519b, 520a,

	520b, 521a, 522a, 525b, 567b, 583a; IV 26b, 68a, 319a, 319b, 320a, 352b, 425a, 425b, 538a, 577a, 580b, 584b, 605b; V 130a, 132a, 133b, 171a, 171b, 184b, 253b, 313b, 389a, 482a, 528a, 534b
People of	I 6a, 54b, 338a, 513b; III 232b, 418a, 540a, 541a; IV 290a, 425a, 505b, 513b, 523b; V 252b, 460b, 470b
Loth, O.	III 475a; IV 193b
Lotus Sutra	IV 560b
Lowin, S.	IV **106b**, **451b**
Lowry, J.	III **176a**; IV **507b**; V **256a**
Lucifer	II 419b
Lucius Verus	I 150a
Lucknow	IV 266a
Ludovicus de Dieu (d. 1642)	IV 246a, 246b
Luke (evangelist)	II 342b; III 13a
Lüling, G.	I 330b, 334b; III 129b; IV 193b, 200a, 200b, 201a, 201b; V 169b, 170a, 426b
Luqmān	III 402a; IV 32a, 68b; V 285b, 437b, 441a, 483a
Luqmān b. ʿĀd	II 463b; III **242a**
Luqmān the Sage [al-Ḥakīm]	I 22a, 62a, 161a, 387b, 532a; II 371b, 441a, 463b; III **242a**, 242b, 243a; IV 159a
Lūṭ	see Lot
Luther, Martin (d. 1546)	IV 242a, 243b, 245b; V 344b
Lutheran School of Technology	V 217a
Lutherans	IV 245a
Luxenberg, Ch.	III 130a, 130b, 131a, 131b; IV 201a; V 69a, 169b, 240b, 241a, 246a, 251a
Luzian	III 242a
Lydda	I 110b
Lyotard, J.	I 413a

M

Maʿadd	V 45b
al-Maʿarrī, Abū l-ʿAlāʾ (d. 449/1057)	I 89b; II 419a; III 221a; IV 23a, 201b
Maʿbad al-Juhanī (d. after 83/703)	IV 72b, 73a

al-Mābiyāt	I 154b
Macdonald, D.	II 479b
Macoraba	II 295b; see also Mecca
Madāʾ	I 150b, 152b
Madāʾin	III 5b
Madāʾin Ṣāliḥ	II 427a, 427b, 428a; V 254a
al-Madāʾinī	I 400b
Madelung, W.	I 471a; II 22b, 533a
Madhabite	V 563a
Madhḥij	I 544a; V 92a
Madigan, D.A.	I **251a**, **487a**; IV **263a**, **447b**
Maʿdīkarib Yaʿfur	V 565b
Madyan	see Midian
Madyanites	see Midianites
Maghrib	I 283b; III 86a, 88a, 260a, 263b, 271a, 432a, 559a, 596a, 600b; IV 233a, 349a, 359a, 360b, 392a; V 559a
Magi	III 244b
Magian(s) [Majūs]	I 222b, 378a, 466b; II 220a; III **244a**, 244b; IV 58a, 399b, 400a, 403a, 403b, 404b, 407b, 408a, 408b, 415b, 511b, 512b, 525a
Magog [Māʾjūj]	I 61b, 110b, 111a, 112b, 398b; II **331b**, 332a, 332b, 333a; III 139a, 143a, 143b, 520a, 543a; IV 210b, 434b; V 375b
Magritte, R.	I 168a
al-Maḥallī, Jalāl al Dīn (d. 864/1459)	I 36a; II 113b; IV 533; V 219b, 346b
Mahdawī (d. after 430/1039)	V 331b
al-Mahdī (r. 158-69/775-85)	I 125b, 126a, 126b; III 557b; IV 105a, 142a; V 371a
[Imām] al-Mahdī (d. 260/874)	see al-ʿAskarī, [Imām] al-Ḥasan (d. 260/874)
al-Mahdī, Muḥammad Aḥmad (d. 1313/1895)	I 111a, 219b; III 112b, 328a
Mahdī b. ʿAlī al-Ṣanawbarī (al-Ṣubunrī) al-Yamanī	see al-Ṣanawbarī (al-Ṣubunrī), Mahdī b. ʿAlī (d. 815/1412)
Mahdiyya (movement)	III 328a
Great Mosque of	III 436b
Maḥmūd (proper name)	II 29a; IV 45a
Maḥmūd, Muṣṭafā Kamāl Maḥmūd	V 10b
Maḥmūd ʿAbbās al-ʿAqqād	V 537a
Maḥmūd al-Ālūsī (d. 1270/1854)	see al-Ālūsī, Maḥmūd
Maḥmūd al-Ḥuṣarī (reciter)	IV 392a

Maḥmūd Khalīl al-Ḥuṣarī see al-Ḥuṣarī, Maḥmūd Khalīl (d. 1980)
Maḥmūd Muḥammad Ṭahā see Ṭahā, Maḥmūd Muḥammad
Maḥmūd Shaltūt Shaltūt, Maḥmūd
Maḥmūd Shihāb al-Dīn al-Ālūsī see al-Ālūsī, Maḥmūd Shihāb al-Dīn (d. 1854)
Maḥmūd b. ʿUmar al-Zamakhsharī see al-Zamakhsharī, Maḥmūd b. ʿUmar (d. 538/1144)
[Wādī] Mahzūr IV 334a
Maimoinides, Moses V 309b
Maʿīn I 152a, 152b; IV 585b; V 86b, 88a, 88b, 92b
Mainz IV 101b
Majanna II 298a; III 411a
Majd al-Dīn al-Mubārak b. al-Athīr (d. 606/1210) II 386b
al-Majlisī, Muḥammad Bāqir (d. 1100/1699 or 1111/1700) II 377b; IV 595a, 596a, 598b, 602a; V 361a, 361b
Maʾjūj see Magog
Majūs see Magians
Makhawān [Makhāʾ] V 565a
[Banū] Makhzūm III 422a; IV 331b; V 508a
al-Mākin, Jirjis b. al-ʿAmīd (d. ca. 1273) V 347b
al-Makkī, Abū Ṭālib (d. 386/996) I 522a; II 409b
Makkī b. Abī Ṭālib al-Qaysī al-Qayrawānī al-Andalusī (d. 437/1045) I 399a; II 109b; III 503b; IV 358b, 359a; V 331a, 332a, 332b, 333a, 335a
al-Maktab al-Islāmī IV 274b, 275a
Malabar III 316a
Malagasy (language) see Sorabe
Malak Ḥinfī Nāṣif II 200b
Malaṭya III 434a
Malay (language) I 136a; II 90a; III 225b V 98a, 99a, 101a, 342a
Malaysia III 316a, 326a, 326b; IV 273b; V 100a, 211b, 214a, 222b, 538b
Universitas Kebangsaan (Malaya) V 224b
Mali III 327a
Mālik b. Anas (d. 179/796) I 17b, 18b, 354a, 391b; II 215a, 337a, 377b, 381b, 386a, 391a, 393b; III 67b, 262a, 307a, 370a, 371a, 502a, 502b; IV 70a, 71b-72a, 73b, 108a, 389b; V 196a, 334b
Mālik b. Dīnār (d. 131/748) V 141a, 307a
Mālikī(s) I 3b, 18b, 19a, 225b, 434a; III 214b,

252b, 307a, 404a, 404b; IV 95a, 110a; V 55b, 415a, 498b
Malikshāh (sultan) III 305a
Malkīkarib Yuhaʾmin V 562b, 563a, 563b, 564a, 567b
Malti-Douglas, F. I **191b**
Maʿmar b. Rāshid (d. 153-4/770) II 107b, 347b; IV 533a; V 33a, 34a, 35a, 37b, 38b
Mambres (Egyptian magician) I 276a
Mamlūk(s) I 125b, 173b, 174a; II 40a; III 308a, 308b, 310b, 311b, 312a, 600b; V 559a
Mamre V 259a, 263a
al-Maʾmūn (r. 196-218/811-33) I 469a, 469b, 471a; II 413a, 420a, 531a, 531b, 538b, 560b; III 302b, 545b, 557b, 558a, 558b; IV 73b, 81b, 142b
Manāf IV 577b
Manasseh III 57a
Manāt I 37b, 95a, 194b, 330a; II 278a, 317b, 329b, 392a, 474a, 483b; V 88a, 88b, 122a, 261a
Manawt V 88b
Manchester V 66a
Mandaeans I 378a; IV 408a, 416b, 512a, 512b
Mandel Khān, G. III **251b**
Mani II 485b; IV 560b
Manichaean(s) II 246a, 421a, 485b, 566b; IV 122b, 216a, 407b, 408a, 512b, 540b; V 293a
Mānkdīm (d. 425/1034) I 470b
al-Manṣūr (r. 136-58/754-75) I 125b, 126a, 126b; IV 142a, 143b; V 33a
Manṣūr b. al-Muʿtamir (d. 132/750) II 382a, 390a
Manṣūr b. Nūḥ (r. 350-66/961-76) IV 59b
Manūchihrī (d. ca. 432/1041) IV 55b
Manuel II Palaiologos (r. 1391-1425) IV 242a
Manzikert, Battle of III 434b
Maqnā V 185a
al-Maqdisī (d. 340/934) V 119a, 306b
al-Maqrīzī (d. 845/1442) III 431a
Marāgha III 601a
al-Marāghī, Muṣṭafā V 99a , 217b, 340b
Marar Trading Company, Baghdad IV 274a
Marburg IV 248b
Marçais, W. II 523b
Marcotte, R. III **538b**

Marcus Aurelius — I 150a
Margoliouth, D. — I 337b; II 530a; IV 535a; V 351a
Mari — III 180a
Mārib/Ma'rib (capital of Saba') — I 151a, 151b, 152a, 214b; IV 258a, 586a; V 86a, 86b, 89b, 563a, 566a
  Dam of — I 44a, 151a, 151b; II 299a, 307b; III 521b, 532b; IV 257b; V 562a
Maʿrifa, [Ayatollah] Muḥammad Hādī — V 329b
Marín, M. — III **574a**
Māriya al-Qibṭiyya (d. 16/638) — see Mary the Copt
Mark (evangelist) — I 109a, 109b; II 342b
Mark of Toledo (Canon Marcus of Toledo) — V 345a
Marlow, L. — II **275a**; III **95b**; IV **540a**
Maronite(s) — IV 237a, 248b
Marracci, Ludovico (d. 1700) — IV 247b, 248a, 248b, 249a, 250a, 265a; V 344b, 345a, 345b, 347a, 348a, 351a
Marrakesh — III 267b, 431b; V 72b
  Great Mosque of — III 303b, 307b
Marshall, D. — IV **322a**; V **340b**, **575b**
Martin, R. — I **107a**, **471b**; II **535b**; IV 578a
Marthad — II 463a, 463b
Martin Luther — see Luther, Martin (d. 1546)
Maruī (Sindhī folk heroine) — V 95a
Mārūt — I 195a; II **404a**, 404b, 405a; III 249b; IV 165a; V 118b, 202b
Marw — IV 63b
Marw al-Rūdh — V 147a
al-Marwa — I 9a, 319b, 353b; II 64a, 179a, 205a, 299b, 513a; III 77a, 339a, 552b; IV 93a, 93b, 94a, 97a, 98a, 105a, 259a, 283b, 491b, 515b, **518a**, 518b, 519b; V 318a, 463a
Marwān I (Marwān b. al-Ḥakam; r. 64-5/684-5) — II 398b; III 429b; IV 239b
Marwān II (Marwān b. Muḥammad; r. 127-32/744-50) — III 423b; IV 52a, 524b
Marwān Suwār — IV 275a
al-Marwazī al-Ḥākim al-Shahīd (d. 334/945) — III 404b
Marx, Karl — V 66a
Mary [Maryam] — I 1b, 2a, 52b, 56a, 59a, 59b, 60a, 87a, 103a, 123b, 124b, 149a, 167a, 203a, 233b, 261b, 298b, 309b, 312a, 312b, 313a, 495a, 512b; II 19a, 156a, 193b, 217a, 278b, 282a, 290b, 291a, 309a,

329b, 341a, 425b, 436b, 439a, 442b, 443a, 443b, 496a, 509a, 569a; III 5b, 7a, 7b, 8b, 11a, 11b, 13a, 13b, 14a, 14b, 15a, 15b, 81a, 81b, 207a, **288b**, 289a, 289b, 290a, 290b, 291a, 291b, 292a, 292b, 293a, 293b, 294a, 294b, 295a, 295b, 300a, 395b, 396b, 441b, 492a, 492b, 519b, 521a, 537a; IV 39b, 40b, 41a, 50b, 70a, 195b, 223a, 241a, 290b, 291a, 292a, 296a, 304b, 308a, 580b, 583b, 585a; V 4a, 54a, 81b, 114a, 114b, 115a, 116a, 117a, 127b, 133b, 188b, 189a, 363b, 369b, 370a, 445b, 449b, 524b, 530a, 532a, 533b, 534a, 534b, 536b, 537a, 574b, 575a, 575b

Mary the Copt [Māriya al-Qibṭiyya] (d. 16/638) — I 57a, 57b, 384a, 396b; II 11a, 398a; V 59a, 508b, 509a, 518a, 518b
Mary the Greater [Maryam al-Kubrā] — V 534b; see also Fāṭima
Mary Magdalene — I 118b; III 493b, 494a; IV 410b, 411a, 505a
Maryam (sister of Moses) — I 2a; II 509a
Marzolph, U. — II **465b**; IV 266b
al-Marzubānī (d. 384/994) — V 13b
al-Marzūqī — I 217a
Mashhad — III 313b; IV 64a; V 499a
al-Mashnī, M.I. — II 112b, 114a
al-Masīḥ al-Dajjāl — see Antichrist
Masik — III 68b
al-Masjid al-Aqṣā — see Aqṣā Mosque
Masjid-i Imām — III 433b
Maslama — V 67b
Masrūq — IV 46a; V 565a, 566b
Massey, K. — III **476b**
Massignon, L. — I 89a, 545a; II 193b; V 354a
Masson, D. — IV 195a; V 354a
al-Masʿūdī, Abū ʿAlī b. al-Ḥusayn (d. 345/956) — I 10a, 58b; II 36a, 36b; IV 525a; V 306b, 562a
Maṣyāf — II 40a
Matthew (evangelist) — II 342b
  pseudo Matthew — III 13b

Mattson, I. II **466b**; III **254b**; V **551a**
al-Māturīdī, Abū Manṣūr Muḥammad b. Muḥammad (d. 333/944) I 483b; II 100b, 115b; III 470a, 470b; V 330a
Māturīdiyya I 483b
Mātūs (of Men of the Cave) IV 351a
Maurice (Byzantine emperor) I 265b
Mauritania I 127b
al-Māwardī, Abū l-Ḥasan (d. 450/1058) II 112b
al-Māwardī, Alī b. Muḥammad (d. 450/1058) III 5b, 6a, 95a, 331b; IV 126a, 143b, 533b, 538b, 539b; V 334a
al-Mawdūdī, Sayyid Abū l-ʿAlāʾ (d. 1979) I 39b, 200a, 200b, 201a, 391b; II 138a, 272b; III 6a, 229a, 241a; IV 145b, 397a, 397b, 535a; V 27a, 27b; V 103b, 228a, 228b, 330a, 405b, 406a, 537b, 538a
Mawlā Fatḥ Allāh Kāshānī II 193b
Mawlānā Jalāl al-Dīn Rūmī see Rūmī, Mawlāna Jalāl al-Dīn
Mawlānā Muḥammad ʿAlī see Muḥammad ʿAlī, Mawlāna (d. 1951)
Mawṣil I 147a; II 206a; III 85b, 86a, 311a
Maybud (province of Yazd, Iran) V 148a
al-Maybudī, Abū l-Faḍl Rashīd al-Dīn Aḥmad (d. 530/1135) II 120a; IV 59b; V 148a, 148b
Mayfaʿ V 87b
Maymūn b. Mihrān (d. 117/735) V 331a
Maymūn b. Qays al-Aʿshā see al-Aʿshā, Maymūn b. Qays
Maymūna bt. al-Ḥarīth V 508a, 516a
Maysara (servant of Khadīja) II 515a; III 80b
Maysara b. ʿAbd Rabbihi (fl. 150/767) I 88b; II 394a
Mayse (of Muʿwiya) V 186b
Mazdaism V 119a
Mazlum, J. I 172a
McAuliffe, J.D. I **5a**, **228b**, **514a**; II **193b**, **409b**; IV **417a**
McDonough, S. I **19b**; II **449b**
McGill University (Canada) V 219a
Mecca [Makka] I 4b, 5b, 7a, 7b, 8a, 9a, 9b, 10a, 14a, 20a, 20b, 22a, 34a, 35b, 40b, 65b, 66a, 88a, 97b, 98b, 110b, 113a, 120b, 125a, 125b, 145b, 148a, 148b, 153b, 154 a, 155a, 156a, 163a, 164a, 164b, 168b, 169a, 170b, 176b, 177a, 196b, 215b, 216a, 217a, 225a, 236b, 263b, 266b, 270b, 271a,

273a, 280b, 290b, 293b, 300b, 306a, 307b, 309b, 311a, 317a, 319b, 320a, 323a, 325a, 328b, 329a, 330b, 337a, 338a, 338b, 340b, 342a, 342b, 353b, 357a, 369a, 372b, 375a, 382a, 382b, 389a, 398a, 399a, 399b, 400a, 405b, 407b, 408a, 408b, 409a, 417a, 422b, 424a, 433b, 459b, 501b, 531a, 547a, 550a, 551a, 551b, 552a; II 8a, 14b, 15a, 15b, 18b, 20a, 20b, 22a, 22b, 33a, 79b, 83b, 84b, 85a, 87a, 88a, 91a, 103a, 105b, 110a, 119b, 148a, 148b, 149b, 159a, 174b, 176a, 178b, 180a, 182a, 190a, 190b, 204a, 204b, 206a, 215b, 218b, 224b, 241b, 256b, 259b, 288b, 294b, 295a, 295b, 296b, 297a, 297b, 298a, 304b, 306b, 307a, 307b, 308b, 309a, 310b, 311a, 312a, 318a, 319a, 338a, 373b, 374a, 378a, 381a, 397b, 403a, 432b, 438b, 439a, 459a, 461a, 461b, 463a, 463b, 464a, 465b, 466a, 466b, 469a, 479a, 479b, 490a, 490b, 495a, 496a, 497a, 504b, 514b, 518b, 520a, 528a, 530a, 530b, 569a; III 3a, 3b, 4a, 4b, 5b, 6a, 7b, 27b, 31a, 35a, 40b, 44a, 75b, 76a, 77a, 78a, 78b, 79a, 79b, 86a, 113a, 123a, 130a, 131b, 150b, 162b, 185b, 213a, 228a, 247a, 247b, 248b, 253b, 275a, 275b, 276a, 278a, 292b, 322b, **337a**, 337b, 338a, 339a, 339b, 340a, 340b, 341a, 367b, 368b, 369b, 370b, 412a, 427a, 428a, 429a, 429b, 430b, 443b, 449b, 455b, 456a, 457a, 461a, 462a, 462b, 486a, 488a, 489b, 491a, 491b, 495b, 525b, 544a, 564b, 568a, 569a, 577a, 577b, 579a, 579b, 581a, 581b, 583b, 589a, 596a, 597a, 600a; IV 21b, 25a, 45a, 45b, 46a,

48b, 54a, 91b, 92b, 93a, 94a, 95b, 96b, 97a, 97b, 98a, 98b, 99b, 104a, 104b, 113a, 114a, 115a, 119b, 130a, 153a, 162b, 209b, 216b, 217b, 218a, 219a, 222a, 226a, 226b, 227a, 227b, 256b, 257b, 259a, 271b, 277a, 281b, 282a, 295a, 305a, 306a, 320b, 321a, 321b, 325b, 326b, 327a, 327b, 328a, 328b, 329a, 329b, 331b, 332a, 332b, 333a, 337a, 340b, 355a, 357a, 373a, 383a, 391b, 399b, 405a, 409a, 410b, 411a, 413a, 416b, 467a, 471b, 491b, 494a, 512b, 514a, 515b, 516a, 518a, 518b, 519a, 519b, 521a, 531a, 531b, 532a, 541b, 572a, 577b, 591a, 598a, 604b; V 20a, 25a, 28b, 44a, 46b, 47a, 58b, 64a, 90b, 104b, 105a, 107a, 107b, 108a, 122a, 127a, 130a, 168a, 169b, 170b, 171b, 175a, 185a, 213b, 225a, 228a, 248a, 248b, 258a, 259a, 261b, 263a, 263b, 272a, 284b, 291a, 303b, 307b, 331a, 352b, 372b, 374a, 374b, 375a, 375b, 389b, 399b, 409b, 423b, 429b, 434a, 435a, 435b, 444b, 448b, 450a, 454b, 463a, 473a, 477b, 507b, 508a, 516b, 522a, 526a, 529b, 550a, 550b, 562a, 565b, 567b, 575b

Grand Shaykh of — I 30b

Great Mosque of — III 75a

Meccan(s) — I 54b, 98b, 160b, 196b, 197a, 209a, 216a, 224b, 242a, 286a, 289a, 319b, 324a, 356b, 406a, 464a, 506b, 530b; II 15b, 16a, 19a, 19b, 20a, 21a, 21b, 30b, 32a, 44b, 134a, 147b, 180a, 184a, 298a, 298b, 299a, 299b, 317a, 317b, 319b, 346a, 390b, 400a, 432a, 466a, 478b, 483b, 514b, 552a; III 4a, 213a, 339b, 340a, 341a, 455b, 456a, 498b, 577a,

578a, 579a, 581b, 592b, 603b; IV 35a, 46a, 219a, 256b, 329b, 330a, 408b, 409a, 415b, 456b, 529a, 604b; V 47b, 184b, 262a, 271b, 272a, 273a, 285b, 291b, 315a, 379b, 435b, 549b, 550a

Emigrants [*muhājirūn*] I 262a, 262b; II **14b**, 518b; III 37a, 207a, 369b, 463a; IV 25b, 26b, 226b, 259a, 455b; V 48a, 59a, 196a, 288a

Mede(s) I 147a; III 390a

Medina [(al-)Madīna(t al-Nabī)] I 14a, 35b, 36b, 54b, 67a, 110b, 119a, 120b, 121a, 121b, 148a, 148b, 153b, 154a, 154b, 155b, 160b, 164a, 168b, 170b, 196b, 210a, 216a, 216b, 217a, 217b, 220a, 222b, 223a, 240b, 262a, 262b, 270b, 273a, 280b, 289a, 289b, 292a, 293b, 300b, 309b, 311a, 320a, 323a, 325a, 325b, 328b, 330b, 331b, 332b, 333a, 337a, 379b, 382b, 384b, 389a, 389b, 398a, 407a, 407b, 408b, 409a, 410a, 417a, 422b, 424a, 433b, 462a, 465a, 466a, 495a, 495b, 505a, 506b, 507a, 531a, 531b, 545b; II 14b, 15a, 15b, 16a, 17a, 18b, 19a, 20a, 21a, 21b, 22b, 25a, 26b, 81b, 110b, 147a, 148b, 150a, 155b, 156b, 167b, 179a, 182a, 184a, 184b, 190b, 204a, 205b, 224b, 264a, 271b, 288b, 294a, 295a, 298b, 299a, 299b, 311a, 374a, 378a, 384a, 397b, 398a, 398b, 427a, 432b, 438b, 439a, 459b, 461b, 466b, 468b, 469a, 469b, 470a, 492a, 494a, 514b, 518b, 524a, 530b, 569a; III 3b, 7b, 29a, 30a, 31a, 32b, 33b, 86b, 131b, 142b, 144a, 150b, 151a, 151b, 152a, 165a, 169a, 195a, 207b, 208a, 238a, 253b, 275a, 275b, 276a, 276b, 278a, 289b, 293a, 294a, 295a, 337b, 339b, 340a, 341a, **367b**, 368a, 368b, 369a, 369b,

370a, 370b, 371a, 412a, 414b, 422b, 428a, 428b, 429b, 430a, 431a, 436a, 437a, 438a, 439a, 455a, 455b, 456a, 456b, 457a, 461a, 498a, 499a, 500b, 502b, 522b, 544a, 564a, 568a, 569a, 571b, 576b, 577a, 577b, 578a, 578b, 579a, 579b, 580a, 581a, 581b, 589a, 591a, 597a, 600a, 606a; IV 19b, 25a, 38b, 42a, 49a, 54a, 63b, 110a, 114a, 115a, 119b, 130a, 140a, 217b, 218b, 219a, 224a, 224b, 225a, 225b, 226a, 226b, 227a, 227b, 228a, 228b, 256a, 272a, 273a, 277a, 305a, 306a, 321b, 323a, 323b, 324a, 325b, 326a, 331b, 332a, 332b, 333a, 333b, 334a, 334b, 340a, 340b, 355a, 357a, 373a, 406a, 410a, 411a, 411b, 412a, 416b, 496b, 512b, 516a; V 20a, 31a, 31b, 33a, 44a, 44b, 45a, 45b, 46b, 47a, 58b, 104b, 105a, 107b, 113b, 168a, 193b, 197b, 198b, 202b, 205b, 213b, 228a, 258a, 262a, 272a, 281b, 292a, 292b, 301a, 314b, 331a, 344a, 352b, 372b, 375b, 376a, 377b, 382a, 389b, 402b, 409a, 414a, 426b, 431a, 435a, 454b, 471a, 477b, 479b, 481b, 507a, 507b, 508a, 511a, 517a, 521a, 526a, 550a, 575a, 575b

Constitution of [*ʿahd al-umma*] I 378b, 398a, 398b; II 17a, 33b, 35a, 40b, 47a, 61a, 65a, 80a; III 128a, 152b, 369b, 491b, 590b; IV 127b; V 193b, 291b

Great Mosque of III 300a

pre-Islamic III 29b; see also Yathrib

Medinan(s) I 262a, 262b, 306a, 353b, 368b; II 14b, 15a, 21a, 21b, 220b, 346a, 382a; III 368b, 462b; V 255b

Helpers [*anṣār*] I 217a, 262a, 262b, 337a, 407a, 408a, 409a, 409b; II **14b**, 15a, 20a, 466a, 466b, 518b; III 37a,

	207a, 369b, 463a, 570a; IV 25b, 26b, 226b, 415a, 455a; V 47b, 48a, 288a
Mediterranean	I 41a, 152a, 152b, 168b; II 566b; III 326b; IV 209b, 259a, 585b
Mediterranean Sea [Baḥr al-Rūm]	I 203b, 439a
Megerlin, D.	V 348b
Meḥmed/Mehmet II (Ottoman sultan)	III 435a; IV 242b
Meier, F.	I 183b
Mekka	see Mecca
Melchert, C.	III **252b**; IV **392b**
Melchizedek	II 155b
Melkites	see Christian(s)
Memphis	IV 66b
Men of the Cave	see Caves; Seven Sleepers
Mendenhall, G.	III 390a
Mereban filius Elhekem	see Marwān I (Marwān b. al-Ḥakam; r. 64-5/684-5)
Meri, J.	IV **497a**
Merv	II 119b; III 596a
MESA	see Middle Eastern Studies Association
Mesgnien Meninski, Franz von (d. 1698)	IV 250a
Mesopotamia	I 8a, 8b, 168b, 195a, 308a, 308b, 340b; II 559b; III 8b, 69a, 306b, 404a, 411b, 500a; V 86b, 129a, 374b
Lower	III 405b
Upper	III 263a
Messiah [al-Masīḥ]	I 102a, 102b, 103a, 106a, 124b, 233b, 309b, 312b, 313a; II 508a; III 7a, 11a, 11b, 12a, 13a, 14b, 15a, 26b, 128b, 143b, 288b, 294a; IV 38b, 40b, 101b; V 41a, 249b
Davidic	III 13a
Metcalf, B.	I **520b**
Micah	I 275b
Michael [Mīkāl, Mikāʾīl]	I 84b, 88a; II 66a, 241a, 278a; III 45a, 117a, 139b, **388a**, 388b, 389a, 389b; IV 301b; V 118b
Michaelis, Johann David (d. 1791)	IV 250a, 250b
Michaud, M.	IV 195b
Middle Ages	I 94a, 116a, 414a; II 349b, 467a, 493b, 538b; III 107a, 405a; IV 391b; V 162b, 344a

Middle East — I 40b, 41b, 43b, 48a, 78b, 103b, 255a, 264a, 307b, 315b, 414b, 494a, 494b, 502a; II 217b, 218a, 219a, 446b; III 258a, 296b, 343b, 346a, 364b, 365a, 366a, 525a; IV 215b, 219b, 241a, 259a, 259b, 260b, 265a, 381b, 383a; V 94a, 98b, 99a, 209b, 210a, 213a, 213b, 217a, 218a, 218b, 225a, 256b, 257b, 359b
Middle Eastern Studies Association — I 418a
Midian [Madyan] — I 41b, 149b, 160b, 261b, 300b; II 212a, 293a, 336b, 399a, 399b, 449a, 459b; III 83a, **389b**, 390a, 390b, 418a, 421a, 496a, 520b, 522a, 588b; IV 53b, 54a, 258a, 352b, 605a, 49a, 606a; V 285b, 312b
People of — III 200b, 390b; V 252b, 468a
Midianites — II 334b; III 381a, 389b, 390a, 390b, 391a, 393b, 520b; IV 288a
Midrash — II 213a, 498a
Rabba — II 482b
Mikāʾīl — see Michael
Minā — I 271a, 293b, 403b; II 298a, 300b; III 4b, 76a, 339a, 341a; IV 96a, 96b, 97a, 97b, 515b
Minaen(s) — I 152b
Ming (dynasty) — III 315a, 315b
Mingana, A. — III 111a, 129a, 129b, 130a, 256b; IV 194b
Ministry of Religious Endowments [*wizārat al-awqāf*] — II 89a
Miquel, A. — I 266a; II 352a
Mir, M. — I **185a**, 186a, 218b, **256b**, **534b**; II 248a, **315b**, **316b**, **345b**, 464b, 465a; III 210a, **226b**, **514b**; IV **162b**; V **276b**, 297a, 297b, **406a**
Mīr Anīs — V 95a
Mīr Dard — I 211a
Mīr Ḥasan — III 224a
Miriam — see Maryam (sister of Moses)
Mirzā ʿAbd al-Wahhāb — IV 266b
Mirzā Abū Faḍl — IV 266a
Mirzā Asad Allāh — IV 266b

Mirzā Ghulām Aḥmad	I 201a
Mīrzā Ḥusayn (calligrapher)	IV 266b
Mīrzā Ḥusayn ʿAlī Nūrī (founder of the Bahāʾī Movement)	I 197a
Mishna	I 476b
Miskawayh	II 440a
Miṣr	see Egypt
Miṣr (son of Nūḥ)	II 10b
Miṣrayim	II 10b
Miṣriyya	III 247b
Mitchell	IV 145a
Mizpah (benediction)	I 379b; IV 530a
Mizzī	see Yūsuf b. ʿAbd al-Raḥmān al-Mizzī
Mkrtič al-Kasīḥ	IV 237a
Moabites	III 390a
Moberg, A.	III 411b
Modern Standard Arabic	see Arabic
Mokha (Red Sea port)	see Makhawān [Makhā]
Moloch	V 106a
Mongols	III 308b, 315a; IV 57b, 146b, 147a, 525a
Īlkhānid	III 311a, 320a
Monophysite(s)	see Christian(s)
Monroe, J.T.	II 254a
[Ayatollah] Montazeri	IV 144b
Montet, E.	V 352b
Moor(s)	I 30b
Moore, K.	IV 554a
Moorish Science Temple	I 30a, 30b, 31b
Moosa, E.	III **241b**
Mopti (Mali)	III 327a
Morabia, A.	I 363b
Mordechai	II 399b
Moritz, B.	I 174a; III 298a
Morocco	I 127b; II 206b, 505b; III 326b, 431a, 558b; IV 271b, 273b, 275b, 378a, 496b; V 72b, 73a, 74b, 75b, 209a, 211a, 450a
Morrison, R.	V **561a**
Moses [Mūsā]	I 1a, 1b, 2a, 5b, 26a, 61b, 62a, 93a, 93b, 98b, 99a, 108b, 117b, 124b, 125a, 157b, 158a, 159a, 160a, 188a, 189a, 219a, 222a, 236a, 236b, 245a, 245b, 247a, 255a, 260a, 260b, 261a, 273b,

274a, 274b, 275a, 275b, 276b, 296a, 296b, 297a, 303a, 303b, 304b, 305b, 306b, 310b, 317b, 324a, 328a, 329b, 330a, 338b, 340b, 345b, 363a, 364a, 365a, 365b, 367a, 376b, 379b, 380b, 387b, 399b, 405a, 464b, 465b, 468b, 478a, 486b, 488a, 492a, 500b, 505a, 507a, 511b, 516b, 518b, 519a, 528b, 532a, 532b, 533b, 534a, 536b, 537a, 553b; II 10a, 11b, 23b, 24a, 43b, 61b, 146a, 176b, 182a, 184a, 199a, 144a, 212a, 212b, 213b, 231a, 240b, 259b, 305a, 305b, 309a, 315b, 316a, 324a, 324b, 330a, 334a, 336b, 338a, 339a, 341b, 342b, 372b, 399a, 407b, 412b, 432b, 433b, 435b, 436a, 437a, 439a, 464b, 481a, 488a, 502b, 507a, 507b, 509a, 509b, 510b, 527b, 534a, 542a, 544a, 544b, 546a, 553a, 558a, 569a, 571b; III 8b, 9a, 17a, 18a, 18b, 21b, 26a, 29a, 50a, 57a, 62b, 65a, 80b, 81b, 82a, 82b, 83a, 83b, 93b, 104a, 104b, 105a, 106a, 106b, 113a, 140a, 143a, 148b, 151a, 184b, 186b, 189b, 190a, 190b, 200b, 208a, 208b, 211a, 211b, 212a, 214a, 219a, 224a, 224b, 225a, 229b, 232a, 233b, 234b, 249a, 249b, 253b, 287a, 289a, 330b, 331b, 340a, 381a, 381b, 382a, 383b, 390a, 390b, 393b, 394a, 394b, 395a, 398a, 400a, **419b**, 420a, 420b, 421a, 421b, 422a, 422b, 423a, 423b, 424a, 424b, 425a, 425b, 426a, 441a, 442a, 444a, 444b, 445a, 450b, 451b, 479b, 480a, 487b, 488a, 494a, 495b, 496a, 496b, 515b, 516a, 518b, 519a, 519b, 520a, 520b, 521a, 521b, 522a, 525b, 529b, 537a, 539b, 540a, 540b, 552b, 562b, 583b, 590b,

592a, 592b; IV 3b, 20a, 21b, 25b, 34a, 35a, 36b, 40b, 49b, 61b, 67a, 67b, 68a, 105b, 106a, 112b, 131a, 138a, 160a, 183a, 210b, 211a, 217a, 218b, 223b, 224a, 225a, 227b, 229b, 241a, 282b, 286b, 291a, 291b, 292a, 292b, 293b, 294b, 296b, 297b, 298b, 299a, 302a, 303a, 305a, 307b, 308a, 313a, 316a, 319b, 341a, 341b, 346a, 348b, 407a, 413a, 421a, 421b, 425b, 429b, 438b, 439b, 440a, 440b, 445a, 446b, 452a, 467a, 483a, 505a, 508a, 508b, 509a, 513a, 513b, 517a, 523b, 524a, 524b, 527a, 528a, 536a, 536b, 538a, 561a, 569b, 574b, 577a, 577b, 578a, 590a, 592a, 604a, 604b, 606a; V 4b, 23a, 28a, 28b, 29a, 41b, 53b, 61b, 68b, 83a, 95b, 107b, 109b, 110a, 110b, 111a, 111b, 127b, 129a, 129b, 136a, 146b, 152a, 155b, 160a, 171a, 171b, 173a, 200b, 201a, 201b, 221a, 239b, 246b, 248a, 259b, 260a, 260b, 261b, 262a, 275b, 276a, 279b, 281b, 285b, 288a, 289a, 300a, 300b, 301a, 301b, 302a, 302b, 303b, 308a, 309a, 317a, 362a, 375a, 375b, 381b, 382a, 395b, 396a, 396b, 455b, 458a, 463b, 464a, 465a, 472b, 525b, 530a, 532a, 532b, 534b, 546b, 547a, 547b, 548b, 549a, 555b, 570b

Moses Maimoinides — see Maimoinides
Mosque of the King — III 432b
Mosul — see Mawṣil
Mother of the Book — see Book
Mother(s) of the Believers — I 56a; II 96a; III 448a, 231b; IV 22a; V 509a, 512b, 515b, 516b, 517b, 535a
Mottahedeh, R. — I **263a**
Motzki, H. — I **259a**, **300a**; III **281a**, **466a**, **516a**; IV 589a; V **455a**
Moubarac, Y. — I 208a, 330b

Mount of Mercy [Jabal al-Raḥma]	I 146a
Mount of Olives	V 184b
Mouton, J.M.	III 309b
Mozambique	III 326b
MSA	see Arabic; Islam
Muʿādh b. Jabl	I 122a; III 570a
Muʿammar (d. 215/830)	III 468a
al-Muʿawwidhatān	II 87b, 92b
Muʿāwiya	II 239b
Muʿāwiya b. Abī Sufyān (first Umayyad caliph; r. 41/661-60/680)	I 125b, 139b, 154a, 539b; II 240b, 385a, 398a, 559b, 560a; III 85a, 88a, 142b, 178b, 429a, 605b; IV 135a, 135b, 136a, 138a, 494a; V 1a, 1b, 2a, 185b, 186b; V 363b
Muʿāwiya b. Rabīʿa (pre-Islamic king)	I 153a
Muʿāwiya b. Yazīd (r. 64/683-84)	II 36b
al-Muʾayyad Dāwūd (Rasūlid ruler)	I 47a
Mubārak Shāh b. Quṭb (of Tabrīz)	III 313a
al-Mubarrad (d. 285/898)	IV 186b
Muḍar	V 364b
Mudāwara	II 295a
al-Mufīd, al-Shaykh (d. 413/1022)	II 422a; IV 594a; V 136a
Muftī of Egypt	see Egypt
Muftic, M.	III 242b
Mughals	III 323b, 559b
al-Mughammas	IV 45a, 45b
Muḥakkima	III 85a
Muhallabids	I 400a, 400b
Muḥammad	passim
Muḥammad II (last Naṣrid ruler of Granada)	III 308a
Muḥammad ʿAbd al-ʿAẓīm al-Zurqānī	V 329b
Muḥammad ʿAbduh	see ʿAbduh, M. (d. 1905)
Muḥammad Abū Zahra	see Abū Zahra, M.
Muḥammad al-Afghānistānī	see al-Afghānistānī, M.
[Shaykh] Muḥammad Aḥmad Kanʿān	IV 274b, 275a
Muḥammad Aḥmad Khalaf Allāh	see Khalaf Allāh, M.
Muḥammad Aḥmad al-Mahdī	see al-Mahdī, M. (d. 1313/1895)
Muḥammad ʿAlī Pasha	IV 268b, 270a, 270b
[Mawlāna/Maulana] Muḥammad ʿAlī (d. 1951)	II 286b; V 99a
[Shaykh] Muḥammad ʿAlī al-Ḥusaynī	IV 272a
Muḥammad Asad (d. 1992)	see Asad, M.
Muḥammad Azharī (of Palembang)	see Azharī, M.
Muḥammad b. ʿAbd al-Raḥmān b. Muḥayṣin	see Ibn Muḥayṣin, Muḥammad b. ʿAbd al-Raḥmān (d. 123/740)

Muḥammad b. Abd al-Raḥmān Qunbul	see Qunbul, Muḥammad b. ʿAbd al-Raḥmān (d. ca. 291/903-4)
Muḥammad b. ʿAbd al-Wahhāb	see IbnʿAbd al-Wahhāb, Muḥammad (d. 1206/1791)
Muḥammad b. ʿAbdallāh b. al-ʿArābī	see Ibn al-ʿArābī, Muḥammad b. ʿAbdallāh Abū Bakr (d. 543/1148)
Muḥammad b. ʿAbdallāh al-Iskāfī	see al-Iskāfī, Muḥammad b. ʿAbdallāh (d. 240/854)
Muḥammad b. Aḥmad al-Iskandarānī	see al-Iskandarānī, Muḥammad b. Aḥmad
Muḥammad b. Aḥmad b. Shannabūdh	see Ibn Shannabūdh, Abū l-Ḥasan Muḥammad b. Aḥmad b. Ayyūb (d. 328/939)
Muḥammad b. Aḥmad al-Tamīmī	see al-Tamīmī, Muḥammad b. Aḥmad (d. late fourth/tenth century)
Muḥammad b. ʿAlī al-Bāqir	see al-Bāqir, [Imām] Muḥammad (d. ca. 114/730)
Muḥammad b. Aybak b. ʿAbdallāh	i 283a; iii 601b, 602a
Muḥammad b. al-Ḥasan b. Miqsam	see Ibn Miqsam, Muḥammad b. al-Ḥasan
Muḥammad b. Ḥusayn al-Sharīf al-Raʾī (d. 406/1015)	iii 469b
Muḥammad b. Ibrāhīm b. Jaʿfar al-Nuʿmānī	see al-Nuʿmānī, Muḥammad b. Ibrāhīm b. Jaʿfar (d. 360/971)
Muḥammad b. Idrīs Abū Ḥātim al-Rāzī	see al-Rāzī, Muḥammad b. Idrīs Abū Ḥātim (d. 277/890-1)
Muḥammad b. ʿĪsā al-Tirmidhī	see al-Tirmidhī, Muḥammad b. ʿĪsā (d. 279/892)
Muḥammad b. Isḥāq	see Ibn Isḥāq, Muḥammad (d. 150/767)
Muḥammad b. Ismāʿīl al-Bukhārī	see al-Bukhārī, Abū ʿAbdallāh Muḥammad b. Ismāʿīl (d. 256/870)
Muḥammad b. Jarīr al-Ṭabarī	see al-Ṭabarī, Abū Jaʿfar Muḥammad b. Jarīr (d. 310/923)
Muḥammad b. Kaʿb al-Quraẓī	see Ibn Kaʿb al-Quraẓī, Muḥammad (d. 118-20/736-8)
Muḥammad b. Mubādir	iii 601b
Muḥammad b. Murtaḍa al-Kāshānī	see Kāshānī, Mullā Muḥsin Fayḍ (d. 1091/1680)
Muḥammad b. al-Mutawakkil Ruways	see Ruways, Abū ʿAbdallāh Muḥammad b. al-Mutawakkil al-Baṣrī (d. 238/852)
Muḥammad b. Nūḥ	i 469b

Muḥammad b. al-Sāʾib Abū-Naḍr al-Kalbī	see al-Kalbī, Muḥammad b. al-Sāʾib Abū-Naḍr (d. 146/763)
Muḥammad b. Shihāb al-Zuhrī	see Ibn Shihāb al-Zuhrī, Muḥammad (d. 124/742)
Muḥammad b. Sunqur al-Baghdādī	see Ibn Sunqur al-Baghdādī, Muḥammad
Muḥammad b. Ṣāliḥ (d. 252/866)	III 131b
Muḥammad b. Sām	III 313a
Muḥammad b. Sayf al-Dīn	III 601b
Muḥammad b. al-Waḥīd	III 601b
Muḥammad b. Yaʿqūb al-Kulaynī (d. 328/939)	II 377b
Muḥammad b. Zakariyya al-Rāzī	see al-Rāzī, Muḥammad b. Zakariyya (d. 313/925)
Muḥammad b. Zanjī (r. 594-616/1197-1219)	III 310b
Muḥammad b. Zayd al-Wāsiṭī (d. 306/918)	III 469a
[Imām] Muḥammad al-Bāqir	see al-Bāqir, [Imām] Muḥammad (d. ca. 114/730)
Muḥammad Bāqir al-Majlisī	see al-Majlisī, Muḥammad Bāqir (d. 1110/1700)
Muḥammad Daud Rahbar	see Rahbar, D.
Muḥammad al-Dhahabī	see al-Dhahabī, Shams al-Dīn Muḥammad b. Aḥmad (d. 748/1348)
Muḥammad Farīd Wajdī	II 130b; V 10a
Muḥammad Fuʾād ʿAbd al-Bāqī	see ʿAbd al-Bāqī , M.F.
Muḥammad Ḥusayn Faḍl Allāh	IV 602b; V 225a
Muḥammad Ḥusayn Haykal (d. 1376/1956)	IV 535a
Muḥammad Ḥusayn Ṭabāṭabāʾī	see Ṭabāṭabāʾī, Muḥammad Ḥusayn
[Mawlānā] Muḥammad Ilyās	V 228a
Muḥammad Ismāʿīl	I 201b
Muḥammad ʿIzza Darwaza	see Darwaza, Muḥammad ʿIzza
Muḥammad Khalafallāh	see Khalaf Allāh, Muḥammad
Muḥammad Muḥyī al-Dīn ʿAbd al-Ḥamīd	II 377a
Muḥammad Rashīd Riḍā	see Rashīd Riḍā, Muḥammad
Muḥammad al-Sabzawārī (d. ca. 1297/1880)	III 376b
[Shāh] Muḥammad Saghir	V 96b
Muḥammad Saʿīd	III 324b
Muḥammad Saʿīd Ṭabāṭabāʾī	see Ṭabāṭabāʾī, Muḥammad Ḥusayn (d. 1403/1982)
Muḥammad Shaḥrūr	see Shaḥrūr, M.
Muḥammad Shams al-Ḥaqq al-ʿAẓīmābādī (fl. 1312/1894)	II 377a, 386b
Muḥammad al-Ṭāhir Ben ʿAshūr	see Ben ʿAshūr, M.
Muḥammad Taqī Sharīʿaṭī Mazīnānī	III 587a
Muḥammad al-Tijānī al-Samāwī	V 225b

Muḥammad ʿUmar al-Bāhilī (d. 300/913) III 469a
Muḥammad ʿUmar al-Wāqidī see al-Wāqidī, Muḥammad ʿUmar (d. 207/823)
[Mawlānā] Muḥammad Zakariyya Kandhalavī I 520b
Muḥammad Zakī see Muḥammad Zakī Ibrāhīm (b. ca. 1905)
[Shaykh] Muḥammad Zakī Ibrāhīm (b. ca. 1905) II 554a, 554b, 555a
Muḥammad Zafrullah Khan V 343b
Muḥammadiyyah V 99a
al-Muḥaqqiq al-Ḥillī see al-Ḥillī, al-Muḥaqqiq (d. 676/1277)
Muḥarram I 518b; II 179b, 204a, 208a; III 411b, 413b
Muḥāsibī (d. 243/857) III 230b, 288a, 373b; V 8b
Muḥsin al-Fayḍ see Kāshanī, [Mulla] Muḥsin Fayḍ (d. 1091/1680)
Muḥyī al-Dīn Ibn al-ʿArabī see Ibn al-ʿArabī, Muḥyī al-Dīn (d. 638/1240)
Muḥyī al-Sunna (d. 516/1122) see al-Baghawī
Muir, W. I 322b; II 150b; IV 190b, 191a, 191b, 535a; V 351a
al-Muʿizz li-Dīn Allāh (r. 344-65/952-75) II 34b; IV 490a, 525a
Muʿizz b. Bādis (r. 407-54/1016-62) I 284a; III 265a
Mujāhid b. Jabr al-Makkī, Abū l-Ḥajjāj (d. 104/722) I 204b, 354a, 400a, 412a; II 103a, 103b, 105a, 105b, 116b, 147a, 150b, 190a, 347b, 389b, 392b, 457a; III 154a, 579a; IV 70a, 110a, 125a, 354a, 354b, 533a, 570a; V 16b, 63b, 322b, 495a
Mujammiʿ b. Jāriya III 439b
Mukarrib I 151b
al-Mukhtār (d. 67/687) III 33a; IV 140b
Mulayka bt. Kaʿb V 509a
Mulder, D.C. IV 484b
Müller, G. II 296b, 298a, 349a, 352a; IV 482b
Müller, F. Max V 351b
Multān III 314b
Mumtāz I 265a
Mumtaz ʿAli V 536a, 536b, 537a, 539a
Mumtāz Maḥall III 324a, 324b
al-Munajjid, Ṣ. III 256a
Mundhir I 308b
Munkar I 90a, 90b, 206a; III 141b; IV 460a; V 499b
al-Muntaṣir II 28a
al-Muqaddasī I 125b, 126a

Muqātil b. Ḥayyān (d. 135/753) II 106b
Muqātil b. Sulaymān al-Balkhī, Abū l-Ḥasan (d. 150/767) I 106a, 114b, 203b, 205a, 266b, 270b, 399a; II 101a, 103b, 106b, 107a, 107b, 109a, 112a, 114a, 146a, 147a, 147b, 148a, 231a, 347b, 389b, 392a, 392b, 509a, 513a, 516a; III 83a, 117a, 142b, 282a, 282b, 438b, 439a, 522a, 579a; IV 14b, 54a, 127b, 130b, 351a, 460b, 533a; V 36a, 39b, 140a, 321b, 322a, 323b, 333a, 435b, 440a, 491a
Muqaṭṭam I 293b
al-Muqawqis II 11a
Muqtadir (r. 295-320/908-32) II 421a
Murād III (r. 982-1003/1574-95) III 320b; IV 268a
Muradabad I 202b
Muranyi, M. II 108a
al-Muraqqish (poet) III 588b
Murata, S. I 89b; V 388a
Murayghān IV 45b
Murdār (d. 226/821) IV 23b
Murjiʾīs/Murjiʾites [Murjiʾa] I 517b, 518a; II 170a; III 469b; IV 72b; V 23b, 24a, 24b, 504b
[Mt.] Murrān I 271a
al-Murrī, Ṣāliḥ (d. ca. 172/788-9) IV 386b
al-Murtaḍa, al-Sharīf (d. 436/1044) II 533a; III 470b; IV 594a; V 136a
Mūsā see Moses
Mūsā b. Manassa b. Yūsuf I 544b
Mūsā b. Masʿūd al-Nahdī al-Baṣrī see Abū Ḥudhayfa (d. 220/835)
Mūsā b. Sayyār al-Aswārī IV 59a
Mūsā b. ʿUbayd Allāh b. Khāqān al-Baghdādī (d. 325/936) III 606b
Mūsā b. ʿUqba al-Asadī (d. 141/758) II 384b; IV 324b, 533a; V 32a, 32b, 42a, 47b
Mūsā b. Yaʿqūb al-Maʾmūn II 41a
Muṣʿab b. ʿUmayr II 20a; V 46b
al-Musāwī, Ḥ (Lebanese leader) II 454b
Musaylima V 67b
Musaylima b. Thumāma b. Kabīr b. Ḥabīb b. al-Ḥārith b. ʿAbd al-Ḥārith [Musaylima b. Ḥabīb al-Kadhdhāb] I 121a, 544a; II 384b, 429a, 530a, 530b, 534b; III 381a, **460b**, 461a, 461b, 462a, 462b, 463a; IV 22b, 23a, 295b; V 45a, 59a, 79a
Musil, A. I 148b
Muslim(s) passim; see Islam

Muslim b. al-Ḥajjāj (d. 261/875) — I 391b; II 110b, 222b, 270b, 377a; III 392a; IV 371a, 489a; V 278a, 330a, 360b, 413a, 471b
Muslim b. Yasār (d. 101/719) — III 154a
Mustaḍʿafūn Foundation — III 582a
Muṣṭafā — II 40b
Muṣṭafā II (r. 1106-15/1695-1703) — III 321a
Mustafa Özcan Güneşdoğdu — III 345a
[Banū l-] Muṣṭaliq — I 56b; II 391b; V 508a, 520a
al-Mustaʿṣimī — I 282b
MUT — see Indonesia
Muʾta — I 266a; II 148b, 240a; V 185a, 185b
Mutafarriqa, I. — IV 268a
[Ayatollah] Muṭahharī — III 286a
Mutalammis — III 589a, 589b
al-Mutanabbī, Abū l-Ṭayyib Aḥmad b. al-Ḥusayn (d. 354/965) — IV 23a, 57b; V 416b
al-Muʿtaṣim (caliph; r. 218-27/833-42) — I 469b; II 538b, 560b; III 558a
al-Mutawakkil (mosque) — III 431a
al-Mutawakkil (r. 232-47/847-61) — I 469a; II 28a, 538b; III 303b
Mutawakkil II (ʿAbd al-ʿAzīz al-Mustaʿīn; d. 903/1497) — II 232a
Muʿtazila/Muʿtazilī(s) — I 74a, 104b, 105a, 106a, 106b, 115b, 117b, 206a, 225b, 275a, 418a, 467b, 468b, 469a, 470a, 484b; II 52b, 53a, 54a, 111a, 114a, 114b, 115a, 115b, 116a, 117b, 160b, 170b, 171a, 171b, 270b, 271a, 286a, 337b, 345b, 413a, 418b, 421a, 421b, 470b, 506a, 531b, 532b, 533b, 534a, 535a, 539a; III 72b, 73a, 87b, 88a, 91a, 149a, 352b, **466b**, 467a, 467b, 468a, 469a, 469b; IV 23b, 71b, 76b, 79b, 81a, 83b, 84a, 84b, 86b, 89a, 123a, 123b, 179a, 313b, 365a, 385b, 432b, 433a, 459a, 460b; V 12b, 16b, 24a, 24b, 111b, 135b, 145b, 404a, 485a
  Baṣran — II 534b; III 468b
  Zaydī — II 533a
Muʿṭim b. ʿAdī — II 20a
al-Muṭṭalib — I 290b; V 508a
Muwaffaq al-Dīn b. Qudāma — see Ibn Qudāma, Muwaffaq al-Dīn (d. 620/1223)
al-Muwaḥḥidūn — see Almohad(s)

Muẓaffar al-Dīn Kokbürü (brother-in-law of Saladin) II 206a, 206b
Muzayna (tribe) II 16a
al-Muzdalifa I 319b; II 205a; IV 96a, 96b, 281b, 515b
Mzāb III 86b
von Mžik, H. V 43a

N

Nabatean (language) I 137b, 138a, 138b, 150a, 490a; II 231a, 231b, 544a
Nabatean(s) I 150b, 152b, 156a, 308a; II 239a, 427b; III 79b; V 82a, 92a, 254a
Nabhan II 204b
Nābigha V 38b
Nablus III 57a; IV 524a, 525a
Nabū V 86b
Nadīm II 37a
[Banū l-] Naḍīr I 251b, 320a, 324b, 409a; II 148b, 149a, 150b, 151a, 262b, 459b, 298b, 469b; III 29a, 29b, 456b, **498a**, 498b, 499a, 579b; IV 41b, 42a, 307b, 323b, 324a, 333b, 406a, 415a; V 43a, 44b, 175b, 292a, 508b
al-Naḍr b. al-Ḥarith II 517a; III 518a; IV 323a
Nadwat al-ʿUlamaʾ [Nahdlatul Ulama] V 212b, 213b, 214a, 214b
Nāfiʿ b. ʿAbd al-Raḥmān (d. 169/785) I 334a; IV 356b 357a, 357b, 358a, 358b, 359a, 359b, 360b, 373a, 389a, 389b, 391b, 392a
Nāfiʿ b. al-Azraq III 86b; IV 139a; V 333a
Nag Hammadi I 488b
Nagel, Michael (d. 1788) I 523b; IV 250b; V 502b
Nagel, T. V **275b**
al-Naḥḥās, Abū Jaʿfar Aḥmad b. Muḥammad (d. 338/950) II 109b, 378a; IV 533b
Nahrawān III 85a; IV 328a
  Battle of III 85b
Nāḥūr III 242a
Nāʾila IV 519a; V 90b
Najadāt I 540a; III 86b
Najaf V 215b, 225a
al-Najāshī see Negus
Najd I 121a, 121b, 529b; II 211a, 294b, 295a; IV 254a
Najda b. ʿĀmir III 86b

al-Najjār, [Shaykh] ʿAlī Muḥammad iv 272b
Najm al-Dīn Dāya [al-]Rāzī (d. 654/1256) ii 120a; v 158b
Najm al-Dīn Kubrā see Kubrā, Najm al-Dīn (d. 617-18/1220-1)
Najm al-Dīn al-Nasafī (d. 537/1142) ii 171b
Najm al-Dīn al-Ṭūfī (d. 716/1316) i 514a; iv 115b
Najrān i 115b, 154a, 307b, 309b, 390a, 399b, 466a; ii 148a, 193a; iii 405b, 406a, **500a**, 500b, 501a, 571b; iv 44a, 352b, 406b, 410a, 411a, 411b, 412b, 578a; v 86b, 88a, 88b, 92a, 397a, 397b, 562a, 565a
 Christians of iv 257b, 411b; v 389b
 Kaʿbat iii 500a
Najrānites iii 500a, 501a, 500b
al-Nakhaʿī i 412a
Nakhla i 461a; ii 149a; iii 590b
al-Nakhjuwānī (d. 920/1514) ii 120b
Nakīr i 90a, 90b, 206a; iii 141b; iv 460a; v 499b
Nallino, C.A. iv 248a; v 297a
Nana Asmaʾu iv 177b
Nāmūs ii 514a; iii **515**
Nanji, A. i **70a**
Napoleon iv 268b
Napoleon III i 198b
Naqshbandiyya (Ṣūfī order) iii 324b
Naqqāsh iii 503b
Nasafī, ʿAbdallāh b. Aḥmad b. Maḥmūd (d. 710/1310) i 205a; iv 496b; v 353a, 462a
al-Nasāʾī, Aḥmad b. Shuʿayb (d. 303/915) ii 22b; ii 110b, 334a, 377a, 389b; iii 392a; iv 232a, 371a; v 330a, 330b
Nashshān (al-Jawf) v 86a
Nashī al-Akbar (d. 239/906) iv 23a
Nashwān al-Ḥimyarī (d. 573/1178) v 397b
Nāṣif, Ḥanafī iv 272a
al-Nasīmī, Maḥmūd Nāẓim iii 366a, 366b
Nāṣir al-Dīn al-Bayḍāwī see al-Bayḍāwī, Nāṣir al-Dīn (d. 716/1315-16)
al-Nāṣir lil-Ḥaqq al-Uṭrūsh (d. 304/917) iv 602b
Nāṣir-i Khusraw (d. ca. 470/1077) i 126a; iv 55b, 61a, 63b
Nāṣir Muḥammad (Mamlūk sultan) ii 35a, 312a; iii 601b
Nasr (pre-Islamic male deity) i 404a; ii 317b, 474a, 483a; v 92a, 92b

Nasr, S.H. ɪᴠ 557a
Naṣr b. ʿĀṣim (d. 89/707) ɪ 140b; ɪɪɪ 606a
Naṣr Ḥāmid Abū Zayd see Abu Zayd, N.
Naṣrids ɪɪɪ 308a, 559a
Nasser, Gamal Abdel (Egypt; r. 1956-70) ɪɪɪ 285b; ɪᴠ 145b
Nasser D. Khalili Collection of Islamic Art ɪɪɪ 264b, 268b, 301a, 305b, 315a, 318a, 322a, 324b, 326a, 328a
Nassau Lees, W. ɪᴠ 266a
Naṣṭūr/Nasṭūrā ɪɪ 515a, 515b; ɪᴠ 236a, 236b; see also Baḥīrā
Nathan ɪᴠ 315b
Nation of Islam see Islam
Nativity ɪɪɪ 538a
Nau, M. ɪᴠ 248b
Nawas, J. ɪ **197a**, **505b**; ɪɪ **539a**; ɪᴠ **54b**; ᴠ **363b**
al-Nawawī (d. 676/1277) ɪᴠ 489a, 492a, 494b, 495a
al-Nawawī Jāwī, Muḥammad ᴠ 98b
Nawdh (land of) ɪ 271a
Mount ɪ 271a
Nawf al-Bikālī ɪɪɪ 142b
[Banū] Nawfal ɪ 290b; ɪɪ 20a
Nayereh Tohidi see Tohidi, N.
Nayrīz ɪɪɪ 433a
Nazarenes see Nazoreans
Nazareth [al-Nāṣira] ɪ 310b, 389b
Naẓīr Aḥmad (1831-1912) ɪɪɪ 223b
Naẓira Zayn al-Dīn ɪɪ 200b
Nazoreans ɪ 310b, 311a, 311b, 312a, 313a, 313b, 314a
al-Naẓẓām, Abū Isḥāq Ibrāhīm b. Sayyār (d. ca. 221/835) ɪɪ 532a, 532b, 533a, 533b; ɪɪɪ 468b; ɪᴠ 74a, 477b; ᴠ 8b
Near East ɪ 102a, 268a, 286a, 307b, 370b, 399b, 433b, 508b; ɪɪ 105b, 267a, 287a, 429a, 432b, 433a, 434b, 436b, 566a; ɪɪɪ 45b, 129a, 315b, 435b; ɪᴠ 128a, 204b, 209b, 458a; ᴠ 129b, 236b, 493b, 542a
Nebes ɪɪ 351b
Nebuchadnezzar ɪ 108b, 195b; ɪɪɪ 4a, 6a, 52a, 52b; ɪᴠ 44a; ᴠ 455b
Nedim ᴠ 394a
Nedjar ɪɪ 350a
Negev ɪ 150a, 155a; ᴠ 366b

Negus [al-Najāshī]	I 4b, 21a, 320a; II 19a; III 8a; IV 411a; V 44a, 47b
Nelson, K.	IV 380b, 381b, 392b
Neoplatonism	I 85a; IV 82b; V 81a
Neoplatonists	IV 74b, 80b, 82b, 83a, 87b, 88a
Nero	I 107b, 109b
Nerreter, D.	V 345b, 347a
Nesin, A.	V 394b
Nestorian(s)	see Christian(s)
Nestorius	V 370b; see also Christians
[The] Netherlands	V 216b, 346b
Netton, I.R.	III **185b**, **535b**
Neuwirth, A.	I 249a, **457b**; II **143b**, 191a, 250b, 251a, 251b, 252a, 253a, 255a, 260b, **264b**, **312b**, 356a; III 196a, 212b, **496b**; IV 7b, 199b, 204b, **347b**, **475b**; V **108a**, **176b**, 299a, **429a**
Neuwirth, K.	II 191a; III 128b; V 425b
Nevo, Y.	I 155a
New Testament	see Testament
New Year	II 181b; IV 340a
New Zealand	I 385b
Newby, G.	I **158b**, **194b**, **518a**; II **244a**, **293b**
Newton, I.	V 71a
Niasse, [Shaykh] Ibrāhīm	I 33b; III 345a
Nicea [Iznīq]	I 308a; III 434b
Second Council of	II 474a
Nicene Creed	II 326b, 329b
Nicholas of Cusa (Nicolaus Cusanus; d. 1464)	IV 236b, 242b, 243a, 245b; V 371b
Nicolson, R.	III 111a, 195b, 222b; V 351b
Nietzsche, F.	I 427a
Nigeria	I 33a; III 327b, 344b; IV 170a, 177b; V 209a, 211b
Night of Power/Destiny/Divine Decree [*laylat al-qadr*]	II 84a, 89a, 181b, 182b, 183a, 216a, 268b, 269b, 381b, 443b; III 222a, 328a, 417b, **537b**; IV 34a; V 272a, 342b, 431b, 475b
Niḥāwand	II 39b, 560a
Niketas of Byzantium	IV 237b, 238a; V 344a
Nikolajev, K.	V 349b
Nile [al-Yamm]	I 29b, 150a, 158a, 345b; II 10b, 83a, 303b, 304a; IV 68a; V 51b, 52a, 96b, 361a, 463b, 466b
Nilometer [*miqyās al-nīl*]	III 303b

Nimrod [Namrūd] I 8b, 192a, 533a; II 279a; III 93a, 224b, 389a, 494b, 522a, 529b, **539a**, 539b; IV 78a, 211a; V 63b, 95b
Nineveh I 195b, 265b; II 514a; III 53a, 53b, 54a, 54b
People of III 207b
Nīsābūr see Nīshāpūr
al-Nīsābūrī, Abū l-Qāsim al-Ḥasan b. Muḥammad b. Ḥabīb (d. 404-6/1014-16) I 70b, 411a; II 57a, 64b; IV 304b, 549b; V 324b, 330b
Nīsābūrian(s) V 325a
Nīshāpūr II 111b, 112b; III 126a, 300b; V 139a, 143b, 325a
Nisisbis IV 74a
Nissel, Johann Georg (d. 1662) IV 246b
Niu Jie (mosque on) III 315a
Niẓām al-Dīn al-Ḥasan b. Muḥammad b. al-Ḥusayn al-Nīsābūrī al-Aʿraj (d. after 730/1329) II 113a; V 330a
[Mulla] Nizam al-Din Muḥammad (d. 1748) V 212a
Niẓām al-Mulk (vizier to the Saljūq sultans; d. 485/1092) III 305a, 433a; V 210b
Niẓāmī (d. 605/1209) I 62a; III 221b; IV 55b, 60a, 61a, 61b; V 122b
Niẓāmiyya IV 58a
Noah [Nūḥ] I 21b, 38b, 59b, 95b, 146b, 147a, 157b, 158a, 160b, 195a, 222a, 236b, 245a, 245b, 261b, 296b, 319a, 379b, 380b, 398b, 437a, 464b, 492a, 511a, 512b, 513a, 518b, 519a, 521b, 532a, 536b, 553b; II 10b, 64a, 145b, 154a, 199b, 212b, 219a, 231a, 259b, 293a, 293b, 318a, 324b, 338a, 339a, 372b, 418a, 423b, 433a, 434a, 434b, 436a, 437a, 439a, 441a, 449b, 462b, 483a, 488a, 504b, 509a, 510b, 544b, 558a; III 2a, 13a, 17a, 18a, 18b, 50a, 63b, 68b, 69a, 118a, 119a, 190a, 200b, 212b, 222a, 231b, 232a, 253b, 289b, 381a, 381b, 393a, 400b, 441a, 441b, 444a, 444b, 479b, 485b, 486a, 486b, 487a, 488a, 514b, 518b, 519a, 519b, 520b, 521a, 521b, 522a, 525b, 536b, 540a, 540b, 541a, 541b, 542a, 542b, 543a, 543b, 549b,

	550b, 567b; IV 6b, 21a, 25b, 32b, 34a, 50b, 68a, 112b, 130b, 160a, 213b, 217a, 218b, 223b, 263b, 291a, 292a, 292b, 293b, 294a, 297b, 302b, 303a, 303b, 304a, 307b, 308a, 309a, 319a, 320a, 321a, 337a, 352b, 425b, 438b, 439b, 523b, 559b, 577a, 592a, 604a; V 5b, 16a, 45b, 92a, 104a, 109b, 126b, 130b, 171b, 262a, 285b, 302a, 313b, 373a, 373b, 430a, 464b, 482a, 534b, 549a, 551b
Ark of	III 521b; IV 581a, 592a; V 373a
Mosque of	III 69a
People of	I 21b; II 474a; III 78a, 522a, 583a; IV 258a, 259a; IV 421a, 605b; V 252b, 261b, 317b, 318a, 389a, 460b, 461a
Noble Drew Ali	see Drew Ali, Noble
Noja, S.	IV 204a
Nöldeke, T.	I 5a, 11a, 19b, 112a, 138a, 208a, 248b, 270b, 322b, 323b, 325b, 331a, 331b, 350b, 351b, 372a, 377b, 400a, 417b, 420b, 531a; II 180a, 191a, 235a, 250a, 250b, 251a, 255a, 255b, 262a, 350a, 350b, 351a, 352b, 354b, 355b, 358a, 359a, 360a, 361a, 361b, 363a, 363b, 366b, 367a, 367b, 496b, 539b; III 7b, 110b, 129a, 131b, 195b, 475a, 476a, 480a; IV 188a, 188b, 189a, 189b, 190b, 191b, 193b, 194b; V 239b, 240a, 297b, 298a, 350a, 350b, 351a, 351b, 353a
North America	see America
Noth, A.	II 296b
NU	see Nadwat al-ʿUlamaʾ
Nubāta b. Ḥanẓala	IV 51b
Nubian	III 242a
[al-Qāḍī] al-Nuʿmān (d. 363/974)	IV 490a, 490b, 602b
Nuʿmān b. Mundhir	I 308b, 309a
al-Nuʿmānī, Muḥammad b. Ibrāhīm b. Jaʿfar (d. 360/971)	II 117a, 396b; IV 602a
[General] Numeiri	I 35a
Nūn	III 8b

Nuovo — IV 265a, 267b
Nūr al-Dīn al-Ṣābūnī al-Bukhārī — see al-Bukhārī, Nūr al-Dīn al-Ṣābūnī (d. 580/1184)
Nūr al-Dīn Zanjī — III 309a
Nurcholish Madjid — IV 149b
Nurculuk — V 216b
Nuremberg — V 346a
al-Nūrī, Abū l-Ḥusayn (d. 295/907) — III 230b, V 140b, 141a
Nūrī al-Ṭabarsī, Ḥusayn Taqī (d. 1320/1902) — IV 595a, 595b
Nursi, Said (d. 1960) — IV 555a; V 216b
Nurosmaniye Library — III 598a
Nuṣayrīs — IV 597b, 598a
Nuṣrat bt. Muḥammad Amīn — see Banū-yi Iṣfahānī (d. 1403/1982)
al-Nuwayhī, M. — I 242a
Nuwayrī (d. 733/1333) — II 338b
Nwyia, P. — V 97b, 140a, 140b, 141a

O

O'Connor, K.M. — I **79a**; IV **181a**
Occultation
  Major — II 117a; IV 602a
  Minor — II 117a
Og [ʿŪj b. ʿAnaq] — II 293b; III 543a
Ölceytü — see Öljeytü
Old Testament — see Testament; Bible
Öljeytü (r. 703-16/1304-16) — I 283a; II 35a; III 311a, 559a
Oman [ʿUmān] — I 22a, 121a, 127b, 495b; II 503b; III 86a, 87a, 140a
Omar ibn Said (d. ca. 1864) — I 30a
Omdurman — III 328a
Orientalist(s) — III 242b, 342a; IV 197b, 249a, 249b, 275b; V 48a
Origen (of Alexandria) — I 104a, 308a
Orion — V 51b
Orthodox Church — IV 71a
Ortiz de la Puebla, V. — V 349b
Ory, S. — I **285b**; III 255b
O'Shaughnessy, T. — I 506b, 508b; IV 196b, 197a
[Mulla] Osman Ismail — III 607a; IV 251a
Ottoman(s) — II 569b; III 272a, 308a, 317a, 317b, 318b, 319b, 321a, 341b, 370b, 434a, 435b, 598b; IV 149a, 267b, 268b, 271b, 361a; V 60a
Ovid — V 52a

Owens, J. III 124a
Oxford IV 249a

P

Padua IV 247a
Padwick II 81b
Pahlavi/Pahlevi (language) I 45b; II 486b; III 223b
Paikuli I 208a
Pakistan I 39b, 50b, 69b; II 15a; III 314a, 365b; IV 273b, 274a; V 94a, 97a, 209a, 211a, 211b, 212a, 212b, 343a, 538b
Palaiologues IV 238a
Palermo III 263a, 263b, 596b, 597a
Palestine I 9a, 43a, 110b, 149a, 150a, 155a, 169a, 171a, 173b, 195b, 214a, 265b, 307b, 308a, 335b, 532b, 557a; II 155b, 343a, 457b, 463b; III 5a, 5b, 52a, 286a, 299a, 368b, 390a, 405a; IV 27a, 253b; V 28b, 107a, 127a, 176a, 185a, 186a, 222b, 263a, 305a, 310a, 564b
Palestinian Authority/State I 128a
Palestinians III 241a
Palmer, E.H. V 351b
Palmyrenians V 88b
Panjabi (language) V 96a
Paraclete III 504a
  Johannine IV 407b
Paret, R. I 36a, 112b, 210b, 288a, 323a, 399a, 417b; II 191a, 493a; III 189a; IV **12a**, 18a, 49b, 52b, 101b, 199a, 477b; V 247a, 296a, 297a, 298a, 299a; V 352b, 353a, 353b, 354a, 398a, 424b
Paris II 137a
Parkinson, D. I 133a, 134a
Parr, P. II 428a
Parrinder, G. IV 195b
Parry, M. II 254a
Parsees V 56a
Parson, T. I 374b
Pashto (language) I 136a
Passover [Pesach] II 184b; III 411a; IV 338a, 338b,

339a, 339b, 340a, 345a, 345b, 346a, 347a
Paton, A.A. IV 269b, 270a
[St.] Paul I 118a, 118b, 307b, 310b, 488a; II 499a; IV 11a; V 47b, 186a
Paul of Antioch (Melkite bishop) V 371b
Paulicians II 475a
Pauthier, J.P.G. V 349b
Pavel I (czar) IV 265b
Pedro (de) Pascual (archbishop of Jaen; d. 1300) IV 240b, 243a
Pellat, C. III 147a
Pennsylvania, University of V 69b
Penrice, J. I 487b; IV 194a; V 296b
Pentakes, G.I. V 351a
Pentateuch I 22b, 367a, 410b, 465a; II 343a; III 248a; IV 37b, 61b; V 260a, 260b, 300b, 308b
People(s) of see below the respective names
Percival David Foundation III 325b
Perho, I. III **366b**
Persia I 48a, 61b, 62a, 173b, 266b, 314a; II 105b, 223a, 296a; III 221b, 275a, 369a, 461b, 596a; IV 44a, 57a, 57b, 329a, 407b, 408a, 413b; V 34a, 45a, 391a
  Academy of Language IV 57a
  Empire I 211a; II 399b; III 91a
  Gulf [Baḥr Fāris] I 155a, 203b, 309a; IV 411b; V 86b
  Language I 136a, 142b, 483a, 490a, 520a; II 90a, 146b, 147b, 229b, 230b, 231a, 231b, 286b, 287a, 544a; III 117b, 223b, 258b, 319a, 325a; IV 56a, 56b, 57b, 58a, 58b, 59b, 62a, 63a, 172b, 266a, 602b; V 94a, 131a, 148b, 188a, 296b, 323b, 346b, 349b, 393a
  Middle Persian IV 56b
Persian(s) I 108a, 265b, 266a, 266b, 267a, 267b, 268a, 268b, 308b, 309a, 487b; II 147a, 147b, 230b, 232a, 240a, 281a, 296b, 438b, 490a; III 405b, 542a, 543a; IV 58a, 59a, 59b, 313a, 257b; V 47a, 80a,

286a, 341a; see also Sasanian(s)/Sasanid(s)
Pesach — see Passover
Peter (apostle of Jesus) — V 189a
Peter Alphonsi (Petrus Alphonsi, Rabbi Moses Sephardi, d. after 1130) — IV 238b, 243b
Peter the Great (czar) — V 347b
Peter the Venerable (abbot of Cluny; d. 1156) — IV 236b, 238b, 239a, 559a; V 344b
Peters, E. — IV 535a; V 49a, 315a
Peters, R. — I **252b**
Peterson, D. — I **480a**; II **245a**, **341b**; III **380a**
Petra — I 150b; III 79b
Petrus Alphonsi — see Peter Alphonsi
Petrus de Pennis — IV 243b
Pharaoh [Firʿawn] — I 1a, 59a, 158a, 159a, 160a, 160b, 161a, 162b, 163a, 190a, 219a, 255a, 294b, 295b, 297a, 302a, 304a, 304b, 306b, 329b, 338b, 340b, 341a, 364a, 365b, 369a, 395b, 405a, 478a, 488a, 489a, 500b, 501b, 511b, 518b, 519a, 532a, 532b, 533b, 536b, 537a, 548b, 552a, 553b; II 24a, 66a,162a, 174a, 182a, 184a, 193b, 199a, 204a, 212b, 241b, 259b, 305b, 319a, 334a, 338a, 338b, 339a, 399a, 399b, 481a, 504b, 541b, 542a, 542b, 558b; III 56a, 81a, 92a, 93a, 104b, 190a, 200b, 211b, 289b, 383b, 393b, 394a, 394b, 420a, 420b, 421b, 422a, 423a, 423b, 425a, 425b, 485b, 487b, 489b, 495b, 496a, 518b, 519a, 520b, 521b, 522a, 539b, 552b, 583a, 583b; IV 49b, **66b**, 67a, 67b, 68a, 105b, 106a, 112b, 131a, 132a, 147a, 160a, 210b, 211a, 225a, 263b, 276b, 286a, 296b, 307b, 309a, 320a, 340b, 348b, 352b, 421b, 452a, 454a, 508a, 509a, 523b, 524a, 592a; V 4b, 6a, 53b, 171a, 171b, 236b, 239b, 252b, 281b, 285b, 317b, 318a, 363a, 375a, 377a, 377b, 389a, 396a,

396b, 416a, 463b, 464b, 468a, 472b, 530a, 532a, 532b, 534a, 553a
Magicians of — I 255a, 488a, 500b; III 211b, 212a, 217a, 249b, 425a, 444b; V 201b
Pharisees — IV 27b
Philippines — II 454b
Philistines — I 496b; II 145b, 335a, 407b, 416a, 417b, 432b, 434b, 435b, 439a; IV 315b, 529a
Philo of Alexandria — I 104a; V 259a, 259b, 260a, 260b, 262b, 266a
Philonenko, M. — III 45a; V 398a
Phocas — I 265b
Pickthall, M. — I 36b, 200a, 391b; II 369b; III 110a, 113b, 189a, 196a, 198b; IV 48a, 566a; V 343a, 354a, 539b
Pietruschka, U. — I **217b**; V **236b**
Pines, S. — IV 406b
Pinhas — II 156b
Pirenne, J. — V 90a
[Pope] Pius II — IV 243a
[Pope] Pius IX — I 198b
Place of Abraham — see Abraham
Plato — III 386b; IV 74b, 581a
Platonist(s) — I 477b
Pleiades (Thurayya) — III 415b; IV 108b
Pleistocene — I 43a
Plessner, M. — III 538a
Pliny (the Elder) — I 499b; II 427a; IV 586a; V 254a
Plotinus — I 104a; IV 80b, 82b, 83b
Plutarch — V 236b
Pococke, Edward (d. 1691) — IV 188a, 249a; V 348a
Poimandres — II 485b
Poonawala, I.K. — IV 490b
Porter, V. — II **41a**
Possessor of the Two Horns [Dhū l-Qarnayn] — I 189a, 295b; II 332a, 332b, 437a; III 81b, 383a, 441b, 520a, 537a; IV 61b, 302a, 540b; V 375b; see also Alexander
Postel, Guillaume (d. 1581) — IV 245a
Pos(t)nikov, P.V. — V 347b
Potiphar — I 19b, 28a, 163a, 255b, 533a; II 335b, 547a; III 181b, 222b, 229b, 492a; IV 62a, 584b; V 82b, 96a

Powers, D. II 524a, 524b, 525a, **526a**; III 98a, 98b, 99a
PPIM see Islam
Preserved Tablet [*lawḥ mahfūẓ*] see Tablet
Pretzl, O. I 322b, 334a, 350b, 417b; IV 189a, 189b, 392b
Prideux, H. V 347a
Princeton University Library IV 265b
Procházka, S. V 297a
Proclus IV 82b
Procopius I 4a, 20b
Procyon V 51b
Progressive Muslims Union (United States) see Islam
Prometheus I 270b; III 242a
Promised Land I 303b, 304b, 305a
Prophet passim
 Companions of the see Companions of the Prophet
 Family of the [*ahl al-bayt*] see House, People of the
Proudfoot, W. IV 269a, 271b, 275b
Psalms [*zabūr/zubur*] I 228b; III 4a, 523b; IV 128a, 304b, **314a**, 314b, 315a, 316b, 317a, 317b, 438b, 474b, 537a, 561a; V 152a, 170b, 171a, 301b, 320b
Psalters V 208b
PSW see Islam
Ptolemy II 295b, 298b; III 337b; IV 586a; V 254a
Punjab I 50a; V 97a, 212b
Punjabi (language) V 342a
Pustaka Nasional V 100a
Pythagoras IV 68b

Q

Qadarī(s) I 74b; II 270b, 271a, 345b; III 33a, 179a, 420b, 425b; IV 72b, 84a; V 504b
al-Qāḍī, W. see Kadi, W.
al-Qāḍī, ʿA. IV 272b
al-Qāḍī, N. IV 274a
al-Qāḍī ʿAbd al-Jabbār see ʿAbd al-Jabbār b. Aḥmad al-Asadābādi al-Qāḍī al-Hamadhānī (d. 414-15/1025)
Qāḍī Aḥmad III 268a
al-Qādir (r. 381-422/991-1031) I 482a; V 147b
 Qādirī Creed [*al-iʿtiqād al-qādirī*] I 482a

al-Qādisiyya ii 560a; v 47a
Qadmān v 86b
[Mt.] Qāf i 62b; ii 95a
Qaḥṭān i 228b; iii 119a
Qalʿat Simʿān i 308b, 336a
al-Qalīs (church) i 155a
al-Qalqashandī (d. 821/1418) i 136a, 280a; ii 36a, 36b, 498a; iv 477b, 479a, 481a, 481b
Qālūn, ʿĪsā b. Minā (d. ca. 220/835) iv 359b, 360b, 390a, 391b
Qānīʾ v 562b
Qarā Memi iii 598b, 599a
al-Qaraḍāwī, Yūsuf ii 281b; iii 176a; iv 144a, 144b, 414b; v 26a, 227a
Qarāḥiṣārī, Aḥmad iii 320b, 321a, 599b
Qarawiyyīn University v 211a
Qardū i 147a; iii 68b
Qarmāṭīs i 540b; ii 560b
Qarmathian Qurʾān iii 598a
Qārūn see Korah
Qaryat al-Fāʾw i 148b, 152b, 156a; v 88a
Qaryat Thamānīn iii 69a
Qaṣba iii 597b
al-Qāshānī, ʿAbd al-Razzāq Kamāl al-Dīn (pseudo Ibn al-ʿArabī; d. 730-1/1329-30) iv 349b, 354b, 355a, 460b; v 156b, 157a, 157b, 158a, 382b, 383a
al-Qāshānī, Muḥammad ʿAlī iv 266a
Qāsim (son of the Prophet and Khadīja) v 507b
[Imām] al-Qāsim b. Ibrāhīm Rassī (d. 246/860) i 116b, 118a; ii 533a; iv 23a, 602b; v 8b, 371b
Qāsim b. Khalīl al-Dimashqī see al-Dimashqī, Qāsim b. Khalīl
al-Qāsimī, Muḥammad Jamāl al-Dīn iii 242b; v 329b; v 536b
al-Qaṣr iv 361a
Qaṣr al-Ḥallābāt iii 432b
Qaṣr al-Ḥamrāʾ i 152b
Qaṣr al-Ḥayr al-Sharqī iii 430b
[Mt.] Qāsyūn i 271a, 293b
Qatabān i 152a; iv 585b; v 85b, 88a, 91a, 91b, 92b, 563a
Qatāda b. Diʿāma al-Sadūsī (d. 117-18/735) i 23b, 257a, 322a, 341a, 412a; ii 103a, 108a, 190a, 387b, 389b, 393b; iii 89a, 142a, 154b, 517b; iv 100b, 387a, 407b, 533a; v 165b
Qaṭar i 127b; iv 273b; v 562a
Qaṭarī b. al-Fujāʾa see Ibn al-Fujāʾa, Qaṭarī
[Banū] Qayla ii 15a
[Banū] Qaynuqāʿ i 150a, 325a; ii 148b, 298b; iii 29a,

29b, 498a, 579b; IV 41b, 227a, **323a**, 323b, 324a, 324b, 333b, 406a; V 43a, 44b

Qayrawān (Tunisia) I 284a; II 40b, 110a, 116b; III 262a, 264a, 265a, 272b, 430b, 432a, 432b, 596a; V 305a

  Great Mosque of III 298a, 428b, 429b, 431a, 599b

al-Qayrawānī (d. 385/996) IV 169b; V 471b

Qays I 529b; V 367a

Qays ʿAyalān IV 51b

Qazvīn [Qazwīn] III 305a

al-Qazwīnī (d. 739/1338) IV 479a

al-Qazwīnī, Abū Yūsuf (d. 488/1095) II 115a

al-Qazwīnī, Zakariyyā b. Muḥammad (d. 682/1283) III 287b, 389a

Qinnesrin IV 74a

al-Qirqisānī, Yaʿqūb V 309a

Qiṭmīr III 321b, 327a; IV 351b

Qlaaji, M. I 168a

Qom/Qumm V 215a, 225a, 225b

Qubāʾ II 20b, 299a; III 439a, 439b; IV 516a

  Mosque of I 342b

Qubbat al-Ṣakhra see Dome of the Rock

Qudāma b. Jaʿfar (d. 337/948) IV 143b

Quedlinburg V 349a

al-Quff IV 323a

al-Qummī, Abū l-Ḥasan ʿAlī b. Ibrāhīm (d. 328/939) I 57a, 268a; II 117a, 147a, 147b; III 65b; IV 591b, 602a, 603a; V 442a

Qumran[Qumrān] IV 195a; V 398a, 398b

  Caves II 485b

  Scrolls II 485b

al-Qūnawī, Ṣadr al-Dīn (d. 673/1274) I 27b; II 119b; III 230b; V 156a

Qunbul, Muḥammad b. ʿAbd al-Raḥmān (d. ca. 291/903-4) IV 359b, 390a

Qurā I 154b

  Wādī I 154b; II 150a; IV 334a

Qurʾān passim

  Kūfic IV 265b

  Ur- I 334b

Quraysh / Qurashī(s) / Qurayshite(s) I 20b, 38b, 63a, 140b, 144b, 256b, 290b, 291a, 333a, 381a, 382a, 406b, 529b, 531b; II 15a, 15b, 17b, 19a, 19b, 20a, 20b, 87b, 147b, 149a, 149b, 176a, 227a, 296b, 297a, 337b, 357a, 384b, 397b, 448a, 464a, 466a, 466b,

489b, 490a, 490b, 513a, 516a, 528a; III 4a, 32a, 35a, 59a, 80a, 88a, 95b, 112a, 112b, 113a, 115a, 115b, 116b, 119a, 119b, 120a, 125b, 162b, 236a, 337b, 338a, 340a, 394a, 398a, 411a, 422b, 455b, 461a, 462b, 464b, 501b, 508b, 545b, 568a; IV 25a, 44b, 45a, 45b, 49b, 53a, 71b, 96b, 162b, **329a**, 329b, 330a, 330b, 331a, 331b, 332a, 332b, 333a, 337a, 337b, 415a, 493a, 512b, 515a, 532a, 532b, 533a, 534a, 572a, 592a; V 37b, 44b, 64b, 65a, 113b, 164a, 263a, 364b, 366a, 373b, 377a, 377b, 401b, 409b, 448b, 471a, 507b, 508a, 508b, 550b

Qurayya — I 149b

[Banū] Qurayẓa — I 289a, 324b; II 148b, 149a, 150a, 150b, 151a, 298b; III 29a, 30a, 456b, 498a, 545b, 579b; IV 25a, 323a, 323b, 324a, **333b**, 334a, 334b, 406a, 412a; V 43a, 44b, 508b

Qureyshi, I. — V 101a

Qurḥ — I 154b

Qurra b. Sharīk — I 139b

al-Qurṭubī, Abū ʿAbdallāh Muḥammad b. Aḥmad (d. 671/1272) — I 176a, 200a, 203b, 204a, 205a, 257a, 268a, 273a, 288a, 409a, 549a, 549b, 551a; II 21b, 88b, 114a, 147a, 271a, 313b, 336b, 468b, 491b, 498b, 500b, 542b; III 240a, 240b, 548b; IV 15a, 109b, 110a, 509a, 509b, 533b, 547b, 550a; V 55b, 160b, 330a, 404a, 466a, 466b, 467a, 549a, 552a

Qurva — III 433a

Quṣayy b. Kulāb — I 406b

al-Qushayrī, Abū l-Qāsim ʿAbd al-Karīm b. Hawāzin (d. 465/1072) — I 176a, 268a, 484a, 550a; II 120a, 452a, 453b; IV 57b, 157a; V 83b, 139b, 143b, 144b, 145a, 145b, 146a, 151a, 151b, 152a

Quss — III 500b

Quṭb, Sayyid — I 39b, 184b, 224b, 293a,

408a, 408b, 428a; II 21a, 130b, 131a, 134b, 137b, 138a, 445a, 468b, 471b, 535b; III 81b, 93a, 194b, 195a, 195b, 201b, 202b, 206a, 208b, 240b, 241a, 285b, 376b, 402b; IV 139b, 143b, 145a, 145b, 414b, 528a, 535a; V 10a, 10b, 27a, 99a, 103b, 206a, 406a, 443a, 538a, 539a
Quṭb al-Dīn al-Shīrāzī II 113a
Quṭb Manār III 314b
Quṭrub (d. 206/821) V 333b
Quwwat al-Islam III 314b
Quzaḥ IV 515b
  Hill of IV 281b

R

al-Rabadha I 154b
Rabbat, N. I **339a**
Rabīʿ I II 20b
[Banū] Rabīʿa II 513b
Rābiʿa al-ʿAdawiyya II 286a
Rabin, Ch. I 531a; II 354b, 356b, 357b, 359b, 366b, 367a; III 122a; IV 194a
Rachel I 226a, 228a
Rada III 312b
Radscheit, M. IV **313b**, **433b**; V **127b**, **190b**, **505a**, **548a**
Radtke, B. IV **520b**; V **484a**
Raḍwān, [Shaykh] Muḥammad IV 266b, 269b
[Shāh] Rafīʿ al-Dīn (d. 1818) III 223b; V 341b
al-Rāghī al-Tūnisī (d. 715/1315) V 346b
al-Rāghib al-Iṣfahānī, Abū l-Qāsim al-Ḥusayn (d. 502/1108) I 261b, 398b; II 231b, 315a; III 10a, 506b, 511a, 513b; IV 12b; V 297b, 330a, 560b, 572a
Ragmat V 88b; see also Najrān
Rahardjo, D. V 101b
Rahbar, D. II 125b, 135a, 140b; III 70a; IV 197a
al-Raḥmān (name for ʿAllāh') II 317b, 318a, 318b; IV 22b, 380a; V 308a
Rahman, F. (d. 1988) I 64a, 87a, 87b; II 135a, 139b, 140b, 187b, 469a; IV 89b; V 26b, 68b, 101b, 298b, 434b
Raḥmānān V 566a, 566b, 567a
Rahmani, Khadim IV 274a, 274b

Rahmat Allah Kayranawi iv 124a
Räisänen, H. iv 195b
Rajab i 398a, 402b, 403a, 403b; ii 179b, 183a, 184a, 169a, 169b, 170a, 170b, 171a; iii 263a, 410a, 410b, 411a, 413b; iv 340a, 340b
Rakhmat, Jalaluddin v 101b
Ramaḍān i 12a, 14a, 33b, 66b, 183a, 196a, 326a, 358a, 359a, 398a, 400a, 444b, 445a, 487a, 503a; ii 81a, 83b, 84a, 84b, 85a, 89a, 91a, 180b, 181a, 181b, 183a, 183b, 204a, 204b, 216a, 381b, 382a, 450b, 546b; iii 161a, 304b, 412b, 413a, 414a, 414b, 415a, 419a, 427a, 496a, 496b, 537b, 538b, 552b; iv 227a, 232b, 293a, **338a**, 338b, 339b, 340a, 341a, 343b, 344a, 345a, 346b, 347a, 379b, 387a, 488a, 490a, 502b, 571b; v 37a, 73b, 141a, 214a, 226a, 227b, 272a, 284b, 372b, 394a, 431b, 475b, 504a, 556a, 556b
Ramadan, T. v 225a
Ramallah i 171a
Ramla ii 11a; iii 5b, 53b; v 508b
Ramla (wife of Umayyad caliph Yazīd I) v 186b
Ramli, Muḥammad v 101a
[Mt.] Ramm i 138a
Rammān v 86b
Ramón Martí see Raymond Martin (d. ca. 1284)
al-Raqīm i 151b; iii 374a, 375a; iv **351a**, 351b; v 185a, 251a
al-Raqqa v 1a
Raqqāda i 284a
Rashīd, S. i 149a
Rashīd Aḥmad Gangōhī i 520b
Rashīd al-Dīn iii 268a
Rashīd al-Dīn al-Maybudī see al-Maybudī, Rashīd al-Dīn
Rashid Khalifa see Khalifa, R.
Rashid Omar, ʿA. v 206b
Rashīd Riḍā, M. i 39b, 52a, 208a; ii 128a, 128b, 130b, 286b, 445a; iii 6a, 229a, 293b, 348b, 376b; v 10a, 99a,

103b, 208a, 228a, 442b, 536b, 537a
al-Rass I 150b; IV 320a, **352a**; V 249a, 250b, 389a
People of IV 352b
Rasūlids III 312b, 370b
Raven, W. III **286b**; IV **461b**; V **49b**
Ravius, Christis (d. 1677) IV 246b, 249a
Rawāfiḍ II 471b; III 547a
Rawḥ b. ʿAbd al-Muʾmin (d. ca. 235/849-50) IV 390a
Raydān V 87b
Rayḥāna bt. Zayd V 508b, 509a, 518b
Rayḥāna al-Quraẓiyya IV 334b
Raymond Lull (d. 1316) IV 240b
Raymond Martin (d. ca. 1284) IV 240a, 243b
Raymund of Pennaforte (d. 1275) IV 240a
Rayy II 106a; III 112b; V 307b
al-Rāzī, Abu Bakr (d. 313/925) II 223a; III 349b; IV 74b
al-Rāzī, Fakhr al-Dīn (d. 606/1210) I 53a, 71b, 80a, 81a, 89a, 111b, 203b, 219b, 225b, 241a, 256b, 288a, 373a, 425b, 427a, 483a, 547a, 548a; II 21b, 113a, 113b, 115b, 116a, 124a, 129b, 136b, 138a, 151b, 188b, 235b, 338b, 415a, 424a, 468b, 495b, 500b, 505a; III 4b, 35b, 91b, 104a, 140b, 173a, 181a, 181b, 236b, 249a, 250b, 293b, 294a, 334b, 424b, 460a, 470a, 470b; IV 13b, 14b, 16a, 83b, 187a, 214b, 285b, 358a, 527b, 528a, 533b, 539b, 543a, 543b, 544a, 544b, 545a, 545b, 547b, 548a, 548b, 549b, 550a, 550b, 551a, 551b, 552a, 578b; V 3b, 9a, 9b, 16b, 17a, 17b, 18a, 83b, 98b, 125a, 202a, 275b, 300b, 346b, 353a, 362b, 401a, 405b, 439b, 440b, 441a, 462a, 485a, 561a
al-Rāzī, Ibn Abī Ḥātim (d. 327/938-9) II 111b, 415a; IV 592b
al-Rāzī, Muḥammad b. Idrīs Abū Ḥātim (d. 277/890-1) I 481b
al-Rāzī, Muḥammad b. Zakariyyā (d. 313/925) III 358b, 359b; IV 169a
Reat, N.L. V 361a
Rebstock, U. II 294a
Reckendorf, H. II 350b, 361b; V 240a, 297b, 350b

Reclam, P. v 352a
Red Sea i 307b, 553b; ii 79b, 294b, 295a, 298b, 527b, 534a, 534b; iii 394a; iv 343a, 604b; v 4b, 246b, 375a, 562a
Redhouse ii 37b
Reed, L. ii 428a
Reformation i 425a
Reineccius, Christian (d. 1752) iv 248a
Reinhart, A. i **412b**, ii **78b**
Reland, Adriaan (d. 1718) iv 249b
Renaissance i 425a
Renan, E. v 48a
Renard, J. i **27b**, **62b**, **519b**, **522a**, iii **83b**
Rephaim iii 543a
Republican Brothers i 34a, 35a
Reşat Nuri Güntekin v 394b
Retsö, J. i 132a
Reuschel, W. ii 351b, 360a; iv 199b
Revelation of John iii 144a
Revolution
French i 418b
October i 418b
Reyahi, B. v **52b**
Reynolds, G.S. v **410b**
Rezvan, E. iii **608a**
Riʾām v 92a, 92b, 389b
Ribāṭ iii 314b
Rice, D. i 282a
Richter, G. ii 352a
Ri(c)coldo da Monte Croce (d. ca. 1320) iv 241a, 241b, 242a, 243a, 245b; v 344b
Richardson, M.E.J. v 353a
Riḍwān (angel) i 89b
Riḍwān, Muḥammad Aḥmad (father of Shaykh Aḥmad Riḍwān of Egypt) ii 452a
Riḍwān, [Shaykh] Aḥmad (of Egypt) ii 451b, 453b
Rifāʿa al-Ṭahṭāwī iv 270b
Riffat Hassan see Hassan, Riffat
[Mt.] Rijām ii 300b
Ringgren, H. ii 565b
Rio de Janeiro v 351b
Rippin, A. i **2b**, **20a**, **103a**, **364b**, 421a, **527b**; ii **236a**, 246a, 249a, **464a**, **473a**, **563a**; iii **2a**, **52b**,

	493a, **554a**, **572b**; IV 192a, 199a, 203a, 204a, 471b, 472a, **511a**, **575b**; V **299b**, **315b**, 469b, **491a**, 502b
Rivlin, Y.	V 350b
Riyadh	I 149a, 153a, 172b; III 607b; IV 273b, 511a; V 39b, 565b
[Mt.] Riyām	V 89b, 92b
Robert, R.	IV 197a
Robert of Ketton (or Robert of Chester, Robertus Cestrensis, Robertus Ketenensis)	IV 238b, 243a, 245b, 265a; V 344b, 345a
Robin, C.J.	I 155a; V **93b**, **398b**, **568a**
Robinson, C.	I **400b**; V **461a**
Robinson, N.	I **111b**, **341a**, **489b**; II 262a; III **20b**, 212b, 474b; IV 116a, 195b, 275b, 529a
Robles, J.G.	V 349b
Robson, J.	II 565b
Roded, R.	V **540b**
Rodinson, M.	I 43a; IV 535a; V 67a, 314a, 349b
Rodrigo Jiménez de Rada (archbishop)	V 345a
Rodwell, A.	IV 190b
Rodwell, J.M.	I 200a; IV 48a, 191b; V 351a, 352b
Roman(s)	I 137b, 150a, 308b, 309a, 487b, 488a, 488b, 499b; II 240a, 499a, 511b; III 3a; IV 516a; V 563b; see also Byzantine(s)
Empire	I 308a, 311a; IV 253b
Law	I 396b
Rome	I 308b; III 409a, 556b; IV 237a, 242a; V 73a
Rosenthal, F.	I 37a; II **441b**; V 336a
Ross, A.	V 345b, 347a
Ross, E.D.	V 345b, 348b
Rotary Club	II 471b
Rowson, E.	II **344b**, **445b**
Rubin, U.	I 5a, **291a**, **307a**, 417b; II 151a, 393a, **398b**, **403b**, 445b, **490b**, **572a**; III **34a**, **457b**, **576a**; IV 153a, 199b, **306a**, **333a**, **337b**, **425b**, **430b**, **516b**; V 35b, 39a, 40a, 41a, 49a, 351a, **412a**
Rückert, F.	V 350a
Rudolf, K.	V 352a
Rudolph, W.	IV 194b

Rufa — I 33b
Rufayʿ b. Mihrān — see Abū l-ʿĀliya al-Riyāḥī (d. 93/711)
al-Ruhnī — V 324a
Rūmān — I 90b; IV 460a
al-Rūm — see Byzantines
al-Rūmī, [Mawlāna] Jalāl al-Dīn (d. 672/1273) — I 86b; II 240a; III 83b, 222b, 223a, 223b, 311a, 311b; IV 57b, 61b, 64a, 64b, 65a, 349a; V 97b
[Wādī] Rumm (in TransJordan) — V 185a
[Wādī] al-Rumma — II 295a
al-Rummānī, ʿAlī b. ʿĪsā (d. 384/994) — II 114b, 533b, 534b; III 325b, 469a, 470b, 471a; IV 477a, 14a; V 324a
Ruqayya (daughter of the Prophet and Khadīja) — III 80b; V 507b
Ruṣāfa (Sergiopolis) — I 308b, 336a
Rushdie, S. — II 392a; IV 535b
Russia — III 607a; IV 250b
  Czarist — III 343b
Russian-Turkish War (1768-74) — IV 250b
Ruṣṭāfa — I 308b; III 405b
Rustam — II 517a
Rūstem Pasha — III 598b
Ruways, Abū ʿAbdallāh Muḥammad b. al-Mutawakkil al-Baṣrī (d. 238/852) — IV 360a, 390a
Ruwwāfa — I 150a
Rūzbihān b. Abī Naṣr al-Baqlī al-Shīrāzī (d. 606/1209) — II 120a; III 187b; V 151b, 152a, 152b, 153a
Rūzbihān Muḥammad — III 602a
du Ryer, André (d. 1672) — IV 249b; V 346b, 347a, 347b, 348a

S

Saʿadyā Gaon (alias Saʿd b. Yūsuf al-Fayyūmī; d. 331/942) — IV 317a; V 306b, 309a
Sabaʿ (near Jerusalem) — I 8b
Sabaʾ — I 214b; II 437b, 558a; III 58b, 472a, 532b; IV 511a; V 85b, 86a, 87a, 89a, 89b, 91b, 92b, 93a, 464a, 562b, 563a; see also Sheba
Sabaeans — I 152b; II 437b; IV 7a, 408a, 511a, 586a, 586b; V 91a, 162b
Ṣabāt — IV 268b, 270a
Sabbagh, T. — IV 471a
Sabbath — I 36b, 98a, 98b, 306a, 366a, 492a, 500b; II 272a; III 520b; IV 132b,

327b, 407a, **510a**, 510b, 511a; v 279b, 285b, 438b, 441a
Sabians [Ṣābiʾūn] i 222b, 378a; ii 566a; iii 22a, 244b, 529b; iv 38a, 399b, 400a, 403a, 403b, 404b, 407b, 408a, 408b, **511a**, 511b, 512a, 525a, 586a; v 268a
Sablukov, G.S. v 351b
al-Ṣābūnī, M. ʿA. ii 557a
Sābūr iii 5b
Sachedina, A. i **3b**; ii 151b
Sacred Mosque i 342b
de Sacy, S. v 349b
Saʿd b. Abī Waqqāṣ (d. after 40/660) i 389a, 408a; ii 520a; v 47a, 47b
Saʿd b. Bakr iii 120a
Saʿd al-Dīn al-Taftazānī see al-Taftazānī, Saʿd al-Dīn (d. 792/1390)
Saʿd b. Jubayr (d. 93/714) iii 438b
Saʿd b. Muʿādh iii 284a; iv 334b
Saʿd b. ʿUbāda ii 17a
Saʿd b. Yūsuf al-Fayyūmī (d. 331/942) see Saʿadyā Gaon
Ṣadaqa iii 53b
Sadat, A. iv 143a, 146a, 147a
Saddam Hussein see Ḥusayn, Ṣaddām
Sadducees iv 27b
Saʿdī iv 57b, 65a
al-Saʿdī, ʿAbd al-Raḥmān i 32a
al-Ṣādiq, [Imām] Jaʿfar see [Imām] Jaʿfar al-Ṣādiq (d. 148/765)
Ṣadr al-Dīn al-Qūnawī see al-Qūnawī, Ṣadr al-Dīn (d. 673/1274)
[Mullā] Ṣadrā Shīrāzī (d. 1050/1640) i 428a; v 159a
al-Sadūsī al-Baṣrī (d. 106/724) see Abū Mijlaz Lāḥiq b. Ḥumayd
Saeed, A. ii **9b**
al-Ṣafā i 9a, 153b, 319b, 353b; ii 64a, 179a, 205a, 299b; iii 77a, 79a, 339a, 552b; iv 93a, 93b, 94a, 97a, 98a, 105a, 259a, 283b, 423b, 491b, 515b, **518a**, 518b, 519b; v 318a, 463a
Ṣafar v 1a
Safavid(s) iii 317b, 433b
al-Saffāḥ (caliph; d. 136/754) ii 26b
Ṣaffār al-Bukhārī (d. 534/1139) iv 424a
al-Ṣāfī Abū l-Faḍāʾil b. al-ʿAssāl iv 236b
Safīd Buland iii 305a

al-Sāfila (of Yathrib) ɪɪ 20b, 21a
Ṣafiyya (wife of the Prophet) ɪɪɪ 498a, 499a; ᴠ 515b, 516b, 518a, 518b
Ṣafiyya (Ḥamza's sister) ɪɪ 400b
Ṣaffūriyya see Sepphoris
Ṣafwān b. al-Muʿaṭṭal al-Sulamī see al-Sulamī, Ṣafwān b. al-Muʿaṭṭal
Safwat Collection ɪɪɪ 328b
Ṣaḥāba see Companions
Saḥar ᴠ 86b
Sahara ɪɪɪ 248a; ᴠ 344a
Sahas, D. ɪɪ **475a**
al-Ṣāḥib Ibn ʿAbbād (d. 385/995) ᴠ 324b
Sahl al-Tustarī see al-Tustarī, Sahl b. ʿAbdallāh (d. 283/896)
Sahm ɪɪ 397b
Said, S.S. ɪɪɪ **337a**
[Khedive] Saʿīd (Egyptian ruler; r. 1854-63) ɪᴠ 270b, 271a
Saʿīd b. ʿAbd al-Malik b. Marwān ɪᴠ 52a
Saʿīd al-Dīn al-Farghānī (d. ca. 700/1300) ɪɪɪ 389a
Saʿīd Ḥawwā see Ḥawwā, Saʿīd
Saʿīd b. Jubayr (d. 95/714) ɪ 73b; ɪɪ 102b, 103b, 106a; ɪɪɪ 117a, 179a, 438b; ɪᴠ 533a; ᴠ 440b
Saʿīd b. Manṣūr al-Khurāsānī (d. 227/842) ᴠ 330a, 330b
Saʿīd b. Saʿīd b. al-ʿĀṣ ɪɪɪ 276a
Saʿīd b. Zayd ɪ 389a
Sajāḥ bt. al-Ḥārith ɪɪɪ 462a, 462b; ᴠ 79a
al-Sakhāwī, ʿAlam al-Dīn (d. 643/1246) ᴠ 327a
al-Sakhāwī (d. 902/1497) ɪɪɪ 371a
Sakkākī ɪ 425b
Sakrān b. ʿAmr ᴠ 508a
Saladin ɪɪ 206b; ɪɪɪ 309a; ᴠ 217a
Salafism ᴠ 100a
Ṣalāḥ al-Dīn (d. 589/1193) see Saladin
Salama b. al-Akwa (d. 74/693) ɪ 12a
Salāma, M.ʿA. ᴠ 329b
Sale, George (d. 1736) ɪ 200a; ɪɪɪ 110a; ɪᴠ 48a, 188a, 249a, 249b; ᴠ 347a, 348a, 348b, 349a
Ṣāliḥ ɪ 98b, 149b, 150b, 152b, 222a, 261b, 286b, 296b, 308a, 401b, 511a, 519a, 532a, 538a; ɪɪ 64a, 293a, 339a, 340b, 427a, 438a, 504b, 558a; ɪɪɪ 18a, 18b, 99b, 118b, 200b, 212b, 219a, 232a, 381a, 381b, 418a, 479b, 519b,

520b, 525b, 534b, 540a, 540b, 551a, 553a, 567b; IV 130b, 258a, 263b, 296a, 319a, **521a**, 521b, 522a, 523b, 529b; V 16a, 253a, 253b, 254a, 313b, 463b

People of — II 338a, 542a; IV 605b

Ṣāliḥ al-Murrī — see al-Murrī, Ṣāliḥ (d. ca. 172/788-9)

el-Salih, S. — IV 197a

Salīm — I 529b

Salīm, ʿA. — IV 272b

Sālim b. Maʿqil (12/634) — V 59a

[Shaykh] Sālim Chistī (d. 980/1572) — III 323b

[Banū] Salima — V 379b

Saljūq(s) — see Seljuq(s)

Sallār b. ʿAbd al-ʿAzīz al-Daylamī (d. 448/1056) — IV 489a

Sallām b. Abī l-Ḥuqayq — III 498b

Sallām the Interpreter — II 333a

Salmān Pāk — I 546a

Salmān al-Fārisī ('the Persian'; d. ca. 35/656) — I 315a; III 32b, 406a; IV 58b, 334a; V 58b

Salome — III 52a

Salsabīl — II 283b; V 62b

Sām — see Shem

Samaria — IV 524a

Samaritans — IV 405a, **524a**, 524b, 525a; V 489a

Samarqand — II 421a; III 314a, 431b

al-Samarqandī, Abū Layth (d. 373-5/983-5) — I 483a; IV 445b; V 330a, 439b

al-Samarqandī, ʿAlāʾ al-Dīn (d. 539/1144) — II 115b

Sāmarrāʾ — II 560b; III 431a

Ṣamaà — II 212a

al-Ṣamawʾal b. ʿĀdiyā — II 447b; IV 111b

al-Ṣamawʾal b. Yaḥyā al-Maghribī (d. 569/1174) — IV 527b; V 305a

al-Samhūdī (d. 911/1506) — III 371a

Samʿī — V 86a, 89b, 90b, 93a

al-Samīn al-Ḥalabī (Aḥmad b. Yūsuf; d. 756/1355) — II 113b; V 327b

al-Sāmirī — I 274a, 274b, 275a, 275b; III 394b; IV 405a, 524b; V 463b

Samiyya — I 408b

Samnanids — I 483a

Samrāʾ bt. Nuhayk al-Asadiyya — III 276a, 276b

Samson [Shamsūn] — III 479b; IV **525b**, 526a, 526b

Samuel — I 460b; II 145b, 240b; IV **526b**, 527b, 528a, 528b, 529b, 530a, 536a, 577b

Samūm ɪɪ 455b
Samawʾal b. ʿĀdiyāʾ (d. ca. 560) ɪᴠ 527b
Samawʾal b. Yaḥyā al-Maghribī ɪᴠ 529b
Ṣanʿāʾ ɪ 4b, 44a, 155a, 348a, 350b; ɪɪ 338b; ɪɪɪ 85b, 257b, 594a; ᴠ 37a, 89a, 89b, 92a, 92b, 167a, 562b, 563b, 565b
Great Mosque of ɪ 137a, 348a; ɪɪɪ 298a, 594a, 598b, 600a; ɪᴠ 362a; ᴠ 295b
Sanacharib ɪɪ 146b
Sanāʾī of Ghazna (d. ca. 525/1131) ɪᴠ 56a, 58a, 63a, 64a
al-Ṣanawbarī (or al-Ṣubunrī), Mahdī b. ʿAlī (d. 815/1412) ɪɪɪ 363b, 364a, 364b, 365a
Sanchez, G. ɪ 48a
Ṣandal ɪɪɪ 600b, 601b
Sanders, P. ɪɪɪ 304a
Sanneh, L. ɪɪ **373a**
Sanskrit ɪɪɪ 245a; ᴠ 52a
al-Sanūsī, Abū ʿAbdallāh Muḥammad b. Yūsuf (d. 892/1486) ɪ 78a; ɪᴠ 169a; ᴠ 499b
Sanyal, U. ɪ **203a**
Sapir, E. ᴠ 70a
Saracen(s) ɪ 125b, 150a; ɪᴠ 243a
Sarah ɪ 6b, 8b, 9a; ɪɪ 341a; ɪɪɪ 148a, 287a; ᴠ 259a, 534a
Sargis-Baḥīrā see Baḥīrā
Sargon II (Assyrian) ᴠ 254a
Sarkīs ɪᴠ 265b, 266a
Saritoprak, Z. ɪᴠ **509b**, **531b**
al-Sarrāj, Abū Naṣr (d. 378/988) ɪɪɪ 83b; ᴠ 141b
Sarwat Anis al-Assiouty see al-Assiouty, Sarwat Anis
Sasanian(s)/Sasanid(s) ɪ 265b, 266a, 308a, 400b; ɪɪ 560a; ɪɪɪ 245a, 405b, 408b, 556a, 573b; ɪᴠ 142a; ᴠ 430b, 562a; see also Persian(s)
Satan ɪ 9b, 15a, 25a, 25b, 31a, 80a, 86b, 91b, 95b, 98b, 108a, 108b, 109a, 160a, 160b, 161a, 167a, 185b, 186a, 378a, 380a, 395b, 411a, 441a, 452a, 460a, 465b, 491b, 511a, 525a, 532a, 536b, 543b, 547b, 548a, 552a; ɪɪ 1a, 23b, 24a, 24b, 54a, 66a, 67b, 72a, 91a, 91b, 95b, 172b, 173a, 196b, 205a, 205b, 219b, 220b, 221b, 241b, 273b, 274b, 280a,

336a, 404b, 417a, 417b, 430b, 436a, 461a, 479a, 482b, 540b, 550b, 556b, 558b, 563a; III 12b, 44b, 46a, 46b, 47a, 47b, 50b, 92b, 179b, 211a, 225b, 248b, 289b, 292a, 420b, 454a, 489a, 490b, 491a, 548a, 563b; IV 25a, 29b, 30a, 78b, 118a, 127a, 138a, 230a, 232a, 263b, 289b, 295a, 301b, 308a, 377b, 503b, 505a, 520a, 531b, 532b, 534b, 535a, 583a; V 25a, 37b, 42b, 82a, 82b, 120a, 130a, 134a, 146a, 243a, 267b, 269b, 278a, 298b, 360a, 363b, 379b, 448b, 456a; V 484a, 487a, 494b, 530a, 538a; see also Iblīs

Saṭīh — III 247a; V 80a, 96a, 120b

Saudi Arabia — I 127b, 148b, 150a, 152b, 154a, 155a, 172b, 491b, 524a, 524b, 525a, 525b, 526a, 526b; III 501a; IV 273a, 273b; V 75b, 215a, 216b, 227b, 397a, 415b, 453a

  Department of Antiquities in — II 428a

Saul [Ṭalūt] — I 79b, 303a, 460b, 496a; II 145b, 198b, 238a, 335a, 403b, 404a, 432b; III 9a, 9b, 92a, 94a, 94b, 395a, 521a, 522b; IV 291a, 315b, 316b, 527a, 528b, 529a, 529b, 530a, **536a**, 536b, 537a, 538a, 590a; V 377a, 455b, 458a, 468a

de Saussure, F. — V 70a

Savary, C.E. — V 348b, 349a, 349b

Savary de Brèves, François (d. 1628) — V 346b

Savignac, R. — II 428a

Savoy — IV 243a; V 341b

Sawda bt. Zamʿa (wife of the Prophet) — V 507b, 516b, 517b, 518a

Sawdā (Urdu poet; d. 1195/1781) — III 224a

Sayāḥ — I 121a

Sayf b. ʿUmar (d. 180/796) — IV 134a

Sayīn — V 86b, 89b, 90a, 91b, 92b

Sayyid Abū l-ʿAlāʾ al-Mawdūdī — see al-Mawdūdī, Sayyid Abū l-ʿAlāʾ (d. 1979)

Sayyid Aḥmad al-Badawī — II 207b

Sayyid Aḥmad Barēlwī	I 201b
[Sir] Sayyid Aḥmad Khān	see Khan, S.A. (d. 1898)
Sayyid-i Ajall	III 315b
Sayyid ʿAlī	IV 266b
Sayyid ʿAlī Muḥammad Shīrāzī	I 197a, 197b
Sayyid Darwīsh	II 88a
al-Sayyid Ibrāhīm al-Mayānjī	II 377b
Sayyid Kasrawī Ḥasan	II 377b
Sayyid Othman	III 344a, 344b, 345a
Sayyid Quṭb	see Quṭb, Sayyid
al-Sayyid, Riḍwān	I 368a, 371a
Scaliger, Joseph Justus (d. 1609)	IV 235a, 245b, 246a; V 344b, 346a
Schacht, J.	I 11a, 28b, 481b; II 389b; IV 589a; V 32a, 32b
Schaeffer, S. [Schneide]	II 38b
Schapiro, I.	IV 194b
Schcheglova, O.	IV 266a, 267a
Schick, R.	I **156b**; IV **105a**, **308b**
Schimmel, A.	III 144a; V 350a, 352a
Schippers, A.	IV **317b**
Schleiermacher, F.	II 139b
Schmidtke, S.	I **485a**, **524a**; III **471a**; IV **8b**
Schneide *ṭarsh*	II 38b
Schneider, I.	II **491b**; III 96b
Schnig, H.	I 288b
Schnurrer, C.	IV 265b
Schöck, C.	I **26b**; III **426b**
Schoeler, G.	II 381b, 438b; IV 589a; V 32a, 49a
Schöller, M.	III **371a**, **499b**, **580a**; IV 199a, **205a**, **324b**, **334b**; V 43a, 48a
Schönig, H.	I **288b**; II **334b**
Schub, M.	V **405a**
Schumann, O.	IV 195b
Schultens, A.	II 235b
Schuon, F.	V 462a
Schwally, F.	I 11a, 248b, 322b, 417b; II 255a, 384a; III 465a; IV 189a, 189b, 193b
Schwarzbaum, H.	I 195b
Schwieger, S.	V 346a
Scottish Rite Mason	I 30b
Scripture	see Book
Seale, M.	IV 193b, 195a
Sears, S.	III **409a**

Second World War	see World War II
Segovia	IV 243a
Seiros Aster	V 52a
Seleucia-Ctesiphon	I 309b
Seleucid (empire)	I 137b
Selim I (Ottoman sultan; r. 1512-20)	IV 244b
Selim III (Ottoman sultan)	I 30b
Selīmiye Mosque	III 429b
Seljuqs	II 421a, 560b; III 265b, 308b, 433b, 434b
Sells, M.	I **180b**; III **374a**; IV 102b, 103a, 383b; V **117a**, 168b, 184a
Semitic (languages)	II 227b, 228a, 235a, 241b, 434b, 483a, 544a; III 49a; IV 111a; V 286b
pre-Islamic	II 482b
Semites	IV 477a
Semitist(s)	III 130b
Senegal	I 30a
Sennacherib [Sanḥarīb]	I 195a; II 562b, 563a
Sepphoris [Ṣaffūriyya]	V 185a
Septuagint	I 192b; III 8b, 390a; V 260b, 308b
Serbo-Croatian (language)	I 136a
Sergiopolis	see Ruṣāfa
Sergius (alias Nestorius)	see Naṣṭūr/Nasṭūrā
[St.] Sergius the Martyr	I 336a; II 405b
Serjeant, R.	II 468a, 543a; IV 204a
Segovia	IV 243a
Sēs	see Usays
Seth	II 412b; III 69a, 118b, 541b, 542b; IV 303b
Seven Sleepers	I 98a, 99a, 292b; II 433b, 435b, 436a, 436b, 437a; III 287a, 321b, 327a, 427a, 520a, 537a; IV 351a; V 251a; see also Cave, Men/People of the
Severus of Antioch	I 312a
Seville	I 48b; II 119a; III 83b; IV 242a
Seyyid Meḥmed Şükrü	III 322b
Sezgin, F.	II 103b, 396b
Shaʿbān	II 181b, 398a, 505b; III 414a; V 2a, 127a
Shaban, M.A.	IV 386b
al-Shaʿbī, ʿĀmīr b. Sharāḥīl (d. ca. 105/725)	II 393b, 538a, 538b
Shabwat	V 89b
Shaḍḍad	I 22a; II 559a, 559b

Shādhī III 601b
Shadīd I 22a
al-Shāfiʿī (d. 204/820) I 11a, 13a, 13b, 18a, 18b, 19a, 67b, 210a, 337b, 344a, 357b, 387a, 388b, 412a, 415a, 483a; II 85b, 90a, 104b, 215a, 225b, 229b, 230a, 389b, 520b, 537a, 553b; III 67b, 125a, 175a, 214b; IV 9b, 110a, 323b, 416b, 564a; V 164b, 165b, 322b, 322b, 323a, 323b, 415a, 496b, 557a
Shāfiʿī(s) II 111b; III 404a, 404b; V 55b
Shāh ʿAbdu l-Laṭif (d. 1752) V 95b, 96a, 97a
Shāh Jāhān see Jāhān
Shaḥar V 86b
Shaḥāta, ʿA.M. III 142b
Shahid, I. A. III **501a**; IV **46b**, 411a, **605a**; V **29a**, **186b**
Shahla Sherkat see Sherkat, Sh.
al-Shahrastānī, Abū l-Fatḥ Muḥammad (d. 548/1153) I 105a, 105b, 118b; IV 414a, 525a; V 268a, 268b, 330a
Shaḥrūr, M. I 428b; V 69b, 70a, 70b, 71a, 71b
Shaked, S. III 144a
Shaker Collection III 326b
Shakespeare, W. II 131b
Shākir, M. I 391b; II 231a
  brothers II 388b
Shakir, M.H. III 189a; IV 46b
Shalabī, H. IV 392b
Shaleh, Q. V 101a
Shaltūt, M. II 125b, 130b; III 230b; V 99a, 217b, 342b
al-Shām see Syria
Shamanism III 247b
Shamma, S. IV 196b
Shammar Yuharʿish V 562b
Shams al-Dīn al-Dhahabī see al-Dhahabī, Shams al-Dīn Muḥammad b. Aḥmad (d. 748/1348)
Shams al-Dīn Muḥammad b. ʿAbd al-Raḥmān b. al-Ṣāʾigh al-Ḥanafī see Ibn al-Ṣāʾigh al-Ḥanafī, Shams al-Dīn Muḥammad b. ʿAbd al-Raḥmān (d. 776/1375)
Shams al-Dīn Muḥammad b. Abī Ṭālib al-Dimashqī see al-Dimashqī, Shams al-Dīn Muḥammad b. Abī Ṭālib (d. 727/1327)
Shams al-Dīn ʿUmar III 315b

Shams-i Tabrīzī (disappeared ca. 645/1248) IV 61b
Shamsūn see Samson
al-Shanfarā II 301b
Shannon, C. II 136a
Shaqīq al-Balkhī V 141a, 383a
Sharaf al-Dīn ʿAlī al-Ḥusaynī al-Astarābādī IV 602b
Sharaḥʾil Yaqbul V 565a
al-Shaʿrānī I 206b, 207a
al-Shaʿrāwī, [Shaykh] Muḥammad Mutawallī (d. 1998) I 185a; IV 212a; V 224a
Shareef, A. I 421a
Sharīʿatī ʿAlī (d. 1977) III 286a, 582a
al-Sharīf al-Murtaḍā see al-Murtaḍa, al-Sharīf (d. 436/1044)
al-Sharīf al-Raḍī (d. 406/1016) II 114b
Sharnūbī III 503a
Sharon, M. I 169a; IV **43a**, **53a**
al-Sharqāwī II 132b
Shaʾs b. Qays IV 323a
al-Shāṭibī (d. 790/1388) II 131a, 132a, 133b; III 164b, 165a, 165b, 166a, 166b, 167a, 167b, 168a; V 407b
Shavuot II 184b
Shawḥaṭān V 563a
al-Shawkānī, Abū ʿAbdallāh Muḥammad b. ʿAlī (d. 1250/1834-9) I 461b; II 113b, 280b; IV 185b, 187a, 530b, 603a; V 434b, 435b, 442b
Shawwāl-Dhū l-Qaʿda V 2a
Shayba II 513b
al-Shaybānī (d. 189/804) III 253b
Shaydhala, Abū l-Maʿālī ʿAzīzī/ʿUzayzī b. ʿAbd al-Malik al-Jīlī (d. 494/1100) V 326a, 331b
Shaykh al-Islām IV 268a, 268b, 271b
al-Shaykh al-Mufīd see al-Mufīd, al-Shaykh (d. 413/1022)
Shaykh Sharaf IV 266b
al-Shaykhlī, [Shaykh] ʿAbdallāh IV 274a
Shayṭān see Iblīs; Satan
Sheba [Sabaʾ] I 60b, 228b, 254b; II 283a, 459b; IV 408a, 511a, 514a, **585a**, 586a, 586b; V 86a, 373b, 532b; see also Sabaʾ
  Kingdom of I 151b
  Queen of I 61a, 100b, 151b, 152a, 162b, 163a, 166a, 229b, 347a, 369a, 532a; II 216a, 291a, 313b, 314a,

318a, 344b, 432b, 437b, 486a, 538a, 558a; III 48b, 61a, 91b, 92a, 212a, 395a, 487b, 520a; IV 586a, 586b; V 77a, 77b, 93a, 277a, 424a, 530a, 532b, 533a, 538a

Sheban(s) I 61a
Shechem IV 524a
Shekhinah I 459b; IV **589b**
Shem [Sām] I 21a; III 542b, 543a
Sheol V 398a
Shepard, W. I **40a**; II **489b**
Sherif, F. V 297b
Sherkat, Sh. V 540b
al-Shiblī, Abū Bakr (d. 334/946) V 141a, 148b
Shihāb al-Dīn al-Ālūsī see al-Ālūsī, Maḥmūd Shihāb al-Dīn (d. 1854)
Shihāb al-Dīn al-Būnī see al-Būnī, Shihāb al-Dīn (d. 622/1225)
Shihāb al-Dīn Yaḥyā b. Ḥabash al-Suhrawardī see al-Suhrawardī, Shihāb al-Dīn Yaḥyā b. Ḥabash (d. 578/1191)
al-Shiḥr I 22a
Shīʿī(s)/Shīʿite(s) [Shīʿa] I 57b, 58a, 59b, 62b, 68b, 69b, 189b, 206b, 210a, 219a, 225a, 225b, 261a, 272a, 306b, 307a, 342a, 390a, 412a, 518a, 540b, 541a; II 12a, 106a, 106b, 111a, 177a, 189a, 193a, 207b, 208a, 243b, 396a, 396b, 398a, 424b, 425b, 426a, 427a, 471a, 471b, 485b, 503b, 504a, 506a, 527b, 538b, 560a, 560b; III 33a, 67a, 68a, 85b, 249a, 282a, 286a, 302b, 346b, 370b, 430b, 547a, 571b; IV 26a, 50a, 50b, 52b, 99a, 129b, 305b, 333a, 387a, 430b, 450a, 489b, 500a, 534a, 582b, **591b, 593a**, 593b, 594b, 595a, 595b, 597b, 599a, 599b, 600a, 601a; V 25b, 192b, 215a, 215b, 222b, 225a, 225b, 232b, 233a, 234a, 320b, 325b, 334b, 404b, 499a, 527b, 534b, 535a
Ismāʿīlī II 503b
Twelver [Ithnāʾ ʿAsharī; Jaʿfarī/Imāmī] I 63a, 68b, 106a, 122b, 307a, 484b,

	540b, 541a; II 117a, 208a, 421b, 503b, 504a, 521b, 532b, 533a; III 467a; IV 144b, 538a, 598a; V 135a, 135b, 232b, 320b
Zaydī	I 105a, 540b; II 421b
Shillong (East Pakistan)	IV 274a
al-Shinqīṭī, Shurayḥ al-Khuzāʿī (d. 1913)	V 418a
Shīrāz (Iran)	I 282a; III 313b, 317b, 319a, 321a, 599b, 602a
Shīrāz Jamāl al-Dīn Abū Isḥāq Injū	see Abū Isḥāq Injū, Shīrāz Jamāl al-Dīn (r. 743-54/1343-53)
al-Shīrāzī (d. 1050/1641)	IV 88b
Shiqq	V 80a
Shuʿayb	I 149b, 261b, 296b, 300b, 511a, 519a, 532a; II 293a, 338a, 449a, 503a, 510, 558a; III 118b, 200b, 212b, 381a, 381b, 390a, 390b, 393b, 401b, 421a, 449a, 479b, 520b, 525b, 567b; IV 53b, 130b, 218a, 258a, 263b, 318b, 319a, 352b, 429b, 508b, 523b, **605a**, 605b, 606a; V 130b, 245a, 246b, 247b, 312b, 313a, 313b, 468a
[Shaykh] Shuʿayb al-Ḥurayfīsh (d. 801/1398-9)	V 220b
al-Shuʿayba	II 295a; IV 604b
Shuʿba b. al-Ḥajjāj (d. 160/776)	II 384a, 385a, 385b, 386b, 387a, 391a, 392a, 393b, 395a, 395b
[Wādī l-] Shuḍayf	V 86b
Shukrī ʿAyyād	II 132b
Shukrī Muṣṭafā	I 293a
Shumen (Bulgaria)	III 602a
Shummnu/Shumen	III 322b
Shurāt	III 84b
Shūrbajī	IV 266b
[Sheikh] Si Hamza Boubakeur	V 343b
Sialkot	IV 266a
Sībawayhi (d. 177/793)	I 131a, 131b, 529b, 530a; II 108b, 229b, 347a, 347b, 348a, 349a, 352a, 355b, 361a, 364a; III 112b, 124a, 202a, 606a
Sicily	V 402a
Siddiqui, M.	II **215a**; V **416a**, **481a**
Sidersky, D.	IV 194b
Sierra Leone	III 327a
Ṣiffīn	I 518a

Battle of	III 84b, 85a; IV 72b, 135b, 365b, 494a; V **1a**
Sijistān	III 86a
al-Sijistānī, Abū Bakr (d. 330/942)	II 231b
al-Sijistānī, Abū Ḥātim (d. 255/869)	II 228b
al-Sijistānī, Aḥmad (d. 399/1008)	IV 169b
al-Sijistānī, Ibn Abī Dāwūd (d. 316/929)	I 348a, 350b, 481b; III 288a; IV 355a, 356b, 362a; V 332a
Sikandara	I 165a; III 323a
al-Silafī, Abū Ṭāhir (d. 576/1180)	V 329a
Silay, K.	V **395a**
Silvestre de Sacy, A.	IV 189b
[St.] Simeon (the Stylite)	I 181b, 336a; III 405a, 405b
Simnānī, ʿAlā al-Dawla (d. 736/1336)	II 120a, 120b; V 158b
Simonsen, J.B.	IV 153a, 153b; V 194b
Simurgh	III 222b
Sīn	V 86b
Sinai	I 214a, 308a, 336a, 465a; II 309a; III 9b, 394a, 405a; IV 510a; V **28a**, 184b, 185a, 366b, 463b
Mount [Ṭūr]	I 179a, 260b, 261a, 534a; II 218b, 256b, 305a, 305b, 306b, 308b, 311a, 316a, 324a; III 5b, 190b, 224a, 394a, 495b, 496a, 496b; IV 132b, 467a, 513b; V 28a, 28b, 29a, 41a, 107a, 259b, 260a, 300a, 362a, 546b
Sinai, N.	V 174a, 421a, 421b
Sinān (architect)	III 435a
Sinān dhū-Ilīm	V 93a
Sinān Pasha (mosque in Cairo)	III 435b
Sind	III 314a
Sindhi (language)	I 136a; V 95a, 96a, 342a
Singapore	III 344b; IV 271b; V 100a
Sinitic, Old (language)	III 244a
Sinkiang	I 172b
Ṣīr Banī Yās	I 155a
Sirius [al-Shiʿrā]	IV 109a; V **51b**, 52a, 52b
Sirius Verse	see Verse
Ṣirwāḥ	V 89a
Sistan	V 503a
al-Sistānī, ʿAlī Ḥusaynī	V 225a
Six Books	II 379a, 381a
Skidmore, Owings and Merrill's Islamic Cultural Center (New York)	III 435b
Slavs	III 543a

Sleepers see Seven Sleepers; Cave, Men/People of the
Smith, J.I. I 89b; II **53b**, **172a**; III 529b
Smith, J.Z. IV 485a
Smith, W.C. II 565a, 565b; IV 383b, 395a
Smith, W. Robertson I 368a, 402a; II 523b; III 96b, 97a, 98a; V 66b, 67a, 362a
Smitskamp, R. IV 267a
Snouck Hurgronje, C. I 8a, 330b; III 343b, 344a, 344b; IV 98a
Socrates V 8b
Sodom II 299b; III 231b, 232a, 232b, 489b; IV 425a, 584b; V 253b, 470b
  People of III 231b
Soekarno V 100a
Sogdiana I 139b
[King] Solomon [Sulaymān] I 52a, 53b, 54a, 61b, 99a, 100b, 101a, 149b, 151b, 152a, 162b, 163a, 165a, 166a, 166b, 168a, 168b, 195a, 207b, 211b, 228b, 229a, 229b, 236b, 245b, 347a, 490b, 496a, 496b, 532a; II 38b, 216a, 275b, 313b, 314a, 318a, 344b, 394b, 404b, 416a, 436a, 436b, 437b, 467b, 476b, 481b, 486a, 537b, 547a, 558a; III 4a, 4b, 12a, 43b, 44b, 48b, 50a, 50b, 61a, 91a, 93a, 93b, 94a, 94b, 95a, 103a, 190a, 208a, 224a, 226a, 242a, 247a, 249a, 249b, 250a, 253b, 395a, 410a, 418a, 444b, 479b, 487a, 487b, 520a, 521a, 522a, 525b, 534b, 546a; IV 61b, 135b, 210b, 213b, 288b, 291a, 294a, 304a, 304b, 307b, 315a, 315b, 316a, 316b, 438b, 509a, 513b, 516b, 524b, 538a, 555a, 577a, 586a, 586b, 604a; V **76b**, 77a, 77b, 108a, 120b, 127b, 200b, 202b, 277a, 281b, 285a, 342b, 373b, 377a, 390a, 412a, 424a, 470b, 475b, 476a, 530a, 532b, 533a, 533b
Solomon Ibn Adret (d. 1310) V 309b
Solvet, Ch. IV 188a

Somalia I 127b; III 326b; IV 360b
Sons of Adam see Adam
Sons of the Covenant I 181b
Son of God III 7a; see also Ezra; Christ; Jesus; Messiah
Sons of Israel see Israel
Soqollu Meḥmed III 322a
Sorabe (language) I 136a
Sorbonne I 425a
Sothis V 52a
Soucek, P. III **328b**; V **78a**
Sourdel, D. II 538
South Africa see Africa
Sozomen/Sozomenos V 90b, 258b, 263a, 263b
Spain II 35a, 343a, 472a; III 296b, 301a, 302, 303a, 303b, 306b, 321b, 432a, 559a; IV 236b, 240a, 244b, 317a, 415b; V 186a, 341b, 344b, 345a, 401b, 402a
    Muslim II 206b; III 263b; IV 317a
    Naṣrid III 308a, 318b
Spaniards V 309b
Spanish (language) see Aljamiado
Spellberg, D. I **60a**
Speyer, H. II 436a; III 4a, 522a; IV 54b, 194b; V 236b
Spitaler, A. II 354b, 361b; III 131b; IV 195b
Sprenger, A. I 323a; IV 192b, 193a, 194b
Sri Lanka IV 273b; V 538b
St. Petersburg IV 250b, 251a, 265b, 362a; V 347b
Starcky, J. I 138a
Station of Abraham see Abraham
Steingass, F. III 110b
Stenhouse, P. IV **525a**
Stephanus Byzantinus (Stephanus of Byzantium) II 298b; II 427a
Stephen (of Acts 7:40-1) I 275b
Stetkevych, J. III 477a, 481b
Stewart, D. I **236a**, **237a, 492b**, II **180a**; IV **104a, 483b**, **585a**; V **63b, 80a**, **232a**
Stewart, T. V 97a
Stoics III 386b; V 8b
Stowasser, B.F. III **81b**, **295b**; V **521b**
Stiegecker, H. III 396b
Strabo II 427a; IV 586a

Strasburg i 42b; iv 243b
Strothmann, R. i 105a
Stuttgart v 352a
Sudan i 33b, 69b, 127b; iii 306b, 326b; iv 176b, 275b, 360b, 538b
 Republic of iii 328a
al-Suddī al-Kabīr, ʿAbd al-Raḥmān (d.127-8/745-7) i 488a, 488b; ii 106a, 151a; iii 224b
Suez v 184b
Ṣūfī(s) [*ahl al-taṣawwuf*] i 51a, 62b, 68b, 176a, 189b, 201b, 206b, 263a, 389b, 481a, 485a, 497a, 520b, 526b, 556b; ii 119a, 120a, 161a, 206b, 215b, 279b, 286a, 286b, 409b, 451a, 451b, 452a, 502a, 527b; iii 67a, 83a, 101a, 167a, 187b, 230b, 236b, 251a, 254a, 305b, 310b, 311a, 317a, 374a, 395b, 397a, 407a, 492a, 507b; iv 77b, 88a, 88b, 157a, 157b, 167b, 169b, 173b, 175a, 232b, 371a, 424a, 424b, 430b, 491a, 494b, 509b, 547a, 573a, 579b; v 13a, 94b, 97b, 100a, **137a**, 137b, 138a, 138b, 139a, 139b, 141a, 141b, 142a, 142b, 143a, 144a, 146b, 147a, 151b, 152b, 153a, 157b, 158a, 220b, 288a, 383b, 384a, 386b, 401a, 467a, 486b, 552b
Ṣufrites i 540a; iii 86a, 87a, 387a, 389b, 400a, 521a; iv 354a, 354b, 355a, 387a
Sufyān b. ʿAbd al-Asad iii 178a
Sufyān b. ʿUyayna (d. 198/814) ii 105b, 387b; iv 390b
Sufyān al-Thawrī al-Kūfī, Abū ʿAbdallāh (d. 161/778) i 277b, 349a, 481a; ii 103b, 105b, 347b, 386b; v 139a, 139b
Ṣuhayb b. Sinān i 289b; v 59a
Suhayl (Canopus) v 51b
al-Suhaylī, Abū l-Qāsim ʿAbd al-Raḥmān b. ʿAbdallāh (d. 581/1185) iv 10b; v 334a
al-Suhrawardī, Abū Ḥafṣ ʿUmar (d. 632/1234) v 143b, 147b, 148a
al-Suhrawardī, Shihāb al-Dīn Yaḥyā b. Ḥabash (d. 587/1191) i 85a; ii 279b; iii 187b, 310a; v 484a
Sukulu Mosque i 285b
al-Sulamī, Abū ʿAbd al-Raḥmān (of Nīshāpūr; d. 412/1021) ii 119b, 120a, 453a; iii 236b; iv 157a; v 139a, 139b, 140a, 141a, 143a, 143b, 147a, 148b, 151b

al-Sulamī, Ṣafwān b. al-Muʿaṭṭal i 56b, 57b
Ṣulayḥids ii 34b
Sulaymān (Umayyad caliph) v 186a
Sulaymān ʿAbd al-Qawī al-Ṭūfī (d. 716/1316) v 334a
Sulaymān b. Khalaf al-Bājīs (d. 474/1081) i 514a
Sulaymān b. Mihrān al-Aʿmash see al-Aʿmash, Sulaymān b. Mihrān (d. 148/765)
Sulaymān b. Muslim b. Jammāz see Ibn Jammāz, Sulaymān b. Muslim (d. after 170/776-7)
Sulaymān b. Tarkhān al-Taymī (d. 143/760-1) ii 390b, 516a; iv 387b
Sulaymān b. Wahb see Ibn Wahb, Sulaymān
Sulaymāniyya complex (Damascus) iii 435b
Süleymān (the Magnificent; r. 926-74/1520-66) iii 320a, 320b, 322a, 599a
Süleymanlis v 225b, 226a
Süleymāniye mosque (Istanbul) iii 435a
Sulṭān Bāhū (d. 1103/1691) iii 225b; v 97a
Sulṭān Walad (d. 712/1312) iv 56a, 58b, 62b
Sulu (language) i 136a
Sulwān v 127a
Sumatra iii 316a
Sumayya bt. Kubbāṭ (d. bef. the *hijra*) v 59a
Sumerians v 52a, 124b
Sumūyadaʿ v 87b, 91b
Sumūyafaʿ Ashwaʿ v 565b, 566a
Sundanese (language) v 101a
Sundermann, W. iii 144a
Sunnīs/Sunnites i 56b, 57b, 59b, 74a, 186b, 342a, 386b, 387a, 388b, 390a, 390b, 418a, 427a, 518a; ii 12a, 113a, 189a, 206a, 111a, 206a, 207b, 208a, 243b, 285a, 422a, 424b, 471b, 504a, 506a, 521b, 527b, 532b, 537b, 538b, 553a; iii 161b, 285a, 285b, 370b; iv 99a, 129b, 265a, 268b, 342a, 387a, 449a, 450a, 450b, 495b, 500a, 593a, 594a, 594b, 598b; v 24a, 24b, 139b, 210b, 217a, 225b, 227a, 233a, 404a, 404b, 527b
Surya v 52a
Sūsa (Tunisia) iii 432b
al-Sūsī, Abū Shuʿayb Ṣāliḥ b. Ziyād (d. ca. 261/874) iv 359a, 359b, 390a
Suwāʿ ii 317b, 474a, 483a; iii 518b
al-Suyūṭī, Jalāl al-Dīn (d. 911/1505) i 33a, 36a, 73b, 78a, 90a, 126a, 200b, 205b, 210a, 358b, 420b, 514a; ii 110b, 113b, 114b, 121a,

229a, 231a, 231b, 232a, 232b, 233b, 271a, 357a, 358b, 378a, 385a, 390a, 394a, 415b, 461a, 468b; III 141b, 215a, 309a, 363a, 363b, 385a, 506a, 561b, 570b, 572b; IV 9b, 15b, 156a, 166b, 212b, 232a, 287a, 351b, 373b, 444b, 477b, 542b, 543a; V 119b, 219b, 221a, 277b, 302a, 302b, 326b, 327a, 328a, 328b, 330b, 332a, 332b, 334a, 334b, 335a, 346b, 434b, 444b, 496a

Swahili (language) I 136a; V 342a
Swanson, M. IV **287b**
Sweeney, A. III 226b
Sword Verse see Verse
Syr V 52a
Syria [(Bilād) al-Shām] I 9a, 9b, 10a, 47a, 108b, 110b, 121a, 127b, 138a, 150a, 153b, 173b, 181b, 210a, 265b, 290b, 307b, 308a, 308b, 332b, 333a, 335b, 336a, 557a; II 22b, 30a, 30b, 39a, 40a, 294b, 384b, 514b, 515a, 515b, 560a; III 3b, 5a, 5b, 9a, 29a, 68b, 85b, 142b, 152b, 153a; III 179b, 263a, 300b, 301a, 308b, 309a, 309b, 310b, 311a, 370a, 405b, 409a, 428b, 429a, 429b, 430a, 432a, 433a, 499a, 500a, 500b, 544a, 556a, 578a; IV 44a, 46a, 111b, 237a, 240b, 325b, 360b, 389a, 389b, 467a, 524b, 525a, 572a; V 2a, 71a, 92a, 137a, **184b**, 185a, 185b, 186a, 186b, 217a, 235a, 263a, 361b, 481b, 516b

Greater [al-Shaʾm/al-Shaʾām] III 180a
Syriac (language) I 45b, 136a, 138a, 138b, 200b, 311a, 313b, 316b, 490a; II 228a, 231a, 231b, 233b, 234a, 235b, 544a; III 1a, 8b, 9a, 9b, 49a, 56a, 57a, 114a, 118a, 118b, 129a, 130a, 130b, 131a, 231a, 244a, 244b, 407b, 518a; IV 257b, 351b, 397a, 517a; V 3a, 241a, 246a, 251a, 306a, 306b, 404b, 551b

Christian — II 236a
Syrian(s) — I 47b, 353b; III 119a, 309a; V 251a
Christian Fathers — III 144a
Szedlmayer, I.B. — V 345b
Szokoly, I. — V 348b

T

[Ayatollah] Ṭāleqānī — III 286a
Tabāla — II 237b
al-Ṭabarī, Abū Jaʿfar Muḥammad b. Jarīr (d. 310/923) — I 2a, 20b, 44b, 45a, 53a, 55a, 57a, 60b, 94b, 113b, 186a, 200a, 200b, 203b, 205a, 208a, 208b, 255b, 257a, 260b, 262b, 266b, 267a, 267b, 277b, 278a, 286b, 354a, 396b, 411a, 412a, 425a, 427a, 439a, 445b, 494b, 527a, 528b, 531a; II 4a, 4b, 21b, 88b, 98b, 99a, 105a, 106b, 110a, 110b, 111a, 111b, 112a, 113a, 113b, 114a, 146b, 147a, 147b, 148a, 150b, 151b, 154b, 156a, 156b, 177b, 178a, 195b, 217b, 219b, 220a, 220b, 221a, 221b, 227b, 230b, 239b, 271a, 278a, 338a, 338b, 357b, 369b, 385a, 388b, 389b, 392b, 400b, 424a, 426b, 435a, 446b, 456b, 468b, 478a, 478b, 488a, 491a, 491b, 495b, 498b, 505a, 517a, 523b, 524a, 530a, 545b, 562b, 563a; III 5b, 6a, 38a, 50b, 52b, 57a, 58b, 67b, 82a, 82b, 91a, 91b, 94b, 95a, 130a, 146a, 181a, 228b, 236a, 239b, 249b, 282a, 282b, 283a, 284a, 294a, 378a, 388b, 402b, 410b, 421b, 423b, 424b, 427a, 459b, 460a, 470a, 470b, 471a, 505b, 506a, 541b, 542a, 565a, 582a; IV 22b, 44b, 47a, 54b, 59a, 59b, 59b, 61a, 69a, 69b, 70a, 76b, 95b, 96a, 96b, 131a, 133b, 134b, 157a, 157b, 212b, 214b, 262a, 262b, 303b, 304a, 315a, 315b, 316a, 316b, 317a, 324a, 327a, 354b,

356a, 397a, 407b, 460b, 496b, 509b, 511b, 519a, 525b, 533b, 536b, 539b, 592a; v 9a, 16b, 17b, 18a, 25b, 31b, 33b, 34a, 34b, 37a, 41a, 46a, 55a, 64a, 83b, 119b, 125a, 131a, 131b, 143b, 157a, 160b, 161a, 164a, 179a, 195a, 219b, 242b, 243a, 277a, 329b, 341a, 353a, 360a, 361b, 377a, 377b, 389b, 398a, 400b, 401a, 435b, 439b, 440b, 441b, 442a, 444a, 448a, 448b, 462a, 466a, 470a, 473a, 473b, 474b, 475a, 476a, 482a, 428b, 491a, 495a, 552a

al-Ṭabarī, ʿAlī b. Sahl Rabban (d. ca. 250/864) — i 118a, 437b; ii 531a; iv 123b, 169a

Ṭabaristān — iii 558b

al-Ṭabarsī, Abū ʿAlī al-Faḍl b. al-Ḥasan (al-Tabrisī; d. 548/1153-4) — i 200a, 225a, 268b; ii 115a, 118a, 188a, 188b, 468b, 505a; iii 5b, 6a, 239b, 240a, 469b, 470a; iv 15a, 594b, 602b; v 330a, 335b, 336a, 360b, 442a

Ṭabāṭabāʾī, Muḥammad Ḥusayn (d. 1403/1982) — i 203b, 204a, 427b; ii 80b, 130b, 468b; iii 6a, 10b, 460b; iv 489b, 536b, 602b

Tabbaa, Y. — iii 310a

Tablet(s) — i 305a, 468b; iv 262b, 425b

  Preserved [*lawḥ mahfūẓ*] — i 92a, 247b; iii 508a, 538a; iv **261b**, 262a, 445b, 447a, 545a, 570a; v 150a, 153b

Ṭabkhānah-yi Sayyidāt-i Kazān — iv 265b

Tablīghī Jamāʿat — i 520b; v 228a

al-Tabrisī [al-Tabrīzī] — see al-Ṭabarsī, Abū ʿAlī al-Faḍl b. al-Ḥasan (al-Tabrisī; d. 548/1153-4)

Tabrīz — iii 268a; iv 266b

Tabūk — i 320a, 398a, 517b; ii 148b, 149a, 151a, 262b, 295a, 339a, 427b, 455a; iii 390a, 457a; iv 153b; v 40a, 40b, 175b, 185a, 472a

Tafrīshī, A. — iv 267a

al-Taftazānī, Saʿd al-Dīn (d. 791-2/1389-90) — i 198a, 483b

Tagalog (language) — v 101a, 101b

[Banū] Taghlib — ii 221a; iii 462a; iv 152a v 416b

Ṭāghūt — iii 26b

Ṭāhā, Maḥmūd Muḥammad i 33b, 34a, 34b, 35a
Ṭāhā Ḥusayn see Ḥusayn, Ṭāhā
al-Ṭaḥāwī (d. 321/933) ii 419a
Ṭahir al-Jazāʾirī v 329b
Ṭāhirids iii 312b
al-Ṭāʾif i 154a, 290b, 319b, 323b, 338b; ii 19b, 20a, 294b, 295a, 298a, 299b, 303a, 388a, 465b, 466a, 466b, 513b, 578b; iv 111b; v 254a, 481b, 565b
Taiwan i 287b
al-Ṭāʾiyyūna i 529b
Tajikistan v 226a
Takim, L. iv **526b**, **537a**
Taʾlab Riyām^um b. Shahrān v 86b, 89b, 92b, 93a, 563a
Ṭalḥa i 389a; ii 148a
Ṭalḥa b. Muṣarrif (d. 112/730) ii 387a
Ṭālibids iv 51a
Talmon, R. i **531a**; ii 351b, 361a, 364a, 365a, **367b**; iv 199b
Talmud ii 213a, 402b; iii 9b, 174a, 539b; iv 484b; v 90b, 495b
  Babylonian ii 241a
  Jerusalem ii 482b
Talshīr iv 266a
Ṭālūt see Saul
Ṭālūt (son-in-law of Labīd b. al-Aʿṣām) i 468a
Tamil (language) v 94a, 342a
[Banū] Tamīm i 110b, 121a, 529b, 530a; iii 460a; v 79a, 199a, 366a
Tamīm b. Ḥuwayṣ iii 89a
Tamīm al-Dārī i 110a
Tamīm wa-Bakr i 529b
Tamīm wa-Rabīʿa i 529b
al-Tamīmī v 334b
al-Tamīmī, Ismāʿīl b. Muḥammad i 554b, 556a
al-Tamīmī, Muḥammad b. Aḥmad (d. late fourth/tenth century) ii 446b
[Shaykh] al-Tamīmī (Muftī of Egypt) iv 270a
Tamlīkhā iv 10b
Tamnaʿ (capital of Qatabān) v 86a
Ṭanṭā ii 207b
Ṭanṭawī, M. i 186b; v 218a
Ṭantāwī Jawharī see Jawharī, Ṭantāwī
Tanūkh i 308a
al-Tanūkhī, ʿĪsā i 554a

Tanzania	v 209a, 218a
Taoism	iii 247b
Taqī al-Dīn b. Taymiyya	see Ibn Taymiyya, Taqī al-Dīn Aḥmad b. ʿAbd al-Ḥalīm (d. 728/1328)
Taqīf	ii 19b
Ṭarafa	iii 588b, 589a, 589b
al-Ṭarafī	iii 542b
Targum	i 146a
Tārīḥ	iii 242a
Tarim Basin	i 172b
Tāriq Rajab Museum	iii 305b
Tariq Ramadan	see Ramadan, T.
Tarquinius Priscus (r. 616-578 BCE)	iv 52a
Tarsus	iii 374b
Tartars	v 350b
Tashī Khātūn	iii 313b
Tasnīm	ii 218a, 283b, 284a
Tathlīth	see Trinity
Tatian	iii 13a
al-Tawḥīdī (d. 414/1023)	i 428a
Tawfīq, Khedive	iv 271a
Tawfīq al-Ḥakīm	see al-Ḥakīm, Tawfīq
al-Ṭawīl, S.R.	v 329b
Tawrāt	see Torah
Ṭāwūs b. Kaysān (d. 106/724)	ii 239a
al-Tawwazī, ʿAbdallāh b. Thābit (d. 308/920)	ii 107a; iii 117a
Ṭayyibī-Mustaʿlī Ismāʿīlī	iv 490a
Taym	i 152b; v 508a
Taymāʾ	ii 150a; iii 588b; iv 111b, 427b
Rabbi of	ii 515a
al-Ṭayy	i 308a
al-Ṭayyib, ʿAbdallāh	i 33b
[Imām] al-Ṭayyib	ii 503b
al-Ṭayyib al-Azraq	iv 267a
Techiman	iii 327b
Tehran	i 172a; iii 347a; v 342a, 540a
Telanissos	iii 405b
Tell el-Maskhūṭa	i 137b
Telugu (language)	v 342a
Temple	ii 155b; iii 4a; v 455b
in Jerusalem [*bayt al-maqdis*]	iv 514a, 516a, 516b
Jewish	i 125b, 303a; iii 2b, 3a
Mount [*al-ḥaram al-sharīf*]	i 125b, 126a, 149b, 156a, 156b; iii 2b, 3a, 3b, 5a, 427a, 429a
University (Philadelphia, PA)	v 69b

Ten Commandements I 365a, 365b, 366a, 366b, 367a, 367b; V 259b
Teraḥ [Tāriḥ, Tārakh] I 192a; V 248b
Termez (Uzbekistan) III 432b
Terrolensis, Johannes Gabriel V 345a
Tertullus (of Acts 24:2) I 310b
Teseo Ambrogio degli Albonesi (d. 1540) IV 245a
Testament
Greek New I 475a; III 12a
New I 42b, 98a, 108b, 109b, 123b, 237b, 303b, 307b, 316a; II 146b, 244b, 269a, 343a, 404b, 566a; III 8a, 8b, 11a, 13a, 23b, 51b, 144a, 147a, 184a, 477b, 519b; IV 236b, 241b, 289a, 298a, 299a, 450b, 586a; V 7a, 129b, 427a, 468b
Old I 109a, 166b, 214a; III 9b, 111a, 480a; IV 122b
See also Bible; Luke; Mark; Matthew; Revelation of John
Thailand V 213a, 215a
Thaʿlaba II 16b
al-Thaʿlabī, Abū Isḥāq Aḥmad b. Muḥammad b. Ibrāhīm (d. 427/1035) I 62a, 366a; II 105b, 111b, 404b, 405a, 462b, 463b, 542a; III 83a, 214a; IV 57b, 303a, 351b, 396b, 533b; V 146b, 147a, 324b, 325a, 329b, 390a
Thamānīn I 146b
Thamūd I 21b, 98b, 149b, 150a, 150b, 152b, 160b, 261b, 286b, 287a, 395b, 505a, 538a; II 43b, 212a, 259b, 293a, 338b, 339a, 340b, 399b, 427a, 427b, 437a, 459b, 541b, 542a, 543a; III 200b, 381a, 417a, 485b, 486a, 518b, 519a, 519b, 520a, 520b, 521b, 522a, 534b, 553a; IV 160a, 258a, 296a, 296b, 309a, 321a, 352a, 352b; V **252b**, 253a, 253b, 254a, 261b, 280a, 318a, 389a, 460b
People of III 443a, 583a; IV 352b, 425a, 454a, 520a, 521b, 522a; V 107b, 164b, 171b, 252b, 317b, 471a
Thamudeni I 150a
Thaqīf II 466a, 513b

Thaʾrān Yuhanʿim	V 563b, 564a
Thatta	III 434a
Thawr	
Cave of	II 20a
Mount	I 271a, 293b
Thawr-Baʿal^{un}	V 90b
al-Thawrī	see Sufyān al-Thawrī al-Kūfī (d. 161/778)
Theodore Abū Qurra (bishop of Ḥarrān; d. 210/826)	IV 71a, 404b, 560a; V 8b
Theodor Bibliander	see Bibliander, Th.
Theodosius	I 293a; III 375a
Theophanes	II 475a
Theophilus the Indian	V 563b, 564a
Thicket, People of the [*aṣḥāb al-ayka*]	II 260a; III 393b, 486a, 519b, 522a; IV **53b**, 54a, 54b, 318b; V 245a, 313a
Thomas, D.	I **118b**, **438a**; V **372a**
Thomas Erpenius	see Erpenius, Thomas (d. 1624)
Thot/Thoth (Egyptian god)	II 485a; V 119a
Throne of God	see God
Throne Verse	see Verse
Tiberias	III 309b, 390a
Tietz, R.	II 352a
al-Tīfāshī	I 439a
al-Ṭighnarī	I 48b
Tigris	I 147a; II 332b, 559b, 560b; III 5b, 53b; V 126b
Tihāma	I 214b, 529b; II 211a, 294b; IV 254a
al-Tijānī, [Shaykh] Aḥmad	I 33b
al-Ṭilimsānī, Ibn al-Ḥājj (d. 737/1336)	I 78a
Timothy I (Nestorian patriarch)	V 371a
Tīmūr (r. 771-807/1370-1405)	III 268a, 313b, 314a, 318a, 320b
Tīmūrids	I 174a, 283a; III 308b, 320a
al-Tirmidhī, Abū ʿĪsā Muḥammad b. ʿĪsā (d. 279/892)	I 389a, 391b; II 270b, 377a; 461a, 554a; III 391b; IV 370a, 371a; V 278a
Titus	II 146b; III 4a, 6a, 539b
Tjokroaminoto	V 99a
TKA	see Islam
Toelle, H.	II **4b**, **213b**; V **65b**, 126b
Toledan(s)	I 48b
Toledo (Spain)	III 432b; IV 236b, 242a
Corpus Toletanum	IV 236b, 239a, 242b, 243, 245a, 245b
Tohidi, N.	V 540b

Tollens, L. v 350a
Toorawa, S. i **347a**; v **376b**
Topkapı Museum i 155b, 283a
Topkapı Sarayı iii 299a, 318b, 320a
Torah [Tawrāt] i 11b, 17b, 100a, 118a, 228b, 245b, 305a, 310b, 312b, 516b; ii 183b, 221a, 235b, 316a, 342a, 342b, 343a, 434a, 485b, 494a, 498a, 499a, 513a, 516b, 544b, 571b; iii 16a, 23b, 24b, 25a, 25b, 26a, 28a, 30b, 31a, 51b, 57a, 65a, 104b, 150b, 151a, 174b, 186b, 190a, 191a, 255b, 260a, 425b, 445a, 445b, 495b, 507a, 507b, 513a, 515a, 593b; iv 3b, 37b, 536b, 561a, 563b; v 15b, 103a, 111a, 152a, 176a, 200b, 231b, 256b, 270a, **300a**, 300b, 301a, 301b, 302a, 302b, 303a, 304a, 304b, 305a, 305b, 306a, 306b, 307a, 307b, 308a, 309a, 309b, 399b, 437b, 463b, 483b
Tornberg, C.J. v 350b
Torrey, C. i 42b; ii 485a; iv 101a, 101b, 104a, 133a, 193a, 195a, 302a, 304a, 314b, 315a, 351b, 399b, 471b; v 311b, 314a, 315a, 315b
Toronto, J. i **186b**
Tottoli, R. i **22a**, **255a**; ii **13b**, **14a**, **155a**, **509b**; iii **105a**, **375b**; iv **44b**, **352a**, **353b**, **522a**, **606a**; v **62a**
Tower of Babel see Babel
TPA see Islam
Traditionalists [*muḥaddithūn*] i 468b
Transjordan i 308b; v 185a
Transoxania i 483a, 518a; ii 106a, 112b, 115b; iii 305a; iv 56b
Transvaal v 56b
Trench see Ditch
Tribes iii 27a
Trinity [*tathlīth*] i 117a, 117b, 223a, 312a, 312b, 313a, 471b; ii 479b; iii 300a; iv 38b, 80b, 121a, 122a, 123a, 412b, 456a; v **368b**, 369a,

	369b, 370a, 371a, 371b, 372a, 573b
Christian	I 378b; II 443a
Tripolitania	III 86b
Troupeau, G.	III **384a**
Tuʿaylib, A.	III 6a
Tubān Abū Karib b. Malkī Karib	V 567b
Tubbaʿ	I 152a; II 437b; IV 320a; V **389a**, 389b, 390a, 390b
People of	III 522a; V 252b, 389a
Tübingen University	II 362a
al-Ṭufayl b. al-Ḥārith	V 508a
Ṭulayḥa b. Khuwaylid (d. 21/642)	I 121a; II 530a; V 79a
Tumīm	II 238a
Tunis	III 597b
Tunisia	I 127b; III 86b, 436b, 596a; IV 349a,. 360b
Ṭūr	see Mount Sinai
Turʿa	V 93a
Turrabān	V 565b
Turfan	I 172b
Turk(s)	I 146b; II 240a; III 543a; IV 242b, 243a; V 350b, 359b
Ottoman	IV 244b
Persophilic	IV 57b
Turkestan	I 293b
Turkey	I 43a, 146b, 147a, 321a; III 325a; IV 486b, 566b; V 209b, 211a, 225b, 342b, 346a, 352a, 394b
Ottoman	III 595b; see also Ottoman(s) [empire]
Turkish (language)	I 483a; II 90a, 287a; IV 517a; V 131a, 343b, 346b, 391a, 393a
Ottoman	I 136a; V 391b
Turpin, François Henri (d. 1799)	IV 250a
al-Ṭūsī, Abū Jaʿfar Muḥammad b. al-Ḥasan (d. 460/1067)	I 225a, 225b, 261a, 546a; II 115a, 117b, 189a, 468b; III 94b, 470a, 470b, 471a; IV 538b, 539b, 594b, 597a, 602b; V 330a, 442a
al-Tustarī, Sahl b. ʿAbdallāh (d. 283/896)	I 86b; II 118b, 119a, 119b, 409b; III 187b, 230b; IV 157b, 158a; V 140b, 141a, 141b, 142a, 143a, 147a, 148b, 153a, 361a
Tutty Alawiya(h)	V 214b, 227a
Ṭuwā	III 421a; IV 282b; V 110a, 248a, **395b**

Tuyuk I 293b
Twelve Tables III 509a
Twelver(s) see Shīʿism
Tyana I 45b
Tyre III 594a; V 558b

U

ʿUbayd b. al-Sabbāq II 383b
ʿUbayd b. Umayr (d. 68/687) II 381a; III 515b
Ubayda b. al-Ḥārith II 400a; V 508a
ʿUbaydallāh b. Jaḥsh II 403a; V 508b
ʿUbaydallāh b. Ziyād (governor of Kūfa; r. 53-9/673-9) III 85b; V 244b
Ubayy (Codex) IV 223a
Ubayy b. Kaʿb (d. 21/642) I 209b, 333a, 348b, 349b, 350a, 350b, 353a, 354a, 355a, 356b, 359a; II 17b, 102b, 190a, 243b, 247a, 378a, 385a, 520a; III 17b, 19b, 257b, 502a; IV 388b; V 238b, 241b
Ubayy b. Khalaf II 147b
Üç Şerefeli mosque III 435a
ʿUdhra I 544a
ʿŪj b. ʿAnaq see Og
Ugarit V 86b, 126b
Ugaritic (language) II 235b
Uḥud I 110b, 320a, 398a, 406a, 407b, 409b, 460b, 461b; II 162a, 241b, 508b, 519a; III 18b, 283a, 369b; V 43a, 379b, 409a, 491a, 508a
  Battle of (3/625) I 54b, 320a, 405b, 407b, 409a, 409b, 461a, 462a, 537a; II 148b, 149a, 221b, 262b, 374a, 397b, 400b, 519a; III 35a, 456b, 498b, 603b; IV 256a, 307b; V 175b, 491a
al-Ujhūrī (1190/1776) III 570b
ʿUkal al-ʿĀliya I 529b
ʿUkāẓ I 154a; II 298a, 529a; III 411a, 500b
al-Ukhdūd I 154a, 154b; III 501a; V **397a**, 397b
ʿUkl I 489a
al-ʿUlā I 150b, 152b, 156a; II 427b
Ulfa, Maria V 214a
Ūljāytū see Öljeytü (r. 703-16/1304-16)
Ullmann, M. II 347a; V 297a

Ullmann, Rabi Lion (Ludwig) Baruch v 350a
Ūlū Cāmiʿ iii 434a
ʿUlyā Tamīm wa-Suflā Qays i 529b
ʿUmān see Oman
ʿUmar II (b. ʿAbd al-ʿAzīz; r. 99-101/717-20) 307a, 307b
ʿUmar al-Aqṭaʿ iii 313b
ʿUmar b. al-Khaṭṭāb (r. 13-23/634-44) i 17b, 18a, 125b, 154b, 189b, 209b, 273a, 320a, 332a, 332b, 333a, 355a, 355b, 356b, 357a, 357b, 358a, 360a, 360b, 388b, 389a, 390a, 398a 408a, 462a, 518a, 540b; ii 12a, 16b, 22a, 22b, 147a, 148b, 183a, 214b, 241a, 278b, 337a, 381a, 382b, 384a, 384b, 385b, 393a, 397b, 398a, 398b, 400a, 403a, 522b, 523a, 523b, 524a, 528b, 555a, 560a; iii 3a, 85a, 153b, 179b, 261a, 429a, 439b, 464b, 500b, 546b, 552b, 570a, 605a; iv 99a, 105a, 125b, 277a, 339b, 386b, 448b, 449a, 582b, 584a, 587b, 599a; v 47b, 59a, 185b, 192a, 196a, 232b, 285a, 334a, 362a, 441b, 472a, 510a, 510b, 516a, 535b
Covenant of [*ʿahd ʿumar*] iv 235a
ʿUmar al-Khayyām (d. bef. 530/1135) iii 222a
ʿUmar al-Murtaḍā iii 267b
ʿUmāra b. Ḥayyān iii 89a
ʿUmāra b. ʿUkayl iii 460b
Umayya b. ʿAbd al-Malik ii 30b
Umayya b. Abī l-Ṣalt iv 111b, 351a; v 36b, 119a, 254a, 427a
Umayya b. Khalaf v 59a
Umayyad(s) i 126b, 306b, 466a; ii 22b, 272b, 560a; iii 6a, 153a, 301a, 302b, 323a, 370a, 423b, 430a, 430b, 605b; iv 52a, 84a, 141a, 333a, 342b, 364a, 364b; v 186b
Umayyad Mosque i 165b, 279b; iii 298a, 309b, 429b; iv 524b, 598b; v 17a, 186a, 186b, 503a, 503b, 505a
Umm Ayman iv 45b
Umm Ḥabība bt. Abī Sufyān v 508b, 516b, 520a
Umm Hāni (Bint Abī Ṭālib) ii 103a

Umm al-Jimāl	I 138a
Umm Kalthūm	II 88a
Umm Kulthūm (daughter of ʿUtba)	V 535a
Umm Kulthūm (daughter of the Prophet and Khadīja)	III 80b; V 507b
Umm Kulthūm (vocalist)	IV 381b
Umm Muḥammad	II 41a
Umm al-Qurā	III 443b
Institute	V 225b
Umm Salama bt. al-Mughīra	II 398b; IV 442a; V 508a, 517b, 518a, 535b
Umm al-Walīd	III 432b
Umm Waraqa	V 535b
ʿUmyānis	II 478b
Unays	IV 45a
Universal House of Justice	see Bahāʾīs
United Arab Emirates	I 127b
United Kingdom	I 202b; IV 23b
United States of America	I 30b, 31a; II 135a; III 286a; IV 23b, 180b, 273b; V 207a, 215b, 216b, 218a, 225a, 226b, 538b
[Banū] ʿUqayl	I 529b
Urarṭu	I 147a; III 68b, 69a
ʿUrayna	IV 364a
Uraz Muḥammad	III 319a
Urdu (language)	I 136a, 520a, 520b; II 90a, 223b; IV 172b; V 94a, 96a, 342a
al-Urdunn	see Jordan
Uriah [Ahriya]	I 496a, 496b, 497a; IV 315b, 317a
Urīm	II 238a
ʿUrwa	I 353b
ʿUrwa b. al-Ward	II 302a
ʿUrwa b. al-Zubayr (d. ca. 94/713)	II 150a, 382a; III 438b; IV 533a; IV 93b; V 31b, 32a, 32b, 33a
Usāma b. Lādin	IV 414b
[Mt.] Usays (Sēs)	I 138a; III 430b
[Banū] Usayyid	III 461b, 462a
[Shaykh] Usman dan Fodio	IV 177b
Usmānī, Sh. (d. 1949)	II 80b
al-Ushmūnī (grammarian)	II 356b
Ussher, James (d. 1656)	IV 249a
al-ʿUṭāridī, Aḥmad b. ʿAbd al-Jabbār (d. 272/886)	V 34a
ʿUtba	II 513b
ʿUthmān	see ʿUthmān b. ʿAffān (r. 23-35/644-56)

ʿUthmān b. ʿAffān (r. 23-35/644-56) ɪ 63a, 154b, 174a, 209b, 247b, 271b, 278b, 331b, 333a, 348a, 355b, 356a, 356b, 357a, 357b, 358b, 359a, 388b, 389a, 462a, 518a, 539b; ɪɪ 169b, 246b, 247a, 383b, 384a, 384b, 386a, 396a, 398a, 464a; ɪɪɪ 85a, 87b, 88a, 123a, 189a, 255b, 256a, 298b, 303a, 323a, 429a, 464b, 465b, 476a, 480b, 595a, 598b, 605a; ɪv 26a, 134a, 134b, 135a, 136b, 139a, 140a, 140b, 201b, 244a, 265b, 270a, 356a, 356b, 384a, 389a, 449a, 449b, 450a, 587b, 593a; v 1a, 2a, 23b, 24a, 24b, 25a, 166b, 324a, **408b**, 409a, 409b, 410a, 535b

ʿUthmānic Codex ɪ 350a; ɪɪ 398b; ɪɪɪ 124b, 307a, 307b, 309b; ɪv 355a, 355b, 356a, 357a, 449a, 492b, 497a,593a, 594b, 600a, 601b; v 167a, 335b, 409a, 410a, 410b

ʿUthmān al-Battī ɪ 482b

ʿUthmān (b.) Ḥusayn (al-)Warrāq ɪ 281b, 282a; ɪɪɪ 264a

ʿUthmān b. al-Ḥuwayrith ɪɪ 403a

ʿUthmān b. Muḥammad ɪɪɪ 601b

ʿUthmān b. Saʿīd b. ʿAbdallāh al-Quṭbī (d. 197/812) ɪv 359b

ʿUthmān b. Saʿīd Warsh see Warsh, ʿUthmān b. Saʿīd (d. 197/812)

ʿUthmān b. Sulaymān al-Battī v 417b

[Mullā] ʿUthmān Ismāʿīl see Osman Ismail

ʿUways, Sayyid ɪɪ 81a

Uyghur ɪ 136a

ʿUzayr see Ezra

Uzbekistan ɪɪ 110b; v 226a

al-ʿUzzā/al-ʿUzzāʾ ɪ 37b, 95a, 194b, 208a, 330a; ɪɪ 278a, 317b, 329b, 392a, 474a, 483b; ɪv 216b, 330a; v 87a, 88a, 122a, 261a, 362a

ʿUzzayān v 88a

V

Vajda, G. ɪ 528a

Valencia ɪ 284b; ɪv 243b

Valéry, P. IV 470a
Varis Shāh V 97a
Varisco, D.M. III **416a**, **555a**
Vatican Library IV 248a
Vedas III 584b
Vedat Dalakoy's State Mosque in Islamabad, Pakistan III 435b
Venice IV 242a, 250a, 265a
Venus II 405a; IV 108b; V 93a
Verevkin, M.I. V 347b
Vernet, J. V 354b
Verse V **419b**
  Challenge II 527a, 532b; III 116a
  Darkness V 182a, 182b
  Light [*āyat al-nūr*] I 199a, 213b; II 218a, 218b; II 31b, 34a, 96a, 96b, 218b, 275b, 276b, 305a, 326a, 326b; III 108a, 187b, 208b, 311b, 387b, 431b, 437a, 534b; IV 380a; V 18a, 138a, 151a, 155a, 181b, 182a, 182b, 361b, 427b
  Satanic IV **531b**
  Sirius V 52b
  Sword II 151a; IV 409b
  Throne [*āyat al-kursī*] I 103b, 171a, 264b; II 32a, 37b, 38a, 38b, 96a, 96b, 275b, 276b, 325b, 408b, 461a, 461b; III 182b, 267b, 437a; IV 173a, 176a, 180a, 380a; V 150b, 151a, 277a, 277b, 371b, 427b
  Victory III 326b, 558a
Versteegh, K. I 128a, 130b, 134a, 231b; II 347a; IV 199b
[Queen] Victoria I 198b
Vienna IV 361b
  Council of IV 240b
Vietnamese (language) V 101a
Vincent of Beauvais (Vincentius Bellovacensis; d. ca. 1264) IV 256b
Violet, B. IV 317a
Virani, N. IV **350b**
Virgil II 240a; III 479b; V 52a
Vizier's Gate [Bāb al-Wuzarāʾ] III 436a
Vollers, K. II 346a, 346b, 357a, 367a; III 123a, 124a, 132a; IV 193b
Vrindavan V 96b

W

Waardenburg, J. — I **510b**
Wadd — II 317b, 474a, 483a; III 518b; V 86b, 87b, 91b
Wadud-Muhsin, A. — II 202a, 203a, 288b; V 227a, 540a
Wagl — V 91b
Wagtendonk, K. — II 181b, 183a, **184b**; III 496b, 538a; IV 197a, 341a, 342b, 344a, 345a; V **431b**
Wahaj, S. — V 206b, 225a
Wahb b. Munabbih (d. 110/728 or 114/732) — I 365b, 366a, 488a, 496b, 544b; II 335a; III 117a, 117b, 374b, 408b; IV 303b, 525b, 586b; V 31a, 31b, 38b, 39a, 47b, 307a, 360b, 390a, 397b
Wahhābī(s) — I 39a, 201b; II 554a, 554b; III 179b, 370b; IV 493b V **452a**, 453a; see also Ibn ʿAbd al-Wahhāb, Muḥammad (d. 1206/1791)
Wahid, A. — V 214b
al-Wāḥidī, Abū l-Ḥasan ʿAlī b. Aḥmad al-Nīsābūrī (d. 468/1076) — I 200a, 321b, 549a; II 112a, 391b, 392a; III 570a, 570b, 571b; IV 15b, 533b; V 143a, 325a
Wahl, S. — V 349a
Waḥshī — II 400b; III 463a
Waḥshī b. Ḥarb (d. 41-50/662-70) — V 59a
Waines, D. — I **49a**, **292a**, **495b**; II **178b**, **223a**, **369b**, **447a**; III **392a**; V **179b**, **362a**, **471a**
Waldman, M. — IV 383b
[Shāh] Walī Allāh al-Dihlawī (d. 1176/1762-3) — I 520a; III 223b; V 158a, 341b
Wali Fard Muhammad — see Fard Muhammad (d. ca. 1934)
al-Walīd I (r. 86-96/705-15) — I 125b, 126b, 156b; II 29b; III 429b
al-Walīd II (al-Walīd b. ʿAbd al-Malik; r. 125-6/743-4) — II 30a; IV 52a, 141b, 305b; II 39b; III 298b, 300a; V 31b, 186a
al-Walīd b. al-Mughīra (d. 218/833) — II 528b; III 247a
Wāliya (one name of Noah's wife) — III 541b
Walker, J. — IV 194b
Walker, P. — II **507b**; III **104a**
Wallace D. Mohammed — see Warith Deen Mohammed
Wansbrough, J. — I 133b, 323a, 334a, 350b, 417b; II 103b, 150a, 245b, 246a, 250b, 384b; III 109a, 124b, 194b, 456b; IV 7b, 27a, 116a, 197b, 199a, 201b, 202a, 202b, 203a,

203b, 204a, 260a, 589a; v 48b, 299a
al-Wāqidī, Muḥammad ʿUmar (d. 207/822-3) ii 145a, 149b, 150a; iv 323b, 324a, 533a; v 34b, 35a, 42a, 42b, 43a, 43b, 45a, 194a, 271b
Waraqa b. Nawfal (cousin of Khadīja) i 315a; ii 241a, 343a, 403a, 514a, 517b; iii 80b, 81a, 515a, 515b, 516a; iv 217a, 408b
Warda (vocalist) iv 381b
Warith Deen Mohammed i 31b
Warqā (d. 160/776) ii 105a
al-Warrāq, Isḥāq Ibrāhīm (d. 286/899-900) iv 390a
Warsh, ʿUthmān b. Saʿīd (d. 197/812) i 334a; ii 247b; iii 607b; iv 356b, 357b, 359a, 359b, 360b, 361a, 361b, 373a, 390a
Wāṣil, [Shaykh Dr.] Naṣr Farīd (mufti of Egypt) v 220a
Wāṣil b. ʿAṭāʾ (d. 131/728-9) iii 466b; iv 74a
Wāsiṭ ii 387b; iii 5b
al-Wāsiṭī, Abū Bakr (d. 320/932) v 141a
al-Wāthiq (r. 227-32/842-7) i 469b; ii 333a, 538b; iv 328a
Watson, A. i 47b, 48a
Watt, W.M. i 38a, 43a, 200b, 248b, 249a, 323a, 368a, 368b, 369a, 370a, 382b, 399a, 417b, 468b; ii 151b, 191a, 296a, 374b; iii 22b, 47a, 107a, 196a, 578b; iv 196a, 199a, 449b, 535a; v 42a, 48b, 298a, 314a, 469b, 502b
al-Waṭwāṭ, Jamāl al-Dīn Muḥammad b. Yaḥyā i 47a
Waugh, E. i **176b**, **238b**; ii **216a**; iv **35b**
al-Wazzān v 329a
Webb, G. i 85b, **92a**; ii **279b**; iii **389b**
Weil, G. i 322b; iv 188a, 188b, 190b, 450a; v 351a
Weiss, B. iv **285b**
Weiss, L. (later Muhammad Asad) v 343a
Weitbrech, H. v 297b
Welch, A. i **36b**; v 424b
Wellhausen, J. i 417b; iii 76a, 411a; iv 98a, 257a, 260b; v 48a
Wensinck, A.J. i 204a, 330b; ii 181b, 488b, 499a; iii 538a; v 502b, 504a

Wheeler, B. I **258a**; II **99b**, **339a**, **340b**; IV **110b**
Wheelocke, Abraham (d. 1653) IV 249a
Whelan, E. III 298b
Wherry, E. IV 529b; V 548b
White Mosque (Ramla) V 186a
Widengren, G. I 248b
Widmanstetter (Widmanstadius), Johann Albrecht von (d. 1557) IV 245a
Wiederhold, L. III **419a**; IV **284a**; V **178b**
Wielandt, R. II **140b**
Wiet, G. I 169a
Wild, S. I 418a, 421a; IV 197a
Wilde, C. IV **215a**, **417a**
William of Tripoli IV 240b, 241a
Winnett, F. II 428a
Winter, T. II **162a**, **448a**; V 350a
Wisnovsky, R. II **413b**
Wittenberg IV 247a
Wolfson, H. I 104a
Wolof (language) I 33a
World War I IV 265b; V 48b
World War II I 148a, 350b, 361a; V 343b, 351b
World Wide Web (WWW) I 391a, 392a, 393a, 393b
Wright, W. II 350b; V 297b

X

Xenophanes I 103b
Xenophon I 147a
Xian, Great Mosque of see China

Y

Yadaʿismuhū V 87b
Yā Sīn IV 353a
Yafʿān V 87b
al-Yāfiʿī (d. 768/1367) I 78a
Yāfith see Japeth
Yaghūth II 317b, 474a, 483a; V 92a
Yahūd II 462b
Yahuda, A.S. V 236a
Yahūdhā see Judah
Yahūdaʾ Yakkuf V 564b
Yahweh III 9b, 10a, 530b; V 500b

Yaḥyā (son of Zechariah) see John the Baptist
Yaḥyā b. Abī Kathīr (d. bet. 129/747 and 132/750) II 381b, 388a; V 165a
Yaḥyā b. ʿAdī (d. 363/974) IV 71b
Yaḥyā b. Maʿīn (d. 233/847) II 384a
Yaḥyā b. Mubārak al-Yazīdi see al-Yazīdi, Yaḥyā b. Mubārak (d. 202/817-8)
Yaḥyā b. Naṣr al-Jamālī al-Ṣūfī III 313a, 313b
Yaḥyā b. Sallām al-Baṣrī (d. 200/815) II 110a, 116b; IV 533a; V 333a, 335a
Yaḥyā b. Yaḥyā al-Tamīmī (d. 226/840) I 470a
Yaḥyā b. Yaʿmur (or Yaʿmar; d. 129/746) III 606a
Yaḥyā Ḥaqqī II 555a
Yaḥyā al-Ṣūfī see Yaḥyā b. Naṣr al-Jamālī al-Ṣūfī
Yaʾjūj see Gog
Yakhṭūb I 529a
Yaksūm IV 46a
Yaʿlā V 90b
Yalmaq V 93a
Yām III 541a; see also Canaan [Kanʿān]
al-Yamāma I 121a, 332a, 332b; II 384b, 388a; III 461b, 462a, 462b, 500a; IV 22b, 254a, 352b; V 79a, 549b
Yamm V 126b
Yaʿqūb see Jacob
Yaʿqūb b. Ibrāhīm b. Saʿd (d. 208/823) II 393a
Yaʿqūb b. Isḥāq al-Ḥaḍramī see al-Ḥaḍramī, Abū Muḥammad Yaʿqūb b. Isḥāq (d. 205/821)
al-Yaʿqūbī, Aḥmad b. Abī Yaʿqūb b. Wāḍiḥ II 343a, 403b; IV 304a, 315b, 316a, 317a, 525a; V 389b, 409b
Yāqūt b. ʿAbdallāh al-Ḥamawī (d. 626/1229) I 147a, 195a; II 338b, 559b; III 68b; V 127a, 362a
Yāqūt al-Mustaʿṣimī (d. ca. 697/1298) I 137a; III 310b, 311a, 313a, 320a, 595b, 597a
Yarmūk V 185b
Yarmouk University I 153a
[Banū] Yaʿrūb III 462a
al-Yasaʿ see Elisha
Yasār II 517a
Yashūʿ b. Nūn see Joshua
Yāsir[um] Yuhanʿim V 562b
Yathill V 89a, 89b
Yathrā III 421a; see also Jethro
Yathrib I 338a, 405b, 407a, 409a; II 15a, 15b, 16b, 20a, 20b, 21a, 148b, 149b, 294b, 295a, 299a, 299b,

303a, 439a; III 131a, 207b, 208a, 367b, 456b, 525b; IV 49a, 259b, 397a, 529a; V 28b, 44b, 87a, 375b, 376a, 389b, 549b; see also Medina

Yaʿūq II 317b, 474a, 483a; V 92a
Yawm al-Furqān see Day of the Criterion
Yazīd III 304b, 433a
Yazīd-i Khwāsi III 433a
Yazīd IV 26a; V 185b
Yazīd I (Umayyad caliph) V 186b
Yazīd II (r. 101-5/720-4) II 474b, 475a
Yazīd b. ʿAbdallāh II 28a
al-Yazīdi, Yaḥyā b. Mubārak (d. 202/817-8) IV 360a, 389b
Yça Gidelli of Segovia see ʿĪsā Dhā Jābir
Yemen [al-Yaman] I 4b, 20b, 44a, 46b, 47b, 67a, 110b, 121a, 122a, 128a, 148b, 168b, 173a, 174b, 290b, 293b; II 19b, 25b, 34b, 148a, 179a, 294b, 317b, 358a, 437b, 454b, 463a, 463b, 559a; III 58b, 180a, 312b, 363b, 369a, 471a, 558b, 559b; IV 11b, 37a, 44a, 45a, 46a, 257b, 329a, 352b, 360b, 407b, 572a; V 31a, 79a, 80a, 88a, 90b, 91a, 92a, 167a, 389a, 389b, 390a, 397a, 481b, 500b, **561b**, 562a, 564a, 565b, 566a, 567b
  Zaydī III 607b
Yemenis/Yemenites II 490a
  Sabaean III 339a
Yerushalmi, Y.H. IV 346a; V 175b
Yeşil Cāmiʿ III 434b
Yiṣḥāq see Isaac
Yoab IV 316a
Yogykarta V 219a
Yom Kippur II 182a, 184b; IV 340a, 340b, 341a, 342a, 343a
Yoruba (language) V 342a
Yuan see China
Yuḥannā al-Ḥawshabī (d. 1632) IV 237a
Yung-lo III 315b
Yunnan (China) see China
Yūnus see Jonah
Yūnus b. Bukayr (d. 199/815) V 34a
Yūnus b. Ḥabīb al-Thaqafī (d. 182/798) II 363a

Yusuf, H. V 206b
Yusuf, I. II **504a**
Yūsuf I (of Spain) II 35a
Yūsuf ʿAlī, ʿA. (1872-1953) I 87a, 176a, 186a, 200a, 200b, 229a, 231b, 369a, 391b, 537a; II 509b; III 182a, 183a, 184b, 189a, 529a, 529b, 530a, 532a, 532b, 539b; IV 274b; V 343a
Yūsuf Asʾar Yathʾar (Dhū Nuwās; Jewish king of the Ḥimyarites) I 309b; III 500a; V 389b, 397b, 565b, 568a
Yūsuf b. ʿAbd al-Raḥmān al-Mizzī (d. 742/1341) II 379a, 389b
Yūsuf b. Tāshufīn III 307a
Yūsuf al-Baṣīr V 136a
Yūsuf al-Hindī III 251a
Yūsuf al-Qaraḍāwī see al-Qaraḍāwī, Yūsuf

Z

Zāb III 423b
Zabad I 138a
al-Ẓabarī I 2a, 20b
Ẓabyān Temple V 89b
Zacharias Graphius IV 250a
Ẓafār (Ḥimyarī capital) V 563a, 565a, 565b
Zaghloul El-Naggar see El-Naggar, Z.
Zaghhūlī, Muḥammad b. al-Ḥusayn al-Aruzzī (d. 559/1164) V 326b
al-Ẓāhir (caliph) I 126b
al-Ẓāhir Ghāzī (r. 582-613/1186-1216) III 310a
Ẓāhirī(s) III 385b; IV 123b
Zahniser, A.M. I **123b**; II 262a, **510b**, **558b**; III 212b, **243a**, **382b**; IV **11b**; V 174b
Zainuddin M.Z.H. V 224b
al-Zajjāj(ī), Abū Isḥaq Ibrāhīm b. Muḥammad b. al-Sarī (d. 311/923) I 257a, 432b; II 109a, 557a; V 243a, 439b, 551b
Zakariyyāʾ Aḥmad II 88a, 88b
Zakariyyāʾ b. Abī Zāʾida (d. 147-9/764-6) II 382b
Zakariyyāʾ b. Muḥammad al-Qazwīnī see al-Qazwīnī, Zakariyyā b. Muḥammad (d. 682/1283)
Zakariyyāʾ b. Yuḥannā III 53b
Zakariyyāʾ Yaḥyā b. al-Khayr al-Jannāwunī (fl. fifth/eleventh century) I 485a
Zakeri, M. I **148a**
Zaki, M. I **204a**, **207a**
al-Zamakhsharī, Maḥmūd b. ʿUmar (d. 538/1144) I 53a, 81b, 82a, 203b, 208a, 225b,

256b, 267a, 378a, 397a, 431b, 439a, 484b, 522a; II 113a, 115a, 116b, 124a, 136b, 138a, 146b, 147b, 151b, 228a, 271a, 278a, 280b, 281a, 313b, 354b, 355a, 365a, 408b, 426b, 468b, 486b, 488a, 500b, 505a; III 3b, 65a, 67b, 73a, 81b, 181a, 183a, 201b, 249b, 401b, 408b, 460a, 469a; IV 3a, 77b, 100b, 186b, 244a, 266a, 358a, 460b; V 16b, 18a, 24b, 25b, 83b, 109b, 110a, 111a, 124b, 160b, 193b, 195a, 300b, 341a, 359a, 359b, 360b, 361b; V 435b, 494b, 496a, 560a

Zaman, M.Q. III **582b**; V **27b**

Zamzam I 9a; II 205a; III 338b, 388b; IV 97b, 519b, 539b, 543a; V 122b, 127a, 463a

Zanj II 560b

Zanzibar III 87a, 328b

al-Zaqqūm I 42a; II 50a, 50b, 415b; III 177a, 383b, 533a; V 359a, 359b, 360a, **571a**, 571b, 572a

Zaria (Nigeria) III 344b

al-Zarkashī, Badr al-Dīn (d. 793-4/1391-2) I 70b, 535a, 514a, 536a; II 121a, 386b; III 207a, 506a; IV 156a, 158a; V 326a, 326b, 327a, 327b, 328a, 328b, 335a, 405b

Zawāra III 86b

Zayd of Jurhum V 90b

Zayd b. ʿAlī Zayn al-ʿAbidīn (d. 122/740) II 347b; V 255a

Zayd b. ʿAmr b. Nufayl II 403a; V 263b

Zayd b. Aslam (d. 136/753) I 257a; II 108a

Zayd b. Ḥāritha (d. 8/630) I 302a, 320a; II 439a; III 283b, 448b; IV 237b; V 59a, 508b, 509b, 510a, 534b

Zayd b. Thābit (d. 45/665) I 331b, 332a, 332b, 333a, 348a, 348b, 355a, 355b, 356a, 356b, 357a, 357b, 358a, 360a, 360b, 388b; II 17b, 102b, 383a, 384b, 396a, 492a, 493a, 523a; III 131a, 131b, 464b, 475a, 476a; IV 394b, 448b, 587b; V 331b, 409b

Zaydī(s)/Zaydites/Zaydiyya i 540b; ii 117a, 421b; iii 467a; iv 23a, 603a
Zayn al-ʿĀbidīn ʿAlī b. al-Ḥusayn (fourth Imām, also called al-Sajjad; d. bet. 92/710 and 99/717) iii 311a; iv 232b
Zaynab iii 234b, 573b
Zaynab (daughter of the Prophet and Khadīja) iii 80b, v 507b
[Sayyida] Zaynab (granddaughter of the Prophet) ii 553b, 555a; v 223a
Zaynab al-Ghazzālī [al-Ghazālī] ii 291b
Zaynab bt. Jaḥsh i 302a; ii 392b; iv 237b, 413b; v 508a, 508b, 509b, 510a, 515b, 516a, 517a, 517b, 518a, 518b, 534b, 550b
Zaynab bt. al-Khuzayma v 508b, 509a
Zaynab bt. Maẓʿūn ii 397b
al-Zaytūna (in Tunis) v 211a
Zebiri, K. iv **124a**
Zechariah [Zakariyyā] i 149a, 165a, 328a, 344b, 477a, 528b; ii 12b, 309a, 340b, 341a; iii 10b, 14b, 15a, 50a, 51b, 52a, 52b, 53a, 204b, 210b, 289a, 289b, 290a, 291b, 294a, 395b, 492a, 519b, 521a, 522a, 525b; iv 31b, 32a, 32b, 211a, 224a, 229a, 229b, 291b, 293b, 516b, 577a; v 280a, 281a, 363a, 546a, 570b, **574a**, 574b, 575a, 575b
Zechendorff, Johannes (d. 1662) iv 246b
Zedekiah ii 562b, 563a
Zetterstéen, K.V. v 352a
Zeus i 108b
Zewi, T. ii 352a
Zilio-Grandi, I. iv 197a
Zimmermann, F. v 24a
Zimmermann, J.G. iv 251a
Zīnat al-Nisāʾ (daughter of Shāh Jahān) iii 324b
Zion ii 312a; v 423b
Mount v 250a
Zionism v 222b
Zia ul-Haq [Ziyā al-Ḥaqq] (president of Pakistan; r. 1977-88) iv 145b; v 212b
Ziyād b. Abī Sufyān (r. 47-55/668-75) iii 556a
Ziyād b. Abīhi (d. 53/673) i 140a; iii 85b, 605a, 605b
Ziyād b. Mundhir Abū l-Jārūd iv 602b
Zoroaster i 509a; iii 245a
Zoroastrian(s) i 316a, 378a; ii 530b, 566b;

	III 377a, 377b; IV 56b, 152a, 228a, 407b, 408a, 416b, 511b; V 56a, 293a
Mazdaean	IV 216a
Zubayr	II 148a; V 32a
Zubayrids	V 502b, 503b
al-Zuhara/Zuhra (Venus)	II 405a; V 93a
al-Zuḥaylī	III 6a
Zuhayr b. Abī Sulmā	I 379a, 389a; IV 111b; V 38b
al-Zuhrī, Ibrāhīm b. Saʿd (d. 183/799)	I 355a; II 383b, 384a, 384b, 391b, 392a
al-Zuhrī, Muḥammad b. Muslim b. Shihāb (d. 124/742)	II 516a; III 178a; IV 588a; V 32a, 32b, 33a, 34a, 199a
Zuleika [Zulaykha]	I 163a, 346b; II 43b; III 234b, 491b; IV 62a, 584b; V 96a, 96b, 152b, 392a, 392b, 531a, 531b, 532a
Zushan (China)	see China
Zwettler, M.	II 254a

INDEX OF ARABIC WORDS AND PHRASES

-alif-

ʾ-b-b
abb v 404b
abjad i 135b, 136a, 138a, 139a, 140a; iii 259a, 261b, 555a, 555b, 596a; iv 175a
ʾ-b-d
abad ii 54a, 54b; v 278b, 475a
abadiya iv 83a
ʾ-b-q
abaqa iii 207b
ʾ-b-l
ibil i 94a, 287a; ii 218b
abābīl i 95a, 100b
ʾ-b-(w)
ab i 42a; iii 212b; iv 20a
ʾ-b-y
abā ii 541b
utrujj ii 387a
ʾ-t-y
atā i 487a, 532b; iv 443b; v 8a
ātiya v 287b
ātā ii 352b, 362b; iii 103a, 524a; iv 294b; v 8a
ʾ-th-th
athāth ii 275a

ʾ-th-r
athar, pl. *āthār* I 275b; II 198b, 199b, 537a; IV 141b, 143b; V 3a, 316b, 317a
ʾ-th-l
athl I 41b; II 305b
ʾ-th-m I 536b
ithm, pl. *āthām* I 271b; II 63b, 67b; III 228a; IV 85a, 93b, 96b; V 19a, 19b, 20b, 178b
ʾ-j-j
ujāj III 530a
ʾ-j-r
ajr, pl. *ujūr* I 258a, 258b; II 374b, 447b; III 451a; IV 452a, 452b, 582b; V 192b, 196b, 312a, 313b, 529a
ʾ-j-l
ajal I 204b, 205a, 448b, 507a, 508a, 508b, 516b, 523a; II 45a, 72a, 186a, 186b, 267b, 269a, 328b, 439b; IV 600b; V 163a, 288a, 289a, 289b, 290a, 454b, 554a
ʾ-ḥ-d
aḥad II 329b, 361a; III 550b
huwa llāhu aḥadu see ʾ-l-h
āḥād III 162a
ʾ-kh-dh
akhadha I 213b, 443b, 464b; III 210a
maʾkhūdh III 127a
ittakhadha I 465b; II 273a, 329a; III 565a; IV 104b, 153b; V 248b
muttakhidh I 299a
akhdh V 5a
ʾ-kh-r
ākhir, pl. *ākhirūn* II 320b; III 177b; V 552b
(al-)ākhira I 205a, 205b, 368b, 449a; II 22a, 44b, 234a, 362b; III 136b, 143a, 418b; IV 14b, 283b; V 105b, 106a, 289a, 340a, 552a, 552b, 554a
taʾkhīr III 45a; V 322a
muʾakhkhar V 333b
taʾakhkhara IV 97a
ʾ-kh-(w)
akh, pl. *ikhwa, ikhwān* I 259b, 261b, 262a, 262b, 263a, 345a–345b, 555a; III 96a, 232a, 486a; V 53a, 53b, 54a
ikhwān al-ṣafāʾ I 263a, 488b; III 555a; V 118a

ukht V 53a, 54a
mu'ākhāt I 262a; II 15b
ʾ-d-b
adab, pl. *ādāb* I 339a; II 87b, 452b, 453a, 453b; III 119a, 175a; IV 369b, 370a, 374b, 377b, 485b, 487b, 492b
adab al-qurʾān IV 374b
ādāb al-tilāwa II 87b
ādāb al-samāʿ II 87b
taʾdīb V 203b
ʾ-d-m
ādam I 349b
banū ādam II 328b
adam, f. *adama* I 22b; II 426b
adīm, pl. *udum* I 22b; IV 587a
ʾ-d-y
adāʾ I 239b
ʾ-dh-n
muʾadhdhin III 303b, 430b
istaʾdhana I 349a
istiʾdhān III 36a
idhn III 395b; V 158b
udhun, pl. *adhān* I 83b; II 1a, 2a, 90b, 241a, 272b; III 430b, 553b; IV 225b, 226a, 375b, 377b, 523a, 566a, 575a; V 219a, 499a, 504b
miʾdhana III 431a
ʾ-dh-y
adhan I 296a
idhā III 376a
ūdhīnā II 257b, 258a
I 296a
ʾ-r-kh
taʾrīkh II 433a; V 483b
ʾ-r-ḍ
arḍ, pl. *arāḍin, araḍūn* I 32a, II 2b, 3a, 3b, 10b, 11a, 62b, 309a, 362a, 410b, 552; III 2b, 3b, 4a, 5b, 78b, 142b, 531b, 532a; IV 127b, 130b, 211a, 364a, 474a, 474b, 513b; V 64b, 107a, 184b, 553a, 553b
al-arḍ allatī bāraknā ḥawlahā/fīhā II 309a; V 107a
al-arḍ al-muqaddasa II 11a, 309a; III 2b, 5b; IV 513b; V 107a, 184b
fasād fī arḍ I 32a; IV 130b, 364a; see also f-s-d
ʾ-r-k
arīka, pl. *arāʾik* II 415b; IV 18a

ʾ-z-r	
āzar	I 192a, 192b
izār	III 403b
ʾ-z-f	
al-āzifa	III 137a
ʾ-z-l	
azal	V 278b
azaliyya	IV 83a
ʾ-s-t-ʾ-dh	
ustādh	II 496a; V 224a
ʾ-s-t-b-r-q	
istabraq	I 347a; II 228b, 231a, 231b
ʾ-s-r	
asara	I 289a
asīr, pl. *asrā, asārā, usārāʾ*	I 289a; IV 277a
ʾ-s-r-ʾ-l	
isrāʾīl	II 571a; IV 67a
banū isrāʾīl	IV 67a; 120b
isrāʾīliyyāt	II 128a; III 138a, 142b; IV 61b, 62a; V 221a
ʾ-s-s	
usus	IV 490b
asās	II 189a
ʾ-s-f	
asaf	V 134a
ʾ-s-w	
asiya	II 510b
uswa	II 439a; III 162b, 447a; V 2b
ʾ-sh-r	
ushar	II 212b
ishār	I 287a
ʾ-ṣ-r	
iṣr	III 228a
ʾ-ṣ-l	
taʾṣīl	II 570b
aṣl, pl. *uṣūl*	I 387a; II 102a, 225b, 412b, 494b; III 155a, 165a, 168b, 424b; IV 261b, 376a; V 210b, 384a, 573a
uṣūl al-fiqh	I 387a; II 225b; III 155a, 168b; V 164b, 210b
aṣīl, pl. *āṣāl*	I 504a; II 80a, 80b; III 418b; IV 223a
ʾ-ṭ-m	
uṭum, pl. *āṭām*	II 298b; III 368b
uṭūm	I 154a

ʾ-f-f
uff II 365b; IV 21a
ʾ-f-q
ufuq, pl. *āfāq* III 534b; IV 107b; V 9b
ʾ-f-k
muʾtafika, pl. *muʾtafikāt* II 299b; III 232b, 521b; IV 584b; V 184b
ifk I 56b; II 344a, 391a; III 181a, 448a; V 511a, 528a, 535a
ʾ-k-l II 216b
akala I 447b; II 220b; III 284b
ākila II 400b
akl I 300a, 301a
ʾ-l-t
alata IV 457b; V 312a
ʾ-l-f II 489b
alifa II 490b
alif I 136b
ilf II 490a
taʾlīf II 382b, 533b
ilāf II **489b**, 490a, 490b; III 59a, 338b
ilāf quraysh II 489b, 490a, 490b
iʾtilāf IV 141a
ʾ-l-m V 132b
alima V 132b
alam IV 241a; V 132b
alīm V 132b
ʾ-l-h
ilāh I 328a, 329a, 329b, 330a; II 316b, 318b, 481a; III 178b, 229b, 557b, 558a, 558b, 586a, 586b; IV 161b, 162b, 375b, 466b, 483a, 488b
ilāh al-nās I 329a
(lā) ilāha (illā llāhu) I 330a; II 91a, 95b, 96a; III 556a; IV 162b, 233a, 375b; V 498b, 499a, 499b, 500a, 500b
ilāhukum ilāhun wāḥidun V 500a
inna ilāhakum la-wāḥidun IV 466b
lā ilāha illā anā I 329b; II 330a; V 500b
lā ilāha illā anta V 500b
(allāh) lā ilāha illā huwa I 329b; V 488b, 500b, 501a
lā ilāha illā llāh wa-musaylima rasūlu llāh III 463a
āliha II 478b, 481b
āliha wa-awthān II 478b

ālihatahum wa-andādahum II 478b
allāh I 198a, 208a, 208b, 209a, 329b; II 85a, 91a, 91b, 92a, 96a, 316b, 317a, 317b, 476b; III 178b, 200a, 225a, 225b, 229b, 230a, 230b, 231a, 265b, 557b, 558a, 558b, 564a, 586b; IV 233a, 233b, 234a, 350b, 440b, 483a, 494a; V 69a, 125a, 145b, 369b, 374a, 489b, 496a, 500a, 500b, 501a; see also r-b-b
allāhu akbar II 91a, 92a; IV 232b, 233b, 250b; see also k-b-r
(al-)ḥamdu lillāhi see ḥ-m-d
(qul) huwa llāhu aḥadun II 361a; IV 387a; V 500a
ṣubḥān allāh IV 233b, 494a
allāhumma II 32b
bi-smi-llāh(i l-raḥmāni l-raḥīm) [basmala] I 78b, 126b, 170a, **207b**, 208a, 208b, 209a, 209b, 210a, 210b, 211a, 211b, 281a, 326b, 329b; II 32b, 39b, 91a, 92a, 92b, 93a, 95b, 96a, 119b, 190b, 191a, 318a, 321b, 354a, 461b; III 145b, 197a, 219b, 220a, 257a, 270b, 301a, 346b, 471b, 474a, 553b, 586b, 595a; IV 5a, 58b, 59a, 60a, 173b, 180b, 214b, 232b, 274b, 377b, 486b; V 52b, 75b, 126a, 144b, 145a, 424a, 424b, 435b, 503a; see also s-m-y
ulūhiyya V 103a, 103b
tallāhi III 561a; IV 217a
ʾ-l-w/ʾ-l-y I 19b
ālā I 19b; III 563a
ālāʾ IV 421a
ulū l-amr see ʾ-m-r
ʾ-m
ama, pl. *imāʾ* I 396a; V 57a, 58a
ʾ-m-d
amad III 335a; V 475a
ʾ-m-r
amara I 245a; II 348a, 366a; V 438a
āmara II 348a
amr, pl. *awāmir* I 87b, 188b, 189b, 241b, 475b,

538a; II 6a, 71b, 170b, 186a, 186b, 224a, 269a, 336b, 340a, 386a, 421b, 443b; III 91b, 159a, 276b, 461a, 466b, 537b; IV 79a, 83a, 125a, 127a, 131b, 149b, 292b, 293b, 490a, 539a, 539b; V 240b, 266a, 266b, 268a, 268b, 270b, 271a, 272a, 272b, 273b, 275a, 287a, 289b, 292a, 321b, 436b, 448b, 542b, 543a, 545a

amr bi-l-maʿrūf (wa-l-nahy ʿan al-munkar) I 241b; II 6a, 62a, 71b, 170b, 224a, 421b; III 276b, 461a, 466b, 496a, 539b; IV 131b, 490a; V 114a, 115b, 142a, 436b

ulū l-amr min[kum] I 189b; III 91b; IV 539b; IV 125a, 147b, 49b, 539b

umūr IV 144a

amīr, pl. *umarāʾ* I 189b, 483a; III 463a; IV 133a, 387a

umarāʾ wa-l-wulāt I 189b; IV 133a

wa-amīr al-muʾminīnāh III 463a

amīriyya IV 272b

imra IV 136a

ammāra V 138b

ʾ-m-s

ams II 364b; V 288b

ʾ-m-l II 448b

imāla V 332b

ʾ-m-m

umm, pl. *ummahāt* I 70b, 75a, 367a, 396b, 467b, 495a; II 83a, 83b, 189a, 299a, 439a, 495a, 557a; III 338a, 482b; IV 20a, 100b, 102a, 103b, 104a, 167a, 233b, 261b, 262b, 285b, 297a, 299b; V 58a, 252a, 399b, 404a, 431a, 528a

fa-ummahu hāwiyah V 252a

umm al-kitāb I 70b, 75a, 367a, 467b, 523a; II 83a, 83b, 189a; IV 233b, 261b, 262b, 297a; see also k-t-b

umm al-qurā II 299a, 439a, 495a; III 338a; IV 299b; V 399b; see also q-r-y

umm al-qurʾān II 189a; IV 167a; see also q-r-ʾ

umma, pl. *umam* I 38a, 66a, 96a, 145b, 261a, 305b, 368a, 370a, 371a, 371b, 372a, 372b, 373a, 373b, 374a, 374b,

375a, 377a, 377b, 378b, 379a, 379b, 380a, 381a, 382a, 385b; II 17a, 22a, 72a, 72b, 73a, 155b, 156a, 162a, 167b, 170a, 179b, 201b, 205b, 307a, 307b, 308a, 334a, 396a, 431b, 432a, 459a, 468a, 493b, 494b, 496a, 496b, 497a, 497b, 498a, 530a, 553a, 558b; III 23a, 33a, 47b, 127b, 381a, 390b, 402a, 402b, 443a, 483b, 488b, 533b, 565a; IV 20a, 25a, 26a, 35b, 67a, 74b, 115b, 126b, 131a, 141b, 188b, 290b, 299b, 303a, 305a, 329b, 336b, 337a, 337b, 398a, 396b, 398a, 401a, 403b, 404a, 438a, 563a, 570a, 600a; V 44b, 54a, 69a, 207b, 231b, 241b, 302a, 386b, 399b, 400a, 437a, 437b, 438b, 439b, 442b, 493a

umma(tun) qāʾima(tun) I 374a; V 431a, 437b

umma wāḥida I 372a; II 432a, 497a; IV 290b, 337a

ummatan wasaṭan I 372a; III 402b

ummatun yadʿūna ilā l-khayri II 496b

khayra ummatin V 437a, 442b

umam khāliya II 307a, 307b, 308a; III 390b, 483b, 485b, 488b; IV 67a, 126b, 141b, 438a, 570a

umam al-kufr II 498a

ummī, pl. *ummi(y)yūn* I 379a; II 73b, 101a, 493a, 493b, 494a, 494b, 495a, 495b, 496a, 496b, 498a, 498b, 499a; III 27a, 127b, 191a, 443b, 508b; IV 299a, 407b; V 302b, **399a**, 399b, 400a, 400b, 401a, 401b, 402a, 402b

imām, pl. *aʾimma* I 39a, 63b, 68a, 68b, 243b, 244a, 252a, 264b, 306a, 348a, 380a, 470a, 540b; II 118a, 118b, 206a, 396a, 396b, 439a, **502a**, 503a, 504a; III 90b, 95a, 95b, 177a, 404b, 437a, 439b, 460a, 581a; IV 3b, 300b, 389b, 485b, 600a, 601b, 602a; V 25a, 25b, 95a, 139b, 207b, 218b, 227a, 442b, 536b

aʾimmata l-kufr III 95b
aʾimmatan wasaṭan IV 600a
khayra aʾimmatin IV 600a; V 442b
imāmiyya II 421b
ʾ-m-n I 218a, 218b, 246b, 381a, 569a; IV 307a, 402a; V 378b, 503b
amana I 375a; II 72b; V 382b, 420a, 503b
amuna II 163a
āmin IV 482b; V 373b
āmana I 113a, 218b, 219a, 221a, 324b; II 22a, 75b, 163a, 164b, 169a, 348a, 362a, 363a, 366a, 366b, 367a; IV 16b, 408a, 431b, 600a; V 378b, 501b, 502a
alladhīna āmanū wa-ʿamilū l-ṣāliḥāt IV 16b, 431b; V 382b
alladhīna lā yuʾminūna I 221a; II 362a
muʾmin, pl. *muʾminūn* I 34a, 218a, 218b, 219a, 220a, 221a, 374a, 375a, 376a, 379a, 422b, 431b; II 72b, 163a, 163b, 164a, 164b, 165a, 165b, 169b, 170a, 170b, 291b, 361b, 363a, 370b, 569b; III 238b, 388a, 388b; IV 17a, 24b, 37b, 307a, 403b; V 158b, 239b, 378a, 383b
muʾmina, pl. *muʾmināt* I 219a; II 165a, 291b, 569a; see also ʾ-m-r
īmān I 185b, 218a, 218b, 219b, 220a, 374a, 375a, 376a, 481a, 493b, 556a; II 7a, 49b, 161b, 163a, 163b, 164b, 166a, 166b, 167a, 168a, 168b, 169a, 169b, 170a, 170b, 171a, 171b, 172a, 196a, 370b, 396b, 502a, 503b, 508a, 567b, 568b, 569a; III 66a, 72b; IV 401b, 403b, 432a, 438a; V 69a, 243b, 270a, 379a, 445b, 491b, 504a; see also k-f-r
īmān mufaṣṣal II 168a, 168b
īmān mujmal II 168a, 171a; see also j-m-l
amn III 76b
amīn, pl. *umanāʾ* IV 98b, 515b, 520b; V 115b
balad al-amīn IV 515b
āmīn II 189a, 190b; IV 103a, 482b
amāna, pl. *amānāt* I 86b, 256b; II 197b; IV 127a, 131b, 147b

ʾ-n-th
unthā, pl. *ināth* II 289a, 292a
ʾ-n-j-l
injīl I 318a; II 235b, 254b, 342a, 342b; III 186b; IV 36b, 37b, 124a, 297b
ahl al-injīl I 310b; IV 37b
ʾ-n-s
istaʾnasa I 349a
uns I 176a
ins V 265b
insān I 62a, 86a, 440b, 449a, 449b; II 75b, 173b, 289a, 291b; III 103a, 157b, 189a; IV 483a; V 83b, 84a, 114b, 277b
insān al-kāmil I 62a; V 277b
ʾ-n-f
anf V 62a
anafa V 435b
ʾ-n-y
inā, pl. *āniya* I 166a, 490a, 490b; II 219a, 276a, 455b
ʾ-h-l
ahl I 50a, 201a, 201b, 207a, 347a, 390a, 463b, 466a, 556a, 556b; II 170b, 174a, 176b, 182a, 193a, 286b, 291b, 351a, 421b, 422a, 452b, 496b, 499a, 504a, 521a, 523b; III 33a, 67b, 118b, 141a, 236a, 240a, 367b, 378a, 381a, 402b, 437a, 484a; IV 36a, 36b, 37a, 37b, 38a, 39a, 39b, 40a, 41a, 41b, 42a, 42b, 43a, 48b, 49a, 49b, 50a, 50b, 51a, 51b, 52a, 52b, 53a, 54a, 120a, 129a, 131a, 151b, 163b, 178a, 230a, 302a, 303b, 309a, 371b, 402b, 403a, 403b, 503a, 560a, 595b, 596a; V 56a, 131b, 143a, 144b, 154a, 157b, 195a, 235a, 281b, 293a, 417b, 437b
ahl al-ʿadl (wa-l-tawḥīd) II 170b, 421b
ahl al-ʿahd I 466a
ahl bayt II 174a; IV 48b, 50a, 51b, 52a

ahl al-bayt	I 50a, 390a; II 174a, 176b, 177a, 193a, 452b; III 236a, 437a; IV 37a, 48b, 49a, 49b, 50b, 51a, 51b, 52a, 52b, 53a, 163b, 178a, 503a, 595b, 596b
ahl baytī	IV 50a
ahl al-dhikr	see dh-k-r
ahl al-dhimma	III 33a, 240a; IV 151b; V 293a
ahl al-ḥadīth	I 201a, 201b, 463b; III 67b
ahl al-injīl	see ʾ-n-j-l
ahl al-kahf	III 321b; IV 230a
ahl al-kashf	V 157b
ahl al-kisāʾ	I 347a, I 390a; II 177a, 193a
ahl al-kitāb	see k-t-b
ahl al-madīna	IV 49a
ahl al-maghfira	III 378a; IV 49a
ahl al-makka	IV 48b
ahl maydan	IV 49a
ahl qarya	IV 49a
ahl al-qurā	IV 37a, 49a, 131a; V 281b
ahl al-qurʾān	IV 36a, 371b
ahl al-sunna wa-l-jamāʿa	I 201a; II 422a, 504a
ahl al-taṣawwuf	II 286b
ahl al-taʾwīl	III 118b
ahl yathrib	III 367b; IV 49a
ʾ-w-b	
awwiba	IV 213a, 428a
awwāb	IV 213b, 214b
tawābīn	IV 428a, 429b
maʾāb	IV 428a
	IV 104a
ʾ-w-f	
āfa	V 61a
ʾ-w-q	
ūqiyya	III 336b; V 474b
ʾ-w-l	
āla	IV 76a
taʾwīl	I 63b, 107a, 348b, 555b, 556a; II 99b, 100b, 101a, 102a, 118a, 127a, 241b; III 159a, 469a; IV 69a, 69b, 72a, 76b, 157a, 157b, 158b, 365b, 366a, 366b, 386b, 597b, 601b; IV 7a; V 150a, 156b, 157a, 322a, 323a, 334b
taʾwīlāt	V 143a

taʾawwala — II 100b
āl — II 174a; IV 291a
āl ibrāhīm — II 174a
awwal — II 54a, 320b, 518b; IV 4b, 599a; V 317b
awwalūn — II 434a, 434b; IV 302b
asāṭīr al-awwalīn — see s-ṭ-r
ūlā, pl. *awāʾil* — I 75a; II 234a; V 46b, 552b
awāʾil al-suwar — I 75a
ʾ-w-n
ān — I 319a
ʾ-w-y — V 3a
āwā — I 405b
maʾwā — II 458a, 458b, 460b; IV 103b
āya, pl. *āyāt* — I 51b, 65b, 70b, 124b, 177b, 202a, 209b, 211a, 246a, 260a, 304a, 318b, 325a, 353a, 365b, 441b, 445b, 446a, 448a, 449a, 473b, 474a, 474b, 489a, 490a, 491a, 497b, 505b, 554a; II 58b, 67a, 83a, 89b, 127b, 147a, 163a, 164a, 165b, 201a, 202a, 258b, 259a, 259b, 262b, 302b, 408b, 409a, 425a, 489a, 520a, 527b, 529a, 547a, 548a; III 40a, 47b, 55b, 96a, 108a, 116a, 185b, 187b, 197a, 204b, 222a, 290b, 372a, 392b, 394a, 396a, 398b; III 96a, 394a, 421b, 422b, 441a, 450a, 523b, 528b, 530b, 531b, 535a, 570a, 594b, 607a, 608a; IV 29b, 50a, 63b, 105b, 167a, 176a, 176b, 179a, 180a, 183a, 234a, 264a, 273b, 286a, 293a, 296a, 296b, 311b, 312a, 313a, 319b, 364b, 365b, 366b, 367a, 371a, 377b, 378a, 395b, 422b, 425a, 428a, 438a, 461b, 477b, 527a, 532b, 561b, 562a, 562b, 584a; V 2b, 3a, 4a, 4b, 5a, 6b, 7a, 7b, 8a, 70b, 115b, 155a, 171a, 171b, 179a, 279b, 280b, 293a, 410a, 419b, 420a, 422a, 423a, 423b, 427b, 438a, 482a, 495b, 497b
āyat al-bayʿat — IV 63b

āyat al-dayn	v 495b
āyat al-jizya	iii 40a
āyat al-kursī	ii 408b; iv 63b, 180a, 234a; v 427b
āyat al-nūr	i 490a, 491a; ii 547a; iii 108a, 187b; v 155a, 427b
āyat al-rajm	iv 584a; v 410a, 497b
āyat al-sayf	i 505b; iii 40a; v 293a
al-āyāt al-bayyināt	i 398b; iv 286a, 286b, 296b; v 8a
āyāt al-ḥarb	iv 176a
āyāt al-ḥifẓ	i 78b; iv 176a, 180a
āyāt al-ḥirāba	iv 365b, 366b, 367a
al-āyāt al-muḥkamāt	i 70b; ii 425a; v 70a
al-āyāt al-mutashābihāt	v 70a
āyāt al-shifāʾ	i 78b; iv 176a
āyāt al-ṣulḥ	iv 63b
āyāt al-taḥaddī	ii 529a; iii 116a; iv 461b
ʾ-y-d	
ayyada	ii 442a
ʾ-y-s	
aysa	iv 82a
muʾayyis	iv 82a
ʾ-y-k	
ayka, pl. *ayk*	i 41b; iv 54a, 54b
ʾ-y-w-ʾn	
īwān	iii 433a, 433b, 434a, 434b
ʾ-y-y	v 3a
āya, pl. *āyāt*	see ʾ-w-y

-bāʾ-

b-ʾ-r	
biʾr	v 461b, 463a
biʾr sabaʿ	i 9a
b-ʾ-s	i 521a
biʾsa	ii 365b, 415a
baʾs	i 458b; iv 210a
baʾsāʾ	i 296b
baʾisa	ii 72a
b-t-r	
batrāʾ	iii 220a
b-t-ʿ	
bitʿ	ii 446b
b-t-l	
batūl	iii 292a, 292b; iv 50b

b-th-th
mabthūtha III 128b
b-ḥ-r
baḥr, pl. *biḥār* I 97a, 203b, 204b, 401b, 446a; II 212b, 213a, 303b; III 531a; V 246b, 462a, 463b
baḥr fāris I 203b
baḥr al-rūm I 203b
baḥrān/baḥrayn I 204a; II 303b; V 464a
baḥīra I 97a, 401b
biḥār II 396a
b-kh-s
bakhasa I
bakhs I 300a, 300b, 301a, 313a
b-kh-ʿ
bakhʿ V 160a, 160b
b-kh-l
bakhila I 191a; V 468b
bukhl I 191b
bakhīl, pl. *bukhalā’*, *bukhkhāl* I 191a
b-d-’ I 478a; see also b-d-w
bada’a I 478a
ibtidā’ II 349b
badā’ I 540b; IV 599b
b-d-ḥ
budūḥ II 38a; III 554b, 555a
b-d-d
tabdīd al-ʿilm I 541b
b-d-r
badr III 414b
b-d-ʿ I 478b; II 421b, 536b
tabdīʿ IV 85a
ibdāʿ IV 82a
mubdiʿ IV 82a
ibtadaʿa V 316b
bidʿ I 478b; II 422a; V 164a, 316b
bidʿa I 481b; II 420b, 422a, 536b, 537a, 537b; III 289b; IV 73b, 148a, 149b, 270a, 493b; V 316a, 316b
ahl al-bidʿa II 537b
badīʿ I 136b, 472a; II 320a, 320b, 327a, 536b; IV 82a
b-d-l
baddala I 15a; II 243a; IV 594a
tabdīl II 243a, 243b; IV 450a, 450b; V 317b

tabaddala II 43b
istabdala I 277a
abdāl IV 62a, 520b
b-d-n
badana, pl. *budn* I 94b, 403b; II 218b
b-d-w
badā I 214a
badūna fī l-aʿrāb I 215a
tabaddī I 215b
abdā III 571a
badw I 214a, 217a
badāʾ I 540b; IV 599b
badawī I 128a, 214a
bādī I 214a, 215a
bādiya I 214a
b-dh-r
tabdhīr II 448a
b-r-ʾ
baraʾa I 478b; II 504b
bāriʾ I 478b; II 151b
barīʾ II 320b, 327a; IV 74b, 82a, 83b
barāʾa II 505a
barāʾat al-dhimma I 209b, 465b; II 504b, 505a, 505b; III 88a; IV 596b; V 144b
II 505b
b-r-j
tabarruj V 512a, 512b
burj, pl. *burūj* IV 107a, 108a, 108b, 550a; V 283b
b-r-d
barada I 275a
bārid II 455b
bard II 455b; IV 3a, 156b
barad V 461b, 463a, 471a
b-r-r
barra II 60b, 447b
birr II 60b; II 74a
I 32a, 209a; II 60b, 61a, 62b, 67a; III 99a, 84b, 90a, 90b, 91a, 99a, 144b; IV 91a
barr, pl. *abrār* II 3a, 321b; III 233b; IV 4b, 5b, 16b, 90a, 281b
burr I 25a
bārr V 436a
b-r-z-kh
barzakh I 90b, 91a, 203a, 203b, 204a, **204b**, 205a, 205b, 206a, 206b, 207a, 232b; II 229a; III 141b, 284a; IV 47b

b-r-ṣ	
baraṣ	I 364a
b-r-gh-th	
barāghīth	II 361b
b-r-q	
barq	II 362a; V 471a
ibrīq, pl. *abārīq*	I 490a; II 219a, 276a
b-r-q-sh	
barāqish	V 52a
b-r-k	
baraka	I 77b, 236a; II 93a, 95a, 189b, 191b, 206a, 207a, 452b, 553b, 555a; IV 163b, 164a, 174a, 174b, 282a, 493b
birka	V 124a
bāraka	I 236a; IV 513b; see also ʾ-r-ḍ
mubārak	I 102b; III 513a; IV 297a, 513b, 514a
tabāraka	I 208b, 237a; II 259b; IV 220b, 470b
baraka, pl. *barakāt*	III 513a; IV 131a, 485b, 486a, 486b
tabarruk	IV 485b, 486b
b-r-m	
ibrām	V 479b
b-r-h-n	
burhān	I 124a; II 67b; III 56b, 186b, 421b; IV 69b, 286b, 287a, 287b, 296a, 296b, 312b, 585a; V 3a
b-r-w-f	
barūfa, pl. *barūfāt*	IV 272b
b-r-y	see also b-r-ʾ
tabarrī	I 540b
b-s-ṭ	
bisāṭ	II 2b, 276a, 460b
b-s-l	
basāla	I 458b, 459a
b-s-m	III 146b
tabassama	III 149a
basmala	see ʾ-l-h
b-sh-r	II 341a, 341b; III 61b, 62a
bushira	II 341a
bashshir	III 444b
mubashshir, pl. *mubashshirūn*	II 341b; III 440b, 503b; IV 3b, 300a; V 460a
mubashshira, pl. *mubashshirāt*	I 53a; 341a
bāshara	I 412a; IV 581b
istabshara	III 62a

bush[u]r I 52b; II 341a
bashar I 22b, 305b; II 289a, 291b, 328b; III 354b, 443b; IV 301a, 578a; V 114b, 115a, 201a, 202b
bashīr II 341a, 341b; III 62a, 223a, 440b, 512a; IV 3b, 63a; V 460a
bushrā I 406a, 546a, 547a, 550a; II 340b, 341a, 341b, 360b; IV 178b
bushrayya II 356b
b-ṣ-r II 153b; IV 574a; V 444b
baṣṣara V 247a
abṣara II 153b; III 208b; IV 574a
mubṣir I 498a
mubṣira III 394a
baṣar, pl. *abṣār* I 81a, 81b; II 153b, 154a, 324a, 402a; IV 64a, 574a; V 153b, 414a, 444a, 444b, 445b, 447a, 544b
baṣīr I 493b; II 1b, 153b, 154a, 320b; III 482b; 82a; IV 444b, 573b, 574a, 574b, 575a; V 445a, 446a
baṣīra, pl. *baṣā᾿ir* III 394a, 512a; IV 287a
b-ṣ-l
baṣal II 217b, 305b
b-ḍ-ʿ
biḍāʿ II 360b; IV 288a
b-ṭ-r
baṭira I 242a
baṭar I 242a
b-ṭ-sh
baṭsh I 458b; III 120b
baṭsha V 64b
b-ṭ-l
bāṭil I 301a; II 98b, 99a, 338a, 340b; III 181b, 424b, 477a, 509b; V 385b, 544b, 545a
b-ṭ-n II 423a
bāṭin I 63b, 541b, 556a; II 118a, 119a, 320b, 422a, 425a, 503b, 556a; III 554b; IV 157b, 158a, 158b, 490a, 572b, 597a; V 140a
baṭn II 295a, 338a; IV 157a; V 156b, 364a
baṭn makka III 338a
baṭā᾿in II 234a
biṭāna II 274a; III 240a

b-ʿ-th
baʿatha v 8a
mabʿūth iv 130a
baʿth i 205a; ii 46a; iii 139a, 140a; iv 435b
tubʿathūna iii 183b
b-ʿ-th-r
baʿthara iv 465b
b-ʿ-d
baʿd ii 434a
buʿd i 491b; ii 363b
b-ʿ-r
baʿīr i 286b; v 411b
b-ʿ-ḍ
baʿūḍa i 95a, 99b; v 57b
baʿḍ iv 272b; v 110a, 155b
baʿḍuhum awliyāʾ baʿḍin i 262b
baʿḍukum min baʿḍin i 262b; v 57b
b-ʿ-l
baʿl, pl. *buʿūla* i 194a, 194b; ii 175b; iii 277a
baʿal v 93a
b-gh-t
baghtatan iii 138a
b-gh-ḍ
abghaḍa i 453a
b-gh-l
bighāl i 95a; iii 534a
b-gh-y ii 420b, 421b; v 432b
ibtaghā i 349a; v 487a
ibtighāʾ i 498a; iv 221a; v 486b
baghy ii 6a; iii 70b, 583a; iv 133b, 598b
baghī, pl. *bughāt* i 299a; iv 365b, 366a, 366b, 585a
b-q-r
baqar i 94b; ii 218b
baqara, pl. *baqarāt* i 94b; ii 189b, 218b
b-q-ʿ
buqʿa iv 513b
b-q-l
baql ii 217a
b-q-y iv 425a, 425b
baqiya v 340a
bāqiya iv 425a
baqāʾ i 91b
bāqin v 340a
abqā v 340a
baqiyya iv 425b

b-k-r I 501b
ibkār I 503b; III 416b; IV 223a
abkār I 501b; III 418b; IV 18a; V 480b
bukra I 501b, 503b, 504a; II 80a; III 416b, 418b; IV 223a; V 281a
bukratan wa-ʿashiyyan II 80a; V 281a
bukratan wa-aṣīlan I 503b; II 80a; V 281a
b-k-k
bakka III 337b; IV 77a, 97a
b-k-m
bukm III 534a
b-k-y
bukāʾ IV 485b
bakkāʾ III 147b
b-l-d
balad I 163a; II 3a, 3b, 4a, 311b; III 339b; IV 54a, 514b; V 107a, 373b
balad āmin I 163a; II 311b; III 339b; V 107a, 373b
balad mayyit II 3b
balad ṭayyib II 4a
bilād al-shām IV 46a
balda II 3a
b-l-gh III 330a; V 208a
balagha I 301b; II 374a, 534a; IV 94b
bāligh III 330a; V 496b
tablīgh V 207b, 208a, 212a, 228a
tablīgh al-daʿwa V 208a
muballigh III 431b; V 207b
ablagh IV 186b
balāgh III 125a, 512a, 512b; IV 300b
b-l-w/b-l-y
balā II 349a; V 133a, 362b
baliya I 29b
ibtilāʾ V 362b
ubtuliya III 423a
balāʾ V 135a
b-n-y I 478a
ibn, pl. *banūn* I 22b, 301b, 345a, 369a; II 61a, 75a, 328b; IV 120b; V 365b; see also ʾ-d-m; ʾ-s-r-ʾ-l
ibn al-sabīl II 61a, 75a
banāt III 48a
b-h-t
buhtān II 344a

b-h-j
bahīj I 212b
b-h-l
mubāhala I 115b, 466a, 492b; II 193a; III 500b; IV 411b; V 498a
ibtahala I 466a, 492b; II 193a
b-h-m
mubham II 128a; V 322a, 334a
mubhamāt IV 595b
b-w-ʾ
bawwaʾa II 458b
b-w-b
bāb, pl. *abwāb* II 60b, 459a
mubawwab IV 588b
b-w-ḥ
ibāḥiyya II 422a
mubāḥ II 225b, 282a; III 159b; IV 518b
b-w-r
būr I 530a
b-w-ʿ
bāʿ V 473a
b-y-t
bayyata III 191a
bayt, pl. *buyūt* I 50a, 67b, 163a, 163b, 165a, 177a, 179a, 215b; II 174a, 201a, 299a, 426a, 426b, 458a, 458b, 459a, 459b, 460b, 461a, 564a; III 2b, 4a, 4b, 6a, 30b, 75a, 76a, 76b, 77a, 77b, 78b, 79a, 79b, 140a, 142b, 313b, 338a, 338b, 340b, 544a; IV 48b, 49b, 50a, 51b, 52b, 56a, 93a, 97a, 282a, 444a, 514a, 514b, 516a, 519a; V 28b, 78b, 92a, 196a, 234b, 235a, 235b, 304a, 556a; see also b-k-k
bayt allāh III 75a; IV 48b
al-bayt al-ʿatīq I 179a; III 77a, 340b; IV 52b, 514b
bayt al-ḥarām I 163b, 179a; IV 52b, 514b
bayt al-ʿizza IV 444a
bayt al-māl I 67b; V 196a
al-bayt al-maʿmūr I 179a, 179b; II 299a; III 77b; IV 52b, 514a
bayt al-maqdis I 177a; III 2b, 4a, 4b, 6a, 140a, 142b; IV 514a
bayt al-maṣāḥif III 313b
bayt al-midrās II 30b; V 304a

bayt al-shaʿr iii 544a; v 235a
bayt al-ṭāʿa ii 201a
ahl (al-)bayt see ʾ-h-l
wa-l-bayt al-ʿarab ashrafuhā iv 51b

b-y-ḍ
ibyaḍḍa i 364a
bayḍ v 125b
abyaḍ i 362a, 363b
bayḍāʾ v 125a

b-y-ʿ
bāyaʿa iii 562b
mubāyaʿa iii 568a
bayʿa i 217a, 433b, 466a; ii 16a, 20a, 299a, 567b; iii 179b, 447b, 562b, 568a; iv 125b, 493a; v 255b, 312b
bayʿa aʿrābiyya i 217a
bayʿa hijriyya i 217a
bayʿat al-ḥarb ii 20b, 299a
bayʿat al-nisāʾ ii 20a; v 255b
bayʿat al-riḍwān iv 125b
bīʿa, pl. *biyaʿ* i

b-y-n i 246b; iii 125a, 186b
bayyana ii 114a, 549a; iii 109a, 112a, 114b, 125a; v 8a, 322b, 422b
mubayyan iii 156b; v 333b
tabyīn iii 108b; v 203b, 322b, 323a, 439b
tibyān iii 124b, 506b; v 319a
abāna iii 109a, 114b, 125a
mubīn i 243a, 244a, 261a; ii 226b, 497b; iii 109a, 113b, 114b, 124b, 125a, 126b, 186b; iii 512b, 514a, 528a; iv 286b; v 430a
kitāb mubīn ii 497b; iii 187a
qurʾān mubīn ii 497b; iii 528a
sulṭān mubīn iv 286b
tabayyana i 445a
mustabīn iii 125a
bayn iv 4b
bayna ii 362a; iv 4a
bayyina, pl. *bayyināt* i 304a; ii 58b, 430b, 497b; iii 187a, 392b, 393a, 421b; iv 39b, 42a, 286a, 286b, 292a, 295b, 296a, 297a, 569b; v 2b, 8a, 115a, 422a, 490a, 569b
āyāt bayyināt see ʾ-w-y

bayān I 197b; II 101a, 103a; III 124b, 125a, 392b, 514a; V 201a, 203b, 319a, 322b, 331b, 423a

-tāʾ-

t-b-b
tabba II 261b; IV 478a
t-b-t
tābūt I 158a; II 207a; III 261b, 420a; IV 425b
t-b-ʿ I 246b
tābiʿ V 78b
tābiʿūn II 102b, 387a, 390b, 392a, 393a; III 142a, 154a; IV 99a, 588a
ittabaʿa III 567a; V 294b
ittibāʿ V 440a
tubbaʿ V 389a, 389b
t-j-r
tājir V 315a
tijāra II 449a; III 275b; V 312b, 315a, 373b, 469b, 549a
t-r-b
turāb, pl. *atriba* I 24a, 230a, 230b, 231a, 476a; II 4a, 4b, 328a, 354b; V 569b
t-r-j-m
tarjama I 520a
t-r-f
mutraf, pl. *mutrafūn* III 583b ; V 468b
t-r-k
taraka II 83b
t-s-ʿ
tisʿa III 552b
t-ʿ-s
taʿs I 491b
t-f-f
tatfīf I 300a, 300b
t-q-n
atqana I 213a
itqān I 212b
t-l-m-dh
tilmīdh, pl. *talāmīdh* I 123a
t-l-w I 246b
talā I 270b; II 312a; III 188b, 189b,

190a, 191a, 441a, 524a, 524b; v 7a, 203a, 400b
atlā iii 440b; iv 297a, 302b
tālī iv 386a
tilāwa ii 119a; iv 367b, 368b, 372a, 372b; iv 386a, 484b, 485b, 488b, 494b, 567b; v 141a, 153b, 157a, 213b, 332b, 557a
t-m-m
atamma iv 94b
tamām v 322a
t-n-r
tannūr ii 213a , 219a, 229a; iii 393a, 540b
t-h-m
tuhma v 177b
t-w-b v 404a
tāba i 25a, 275a, 436b, 450a; ii 550b; iii 118b, 424a; iv 25b, 426b, 427a, 427b, 428b, 429a, 429b
tāʾibūn iv 426b
tāʾibāt iv 426b
tawb iv 426a
tawba i 25b; ii 314b, 550b, 551a; iii 68a, 424a; iv 426a, 428b
tawwāb, pl. *tawwābūn* i 209a; ii 244b, 321a, 350a; iv 5b, 6a, 342b, 426a, 427b, 428b, 429a; v 483a
t-w-r
tawrāt [tawrāh] ii 235b, 254b, 342a, 353a; iii 424b; iv 36b, 37b, 297b; v 300a, 300b, 301a, 307a
t-y-n
tīn ii 217b, 305b; v 107a
wa-l-tīn wa-l-zaytūn v 107a
tīna i 25a

-thāʾ-

th-ʾ-r
thaʾr iii 183b
th-b-t
thābit v 16b
tathbīt i 118b; ii 532a

th-r-y
tharā II 4a
thurayyā III 415b
th-ʿ-b-n
thuʿbān, pl. *thaʿābīn* I 95a, 90a
th-q-b
thāqib IV 108b
th-q-f
thaqāfa III 188a
th-q-l III 333a, 334a, 334b
thaqula III 334b; V 183b, 184a
thaqalān IV 596b, 597a
athqāl III 228a
mithqāl II 545b; III 334b, 408b, 409a; V 312a, 473a, 473b, 474b
mithqāl dharratin II 545b; III 309a
mithqāl ḥabbatin min khardalin III 409a
mithqāl khardal II 545b
th-l-b
mathālib V 46b, 47b
th-l-th
thālith I 312b; IV 413a; V 369a
thālith thalāthatin I 312b; II 364a; V 369a
thalātha II 364a; III 550b; V 371b
thuluth I 136b, 137a, 142a, 283b, 285b; III 265a, 599a
thulth III 265a, 321a
thalāthin IV 413a
th-m-r
thamar I 41a, 42b
thamara, pl. *thamarāt* II 304b, 305b; IV 18a
th-m-n
thaman IV 583b; V 312b
thamāniya III 552b
th-n-y III 574b
thanā III 575a
thānī IV 599a
thanāʾ I 27a; III 146a, 574b
thannā III 574b, 575a
athnā II 83a
istathnā III 575a; IV 63a
istithnāʾ III 564a
ithnān III 575a
ithnaynī thayni II 348b
thāniya II 364a
thāniya thnayni II 364a

thanawiyya I 470a
ithnatā ʿashrata II 364a
ithnā ʿashariyya II 421b
mathnā, pl. *mathnāt* III 549b, 574b
mathānī III 446b, 509b, 552b, 574b, 575a, 575b, 576a; V 424b, 425a, 425b
sabʿ mina l-mathānī V 424a, 425a, 425b
th-w-b III 63a
thawāb II 83a; IV 452b, 457b; V 312a
thiyāb I 346a
mathāba IV 515b; V 448b
mathūba IV 452b; V 312a
th-w-r
athāra, pl. *athārāt* I 40b; II 239b
th-w-y
thawā II 458b
mathwā I 163b; II 458a, 458b, 460b; IV 103b
th-y-b
thayyibāt V 480a, 480b

-jīm-

j-b-b
jubb V 461b, 463a
j-b-t
jibt II 229a, 477b, 481a, 482a, 482b; III **34b**, 35a, 35b; IV 599a; V 119b, 120a, 248a, 248b
jibt wa-l-ṭāghūt III 35a; IV 599a
j-b-r II 541b
jabr IV 141a
jabriyya I 74a; IV 73a, 84b
jabarūt V 157b, 158b
jabbār, pl. *jabābira* I 160a, 161a; II 320b, 432b, 484b, 541b; III 504b; IV 137b, 264a, 264b
jabbārīn V 455b
ijbār V 292b
j-b-s
jibsun III 35a
j-b-l
jabal, pl. *jibāl* III 78b; IV 96a
jabal makka III 78b

j-b-h
jibāh I 81b
j-b-y II 11b, 12a
ijtabā I 26a, 455a; II 11b,12a; IV 291a, 291b
j-ḥ-d
jaḥada V 6a
j-ḥ-m
jaḥīm II 49b, 50a, 210a, 212a, 414b, 419a; III 203b; V 181a
j-d-b
jadūb II 178a
j-d-th
ajdāth I 263b
j-d-r
judarī II 212b; III 364b
j-d-l I 511b, 513b
jadala I 511b, 512a, 512b, 513a; IV 309b
jādala I 512a, 512b, 513a, 513b; IV 115a
alladhīna yujādilūna fī āyāti llāhi I 512a
mā yujādilu fī āyāti llāhi illā lladhīna kafarū I 512a, 512b
qad jādaltanā fa-aktharta jidālanā I 513a
wa-jādilhum bi-llatī hiya aḥsanu I 513b
mujādala III 48a
mujādila I 513a
jidāl I 511b; III 178a; V 6b
jadal I 512b, 513b, 514a; III 522b; IV 115b; V 321a, 334a
j-dh-ʿ
jidhʿ, pl. *judhūʿ* I 494b
j-r-b
jarīb III 336b
tajriba I 46a
mujarrabāt I 77b; IV 169a, 170b, 495a
j-r-ḥ V 253a
jāriḥa, pl. *jawāriḥ* I 95a; II 159a, 467a
j-r-d
jarrada V 145a
tajarrud V 157b
arād I 95a
j-r-sh
jawārish II 447a
j-r-m V 19a
jurm II 63b, 64a; V 19a
ajrama I 112b; V 420a
mujrim, pl. *mujrimūn* I 375b; II 64a, 551a; III 70b; V 19a

j-r-y
jarā v 106b
jāriya, pl. *jāriyāt, jawārī* i 55a; iv 604a; v 58a, 412b
j-z-ʾ
juzʾ, pl. *ajzāʾ* ii 94a, 125a, 262b; iii 261b, 264b, 265a, 268a, 271a, 271b, 272b; iii 596b, 602a; iv 269b, 270a, 272a, 347a,378a, 379b, 380a; v 99b
j-z-r
jazīra iv 253b
jazīrat al-ʿarab iv 253b
jazūr ii 280b, 281a
jazūr alladhī kānū yataqāmarūna ʿalayhi ii 280b
j-z-y iii 63a
jazā ii 361b, 362a, 366b
ajzā i 54a
jazāʾ i 187a, 294b, 295a; iii 76b, 141b; iv 152b, 452b, 457b
jizya i 224a, 252b, 312a, 336a, 397b; ii 401b; iii 29a, 40a, 41b; iv 151b, 152a, 152b, 153a, 153b, 154a, 408a, 409b, 415b, 416b, 524b, 525a; v 192b, 193b, 291b, 457a, 458b
āyat al-jizya see ʾ-w-y
j-s-d
jasad i 80a, 124b, 274b, 275a
j-s-m
tajsīm i 24b, 103b, 184b; iii 139b
mujassima ii 160b
jism, pl. *ajsām* i 79b, 80a, 103b; v 447a
j-ʿ-l i 477b
jaʿala i 442b, 443b, 446b, 448a, 449a. 450b, 452b, 478a; ii 252b, 259a, 366b, 367a, 374a; iv 277b, 592a; v 373a, 467b, 543b
jāʿil i 22b, 455b; ii 330a
j-f-r
jafr iv 175a
j-f-n
jafna, pl. *jifān* i 162b, 165a, 490b; ii 219a; v 77a
j-l-b-b
jilbāb, pl. *jalābīb* i 346b, 384a; v 413b, 414b, 415a, 510b, 526a
j-l-d ii 214a

jalada II 214a
jald II 214a; IV 584a
jild, pl. *julūd* I 215b; II 426a; IV 587a; V 235b
j-l-s
majālis III 88b
j-l-l
jalla III 323b
tajallī V 154b
majalla IV 587b
jalal II 315b
jalāl II 321; V 265b
jalīl I 136b; II 315b
j-l-w
tajallā II 316a; V 275b
tajallī II 161a; V 277b
j-m-r
jamra, pl. *jamarāt* I 9b
j-m-ʿ
jāmiʿ II 320b; IV 76b, 588b
jimāʿ I 412a; III 120b
jamāʿa I 201a, 375a, 538b; II 57a, 83b, 174a; IV 26a; V 166a, 377a
jamāʿat-i islāmī I 201a
ijmāʿ I 11b, 122b; II 90a; IV 359a
ijtimāʿ IV 147a
jamʿ II 247a, 382b
jamʿiyya V 442b
jumʿ V 331b
majmaʿ I 78a, 204a
majmaʿ al-baḥrayn I 204a
j-m-l I 286b
jummal I 286b
mujmal III 156b, 157a; V 143a, 333b
īmān mujmal III 168a, 171a
jumla I 250b; II 412b; IV 444a
jumlatan wāḥidatan I 250b; IV 444a
jamal, pl. *jimāl* I 94a, 212b, 213a, 286b
jimāla I 94a, 99b
jimāla ṣufr I 99b
j-n-b I 411a
ijtanaba I 411a
janb II 324b; V 131a, 131b, 132a
fī janbi llāhi II 324b
ṣāḥib bi-l-janbi V 131a, 131b, 132a
junub I 341a, 341b, 411b; IV 225b, 492a,

	499b, 501b, 502a, 504b, 506a; v 131a, 131b
al-jār al-junubi	v 131a, 131b
janāba	iv 491b, 506b
ajnabī	v 131a
j-n-ḥ	i 536b
junāḥ	i 353b; ii 60a, 61b, 63b, 64a, 538a; iii 173b, 93a, 93b; v 19a
j-n-d	
jund, pl. *junūd*	ii 365b; iii 423a, 423b; v 377a, 377b, 378a
j-n-z	
janā'iz	i 263b; iv 488b, 490a
j-n-s	
jins	ii 288a, 534b
j-n-n	iii 49a; iv 12b; v 120a
jānn	iii 46b; v 120a
majnūn	i 324a, 447a, 542b, 544a; ii 528a, 539b, 540a, 540b; iii 44a, 246b, 450a, 450b, 541b, 542b; iv 67b, 112a, 112b, 113b, 295a, 301a, 311b, 463a; v 420b
jinn (coll.)	i 23a, 61b, 86b, 99a, 115a, 162b, 229a, 213b, 236a, 440b, 446a, 446b, 447a, 447b, 451b, 476a, 490b, 524a, 526b, 527a, 544a, 544b; ii 2a, 50b, 82a, 87a, 127b, 190a, 315a, 317b, 328a, 388a, 404b, 476b, 486a, 486b, 487a, 539b, 540a; iii **43a**, 43b, 44a, 44b, 45a, 45b, 46a, 46b, 47a, 47b, 48a, 48b, 49a, 49b, 55b, 97b, 199b, 250a, 253b, 295a, 395b, 399a, 443b, 450a; iv 15a, 22b, 112a, 130b, 164a, 164b, 165b, 211a, 216b, 280b, 280b, 299b, 301b, 308a, 336b, 337a, 463a, 495b, 576a, 578b; v 77a, 77b, 82a, 118a, 120a, 120b, 122a, 179a, 248b, 265b, 274b, 313a, 363a, 373b, 390a, 445b, 460a, 478b, 494b, 547b, 555b
jinna	ii 540b; iii 450b; iv 112a; v 248b
janna, pl. *jannāt*	i 25a, 41a, 42b, 113a, 177b, 447b, 449a, 527a, 550a; ii 33a, 51a,

54b, 209b, 258b, 282b, 283a, 286b, 304a, 556a; III 136a, 203b, 493a, 493b, 495b, 532b, 533a, 534a, 564a; IV 7b, 12b, 13a, 13b, 14a, 14b, 15a, 15b; V 104b, 106a, 106b, 360b, 408a, 554b
janna ʿāliya IV 14a
janna bi-rabwatin V 408a
jannat al-khuld II 54b, 282b; IV 13a, 14b
jannat/jannāt [al-]maʾwā I 177b; II 282b; III 495b; IV 13a, 14a
jannat/jannāt [al-]naʿīm II 33a, 282b; III 203b, 533a; IV 13b, 14b
jannatān IV 7b
jannāt adan I 550a
jannāt ʿadn III 534a; IV 13a, 14b
jannāt alfāf I 41b
jannāt [al-]firdaws III 203b; IV 13a
junūn II 540b
jinniyya I 271a
j-n-y
janā I 494b
jināya II 511b
j-h-d II 144a, 152a; III 35b, 36a, 36b, 37a, 37b, 38a, 38b; V 432b, 455a
jāhada II 72b; II 144b; III 38a; IV 30a, 30b; V 432b
mujāhid, pl. *mujāhidūn* I 32b, 123a; II 144b; III 36b; IV 30a; V 432b
jihād I 34b, 224b, 324b, 369b, 398a, 437b, 458b, 507b, 540a; II 6b, 144b, 151b, 340a, 457b, 484b, 569a; III 34a, **35b**, 36a, 36b, 37a, 37b, 38a, 38b, 42a, 42b, 285b, 361b, 407a, 454b; IV 28a, 30a, 30b, 34a, 129b, 146a, 148a, 154a, 490a; V 193b, 220b, 432b, 458a, 521a
jihād fī llāhi II 340a
jihād fī sabīl allāh IV 30b; V 458a
jihād al-nafs III 37a
jihād al-shayṭān III 37a
wa-āhidū fī llāhi ḥaqqa jihādihi III 38a

ijtihād I 25b, 539b; II 129a, 200a, 572a; IV 9b, 148b, 149b; V 25a, 222b, 538b, 540b
mujtahid II 504a; V 215a
jahd II 144a; III 35b
jāhid II 144b; III 36b
j-h-r
jahara IV 221b–222a, 229b; V 479b
jahr IV 229b; V 479a
j-h-ḍ
ijhāḍ I 2b
j-h-l I 37a; II 487b, 488a, 488b
jahila II 487b; V 203b
jāhil, pl. *jāhilūna* I 37a, 75a, 191b; II 488a
jāhilī I 37b, 39b, 145a, 450b; III 96b, 98a; IV 52a, 91a, 254b, 258a, 260b, 339b, 477a, 503a; V 318a, 435b, 436a, 439a, 443a
ḥukm jāhilī I 37b
(al-)jāhiliyya I 37a, 37b, 38b, 39a, 39b, 40a, 301b, 444a, 444b, 446b, 450b, 508a, 543a; II 219b, 220a, 395a, 403a, 479a, 482a, 483a, 487b, 488a, 488b, 489a, 494b, 568a; III 73b, 76a, 78b, 97a, 402a, 448a, 477b, 483b, 501b, 565a; IV 51b, 96b, 109a, 145b, 253b, 254a, 254b, 255a, 255b, 256a, 256b, 257a, 258b, 259b, 260a, 260b, 590b; V 27b, 117b, 257a, 286a, 286b, 318a, 416b, 435b, 486a, 512a, 512b, 519a
al-jāhiliyya al-ūlā I 37b; V 286b, 512a
jāhiliyyat al-fusūq I 39a
jāhiliyyat al-kufr I 39a
ḥamiyyat al-jāhiliyya I 37b; V 286b
ḥukm al-jāhiliyya V 286b
ḥann al-jāhiliyya V 286b
jahāla II 66b, 488b
jahl II 487b, 488a; III 102b, 349b, 483b; V 316b, 436a
juhhāl I 557a
j-h-m
juhum II 322a
jahīm I 113a; V 106a

j-h-n-m
jahannam I 113a, 294a, 449a; II 49a, 49b, 50a, 50b, 52b, 210a, 258b, 414b, 417b, 419a; III 5a, 63b, 136a, 529b; IV 42b, 186b; V 104b, 106a, 106b, 181a, 267b, 478v
j-w-b
ajāba V 108b
ijāba V 499a
jawāb I 250b; V 322a
j-w-d IV 373b
tajwīd I 520a, 520b; II 88a, 88b, 93b; III 585a; IV 163a, 170b, 172a, 275a, 367b, 369a, 372a, 372b, 373b, 374a, 374b, 375a, 375b, 376b, 377b, 379b, 382b, 567b; V 100b, 210a, 327a, 332b
mujawwad IV 377b, 378b, 380b, 381a, 381b, 382b, 383a
j-w-r IV 307a
ajāra I 369b, 519b
jār I 344a, 369b; V 131a
al-jār dhī l-qurbā V 131a
jawr III 70b
j-w-z
jawāz IV 79a
jāʾiz II 108b; IV 376a, 391a
ijāza II 298a
majāz II 108b; III 384a; V 151a
j-w-ʿ
jāʿa I 454a
j-w-f
jawf III 284b
j-w-w
jaww I 51b; III 195b
j-w-y
ajwā V 479b
j-y-ʾ
jāʾa I 52a; V 8a
ajāʾa I 530a
j-y-b
jayb, pl. *juyūb* V 414a, 510b
j-y-sh
jaysh V 552a

-ḥāʾ-

ḥ-b-b
- *ḥabbaba* III 235a
- *aḥabba* III 235b
- II 322a; III 233a, 234a, 235a; IV 482a, 489b
- *ḥabb* I 42a, 42b, 44a; II 3b, 305a
- *ḥabba* II 305a, 322a; V 473b
- *ḥubb* III 233a, 234a, 234b, 235a; III 237b; V 383b
- *aḥabbu* III 234b
- *ḥabīb*, pl. *aḥibbāʾ* II 324a; III 233b, 503b; IV 292a
  - *ḥabīb allāh* II 324a; IV 292a
- *maḥabba* III 233b; V 383b

ḥ-b-t-r
- *ḥabtar* IV 599a

ḥ-b-r
- *ḥabr*, pl. *aḥbār* II 156a; III 406a; IV 404a; V 202a, 389b

ḥ-b-s
- *ḥabasa* IV 277a
- *ḥabs* V 378b
  - *ḥabs al-rūḥ* V 378b

ḥ-b-ṭ
- *ḥubūṭ al-ʿamal* II 161b

ḥ-b-k
- *ḥubuk* II 411a

ḥ-b-l
- *ḥabl*, pl. *ḥibāl* I 374b, 465a; II 546a, 546b; III 512b; V 165b, 166a
  - *ḥabl allāh* I 374b, 465a; III 512b
  - *ḥabl al-warīd* II 546b

ḥ-j-b V 312b
- *ḥājib* V 78b
- *ḥijāb* I 56a, 203a, 203b, 205a, 346b, 384a, 384b; II 35b, 52a, 276a, 324a, 392b, 393a; IV 47a, 294a, 411a; V 244a, 412b, 413a, 413b, 414b, 415a, 510a, 510b, 512b, 515b, 518b, 525b, 526a, 526b, 536b, 537a
  - *ḥijāban mastūran* I 203b; V 412b
  - *min warāʾi ḥijāb[in]* I 56a; II 324a; V 413b

ḥ-j-j IV 92a
- *ḥajja* IV 92a, 92b

iḥtajja — IV 141b

ḥajj — I 65a, 290b, 293b, 404a, 525a; II 6b, 64a, 84b, 85a, 168a, 178b, 179a, 180b, 205a, 205b, 239a, 297b, 298a, 450b, 458b, 460a, 461b, 462a, 466b; III 3a, 58b, 75b, 76a, 76b, 77a, 78a, 79a, 115b, 278b, 372a, 410a, 410b, 411a, 411b, 413b, 494b, 553a; IV 91b, 92a, 92b, 93a, 93b, 94a, 94b, 95a, 96a, 96b, 97a, 97b, 98a, 98b, 99a, 99b, 115a, 175b, 282a, 339b, 342b, 379b, 484b, 485b, 486a, 487a, 488a, 489a, 489b, 490a, 490b, 491a, 491b, 517a, 518a, 518b, 571b; V 175a, 210a, 285a, 318a, 414b, 448b, 450a, 556b, 557a

ḥijj — IV 92a, 92b, 94a, 95b

ḥijja — IV 517a

dhū l-ḥijja — IV 517a

ḥujja — I 261a; II 57a, 329a, 349a, 532a; III 421b; IV 42b, 287a, 565b

ḥijaj — V 289a

ḥujaj — IV 490b

ḥujjiyya — III 155a

ḥ-j-r

maḥjūr — III 173b

ḥijr — I 402b; II 295b, 339a; III 75b, 173b; IV 227a; V 89a

ḥijrī — III 414b

ḥajar, pl. *ḥijāra* — II 4a; II 295b; III 75a, 232a, 383b; V 128b, 129a, 130a, 470b

ḥujūr — II 266b

ḥ-j-z

ḥājiz — I 203b, 205a

ḥijāzī — I 139b, 142a, 280b, 281a

ḥ-d-th — II 536b

muḥaddith, pl. *muḥaddithūn* — I 104b, 106b, 468b; IV 89a, 565a; V 147a

aḥdatha — II 424b, 536a

muḥdath — I 411b, 470a, 470b; II 536b; III 468a; IV 79a, 424a

muḥdith — IV 79a, 82a, 492a

iḥdāth — IV 81b, 82a, 82b

ḥadīth, pl. *aḥādīth* I 2a, 3a, 11a, 13b, 15b, 16a, 23a, 26a, 27a, 36a, 38b, 39a, 44a, 45a, 58a, 58b, 59a, 63a, 67a, 76a, 77b, 78a, 87a, 89b, 97b, 100b, 104b, 105b, 106a, 106b, 110a, 110b, 111a, 113b, 114a, 114b, 121b, 122a, 135a, 146a, 159b, 181b, 201b, 234a, 257a, 271a, 271b, 291b, 314b, 315a, 321a, 321b, 337b, 349b, 352a, 360a, 378a, 388a, 389a, 391b, 399b, 461a, 463b, 480a, 489a, 495a, 499b, 518b, 520a, 521b, 535a, 538b, 539a, 544a, 545a, 546b, 548a, 549a, 552a, 552b; II 5a, 11a, 14b, 22b, 24b, 80a, 86b, 92b, 103b, 108a, 110a, 111a, 112b, 117b, 138a, 144b, 154b, 160b, 191a, 191b, 193b, 204a, 205b, 214b, 222a, 227b, 237b, 239b, 240a, 243b, 254b, 266b, 278b, 284b, 285a, 285b, 323a, 324a, 325a, 331b, 344a, **376a**, 376b, 377b, 378a, 378b, 391a, 391b, 394b, 395b, 396a, 396b, 419a, 429a, 435b, 441a, 444b, 446a, 450a, 451b, 461a, 470b, 471b, 488b, 491a, 493a, 501a, 502a, 506a, 511a, 511b, 517a, 520b, 529b, 537a, 540a, 544a, 549b, 551b, 552b, 553a, 557a, 560b; III 10a, 37a, 59a, 82a, 82b, 83a, 91a, 101a, 107b, 136a, 137b, 141a, 156a, 168a, 175a, 179a, 232b, 250a, 254a, 284b, 285a, 305a, 308b, 314b, 321a, 352a, 357a, 361a, 389a, 402b, 407a, 413b, 415b, 426a, 451b, 457b, 502a, 502b, 505a, 512a, 517a, 517b, 524a, 568a, 573b, 584b, 586b; IV 40a, 43b, 50a, 56a, 61a, 62a, 71a, 73a, 93b, 104b, 125b, 141a, 144b, 167b, 171b, 174a, 178a, 180a, 209b, 232a, 302b, 303a, 312b,

313a, 315b, 316b, 323a, 326b, 351b, 369a, 369b, 372b, 378b, 384a, 387a, 388a, 389b, 390b, 391b, 401b, 405a, 407a, 407b, 416b, 423a, 442a, 449b, 452a, 458b, 459a, 459b, 460b, 488b, 495a, 506b, 534a, 564a, 565a, 566a, 571b, 572b, 581b, 582b, 583a, 583b, 588a, 588b, 589a, 593a, 595a, 597a; v 2b, 21b, 30b, 32b, 33a, 34b, 35a, 35b, 37a, 46a, 47b, 62a, 79b, 113b, 117b, 120a, 125b, 134b, 164b, 193b, 207a, 221b, 223a, 226a, 232b, 277b, 293b, 307a, 319b, 329a, 330a, 332b, 360b, 361a, 391b, 392b, 415a, 419a, 434b, 448b, 450b, 452a, 453a, 455a, 460a, 466b, 471b, 477a, 486b, 502b, 504a, 504b, 507a, 507b, 510a, 511a, 514a, 514b, 516a, 518b, 520b, 521b, 523a, 526b, 528a, 534a, 535a, 550a

ḥadīth al-ifk ii 344a, 391b
ḥadīth al-kisā' iv 50a
ḥadīth qudsī i 159b, 391b; ii 191b, 395b, 396a; iv 566a; v 134b, 486b
ḥadīth al-thaqalayn iv 596b, 597a
ḥadīthan yuftarā ii 435b
ahl al-ḥadīth i 105a, 463b; ii 471b
aḥsan al-ḥadīth iii 512a
aṣḥāb al-ḥadīth i 105a
bi-ḥadīthin mithlihi ii 529b; iv 312b
hal atāka ḥadīth iii 524a
aḥādīth wa-āthār iv 144b
ḥadath iv 491b, 501a, 506a
ḥidthān ii 241b
ḥudūth iv 79a, 80a, 83b
ḥawādith v 316a

ḥ-d-d
ḥādda iv 309b
maḥdūd v 496b
ḥadd, pl. *ḥudūd* i 28a, 29b, 72a, 252b, 253a, 253b, 536b; ii 63a, 214a, 214b, 215a, 460a; iii 72a; iv 143b, 157b,

581b, 598a; V 19b, 20a, 21a, 26a, 70b, 71a, 158b, 254b, 255a, 322a, 323a, 433a, 490a, 495b, 496b, 497a

ḥudūd allāh I 253b, 536b, 460a; III 72a; IV 581b

ḥadīd III 383a; IV 158a

ḥadīda V 161b

ḥ-d-r

ḥadr IV 377b

ḥ-d-q

ḥadīqa, pl. *ḥadāʾiq* I 41a; II 304a

ḥ-d-w

taḥaddin, taḥaddī II 229b; III 398b; IV 312b, 313a, 313b

ḥ-dh-r II 194b

ḥidhr II 194b, 197a, 197b; III 210a

ḥ-dh-f

ḥadhf III 207b

maḥdhūf V 462a

ḥ-r-b II 144a, 208b; V 432b

ḥaraba II 144a

ḥāraba II 144a, 208b

muḥāribūn IV 367a

ḥarb I 369b; II 144a, 208b; III 422b; V 455a

ḥurūb al-ridda V 502b

miḥrāb, pl. *maḥārīb* I 126a, 126b, 149a, 162b, 163b, 164b, 165a, 165b, 171a, 172b, 284b, 285b; II 299b; III 290a, 303a, 303b, 304b, 309b, 310a, 315b, 325b, 429b, 430a, 430b, 433a, 433b, 435a, 435b, 559b; IV 227b, 516b; V 77a, 184b

ḥ-r-th I 40b

ḥarth I 41a, 41b, 402b; II 63a, 304a, 304b

nisāʾukum ḥarthun lakum fa-ʾtū ḥarthakum annā shiʾtum II 304b

ḥ-r-j

ḥaraj V 19a

ḥ-r-d

taḥrīd V 194a

ḥ-r-r

ḥarra II 295a, 298b

ḥarr II 455a

ḥurr V 58a, 496b

ḥarūr	II 455a
ḥarīr	I 347a; V 11b
ḥarāra	III 354a
ḥarāra gharīziyya	III 354a
ḥ-r-z	
ḥirz	II 35b
iḥtirāz	II 196a
ḥ-r-ṣ	
ḥirṣ	I 191b
ḥ-r-f	
ḥarrafa	I 440a; II 243a, 363a; IV 594a
taḥrīf	I 318a; II 243a, 243b, 342b; III 25a; IV 103b, 124a, 241b, 450a, 450b, 451a, 593a, 595a, 595b; V 143a, 304b
taḥrīf al-ma'ānī	IV 451a
taḥrīf al-naṣṣ	IV 451a
taḥrīf wa-qarmaṭa	V 143a
taḥrīfāt	II 396a
ḥarf, pl. *ḥurūf*, *aḥrūf*	I 326b, 334a; II 93a, 101a, 376a, 385b, 386b; III 115a, 118a, 472b, 522b; IV 157b, 354a, 354b, 355a, 356b, 358a, 372b, 390b, 477b, 572a, 572b; V 244b, 319a, 320a, 320b, 321a, 321b, 322b, 323a, 325b, 327b, 330a
ḥurūf al-fawātiḥ	III 472b
ḥurūf al-muqaṭṭ'a	I 326b; II 93a; III 472b; IV 572a, 572b
aḥruf al-sab'a	II 101a; V 325b
ḥ-r-q	
ḥarraqa	I 275a
ḥirq	II 571b
ḥirq al-nasā	II 571b
ḥ-r-k	
ḥaraka	IV 374b, 376b
ḥarakāt	III 605a; IV 375b, 376a
ḥ-r-m	II 223b, 224a, 225a; III 172a, 172b, 173a, 174a, 174b, 175a; IV 281b, 282b, 282a, 283b
maḥrūm, pl. *maḥrūmūn*	III 211a
ḥarrama	II 223b, 224a, 267a; III 172b, 173a, 174a, 175a, 182a, 339b; IV 282a, 283a, 504b, 514a; V 308a
taḥrīm	II 225b; III 175a, 565b, 566a; V 433a

muḥarram	IV 270a, 504b, 514b
iḥrām	I 187a, 291b, 404a; II 179a, 183a, 224b, 225a; III 76b; IV 91b, 94b, 98b, 282a, 282b, 283a, 491b
muḥrim	III 76b, 79a
ḥaram, pl. *aḥrām*	I 125a, 156a, 156b, 404a, 444b; II 209a, 263b, 295b, 297a, 297b, 298a, 459a, 490a; III 2b, 183b, 339b, 449b, 461b, 566a; IV 96a, 96b, 104b, 105a, 256a, 282a, 283b, 329b, 467a, 493a, 502b, 504a, 515b; V 78b, 448b
ḥaram āmin	III 339b, 449b; IV 282a, 515b; V 89a, 90b172a
al-ḥaram al-sharīf	I 125a, 156a; III 2b
ḥurum	II 209a; IV 282a, 282b, 283a, 502b
al-ashhur al-ḥurum	II 209a; IV 282b
ḥurumāt	IV 282a
ḥirm	III 173a
ḥarīm	II 225a
ḥurma, pl. *ḥuram, ḥurumāt, ḥuramāt*	II 225a, 225b, 298a; III 172b, 173a, 174b, 460a; IV 22a
ḥarām, pl. *ḥurūm*	I 72a, 125a, 156a, 163b, 344a, 402a; II 209a, 223b, 224a, 224b, 225a, 281b, 282a, 306b, 386a; III 76a, 172a, 172b, 173a, 173b, 175a, 175b, 176a, 366a, 366b; IV 95a, 131b, 282a, 282b, 283a, 514b; V 56a
bayt al-ḥarām	II 224a; IV 514b
masjid al-ḥarām	II 224a
shahr al-ḥarām	II 224b; III 172b; IV 282a, 283a
maḥram, pl. *maḥārim*	I 28a, 152a, 383b; II 225a
ḥ-r-m-l	
ḥarmal	II 212b
ḥ-z-z	
iḥtazza	II 3a
ḥ-z-b	
ḥizb, pl. *aḥzāb*	I 375a, 377b, 380a, 432a; II 72a, 94a, 430a, 431b, 432a; III 271a, 456b, 596b; IV 24b, 25a, 25b, 26a, 26b, 332b, 388b, 403b; V 430b
ḥizb allāh	I 375a, 380a; II 72a, 430b; III 270b; IV 24b, 25a, 26a; V 430b
ḥizb al-shayṭān	II 430b; IV 25a

ḥizāb III 240b
ḥizāb allāh III 240b
ḥ-s-b II 447b
ḥasiba I 245a, 449b; III 550a
ḥasaba II 367a, 478b
muḥāsaba III 140b
muḥtasib I 300b; III 276a, 276b, 336b; IV 65a
ḥasb III 300b, 301a
ḥasīb IV 457b
ḥisāb II 48a, 64b, 187a, 320b; III 64b, 66b, 176b, 178a, 275b ; IV 457b; V 284a, 312a
ḥisāb yasīr III 178a
ḥisābiya IV 101a
ḥusbān IV 108a; V 163a, 283b
ḥ-s-d
ḥasada II 25a
ḥāsid II 25a
ḥasad II 24b, 25a, 154b
ḥ-s-r
ḥasra, pl. *ḥasarāt* IV 430a
ḥ-s-s
aḥassa II 405b
ḥasīs V 478b
ḥ-s-n II 61b, 447b
taḥsīniyyāt V 407b
aḥsana I 213a; II 60a, 61b, 73b; IV 17b
aḥsana ṣuwwarakum I 213a
alladhī aḥsana II 61b
lilladhīna aḥsanū IV 17b
muḥsin, pl. *muḥsinūn* III 234a
muḥsan I 28b
iḥsān I 220a, 300a; II 61b, 62a, 75b, 77b, 78a, 447b; III 70a, 563b; IV 90a; V 438a
bi-l-wālidayni iḥsānan II 61b
iḥtisān III 73b
istiḥsān III 168b, 403b; IV 143a
ḥusn I 71a, 212b; II 336a, 339b
ḥasan I 350a; II 336a, 339b; V 179a
ḥasana, pl. *ḥasanāt* II 69a, 98a, 336a, 339b, 537a; III 177b
aḥsan II 100a, 321a
ḥusnā IV 13a, 15a, 17b
ḥ-sh-sh
ḥashīsh II 369b

ḥ-sh-r
ḥashara I 506a; II 361b; III 140a, 140b
ḥāshir II 148b
ḥashr II 47a, 47b; III 140a, 499b; IV 434a
maḥshar III 139a
ḥ-sh-w
ḥashwa I 105b
ḥashwiyya I 105b, 470b; II 160b, 422b
ḥ-ṣ-b
ḥāṣib I 52b, 54a, 54b; III 232a; IV 530b, 531a; V 133a
ḥaṣab V 241b
ḥaṣaba II 212b
ḥ-ṣ-d
ḥaṣīd I 42a
ḥ-ṣ-r
aḥṣara IV 94b, 95b
ḥāṣir IV 277b
ḥaṣr II 363a
ḥaṣūr III 51b; IV 291b
ḥ-ṣ-n
aḥṣana I 298b, 299a; III 96a
iḥṣān IV 583b
muḥṣin I 299a; V 158b
muḥṣan IV 584a
muḥṣana III 279a; IV 584a
muḥṣanāt II 374b
taḥaṣṣun IV 583b
taḥaṣṣan I 298b
ḥ-ṣ-y
aḥṣā III 550a; IV 457b; V 312a
muḥṣī IV 457b
ḥ-ḍ-r
ḥāḍir I 214a; II 503b
ḥaḍar I 215b
ḥaḍarī I 128b; V 323a
ḥaḍrā IV 234a
ḥ-ḍ-n
ḥaḍāna III 107b
ḥ-ṭ-ṭ
ḥaṭṭa V 242a
ḥiṭṭa [ḥiṭṭah] I 305a; IV 429a; V 242a
ḥ-ṭ-m
ḥāṭima IV 103b
al-ḥuṭama II 210b, 211a, 414b, 415a, 419a;

	III 203a, 203b; IV 102b, 103b; V 106a, 181a
ḥuṭām	I 42a, II 3b, 49b, 369b
ḥaṭīm	III 75b; IV 227a
ḥaṭṭāma	IV 103b
ḥ-ẓ-r	
maḥẓūr	II 223b, 225a; III 175a
ḥ-ẓ-ẓ	
ḥaẓẓ	I 528a
ḥ-f-ẓ	IV 307a
ḥafiẓa	I 245a, 298b; II 493a; III 564b; IV 583b
ḥāfiẓ, pl. *ḥāfiẓūn*/*aḥfāẓ*/*ḥuffāẓ*	I 243b; V 74b, 118b, 493a
ḥāfiẓ[a]	I 243b, 520b; II 86b; III 585b; IV 386a; V 214a
taḥfīẓ	IV 368b, 378a
ḥifẓ	I 357b, 541b; III 585b
ḥifẓ al-sirr	I 541b
ḥifẓ al-qurʾān	III 585b
ḥafīẓ	I 243a; II 320b; IV 271a, 307a
ḥafaẓa	V 118b, 118b, 493a
ḥuffāẓ	IV 378a
ḥ-f-y	
ḥufātan	III 140b
ḥ-q-b	
aḥqāb	II 439b
ḥ-q-q	I 246b
ḥaqqa	V 547a, 547b
taḥqīq	III 123a; IV 158a; V 140b
muḥaqqaq	I 137a, 141a, 142a, 283a; III 265a, 311a, 315a; V 559a
muḥaqqiqa	IV 26a
ḥāqqa	III 137a, 203a; IV 102b, 103a
ḥaqq	I 64b, 71a, 414a, 442a, 453a, 542a; II 57b, 58a, 58b, 99a, 214a, 321b, 435b, 489a; III 69b, 70a, 70b, 181a, 182a, 424b, 451a, 477a; IV 71b, 133b, 209b, 297a, 441a, 600a; V 154b, 178a, 385b, 386a, 386b, 387b, 388b, 469a, 544b
ḥaqq allāh	II 214a
ḥaqq maʿlūm	IV 209b
ḥaqq wa-l-ṣidq	I 71a
ḥaqq al-yaqīn	V 387b

āl muḥammad ḥaqqahum iv 600a
anā l-ḥaqq i 542a
bi-l-ḥaq[i] ii 435b; ii 57b, 58b; iii 182a, 451a
illā bi-l-ḥaqqi wa-ajalin musamman i 442a
khalaqa l-samāwāti wa-l-arḍa bi-l-ḥaqq iii 70a
qawla l-ḥaqq v 544a
wa-l-waznu yawmaʾidhin al-ḥaqq iii 70a
ḥaqīqa ii 100b; iii 246a, 384a; iv 555b; v 146b, 151a
ḥaqāʾiq iv 158a; v 140a
aḥaqq iv 305a
ḥ-k-m i 147b, 246b; iii 64b; v 102b
ḥakama i 147b, 148a, 246a, 399a; ii 30b, 321a; iii 65a; v 102b, 103a
fa-ḥkum i 148a
ḥākim, pl. ḥākimūn, ḥukkām i 147b, 399a, 516a; ii 321a; iii 64b, 102a, 246b; v 102b
ḥākimiyya ii 138a; iv 143a, 145b; v 102b, 103a
ḥakkama iii 65a, 65b
taḥkīm v 422b
aḥkima i 70b
muḥkam i 70b, 71b, 72a, 72b, 73a, 74a, 74b, 75a, 76a, 76b; ii 386a; iii 156a, 386a, 523a; iv 158b; v 323a
muḥkamāt i 70b, 103b, 248a; ii102a; iii 470b; iv 3b, 69b, 70a, 76b, 77a, 157a
ḥukm, pl. aḥkām i 23a, 37b, 132a, 145a, 147b, 188b, 205b, 365b, 452b, 516a, 516b; ii 29a, 83a, 321a, 321b, 382b, 537a, 570b; iii 64b, 64b, 65a, 66a, 72a, 85a, 113b, 175a, 557a; iv 3b, 127b, 133b, 135a, 136a, 140b, 144b, 315b, 364b, 365b, 482b, 489a, 538a; v 2a, 103a, 143a, 147b, 322a, 323a, 325a
ḥukm jāhilī i 37b; ii 321a
lā ḥukm(a) illā lillāh(i) iii 85a, 557a; iv 2a
ḥakam, pl. ḥukkām i 147b, 148a, 516a; ii 321b; iii 64b, 150b, 246b; iv 128a; v 102b
ḥikma i 85b, 246a, 496a, 516a; ii 311b, 342a; iii 64b, 100b, 512a, 513a, 514a; iv 68b, 88b, 294b, 315b, 538a; v 77a, 165b, 483a, 483b, 484a

ḥukuma IV 144b
ḥakīm, pl. *ḥukamāʾ* I 516a; II 320b; III 208a, 513a; IV 5b, 141b; V 102b, 483a, 483b
aḥkam I 516a; II 321a
ḥ-k-y
hikāya, pl. *ḥikāyat* III 226a, 517a; IV 446b; V 111b
ḥ-l-f III 562a, 566a
ḥalafa III 562a, 563a; IV 492b; V 449a
ḥalf IV 492b
ḥilf, pl. *aḥlāf* I 257a, 379b, 432a, 466a; III 564a
ḥilf al-fuḍūl I 379b
ḥalīf, pl. *ḥulafāʾ* I 289b
ḥallāf III 563b
ḥallāf mahīn III 563b
aḥālif III 561b
qurā al-aḥālif III 561b
ḥ-l-q
ḥalq IV 374b
ḥalqa II 88b
ḥ-l-l III 172a, 173b, 174a, 174b, 175a; IV 283a, 283b
ḥalla III 172a, 172b; IV 283a
idhā ḥalaltum III 172a; IV 283a
taḥlīl IV 486a
aḥalla II 224a; III 172b, 174a, 174b, 175a; IV 283a, 517b
muḥill IV 283a
istaḥalla IV 283a
ḥill II 297b, 306a, 538a; III 172b, 173a; IV 283a
ḥilla I 458b; II 297b, 298a
ḥalāl I 72a, 96b, 344a, 411a, 557a; II 7a, 9a, 100b, 224a, 386a, 467a; III 172a, 172b, 173a, 175b, 176a, 566a; IV 131b, 167a, 283a, 487b, 504a; V 320a
ḥalāl wa-ḥarām I 557a; II 9a, 100b; III 175a; V 321b
ḥ-l-m II 487b, 488a, 488b
ḥālim IV 152a
ḥilm I 37a, 459a; II 61b, 487b, 488a; III 401b, 483b; V 436a
ḥulum III 278b
ḥalīm I 5b; II 320b, 372b; III 401b; IV 5b, 21a; V 192b

ḥulm, pl. *aḥlām* I 543b, 546b, 548b, 550a, 552a; II 241b
alghāth aḥlām I 546b, 548b, 550a, 552a
ḥ-l-w/ḥ-l-y
ḥilya I 142b, 212b, 346a, 439a; IV 604a
ḥulī I 274a
ḥulwān V 79a
ḥ-m-ʾ
ḥamaʾ, pl. *ḥamaʾāt* I 24a; III 328a, 383b
ḥamāʾ II 328a
ḥ-m-d I 27a, 27b; IV 213a, 213b; V 555b
ḥamada II 83a
ḥāmidūn IV 214a; V 437a
maḥmūd I 514a; II 29a; III 504b
maqām maḥmūd II 29a
muḥammad III 502a, 504b
taḥmīd III 220b; IV 180b
ḥamd I 27a, 27b, 237a; II 82a, 82b, 83a, 85a, 93a, 93b, 189a, 191b, 314b, 315a, 370a, 371b; III 145b, 146a, 220a; IV 58a, 60a, 213a, 213b, 214b, 220b, 474a; V 387b, 425b
ḥamdu lillāh[i] I 27a, 237a; II 189a, 190b, 371b; III 145b, 220a; IV 214b, 220b, 232b, 474a; V 387b
ḥamīd I 27a; IV 5b, 213a; V 483a
aḥmad III 505a
anā aḥmad bi-lā mīm III 505a
ḥ-m-d-l
ḥamdala IV 215a, 232b; V 219b
ḥ-m-r
aḥmar, pl. *ḥumr* I 362a; III 10b
ḥimār, pl. *ḥumur*, *ḥamīr* I 94b; III 534a
ḥ-m-s V 432b
ḥams V 432a
ḥums I 458b; II 297a, 297b, 298a
ḥamāsa I 458b, 459a
ḥ-m-l I 94b; III 227b
ḥāmila, pl. *ḥāmilāt* I 55a
ḥammala I 276a
ḥaml I 286b; III 227b
ḥamlu baʿīrin I 286b
ḥiml V 473b
ḥiml baʿīr V 473b
ḥamūla I 94b

ḥ-m-m
ḥamma, pl. *ḥammāt* v 121b
ḥamīm ii 415a, 455b; iii 96a, 531b; v 65a, 121b, 462a, 464b
yaḥmūm ii 415a; v 64a, 65a
ḥ-m-y
ḥāmī i 97a, 402a
aḥmā ii 455b
muḥamin iii 504a
ḥamiyya i 37b, 459b; ii 455b; v 435a, 435b
ḥamiyyat al-jāhiliyya i 37b, 459b
ḥimā i 154b
ḥ-n-th iii 563a
ḥanatha iii 563b
taḥannuth i 182a; ii 181a, 183a; iv 217b; v 284b
ḥinth iii 177a, 363b, 563b
ḥ-n-dh
ḥanadha ii 219a
ḥanīdh ii 219a
ḥ-n-ṭ
ḥinṭa i 25a
ḥ-n-ẓ-l
ḥanẓal ii 212b
ḥ-n-f ii 402b
ḥanīf, pl. *ḥunafāʾ* i 5b, 6a, 7b, 22b, 310a, 315a, 325a, 330b, 337b, 372b, 373a, 377b, 381a, 543a; ii 163a, 163b, 164a, 295b, 329a, **402b**, 403a, 403b, 480a, 569b; iii 27b, 340b, 445b, 446a, 494b; iv 37a, 217a, 255a, 299b, 400a, 401b, 402a, 402b, 403b, 404b, 407b, 408a, 408b, 413a; v 258b, 263a, 263b, 268a, 268b, 270b, 271a, 273a
ḥanīf muslim i 7b, 310a; ii 569b
ḥ-n-n
ḥanān iii 234a
ḥ-w-b
ḥūb ii 231a
ḥ-w-t
ḥūt, pl. *ḥītān* i 95b, 99a; ii 218b
ḥ-w-j iv 92a
ḥāja v 404a
ḥājiyyāt v 407b

ḥ-w-r II 348b; V 125b
ḥāra I 123a
ḥūriya, pl. *ḥūr* I 166a, 271a, 384b; II 52a, 284a, 348b, **456b**; III 139b, 493a
ḥūr ʿīn II 348b, 456b; III 139b, 493a; IV 18a; V 12a, 125b
ḥūrī III 493a
ḥawrāʾ, pl. *ḥūr* II 154a, 456a; IV 585a; V 540a
ḥawārī, pl. *ḥawāriyūn* I 123a, 123b, 311a; III 392b
miḥwar V 406a
ḥ-w-z / ḥ-y-z
ḥāzī II 239b
ḥawza V 215a
ḥawza ʿilmiyya V 215a
ḥ-w-ṣ-l
ḥawṣala III 284b
ḥ-w-ḍ
ḥāḍa III 148a
ḥawḍ II 395a; III 141a; v124a, 125a
ḥ-w-ṭ
ḥawṭa I 152a
ḥ-w-q
ḥāqa IV 310a
ḥ-w-l
ḥāʾil I 203b, 205a
taḥwīl V 317b
ḥawl II 91a, 92a, 95b; V 285b
ḥawlayn V 285b
ḥāl II 313b
aḥwāl V 383b
muḥāl I 131b
ḥ-y-s
ḥays I 495a
ḥ-y-ḍ
ḥayḍ IV 491b, 501b
ḥāʾiḍ I 81a; IV 492a
ḥayāḍ III 278b
maḥīḍ I 81a; II 85b; III 376a, 377a; IV 501b
ḥ-y-n
ḥīn I 319a; IV 224a; V 288b
ḥīna I 328b, 444a, 504a, 504b; IV 224a, 224b, 224b; V 281a, 288b
ḥīnaʾidhin V 288b

ḥ-y-y
aḥyā I 270a, 270b, 272a, 447b, 455a, 489a; III 148b, 283a; IV 435b; V 545a
muḥyī IV 435b
istaḥyā III 403b
istiḥyāʾ III 403b
ḥayy I 22b, 507a; II 320a; III 97a, 182b, 183a; IV 6a, 172b; V 364a
ḥayy al-qayyūm IV 6a, 172b
ḥayya, pl. *ḥayyāt* I 95a, 99a
ḥayāt [ḥayāh] I 86b, 241b, 368b; II 353a; III 182a, 182b, 183a, 183b, 530b; IV 435b; V 104b, 105a, 106a, 339b, 340a; V 552a
ḥayāt al-ākhira V 104b, 105a
ḥayāt al-dunyā I 241b, 368b; III 182a, 183b; V 104b, 105a, 339b, 340a, 552a, 552b
ḥayawān I 94a; IV 15a

-khāʾ-

kh-b-ʾ
khabʾ I 541a
kh-b-th I 440a; II 63a
khabīth, pl. *khabīthūn* I 343b, 440a; II 63a; III 533a; IV 499a, 504a
kalima khabītha III 533a
shajara khabītha III 533a
khabītha, pl. *khabīthāt* I 299a, 440a
khabāʾith II 63a
kh-b-r
ikhbār V 496b
ikhtibārī IV 376b; V 499a
khubr III 536b
khabar, pl. *akhbār* II 144b, 391b, 392a, 435b, 451a; III 126b, 286a, 517b, 518a, 536b; IV 56a, 326a, 588a; V 292b, 320b, 322a, 323a
khabīr II 320b, 435b; V 483a
kh-b-z
ikhtabaza II 217b
khubz I 255b; II 218a

kh-t-l
mukhtāl I 395a
kh-t-m
khatama I 83b, 264b; II 407a
khātam, pl. *khawātīm* II 148b, 189b, 544b; III 444a; IV 170a, 299a
khātam al-nabiyyīn II 544b; III 444a
khawātīm al-baqara II 189b
khatm IV 378a, 494b
khatma II 461a; IV 387b
khātima III 260b; IV 346b
kh-t-n
ikhtatana I 337b
khitān I 336b, 337b; IV 488b
kh-d-d
ukhdūd, pl. *akhādīd* V **398a**
kh-d-ʿ
khadʿ V 479b
kh-d-m
khidma, pl. *khidam* II 452b
khādim V 58a
kh-dh-ʾ
istikhdhāʾ III 146a
kh-dh-b
takhdhīb I 235a, 235b
kh-dh-l
khadhūl III 46b
kh-dh-n
khidhn V 119b
kh-r-b
kharābāt IV 58a
kh-r-j II 18b, 63a; III 84a
kharaja I 507a; II 349a, 415b
khārij II 349a, 349b
akhraja I 455a; II 3a; III 449a
istikhrāj III 215a
khurūj IV 363b; V 193b
kharj IV 452b
kharāj I 252b; III 336a; IV 154a, 452b, 524b; V 192b, 196a
makhraj, pl. *makhārij* I 486b; IV 374a, 374b
makhārij al-ṣawt IV 374a
kh-r-d-l
khardal II 217b, 305b

kh-r-r
kharra II 159b
kh-r-s
khars II 165a
kh-r-ṣ
kharaṣa II 360a
kh-r-ʿ
ikhtirāʿ IV 79b
kh-r-f
khurāfa III 517a
kh-r-q III 181a
kharaqa I 330a; III 181b
kharq III 293b
khirqa III 83b
kh-r-y
akhrā II 465a
kh-z-n
khāzin II 505b
kh-z-y
akhzā II 465a
khizy IV 453b
kh-s-r II 161b
khasira III 335a; V 312a
akhsara III 335b
khusr II 173b; IV 457a
khusrān I 185b
kh-s-f
khasafa III 416a; IV 107a
khusūf IV 218b
kh-sh-ʿ
khāshiʿa II 363b
khushshaʿ II 363b
kh-sh-y II 194b
khashya II 194b, 196b, 197a, 197b
kh-ṣ-ṣ
khaṣṣa V 145a
takhṣīṣ I 18a; III 158a
khāṣṣ IV 39b; V 255a
khaṣṣa, pl. *khawāṣṣ* I 123a, 416a; II 422b; III 39a; IV 169a, 179b; V 140a, 145a, 334b
kh-ṣ-l
khaṣla V 335a
kh-ṣ-m I 513b
takhāṣum I 452b, 453a

ikhtaṣama I 513a, 513b
khuṣūma V 322a
kh-ḍ-r
mukhḍarra I 362b
khaḍir I 42b, 362b; II 3b
akhḍar, pl. *khuḍr* I 362a, 362b
kh-ḍ-ʿ
khāḍiʿūna II 363b
kh-ṭ-ʾ
khaṭaʾa II 64a; V 19a
khaṭiʾ, pl. *khāṭiʾūn* III 482b; V 174a, 428a
khiṭʾ II 75a; V 21a
khaṭaʾ I 25b; II 63b, 64a, 422a; V 24b
khaṭīʾa V 19a, 19b
kh-ṭ-b
khiṭāb V 143a
khiṭba III 278a
khuṭba I 146a; II 83b, 271b, 272b; IV 226a; V 205b, 206b, 207a, 208a, 216a, 219a, 219b, 220a, 221b, 222b, 224a
al-khuṭba al-naʿtiyya V 219b
al-khuṭba al-waʿẓiyya V 219b
khuṭbat al-jumʿa II 272b; V 207a
khaṭīb I 543a; III 127b, 587b, 588a, 589b; IV 62a;V 205b, 207a, 207b, 208a, 208b, 211a, 219b, 222a
khaṭibāt V 226b
kh-ṭ-r
khāṭir IV 433a
kh-ṭ-ṭ V 558a
khaṭṭa III 190b; V 558a
khaṭṭ, pl. *khuṭūṭ* I 173a, 278a, 282a; II 95b, 239b; III 195a, 605a
kh-ṭ-f
khaṭifa II 348a
takhaṭṭuf III 338b
kh-f-t
tahkāfata V 479a
takhāfut V 479b
kh-f-ḍ
khafḍ I 336b
kh-f-f III 333a, 334a, 334b
khaffa V 184a
takhfīf II 386a; III 123a

khaffa	III 334a; V 183b
kh-f-y	IV 572b
akhfā	III 571a; IV 573a
ikhfāʾ	I 541b; IV 375a
mustakhfā	I 498a
khafī	IV 573a
khufya	IV 229b
kh-l-d	II 439b
khālidīna fīhā	II 418b; V 340a
khuld	I 25a; V 11b
shajarat al-khuld	see sh-j-r
khālid, pl. *khālidūn*	II 52b, 418b; V 340a
khulūd	II 54a; V 289a
kh-l-ṣ	II 550a
ikhlāṣ	II 478a, 550a; III 444a; V 221b
mukhliṣ	II 550a; IV 577a
mukhlaṣ pl. *mukhlaṣūn*	IV 291b, 577a; V 267b
ikhtilāṣ	III 215a
khalāṣ	IV 522b
khalīṣ, pl. *khulaṣāʾ*	I 123a
kh-l-ṭ	
khālaṭa	III 121a
kh-l-ʿ	
khulʿ	V 453a, 528b
kh-l-f	III 90b
khalafa	I 277a, 488b, 489a
mukhallafūn	I 216b; III 36a; V 375b
khālafa	III 377a
ikhtalafa	I 539a
mukhtalif	I 535a; II 363b
ikhtilāf	I 11a, 305a, 497b, 535a, 538a, 539a, 539b; V 333b
istakhlafa	I 277a
khalīfa, pl. *khalāʾif*, *khulafāʾ*	I 22b, 23a, 86a, 189a, 125b, 137b, 276b, 277a, 277b, 278a, 456a, 457a, 496a; II 9a, 12a, 29b, 327b, 383a; III 90b, 94a, 487b; IV 127a, 130b, 185a; V 152b, 274b, 409b
khalīfa fī l-arḍ	I 496a; III 94a
khalīfāt allāh	I 278a
khalīfāt rasūl allāh	I 278a
yamīn al-khalīfa	II 29b
al-khulafāʾ al-rāshidūn	I 153b; II 383a; V 409b
khilāfa	I 449b; II 202b

kh-l-q — I 22b, 476a, 478a; II 327b; V 549a
khalaqa — I 442a, 443a, 445b, 446a, 446b, 448b, 450a, 451a, 467a, 476a, 477b, 478a; II 328a; V 543b
khāliq — I 22b, 467b; II 320b, 327b, 330b; III 416a; IV 82a, 433b; V 500a
khāliq afʿāl al-ʿibād — IV 433b
makhlūq — I 468a, 470b; II 465a; IV 89a, 143b
mukhallaq — I 231a
akhlāq — II 59b, 452b; IV 132b; V 435b
khalq — I 440b, 443a, 449a, 467a, 467b, 470a, 472a, 477a; II 328a, 531b; III 467b, 512a; IV 73b, 82a, 82b; V 287a
khalq al-qurʾān — I 467b, 470a; II 531b; III 467b; IV 73b
khuluq — II 434a
khallāq — II 320b, 327b; IV 6a
kh-l-l
khalīl — I 5b, 330b; II 273a, 324a; III 99b, 494b; IV 112a, 291b
khalīl allāh — I 5b; II 324a; III 494b
kh-l-w
khallā — IV 233a
khalwa — I 34a
umam khāliya — see ʾ-m-m
kh-m-d
khumūd — I 204b
kh-m-r
khammara — I 24b; II 221b
khamr — I 411a; II 67b, 85b, 281b, 556a, 556b, 557a; III 152a, IV 18a, 500a; V 481b, 482a, 482b
khamr mā khāmara al-ʿaql — II 557a
khamr wa-l-maysir — II 85b
shajarat al-khamr — I 25a
khamriyya — IV 527b
khimār, pl. *khumar* — II 221b, 557a; V 414a, 414b, 415a, 510b, 515b, 526a
kh-m-s
khums — IV 489b, 490a; V 194b
khamsa — III 251a, 551b
kh-m-ṣ
makhmaṣa — II 177b

kh-m-ṭ
khamṭ II 305b
kh-n-z-r
khinzīr, pl. *khanāzīr* I 95a
kh-n-s
khannās I 526a; V 479a
kh-n-q
munkhaniqa II 220b
khānāq IV 281a
khānqāh II 452a; III 311b, 312a
kh-w-b
khāba II 162a
kh-w-ḍ
khāḍa II 367a; IV 309b
kh-w-f II 194b
khāfa I 405a; II 195b, 196b, 197a
takhwīf IV 423b
khawf I 460a; II 194b, 196b, 197a, 197b, 365a, 448b
kh-y-b
khāʾib, pl. *khāʾibūn* II 162a
kh-y-r II 11b
ikhtāra I 304a; II 11b; III 304a; IV 291b
khayr I 65a, 516a, 516b; II 61a, 61b, 72a, 78a, 237b, 321a, 336a, 336b, 367a, 367b; III 532a; IV 42b, 84b, 85a, 209a, 288b, 465a; V 336a
khayr al-ḥākimīn I 516a; II 321a
khayra ummatin/aʾimmatin see ʾ-m-m
akhyār II 14a
khayrāt II 61a, 63b, 73a
ikhtiyār II 11b, 12a, 12b; III 376b, 606b; IV 147b, 390b, 432b; V 292b
ikhtiyārāt II 12b
mukhtār III 503b
istikhāra III 317b; IV 163a, 165b, 178a, 179a, 179b, 232b
khiyār III 402b
khīra II 11b, 12a
kh-y-sh
khaysha V 483b
kh-y-ṭ
khayṭ II 546b
khiyāṭ II 546b
kh-y-l
mukhtālan I 241b

khayl I 94b; III 534a; V 374a
khayāl III 246a
kh-y-m
khayma, pl. *khiyām* I 166a, 234b; V 235b

-dāl-

d-ʾ-b
daʾb V 317b, 318a
d-b-b
dābba, pl. *dawābb* I 94a, 95b, 96a, 99a, 99b, 100b; III 138b, 144a, 533b, 534b; IV 434b
dābbat al-arḍ I 95b, 99a, 100b
d-b-r IV 394b
dabbara I 443b; V 203b
tadbīr IV 127a
mudabbirāt V 118a
mudabbar V 58a
idbār I 503b; III 417b; V 282b
idbār al-nujūm I 503b; III 417b; V 282b
tadabbur II 201b
dubur, pl. *adbār* I 80a, 80b
d-th-r
dithār I 346b
muddaththir III 440b; V 95b
d-j-l
dajala I 107b, 108a
dajjāl I 107b, 108a; III 138b, 139a; IV 434b
masīḥ al-dajjāl I 107b; III 138b
d-ḥ-w
daḥā II 2b
d-kh-l
adkhala I 436a
dakhal II 266b; III 564b, 565b
dukhūl IV 485b
madkhal II 33a
d-kh-n
dukhān II 410b; IV 434b; V 64a, 64b, 65a
d-r-b
darb IV 45a
darb al-fīl IV 45a
d-r-j
daraja II 284b

dārija I 128a
istadraja II 322a
darj IV 587b
darajāt IV 14a, 285b; V 191b
d-r-r
durra V 125a
d-r-z
durzī, pl. *durūz* I 554a
d-r-s
darasa I 246a
dirāsa V 203a
dars V 207a, 224a
madrasa, pl. *madāris* I 171b, 284b; II 90b, 275b, 560b; III 310a, 312a; IV 392a; V 73a, 205b, 207b, 208b, 209a, 209b, 210a, 210b, 211a, 211b, 212a, 212b, 213a, 215a, 215b, 218a, 220b, 225b
khānqāh-madrasa III 310a
idrīsin II 364a
d-r-k
adraka I 506a; II 324a; v163a
d-r-h-m
dirham, pl. *darāhim* II 545b; III 335a, 336b, 408a, 408b, 430a; IV 288b; V 474a, 474b
d-r-y
darā V 203b, 376b
adrā V 183a, 183b, 203a
mā adrāka V 183a, 183b, 203a
diraya II 100b
d-s-r
disār, pl. *dusur* I 494b; II 546b; IV 604a
d-s-y
dassā II 162a
d-ʿ-w / d-ʿ-y
daʿā I 437a, 437b; II 142b, 189a, 352b; IV 229a, 229b
ummatun yadʿūna ilā l-khayri II 496b
dāʿī, pl. *duʿāt* I 555a; II 503b, 558b; III 440b, 503b; IV 229a, 602a, 602b; V 207b, 218a, 221b, 224b
daʿwa II 557b; IV 229a, 381b, 382a, 383b; V 206b, 207b, 212a, 218a, 218b, 222a, 227b, 228a
duʿāʾ, pl. *adʿiyya* I 77a; II 1b, 40b, 82a, 82b, 85a, 93b, 388a, 550a; III 220b, 317b;

iv 163a, 175a, 215b, 228b, 229a, 229b, 230b, 233a, 491a; v 219b
duʿāʾ al-talbiya ii 85a
duʿā-i khātim iii 317b
samīʿu l-duʿāʾ iv 229a
wa-taqabbal duʿāʾī iv 229b
daʿī, pl. *adʿiyāʾ* ii 491b
dāya v 224b
adʿiyā v 57a
duʿa iv 232a, 232b
d-gh-m
idghām iii 124a; iv 375b
d-f-t-r
daftar, pl. *dafātir* iv 587b
d-f-ʿ
dafaʿa i 345a; ii 281a
difʿ ii 455b
daffāʿ iv 96b
d-f-f
daffa iv 587b
d-f-q
indifāq iii 363a
d-q-q
mudaqqiq iv 275a
d-k-k
dikka iii 431b
d-l-k
dalaka iii 546b
dulūk i 504b; v 163a, 556b
d-l-l
dalla ii 424a; v 552a
dalāla, pl. *dalālāt* i 470b; iv 89b, 556a
dalīl, pl. *dalāʾil* iv 544b, 546b; v 3a, 3b, 9b, 410a
d-l-w
dalw i 490b
d-m
dam, pl. *dimāʾ* i 80b, 137b, 240a, 241a, 347a
dam kadhib i 347a
lā tasfikūna dimāʾakum 241a
safk al-dimāʾ i 240a
yasfiku l-dīmāʾ i 240a
d-m-d-m
damdama v 253a
d-m-r
dāmir v 375a

d-m-ʿ
damʿ v 462a
d-m-m
damm ii 220a; iii 99a
damm masfūḥ ii 220a
d-n-w / d-n-y iv 283a, 283b
adnā iii 403a; v 321a
dunyā i 91a, 91b, 105a, 205b, 445b, 449a, 506a; ii 36b, 44b, 527b, 567b; iii 424a, 425b; iv 14b, 283a, 283b; v 106a, 106a, 289a, 552a, 552b, 553a, 554a, 561a
d-h-r
dahr i 36a, 318b, 448b, 506a, 507b, 508a, 509a, 509b; ii 54a, 267b, 268a, 302a; v 287a, 475a, 486a
dahriyya ii 422a; iv 122b
d-h-n
duhn i 102a, 102b, 362a; ii 218b; v 362a
dihān i 362a
d-h-y
adhā iv 501b
d-w-r
idāra iv 144b
madār iv 543b
dār, pl. *diyār* i 163b, 165a, 338a, 406b, 540b; ii 52a, 52b, 283a, 321b, 458a, 458b, 460b; iii 136b, 240a, 336b; iv 13a, 14a, 14b, 15b, 392a; v 11b, 292b, 362b, 352b, 553b
dār al-ʿalāniyya i 540b
dār [al-sāʿa] al-ākhira ii 283a, 460b; iii 136b; iv 13a, 14b; v 552b, 553b
dār al-bawār ii 460b
dār al-dunyā v 362b
dār al-ḥarb iii 240a
dār al-ibtilāʾ v 292b
dār al-ʿiyār iii 336b
dār al-khuld ii 52b, 460b; iv 13a, 14b
dār al-khulūd iv 14b
dār al-kufr i 540b
dār al-maʾwā iv 15b
dār al-muqām ii 460b
dār al-muqāma ii 283a; iv 13a

dār al-muttaqīn	II 460b; IV 13a, 14b
dār al-nadwa	I 406b
dār al-qarār	II 283a, 460b; IV 13a, 14b
dār al-qurʾān	IV 392a
dār al-salām	II 52a, 283a, 321b, 460b; IV 13a, 14a; V 11b
dār al-taqiyya	I 540b
sūʾ al-dār	II 460b
diyārāt	I 336a
diyāriyyāt	III 407b
d-w-l-ʾ-b	
dūlāb	I 43b
d-w-m	
dāʾim	II 54b; IV 81b
dawm	IV 54a
dawām	III 505a; V 278b
daymūmiyya	I 27b
d-w-n	
dīwān	II 500b; IV 271a, 274a
d-w-y	
dawāʾ	IV 172a
d-y-n	
dāna	I 246b; III 141b; IV 396b
tadayyun	II 73b; III 66a
dayn	IV 577b
dīn, pl. *adyān*	I 514b; III 66a
	I 90a, 91a, 224a, 262a, 338a, 373b, 375b, 380a, 380b, 481b, 538b; II 72b, 73a, 228a, 329a, 567b; III 64b, 66a, 66b, 141b, 142a, 240a, 323a, 424b, 531a; IV 8b, 71a, 145b, 152b, 255a, 395a, 395b, 396a, 396b, 397a, 397b, 398a, 398b, 400a, 400b, 401a, 401b, 415a, 415b; V 263b, 291b, 292b, 433a, 501b
dīn allāh	IV 397b; III 323a
dīn ʿatīq	I 481b
dīn al-fiṭra	IV 71a
dīn al-ḥaqq	I 538b; III 66b; V 433a, 501b, 502a
dīn ibrāhīm	IV 255a
dīn al-malik	IV 397b
dīn muḥammad	IV 152b
al-dīn al-qayyim	II 329a
lā ikrāha fī l-dīn(i)	I 224a; III 531a; V 291b
lakum dīnakum wa-liya dīn	I 373b

lil-yahūd dīnuhum wa-lil-muʾminīna dīnuhum	V 291b
yawm al-dīn	III 66b; IV 395b, 396a
dayyān	I 338a; III 66a
diyāna, pl. *diyānāt*	II 313b, 398a
diyānatan	II 313b
madīna, pl. *madāʾin*	I 163a, 338a, 338b, 339a, 530b; II 10b, 298b, 339a; III 367b, 368a; V 28b
al-madīna al-munawwara	III 368a
al-madīna al-sharīfa	III 368a
madīnat al-nabī	III 368a
madīnat rasūl allāh	I 338a, 338b
wa-ahl al-madīna yaqraʾūna hīta	I 530b
madāʾin ṣāliḥ	II 339a
madanī	I 128b
madaniyya	I 338a
d-y-n-ʾ-r	
dīnār, pl. *danānīr*	II 73b, 545b; III 335a, 336b, 408b; IV 288b; V 474a, 474b

-dhāl-

dh-ʾ	
hādhā, f. *hādhihi*	I 23b
dh-ʾ-b	
dhiʾb	I 95a
dh-b-b	
dhubāb	I 95a, 99b
dh-b-ḥ	IV 516b, 517a; V 555b
dhabaḥa	IV 517b
dhabḥ	I 403a, 403b; V 55a
dhabḥ al-ʿatāʾir	I 403a
dhabḥ al-manāsik	I 403b
dhabīḥ	I 6b; II 562a, 564b; IV 517b
dhabīḥa	V 54b
dh-r-ʾ	
dharaʾa	III 549b
dh-r-r	
dharra	I 95a, 99b; V 473b
mithqāl dharra	V 473b
dhurriyya	I 301b, 453b; III 486b; IV 297b, 291a
dh-r-ʿ	III 333a
dharʿ	III 333a
dhirāʿ	III 333a, 336b; V 473a

dh-r-w / dh-r-y
dharā I 52a; II 143a; III 453b; V 480a
dhāriya, pl. *dhāriyāt* I 53a, 55a
dhura I 46b
dh-k-r I 208a, 246b; II 434b; III 372a, 441b, 443a; IV 302a, 368b, 419b, 422b, 470a, 555b
dhakara II 205b; III 372a, 441b, 510a, 524b; IV 229b, 230a, 302a, 368b, 421a, 421b, 470a; V 55b, 203a
dhakkara II 363b; III 246b; IV 470a; V 8a, 203a, 460a
mudhakkir III 440b, 524b; V 460a
tadhkira II 142b, 435a; III 372a, 529a; IV 230a, 419b, 422a; V 422a
tadhakkara I 246a; III 372a, 373a
dhakar, pl. *dhukūr, dhukrān* II 289a, 292a
dhikr I 86b, 211a, 249a; II 82a, 82b, 94a, 163a, 204b, 207a, 272b, 314b, 371a; III 4a, 17b, 22b, 372a, 372b, 373a, 373b, 374a, 393a, 441b, 505b, 509b, 510a, 530a; IV 129b, 166b, 170b, 172a, 172b, 173a, 175a, 176a, 215a, 215b, 228b, 229b, 230a, 230b, 234a, 365b, 366a, 368a, 380a, 393b, 394b, 419b, 423b, 424a, 424b, 466a, 474a, 485b, 487b, 488a; V 70b, 105b, 138b, 142b, 153b, 269a, 301b, 499b, 557a, 557b
dhikr allāh II 272b, 230a
dhikr bi-lisān III 510a
dhikr bi-qalb III 510a
ahl al-dhikr III 372b; IV 49a, 129b, 230a, 302a
dhikrā II 409a; III 372a, 372b; IV 129b, 230a, 419b, 422b, 466a
dh-k-w/dh-k-y V 54b
dhakā V 54b, 55a
dhakkā IV 504b; V 54b, 55a
tadhkiya V 54b, 55a, 55b
dh-l-l IV 453b
istidhlāl IV 131a
dh-m-m
madhmūm I 514a
mudhammam III 502a

mudhāmm — I 41b, 362b, 364b; II 283b
dhimma — I 216b, 224a, 336a; III 33a; IV 152b, 153a, 153b, 402b, 403a, 403b, 407b, 408a, 416b
ahl al-dhimma — III 33a; IV 403a
dhimmī — III 33b; IV 235b, 403a
adham — I 362b
dh-n-b — I 536b
dhanb, pl. dhunūb — II 63b, 64a, 98a; III 228a, 424a; V 19a, 19b, 22b
dh-h-b
dhahaba — I 83b; III 54a
tadhhīb — III 601b
adhhaba — I 277a
dhahab — II 333b, 383b; III 409a; IV 354b; V 474b
madhhab, pl. madhāhib — I 554a, 557a; II 531b; III 66b, 115a, 240a; IV 73b, 99a
dh-w
dhū — II 315ab, 542a
dhū l-awtād — II 542a
dhāt — II 83a, 317a, 319a, 323b, 352b; IV 81a
dh-w-q
dhawq — III 100b

-rāʾ-

r-ʾ-s
raʾs, pl. ruʾūs — I 81b; II 211b; IV 152a, 372b, 477b; V 65a, 407b
ka-l-raʾs al-ḥanīdh — V 65a
ruʾūs amwālikum — V 407b
ruʾūs al-shayāṭīn — II 211b
riyāsa — I 261a; V 442b
r-ʾ-f
raʾfa — III 234a
raʾūf — II 321a; III 234a; IV 5b
r-ʾ-y — V 444a, 446b
raʾā — I 241b, 440b, 534a; II 253a, 259a, 259b, 559a; III 208b, 442a, 524a; IV 470a, 574b; V 171b, 445b, 446b, 447a
ruʾya — II 160b, 324a; III 424a; V 495a

ruʾyat allāh II 160b, 324a
ruʾyat al-hilāl V 495a
rāʾā II 71a
riʾāʾ II 468b; IV 119b
arā IV 574b; V 444b, 446a
raʾy I 76a; II 116a; III 64b, 67b; IV 142b, 143a, 143b, 144a, 157a
ruʾyā I 177a, 444b, 546b, 547b, 548a, 549a, 550a, 551a, 551b, 552a; II 240b, 241b; III 340a; IV 163a, 169b, 179a, 294b; V 444a, 444b, 445b
rayʾ II 101b
riyāʾ II 468b
r-b-b
rabba III 229b
marbūb III 230b
rabb, pl. *arbāb* I 188b, 329a, 329b, 330a, 446a, 447b, 448b, 502a, 555a; II 82b, 196a, 318b, 319a, 324a, 330a, 364a, 364b, 371a; III 43a, 71a, 77a, 229a, 229b, 230a, 231a, 338a, 418a, 489b, 561a; IV 4b, 20b, 68a, 184a, 213b, 217a, 222b, 288a, 474b, 481a, 578a; 94b, 105a; V 94b, 105b, 169b, 202a, 282b, 378b, 500b, 553a
rabb al-ʿālamīn I 188b; III 229b, 230a, 230b, 231a, 338a, 406a, 420a, 489b; IV 213b, 288a; V 105a, 500b, 553a
rabb al-falaq I 502a; III 418a
rabb hādhā l-bayt I 329a; II 319a; IV 288a
rabb al-mashriq[mashāriq/mashriqayn] wa-l-maghrib [maghārib/maghribayn] II 364a; IV 4b
rabb al-nās I 329a
rabb al-samāwāt(i) wa-l-arḍ(i) IV 288a; V 5553
anā rabbukum I 329b, 330a
fa-bi-ayyi ālāʾi rabbikumā tukadhdhibān I 448b; IV 474b, 481a
innanī anā rabbuka I 329b
iqraʾ bi-smi rabbika lladhī khalaq V 169b
(al-)rabba II 319a; III 43a
rabība, pl. *rabāʾib* II 266a
rabbānī IV 540a; V 202a
rabbāniyyūn II 569a; IV 404a, 539b, 578a; V 201b, 202a

rubūbiyya III 230b
r-b-ḥ
rabīḥa V 312b
r-b-ṣ
tarabbaṣa V 38b, 453b
tarabbuṣ V 453b
r-b-ṭ
rabaṭa I 405a; IV 277a
rābaṭa II 70b
marbūṭ II 353a
r-b-ʿ
murabbaʿ III 75a
arbaʿ III 551a
arbaʿūn V 75a
rubʿ II 94a; IV 244a
rubāʿī IV 480a
rabʿa III 254b
r-b-w
rabā II 3a
ribā I 301a, 434a; II 5b, 8a, 8b, 9b, 353a; IV 208b; V 198b, 269b, 406b, 407a, 407b, 408a, 408b, 469b
rabwa II 5b
ribwa II 10b
arbā III 565a
r-t-b
rutba V 384a
tartīb al-āyāt V 101b
martaba, pl. *marātib* II 195b
r-t-q
ratq II 327b
r-t-l
rattala III 116b
tartīl II 88a, 89a, 93b, 386b; III 116b; IV 367b, 368b, 373b, 377b; V 423a, 431a
rattil III 440b
murattal IV 377b
r-j-ʾ I 517b
irjāʾ I 517b
murjiʾa II 170a
murjawna I 517b
murjaʾūnā I 517b
r-j-b
rajabiyyūn II 183a

r-j-j
rujja I 113a
r-j-z
rijz III 232a; IV 454a, 499a, 502b, 503a, 503b
rujz IV 454a, 499a, 502b, 503b
rajaz I 542b; IV 317a
rijāz I 305a
urjūza, pl. *arājīz* I 48b
r-j-s
rijs I 410b, 411a, 411b; II 481b; IV 132b, 454a, 499a, 502b, 503a, 503b, 504a
r-j-ʿ
rajaʿa IV 428a, 429a, 429b
tarjīʿ II 386b
marjaʿ V 225a
marājiʿ V 215a, 225a
rajʿa I 206b; II 106a
rujuʿ I 205a
r-j-f I 113a
rajfa II 212a, 212b; IV 103b; V 133a, 253a
rājifa IV 103b
r-j-l II 199a
rajil, pl. *rijāl* II 198b, 289b, 290a, 290b; III 451b, 47a; IV 296a, 388a; V 375a
rajul II 328a; V 57a
rijl, pl. *arjul* II 198b, 199a, 199b; IV 372a
urkuḍ bi-rijlika II 199b
r-j-m
rajama V 129b
rajīm I 525a; II 543a; III 30b; V 130a, 267b
r-j-w I 517b; II 448b, 449a
rajāʾ I 522a, 530a
arjā V 334b
r-ḥ-b
marḥaban I 491b
lā marḥaban bikum I 491b
r-ḥ-q
raḥīq II 218a, 229a, 556a; V 62b, 482a
r-ḥ-l III 58b
raḥl, pl. *riḥāl* III 58b, 308b; IV 494b
riḥla I 290b; III 58b, 59a, 184b; IV 572a
raḥīl IV 55a, 472a

r-ḥ-m
raḥma I 237a, 449b; II 244b, 275a, 322a, 345a, 352b, 502a; III 68a, 372a, 377b, 426a, 442b, 504b, 512a; IV 300b; V 191b, 522a, 574b
raḥīm I 208b, 209a; II 244a, 244b, 318a; III 378a; IV 5b, 482a, 483a; V 126a, 381a, 522a
raḥmān I 208b, 209a, 329a; II 83a, 244a, 244b, 318a, 321b; III 233b, 378a, 378b, 380a, 460b, 461b, 474a; IV 5a, 258a; V 126a, 424a, 424b, 500b, 501a, 522a
al-raḥmān al-raḥīm II 83a; III 378a, 380a; IV 5a; V 501a
raḥmān al-yamāma III 461b
raḥim, pl. *arḥām* II 174b, 321b; III 95b, 378a, 378b, 474a; IV 20b, 177b; V 522a
ūlū l-arḥam II 174b; IV 20b
riḥm V 522a
r-kh-ṣ
murakhkhaṣ IV 377a
r-kh-w
rukhāʾ I 52b
rikhwa IV 374b
r-d-d
radda I 120a
murtadd I 119b
irtidād I 119a, 119b, 120a
radd IV 122b; V 410a
ridda I 120b, 217b, 544a; II 148a; III 462a, 464b
ḥurūb al-ridda I 120b
r-d-y
mutaraddiya II 220b
r-z-q V 178b
razaqa II 205b, 511a; V 545a
rizq I 86b; II 186a, 186b, 217a, 267b, 268a, 304b, 447b; III 152a, 183a, 210a; IV 2a, 18b; V 178b, 268b, 269b, 454b, 468a, 469a
razzāq II 320b
r-s-kh
rāsikh, pl. *rāsikhūn* I 72b, 75b, 349a; II 409a, 425a, 425b

al-rāsikhūn fī l-ʿilm	I 72b, 75b, 349a; II 409a, 425a, 425b
r-s-s	
rass	IV 352a, 352b
aṣḥāb al-rass	IV 352a
r-s-l	I 246b
rasala	I 52a, 189b
arsala	I 52a, 189b; II 365a; III 524a; IV 295a; V 8a, 130a
mursal, pl. *mursalūn*	III 232a, 380b, 381a, 382b; IV 289b, 297b
mursala, pl. *mursalāt*	I 53a, 55a; II 390b; III 382b
rasūl, pl. *rusul*	I 62a, 243b, 245b, 513a, II 12a, 95b, 363b, 462b, 497b, 563b; III 16a, 207a, 232a, 293a, 341a, 380b, 381a, 381b, 382b, 440a, 440b, 486a, 502a, 528a, 556a, 558a, 558b; IV 128b, 289b, 290a, 290b, 291a, 295a, 296a, 297a, 297b, 298a, 306a, 375a; V 28b, 83a, 96b, 115a, 116a, 174b, 437b, 438a, 493a, 498b, 501a, 501b
rasūl karīm	IV 290a; V 116a
al-rasūl al-nabī al-ummī	V 437b
allāhu wa-rasūluhu	V 174b
anna l-rasūla ḥaqqun	V 502a
muḥammad rasūl allāh	II 95b; III 556a, 558a, 558b; V 498b
risāla, pl. *risālāt*, *rasāʾil*	I 554a; II 22a, 270b; III 83b, 528a; IV 128b, 289b, 441b; V 378a, 534a
r-s-m	
rasm	I 348b, 349b, 350b; III 259b, 605a; IV 272a, 273b, 354a, 354b, 355a, 356a, 357b, 391b, 446b, 447b; V 238a, 239b, 248b, 249b
rasm ʿuthmānī	III 605a
r-s-w	
rāsin, pl. *rawāsin*	II 2b
r-sh-d	
arshada	I 348b; II 189b
rāshid, pl. *rāshidūn*	I 388b; II 471b; IV 588b; V 409a
rushd	II 374a; III 64b, 67b, 330a, 331b
rashad	III 64b; III 67b
r-ḍ-ʿ	V 476b

arḍaʿa III 106a
murḍiʿa III 106a; V 476b
raḍāʿ III 107b
marāḍiʿ III 106a
r-ḍ-y
raḍiya II 58a
rāḍiya IV 103b; V 183b
marḍiyya IV 103b
riḍwān I 89b; II 52a, 285b, 321b; IV 17a, 264a, 523a; V 430a
marḍāt II 352b
riḍā IV 141a; V 135a
r-ṭ-b
muraṭṭab I 137a
ruṭab I 495a; II 305b
r-ṭ-l
raṭl III 336b
r-ʿ-b
ruʿb II 194b, 198a
r-ʿ-d
raʿd V 471a
r-ʿ-w
irʿawā II 346b
r-ʿ-y
marʿā I 41a
rāʿinā I 440b
r-gh-b
targhīb II 558a; IV 527b; V 321a
r-gh-d
raghadan I 436a
r-f-t
rufāt II 4b
r-f-th
rafth IV 502b
rafath I 511b; IV 583a
r-f-r-f
rafraf II 276a; IV 18a
r-f-ḍ
rāfiḍa, pl. *rawāfiḍ* II 421b
r-f-ʿ IV 47b
rafaʿa I 442b; III 19b, 76b; V 64b, 544a
rāfiʿ III 19b
marfūʿa III 128b, 513a
rafʿ I 358a
r-f-q
rafīq V 41b

r-q-b
raqīb II 320b; V 118b, 493a
raqaba, pl. *riqāb* I 289a, 289b; II 307a; IV 227a; V 57a, 58a
r-q-d
rāqid, pl. *ruqūd* IV 351b; V 251b
r-q-ʿ
riqāʿ I 137a
r-q-q
tarqīq IV 374b
raqq II 544b, 545a; III 591a; IV 587a
riqq IV 587a; V 57a
raqīq V 58a
r-q-m IV 351a; V 558a
marqūm V 558a
raqīm V 251a
r-q-y
ruqā IV 173a
ruqī I 177a
ruqya, pl. *ruqan, ruqā* I 77a; III 361b; IV 163a, 165b, 170b, 173a, 173b
rāqiya II 189a
r-k-b
rikāb I 94b; V 411b
r-k-z
rikz V 479a, 479b
r-k-ʿ V 555b
rakaʿa I 254a; IV 220a
rākiʿan I 254b; IV 219b
rakʿa II 82b, 272b, 388a; III 546b; IV 105a, 178b; V 499a
rukūʿ I 254a; III 596b; IV 219b, 486a, 490b; V 170b, 556a
rakāt V 208a
r-k-n
rukn, pl. *arkān* II 168b; III 136a, 178b; IV 30b, 487a; V 504a
r-m-ḥ
rumḥ, pl. *rimāḥ* II 546a
r-m-d
ramida I 184b
rammada I 184b
ramad III 356b
ramād I 184a, 184b
r-m-z
ramz IV 439b

r-m-ḍ
ramaḍa II 219a
ramaḍān I 12a, 14a, 66b
r-m-l
raml IV 530b, 531a
ramal IV 64a
r-m-n
rummān I 42b, 44b; II 217b, 305b
r-m-y
ramā III 398a; IV 64a; V 130a
r-n-d
rind IV 65a
r-h-b
ruhbān II 156a; III 406a; IV 404a
tarhīb II 558a
irhāb II 197b
rahab II 194b, 197b
rahba II 197b
rahb II 197b
rahbāniyya I 181a, 183b; II 408b, 536b; III 406a
r-h-ṭ
rahṭ V 552a
r-h-n II 454a
murāhana I 267b
rahn IV 109b
ruhn IV 109b
ruhun IV 109b
rihān II 454a; IV 109b; V 204a, 312b
rahīn II 454a; IV 109b; V 312b
rahīna II 454a; IV 109b
rahāʾin II 454a
r-h-w
rahwan V 247a
r-w-ḥ / r-y-ḥ III 573a
tarāwīḥ IV 347a, 379b
rāʾiḥa I 288a
rūḥ, pl. *arwāḥ* I 3a 52a 52b, 82a, 87a, 114a, 178b, 230b, 508a, 508b; II 442b, 443a, 443b; III 15b, 186b, 292b, 293a, 442a, 504a, 512a, 537b; IV 293a, 294a, 294b, 296a, 573a; V 81a, 81b, 83b, 84a, 114a, 114b, 115a, 116a, 116b, 117a, 118b, 119a, 122a, 144b, 154b, 271a, 546a

rūḥ al-amīn II 443b; III 442a; IV 293a
rūḥ al-ḥaqq III 504a
rūḥ al-qudus I 87a; II 442b, 443a; III 293a, 442a, 504a; IV 293a; V 81a, 115a, 118b
rīḥ, pl. *riyāḥ* I 42a, 51b, 52a, 52b, 54b; III 529b, 573a, 573b, 574a; IV 590b, 591a; V 62a, 63a, 63b, 133a, 462b, 470b, 471a
rawḥ V 63b
rawāḥ I 504a; V 476a
rayḥān I 44a, 137a, 142a, 448b; II 305b; III 265a, 573a; V 62b
rayḥānī I 282b, 283a; III 265a
rūḥāniyyūn V 118a
r-w-d II 550a
rāwada II 444b
arāda I 271b; V 485a, 485b, 486b, 487a, 543a
irāda IV 433b
murīd V 142b
r-w-s
tarwīs I 137a
r-w-ḍ
rawḍa, pl. *rawḍāt* I 41a; II 283a, 304a; IV 13a
r-w-m
rūm V 286a, 430b
baḥr al-rūm I 203b
r-w-y
riwāya I 334a; II 100b; III 517a, 606b; IV 275a, 359b
rāwin, *rāwī*, pl. *ruwāt* IV 358a, 359b, 360a, 389b, 390a
tarwiya V 214a
r-y-b V 177b
irtāba V 178b
rayb II 185a; IV 113a, 391a; V 287a, 404a
rayb al-manūn II 185a; IV 113a; V 287a
r-y-ḥ see r-w-ḥ
r-y-sh
rīsh I 346a, 346b; V 3b

-zāʾ-

z-b-d	
zubd	V 359b
z-b-r	
zabūr, pl. *zubur*	I 243b, 245b; II 434a, 504b; III 4a, 24b, 591a; IV 24b, 25a, 36b, 296b, 297a, 297b, 304b, 315a, 316a, 403b, 569b; V 301b
z-b-n	
zabāniya	II 417b; V 119a
z-j-j	
zujāja	I 490a, 491a
z-j-r	
muzdajar	II 441a
zajr	II 239b, 386a; V 321a
z-ḥ-m	
izdiḥām	IV 97a
z-kh-r-f	
zukhruf	I 212b, 213a, 213b, 543b; II 3b, 459a; IV 354b
z-r-b	
zarābī	II 276a
z-r-ʿ	I 40b
zarʿ, pl. *zurūʿ*	I 42a; II 3b, 304b
z-r-q	
azraq, pl. *zurq*	I 363a
zarq	I 363a
zurayq	IV 599a
z-q-m	V 572a
zaqqūm	II 211a
z-k-m	
zakma	V 65a
zukām	V 65a
z-k-w / z-k-y	I 343b; IV 208b, 499a, 505b
zakā	I 66a, 343b; II 311b
zakkā	IV 505a, 505b
tazkiya	I 404a
muzakkī	IV 490b
tazakkā	IV 505b; V 196b
zakāt/zakāh	I 64a, 64b, 65a, 66a, 66b, 67a, 67b, 68a, 263a, 328a, 403b; II 7a, 61a, 62a, 65b, 148a, 168a, 176b, 353a, 450a; III 16a, 252b, 336a, 372a, 373a; IV 6b, 42b, 208b,

221b, 225a, 485b, 486a, 487a, 488a, 489a, 489b, 490a, 490b, 491a, 598a; v 196b, 197a, 197b, 198a, 198b, 199a, 452b, 523a, 549b, 556a, 556b, 564b
zakāt al-mafrūḍa v 196b
ayāt al-zakāt v 197b
iqāmat al-ṣalāt wa-ītā' al-zakāt v 197a
zakiyy iv 505a
azkā ii 460a; iv 505b, 506a
z-l-z-l
zalzala ii 148a
z-l-f
zulaf i 503a; ii 79b; v 282b, 431a, 432a
z-l-l
zalla ii 199a
azalla i 25b
z-l-m
zalam, pl. *azlām* i 411a; ii 281b, 546b; iv 259b; v 78b
z-m-r
mazmūr iv 314a
zumra, pl. *zumar* v 377a
mizmār iv 314a
z-m-z-m
zamzam i 179b
z-m-k
zammaka iii 601b
z-m-l
muzzammil iii 440b; v 95b
z-m-n
zamān i 319a; ii 267b; v 278b
z-n-j-b-l
zanjabīl i 490b; ii 217b, 229a, 305b; v 62b, 464b
z-n-d-q
zindīq, pl. *zanādiqa* i 122a; ii 422a, 471a; iv 399b, 512b
zandaqa i 470a; ii 420b, 422a; iv 122b
z-n-m
zanīm ii 491a, 491b
z-n-n
zānin i 299a
z-n-y
zanā iv 580b

zānī, f. *zāniya*	I 299a; IV 580b; V 254b
zinā	I 28a, 366b; II 63a, 445a; IV 285a, 580b; V 497b, 540a
zināʾ	I 28a; II 214a, 214b; III 492a; IV 580b
z-h-d	
zuhd	I 181a; III 138a; IV 90a
zāhid	IV 65a; V 148b
zuhhād	IV 387a
z-w-j	
zawwaja	III 96a, 277a; IV 354b
tazwīj	V 232a
izdiwāj	III 220b; IV 481b
zawj, pl. *azwāj*	II 290b, 291a, 292a, 292b, 362b; III 95b, 277a, 363a; IV 18a, 22a, 505b
zawja, pl. *zawjāt*	I 24b; II 362b; III 95b
z-w-r	V 448a
zāra	V 448a
zūr	III 70b
ziyāra	II 206b; III 370b; IV 92a; V 448a
mazārāt	V 186b
z-w-l	
zawāl	I 504a
z-w-y	
zāwiya	III 434b
z-y-t	
zayt	I 102b; II 218b
zaytūn	I 42b; II 4a, 217b, 305b; III 4b
z-y-d	
zāda	III 549b
ziyāda	II 324a; IV 17b
mazīd	II 324a
z-y-gh	
zāgha	I 177b; II 59a
azāgha	II 59a
zaygh	III 31a
z-y-n	
zayyana	I 213a, 442b; II 387a
izzayyana	I 213b; II 347a
zīna	I 212a, 213a, 346a, 442b; II 3b; III 534a, 534b, 535b; IV 256b; V 414a, 510b, 526a, 528a

-sīn-

s-ʾ-l
saʾala I 444b; II 85b; IV 431a; V 108b, 247a
sāʾil, pl. *sāʾilūn* III 528b; V 197a
tasāʾala II 364a
masʾūliyya IV 431a
musāʾala III 141a; IV 460a
masʾala, pl. *masāʾil* II 116a; IV 527b
suʾāl II 189a
s-b-b
sabba IV 309b
musabbab IV 444b; V 383a
sabab, pl. *asbāb* I 321b, 513a, 552b; II 130b, 133a, 135a; II 193a, 377a, 378b, 388b, 390a, 391b, 392b, 393a, 519a; III 55b, 164b, 353a, 377a, 457a, 457b, 569a, 569b, 570b, 571a, 571b, 572a, 572b; IV 155a, 255b, 399a, 444b, 447a, 532b; V 292a, 326a; V 404a, 509b, 513a, 526a, 535a
sabab al-nuzūl I 513a; II 130b, 193a, 377b; III 457a, 457b, 569a, 569b, 570a; IV 532b
asbāb al-nuzūl I 321b, 552b; II 133a, 135a, 377b, 378b, 388b, 390a, 391b, 392b, 393a, 519a; III 55b, 164b, 377a, 569a, 569b, 570b, 571a, 571b, 572a, 572b; IV 155a, 255b, 444b, 447a; V 292a, 326a, 404a, 509b, 526a, 535a
s-b-t IV 510b
sabata IV 510a, 511a
sabt IV 510a, 511a
subāt I 498a; IV 511a
s-b-ḥ I 27a; II 314b; IV 213a; V 555b
sabaḥa I 27a, 237a, 442a; II 92b, 315a; IV 214b
sābiḥāt II 315a; V 396b
sabbaḥa I 455b; II 214b, 215a, 314b, 315a; III 443a, 546b; IV 220a, 220b, 221a; V 170b, 426a
tasbīḥ I 27a, 86b, 180b, 502b; II 82a, 82b,

	93b, 314b, 315a; III 373a, 404b, 418b; IV 220a; V 75a
subḥān	I 27a, 237a; II 214b, 371a; III 220a, 404b; IV 215a, 220a, 220b, 474a; V 376a
subḥāna llāhi	I 27a, 237a; II 92b, 214b, 376a; III 220a, 404b; IV 215a, 220a 474a
subḥāna rabbī	IV 220a
subḥāna rabbika	IV 220b
subḥāna rabbinā	IV 220b, 474a
subḥānaka	I 237a; II 214b, 314b; IV 220b
musabbiḥ, pl. *musabbiḥūn*	II 315a; III 54b
musabbiḥāt	II 394a
s-b-ṭ	
sabaṭ	V 364a
sibṭān	IV 334a
asbāṭ	III 50a; V 364a, 364b
s-b-ʿ	
sabʿ	I 210b; II 36a, 189a, 190b, 191a, 385b, 396b; V 424b
sabʿat aḥruf	II 385b, 396b
sabʿan min al-mathānī	I 210b, II 36a, 189a, 190b, 191a
sabʿa	III 552a
sabuʿ	I 95a
subʿ, pl. *asbāʿ*	III 576a, 596b
usbūʿ	V 285b
s-b-gh	
sābigha, pl. *sābighāt*	II 546a
s-b-q	
sābiq, pl. *sābiqūn*	III 67a, 177b; IV 2b, 15b, 16a, 16b, 332b
sābiqa	II 16b
s-b-l	
sabīl, pl. *subul, asbila*	I 324b, 506a; II 72b, 176a, 177b, 209a; III 38b, 58a, 282b; IV 2a, 28a, 28b, 29a, 29b, 30a, 129b, 209a, 431b; V 124a, 193b, 194b, 373a, 374a, 455a
(fī) sabīl allāh	I 324b, 506a; II 72b, 177b, 209a; III 38b, 58a, 282b; IV 28a, 29a, 30a, 129b, 431b, 455a; V 193b, 374a, 455a
fī sabīl al-shayṭān	V 193b
fī sabīli	IV 30a
ibn al-sabīl	II 176a; IV 28b, 209a; V 194b

s-t-t
sitta III 552a
s-t-r
satara II 557a
istatara I 29bb
satr I 203a
s-j-d
sajada I 26b, 254b; II 369b; IV 221a; V 169b, 221b, 555b
sājid, pl. *sājidūn* IV 305a
sujjad I 254b; IV 219b, 221b
sujūd IV 219a, 219b, 254a, 254b, 486a, 491a; V 471b
sajda I 254a, 254b; II 390b; III 427a, 596b; IV 377a, 377b, 378a, 388b; V 170b
masjid, pl. *masājid* I 81b, 125a, 163b, 164a, 164b, 165a, 171a, 173a, 176b, 335b; II 299a, 299b, 309b, 311a, 349a, 458b; III 3a, 4b, 75a, 77a, 77b, 78a, 79a, 79b, 340a, 427a, 427b, 429b, 436a, 438a, 491b; IV 92b, 226b, 259a, 281b, 327b, 404a, 514a, 515a, 516a, 516b; V 104b, 184b, 501b, 556a, 556b, 567b
al-masjid al-aqṣā I 125a, 125b, 164a, 176b; II 299b, 309b; III 3a, 427a, 491b; IV 325a, 514a; V 104b
al-masjid al-ḥarām I 81b, 125a, 176b, 225a; II 299a, 309b, 311a; III 75a, 77a, 77b, 78a, 79a, 79b, 340a, 427a, 429b, 436a; IV 92b, 226b, 259a, 281b, 325a, 327b, 515a; V 104b, 501b, 556b
masjid al-nifāq III 438a
wa-anna l-masājida bi-llāhi fa-lā tadʿū maʿa llāhi abadan II 349a
s-j-ʿ
sajʿ, pl. *asjāʿ* I 316b, 542b; II 251b, 253a, 320a, 385a, 528b; III 148b, 196b, 207b, 220b, 221b, 246b, 481a, 489b; IV 60a, 217a, 463a, 463b, 464a, 476b, 477a, 477b, 478a, 478b, 479a, 479b, 480a, 480b, 481a, 481b, 482a; V 67b, 79a, 168b, 173b, 253a, 425b, 426a, 427b

saj'a, pl. *saj'āt* IV 476b, 477b, 479a, 479b, 480a, 480b, 481a, 482a

s-j-l
sijill V 242a
sijjīl I 339a, 339b, 340a, 340b; II 411a, 545a; III 383b, 591a

s-j-n
masjūn IV 276a
sijn IV 276a
sijjīn I 205b; IV 2b, 102b, 103a

s-j-w
sajā V 36a

s-ḥ-b
saḥāb V 461b, 462b, 471a

s-ḥ-t
suḥt II 173b, 174a

s-ḥ-r
ṣaḥara III 246a
sāḥir I 530b, 542b; II 540a; III 44a, 246b, 247a; IV 301a, 311b; V 239b
sāḥira III 246a
masḥūr I 542b; III 44a, 247a; IV 67b
siḥr I 542b; III 246a, 356a; IV 163a, 164a, 164b, 165a, 172a
saḥar, pl. *asḥār* I 503b; III 417a; IV 222b; V 281a
saḥḥār III 246a, 246b

s-ḥ-q
saḥq IV 584a
siḥāq IV 584a; V 497b, 528a
suḥq I 491b

s-ḥ-l
misḥal IV 112a

s-kh-r III 400a, 400b, 401a
sakhira II 322a; IV 309b
sakhkhara I 442b, 443a, 498a
taskhīr IV 549b
musakhkharāt IV 107b
sukhrī III 253a

s-kh-ṭ
sakhaṭ II 321a

s-d-r
sidra, coll. *sidr* I 41b, 177b; II 51b, 283b, 305b, 324b, 411b; III 285a, 442a, 532a; V 126a, 360b, 361a, 361b, 466b
sidrat al-muntahā I 177b, 180a; II 51b, 283b, 324b,

	411b, 500b; III 285a, 442a, 532a; V 125a, 360b, 361a, 361b, 466b
sādin	II 238a; V 78b
s-r-b	
sārib	I 498a
sarab	III 426a
s-r-b-l	
sarābīl	I 346b; II 455a
s-r-j	
sirāj	II 275b, 547a; III 107b, 108a, 186a, 186b, 187a, 440b, 503b; V 163a
s-r-ḥ	
sariḥa	III 284b; III 417b, 418b
s-r-d	
sarada	II 546a
sard	II 546a
s-r-d-q	
surādiq	V 234b, 236b
s-r-r	II 423a; III 62b; IV 572b
masrūr	III 62b
asarra	V 479b
sirr, pl. *asrār*	II 118a; III 571a; IV 424b, 572b, 573a; V 141b, 144b, 479a, 479b
sirār	III 414b
sarīr, pl. *surur*	I 166a; II 276a, 459a; IV 18a
surriyya	I 396a
s-r-ṭ	
sirāṭ	I 348b; II 395a, 415a; III 143a; IV 523a
s-r-ʿ	
sarīʿ	IV 60b
sirāʿan	III 185a
s-r-f	
asrafa	V 22b
musrifīn	II 418a; V 257b
isrāf	II 7b
s-r-q	
saraqa	III 208b
istaraqa	I 442b
sariqa, pl. *sariqāt*	III 215a; V 255a
s-r-m-d	
sarmad	I 498a; V 279a, 475a
s-r-y	
sarā	V 282a
asrā	I 88a; IV 64a, 246b, V 376a

asrā bi-ʿabdihi (laylan) I 88a; V 376a
isrāʾ I 551b; II 215b, 240b, 241b, 324b, 392b, 484a; III 3a, 4a, 5b, 388b, 487b, 488a, 491b, 496a, 546a; IV 179a, 295a; V 185a, 376a
sarī III 395b; V 127b
suryānī II 228a
s-ṭ-r V 558a
saṭara II 512b; III 190b, 518a; V 558a
masṭūr V 558a
usṭūr II 492b
mustaṭar III 191a; V 558a
saṭr, pl. *asāṭīr, suṭūr, asṭur, asṭār,* I 209b; II 492b; III 188b, 190a, 509b; IV 302b, 463a; V 400b
asāṭīr al-awwalīn II 434a, 492b; III 188b, 190a, 190b, 518a; IV 463a; V 400b
usṭūra, pl. *asāṭīr* II 430a, 493a, 512b; III 517a, 518a
s-ʿ-r
saʿīr II 49b, 210a, 414b, 419a; III 203b, 529b; V 106a
s-ʿ-y
saʿy I 9a, 353b; III 79a; IV 93a, 93b, 94a, 105a, 518a, 518b, 519b; V 463a
s-gh-b
masghaba II 177b, 307a
s-f-ḥ
masfūḥ I 411a
musāfiḥūn I 299a
musāfiḥāt I 299a
s-f-r III 57b
tasfīr II 100a
sifr, pl. *asfār* II 544b; III 58b; V 15b
safar III 58a; V 323a, 373b
ʿalā safarin III 58a; V 373b
safara I 247b; II 387b; III 189b; IV 444a
s-f-l
istisfāl IV 374b
sāfila III 439a
s-f-h
safiha II 364a
safah IV 433b
safāha II 462b
sufahāʾ II 1a, 7b, 374a
s-f-y-n
safīna I 157b; IV 604a, 604b

s-q-r
saqar II 49b, 210a, 414b, 419a; III 177b, 203a; IV 102b, 103a
s-q-ṭ
saqaṭa IV 428b
isqāṭ I 2b
s-q-f
saqf, pl. *suquf* II 363b, 459a, 459b, 460b; V 277b
al-saqf al-marfūʿ V 277b
usquf III 501b
s-q-y
saqā V 462a
sāqiya I 43b
istisqāʾ V 89b
siqāya I 490a, 491a
s-k-r
sukr II 557a, 557b
muskir II 556a
sakar II 556a; V 482a
sakrān, pl. *sukārā* I 341a; II 221b, 556a, 557a; IV 225b
s-k-n IV 589b
sakana I 52a, 277a; II 458b
sākin IV 376a
taskīn IV 478a
sukūn I 141a; III 260a, 264a; V 145a
sakan II 458a, 458b, 459a
sakina II 62a; IV 34a
sikkīn II 547a
sakīna I 158a, 405b, 459b; II 466a; III 454a, 586a; IV 441b, 536a, 536b, 589b, 590a, 590b, 591a; V 404b, 435a, 435b, 436a
maskan, maskin, pl. *masākin* I 163a, 165b, 498a; II 458a, 458b, 460b; IV 424a; V 194b, 197a
s-l-b
salab I 252a
s-l-ḥ
silāḥ, pl. *asliḥa* II 545b; III 210a
s-l-kh
salakha I 497b
s-l-s-b-l
salsabīl V 124b, 464b, 466b
s-l-s-l
silsila, pl. *salāsil* II 544b, 547a
musalsal I 136b; II 125a, 125b, 138b

s-l-ṭ
sulṭa I 188b
sulṭān I 188b, 189a, 190a, 260a, 261a, 278a; III 43b, 90b, 157a, 177a, 421b; IV 142a, 143b, 210a, 287a, 312b; V 3a
sulṭāniya IV 101a
s-l-ʿ
silʿāt III 246b
s-l-f
aslafa V 312b
salaf I 471a; II 270b; III 54b; IV 69b, 493b, 495b
salafiyya V 536b
s-l-k
maslak I 556a, 556b
s-l-l
sulāla I 340a, 476a; II 328a
s-l-m I 246b, 381a; II 91b, 164b, 565a, 567a; IV 34a
sallama III 567a
taslīm IV 225a
aslama I 218b, 375a; II 72b, 169a, 402b, 459a, 568b; III 444a, 567a; IV 299a; V 263a, 263b
aslama wajhahu lillāhi II 568b
muslim, pl. *muslimūn* I 223b, 374a, 376a, 506a, 556a, 556b; II 163b, 164b, 170a, 186a, 311b, 402b, 459a, 561b, 565a, 568a, 568b; III 71b, 157b, 340b, 507b; IV 37b, 67b, 402a, 403b; V 158b
muslima, pl. *muslimāt* II 568b
islām I 27a, 37a, 37b, 220a, 374a, 375a, 376a, 472a; II 73a, 163b, 164b, 167a, 167b, 168a, 168b, 169a, 169b, 170b, 172b, 562a, 565a, 565b, 566a, 567b, 568a, 568b, 569a; III 483b, 525a; IV 254a, 263b, 397a, 398a, 401b, 402a, 403b, 404a, 438a; V 69a, 145a, 271b, 381a, 436a, 504a, 555a
istilām III 179a
istaslama V 378a
salm III 39b

silm III 39b
salam 434a
salām I 32a, 237a; II 91a, 91b, 164b, 283b, 321b; III 31b, 178b, 529b; IV 14a, 33b, 34a, 225a, 377b; V 117a, 144b, 219a
(al-)salām(un) ʿalayka III 31b; IV 225a
(al-)salām(un) ʿalaykum I 237a; II 91a, 91b; IV 225a; V 219a
salīm II 408a
s-l-w
salwā I 95a
sulwān IV 583b
s-m-d
sāmidūna III 147a
wa-antum sāmidūna III 147a
s-m-r
samar III 517a
s-m-ṭ
simāṭ V 188a
s-m-ʿ
samiʿa II 1b, 405b, 406a
I 32a, 83a, 83b, 537a; II 1b, 2a, 405b, 406a, 548a; III 27a; V 502a
asmaʿa II 405b
issammaʿa II 405b
issamaʿa II 405b
istamaʿa II 2a
samʿ, pl. *asmāʿ* I 83b; II 91b, 94a, 95b, 406a, 506b; V 478b
samʿ wa-l-ṭāʿa II 406a; IV 506b
samāʿ II 87b; IV 172b, 380b, 391a, 391b, 588a
samīʿ II 1b, 320b, 323a, 405b, 406a; III 102a; IV 5b, 82a, 444b, 573b, 574b
s-m-k
samk II 460b
s-m-m
samm, pl. *samūm* I 286b; II 415a; III 48b
fī sammi l-khiyāṭ I 286b
summ I 286b
s-m-w
al-samʾ II 410a
samāʾ, pl. *samāwāt* II 410a
I 440b, 462b; II 362a, 363a, 364a, 410a, 411b; III 531b, 546b; IV 4a, 107b, 108b, 217a; V 64a, 104b, 105b, 108a, 553a

samāʾ al-dunyā I 462b; V 105b
samāʾ wa-l-arḍ III 531b; V 104b; 553a
samāʾwāt wa-l-arḍ I 440b; V 104b, 553a
s-m-y
tasmiya I 207b; V 55b
ism, pl. *asmāʾ* I 23b, 78b, 103b, 170a, 207b, 208a, 208b, 210b, 330a, 516a; II 253a, 317a, 318a, 319b; III 11a, 178b, 302a, 304b, 305a, 306a, 312a, 319b, 327b, 503a; IV 165b, 170a, 170b, 174a, 232b, 239a, 366a, 377b, 380a, 482a; V 126a, 382b, 424a, 493a, 552a
bi-smi llāh[i] I 207b, 208a, 209b; II 318a; III 536a, 554b, 556a; IV 232b, 377b; V 424a; see also ʾ-l-h
asmāʾ [allāh] al-ḥusnā I 78b, 330a, 516a; II 91b, 94a, 95b, 253a, 317a, 319b; III 178b, 302a, 304b, 305a, 306a, 312a, 319b, 327b; IV 165b, 170a, 239a, 380a, 482a; 493a, 501a
s-n
sana, pl. *sinīn(a)* III 335a; V 285b, 286a, 475a, 475b, 560a, 560b
s-n-b-l
sunbul, pl. *sanābil* I 42a; II 217b, 218a
sunbula, pl. *sunbulāt* I 25a
sanjaq III 318b
s-n-d
isnād I 357a, 358a, 358b, 388a, 391b; II 102a, 102b, 376b, 378a, 378b, 379a, 379b, 381a, 381b, 382b, 383a, 383b, 384a, 385a, 387a, 387b, 388a, 389a, 390a, 390b, 391b, 392a, 392b, 394a, 394b, 395b, 396a; IV 534b; V 35a, 504b
musnad I 153a; IV 588b, 589a; V 31a
sundus I 347a; V 11b
s-n-m
tasnīm V 124b, 464b
s-n-n II 348a
masnūn I 24a
ṣalṣāl min ḥamaʾ masnūn I 24a
sinn V 231a

sunna, pl. *sunan*	I 11a, 11b, 13a, 13b, 18a, 62b, 121b, 201a, 306b, 337b, 353b, 354a, 387a, 390b, 403b, 482a, 544b; II 9a, 78b, 83b, 84a, 230a, 270a, 400b, 422a, 434a, 567b; III 37a, 85a, 152b, 158a, 161b, 163a, 163b, 166a, 166b, 167a, 167b, 169a, 350a, 590b; IV 9b, 126b, 140b, 141b, 147a, 152a, 174b, 232a, 301b, 369a, 434b, 445b, 459a, 460b, 487b, 488b, 541b, 556a, 584a, 588a, 594a; V 1b, 2a, 20a, 30a, 46b, 138b, 139a, 154a, **163b**, 164a, 164b, 165a, 165b, 166a, 195b, 199a, 316a, 317b, 318a, 386b, 507a, 509b, 514b, 515a, 556b
al-sunna al-kawniyya	IV 556a
sunnat allāh	IV 126b; V 317b, 509b, 514b
sunnat al-awwalīn	V 317b
sunnat al-nabī	IV 596b; V 165b, 166a
sunnat rasūl allāh	V 165b
ahl al-sunna wa-l-jamāʿa	II 422a
sanna	I 271b; IV 137b
sunnī	I 14b, 26a
s-h-r	
sāhira	III 5a, 6a
s-h-l	
tashīl	II 386a
sahl	III 115a
s-h-m	
sāhama	II 282a
s-h-w	
istahā	V 374b
s-w-ʾ	II 64a
sāʾa	II 64a; III 336b
sāʾa mā yaḥkumūna	II 64a, 64b
sawʾ	II 64a
sūʾ	II 64a, 64b, 336a, 336b; V 439a, 441a
sawʾa, pl. *sawʾāt*	I 84a, 346b; II 364a; III 548a, 548b; IV 581a, 584a
sayyiʾ	II 64a; V 21a
sayyiʾa, pl. *sayyiʾāt*	II 69a, 98a; V 19a, 19b, 22a, 198a

s-w-ḥ
sāʾiḥūn v 374a
sāʾiḥāt v 374a
s-w-d i 364b
muswadd i 364b
aswad i 362a, 364a, 364b
sayyid i 344b, 369a; ii 175b, 319a, 400b, 503b; iv 291b
sayyida ii 96b
s-w-r v 247b
sūr i 203a; iv 47a
sūra, pl. *suwar* i 12a, 20a, 27a, 36a, 44b, 202a, 207b, 208a, 209b, 210b, 211a, 226b, 293b, 318b, 344b, 345a, 359a, 367a, 375b, 382b, 444b, 452a, 452b, 453b, 454b, 455b, 502a, 505a, 533a, 543b, 548b; ii 72b, 133a, 188b, 189a, 190b, 191a, 217a, 218b, 220a, 246a, 246b, 248a, 251b, 258a, 263a, 307a, 372a, 385a, 393b, 394b, 437a, 494a, 505a, 527b; iii 8a, 55a, 55b, 56a, 57a, 96a, 106a, 165a, 194b, 195a, 196a, 199b, 251a, 258b, 259a, 260a, 346b, 374b, 451b, 457a, 473a, 485b, 521b, 575a, 594b, 597b; iv 15b, 22b, 44b, 45a, 45b, 54a, 59a, 100b, 103b, 159a, 172b, 191b, 239a, 244a, 249a, 293a, 312b, 313a, 327b, 371a, 436a, 445a, 453b, 467b, 468b, 469a, 472a, 472b, 473a, 481a, 532a, 586a, 601b; v 28b, 43a, 65a, 145a, 163a, **166b**, 167a, 167b, 174b, 175b, 183b, 247b, 261a, 296b, 322a, 325b, 375b, 419b, 420a, 420b, 457b , 504b
bi-ʿashri suwarin mithlihi iv 312b
fa-ʾtū bi-sūratin mithlihi iv 312b; v 167a
fawātiḥ al-suwar iii 473a
s-w-s
sāʾis iv 45a
sawwās ii 213a
siyāsa iv 126a, 127a

s-w-ʿ
sāʿa I 85b, 89b, 319a, 500b, 501a, 503a; II 363a; III 66b, 137a, 138a, 335b; IV 12a, 25b, 434a; V 287a, 287b, 288a, 476b

s-w-q
sāʾiq V 118b, 494a
sāq II 324b
aswāq III 275a

s-w-k
siwāk III 563a; V 359a

s-w-m
musawwama II 212b

s-w-y
sawwā II 328b; V 114b, 543b
istawā I 442a, 443b, 450a; II 410b, 411a
sawāʾ IV 29a
taswiya, pl. *taswiyāt* V 114b, 323a

s-y-b
sāʾiba I 97a, 401b

s-y-ḥ
sāḥa I 183a; III 12b
sāʾiḥ, pl. *sāʾiḥūn* II 181a; III 58a
sāʾiḥa, pl. *sāʾiḥāt* II 181a
siyāḥa I 182a, 183a

s-y-r
sāra I 290a; III 57b, 58a
sayr V 29b, 373b, 376a
sīra, pl. *siyar* III 58a

I 266a, 314b, 388a, 399b; II 11a, 24b, 241a, 241b, 245b, 246a, 248a, 263a, 528b, 567b; III 29a, 38b, 80a, 138a, 371a, 406a, 455a, 457a, 457b, 515a, 568a, 577a, 578b, 579b, 590b, 593a; IV 26b, 62a, 113b, 116a, 141b, 155a, 174a, 202b, 209b, 244a, 323a, 324b, 334a, 405a, 407a, 407b, 442b, 533a, 534b, 535b; V **29b**, 30a, 31a, 31b, 33a, 33b, 34a, 34b, 35a, 35b, 36a, 36b, 37a, 37b, 38a, 39a, 39b, 40a, 40b, 41b, 42a, 43b, 44a, 44b, 45a, 45b, 46a, 46b, 47a, 47b, 48a, 48b, 49a, 175b, 190a, 257a, 268a, 459b

sīrat rasūl allḥ v 29b
siyar al-mulūk al-awwalīn iv 141b
sayyāra i 290a
s-y-l
sayl ii 437b; iii 532b; v 462a, 463a, 464a
sayl al-ʿarim ii 437b; iii 532b
sīmīyā iv 175a

-shīn-

sh-ʾ-m
shām v 561b
shāmiyya v 51b
shuʾm iii 180a
mashʾama iii 176b
sh-b-ʿ
ishbāʿ ii 386b
sh-b-h i 70b, 103b; v 177b
shabbaha i 124b, 312a; iii 19a
mushabbihūn i 103b
tashbīh i 24b, 103a, 104b; iii 384b; iv 471a, 471b; v 13b, 14a, 18b
ṭashābaha i 103b
mutashābih, pl. *mutashābihāt* i 70b, 71b, 72a, 72b, 73a, 73b, 74a, 74b, 75a, 76a, 76b, 103b, 106b, 248a, 535b; ii 101b, 102a, 323a, 386a, 425a; iii 31a, 156a, 294b, 386a, 470b, 522b, 523a, 574b; iv 3b, 69b, 70a, 76b, 136a, 157a, 158b, 297a
shibh iii 19a
shabah iv 76a
shubha, pl. *shubuhāt* ii 422a; iii 176a
ashbāh v 322a
sh-j-r
shajar ii 213a, 305a; v 358b, 359a
shajara i 25a, 447b, 454a, 466a; ii 54a, 219b, 305a; iii 421a, 533a; v 358b, 359a, 360a, 361a, 361b, 362a, 571b
shajara khabītha v 361b
shajarat al-khuld i 454a; ii 54a, 219b; v 360a
shajara min yaqṭīn v 361b

shajara mubāraka zaytūna	II 305a
shajara ṭayyiba	V 361b
shajarat al-ʿinab	I 25a
shajarat al-khamr	I 25a
shajara al-malʿūna (fī l-qurʾān)	III 533a; V 571b
shajarat al-ṭūbā	V 361a
shajarat al-zaqqūm	II 305a; V 359a
sh-j-ʿ	
shajāʿa	I 458b, 459a; V 382b
sh-ḥ-ḥ	
shuḥḥ	I 191b
sh-ḥ-m	
shaḥm, pl. *shuḥūm*	II 218a
sh-kh-ṣ	
shakhṣ, pl. *ashkhāṣ*	I 25b; V 372a
shākhiṣa	II 361a
sh-d-d	
shadda	II 407a; III 330a
tashdīd	I 141a
ishtadda	I 52a
shadd	I 141a
shadda	III 260a, 264a
shidda	II 177b
shidād	II 178a
shadīda	IV 374b
ashadd	I 216b, 356b; II 259a
ashudd	III 330a
shādūf	I 43b
sh-dh-dh	
shādhdh, pl. *shawādhdh*	II 109b, 357a; IV 362a; V 238b, 249a
shādhdha	IV 357b, 359a, 359b
sh-r-b	II 216b
shariba	I 288a
shurb	II 214b
sharāb	I 284a; III 349b; IV 18b
sh-r-ḥ	V 203b
sharaḥa	III 495b, 496a
sharḥ	II 99b, 115b; V 203b
sh-r-dh-m	
shirdhima	V 377a
sh-r-r	
sharr	II 25a; II 336a; III 535a
sh-r-ṭ	
sharṭ, pl. *shurūṭ*	I 336a; III 158a

sharaṭ, pl. *ashrāṭ* I 113b; II 46a, 395b; III 138a, 143a, 144a; IV 183a; V 287b
ashrāṭ al-sāʿa II 46a; III 138a, 143a, 144a; IV 183a
sh-r-ʿ
shāriʿ IV 489b
sharʿ II 313b; IV 56a, 75b, 77a, 87b, 142b
sharʿī IV 87b
shirʿa IV 145b
sharīʿa I 34a, 69a, 369b, 556a; II 5a, 340a; III 6b, 27a, 96a, 98b, 149b, 150a, 150b, 166a, 167b, 168b, 201a, 201b, 336a, 344b, 381a, 453b; IV 28a, 87b, 91a, 126a, 144a, 149a, 149b, 289b, 292b, 304b, 401b, 402b, 403b, 414b; V 26a, 104a, 143b, 146b, 164b, 222a, 264b, 274b, 311b
sh-r-f II 447b
sharaf IV 51b
ashrāf V 550b
sh-r-q
mushriqūn I 503b; III 417b, 418b; V 282b
ishrāq I 85a, 503b; III 417b, 418b; V 282b
mashriq, pl. *mashāriq* II 311a; IV 4b, 107a; V 282b
mashriqayn V 282b
sh-r-k II 476a; IV 258b
ashraka I 221b; II 476a; III 26b; IV 220b
mushrik, pl. *mushrikūn* I 74a, 221a, 221b, 224a, 225a, 263a, 330b, 373a, 376a, 410b, 411a; II 99a, 149b, 151a, 163b, 164a, 402b, 403a, 471a, 476a, 476b, 477a, 477b, 478a, 479a, 479b, 482a, 483b, 494b, 569a; III 22a, 26b, 32b, 33a, 33b, 40a, 181a, 338b, 443a, 444a, 445b, 446a, 563b, 564a; IV 25b, 27a, 36b, 38a, 40a, 43a, 118a, 118b, 119b, 129a, 132a, 132b, 152b, 153b, 159a, 160b, 161a, 260a, 286b, 300a, 309a, 403b, 409a, 412b, 415a, 502b, 503a, 516a; V 15a, 131a, 131b, 197a, 377b
ishrāk IV 137b
shirk I 37b, 45a, 159a, 221a, 221b, 235b,

	271b, 375b, 376a, 381b; II 43b, 156a, 163b, 164a, 195b, 242a, 329a, 329b, 474a, 476a, 476b, 477a, 477b, 478a, 478b, 479a, 479b, 482a, 489a; III 79a, 181a, 358a, 360a, 444a, 543a; IV 118a, 118b, 119b, 120b, 121a, 159a, 159b, 160a, 160b, 161a, 161b, 167a, 178b, 256a, 256b, 258b, 260a, 263b, 300a, 312a, 503b, 534a; V 20b, 21a, 22b, 23a, 27a, 369b, 380b, 440a, 555a
sharīk, pl. *shurakāʾ*	II 34a, 85a, 329a, 366a, 476a, 476b, 478b, 479a, 443b, 444a; III 48a, 556a; IV 80b, 184b, 312b; V 489b, 494a
sh-r-y	
sharā	V 312a
ishtarā	II 43b; V 312a
shirāʾ	IV 138b
shārin, pl. *shurāt*	I 462a
sh-ṭ-ḥ	
shaṭḥ	I 541b
shaṭranj	II 281a
sh-ʿ-b	
shaʿb, pl. *shuʿūb*	I 369a; II 71b, 431b; IV 336b; V 364a, 364b
shuʿūban wa-qabāʾila	V 364b
shuʿūbiyya	IV 313a, 337a
shiʿb	II 295a
sh-ʿ-r	V 52a
shaʿara	II 548b; V 203b
shāʿir, pl. *shuʿarāʾ*	I 542b; II 528a, 540a; III 121a, 246b, 587b, 589b; IV 112a, 112b, 113b, 164b, 259b, 301a, 311b, 462b, 463a, 477a; V 420b
shāʿir majnūn	II 540a, 540b; IV 112b
ishʿār	I 403b
shuʿūr	III 100b, 102a
shiʿr	III 121a; IV 56a, 110b, 112a
ashʿār	II 426a
shaʿīra, pl. *shaʿāʾir*	I 97a, 403b; III 77a, 339a; IV 93a, 515b, 518b; V 3a
mashʿar, pl. *mashāʿir*	IV 95b, 96a, 281b, 515b
shiʿrā	IV 108b, 109a; V 51b

sh-ʿ-ʿ
shuʿāʿ III 357a

sh-ʿ-l
ishtaʿala III 204b

sh-gh-r
shighār IV 582b

sh-f-ʿ
shafaʿa II 552b
shāfiʿ II 551a
istashafaʿa II 554a
shafʿ III 549b
shafīʿ II 273a
shafāʿa I 465b; II 49a, 49b, 117b, 551a, 552a, 555a; III 68a, 141a; IV 163b, 599b; V 117b

sh-f-q II 194b, 197b
ashfaqa II 197b
ishfāq II 194b, 197b
mushfiq, pl. *mushfiqūn* II 197b
shafaq I 503a; II 79b; IV 217a; V 281b, 282a

sh-f-w
shafawī I 82b; IV 374b

sh-f-y
shifāʾ I 77b, 118b; II 189a, 501b, 502a, 512a; III 349b; IV 166b

sh-q-q
shaqqa II 3a
shāqqa IV 309b
shaqāʾiq IV 581b
ashaqq III 546a

sh-q-w / sh-q-y
shaqāʾ I 185b
shiqwa V 430b
shaqī I 161a

sh-k-r IV 213a
shakara II 370a
shākir II 370b, 372a, 572a; IV 6a, 213a
shukr I 441b, 445b; II 58a, 302b, 345a, 370a; III 146a, 422b; V 382b, 384b, 385a
mashkūr II 373a
shakūr II 321a, 372b; IV 6a, 213a; V 382b

sh-k-k V 177b
shakk III 359a; V 404a
sh-k-l
shakala III 466a
tashkīl III 605a
ishkāl I 241a; III 605a
shakl III 605a
mushkil I 535a; V 333b
mushkilāt V 143a
sh-k-w
mishkāt [mishkāh] I 171a; II 353a; III 187a
sh-m-ʾ-z
ishmaʾazza III 62a
sh-m-s
shams I 36a, 503b, 504a; II 212a; III 108a, 414b; IV 107a, 107b, 108b, 217a, 219a, 222b, 550b; V 163a, 163b, 282b
sh-m-l
shimāl, pl. *shamāʾil* II 401b; III 176b, 179b
sh-n-ʾ
shāniʾ II 362b; III 32a
sh-h-b
shihāb, pl. *shuhub* III 48b; IV 107a, 108a, 108b
sh-h-d V 446b, 490a, 492a, 492b
shahida I 444b, 466b; II 171a; IV 600a; V 488a, 492a, 492b, 497b, 498a, 499a, 502a
shāhid, pl. *shuhūd, shuhadāʾ, shāhidūn, ashhād* I 244a; II 320b, 340b; III 139a, 139b, 282a, 282b, 402a, 440b, 447a, 456b; IV 13b, 14a, 17b, 290b, 312a, 312b; V 118b, 158b, 445a, 490b, 491a, 492a, 493b, 494a, 494b, 495b, 497a, 497b, 499a
mashhūd IV 221b
mushāhada IV 573a
tashahhud IV 233b; V 499a, 503a, 504b
shawāhid II 104a, 108b; III 121a
istashhada V 497b
istishhād III 215a
shahāda I 219a; II 83b, 84b, 95b, 168a, 171a, 191b, 317a, 471a; III 300b, 323a, 324b, 504b, 555a, 556a, 556b, 557b, 558a, 559b; IV 30b,

331a, 375b, 424b, 485b, 496a, 487a, 488a, 502a; v 16b, 108a, 219b, 435b, 446b, 488a, 488b, 489a, 489b, 490a, 490b, 491a, 491b, 492b, 496a, 497a, 498b, 499a, 499b, 500a, 502a, 502b, 503a, 503b, 504a, 504b, 505a, 543a

shahīd, pl. *shuhadāʾ* ii 360a; iii 285a, 382a, 503b; iv 300b, 490a, 492b, 493a, 493b, 494b

mashāhīd v 186b

sh-h-r iii 412b

shahr, pl. *ashhur, shuhūr* i 444b; iii 409b, 410a, 410b, 412b; v 284a, 284b, 285a, 285b, 475b

shahr al-ḥarām iii 410a, v 285b

shahr ramaḍān alladhī unzila fīhī l-qurʾan i 444b

ashhur al-ḥurum i 444b; iii 410b; v 284b

tashhīr v 495a

mashhura iv 358b, 359b

sh-h-w

shahwa ii 444b; ii 359a

sh-w-r

ishāra, pl. *ishārāt* i 198a; ii 120b; iii 215a, 511a; iv 158a; v 140a, 141b, 148a

tashāwur i 407a

shūrā i 406a, 406b, 407a, 408a; ii 12a, 139a; iv 144a, 146a

shāra i 406b

shāwir i 407a

sh-w-q

tashawwuq iii 371a

sh-w-k

shawka iv 366b

sh-y-ʾ

shāʾa ii 96a, 327b, 481b; iv 63a; v 450b, 484b, 485a, 485b

ashāʾa i 530a

shayʾ, pl. *ashyāʾ* i 23b, 95b, 105a, 475b, 477a, 530a; ii 92a, 92b, 322a, 323a, 365a; iii 148a, 189a; iv 185a, 211a, 214a, 214b, 288a, 592a; v 381b, 428a, 484b, 500a, 543a

laysa ka-mithlihi shayʾun ii 323a; v 500a

wa-allāh ʿalā kulli shayʾin qadīrun v 484b

sh-y-kh
shaykh, pl. *shuyūkh* I 90a; II 88b, 94a, 131b, 360b, 403a, 452b, 554a; III 83b, 230b, 345a, 421a; IV 134a, 361a; V 72b, 207b, 209a, 222a, 224a, 225a, 569b, 570b
shaykh al-islām IV 134a
shaykh al-maqāriʾ IV 361a
shaykh al-naṣrānī II 403a
sh-y-ṭ-n
shayṭān, pl. *shayāṭīn* I 240b, 262b, 447a, 447b, 451b, 452a, 453b, 454b, 455a, 456a, 512b, 526a, 544b; II 344a, 411a, 487a; III 31b, 44a, 44b, 45a, 46a, 46b, 420b, 491a; IV 29b, 30a, 112a, 113b, 130a, 210b, 262a, 295a, 439b, 443a, 598b; V 77a, 113a, 117b, 118a, 119b, 120b, 130a, 202b, 379b, 381a, 478b, 479a, 480a, 487a
sh-y-ʿ
shāʿa IV 591b
shīʿa, pl. *shiyaʿ*, *ashyāʿ* I 58b, 380a, 541a; II 431b; III 583b; IV 24b, 25a, 25b, 26a, 403b, 591b, 592a, 592b

-ṣād-

ṣ-b-ʾ
ṣābiʾ IV 512b, 560a
ṣābī IV 512b
ṣābiʾūn IV 511a
ṣ-b-b
aṣabb III 413b
ṣ-b-ḥ III 416b, 417a; see also ʾ-l-h
ṣabbaḥa I 504a; III 417a
aṣbaḥa I 504a; II 361b; III 417a
muṣbiḥīna I 504a; III 417a, 418b
iṣbāḥ I 504a; III 417a
ṣubḥ I 504a; II 388a; III 204a, 204b, 417a, 418b; IV 465a; V 281a, 282a
ṣubḥān allāh see ʾ-l-h

ṣabāḥ	I 504a; III 416b, 417a; V 281a
miṣbāḥ, pl. *maṣābīḥ*	II 275b, 276a, 547a; III 107b, 108a, 186a; V 64a
ṣ-b-r	II 70b; V 378b
ṣabara	II 70b, 450a; II 364b; III 422b, 452b; V 379a, 381b, 382a, 441a
ṣābir, pl. *ṣābirūn*	II 61a, 165a; IV 21a; V 379a, 381a, 383b
ṣābara	II 70b
iṣṭabara	V 379a
ṣabr	I 458b, 459a, 461a; II 70b, 165a; III 361b, 422b, 483a; V 135a, 378b, 379a, 380b, 381a, 381b, 382a, 382b, 384b, 385a, 434b
ṣabbār	III 423a; V 379a, 382b
ṣ-b-gh	
ṣibgh	V 362a
ṣibgha	I 200a, 200b, 466b; V 243b
ṣibghat allāh	V 243b
ṣ-b-w / ṣ-b-y	
ṣabā	IV 512b
ṣabī	I 301b
aṣbu	III 234b
ṣ-ḥ-b	I 386b, 387b
ṣaḥiba	I 387b
ṣāḥib, pl. *aṣḥāb*, *ṣaḥāba*	I 386b, 387a, 387b, 528a, 539a, 543b; II 198a, 260a, 438a, 553a; III 53a, 95b, 142a, 177a, 178a, 178b, 219a, 374a, 390b, 450b, 558a, 564a; IV 2a, 2b, 15b, 16a, 16b, 43b, 45a, 47a, 53b, 102b, 352a, 509b; V 131b, 185a, 185b, 244a, 244b, 245a, 245b, 246b, 250b, 251a, 252b, 375b, 397a, 397b, 398b, 565b
ṣāḥib ʿaṣā l-nabī	IV 509b
ṣāḥib bi-l-janbi	V 131b
ṣāḥib al-ḥūt	III 53a
ṣāḥib al-shafāʿa	II 553a
ṣāḥib al-ukhdūd	IV 43b; V 397a, 398a
ṣāḥib al-zanj	III 558a
aṣḥāb amīr al-muʾminīn	III 178b
aṣḥāb al-aʿrāf	IV 46b, 47a; V 244a, 244b
aṣḥāb al-ayka	II 260a, 438a; III 390b, 393b; IV 53b, 54a; V 245a, 245b, 246b
aṣḥāb al-fīl	IV 44b, 45a; V 565b

aṣḥāb al-ḥijr II 260a, 438a
aṣḥāb al-janna II 260a; III 564a; IV 16b
aṣḥāb al-kahf II 198a; III 219a, 374a; V 375b
aṣḥāb al-mashʾama III 177b; IV 2a, 2b, 102b; V 183a
aṣḥāb al-mayama III 177b; IV 2a, 2b, 15b, 102b; V 183a
aṣḥāb al-nabī I 386b, 387a
aṣḥāb al-rass II 438a; IV 352a; V 250b, 252b
aṣḥāb al-shimāl III 177b, 178a, 178b; IV 2a, 102b; V 183a
aṣḥāb al-yamīn III 177b, 178a, 178b; IV 2a, 15b, 16a, 102b; V 183a
ṣāḥiba II 329b; III 95b, 99b
muṣāḥib V 119b
ṣ-ḥ-ḥ
muṣaḥḥiḥūn IV 270b
ṣaḥīḥ I 77b; IV 534b
ṣ-ḥ-f
ṣaḥfa, pl. *ṣiḥāf* I 490a, 491a; II 276a
ṣaḥīfa, pl. *ṣuḥuf*, *ṣaḥāʾif* II 104b, 228b, 245b, 330a, 332a; II 382b, 384b, 430a; II 434a, 484b, 544b, 545a; III 140b, 177b, 188a, 189b, 190a, 425b, 441a, 463b, 464b, 513a, 591a, 592b, 605a; IV 42a, 42b, 296b, 304a, 505b, 569b, 570b, 587a, 587b, 588a, 588b, 589a; V 301a, 421b, 422a
ṣuḥuf ibrāhīm wa-mūsā III 189b
ṣuḥuf mūsā III 425b
ṣuḥuf al-ūlā I 245b; II 434a; III 425b
muṣḥaf, pl. *maṣāḥif* I 141a, 209b, 210a, 332a, 333b, 347b, 352a, 352b, 353a, 353b, 354a, 354b, 355a, 356a, 357a, 357b, 358b, 359a, 359b, 360a, 360b, 424a, 441a, 451b; II 92a, 94b, 95a, 247a, 247b, 276a, 276b, 382b, 384b, 386b, 393b, 398a, 568a; III 254b, 345b, 346a, 347a, **463b**, 464a, 465a, 465b, 466a; IV 134a, 135a, 270a, 271a, 273a, 275b, 355b, 356a, 358b, 359a, 361a, 361b, 362a, 391b, 486b, 492b, 493a, 493b, 570b, 601b; V 390a, 409a, 409b, 410a, 419b

muṣḥaf fāṭima IV 601b
ṣ-kh-kh
ṣākhkha I 113a; III 137a, 203a
ṣ-kh-r
ṣakhr I 114a
ṣakhra III 3b
ṣ-d-d
ṣadda IV 29b, 456a
ṣadd V 375a
ṣadīd V 462a
ṣ-d-r
ṣadr, pl. *ṣudūr* II 407a, 413b, 502a, 550b; III 404a, 509b; IV 82b, 465b
ʿalimun bi-dhāti l-ṣudūri II 550b
mā fī l-ṣuddūri IV 465b
maṣdar II 195a, 357a; III 506a, 586a; IV 443a; V 378a, 378b
maṣdariyya II 367a
ṣ-d-f
ṣadaf V 149b
ṣ-d-q I 65a; II 70b, 447b, 450a
ṣadaqa I 64a, 64b, 65a, 65b, 66a, 67a, 67b, 68a, 217a; II 7a, 61a, 70b, 176b; IV 208b, 377b, 496b, 505b; V 193b, 385b, 434a, 556a
ṣādiq, pl. *ṣādiqūn* II 70b, 72b, 362a, 362b, 564a; III 237b, 425a; IV 291b, 520b; V 434a
ṣādiq al-waʿd II 564a; IV 291b
ṣaddaqa II 253a
muṣaddiq III 445a, 512b, 513b, 514b; IV 36b, 298a, 439a
taṣdīq I 218b; II 169a, 502a, 529b; IV 438a, 440a
taṣaddaqa V 198a
muṣṣaddiqīna II 366b
ṣidq I 522a; II 70b; III 69b, 70a, 421b; V 385b, 434a
ṣadāq I 258b, 259a; IV 582a; V 198b
ṣadaqa, pl. *ṣadaqāt* II 343b; IV 152b, 209a; V 196b, 198a, 198b, 199a, 199b, 556b
farāʾiḍ al-ṣadaqa V 199a
ṣaduqa, pl. *ṣaduqāt* I 258a, 258b, 530a; II 374b
ṣadīq I 65a, 345a; II 71a, 273a, 273b; III 236a

ṣiddīq, pl. *ṣiddīqūn* I 5b, 65a, 330a; II 71a, 340b, 552b; IV 290b, 291b; V 154a, 198b, 404b, 434a
ṣiddīqan nabiyyan I 330a; II 71a
min al-ṣiddīq IV 291b
ṣudqāt I 530a
ṣ-d-y
taṣdiya III 777
ṣ-r-ḥ
ṣarḥ I 162b, 165a, 168a; II 458b; III 487b
ṣ-r-r
ṣarra I 52b
ṣirr I 52b, 54b
ṣ-r-ṣ-r
ṣarṣar I 52b, 53a, 54b; II 338b, 455b
ṣ-r-ṭ
ṣirāṭ I 185a; II 49a, 83a, 234a, 311a, 329a, 415b; III 141a, 184b; IV 28a, 28b, 29a, 29b, 396a, 396a; V 182b, 374b
ṣirāṭ allāh IV 29a
ṣirāṭ al-jaḥīm II 49a, 415a; V 374b
al-ṣirāṭ al-mustaqīm I 185a, II 49a, 83a, 311a, 329a; III 184b, 185a; IV 29b, 396a; V 182b, 374b, 523a
ṣīraṭ rabbika IV 29a
ṣ-r-f
ṣarrafa III 212a; V 8a
taṣrīf I 52a; III 212a
taṣarruf V 380a
ṣarf II 348a, 349a; III 246a
ṣarfa II 532b, 533a, 533b, 534a, 535a; III 468b
ṣ-r-m
ṣarīm I 41b, 494b
ṣ-ʿ-d
ṣaʿīd II 3b
ṣ-ʿ-q
ṣāʿiqa, pl. *ṣawāʿiq* II 212a ; III 140a; V 253a, 471a
ṣ-gh-r
[wa-hum] ṣāghirūn IV 153b
ṣaghīr I 301b
ṣaghīra, pl. *ṣaghāʾir* V 19a, 25b
ṣaghār IV 152a, 152b

aṣghar I 24b
ṣ-gh-w
aṣghā II 405b
ṣ-f-ḥ III 65b
ṣafaḥa III 453a
ṣafḥ V 291a
ṣ-f-d
ṣafad, pl. *aṣfād* II 546a
ṣ-f-r
aṣfar I 362a, 363a
ṣ-f-f
ṣāffūna IV 348b, 349a
ṣaffāt IV 348b
maṣfūfa III 128b
ṣaff, pl. *ṣufūf* IV 348a, 348b, 349a, 349b, 350a, 350b; V 116b
ṣaffan V 116b
ṣuffa I 389b, 408a; III 428a
ṣ-f-w II 11b, 12a
ṣafā IV 518a
ṣāfin/ṣāfī V 194a
iṣṭafā I 256; II 11b, 12a; III 445a, 446a; IV 291a, 529b
muṣṭafā II 11b, 12a; III 125b, 503b; IV 518a
ṣafwa II 12a
ṣafwān II 4a
aṣfiyāʾ V 144a, 144b
ikhwān al-ṣafāʾ see ʾ-kh-(w)
ṣ-l-b
ṣalaba I 487b
ṣallaba I 487b
ṣalīb I 487b; III 138b
ṣ-l-ḥ
ṣalaḥa II 60a, 167a
ṣāliḥ, pl. *ṣāliḥūn* I 374a; II 60a, 60b, 62b, 63b, 73a, 336b, 338a, 340b, 552b; IV 21a, 290b, 291b, 520a; V 70b, 436a
ṣāliḥāt II 58b, 61b, 70b, 76a, 167a, 339b; IV 16b; V 436a, 548b
aṣlaḥa II 66b; IV 63b; V 195a
iṣlāḥ I 474b; IV 135a
istiṣlāḥ III 168b, 403b
ṣulḥ I 400a; IV 63b, 437a; V 195b, 417a
ṣalāḥ IV 432b, 490b
aṣlaḥ IV 432b; V 274b

maṣlaḥa, pl. maṣāliḥ — II 201a; III 73b, 168b; IV 130a, 143a, 144a; V 452b, 453a

ṣ-l-ṣ-l

ṣalṣala — I 339b

ṣalṣāl — I 24a, 230b, 231a, 240a, 339a, 339b, 476a; II 4a, 4b, 328a, 354b; III 383b, 532a

(min) ṣalṣāl min ḥamā'in masnūnin — I 24a, 240a, 476a; II 4b; III 532a

ṣalṣālin ka-l-fakhkhār — I 24b, 476a; II 4a, 4b

ṣ-l-w

ṣallā — I 327b, 551b; II 32b, 210b, 551b; IV 217b, 218a

muṣallā — III 427a, 427b; IV 218b

aṣlā — II 210b

ṣalāt [ṣalāh], pl. ṣalawāt — I 35b, 164a, 209a, 210a, 217a, 327b, 328a, 328b, 335b, 502a, 502b, 528a; II 7b, 62a, 65b, 69b, 82a, 82b, 83b, 84a, 89a, 91a, 168a, 188a, 188b, 189a, 190a, 190b, 191a, 191b, 204b, 228a, 271b, 272b, 353a, 388a, 391b, 402a; III 76a, 77a, 79a, 275b, 336a, 361b, 372a, 373a, 418b, 427a, 431b, 545a, 546a, 585a, 586a, 586b; IV 42b, 58b, 163a, 215b, 217b, 218a, 218b, 219a, 219b, 220a, 220b, 221a, 221b, 222a, 223b, 224a, 224b, 225a, 225b, 226a, 227a, 227b, 228a, 228b, 229a, 229b, 230a, 230b, 233a, 347a, 348b, 350b, 357b, 359a, 367b, 377b, 379b, 389a, 404a, 424b, 484b, 485b, 486a, 487a, 488a, 488a, 488b, 489a, 490a, 490b, 497a, 516b, 523a, 566a, 567a, 567b; V 163a, 170b, 175a, 208a, 219b, 220a, 263b, 278b, 281b, 431a, 457a, 488a, 494a, 496a, 498b, 499a, 502b, 504b, 505a, 555b, 556a, 556b, 557a, 564b

ṣalāt ʿalā l-mayyit — IV 233a

ṣalāt al-ʿaṣr — I 36a, 36b, 502b; IV 219a, 223b, 224b, 227b, 228a

ṣalāt al-ḍuḥā — IV 218b, 223b

ṣalāt al-fajr	I 502b; III 418b; IV 224a, 227b
ṣalāt al-hajīri	III 546a
ṣalāt al-ʿīdayn	II 83b; IV 218b
ṣalāt al-ʿishāʾ	IV 224a, 227b, 228a, 281b
ṣalāt al-istisqāʾ	IV 218b, 233a
ṣalāt al-janāza	II 89a; IV 218a
ṣalāt al-jumʿa	II 83b
ṣalāt al-jumuʿa	II 83b, 271b; IV 497a; V 175a
ṣalāt al-khawf	IV 224b, 233a
ṣalāt al-maghrib	I 502b; IV 227b, 228a
ṣalāt al-qiyām	II 84a, 91a
ṣalāt al-ṣubḥ	I 502b
ṣalāt al-tarāwīḥ	II 204b
ṣalāt al-witr	IV 227b
ṣalāt al-wusṭā	I 35b, 328b; III 545a; IV 224a; V 278b, 556b
ṣalāt al-ẓuhr	I 36a, 502b; IV 224b, 227b, 228a
taṣliya	III 270b; IV 180b, 218a
ṣ-l-y	
ṣalā	II 218b, 219a
ṣ-m-t	
ṣamt	II 180b
ṣ-m-d	
ṣamad	II 54a, 321b; IV 238a, 482b; V 264a
ṣāmid	IV 482b
ṣamūd	IV 482b
ṣ-m-ʿ	see ṣ-w-m-ʿ
ṣ-m-m	II 406a
ṣumm	II 406b; III 534a
aṣamm	III 413b
ṣ-n-d-w-q	III 261b
ṣundūq	III 261b
ṣ-n-ʿ	V 549a
ṣanaʿa	I 345b, 450a
ṣāniʿ	IV 82a; V 318a
iṣṭanaʿa	I 345b; IV 291b
muṣṭanaʿ	I 346a
ṣanʿa	I 346b
ṣanīʿ	I 346a
ṣanīʿa	I 346a
ṣināʿa	V 497a
maṣāniʿ	V 340a
maṣnūʿa	IV 75b
ṣ-n-f	
muṣannaf	IV 588b

ṣinf	I 23a
ṣ-n-m	
ṣanam, pl. *aṣnam*	I 167a, 167b; II 476b, 478a, 481a, 481b; IV 409a; V 89b
ṣ-h-r	
muṣāhara	III 96a
ṣihr	I 368b; II 174b; III 96a
ṣ-w-b	II 550a
aṣāba	V 441b
ṣawāb	V 385b
ṣayyib	V 16b, 470b
ṣ-w-t	
ṣawt, pl. *aṣwāt*	I 82b; V 111b
ṣ-w-kh	
aṣākha	II 405b
ṣ-w-r	II 481a
ṣāra	V 242a, 242b
ṣawwara	I 446b; II 323a; IV 177b
taṣwīr	I 184b; III 201b
muṣawwir	II 320b, 327b, 474a
ṣūra, pl. *ṣuwar*	I 167b; II 323a, 328a; III 246a; IV 65a
ʿalā ṣūratihi	II 323a
fī aḥsana ṣuwarakum	II 323a
ṣūr	I 112b; II 47a, 547a; III 139a, 140a, 143b; IV 434b
ṣ-w-ʿ	III 333a, 334a
ṣāʿa	I 491a; III 336a
ṣuwāʿ	I 490a, 491a; II 219a; III 334a
ṣ-w-f	
aṣwāf	II 426a
ṣūfī	I 389b
taṣawwuf	III 606b; V 137a, 213b; V 391b
ṣ-w-m	
ṣāma	I 183a; II 366b
ṣawm	II 180b; III 361b; IV 489a, 490a, 490b, 598a
ṣiyām	II 83b, 180b; IV 341a, 485b, 486a, 487a, 488a
ṣ-w-m-ʿ	
ṣawmaʿa, pl. *ṣawāmiʿ*	I 164a, 335b; IV 404a, 516b
ṣ-y-ḥ	
ṣayḥa	II 212a, 212b, 338b; III 203a; IV 435a, 453a, 454a, 605b; V 253a, 545a

ṣ-y-d
ṣayd i 95a, 187a; ii 218b, 467a
ṣayd al-baḥr ii 218b
ṣ-y-r
ṣāra v 287a
taṣīru l-umūr v 287a
maṣīr v 287a
ṣ-y-ṣ-y
ṣayāṣin iv 41b
ṣ-y-f
ṣayf iii 338b

-ḍād-

ḍ-ʾ-n
ḍaʾn i 94b; ii 218a
ḍ-b-b
ḍabba i 441a
ḍ-b-ṭ
ḍābiṭ, pl. *ḍābiṭūn* iv 185a, 185b
ḍabṭ iii 605a
ḍ-j-ʿ
maḍājiʿ ii 76a, 276
ḍ-ḥ-k iii 146b
ḍaḥika i 6b; iii 148a; iv 309b
aḍḥaka iii 148b
ḍ-ḥ-y
ḍaḥā v 281b
ḍuḥan/ḍuḥā i 36a, 444a, 504a; iii 416b, 417a, 418a; iv 217a, 516b, 517a; v 281b, 282a, 476a
ḍaḥāya i 401b, 403b
aḍḥā i 401b, 403b
ḍ-d-d
taḍādd iii 220b
ḍ-r-b iii 57b, 58a; v 432b
ḍaraba ii 1a, 260a; iii 50b, 58a, 524b; iv 9a
ḍarb ii 237b
ḍ-r-r
ḍarra iv 5a
ḍirār iii 238a; iv 516a
iḍṭarra v 55a
iḍṭirārī iv 376b

ḍurr v 381a
ḍarūra v 55a
ḍarūriyyāt v 407b
maḍārr i 288a
ḍ-r-ʿ
taḍarraʿa iv 495a
taḍarruʿ iv 485b
ḍarīʿ i 41b; ii 211a, 305b
muḍāriʿ v 286b
ḍ-ʿ-f
ḍāʿafa ii 507b; iii 580b
istaḍʿafa iii 549b
mustaḍʿaf, pl. *mustaḍʿafūn* iii 95a, 581a
i 159a, 161a; ii 273b; iii 580b, 581a, 581b, 582a, 582b, 583a, 583b; iv 132a, 332b
istiḍʿāf iii 583a
ḍiʿf i 528a; iii 549b
ḍaʿīf, pl. *ḍuʿafa* iii 580b, 581a, 582a
ḍ-gh-th
ḍighth, pl. *aḍghāth* i 41b; ii 241b, 369b; iii 56a; iv 178b, 301a
aḍghāth aḥlām iii 56a; iv 178b, 301a
ḍ-f-d-ʿ
ḍafādiʿ i 95b
ḍ-l-ʿ
ḍilʿ i 24b
ḍ-l-l
ḍalla i 185a; ii 66a
ḍāllūn i 185a; ii 43a, 66a; iii 211a
i 381b; ii 43b, 190b; iii 177a; iv 498b
taḍlīl iv 103a, 482b; v 480a
ḍālilīn iv 376a
aḍalla i 186a; ii 59a; iii 425a; iv 29b
muḍill iii 420b
iḍlāl iii 425a, 425b
ḍallin i 185a, 185b
ḍalāl i 185b, 272a; ii 43a, 43b, 44a, 99a, 421b, 422a; iii 525a; iv 103a, 482b; v 24b, 480a
ḍalāla i 185b, 493b; ii 43a, 421b, 422a; iv 29b
ḍ-m-r
ḍāmir i 94a; ii 362b, 363b
iḍmār v 322a, 335a

ḍ-m-m
ḍamma I 279a
ḍ-m-n
taḍmīn III 215a; IV 60b
ḍamān IV 431a
ḍ-w-ʾ
aḍāʾa II 362a
ḍiyāʾ III 186a, 186b, 187a, 208a; V 163a
ḍ-y-ʿ
aḍāʿa IV 457b
ḍ-y-f
ḍāfa V 145b
iḍāfa I 198a; II 366a, 481b
muḍāf II 352b
ḍayf V 132a

-ṭāʾ-

ṭāwula V 188a
ṭ-b-b
ṭibb I 78a; II 222b; 308b; III 350a, 350b; IV 166a, 180a
ṭibb al-aʾimma I 78a
ṭibb al-nabawī I 78a; II 222b; III 308b, 309q, 350a, 350b; IV 165a, 180a
ṭ-b-ʿ
ṭabīʿa, pl. *ṭabāʾiʿ* III 353a; V 371b
maṭbaʿa IV 271a
ṭ-b-q
ṭabaqāt I 388a
ṭibāq I 442a; III 184a, 184b; IV 107b
ṭ-r-ḥ
ṭarḥ I 2b
ṭ-r-sh
ṭarsh II 38b
ṭ-r-f
muṭarraf III 128a
taṭarruf V 573b
ṭaraf IV 405b
aṭrāf V 282b
ṭirāf III 544a
ṭ-r-q
ṭarq II 239b
ṭāriq IV 108b

ṭarīq, pl. *ṭuruq* iv 28a, 28b, 29a, 102b, 390a; v 140a
ṭarīqa, pl. *ṭarāʾiq*, *ṭuruq* i 201a, 201b; ii 51a; iii 247b, 250b; iv 28b, 107b, 403b; v 137a
ṭ-ʿ-m ii 216b
aṭʿama ii 217a, 450b
taʿām i 47b; ii 211b, 217a, 450b; v 56a
ṭ-ʿ-n
ṭāʿūn iii 364b
ṭ-gh-r
ṭughrāʾ i 211b
ṭughrāʾī iii 314b
ṭ-gh-w/ṭ-gh-y ii 541b; iii 70b; v 253a
ṭaghā ii 541b
ṭāghiya ii 212a, 212b; iv 103b; v 253a, 471a
ṭughyān ii 6a; iii 583a; iv 103b
ṭāghūt, pl. *ṭawāghīt* i 533a, 533b; ii 474a, 477b, 481a, 482a, 482b; iii 35a, 35b; iv 29b, 30a, 138a; v 119b, 120a, 248a, 248b, 458a
jibt wa-l-ṭāghūt iii 35a; iv 599a
ṭ-f-l
ṭifl, pl. *aṭfāl* i 301b; iii 178b; v 569b
ṭufaylī ii 465a
ṭ-l-b
ṭālib v 72b
ṭalab ii 225b; iii 37a; iv 131a
ṭ-l-ḥ
ṭalḥ i 41b; iii 532b; v 360b
ṭilasm, pl. *ṭalismāt*, *ṭalāsim* i 77a; ii 35b; iv 163a
ṭ-l-ʿ
ṭalaʿa ii 424b; iv 107a
muṭālʿa ii 495b
iṭṭalaʿa ii 366a, 415b
muṭṭalaʿ v 158b
ṭalʿ i 494b; v 571a
ṭulūʿ i 503b; iii 417a; iv 107a; v 163a
maṭlaʿ i 503b; iv 107a, 158a, 479b, 480b; v 158b
maṭliʿ iv 107b
ṭ-l-q
ṭallaqa iii 96a, 277a
muṭlaq i 141a; iii 158a; v 333b
ṭalāq iii 96a, 277a, 279b, 280a; v 453a

ṭ-l-l
ṭall i 42a; v 461b
ṭalal, pl. *aṭlāl* i 148b, 152b; ii 300a, 308b
ṭ-m-th
ṭamatha ii 456b
ṭ-m-r
ṭumār i 137a
ṭ-m-s
ṭams i 137a
ṭ-m-m
ṭāmma i 113a; iii 137a; iv 103a
ṭ-h-r i 343b, 498b, 499a, 499b, 502a, 503b, 505b
ṭahara iv 501b; iii 76b; v 55a
ṭāhira iv 50b
ṭahhara iii 76b; iv 505a, 505b
muṭahharūn i 342b; iv 225b, 492a
muṭahhara iii 513a; iv 491a, 505b
taṭhīr iii 291b; iv 152b, 490b
ṭahāra i 336b, 556b; iii 291a, 291b, 376a; iv 50b, 270a, 485b, 488a, 489a, 490a, 491a, 491b, 506a, 506b
taṭaharra iv 501b, 505b
taṭahhur iv 490a
iṭṭahhara i 341b
ṭahūr iv 491b, 505b
aṭhar iv 505b, 506a
maṭāhir v 124a
ṭ-w-b
ṭūbā i 406a; ii 284b; iv 13a, 15a, 430a; 361a, 361b
ṭ-w-ḥ
ṭāḥa ii 231a
ṭ-w-r
ṭawr, pl. *aṭwār* i 476b; iii 128a; v 280a
ṭūr iv 513b; v 28a, 28b, 29a
ṭūr sīnīn v 28b
ṭ-w-ʿ i 246b; iii 566b
ṭāʿa i 189a, 189b; ii 65b; iv 487a, 489b; v 378b, 379b, 450a
aṭāʿa i 189b; iii 566b, 567a; iv 301a; v 501b
taṭawwaʿa iv 93a
istaṭāʿa iv 83b, 92a, 210a, 432b; v 191a
ṭawʿ ii 351a

ṭāʿāt	IV 84b
ṭ-w-f	V 555b
ṭāfa	V 448b
ṭāʾif	V 448b
ṭāʾifiyya	IV 26a
ṭāʾifa, pl. *ṭawāʾif*	II 431b; IV 24b, 25a, 25b, 26a, 222a, 403b; V 495a
iṭṭawwafa	IV 93b, 518b
ṭūfān	III 540b; V 133a
ṭawāf	II 85a, 297b; III 75a, 79a, 338b, 339a; IV 92a, 93b, 94a, 98a, 105a, 219a, 492a, 515a, 515b; V 557a, 557b
ṭ-w-q	
ṭāqa	IV 210a
ṭ-w-l	III 333a
ṭāla	V 288b
ṭūl	III 333a, 333b
ṭiwāl	II 247b
ṭāwila	II 281a
ṭ-w-y	
ṭuwan/ṭuwā	IV 513a; V 395b, 396b
ṭ-y-b	III 174b
ṭāʾibūn	IV 214a
ṭayyib	I 212b, 343b, 440a; II 63a, 78a; III 504b; IV 499a, 504a
ṭayyibāt	I 96b; II 467a; III 174b; V 179a
ṭīb	I 288a; III 573b
ṭayba	III 368a
ṭ-y-r	
ṭāʾir	I 95a, 523a; II 242a
taṭāyur	III 178a
ṭayr	I 95a; II 237a, 237b
ṭīra	II 242a, 242b
ṭ-y-n	
ṭāna	I 339a, 339b
ṭīn, pl. *aṭyān*	I 24a, 230b, 231a, 339a, 340a, 447a, 476a; II 4a, 4b, 328a; III 45b, 354b, 383b, 532a
ṭīn lāzib	I 24a, 476a; II 4a, 4b, 328a, 383b
ṭīn yābis	I 24a

-ẓāʾ-

ẓ-f-r	
ẓufur	I 403a
ẓ-l-l	
ẓalla	II 363b
ẓilāl	II 455a
ẓulla, pl. *ẓulal*	V 234b, 235b, 236a
ẓ-l-m	II 64b, 65a, 98a; IV 600a; V 432b, 433a
ẓalama	II 65a, 360b; III 71a, 72a; IV 457b; V 6a, 312a, 432b
ẓālim, pl. *ẓālimūn*, *ẓalama*	I 206a; II 64b, 65a, 65b, 407b; III 54a, 70b, 71a, 234a, 581b; IV 129a, 133a, 133b, 430a; V 312a, 432b
aẓlama	I 493a; II 362a
muẓlim	I 493a
ẓulm	I 32a, 159a, 161a, 220b, 493b; II 6a, 8a, 64b, 65a; III 69b, 70b, 71a, 71b, 72a, 72b, 583a
ẓulma, *ẓuluma*, pl. *ẓulumāt*	I 231b, 493a, 494a; III 186a, 187b, 535a, 554b
ẓallām	III 71a
aẓlam	I 493a; II 64b
ẓ-n-n	II 488b, 489a; V 177b, 178a
ẓanna	I 452b; III 54b; V 177b, 178a
ẓann	I 37b; II 72b, 165a; III 66a, 162a; IV 287a; V 21a, 178a, 178b
ẓ-h-r	III 545a
ẓahara	I 187b, 198b, 328b, 444a
ẓāhir, pl. *ẓāhirūn*	I 541b, 556a; II 118a, 119a, 320b, 425a; III 157b, 159a, 239b, 554b; IV 4b, 157b, 158a, 158b, 285a, 572b, 597a; V 140a
ẓāhara	II 75a; III 96a; III 563a
aẓhara	III 546a; V 282b
iẓhār	III 548b; IV 37
ẓahr, pl. *ẓuhūr*	II 57a; III 177b, 563a; IV 157b; V 156b
ẓuhr	I 36a, 444a, 502b; II 271b, 388a, 388b, 545a; III 547b
ṣalāt al-ẓuhr	I 36a; II 388b
ẓahīra	I 504a; III 545b; IV 224a; V 282b
aẓhar	III 546a

ẓihār I 187b; II 180b; III 158b, 159a, 279b, 280a, 363a, 566a; IV 582a

-ʿayn-

ʿ-b-th
ʿabath IV 433b
ʿ-b-d I 375b, 376a; IV 401a, 401b, 487a, 576b; V 555a
ʿabada II 31b, 58a, 83a, 362a, 362b, 386a; III 193a; IV 300a, 483a, 576a, 578b; V 555a, 555b
ʿabada l-ṭāghūt II 386a; IV 576a
ʿābid IV 578b
ʿabd, pl. *ʿibād, ʿabīd* I 161a, 188b, 375b, 452a, 453b; II 83a, 196a, 360a; III 50b, 117a, 230a, 426a, 440b; IV 187a, 292b, 341b, 445a, 538b, 576a, 576b, 577a, 577b, 578a, 579a, 579b; V 57a, 58a, 153b, 284b, 555a
ʿibāda, pl. *ʿibādāt* I 375b, 508b, 510a; II 7a, 49b, 82a, 83b, 223a, 336b, 340a, 370a, 476b, 478b, 481b, 550a; III 47b, 48a, 73a, 338a, 586b; IV 129b, 132b, 149b, 158a, 284a, 400a, 401a, 403b, 487a, 487b, 488b, 489a, 489b, 490a, 490b, 491a, 494b, 495a; V 208a, 450a, 555a, 556b, 557a
ʿubūdiyya V 57a
ʿ-b-r IV 394b
ʿābir I 341b
maʿbūr V 153b
ʿabbara IV 445b
taʿbīr I 549b, 552b, 553a; IV 163a, 165b, 179a; V 150a
iʿtabara IV 70b, 394b
iʿtibār V 153b
ʿabūr V 52a
ʿibra, pl. *ʿibar* I 497b; II 435b, 441a, 441b; V 2b, 5a, 153b, 171a
ʿibāra, pl. *ʿibārāt* II 120b; IV 158a, 446b; V 112a, 140a

ʿ-b-q-r	
ʿabqarī	II 276a
ʿ-t-r	
ʿitra	I 390b
ʿatāʾir	I 402b, 403a, 403b; II 183a; IV 339b
ʿ-t-q	III 76a
ʿitq	V 58b
ʿatīq	III 76a
ʿ-t-l	
ʿutull	II 491a
ʿ-t-m	
ʿatma	II 80a
ʿ-t-w	
ʿatā	I 395b
ʿātiya	I 52b, 247b
ʿutuww	I 395b
ʿataw	IV 264a
ʿ-j-b	II 527b; III 287a
aʿjaba	I 213a; III 148a
iʿjāb	I 212b
taʿajjub	III 148a
ʿajab	I 213b; II 527b; III 49a, 392b, 394b, 399a, 506b
ʿajīb	I 174a; III 287b
ʿajība, pl. *ʿajāʾib*	II 505a, 527b; III 287a, 288a
aʿjab	III 546a
ʿ-j-z	II 533a
ʿajaza	II 527a, 533a
ʿājaza	II 527a
muʿājizūn	II 527a
aʿjaza	II 526b
iʿjāz	I 71a, 213b, 425b; II 108b, 129b, 130a, 131a, 133b, 146a, 243a, 526b, 527a, 528b, 529a, 531a, 532a, 533a, 535a, 535b, 566b; III 199a, 385a, 385b, 396b, 397a, 398b, 468b, 469a; IV 22b, 89b, 119a, 313a, 378b, 442b, 450b, 461b, 462a, 553b, 555b, 556a, 565a, 565b, 566b; V 401a
iʿjāz al-qurʾān	I 71a; II 243a, 526b, 527a, 528b, 529a, 531a, 533a, 535b; III 199a; IV 450b, 461b
ʿājiz	II 533a

muʿjiz II 526b, 527a, 533a
muʿjiza, pl. *muʿjizāt* I 24a; II 495b, 527a; III 396a, 396b, 397a; IV 22b, 156b, 565a; V 401a
ʿajuz, pl. *aʿjāz* I 494b; V 570b
ʿ-j-l
ʿajila III 441b
taʿajjala IV 97a
taʿjīl III 547a
ʿijl I 94b, 273b; II 218b; IV 40b
ʿijl ḥanīdh II 218b
ʿijl samūn II 218b
ʿ-j-m
iʿjām I 139b; III 605a
ʿajm III 605a
aʿjamī, pl. *aʿjām* I 132a, 145a; II 226b, 227a, 513a; III 109a, 114a, 114b, 122a, 507a; IV 337b, 444a; V 131b
ʿ-j-n
ʿajana I 24b
maʿjūn II 447a
ʿajwa I 495a; V 572a
ʿ-d-d III 550a; V 191a
ʿadda III 550a
aʿadda V 554b
istiʿdād V 192a
ʿadad II 225b; V 284a, 475a
ʿidda I 28b, 383a, 442b; II 175b; III 280b, 376a; IV 256a, 283b; V 233b, 453b, 480b, 481a, 495b
ʿ-d-s
ʿadas II 217b, 305b
ʿ-d-l V 433a
ʿadala II 328a; III 71a, 71b, 72b
taʿdīl V 496b
iʿtidāl IV 479b
muʿtadil IV 476b
ʿadl I 23a, 470b; II 5b, 70a, 70b, 321a, 321b; III 69b, 70a, 70b, 72a, 178b, 402b, 466b; IV 133b, 141a, 432b, 433a; V 195b, 496a, 496b
ʿadīl II 321a
ʿadāla I 358a; V 20a, 496b, 497a
ʿ-d-m
ʿadam V 151a

ʿ-d-n IV 13b
ʿadn II 282b; IV 13b, 15b
maʿdan IV 13b
maʿdin III 383a
ʿ-d-w II 23a; V 432b
iʿtadā I 536b; II 151a; IV 309b
muʿtadūn III 234a
iʿtidāʾ II 66b
ʿadwiya III 361b
ʿaduww, pl. aʿdāʾ I 32a, 454a, 455a; II 23a, 23b, 24a, 24b, 44b; IV 118a, 520a; V 15a, 432b
ʿadwāʾ III 356b, 357a, 357b
ʿudwān I 32a, 536b; II 6a; III 583a
ʿ-dh-b III 63a
ʿadhb I 446a; V 126a
ʿadhāb I 178b, 179a, 294b, 295a; II 210a, 210b, 212a, 414b, 415a, 415b, 416a, 418b; III 141b, 143a, 253b; IV 31a, 131a, 277b, 452b, 453a, 453b, 454a, 460a, 503b; V 119a, 132b, 133a
ʿadhāb alīm II 416a; IV 277b; V 133a
ʿadhāb al-qabr III 141b, 143a; IV 453a, 460a
ʿ-dh-r
maʿādhīr III 178a
ʿ-r-b I 214a
iʿrāb I 132b, 530b; II 346a, 348b, 349a, 359a, 394a; III 122b, 123a, 123b; IV 376b, 387b; V 143a, 323a, 326a, 333a
muʿarrab II 228b
taʿarraba I 217a
ʿarab, pl. aʿrāb I 132b, 135b, 144b, 145a, 214a, 214b, 215a, 216b, 217a, 221b; III 128a, 128b, 544a, 544b, 545a, 578a, 589a; IV 259a; V 35b, 42b, 198b
ayyām al-ʿarab see y-w-m
ʿarabī I 132a, 144b, 145a; III 114a, 507a, 514a, 545a; IV 259a, 443b
ʿarabiyya I 127b, 128a, 140b; II 231b; III 129b; IV 471a
aʿrab III 119b, 120a

ʿ-r-j — I 178b
ʿaraja — I 178b
aʿraj — V 249a
ʿurūj — III 46a; V 118b
miʿrāj, pl. *maʿārij* — I 85b, 88a, 88b, 176b, 178b, 206a, 367a; II 183a, 215b, 240b, 241b, 324b, 392b, 411b, 459a; III 3a, 19b, 388b; IV 60b, 64a, 179a, 228a, 295a, 349a; V 125a, 126a, 185a, 376a, 445b
ʿ-r-j-n
ʿurjūn — I 494b
ʿ-r-s
ʿurs — II 206a, 206b; III 324a
ʿ-r-sh
ʿarsh, pl. *ʿurūsh* — I 166a, 442a, 442b, 446a; II 284b, 325b, 410b; III 202a, 302a; V 276b, 277a, 277b
ʿ-r-ṣ
ʿaraṣāt — III 177b
ʿ-r-ḍ — II 447b; III 333a
ʿāriḍ — V 471a
muʿāraḍa — II 528b, 529a; III 214a; IV 22a, 313b
aʿraḍa — IV 309b
istiʿrāḍ — III 86b; IV 138b
ʿarḍ — III 140b, 178a, 333b; IV 391b, 588b; V 461b
aʿrāḍ — III 352b; IV 9a, 9b
ʿurūḍ — III 178a
ʿurḍa — III 564b, 565b
aʿriḍ — III 453b
ʿirḍ — I 458b; II 568b; III 119b
ʿ-r-f — I 146a; IV 47a, 47b
ʿarafa — I 146a; II 489a; III 101b; IV 47a, 95b, 597a
ʿārif, pl. *ʿārifūn* — IV 65a; V 140b, 151a, 154a, 154b
maʿrūf — II 60a, 61a, 61b, 62a, 63b, 65b, 72a, 75b, 77b, 78a, 290a; II 75b, 453a, 489a; III 359b; IV 84b, 85a, 316b; V 434b
al-amr bi-l-maʿrūf wa-l-nahy ʿan al-munkar — see ʾ-m-r
ʿarrafa — I 146a
taʿārafa — I 146a
ʿirāfa — II 239b; III 246b
ʿurf, pl. *aʿrāf* — II 52a, 395a, 415b; IV 46b, 47a,

	47b, 48a, 142b; v 244a, 316b, 419a
aṣḥāb al-aʿrāf	see ṣ-ḥ-b
ʿarafāt	iii 339b
ʿarrāf	iii 246b
maʿrifa	i 198a; ii 372b, 100b, 102a; iii 188a; iv 432b, 539a; v 72b, 140b, 141b, 142a, 149a
maʿrifat al-qirāʾa wa-l-kitāba	iii 188a
maʿrifa qalbiyya	i 198a
ʿ-r-q	
ʿirāqī	i 136b
ʿ-r-m	
ʿarima, pl. *ʿarim*	i 60b, 61a; v 464a
sayl al-ʿarim	i 60b, 61a
ʿ-r-w	
ʿurwa	i 374b, 465a; iii 503b; v 68a, 405a
ʿurwa(tu)(l-)wuthqā	i 374b, 465a; iii 503b; v 68a, 405a
ʿ-r-y	
ʿariya	i 84a
ʿ-z-r	
taʿzīr	ii 214a, 215a
ʿuzayr	iv 39a
ʿ-z-z	i 27a; ii 447a
ʿizza	i 453a; ii 274b; iv 210a
ʿazīz	i 209a; ii 10a, 29a, 320a, 447a; iii 200a, 208a, 509b; iv 6a; v 266b, 483a
ʿ-z-l	
iʿtazala	i 342b; iii 377a
ʿazl	i 234a, 234b; ii 511b
ʿ-z-m	
ʿazm	i 496a; iv 292a
ʿazāʾim	iv 492a
ʿ-z-w / ʿ-z-y	
ʿazāʾ	ii 89a
taʿziya, pl. *taʿāzī*	ii 94a, 208a; iv 56b
ʿ-s-r	
ʿusrā	iii 179b
ʿ-s-l	
ʿasal	ii 218a, 445b
ʿ-s-y	iii 8b
ʿasā	ii 367a; iii 10b

ʿ-sh-b
ʿushb II 369b
ʿ-sh-r
ʿushr V 192b, 197b
ʿishār I 94a
ʿashīra I 262b, 422b; II 174a, 431b; III 95b, 97a, 443a; V 364a
ʿāshūrāʾ IV 340b, 341a
ʿushar II 213a
ʿ-sh-q
ʿāshiq IV 65a
ʿishq III 360a; IV 234a
ʿ-sh-y
ʿashī / ʿashiyy I 503a, 503b, 504a; II 79b; III 418b; IV 223a; V 281a, 281b
ʿashiyya I 503a; V 476a
ʿishāʾ I 444a, 498a, 502b, 503a; II 79b, 80a; III 547a; V 281b
ṣalāt al-ʿishāʾ I 503a; II 79b
ʿ-ṣ-b
ʿaṣaba II 521a, 521b, 523b
ʿaṣabiyya I 38a; IV 365b; V 367a
ʿ-ṣ-r
ʿaṣr I 36a, 36b, 444a, 502b, 504a; II 80b, 388a, 388b; III 547a; IV 219a, 281b, 282a
ṣalāt al-ʿaṣr I 36a; II 388b; IV 219a
wa-l-ʿaṣr I 36, 444a
muʿāṣira I 128a
muʿāṣirāt V 461b
ʿ-ṣ-f
ʿāṣif I 52b, 53a; V 470b
ʿāṣifa I 52b, 53b
ʿaṣf I 41b, 44a, 44b
ʿ-ṣ-m I 19b; IV 307a
maʿṣūm II 506a
iʿtaṣama I 465a
istaʿṣama I 19b
ʿiṣma I 25b, 274a; II 117b, 505b, 506a, 506b; III 292a; IV 534a, 534b, 565b, 599b
ʾ-ṣ-w
ʿaṣā, pl. *ʿiṣiyy* II 544a, 546a; III 208a; IV 508a
ʿ-ṣ-y II 65b, 98a
ʿaṣā II 98a, 243a; III 2a

maʿṣiya, pl. *maʿāṣī* ii 98a; iii 420b; iv 84b; v 19a, 19b
ʿiṣyān ii 66a, 98a
ʿ-ṭ-r
ʿiṭr iii 573b
ʿ-ṭ-l
taʿṭīl i 104b
ʿ-ṭ-y
aʿṭā ii 313a, 313b
ʿaṭāʾ ii 16b, 313a
ʿaṭiyya ii 313b
ʿ-ẓ-r
taʿzīr ii 445a
ʿ-ẓ-m i 27a
ʿaẓama i 159b; iii 288a
taʿẓīm iii 288a
iʿẓām ii 4b
ʿaẓīm ii 320b; iii 449b, 504a; v 430a, 483a
ʿaẓm iii 54b, 382a
ʿ-f-r ii 486b
ʿifr ii 486b
ʿifriya ii 486b
ʿafār ii 213a; v 359a
ʿ-f-r-t
ʿifrīt, pl. *ʿafārīt* ii 486a, 486b, 487a; iii 48b, 487b; v 120b
ʿ-f-f i 19b
iʿfāf iii 252b
istaʿaffa i 19b, 298b; iv 600b
ʿ-f-w
ʿafā iii 65b
ʿafw ii 244b
ʿafuww ii 244b, 321a; iv 5b, 6a
ʿ-q-b iii 63a; iv 453a; v 432b
ʿāqiba iii 422b; iv 425a
ʿaqqaba v 118b
muʿaqqibāt v 118b
ʿāqaba iv 453a; v 118b
ʿiqāb i 294b, 295a; iv 453a
(al-)ʿaqaba ii 306a, 306b, 307a; iv 102b; v 182b, 183a
ʿaqb iii 2a
ʿuqbā ii 69b
ʿuqūba iii 54b, 401b

ʿ-q-d	I 433a
ʿaqada	I 432b
ʿaqqada	I 187a
iʿtiqād	I 481b
ʿaqd, pl. *ʿuqūd*	I 256b, 431a, 432b, 433b, 464a; III 215a; IV 489a; V 232b
ʿaqīda, pl. *ʿaqāʾid*	I 427a, 480a; III 64a, 241a; IV 149b; V 499b
ʿuqda	I 432b, 464a; III 278a; V 527a
ʿuqdat al-nikāḥ	I 464a; III 278a; V 527a
ʿ-q-r	V 253a
ʿāqir	V 253a
ʿaqr	V 55b
ʿ-q-q	
ʿaqīqa	I 403b
ʿ-q-l	I 246b; II 67a, 547b, 548a
ʿaqala	I 246a, 411b; II 67a, 67b, 547b, 548a, 548b, 549a; IV 71a; V 203b, 204b
ʿaql	I 198a, 466b; II 67a, 67b, 69b, 164a, 413b, 547b, 549a; IV 69a, 142b, 144a, 438a; V 73b, 140b
ʿāqil, pl. *ʿuqqāl*	I 23a, 557a; III 332a; V 496b
ʿ-q-m	
ʿaqīm	I 52b, 53a, 54b
ʿ-k-f	V 555b
ʿākif	I 215a; II 474a
ʿākifa	II 182b
iʿtikāf	II 84a, 180b, 182b, 183a, 204b; III 538b; IV 342b, 346b, 490a; V 431b
ʿukūf	IV 340a
ʿ-l-q	
ʿalaqa	III 284b
taʿlīq	I 142b
muʿallaqa, pl. *muʿallaqāt*	I 94b; II 529a; III 284b, 589a
ʿalaqa, coll. *ʿalaq*, pl. *ʿalaqāt*	I 3a, 81a, 230b, 231a, 238a, 240a, 476b; II 328a; V 522b
ʿ-l-l	
ʿilla	IV 76a
ʿallāt	IV 304b
ʿ-l-m	I 246b; II 487b, 488b; IV 537b
ʿalima	I 246a, 272a, 272b 349a; II 366b, 424b, 425b, 548b; III 101b,

102b; IV 537b, 538a, 538b; V 203b
ʿālim, pl. *ʿālimūn* II 90b, 548b; III 102a, 382b; IV 299b, 537b, 538b; V 146b, 485a
ʿallama I 246a; III 44a, 102b; IV 473b; V 200a, 200b, 381b
taʿlīmāt V 71a
muʿallam V 78b, 202b
taʿallum V 203a
ʿilm, pl. *ʿulūm* I 24a, 25a, 37a, 75a, 198a, 201b, 206b, 211a, 246b, 247b, 480a, 483a, 496a, 519b, 520a; II 75b, 96b, 99b, 130a, 165a, 247b, 367b, 430b, 488a, 488b, 489a, 495b, 520a, 520b, 521a, 522a, 523b, 525a, 525b, 526a, 567b; III 17b, 59a, 98b, 100b, 102a, 102b, 125a, 401b, 426a, 570b, 604b, 605b, 606b; IV 125b, 156a, 164b, 165a, 165b, 169b, 170a, 175a, 312b, 315b, 397a, 414a, 433b, 490a, 536b, 537b, 538a, 538b, 539a, 579a; V 77a, 141b, 143a, 150a, 177b, 203b, 208b, 277b, 318b, 319a, 321a, 321b, 381b, 442b, 497a
ʿilm al-balāgha I 198a; III 125a
ʿilm al-bayān I 198a; III 125a
ʿilm al-farāʾiḍ II 520a, 520b, 521a, 522a, 523b, 525a, 525b, 526a; III 98b
ʿilm al-ghayb I 201b
ʿilm al-ḥurūf IV 169b, 170a, 175a
ʿilm al-ishāra V 141b
ʿilm al-khawāṣṣ IV 165b, 169b
ʿilm maʿrifat llāh II 96b
ʿilm al-qirāʾāt II 247b; III 604b
ʿilm al-siyāsa V 442b
ʿilm al-tajwīd II 247b; III 604b, 606b
alladhīna ūtū l-ʿilm I 247b; IV 537b, 538a, 538b
rāsikhūn fī l-ʿilm III 102a, 102b; IV 539a
tabdīd al-ʿilm I 541b
ṭalab al-ʿilm III 100b
ūlū l-ʿilm IV 536b, 538b; V 203b
ʿulūm al-awwalīn wa-l-ākhirīn II 495b
ʿulūm al-qurʾān II 99b; III 604b; IV 156a, 397a; V 319a

dār al-ʿulūm	I 519b
ʿalam, pl. *aʿlām*	I 244a; II 528a; III 5a, 17b, 44a, 506a; V 322b, 552a
ʿālim, pl. *ʿulamāʾ*	I 32a, 189b, 201a, 201b, 234b, 278b, 279a, 393b, 469b, 519b, 520a, 539a, 539b, II 1b, 84a, 133b, 134a, 140a, 156b, 320b, 372a, 497a, 538b, 539a, 552b; III 100b, 102a, 102b, 121b, 347a, 347b, 416a; IV 5b, 6a, 56a, 130b, 168b, 270a, 270b, 271a, 275b, 444b, 537b, 538b, 539a, 539b, 575a; V 26a, 26b, 71b, 100b, 165a, 205b, 208b, 210a, 211b, 218a, 220a, 222a, 226a, 233a, 483a, 518b
ʿallām	III 102a; IV 537b
ʿalāma, pl. *ʿalāmāt*	II 36b; V 552a
maʿlam	IV 96a
ʿālam, pl. *ʿālamūn*	I 24b, 87b; II 190a, 193b; III 443b; IV 538b; V 105b, 118a, 156a, 157b, 551b, 552a, 553a
ʿ-l-n	
aʿlana	V 479b
ʿalāniya	II 168b; III 571a
ʿ-l-w / ʿ-l-y	II 541b
ʿalā	V 492a
taʿālā	I 237a, 237b; IV 220b
mutaʿālī	I 158b; II 320b
istiʿlāʾ	IV 374b
ʿālin	II 541b, 542a
ʿalī/ *ʿaliyy*	I 158b; II 320a; III 513a; IV 5b; V 483a
ʿuluww	II 541b
ʿilliyy / *ʿilliyyūn*	I 205b; II 51a, **500a**, 500b, 501a; IV 2b, 13a, 14a, 102b, 103a
ʿ-m-d	
iʿtamada	V 378a
ʿimād	II 83b, 559a
ʿamūd	IV 8b
ʿ-m-r	IV 92a
ʿamara	I 164a; V 203a
iʿtamara	IV 92a, 92b; V 448a
ʿumra	I 290b, 404a; II 64a, 85a, 149b, 179a, 183a; III 58b, 75b, 76a,

76b, 77a, 78a, 79a, 115b, 410a, 410b, 553a; IV 91b, 92a, 93a, 93b, 94a, 94b, 95a, 95b, 97b, 98a, 98b, 99a, 99b, 282a, 338b, 339b, 340a, 518a, 518b; V 435a, 448a, 448b, 450a, 556a, 556b
ʿumariyyatān II 525a
ʿ-m-l V 548b
ʿamila I 113a; II 60a
muʿāmalāt II 223a; III 73a; IV 132b, 284a, 284a, 485b, 486a, 488b, 489a
aʿmāl II 166b; III 39a; IV 432a, 494b
ʿamal I 220a; II 6b; IV 132b, 487b, 539a
ʿamal al-ṣāliḥāt I 220a; see also ʾ-m-n
ʿamaliyya, pl. *ʿamaliyyāt* I 520b
ʿ-m-m
ʿāmm III 39a, 39b, 157b, 159a
ʿāmmiyya I 128a, 133b
ʿawāmm I 416a; II 422b; V 140a
ʿ-m-y
aʿmā V 447a, 447b
ʿ-n-b
ʿinab, pl. *aʿnāb* I 25a, 42b; II 217b, 305b
ʿ-n-d II 541b
ʿinda III 398b; V 458b
ʿanīd II 541b
ʿ-n-z
ʿanaza III 428b
ʿ-n-f V 432b
ʿunf V 432a
ʿ-n-q
muʿāniqa IV 377a
aʿnāq II 363b
ʿ-n-k-b
ʿankabūt I 95a; V 113a
ʿ-n-w
ʿanwa V 195b
ʿ-n-y
maʿnā, pl. *maʿānin* I 71a; II 109a, 109b, 554a; III 125a; IV 65a, 445b, 564a; V 141b, 112a, 323a, 326a, 329b, 332b, 341a
ʿ-h-d
ʿahida I 25a, 448a, 464a, 465a

ʿāhada I 464b; III 564b
aʿhada I 448a
taʿāhud V 336a
ʿahd, pl. ʿuhūd I 256b, 304b, 379a, 379b, 381a, 431a, 431b, 432b, 464a, 464b, 465a, 465b, 466a, 466b; II 8b, 61a, 552b; III 239a, 564b; V 291b, 292b, 449b
maʿāhid V 218a
ʿ-h-n
ʿihn I 178b, 346b; V 183b
ʿ-w-j
ʿiwaj III 513a; IV 297a
ʿ-w-d
ʿāda III 141b, 352b
ʿādda, pl. awāʿid I 401b
ʿūd IV 381a
ʿīd I 66b; II 40b, 192a, 203b, 204b, 298a; III 396a; IV 218a, 346b, 517a; V 190a
ʿīd al-aḍḥā I 66b; II 192a, 203b, 204b, 298a; IV 218b, 517a
ʿīd al-fiṭr I 66b; II 192a, 203b, 204a; IV 218b, 346b
ʿīd al-qurbān IV 517a
maʿād II 83a; III 66b, 139a, 140a; IV 88a, 435a
ʿ-w-dh IV 307a
ʿādha II 92a; IV 233b, 234a, 377b
taʿwīdh IV 163a
taʿawwudh I 391a; IV 377b
muʿawwidhatān I 77a; II 189a, 190b, 393b; IV 233b, 295a
istaʿādha I 78b, 525a; II 91a, 91b, 92a, 92b, 95b
ʿawdh III 48a
ʿ-w-r
istiʿāra III 384a, 384b; V 13a
ʿawra, pl. ʿawrāt I 84a; III 403b, 404a, 404b, 548a, 548b, 549a; V 414b, 415a
ʿ-w-l
ʿāʾilan IV 209a
taʿwīl I 198a; IV 534b
ʿawl II 523a, 525a
ʿiyāl V 323b

ʿ-w-m
ʿām iv 45a; v 285b, 475a, 475b, 560a, 560b

ʿ-w-n
aʿwān iii 239b
istaʿāna v 441b
ʿ-y-b
ʿayb i 397a
ʿ-y-d see ʿ-w-d
ʿ-y-sh
ʿīsha iii 275b
maʿāsh i 498a
maʿīsha ii 217a
ʿ-y-n ii 153b, 348b
taʿyīn v 334a
ʿayn, pl. *ʿuyūn, aʿyun [aʿyān]* i 42a, 81a, 212b, 288a, 410b; ii 153b, 154a, 154b, 212a, 324b; iii 157a, 202a, 409a, 456a; iv 424a, 574a, 585a; v 121b, 124a, 125b, 127b, 461b, 464b, 466a
maʿīn v 121b, 127b, 482a
ʿ-y-y
ʿayya i 443b

-ghayn-

gh-b-r
ghubār i 136b, 137a, 142b; iii 271b, 318a, 318b, 321a

gh-b-n
taghābun i 300a, 301a
gh-th-ʾ
ghuthāʾ i 364b
gh-d-w iii 417a
ghadā i 504a
ghadan v 281a
ghadāt [ghadāh] i 503b, 504a; ii 80a, 353a; iii 417a, 418b; iv 223a; v 281b
ghuduww i 503b, 504a; ii 80a; iii 417a, 418b; iv 223a; v 276a, 281b, 285a
ghadāʾ i 504a; iii 417b
gh-r-b
gharaba iv 107a

ghurāb I 95a
gharīb II 108b, 231b, 419a; III 115a, 287b; IV 155b; V 131a, 332b
gharā'ib II 108a
ghurūb I 444a, 504b; IV 107a, 223a; V 163a
maghrib, pl. *maghārib* I 140a, 142a, 444a, 498a, 502b; II 80a, 311a, 388b; IV 107a; V 282b

gh-r-b-b
gharābīb II 217b

gh-r-r
gharūr I 526a; V 360a
ghurūr I 543b

gh-r-f
ghurfa, pl. *ghuraf* I 165b; II 458a, 458b, 460b

gh-r-q
mughraq I 553b
aghraq I 553b
gharaq I 553b

gh-r-l
aghral I 337a
gharānīq I 95a; IV 532a; V 122a

gh-z-l
ghazal III 224a; IV 57a, 58a

gh-z-w II 144a
ghazw I 216a, 369b
ghazwa, pl. *ghazawāt* II 256b; IV 465a, 465b; V 194a
maghzāt, pl. *maghāzī* I 321a, 399b; II 144b, 145a, 149a, 149b, 150a; III 455b; IV 209b; V 30a, 32a, 32b, 35a, 42a, 42b, 43a, 194a

gh-s-q
ghāsiq III 247b
ghasaq I 503a; II 79b; V 282b
ghassāq II 211a

gh-s-l IV 498b, 499b
ghasala V 462a
ightasala I 341b
ghusl I 328b, 341b, 411a; II 89a; IV 225b, 485b, 488b, 491b, 492a, 506b

gh-s-l-n
ghislīn II 211a

gh-sh-y
ghashiya I 497b; V 64b
ghāshiya III 137a; IV 103a
aghshā V 544a

gh-ḍ-b	
ghaḍiba	III 25a
maghḍūb	II 190b; IV 589b; V 374b
ghaḍb	I 411b
ghaḍab	I 491b; III 25a, 33a; IV 310a
gh-ṭ-ṭ	
mughaṭṭa	III 428a
gh-f-r	III 378a
ghafara	II 245a; III 65b
ghāfir	II 321a; III 378b
istaghfara	I 442a; II 95b, 551b
istighfār	II 91a, 91b
ghafūr	I 209a; II 321a; IV 5b, 6a
ghaffār	II 244b; II 321a
maghfira	II 244b
gh-f-l	II 488b
ghafala	V 203b
ghafla	I 206b
gh-l-b	I 399b; II 144a, 147a; IV 210a; V 429b, 430b
ghalaba	I 265a, 265b, 266b, 267b; II 144a
ghālib, pl. *ghālibūn*	III 308a; IV 212a; V 377b, 430b
taghlīb	II 363b, 364a
ghalab	II 144a
gh-l-f	
aghlaf, pl. *ghulf*	I 336b, 337a
gh-l-l	
ghalla	IV 291b
ghull, pl. *aghlāl*	II 544b, 546a, 547a
gh-l-m	
ghulām, pl. *ghilmān*	I 301b; II 284a, 445a; IV 18a, 585a; V 58a
gh-l-w	
ghalā	V 573a
ghuluww	V 573b
ghulāt	I 555a; II 422a
gh-m-m	
ghamām	V 461b, 463a
gh-m-ṣ	
ghumayṣāʾ	V 51b
gh-n-j	
ghunj	IV 583a
gh-n-m	
ghanima	I 251b; V 194a, 194b
ghanam	I 94b

ghanīma, pl. *ghanāʾim* I 251b, 252a; II 6b; V 146a, 195a
maghnam, pl. *maghānim* I 251b; V 194a
gh-n-n
ghunna IV 375a
gh-n-y II 507b
aghnā I 405b; V 467b
taghannā IV 369a
istighnāʾ I 159a
ghaniyy I 27a; II 320a, 330a; IV 6a; V 272b, 408a, 467b
ghināʾ II 93b, 280b; V 467b
gh-w-r II 144a
mughīr II 144a
ghār I 292b, 293b
maghārāt I 292b, 294a
gh-w-ṣ
ghawwāṣ II 467b
gh-w-l
ghūl V 120b
ghawl, pl. *ghīlān* V 120b, 122a
gh-w-y II 66a
ghawā I 536b; II 43a, 66a; V 267b
mughawwī III 45a
aghwā I 453a; V 267b
ighwāʾ I 185b
mughwī III 45a
gh-y-b
ightāba II 343b
ightiyāb II 343b
ghayb, pl. *ghuyūb* I 84a, 219a, 219b, 461b; II 423a, 423b, 424a, 425b; III 43b, 102a, 452a; IV 4a, 179a, 291b, 443a, 509a, 572b; V 79a, 108a, 445a, 492b, 543a
ghayba I 68b; II 424a, 503b, 504a; IV 602a
gh-y-th
ghayth I 42a; II 212a; V 470b
gh-y-r
ghayyara IV 594a
mughīrāt IV 465a
ghayr I 470b; IV 564b; V 404a, 496a
ghayra III 113a; V 247a
gh-y-y IV 23a
ghāya, pl. *ghāyāt* IV 23b; V 475a
ghayy IV 29a

-fāʾ-

f-ʾ	
fiʾa	II 421b, 431b
f-ʾ-d	
fuʾād	II 324a, 407a, 547b; III 442a
f-ʾ-r	
faʾra	I 61a
f-ʾ-l	
faʾl	II 242a, 242b; IV 163a, 165b, 178b, 179a, 179b
fāl-nāma	III 317b, 318a, 318b, 266b, 269b
f-t-ḥ	I 397b, 398b, 399a, 400a; II 144a, 152a, 429b, 430b
fataḥa	I 32a
mufattaḥa	II 361b, 363b
fatḥ, pl. *futūḥ*	I 78b, 397b, 398a, 399a, 399b, 400a, 400b; III 340a, 454a; IV 176a, 180a, 332b, 495b, 590a; V 429b
fatḥa	I 279a; II 191b
fattāḥ	I 399a; II 320b; IV 6a
miftāḥ, pl. *mafātīḥ*	II 546b; III 104a
fātiḥa, pl. *fawātiḥ*	I 75b, 209b, 210a, 210b, 248a; II **188a**, 189a, 378a; III 260b; IV 601b
f-t-r	
fatra, pl. *fatarāt*	I 405b; II 436b; III 201b, 443b; IV 297b, 441b
f-t-q	
fataqa	V 544a
f-t-n	II 144a, 152a
fatana	V 362b
maftūn	II 540b
fitna, pl. *fitan*	I 212b, 241a, 370b, 397b, 539b, 551b, 552a; II 69a, 74a, 75a, 144a; III 41b, 72b, 139a , 487b, 545b; IV 26a, 289a, 365a; V 24a, 292b, 362b, 363b, 456b, 458b, 516a
f-t-w / f-t-y	
fatiya	III 425b, 426a; V 58a, 200b
aftā	V 321a
muftī	IV 144a
istafā	V 203b

fatwā, pl. *fatāwā* I 29b, 202a; II 281b; III 344a, 344b, 345a, 366a; IV 59b, 268a, 494a; V 56a, 214a, 214b, 222a, 224a, 227a, 232b, 305a, 305b

lajnat al-fatāwā I 29b

fatayāt I 396a; V 57a

f-j-j

fajj V 375a

f-j-r

fājir II 66b; IV 147b

fajjara V 126a

fajr I 36a, 444a, 503b; III 417a, 417b; IV 107a, 217a; V 163a, 281a, 282a, 556b

maṭlaʿ al-fajr V 282b

qurʾān al-fajr V 281a

ṣalāt al-fajr III 417a; V 281a, 282b

wa-l-fajr I 444b; IV 217a

fujjār IV 481b, 598b

f-ḥ-sh II 63a; V 19a

fāḥish II 491a

fāḥisha, pl. *fawāḥish* I 28a; II 444b, 445a; IV 32a, 277a, 580b, 584b; V 19a, 20a, 21a, 528a

faḥshāʾ III 69b, 70b; IV 580b, 598b, 599a; V 269a

f-kh-r

fakhara I 339b

fakhkhār I 24b, 339a, 339b

ṣalṣāl ka-l-fakhkhār I 24b

tafākhur I 241b

mufākharāt III 247a

fakhr II 301b; III 120a; IV 472b

fakhūr I 241b, 395a

f-kh-m

tafkhīm IV 374b

f-d-n

faddān III 336b

f-d-y

fadā IV 517b

fidāʾ I 404b; IV 533b

iftadā III 280a

iftidāʾ III 279b

fidya I 187b; II 182b; IV 94a, 343b, 344a, 523b

f-r-t	
furāt	I 443a
f-r-j	
farj, pl. *furūj*	I 84a, 298b; III 14a, 548a; IV 580b; V 115a
f-r-ḥ	III 60b
faraḥ	III 62a
farḥa	III 61a, 61b
fariḥīn	III 61b
f-r-d	
mufradāt	V 334b
f-r-d-s	
firdaws	II 51a, 51b, 229a, 231a, 283a, 284b, 411b; IV 13a, 13b, 14b, 15b; V 466b
f-r-z	
ifrāz	III 376b
f-r-sh	
farasha	II 2b
farsh	I 94b
farāsh	I 95a; V 183b
firāsh, pl. *furush*	II 2b, 276a; IV 18a, 547a, 547b
f-r-ḍ	
faraḍa	I 245a
farḍ, pl. *furūḍ*	II 71b; III 41a, 92a, 94a; IV 378a; V 439b, 450a
farḍ ʿalā l-aʿyān	V 439b
farḍ kifāya	II 71b; III 42a; IV 378a; V 439b
farḍ wājib	IV 94a
furūḍ al-islām	V 450a
farīḍa, pl. *farāʾiḍ*	I 72a, 257a, 258a; II 262b, 313b, 351a; IV 594a; V 196a, 197a, 198b, 320a, 322a
f-r-ṭ	
faraṭ	II 395a
f-r-ʿ	
furūʿ	III 424b; V 329b
farāʾiʿ	I 402b, 403a, 403b
f-r-ʿ-n	
firʿawn	IV 66b, 67a, 105b
f-r-gh	
faragha	II 252a, 252b
f-r-q	I 486b; II 184a; IV 24b, 25b, 345b, 403b
faraqa	I 250b, 486b, 487a; II 184a; III 424b, 425a, 514b; IV 343a

mufarraqan IV 444a
tafarruq I 538a
iftaraqa IV 597a
iftirāq III 86a
farq I 487a; III 424b
firqa, pl. *firaq* II 115b, 420b; III 86a; IV 24b, 25b, 26a
farīq II 351a, 431b; IV 25b, 403b
furqān I 1a, 196b, 486a, 486b, 487a, 500b; II 183b, 184a, 186b; III 424b, 425a, 442a, 496b, 505b, 507b, 508a, 514b; IV 37b, 293b, 343a, 344a, 345a, 345b, 346a, 443b; V 37a, 301b
firāq V 381b
f-r-n
furn II 219a
f-r-y
iftarā I 235b; II 529b; III 116a, 181a; IV 309b, 311b
f-z-ʿ II 194b
fazaʿ II 194b, 197b, 198a
f-s-d I 439b, 440a; V 432b
fasada I 440a, 474b; II 62b; IV 366b
fāsid I 530a
afsada I 440a
mufsid, pl. *mufsidūn* I 240b; II 62b; IV 364a, 364b, 598b
mufsidūn fī l-arḍ IV 364a, 364b, 598b
fasād I 32a, 440a, 441a; II 7b, 62b; III 458b; IV 127b, 129a; V 255a
(al-)fasād fī arḍ I 32a, 439b; III 458b, 459a
f-s-r
fassara II 100a
tafsīr, pl. *tafāsīr* I 32a, 65b, 76a, 106a, 198a, 230a, 238b, 331b, 335b, 339a, 341b, 347b, 349a, 371b, 381b, 391b, 393b, 461a, 480a, 520a, 525a, 528a, 547a, 548a, 549b, 553a; II 99b, 100a, 100b, 101a, 101b, 102b, 103a, 103b, 104a, 104b, 105a, 105b, 106a, 108a, 110a, 113a, 117a, 118a, 125a, 125b, 126b, 128a, 129a, 130a, 130 b, 131a, 138b, 139a, 145a, 149a, 150b, 191b, 201b, 231a, 233b, 237b, 268b, 271a, 284b, 333b,

347a, 377a, 388b, 389a, 389b, 390a, 393a, 396b, 429a, 441a, 478a, 478b; III 2b, 3a, 6a, 6b, 30a, 32a, 53a, 55b, 81a, 137b, 139a, 230a, 232b, 268b, 269a, 283a, 284b, 290a, 290b, 291b, 375a, 399a, 469a, 535b, 539a, 570b, 579a; IV 45a, 61a, 61b, 69a, 69b, 157a, 157b, 158b, 202b, 257b, 262a, 266a, 349a, 386b, 460a, 531b, 533a, 534b, 535b, 543b, 549a, 549b, 550a, 555b, 593b, 595a, 602a, 602b, 603a; V 31a, 36a, 52a, 52b, 74a, 98a, 98b, 99b, 100a, 139b, 140a, 143a, 143b, 146b, 147a, 147b, 148a, 148b, 149b, 156b, 157a, 158a, 165b, 203b, 210b, 213b, 219b, 222a, 224a, 226a, 277b, 297b, 298a, 307a, 318b, 321b, 322a, 326a, 341a, 413b, 414b, 452a, 507a, 510a, 514a, 515a, 522b

tafsīr bi-l-ʿilm I 76a

tafsīr bi-l-maʾthūr II 110a; V 147a, 147b

tafsīr al-fātiḥa II 128a

tafsīr ʿilmī I 230a, 238b; II 129a, 130a, 130b, 131a; III 399a; V 52a, 52b

tafsīr mawḍūʿī II 125b, 138b, 139a

tafsīr musalsal II 125a

tafsīr al-qurʾān I 332a

tafsīr al-qurʾān bi-l-qurʾān IV 45b

tafsīr al-ẓāhir V 149b

uṣūl al-tafsīr I 520a; II 126b

mufassir, pl. *mufassirūn* I 321a; II 364b; III 3a

mufassirāt II 201b

mufassar III 156b; V 322a

fasāṭīṭ II 426b

f-s-q II 63a, 62b

fāsiq, pl. *fāsiqūn* I 119b; II 63a, 170b, 258b, 407b, 470b; IV 129a, 133a, 133b; V 24a

fisq I 119b, 120a, 220b; III 547a

fusūq I 511b; II 57a, 66a

f-ṣ-ḥ
faṣīḥ III 120a
faṣāḥa III 198a, 198b, 468b
afṣaḥ III 112a, 112b, 113a, 113b, 120a
fuṣḥā I 128a, 129a, 132b, 133b; II 89b; III 112a
f-ṣ-l
fāṣil, pl. *fāṣilūn* I 246b
faṣṣala I 516b
mufaṣṣal II 226b, 497b; III 114a, 114b; V 8a
īmān mufaṣṣal I 202a; III 159a
tafṣīl II 168a, 168b
munfaṣil I 365a; II 529b; III 506b; V 203b, 422b, 423b
faṣl, pl. *fuṣūl* IV 376a
mafṣūl I 486b, 496a, 516a, 516b; II 353b; III 424b; IV 23b, 476b, 477b, 480b
fiṣāl V 332b
fāṣila, pl. *fawāṣil* III 106a, 106b
III 128b, 197a; IV 476b, 477b, 481a; V 168b
f-ḍ-ḍ
fiḍḍa III 383b, 409a
f-ḍ-l
fāḍil V 334a
faḍḍala I 304a; II 14a, 202b, 203a; III 94b; V 191b, 540a
faḍl II 96a, 344b, 345a, 345b, 371a; IV 209a; V 198a, 468a, 469a
faḍīla, pl. *faḍāʾil* I 33b, 388a, 497a, 539b; II 110b, 389b, 390a; III 2b, 3a; V 46b, 47b, 324a, 333b
afḍal II 285b; V 334a
f-ṭ-r
faṭara II 402b; V 258b, 263a
fāṭir IV 82a, 213b
ifṭār IV 347b
munfaṭir II 363a
fiṭra I 26a, 337a, 337b, 466b; II 329a, 402a, 402b; III 376b, 446a, 510b; V 268a, 268b, 269b
fiṭriyya III 376b
f-ʿ-l
faʿala I 32a; II 259b, 360b, 363a, 365b; IV 483b; V 3a, 171b

fāʿil II 360b
mafʿūl II 313b, 351a, 351b
fiʿl, pl. *afʿāl* II 83a, 502a; III 162a; IV 433a; V 318a
fāʿila IV 103a
fāʿilāt II 256a, 257a; IV 464b, 466a, 466b, 468b
faʿīl II 363a
afʿal I 192b
f-q-d II 537b
tafaqqada II 537b
f-q-r II 507b
faqr IV 547a
fiqra, pl. *fiqar* IV 476b
faqār III 322b
faqīr, pl. *fuqarāʾ* IV 209a, 494b, 495a; V 467b
f-q-ʿ
fāqiʿ I 363a
f-q-h
faqiha II 548b
tafaqqaha III 103b
fiqh I 131b, 198a, 201b, 234b, 239b, 263b, 264a, 339a, 341b, 343b, 391b, 412b, 502b; II 5a, 205a, 215a, 511b, 549b; III 100b, 102a, 107a, 307a, 366a; IV 59b, 93b, 123a, 125b, 149b, 488b, 506a, 506b; V 55a, 193b, 205b, 206a, 209b, 213b, 214b, 215a, 220a, 222a, 223a, 226a, 329a, 477a, 514a, 515a; see also ʾ-ṣ-l
faqqih II 390a
faqīh, pl. *fuqahāʾ* I 189b, 201b, 231a, 320b; II 101a, 230a, 390b, 393b; IV 65a, 156a, 176b, 525a; V 150a, 293a, 293b, 499b
fqīh V 72a, 73a, 73b
f-k-r I 246b; II 67b; IV 393b, 394a, 394b
fakkara II 548b
tafakkara I 246a; II 67b, 548a
tafakkur IV 69a, 393b, 394b
fikr II 69b; IV 394b, 424a
f-k-k
fakka I 289b
fakk V 57b

f-k-h
fākih II 304b; III 63a
fākiha, pl. *fawākih* III 63a
I 42a, 44b; II 217b, 304b, 364b; IV 18a
f-l-j
falaj I 43b
f-l-ḥ
aflaḥa I 40a, 376b; II 162a
mufliḥ, pl. *mufliḥūn* I 40b; II 31a; IV 523a
falāḥ I 376b, 380a; IV 127b, 523a, 523b
filāḥa I 376b; IV 523a
I 40b
f-l-s
fals III 336b
f-l-s-f
mutafalsifūn II 286b
falsafa I 85a, 198a, 480a; II 185a; III 100b; IV 287a; V 483b
falāsifa III 185b
f-l-q III 417a
fāliq I 502a, 503b; III 418a; V 281a
fāliq al-iṣbāḥ I 502a, 503b; III 418a; V 281a
infalaqa III 423b
falaq I 503b; III 247b, 417a; V 281a
rabb al-falaq I 503b; III 417a
f-l-k
falak, pl. *aflāk* I 445b; IV 107a; V 163a
fulk I 157b; III 486a, 542b; IV 604a, 604b
f-l-n
fulān II 379b
f-m
fam, pl. *afwāh* I 82b
funduq V 213a
f-n-y
fānin V 340a
fanā' I 88b; II 47b, 94b; IV 86a, 434a
f-h-d
fahd V 246a
f-h-m
mafhūm V 333b
fahm V 74a, 320a
f-w-j
fawj, pl. *afwāj* II 431b; V 377a
f-w-r
fāra V 126b

fawwāra, pl. *fawwārāt* v 121b
f-w-z v 429b, 430a
fāʾiz, pl. *fāʾizūn* iv 523a; v 430a
fawz iv 18b, 522b; v 430a
f-w-ḍ
tafwīḍ iv 549b
mufawwiḍa ii 422a
f-w-m
fawwama ii 217b
fūm i 529b; ii 217a, 217b; ii 305b
f-y-ʾ
fāʾa iii 563a
fayʾ, pl. *afāʾa* i 251b, 252a, 252b; ii 149a; v 194a
f-y-d
fawāʾid v 143a
f-y-ḍ
afāḍa iv 95b
ifāḍa iv 95b, 96a, 96b, 515b
fayḍ iv 82b
f-y-l
fīl i 95a; iv 44b, 46a

-qāf-

q-b-b
qubba iii 299b, 544a
qubbat al-ṣakhrā iii 299b
q-b-ḥ
qabīḥ i 411a; iii 548b
qabāʾiḥ iv 503b
q-b-r
aqbara i 263b
qubūr i 263b; iv 465b
q-b-s
iqtibās iii 214a, 215a; iv 56a; v 392b
q-b-ḍ
qabḍa i 275b; ii 325a; v 474b
q-b-l
taqbīl iv 485b
mutaqābilūn ii 159a
qabl ii 433b; v 317b
qibla i 12b, 153b, 163b, 164b, 328b, 330b, 378b; ii 159a, 182a, 182b, 190b, 261a, 263b, 309b, 310a,

311a; III 3a, 27b, 31a, 34a, 76a, 77b, 79a, 179b, 300a, 303a, 305a, 307b, 314b, 340a, 427b, 428a, 429a, 430a, 430b, 433b, 434a, 446b, 572a; IV 16a, 104b, 217b, 219a, 224a, 226a, 226b, 228b, 283b, **325a**, 325b, 326a, 326b, 327a, 327b, 377b, 407a, 413a, 515a, 516a, 519b, 541a; V 55a, 107b, 172b, 175a, 185a, 556a, 556b
qabūl I 433b; V 192a
qabīla, pl. *qabāʾil* II 71b, 431b; IV 336b; V 364a, 364b
q-t-l II 144b, 208b; III 38a, 38b; V 432b, 433a, 455a
qatala I 270a, 271b, 276b, 449b, 489a, 491b, 508a; II 144b, 151a, 261b; III 139b, 458b; IV 30b, 483a; V 160a, 160b
qātil II 144b
muqātil II 106b
qitāl I 398a; II 144b, 208b, 209a; III 38a, 38b, 422b
qātala II 155b, 208b, 274a; IV 30a
qatl II 366a; III 193a; V 161a
q-th-ʾ
qiththāʾ II 217a
q-ḥ-ṭ
qaḥṭ II 178a
q-d-ḥ
qidḥ, pl. *aqdāḥ* II 281a; V 78b
q-d-r II 185b, 186a, 507b; III 333a, 334a, 334b, 335a
qādir I 507a; II 185b, 320a; III 92a; IV 212a
qadara II 185b, 349a; III 54b
qaddara I 273a, 442b, 507a; II 185b, 328b; III 333a, 334a
qadr I 159a; II 168a, 185b, 268b, 334b; III 537b, 538a, 538b; V 116a
laylat al-qadr II 185b, 268b
taqdīr I 159a; II 59a
muqtadir II 320b
qadar I 159a, 516b; II 59a, 168b, 185a,

185b, 186a, 186b, 267a, 267b, 268b, 269a, 270b, 328b; III 87b, 178b, 334a, 334b, 335a, 538a; IV 72b, 73a, 85b, 95b, 380a, 380b, 450b
qadarī II 105a
qadariyya I 74b; II 422a
qidr, f. *qidra*, pl. *qudūr* I 162, 165ab, 490b; II 219a
qudra III 538a; IV 433b
qadīr I 507a; II 185b, 268b; III 200b; V 174a, 380b
miqdār III 333a, 334b, 335a; V 286a
q-d-s IV 282b, 283b
muqaddas III 504a; IV 282b, 283b, 513a, 513b; see also ʾ-r-ḍ
qudus II 443b; IV 282b; see also r-w-ḥ
qudsī II 285b, 376b, 396a; III 505a
q-d-m II 198b
taqdīm V 322a
muqaddima III 470b
muqaddam I 72a; V 333b
qadam, pl. *aqdām* II 198b, 199a, 325a; IV 14b
al-qadam al-ṣidq II 199a; IV 14b
qidam I 319a; IV 83a; V 278b
qadīm I 471a; IV 81b, 89b
qadūm I 337b
aqdamūna II 434a
q-d-w
iqtidāʾ II 196a
q-dh-r
qadhir I 411a
q-dh-f
qadhafa II 198a
maqdhūf II 214b
qadhf II 214a, 214b, 344a; III 153b; V 498a
q-r-ʾ I 246b; III 506b, 585b; IV 368a
qaraʾa I 245b, 326a, 451a, 554b; II 81b, 86b, 87a; III 123a, 188b, 190b, 440b, 443a, 584b; IV 217b, 354b, 403a, 449b, 470a; V 203a
qāriʾ, pl. *qurrāʾ* I 131b, 332a, 334a, 347b, 350a, 520a, 520b; II 17b, 86b, 88a, 90a, 93b, 94a, 147a, 276b;

III 123b, 506b; IV 134a, 371b, 386a, 386b, 387b, 388a; V 1b, 505a

maqrū' IV 446b

aqra'a II 493a

muqri', pl. *muqri'ūn* IV 386a, 392a

qurū' V 435a, 495b

qirā'a, pl. *qirā'āt* I 333b; II 10a, 87b, 88a, 88b, 93a, 108a, 109b, 190b, 247a, 247b, 376a, 398a, 520a, 524a; III 123a, 124a, 131b, 302a, 605a, 606b, 607a, 607b; IV 135a, 189a, 353b, 354a, 354b, 355a, 355b, 356a, 356b, 357a, 359a, 367b, 369a, 372a, 372b, 373a, 377a, 380b, 386a, 388b, 390b, 391b, 446a, 450a, 599b, 601b; V 111b, 112a, 143a, 213b, 295b, 326a

qirā'a bi-l-alḥān IV 380b

qirā'at al-fātiḥa II 93a

al-qirā'āt al-mutawātira II 109b, 247a

qirā'āt al-sab' II 247b

al-qirā'āt (al-)shādhdha I 347b, 350a; II 247a

qawā'id al-qirā'āt III 605a, 606b, 607a

qar' IV 386b

qur' IV 386b

qur'ān I 63b, 248b, 325a, 372b, 441a, 502b; II 2a, 82a, 118a, 254a, 254b, 257b, 499b; III 49a, 113b, 114a, 440b, 505b, 506a, 506b, 507b, 508a, 509b, 510b, 514b, 524b, 584b, 585a, 586a, 591b; IV 63a, 148a, 221b, 293a, 310b, 312b, 313a, 344a, 368b, 386a, 440a, 443b, 468b, 470a, 560b, 562a, 566a; V 419b, 422a, 422b, 423a, 425a, 425b, 483a, 556b

qur'ān 'ajab II 2a

qur'ān 'ajamiyy III 114a

qur'ān 'arabiyy/ 'arabī III 585a; IV 566a

qur'ān dhī l-dhikr II 257b

qur'ān al-fajr I 502b; II 82a; IV 221b

qur'ān al-majīd II 257b

qur'ān al-nāṭiq I 63b; II 118a

ahl al-qurʾān	IV 386a
umm al-qurʾān	II 189a; IV 167a
q-r-b	IV 516b
qariba	I 447b
qarraba	IV 292a
muqarrabūn	III 67a, 204a; IV 2b, 15b, 16a, 16b, 220a; V 124a
aqraba	II 174b
taqarrub	IV 489b
qurb	I 176a; V 196b
qarīb	I 345a; IV 5b
qarāba	I 345a; II 521b; III 97a
aqraba	III 236a
qurbā	II 75a, 174b; III 95b; IV 209a, 489b
dhawū l-qurbā	II 176a
dhū l-qurbā	II 75a, 174b, 176a; IV 209a
ūlū l-qurbā	II 174b, 176a
maqraba	II 174b, 307a
dhū maqraba	II 174b
qurbān	IV 517a
q-r-d	
qirada	I 95a, 475b
q-r-r	
aqarra	I 405a
iqrār	II 169a
mustaqarr	II 458b; IV 550b, 556a; V 163a, 283b
qurrāt	I 212b; III 235a
qarār	III 13b
qārūra, pl. *qawārīr*	I 166a, 490a, 490b; II 219a, 276a
q-r-ḍ	
qaraḍa	V 312b
qarḍ	I 65a; II 8a
q-r-ṭ-s	
qirṭās, pl. *qarāṭīs*	I 247a; II 430a, 544b, 545a; III 25b, 591a; IV 587b; V 558a
q-r-ʿ	I 246b
qaraʿa	II 280a
qāriʿa	I 113a; II 365b; III 137a, 203a; IV 102b, 103a; V 183b
qurʿa	II 237b, 239b, 240a
qarmaṭa	I 136b
q-r-n	
qarn, pl. *qurūn*	II 292b, 293a, 434a; III 190a; IV 425a

dhū l-qarnayn III 190a
quranāʾ V 119b
qarīn V 119b, 494a
qarīna, pl. *qarāʾin* III 159b; IV 476b, 477b, 481a; V 20a
qarna V 525b
qirna V 525b
q-r-y
qarya, pl. *qurā* I 163a, 217a, 338a, 338b; II 295a, 299a, 308a, 363b; III 5a, 338a; IV 386b, 513b; see also ʾ-m-m
qarawī I 128b
q-s-s
qissīsīn III 406a; IV 404a
q-s-r V 432b
qasr V 292b
q-s-ṭ II 70b
qāsiṭūn III 71a
muqsiṭ, pl. *muqsiṭūn* III 234a
qisṭ II 70a, 70b, 76b, 234a, 321b; III 69b, 70a, 335b, 336b, 402b, 437a; IV 84b, 133b; V 440b
q-s-ṭ-s
qisṭās II 231a, 231b, 234a, 544b, 545b; III 334b, 336a
q-s-m III 562a
qasama II 83a; III 549b
qāsama III 563b
aqsama II 255b, 256a; III 562a, 562b, 564a; IV 217a; V 449a
istiqsām II 237b, 239a
qism, pl. *aqsām* I 72a; IV 272b; V 193b
qasam I 466a; II 255b; III 562a; IV 492b; V 498a
wāw al-qasam II 255b
qasāma III 562b; V 498b
q-s-w
qasā II 407a, 407b
qāsiya II 363b, 407a
q-s-w-r
qaswara I 95a, 100a; V 245b, 246a, 247b
q-ṣ-ṣ II 428b, 435b; V 432b
qaṣṣa III 517b, 524a; IV 302b, 443b; V 8a, 111a, 541b
qaṣṣ III 589b; V 207a

qiṣṣa, pl. *qiṣaṣ* I 62a, 239a, 496b, 533b; II 11a, 279a, 335a, 337a, 376b, 394b, 404b, 435b, 448a, 509a, 562b; III 2a, 53a, 80a, 81a, 83a, 138a, 290a, 290b, 291a, 517a, 517b, 539a, 541a, 542a, 542b; IV 61a, 61b, 436a, 436b, 437a, 531b, 606a; V 30b, 31b, 32a, 41a, 44a, 147b, 417a, 495b, 497a

qiṣaṣ al-anbiyāʾ I 62a, 228a, 496b; II 11a, 279a, 335a, 337a, 376b, 392b, 394b, 404b, 509a, 562b; III 2a, 53a, 80a, 81a, 83a, 138a, 253b, 290a, 290b, 291a, 388b, 539b, 570b, 606a; IV 315a; V 221a

qiṣās al-gharānīq IV 531b

qaṣaṣ III 55b, 512a, 512b, 517b, 522b, 541a; IV 61a, 61b, 62a, 302b, 386b

qiṣāṣ III 193a, 253b, 388b, 570b; IV 315a; V 221a, 231b, 432b, 514b

qāṣṣ, pl. *quṣṣāṣ* I 497a; II 102a, 106b, 381a; III 177b, 515b, 587b; IV 62b; V 30b, 221a

q-ṣ-b

qaṣaba III 336b

q-ṣ-d III 402a

qaṣada III 402a

muqtaṣid III 402a, 402b

qaṣīda II 300a, 301a, 301b, 302a, 528b; III 115b, 196b, 219b, 224a, 408b, 584b; IV 55b, 57a, 57b, 471a, 472a, 473a

maqāṣid IV 144a

q-ṣ-r

qaṣura V 246a

qāṣirāt II 456a; V 125b

qaṣr, pl. *quṣūr* I 163b, 165b; II 210b, 458b; IV 376a

qaṣar II 210b

qaṣṣār I 123a

qiṣār II 262b

quṣayrā I 24b

maqṣūra II 207a; III 429a, 429b, 430a, 430b, 433a, 433b

q-ṣ-f
qāṣif I 52a, 53a, 54a; IV 531a
q-ṣ-w
aqṣā I 125a; IV 64a
q-ḍ-b
qaḍb I 41b; II 4a, 305b
q-ḍ-y II 268b; III 65a
qaḍā I 399a, 442a, 446b; II 185a, 186b, 362b; III 65a, 65b; IV 65a; V 542b, 543a, 544a
qaḍāʾ I 225b, 442a, 446b, 507a, 516a, 516b, 517a; II 59a, 185a, 186b, 267b, 268b, 269a, 508b; III 64b, 65a; IV 72b, 84a, 86a; V 380a
qaḍāʾ wa-(l-)qadar I 225b; II 508b; IV 72b, 86a
qāḍī, pl. *quḍāt* I 33a; III 65a, 252b; IV 386b, 388b, 490a, 575b; V 217b, 305b, 496b
q-ṭ-b
quṭb, pl. *aqṭāb* IV 62a; V 154b
q-ṭ-r
qiṭr II 210b; III 383a
qaṭirān II 210b
q-ṭ-r-b
quṭrubī III 246b
q-ṭ-ṭ
qaṭṭ IV 130a
q-ṭ-ʿ
maqṭūʿ V 335a
munqaṭiʿ II 367a; IV 81b
qaṭʿ I 122a; II 162a
qaṭʿiyya IV 144a
qiṭʿ I 501a
quṭṭāʿ IV 364b
maqṭaʿ, pl. *maqāṭiʿ* IV 481a
q-ṭ-f
qiṭf, pl. *quṭūf* I 41b
q-ṭ-m-r
qiṭmīr I 494b; V 474b
q-ṭ-n
yaqṭīn II 217a, 305b; III 395b
q-ʿ-d III 84a; IV 14b
qaʿada II 569a
qāʿidūn III 36a
qaʿīd III 177b
quʿūd IV 485b

maqʿad IV 13a, 14b
q-f-r
qāfūr I 287b
qaf[f]ūr I 287b
q-f-l
qufl, pl. *aqfāl* II 546a
q-f-w
qaffā IV 291a
qāfiya IV 477b; V 168b
q-l-b
qalaba I 497b
iqlāb IV 375a
taqallub IV 305a
qalb, pl. *qulūb* I 82a, 87b, 91b; II 64b, 161a, 324a, 364a, 387a, 394b, 406b, 407a, 408a, 409a, 409b, 502a, 547b; III 358b, 359a, 442a; IV 117b, 293a, 375a, 573a; V 277b
q-l-d
taqlīd V 316b
muqallida II 422b
qilāda, pl. *qalāʾid* I 403b; III 76b
miqlād, pl. *maqālīd* II 231a, 546b
q-l-l
aqalla II 367a
aqall II 422b
q-l-m
qalam, pl. *aqlām* I 137a; II 186b, 257b, 413b, 484b, 544b, 545a; III 189a, 191b, 591a; V 558a
q-l-w
qalā II 219a
q-m-r
qamar III 414b; IV 107a, 108b, 217a
qimār II 280b, 282a
q-m-ṣ
qamīṣ I 346b
q-m-ʿ
miqmaʿa, pl. *maqāmiʿ* II 546a
q-m-l
qummal I 95a
q-n-t
qanata V 556a
qānit, pl. *qānitūn* IV 223a
qānitāt II 291a; IV 222b, 223a
qunūt II 76a; III 236b; V 540a
IV 222b; V 222b

sūrat al-qunūt IV 223a
q-n-ṭ
qaniṭa I 521a, 522a
qanūṭ III 224a
q-n-ṭ-r I 522a
qinṭār, pl. *qanāṭīr* I 259a; II 234a, 545b; III 335a, 336b; V 474a, 474b
q-n-n
qinn V 58a
q-n-w / q-n-y
qinwān I 42b, 494b
qanat I 43b
q-h-r
qāhir, pl. *qāhirūn* III 583b, 584a
qahr III 583a, 583b; IV 210a
qahhār II 320b; III 584a; IV 142b, 212a
taqhar III 584a
q-w-b
qāb I 177b; III 333a; IV 60b; V 473a
qāba qawsayn I 177b; IV 60b; V 473a
q-w-t
muqīt II 217a
qūt, pl. *aqwāt* II 217a; V 178b
q-w-s III 332b, 333a
qāsa III 333a
qaws II 545b, 546a; III 332b, 333a; V 473a
qawsayn II 545b; III 333a
q-w-l I 246b; II 2a; III 109b; V 541b, 547a
qāla I 32a, 235b, 250b, 274b, 324a, 421b, 449b, 453a, 454a, 455b; II 2a, 258b, 261b, 351a, 365b, 366a, 386a; III 108b, 585b; IV 310b, 311a, 387a, 442a, 446b, 463a, 463b, 483a; V 108b, 109b, 247b, 541b, 544a, 547a, 501a
qul I 250b, 324a; II 2a; III 585b; IV 310b, 442a
qul huwa llāhu aḥad see ʾ-l-h
wa-yaqūlūn… fa-qul II 261b; IV 311a
taqawwala II 529b; III 116a
qawl, pl. *aqwāl*, *aqāwīl* I 447a; II 390b, 393a, 481b, 532a; III 15a, 15b, 162a, 513a, 528a; IV 141b, 290a, 441b; V 21a, 78b, 541b, 547a, 547b
maqāla, pl. *maqālāt* II 420b

q-w-m IV 434a
qāma V 287b
maqāma III 517b
qāʾim I 502b; IV 229b, 601b
umma(tun) qāʾima(tun) I 374a; V 431a, 437b
taqwīm II 327b
aqāma III 495b
muqīm III 504a
iqāma IV 144b; V 499a, 556a
istaqāma V 485a
mustaqīm I 131b; IV 29a
qawm I 261b, 369a, 375b, 377a, 422b, 512b; II 59a, 448b, 462b, 510b; III 53a, 97a, 109a, 232a, 381a, 421b, 425a, 443a, 486b; IV 299b, 425a, 538b, 584b; V 364a, 389a
qawm al-fāsiqīn II 59a, 510b
qawm khaṣimūn I 512b
al-qawm al-khāsirūn I 377a
qawm al-ṣāliḥīn II 448b
qawm tubbaʿ V 389a
qawm yūnus III 53a
qiyām I 465b; III 140b; IV 219b, 493b
qiyāma I 86a, 204b, 206a; II 47a; III 136a, 139a, 141b; IV 530b
qayyim III 513a, 513b; IV 482b; V 385b
qayyima IV 482b
qayyūm II 320a; III 141b, 182b, 183a, 513b; V 500b
qawwām, pl. *qawwāmūn* II 76a, 202b, 203a, 290a; V 539b
aqwam I 356b
maqām, pl. *maqāmāt* II 205a, 326a, 458b, 552b; III 76b, 78b, 340b, 427a, 446b; IV 13a, 14b, 104b, 350a, 380b, 381a, 381b, 383a, 476b, 514a, 514b; V 135a, 141b
maqām amīn IV 13a, 14b
maqām ibrāhīm II 205a; III 76b, 78b, 340b, 427a; IV 104b, 514a, 514b; V 141b, 383b
maqām maḥmūd II 326a, 552b; III 446b
maqām maʿlūm IV 350a
maqāmahu wa-martabatahu IV 350a
q-w-y
quwwa, pl. *quwan* I 188b; II 322a, 353a; IV 147b, 210a

qawiyy, qawī II 320a, 322a; IV 5b, 212a

q-y-d

taqyīd III 158a

muqayyad V 333b

q-y-s III 332b, 333a

qays III 332a

qiyās I 11b, 160a, 198a; II 556a; III 67b, 155a, 161b, 163a, 164a, 168b, 332b; IV 75b, 76a, 76b, 144a

miqyās III 303b, 333a

miqyās al-nīl 303b

q-y-n

qayn II 516b

qayna V 58a

-kāf-

kārīz I 43b

k-ʾ-s

kaʾs I 166a, 490a, 490b; II 219a, 276a; IV 18b

kāghadh IV 587a

k-b-d II 447b

kabad II 306a

k-b-r II 541b

kabura II 365b

takbīr II 82b, 85a, 92a; IV 180b, 219a, 220a, 220b, 232b, 350b, 378a

takbīra II 92a

takabbara I 395b; II 43b, 541b; IV 130b

mutakabbir, pl. *mutakabbirūn* I 158b, 159a, 159b, 160a, 241b, 382a, 395b; III 583b; IV 263b, 264a, 264b

takabbur I 159b, 160a

istakbara I 159a, 160b, 161a, 395b, 453a; II 541b, 542a, 543a; IV 263b, 309b, 482b; V 6a, 468b

mustakbir, pl. *mustakbirūn* I 161a, 161b; II 541b; III 583a; IV 263b

istikbār I 159a, 159b, 160a, 161a, 161b, 220b, 395b; IV 263b

kibr I 159a, 159b, 395b; III 543a

kibar V 573b

kabīr, pl. *kubarāʾ* I 158b, 159b; II 82b, 320a; IV 5b, 130b, 263b; V 430a

kabīra, pl. *kabāʾir* — I 23a, 159b; IV 72b, 74b; V 19a, 19b, 20a

akbar — II 82b; IV 220b, 378a

allāhu akbar — II 82b; IV 220b, 378a; see also ʾ-l-h

kubrā — II 193b

kibriyāʾ — I 158b, 159a, 159b, 242a; IV 264b

k-t-b — I 244b; II 26a; III 591b, 592b; V 402b, 558a

kataba — I 242b, 243b, 244b, 245a; II 67b, 68a, 83b, 262b, 322a; III 190b, 191a, 424b, 591b, 592b, 605a; IV 594a; V 175a, 402b

kātib — III 191b, 310b; V 204a

maktūb — I 29b; II 493a; V 307a

mukātab — I 289b; V 58a, 469a

iktaba — II 492b, 493a; III 188b

katb — II 93a

kitāb, pl. *kutub* — I 14b, 70b, 140a, 189a, 222b, 242b, 243a, 243b, 244a, 244b, 245a, 245b, 246a, 246b, 247a, 247b, 248a, 249a, 249b, 250a, 250b, 251a, 325b, 328b, 372a, 372b, 388a, 392a, 392b, 403b, 486b, 522b, 523a; II 27a, 82a, 108a, 111a, 186b, 254a, 254b, 255a, 257b, 269a, 310a, 311b, 342a, 376b, 412a, 420b, 423b, 492b, 495a, 499a, 500b, 544b; III 30b, 124b, 140b, 177a, 177b, 178a, 178b, 186b, 188a, 189b, 190a, 191a, 255b, 275b, 288a, 404a, 424b, 425b, 441a, 441b, 442a, 442b, 452a, 482a, 486a, 505b, 508a, 508b, 509a, 509b, 514b, 566a, 585a, 591a, 591b, 592a, 592b, 593a, 605a; IV 2b, 3b, 36a, 36b, 37a, 37b, 38b, 41b, 42b, 102b, 120a, 127b, 152b, 153a, 153b, 166a, 169a, 224a, 261b, 293b, 296b, 297a, 297b, 303a, 312b, 351a, 355a, 403b, 438b, 439a, 440a, 457a, 468b, 559a, 559b, 560a, 560b, 561a, 561b, 562a, 569b, 587b, 597a; V 19a, 44b, 68b, 167a, 173a, 173b,

197a, 271b, 284b, 317b, 320a, 400b, 401b, 419b, 422a, 425a, 446a, 483a, 493a

kitāb allāh II 27a; IV 560a, 596b

kitāb allāh al-nāṭiq IV 597a

kitāb kalām allāh III 514a, 514b

kitāb maknūn II 412a, 423b; IV 261b

kitāb marqūm II 500b; III 591a; IV 102b

kitāb mawqūt I 328b; IV 224a

kitāb muʾajjal I 244a; II 269a

kitāb mubīn I 523a; II 257b; III 186b, 592a; V 284b

al-kitāb al-munīr IV 297a

kitāb mūsā III 425b; IV 3b

kitāb mutashābih I 70b; III 509b

kitāb wa-l-ḥikma IV 3b; V 317b

kitāban anzalnāhu ilayka III 508a

ahl al-kitāb I 207a, 247a, 247b, 309b, 325a, 377b; II 182a, 496b, 499a, 544b; III 141a, 189b, 484a, 508b; IV 36a, 37b, 38a, 39a, 39b, 40a, 40b, 41a, 42a, 42b, 43a, 120a, 129a, 151b, 153a, 303b, 309a, 402b, 403a, 403b, 560a; V 56a, 131b, 417b, 437b

alladhīna ātaynāhum al-kitāb I 222b

alladhīna ūtū l-kitāb I 222b, 247a; IV 36a, 38b, 42b, 120a, 152b, 153b

alladhīna ūtū naṣīban mina l-kitābi III 30b; IV 36a

umm al-kitāb I 247b, 248a, 523a; II 412a, 423a; IV 297a, 560b; see also ʾ-m-m

kitābiya IV 101a

kitāba III 189b, 605a; V 58a, 60a

kuttāb I 140a; III 591a; V 209b, 225b, 536a

maktab V 209b, 536a

k-t-m I 540a; IV 572b

katama I 540a; V 479b

katm I 541b; V 479b

kitmān I 540a, 541a, 541b

k-th-b

kathīb IV 530b, 531a

k-th-r

kaththara III 549b

kathīr V 125a

kawthar I 88b; III 141a, 446b; IV 61a; V 36b, 37a, 125a, 466b
akthar II 422b
k-d-ḥ
kādiḥ III 184a
k-dh-b I 381b; II 58b, 181a; V 434b
kadhaba I 235b; III 181a; IV 309b
kādhib, pl. *kādhibūn* II 462b; III 425a; IV 103b, 483b
kādhiba IV 103b
kadhdhaba II 251b, 370b; III 181b, 524a; IV 309b, 319a, 474a; V 6a
mukadhdhib, pl. *mukadhdhibūn* I 381b
takdhīb I 220b; V 440a
kadhdhāb, pl. *kadhdhābūn* II 530a, 540a; III 460b; IV 22b
sāḥir kadhdhāb II 540a, 540b
k-r-b
mukarrib I 151b
k-r-s
kursī I 446a; II 275b, 276b, 325b, 410b; III 307b, 308b, 431b; V 276b, 277a
āyat al-kursī V 277a, 277b
kurrāsa, pl. *karārīs* IV 587b
k-r-m II 447a
karrama II 447b
mukarrama III 513a
mukram II 447b
mukramīn II 447b
karma I 25a
karāma, pl. *karāmāt* II 555a; III 396a, 396b, 397a, 460a, 575b
karīm, pl. *karāʾim* I 212b; II 320b, 447b; III 506b, 513a; V 179a, 320a, 594a
maqām karīm II 447b
kirām V 118b
makruma II 448a
k-r-h
kariha II 225b
makrūh II 225b; III 175a, 366a, 366b; IV 270a, 492a, 495a, 495b
karraha III 235b
ikrāh V 290b, 292b; see also d-y-n
karāha II 282a
k-s-b
kasaba IV 85a, 86b, 431a, 432a, 433b,

459a, 273b; V 268a, 312a

iktasaba III 121a; IV 85a, 86b, 432b

iktisāb I 517a; III 254a; V 549a

muktasib IV 433b

kasb I 517a; III 254a; IV 431a, 431b, 433b; V 268a, 269a, 487b

k-s-r

kasra I 279a

k-s-f

kusūf IV 218b

k-s-w

kiswa IV 175b; V 91a, 390a

kisāʾ, pl. *aksiya* I 390a; II 177a; IV 50a

ahl al-kisāʾ I 390a; II 177a

k-sh-f

kāshifa IV 103b

takshīf II 100a

kashf I 92a; IV 103b; V 154a

k-ʿ-b

kaʿba III 76b, 79b; V 78b

k-f-ḥ

kifāḥ I 161a

k-f-r I 119b, 218a

kafara I 119a, 119b, 120b, 221a; II 57b, 154a, 166a, 171b, 510a; III 31b; V 6a, 293b, 369a, 379b

kāfir, pl. *kāfirūn, kuffār* I 110a, 112b, 120a, 158b, 160a, 218a, 221a, 266b, 268b, 375b, 381b, 422b, 493a; II 24a, 45b, 53a, 66a, 74a, 149b; II 165b, 166a, 166b, 170a, 170b, 258b, 415b, 417b, 471a, 489a, 538a; III 24b, 26a, 27a, 47a, 239b, 338b, 529a, 558b; IV 89b, 118b, 120b, 129a, 133a, 133b, 309a; V 15a, 380a, 418a, 436a

takfīr IV 83a, 531b; V 198a

kufr I 77b, 119a, 119b, 120, 158b, 160a, 218a, 220b, 221a, 221b, 235b, 297b, 375b, 376a, 381a, 493a, 493b, 540b; II 43a, 57a, 62b, 63b, 66a, 137a, 165b, 166a, 166b, 370a, 422a, 488a, 489a, 501b, 503a, 510a; III 70b, 181a, 531b, 564a; IV 75a, 118b, 120b,

121a, 133a, 166a, 166b, 172a, 255b, 283a, 409b, 488a, 534a; v 20b, 446b
umam/a'imma al-kufr ii 498a; iii 95b
kaffār i 221a
kaffāra i 186b, 187a, 188a; iii 563a, 565b, 566a; iv 148a; v 449a
kafūr i 221a, 287b, 288a, 490b; v 62b
k-f-f
kaff ii 401a
k-f-l i 528a
kafala i 528a
kaffala i 528a
wa-kaffalahā zakariyyā i 528b
takaffala i 528a, 528b
kifl i 528a
kafāla iv 431a
kafīl i 379b, 528b
k-f-y
kāfin ii 385b
kāfiya ii 189a
k-l-l
kull ii 363a
kulla i 23b
kall iii 228a
kalāla ii 385a, 519b, 523b, 524a, 524b; iii 98a, 98b, 99a
k-l-b
kālib i 546a
mukallabīn i 545b
kalb i 95a, 545b, 546a; v 52a
k-l-f
kallafa iv 431a, 432b
mukallaf i 122a; v 135b
taklīf i 555b, 556a; iv 73a, 431a, 432b, 433a, 433b; v 135b
takālīf i 555b
k-l-m i 246b; iii 109b; v 108b, 541b, 547a
kallama iii 423b, 511a, 511b; iv 292a, 292a, 440b; v 108b, 110a, 110b, 541b, 546a, 546b, 547b
taklīm iv 440b; v 111a
mutakallim, pl. *mutakallimūn* i 90a, 104b, 115b, 436b, 463b, 468a, 469a; ii 111a, 270a, 527b, 531a, 532a, 532b, 533b, 534b;

iv 75b, 80a, 82a, 82b, 83a, 83b, 87a, 88b, 287b, 549a, 564b, 565a; v 111b, 150a, 309b

takallama v 108b, 111a

kalima pl. *kalimāt* i 25b; ii 443b; iii 14b, 15a, 41b, 29, 294b, 531a, 533a, 556b; iv 296a, 476b; v 16b, 289b, 435a, 435b, 498b, 499b, 501a, 502b, 503a, 503b, 504b, 541b, 545b, 546a, 547b

kalām i 85a, 106a, 160a, 198a, 436b, 471a, 529b, 530a; ii 74b, 95a, 114a, 116a, 185a, 186b, 527a, 527b, 531a, 532b, 533b; iii 100b, 115a, 120a, 125b, 126b, 424a, 467a, 511a, 511b, 514a; iv 67b, 72a, 84a, 125b, 133b, 445a; v 108b, 110a, 111a, 112a, 150a, 224a, 306b, 387b, 541b, 547b

kalām allāh i 471a; ii 95a; iii 125b, 467a, 511a; iv 133b, 262b, 287a, 413b, 445a, 493b; v 111a, 541b, 547b

kalīm ii 324a; iv 292a

kalīm allāh ii 324a; iv 292a

k-m-m

kumm, pl. *akmām* i 494b

k-n-d

kanūd ii 372a

k-n-z

kanz ii 189a

k-n-s

kanīsa i 335b; v 567b

k-n-y

kunya iii 501b, 502a

k-h-f

kahf i 292b

k-h-n iii 246b

kahana iii 246b

kāhin, pl. *kuhhān*, *kahana* i 148a, 324a, 542b, 543a, 543b, 544b; ii 238a, 255b, 256a, 319a, 320a, 528a, 528b, 540a; iii 127b, 220b, 231a, 246b, 247a, 451a, 480b, 489b, 498a, 578b, 587b, 588a, 589b; iv 112a, 112b, 113a, 164b, 216b, 255b, 259b, 295a, 311b, 334a, 462b, 463a,

	463b, 464a, 465b, 473a, 477a; v 78a, 168b, 172a, 420b, 426a, 426b
kāhina	III 246b
kihāna	I 542b, 544b; II 239b
kahāna	III 246b
k-w-b	
kūb, pl. *akwāb*	I 166a, 490a, 490b; II 276a; V 123a
k-w-d	
kāda	IV 309b
k-w-k-b	
kawkab, pl. *kawākib*	III 202b, 415b; IV 106b, 107a, 108b, 109a
k-w-n	
kāna	I 230b, 244b, 288a, 447a, 453a, 474b, 475b, 516b, 535b; II 258b, 327b, 366b, 425a; III 395b; IV 61a, 354b, 483a; V 109a, 290a, 437a, 542b, 543a, 544a
kun fa-yakūn	I 474b, 475b, 516b; II 327b; IV 61a
kāʾin	II 100b; V 322a
kawn	III 187b
makān	I 114a; III 3b; V 475a
k-y-d	
kayd	II 162a; III 492a; V 479b, 531a
kayd al-nisāʾ	III 492a
k-y-f	
kayf	I 105b; II 160b, 286a; III 385b
bi-lā kayf	I 105b; II 286a; III 385b
bi-lā kayf wa-lā tashbīh	II 160b
k-y-l	IV 333a, 334a
kāla	III 334a
ikyāl	I 490b; II 544b
iktāla	III 334a
kayl	II 545a; III 334a, 335b; V 473b, 474a
kayl baʿīr	III 334a; V 473b, 474a
mikyāl	II 545a; III 334a; V 313a
kīmiyā	III 247b; IV 165b

-lām-

l-ʾ-t	
lāt	II 352b

l-ʾ-k
malak, pl. *malāʾika* — i 84b, 178b; ii 404a; iii 45a, 45b; iv 376a; v 118a
l-ʾ-l-ʾ
luʾluʾ — i 438b, 439a; iii 384a; v 125b
l-ʾ-m
luʾm — i 191b
laʾīm — ii 491a
lāhūt — i 555a, 555b; v 149a, 158b
l-b-b
lubb, pl. *albāb* — ii 407a, 409a, 548b; iii 102a, 102b, 373a
ūlū l-albāb — ii 407a, 409a, 548b; iii 102a, 102b, 373a
l-b-s
labasa — iv 591b
talbīs — i 541b; iv 75a
libās — i 346a, 498a; ii 175a; iii 548b
l-b-n
talbīna — ii 446b
laban — ii 218a; iii 391a, 392a
l-b-y
labbaya — ii 85a; iv 233a
labbayka allāhumma labbayka — ii 85a; iv 233a
talbiya — ii 297a, 297b, 480a; iv 233a, 532a
l-t-ẓ
latẓ — iii 125a
l-t-f
lutf — iv 74a
l-ḥ-d — ii 420b; iii 114a, 280a
alḥada — iii 114a
ilḥād — ii 137a, 531a; iv 122b
mulḥid, pl. *malāḥida* — ii 471b, 531a
l-ḥ-q
alḥiqa — ii 33a
l-ḥ-m
laḥm — i 80a; ii 218b, 220a
luḥūm — i 80b
malāḥim — ii 101b, 242a; iii 139a
l-ḥ-n — iii 109b
laḥn — i 82b; iii 109b, 120a; iv 356a
l-kh-ṣ
talkhīṣ — ii 378a
l-z-b
lāzib — i 24a

l-z-m
lāzim IV 374b, 376a
ilzām V 449b
l-s-n III 109b
lisān, pl. *alsina, alsun* I 82b, 83a, 132a, 203b; II 210a, 226b; III 108a, 108b, 109a, 110a, 112a, 113a, 113b, 114a, 114b, 117a, 124b, 443a, 473a; IV 299b, 374b, 439b, 566a
lisān al-ʿarab II 210a
lisān ʿarabī III 109a, 124b; IV 566a
bi-lisānin ʿarabiyyin mubīnin III 110a, 113b, 114b, 473a; IV 439b
lisn I 132a
l-ṭ-f
luṭf II 506b
laṭīf II 320b; V 145b
laṭāʾif IV 158a, 573a; V 140a, 141b, 144a, 145b, 148a, 159a
l-ẓ-y
talaẓẓa II 414b
laẓā II 49b, 210a, 414b, 419a; III 203b
l-ʿ-b II 280a, 281b; III 400b
laʿiba IV 309b
laʿib III 182a
luʿb II 281a, 281b
l-ʿ-n
laʿana I 491b
laʿna I 29a
liʿān I 29a, 492a; II 520b; III 279b; V 498a
l-gh-b
lughūb I 443b
l-gh-w III 109b
laghw I 187a; III 108a, 562a, 565a, 565b; IV 103a, 482b
lugha, pl. *lughāt* I 529b, 530a; III 108a, 109b, 112a, 112b, 115a, 117a, 122a, 124a, 125b; V 143a, 333a
lāghiya III 108a; IV 103a, 482b
l-f-ẓ
lafẓ I 71a; III 159a, 511a, 605a; IV 445b, 447b, 564a; V 112a, 160b
lafẓa IV 476b
tallaffuẓī IV 376a
l-q-b
laqab III 12a, 12b

l-q-m
laqima III 242b
l-q-n
talqīn I 264b
l-q-y
alqā IV 294b, 295a, 296a
ilqāʾ I 2b
mulqiyāt IV 294b
talaqqā I 448a, 456a
mutalaqqiyān(i) III 177b; V 119a
liqāʾ 91b
l-m-ḥ
talmīḥ III 215a; V 392b
talmīḥāt IV 56a
lamḥ III 138a; V 287b, 288a
ka-lamḥi l-baṣar III 138a; V 288a
lamḥ bi-l-baṣar V 287b
l-m-z
lamaza II 344a; IV 309b
lamz II 343b
lumaza II 344a
l-m-s
lamasa I 412a
lāmasa I 412a; IV 501a
l-m-m
lamam I 29a; V 19a, 19b
l-h-b
lahab II 414b
l-h-j
lahja, pl. *lahjāt* I 128a
l-h-m IV 294b
alhama IV 294b; V 409b
ilhām I 46a; IV 442a; V 109b
l-h-w
lahw I 160b
l-w-ḥ
talwīḥ III 215a
lawḥ [lūḥ], pl. *alwāḥ* I 14b, 87b, 157b, 160b, 365a, 467b; II 95a, 186b, 413b, 544b, 546b; III 189b, 424a, 424b, 591a; IV 261b, 270b, 297a, 570a, 587b, 604a; V 73a, 150a, 301a, 404a, 422a
(al-)lawḥ (al-)maḥfūẓ I 87b, 92a, 467b; II 95a, 413b; III 189b; IV 261b, 297a, 570a; V 150a, 404a

lawwāḥa II 414b
l-w-ṭ
lāʾiṭ III 232b
lūṭiyya III 232b; IV 584b
liwāṭ IV 584b
l-w-n
lawn, pl. *alwān* I 212b, 361b, 362a
l-y-s
laysa I 466b; IV 82b
l-y-l
layl, pl. *layālin* I 36a, 328a, 498a, 499a, 499b, 501a, 503a; III 335a, 417b; IV 102b, 217a, 222a, 222b, 279a, 342b; V 280b, 282a, 282b, 476a, 556b
(min) ānāʾ al-layl I 328a, 498a; IV 220b, 222a; V 282b
layla, pl. *layālin* I 178a, 326a, 444a, 445a, 449a, 501b, 503a; II 84a, 89a, 91a, 269b, 412b; III 222a, 410a, 413b, 414a, 417b, 442a, 537b; IV 222a, 293a, 340a, 342b, 343a, 343b, 346b; V 127a, 279a, 284a, 284b, 431b, 476a
layla mubāraka III 414a; IV 343a
laylat al-barāʾa III 414a; V 127a
laylat al-qadr I 178a, 326a, 501b; II 84a, 89a, 91a, 181b, 182b, 183a, 204a, 269b, 381b, 412b; III 222a, 410a, 413b, 414a, 417b, 442a, 537b; IV 102b, 293a, 340a, 342b, 343b, 346b; V 284b, 431b
l-y-n
līna I 494b
layyin III 115a

-mīm-

m-t-ʿ III 60a; V 232a
tamattaʿa IV 98b
tamattuʿ II 180b; IV 98b, 99a
istamtaʿa IV 99a, 582b; V 232b
istimtāʿ IV 98b; V 232a
mutʿa IV 98b, 99a, 99b, 582b, 600b; V 232a, 232b, 233a, 527b

matāʿ, pl. *amtiʿa* i 398b; ii 275a, 275b; iii 59b, 60a, 60b, 182a; v 454b

m-t-n

matn i 388a; ii 376b, 385b

matīn ii 320b

m-th-l

tamthīl i 106b; ii 96b; iii 384b; iv 88b

mumaththilūn i 106b

mumāthala iii 128b

tamaththala v 445b

mithl iii 201b; v 18b

laysa ka-mithlihi shayʾ(un) iii 201b; v 18b

mathal, pl. *amthāl* i 54b, 72a, 512b; ii 386a, 434b; iii 517b; iv 6b, 9a, 10a, 10b, 11a; v 3a, 13b, 14a, 14b, 15b, 16a, 124b, 125a, 182a, 321a, 322a, 333b

mathalu l-jannati v 124b

mathula, pl. *mathulāt* i 530a; iv 453b; v 164a

muthlāt i 530a

mithāl iv 77a

timthāl, pl. *tamāthīl* i 162b, 165a, 167b; ii 43b, 476b, 481a, 481b; v 77a

m-j-d i 27a

majjada ii 83a

majd ii 315b; iii 504b

majīd ii 315b, 320a; iii 506b, 513a

m-j-s

majūs ii 22a; iii 244a, 246b; iv 152a, 407b, 511b; v 56a

m-ḥ-d

tamḥīd iv 220a, 220b

m-ḥ-ṣ

maḥḥaṣa v 362b

m-ḥ-ḍ-r-m

muḥaḍram iv 474b

m-ḥ-n ii 537b, 538a

imtaḥana ii 538a; v 362b

miḥna i 469b, 471a; ii 413a, 531b, 538a, 538b, 539a; iii 468a; iv 73b, 81b, 142b; v 18a

m-ḥ-w

maḥw i 77a; iv 163a, 174a

m-kh-kh

mukhkh ii 83b

m-d-ḥ
madīḥ, pl. *madā'iḥ* ii 93b
m-d-d
madda i 504a; ii 2b; v 282b, 544a
amadda iv 354b
madda iv 376a
madd ii 386b; iv 375b, 376a
madad ii 555a
mudda v 278b
midād ii 544b, 545a; iii 191b, 531a, 591a; v 558a
m-d-n
madīna, pl. *madā'in/mudun* see d-y-n
m-r-'
imra' i 299a
imru' v 92a
mar' ii 289b
imra'a ii 289b, 290a, 290b, 291a, 292b, 352b; iii 92a, 95b
muruwwa i 458b; ii 70a, 301b, 450a; iv 111a, 255a, 395a, 400b
m-r-j
maraja i 443a, 445b; iv 7a
mārij iii 48b
marj ii 213a
m-r-j-n
marjān i 438b, 439a; iii 384a
m-r-kh
markh ii 213a, v 359a
m-r-d
mārid ii 487a; v 486b
mumarrad i 162b
m-r-r
mirra iii 495b
m-r-ḍ
mariḍa ii 501b
maraḍ, pl. *amrāḍ* ii 407b, 501a, 501b, 502a; iii 349b, 358a
marīḍ, pl. *marḍā* ii 501b; iii 349b
m-r-w
marwa iv 518a
m-z-j
mizāj i 288a
m-z-n
muzn v 461b, 462b

m-s-ḥ III 333a, 333b; IV 498b, 499b
masaḥa III 10b, 12a, 12b; IV 372a, 372b
masḥ III 333b
massāḥ III 333b, 334a
misāḥa III 333b
masīḥ I 102a; II 156a, 508a; III 10b, 11b, 12a, 12b, 138b, 294a; IV 38b, 39a; V 251a
al-masīḥ al-dajjāl III 138a
masīḥiyya IV 406b
m-s-d
masad I 494b; II 546b
m-s-s I 412a
massa II 348
misās I 274b; IV 524b
mass II 540b
m-s-k IV 277a
masaka I 443a
misk V 62b
miskīn, pl. *masākīn* III 63a; IV 129a, 209a
m-s-y see also ʾ-m-s
amsā I 504b
masāʾ I 504a
m-sh-q
mashq I 136b, 141a
m-sh-y
mashā I 241b
mashshāʾ II 344a
m-ṣ-r
miṣr III 208b
amṣār I 217b, 333a
maṣīr II 31a
m-ḍ-gh
muḍgha I 3a, 230b, 231a; II 328a; V 522b
m-ḍ-y
maḍā II 434b
māḍī V 286b
m-ṭ-r V 470b
amṭara V 130a, 470b
maṭar V 461b, 465b, 470b
m-ʿ-z
maʿz I 94b; II 218a
m-q-l
muql IV 54a

m-k-th
mukth I 250b
m-k-r
makara III 18a; IV 309b
makr I 376b, 377a; II 322a; IV 471b; V 479b
makr allāhī II 322a
m-k-k
makka III 337b
m-k-n
tamkīn V 292b
imkān IV 79a

m-l-ʾ
malaʾ, pl. *amlāʾ* I 22b, 297a, 369a, 406b, 462b, 463a; II 296b, 432b; III 338a, 420b, 421b, 422a, 422b, 423a, 583a, 583b; IV 130b, 131a
m-l-ḥ
milḥ I 446a; II 212b, 217b; V 126a
milḥ ujāj I 446a; II 212b; V 126a
m-l-ṣ
imlāṣ I 2b
m-l-q
imlāq III 182a
malaq III 121a
m-l-k III 90b; V 103b
malaka II 29b; IV 184a, 288a; V 57a
mālik, pl. *mālikūn* I 89b; II 83a, 189b, 321b; III 91a, 184a, 184b, 185b, 186b; IV 186b, 187a; V 119b
mamlūk IV 184b, 185a
malk II 189b
milk, pl. *amlāk* II 226a; IV 185b
mulk I 27b, 188b, 496a; III 90b, 91a, 91b, 92a, 92b, 93a, 93b, 94a, 267b, 504b; IV 127b, 142a, 184a, 185a, 186b, 210a, 212a; V 103b
malak II 404a; III 139b
malik, pl. *mulūk* II 29b, 91b, 189b, 321b; III 90b, 91a, 91b, 92a, 93b; IV 128a, 130a, 184a, 186b, 187a; V 145b
malakūt III 90b; IV 127b, 184a; V 157b, 158b, 258a

m-l-l see also m-l-y

amalla III 592b
milla, pl. *milal* I 6a, 118b, 200a, 325a, 330b, 373a, 373b, 462b; II 274b, 313b, 329a, 402b, 431b, 569b; III 27b, 38a, 340b, 445b; IV 130b, 396a, 400a, 401a, 401b, 403b, 414a; V 243b, 263b
millat ibrāhīm I 6a, 325a, 330b, 373a, 381a; II 569b; III 38a, 340b; IV 396a; V 243b

m-l-y see also m-l-l
amlā II 492a, 492b, 493a; III 188b; V 400b
*imlā*ʾ II 493b; IV 588a

m-n-j
manj II 213a

m-n-ʿ IV 307a
manaʿa I 450a, 453a
māniʿ IV 307b

m-n-n
mann II 217b
minna V 144b
manūn II 302a

m-n-y
tamannā IV 532b
*istimnā*ʾ IV 584a
manāyā II 302a
manāh [manāt] II 353a
umniyya IV 532b

m-h-d
mahd II 2b, 276a
mihād II 2b, 276a; IV 103b

m-h-r
mahr I 258b, 259a, 434b; IV 582a, 582b, 583b; V 79a, 313b, 453a, 481a, 528b, 529a

m-h-l
muhl II 211b; III 203a, 203b, 383a; V 572a

m-w-t/m-y-t
māta III 140a
amāta I 508a; III 148b; V 545a
mawt I 205a, 505b; II 45b; IV 486a
mayta I 291a, 291b; II 220a, 220b; V 55a
mumīt IV 435b

m-w-j
māja III 185a
mawj V 462a, 464b
m-w-l
māl, pl. *amwāl* II 334a; IV 3b, 288a, 288b, 289a; V 160b, 197a, 457b, 467b, 469a, 469b, 474b
m-w-h
māʾ I 42a; II 3a, 211a, 212a; III 203b, 263a, 530b; V 64a, 461b, 462a, 462b, 463a, 464b
māʾ dāfiq V 462a, 462b
māʾ mahīn V 462a, 462b
māʾ min al-samāʾ V 461b
māʾ ṣadīd II 211a; III 203b
[anzala] min al-samāʾ māʾ I 42b; V 462b
wa-jaʿalnā min al-māʾ kulla shayʾin ḥayyin III 530b
m-y-d
māda II 2b; III 16b
māʾida II 176a; III 16b, 396a; V 188a, 189b, 190a
m-y-z
tamyīz III 112a
m-y-l
māʾil I 136b, 348a

-nūn-

n-ʾ-s
nās I 324b, 377a, 397a, 416b, 422b; II 22a, 264a, 289a, 291b; III 229b, 425a, 443b; IV 96b, 299b, 304b, 490b; V 174b, 268b, 369b, 440a, 479a
nāsūt I 555a, 555b; V 158b
n-b-ʾ II 435b; III 536a
nabbaʾa I 442b, 452a; III 524b, 534a, 536a; IV 473b, 474a; V 108b, 541b
anbaʾa III 536b; V 110b
istanbaʾa III 536b
nabaʾ, pl. *anbāʾ* I 452b; II 435b; III 441a, 441b, 517b, 518a, 519a, 520b, 524a, 524b, 536b, 537a; IV 131b, 294b, 302b, 438b

anbāʾ al-ghayb II 241b; III 441a, 441b, 537a; IV 294b, 302b, 438b

n-b-t

anbata II 3b, 328a

nābita I 105a

nabāt I 40b, 42b, 440b; II 304b, 369b

n-b-dh

nabīdh V 481b

n-b-r

minbar, pl. *manābir* II 272b; III 6a, 307b, 428b, 429b, 430a, 430b, 435a; IV 226a; V 208a, 219a, 220b, 227a

n-b-ṭ

istinbāṭ III 215a; V 141b

mustanbaṭāt V 141b

nabaṭī II 228a

n-b-ʿ I 246b

yanbūʿ, pl. *yanābīʿ* I 42a; V 121b, 127b, 461b, 463b

n-b-h

tanabbuh IV 424a

n-b-y V 445b

nabī [nabiyy], pl. *nabiyyūn, anbiyāʾ* I 62a, 245b, 261a, 325a; II 264a, 353a, 499a, 563b, 567a; III 16a, 55b, 188b, 207a, 382b, 440b, 445a, 463a, 485b, 486b, 502a, 502b, 503a, 503b; IV 289a, 526b, 561a; V 69a, 96b, 140a, 174b, 402b, 445b, 501a, 574a

al-nabī al-ummī I 325a; II 499a; III 188b, 445a, 503b, 528a; IV 289a, 289b, 306a, 375a

nubuwwa I 371a; III 82b, 421b; IV 127b, 289b, 297a, 297b, 441b; V 534a, 574a

n-t-f

nutfa I 3a, 230b, 231a, 476b; II 328a; III 354b, 597a; V 267a, 462a, 522b

n-j-d

najd II 306a, 306b; IV 2a

najdān/najdayn II 306a, 306b; IV 2a

n-j-s

najas I 342b, 410b, 411a; III 33b; IV 132b, 499a, 502b, 504a

najāsa I 411a

najis I 344a, 411a; III 376b

najāshī IV 411a
n-j-m
najm, pl. *nujūm* I 36a, 204a; II 369b; III 202b, 561b; IV 102b, 106b, 107a, 108b, 109a, 217a; V 51b
najūman IV 444a
munajjaman I 250b; II 85b; IV 444a
n-j-w IV 523b
najjā I 518b, 519a; IV 523b
anjā I 518b, 519b; IV 523b
tanājī V 479b
najāt [najāh] I 486b; II 184a, 353a; III 423a; IV 524a
najwā II 63b; IV 496b; V 198a, 479b
munājāh, pl. *munājāt* I 86b; IV 292a; V 379b
n-ḥ-b
naḥb IV 485b, 486a
n-ḥ-r V 555b
naḥr III 339a; V 55a
n-ḥ-s
nuḥās II 546a; III 383a
n-ḥ-l
naḥala II 313b
intaḥala II 313b
naḥl I 95a
niḥla I 258b; II 313a, 313b
n-kh-l
nakhl I 42b, 44b, 494b; II 305a, 305b
nakhla, pl. *nakhīl* I 494b; II 305a, 305b
n-d-b
mandūb II 225a; III 159b, 175a
n-d-d
nidd, pl. *andād* II 476b, 478b
n-d-r
nadr II 362b
nādira III 517a
n-d-m
nādim, pl. *nādimūn* IV 428b
nadām IV 430b
n-d-y
nādā II 558b; IV 225b; V 110a, 541b
nādī II 558b; III 128a; V 36b
nādaya V 110a
tanādī II 558b
munādī I 113b; II 558b

nadwa	I 201a
n-dh-r	I 246b
nadhara	II 82b; III 562b
andhara	V 459b, 460a
nadhr, pl. *nudhūr*	I 403a; III 562b; IV 485b, 486a; V 449b, 460a
nadhīr	II 341b; III 382a, 440b, 442b, 503b, 512a; IV 3b, 486a; V 459b, 460a
nadhīr al-jaysh	V 459b
nadhīr al-qawm	V 459b
nadhīr al-ʿuryān	V 460a
mundhir	IV 3b; V 459b
n-r-d	
nard	II 281a, 281b
n-z-ʿ	I 513b
nāziʿāt	V 396b
nāzaʿa	I 513a
intizāʿ	III 215a
n-z-f	
anzafa	II 556a
n-z-l	I 246b; III 442a; IV 292b, 443a, 443b
nazala	I 530b; IV 292b, 293a; V 322b, 465b
nazzala	I 87a, 87b, 178b, 245b, 487a; II 424b, 442a; III 440a, 550b; IV 292b, 293a, 443a; V 8a, 115b, 302b, 423a
tanzīl	I 85b, 424b, 555b, 556a; III 505b, 506a, 510b, 511a, 514b; IV 36a, 292b, 437b, 443a, 443b, 444b, 446a; V 115b, 271b, 323b, 328a, 330b, 422a, 465b
anzala	I 42a, 42b, 245b, 346b, 400b, 487a, 554b; II 302b, 303a, 561b; III 103a; IV 292b, 293a, 295a, 295b, 443a; V 8a, 116a, 302a, 322b, 545a
inzāl	III 413a; IV 292b; V 330b
tanazzala	IV 292b
tanazzul	V 115b
nazla	I 177b
nuzūl	V 327b, 328a, 330b
manzil, pl. *manāzil*	I 272b; II 458b, 461a; III 413a, 415b; IV 107a, 108a

manāzil al-qamar I 272b; III 415b; IV 571b
manzila, pl. *manāzil* II 170b; III 466b; IV 347a, 571b; V 283b, 560b
manzila bayna l-manzilatayn II 170b; III 466b
n-z-h
tanzīh I 106b; II 160b, 373a; V 18b
nuzha I 203a
n-s-ʾ
nasaʾa I 16a, 34a; II 547a; III 412a
nasīʾ II 179b, 432b; III 339b, 411b, 412a, 415a; IV 255b, 259b, 571b; V 285a
minsaʾa II 544a, 547a; III 208a; IV 509a
n-s-b
munāsaba III 126a, 194b; IV 482b; V 405b
tanāsub III 194b; V 405b
nasab I 368b; II 11a, 48a, 174b; III 96a, 97a, 99b; V 248b
nasīb II 300b; IV 55a, 472b
nisba II 496b, 498a; IV 406b; V 105b
n-s-t-ʿ-l-y-q
nastaʿlīq III 265a
n-s-kh I 14b
nasakha I 14b, 15a, 353a; IV 532b; V 497b
nāsikh I 72a, 248a, 320b, 535a, 554b, 556b; II 135a, 378b, 388b, 389a; III 570b; IV 449a; V 143a, 323a
(al-)nāsikh wa-(l-)mansūkh I 72a, 320b, 535a; II 135a, 378b, 388b, 389a; III 570b; IV 449a; V 143a
nāsikhāt I 72a
mansūkh I 342a, 342b, 554b, 556b; V 130b, 291a, 323a
mansūkhāt I 72a
tanāsukhiyya II 422a
istansakha I 14b; II 493a
naskh I 11b, 14b, 16a, 17a, 137a, 142a, 251a, 349b, 351a; II 382b, 388b; III 39a, 160a, 265a, 319a, 320b, 321a, 326b, 328a, 328b, 595a, 598b, 599a; IV 325b, 326a, 327a; V 146a, 165a, 326a, 514a
naskh al-tilāwa dūna l-ḥukm I 349b–350a
naskhī I 136b, 282b, 283a; III 262b, 263a, 263b, 265a

nuskha, pl. *nusakh* I 14b; II 544b, 545a; IV 588b
n-s-k V 555b
nask I 181a
nusk I 181a
nusuk I 181a, 403b
nussāk IV 387a
mansik, pl. *manāsik* I 7a, 403b; IV 518a, 519a
mansak I 372a; II 205a, 432a; IV 132b
n-s-l
nasl II 63a
n-s-w
niswa, pl. *nisāʾ* II 289b, 291a; IV 501a
n-s-y
nasiya I 16a, 16b, 34a, 348b; II 322a
n-sh-ʾ
anshaʾa I 479 a; II 3b
inshāʾ III 126b, 127a, 145b; V 499a
n-sh-d
inshād II 93b
munshid II 94a; IV 172b
n-sh-r
nāshirāt I 53a, 55a
nashr I 52a, 53a, 55a
nushr I 53a
nushra I 52a, 53a, 77a; IV 163a, 170b, 171b, 174a
nushūr I 498a; III 139a; IV 434a
n-sh-z
nāshiz II 292a
nāshiza II 292a
nushūz II 76a, 291b, 292a; V 540a
n-ṣ-b
naṣaba II 482b
nuṣub II 481a, 482b, 483a, 547a; III 5a; IV 517b
naṣb II 349a, 360b
nuṣb, pl. *anṣāb* I 167a, 167b, 404b, 411a; II 281b, 481a, 482b, 483a; IV 259b
naṣab III 254b
naṣīb I 528a; II 76a; III 69b
n-ṣ-t
anṣata II 405b
inṣāt II 87a
n-ṣ-ḥ
nuṣḥ IV 130b

naṣīḥa	iv 130b
*nuṣaḥā*ʾ	iv 520b
n-ṣ-r	i 311a; v 429b, 430a
naṣara	i 389b
nāṣir, pl. *anṣār*	i 123a, 217a, 256b, 311a, 324b, 337a, 345a, 389a, 389b, 422b, 432a; ii 14b, 15a, 16a, 17a, 17b, 20a, 273a, 274a, 518b; iii 17a, 37a, 239b, 369b; iv 26b, 27a, 430a
naṣr	i 398a, 400b; ii 96a; iii 308a, 425a; iv 295b, 590b
naṣrānī, pl. *naṣārā*	i 310b, 311a, 389b; iv 152a, 405a, 406b, 511b, 512b
naṣīr	v 430a
n-ṣ-ṣ	
naṣṣ	ii 12a, 136a; iii 157a, 157b; iv 146a
n-ṣ-f	
inṣāf	iii 73b
n-ḍ-j	
naḍija	ii 210b, 218b
n-ḍ-d	
minḍada	v 188a
n-ḍ-r	
nāḍira	iv 435a
n-ṭ-ḥ	
naṭīḥa	ii 220b
n-ṭ-ʿ	
*anṭā*ʿ	ii 426b
n-ṭ-q	
naṭaqa	v 108b, 110b, 111a
manṭūq	v 333a
nuṭq	iii 605a; v 201a
manṭiq	v 200b
n-ẓ-r	v 446b
naẓara	i 548a; ii 259a; iii 208b; iv 574a
nāẓira	iv 435a, 574b
munāẓara	iii 222a
inẓār	iii 45a
munẓarīn	v 267b
intiẓār	iv 377a
naẓar	i 91b; iii 404a; iv 69a
naẓāʾir	iv 143b, 155b, 156a; v 323a
n-ẓ-m	

naẓm	II 533b, 535a; III 115b, 126a, 127a, 194b, 198b; V 326a
niẓām	II 137b; IV 127a, 145b
n-ʿ-t	
naʿt	II 363b; IV 60b; V 302b, 394a
n-ʿ-j	
naʿja, pl. *niʿāj*	I 94b
n-ʿ-r	
nāʿūra	I 43b
n-ʿ-l	
naʿl	I 346b
n-ʿ-m	III 62a
niʿma	I 236a, 304a, 304b, 305b; II 6b, 352b, 365b, 367a; III 62b, 372a, 423a, 451a; IV 290b, 420b, 421a, 506b
niʿimmā	II 365b
anʿama	I 236a; II 190b
naʿam, pl. *anʿām*	I 94a, 99b, 402b, 441a; III 76b, 534a; IV 3b; V 14b, 373b, 548b
anʿām wa-banūn	IV 3b
bahīmat al-anʿām	I 94a
ūlāʾika ka-l-anʿām	V 14b
niʿam	IV 14b, 186a
naʿīm	II 51a; III 62a, 62b; IV 14b, 15b; V 62b
n-f-th	
naffāthāt	IV 486b
naffāthāt fī l-ʿuqad	IV 486b
n-f-ḥ	
nafḥa	II 452b
n-f-kh	
nafakha	I 446b; II 362a; III 203a; V 116b
nafkh	III 139b, 140a
n-f-d	
nafida	V 340a
n-f-dh	
nufūdh	IV 210a
n-f-r	
nafara	III 36a; V 374a
munāfarāt	III 247a
nāfūra	V 121b
n-f-s	
nafusa	V 81b

tanaffasa — I 52b, 55a
tanaffus — V 64b
nafs, pl. *nufūs*, *anfus* — I 24b, 87a, 91b, 92a, 357b, 476b; II 161b, 162a, 202b, 290b, 292a, 323b, 328b, 413b, 424b; III 182a, 224a, 359a, 443b, 459b; IV 173b, 573a; V 81a, 81b, 82a, 82b, 83a, 83b, 84a, 96b, 111b, 136b, 138b, 142b, 160b, 442a
nafs al-ʿaql wa-l-tamyīz — V 83b
al-nafs al-lawwāma — V 83a, 96b
al-nafs al-muṭmaʾinna — V 83a, 96b, 136b
al-nafsa la-ammāratum bi-l-sūʾi — III 224a; V 82b, 96b
nafas — V 81b
anfas — I 357b

n-f-q — II 71a, 420b, 421b, 450a, 468a, 468b
nafaqa — I 65a; II 61a; III 252a, 252b; V 193b, 232b, 454b
nāfaqa — IV 42a
munāfiq, pl. *munāfiqūn* — I 160b, 216b, 221b, 324b, 381a, 409a, 422b, 493b, 551a; II 24a, 71a, 73b, 166b, 387b, 468a, 468b, 470b, 471a, 471b, 501b; III 30a, 31b, 47a, 181b, 439a, 453b, 456b, 563b, 564a, 578a; IV 25a, 27a, 119b, 129a, 218a, 309a, 399a, 427a; V 14b, 164a, 380a
anfaqa — IV 30b
infāq — II 85b
munfiq — V 193b
nafaq — II 468a
nufaqa — II 468a
nāfiqāʾ — II 468a
nafaqa — II 468b; V 198a, 199a
nifāq — I 493b; II 166b, 468a, 468b, 501b; IV 119b

n-f-l
nafl, pl. *anfāl* — I 252a; II 85b; III 447b; V 194a, 195a
nāfila, pl. *nawāfil* — I 182b; II 82b, 552a; IV 222a; V 431a

n-f-y
nāfiya — II 365a

nifāʾ ii 502a
nafy v 496b
n-q-b
niqāb v 415a
naqīb, pl. *nuqabāʾ* i 307a; ii 16b, 432b
manāqib i 388a; v 46b, 47b
n-q-dh
anqadha i 518b, 519a, 519b; iv 523b
n-q-r
nāqūr i 112b; ii 47a; iii 139b, 140a, 143b
naqīr i 494b
n-q-sh
naqqāsh iii 601b
n-q-ṣ
naqaṣa iii 335b; v 312a, 313a
n-q-ḍ iii 563a
naqḍ ii 534a, 534b; iii 287b
naqāʾiḍ ii 529a
n-q-ṭ
naqaṭa iii 466a
naqṭ i 139b; iii 605a
n-q-l
naqala i 15a
naql i 466b; v 140b
naqqāla iii 357b
n-q-m v 416a
naqama ii 147b
muntaqim iv 453b
intiqām iv 310a, 453a
n-k-th iii 563a, 564b
nakatha iii 562b, 564a
n-k-ḥ
nakaḥa iii 96a, 277a
ankaḥa iii 277a
nikāḥ i 432b; iii 96a, 277a, 279a; iv 486a, 488b, 580b, 584a; v 232a, 232b
n-k-d
nakid iii 191a
n-k-r ii 63b, 488b, 489a
ankara ii 489a
munkar ii 62a, 63b, 72a, 489a; iii 70b, 84b, 85a; iv 598b; v 119a, 269a, 316b, 438a, 438b, 439a
al-amr bi-l-maʿrūf wa-l-nahy ʿan al-munkar see ʾ-m-r
munkarūn ii 489a

nakīr v 119a
n-k-f
istankafa i 161a, 241b
n-k-l
tankīl iv 453b
nakāl i 294b, 295a; iv 453b, 454a; v 254b
nikl, pl. *ankal* ii 546a
n-m-r-q
namāriq ii 229a, 276a
n-m-z
namāz iv 58b
n-m-s
nāmūs iii **515a**, 515b, 516a
n-m-l
naml, f. *namla* i 95a; ii 372b; v 342b
n-m-m
namīm ii 343b
n-m-w
numuww iv 490b
n-h-j
manhaj ii 137b; iv 145b
minhāj iv 28a, 28b
n-h-r
nahr, pl. *anhār* iii 335a, 531a; v 184b, 462a, 463b, 466a, 467a
nahār i 497b, 498a, 499a, 503b; iv 222a, 223a; v 279a, 280b, 282a, 282b, 476a, 476b
n-h-ḍ
nahḍa ii 549a
n-h-y ii 224a
nahā v 108b, 438a, 438b, 439a
tanāhā v 438b, 441a
intahā iv 428a; v 438b
nahy iii 159a, 175a; v 321a
al-amr bi-l-maʿrūf wa-l-nahy ʿan al-munkar see ʾ-m-r
n-w-ʾ
nāʾa v 283b
nawʾ, pl. *anwāʾ* i 272b, 273a; iii 415b; iv 107a; v 283b, 561a
n-w-b iv 427b
anāba i 437a; iv 427b, 428a, 429b, 430a
munīb ii 408a
nawba v 148b

n-w-ḥ
nāḥa III 542a
n-w-r I 246b
munawwar III 104b
nūr I 91b, 493b; II 189a, 326a, 326b; III 45b, 186a, 186b, 187a, 187b, 208a, 425a, 504a, 511b, 534b, 554b; IV 3b, 304b; V 118a, 427b
nār I 476a; II 49b, 50a, 210a, 212a, 258b, 414b, 503a; III 45b, 47b, 48b, 203b, 529a, 529b, 530a; IV 4a, 100b, 102b, 103a, 104a, 293b; V 106a, 118a, 181a, 183b, 359a
nār ḥāmiya II 414b; IV 103a; V 183b
manāra III 431a
n-w-ʿ
nawʿ I 25b; II 225b
n-w-q
nāqa I 94a, 286b, 287a, 401b; III 534b; IV 296b
nāqat allāh I 401b
n-w-l
munāwala IV 588b
n-w-m
nawm V 60b, 61b
manām I 498a, 546b, 547b, 548a, 550b, 552a; II 241b; IV 179a; V 61a, 61b
n-w-n
tanwīn I 140b
nūn I 95b, 99a
n-w-y
nawā I 494b
niyya II 502a, 549b, 550a, 550b, 551a; IV 378a, 487b, 490a, 493a
n-y-k
nikāh I 556b

-hāʾ-

h-b-ṭ
habaṭa II 23b; III 490a
hubūṭ III 45a

h-b-w
habāʾa I 184b
h-j-d
tahajjada II 552b; V 430b
tahajjud I 182a, 327b, 328a; IV 222a, 485b, 488a; V 430b
h-j-r I 19b; II 18b
hajara I 19b
hājira III 546a, 546b
muhājir, pl. *muhājirūn* I 217a, 262a, 324b, 379b, 389a, 389b, 422b; II 14b, 15a, 16a, 17a, 17b, 20a, 274a, 518b; III 37a, 369b; IV 26b, 27a, 226b, 333a; V 59a, 196a, 382a, 409a
ahjara II 310b; III 453a
hijra I 20b, 164a, 217a, 273a, 289a, 293a, 293b, 320a, 321b, 325b, 328a, 338a, 338b, 379b, 398a, 407a; II 15a, 15b, 16a, 16b, 17b, 18b, 20a, 21b, 22a, 22b, 145a, 155b, 167b, 178b, 182a, 204a, 298b, 299a, 310b, 374a, 386a, 390b, 469a, 518b, 530b; III 4a, 6a, 37a, 40b, 54a, 61a, 80a, 144a, 412a, 456a, 488a, 494b, 496a, 522b, 568a, 590a; IV 17a, 224a, 226b, 227a, 305a, 306a, 321b, 331b, 332a, 333a, 340b, 406a; V 37b, 113b, 169b, 258a, 271b, 285a, 291a, 291b, 372b, 375b, 508a, 509b, 510b, 511a, 511b, 562b
hijrī II 432b; III 320a, 322a, 557a
h-j-n
tahjīn III 121a
h-j-w
hijāʾ II 263a
h-d-d
tahdīd I 206a, 511a
h-d-h-d
hudhud I 95a; III 222b
h-d-y I 246b; V 555b
hadā I 348b, 405b; II 44a, 561b; III 222b, 425a; IV 29b, 30a
hādī I 554b; II 320b

ihtidāʾ I 185b; IV 107a, 108a
hady I 97a, 187a; III 76b; IV 95a, 98b
hudā I 25b, 185b, 435b; II 270a, 502a; III 27b, 102b, 186b, 424b, 425a, 425b, 511b, 514a, 525a; IV 3b, 28a, 300b, 391a; V 374b
hadiyya II 313a, 313b, 314a
hadī I 403b, 404a, 404b
hidāya II 127b; II 503a; IV 28a, 131a
mahdī I 555a; II 47a, 424a; III 138b; IV 140b

h-dh-dh
hadhdha II 386b

h-r-q
harāqa II 346b

h-r-m
haram III 392a

h-z-ʾ III 400a, 400b, 401a
istahzaʾa II 322a; III 400a, 400b; IV 309b
mustahziʾūn IV 415a
huzuʾ III 400a

h-sh-m
hashīm I 41b; II 3b, 369b

h-ḍ-m III 70b
haḍīm I 494b

h-l-k
ahlaka I 327b; II 307a, 307b; III 422b
halāk III 423a

h-l-l IV 517b
tahlīl III 374a
uhilla IV 517b
hilāl, pl. *ahilla* I 273; 444b; III 412b, 414b; IV 108a; V 284a

h-m-d
hāmida I 364b

h-m-z
hamz I 140b; II 343b
hamza, pl. *hamazāt* II 344a, 355a, 355b, 356a, 356b; III 123a, 259b, 270a
hammāz II 344a

h-m-s
hams V 479a

h-m-l
muhmal IV 588b

h-w-d — III 21b
hāda — III 21b
hawwada — III 21b
hūd — III 21b
yahūd — III 21b; IV 42a, 42b, 152a, 405a
yahūdiyya — III 21b
h-w-n
hawn — II 488a; III 403a
h-w-y
hawā — I 52a, 177b; II 489a; IV 100a, 100b, 101a, 108b, 133b, 141b
hāwiya — II 49b, 414b, 419a; IV 100a, 100b, 101a, 101b, 103a, 103b, 104a; V 181a
muhawwi — IV 82b
huwwa — IV 103a
hawāʾ, pl. *ahwiya, ahwāʾ* — I 51b, 185b; II 422a; III 27a, 453b, 529b; V 486b
mahwan, mahwā — IV 103a
h-y-ʾ
hayʾa — I 167b
h-y-t
hayta — I 530b
h-y-m
hīm — I 94b, 99b; III 531b
h-y-m-n — IV 307a
muhaymin — III 512b, 514b; IV 307a
hayhāt — II 352b

-wāw-

w-ʾ-d
waʾd — I 234a; II 511a, 511b; IV 255b
w-b-r
awbār — II 426a
w-b-l
wābil — I 42a, II 4a
w-t-d
watad, pl. *awtād* — V 236b
dhū l-awtād — V 236b
w-t-r
tawātur — III 155b, 156a; IV 534b; V 309a
mutawātir — III 162a
mutawātira — IV 357b, 358b
tatrā — IV 291a

watr III 549b
w-th-q
wathiqa I 465a
thiqa, pl. *thiqāt* I 380b, 464a; V 378a
mawthiq IV 358b; V 140a
mīthāq, pl. *mawāthīq* I 465a
I 26a, 188b, 240b, 256b, 304b, 349a, 379b, 380b, 431b, 464a, 464b, 465a, 466a, 466b; II 57b, 63b, 567a, 569b; III 278b, 568b; IV 128b, 292a, 298b; V 138b, 197a, 446a, 502a
mīthāq alladhīna ūtū l-kitāb I 349a
mīthāq al-awwal ʿalā l-fiṭra II 57b
mīthāq ghalīẓ I 464b; III 278b
mīthāq al-kitāb I 465a
mīthāq al-nabiyyīn I 349a, 379a
wuthqā I 465a
w-th-n
wathan, pl. *awthān* II 476b, 478a, 481a, 481b; IV 503b
w-j-b
wājib I 337b; II 225a; III 159b, 175a, 175b; III 182b; IV 376a; V 449b
wājiba II 313b
mujīb II 321a
w-j-d
wajada V 374b
ījād I 421b; IV 82a
w-j-z
ījāz III 207b
mūjaz I 71b
w-j-ʿ
wajaʿ V 132b
w-j-h
wajh, pl. *wujūh*, *awjuh* II 53a, 100b, 101a, 159a, 159b, 258b, 323a, 323b; III 417b, 418b; IV 155b, 156a, 156b, 157a, 221a, 495a; V 321b, 322a, 323a, 333a, 440a
wajh allāh II 53a, 159a, 159b; IV 221a
wajh rabbihim II 159b
wajh rabbika II 159a
al-wujūh wa l-naẓāʾir V 333a
w-ḥ-d
wāḥid II 320a, 329b, 330a; III 550b; IV 6a; V 489b, 500b

umma wāḥida see ʾ-m-m
tawḥīd i 117a, 554b, 555b, 556a; ii 22a, 44a, 163a, 202b, 279a, 328b, 474a, 478a; iii 3a, 183a, 466b, 467a; iv 130b, 149b, 159a, 161a, 162a, 166a, 166b, 396a, 398a, 460b, 573a; v 16b, 213b, 283a, 383a, 383b, 384a, 440a, 452a
muwaḥḥidūn i 554b, 555b, 556a, 556b
muwaḥḥidāt i 556b
waḥd iii 556a; v 503a
waḥda v 156b, 489b
waḥdāniyya i 27b
w-ḥ-sh
waḥshī iii 115a
w-ḥ-y i 246b; iii 511a; v 270b, 271a
waḥā i 245a; iv 293b
awḥā i 245a; ii 11b; iii 441b, 442b, 444b, 511b, 592a; iv 293b, 294a, 294b, 295a, 297a, 438b, 439a, 439b, 440a, 440b, 441b; v 271a, 274a, 483a, 546a
waḥy i 46a, 245b, 260a, 451a, 470b, 547b, 548a, 549a; ii 86b, 381a, 395b, 561b; iii 82b, 441b, 442b, 511a, 511b, 514b; iv 179a, 293b, 294a, 294b, 295a, 311b, 437b, 439a, 439b, 440a, 440b, 441a, 441b, 546a, 546b; v 69b, 478b
w-d-d iii 233a
wadda iii 235b
wudd iii 233b
wadūd ii 321a, 322a; iii 233b
mawadda ii 275a; iii 235a, 235b, 236a, 241a, 279a
w-d-ʿ
waddaʿa ii 178b
wadāʿ ii 178b
wadīʿa v 378b
w-d-q
wadq i 42a; v 461b, 463a, 465b, 470b
w-d-y
diya i 3b, 122b, 239a, 239b, 369b; iv 436b, 437a; v 417b, 418a, 418b

wādī, pl. *awdiya*	II 295a; III 495b; IV 513a, 519a; V 17a, 17b, 248a
al-wādī l-muqaddas ṭūwan	III 495b; IV 513a; V 248a
w-r-th	
awratha	I 277a; II 65a, 519b; IV 297b
irth	III 336a
turāth	III 96a; V 70a
mīrāth	III 96a
w-r-d	
wird	IV 175a
awrād	V 157a
wāridāt	II 371b
ward	I 362a
warīd	I 175b, 362a; V 154b
w-r-ʿ	
waraʿ	III 175b; IV 90a; V 483b
w-r-q	
waraqa, coll. *waraq*	I 41b, 346b; III 408b; IV 587b
wariq	III 408b
warrāq	III 265a
warraq	III 598a
w-r-y	V 300b
warāʾa	IV 285a
w-z-r	
wāzira	III 228a
wizr, pl. *awzār*	III 228a; IV 85a; V 249a, 474a
wazīr	I 1a, 260a, 261a; III 558a
wizāra	II 89a
w-z-ʿ	
awzaʿa	V 377a
w-z-n	III 333a, 334a, 334b
wazana	III 334a; V 312a, 313b
mawzūn	III 334b
muwāzana	III 128b; IV 476b, 477a, 481b
wazn	III 128a, 128b, 334b; IV 481a
mīzān, pl. *mawāzīn*	I 491a; II 48b, 544b, 545a, 545b; III 69b, 70a, 140b, 334b, 389b; IV 170a, 312a, 313a, 313b
w-z-y	
mutawāzī	III 128b
w-s-ṭ	III 402a
mutawassiṭ	I 205b
wasaṭ	III 402a, 402b
ummatun/aʾimmatan wasaṭan	see ʾ-m-m
wisāṭa	II 554a
awsaṭ	III 402a

wusṭā	I 35b
w-s-ʿ	
wasiʿa	I 443b, 446a
wāsiʿ	II 320a; IV 6a; V 483a
wusʿ	IV 432b
w-s-q	
wasq	III 336b
w-s-l	
wasīla	II 554a; IV 163b
w-s-m	
mawsim, pl. *mawāsim*	I 349a; II 298a; IV 571b
w-s-w-s	V 479a
waswasa	II 550b; IV 295a; V 479a
waswās	V 479a
w-ṣ-f	
waṣafa	IV 220b
mawṣūf	II 360a
ṣifa, pl. *ṣifāt*	I 469a; II 83a, 195a, 319a, 319b, 348b, 395a, 534b; III 158a, 187b; IV 88a, 187a, 374a
w-ṣ-l	
mawṣūl	V 332b, 335a
ittiṣāl	IV 87b
muttaṣil	IV 376a
ṣila, pl. *ṣilāt*	IV 376a; V 322a, 522a
waṣl	I 140b; II 354a
waṣla	III 270a
waṣīla	I 97a, 401b
w-ṣ-y	
awṣā	III 220b
waṣī, pl. *awṣiyāʾ*	II 118a, 374a; IV 304a
waṣiyya	II 518b, 520b; IV 304a
waṣāya	IV 601b
w-ḍ-ʾ	
tawaḍḍaʾ	IV 506b
wuḍūʾ	I 328b, 341b, 410b; II 391b, 402a; III 431a; IV 485b, 488b, 491a, 491b, 492a, 506b; V 210a, 465a
mayāḍiʾ	V 124a
w-ḍ-ḥ	
wāḍiḥ	III 115a
w-ḍ-ʿ	
mawḍūʿ	I 539a; III 195a; V 101b
mawḍūʿa	III 128b

w-ʿ-d
waʿada v 108b
waʿd iii 466b; iv 423b; v 478b
waʿīd v 321b
w-ʿ-ẓ
waʿẓ v 207a
waʿẓa v 207a
wāʿiẓ iv 62a, 65a; v 207a
mawʿiẓa i 365a; ii 142b, 502a, 511b
w-f-ḍ
awfaḍa iii 185a
w-f-q
wāfaqa ii 229b, 230a, 230b
ittafaqa ii 230b
wafq ii 38a
muwāfaqa ii 86a; v 145a
w-f-y ii 447b
wafā i 379a
wāfī iii 336b
wāfiya ii 189a
waffā i 5b; iv 457b; v 312a
awfā ii 447b, 448a, 562b; v 434a
īfāʾ iii 239a
tawaffā i 443b, 506a, 507a; iii 18b, 20a; v 289b
wafāʾ i 379a; iii 337a; v 434a
wafāt i 505b
w-q-t
waqqata v 283a, 288a
waqt i 272b, 319a; v 288a, 288b
mīqāt, pl. *mawāqīt* i 272b, 502a; iv 223a, 227b, 228a; v 146b, 284a, 288a, 288b
w-q-dh
mawqūdha ii 220b
w-q-r
waqr v 474a
wiqr v 474a
waqār ii 128a; v 435b
w-q-ʿ
wāqiʿ ii 134a
wāqiʿa iv 103a
tawqīʿ i 137a
īqāʿ iii 195b
īqāʿāt iv 489a
mawāqiʿ iv 108b

w-q-f
waqafa I 146a
waqf, pl. *awqāf* I 279b; II 526a; III 607a; IV 273b, 275a, 275b, 376b, 391a, 494b; V 325a, 326a, 327a
al-waqf al-ḥasan IV 376b
al-waqf al-kāfī IV 376b
al-waqf al-qabīḥ IV 376b
al-waqf al-tāmm IV 376b
waqf wa-(l-)ibtidāʾ III 607a, IV 376b, 391a
waqf wa-l-itmām V 326a
waqfiyya, pl. *waqfiyyāt* III 261b, 268a, 594a; V 558b
wuqūf II 183a; III 75b, 76a; IV 95b, 97b, 340a
mawqūfāt II 390b, 393a
w-q-y I 540a; II 60b, 164b, 194b, 195a; IV 307a
waqā I 518b, 519a; V 436a
atqā II 72a; V 436b
ittaqā I 540a; II 31a, 164b, 195b, 204a, 510a; III 195a; IV 16b, 90b; V 436a
muttaqī, pl. *muttaqūn* I 263a, 379a; II 61a, 195a, 196a; IV 3a, 16b, 90a, 90b, 520a
tuqā I 540a
waqyā/waqyān II 195a
taqiyya I 224b, 540a, 540b, 541a; II 505a; III 86b, 238b; IV 597b
taqwā I 37b, 90a, 460a, 538a; II 60b, 152a, 164b, 194a, 194b, 195a, 195b, 196a, 196b, 197a, 197b, 202b, 336b, 337a, 408a, 510a, 550a; IV 90a, 91a, 516a, 518a, 590b; V 26b, 379b, 434b, 436a, 522b
taqyan/taqyā II 195a
wāqiya II 189a
w-k-d
tawkīd II 360a, 362b; IV 287a
w-k-l V 378a, 378b
mawkūl V 380a
mawkūlāt V 118a
tawwakala II 96a; III 352a, 388b; IV 234a; V 378b, 379a, 380a, 384a
mutawakkil III 503b; V 378b, 383b
tawakkul II 164b, 279a; V 135a, 140a, 378a,

378b, 379a, 379b, 380b, 382a, 383b, 384a, 384b, 385a
wakīl II 320b; V 378a, 378b, 380a
w-l-j
walaja I 507a
awlaja I 497b
w-l-d
walada II 54a, 217a, 329b
lam yalid wa-lam yūlad II 217a, 329b
wālida IV 20a
wālidayn III 252a
mawlūd I 301b; II 175b; IV 20a
mawlūd lahu II 175b; IV 20a
walad, pl. *awlād* I 301b; II 175b, 329b, 366a, 491b
walīd, pl. *wildān* I 301b; II 284a, 445a; III 139b; IV 20a, 20b, 585a
wild IV 18a
mawlid II 206a, 206b, 207a, 207b, 452b
mawlid al-nabī II 206a
mīlād IV 486a
w-l-y
waliya I 345a, 432a; IV 307a
wallā I 19b; III 237a
muwālā II 466a
īlāʾ III 237a, 238a, 240b
tawallā I 19b; III 279b, 563a, 566a
tawallī III 453a
walī [waliyy], pl. *awliyāʾ* I 540b
I 259b, 262a, 370a, 432a, 432b, 434b, 466a; II 24b, 52a, 59a, 65b, 73a, 93a, 203a, 206a, 273a, 274b, 320b; III 27a, 43a, 47a, 229a, 231a, 231b, 235b, 236a, 237a, 238a, 331b, 558b, 559a, 559b; IV 5b, 307a, 371b, 490b, 520a, 520b; V 53b, 138a, 140a, 142a, 144b, 317a, 430a, 498b, 507b, 527a
walī al-ʿahd I 466a
walī allāh III 558b, 559a, 559b
awliyāʾ allāh IV 371b; V 142a
awliyāʾ al-shayṭān II 24b
walāya, pl. *walāyāt* III 235b, 236b; IV 485b, 490a, 490b, 520b, 596b, 600a, 600b
walāʾ I 344b, 345a, 345b, 432a, 466a; III 46b; V 58b

wilāya II 505a; III 65b, 83b; IV 147a, 371b, 520b; V 152b
wulāt I 277b
umarāʾ wa-l-wulāt I 189b; IV 133a
mawlan IV 5b
mawlā, pl. *mawālī* I 262a, 289b, 344a, 344b, 345a, 412a; II 17a, 379a, 381b, 382b, 384a, 385a, 386b, 387b, 388a, 389b, 392b, 393b, 394a, 395a, 395b, 398a, 521a; III 229a, 231a; IV 104a, 389b; V 365a
w-h-b V 191a
wahaba II 313b
hiba II 313b; V 507b, 509a
wahhāb II 320b
mawhaba IV 126b
w-h-n I 521a
wahana, wahina I 406a; V 383a
w-y-l
wayl II 261b; IV 470a; V 424a

-yāʾ-

yāqūt I 439a; III 384a
y-b-s
yābis I 24a, 137a, 204a
y-t-m
yatīm, pl. *yatāmā* I 302b; II 85b, 373b; III 603a
y-d(-y)
yad, pl. *aydī* II 151a, 325a, 374b, 401a, 401b, 402a
ʿan yadin II 151a, 401b
y-s-r II 280b; III 179b
yāsir II 281a
taysīr I 186a
tayassara V 176b
istaysara IV 94b
yasār II 280b
yusrā II 280b; III 179b
maysir II 67b, 162a, 237b, 238b, 239a, 280a, 280b, 281a, 281b, 282a, 482b; III 152a, 570a; IV 259b
maysar I 411a
y-gh-th
yaghūth V 92a

y-q-n
yaqīn II 416a; III 162a; IV 171b; V 140a, 384b, 387b, 404a
II 550a
y-m-m
tayammama IV 501a, 501b
tayammum I 328b, 341b, 342a, 411b; II 391a; IV 225a, 485b, 488b, 491b, 492a, 500a, 501a, 506b; V 161a
II 213a, 231a; V 462a, 463b
yamm II 401a; III 562a, 566a
y-m-n
yaman V 561b
yamīn, pl. *aymān* I 187a, 256b, 379b, 396a, 466a; II 325a, 401a; III 176b, 179a, 179b, 563b, 564a, 564b, 566a; IV 312b; V 498a
yamīna III 180a
ayman IV 513b
maymana III 176b
yamāniyya V 51b
y-w-m
II 258a; V 278b, 283a, 283b, 374a
yawm, pl. *ayyām* I 91a, 178b, 197b, 319a, 328b, 443b, 449a, 480b, 499a, 499b, 500a, 500b, 505a, 505b, 516b; II 44a, 46a, 182a, 251b, 258a, 271b, 366b, 429b, 431a, 439a, 449a, 558b; III 66b, 136a, 136b, 137a, 137b, 138a, 141b, 142a, 177a, 183b, 199b, 203a, 335a, 416a, 423a, 566a; IV 12a, 96b, 102b, 153a, 226a, 343b, 434a; V 80a, 113a, 126b, 194b, 278b, 279a, 279b, 280a, 281b, 282a, 282b, 283a, 283b, 284b, 285b, 286a, 374a, 476a
yawm ʿabūs qamṭarīr I 500a
yawm al-aḥzāb I 500a
yawm al-ākhir I 500a; II 449a, III 136b, 137a; IV 12a, 153a; V 279a, 279b, 280a, 280b, 282a
yawm alīm I 500a
yawm ʿaqīm I 500a; III 137a
yawm ʿaṣīb I 500b
yawm ʿāṣif I 500a
yawm ʿasir I 500a
yawm al-āzifa I 500a; III 66b, 137a
yawm ʿaẓīm I 500a; III 137a

yawm al-baʿth III 137a, 141b
yawm buʿāth V 279b
yawm al-dīn I 178b, 480b, 500a, 516b; III 66b, 136a, 136b, 137a, 141a, 142a, 177a; IV 12a, 434a; V 114a, 279a
yawm al-faṣl I 500, 516b; III 66b, 137a, 199b, 203a; IV 102b; V 279a, 283a
yawm al-fatḥ I 500a
yawm al-furqān I 196b, 500b; V 194b, 279a, 284b
yawm al-ḥajj al-akhbar I 500b; V 279a
yawm al-ḥaṣād I 500b
yawm al-ḥasra I 500a; III 137a
yawm al-ḥisāb I 500a; III 66b, 137a; IV 12a, 434a; V 279a
yawm al-jamʿ I 500a; III 137a
yawm al-jumʿa I 328b, 500b; II 271b
yawm al-jumuʿa II 271b; IV 226a; V 279a, 285a
yawm kabīr I 500a
yawm al-khulūd I 500a; II 54b; III 137a
yawm al-khurūj I 500a; III 137a
yawm maʿlūm I 500a, 500b; V 280a
yawm al-mawʿūd I 500a; III 137a; V 282b
yawm muḥīṭ I 500a; II 46b
yawm al-qiyāma I 91a, 480b, 500a; II 44a; III 66b, 136a, 136b, 137a, 137b, 138a, 183b, 416a; IV 12a, 434a; V 279a, 282a
yawm sabtihim I 500b
yawm al-taghābun I 500a; III 137a
yawm al-talāq I 500a; III 137a
yawm al-tanādi I 500a; II 558b; III 66b, 137a
yawm thaqīl I 500a
yawm al-waʿīd I 500a; III 137a
yawm al-wāqiʿa III 137a
yawm al-waqt al-maʿlūm I 500a
yawm al-zīna I 500b; V 281b
yawma tabyaḍḍu wujūhun wa-taswaddu wujūhun III 137b
yawma zaʿnikum wa-yawma iqāmatikum V 374a
ayyām allāh I 505a, 505b; III 423a; V 279b
ayyām maʿdūdāt II 182a; IV 96b, 342b; V 280b, 284b
ayyām al-tashrīq IV 96b, 97a
ayyām-i buṭūn I 197b
yawmaʾidhin I 499b; II 258a, 366a, 366b; V 80a, 279a

INDEX OF QUR᾽ĀN CITATIONS

Sūrat al-Fātiḥa (1)

I 209b, 210b (Basmala); 264a (Burial); 322b (Chronology and the Q); 381b (Community and Society in the Q)

II 87b (Everyday Life, Q In); 119a (Exegesis of the Q: Classical and Medieval); 388a (Ḥadīth and the Q)

III 194b (Literary Structures of the Q); 575a (Oft-Repeated); 598b (Ornamentation and Illumination)

IV 58a (Persian Literature and the Q); 176a (Popular and Talismanic Uses of the Q); 241a, 244a, 245a, 246b, 250b (Pre-1800 Preoccupations of Q Studies); 376a (Recitation of the Q)

V 127b, 172a (Springs and Fountains); 100b (Southeast Asian Q Literature); 308b (Torah); 334b (Traditional Disciplines of Q Studies); 551b (World)

1 I 207b, 210b (Basmala); 237a (Blessing)
II 190b (Fātiḥa); 317a (God and his Attributes)

1-7 IV 221b, 229a (Prayer)

2 I 188b (Authority)
II 36b (Epigraphy); 190a (Fātiḥa); 462a (House, Domestic and Divine)
III 145b (Laudation); 305b (Material Culture and the Q); 586b (Orality)
IV 78b (Philosophy and the Q); 184b (Possession and Possessions); 214b (Praise); 220b (Prayer); 288a (Property)
V 378b (Trust and Patience)

2-4 IV 479b (Rhymed Prose)

2-5 II 190b (Fātiḥa)

3 I 209a, 210b (Basmala)
IV 5a (Pairs and Pairing)

4 I 500a (Day, Times of); 516b (Decision)
II 189b (Fātiḥa); 321b (God and his Attributes)
III 136b, 142a (Last Judgment)
IV 78b (Philosophy and the Q); 184b (Possession and Possessions); 372a (Recitation of the Q)

5 I 435a (Conversion)
II 189b (Fātiḥa); 345b (Grace); 357a, 362b (Grammar and the Q)
III 193a (Literary Structures of the Q)
IV 167a (Popular and Talismanic Uses of the Q); 483a (Rhymed Prose); 487a (Ritual and the Q)

6 I 185a (Astray); 348b (Codices of the Q)
II 189b (Fātiḥa)
IV 431b (Responsibility)
V 182b (Symbolic Imagery); 374b (Trips and Voyages); 386b (Truth)

6-7 I 381b (Community and Society in the Q)
II 190b (Fātiḥa)

7 I 93a (Anger); 186a (Astray); 529b (Dialects)
II 190a (Fātiḥa); 362a, 363b (Grammar and the Q)
III 33a (Jews and Judaism)
IV 29a (Path or Way); 310a (Provocation)
V 374b (Trips and Voyages)

Sūrat al-Baqara (2)

I 93b (Animal Life); 306a (Children of Israel); 328a (Chronology and the Q); 353a (Collection of the Q); 408b (Consultation)
II 264a (Form and Structure of the Q); 394a, 396b (Ḥadīth and the Q); 461a (House, Domestic and Divine)
III 165a (Law and the Q); 194a, 195a (Literary Structures of the Q); 235a (Love and Affection); 395a (Miracles); 472b (Mysterious Letters); 496b (Myths and Legends in the Q); 521a (Narratives); 534a (Nature as Signs); 598b, 599a (Ornamentation and Illumination)
IV 237b, 238a, 241a, 244a, 245a (Pre-1800 Preoccupations of Q Studies); 327a, 327b (Qibla); 371a (Recitation of the Q); 436a (Retaliation); 494b (Ritual and the Q); 529a (Samuel); 594b (Shīʿism and the Q)
V 174b (Sūra); 272a (Theology and the Q); 453b (Waiting Period); 528a (Women and the Q)

1 I 249b (Book)
II 262a (Form and Structure of the Q)
III 473a (Mysterious Letters)
V 393a (Turkish Literature and the Q)

1-2 I 249b (Book)

1-5 I 376b (Community and Society in the Q)

1-14 IV 250b (Pre-1800 Preoccupations of Q Studies)

1-79 IV 250b (Pre-1800 Preoccupations of Q Studies)

2 I 249b (Book)
II 195a, 195b (Fear); 263b (Form and Structure of the Q)
III 508a, 509a (Names of the Q)
IV 377a (Recitation of the Q); 391a (Reciters of the Q)
V 172a (Sūra); 393a (Turkish Literature and the Q); 404a (Uncertainty)

2-3 II 424a (Hidden and the Hidden)

2-4 I 372a (Community and Society in the Q)

2-7 IV 117a (Polemic and Polemical Language)

3 I 218b, 219a (Belief and Unbelief)
II 424a (Hidden and the Hidden)
IV 357b (Readings of the Q)

4 II 433b (History and the Q)
III 136b (Last Judgment)
IV 438b (Revelation and Inspiration)

4-5 I 435b (Conversion)

5 I 220b (Belief and Unbelief)
IV 282a (Profane and Sacred); 523a (Salvation)

6 I 220b (Belief and Unbelief)
II 510b (Indifference)

6-7 I 523a (Destiny)
II 508b (Impotence); 510b (Indifference)
III 31b (Jews and Judaism)

7 I 82a, 83b (Anatomy)
II 154a (Eyes); 187a (Fate); 407a, 408b (Heart); 416a (Hell and Hellfire)
III 380a (Mercy)
IV 118a (Polemic and Polemical Language); 391a (Reciters of the Q)
V 444b (Vision)

8 I 500a (Day, Times of)
II 439b (History and the Q)
III 136b (Last Judgment)
V 502a (Witnessing and Testifying)

8-18 I 240b (Bloodshed)

8-20 II 468b (Hypocrites and Hypocrisy)

10 II 407b (Heart); 416a (Hell and Hellfire); 470a (Hypocrites and Hypocrisy); 501b (Illness and Health)
III 359b (Medicine and the Q); 380a (Mercy)
IV 309b (Provocation)
V 447a (Vision and Blindness)

11-12	II	98b (Evil Deeds); 337b (Good and Evil)
13	II	1a (Ears)
14	I	526b (Devil)
	II	355a (Grammar and the Q)
	III	31b (Jews and Judaism); 48a (Jinn)
	IV	309b (Provocation)
	V	120b (Spiritual Beings); 502a (Witnessing and Testifying)
14-15	IV	310a (Provocation)
15	II	322a (God and his Attributes); 355a (Grammar and the Q)
	III	380a (Mercy); 400b (Mockery)
16	II	43b (Error); 356b (Grammar and the Q)
	III	46b (Jinn); 209a (Literature and the Q); 275b (Markets)
17	II	43b (Error)
	III	186a (Light); 225b (Literature and the Q)
	IV	10a (Parable)
	V	14b, 16a (Simile); 181a (Symbolic Imagery)
17-18	III	209b (Literature and the Q)
17-20	I	493b (Darkness)
18	I	226a (Belief and Unbelief)
	II	406b (Hearing and Deafness)
	IV	118a (Polemic and Polemical Language); 391a (Reciters of the Q)
19	II	1a (Ears); 406b (Hearing and Deafness)
	IV	10a (Parable); 575a (Seeing and Hearing)
	V	14b, 16b (Simile); 470b (Weather)
19-20	V	471a (Weather)
20	I	83b (Anatomy); 480b (Creeds); 493a (Darkness)
	II	320a (God and his Attributes); 348a, 357b, 361a, 362a (Grammar and the Q)
	III	200b (Literary Structures of the Q)
20-22	V	444b (Vision)
21	I	45a (Agriculture and Vegetation); 472a, 476a, 476b (Creation)
	II	31a (Epigraphy); 433b (History and the Q)
	IV	487a (Ritual and the Q)
21-22	I	44b (Agriculture and Vegetation)
22	I	44b (Agriculture and Vegetation); 472b, 473a, 478a (Creation)
	II	2b, 3a (Earth); 276a (Furniture and Furnishings); 304b (Geography); 411a (Heaven and Sky); 476b (Idolatry and Idolaters)
	III	379a (Mercy)
	IV	544b, 547a, 547b, 549a (Science and the Q)
	V	179a (Sustenance); 279b (Time)

23 III 116a (Language and Style of the Q); 398b (Miracles)
IV 312b (Provocation); 443a (Revelation and Inspiration); 577a (Servants)
V 167a (Sūra); 494a (Witnessing and Testifying)

23-24 I 115a (Apologetics)
II 527a, 529b (Inimitability)
III 468a (Muʿtazila)
IV 119a (Polemic and Polemical Language)

24 I 222a (Belief and Unbelief)
II 210b (Fire); 414b, 415a, 417b (Hell and Hellfire)
III 383b (Metals and Minerals)
III 383b (Stone)

25 I 41a (Agriculture and Vegetation); 220b (Belief and Unbelief); 343b (Cleanliness and Ablution)
II 60a (Ethics and the Q); 175a (Family); 341a, 341b (Good News); 456b (Houris)
III 277a (Marriage and Divorce); 444b (Muḥammad)
IV 16b, 18a (Paradise); 431b (Responsibility); 505b (Ritual Purity)
V 123a (Springs and Fountains)

26 I 99b (Animal Life)
II 270a (Freedom and Predestination)
IV 63a (Persian Literature and the Q); 538a (Scholar)
V 15b, 17a (Simile); 485b (Wish and Desire)

27 I 240b (Bloodshed); 464b (Covenant)
II 8b (Economics)
IV 129a (Politics and the Q); 413a (Religious Pluralism and the Q)

27-28 I 431b (Contracts and Alliances)

28 II 45a (Eschatology)
IV 435b (Resurrection)
V 545b (Word of God)

28-29 I 455b (Cosmology)

28-31 I 447a (Cosmology)

28-39 I 448a, 455b, 457a (Cosmology)

29 I 95b (Animal Life); 189a (Authority); 473a (Creation)
II 68b (Ethics and the Q); 410b (Heaven and Sky)
III 379a (Mercy)
IV 107b (Planets and Stars); 186a (Possession and Possessions); 547b (Science and the Q)
V 64a (Smoke); 543b, 544a (Word of God)

30 I 22b, 23a (Adam and Eve); 27a (Adoration); 86a (Angel); 237b (Blood and Blood Clot); 240a (Bloodshed); 277a (Caliph); 435a (Conversion); 449b, 453a, 455b (Cosmology); 474a (Creation)
II 172b (Fall of Man); 187a (Fate); 327b, 330a (God and his Attributes)

	III	523b (Narratives)
	IV	127a (Politics and the Q); 213a (Praise)
	V	109a (Speech); 257a, 274b (Theology and the Q)
30-31	I	240a (Bloodshed)
30-33	I	463a (Court); 532b (Dialogues)
30-34	I	189a (Authority); 474a (Creation)
	III	211a (Literature and the Q)
	IV	9b (Parable)
30-37	V	530a (Women and the Q)
30-39	I	240a (Bloodshed); 525b (Devil)
	III	521a (Narratives)
31	I	23b (Adam and Eve)
	III	102b (Knowledge and Learning); 118b (Language and Style of the Q); 537a (News)
	V	109a (Speech); 200b (Teaching)
31-32	I	23b (Adam and Eve)
	II	327b (God and his Attributes)
	IV	71a (Philosophy and the Q)
31-33	I	86a (Angel)
	V	270b (Theology and the Q); 547a (Word of God)
32	II	320b, 321a (God and his Attributes)
	III	102b (Knowledge and Learning)
	IV	220a, 220b (Prayer); 537b, 538a (Scholar)
	V	201b (Teaching)
33	I	455b (Cosmology)
	III	537a (News)
	IV	4a (Pairs and Pairing); 572b (Secrets)
	V	547a (Word of God)
34	I	24a (Adam and Eve); 86a (Angel); 190b (Authority); 255a (Bowing and Prostration); 395b (Conceit); 447a (Cosmology); 525a, 527a (Devil)
	II	166b (Faith); 172b (Fall of Man); 543a (Insolence and Obstinacy)
	III	45a (Jinn); 523b (Narratives); 532a (Nature as Signs)
	IV	220a (Prayer); 263b (Pride)
	V	109a (Speech)
34-39	I	532a (Dialogues)
35	I	25a (Adam and Eve); 447b, 456a (Cosmology)
	II	54b (Eternity); 172b (Fall of Man); 175a (Family); 219b (Food and Drink); 283a (Garden); 335b (Good and Evil); 356b, 357a, 362b (Grammar and the Q)
	III	70b (Justice and Injustice)
	IV	13a (Paradise); 589b (Shekhinah)
	V	109b (Speech); 360a (Tree)

35-37 V 25a (Sin, Major and Minor)

36 I 25a, 25b (Adam and Eve); 447b (Cosmology); 526a (Devil)
II 23b, 24a (Enemies); 173a (Fall of Man)

37 I 448a, 456a (Cosmology)
II 321a (God and his Attributes)
III 379a (Mercy)
IV 429a (Repentance and Penance)
V 541b, 548a (Word of God)

37-38 I 25b (Adam and Eve)

38 II 173a (Fall of Man); 196b (Fear); 356b (Grammar and the Q)
III 303a (Material Culture and the Q); 425b (Moses)
V 109b (Speech); 138a (Ṣūfism and the Q)

39 II 418a (Hell and Hellfire); 439b (History and the Q)

40 I 236b (Blessing); 306a (Children of Israel); 381a (Community and Society in the Q); 465b (Covenant)
II 197b (Fear); 447b (Honor)
III 239a (Loyalty); 373b (Memory)
IV 116b, 120b (Polemic and Polemical Language)
V 434a (Virtue)

40-41 IV 310b (Provocation)

40-43 I 304b (Children of Israel)

40-48 III 579b (Opposition to Muḥammad)

40-74 I 240b (Bloodshed)

41 III 276a (Markets)
IV 292b, 298a (Prophets and Prophethood); 439a (Revelation and Inspiration)

42 III 25b (Jews and Judaism); 181b (Lie)
IV 450b (Revision and Alteration)
V 304b (Torah)

43 I 254a (Bowing and Prostration)
II 340a (Good Deeds)
III 159b (Law and the Q)
IV 219b (Prayer); 487a (Ritual and the Q)

44 I 245b (Book)
II 60b, 67a (Ethics and the Q)
III 189b, 190a (Literacy); 508a (Names of the Q); 591b (Orality and Writing in Arabia)
V 204b (Teaching)

45 II 181a (Fasting)
IV 487a (Ritual and the Q)
V 404b (Uncertainty)

47 I 236b (Blessing); 304b, 307a (Children of Israel)
II 299a (Geography); 345a (Grace); 434b (History and the Q)
III 379a (Mercy); 425a (Moses)
IV 421b (Remembrance)
V 393a (Turkish Literature and the Q); 551b (World)

48 II 49a (Eschatology); 366b (Grammar and the Q); 552a (Intercession)

49 I 295b (Chastisement and Punishment); 302a (Children); 518b (Deliverance)
II 416a (Hell and Hellfire); 542a (Insolence and Obstinacy)
III 422b, 425a (Moses)
IV 421b (Remembrance); 517a (Sacrifice); 523b (Salvation)
V 362b, 363a (Trial)

49-50 II 184a (Fasting)

49-70 III 521a (Narratives)

49-73 IV 421b (Remembrance)

49-74 II 182a (Fasting)

50 I 553b (Drowning)
II 213a (Fire); 542b (Insolence and Obstinacy)
III 423a, 423b (Moses)
IV 210b (Power and Impotence); 343a (Ramaḍān); 523b (Salvation)
V 464b (Water)

51 I 274a (Calf of Gold); 499b (Day, Times of)
II 218b (Food and Drink)
III 210a (Literature and the Q); 423b (Moses)

51-54 I 99a (Animal Life); 236a (Blasphemy)
III 496a (Myths and Legends in the Q)

52 I 274a (Calf of Gold)

53 I 245a, 245b (Book); 486b (Criterion); 500b (Day, Times of)
III 189b (Literacy); 424b, 425a (Moses); 442a (Muḥammad); 496b (Myths and Legends in the Q); 507b (Names of the Q)
IV 346a (Ramaḍān)
V 301a, 301b, 302a (Torah)

54 I 188a (Atonement); 274a, 275a, 276b (Calf of Gold); 472a, 478b (Creation)
II 218b (Food and Drink); 320b, 327a (God and his Attributes)
IV 428b (Repentance and Penance)
V 22b (Sin, Major and Minor); 159b, 160a (Suicide)

55 III 394a (Miracles)

55-56 I 507a (Death and the Dead)

57 I 98a (Animal Life)
II 215b (Flying)
III 71a (Justice and Injustice); 394a (Miracles)

	IV	443b (Revelation and Inspiration)
	V	190b (Table); 463a (Water)
58	I	149a (Archaeology and the Q); 254b (Bowing and Prostration)
	III	5a (Jerusalem)
	IV	219b (Prayer)
	V	110b (Speech); 242a (Textual Criticism of the Q)
58-59	I	305a (Children of Israel)
	IV	428b (Repentance and Penance)
59	II	243a (Forgery); 411a (Heaven and Sky)
	IV	450b (Revision and Alteration); 454a (Reward and Punishment); 503a (Ritual Purity)
	V	302b (Torah)
60	II	4a (Earth); 7b (Economics); 546a (Instruments)
	III	208a, 219a (Literature and the Q); 383b (Metals and Minerals); 553a (Numbers and Enumeration)
	IV	218b (Prayer); 508b (Rod)
	V	121b (Spiritual Beings); 127b (Springs and Fountains); 178b (Sustenance); 463b (Water)
61	I	93a (Anger); 305a (Children of Israel); 529b (Dialects); 536b, 537a (Disobedience); 541a (Dissimulation)
	II	3b (Earth); 10a (Egypt); 217a, 217b (Food and Drink); 305b (Geography); 527b (Inimitability)
	III	24a (Jews and Judaism); 208b (Literature and the Q); 382a (Messenger)
	IV	301a (Prophets and Prophethood)
62	I	219a, 222b (Belief and Unbelief); 312a (Christians and Christianity)
	II	439b (History and the Q)
	III	22a (Jews and Judaism); 39b, 40a (Jihād); 136a, 136b (Last Judgment); 244a (Magians)
	IV	38a (People of the Book); 120b (Polemic and Polemical Language); 404a, 404b, 405a, 408a (Religious Pluralism and the Q); 455b (Reward and Punishment); 511b (Sabians); 586a (Sheba)
	V	313b (Trade and Commerce)
63	I	240b (Bloodshed); 304b (Children of Israel); 431b (Contracts and Alliances); 465a (Covenant)
	II	316a (Glory)
	III	394a (Miracles)
	IV	128b (Politics and the Q); 422a (Remembrance)
	V	302b (Torah); 546b (Word of God)
63-64	II	311a (Geography)
	III	379a (Mercy)
	IV	413a (Religious Pluralism and the Q)
63-93	II	215b (Flying)

64	II	344b, 345a (Grace)
	V	302b (Torah)
65	I	98b (Animal Life); 305a, 306b (Children of Israel); 475b (Creation)
	III	25a (Jews and Judaism)
	IV	413a (Religious Pluralism and the Q); 510b (Sabbath)
	V	285b (Time); 545a (Word of God)
66	IV	247a (Pre-1800 Preoccupations of Q Studies); 454a (Reward and Punishment)
67	II	218b (Food and Drink); 488a (Ignorance)
	III	400a (Mockery); 425a (Moses)
	IV	308a (Protection); 413a (Religious Pluralism and the Q); 517a (Sacrifice)
67-71	I	99a (Animal Life)
	III	562b (Oaths)
67-74	III	394b (Miracles)
67-80	IV	528b (Samuel)
68	III	521a (Narratives)
69	I	213a (Beauty); 361b, 363a (Colors)
	III	62b (Joy and Misery)
70	I	103b (Anthropomorphism)
71	IV	517a (Sacrifice)
	V	288b (Time)
72-73	I	489a (Crucifixion)
72-74	IV	121a (Polemic and Polemical Language)
72-75	I	489a (Crucifixion)
74	II	4a (Earth); 370b (Gratitude and Ingratitude); 407a (Heart); 510b (Indifference)
	III	225b (Literature and the Q); 383b (Metals and Minerals)
	V	127a (Springs and Fountains); 129a (Stone); 465b (Water)
75	I	118a (Apologetics); 310b (Christians and Christianity); 497a (David)
	II	243a, 243b (Forgery)
	III	25a (Jews and Judaism); 143a (Last Judgment); 511a (Names of the Q); 579b (Opposition to Muḥammad)
	IV	120b (Polemic and Polemical Language)
	V	111a (Speech); 541b, 547b (Word of God)
75-79	IV	450b (Revision and Alteration)
	V	304b (Torah)
76	III	25b, 30b (Jews and Judaism)
	V	502a (Witnessing and Testifying)
77	IV	4a (Pairs and Pairing); 572b (Secrets)
	V	479b (Whisper)
77-79	IV	413a (Religious Pluralism and the Q)

78 I 246a (Book); 325a (Chronology and the Q)
II 489a (Ignorance); 494b, 498b (Illiteracy)
V 243a (Textual Criticism of the Q); 399a, 400a (Ummī)

78-79 III 191a (Literacy)

79 II 244a (Forgery); 401b (Hand)
III 25a (Jews and Judaism); 592b (Orality and Writing in Arabia)
IV 116b (Polemic and Polemical Language); 593b, 594a (Shīʿism and the Q)

79-80 III 24a (Jews and Judaism)

80 I 465b (Covenant)
IV 120b (Polemic and Polemical Language); 246b (Pre-1800 Preoccupations of Q Studies); 311a (Provocation)

81 II 439b (History and the Q)
IV 310a (Provocation); 432a (Responsibility)
V 19a, 19b (Sin, Major and Minor)

81-82 V 340a (Transitoriness)

82 I 220a (Belief and Unbelief)
II 167a (Faith)
IV 16b (Paradise)
V 393a (Turkish Literature and the Q)

83 I 350a (Codices of the Q); 465a (Covenant)
II 7a (Economics); 61b, 75b (Ethics and the Q); 174b (Family); 447b (Honor); 453a (Hospitality and Courtesy)
III 40b (Jihād); 603b (Orphans)
IV 20b (Parents); 129a (Politics and the Q); 487a (Ritual and the Q)
V 197a (Taxation); 204b (Teaching); 302b (Torah)

83-84 I 304b (Children of Israel)

83-85 II 418a (Hell and Hellfire)

84 I 237b (Blood and Blood Clot); 240a (Bloodshed); 464b (Covenant)
II 63b (Ethics and the Q)
III 499a (Naḍīr, Banū al-)
IV 324b (Qaynuqāʿ, Banū); 333b, 335a (Qurayẓa, Banū al-)
V 502a (Witnessing and Testifying)

84-85 I 241a (Bloodshed)

85 I 500a (Day, Times of)
II 63b (Ethics and the Q)
III 24b, 28b, 29a (Jews and Judaism)
IV 298b (Prophets and Prophethood); 457a (Reward and Punishment)

86 I 368b (Community and Society in the Q)
III 276a (Markets); 379b (Mercy)
V 138a (Ṣūfism and the Q)

87	I	245a, 245b (Book); 305a (Children of Israel)
	II	351a (Grammar and the Q); 442a (Holy Spirit); 499a (Illiteracy)
	III	7b, 8a, 16a (Jesus); 24a (Jews and Judaism); 293a (Mary); 382a (Messenger); 424b (Moses); 502b (Names of the Prophet); 508a (Names of the Q)
	IV	36b (People of the Book); 282b (Profane and Sacred); 286a (Proof); 291a, 294b, 295b, 297b (Prophets and Prophethood); 413a (Religious Pluralism and the Q); 482b (Rhymed Prose)
	V	81a (Soul); 115a (Spirit); 301a (Torah)
88	I	337a (Circumcision); 492a (Curse)
	II	408a (Heart)
89	I	398b (Conquest)
	III	449a (Muḥammad)
	IV	439a (Revelation and Inspiration)
	V	300b (Torah)
89-90	III	26a (Jews and Judaism)
89-91	III	26b (Jews and Judaism); 579b (Opposition to Muḥammad)
90	I	93a (Anger)
	II	345a (Grace); 420b (Heresy)
	III	25a (Jews and Judaism); 276a (Markets)
	IV	453b (Reward and Punishment)
91	I	305a (Children of Israel)
	III	24a (Jews and Judaism); 382a (Messenger); 449a (Muḥammad)
	IV	301a (Prophets and Prophethood); 439a (Revelation and Inspiration); 600a (Shīʿism and the Q)
92	I	274a (Calf of Gold)
	II	510a (Indifference)
	III	421b (Moses)
92-93	I	99a (Animal Life)
93	I	83b (Anatomy); 274a, 275a (Calf of Gold); 304b (Children of Israel); 465a (Covenant); 537a (Disobedience)
	II	218b (Food and Drink); 311a (Geography); 316a (Glory); 406a (Hearing and Deafness); 408b (Heart)
	III	394a (Miracles)
	IV	128b (Politics and the Q)
	V	190a (Table); 302b (Torah); 502a (Witnessing and Testifying); 546b (Word of God)
94	II	283a (Garden)
	III	24a (Jews and Judaism)
	IV	311a, 312a (Provocation)
96	I	378a (Community and Society in the Q); 480b (Creeds)
	IV	483a (Rhymed Prose); 524b (Samaritans)
	V	286a (Time)

97 I 87a, 87b, 89a (Angel); 447a (Cosmology)
II 278a (Gabriel); 341a, 341b (Good News); 409a (Heart)
III 13b (Jesus); 117a (Language and Style of the Q); 293b (Mary); 442a (Muḥammad); 511b, 513b (Names of the Q); 516a (Nāmūs)
IV 228a (Prayer); 293a (Prophets and Prophethood); 439a, 445a (Revelation and Inspiration)
V 81a (Soul); 201a (Teaching); 300b (Torah)

97-98 I 84b (Angel)
II 23b (Enemies)
III 26a (Jews and Judaism)
IV 217a (Prayer)

98 II 24a (Enemies); 278a (Gabriel); 66a (Ethics and the Q)
III 380a (Mercy); 388a (Michael)
IV 128a (Politics and the Q); 301b (Prophets and Prophethood)

99 III 441a (Muḥammad)
IV 286a (Proof)
V 6a, 8a (Signs); 422b (Verse)

100 I 431b (Contracts and Alliances)

101 III 24b (Jews and Judaism); 449a (Muḥammad); 579b (Opposition to Muḥammad)
IV 120b (Polemic and Polemical Language); 439a (Revelation and Inspiration)
V 300b, 303b (Torah)

101-102 III 189b (Literacy); 249b (Magic)

102 I 195a (Babylon); 526b (Devil)
II 115b (Exegesis of the Q: Classical and Medieval); 404a, 404b (Hārūt and Mārūt)
III 44a (Jinn); 94a (Kings and Rulers); 103b (Knowledge and Learning); 190a (Literacy); 246a (Magic)
IV 165a (Popular and Talismanic Uses of the Q)
V 103b (Sovereignty); 202b, 203a (Teaching); 118b, 120b (Spiritual Beings)

103 II 195b (Fear)

104 II 439a (History and the Q)
III 25b (Jews and Judaism)

105 I 222b (Belief and Unbelief)
II 345a (Grace); 365a (Grammar and the Q)
III 26a (Jews and Judaism); 380a (Mercy)
IV 120b (Polemic and Polemical Language); 40a (People of the Book); 409b (Religious Pluralism and the Q)

105-109 IV 38a (People of the Book)

106 I 15a, 15b, 16a, 16b, 17a (Abrogation); 34a (African Literature); 321a (Chronology and the Q); 348b (Codices of the Q); 353a (Collection of the Q); 480b (Creeds)

Verse	Vol.	References
	II	322a (God and his Attributes)
	III	160a, 162a, 163a (Law and the Q); 467b (Muʿtazila)
	IV	447b (Revelation and Inspiration)
	V	6b, 8a (Signs); 303a (Torah); 422b (Verse)
107	I	432b (Contracts and Alliances)
	II	274b (Friends and Friendship)
108	I	120a (Apostasy)
	II	43b (Error); 358a (Grammar and the Q)
	IV	301a (Prophets and Prophethood); 309b (Provocation)
109	I	120a (Apostasy); 222b, 223b (Belief and Unbelief); 480b (Creeds)
	II	25a (Envy)
	III	26a, 28a (Jews and Judaism); 40a (Jihād); 65b (Judgment)
	IV	40a (People of the Book); 120b (Polemic and Polemical Language)
	V	152b (Ṣūfism and the Q)
110	I	480b (Creeds)
	II	340a (Good Deeds)
	V	196b (Taxation)
111	III	24a (Jews and Judaism)
	IV	116b (Polemic and Polemical Language); 286b, 287b (Proof); 311a, 312a, 312b (Provocation); 405a (Religious Pluralism and the Q)
112	I	170b (Art and Architecture and the Q)
	II	323b (God and his Attributes)
	IV	17a (Paradise)
	V	313b (Trade and Commerce)
113	I	245b (Book); 538b (Dissension)
	II	321a (God and his Attributes)
	III	24a (Jews and Judaism); 190a (Literacy); 591b (Orality and Writing in Arabia)
	IV	405a (Religious Pluralism and the Q)
	V	301a, 304b (Torah); 573b (Zealotry)
114	II	64b (Ethics and the Q)
	III	4a, 6a (Jerusalem); 572a (Occasions of Revelation)
	IV	230b (Prayer); 457a (Reward and Punishment); 516a (Sacred Precincts)
114-115	III	572a (Occasions of Revelation)
115	II	53a (Eschatology); 159a (Face); 160a (Face of God); 323b (God and his Attributes)
	III	572a (Occasions of Revelation)
	IV	4b, 6a (Pairs and Pairing); 107a (Planets and Stars); 128a (Politics and the Q); 221a (Prayer); 325b (Qibla)
	V	137b (Ṣūfism and the Q); 282b (Time); 393b (Turkish Literature and the Q)
116	I	99b (Animal Life)
	II	314b (Glorification of God); 329b (God and his Attributes)

	III	571b (Occasions of Revelation)
	IV	4a (Pairs and Pairing); 220b, 223a (Prayer)
117	I	319a (Chronology and the Q); 472a, 475b (Creation); 516b (Decision)
	II	185b (Fate); 269a (Freedom and Predestination); 327a, 327b (God and his Attributes); 536b (Innovation)
	IV	4a (Pairs and Pairing); 61a (Persian Literature and the Q); 79a, 82a (Philosophy and the Q)
	V	109a (Speech); 287a (Time); 542b (Word of God)
118	III	453a (Muḥammad)
	IV	296a (Prophets and Prophethood); 311b (Provocation)
	V	422b (Verse); 547b (Word of God)
119	II	341b (Good News); 414b (Hell and Hellfire)
	III	440b, 451a (Muḥammad)
	IV	3b (Pairs and Pairing)
120	I	312a (Christians and Christianity)
	II	274b (Friends and Friendship)
	III	27b (Jews and Judaism); 449a (Muḥammad)
	IV	401a, 405a (Religious Pluralism and the Q)
121	I	245b (Book)
	III	591b (Orality and Writing in Arabia); 190a (Literacy)
	IV	402b (Religious Pluralism and the Q)
	V	301a (Torah)
121-122	III	379a (Mercy)
122	I	236b (Blessing); 304b (Children of Israel)
	II	345a (Grace); 434b (History and the Q)
	IV	421b (Remembrance)
123	II	366b (Grammar and the Q); 552a (Intercession)
	III	137b (Last Judgment); 379b (Mercy)
124	I	7a, 7b (Abraham); 465b (Covenant)
	II	502b (Imām)
	III	95a (Kings and Rulers)
	V	109b (Speech); 363a (Trial); 548a (Word of God)
124-125	I	6a (Abraham)
124-134	IV	421b (Remembrance)
124-141	I	330b (Chronology and the Q)
125	I	7b (Abraham); 163b (Art and Architecture and the Q); 254a (Bowing and Prostration)
	II	179a (Farewell Pilgrimage); 205a (Festivals and Commemorative Days); 564a (Ishmael)
	III	4b (Jerusalem); 76b, 78b (Kaʿba); 340b (Mecca); 427a (Mosque)

IV 52b (People of the House); 104b, 105a (Place of Abraham); 218a, 219b (Prayer); 485b, 488a (Ritual and the Q); 505b (Ritual Purity); 514b, 515b (Sacred Precincts)
V 374b (Trips and Voyages); 448b (Visiting)

125-127 I 6a (Abraham)
II 84b (Everyday Life, Q In); 460a (House, Domestic and Divine)

125-128 II 459a (House, Domestic and Divine)
III 340b (Mecca)
IV 327b (Qibla)

125-136 III 38a (Jihād)

126 I 221b (Belief and Unbelief); 236b (Blessing)
II 3a (Earth); 311b (Geography)
III 136a, 136b (Last Judgment)
IV 514b, 516a (Sacred Precincts)
V 108a (Spatial Relations); 287a (Time)

127 II 1b (Ears); 205a (Festivals and Commemorative Days); 320b (God and his Attributes); 564a (Ishmael)
III 76b, 78a (Kaʿba)
IV 5b (Pairs and Pairing); 52b (People of the House); 227a (Prayer); 514b (Sacred Precincts); 575a (Seeing and Hearing)

127-128 I 7a (Abraham)
IV 329b (Quraysh); 337b (Races); 519a (Ṣafā and Marwa)

127-129 III 446a (Muḥammad)

128 I 372a (Community and Society in the Q)
II 72a (Ethics and the Q); 354b (Grammar and the Q)
IV 337b (Races); 429a (Repentance and Penance)

128-129 V 423b (Verse)

129 I 245b, 246a (Book)
II 312a (Geography); 320a, 320b (God and his Attributes)
III 190a, 191a (Literacy); 341a (Mecca); 441a (Muḥammad); 491b (Myths and Legends in the Q)
IV 6a (Pairs and Pairing); 301a (Prophets and Prophethood); 505a (Ritual Purity)
V 7a (Signs); 165b (Sunna); 201b (Teaching); 484a (Wisdom)

130 I 6a (Abraham); 330b (Chronology and the Q); 373a (Community and Society in the Q)
II 11b (Election); 364b (Grammar and the Q)
IV 291a (Prophets and Prophethood); 401a (Religious Pluralism and the Q)

130-135 IV 32b (Patriarchy)

130-141 II 561b (Isaac)

131 IV 288a (Property)
V 547a (Word of God)

132	I	8a (Abraham)
	II	11b (Election); 366a (Grammar and the Q)
	III	1a (Jacob)
	IV	397a (Religion)
133	II	561b (Isaac); 563b (Ishmael)
	III	1b (Jacob); 507b (Names of the Q)
135	I	5b, 6a (Abraham); 330b (Chronology and the Q); 373a (Community and Society in the Q)
	II	164a (Faith); 402b (Ḥanīf)
	III	27b (Jews and Judaism); 446a, 449a, 453b (Muḥammad)
	IV	299b (Prophets and Prophethood); 401a, 405a (Religious Pluralism and the Q)
	V	243b (Textual Criticism of the Q)
135-141	III	7b (Jesus)
136	I	8a (Abraham); 480b (Creeds)
	II	561b (Isaac); 563b (Ishmael)
	III	1a (Jacob); 8a, 17a (Jesus); 300a (Material Culture and the Q); 382a (Messenger); 428a (Mosque); 445a (Muḥammad)
	IV	298a (Prophets and Prophethood); 438b (Revelation and Inspiration)
	V	364a (Tribes and Clans)
137	II	1b (Ears)
	III	321b (Material Culture and the Q); 454b (Muḥammad); 559a (Numismatics)
	IV	575a (Seeing and Hearing)
137-138	V	243b (Textual Criticism of the Q)
138	I	200a (Baptism); 466b (Covenant)
	V	243b (Textual Criticism of the Q)
139	I	170b (Art and Architecture and the Q)
	II	550a (Intention)
	III	39a, 40a (Jihād); 579b (Opposition to Muḥammad)
	IV	115b (Polemic and Polemical Language)
	V	291a (Tolerance and Coercion)
140	I	7b, 8a (Abraham); 118a (Apologetics)
	II	561b (Isaac); 563b (Ishmael)
	III	1a (Jacob); 27b (Jews and Judaism)
	IV	405a (Religious Pluralism and the Q)
	V	364a (Tribes and Clans); 492b (Witnessing and Testifying)
141	III	209a (Literature and the Q)
142	III	27b, 31a (Jews and Judaism)
	IV	4b (Pairs and Pairing); 128a (Politics and the Q); 226b (Prayer); 413a (Religious Pluralism and the Q); 431b (Responsibility)
	V	282b (Time)

142-143 IV 226b (Prayer); 326b (Qibla)

142-144 I 320a (Chronology and the Q)
II 311a (Geography)
V 108a (Spatial Relations)

142-145 IV 519b (Ṣafā and Marwa)

142-147 I 163b (Art and Architecture and the Q)

142-150 I 12b (Abrogation)
III 3a (Jerusalem)
IV 226b (Prayer); 325a, 327a, 327b (Qibla)

142-151 III 340a (Mecca)

142-152 I 328b (Chronology and the Q)

143 I 12b (Abrogation); 372a (Community and Society in the Q)
II 321a (God and his Attributes); 396a (Ḥadīth and the Q)
III 197b (Literary Structures of the Q); 377b (Menstruation); 402a, 402b (Moderation); 447a (Muḥammad); 502a (Names of the Prophet)
IV 5b (Pairs and Pairing); 327a (Qibla); 600a (Shīʿism and the Q)
V 175a (Sūra); 490b (Witness to Faith); 493b (Witnessing and Testifying); 572b, 573a (Zealotry)

144 I 222b (Belief and Unbelief); 246a (Book)
II 32a (Epigraphy); 159a (Face); 299a (Geography)
III 77b, 79a (Kaʿba); 162b (Law and the Q); 340a (Mecca); 446b (Muḥammad)
IV 226b (Prayer); 281b (Profane and Sacred); 327a (Qibla); 515a (Sacred Precincts)
V 303b (Torah)

144-145 IV 36a (People of the Book)
V 556b (Worship)

145 I 222b (Belief and Unbelief)
III 27b (Jews and Judaism)
V 301a (Torah)

146 I 222b (Belief and Unbelief); 245b, 246a (Book)
II 243a (Forgery)
III 25b (Jews and Judaism)
IV 36a (People of the Book)
V 301a (Torah)

148 II 61a (Ethics and the Q)
III 197b (Literary Structures of the Q)

149 II 224a (Forbidden); 299a (Geography)
III 77b (Kaʿba); 340a (Mecca)
IV 226b (Prayer)

149-150 IV 8a (Pairs and Pairing); 281b (Profane and Sacred)

150 I 320a (Chronology and the Q)

	II	224a (Forbidden); 299a (Geography)
	III	77b (Kaʿba); 162b (Law and the Q); 340a (Mecca)
	IV	226b (Prayer)
151	I	245b, 246a (Book)
	II	335a (Goliath)
	III	189b, 190a, 191a (Literacy); 441a, 442b, 443b (Muḥammad); 524a (Narratives)
	IV	301a (Prophets and Prophethood); 505a (Ritual Purity)
	V	7a (Signs); 201b (Teaching); 483b (Wisdom)
152	I	220b (Belief and Unbelief)
	II	166a (Faith); 434b (History and the Q)
	III	373b (Memory)
	IV	2a (Pairs and Pairing); 230a (Prayer); 424a (Remembrance); 487b (Ritual and the Q)
152-153	II	372a (Gratitude and Ingratitude)
152-157	V	362b (Trial)
153	I	458b (Courage)
	II	165a (Faith); 181a (Fasting)
153-155	I	461a (Courage)
153-156	V	434b (Virtue)
154	I	506a (Death and the Dead)
	II	45b (Eschatology); 209b (Fighting)
	III	282b, 283a, 286a (Martyrs); 41a (Jihād)
	IV	30b (Path or Way)
	V	457a (War)
155	I	458b (Courage)
	II	6b (Economics); 341a (Good News)
	III	184b (Life); 579a (Opposition to Muḥammad)
	IV	289a (Property)
	V	83a (Soul); 133b (Suffering); 363a (Trial)
155-156	III	37b (Jihād)
155-157	V	363a (Trial)
156	II	28b (Epigraphy); 91b (Everyday Life, Q In)
	IV	63a (Persian Literature and the Q)
	V	133b (Suffering); 374b (Trips and Voyages)
156-157	III	359b (Medicine and the Q)
157	IV	218a (Prayer)
158	I	353b, 354a (Collection of the Q)
	II	64a (Ethics and the Q); 85a (Everyday Life, Q In); 179a (Farewell Pilgrimage); 299b (Geography); 340a (Good Deeds); 372a (Gratitude and Ingratitude)
	III	77a, 79a (Kaʿba); 128a (Language and Style of the Q); 338b, 339a (Mecca)

	IV	52b (People of the House); 92b, 93a, 98a (Pilgrimage); 213a (Praise); 259a (Pre-Islamic Arabia and the Q); 283b (Profane and Sacred); 515b (Sacred Precincts); 518b, 519b (Ṣafā and Marwa)
	V	318a (Tradition and Custom); 448a (Visiting); 463a (Water)
159	I	305a (Children of Israel); 492a (Curse)
	III	25b (Jews and Judaism); 509a (Names of the Q)
	V	479b (Whisper)
160	II	330a (God and his Attributes)
	IV	427b (Repentance and Penance)
161	I	120b (Apostasy); 492a (Curse)
	IV	116b (Polemic and Polemical Language)
161-162	II	418a (Hell and Hellfire)
162	II	553a (Intercession)
163	I	209a (Basmala); 329b (Chronology and the Q)
	II	320a, 329b (God and his Attributes)
	III	304b (Material Culture and the Q)
	IV	5a (Pairs and Pairing)
	V	488b (Witness to Faith); 500a, 500b, 501a (Witnessing and Testifying)
163-238	III	210a (Literature and the Q)
164	I	45a (Agriculture and Vegetation); 52a, 53b (Air and Wind); 95b (Animal Life); 443a (Cosmology); 474a (Creation); 501a, 501b (Day, Times of)
	II	3a (Earth)
	III	212a (Literature and the Q); 379a (Mercy); 528b, 530b, 531b (Nature as Signs)
	IV	70b (Philosophy and the Q); 438a (Revelation and Inspiration); 604a (Ships)
	V	280b (Time); 373a (Trips and Voyages); 412a (Vehicles); 471a (Weather)
164-165	I	472b (Creation)
165	II	476b (Idolatry and Idolaters)
	III	235b, 236b (Love and Affection)
	V	486b (Wish and Desire)
165-166	III	197b (Literary Structures of the Q)
167	I	298a (Chastisement and Punishment)
	III	197b (Literary Structures of the Q); 379a (Mercy)
	IV	430b (Repentance and Penance)
168	I	526a (Devil)
	II	23b (Enemies); 219b (Food and Drink)
169	IV	580b (Sex and Sexuality)
	V	19a (Sin, Major and Minor)
170	I	221b (Belief and Unbelief)
	III	31b (Jews and Judaism)
	IV	32b (Patriarchy)
	V	317a (Tradition and Custom)

171 I 100a (Animal Life); 226a (Belief and Unbelief)
II 370b (Gratitude and Ingratitude); 406b (Hearing and Deafness)
IV 10a (Parable)

172 I 96b (Animal Life)
II 219b (Food and Drink); 462a (House, Domestic and Divine); 467a (Hunting and Fishing)

172-173 III 174b (Lawful and Unlawful)

173 I 96b, 97a (Animal Life); 237b (Blood and Blood Clot); 291b (Carrion)
II 68b (Ethics and the Q); 220a, 220b, 221a (Food and Drink); 224a (Forbidden); 321a (God and his Attributes)
III 173a, 174a (Lawful and Unlawful)
IV 5b (Pairs and Pairing); 282a (Profane and Sacred); 483b (Rhymed Prose); 504a (Ritual Purity); 517b (Sacrifice)
V 19a (Sin, Major and Minor); 55a (Slaughter)

174 I 245b (Book); 298a (Chastisement and Punishment); 305a (Children of Israel)
II 416a (Hell and Hellfire)
III 25b (Jews and Judaism)
IV 36b (People of the Book); 505a (Ritual Purity)
V 110b (Speech); 547b (Word of God)

175 II 43b (Error)
III 276a (Markets)

176 I 245b (Book)
III 579b (Opposition to Muḥammad)

177 I 66a (Almsgiving); 189a (Authority); 219a (Belief and Unbelief); 289a, 289b (Captives)
II 7a, 8b (Economics); 60b, 61a, 70b, 71b, 75b (Ethics and the Q); 174b, 176a (Family); 340a (Good Deeds); 359a (Grammar and the Q)
III 63b (Joy and Misery); 136a, 136b (Last Judgment); 210a (Literature and the Q); 603b (Orphans)
IV 90b (Piety); 288b (Property); 298b (Prophets and Prophethood)
V 57a, 58a, 59b (Slaves and Slavery); 132a (Strangers and Foreigners); 132a (Suffering); 196b, 197a (Taxation); 282b (Time); 305a (Torah); 501b (Witnessing and Testifying)

178 I 38a (Age of Ignorance); 239a, 239b (Blood Money); 244b (Book); 260a (Brother and Brotherhood); 369b (Community and Society in the Q)
II 61b, 62a (Ethics and the Q)
III 459a (Murder); 499a (Naḍīr, Banū al-)
IV 436a (Retaliation); 453a (Reward and Punishment)
V 58a (Slaves and Slavery); 417a, 417b (Vengeance); 438a (Virtues and Vices, Commanding and Forbidding); 525a (Women and the Q)

178-179 III 183b (Life)

179 II 409a (Heart)
III 193a (Literary Structures of the Q)

	IV	436b (Retaliation)
	V	417a (Vengeance)
180	I	12a, 12b (Abrogation); 244b (Book); 321a (Chronology and the Q)
	II	75a (Ethics and the Q); 174b (Family); 518b (Inheritance)
	III	163b, 164a, 164b (Law and the Q)
	IV	21b (Parents); 32a (Patriarchy); 288b (Property); 449a (Revision and Alteration)
	V	438a (Virtues and Vices, Commanding and Forbidding)
181	I	480b (Creeds)
	II	1b (Ears); 32a (Epigraphy); 519a (Inheritance)
	IV	5b (Pairs and Pairing); 575a (Seeing and Hearing)
181-182	V	19a (Sin, Major and Minor)
182	II	519a (Inheritance)
	IV	5b (Pairs and Pairing); 483b (Rhymed Prose)
183	I	244b (Book)
	II	83b (Everyday Life, Q In); 182a (Fasting)
	III	23a (Jews and Judaism)
	IV	340b, 341a (Ramaḍān)
183-184	II	182a (Fasting)
	IV	487a (Ritual and the Q)
183-185	IV	227a (Prayer); 413a (Religious Pluralism and the Q); 485b (Ritual and the Q)
	V	284b (Time)
183-186	IV	340a (Ramaḍān)
183-187	I	253a (Boundaries and Precepts)
	II	180b (Fasting); 262b (Form and Structure of the Q)
	IV	341a, 346b (Ramaḍān)
	V	175a (Sūra); 556a, 556b (Worship)
184	I	12a (Abrogation); 187b (Atonement); 358a (Collection of the Q)
	II	182b, 183b (Fasting); 450a (Hospitality and Courtesy); 501b (Illness and Health)
	III	57b (Journey); 353b (Medicine and the Q)
	IV	342b, 343b (Ramaḍān); 523b (Salvation)
	V	284b (Time); 373a (Trips and Voyages)
184-185	II	340a (Good Deeds)
	III	57b (Journey)
	IV	8a (Pairs and Pairing)
	V	280b (Time)
185	I	12a (Abrogation); 183a (Asceticism); 289a (Captives); 444b (Cosmology); 486b (Criterion)
	II	82b, 84a (Everyday Life, Q In); 181a, 182a, 183a, 183b, 184a (Fasting); 187a (Fate); 204a (Festivals and Commemorative Days); 219a (Food and Drink); 366b (Grammar and the Q); 501b (Illness and Health)

	III	57b (Journey); 160b, 161a (Law and the Q); 378b (Mercy); 412b, 413a (Months); 415a (Moon); 442a (Muḥammad); 496b (Myths and Legends in the Q); 507b (Names of the Q); 537b (Night of Power)
	IV	293a (Prophets and Prophethood); 343b, 344a, 344b (Ramaḍān); 443b (Revelation and Inspiration); 571b (Seasons)
	V	272a (Theology and the Q); 284b (Time); 373a (Trips and Voyages); 475b (Weights and Measures); 492a, 495a (Witnessing and Testifying)
186	I	445a (Cosmology)
	IV	229a (Prayer); 341b, 342a (Ramaḍān); 229a (Ṣūfism and the Q)
187	I	244b (Book); 252b, 253a (Boundaries and Precepts); 346b (Clothing); 364a, 364b (Colors); 445a (Cosmology); 500b, 503a, 503b (Day, Times of)
	II	175a (Family); 182b (Fasting); 546b (Instruments)
	III	209a, 222a (Literature and the Q); 235a (Love and Affection); 278b (Marriage and Divorce); 417a, 419a (Morning)
	IV	107a (Planets and Stars); 283b (Profane and Sacred); 344b (Ramaḍān); 485b, 486a (Ritual and the Q); 502b (Ritual Purity); 581b, 583a (Sex and Sexuality)
	V	7a (Signs); 281a, 288b (Time); 526b (Women and the Q)
187-190	III	496b (Myths and Legends in the Q)
188	I	301a (Cheating)
	II	6b (Economics)
	III	65b (Judgment)
	V	469b (Wealth)
189	I	272b, 273a (Calendar); 444b (Cosmology)
	II	31a (Epigraphy); 60b (Ethics and the Q); 182b (Fasting)
	III	223a (Literature and the Q); 412b (Months); 414b, 415a (Moon); 571b (Occasions of Revelation)
	IV	90b (Piety); 91b (Pilgrimage); 108a (Planets and Stars); 228a (Prayer); 256a (Pre-Islamic Arabia and the Q); 330b (Quraysh); 487a (Ritual and the Q)
	V	284a (Time); 318a (Tradition and Custom); 475b (Weights and Measures)
190	I	397b (Conquest); 461a (Courage)
	II	151a (Expeditions and Battles); 209a, 209b (Fighting); 322b (God and his Attributes)
	III	38a, 39a, 40a (Jihād); 58a (Journey)
	IV	30a (Path or Way); 35a (Peace); 482a (Rhymed Prose)
	V	456a, 456b (War)
190-191	II	209a (Fighting)
190-193	I	225a (Belief and Unbelief)
	III	36b (Jihād); 577b (Opposition to Muḥammad)
190-195	III	339b (Mecca)
191	I	14a (Abrogation)
	II	144a (Expeditions and Battles); 209a (Fighting); 224a (Forbidden); 299a (Geography)

	III	39a (Jihād); 77b (Kaʿba); 449b (Muḥammad)
	IV	281b (Profane and Sacred); 515b (Sacred Precincts)
	V	456b, 458b (War)
191-194	III	40a (Jihād)
192	III	41b (Jihād); 379b (Mercy)
	IV	5b (Pairs and Pairing)
192-193	IV	428a (Repentance and Penance)
193	I	397b (Conquest); 461a (Courage)
	II	144a (Expeditions and Battles)
	III	39a, 41b (Jihād)
	IV	416a (Religious Pluralism and the Q)
	V	292b (Tolerance and Coercion); 456b, 458b (War); 543a (Word of God)
194	II	209a (Fighting); 224b (Forbidden)
	III	172b (Lawful and Unlawful); 183b (Life); 39a (Jihād); 410a (Months)
	IV	282a (Profane and Sacred); 436a (Retaliation)
	V	285a (Time); 417a (Vengeance); 456b (War); 475b (Weights and Measures)
195	II	209b (Fighting); 322a (God and his Attributes)
	III	42a (Jihād)
	IV	30b (Path or Way); 64b (Persian Literature and the Q)
	V	159b, 161a, 162a (Suicide); 486b (Wish and Desire)
196	I	65a (Almsgiving); 81b (Anatomy); 187b (Atonement)
	II	85a (Everyday Life, Q In); 180b (Fasting); 205b (Festivals and Commemorative Days); 299a (Geography); 450a (Hospitality and Courtesy); 501b (Illness and Health)
	III	77b (Kaʿba); 128a (Language and Style of the Q); 339a (Mecca); 353b (Medicine and the Q); 376a (Menstruation); 551a, 553a (Numbers and Enumeration)
	IV	91b, 94a, 94b, 95a, 95b, 98b (Pilgrimage); 281b (Profane and Sacred); 485b, 487a (Ritual and the Q); 523b (Salvation)
	V	175a (Sūra); 198a (Taxation); 280a (Time); 375a (Trips and Voyages); 448a (Visiting); 556b (Worship)
196-203	II	340a (Good Deeds); 460a (House, Domestic and Divine)
197	I	511b (Debate and Disputation)
	II	84b (Everyday Life, Q In)
	III	278b (Marriage and Divorce); 410b (Months)
	IV	91b (Pilgrimage); 583a (Sex and Sexuality)
	V	285a (Time); 475b (Weights and Measures)
197-199	III	339b (Mecca)
197-200	IV	423b (Remembrance)
198	I	146a (ʿArafāt); 349a (Codices of the Q)
	II	6b (Economics)

III 173b (Lawful and Unlawful); 372a (Memory)
IV 95b, 96b (Pilgrimage); 259a (Pre-Islamic Arabia and the Q); 281b (Profane and Sacred); 421a (Remembrance); 515b (Sacred Precincts)
V 19a (Sin, Major and Minor); 318a (Tradition and Custom)

198-199 IV 95b (Pilgrimage)

199 III 379b (Mercy)
IV 5b (Pairs and Pairing); 96b (Pilgrimage); 330b (Quraysh); 482a, 483b (Rhymed Prose)

200 II 434b (History and the Q)
IV 487b (Ritual and the Q)
V 317a (Tradition and Custom)

201 V 552a (World)

202 III 66b (Judgment)

203 I 499b (Day, Times of)
IV 96b (Pilgrimage)
V 280a (Time)

204-205 I 440a (Corruption)

205 I 32a (African Literature)
II 63a (Ethics and the Q); 322b (God and his Attributes)

206 II 414b, 415a (Hell and Hellfire); 448a (Honor)
IV 104a (Pit)

207 IV 577a (Servants)
V 441b (Virtues and Vices, Commanding and Forbidding)

208 I 526a (Devil)
II 23b, 24a (Enemies)
III 39b, 40a (Jihād)

209 IV 6a (Pairs and Pairing); 286b (Proof)

210 I 463a (Court)
II 316a, 316b (Glory); 325b (God and his Attributes)
V 543a (Word of God); 554a (World)

211 I 236b (Blessing); 304a (Children of Israel)
IV 286a (Proof)
V 4b, 8a (Signs)

212 III 401a (Mockery)
V 340a (Transitoriness)

213 I 222b (Belief and Unbelief); 245a, 245b (Book); 372a, 377a (Community and Society in the Q); 538a (Dissension)
II 321a (God and his Attributes); 341b (Good News); 431b, 432a (History and the Q)
III 444b (Muḥammad); 509a (Names of the Q)

	IV	3b (Pairs and Pairing); 127b, 133b (Politics and the Q); 290b, 301a (Prophets and Prophethood); 337a (Races)
214	I	220b (Belief and Unbelief)
	II	282b (Garden)
	III	37b (Jihād); 63b (Joy and Misery)
	IV	335a (Qurayẓa, Banū al-)
215	II	75a (Ethics and the Q); 85b (Everyday Life, Q In); 174b (Family); 450a (Hospitality and Courtesy)
	III	604a (Orphans)
	IV	21b (Parents); 209a (Poverty and the Poor)
	V	132a (Strangers and Foreigners); 204b (Teaching)
215-216	III	252a (Maintenance and Upkeep)
216	I	14a (Abrogation); 224a (Belief and Unbelief); 244b (Book)
	II	68a (Ethics and the Q); 151a (Expeditions and Battles); 209a, 209b (Fighting); 340a (Good Deeds); 367a (Grammar and the Q)
	III	41b (Jihād); 235b (Love and Affection); 577b (Opposition to Muḥammad)
	V	456b, 457a (War)
217	I	120b (Apostasy); 397b (Conquest)
	II	69a (Ethics and the Q); 85b (Everyday Life, Q In); 144a, 149a (Expeditions and Battles); 209a (Fighting); 224b (Forbidden); 299a (Geography); 358a (Grammar and the Q); 431a (History and the Q)
	III	40a, 41b (Jihād); 77b (Kaʿba); 183b (Life); 339a (Mecca); 410a (Months); 449a (Muḥammad); 579b (Opposition to Muḥammad)
	IV	282a (Profane and Sacred); 332a (Quraysh); 456a (Reward and Punishment); 515a (Sacred Precincts)
	V	285a (Time); 293b (Tolerance and Coercion); 375a (Trips and Voyages); 456b, 458b (War); 475b (Weights and Measures)
218	I	225a (Belief and Unbelief); 320a (Chronology and the Q)
	II	449a (Hope)
	III	37a (Jihād); 58a (Journey)
	IV	5b (Pairs and Pairing); 17a (Paradise); 30a (Path or Way)
	V	375b (Trips and Voyages)
219	I	321a (Chronology and the Q)
	II	7a (Economics); 67b (Ethics and the Q); 85b (Everyday Life, Q In); 221b (Food and Drink); 237b, 238b (Foretelling in the Q); 280a (Gambling); 556a, 556b, 557a (Intoxicants)
	III	152a, 169a (Law and the Q); 252b (Maintenance and Upkeep); 570a (Occasions of Revelation); 579b (Opposition to Muḥammad)
	IV	500a (Ritual Purity)
	V	19a (Sin, Major and Minor); 481b (Wine)
220	I	261b (Brother and Brotherhood)
	II	62b, 75b (Ethics and the Q); 85b (Everyday Life, Q In)

III 96a (Kinship); 604a (Orphans)
IV 6a (Pairs and Pairing); 488b (Ritual and the Q)

221 I 213a (Beauty); 299a (Chastity); 396a, 397a (Concubines); 437a (Conversion)
II 245a (Forgiveness); 558b (Invitation)
III 277a, 277b, 278a (Marriage and Divorce)
IV 580b, 582a (Sex and Sexuality)
V 7a (Signs); 57a, 58a (Slaves and Slavery); 293a (Tolerance and Coercion)

222 I 81a (Anatomy); 342b (Cleanliness and Ablution)
II 85b (Everyday Life, Q In); 322a (God and his Attributes)
III 376a, 377a (Menstruation)
IV 426a (Repentance and Penance); 491a (Ritual and the Q); 501b, 502a (Ritual Purity); 583a (Sex and Sexuality)
V 524b (Women and the Q)

222-223 III 278b (Marriage and Divorce)

223 I 235a (Birth Control)
II 76a (Ethics and the Q); 175b (Family); 304b (Geography); 341a (Good News)
IV 582b (Sex and Sexuality)
V 71a (Social Sciences and the Q); 524b, 540a (Women and the Q)

224 I 480b (Creeds)
II 60b (Ethics and the Q)
III 564b (Oaths)
IV 5b (Pairs and Pairing); 575a (Seeing and Hearing)
V 393a (Turkish Literature and the Q)

225 III 109b (Language and Style of the Q); 401b (Moderation); 565a, 565b (Oaths)
IV 5b (Pairs and Pairing); 573a (Secrets)
V 334a (Traditional Disciplines of Q Studies); 393a (Turkish Literature and the Q)

226 I 19b (Abstinence)
III 279b (Marriage and Divorce); 551b (Numbers and Enumeration)
IV 5b (Pairs and Pairing); 583b (Sex and Sexuality)
V 285a (Time); 453b, 454a, 454b (Waiting Period); 476a (Weights and Measures)

226-227 III 280a (Marriage and Divorce); 562b (Oaths)

227 III 96a (Kinship)
IV 5b (Pairs and Pairing)

227-232 II 68b (Ethics and the Q)

228 I 194a, 194b (Baal)
II 76a (Ethics and the Q); 175b (Family)
III 136b (Last Judgment); 278b, 279a, 280b (Marriage and Divorce)
IV 6a (Pairs and Pairing); 501b (Ritual Purity)
V 438a (Virtues and Vices, Commanding and Forbidding); 453b, 454a, 454b (Waiting Period); 480b (Widow); 495b (Witnessing and Testifying); 522a (Womb); 525a, 528b, 537a (Women and the Q)

228-230	IV	283a (Profane and Sacred)
229	I	252b, 253b (Boundaries and Precepts)
	II	23b (Enemies); 61b, 64b (Ethics and the Q)
	III	280a (Marriage and Divorce); 96a (Kinship)
	IV	7a (Pairs and Pairing); 237b (Pre-1800 Preoccupations of Q Studies)
	V	438a (Virtues and Vices, Commanding and Forbidding); 528b (Women and the Q)
229-230	I	253a, 253b (Boundaries and Precepts)
	IV	581b (Sex and Sexuality)
	V	528b (Women and the Q)
230	I	253a, 253b (Boundaries and Precepts)
	III	172b (Lawful and Unlawful); 280b (Marriage and Divorce)
	IV	538b (Scholar); 580b (Sex and Sexuality)
231	I	245b (Book); 305b (Children of Israel)
	III	71a, 72a (Justice and Injustice); 279b (Marriage and Divorce); 400a, 401a (Mockery)
	IV	3b (Pairs and Pairing)
	V	7a (Signs); 317b (Tradition and Custom); 454b (Waiting Period); 483b (Wisdom)
231-235	V	289a (Time)
232	I	343b (Cleanliness and Ablution)
	III	136b (Last Judgment); 235a (Love and Affection)
	IV	505b (Ritual Purity); 580b (Sex and Sexuality)
232-233	IV	20a (Parents)
233	I	234b (Birth Control); 302a (Children); 407a, 408b (Consultation)
	II	76a (Ethics and the Q); 175b (Family); 290a (Gender)
	III	106a, 106b, 107a, 107b (Lactation); 252b (Maintenance and Upkeep); 278b, 279a, 280b (Marriage and Divorce)
	IV	7a (Pairs and Pairing); 432b (Responsibility)
	V	204b (Teaching); 285b (Time); 476b, 477a, 477b, 478a (Wet-Nursing); 549a (Work); 570a (Youth and Old Age)
234	I	353a (Collection of the Q)
	III	551b (Numbers and Enumeration)
	V	285b (Time); 453b, 454a, 454b (Waiting Period); 476a (Weights and Measures)
234-235	V	480a (Widow)
235	I	244b (Book); 464a (Covenant)
	III	96a (Kinship); 235a (Love and Affection); 278a (Marriage and Divorce); 401b (Moderation)
	IV	5b (Pairs and Pairing); 580b (Sex and Sexuality)
	V	19a (Sin, Major and Minor); 438a (Virtues and Vices, Commanding and Forbidding); 454b (Waiting Period); 480b (Widow)

236 III 60b (Joy and Misery)
V 438a (Virtues and Vices, Commanding and Forbidding)

236-237 I 258b (Bridewealth)
II 313b (Gift-Giving)
III 278b, 281a (Marriage and Divorce)

237 I 258b (Bridewealth); 412a (Contamination); 464a (Covenant)
II 195b (Fear); 374b (Guardianship)
III 96a (Kinship); 278b (Marriage and Divorce)
IV 580b (Sex and Sexuality)
V 527a (Women and the Q)

238 I 35b, 36a (Afternoon); 44b (Agriculture and Vegetation); 328b (Chronology and the Q); 502b (Day, Times of)
III 158a (Law and the Q); 210a (Literature and the Q); 419a (Morning); 545a (Noon)
IV 219b, 222b, 224a, 224b (Prayer); 308a (Protection)
V 278a (Time); 556a, 556b (Worship)

239 II 198b (Feet)
III 42a (Jihād)
IV 233a (Prayer Formulas); 421a (Remembrance)
V 201a, 201b (Teaching)

240 I 12a (Abrogation); 352b (Collection of the Q)
II 519a (Inheritance)
III 60b (Joy and Misery); 252a (Maintenance and Upkeep); 278b (Marriage and Divorce)
IV 6a (Pairs and Pairing)
V 454b (Waiting Period); 481a (Widow)

241 III 60b (Joy and Misery); 280b (Marriage and Divorce)
V 454b (Waiting Period)

242 II 67a, 67b (Ethics and the Q)

243 I 506b (Death and the Dead)
II 154b (Ezekiel)
III 5b (Jerusalem); 364b (Medicine and the Q); 379a (Mercy); 524a (Narratives)
V 109a (Speech); 455b (War); 545a (Word of God)

243-252 III 521a (Narratives)

244 I 225a (Belief and Unbelief); 461a (Courage)
II 209b (Fighting); 340a (Good Deeds)
III 39a, 40a (Jihād)
V 457a (War)

245 I 65a (Almsgiving)
II 8b (Economics); 354a (Grammar and the Q)
III 209a (Literature and the Q)

IV 6b (Pairs and Pairing); 457a (Reward and Punishment)
V 457a (War)

246 I 244b (Book); 369a (Community and Society in the Q)
II 355b, 367a (Grammar and the Q); 432b (History and the Q)
III 524a (Narratives)
IV 527a, 527b, 528a (Samuel)
V 457a (War)

246-248 IV 526b, 527a, 527b, 528b, 530a (Samuel); 590a (Shekhinah)

246-251 III 522b (Narratives)
IV 536a (Saul)
V 455b (War)

246-252 I 303a (Children of Israel)

247 I 80a (Anatomy)
II 6b (Economics); 11b (Election); 320a (God and his Attributes); 354a (Grammar and the Q)
III 94a (Kings and Rulers)
IV 6a (Pairs and Pairing); 128a, 130a (Politics and the Q); 291a (Prophets and Prophethood); 527a, 529a, 529b (Samuel); 538a (Scholar)
V 468a (Wealth)

247-251 II 145b (Expeditions and Battles); 404a (Hārūt and Mārūt)

248 I 158a (Ark)
III 94b (Kings and Rulers); 395a (Miracles)
IV 425b (Remnant); 527a, 529a (Samuel); 590b (Shekhinah)
V 404b (Uncertainty)

249 II 335a (Goliath)
IV 529b (Samuel)
V 43a (Sīra and the Q); 184b (Syria); 377a (Troops)

249-250 I 461a (Courage)
V 434b (Virtue)

249-251 II 334b (Goliath)
IV 529a (Samuel)

250 II 70b (Ethics and the Q); 198b (Feet)

251 I 439b (Corruption); 496a (David)
II 62b (Ethics and the Q); 431a (History and the Q)
III 94a (Kings and Rulers)
IV 128a, 128b (Politics and the Q); 536b (Saul)
V 103b (Sovereignty); 200b (Teaching); 457a (War); 483a (Wisdom); 553a (World)

251-252 V 4a (Signs)

252 II 119b (Exegesis of the Q: Classical and Medieval)
III 190a (Literacy); 441a, 451a (Muḥammad)

IV 297b (Prophets and Prophethood)
V 421b (Verse)

252-253 III 7b (Jesus)

253 I 480b (Creeds); 538b (Dissension)
II 430b (History and the Q); 442a (Holy Spirit)
III 8a, 16a, 17a, 19b (Jesus); 293a (Mary); 382a (Messenger)
IV 282b (Profane and Sacred); 286b (Proof); 292a, 295b (Prophets and Prophethood)
V 81a (Soul); 110a (Speech); 115a (Spirit); 533b (Women and the Q); 546b, 547b (Word of God)

254 I 500a (Day, Times of)
III 141a (Last Judgment)

255 I 103b (Anthropomorphism); 115a (Apologetics); 170b, 171a (Art and Architecture and the Q); 264b (Burial); 329b (Chronology and the Q); 443b, 446a (Cosmology); 472b (Creation); 480b (Creeds)
II 28b, 30b, 33b, 37b, 38b (Epigraphy); 96a (Everyday Life, Q In); 275b (Furniture and Furnishings); 320a, 320b, 325b, 326a (God and his Attributes); 408b (Heart); 410b (Heaven and Sky); 461a (House, Domestic and Divine); 552b (Intercession)
III 182b (Life); 197b (Literary Structures of the Q); 267b (Manuscripts of the Q); 300a, 304b, 319a, 321b, 322a, 327a, 327b (Material Culture and the Q); 437a (Mosque); 513b (Names of the Q)
IV 4a, 4b, 5b, 6a (Pairs and Pairing); 63b (Persian Literature and the Q); 163b, 172b, 173a, 176a, 180a (Popular and Talismanic Uses of the Q); 184a (Possession and Possessions); 234a (Prayer Formulas); 380a (Recitation of the Q); 435b (Resurrection)
V 61a (Sleep); 61a (Ṣūfism and the Q); 277a (Throne of God); 371b (Trinity); 427b (Verse); 488b (Witness to Faith); 500b, 501a (Witnessing and Testifying)

256 I 224a (Belief and Unbelief); 374b (Community and Society in the Q); 465a (Covenant)
II 152a (Expeditions and Battles)
III 40a (Jihād); 197b (Literary Structures of the Q); 325b (Material Culture and the Q); 499a (Naḍīr, Banū al-); 503b (Names of the Prophet); 531a (Nature as Signs)
IV 121b, 122a (Polemic and Polemical Language); 142a (Politics and the Q); 238b (Pre-1800 Preoccupations of Q Studies); 415a, 415b (Religious Pluralism and the Q)
V 68a (Social Sciences and the Q); 291b, 292b, 293a, 293b, 294a (Tolerance and Coercion); 362b (Trial); 393a, 393b (Turkish Literature and the Q); 405a (Uncertainty); 573b (Zealotry)

256-258 III 314b (Material Culture and the Q)

257 I 533a (Dialogues)
II 273a, 273b (Friends and Friendship); 482a (Idols and Images)

	III	70b (Justice and Injustice); 186a (Light); 231b (Lord)
	V	120a (Spiritual Beings); 182a (Symbolic Imagery)
258	I	295b (Chastisement and Punishment)
	II	330a (God and his Attributes)
	III	93a (Kings and Rulers); 524a (Narratives); 539a, 539b (Nimrod)
	IV	78a (Philosophy and the Q); 107a (Planets and Stars); 160a, 161a (Polytheism and Atheism); 184a (Possession and Possessions); 211a (Power and Impotence)
	V	103b (Sovereignty); 282b (Time)
258-260	III	494b (Myths and Legends in the Q)
259	I	98a (Animal Life); 166a (Art and Architecture and the Q)
	II	348a (Grammar and the Q)
	III	5b (Jerusalem); 396b (Miracles)
	V	4b, 5a (Signs); 286a (Time)
260	I	6a (Abraham); 98a (Animal Life); 532a (Dialogues)
	II	409a (Heart)
	III	117b (Language and Style of the Q); 396a (Miracles)
	IV	6a (Pairs and Pairing)
	V	242a (Textual Criticism of the Q)
261	I	42a (Agriculture and Vegetation)
	III	399a (Miracles)
	IV	6a, 6b (Pairs and Pairing); 10a (Parable); 30b (Path or Way)
261-262	II	209b (Fighting)
261-265	V	469a (Wealth)
262	III	58a (Journey); 376a (Menstruation)
	IV	30b (Path or Way); 455a (Reward and Punishment)
	V	138a (Ṣūfism and the Q); 313b (Trade and Commerce)
263	I	65b (Almsgiving)
	II	320a (God and his Attributes); 453a (Hospitality and Courtesy)
	III	376a (Menstruation); 378b (Mercy)
	IV	6a (Pairs and Pairing)
263-264	V	198b (Taxation)
264	I	65b (Almsgiving); 184b (Ashes); 435b (Conversion)
	II	4a (Earth); 468b (Hypocrites and Hypocrisy)
	III	136b (Last Judgment); 225b (Literature and the Q); 376a (Menstruation)
	IV	10a (Parable)
	V	129b (Stone); 129b (Ṣūfism and the Q); 268b (Theology and the Q); 434a (Virtue); 469a (Wealth)
264-265	III	209b (Literature and the Q)
	IV	13a (Paradise)
265	I	42a (Agriculture and Vegetation); 65a, 66b (Almsgiving)
	II	4a (Earth)

	IV	6b (Pairs and Pairing); 10a (Parable)
	V	252a (Textual Criticism of the Q); 407b, 408a (Usury)
265-266	II	283a (Garden)
266	I	246a (Book)
	II	304a (Geography)
	III	580b (Oppressed on Earth)
	V	5b (Signs); 127b (Springs and Fountains); 464b (Water); 570b (Youth and Old Age)
267	II	330a (God and his Attributes)
	IV	6a (Pairs and Pairing)
	V	408a (Usury)
268	I	526a (Devil)
	II	245a (Forgiveness)
	IV	6a (Pairs and Pairing); 580b (Sex and Sexuality)
269	II	434b, 435a (History and the Q)
	IV	68b (Philosophy and the Q)
	V	483a (Wisdom)
270	V	193b (Taxation); 449b (Vow)
271	I	65b (Almsgiving)
	II	7a (Economics); 450a (Hospitality and Courtesy)
	III	571a (Occasions of Revelation)
	IV	209a (Poverty and the Poor)
	V	198a (Taxation)
271-272	V	198b (Taxation)
271-273	V	199a, 199b (Taxation)
272	I	65b (Almsgiving); 435b (Conversion)
	II	110b (Exegesis of the Q: Classical and Medieval); 159a (Face); 160a (Face of God); 323b (God and his Attributes)
	IV	221a (Prayer)
	V	198b (Taxation); 487a (Wish and Desire)
273	I	66a (Almsgiving)
	II	450a (Hospitality and Courtesy)
	III	58a (Journey)
	IV	209a (Poverty and the Poor)
	V	198b (Taxation)
273-274	I	389b (Companions of the Prophet)
274	I	65b (Almsgiving); 501a (Day, Times of)
	II	450a (Hospitality and Courtesy)
	III	571b (Occasions of Revelation)
	V	313b (Trade and Commerce); 469b (Wealth)

274-275	V	407b (Usury)
275	II	6b (Economics); 142b (Exhortations); 418a (Hell and Hellfire); 540b (Insanity)
	III	174b (Lawful and Unlawful)
	IV	282a, 283a (Profane and Sacred)
	V	438b (Virtues and Vices, Commanding and Forbidding)
275-276	V	21b (Sin, Major and Minor)
275-280	II	8a (Economics)
276	I	221a (Belief and Unbelief)
	II	322b (God and his Attributes)
	III	380a (Mercy)
	V	198b (Taxation)
277	I	220a (Belief and Unbelief)
	II	60b (Ethics and the Q); 340a (Good Deeds)
	III	184a (Life)
	IV	17a (Paradise); 487a (Ritual and the Q)
	V	196b (Taxation); 313b (Trade and Commerce)
278	I	326a (Chronology and the Q)
	V	456a (War)
278-279	IV	427a (Repentance and Penance)
	V	21b (Sin, Major and Minor)
279	II	8a (Economics); 144a (Expeditions and Battles)
	V	407a (Usury); 455a (War)
280	II	8a (Economics); 450a (Hospitality and Courtesy)
	V	198a (Taxation); 543a (Word of God)
281	IV	85a (Philosophy and the Q); 432b (Responsibility)
	V	268a (Theology and the Q)
282	I	300b (Cheating); 433a (Contracts and Alliances); 514b (Debt)
	II	8b (Economics); 70a, 70b (Ethics and the Q); 358a (Grammar and the Q)
	III	71b (Justice and Injustice); 158b (Law and the Q); 189a (Literacy); 550b (Numbers and Enumeration); 580b (Oppressed on Earth)
	IV	7a (Pairs and Pairing)
	V	201a, 201b (Teaching); 289a (Time); 312b (Trade and Commerce); 490a (Witness to Faith); 492b, 495a, 495b, 497a, 498b (Witnessing and Testifying); 525a (Women and the Q)
282-283	III	191b (Literacy); 590b, 592b, 593a (Orality and Writing in Arabia)
	V	204a (Teaching)
283	II	8b (Economics); 454a (Hostages)
	III	57b, 58a (Journey); 66a (Judgment)
	IV	109b, 110a (Pledge); 573a (Secrets)
	V	21a (Sin, Major and Minor)

284 I 298a (Chastisement and Punishment)
II 244b (Forgiveness)
III 200b (Literary Structures of the Q)
IV 4a (Pairs and Pairing); 457b (Reward and Punishment); 572b, 573a (Secrets)
V 22a (Sin, Major and Minor); 553b (World)

285 I 189a (Authority); 219a (Belief and Unbelief); 247a (Book); 480b (Creeds)
II 360a, 363a (Grammar and the Q); 406a (Hearing and Deafness)
III 17a (Jesus); 445a (Muḥammad); 568b (Obedience)
IV 298b (Prophets and Prophethood)
V 287a (Time); 305a (Torah); 393b (Turkish Literature and the Q); 501b (Witnessing and Testifying)

285-286 II 189b (Fātiḥa)

286 I 11b (Abrogation); 344b (Clients and Clientage)
II 59b, 64a (Ethics and the Q); 244a, 244b (Forgiveness); 330b (God and his Attributes); 508b (Impotence)
III 12b (Jesus); 231a (Lord); 303a (Material Culture and the Q)
IV 85a (Philosophy and the Q); 128a (Politics and the Q); 307b (Protection); 432b (Responsibility)
V 22a (Sin, Major and Minor)

Sūrat Āl ʿImrān (3)

I 409a (Consultation)
II 176b (Family of the Prophet); 264a (Form and Structure of the Q)
III 10b, 13a, 18a (Jesus); 283b (Martyrs); 294b (Mary); 472b (Mysterious Letters)
IV 177a (Popular and Talismanic Uses of the Q); 241a (Pre-1800 Preoccupations of Q Studies)
V 174b (Sūra); 575a (Zechariah)

1 I 170b (Art and Architecture and the Q)
II 262a (Form and Structure of the Q)

1-17 III 304b (Material Culture and the Q)

2 II 320a (God and his Attributes)
III 182b (Life)
IV 6a (Pairs and Pairing); 172b (Popular and Talismanic Uses of the Q)
V 500b, 501a (Witnessing and Testifying)

2-4 V 7a (Signs)

3 II 235b (Foreign Vocabulary)
III 303a (Material Culture and the Q); 445a (Muḥammad)
IV 439a (Revelation and Inspiration)
V 300b, 302b, 307b (Torah); 386b (Truth)

3-4 I 117b (Apologetics)
IV 37b (People of the Book); 293b, 298a (Prophets and Prophethood)

4 I 486b (Criterion)
II 416a (Hell and Hellfire)
III 380a (Mercy)
IV 293b (Prophets and Prophethood); 310a (Provocation); 343a (Ramaḍān); 443b (Revelation and Inspiration); 453b (Reward and Punishment)
V 416a (Vengeance)

5 I 198a (Bahāʾīs)

6 I 329b (Chronology and the Q); 446b (Cosmology); 476b (Creation)
II 328a (God and his Attributes)
IV 6a (Pairs and Pairing); 177b (Popular and Talismanic Uses of the Q)
V 522a (Womb)

7 I 70b, 71b, 72b, 73b, 75a, 75b, 77a (Ambiguous); 103b (Anthropomorphism); 113b (Apocalypse); 247b, 248a (Book); 349a (Codices of the Q)
II 100a, 102a (Exegesis of the Q: Classical and Medieval); 189a (Fātiḥa); 323a (God and his Attributes); 409a (Heart); 425a, 425b (Hidden and the Hidden); 434b, 435a (History and the Q)
III 31a (Jews and Judaism); 303a (Material Culture and the Q); 386a (Metaphor)
IV 3b (Pairs and Pairing); 69b, 70a, 76b, 81a (Philosophy and the Q); 157a (Polysemy in the Q); 261b (Preserved Tablet)
V 7a (Signs); 70a (Social Sciences and the Q); 180a (Symbolic Imagery); 422b (Verse)

8 I 492a (Curse)
II 320b (God and his Attributes); 408b (Heart)
III 303a (Material Culture and the Q)

9 II 320b (God and his Attributes)
III 66b (Judgment)

10 I 221b (Belief and Unbelief); 302b (Children)
II 150a (Expeditions and Battles); 415a (Hell and Hellfire)
IV 31b (Patriarchy)
V 468a (Wealth)

10-11 IV 320b (Punishment Stories)

11 II 174a (Family)
III 380a (Mercy)
IV 67a (Pharaoh); 453a (Reward and Punishment)
V 4b (Signs); 19a (Sin, Major and Minor); 317b (Tradition and Custom)

12 II 276a (Furniture and Furnishings)
III 29b (Jews and Judaism)
IV 104a (Pit); 324b (Qaynuqāʿ, Banū); 406a (Religious Pluralism and the Q)

13 I 81a (Anatomy); 124b (Apparition); 550b, 551a (Dreams and Sleep)
III 42b (Jihād); 455a (Muḥammad)
IV 30a (Path or Way); 185a (Possession and Possessions)
V 5a (Signs); 393b (Turkish Literature and the Q)

14 I 41b (Agriculture and Vegetation); 96a (Animal Life)
II 304a (Geography); 333b, 334a (Gold); 545b (Instruments)
III 60a (Joy and Misery); 235b (Love and Affection); 383b (Metals and Minerals)
IV 580a (Sex and Sexuality)
V 393a, 393b (Turkish Literature and the Q); 434b (Virtue); 474a (Weights and Measures); 486b (Wish and Desire)

15 I 220b (Belief and Unbelief); 343b (Cleanliness and Ablution); 480b (Creeds)
II 175a (Family); 321b (God and his Attributes); 353b (Grammar and the Q); 456b (Houris)
III 536b (News)
IV 17a, 18a (Paradise); 505b (Ritual Purity); 574b (Seeing and Hearing)
V 123a (Springs and Fountains)

15-18 III 312b (Material Culture and the Q)

16 V 19a (Sin, Major and Minor)

16-17 IV 221a (Prayer)

17 I 503b (Day, Times of)
III 417a (Morning)
V 281a (Time); 556a (Worship)

18 I 329b (Chronology and the Q)
II 28b, 33b (Epigraphy); 321b (God and his Attributes)
III 437a (Mosque)
IV 6a (Pairs and Pairing); 538b, 539a (Scholar)
V 490b (Witness to Faith); 492a, 492b, 500b, 501a (Witnessing and Testifying)

18-19 I 170b (Art and Architecture and the Q)
II 276b (Furniture and Furnishings)

19 I 200a (Baptism); 222b (Belief and Unbelief); 305a (Children of Israel)
II 31a (Epigraphy); 329a (God and his Attributes); 569b (Islam)
III 40a (Jihād); 66b (Judgment); 303a (Material Culture and the Q); 507b (Names of the Q)
IV 120a (Polemic and Polemical Language); 396b, 397a, 397b, 398a (Religion); 401b, 404a (Religious Pluralism and the Q)
V 301a (Torah); 436a (Virtue)

19-20 IV 36a (People of the Book); 487a (Ritual and the Q)

20 I 222b (Belief and Unbelief); 325a (Chronology and the Q); 437b (Conversion)
II 158a (Face); 323b (God and his Attributes); 494b, 495a, 498b (Illiteracy)
III 28a (Jews and Judaism); 40a (Jihād); 567a (Obedience)
IV 115b (Polemic and Polemical Language)
V 399a, 400a (Ummī)

21 I 305a (Children of Israel)
II 418a (Hell and Hellfire); 431a (History and the Q)
III 382a (Messenger)

	IV	456a (Reward and Punishment)
	V	6a (Signs); 440b (Virtues and Vices, Commanding and Forbidding); 575a (Zechariah)
21-22	IV	431b (Responsibility)
23	III	30b (Jews and Judaism)
	IV	24b (Parties and Factions); 36a (People of the Book); 133b, 134b (Politics and the Q)
	V	231b (Teeth); 301a, 303b, 304a (Torah)
23-24	III	24a (Jews and Judaism)
24	II	418b (Hell and Hellfire)
	V	280b (Time)
25	III	379b (Mercy)
	V	268a (Theology and the Q)
26	I	170b (Art and Architecture and the Q); 443a (Cosmology)
	II	35a (Epigraphy); 61a (Ethics and the Q); 321b, 331a (God and his Attributes)
	III	91a, 91b, 93a, 93b (Kings and Rulers); 300a (Material Culture and the Q); 559a (Numismatics)
	IV	128a (Politics and the Q); 184a, 184b (Possession and Possessions); 210b, 212a, 212b (Power and Impotence)
	V	103b (Sovereignty)
26-27	II	276b (Furniture and Furnishings)
	IV	211b (Power and Impotence)
27	I	98a (Animal Life); 501b (Day, Times of)
	IV	212a (Power and Impotence)
28	I	224b (Belief and Unbelief); 540a (Dissimulation)
	II	274a (Friends and Friendship)
	III	40a (Jihād); 231b (Lord); 238a, 238b, 239b (Loyalty)
	IV	573a (Secrets)
	V	251b (Textual Criticism of the Q); 287a (Time)
29	V	428a (Verse); 553b (World)
30	III	335a (Measurement)
	V	241b (Textual Criticism of the Q); 288b (Time); 475a (Weights and Measures)
30-31	I	2b (Aaron)
31	II	74b (Ethics and the Q)
	III	233b, 236b (Love and Affection); 447a (Muḥammad); 567a (Obedience)
	IV	5b (Pairs and Pairing)
	V	137b (Ṣūfism and the Q)
32	I	189b (Authority)
	II	65b, 74b (Ethics and the Q); 322b (God and his Attributes)
	III	380a (Mercy); 447a (Muḥammad); 502a (Names of the Prophet)
	V	272b (Theology and the Q)

33 I 526a (Devil)
II 11b (Election); 509a (ʿImrān)
III 289b (Mary); 486b (Myths and Legends in the Q); 540a (Noah)
V 552a (World)

33-34 IV 291a (Prophets and Prophethood); 337a (Races)

33-37 III 289a (Mary)

33-45 III 13a (Jesus)

33-58 V 575a (Zechariah)

34 I 480b (Creeds)
IV 5b (Pairs and Pairing); 575a (Seeing and Hearing)

35 I 1b (Aaron)
II 509a (ʿImrān)
III 519b (Narratives); 562b (Oaths)
IV 5b (Pairs and Pairing)
V 449b (Vow)

35-36 I 233b (Birth)
III 289b (Mary)
V 575a (Zechariah)

35-47 V 533b (Women and the Q)

36 I 233b (Birth)
II 92b (Everyday Life, Q In)
III 292a (Mary)
IV 221b (Prayer); 308a (Protection)
V 130a (Stoning)

37 I 149a (Archaeology and the Q); 165a (Art and Architecture and the Q); 528b (Dhū l-Kifl)
II 299b, 309a (Geography)
III 289b (Mary); 395b (Miracles)
IV 227b (Prayer); 516b (Sacred Precincts)
V 184b (Syria); 575a (Zechariah)

37-44 V 574a, 574b (Zechariah)

38 IV 229a (Prayer); 575a (Seeing and Hearing)
V 575a (Zechariah)

38-39 IV 224a, 229a, 229b (Prayer)

38-40 V 545b (Word of God)

38-41 III 289a, 290a (Mary)

39 I 149a (Archaeology and the Q); 165a (Art and Architecture and the Q); 233a (Birth)
II 299b, 309a (Geography); 341a, 341b (Good News); 355a (Grammar and the Q)
III 14b (Jesus); 51b, 52a, 51b (John the Baptist); 289a (Mary); 395b (Miracles)

	IV	227b (Prayer); 291b (Prophets and Prophethood); 439a (Revelation and Inspiration); 516b (Sacred Precincts)
	V	184b (Syria); 545b (Word of God); 575a, 575b (Zechariah)
39-41	V	575a (Zechariah)
40	I	480b (Creeds)
	III	289a (Mary)
41	I	503a, 503b (Day, Times of)
	II	82a (Everyday Life, Q In); 314b (Glorification of God)
	III	373a (Memory); 416b (Morning)
	IV	439b (Revelation and Inspiration); 487b (Ritual and the Q)
	V	280a, 281a (Time); 546a (Word of God)
42	I	59a, 59b (ʿĀʾisha bint Abī Bakr); 233b (Birth)
	II	11b (Election); 193b (Fāṭima); 291a (Gender)
	III	81a (Khadīja); 290a, 290b (Mary)
	IV	291a (Prophets and Prophethood); 505a (Ritual Purity)
	V	105b (Spatial Relations); 533b, 534a (Women and the Q)
42-47	III	13a (Jesus)
42-48	I	87a (Angel)
42-51	III	289a (Mary)
42-64	III	7b (Jesus)
43	I	254a (Bowing and Prostration)
	III	290a (Mary)
	IV	219b, 223a (Prayer)
	V	534a (Women and the Q)
44	I	513b (Debate and Disputation)
	II	280a, 282a (Gambling); 423b, 425a (Hidden and the Hidden); 545a (Instruments)
	III	290a (Mary); 441b (Muḥammad); 537a (News)
	IV	165b (Popular and Talismanic Uses of the Q); 302b (Prophets and Prophethood); 438b (Revelation and Inspiration)
	V	271a (Theology and the Q); 575a, 575b (Zechariah)
44-48	IV	36b (People of the Book)
45	I	102b, 103a (Anointing); 233b (Birth)
	II	341a, 341b (Good News)
	III	8a, 14b, 16a (Jesus); 289a, 294a, 294b (Mary)
	IV	16b (Paradise)
	V	545b (Word of God)
45-46	III	395b (Miracles)
45-47	II	342a (Gospel)
	III	295a (Mary)
45-49	I	313a (Christians and Christianity)
45-51	III	294a (Mary)

45-57	v	575a (Zechariah)
46	i	149a (Archaeology and the q)
	ii	276a (Furniture and Furnishings)
	iii	13a (Jesus)
47	i	233b (Birth); 319a (Chronology and the q); 475a, 475b (Creation); 516b (Decision)
	ii	185b (Fate); 269a (Freedom and Predestination); 327b (God and his Attributes)
	iii	289a, 294a (Mary)
	v	109a (Speech); 287a (Time); 542b (Word of God)
47-49	i	167a (Art and Architecture and the q)
48	i	245a, 245b (Book)
	ii	342a (Gospel)
	iii	16a (Jesus)
	iv	68b (Philosophy and the q)
	v	300b (Torah); 483b (Wisdom)
48-49	iii	191a (Literacy)
	v	200b (Teaching)
48-58	iii	295a (Mary)
49	i	98a (Animal Life); 163a, 167b (Art and Architecture and the q); 340b (Clay); 476a (Creation); 507a (Death and the Dead)
	ii	4a (Earth); 355a (Grammar and the q)
	iii	16a (Jesus); 226a (Literature and the q); 381b (Messenger); 396a, 398a (Miracles); 537a (News)
	iv	178b (Popular and Talismanic Uses of the q); 183a (Portents); 295b (Prophets and Prophethood); 435b (Resurrection)
	v	133b (Stoning)
49-57	ii	558a (Invitation)
50	i	11b (Abrogation); 97a (Animal Life); 189a (Authority)
	iii	16a (Jesus); 174b (Lawful and Unlawful); 445a (Muḥammad)
	iv	283a (Profane and Sacred); 439a (Revelation and Inspiration)
	v	300b, 303a (Torah)
51	i	118b (Apologetics)
	iii	230a (Lord)
52	i	123a (Apostle); 389b (Companions of the Prophet); 446a (Cosmology)
	ii	405b (Hearing and Deafness)
	iii	8a (Jesus); 382b (Messenger)
	iv	26b (Parties and Factions)
	v	430a (Victory); 436a (Virtue)
52-53	i	123b (Apostle)
	iii	382b (Messenger)

53	I	243b (Book)
	III	16a (Jesus); 567a (Obedience)
	V	490b (Witness to Faith); 492b (Witnessing and Testifying)
54	II	322a (God and his Attributes)
	III	18a, 18b (Jesus)
	IV	117b (Polemic and Polemical Language); 471b (Rhetoric and the Q)
55	I	51a (Aḥmadiyya); 111a (Antichrist); 488b (Crucifixion)
	II	216a (Flying)
	III	8a, 18a, 19b, 20a (Jesus)
	IV	505a (Ritual Purity)
	V	109b (Speech); 375b (Trips and Voyages); 547a (Word of God)
57	I	220a (Belief and Unbelief)
	II	68b (Ethics and the Q); 322b (God and his Attributes)
	III	380a (Mercy)
58	III	190a (Literacy); 441a, 510a (Muḥammad)
	IV	230a (Prayer)
	V	4a (Signs)
59	I	24a (Adam and Eve); 233b (Birth); 312a, 313a (Christians and Christianity); 319a (Chronology and the Q); 446b (Cosmology); 475a, 475b, 476a (Creation)
	II	4b (Earth); 327b, 328a (God and his Attributes); 443b (Holy Spirit)
	III	8a, 15a (Jesus); 295a (Mary)
	V	109a (Speech); 287a (Time); 542b, 545b, 547a, 547b (Word of God)
61	I	115b (Apologetics); 314a (Christians and Christianity); 466a (Covenant); 492a (Curse)
	II	193a (Fāṭima)
	IV	411a, 411b (Religious Pluralism and the Q)
	V	82a (Soul); 498a (Witnessing and Testifying)
61-62	I	309b (Christians and Christianity); 347a (Clothing)
62	II	435b (History and the Q)
	III	517b (Narratives)
	IV	6a (Pairs and Pairing)
	V	488b (Witness to Faith)
63	II	62b (Ethics and the Q)
64	I	222b (Belief and Unbelief)
	III	22b, 32b (Jews and Judaism); 40a (Jihād); 229b (Lord)
	IV	38b, 40a (People of the Book); 403a (Religious Pluralism and the Q)
	V	436a (Virtue); 490b (Witness to Faith)
64-115	I	378b (Community and Society in the Q)
65	I	222b (Belief and Unbelief)
	II	434a (History and the Q)
	III	28a (Jews and Judaism); 445b (Muḥammad); 508b (Names of the Q); 579b (Opposition to Muḥammad)

	IV	40a (People of the Book); 403a (Religious Pluralism and the Q)
	V	300b, 304a (Torah)
65-68	I	330b (Chronology and the Q)
65-70	I	7b (Abraham)
66	III	102b (Knowledge and Learning)
	V	203b (Teaching)
67	I	5b (Abraham); 310a (Christians and Christianity); 330b (Chronology and the Q); 373a, 377b (Community and Society in the Q)
	II	31b (Epigraphy); 402b (Ḥanīf); 569b (Islam)
	III	340b (Mecca); 445b (Muḥammad)
	IV	255a (Pre-Islamic Arabia and the Q); 405a, 408b, 413a (Religious Pluralism and the Q)
	V	436a (Virtue)
67-68	II	163b (Faith)
	III	28a (Jews and Judaism)
	IV	37a (People of the Book)
68	I	370a (Community and Society in the Q)
	II	273a (Friends and Friendship)
	III	231b (Lord); 381b (Messenger); 445b (Muḥammad); 502a (Names of the Prophet)
69	I	222b (Belief and Unbelief)
	III	26a (Jews and Judaism)
	IV	26a (Parties and Factions); 40a (People of the Book); 120a (Polemic and Polemical Language)
70	I	222b (Belief and Unbelief)
	IV	120b (Polemic and Polemical Language)
	V	301a (Torah)
70-71	IV	40a (People of the Book)
71	I	222b (Belief and Unbelief)
	II	243a (Forgery)
	III	25b (Jews and Judaism)
	IV	450b (Revision and Alteration)
	V	301a, 304b (Torah)
72	I	222b (Belief and Unbelief); 503b (Day, Times of)
	III	26a (Jews and Judaism); 417b, 418b (Morning)
	IV	26a (Parties and Factions)
	V	282b (Time)
73	I	103b (Anthropomorphism)
	II	323b, 325a (God and his Attributes); 401b (Hand)
	III	201b (Literary Structures of the Q)
73-74	IV	311a (Provocation)
74	II	345a (Grace)

Verse	Vol.	Entries
75	I	222b (Belief and Unbelief); 235b (Blasphemy); 325a (Chronology and the Q)
	II	8b (Economics); 73b (Ethics and the Q); 494b, 495a, 498a, 498b (Illiteracy); 545b (Instruments)
	III	27a, 32a (Jews and Judaism); 335a (Measurement); 408b (Money)
	IV	40a (People of the Book); 120a (Polemic and Polemical Language)
	V	400a (Ummī); 474a (Weights and Measures)
76	I	379a (Community and Society in the Q)
	II	322a (God and his Attributes); 447b (Honor)
	V	137b (Ṣūfism and the Q)
77	I	298a (Chastisement and Punishment)
	II	416b (Hell and Hellfire)
	III	276a (Markets); 563b (Oaths)
	IV	505a (Ritual Purity)
	V	110b (Speech); 547b (Word of God)
78	I	118a (Apologetics); 170b (Art and Architecture and the Q); 235b (Blasphemy)
	II	353a (Grammar and the Q)
	III	25b, 32a (Jews and Judaism)
	IV	280b (Profane and Sacred); 450b (Revision and Alteration)
	V	304b (Torah)
79	I	246a (Book)
	III	398a (Miracles); 451b (Muḥammad)
	IV	127b (Politics and the Q); 281a (Profane and Sacred); 292b (Prophets and Prophethood); 539b (Scholar); 578b (Servants)
	V	202a, 203a (Teaching)
80	V	203a (Teaching)
81	I	245a (Book); 349a (Codices of the Q); 380a (Community and Society in the Q); 464b (Covenant)
	II	360a (Grammar and the Q)
	III	228a (Load or Burden); 445a (Muḥammad)
	IV	128b (Politics and the Q); 298b (Prophets and Prophethood); 439a (Revelation and Inspiration)
	V	492a, 502a (Witnessing and Testifying)
81-82	II	63b (Ethics and the Q)
81-85	III	7b (Jesus)
83	I	437b (Conversion)
	II	91b (Everyday Life, Q In); 351a (Grammar and the Q); 420b (Heresy)
84	I	8a (Abraham); 189a (Authority); 480b (Creeds)
	II	561b (Isaac); 563b (Ishmael)
	III	1a (Jacob); 8a, 17a (Jesus); 300a (Material Culture and the Q); 445a (Muḥammad)
	V	302a, 303b (Torah); 364a (Tribes and Clans)
84-85	II	73a (Ethics and the Q)

85	II	34b (Epigraphy); 569b (Islam)
	III	307a (Material Culture and the Q); 559a (Numismatics)
	IV	396b, 397a, 397b, 398a (Religion); 404a (Religious Pluralism and the Q)
85-91	III	380a (Mercy)
86	I	435b (Conversion)
	II	270a (Freedom and Predestination); 371a (Gratitude and Ingratitude)
	III	502a (Names of the Prophet)
	IV	286b (Proof)
	V	293b (Tolerance and Coercion); 490b (Witness to Faith); 502a (Witnessing and Testifying)
86-89	IV	427a (Repentance and Penance)
	V	498a (Witnessing and Testifying)
86-91	II	418a (Hell and Hellfire)
87	I	120a (Apostasy)
87-88	II	418b (Hell and Hellfire)
90	I	120b (Apostasy); 381b (Community and Society in the Q)
	IV	426a (Repentance and Penance)
	V	293b (Tolerance and Coercion)
91	I	120b (Apostasy)
	II	333b, 334b (Gold); 371a (Gratitude and Ingratitude)
92	II	60b, 61a (Ethics and the Q)
93	I	197b (Bahāʾīs)
	II	221a (Food and Drink); 571a, 571b (Israel)
	III	2a (Jacob); 25a (Jews and Judaism); 174b (Lawful and Unlawful); 190a (Literacy)
	IV	282a (Profane and Sacred); 312a, 312b (Provocation)
	V	300b, 303a (Torah)
95	I	5b, 6a (Abraham); 330b (Chronology and the Q); 337b (Circumcision); 373a (Community and Society in the Q)
	II	70b (Ethics and the Q); 402b (Ḥanīf)
	III	445b (Muḥammad)
	IV	401a (Religious Pluralism and the Q)
95-97	I	330b (Chronology and the Q)
95-98	I	7b (Abraham)
96	I	155a (Archaeology and the Q)
	II	299b, 311b, 312a (Geography)
	III	77a, 78a (Kaʿba); 337b (Mecca)
	IV	54a (People of the Thicket); 97a (Pilgrimage); 259a (Pre-Islamic Arabia and the Q); 327b (Qibla)
	V	374b (Trips and Voyages); 552a (World)

96-97 I 7b (Abraham)
II 84b (Everyday Life, Q In); 34a (Epigraphy); 458b, 462a (House, Domestic and Divine)
III 340b (Mecca)
IV 514a (Sacred Precincts)

97 II 340a (Good Deeds); 460a (House, Domestic and Divine)
III 77a, 79a (Kaʿba); 158a (Law and the Q); 305a (Material Culture and the Q); 340b (Mecca)
IV 52b (People of the House); 92a, 94b (Pilgrimage); 104b (Place of Abraham); 286a (Proof); 515b (Sacred Precincts)
V 8a (Signs); 467b (Wealth); 556b (Worship)

98 I 222b (Belief and Unbelief)
II 320b (God and his Attributes)
IV 120a (Polemic and Polemical Language)
V 301a (Torah); 493a (Witnessing and Testifying)

98-100 IV 40a (People of the Book)

98-199 I 223b (Belief and Unbelief)

99 I 222b (Belief and Unbelief)
II 420b (Heresy)
IV 120a (Polemic and Polemical Language)
V 492b (Witnessing and Testifying)

99-100 I 224b (Belief and Unbelief)
III 26a (Jews and Judaism)

100 I 222b (Belief and Unbelief)
II 65b (Ethics and the Q)
III 567b (Obedience)
IV 120b (Polemic and Polemical Language)

100-114 IV 40a (People of the Book)

101 I 465a (Covenant)
III 190a (Literacy)
IV 562b (Scripture and the Q)

101-103 II 17a (Emigrants and Helpers)

102 II 195b (Fear)
V 251b (Textual Criticism of the Q)

102-103 IV 134b (Politics and the Q)

102-104 I 374a (Community and Society in the Q)

103 I 262b (Brother and Brotherhood); 305b (Children of Israel); 435b (Conversion); 465a (Covenant); 519b (Deliverance); 538b (Dissension)
II 21b (Emigration); 23b (Enemies); 408a, 408b (Heart); 546b (Instruments)
III 99b (Kinship); 512b (Names of the Q)

	IV	25b (Parties and Factions); 142a (Politics and the Q); 523b (Salvation)
	V	7b (Signs); 54a (Sister); 166a (Sunna); 365a (Tribes and Clans)
103-112	V	393b (Turkish Literature and the Q)
104	I	220b (Belief and Unbelief)
	II	72a (Ethics and the Q); 170b (Faith); 224a (Forbidden); 453a (Hospitality and Courtesy); 497a (Illiteracy)
	IV	85a (Philosophy and the Q); 127b (Politics and the Q); 490a (Ritual and the Q); 523a (Salvation)
	V	207b (Teaching and Preaching the Q); 316b (Tradition and Custom); 436b, 438a, 439a, 440a, 440b, 441a, 441b, 442b, 443b (Virtues and Vices, Commanding and Forbidding)
105	I	538b (Dissension)
	III	32b (Jews and Judaism)
	IV	25b (Parties and Factions)
106	I	363b, 364b (Colors)
	III	137b (Last Judgment); 380a (Mercy)
107	I	363b (Colors)
108	III	71a (Justice and Injustice); 190a (Literacy); 441a (Muḥammad)
	V	552a (World)
110	I	64a (Almsgiving); 145b (Arabs); 219a, 222b, 223b (Belief and Unbelief); 374a (Community and Society in the Q)
	II	170b (Faith); 396a (Ḥadīth and the Q); 497a (Illiteracy)
	III	23a (Jews and Judaism)
	IV	120a, 120b (Polemic and Polemical Language); 490a (Ritual and the Q); 600a, 600b (Shīʿism and the Q)
	V	209a (Teaching and Preaching the Q); 301a, 303b (Torah); 437a, 438a, 440a, 440b, 442a, 442b (Virtues and Vices, Commanding and Forbidding); 458a (War); 573a (Zealotry)
111	I	80b (Anatomy)
	III	40a, 40b (Jihād); 377a (Menstruation)
112	I	93a (Anger); 264b (Burial); 305a (Children of Israel); 465a (Covenant); 536b, 537b (Disobedience)
	II	546b (Instruments)
	III	382a (Messenger)
	IV	309b (Provocation)
	V	575a (Zechariah)
113	I	182b (Asceticism); 222b, 223b (Belief and Unbelief); 254b (Bowing and Prostration); 328a (Chronology and the Q); 502b (Day, Times of); 530a (Dialects)
	III	32a (Jews and Judaism); 190a (Literacy)
	IV	222b (Prayer)
	V	7a (Signs); 282b (Time); 301a, 303b (Torah); 430b (Vigil); 437b, 438a (Virtues and Vices, Commanding and Forbidding)

113-114 I 306a (Children of Israel); 374a (Community and Society in the Q)
II 63b, 73a (Ethics and the Q)
III 23a (Jews and Judaism)
IV 368b (Recitation of the Q)

113-115 I 219a (Belief and Unbelief)

114 II 63b (Ethics and the Q)
III 136a, 136b (Last Judgment)
IV 85a (Philosophy and the Q)
V 437b, 438a, 440a, 440b (Virtues and Vices, Commanding and Forbidding)

115 I 220b (Belief and Unbelief)
III 379a (Mercy)

116 I 221b (Belief and Unbelief); 302b (Children)
IV 31b (Patriarchy)
V 468a (Wealth)

117 I 41b (Agriculture and Vegetation); 52b, 54b (Air and Wind); 184b (Ashes)
II 65a (Ethics and the Q)
III 71a (Justice and Injustice)
IV 10a (Parable); 310a (Provocation)
V 82b (Soul); 470b (Weather)

118 I 82b (Anatomy); 224b (Belief and Unbelief)
II 73a (Ethics and the Q); 274a, 275a (Friends and Friendship)
III 240a (Loyalty)
IV 24b (Parties and Factions)

118-120 II 468b (Hypocrites and Hypocrisy)

118-174 I 409a, 409b (Consultation)

119 I 93b (Anger)
II 550b (Intention)
III 26a (Jews and Judaism)
IV 442a (Revelation and Inspiration)

120 III 61b (Joy and Misery); 579a (Opposition to Muḥammad)

121 I 501b, 504a (Day, Times of)
III 417b (Morning)
IV 5b (Pairs and Pairing)

121-122 III 456b (Muḥammad)

122 II 161b (Failure)
V 379a, 379b (Trust and Patience)

123 I 196a, 196b (Badr)
II 262b (Form and Structure of the Q); 299b (Geography); 508a (Impotence)
III 455a (Muḥammad); 579a (Opposition to Muḥammad)
IV 226b (Prayer)
V 175b (Sūra); 284b (Time); 430a (Victory)

123-125	II	209b (Fighting)
	III	183a (Life)
123-127	III	42b (Jihād)
123-128	III	456a (Muḥammad)
	IV	332a (Quraysh)
124	IV	335a (Qurayẓa, Banū al-)
124-125	I	463a (Court)
	II	411b (Heaven and Sky)
	V	378a (Troops)
124-126	III	398a (Miracles)
125	III	552a (Numbers and Enumeration)
126	II	35a (Epigraphy); 341b (Good News)
	IV	6a (Pairs and Pairing)
127	II	162a (Failure)
	IV	403b (Religious Pluralism and the Q)
128	II	186a (Fate)
	IV	427a (Repentance and Penance)
129	II	244b (Forgiveness)
	IV	5b (Pairs and Pairing); 457b (Reward and Punishment)
	V	553b (World)
130	II	8a (Economics); 31a (Epigraphy)
	IV	284a (Profane and Sacred)
	V	407a (Usury)
130-131	V	21b (Sin, Major and Minor)
130-135	IV	455a (Reward and Punishment)
131	V	554b (World)
132	I	189b (Authority)
	IV	17a (Paradise)
	V	272b (Theology and the Q)
133	III	333b (Measurement)
	IV	15b (Paradise); 64b (Persian Literature and the Q)
	V	554b (World)
133-134	III	359a (Medicine and the Q)
134	I	93b (Anger)
	II	244b (Forgiveness); 322a (God and his Attributes)
	III	65b (Judgment)
	IV	17a (Paradise)
	V	137b (Ṣūfism and the Q)
135	II	244b (Forgiveness)
	III	373b (Memory); 510a (Names of the Q)

	IV	580b (Sex and Sexuality)
	V	204b (Teaching)
136	II	245a (Forgiveness)
	IV	17a (Paradise)
137	IV	425a (Remnant)
	V	164a (Sunna); 376a (Trips and Voyages)
138	II	142b (Exhortations)
	III	124b (Language and Style of the Q)
139	I	461a, 461b (Courage); 521b (Despair)
139-140	I	406a (Consolation)
139-144	II	162a (Failure)
139-175	III	40a, 41a (Jihād)
140	II	322b (God and his Attributes); 429b, 431a (History and the Q); 448a (Honor)
	III	282a (Martyrs); 380a (Mercy)
	V	280a (Time); 458b (War); 490b, 491a (Witness to Faith)
140-142	I	460b (Courage)
141	I	461b (Courage)
	V	362b (Trial)
142	I	458b, 461a (Courage)
	III	37a, 37b (Jihād)
143	I	461b (Courage)
144	I	310b (Christians and Christianity)
	II	372a (Gratitude and Ingratitude)
	III	18b (Jesus); 381b (Messenger); 440a, 444a (Muḥammad); 501b (Names of the Prophet)
	IV	17a (Paradise); 259a (Pre-Islamic Arabia and the Q); 298a (Prophets and Prophethood)
	V	41b (Sīra and the Q); 489a (Witness to Faith); 501b (Witnessing and Testifying)
145	I	244a (Book); 523a (Destiny)
	II	269b (Freedom and Predestination); 360a (Grammar and the Q); 372a (Gratitude and Ingratitude)
	IV	452b, 456b (Reward and Punishment)
	V	83a (Soul)
145-151	V	383a (Trust and Patience)
146	I	458b, 461a (Courage); 521b (Despair)
	II	322a (God and his Attributes); 352b (Grammar and the Q)
	III	577b (Opposition to Muḥammad)
	IV	300a (Prophets and Prophethood)
	V	137b (Ṣūfism and the Q); 383b (Trust and Patience); 455b (War)

147 II 370b (Gratitude and Ingratitude)

148 I 460a (Courage)
IV 176b (Popular and Talismanic Uses of the Q); 452b, 456b (Reward and Punishment)
V 137b (Ṣūfism and the Q)

149 III 41b (Jihād); 567b (Obedience)

149-152 I 460b (Courage)

150 I 344b (Clients and Clientage); 461a (Courage)
III 231a (Lord)
IV 307b (Protection)

151 II 198a (Fear); 460b (House, Domestic and Divine)
IV 103b (Pit); 287a (Proof)

152 I 537b (Disobedience)
II 161b (Failure)
IV 148a (Politics and the Q)
V 434b (Virtue); 552b (World)

152-155 II 162a (Failure); 508b (Impotence)

152-158 II 468b (Hypocrites and Hypocrisy)

153 IV 452b (Reward and Punishment)

154 I 37b (Age of Ignorance); 244a (Book); 460b (Courage)
II 269b (Freedom and Predestination); 489a (Ignorance); 550b (Intention)
IV 26a (Parties and Factions); 442a (Revelation and Inspiration)
V 178a (Suspicion); 286b (Time); 362b (Trial)

154-155 III 38a (Jihād)

155 I 526a (Devil)
IV 5b (Pairs and Pairing)
V 457b (War)

155-174 II 262b (Form and Structure of the Q); 175b (Sūra)

156 II 144a, 144b (Expeditions and Battles)
III 58a (Journey)
IV 435b (Resurrection); 483a (Rhymed Prose); 574b (Seeing and Hearing)
V 458a (War); 545a (Word of God)

157 II 245a (Forgiveness)
III 379b (Mercy)
IV 30b (Path or Way)

157-158 I 506a (Death and the Dead)
II 209b (Fighting)
III 282b (Martyrs)

158 II 209b (Fighting)

159	I	235a (Birth Control); 407a, 409a, 409b, 410a (Consultation)
	II	245a (Forgiveness); 322a (God and his Attributes); 408b (Heart)
	III	447a (Muḥammad); 567a (Obedience)
	IV	139a, 149b (Politics and the Q)
	V	137b (Ṣūfism and the Q); 221b (Teaching and Preaching the Q); 383b (Trust and Patience)
160	II	462a (House, Domestic and Divine)
161	I	522b (Destiny)
	IV	291b (Prophets and Prophethood)
162	I	93a (Anger)
	II	321b (God and his Attributes)
	IV	103b (Pit)
163	IV	574b (Seeing and Hearing)
164	I	32a (African Literature); 245b, 246a (Book)
	II	43a (Error); 497b (Illiteracy)
	III	190a, 191a (Literacy); 441a, 442b (Muḥammad)
	IV	301a (Prophets and Prophethood); 505a (Ritual Purity)
	V	434a (Virtue)
165-167	II	162a (Failure)
166	I	460b (Courage)
	V	458a (War)
166-167	II	209b (Fighting)
	III	38a (Jihād)
166-168	II	469b (Hypocrites and Hypocrisy)
167	I	82a, 82b (Anatomy); 461a (Courage)
	II	71a (Ethics and the Q); 468b, 470a (Hypocrites and Hypocrisy)
	III	181b (Lie)
	V	457b, 458a (War)
168	III	567a (Obedience)
169	I	114a (Apocalypse); 264b (Burial); 488b (Crucifixion); 506a (Death and the Dead)
	II	45b (Eschatology); 209b (Fighting)
	III	18b, 19a (Jesus); 62a (Joy and Misery); 139b (Last Judgment); 282b, 283a, 283b (Martyrs)
	IV	30b (Path or Way); 459b (Reward and Punishment)
	V	491a (Witness to Faith)
169-170	III	285a (Martyrs)
169-171	III	456b (Muḥammad)
170	II	554b (Intercession)
	III	61a, 62a (Joy and Misery)
	V	138a (Ṣūfism and the Q)

170-171	II	45b (Eschatology)
171	III	62a (Joy and Misery)
172	II	61b (Ethics and the Q)
172-175	I	460a (Courage)
173	I	220b (Belief and Unbelief)
	II	32b (Epigraphy); 320b (God and his Attributes); 351a (Grammar and the Q)
	III	299a, 300b (Material Culture and the Q)
175	I	526a (Devil)
	II	273b (Friends and Friendship)
	III	231b (Lord)
175-177	I	405b (Consolation)
176	II	510b (Indifference)
	III	452b (Muḥammad)
176-177	I	120a (Apostasy)
	IV	456a (Reward and Punishment)
176-179	II	468b (Hypocrites and Hypocrisy)
177	III	276a (Markets)
178	II	416a (Hell and Hellfire)
179	I	202a (Barēlwīs)
	II	11b (Election); 423a (Hidden and the Hidden)
	IV	291b (Prophets and Prophethood)
180	I	64b (Almsgiving); 191a (Avarice)
	II	367a (Grammar and the Q)
181	I	243b (Book); 305a (Children of Israel)
	II	210b (Fire); 414b (Hell and Hellfire)
	III	24a (Jews and Judaism); 382a (Messenger)
	IV	324b (Qaynuqāʿ, Banū)
	V	493a (Witnessing and Testifying); 575a (Zechariah)
182	I	522b (Destiny)
	III	71a (Justice and Injustice)
	IV	84a (Philosophy and the Q)
183	II	211b (Fire); 350b (Grammar and the Q)
	III	24a (Jews and Judaism); 450a (Muḥammad)
	IV	517a (Sacrifice)
	V	575a (Zechariah)
184	I	245b (Book)
	III	232a (Lot); 453a (Muḥammad)
	IV	296a, 296b, 297a, 301a (Prophets and Prophethood); 316a (Psalms); 570b (Scrolls)
	V	300b, 301b, 303b (Torah)

185	I	264b (Burial)
	II	36b (Epigraphy)
	III	300b (Material Culture and the Q)
	IV	486a (Ritual and the Q)
	V	83a (Soul); 552a, 552b (World)
186	I	83b (Anatomy); 220b, 222b (Belief and Unbelief)
	III	26b, 32a (Jews and Judaism); 184b (Life); 579a (Opposition to Muḥammad)
	V	362b, 363a (Trial)
187	I	222b (Belief and Unbelief); 304b, 305a (Children of Israel); 464b (Covenant)
	IV	129a (Politics and the Q)
	V	303b, 304b (Torah)
187-188	III	24b (Jews and Judaism)
188	III	61b (Joy and Misery)
	IV	213b (Praise)
189	IV	127b (Politics and the Q)
190	I	501b (Day, Times of)
	III	528b, 531b (Nature as Signs)
	V	280b (Time)
190-191	I	473a, 474a (Creation)
	II	372a (Gratitude and Ingratitude)
	III	373b (Memory)
	IV	70b (Philosophy and the Q); 438a (Revelation and Inspiration); 545b (Science and the Q)
191	II	37a (Epigraphy); 82a (Everyday Life, Q In); 314b (Glorification of God)
	III	373a (Memory)
192	II	465a (Humor)
	III	379b (Mercy)
	IV	453b (Reward and Punishment)
193	I	506a (Death and the Dead)
	III	18b (Jesus)
	IV	486a (Ritual and the Q)
	V	19a, 19b (Sin, Major and Minor)
193-195	V	22a (Sin, Major and Minor)
194	IV	298b (Prophets and Prophethood)
195	I	262b (Brother and Brotherhood)
	II	209b (Fighting); 289b (Gender)
	III	41a (Jihād)
	IV	17a, 17b (Paradise); 30b (Path or Way)
	V	134b (Suffering); 526b (Women and the Q)
196-197	I	221b (Belief and Unbelief)

197 II 276a (Furniture and Furnishings)
III 60a (Joy and Misery)
IV 103b, 104a (Pit)

199 I 219a, 222b, 223b (Belief and Unbelief); 306a (Children of Israel)
III 23a (Jews and Judaism); 66b (Judgment)
IV 40b (People of the Book); 455b (Reward and Punishment)
V 301a (Torah)

200 II 31a (Epigraphy); 70b (Ethics and the Q)
V 134b (Suffering)

Sūrat al-Nisāʾ (4)

I 328a (Chronology and the Q); 383a (Community and Society in the Q)
II 264a (Form and Structure of the Q)
III 19a (Jesus); 235a (Love and Affection); 549a (Numbers and Enumeration)
IV 237b (Pre-1800 Preoccupations of Q Studies)
V 21a (Sin, Major and Minor); 166b, 174b (Sūra); 369a (Trinity); 522b (Womb); 523a, 528b (Women and the Q)

1 I 24b (Adam and Eve); 233a, 233b (Birth); 235a (Birth Control); 447b (Cosmology); 474b, 476b (Creation)
II 31a (Epigraphy); 75b (Ethics and the Q); 202b (Feminism and the Q); 290b (Gender); 320b, 328b (God and his Attributes); 364a (Grammar and the Q); 432a (History and the Q)
III 229b (Lord); 277b (Marriage and Divorce)
IV 20b (Parents); 581b (Sex and Sexuality)
V 84a (Soul); 522a (Womb); 524a, 530a (Women and the Q)

1-42 IV 32a (Patriarchy)

2 II 68a (Ethics and the Q); 374a (Guardianship)
III 169b (Law and the Q); 604a (Orphans)
V 570a (Youth and Old Age)

2-3 V 524b (Women and the Q)

3 I 383a (Community and Society in the Q); 396b (Concubines)
II 70a (Ethics and the Q); 175b (Family); 348b (Grammar and the Q); 374a (Guardianship)
III 70a, 71b (Justice and Injustice); 169b (Law and the Q); 235a (Love and Affection); 277b, 278a (Marriage and Divorce); 549b, 551b (Numbers and Enumeration); 604a (Orphans)
IV 32a (Patriarchy); 186b (Possession and Possessions); 237b (Pre-1800 Preoccupations of Q Studies); 256a (Pre-Islamic Arabia and the Q); 288a (Property); 580b, 582a (Sex and Sexuality)
V 183a (Symbolic Imagery); 424b (Verse); 506b (Wives of the Prophet); 527a, 527b (Women and the Q)

3-4 V 183a (Ṣūfism and the Q)

4	I	258b (Bridewealth); 530a (Dialects)
	II	76a (Ethics and the Q); 313b (Gift-Giving); 354b (Grammar and the Q); 374b (Guardianship)
	IV	582b (Sex and Sexuality)
	V	529a (Women and the Q)
4-6	IV	186a (Possession and Possessions)
5	II	7b (Economics); 374a (Guardianship)
	III	331b (Maturity); 604a (Orphans)
	V	467b, 469b (Wealth)
6	I	19b (Abstinence)
	II	62a (Ethics and the Q); 374a (Guardianship)
	III	67b (Judgment); 278b (Marriage and Divorce); 330b, 331b (Maturity); 604a (Orphans)
	IV	580b (Sex and Sexuality)
	V	495a, 495b (Witnessing and Testifying)
6-10	V	570a (Youth and Old Age)
7	II	76a (Ethics and the Q); 519a (Inheritance)
	IV	21b (Parents)
7-20	V	529a (Women and the Q)
8	II	174b (Family)
	III	604a (Orphans)
	IV	209a (Poverty and the Poor)
	V	179b (Sustenance)
9	III	580b (Oppressed on Earth)
10	II	64b (Ethics and the Q); 374a (Guardianship); 414b, 418a (Hell and Hellfire)
	III	71b (Justice and Injustice); 604a (Orphans)
10-11	I	321a (Chronology and the Q)
11	I	259b (Brother and Brotherhood); 480b (Creeds)
	II	76a (Ethics and the Q); 351a (Grammar and the Q); 519b, 520a, 522a, 522b (Inheritance)
	III	164a, 164b (Law and the Q)
	IV	5b, 7a (Pairs and Pairing); 21b (Parents); 32a (Patriarchy); 449a (Revision and Alteration); 537b (Scholar)
	V	53a (Sister)
11-12	I	12a, 12b (Abrogation); 515b (Debt)
	II	7b (Economics); 519a, 520b (Inheritance)
	IV	284a (Profane and Sacred)
11-13	I	253b (Boundaries and Precepts)
12	I	12a (Abrogation)
	II	320b (God and his Attributes); 519b, 520a, 520a, 522a, 522b, 523b, 524a, 524b, 525a, 525b (Inheritance)

	III	98a (Kinship); 278b (Marriage and Divorce); 552b (Numbers and Enumeration)
	V	53a (Sister); 481a (Widow); 529a (Women and the Q)
12-14	II	418a (Hell and Hellfire)
	IV	581b (Sex and Sexuality)
13	I	13a (Abrogation)
	IV	17a, 18b (Paradise); 522b (Salvation)
	V	123a (Springs and Fountains); 489a (Witness to Faith)
13-14	I	253a (Boundaries and Precepts)
14	I	537b (Disobedience)
15	I	18a (Abrogation); 28a (Adultery and Fornication)
	II	63a, 68a (Ethics and the Q); 214b (Flogging)
	III	551b (Numbers and Enumeration)
	IV	277a (Prisoners); 580b, 584a (Sex and Sexuality)
	V	490a (Witness to Faith); 497b (Witnessing and Testifying); 528a (Women and the Q)
15-16	I	17a (Abrogation); 28b (Adultery and Fornication); 299b (Chastity)
	II	444b (Homosexuality)
	IV	32a (Patriarchy); 449a (Revision and Alteration)
16	I	28a (Adultery and Fornication)
	III	379b (Mercy)
	IV	5b (Pairs and Pairing); 427b (Repentance and Penance)
	V	528a (Women and the Q)
17	I	450a (Cosmology); 480b (Creeds)
	II	245a (Forgiveness); 488b (Ignorance)
	III	378b (Mercy)
	IV	5b (Pairs and Pairing); 427a (Repentance and Penance); 537b (Scholar)
	V	24b (Sin, Major and Minor)
17-18	II	64b (Ethics and the Q)
18	II	245a (Forgiveness); 542b (Insolence and Obstinacy)
	III	379b (Mercy)
	IV	67b (Pharaoh); 426a (Repentance and Penance)
	V	288b (Time)
19	I	299b (Chastity)
	II	76a (Ethics and the Q)
	III	279b (Marriage and Divorce)
	IV	580b, 582a (Sex and Sexuality)
19-20	IV	32b (Patriarchy)
	V	529b (Women and the Q)
20	I	258b, 259a (Bridewealth)
	II	76a (Ethics and the Q); 292b (Gender); 374b (Guardianship); 545b (Instruments)
	V	19a (Sin, Major and Minor); 474a (Weights and Measures)

21	I	258b (Bridewealth); 380b (Community and Society in the Q); 464b (Covenant)
	III	278b (Marriage and Divorce)
22	II	266b (Fosterage); 460a (House, Domestic and Divine)
	III	277b (Marriage and Divorce)
	IV	580b, 582a (Sex and Sexuality)
	V	19a (Sin, Major and Minor)
22-24	I	383a, 383b (Community and Society in the Q)
	III	174a (Lawful and Unlawful)
	IV	284b, 285a, 285b (Prohibited Degrees)
23	I	18b (Abrogation); 259b (Brother and Brotherhood); 302a (Children)
	II	225a (Forbidden); 266a, 266b (Fosterage); 374b (Guardianship)
	III	106a, 107a, 107b (Lactation); 277b (Marriage and Divorce)
	IV	5b (Pairs and Pairing); 22a (Parents); 582a (Sex and Sexuality)
	V	53a (Sister); 477a (Wet-Nursing); 512b (Wives of the Prophet)
23-24	III	207a (Literature and the Q)
24	I	244b (Book); 258a, 258b (Bridewealth); 480b (Creeds)
	II	64a (Ethics and the Q); 313b (Gift-Giving); 374b (Guardianship)
	III	279a (Marriage and Divorce)
	IV	99a (Pilgrimage); 288a (Property); 537b (Scholar); 582a, 582b, 583b (Sex and Sexuality); 600b (Shīʿism and the Q)
	V	232a, 232b (Temporary Marriage); 469a (Wealth); 527b (Women and the Q)
24-25	III	277a, 278a (Marriage and Divorce)
	IV	32a (Patriarchy); 452a (Reward and Punishment)
	V	183a (Symbolic Imagery); 313b (Trade and Commerce); 527b (Women and the Q)
25	I	18a (Abrogation); 28b (Adultery and Fornication); 258a (Bridewealth); 299a, 299b (Chastity); 396a, 396b (Concubines)
	II	63a (Ethics and the Q); 374b (Guardianship)
	III	279a (Marriage and Divorce); 378b (Mercy)
	IV	5b (Pairs and Pairing); 186b (Possession and Possessions); 288a (Property); 580b, 581b, 582a, 583b, 584a (Sex and Sexuality)
	V	57a, 57b, 58a (Slaves and Slavery)
25-28	V	139a (Ṣūfism and the Q)
26	IV	5b (Pairs and Pairing); 537b (Scholar); 164b (Sunna)
26-27	IV	427b (Repentance and Penance)
28	I	435a (Conversion)
	II	56b (Ethics and the Q)
	IV	128b (Politics and the Q)
29	I	301a (Cheating); 434a (Contracts and Alliances)
	II	359b (Grammar and the Q)
	III	275b (Markets); 366b (Medicine and the Q)
	V	159b, 160b, 162a (Suicide); 417a (Vengeance); 469b (Wealth)

29-30 II 418a (Hell and Hellfire)

30 I 32a (African Literature)

31 I 217a (Bedouin)
II 33a (Epigraphy)
IV 431b (Responsibility)
V 19a, 19b, 21a, 21b, 27a (Sin, Major and Minor)

32 II 290a (Gender)
V 526b (Women and the Q)

33 I 344b (Clients and Clientage)
V 493a (Witnessing and Testifying)

33-36 V 183a (Symbolic Imagery)

34 I 84a (Anatomy); 158b (Arrogance)
II 18b (Emigration); 76a (Ethics and the Q); 82b (Everyday Life, Q In); 175b (Family); 202b (Feminism and the Q); 276a (Furniture and Furnishings); 290a, 292a (Gender); 395b (Ḥadīth and the Q)
III 236b (Love and Affection); 278b, 279b (Marriage and Divorce); 567a (Obedience)
IV 5b (Pairs and Pairing); 32a (Patriarchy); 308a (Protection); 583b (Sex and Sexuality)
V 191b (Talent); 467b (Wealth); 525a, 529a, 536a, 539b (Women and the Q)

35 I 147b (Arbitration)
II 76a (Ethics and the Q)
III 64b (Judgment); 279b (Marriage and Divorce)
IV 5b (Pairs and Pairing); 136a (Politics and the Q)
V 103a (Sovereignty); 528b (Women and the Q)

36 I 241b (Boast); 369b (Community and Society in the Q); 395a (Conceit)
II 7a (Economics); 61b, 67a, 71b, 75a (Ethics and the Q); 174b, 176a (Family); 447b (Honor); 453a (Hospitality and Courtesy)
III 252a (Maintenance and Upkeep); 603b (Orphans)
IV 20b (Parents); 186b (Possession and Possessions); 209a (Poverty and the Poor); 288a (Property)
V 57b (Slaves and Slavery); 131a, 132a, 130b (Strangers and Foreigners); 204b (Teaching); 523a (Womb)

36-38 V 468b (Wealth)

37 III 25b (Jews and Judaism)

38 I 526a (Devil)
II 71a (Ethics and the Q); 450a (Hospitality and Courtesy); 468b (Hypocrites and Hypocrisy)
III 136b (Last Judgment)
V 119b (Spiritual Beings); 494b (Witnessing and Testifying)

39 III 136b (Last Judgment)

40 I 99b (Animal Life)
II 545b (Instruments)

III 72a (Justice and Injustice); 334b (Measurement); 379b (Mercy); 409a (Money)
IV 6b (Pairs and Pairing); 458b (Reward and Punishment)
V 473b (Weights and Measures)

41 III 382a (Messenger); 447a (Muḥammad)
IV 300b (Prophets and Prophethood)
V 493b (Witnessing and Testifying)

42 I 537a (Disobedience)

43 I 321a, 328b (Chronology and the Q); 341a, 342a, 342b (Cleanliness and Ablution); 411b, 412a (Contamination)
II 158a (Face); 221b (Food and Drink); 321a (God and his Attributes); 391a (Ḥadīth and the Q); 501b (Illness and Health); 556a, 557a (Intoxicants)
III 12a (Jesus); 57b, 58a (Journey); 152a, 169a (Law and the Q); 333b (Measurement); 353b (Medicine and the Q); 375b (Menstruation); 378b (Mercy)
IV 5b (Pairs and Pairing); 225b (Prayer); 376b, 377a (Recitation of the Q); 485b (Ritual and the Q); 499a, 499b, 500a, 500b, 501a, 501b, 506b (Ritual Purity)
V 373a (Trips and Voyages); 465a (Water); 482a (Wine); 524b (Women and the Q)

44 I 222b (Belief and Unbelief)
II 43a (Error)
IV 24b (Parties and Factions); 36a (People of the Book)

45 I 432a (Contracts and Alliances)
II 23b (Enemies); 273a (Friends and Friendship)
III 47a (Jinn); 231b (Lord)

46 I 83a (Anatomy); 118a (Apologetics); 305a (Children of Israel); 440a (Corruption); 497a (David); 537a (Disobedience)
II 243a (Forgery); 342b (Gospel); 363a (Grammar and the Q); 406a (Hearing and Deafness)
III 22b, 25a, 25b, 32a (Jews and Judaism); 143a (Last Judgment)
IV 36b (People of the Book); 450b (Revision and Alteration)
V 304b (Torah); 393b (Turkish Literature and the Q); 502a (Witnessing and Testifying)

47 I 222b (Belief and Unbelief); 492a (Curse)
III 449a (Muḥammad)
IV 36a (People of the Book); 120b (Polemic and Polemical Language); 153b (Poll Tax); 298a (Prophets and Prophethood); 439a (Revelation and Inspiration); 510b (Sabbath)
V 285b (Time); 300b (Torah); 545a (Word of God)

48 I 37b (Age of Ignorance); 221b (Belief and Unbelief)
II 244b (Forgiveness); 419a (Hell and Hellfire)
III 37b (Jihād); 380a (Mercy)
IV 119b (Polemic and Polemical Language); 159a (Polytheism and Atheism); 399a (Religious Pluralism and the Q)
V 19a, 20b, 22b (Sin, Major and Minor); 487a (Wish and Desire)

48-49 III 380a (Mercy)

49 III 24a (Jews and Judaism)
IV 505a (Ritual Purity)

50 V 19a (Sin, Major and Minor)

51 I 222b (Belief and Unbelief)
II 229a (Foreign Vocabulary); 482a (Idols and Images)
III 26b (Jews and Judaism); 35a (Jibt); 499a (Naḍīr, Banū al-)
IV 24b (Parties and Factions)
V 119b (Spiritual Beings); 248a (Textual Criticism of the Q)

51-52 III 32a (Jews and Judaism)

52 I 209b (Basmala); 492a (Curse)

53 I 494b (Date Palm)
IV 185a (Possession and Possessions)

53-54 III 92b (Kings and Rulers)

54 I 189a (Authority); 245b (Book)
II 25a (Envy); 174a (Family)
III 26a (Jews and Judaism)
IV 3b (Pairs and Pairing)
V 302a (Torah); 483a (Wisdom)

54-55 I 7b (Abraham)

56 I 222a (Belief and Unbelief)
II 50a (Eschatology); 210b (Fire); 218b (Food and Drink); 416a (Hell and Hellfire); 426a (Hides and Fleece)
III 203b (Literary Structures of the Q)
V 4b (Signs); 133a (Suffering)

57 I 220a (Belief and Unbelief); 343b (Cleanliness and Ablution)
II 54b (Eternity); 456b (Houris)
IV 18a, 18b (Paradise); 505b (Ritual Purity)
V 554a (World)

58 I 480b (Creeds)
II 1b (Ears); 5b, 8b (Economics); 70a (Ethics and the Q)
III 65b (Judgment); 70a, 71b (Justice and Injustice)
IV 5b (Pairs and Pairing); 133b (Politics and the Q)

58-59 IV 147b (Politics and the Q)

58-69 III 568b (Obedience)

59 I 188b, 189b (Authority)
II 65b, 74b (Ethics and the Q)
III 91b (Kings and Rulers); 136b (Last Judgment); 166b (Law and the Q); 447a (Muḥammad); 567a (Obedience)

	IV	125a, 128b, 149b (Politics and the Q); 364a (Rebellion); 539b (Scholar); 596a (Shīʿism and the Q)
	V	272b (Theology and the Q); 501b (Witnessing and Testifying)
60	I	185b (Astray); 526a (Devil)
	II	482a (Idols and Images)
	III	499a (Naḍīr, Banū al-)
	IV	438b (Revelation and Inspiration)
	V	120a (Spiritual Beings); 487a (Wish and Desire)
60-61	II	166b (Faith)
60-63	II	469b (Hypocrites and Hypocrisy)
60-65	IV	144b (Politics and the Q)
61	II	468b (Hypocrites and Hypocrisy)
62	II	61b (Ethics and the Q)
	III	563b (Oaths)
63	II	563b (Ishmael)
	III	40a, 40b (Jihād)
	V	334a (Traditional Disciplines of Q Studies)
64	I	189b (Authority)
	II	245a (Forgiveness)
	III	68a (Judgment); 382a (Messenger); 447a (Muḥammad)
	IV	5b (Pairs and Pairing); 301a (Prophets and Prophethood); 426b (Repentance and Penance)
	V	501b (Witnessing and Testifying)
65	I	13a, 14b (Abrogation); 516a (Decision)
	III	65a (Judgment); 443b (Muḥammad); 561a (Oaths); 567a (Obedience)
	IV	217a (Prayer); 402a (Religious Pluralism and the Q)
	V	103a (Sovereignty)
65-66	V	334a (Traditional Disciplines of Q Studies)
66	I	244b (Book)
	II	18b (Emigration)
	III	38a (Jihād)
	V	159b, 160a (Suicide)
66-78	IV	138a (Politics and the Q)
69	II	340b (Good Deeds)
	III	282a (Martyrs)
	IV	290b (Prophets and Prophethood)
	V	41b (Sīra and the Q); 490b, 491a (Witness to Faith)
71	III	41b (Jihād)
	V	457a (War)
72	V	457b, 458a (War); 492b (Witnessing and Testifying)

73 IV 522b (Salvation)

74 II 209b (Fighting)
III 41a (Jihād); 282b (Martyrs)
IV 457a (Reward and Punishment)
V 457a (War)

74-76 I 225a (Belief and Unbelief)
II 209b (Fighting)

75 I 159a, 161a (Arrogance); 432a (Contracts and Alliances)
II 273b (Friends and Friendship); 363b (Grammar and the Q)
III 41b (Jihād); 577b (Opposition to Muḥammad); 580b, 581a (Oppressed on Earth); 583b (Oppression)
IV 30a (Path or Way); 332b (Quraysh)
V 456a, 457b, 458b (War); 524b (Women and the Q); 570a (Youth and Old Age)

76 I 461a (Courage); 526a (Devil)
II 209b (Fighting); 274a (Friends and Friendship); 431a (History and the Q); 482a (Idols and Images)
IV 29b, 30a (Path or Way); 431b (Responsibility)
V 120b (Spiritual Beings); 456a, 458a (War); 480a (Whisper); 487a (Wish and Desire)

76-77 III 37b (Jihād)

77 I 244b (Book)
II 275b (Furniture and Furnishings)
III 41a (Jihād); 59b (Joy and Misery)
IV 225a (Prayer)
V 457a, 457b (War)

78 I 506a (Death and the Dead)
IV 107a (Planets and Stars); 311a (Provocation); 486a (Ritual and the Q)
V 103a (Sovereignty); 458a (War)

79 II 330b (God and his Attributes)
III 443b (Muḥammad)
IV 299b (Prophets and Prophethood)
V 493a (Witnessing and Testifying)

80 I 13a (Abrogation); 189b (Authority)
II 74b (Ethics and the Q)
III 382a (Messenger); 447a (Muḥammad); 577a (Opposition to Muḥammad)
IV 128b (Politics and the Q); 308b (Protection)
V 272b (Theology and the Q); 501b (Witnessing and Testifying)

80-81 III 40a (Jihād)

81 I 243b (Book)
III 191b (Literacy)

82 I 71b (Ambiguous); 535a (Difficult Passages)
IV 394b (Reflection and Deliberation)
V 203b (Teaching)

83 I 526a (Devil); 541a (Dissimulation)
III 567a (Obedience)
IV 128b (Politics and the Q); 539b (Scholar)
V 141b (Ṣūfism and the Q)

84 I 225a (Belief and Unbelief); 461a (Courage)
II 209b (Fighting); 431a (History and the Q)
III 41a, 41b (Jihād); 577b (Opposition to Muḥammad)
IV 432b (Responsibility)
V 456a, 457a, 458a (War)

85 II 217a (Food and Drink); 449b (Hospitality and Courtesy)

86 II 452b (Hospitality and Courtesy); 320b (God and his Attributes)

87 V 501a (Witnessing and Testifying)

88 I 186a (Astray); 435b (Conversion)
II 59a (Ethics and the Q); 468b (Hypocrites and Hypocrisy)

89 I 432a, 432b (Contracts and Alliances)
II 209b (Fighting); 274a (Friends and Friendship)
III 41b (Jihād); 231b (Lord); 238a (Loyalty); 577b (Opposition to Muḥammad)
V 68a (Social Sciences and the Q)

90 I 431b (Contracts and Alliances); 464b (Covenant)
II 431a (History and the Q)
III 40a, 41a (Jihād)
V 456b (War)

90-91 I 225a (Belief and Unbelief)

91 II 110b (Exegesis of the Q: Classical and Medieval)
III 40a, 41b (Jihād)
IV 35a (Peace)

92 I 239a, 239b (Blood Money); 464b (Covenant); 536b (Disobedience)
II 23b, 24a (Enemies); 64a (Ethics and the Q); 174a (Family); 180b, 184b (Fasting)
III 158b, 159a (Law and the Q)
IV 5b (Pairs and Pairing); 426a (Repentance and Penance); 537b (Scholar)
V 24b (Sin, Major and Minor); 57a (Slaves and Slavery); 198a (Taxation); 252a (Textual Criticism of the Q); 285a (Time); 417a (Vengeance); 475b (Weights and Measures)

92-93 I 239a, 239b (Blood Money)

93 I 93a (Anger); 239a (Blood Money); 492a (Curse)
II 390a (Ḥadīth and the Q)
III 459a, 459b, 460a (Murder)
IV 456a (Reward and Punishment)
V 24b (Sin, Major and Minor); 162a (Suicide); 417a (Vengeance)

94 I 251b, 252a (Booty)
III 42a (Jihād); 58a (Journey)

	IV	35a (Peace)
	V	194a (Taxation); 374a (Trips and Voyages)
95	I	225a (Belief and Unbelief)
	III	36a (Jihād)
	IV	15a, 17a (Paradise); 30b (Path or Way); 455a, 458b (Reward and Punishment)
	V	191b (Talent); 457a (War); 469a (Wealth)
95-96	III	37b (Jihād); 322b (Material Culture and the Q)
	IV	35a (Peace)
96	II	245a (Forgiveness)
	IV	482a, 483a (Rhymed Prose)
	V	270a (Theology and the Q)
97	I	161a (Arrogance)
	II	18b, 22b (Emigration); 418a (Hell and Hellfire)
	IV	103b (Pit)
	V	83b (Soul); 287a (Time)
97-98	III	580b (Oppressed on Earth)
97-99	III	581b (Oppressed on Earth)
98	V	524b (Women and the Q)
98-99	III	378b (Mercy)
99	IV	5b (Pairs and Pairing)
100	I	163a (Art and Architecture and the Q)
	II	14b (Emigrants and Helpers); 459b (House, Domestic and Divine)
	III	38b (Jihād); 579a (Opposition to Muḥammad)
	IV	455a (Reward and Punishment); 483a (Rhymed Prose)
101	II	23b, 24a (Enemies)
	III	58a (Journey)
	IV	225b (Prayer); 233b (Prayer Formulas)
	V	373a (Trips and Voyages)
101-103	III	42a (Jihād)
	IV	233a (Prayer Formulas)
102	I	254a (Bowing and Prostration); 328b (Chronology and the Q)
	II	501b (Illness and Health); 545b (Instruments)
	III	60b (Joy and Misery); 210a (Literature and the Q); 376a (Menstruation)
	IV	26a (Parties and Factions); 219b, 224b (Prayer)
	V	19a (Sin, Major and Minor); 470b (Weather)
103	I	244b (Book); 272b (Calendar); 328b (Chronology and the Q)
	III	373a (Memory)
	IV	224a, 230a (Prayer)
104	I	461a (Courage)
	II	449a (Hope)
	III	40a, 41a (Jihād)

	IV	5b (Pairs and Pairing); 537b (Scholar)
	V	132b (Suffering); 363a (Trial)
105	I	148a (Arbitration)
	III	65a (Judgment); 441a, 443b (Muḥammad); 509a (Names of the Q)
	IV	36b (People of the Book); 133b (Politics and the Q); 301a (Prophets and Prophethood)
	V	103a (Sovereignty); 446a (Vision and Blindness)
105-107	I	513b (Debate and Disputation)
106	III	379b (Mercy); 446b (Muḥammad)
107	I	511b (Debate and Disputation)
	III	380a (Mercy)
109	I	511b (Debate and Disputation)
	III	68a (Judgment); 379b (Mercy)
110	II	335b (Good and Evil)
110-112	I	522b (Destiny)
111	IV	5b (Pairs and Pairing); 537b (Scholar)
112	I	536b (Disobedience)
	V	19a (Sin, Major and Minor)
113	II	345a (Grace)
	III	103a (Knowledge and Learning); 189b, 191a (Literacy); 379a (Mercy); 442a, 454a (Muḥammad)
	IV	3b (Pairs and Pairing); 68b (Philosophy and the Q)
	V	200b, 201b (Teaching); 317b (Tradition and Custom); 483a (Wisdom)
114	V	198b (Taxation)
115	II	187a (Fate)
	III	454b (Muḥammad)
	IV	309b (Provocation)
	V	287a (Time)
116	II	43b (Error); 244b (Forgiveness)
	III	380a (Mercy)
	IV	119b (Polemic and Polemical Language); 159a (Polytheism and Atheism); 159a, 399a (Religious Pluralism and the Q)
117	I	524b (Devil)
	IV	228b (Prayer)
118	I	492a (Curse)
119	I	95b (Animal Life)
	II	1a (Ears); 274a (Friends and Friendship)
120	V	487a (Wish and Desire)
121	IV	103b (Pit)

121-122 I 232b (Biology as the Creation and Stages of Life)

122 I 220a (Belief and Unbelief)
II 54b (Eternity)

122-124 IV 16b (Paradise)

123 I 222b (Belief and Unbelief); 432a (Contracts and Alliances)
II 273b (Friends and Friendship); 335b (Good and Evil)
III 379b (Mercy)
IV 5b (Pairs and Pairing)

123-124 IV 40b (People of the Book)

124 I 494b (Date Palm)
II 128a (Exegesis of the Q: Early Modern and Contemporary); 289b (Gender)
III 492b (Myths and Legends in the Q)
V 524a (Women and the Q)

125 I 5b, 6a (Abraham); 310a (Christians and Christianity); 330b (Chronology and the Q); 373a (Community and Society in the Q)
II 273b (Friends and Friendship); 323b (God and his Attributes); 402b (Ḥanīf)
III 99b (Kinship); 239a (Loyalty)
IV 291b, 299b (Prophets and Prophethood); 401a (Religious Pluralism and the Q)
V 263b (Theology and the Q)

126 I 6a (Abraham)

127 I 244b (Book)
II 374a (Guardianship)
III 169b (Law and the Q); 190a (Literacy); 277b (Marriage and Divorce); 604a (Orphans)
IV 580b (Sex and Sexuality)
V 139a (Ṣūfism and the Q); 203b (Teaching); 524b (Women and the Q)

127-130 IV 32a (Patriarchy)

128 I 194a, 194b (Baal)
II 175b (Family); 290a, 292a (Gender)
IV 63b (Persian Literature and the Q)
V 82b (Soul)

129 I 94b (Animal Life)
II 70a (Ethics and the Q)
III 70a, 71b (Justice and Injustice); 170a (Law and the Q); 235a (Love and Affection); 278a, 279b (Marriage and Divorce)
V 527a (Women and the Q)

130 IV 6a (Pairs and Pairing)

131 I 222b (Belief and Unbelief)
IV 6a (Pairs and Pairing); 36a (People of the Book)
V 301a (Torah)

133 I 277a (Caliph); 474b (Creation)

134 I 480b (Creeds)
II 1b (Ears)
IV 5b (Pairs and Pairing); 456b (Reward and Punishment)

135 II 70b, 76b (Ethics and the Q); 174b (Family)
III 65b (Judgment); 70a, 71b (Justice and Injustice)
IV 21a (Parents)

136 I 219a (Belief and Unbelief); 247a (Book); 480b (Creeds)
II 43a (Error)
III 136a, 136b (Last Judgment)
IV 298b (Prophets and Prophethood); 439a (Revelation and Inspiration)
V 305a (Torah); 489a (Witness to Faith); 501b (Witnessing and Testifying)

137 II 245a (Forgiveness)
III 380a (Mercy)
V 293b (Tolerance and Coercion)

138 II 468b (Hypocrites and Hypocrisy)
IV 119b (Polemic and Polemical Language); 399a (Religious Pluralism and the Q); 456a (Reward and Punishment)

139 II 36a (Epigraphy); 274a, 274b (Friends and Friendship)
III 238a (Loyalty)

140 I 115b, 118a (Apologetics); 224b (Belief and Unbelief); 381a (Community and Society in the Q)
II 320b (God and his Attributes); 418a (Hell and Hellfire); 468b (Hypocrites and Hypocrisy)
III 400b (Mockery)
IV 119b (Polemic and Polemical Language); 456a (Reward and Punishment)

140-146 II 469b (Hypocrites and Hypocrisy)

141 I 399a (Conquest)
II 321a (God and his Attributes)
IV 308b (Protection)
V 456a (War)

141-147 IV 2a (Pairs and Pairing)

142 II 71a (Ethics and the Q); 82a (Everyday Life, Q In); 322a (God and his Attributes); 468b (Hypocrites and Hypocrisy)
IV 117b (Polemic and Polemical Language); 230a (Prayer); 471b (Rhetoric and the Q)

143 II 470a (Hypocrites and Hypocrisy)

144 I 189a (Authority); 224b (Belief and Unbelief); 432b (Contracts and Alliances)
II 274a, 274b (Friends and Friendship)
III 231b (Lord); 238a (Loyalty)

145 II 468b (Hypocrites and Hypocrisy)
IV 399a (Religious Pluralism and the Q); 456a (Reward and Punishment)

145-146 IV 427a (Repentance and Penance)

146 I 436b (Conversion); 465a (Covenant)
II 352b (Grammar and the Q)

147 IV 6a (Pairs and Pairing)

148 IV 5b (Pairs and Pairing)

149 III 586a (Orality)
IV 6a (Pairs and Pairing)

150-152 III 382a (Messenger)

151 III 24a (Jews and Judaism)

152 III 17a (Jesus); 577a (Opposition to Muḥammad)
IV 455b (Reward and Punishment); 483a (Rhymed Prose)

153 I 222b (Belief and Unbelief); 274a (Calf of Gold)
II 218b (Food and Drink)
III 26a (Jews and Judaism); 421b (Moses); 450a (Muḥammad)
IV 128b (Politics and the Q); 443b (Revelation and Inspiration); 569b (Scrolls)
V 276a (Theophany); 303b (Torah)

153-155 II 311a (Geography)
IV 39b (People of the Book)

153-159 IV 40b (People of the Book)

154 I 254b (Bowing and Prostration); 304b (Children of Israel); 465a (Covenant)
II 215b (Flying)
III 394a (Miracles); 586a (Orality)
IV 129a (Politics and the Q); 510a (Sabbath)
V 197a (Taxation); 285b (Time); 302b (Torah); 546b (Word of God)

155 I 305a (Children of Israel); 337a (Circumcision)
II 321a (God and his Attributes); 408a (Heart)
III 24a (Jews and Judaism); 382a (Messenger)
IV 129a (Politics and the Q)
V 302b (Torah)

156 III 9a, 13b (Jesus)
V 533b (Women and the Q)

156-159 III 7b (Jesus)

157 I 51a (Aḥmadiyya); 102b (Anointing); 103b (Anthropomorphism); 124b (Apparition); 312a (Christians and Christianity); 487b, 488a, 488b (Crucifixion)
II 367b (Grammar and the Q); 474b (Iconoclasm); 489a (Ignorance)
III 8a, 19a (Jesus)
IV 40b (People of the Book); 238b (Pre-1800 Preoccupations of Q Studies)

157-158	IV	121a (Polemic and Polemical Language)
157-159	III	19a, 20a (Jesus)
158	II	216a (Flying)
	III	19b (Jesus); 396a (Miracles)
	IV	357a (Readings of the Q)
159	I	111a (Antichrist); 222b (Belief and Unbelief)
	III	19b (Jesus); 141a (Last Judgment)
	V	493b (Witnessing and Testifying)
160	I	11b (Abrogation); 97a (Animal Life)
	II	224a (Forbidden); 571b (Israel)
	III	173a, 174b (Lawful and Unlawful)
	V	303a (Torah)
160-161	III	25a (Jews and Judaism)
	V	469b (Wealth)
161	II	8a (Economics)
	V	304b (Torah)
162	II	340a (Good Deeds); 359a (Grammar and the Q)
	III	22b, 32a (Jews and Judaism); 136a, 136b (Last Judgment)
	IV	17a (Paradise); 438b (Revelation and Inspiration); 539a (Scholar)
	V	196b (Taxation)
163	I	1a (Aaron); 8a (Abraham); 115a (Apologetics); 245b (Book); 496a (David)
	II	561b (Isaac)
	III	1a (Jacob); 8a, 17a (Jesus); 50a (Job); 53a (Jonah); 381b (Messenger); 444b (Muḥammad); 514b (Names of the Q)
	IV	36b (People of the Book); 294a, 297b (Prophets and Prophethood); 315a, 316a (Psalms); 438b (Revelation and Inspiration)
	V	364a (Tribes and Clans); 380b (Trust and Patience); 546b (Word of God)
163-165	III	7b (Jesus); 522a (Narratives)
164	I	480b (Creeds)
	II	436b (History and the Q)
	III	424a (Moses); 517b (Narratives)
	IV	292a, 302b (Prophets and Prophethood); 312a (Provocation); 440b (Revelation and Inspiration)
	V	110a (Speech); 302b (Torah); 546b, 547b (Word of God)
165	II	341b (Good News)
	IV	3b (Pairs and Pairing); 300a (Prophets and Prophethood)
166	III	451a (Muḥammad)
	IV	600a (Shīʿism and the Q)
	V	492b, 493a (Witnessing and Testifying)
167	I	120a (Apostasy)

168	II	245a (Forgiveness)
	IV	28b (Path or Way)
168-169	I	232b (Biology as the Creation and Stages of Life)
169	II	54b (Eternity)
	IV	28b, 29b (Path or Way)
170	III	451a (Muḥammad)
	IV	5b (Pairs and Pairing); 537b (Scholar)
171	I	102b (Anointing); 115a, 117a (Apologetics); 222b, 223a (Belief and Unbelief); 312a, 313a (Christians and Christianity)
	II	329b (God and his Attributes); 443a, 443b (Holy Spirit)
	III	8a, 14b, 15a, 15b, 16a (Jesus); 293a, 294a, 294b, 295a (Mary); 551a (Numbers and Enumeration)
	IV	33a (Patriarchy); 39b, 41a (People of the Book); 120a, 121a (Polemic and Polemical Language); 160b (Polytheism and Atheism); 296a (Prophets and Prophethood); 416a (Religious Pluralism and the Q); 428a (Repentance and Penance)
	V	81b (Soul); 115b (Spirit); 369a, 370b, 371b (Trinity); 500a (Witnessing and Testifying); 533b (Women and the Q); 541b, 545b (Word of God)
171-172	I	170b (Art and Architecture and the Q)
	III	7b (Jesus); 295a (Mary); 300a (Material Culture and the Q)
172	I	102b (Anointing); 160b, 161a (Arrogance)
	III	16a (Jesus)
	IV	16b (Paradise); 220a (Prayer); 579a (Servants)
173	I	161a (Arrogance); 220a (Belief and Unbelief); 241b (Boast); 396a (Conceit); 432a (Contracts and Alliances)
	II	273b (Friends and Friendship); 345a (Grace)
	IV	5b (Pairs and Pairing); 264a (Pride); 458b (Reward and Punishment)
174	I	326a (Chronology and the Q)
	II	326b (God and his Attributes)
	III	186b (Light); 511b (Names of the Q)
	IV	286b (Proof); 296a (Prophets and Prophethood)
	V	3a (Signs); 182a (Symbolic Imagery)
175	I	465a (Covenant)
	V	529a (Women and the Q)
176	I	259b (Brother and Brotherhood)
	II	7b (Economics); 385a (Ḥadīth and the Q); 519b, 520a, 524a, 525b (Inheritance)
	III	98a (Kinship); 194a (Literary Structures of the Q)
	IV	284a (Profane and Sacred)

Sūrat al-Māʾida (5)

I 328a (Chronology and the Q)
II 180a (Farewell Pilgrimage); 220a (Food and Drink); 264a (Form and Structure of the Q); 467a (Hunting and Fishing)
III 6b (Jerusalem); 13a (Jesus); 521b (Narratives)
IV 237b (Pre-1800 Preoccupations of Q Studies); 501b (Ritual Purity)
V 174b (Sūra); 190a (Table); 330a (Traditional Disciplines of Q Studies); 369a (Trinity)

1 I 96b, 97b (Animal Life); 256b, 257a (Breaking Trusts and Contracts); 432b (Contracts and Alliances); 464a (Covenant)
II 8b (Economics); 218b (Food and Drink); 321a (God and his Attributes); 467a (Hunting and Fishing)
III 157a (Law and the Q); 172b (Lawful and Unlawful); 190a (Literacy)
IV 282a (Profane and Sacred); 502b (Ritual Purity)

1-3 II 262b (Form and Structure of the Q)
V 175b (Sūra)

1-5 I 344a (Cleanliness and Ablution)

1-10 II 180a (Farewell Pilgrimage)

2 I 32a (African Literature); 97a (Animal Life)
II 60b, 72a (Ethics and the Q); 196a (Fear); 224b (Forbidden); 299a (Geography); 340a (Good Deeds); 458b, 460a (House, Domestic and Divine); 467a (Hunting and Fishing)
III 77a, 77b (Kaʿba); 159b (Law and the Q); 172a (Lawful and Unlawful); 340b (Mecca); 380a (Mercy); 410a (Months)
IV 52b (People of the House); 91a (Piety); 281b, 282a, 283a (Profane and Sacred); 486a (Ritual and the Q); 514b, 515a (Sacred Precincts)
V 285a (Time); 475b (Weights and Measures)

3 I 96b (Animal Life); 155b (Archaeology and the Q); 237b (Blood and Blood Clot); 291b (Carrion); 305b (Children of Israel); 320b, 326b (Chronology and the Q); 521b (Despair)
II 31a (Epigraphy); 63b, 68b (Ethics and the Q); 177b (Famine); 180a (Farewell Pilgrimage); 197a (Fear); 220a, 220b (Food and Drink); 237b (Foretelling in the Q); 482b (Idols and Images); 546b (Instruments)
III 158a, 165b (Law and the Q); 173a, 174a (Lawful and Unlawful); 378b (Mercy); 457a (Muḥammad)
IV 259b (Pre-Islamic Arabia and the Q); 401b, 404a, 416a (Religious Pluralism and the Q); 504b (Ritual Purity); 517b (Sacrifice)
V 54b, 55a (Slaughter); 190a (Table)

3-4 II 220a (Food and Drink)

4 I 292a (Carrion); 545b (Dog)
II 85b (Everyday Life, Q In); 467b (Hunting and Fishing)
III 579b (Opposition to Muḥammad)

	IV	420b (Remembrance)
	V	55b (Slaughter); 201b, 202b (Teaching); 549a (Work)
4-5	I	343b (Cleanliness and Ablution)
5	I	11b (Abrogation); 222b (Belief and Unbelief); 258a (Bridewealth); 299a (Chastity)
	II	161b (Failure); 221a (Food and Drink); 374b (Guardianship)
	III	23a (Jews and Judaism); 172b, 174b (Lawful and Unlawful); 277a, 278a (Marriage and Divorce)
	IV	36a (People of the Book); 285a (Prohibited Degrees); 431b (Responsibility); 452a (Reward and Punishment); 583b (Sex and Sexuality)
	V	56a (Slaughter); 303a (Torah); 313b (Trade and Commerce)
6	I	81b (Anatomy); 328b (Chronology and the Q); 341a, 341b, 342a, 342b, 343a (Cleanliness and Ablution); 358b (Collection of the Q); 411b (Contamination)
	II	199b (Feet); 391a (Ḥadīth and the Q); 402a (Hand); 501b (Illness and Health)
	III	12a (Jesus); 57b, 58a (Journey); 333b (Measurement); 375b (Menstruation); 378b (Mercy)
	IV	225b (Prayer); 372a (Recitation of the Q); 485b, 488a, 491b (Ritual and the Q); 499a, 499b, 500a, 500b, 501a, 501b, 502a, 505a, 506b (Ritual Purity)
	V	465a (Water)
7	I	236a (Blessing); 256b (Breaking Trusts and Contracts); 305b (Children of Israel); 343a (Cleanliness and Ablution)
	II	406a (Hearing and Deafness); 550b (Intention)
	III	568b (Obedience)
	IV	128b (Politics and the Q); 420b (Remembrance)
	V	190a (Table); 393b (Turkish Literature and the Q); 502a (Witnessing and Testifying)
8	II	70b (Ethics and the Q); 152a (Expeditions and Battles)
	III	65b (Judgment); 70a, 71b (Justice and Injustice)
9	I	220a (Belief and Unbelief)
	II	245a (Forgiveness)
	IV	431b (Responsibility)
9-10	IV	1b (Pairs and Pairing)
10	I	235b (Blasphemy)
	V	6a (Signs)
11	I	305b (Children of Israel)
	III	29b (Jews and Judaism); 499a (Naḍīr, Banū al-); 577b (Opposition to Muḥammad)
	IV	420b (Remembrance)
	V	39b (Sīra and the Q); 379a, 379b (Trust and Patience)
12	I	304b, 307a (Children of Israel); 465a (Covenant)
	II	432b (History and the Q)
	III	553a (Numbers and Enumeration)
	IV	128b (Politics and the Q)
	V	110b (Speech); 123a (Springs and Fountains); 190a (Table); 197a (Taxation)

12-14	IV	421b (Remembrance)
13	I	305a (Children of Israel); 497a (David)
	II	243a (Forgery); 342b (Gospel); 407a, 408b (Heart)
	III	25a (Jews and Judaism); 40a (Jihād); 143a (Last Judgment)
	IV	36b (People of the Book); 450b (Revision and Alteration)
	V	190a, 190b (Table); 302b, 304b (Torah)
14	I	464b (Covenant)
	III	536b (News)
	IV	120b (Polemic and Polemical Language); 128b (Politics and the Q); 405a (Religious Pluralism and the Q)
	V	190a (Table)
15	I	118a (Apologetics); 222b (Belief and Unbelief)
	II	326b (God and his Attributes)
	III	25b (Jews and Judaism); 124b (Language and Style of the Q); 186b, 187a (Light); 443b (Muḥammad); 504a (Names of the Prophet)
	IV	41a (People of the Book); 120a, 120b (Polemic and Polemical Language)
	V	182a (Symbolic Imagery); 300b (Torah)
15-16	III	511b, 512b (Names of the Q)
15-38	I	270b (Cain and Abel)
16	I	435b (Conversion)
	III	186a (Light)
17	I	102b (Anointing); 312a, 313a (Christians and Christianity); 474b (Creation)
	II	327b (God and his Attributes); 508a (Impotence)
	III	16a (Jesus); 92a (Kings and Rulers); 295a (Mary)
	IV	33a (Patriarchy); 121a (Polemic and Polemical Language); 311a (Provocation)
	V	190a (Table); 484b (Wish and Desire); 533b (Women and the Q)
17-18	III	7b (Jesus)
	IV	127b (Politics and the Q)
18	I	305b (Children of Israel); 476a (Creation)
	II	244b (Forgiveness)
	III	16b (Jesus); 24a (Jews and Judaism); 99a (Kinship); 233b (Love and Affection)
	IV	2a (Pairs and Pairing); 120b (Polemic and Polemical Language); 184a (Possession and Possessions); 405a (Religious Pluralism and the Q); 457b (Reward and Punishment)
	V	287a (Time)
18-19	IV	311a (Provocation)
19	I	222b (Belief and Unbelief)
	II	321b (God and his Attributes); 341b (Good News); 436b (History and the Q); 497b (Illiteracy)
	III	201b (Literary Structures of the Q); 443b (Muḥammad); 592a (Orality and Writing in Arabia)

IV 3b (Pairs and Pairing); 36b, 41a (People of the Book); 297b (Prophets and Prophethood)
V 300b (Torah)

20 I 236b (Blessing); 304b (Children of Israel)
III 93b, 94b (Kings and Rulers)
IV 128a (Politics and the Q); 290b (Prophets and Prophethood); 421a (Remembrance)

20-25 I 532b (Dialogues)

20-26 I 305a (Children of Israel)
III 522b (Narratives)
V 190a (Table)

21 I 244b (Book)
II 309a (Geography)
III 5b (Jerusalem)
IV 282b (Profane and Sacred); 513b (Sacred Precincts)
V 107a (Spatial Relations); 184b (Syria); 375a (Trips and Voyages)

21-26 V 455b (War)

22-29 II 145b (Expeditions and Battles)

23 IV 7a (Pairs and Pairing)

24 I 461a (Courage)
II 268a (Freedom and Predestination)

25 I 260a (Brother and Brotherhood)

26 II 433b (History and the Q); 510b (Indifference)
V 285b (Time); 375a (Trips and Voyages)

27 I 270b (Cain and Abel)
III 190a (Literacy); 441a (Muḥammad); 518a, 524b (Narratives); 536b (News)
IV 302b (Prophets and Prophethood); 517a (Sacrifice)

27-31 IV 9b (Parable)

27-32 I 26a (Adam and Eve); 270a (Cain and Abel)
II 418a (Hell and Hellfire)
III 521b (Narratives)

28 I 271a (Cain and Abel)
IV 288a (Property)

29 I 270a, 271b (Cain and Abel)
II 353b (Grammar and the Q)

30 V 82b (Soul)

31 I 98b, 101a (Animal Life); 264a (Burial)
III 548b (Nudity)
IV 428b (Repentance and Penance)

32	I	2b (Abortion); 32a (African Literature); 244b (Book); 270a (Cain and Abel); 304a (Children of Israel); 439b (Corruption); 533b (Dialogues)
	III	458b, 459a, 460a (Murder)
	V	162a (Suicide); 204a (Teaching); 302b (Torah); 417a (Vengeance)
33	I	439b (Corruption); 487b, 489a (Crucifixion)
	II	144a (Expeditions and Battles); 199a (Feet); 353b (Grammar and the Q)
	III	41b (Jihād)
	IV	142a (Politics and the Q); 364a (Rebellion); 453b (Reward and Punishment)
	V	255a (Theft); 455a (War); 552a (World)
33-34	II	208b (Fighting)
	IV	140a (Politics and the Q)
	V	498a (Witnessing and Testifying)
34	IV	426b (Repentance and Penance)
35	I	461a (Courage)
	II	554a (Intercession)
	III	37a (Jihād)
	IV	30a (Path or Way); 163b (Popular and Talismanic Uses of the Q)
35-36	IV	1b (Pairs and Pairing)
36	IV	453a (Reward and Punishment)
	V	133a (Suffering)
37	II	418b (Hell and Hellfire)
	III	73b (Justice and Injustice)
38	I	295a (Chastisement and Punishment)
	II	401b (Hand)
	III	200a (Literary Structures of the Q)
	IV	287b (Property); 454a (Reward and Punishment)
	V	254b, 255b (Theft); 525a (Women and the Q)
38-39	III	70b (Justice and Injustice)
	V	498a (Witnessing and Testifying)
39	II	6a (Economics)
	IV	427b (Repentance and Penance)
40	I	188b (Authority)
	II	244b (Forgiveness)
	IV	2a (Pairs and Pairing); 457b (Reward and Punishment)
40-42	IV	1b (Pairs and Pairing)
41	I	82b (Anatomy); 118a (Apologetics); 305a (Children of Israel); 405b (Consolation); 497a (David)
	II	243a (Forgery); 510b (Indifference)
	III	143a (Last Judgment); 452b (Muḥammad)
	IV	36b (People of the Book); 120b (Polemic and Polemical Language); 450b (Revision and Alteration); 457a (Reward and Punishment)
	V	134a (Suffering); 485b (Wish and Desire)

41-43 III 25a, 25b, 30b (Jews and Judaism)

41-44 IV 36b (People of the Book)

41-82 II 73a (Ethics and the Q)

42 I 148a (Arbitration)
III 65b (Judgment); 173b, 174a (Lawful and Unlawful); 499a (Naḍīr, Banū al-)
IV 133b (Politics and the Q); 335a (Qurayẓa, Banū al-)

42-43 III 443b (Muḥammad)
V 303b (Torah)

42-50 V 231a (Teeth)

43 III 151a (Law and the Q)
V 300b, 304a (Torah)

44 I 516b (Decision)
II 197a (Fear)
III 24b (Jews and Judaism); 65a (Judgment); 151a (Law and the Q); 186b (Light)
IV 3b (Pairs and Pairing); 120b (Polemic and Polemical Language); 133a, 133b, 146b (Politics and the Q); 297b, 299a, 301a (Prophets and Prophethood); 404a (Religious Pluralism and the Q)
V 103a (Sovereignty); 202a (Teaching); 231b (Teeth); 300b, 304a (Torah)

44-47 IV 133a (Politics and the Q)

44-50 III 568b (Obedience)

45 I 187a (Atonement); 239a (Blood Money); 244b (Book); 369b (Community and Society in the Q)
II 1a (Ears); 153b (Eyes)
III 378b (Mercy)
IV 132b, 133a, 133b (Politics and the Q); 436b (Retaliation)
V 23a (Sin, Major and Minor); 83a (Soul); 198a (Taxation); 231a, 231b (Teeth); 307b (Torah); 393a, 393b (Turkish Literature and the Q); 416b, 417a (Vengeance)

46 II 142b (Exhortations); 342a (Gospel)
III 8a, 16a (Jesus); 151a (Law and the Q); 186b (Light); 445a (Muḥammad); 502b (Names of the Prophet)
IV 3b (Pairs and Pairing); 297b, 298a (Prophets and Prophethood); 439a (Revelation and Inspiration)
V 300b (Torah); 316b (Tradition and Custom); 533b (Women and the Q)

46-47 III 7b (Jesus)
IV 120b (Polemic and Polemical Language)

46-49 I 147b (Arbitration)

47 I 73b (Ambiguous); 310b (Christians and Christianity); 516b (Decision)
II 342a (Gospel)
III 65a (Judgment); 151a (Law and the Q); 558b (Numismatics)
IV 37b (People of the Book); 120b (Polemic and Polemical Language); 133a, 133b (Politics and the Q); 402b (Religious Pluralism and the Q)
V 231b (Teeth)

48	I	117b (Apologetics); 245a (Book); 377a (Community and Society in the Q)
	II	61b, 72a (Ethics and the Q); 430b, 435b (History and the Q); 497a (Illiteracy)
	III	151b (Law and the Q); 441a, 443b, 445a (Muḥammad); 512b (Names of the Q); 536b (News)
	IV	29a (Path or Way); 36b (People of the Book); 128a, 149a (Politics and the Q); 307a, 307b (Protection); 337a (Races); 439a (Revelation and Inspiration)
	V	133b (Suffering); 231b (Teeth); 300b (Torah); 363a (Trial)
48-49	III	453b (Muḥammad)
48-50	IV	145b (Politics and the Q)
49	II	59a (Ethics and the Q); 351b (Grammar and the Q)
	III	27a (Jews and Judaism); 443b (Muḥammad)
49-50	III	151b (Law and the Q)
50	I	37b, 39b (Age of Ignorance); 516a (Decision)
	II	321a (God and his Attributes)
	III	64b (Judgment); 72a (Justice and Injustice)
	IV	146b (Politics and the Q)
	V	286b (Time)
51	I	224b (Belief and Unbelief); 312a (Christians and Christianity)
	II	73a (Ethics and the Q); 274a (Friends and Friendship)
	III	27a, 29b (Jews and Judaism); 231b (Lord); 236a (Love and Affection); 238a, 238b, 240b (Loyalty)
	IV	24b (Parties and Factions); 324b (Qaynuqāʿ, Banū); 335a (Qurayẓa, Banū al-); 405a, 413a (Religious Pluralism and the Q)
51-56	IV	324a (Qaynuqāʿ, Banū); 406a (Religious Pluralism and the Q)
51-58	V	43a (Sīra and the Q)
52	I	399a (Conquest)
	II	407b (Heart); 470a (Hypocrites and Hypocrisy)
	V	447a (Vision and Blindness)
53	I	39b (Age of Ignorance)
54	II	322a (God and his Attributes); 358a (Grammar and the Q)
	III	36a (Jihād); 58a (Journey); 233b, 236b (Love and Affection)
	IV	6a (Pairs and Pairing)
	V	137b (Ṣūfism and the Q); 29b (Tolerance and Coercion)
54-55	IV	520a (Saint)
55	I	254a (Bowing and Prostration)
	II	340a (Good Deeds)
	III	231b (Lord); 236b (Love and Affection); 304b (Material Culture and the Q)
55-56	II	273a, 274a (Friends and Friendship)
56	II	72a (Ethics and the Q); 150a (Expeditions and Battles); 430b (History and the Q)
	IV	25a (Parties and Factions)
	V	430b (Victory)

57 II 148a (Expeditions and Battles); 274a (Friends and Friendship)
III 27a (Jews and Judaism); 238a (Loyalty)
IV 36a (People of the Book)

57-58 III 400a, 400b (Mockery)

58 I 328b (Chronology and the Q)
IV 225b (Prayer)
V 556a (Worship)

59 I 222b (Belief and Unbelief)
III 26a (Jews and Judaism)
IV 41a (People of the Book); 120a (Polemic and Polemical Language); 453b (Reward and Punishment)
V 301a (Torah)

59-60 I 93a (Anger)

60 I 93a (Anger); 98b (Animal Life); 306b (Children of Israel); 478a (Creation); 492a (Curse)
II 386a (Ḥadīth and the Q)
III 25a, 26b (Jews and Judaism); 536b (News)
IV 401b (Religious Pluralism and the Q); 510b (Sabbath); 576a (Servants)

61 IV 116b (Polemic and Polemical Language)

62-63 II 73b (Ethics and the Q)
III 174a (Lawful and Unlawful)

63 V 202a (Teaching)

64 I 103b (Anthropomorphism); 491b (Curse)
II 144a (Expeditions and Battles); 211b (Fire); 323b, 325a (God and his Attributes); 508a (Impotence)
III 25a, 28b (Jews and Judaism); 70b (Justice and Injustice); 201b (Literary Structures of the Q); 378b (Mercy)
IV 405a (Religious Pluralism and the Q)
V 455a (War)

65 IV 14b (Paradise); 41a (People of the Book)
V 301a (Torah)

65-66 I 306a (Children of Israel)
III 24b (Jews and Judaism)

66 I 219a, 223b (Belief and Unbelief)
III 23a, 32a (Jews and Judaism); 402a (Moderation); 513a (Names of the Q)
V 300b, 304b (Torah)

67 III 454a (Muḥammad)
IV 307b (Protection)

68 I 222b (Belief and Unbelief)
II 510b (Indifference)
III 24b, 31a (Jews and Judaism)

	IV	36b, 41a (People of the Book)
	V	300b, 304b (Torah)
69	I	222b (Belief and Unbelief)
	II	60b (Ethics and the Q); 350b, 359a (Grammar and the Q)
	III	22a (Jews and Judaism); 40a (Jihād); 136a, 136b (Last Judgment)
	IV	120b (Polemic and Polemical Language); 404b, 405a, 408a (Religious Pluralism and the Q); 455b (Reward and Punishment); 511b (Sabians)
70	I	304b, 305a (Children of Israel); 465a (Covenant)
	III	24a (Jews and Judaism); 382a (Messenger)
	V	190a (Table); 302b (Torah)
70-71	IV	129a (Politics and the Q)
71	I	530a (Dialects)
	II	361b (Grammar and the Q); 406b (Hearing and Deafness)
72	I	102b (Anointing); 312a (Christians and Christianity)
	II	224a (Forbidden)
	III	16a (Jesus); 295a (Mary)
	IV	100b, 103b (Pit); 282a (Profane and Sacred)
	V	369b (Trinity)
72-73	III	295a (Mary)
	IV	121a (Polemic and Polemical Language)
72-75	V	369a (Trinity)
72-76	V	190a (Table)
72-78	III	7b (Jesus)
73	I	115a, 117a (Apologetics); 312a, 312b (Christians and Christianity)
	II	329b (God and his Attributes); 364a (Grammar and the Q)
	III	295a (Mary)
	IV	118a, 121a (Polemic and Polemical Language); 160b (Polytheism and Atheism); 413a (Religious Pluralism and the Q); 428a (Repentance and Penance); 456a (Reward and Punishment)
	V	369a, 369b, 370b (Trinity)
75	I	102b (Anointing); 223a (Belief and Unbelief); 312a, 312b (Christians and Christianity)
	II	217a (Food and Drink)
	III	16a (Jesus); 444b (Muḥammad)
	IV	33a (Patriarchy); 298a (Prophets and Prophethood)
	V	8a (Signs); 369b (Trinity); 422b (Verse); 533b (Women and the Q)
75-76	III	295a (Mary)
76	IV	5a, 5b (Pairs and Pairing); 401b (Religious Pluralism and the Q)
77	I	185b (Astray); 222b (Belief and Unbelief); 312a, 312b (Christians and Christianity)

	IV	41a (People of the Book); 416a (Religious Pluralism and the Q)
78	I	305a (Children of Israel); 492a (Curse); 496a (David); 536b, 537b (Disobedience)
	III	8a, 13a, 16a (Jesus)
	IV	309b (Provocation)
	V	533b (Women and the Q)
78-79	V	438b (Virtues and Vices, Commanding and Forbidding); 446a (Vision and Blindness)
78-82	IV	121a (Polemic and Polemical Language)
79	V	438a, 441a, 443a (Virtues and Vices, Commanding and Forbidding)
80-81	II	274a (Friends and Friendship)
	III	238a (Loyalty)
81	III	502a (Names of the Prophet)
	IV	120b (Polemic and Polemical Language)
	V	501b (Witnessing and Testifying)
82	I	183b (Asceticism); 311b (Christians and Christianity); 378a, 378b (Community and Society in the Q)
	II	73a (Ethics and the Q); 150a (Expeditions and Battles)
	III	26b (Jews and Judaism); 40a (Jihād); 236a (Love and Affection); 406a (Monasticism and Monks)
	IV	264a (Pride); 404a, 405a, 405b, 412b (Religious Pluralism and the Q)
	V	139a (Ṣūfism and the Q); 431a (Vigil)
82-83	I	223a (Belief and Unbelief)
83	I	81a (Anatomy); 160b (Arrogance); 219a (Belief and Unbelief); 243b, 247a (Book)
	II	153a (Eyes)
	IV	369a (Recitation of the Q)
	V	490b (Witness to Faith)
84	II	448b (Hope)
85	IV	452b, 455b (Reward and Punishment)
86	V	6a (Signs)
87	III	174b (Lawful and Unlawful)
	IV	283a (Profane and Sacred)
	V	573a (Zealotry)
89	I	17a (Abrogation); 187a, 188a (Atonement); 289a (Captives); 354b (Collection of the Q)
	II	180b (Fasting); 450a (Hospitality and Courtesy)
	III	109b (Language and Style of the Q); 551a, 553a (Numbers and Enumeration); 562a, 563a, 564b, 565a, 565b (Oaths)
	IV	208b (Poverty and the Poor); 308a (Protection)
	V	7b (Signs); 57b (Slaves and Slavery); 280b (Time); 422b (Verse); 449b (Vow)

90 I 38b (Age of Ignorance); 155b (Archaeology and the Q); 167a (Art and Architecture and the Q); 321a (Chronology and the Q); 411a (Contamination); 526a (Devil)
II 7a (Economics); 221b, 221b (Food and Drink); 237b, 238b (Foretelling in the Q); 482b (Idols and Images); 546b (Instruments)
IV 165b (Popular and Talismanic Uses of the Q); 259b (Pre-Islamic Arabia and the Q); 503b (Ritual Purity)
V 183a (Spiritual Beings)

90-91 II 7a (Economics); 237b (Foretelling in the Q); 280a (Gambling); 556a, 556b, 557a (Intoxicants)
III 152a, 169a, 169b (Law and the Q); 361b (Medicine and the Q)
IV 500a (Ritual Purity)
V 481b (Wine)

91 I 526a (Devil)
II 238b (Foretelling in the Q)
IV 230a (Prayer)
V 487a (Wish and Desire)

92 III 125a (Language and Style of the Q); 166b (Law and the Q); 382b (Messenger)
V 501b (Witnessing and Testifying)

93 I 220a (Belief and Unbelief)
II 60a, 61b (Ethics and the Q); 221b (Food and Drink)
V 137b (Ṣūfism and the Q)

94 II 196b (Fear); 218b (Food and Drink); 467a (Hunting and Fishing); 546a (Instruments)

94-95 I 404a (Consecration of Animals)
V 549a (Work)

94-96 I 97b (Animal Life)

95 I 97b (Animal Life); 187a, 187b (Atonement); 404b (Consecration of Animals)
II 180b (Fasting); 216b, 218b (Food and Drink); 450a (Hospitality and Courtesy); 467a (Hunting and Fishing)
III 71b (Justice and Injustice); 75a, 76a, 76b, 79a (Kaʿba); 338b, 339a (Mecca)
IV 7a (Pairs and Pairing); 133b (Politics and the Q); 208b (Poverty and the Poor); 259a (Pre-Islamic Arabia and the Q); 453b (Reward and Punishment)
V 103a (Sovereignty); 416a (Vengeance); 496b (Witnessing and Testifying)

95-96 IV 282a (Profane and Sacred)

96 II 218b (Food and Drink); 467a, 467b (Hunting and Fishing)
III 60b (Joy and Misery); 174a (Lawful and Unlawful)
IV 502b (Ritual Purity)

96-97 I 163b (Art and Architecture and the Q)

97 I 97a (Animal Life); 404b (Consecration of Animals); 465b (Covenant)
II 224a (Forbidden); 458b (House, Domestic and Divine)

	III	75a, 76a, 76b, 79b (Kaʿba); 338b, 339a (Mecca); 410a (Months)
	IV	4a (Pairs and Pairing); 52b (People of the House); 259a (Pre-Islamic Arabia and the Q); 282a (Profane and Sacred); 514b (Sacred Precincts)
	V	285a (Time); 475b (Weights and Measures)
98	III	380a (Mercy)
	IV	453a (Reward and Punishment)
99	III	40a (Jihād); 452b (Muḥammad)
100	II	31a (Epigraphy); 63a (Ethics and the Q)
	V	393b (Turkish Literature and the Q)
101	IV	5b (Pairs and Pairing)
101-102	III	303a (Material Culture and the Q)
101-104	IV	32b (Patriarchy)
103	I	97a (Animal Life); 236a (Blasphemy); 401b (Consecration of Animals)
104	V	317a (Tradition and Custom)
105	III	40a (Jihād)
	V	442a (Virtues and Vices, Commanding and Forbidding)
106	III	58a (Journey); 71b (Justice and Injustice)
	V	373a (Trips and Voyages); 492b, 496a, 496b (Witnessing and Testifying); 525a (Women and the Q)
106-107	II	519a (Inheritance)
	III	562b (Oaths)
	IV	7a (Pairs and Pairing)
106-108	V	495a, 495b (Witnessing and Testifying)
108	II	2a (Ears)
109	III	141a (Last Judgment)
	IV	300b (Prophets and Prophethood); 537b (Scholar)
	V	188b (Table); 369b (Trinity)
109-118	III	7b (Jesus)
110	I	98a (Animal Life); 149a (Archaeology and the Q); 167b (Art and Architecture and the Q); 236b (Blessing); 245a, 245b (Book); 314b (Christians and Christianity); 340b (Clay); 476a (Creation); 507a (Death and the Dead)
	II	4a (Earth); 276a (Furniture and Furnishings); 342a (Gospel); 442a (Holy Spirit)
	III	8a, 13a, 16a, 16b, 18b (Jesus); 191a (Literacy); 246a (Magic); 293a (Mary); 373b (Memory); 396a (Miracles)
	IV	3b (Pairs and Pairing); 36b (People of the Book); 68b (Philosophy and the Q); 178b (Popular and Talismanic Uses of the Q); 282b (Profane and Sacred); 286b (Proof); 435b (Resurrection)
	V	81a (Soul); 95b (South Asian Literatures and the Q); 115a (Spirit); 133b (Suffering); 188b (Table); 200b (Teaching); 300b (Torah); 371b (Trinity); 483a, 483b (Wisdom); 533b (Women and the Q)

110-116	III	521b (Narratives)
111	I	123a (Apostle)
	III	382b (Messenger)
	IV	439b, 440a (Revelation and Inspiration)
	V	188b, 190a (Table); 489a (Witness to Faith)
112	I	123a, 123b (Apostle)
	II	276a (Furniture and Furnishings); 364b (Grammar and the Q); 411b (Heaven and Sky)
	III	8a (Jesus)
	V	188a, 188b (Table); 533b (Women and the Q)
112-113	III	382b (Messenger)
112-114	V	190a (Table)
112-115	III	16b (Jesus)
	IV	9b (Parable)
113	V	188b (Table)
113-114	III	396a (Miracles)
114	II	215b (Flying); 276a (Furniture and Furnishings)
	III	8a (Jesus)
	V	178b (Sustenance); 188a, 189a (Table); 533b (Women and the Q)
115	III	16b (Jesus)
	V	110b (Speech); 188a, 189a, 190b (Table)
116	I	115a (Apologetics); 223a (Belief and Unbelief); 312a, 313b (Christians and Christianity)
	III	8a, 16a, 16b (Jesus); 295a (Mary)
	IV	537b (Scholar)
	V	369b (Trinity); 533b (Women and the Q); 547a (Word of God)
116-117	III	295a (Mary)
	V	189a, 190a (Table); 493b (Witnessing and Testifying)
117	I	312a (Christians and Christianity)
	III	16a, 20a (Jesus)
	V	493a (Witnessing and Testifying)
118	II	244b (Forgiveness)
	IV	458a (Reward and Punishment); 578b (Servants)
	V	189a (Table)
119	II	54b (Eternity)
	III	203b (Literary Structures of the Q)
	IV	18b (Paradise); 522b (Salvation)

Sūrat al-Anʿām (6)

I 93b (Animal Life); 230b (Biology as the Creation and Stages of Life)
III 165a (Law and the Q); 272a (Manuscripts of the Q); 320b, 321a (Material Culture and the Q); 534a (Nature as Signs)
IV 244a (Pre-1800 Preoccupations of Q Studies); 495b (Ritual and the Q); 591b (Shīʿa)
V 174b (Sūra); 262b, 263a (Theology and the Q); 308a (Torah)

1 I 74a (Ambiguous); 115a (Apologetics); 472a, 472b, 477b (Creation); 494a (Darkness)
III 71a (Justice and Injustice); 534b (Nature as Signs)
IV 118b (Polemic and Polemical Language)
V 308a (Torah); 544a (Word of God); 553a (World)

1-7 III 304b (Material Culture and the Q)

2 I 231a, 232a (Biology as the Creation and Stages of Life); 339b (Clay); 446a, 446b (Cosmology); 474b, 476a (Creation); 516b (Decision)
II 4a, 4b (Earth); 45a (Eschatology); 186a (Fate); 269a (Freedom and Predestination); 328a, 328b (God and his Attributes)
III 185a (Life); 354b (Medicine and the Q)
V 289a (Time); 393a (Turkish Literature and the Q); 554a (World)

3-4 V 198b (Taxation)

5 III 400b (Mockery); 536b (News)

5-11 II 510a (Indifference)

6 I 473a, 479a (Creation)
II 293a (Generations); 508a (Impotence)
III 520b (Narratives)
IV 320a (Punishment Stories)

7 I 250a (Book); 412a (Contamination)
II 38b (Epigraphy); 545a (Instruments)
III 246a (Magic); 448b (Muḥammad); 585b (Orality)
IV 311b (Provocation); 443b (Revelation and Inspiration); 569b (Scrolls)
V 272a (Theology and the Q); 558a (Writing and Writing Materials)

7-8 III 397b (Miracles)

8 V 39b (Sīra and the Q); 543a (Word of God)

8-9 III 450a (Muḥammad)

10 III 400a, 400b (Mockery); 453a (Muḥammad)
IV 309b, 310a (Provocation)
V 272a (Theology and the Q)

11 IV 320b (Punishment Stories); 425a (Remnant)

12 I 170b (Art and Architecture and the Q); 244b (Book)
II 161b (Failure); 322a (God and his Attributes)
III 300a (Material Culture and the Q)
V 82a (Soul)

13 I 501a (Day, Times of)

14 I 472b (Creation)
II 217a (Food and Drink)
III 231b (Lord); 444a, 446b (Muḥammad)

15 I 500a (Day, Times of); 538a (Disobedience)
III 137a (Last Judgment)

16 III 379b (Mercy)
IV 522b (Salvation)
V 430a (Victory)

17 V 485b (Wish and Desire)

18 II 320b (God and his Attributes)
IV 5b (Pairs and Pairing)

19 I 250a (Book)
II 322a, 329b (God and his Attributes)
III 440b, 442b (Muḥammad); 506b (Names of the Q)
IV 487a (Ritual and the Q)
V 461a (Warner); 489b (Witness to Faith); 492b, 493a, 500a (Witnessing and Testifying)

20 I 222b (Belief and Unbelief)
IV 20b (Parents); 36a (People of the Book)
V 301a, 303b (Torah)

21 I 235b (Blasphemy)
II 162a (Failure)
III 70b (Justice and Injustice); 181a (Lie)
IV 523a (Salvation)
V 6a (Signs)

22 II 477b (Idolatry and Idolaters)

24 I 236a (Blasphemy)
II 99a (Evil Deeds)

25 I 82a (Anatomy); 226a (Belief and Unbelief); 512a (Debate and Disputation)
II 370b (Gratitude and Ingratitude); 408b (Heart); 430a (History and the Q)
III 518a (Narratives); 578b (Opposition to Muḥammad)
IV 115b (Polemic and Polemical Language); 309b (Provocation)
V 6b (Signs); 447a (Vision and Blindness); 474a (Weights and Measures)

25-26 III 450a (Muḥammad)

26 II 355a (Grammar and the Q)

27 IV 281a (Profane and Sacred); 430a (Repentance and Penance)

28 II 224a (Forbidden)

29 I 506a (Death and the Dead)

31	I	235b (Blasphemy); 501a (Day, Times of)
	III	137a, 138a (Last Judgment)
	V	287b (Time)
32	II	44b (Eschatology)
	III	136b (Last Judgment); 147b (Laughter); 182a (Life)
	V	552b (World)
33	IV	310a (Provocation)
	V	6a (Signs); 134a (Suffering)
33-34	III	453a (Muḥammad)
33-35	I	405b (Consolation)
34	I	222a (Belief and Unbelief)
	III	518a (Narratives); 536b (News)
	IV	309b (Provocation)
	V	134a (Suffering); 430a (Victory); 434b (Virtue); 548a (Word of God)
35	II	59a (Ethics and the Q); 468b (Hypocrites and Hypocrisy); 510b (Indifference)
	III	102b (Knowledge and Learning); 453a (Muḥammad)
	IV	311b (Provocation)
36	I	480b (Creeds)
	II	91b (Everyday Life, Q In)
	III	397b (Miracles)
	IV	435b (Resurrection)
37	III	452a (Muḥammad)
	IV	311b (Provocation); 538a (Scholar)
	V	8a (Signs)
37-38	III	398b (Miracles)
38	I	96a (Animal Life); 243a (Book); 371b (Community and Society in the Q); 523a (Destiny)
	II	269b (Freedom and Predestination); 497a (Illiteracy); 544b (Instruments)
	III	140a (Last Judgment); 533b (Nature as Signs)
	IV	401a (Religious Pluralism and the Q)
	V	319a (Traditional Disciplines of Q Studies)
39	I	226a (Belief and Unbelief)
	II	330b (God and his Attributes); 406b (Hearing and Deafness)
	III	534a, 535a (Nature as Signs)
	IV	2a (Pairs and Pairing)
	V	6a (Signs)
40	I	501a (Day, Times of)
	III	67b (Judgment); 137a (Last Judgment)
	V	287b (Time)
42	III	63b (Joy and Misery)
	IV	487b (Ritual and the Q)
	V	133a (Suffering)

42-45 IV 320b (Punishment Stories)

43 II 407a (Heart)
IV 487b (Ritual and the Q)

44 I 398b (Conquest); 522a (Despair); 524b (Devil)
III 61b (Joy and Misery)

45 IV 288a (Property); 425a (Remnant)

46 I 81a, 82a (Anatomy)
II 407a, 408b (Heart)
IV 574b (Seeing and Hearing)
V 8a (Signs); 444b (Vision); 446b (Vision and Blindness)

48 II 341b (Good News)
III 444b (Muḥammad)
IV 3b (Pairs and Pairing); 300a (Prophets and Prophethood)
V 460b (Warner)

50 III 398a (Miracles); 452a (Muḥammad)
IV 216b (Prayer); 311b (Provocation)
V 447b (Vision and Blindness)

51 II 273b (Friends and Friendship)
IV 5b (Pairs and Pairing); 307b (Protection)

52 I 389b (Companions of the Prophet); 503a, 503b (Day, Times of)
II 80a (Evening); 323b (God and his Attributes)
III 417a, 418b (Morning)
IV 223a, 229b (Prayer)
V 281b (Time); 487a (Wish and Desire)

54 I 237a (Blessing); 244b (Book)
II 66b (Ethics and the Q); 91b (Everyday Life, Q In); 322a (God and his Attributes); 335b (Good and Evil); 452b (Hospitality and Courtesy); 488b (Ignorance)
IV 427a (Repentance and Penance)
V 5b (Signs); 24b (Sin, Major and Minor)

55 IV 29b (Path or Way); 431b (Responsibility)

56 I 147b (Arbitration); 185b (Astray)

57 I 148a (Arbitration); 516a, 516b (Decision)
II 30a (Epigraphy)
III 517b (Narratives); 557a (Numismatics)
IV 128a (Politics and the Q); 128a, 286a (Proof)
V 2a (Ṣiffīn, Battle of)

58 III 65a (Judgment)
V 543a (Word of God)

59 I 41b (Agriculture and Vegetation); 219b (Belief and Unbelief); 243a (Book); 522b (Destiny)
II 3a (Earth); 269b (Freedom and Predestination); 305a (Geography); 423a (Hidden and the Hidden); 546b (Instruments)

III 124b (Language and Style of the Q); 508a (Names of the Q)
IV 179b (Popular and Talismanic Uses of the Q); 560a (Scripture and the Q)

60 V 83b (Soul); 280b, 289a (Time)
I 502a (Day, Times of)
III 18b (Jesus); 184b (Life)

61 IV 290a (Prophets and Prophethood); 307b (Protection)
V 118b (Spiritual Beings); 493a (Witnessing and Testifying)

62 I 148a (Arbitration); 344b (Clients and Clientage)
III 231a (Lord)
IV 307b (Protection)

63 I 494a (Darkness)
II 3a (Earth)
IV 108a (Planets and Stars); 523b (Salvation)
V 464a (Water)

63-64 I 519a (Deliverance)

64 III 63b (Joy and Misery)

65 III 212a (Literature and the Q)
IV 591b, 592a (Shīʿa)

66 III 40a (Jihād)

66-70 III 577b (Opposition to Muḥammad)

67 III 537a (News)
IV 541b (Science and the Q)

68 I 526a (Devil)
IV 309b (Provocation)

68-69 I 118a (Apologetics)

68-70 I 115b (Apologetics)

69 III 40a (Jihād)

70 II 211a (Fire); 273b (Friends and Friendship); 416a, 418a (Hell and Hellfire); 455b (Hot and Cold)
III 12b (Jesus); 40a (Jihād); 71a (Justice and Injustice)
IV 5b (Pairs and Pairing); 422b (Remembrance)
V 121b (Springs and Fountains)

71 I 437b (Conversion); 526b (Devil)
IV 5a (Pairs and Pairing)
V 120b (Spiritual Beings); 374b (Trips and Voyages)

71-72 II 366a (Grammar and the Q)

72 III 184b (Life)

73 I 318b (Chronology and the Q); 472b, 473a, 475a (Creation)
II 327b (God and his Attributes); 435b (History and the Q); 474a (Iconoclasm); 547a (Instruments)

	III	71b (Justice and Injustice)
	IV	4a, 5b (Pairs and Pairing); 537b (Scholar)
	V	109a (Speech); 287a (Time); 386b (Truth); 492b (Witnessing and Testifying); 542b, 544b, 547a (Word of God)
74	I	7a (Abraham); 166b (Art and Architecture and the Q); 192a (Āzar)
	II	481a (Idols and Images)
	V	95b (South Asian Literatures and the Q); 162b (Sun); 248b (Textual Criticism of the Q)
74-79	I	438a (Conversion)
74-81	IV	159b, 161a (Polytheism and Atheism)
74-83	III	521b (Narratives)
	V	258a, 269a (Theology and the Q)
74-84	I	6b (Abraham); 330a (Chronology and the Q)
	III	239a (Loyalty); 494a, 494b (Myths and Legends in the Q)
75	III	90b (Kings and Rulers)
	IV	127b (Politics and the Q)
	V	262b (Theology and the Q); 553a (World)
75-79	I	7a, 8b (Abraham); 474b (Creation)
	II	402b (Ḥanīf)
76	IV	107a, 108b (Planets and Stars)
77	III	415a (Moon)
	IV	107a (Planets and Stars)
78	I	503b (Day, Times of)
	V	162b (Sun); 282b (Time)
79	I	5b (Abraham)
	II	323b (God and his Attributes); 402b (Ḥanīf)
	III	446a (Muḥammad)
	V	263a (Theology and the Q)
80	I	472a, 472b (Creation)
	II	197a (Fear); 322a (God and his Attributes)
81	V	263a, 274b (Theology and the Q)
83	I	438a (Conversion)
	II	33a (Epigraphy)
	IV	5b (Pairs and Pairing); 537b, 539a (Scholar)
83-87	III	50a (Job); 522a (Narratives)
83-88	III	380a (Mercy)
83-89	III	381b (Messenger)
83-90	III	7b (Jesus); 50a (Job)
	V	302a (Torah)

84 I 1a (Aaron); 7b (Abraham); 496a (David)
II 434a (History and the Q); 561b, 562a (Isaac); 563b (Ishmael)
III 1a (Jacob); 57a (Joseph); 520a (Narratives)
IV 291a (Prophets and Prophethood); 452b (Reward and Punishment)
V 380b (Trust and Patience)

84-86 II 561b (Isaac)
III 17a (Jesus)

84-90 III 525b (Narratives)

85 I 194a (Baal)
II 12b (Elijah); 340b (Good Deeds)
III 8a (Jesus); 51b (John the Baptist); 53a (Jonah)
IV 291b (Prophets and Prophethood); 482b (Rhymed Prose)
V 574a (Zechariah)

85-86 III 53a (Jonah)

86 I 8a (Abraham)
II 14a (Elisha); 564a (Ishmael)

86-87 II 12a (Election)

87 II 11b (Election)

88 II 161b (Failure)
IV 159a (Polytheism and Atheism); 431b (Responsibility)

89 I 222b (Belief and Unbelief)
IV 127b (Politics and the Q)
V 574a (Zechariah)

90 III 510a (Names of the Q)
IV 230a (Prayer); 452a (Reward and Punishment)

91 I 245b, 247a (Book); 305a (Children of Israel)
II 430a (History and the Q); 545a (Instruments)
III 25b (Jews and Judaism); 186b (Light); 189b (Literacy); 425a (Moses); 449b, 451b (Muḥammad); 590b, 592a (Orality and Writing in Arabia)
IV 3b (Pairs and Pairing); 36b (People of the Book); 297b (Prophets and Prophethood); 450b (Revision and Alteration)
V 201b (Teaching); 300b, 301a, 304b (Torah); 558a (Writing and Writing Materials)

91-92 IV 36a, 36b (People of the Book)

92 I 117b (Apologetics); 338b (City)
II 299a (Geography); 495a (Illiteracy)
III 338a (Mecca); 442b, 443b, 445a (Muḥammad)
IV 224b (Prayer); 299b (Prophets and Prophethood); 439a (Revelation and Inspiration); 561b (Scripture and the Q)
V 303b (Torah)

93 I 89b (Angel); 159a, 160b (Arrogance); 236a (Blasphemy); 506b (Death and the Dead)

	II	45b (Eschatology); 514b (Informants)
	III	181a (Lie)
	IV	264a (Pride); 295a (Prophets and Prophethood); 309b (Provocation); 457a (Reward and Punishment)
	V	83b (Soul); 300b (Torah); 546a (Word of God)
94	I	476a (Creation)
	II	362a (Grammar and the Q); 416b (Hell and Hellfire)
	V	117b (Spiritual Beings); 371a (Trinity); 494a (Witnessing and Testifying)
94-95	IV	119a (Polemic and Polemical Language)
95	I	476b, 479a (Creation); 494b (Date Palm)
	II	305a (Geography)
	IV	435a (Resurrection)
95-99	IV	438a (Revelation and Inspiration)
	V	554a (World)
96	I	472a, 477b (Creation); 500b, 502a, 503b, 504a (Day, Times of)
	III	415a (Moon); 417a, 418a (Morning)
	IV	6a (Pairs and Pairing); 108a (Planets and Stars); 589b (Shekhinah)
	V	163a (Sun); 281a, 283b (Time)
96-97	I	442b (Cosmology); 473a, 474a (Creation)
97	I	442b (Cosmology); 494a (Darkness)
	II	3a (Earth); 327b (God and his Attributes)
	IV	108a (Planets and Stars); 538b (Scholar)
	V	373a (Trips and Voyages); 464a (Water)
97-99	IV	287a (Proof); 538a (Scholar)
98	I	479a (Creation)
	II	328b (God and his Attributes)
	III	362a (Medicine and the Q)
	IV	538b (Scholar)
99	I	41a, 42b, 44b, 45a (Agriculture and Vegetation); 362b (Colors); 476b (Creation); 494b (Date Palm)
	II	3a, 3b, 4a (Earth); 305a, 305b (Geography)
	V	5b (Signs)
100	I	236a (Blasphemy); 330a (Chronology and the Q)
	II	317b (God and his Attributes)
	III	48a (Jinn); 181a (Lie)
	IV	220b (Prayer)
	V	120b (Spiritual Beings); 369a (Trinity)
100-101	I	115a (Apologetics)
101	I	472a (Creation)
	II	320b, 327a, 329b (God and his Attributes); 536b (Innovation)

III 300a (Material Culture and the Q)
V 370a (Trinity)

101-103 I 472b (Creation)

102 I 435a (Conversion); 467b (Createdness of the Q)
IV 280b (Profane and Sacred)
V 501a (Witnessing and Testifying)

103 II 53a (Eschatology); 284a (Garden); 324a (God and his Attributes)
V 275b (Theophany); 444b (Vision); 445b (Vision and Blindness)

104 III 40a (Jihād)
IV 287a (Proof)

105 IV 538b (Scholar)
V 203a (Teaching)

106 I 170b (Art and Architecture and the Q)

107 III 452b (Muḥammad)

108 II 432a (History and the Q); 497a (Illiteracy)
IV 228b (Prayer); 309b (Provocation); 331a (Quraysh); 483b (Rhymed Prose)

109 I 329b (Chronology and the Q)
II 317a (God and his Attributes); 354b (Grammar and the Q)
III 398b (Miracles); 562a, 563b (Oaths)
IV 119a (Polemic and Polemical Language); 311b (Provocation); 562b (Scripture and the Q)
V 3a (Signs)

110 V 444b (Vision)

111 II 488a (Ignorance)

112 I 213b (Beauty); 526a (Devil)
II 23b (Enemies)
III 46b (Jinn); 299b, 300a (Material Culture and the Q)
IV 295a, 301b (Prophets and Prophethood); 439b (Revelation and Inspiration)
V 363a (Trial); 494b (Witnessing and Testifying); 546a (Word of God)

114 I 147b (Arbitration); 222b (Belief and Unbelief); 250a (Book)
II 321b (God and his Attributes)
V 301a (Torah)

115 II 321b (God and his Attributes)
III 70a, 71b (Justice and Injustice); 267b (Manuscripts of the Q)
V 547b (Word of God)

116 III 567b (Obedience)
V 178a (Suspicion); 573a (Zealotry)

117 IV 29a (Path or Way)

118 II 220a (Food and Drink)
V 55b (Slaughter)

118-119 I 96b (Animal Life)
V 303a (Torah)

119 I 96b, 97a (Animal Life); 210b (Basmala)
III 102b (Knowledge and Learning)
IV 420b (Remembrance)
V 55b (Slaughter)

119-121 II 85b (Everyday Life, Q In)

120 II 63b (Ethics and the Q)

121 I 96b (Animal Life); 190b (Authority); 512b (Debate and Disputation); 526b (Devil)
II 273b (Friends and Friendship)
III 48a (Jinn); 567a (Obedience)
IV 295a (Prophets and Prophethood); 309b (Provocation); 420b (Remembrance); 439b (Revelation and Inspiration)
V 55b (Slaughter); 546a (Word of God)

123 IV 309b (Provocation)

124 II 345a (Grace)
IV 128a (Politics and the Q); 311b (Provocation)

125 I 225b (Belief and Unbelief); 330b (Chronology and the Q); 436a (Conversion); 523a (Destiny)
II 59a (Ethics and the Q); 215b (Flying); 270a (Freedom and Predestination); 330b (God and his Attributes)
IV 454a (Reward and Punishment); 503a (Ritual Purity)
V 485b (Wish and Desire)

125-127 IV 34a (Peace)

126 IV 29a (Path or Way)

127 II 52a (Eschatology); 273a (Friends and Friendship); 283a (Garden); 321b (God and his Attributes)
IV 14a (Paradise)

128 I 330a (Chronology and the Q)
II 52b (Eschatology)
III 46b, 47b (Jinn)
IV 5b (Pairs and Pairing); 103b (Pit); 216b (Prayer); 537b (Scholar)

129 IV 128b (Politics and the Q)

130 III 46b, 47b (Jinn); 141a (Last Judgment)
IV 299b (Prophets and Prophethood)
V 8a (Signs); 82a (Soul); 492a, 494b (Witnessing and Testifying)

131 II 488b (Ignorance)
III 71a, 72a (Justice and Injustice)

133 I 277a (Caliph); 479a (Creation)
V 467b (Wealth)

135 III 162b (Law and the Q)
IV 523a (Salvation)

136 I 41a (Agriculture and Vegetation); 402b (Consecration of Animals)
II 64a (Ethics and the Q); 478b (Idolatry and Idolaters)
V 449b (Vow)

136-145 I 236a (Blasphemy)

137 I 236a (Blasphemy); 301b (Children)
II 366a (Grammar and the Q); 511a (Infanticide)
III 42b (Jihād)
IV 255b (Pre-Islamic Arabia and the Q)
V 318a (Tradition and Custom); 570a (Youth and Old Age)

138 I 97a (Animal Life); 402b (Consecration of Animals)
II 220b (Food and Drink)
III 173b (Lawful and Unlawful)
V 411b (Vehicles)

138-139 I 402a (Consecration of Animals)

138-150 III 174b (Lawful and Unlawful)

139 I 291b (Carrion); 402b (Consecration of Animals)
IV 5b (Pairs and Pairing); 537b (Scholar)

140 I 235a (Birth Control); 301b (Children)
II 511a (Infanticide)
III 174b (Lawful and Unlawful); 458b (Murder)
IV 255b (Pre-Islamic Arabia and the Q)
V 318a (Tradition and Custom); 570a (Youth and Old Age); 573a (Zealotry)

141 I 41a (Agriculture and Vegetation); 478b (Creation); 500b (Day, Times of)
II 3b, 4a (Earth); 69b (Ethics and the Q); 217b (Food and Drink); 304b, 305b (Geography)
IV 482a (Rhymed Prose)
V 7b (Signs); 197b (Taxation)

142 I 94b, 96a (Animal Life); 403a (Consecration of Animals); 526a (Devil)
II 23b, 24a (Enemies); 219b, 220b (Food and Drink)
V 411b (Vehicles)

142-145 II 220a (Food and Drink)

143 II 218a (Food and Drink); 352b (Grammar and the Q)
III 537a (News)

143-144 I 94a, 95b (Animal Life); 403a (Consecration of Animals)
IV 6a (Pairs and Pairing)

144 I 287a (Camel)
II 218b (Food and Drink)
III 181a (Lie)

145	I	237b (Blood and Blood Clot); 291b (Carrion); 403a (Consecration of Animals); 411a (Contamination)
	II	220a, 220b (Food and Drink)
	III	173a, 174a (Lawful and Unlawful); 378b (Mercy)
	IV	503b, 504a (Ritual Purity); 517b (Sacrifice)
146	I	11b (Abrogation); 97a (Animal Life); 403a (Consecration of Animals)
	II	218a (Food and Drink); 571b (Israel)
	III	25a (Jews and Judaism); 173a, 174b (Lawful and Unlawful)
	V	55a (Slaughter); 303a (Torah)
147	I	375b (Community and Society in the Q)
	III	380a (Mercy)
	V	19a (Sin, Major and Minor)
148	III	174b (Lawful and Unlawful)
	IV	309b, 312b (Provocation)
	V	317a (Tradition and Custom)
148-149	IV	287a (Proof)
148-151	IV	311a (Provocation)
149	I	435b (Conversion)
	II	33a (Epigraphy); 329a (God and his Attributes)
150	II	359a (Grammar and the Q)
	III	71a (Justice and Injustice)
	V	6a (Signs); 492b (Witnessing and Testifying)
151	I	29a (Adultery and Fornication); 234b (Birth Control); 239a (Blood Money); 301b (Children); 367a (Commandments)
	II	61b, 75b (Ethics and the Q); 447b (Honor); 453a (Hospitality and Courtesy); 511a (Infanticide)
	III	190a (Literacy); 252a (Maintenance and Upkeep)
	IV	20b (Parents); 255b (Pre-Islamic Arabia and the Q); 580b (Sex and Sexuality)
	V	162a (Suicide); 179b (Sustenance); 204b (Teaching); 308a (Torah); 318a (Tradition and Custom); 417a (Vengeance); 528a (Women and the Q); 570a (Youth and Old Age)
151-152	V	21a (Sin, Major and Minor)
151-153	I	366b, 367a (Commandments)
	III	447b (Muḥammad)
	V	27b (Sin, Major and Minor)
152	II	5b, 8b (Economics); 75b (Ethics and the Q); 374a (Guardianship); 545a (Instruments)
	III	65b (Judgment); 71b (Justice and Injustice); 276a (Markets); 330a (Maturity); 334a, 334b, 335b (Measurement); 603b (Orphans)
	IV	432b (Responsibility)
	V	313a (Trade and Commerce)

153	III	379a (Mercy)
	IV	25b (Parties and Factions); 29a, 29b (Path or Way); 128a (Politics and the Q)
154	II	61b (Ethics and the Q); 367a (Grammar and the Q)
	III	424b (Moses)
	IV	3b (Pairs and Pairing)
	V	301a (Torah)
154-157	IV	36a (People of the Book)
155	I	367b (Commandments)
	III	162b (Law and the Q)
	IV	297a (Prophets and Prophethood)
156	II	488b (Ignorance)
	III	21b (Jews and Judaism)
	V	203a (Teaching)
157	II	335b (Good and Evil)
	III	181a (Lie); 379a (Mercy); 450b (Muḥammad)
	V	5b (Signs)
158	II	325b (God and his Attributes)
	III	379b (Mercy)
	IV	434b (Resurrection)
	V	8a (Signs)
159	III	32b (Jews and Judaism)
	IV	25b (Parties and Factions); 403b (Religious Pluralism and the Q); 592a (Shīʿa)
160	III	379b (Mercy); 553a (Numbers and Enumeration)
	IV	458b (Reward and Punishment)
161	I	5b, 6a (Abraham); 330b (Chronology and the Q); 373a (Community and Society in the Q); 465b (Covenant)
	II	329a (God and his Attributes); 402b, 403b (Ḥanīf)
	IV	396a (Religion)
162	I	506a (Death and the Dead)
	II	356b (Grammar and the Q)
162-163	II	329a (God and his Attributes)
	III	444a, 446b (Muḥammad)
163	II	33b, 34a (Epigraphy)
	III	299a, 299b, 300b (Material Culture and the Q); 556a (Numismatics)
	V	369a (Trinity); 489b (Witness to Faith)
164	I	271b (Cain and Abel)
	II	420b (Heresy)
	III	228a (Load or Burden)
	IV	432a (Responsibility)
	V	22a (Sin, Major and Minor)

165 I 277a (Caliph)
III 380a (Mercy)
IV 127a, 128b (Politics and the Q); 185b (Possession and Possessions); 453a (Reward and Punishment)
V 133b (Suffering); 363a (Trial)

Sūrat al-Aʿrāf (7)

I 297a (Chastisement and Punishment); 304b (Children of Israel); 454b (Cosmology)
II 415b (Hell and Hellfire)
III 67a (Judgment); 200b (Literary Structures of the Q); 472b (Mysterious Letters); 490b (Myths and Legends in the Q); 520b (Narratives)
IV 48a (People of the Heights); 59a (Persian Literature and the Q); 130a, 131b, 141a (Politics and the Q); 244a (Pre-1800 Preoccupations of Q Studies); 288a (Property); 601b (Shīʿism and the Q)
V 174b (Sūra)

1-10 III 520b (Narratives)

1-22 III 304b (Material Culture and the Q)

2 I 245a (Book)
III 442b, 452b (Muḥammad)
IV 293b (Prophets and Prophethood)
V 203a (Teaching); 461a (Warner)

3 IV 130a, 131b, 139a (Politics and the Q)

4 II 431a (History and the Q)
III 520b (Narratives)

4-5 IV 320b (Punishment Stories)

6 III 141a (Last Judgment)
IV 300b (Prophets and Prophethood); 431a (Responsibility)

7 III 517b (Narratives)
IV 131a (Politics and the Q)

7-8 V 313b (Trade and Commerce)

8 III 70a (Justice and Injustice); 178a (Left Hand and Right Hand); 334b (Measurement)
IV 523a (Salvation)

8-9 I 522b (Destiny)
III 70a (Justice and Injustice); 140b (Last Judgment); 275b (Markets); 334b (Measurement)
IV 2b (Pairs and Pairing); 130a (Politics and the Q)
V 493a (Witnessing and Testifying)

9 II 161b (Failure)
III 178a (Left Hand and Right Hand); 334b (Measurement)
V 6a (Signs)

10	I	446b (Cosmology); 472a (Creation)
	II	371a (Gratitude and Ingratitude)
	IV	117a (Polemic and Polemical Language); 210b (Power and Impotence)
10-34	I	448a (Cosmology)
11	I	447a (Cosmology); 476a (Creation); 525a (Devil)
	II	172b (Fall of Man); 323a (God and his Attributes)
	III	45a (Jinn)
	V	96a (South Asian Literatures and the Q); 109a (Speech)
11-12	I	24a (Adam and Eve); 255a (Bowing and Prostration); 511a (Debate and Disputation)
	IV	220a (Prayer)
11-15	V	145a (Ṣūfism and the Q)
11-18	II	417b (Hell and Hellfire)
11-25	I	525b (Devil)
	III	520b (Narratives)
	V	530a (Women and the Q)
12	I	24a (Adam and Eve); 339b (Clay); 353b (Collection of the Q); 476a (Creation)
	II	4a, 4b (Earth)
	III	355a (Medicine and the Q); 532a (Nature as Signs)
12-18	V	109a (Speech)
13	I	160a (Arrogance)
	II	172b (Fall of Man)
	V	547a (Word of God)
15-16	I	447b (Cosmology)
16	IV	29a (Path or Way); 103b (Pit)
16-17	I	526a (Devil)
	II	172b (Fall of Man); 336a (Good and Evil)
	IV	130b (Politics and the Q)
16-22	I	190b (Authority)
17	II	372a (Gratitude and Ingratitude); 401b (Hand)
18	I	235a (Birth Control)
	II	353b (Grammar and the Q)
18-19	III	425b (Moses)
19	I	25a (Adam and Eve); 447b (Cosmology)
	II	172b (Fall of Man); 175a (Family); 219b (Food and Drink); 283a (Garden); 362b (Grammar and the Q)
19-22	V	360a (Tree)
19-27	III	548a (Nudity)

20 I 25a (Adam and Eve); 526a (Devil)
II 173a (Fall of Man); 224a (Forbidden); 364a (Grammar and the Q)
III 211a (Literature and the Q)
IV 295a (Prophets and Prophethood); 581a (Sex and Sexuality)
V 479a (Whisper); 487a (Wish and Desire)

20-22 I 25a (Adam and Eve); 447b (Cosmology); 525a (Devil)
IV 584a (Sex and Sexuality)

21 III 563b (Oaths)

22 I 41b (Agriculture and Vegetation); 346b (Clothing); 447b (Cosmology); 526a (Devil)
II 23b, 24a (Enemies); 66a (Ethics and the Q); 173a (Fall of Man)
III 490b (Myths and Legends in the Q); 548a (Nudity)
IV 581a (Sex and Sexuality)

22-23 V 25a (Sin, Major and Minor)

22-24 IV 130a (Politics and the Q)

23 I 25b (Adam and Eve); 447b (Cosmology)
II 65a (Ethics and the Q); 245a (Forgiveness)
V 530a (Women and the Q)

24 II 23b, 24a (Enemies); 173a (Fall of Man)
III 60a (Joy and Misery)
IV 130b (Politics and the Q)

24-25 I 25a (Adam and Eve)
II 173a (Fall of Man)

25 I 447b, 455a (Cosmology)

26 I 346b (Clothing)
III 403a (Modesty); 548b (Nudity)
IV 581a (Sex and Sexuality)
V 4a (Signs)

26-27 II 328b (God and his Attributes)

26-58 III 520b (Narratives)

27 I 526a, 526b (Devil)
II 72a (Ethics and the Q); 273b (Friends and Friendship)
III 46b (Jinn); 490b (Myths and Legends in the Q)
IV 130a (Politics and the Q); 581a (Sex and Sexuality)
V 487a (Wish and Desire)

28 I 523a (Destiny)
II 439a (History and the Q)
IV 580b (Sex and Sexuality)
V 317a (Tradition and Custom)

29 I 164a (Art and Architecture and the Q); 478a, 479a (Creation)
II 550a (Intention); 557b (Invitation)
III 140a (Last Judgment)

30	I	435b (Conversion)
	II	273b (Friends and Friendship)
	III	46b (Jinn)
	IV	2a (Pairs and Pairing)
31	II	216b, 222b (Food and Drink); 328b (God and his Attributes)
31-32	I	213a (Beauty)
	IV	256b (Pre-Islamic Arabia and the Q)
31-33	V	145a (Ṣūfism and the Q)
32	III	174b (Lawful and Unlawful)
	IV	538b (Scholar)
	V	179a (Sustenance); 573a (Zealotry)
33	IV	130b (Politics and the Q); 580b, 583b (Sex and Sexuality)
	V	19b (Sin, Major and Minor)
34	I	501a (Day, Times of)
	II	45a (Eschatology); 72a (Ethics and the Q); 269a (Freedom and Predestination)
	III	185a (Life); 335b (Measurement)
	V	288a, 289a (Time)
35	II	328b (God and his Attributes)
35-36	V	145a (Ṣūfism and the Q)
36	I	396a (Conceit)
	II	418a (Hell and Hellfire)
	IV	264a (Pride)
	V	6a (Signs)
37	III	181a (Lie)
	IV	290a (Prophets and Prophethood)
	V	494b (Witnessing and Testifying)
38	I	492a (Curse)
	II	98b (Evil Deeds); 416b (Hell and Hellfire)
	III	46b, 47b (Jinn)
	IV	6b, 7b (Pairs and Pairing); 130b (Politics and the Q); 336b (Races); 438a (Revelation and Inspiration); 458b (Reward and Punishment)
	V	54a (Sister)
38-39	I	532a (Dialogues)
39-40	V	145a (Ṣūfism and the Q)
40	I	98b, 100a (Animal Life); 286b (Camel); 398b (Conquest)
	II	546b (Instruments)
	IV	264a (Pride); 474a (Rhetoric and the Q)
	V	6a (Signs); 19a (Sin, Major and Minor); 468b (Wealth)
40-41	III	70b (Justice and Injustice)
41	II	276a (Furniture and Furnishings); 415a (Hell and Hellfire)
	IV	104a (Pit)

42	I	220a (Belief and Unbelief)
	IV	432b (Responsibility)
43	I	435b (Conversion)
	II	282b, 283b, 284a (Garden); 465a (Humor)
	III	303a (Material Culture and the Q)
	IV	300b (Prophets and Prophethood)
44	I	385a (Community and Society in the Q)
	II	415b (Hell and Hellfire)
44-50	II	417a (Hell and Hellfire)
46	I	203a (Barrier)
	II	52a (Eschatology); 91b (Everyday Life, Q In); 276a (Furniture and Furnishings); 415b (Hell and Hellfire); 448b (Hope); 553a (Intercession)
	IV	46b, 47a, 47b, 48a (People of the Heights)
	V	244a (Textual Criticism of the Q); 412b (Veil)
46-47	III	67a (Judgment)
46-49	II	415b (Hell and Hellfire)
47	IV	47b (People of the Heights)
48	IV	46b, 48a (People of the Heights)
	V	244a (Textual Criticism of the Q); 468b (Wealth)
49	III	204a (Literary Structures of the Q)
	IV	34b (Peace)
50	I	222a (Belief and Unbelief)
	II	415b (Hell and Hellfire)
	III	203b (Literary Structures of the Q)
	V	464b (Water)
52	IV	3b (Pairs and Pairing)
53	II	99a (Evil Deeds)
	III	141a (Last Judgment)
	IV	300b (Prophets and Prophethood); 430a (Repentance and Penance)
54	I	188b (Authority); 318b (Chronology and the Q); 442a, 443b, 450a (Cosmology); 472b, 473b, 476a (Creation); 499b, 501a, 501b (Day, Times of)
	II	325b, 327a, 327b (God and his Attributes); 410b (Heaven and Sky)
	III	202a (Literary Structures of the Q); 512a (Names of the Q)
	IV	73b, 82a (Philosophy and the Q); 107b (Planets and Stars); 128a, 130b (Politics and the Q); 220b (Prayer); 511a (Sabbath); 543b, 545b (Science and the Q)
	V	103a (Sovereignty); 163a (Sun); 265a, 266b (Theology and the Q); 279b, 280b, 287a (Time); 544a (Word of God)
54-56	I	472b (Creation)
55	IV	229b (Prayer)

56	I	474b (Creation)
	II	448b (Hope)
	IV	130b (Politics and the Q)
57	I	52b, 53a, 55a (Air and Wind); 479a (Creation)
	II	341a (Good News)
	III	530a (Nature as Signs)
	IV	435a (Resurrection)
	V	463a (Water); 471a (Weather)
57-58	II	3a (Earth)
58	I	46b (Agriculture and Vegetation)
	II	3a, 4a (Earth)
	V	5b (Signs)
59	IV	162a (Polytheism and Atheism); 310b (Provocation)
59-64	II	558a (Invitation)
59-93	I	296b (Chastisement and Punishment)
	III	381b (Messenger)
59-102	III	212b (Literature and the Q); 520b (Narratives)
59-136	I	190b (Authority)
59-137	IV	320a (Punishment Stories)
60	I	297a (Chastisement and Punishment)
	II	355b (Grammar and the Q)
	IV	130b (Politics and the Q)
61-62	IV	130b (Politics and the Q)
63	III	379a (Mercy); 399a (Miracles)
	IV	230a (Prayer)
64	I	519a (Deliverance); 553b (Drowning)
65	I	21b (ʿĀd); 261b (Brother and Brotherhood)
	II	541b (Insolence and Obstinacy)
	IV	310b (Provocation)
65-72	II	462a (Hūd); 558a (Invitation)
	IV	586b (Sheba)
66	I	297a (Chastisement and Punishment)
	II	462b (Hūd)
	IV	130b (Politics and the Q)
67-68	IV	130b (Politics and the Q)
69	I	21b (ʿĀd); 277a (Caliph)
	II	327b (God and his Attributes); 434b (History and the Q)
	III	393a, 399a (Miracles); 486a (Myths and Legends in the Q)
	IV	131a (Politics and the Q); 421a (Remembrance)

70	III	556a (Numismatics)
70-71	I	21b (ʿĀd)
71	I	93a (Anger); 190a (Authority); 411b (Contamination); 512b (Debate and Disputation)
	IV	313a (Provocation); 454a (Reward and Punishment); 503a, 503b (Ritual Purity)
	V	547a (Word of God)
71-72	II	542a (Insolence and Obstinacy)
72	I	21b (ʿĀd)
	III	379a (Mercy)
	IV	425a (Remnant); 523b (Salvation)
73	I	261b (Brother and Brotherhood); 287a (Camel)
	II	335b (Good and Evil)
	III	219a (Literature and the Q); 393a (Miracles); 534b (Nature as Signs)
	IV	237b (Pre-1800 Preoccupations of Q Studies); 521a, 521b (Ṣāliḥ)
	V	8a (Signs); 253a (Thamūd)
73-79	I	98b (Animal Life); 149b (Archaeology and the Q)
	II	340b (Good Deeds); 427a (Ḥijr); 558a (Invitation)
	IV	521a (Ṣāliḥ)
73-84	I	395b (Conceit)
	III	534b (Nature as Signs)
74	I	150b (Archaeology and the Q); 189a (Authority); 277a (Caliph)
	II	7b (Economics); 434b (History and the Q)
	IV	131a (Politics and the Q); 421a (Remembrance)
	V	253a (Thamūd)
74-79	II	459b (House, Domestic and Divine)
75	I	159a, 161a (Arrogance)
	III	581a (Oppressed on Earth); 583a (Oppression)
	IV	130b, 132a (Politics and the Q); 263b (Pride); 521b (Ṣāliḥ)
75-76	I	160b (Arrogance)
75-77	I	297a (Chastisement and Punishment)
75-92	I	190a (Authority)
76	II	542a (Insolence and Obstinacy)
	IV	263b (Pride)
77	III	219a (Literature and the Q)
	IV	521b (Ṣāliḥ)
	V	253a (Thamūd)
77-78	I	287a (Camel)
	II	212a (Fire)
78	I	113a (Apocalypse); 504a (Day, Times of)
	II	542a (Insolence and Obstinacy)

	III	418a (Morning)
	IV	521b (Ṣāliḥ)
	V	253a (Thamūd)
79	IV	130b (Politics and the Q)
80	II	444b (Homosexuality)
	IV	580b (Sex and Sexuality)
	V	552a (World)
80-82	IV	584b (Sex and Sexuality)
80-84	III	232a (Lot)
81	II	76a (Ethics and the Q); 444b (Homosexuality)
	V	528a (Women and the Q)
82	I	343b (Cleanliness and Ablution)
	II	360b (Grammar and the Q)
	III	449a (Muḥammad)
	IV	505b (Ritual Purity)
83	IV	523b (Salvation)
84	II	212b (Fire)
	V	470b (Weather)
85	I	149b (Archaeology and the Q); 261b (Brother and Brotherhood); 300b (Cheating)
	II	5b, 8b (Economics); 308a (Geography); 545a (Instruments)
	III	334a, 334b, 335b, 336a (Measurement); 390b (Midian)
	IV	130b (Politics and the Q); 288a (Property); 605a (Shuʿayb)
	V	312b (Trade and Commerce)
85-92	II	459b (House, Domestic and Divine)
85-93	II	558a (Invitation)
	III	390b (Midian)
	IV	605a (Shuʿayb)
86	I	235a (Birth Control)
	II	7b (Economics); 62b (Ethics and the Q)
	III	549b (Numbers and Enumeration)
	IV	28b (Path or Way)
87	I	516a (Decision)
	II	321a (God and his Attributes)
	III	64b (Judgment)
88	I	160b (Arrogance)
	III	393b (Miracles); 449a (Muḥammad)
	IV	130b (Politics and the Q); 263b (Pride); 605b (Shuʿayb)
88-89	IV	401a (Religious Pluralism and the Q)
89	I	236a (Blasphemy); 398b (Conquest)
	II	322a (God and his Attributes)
	IV	605b (Shuʿayb)

90	II	161b (Failure)
91	I	113a (Apocalypse); 504a (Day, Times of)
	IV	605b (Shuʿayb)
91-92	II	361b (Grammar and the Q)
92	II	162a (Failure)
93	II	510b (Indifference)
	IV	130b (Politics and the Q)
94	I	296b (Chastisement and Punishment)
	III	63b (Joy and Misery)
	IV	301b (Prophets and Prophethood)
	V	133a (Suffering)
94-95	V	340a (Transitoriness)
94-102	I	376b (Community and Society in the Q)
95	I	296a, 296b (Chastisement and Punishment)
96	I	398b (Conquest)
	II	195b (Fear)
	III	513a (Names of the Q)
	IV	34b (Peace); 131a (Politics and the Q)
	V	126b (Springs and Fountains)
96-97	V	61a (Sleep)
96-98	IV	37a (People of the Book); 49a (People of the House)
97-98	V	281b (Time)
97-100	I	297a (Chastisement and Punishment)
98	I	504a (Day, Times of)
	III	416b, 418a (Morning)
98-99	IV	308a (Protection)
99	I	377a (Community and Society in the Q)
	II	322a (God and his Attributes)
	III	18a (Jesus)
100	II	406b (Hearing and Deafness)
100-101	II	408b (Heart)
100-141	IV	105b (Plagues)
101	I	82a (Anatomy)
	II	435b (History and the Q)
	III	441a (Muḥammad); 536b (News)
	IV	302b (Prophets and Prophethood)
102	I	431b (Contracts and Alliances); 465b (Covenant)
103	III	421b (Moses); 537a (News)
	IV	106a (Plagues); 131a (Politics and the Q)

103-106	V	4b (Signs)
103-129	II	558a (Invitation)
103-133	I	304b (Children of Israel)
103-137	I	296b (Chastisement and Punishment)
103-162	III	520b (Narratives)
104	III	381b (Messenger)
104-109	III	422a (Moses)
105	III	421b (Moses)
	V	8a (Signs)
106	IV	296b (Prophets and Prophethood)
106-108	IV	183a (Portents)
107	I	99a (Animal Life)
	II	546a (Instruments)
	III	219a (Literature and the Q)
107-108	I	297a (Chastisement and Punishment)
	IV	106a (Plagues)
107-109	IV	296b (Prophets and Prophethood)
108	I	364a (Colors)
109	V	239b (Textual Criticism of the Q)
109-110	I	297a (Chastisement and Punishment)
113-114	I	500b (Day, Times of)
113-126	III	211b (Literature and the Q); 422a (Moses)
115-126	III	393b (Miracles)
116	III	246a (Magic)
117	II	546a (Instruments)
	III	208a, 219a (Literature and the Q)
	IV	293b (Prophets and Prophethood); 440a (Revelation and Inspiration); 508b (Rod)
	V	271a (Theology and the Q); 546a (Word of God)
117-119	I	297a (Chastisement and Punishment)
119	II	144a (Expeditions and Battles)
120	I	255a (Bowing and Prostration)
121-122	II	199a (Feet)
122	I	1a (Aaron)
	III	229b (Lord)
	IV	483a (Rhymed Prose)
123	II	10b (Egypt); 348a (Grammar and the Q)
	III	367b (Medina)

124	I	487b, 488a (Crucifixion)
	II	199a (Feet)
	IV	67b (Pharaoh)
126	I	506a (Death and the Dead)
	II	70b (Ethics and the Q)
	IV	453b (Reward and Punishment)
127	I	297a (Chastisement and Punishment); 302a (Children)
	II	10b (Egypt)
	III	421b (Moses); 583b (Oppression)
	IV	67a (Pharaoh); 131a (Politics and the Q)
127-129	III	422b (Moses)
128	V	434b (Virtue)
129	I	277a (Caliph); 296a (Chastisement and Punishment)
	II	10b (Egypt); 23b (Enemies)
	IV	131a (Politics and the Q)
130	II	304b (Geography)
	IV	106a (Plagues)
	V	285b (Time)
130-135	IV	296b (Prophets and Prophethood)
131	II	242a (Foretelling in the Q)
	IV	538a (Scholar)
133	I	98b (Animal Life); 160a (Arrogance); 237b (Blood and Blood Clot)
	III	520b (Narratives)
	IV	105b, 106a (Plagues); 264a (Pride)
	V	6a (Signs)
133-134	I	297a (Chastisement and Punishment)
133-136	V	133a (Suffering)
134	I	379b (Community and Society in the Q); 465b (Covenant)
	IV	503b (Ritual Purity)
134-135	IV	454a (Reward and Punishment); 503a (Ritual Purity)
134-136	I	304b (Children of Israel)
135-136	IV	210b (Power and Impotence)
136	I	297a (Chastisement and Punishment); 553b (Drowning)
	II	10b (Egypt); 213a (Fire)
	IV	453b (Reward and Punishment)
	V	6b (Signs); 126b (Springs and Fountains); 416a (Vengeance); 463b (Water)
136-137	III	423a (Moses)
137	I	304b (Children of Israel)
	II	309a (Geography)

III 3b (Jerusalem); 488a (Myths and Legends in the Q); 583a (Oppression)
IV 131a, 132a (Politics and the Q); 513b (Sacred Precincts)
V 107a (Spatial Relations); 282b (Time); 547b (Word of God); 549a (Work)

138 I 478a (Creation)
II 213a (Fire); 474a (Iconoclasm); 481a (Idols and Images); 488a (Ignorance)
III 423a (Moses)
V 375a (Trips and Voyages); 464b (Water)

138-151 I 305a (Children of Israel)

141 I 302a (Children)
II 184a (Fasting); 335b (Good and Evil); 542a (Insolence and Obstinacy)
IV 67a (Pharaoh); 523b (Salvation)

142 I 260b (Brother and Brotherhood); 499b (Day, Times of)
III 423b (Moses)
IV 29b (Path or Way); 431b (Responsibility)
V 288a (Time)

142-143 IV 227b (Prayer)
V 302a (Torah)

143 I 272b (Calendar); 532a (Dialogues)
II 315b (Glory); 324a (God and his Attributes); 507a (Impeccability)
III 224a (Literature and the Q); 394a (Miracles); 424a (Moses); 444a (Muḥammad)
IV 429b (Repentance and Penance)
V 95b (South Asian Literatures and the Q); 140b, 146b (Ṣūfism and the Q); 275b, 276a (Theophany); 288a (Time); 445b (Vision and Blindness); 546b, 547a, 547b (Word of God)

143-144 V 109b (Speech)

144 II 11b, 12a (Election)
III 424a (Moses)
IV 291a (Prophets and Prophethood)
V 110a, 111a (Speech); 547b (Word of God)

144-145 III 424a (Moses)

145 I 365a, 365b, 366a (Commandments)
II 142b (Exhortations); 544b (Instruments)
III 190b (Literacy); 394b (Miracles); 424b (Moses)
V 301a (Torah)

146 I 160b (Arrogance); 190a (Authority)
II 43b (Error); 489a (Ignorance)
IV 2a (Pairs and Pairing); 29b (Path or Way); 431b (Responsibility)

148 I 99a (Animal Life); 124b (Apparition); 274a, 274b, 276a (Calf of Gold)
IV 29a (Path or Way)

148-149 III 424b (Moses)

148-153	I	274a (Calf of Gold)
148-155	V	155b (Ṣūfism and the Q)
148-157	I	1a (Aaron)
149	I	274a (Calf of Gold)
	II	245a (Forgiveness)
	IV	428b (Repentance and Penance)
150	I	93b (Anger); 260b (Brother and Brotherhood); 276a (Calf of Gold); 534a (Dialogues)
	II	23b (Enemies); 544b (Instruments)
	III	424b (Moses); 583a (Oppression)
	IV	20a (Parents)
	V	301a (Torah); 524b (Women and the Q)
150-151	I	274a (Calf of Gold)
151	I	260b (Brother and Brotherhood); 274a (Calf of Gold)
	III	378a, 379b (Mercy)
152	I	93a (Anger); 99a (Animal Life); 236a (Blasphemy); 274a (Calf of Gold)
	II	218b (Food and Drink)
152-153	IV	428b (Repentance and Penance)
152-155	I	376b (Community and Society in the Q)
153	I	274a (Calf of Gold)
	V	19a, 19b (Sin, Major and Minor)
154	I	14b (Abrogation); 93b (Anger)
	II	544b, 545a (Instruments)
	III	424b (Moses)
	IV	3b (Pairs and Pairing)
	V	301a (Torah)
155	I	113a (Apocalypse); 435b (Conversion)
	II	11b (Election); 244b (Forgiveness); 273a (Friends and Friendship); 321a (God and his Attributes)
	III	231b (Lord); 378a, 379b (Mercy)
	IV	227b (Prayer)
	V	288a (Time)
156	I	170b (Art and Architecture and the Q); 244b (Book)
	III	21b (Jews and Judaism); 300a (Material Culture and the Q)
	V	6a (Signs); 399a (Ummī); 552a (World)
157	I	96b (Animal Life); 223a (Belief and Unbelief)
	II	6a (Economics); 326b (God and his Attributes); 342a (Gospel); 467a (Hunting and Fishing); 494a, 494b, 495a, 495b, 496a, 499a (Illiteracy)
	III	25b (Jews and Judaism); 127b (Language and Style of the Q); 172b (Lawful and Unlawful); 186b (Light); 228a (Load or Burden); 526a (Narratives)

	IV	290a, 299a (Prophets and Prophethood); 504a (Ritual Purity); 523a (Salvation)
	V	28b (Sinai); 300b, 301a, 302b, 303a, 305b (Torah); 399a, 399b (Ummī); 437b (Virtues and Vices, Commanding and Forbidding)
157-158	I	325a (Chronology and the Q)
	III	445b (Muḥammad); 503b (Names of the Prophet)
	IV	17a (Paradise); 131b (Politics and the Q)
158	I	480b (Creeds)
	II	494a, 496a, 499a (Illiteracy)
	III	127b (Language and Style of the Q); 382b (Messenger); 443b (Muḥammad)
	IV	4a (Pairs and Pairing)
	V	399a, 399b (Ummī); 489a (Witness to Faith); 501b (Witnessing and Testifying); 548a (Word of God)
159	I	305b (Children of Israel)
	II	431b (History and the Q)
	IV	131a (Politics and the Q)
	V	386b (Truth)
160	I	98a (Animal Life)
	II	4a (Earth); 215b (Flying); 364a (Grammar and the Q); 546a (Instruments)
	III	219a (Literature and the Q); 383b (Metals and Minerals); 394a (Miracles); 553a (Numbers and Enumeration)
	IV	131a (Politics and the Q); 440a, 443b (Revelation and Inspiration); 508b (Rod)
	V	127b (Springs and Fountains); 129a (Stone); 140b (Ṣūfism and the Q); 271a (Theology and the Q); 364a (Tribes and Clans)
161	I	149a (Archaeology and the Q); 254b (Bowing and Prostration)
	IV	219b (Prayer)
	V	242a (Textual Criticism of the Q)
161-162	I	305a (Children of Israel)
	IV	428b (Repentance and Penance)
162	II	243a (Forgery)
	IV	450b (Revision and Alteration); 454a (Reward and Punishment); 503a (Ritual Purity)
	V	302b (Torah); 547b (Word of God)
163	I	154b (Archaeology and the Q); 500b (Day, Times of)
	IV	510a, 510b (Sabbath)
	V	279b, 285b (Time)
163-166	V	438b, 441a (Virtues and Vices, Commanding and Forbidding)
163-167	I	305a (Children of Israel)
	IV	511a (Sabbath)
163-168	III	520b (Narratives)
163-171	II	337a (Good and Evil)
164	I	371b (Community and Society in the Q)

165	II	335b (Good and Evil)
	V	439a (Virtues and Vices, Commanding and Forbidding)
166	I	98b (Animal Life); 306b (Children of Israel); 475b (Creation); 496a (David)
	III	25a (Jews and Judaism)
	IV	510b (Sabbath)
	V	545a (Word of God)
167	II	335b (Good and Evil)
	III	380a (Mercy)
	IV	453a (Reward and Punishment)
168	IV	131a (Politics and the Q)
169	I	465a (Covenant)
	II	283a (Garden)
	IV	129a (Politics and the Q)
	V	203a (Teaching); 552b (World)
169-174	III	520b (Narratives)
170	II	362b (Grammar and the Q)
171	II	311a (Geography); 316a, 316b (Glory)
	V	235b (Tents and Tent Pegs); 302b (Torah)
172	I	26a (Adam and Eve); 86b (Angel); 189a (Authority); 466b (Covenant)
	II	44b (Eschatology); 57a (Ethics and the Q); 171a (Faith); 328b (God and his Attributes); 488b (Ignorance)
	III	72a (Justice and Injustice)
	IV	127a (Politics and the Q)
	V	94b (South Asian Literatures and the Q); 138a, 142a, 157b (Ṣūfism and the Q); 393a (Turkish Literature and the Q); 446b (Vision and Blindness); 492a, 502a (Witnessing and Testifying); 545b (Word of God)
172-173	II	98a (Evil Deeds); 337a (Good and Evil); 339b (Good Deeds)
	IV	162a (Polytheism and Atheism)
	V	317a (Tradition and Custom); 530b (Women and the Q)
173	II	337a (Good and Evil)
174	IV	428a (Repentance and Penance)
	V	8a (Signs)
175	III	190a (Literacy); 225b (Literature and the Q); 518a, 524b (Narratives)
175-176	III	520b (Narratives)
175-186	II	261b (Form and Structure of the Q)
176	I	100a (Animal Life); 545b (Dog)
	III	224a (Literature and the Q); 517b (Narratives)
	IV	10a (Parable); 117a (Polemic and Polemical Language); 131a (Politics and the Q)
	V	15a (Simile); 485b (Wish and Desire)

176-177	V	6a (Signs)
177-179	I	523a (Destiny)
177-206	III	520b (Narratives)
178	I	225b (Belief and Unbelief); 435b (Conversion)
	II	59a (Ethics and the Q)
	IV	2a (Pairs and Pairing)
179	I	81a, 83b (Anatomy); 99b (Animal Life); 385a (Community and Society in the Q)
	II	2a (Ears); 406a (Hearing and Deafness); 408b (Heart)
	III	46b, 47b (Jinn); 222b (Literature and the Q)
	IV	574a (Seeing and Hearing)
	V	14b (Simile); 393b (Turkish Literature and the Q); 446a (Vision and Blindness)
180	II	319b (God and his Attributes); 420b (Heresy)
	III	40a (Jihād)
	IV	185a (Possession and Possessions); 280a (Profane and Sacred)
181	V	386b (Truth)
182	II	322a (God and his Attributes)
	V	6a (Signs)
183	II	358a (Grammar and the Q)
184	I	387b (Companions of the Prophet)
	II	540a (Insanity)
	III	450b (Muḥammad)
	IV	112a (Poetry and Poets); 216b (Prayer)
185	IV	4a (Pairs and Pairing); 70b, 80a (Philosophy and the Q)
	V	553a (World)
186	I	225b (Belief and Unbelief)
187	I	111a (Antichrist); 113b (Apocalypse); 501a (Day, Times of)
	II	148b (Expeditions and Battles); 439b (History and the Q)
	III	31b (Jews and Judaism); 137a, 138a (Last Judgment); 579b (Opposition to Muḥammad)
	IV	434b (Resurrection); 538a (Scholar)
	V	288a, 288b (Time)
187-188	III	452a (Muḥammad)
188	II	336b (Good and Evil); 341a, 341b (Good News)
	IV	3b (Pairs and Pairing)
189	I	24b, 25a (Adam and Eve); 447b (Cosmology); 476a, 476b (Creation)
	II	328b (God and his Attributes)
	III	227b (Load or Burden); 277b (Marriage and Divorce)
	IV	20b (Parents); 581b, 584b (Sex and Sexuality)
	V	84a (Soul); 524a, 530a (Women and the Q)

189-190	I	302b (Children)
	IV	161b (Polytheism and Atheism)
190	I	237a (Blessing)
191	I	472b (Creation)
193	I	437a (Conversion)
194	I	472b (Creation)
	IV	228b (Prayer); 577a (Servants)
194-195	IV	312b (Provocation)
195	II	199a (Feet)
	III	212b (Literature and the Q)
	IV	309b, 312b (Provocation)
196	II	274b (Friends and Friendship)
	IV	131b (Politics and the Q)
197	IV	228b (Prayer)
	V	430a (Victory)
197-199	II	488a (Ignorance)
198	I	83b (Anatomy)
	III	208a (Literature and the Q)
199	III	40a (Jihād); 378a (Mercy)
	V	316b (Tradition and Custom)
200	II	92b (Everyday Life, Q In)
	IV	308a (Protection); 309b (Provocation)
201	II	153b (Eyes)
	V	448b (Visiting)
203	II	11b (Election)
	III	450a (Muḥammad); 512a (Names of the Q)
	IV	3b (Pairs and Pairing); 287a (Proof)
	V	3a (Signs)
204	II	87a (Everyday Life, Q In); 405b (Hearing and Deafness)
	III	379b (Mercy)
	IV	222a (Prayer)
	V	203b (Teaching)
204-205	I	328b (Chronology and the Q)
204-206	I	328a (Chronology and the Q)
	IV	224a (Prayer)
205	I	171a (Art and Architecture and the Q); 502b, 504a (Day, Times of)
	II	80a (Evening); 196b (Fear)
	III	372a, 373a (Memory); 401b (Moderation); 417a, 418b, 419a (Morning)
	IV	223a, 229b (Prayer); 487b (Ritual and the Q)
	V	281b (Time)

206 I 160b (Arrogance); 254b (Bowing and Prostration)
II 371b (Gratitude and Ingratitude)
IV 219b (Prayer); 264a (Pride); 378a (Recitation of the Q)
V 393a (Turkish Literature and the Q); 555b (Worship)

Sūrat al-Anfāl (8)

I 209b (Basmala); 322a (Chronology and the Q); 397b (Conquest); 505b (Days of God)
II 183b (Fasting); 264a (Form and Structure of the Q)
III 18a (Jesus)
IV 131b (Politics and the Q); 321b (Punishment Stories)
V 43a (Sīra and the Q); 174b (Sūra); 194a (Taxation)

1 I 252a (Booty); 480b (Creeds)
II 65b (Ethics and the Q); 85b (Everyday Life, Q In)
III 42a (Jihād); 447b (Muḥammad)
V 194a, 195a (Taxation)

1-13 III 304b (Material Culture and the Q)

1-19 III 456a (Muḥammad)
IV 332b (Quraysh)

2 I 220b (Belief and Unbelief)
II 163a (Faith); 198a (Fear)
III 190a (Literacy); 372a, 373b (Memory)
IV 384b (Recitation of the Q)

2-4 I 219b (Belief and Unbelief)
III 379b (Mercy)
IV 17a (Paradise)

4 II 245a (Forgiveness)
III 183a (Life)
V 179a (Sustenance)

6 I 512a (Debate and Disputation)
IV 115b (Polemic and Polemical Language)

7 I 196b (Badr)
V 386b (Truth); 547b (Word of God)

7-8 V 387b (Truth)

7-12 III 42b (Jihād)

9 I 196b (Badr); 463a (Court)
III 183a (Life)

9-13 III 398a (Miracles)

10 I 406a (Consolation)
II 341b (Good News)

11	I	196b (Badr); 526a (Devil)
	II	408b (Heart)
	IV	491b (Ritual and the Q); 503b, 505a (Ritual Purity)
	V	126b (Springs and Fountains); 465a (Water)
12	I	196b (Badr); 397b (Conquest)
	II	198a (Fear); 408b (Heart)
	IV	293b (Prophets and Prophethood); 310a (Provocation); 439b, 440a (Revelation and Inspiration)
12-13	III	454b (Muḥammad)
13	II	358a (Grammar and the Q)
	IV	309b (Provocation); 456a (Reward and Punishment)
15	V	457b (War)
15-16	I	80b (Anatomy); 225a (Belief and Unbelief)
	III	42a (Jihād)
16	I	93a (Anger)
	II	418a (Hell and Hellfire)
17	I	196b (Badr)
	II	186b (Fate); 209b (Fighting)
	III	398a (Miracles); 454a (Muḥammad)
	IV	64a (Persian Literature and the Q)
	V	393a, 393b (Turkish Literature and the Q)
17-19	III	42b (Jihād)
19	I	398b, 399a (Conquest)
	IV	428a (Repentance and Penance)
20-24	II	370b (Gratitude and Ingratitude)
20-32	II	184a (Fasting)
21	II	406a (Hearing and Deafness)
22	I	99b (Animal Life); 226a (Belief and Unbelief)
	II	406b (Hearing and Deafness)
24	I	82a (Anatomy)
	II	355b (Grammar and the Q)
	V	140b (Ṣūfism and the Q); 272b (Theology and the Q)
26	I	406a (Consolation)
	III	42b (Jihād); 449b, 454b (Muḥammad); 581a (Oppressed on Earth); 583b (Oppression)
	IV	131b (Politics and the Q)
26-46	IV	345b (Ramaḍān)
27	IV	335a (Qurayẓa, Banū al-)
	V	272b (Theology and the Q)

28	I	302b (Children)
	II	6b (Economics); 75a (Ethics and the Q)
	IV	31b (Patriarchy)
	V	362b (Trial); 468a (Wealth); 570a (Youth and Old Age)
29	I	486b (Criterion); 500b (Day, Times of)
	II	183b, 184a (Fasting)
	IV	345a (Ramaḍān)
30	II	18b, 20b (Emigration)
	III	18a (Jesus); 449a (Muḥammad); 577b (Opposition to Muḥammad)
	IV	117b (Polemic and Polemical Language); 331b (Quraysh)
	V	37b (Sīra and the Q); 458b (War)
31	II	430a (History and the Q)
	III	190a (Literacy); 450a (Muḥammad); 518a (Narratives)
	V	6b, 8a (Signs)
32	II	411a (Heaven and Sky)
	III	383b (Metals and Minerals)
	V	129a (Stone); 130a (Stoning); 470b (Weather)
33	II	184a (Fasting)
34	II	195b (Fear); 299a (Geography)
	III	77b (Kaʿba); 340b (Mecca)
	IV	281b (Profane and Sacred); 332a (Quraysh); 515a (Sacred Precincts); 538b (Scholar)
	V	138a (Ṣūfism and the Q)
34-35	II	458b (House, Domestic and Divine)
	III	338b (Mecca)
34-36	II	459a (House, Domestic and Divine)
35	III	77b, 79a (Kaʿba)
	IV	52b (People of the House); 218a (Prayer); 256b (Pre-Islamic Arabia and the Q); 330a (Quraysh); 515a (Sacred Precincts)
	V	182a (Symbolic Imagery)
36	III	252a (Maintenance and Upkeep)
	IV	456a (Reward and Punishment)
	V	468a (Wealth)
37	I	440a (Corruption)
38	II	74b (Ethics and the Q); 245a (Forgiveness); 434a (History and the Q)
	V	164a (Sunna); 438b (Virtues and Vices, Commanding and Forbidding)
38-39	IV	428a (Repentance and Penance)
39	I	224a (Belief and Unbelief); 397b (Conquest); 461a (Courage)
	II	74a (Ethics and the Q); 144a (Expeditions and Battles); 209b (Fighting)
	III	39a, 41b (Jihād); 577b (Opposition to Muḥammad)

	IV	132a (Politics and the Q)
	V	292b (Tolerance and Coercion); 456b, 458b (War); 543a (Word of God)
40	I	344b (Clients and Clientage)
	III	231a (Lord)
	IV	307b (Protection)
41	I	196b (Badr); 251b (Booty); 302b (Children); 486b, 487a (Criterion); 500b (Day, Times of)
	II	6b (Economics); 149a (Expeditions and Battles); 161b (Failure); 176a (Family); 176a (Family of the Prophet); 184a (Fasting)
	III	42a (Jihād); 425a (Moses); 448a (Muḥammad); 496b (Myths and Legends in the Q); 507b (Names of the Q); 604a (Orphans)
	IV	132a (Politics and the Q); 209a (Poverty and the Poor); 345a, 346a (Ramaḍān)
	V	37a (Sīra and the Q); 146a (Ṣūfism and the Q); 194a, 194b (Taxation); 279a, 284b (Time)
41-44	IV	345a, 346b (Ramaḍān)
42	IV	74a (Philosophy and the Q)
43	I	546b, 550b (Dreams and Sleep)
	II	161b (Failure); 550b (Intention)
	V	61b (Sleep)
43-44	II	241b (Foretelling in the Q)
	III	128b (Language and Style of the Q)
	IV	479a (Rhymed Prose)
44	IV	346a (Ramaḍān)
45	I	461a (Courage)
	V	138b (Ṣūfism and the Q)
45-46	I	225a (Belief and Unbelief)
46	I	52a (Air and Wind); 458b (Courage)
	II	161b (Failure)
	III	305b (Material Culture and the Q)
	IV	131b (Politics and the Q)
47	I	242a (Boast)
	II	468b (Hypocrites and Hypocrisy)
48	II	196b (Fear)
	V	487a (Wish and Desire)
49	II	407b (Heart); 468b, 470a (Hypocrites and Hypocrisy)
	IV	117b, 119b (Polemic and Polemical Language)
	V	447a (Vision and Blindness)
49-55	II	468b (Hypocrites and Hypocrisy)
50	I	222a (Belief and Unbelief)
	II	46a (Eschatology); 210b (Fire)

52	IV	67a (Pharaoh); 132a (Politics and the Q)
	V	317b (Tradition and Custom)
53	I	236b (Blessing)
54	I	553b (Drowning)
	II	174a (Family); 184a (Fasting); 213a (Fire); 542b (Insolence and Obstinacy)
	III	423a (Moses)
	IV	67a (Pharaoh)
	V	6a (Signs); 19a (Sin, Major and Minor); 317b (Tradition and Custom)
55	I	99b (Animal Life)
55-58	II	150b (Expeditions and Battles)
	III	30a (Jews and Judaism); 456b (Muḥammad)
56	I	431b (Contracts and Alliances)
	IV	132a (Politics and the Q); 335a (Qurayẓa, Banū al-)
56-58	III	42a (Jihād)
56-60	V	456b (War)
57	I	225a (Belief and Unbelief)
	II	144a (Expeditions and Battles)
	V	455a (War)
58	II	150a (Expeditions and Battles)
	IV	324a, 324b (Qaynuqāʿ, Banū)
59	II	527a (Inimitability)
60	I	98b (Animal Life)
	II	23b (Enemies); 209b (Fighting)
	III	42a (Jihād)
	IV	30b (Path or Way)
	V	457a (War)
61	I	225a (Belief and Unbelief)
	III	39b, 40a, 41a (Jihād)
	IV	35a (Peace)
	V	456b (War)
61-62	IV	34b (Peace)
63	II	21b (Emigration); 408b (Heart)
	III	446b (Muḥammad)
	V	365a (Tribes and Clans)
64	III	440b (Muḥammad)
65	I	225a (Belief and Unbelief); 321a (Chronology and the Q); 458b, 461a (Courage)
	III	41a, 42a (Jihād); 577b (Opposition to Muḥammad)
	V	457a (War)
65-66	II	209b (Fighting)

66	I	321a (Chronology and the Q)
	III	42a (Jihād); 549b (Numbers and Enumeration)
	V	288b (Time)
67	I	289a (Captives); 398a (Conquest)
	III	42a (Jihād)
	IV	5a (Pairs and Pairing)
67-69	IV	277b (Prisoners)
67-71	V	195b (Taxation)
68	I	244b (Book)
	III	508a (Names of the Q)
	IV	132a (Politics and the Q)
	V	289a (Time)
68-69	III	42a (Jihād)
69	I	251b (Booty)
	III	172b (Lawful and Unlawful)
	V	194a (Taxation)
70	II	61b (Ethics and the Q)
70-71	III	42a (Jihād)
71	III	577b (Opposition to Muḥammad)
	IV	5b (Pairs and Pairing); 537b (Scholar)
72	I	220a (Belief and Unbelief); 389b (Companions of the Prophet); 437b (Conversion); 464b (Covenant)
	II	15a (Emigrants and Helpers); 21a (Emigration); 72b (Ethics and the Q); 274a (Friends and Friendship); 518b (Inheritance)
	III	36b (Jihād)
	IV	30b (Path or Way); 132a (Politics and the Q)
	V	469a (Wealth)
72-74	II	209b (Fighting)
72-75	III	36b, 37a (Jihād)
73	I	224b (Belief and Unbelief)
74	I	219b, 220a (Belief and Unbelief)
	II	15a (Emigrants and Helpers); 21a (Emigration); 245a (Forgiveness)
	III	36b (Jihād)
	IV	17a (Paradise); 30a (Path or Way)
75	II	174b (Family); 518b (Inheritance)
	III	36b (Jihād)
	IV	20b (Parents); 132a (Politics and the Q)
	V	522a (Womb)

Sūrat al-Tawba (9)

I 209b (Basmala); 322a, 328a, 329b (Chronology and the Q); 353a, 355a, 355b (Collection of the Q); 417b (Contemporary Critical Practices and the Q); 505b (Days of God)

II 149a (Expeditions and Battles); 180a (Farewell Pilgrimage); 244a (Forgiveness); 264a (Form and Structure of the Q); 318a (God and his Attributes); 385a (Ḥadīth and the Q); 569a (Islam)

III 564a (Oaths)

IV 131b, 146b (Politics and the Q); 154a (Poll Tax); 244a (Pre-1800 Preoccupations of Q Studies); 456a (Reward and Punishment)

V 40b (Sīra and the Q); 174b (Sūra); 424b (Verse)

1 I 431b (Contracts and Alliances); 464a, 465b (Covenant)

1-2 IV 177b (Popular and Talismanic Uses of the Q)

1-5 II 151a (Expeditions and Battles)

1-14 III 40b (Jihād)

1-16 V 68a (Social Sciences and the Q)

1-23 V 456b, 457a (War)

2 II 527a (Inimitability)
III 12b (Jesus); 339b (Mecca); 551b (Numbers and Enumeration)
V 284b (Time); 475b (Weights and Measures)

3 I 500b (Day, Times of)
II 84b (Everyday Life, Q In); 527a (Inimitability)
III 76a (Kaʿba)
IV 2a (Pairs and Pairing); 91b, 97a (Pilgrimage); 426b (Repentance and Penance)
V 279b (Time); 456b (War)

3-4 IV 132a (Politics and the Q)

4 I 256b (Breaking Trusts and Contracts)
V 456b (War)

4-6 II 74a (Ethics and the Q)

5 I 224a (Belief and Unbelief); 321a (Chronology and the Q); 444b (Cosmology); 505a, 505b (Days of God)
II 74a (Ethics and the Q); 151a (Expeditions and Battles); 151a (Fighting)
III 39a, 40a, 40b, 41a, 41b, 42a (Jihād); 239a (Loyalty); 339b (Mecca); 410b (Months)
IV 38a (People of the Book); 136a (Politics and the Q); 244a (Pre-1800 Preoccupations of Q Studies); 282b (Profane and Sacred); 409b, 414b, 416a (Religious Pluralism and the Q); 426b (Repentance and Penance)
V 197a (Taxation); 284b (Time); 292a, 293a, 294a (Tolerance and Coercion); 434a (Virtue); 456b (War)

6 I 492a (Curse)
II 74b (Ethics and the Q)

	III	511a (Names of the Q)
	IV	308b (Protection); 446a (Revelation and Inspiration)
	V	111a (Speech); 547b (Word of God)
7	I	431b (Contracts and Alliances)
	II	65b (Ethics and the Q); 299a (Geography)
	III	77b (Kaʿba)
	IV	281b (Profane and Sacred); 515a (Sacred Precincts)
7-15	III	33a (Jews and Judaism)
8	II	98a (Evil Deeds); 339b (Good Deeds)
	IV	403a (Religious Pluralism and the Q)
	V	456a (War)
9	III	276a (Markets)
10	IV	403a (Religious Pluralism and the Q)
11	I	263a (Brother and Brotherhood); 436b (Conversion)
	IV	426b (Repentance and Penance); 538b (Scholar)
	V	8a (Signs); 197a (Taxation); 456b (War)
12	I	461a (Courage)
	II	503a (Imām)
	III	95b (Kings and Rulers)
	V	456a (War)
12-13	III	41b (Jihād); 564a (Oaths)
13	II	196b (Fear)
	III	449a (Muḥammad); 577b (Opposition to Muḥammad)
	V	434a (Virtue); 458b (War)
13-14	II	74a (Ethics and the Q)
	V	456a (War)
13-18	II	197a (Fear)
14	I	461a (Courage)
	II	209b (Fighting); 408b (Heart)
	III	42b (Jihād)
	IV	321b (Punishment Stories)
	V	455b, 458b (War)
14-15	IV	427a (Repentance and Penance)
15	I	93b (Anger)
	II	244b (Forgiveness)
	IV	537b (Scholar)
16	III	37a, 37b (Jihād)
17	I	164a, 173a (Art and Architecture and the Q)
	II	418a (Hell and Hellfire)
17-18	IV	283b (Profane and Sacred); 516a (Sacred Precincts)

18 I 164a, 171a (Art and Architecture and the Q)
II 28b (Epigraphy)
III 136a, 136b (Last Judgment); 304b, 312b (Material Culture and the Q); 436b (Mosque)

19 I 163b (Art and Architecture and the Q); 491a (Cups and Vessels)
II 34a (Epigraphy); 299a (Geography)
III 77b (Kaʿba); 37a (Jihād); 136b (Last Judgment)
IV 92b (Pilgrimage); 281b (Profane and Sacred); 330a (Quraysh); 515a (Sacred Precincts)

19-20 II 209b (Fighting)
III 184a (Life)

20 I 225a (Belief and Unbelief)
II 340a (Good Deeds)
III 36b, 37a (Jihād)
IV 17a (Paradise); 30a (Path or Way); 523a (Salvation)
V 83a (Soul); 430a (Victory); 457a (War)

20-21 II 341b (Good News)

21 I 89b (Angel)

22 II 54b (Eternity)

23 II 274b (Friends and Friendship)
V 317a (Tradition and Custom)

23-24 I 224b (Belief and Unbelief)

24 I 262a (Brother and Brotherhood); 302b (Children)
II 174b (Family)
III 37a, 37b (Jihād)
IV 30b (Path or Way)
V 364a (Tribes and Clans); 458a (War)

25 I 500b (Day, Times of)
II 299b (Geography); 439a (History and the Q); 465b, 466a (Ḥunayn)
III 579a (Opposition to Muḥammad)
V 279a (Time); 393a, 393b (Turkish Literature and the Q); 430a (Victory)

25-26 I 405b (Consolation)
II 209b (Fighting)
III 42b (Jihād); 398a (Miracles); 456a (Muḥammad)

25-27 II 465b (Ḥunayn)

26 I 459b (Courage)
II 466a (Ḥunayn)
IV 34a (Peace); 443b (Revelation and Inspiration); 457a (Reward and Punishment); 590a (Shekhinah)
V 377b (Troops)

27 II 244b (Forgiveness)
IV 427a (Repentance and Penance)

28 I 2 (Belief and Unbelief); 342b (Cleanliness and Ablution); 410b (Contamination)
II 299a (Geography)
III 77b (Kaʿba); 33b (Jews and Judaism); 338b (Mecca)
IV 119b (Polemic and Polemical Language); 132b (Politics and the Q); 153a (Poll Tax); 209a (Poverty and the Poor); 281b (Profane and Sacred); 416b (Religious Pluralism and the Q); 502b, 504b (Ritual Purity); 515a (Sacred Precincts); 537b (Scholar)
V 286a (Time); 468a (Wealth)

29 I 222b, 224a (Belief and Unbelief); 312a (Christians and Christianity); 336a (Church); 397b (Conquest); 461a (Courage)
II 73b (Ethics and the Q); 151a (Expeditions and Battles); 401b (Hand)
III 29a (Jews and Judaism); 39a, 40a, 40b, 41a, 41b (Jihād); 136a, 136b (Last Judgment); 174b (Lawful and Unlawful); 577b (Opposition to Muḥammad)
IV 38a, 38b (People of the Book); 121b (Polemic and Polemical Language); 132a (Politics and the Q); 152a, 152b, 153a, 153b, 154a (Poll Tax); 409b, 416a, 416b (Religious Pluralism and the Q); 525a (Samaritans)
V 192b (Taxation); 292a, 294a (Tolerance and Coercion); 456a, 457a, 458b (War)

29-35 II 262b (Form and Structure of the Q)
V 175b (Sūra)

30 I 102b (Anointing); 115a, 117a (Apologetics); 223a (Belief and Unbelief); 313a (Christians and Christianity); 491b (Curse)
II 155b (Ezra)
III 16a (Jesus)
IV 33a (Patriarchy); 38b (People of the Book); 120a (Polemic and Polemical Language); 153a (Poll Tax); 160b (Polytheism and Atheism); 405a, 412b (Religious Pluralism and the Q)
V 249b (Textual Criticism of the Q); 457a (War)

30-31 III 7b (Jesus); 26b (Jews and Judaism)
IV 132a (Politics and the Q)

31 I 102b (Anointing); 311b (Christians and Christianity)
II 156a (Ezra)
III 229b (Lord); 406a (Monasticism and Monks)
IV 120b (Polemic and Polemical Language); 153b (Poll Tax); 404a, 409b (Religious Pluralism and the Q)
V 139a (Ṣūfism and the Q); 431a (Vigil); 500b (Witnessing and Testifying); 533b (Women and the Q)

31-34 I 184a (Asceticism)

32 I 82b (Anatomy)
II 326b (God and his Attributes)
III 187a (Light)

33 I 117b (Apologetics); 170a, 170b, 171a (Art and Architecture and the Q); 397b (Conquest)
II 29a, 30b, 33b, 34a (Epigraphy); 557b (Invitation)
III 41b (Jihād); 299a, 299b, 304b (Material Culture and the Q); 451a (Muḥammad); 557a, 558a (Numismatics)
IV 300a (Prophets and Prophethood); 427b (Repentance and Penance)
V 458b (War); 489b (Witness to Faith); 503b (Witnessing and Testifying)

34 I 301a (Cheating); 311b (Christians and Christianity)
II 333b, 334a (Gold)
III 383b (Metals and Minerals); 406a, 406b (Monasticism and Monks)
IV 30b (Path or Way); 404a (Religious Pluralism and the Q); 490b (Ritual and the Q)
V 431a (Vigil)

34-35 II 7b (Economics)
IV 186b (Possession and Possessions)

35 I 81b (Anatomy); 222a (Belief and Unbelief)
II 210a (Fire); 416a (Hell and Hellfire); 455b (Hot and Cold)
V 133a (Suffering)

36 I 272b (Calendar); 397b (Conquest); 442b (Cosmology); 461a (Courage); 499a (Day, Times of); 505b (Days of God)
II 209a (Fighting)
III 39a, 40a (Jihād); 339b (Mecca); 410b, 411a (Months); 550a, 551b, 553a (Numbers and Enumeration)
IV 4a (Pairs and Pairing); 282b (Profane and Sacred); 482b (Rhymed Prose)
V 284b (Time); 456a, 456b, 457a (War); 475b (Weights and Measures)

36-37 II 180a (Farewell Pilgrimage)

37 I 213a (Beauty)
II 224a (Forbidden); 335b (Good and Evil); 432b (History and the Q)
III 172b, 174b (Lawful and Unlawful); 339b (Mecca); 411b, 412a (Months); 415a (Moon)
IV 255b (Pre-Islamic Arabia and the Q); 283a (Profane and Sacred); 571b (Seasons)
V 285a (Time); 475b, 476a (Weights and Measures)

38 I 368b (Community and Society in the Q)
III 59b (Joy and Misery)
V 457b (War)

38-39 III 41a (Jihād)

38-41 III 36b (Jihād)

38-57 III 568b (Obedience)

39 IV 456a (Reward and Punishment)
V 458a (War)

39-41 III 41b (Jihād)

40	I	292b, 293b (Cave); 387b (Companions of the Prophet); 405b (Consolation); 459b (Courage)
	II	18b, 20b (Emigration); 364a (Grammar and the Q)
	III	41b, 42b (Jihād); 454a, 456a (Muḥammad)
	IV	34a (Peace); 63b (Persian Literature and the Q); 590a (Shekhinah)
	V	140a (Ṣūfism and the Q); 376a (Trips and Voyages); 377b (Troops); 404b (Uncertainty); 458b (War)
40-41	II	310b (Geography)
41	I	458b, 461a (Courage)
	III	36a, 36b (Jihād); 58a (Journey)
	IV	30b (Path or Way)
	V	83a (Soul); 374a (Trips and Voyages); 457a (War)
42	V	457b (War)
43-88	V	458a (War)
44	III	36a, 36b, 37b (Jihād); 136b (Last Judgment)
	V	83a (Soul); 458a (War); 469a (Wealth)
44-45	V	434a (Virtue)
44-46	III	36b (Jihād)
45	III	136b (Last Judgment)
46	III	84a (Khārijīs)
49	II	418a (Hell and Hellfire)
	V	40a (Sīra and the Q); 457b (War)
50	III	61b (Joy and Misery)
51	I	244b (Book); 344b (Clients and Clientage); 523a (Destiny)
	II	186b (Fate); 269b (Freedom and Predestination)
	III	231a (Lord); 327b (Material Culture and the Q); 352a (Medicine and the Q)
52	V	455b, 458b (War)
54	I	224b (Belief and Unbelief)
54-59	I	67a (Almsgiving)
55	IV	3b (Pairs and Pairing)
	V	468a (Wealth)
57	I	292b, 294a (Cave)
	V	376a (Trips and Voyages)
58	I	93b (Anger)
	II	343b (Gossip)
	IV	309b (Provocation)
59	III	300b (Material Culture and the Q)
60	I	66a (Almsgiving); 289a, 289b (Captives)
	II	7a (Economics); 262b (Form and Structure of the Q); 351a (Grammar and the Q); 450a (Hospitality and Courtesy); 466b (Ḥunayn)

IV 132a (Politics and the Q); 208b (Poverty and the Poor); 537b (Scholar)
V 57a, 58a, 59b (Slaves and Slavery); 198b (Taxation); 556b (Worship)

61 II 1a (Ears)
III 299a (Material Culture and the Q)
IV 116b (Polemic and Polemical Language); 456a (Reward and Punishment)

62 III 210b (Literature and the Q)

63 I 294a (Cave)
II 418a (Hell and Hellfire)
IV 131b (Politics and the Q); 309b (Provocation); 453b, 456a (Reward and Punishment)

64 II 468b, 470a (Hypocrites and Hypocrisy)
III 537a (News)
V 167a (Sūra)

64-66 III 400b (Mockery)

65 IV 309b (Provocation)
V 5b (Signs)

66 V 19a (Sin, Major and Minor)

67 II 322a (God and his Attributes); 468b (Hypocrites and Hypocrisy)
IV 117b (Polemic and Polemical Language)
V 437a, 440b (Virtues and Vices, Commanding and Forbidding); 523b (Women and the Q)

67-68 II 470a (Hypocrites and Hypocrisy)

67-72 IV 1b (Pairs and Pairing)

68 I 294a (Cave); 381a (Community and Society in the Q)
II 210a (Fire); 417a (Hell and Hellfire); 468b, 470a (Hypocrites and Hypocrisy)
IV 399a (Religious Pluralism and the Q)
V 523b (Women and the Q)

69 II 352a, 367a (Grammar and the Q)
IV 31b (Patriarchy); 3b (Pairs and Pairing); 309b (Provocation)
V 468a (Wealth); 552a (World)

70 I 21b (ʿĀd)
II 299b, 308a (Geography)
III 390b (Midian); 486b (Myths and Legends in the Q); 518a, 522a (Narratives); 537a (News); 540a (Noah)
IV 131b (Politics and the Q); 286b (Proof); 302b (Prophets and Prophethood); 320b (Punishment Stories)

71 I 220a (Belief and Unbelief); 262b (Brother and Brotherhood)
II 62a, 72b, 75b (Ethics and the Q); 6a (Economics); 165a (Faith); 203a (Feminism and the Q); 274a (Friends and Friendship)
IV 132a (Politics and the Q)
V 53b (Sister); 197b (Taxation); 437a, 438a, 440a, 440b, 443a (Virtues and Vices, Commanding and Forbidding); 501b (Witnessing and Testifying); 523b (Women and the Q)

71-72	I	219a (Belief and Unbelief)
72	I	220b (Belief and Unbelief)
	II	52a (Eschatology); 417a (Hell and Hellfire)
	IV	18b (Paradise); 522b (Salvation)
	V	393b (Turkish Literature and the Q); 430a (Victory); 523b (Women and the Q)
73	I	202b (Barēlwīs); 294a (Cave); 461a (Courage)
	II	468b, 470a (Hypocrites and Hypocrisy)
	III	36b (Jihād); 454b (Muḥammad); 577b (Opposition to Muḥammad)
	IV	103b (Pit)
	V	292a, 294a (Tolerance and Coercion); 456a (War)
73-74	V	468a (Wealth)
74	I	120a (Apostasy); 432b (Contracts and Alliances)
	II	273b (Friends and Friendship); 470a (Hypocrites and Hypocrisy); 552a (Intercession)
	III	578a (Opposition to Muḥammad)
	IV	404a (Religious Pluralism and the Q); 427a (Repentance and Penance); 453b, 456a, 457a (Reward and Punishment)
	V	133a (Suffering); 293b (Tolerance and Coercion); 430a (Victory)
75	I	465b (Covenant)
	V	198a (Taxation)
75-78	V	449b (Vow)
77	II	468b (Hypocrites and Hypocrisy)
	III	181b (Lie)
78	IV	537b (Scholar)
79	I	65b (Almsgiving)
	II	322a (God and his Attributes); 343b (Gossip)
	III	147a (Laughter); 400b, 401a (Mockery)
	IV	309b, 310a (Provocation); 456a (Reward and Punishment)
	V	193a, 198a (Taxation)
80	II	245a (Forgiveness); 552a (Intercession)
	IV	300b (Prophets and Prophethood)
80-83	II	24b (Enemies)
81	I	225a (Belief and Unbelief); 458b (Courage)
	II	455a (Hot and Cold)
	III	36a (Jihād); 61a (Joy and Misery)
	IV	30b (Path or Way)
	V	83a (Soul); 457b (War); 469a (Wealth)
81-83	I	460a (Courage)
81-85	IV	456a (Reward and Punishment)
81-106	III	568b (Obedience)

82 III 146b, 147a (Laughter)
V 472a (Weeping)

83 II 23b (Enemies)

84 I 224b (Belief and Unbelief); 264a (Burial)
II 551b (Intercession)
III 379b (Mercy)
IV 218a (Prayer); 233a (Prayer Formulas); 300b (Prophets and Prophethood)

85 I 221b (Belief and Unbelief)
IV 31b (Patriarchy)
V 468a (Wealth)

86 I 461a (Courage)
III 36a (Jihād)
IV 293a (Prophets and Prophethood)
V 167a (Sūra); 457a, 457b (War)

87 I 82a (Anatomy)
II 408b (Heart)
V 457b (War)

87-92 III 36b (Jihād)

88 III 36b, 37b (Jihād)
IV 523a (Salvation)
V 83a (Soul); 469a (Wealth)

88-89 III 41a (Jihād)
IV 455a (Reward and Punishment)

89 II 209b (Fighting)
IV 18b (Paradise); 522b (Salvation)

90 I 216a, 216b (Bedouin)
III 544b (Nomads)
IV 456a (Reward and Punishment)

90-93 III 41b (Jihād)

90-94 III 37b (Jihād)

91 II 501b (Illness and Health)
III 580b (Oppressed on Earth)
V 19a (Sin, Major and Minor); 457b (War)

91-92 III 378b (Mercy)

93 I 82a (Anatomy)
II 510b (Indifference)
V 457b (War)

94 II 435b (History and the Q)
III 518a (Narratives); 536b, 537a (News)
IV 4a (Pairs and Pairing); 537b (Scholar); 574b (Seeing and Hearing)
V 492b (Witnessing and Testifying)

95 IV 103b (Pit); 503a (Ritual Purity)
V 458a (War)

97 I 216b (Bedouin); 382a (Community and Society in the Q)
II 468b (Hypocrites and Hypocrisy)
IV 34b (Peace); 456a (Reward and Punishment); 537b (Scholar)
V 502a (Witnessing and Testifying)

97-99 I 216b (Bedouin)
III 578a (Opposition to Muḥammad)

97-101 II 470a (Hypocrites and Hypocrisy)
III 544b (Nomads)

98 II 407a (Heart)

99 I 436a (Conversion)
III 136b (Last Judgment)
IV 218a (Prayer)
V 196b (Taxation)

100 I 389b (Companions of the Prophet)
II 15a (Emigrants and Helpers); 54b (Eternity); 61b (Ethics and the Q); 283b (Garden)
IV 16a, 18b (Paradise); 332b (Quraysh); 455b (Reward and Punishment); 522b (Salvation)
V 47b (Sīra and the Q)

101 I 216b (Bedouin); 338a, 338b (City)
II 298b (Geography); 468b (Hypocrites and Hypocrisy)
III 367b (Medina)
IV 49a (People of the House); 6b (Pairs and Pairing); 37a (People of the Book); 456a, 460a (Reward and Punishment)

101-102 I 517b (Deferral)
IV 427a (Repentance and Penance)

102-103 II 551b (Intercession)

102-104 III 379b (Mercy)

103 I 343b (Cleanliness and Ablution)
IV 208b (Poverty and the Poor); 218a (Prayer); 487a, 490b (Ritual and the Q); 505b (Ritual Purity)
V 193b, 198a, 199b (Taxation)

104 II 244b (Forgiveness)
IV 5b (Pairs and Pairing); 426a (Repentance and Penance)
V 199a (Taxation)

104-105 I 65a (Almsgiving)

105 IV 4a (Pairs and Pairing); 537b (Scholar); 574b (Seeing and Hearing)

106 I 517a, 517b (Deferral)
III 578a (Opposition to Muḥammad)
IV 427a (Repentance and Penance); 537b (Scholar)

107 II 144a (Expeditions and Battles)
III 438a (Mosque of the Dissension); 457a (Muḥammad)
IV 403b (Religious Pluralism and the Q); 516a (Sacred Precincts)
V 455a (War)

107-110 II 468b (Hypocrites and Hypocrisy)

108 I 342b (Cleanliness and Ablution)
III 234a (Love and Affection); 4b (Jerusalem); 438b (Mosque of the Dissension)
IV 505b (Ritual Purity); 516a (Sacred Precincts)

110 IV 537b (Scholar)

111 I 310b (Christians and Christianity); 459b, 462a (Courage)
II 209b (Fighting); 342b (Gospel)
III 41a (Jihād); 58a (Journey); 62a (Joy and Misery); 209a (Literature and the Q); 276a (Markets); 282b (Martyrs); 558b (Numismatics); 568b (Obedience)
IV 30a (Path or Way); 457a (Reward and Punishment); 522b (Salvation)
V 269b, 271b (Theology and the Q); 300b, 302b (Torah); 457a (War); 469a (Wealth)

111-112 V 442a (Virtues and Vices, Commanding and Forbidding)

112 I 183a (Asceticism); 219b (Belief and Unbelief); 253a (Boundaries and Precepts); 254a (Bowing and Prostration)
II 181a (Fasting)
III 12b (Jesus)
IV 214a (Praise); 219b (Prayer); 426b (Repentance and Penance)
V 374a (Trips and Voyages); 437a, 437b, 438a, 440a, 440b (Virtues and Vices, Commanding and Forbidding)

113 II 244b (Forgiveness)
III 454b (Muḥammad)
IV 300b (Prophets and Prophethood); 331a (Quraysh)

113-114 I 7a (Abraham)
III 379b (Mercy)

114 I 5b (Abraham); 193a (Āzar)
II 23b (Enemies)
III 401b (Moderation)
IV 21a (Parents); 33a (Patriarchy)

116 I 188b (Authority)
II 273a (Friends and Friendship)
IV 4a, 4b (Pairs and Pairing)
V 430a (Victory)

117 I 389b (Companions of the Prophet); 436b (Conversion); 501a (Day, Times of)
II 15a (Emigrants and Helpers)
III 335b (Measurement)
IV 5b (Pairs and Pairing); 25b (Parties and Factions); 430a (Repentance and Penance)
V 288a (Time); 430a (Victory)

118	I	436b (Conversion)
	IV	5b (Pairs and Pairing); 426b, 427b (Repentance and Penance)
119	V	434b (Virtue)
120	I	216b (Bedouin); 338a, 338b (City)
	II	23b, 24b (Enemies); 177b (Famine); 298b (Geography)
	III	41b (Jihād); 337b (Mecca); 367b (Medina); 544b (Nomads)
	IV	37a (People of the Book)
120-121	I	243b (Book)
121	I	243b (Book)
	II	365a (Grammar and the Q)
	IV	452b (Reward and Punishment)
122	III	41b (Jihād); 103b (Knowledge and Learning)
	IV	25b (Parties and Factions)
123	I	461a (Courage)
	II	209b (Fighting)
	III	40a (Jihād); 577b (Opposition to Muḥammad)
	V	456a, 457a (War)
123-127	IV	138a (Politics and the Q)
124	III	62a (Joy and Misery)
	V	167a (Sūra)
125	I	411b (Contamination)
	II	407b (Heart); 470a (Hypocrites and Hypocrisy); 502a (Illness and Health)
	IV	132b (Politics and the Q); 503a (Ritual Purity)
126	V	286a (Time)
127	II	36a (Epigraphy); 408b (Heart); 465a (Humor)
	IV	133a (Politics and the Q)
128	I	357b (Collection of the Q)
	III	234a (Love and Affection); 378a (Mercy); 443b, 447a (Muḥammad)
	IV	5b (Pairs and Pairing)
128-129	I	326a (Chronology and the Q)
129	I	446a (Cosmology)
	II	31a, 36a (Epigraphy); 96a (Everyday Life, Q In)
	III	300b, 301a (Material Culture and the Q); 453b (Muḥammad)
	IV	184a (Possession and Possessions)
	V	277a (Throne of God); 500b (Witnessing and Testifying)

Sūrat Yūnus (10)

III 472b (Mysterious Letters)
V 174b (Sūra)

1 II 263b (Form and Structure of the Q)
III 441a (Muḥammad); 509a (Names of the Q)
V 6b (Signs); 172a (Sūra)

1-2 II 527b (Inimitability)

2 II 199a (Feet); 341a, 341b (Good News)
III 247a (Magic); 399a (Miracles); 450a (Muḥammad)
IV 3b (Pairs and Pairing); 14b (Paradise); 311b (Provocation); 455b (Reward and Punishment)
V 239b (Textual Criticism of the Q)

3 I 318b (Chronology and the Q); 442a, 443b (Cosmology); 472a, 476a (Creation)
II 325b, 327b (God and his Attributes); 410b (Heaven and Sky)
III 141a (Last Judgment); 202a (Literary Structures of the Q); 379b (Mercy)
IV 4a (Pairs and Pairing); 73b, 82a (Philosophy and the Q); 127a (Politics and the Q); 163b (Popular and Talismanic Uses of the Q); 511a (Sabbath)
V 4a (Signs); 265a, 266a (Theology and the Q); 279b, 287a (Time)

4 I 473b, 478a, 479a (Creation)
II 455b (Hot and Cold)
IV 6b (Pairs and Pairing)
V 121b (Springs and Fountains)

5 I 272b, 273a (Calendar); 442b (Cosmology)
II 433a (History and the Q)
III 187a (Light); 208a (Literature and the Q); 412b, 413a (Months); 550a (Numbers and Enumeration)
IV 4b (Pairs and Pairing); 107a, 108a (Planets and Stars); 538b (Scholar); 571b (Seasons)
V 163a (Sun); 283b, 284a (Time); 475b (Weights and Measures); 560b (Year)

5-6 V 10a (Signs)

5-7 IV 438a (Revelation and Inspiration)

6 I 501b (Day, Times of)
IV 4b (Pairs and Pairing)
V 280b (Time)

6-7 I 473b (Creation)

7 I 530a (Dialects)
II 449a (Hope)
V 6b (Signs)

7-8 II 418a (Hell and Hellfire)

7-9 IV 1b (Pairs and Pairing)

8 IV 103b (Pit)

9 II 282b (Garden)
III 62b (Joy and Misery)
IV 431b (Responsibility)

9-11	IV	17b (Paradise)
10	I	237a (Blessing); 385a (Community and Society in the Q)
	II	91b (Everyday Life, Q In)
11	I	516b (Decision); 530a (Dialects)
	II	269a (Freedom and Predestination)
12	I	213a (Beauty)
13	II	293a (Generations); 350b (Grammar and the Q); 434a (History and the Q)
	IV	128b (Politics and the Q)
13-14	IV	320a (Punishment Stories)
14	I	277a (Caliph)
	II	355b (Grammar and the Q)
	IV	127a (Politics and the Q)
15	I	530a (Dialects); 538a (Disobedience)
	II	353b (Grammar and the Q); 449a (Hope)
	III	137a (Last Judgment); 190a (Literacy); 449a (Muḥammad)
	IV	128b (Politics and the Q)
	V	7a (Signs)
15-16	III	451b (Muḥammad)
16	III	190a (Literacy)
	V	203a (Teaching)
17	II	64a (Ethics and the Q); 162a (Failure)
	III	181a (Lie)
	IV	523a (Salvation)
	V	19a (Sin, Major and Minor)
18	I	236a (Blasphemy)
	IV	5a (Pairs and Pairing); 220b (Prayer); 311a (Provocation)
	V	117b (Spiritual Beings); 369a (Trinity)
19	I	538a (Dissension)
	II	72a (Ethics and the Q); 497a (Illiteracy)
	IV	337a (Races)
	V	289b (Time); 547b (Word of God)
20	II	261b (Form and Structure of the Q)
	III	399a (Miracles); 452a (Muḥammad)
	IV	311a, 311b (Provocation)
	V	8a (Signs)
21	I	243b (Book)
	III	18a (Jesus); 191a (Literacy); 382b (Messenger)
	IV	290a (Prophets and Prophethood)
	V	493a (Witnessing and Testifying)
22	I	52a, 52b, 54a (Air and Wind); 213a (Beauty)
	II	3a (Earth); 317a (God and his Attributes); 550a (Intention)

III 61a (Joy and Misery)
IV 4b (Pairs and Pairing)
V 411a (Vehicles); 464a (Water)

22-23 I 519a (Deliverance)
IV 161b (Polytheism and Atheism)

23 II 420b (Heresy)
III 60a (Joy and Misery)
V 374b (Trips and Voyages)

24 I 41b, 42a (Agriculture and Vegetation); 96b (Animal Life); 213b (Beauty); 349b (Codices of the Q); 501a (Day, Times of)
II 3a, 3b (Earth); 366b (Grammar and the Q)
III 183b (Life)
IV 10a (Parable); 394a (Reflection and Deliberation)
V 5b (Signs); 288b (Time); 339b (Transitoriness)

25 I 435b (Conversion)
II 283a (Garden); 321b (God and his Attributes); 558b (Invitation)
IV 14a (Paradise)

26 II 284a (Garden); 324a (God and his Attributes)
III 379b (Mercy)
IV 15a, 16b, 17b (Paradise); 453b (Reward and Punishment)

27 I 493a (Darkness); 501a, 501b (Day, Times of)
II 416b (Hell and Hellfire)
III 379b (Mercy)

28 II 477b (Idolatry and Idolaters)
V 494a (Witnessing and Testifying)

28-29 V 369a (Trinity)

30 I 236a (Blasphemy); 344b (Clients and Clientage)
II 99a (Evil Deeds)

31 IV 4a, 4b (Pairs and Pairing); 127a (Politics and the Q); 160b (Polytheism and Atheism); 312a (Provocation); 435a (Resurrection)

32 I 472b (Creation)

34 I 478a (Creation)
IV 6b (Pairs and Pairing)

35 I 472b (Creation)

36 II 489a (Ignorance)
V 178a (Suspicion)

37 I 117b (Apologetics)
II 529b (Inimitability)
IV 280b (Profane and Sacred); 439a (Revelation and Inspiration); 560b (Scripture and the Q)

38	I	115a (Apologetics)
	II	527a, 529b (Inimitability)
	III	116a (Language and Style of the Q); 199a (Literary Structures of the Q); 398b (Miracles); 451b (Muḥammad); 468a (Muʿtazila)
	IV	22b (Parody of the Q); 119a (Polemic and Polemical Language); 311b, 312b (Provocation); 443a (Revelation and Inspiration)
	V	167a (Sūra)
39	IV	309b (Provocation)
41	III	39a, 39b (Jihād); 453b (Muḥammad)
42-43	IV	8a (Pairs and Pairing)
45	I	235b (Blasphemy); 501a (Day, Times of)
	III	335b (Measurement)
	IV	435a (Resurrection)
	V	287b (Time); 476b (Weights and Measures)
45-46	III	184b (Life)
46	III	18b (Jesus)
47	I	372a (Community and Society in the Q)
	II	72a (Ethics and the Q); 497a, 497b (Illiteracy)
	III	382a (Messenger)
	IV	299b (Prophets and Prophethood)
48-51	IV	311a (Provocation)
49	I	501a (Day, Times of); 523a (Destiny)
	II	45a (Eschatology); 269a (Freedom and Predestination)
	III	185a (Life); 335b (Measurement)
	V	288a, 289a (Time)
51	V	288b (Time)
52	II	54b (Eternity)
53	III	536b (News)
54	III	203b (Literary Structures of the Q)
	IV	430b (Repentance and Penance)
55	IV	4a (Pairs and Pairing); 538b (Scholar)
55-56	I	479a (Creation)
56	IV	4b (Pairs and Pairing)
57	II	38a (Epigraphy); 142b (Exhortations); 408b (Heart); 502a (Illness and Health)
	III	511b, 512a, 514b (Names of the Q)
	IV	3b (Pairs and Pairing); 171b (Popular and Talismanic Uses of the Q)
58	III	61a (Joy and Misery)
	V	468a (Wealth)

59	I	236a (Blasphemy)
	III	173a, 174b (Lawful and Unlawful)
	V	545a (Word of God); 573a (Zealotry)
61	I	99b (Animal Life); 243a, 243b, 244a (Book)
	II	269b (Freedom and Predestination); 544b, 545b (Instruments)
	III	124b (Language and Style of the Q); 190a (Literacy); 334b (Measurement); 409a (Money)
	IV	4a (Pairs and Pairing); 58b (Persian Literature and the Q); 368b (Recitation of the Q)
	V	473b (Weights and Measures)
61-65	I	522b (Destiny)
62	II	65b (Ethics and the Q); 273b (Friends and Friendship)
	V	138a (Ṣūfism and the Q)
62-64	I	370a (Community and Society in the Q); 550a (Dreams and Sleep)
	II	341a, 341b (Good News)
	IV	520b (Saint)
64	I	546b (Dreams and Sleep)
	IV	178b (Popular and Talismanic Uses of the Q); 522b (Salvation)
	V	548a (Word of God)
65	I	405b (Consolation)
	III	452b (Muḥammad)
	V	134a (Suffering)
66	II	477b (Idolatry and Idolaters)
	IV	4a (Pairs and Pairing); 228b (Prayer)
67	I	83b (Anatomy); 473a, 473b, 477b (Creation); 502a (Day, Times of)
	II	406a (Hearing and Deafness)
	IV	4b (Pairs and Pairing); 589b (Shekhinah)
68	IV	4a (Pairs and Pairing); 312a, 312b (Provocation)
68-69	I	236a (Blasphemy)
	IV	311a (Provocation)
69	I	472b (Creation)
71	I	516b (Decision)
	II	96a (Everyday Life, Q In)
	III	65a (Judgment); 190a (Literacy); 441a (Muḥammad); 518a, 524b (Narratives); 536b (News)
	IV	302b (Prophets and Prophethood)
	V	8a (Signs)
71-74	III	486a (Myths and Legends in the Q)
71-92	IV	320a (Punishment Stories)
72	III	444a (Muḥammad)

73	I	277a (Caliph); 519a (Deliverance)
74	I	82a (Anatomy)
75	I	1a (Aaron); 160a (Arrogance); 190a (Authority); 369a (Community and Society in the Q)
	IV	106a (Plagues); 264a (Pride); 483a (Rhymed Prose)
	V	6a, 6b, 8a (Signs)
75-76	II	542b (Insolence and Obstinacy)
76	I	532b (Dialogues)
	III	246a (Magic)
77	II	162a (Failure)
	III	246a (Magic)
	IV	523a (Salvation)
78	I	159a (Arrogance)
	V	317a (Tradition and Custom)
81	III	246a (Magic)
82	V	386b (Truth); 547b (Word of God)
83	II	542a (Insolence and Obstinacy)
84	I	218b (Belief and Unbelief)
84-86	II	558a (Invitation)
86	I	518b (Deliverance)
	IV	524a (Salvation)
87	I	260a (Brother and Brotherhood)
	II	10a (Egypt); 341a, 341b (Good News)
	IV	224a (Prayer); 440a (Revelation and Inspiration); 516a (Sacred Precincts)
	V	107b (Spatial Relations); 258a (Theology and the Q); 546a (Word of God)
88	I	492a (Curse)
	II	407b, 408b (Heart)
	IV	29a (Path or Way)
	V	468a (Wealth)
89	IV	29b (Path or Way); 431b (Responsibility)
	V	547a (Word of God)
90	I	553b (Drowning)
	II	31b (Epigraphy); 184a (Fasting); 213a (Fire); 542b (Insolence and Obstinacy)
	III	423a (Moses)
	IV	67a, 67b (Pharaoh)
	V	375a (Trips and Voyages); 377a (Troops); 464b (Water)
90-92	II	542b (Insolence and Obstinacy)
91	I	537a (Disobedience)
	V	288b (Time)

92 I 519a (Deliverance)

93 I 305a (Children of Israel)
II 185b (Fate)

94 I 222b (Belief and Unbelief); 245b (Book)
III 22b, 32a (Jews and Judaism); 189b (Literacy); 451a (Muḥammad)
IV 120b (Polemic and Polemical Language); 217a (Prayer); 403a (Religious Pluralism and the Q)
V 303b (Torah)

95 V 6a (Signs)

96 V 547b (Word of God)

96-97 I 225b (Belief and Unbelief)

98 II 293a (Generations)
III 53a, 55a (Jonah)
IV 319b (Punishment Stories); 429a (Repentance and Penance)

98-103 I 523a (Destiny)

99 I 225b (Belief and Unbelief)
III 40a (Jihād); 531a (Nature as Signs)
IV 238b (Pre-1800 Preoccupations of Q Studies)
V 68b (Social Sciences and the Q); 294a (Tolerance and Coercion)

99-100 V 291a (Tolerance and Coercion)

100 I 411b (Contamination)
II 59a (Ethics and the Q)
IV 454a (Reward and Punishment); 503a (Ritual Purity)

101 IV 545b (Science and the Q)

102 V 280a (Time)

103 I 519b (Deliverance)
IV 301b (Prophets and Prophethood)

104 III 453b (Muḥammad)
IV 401b (Religious Pluralism and the Q)

105 I 5b (Abraham)
II 323b (God and his Attributes); 402b (Ḥanīf)
III 446a (Muḥammad)

106 IV 5a (Pairs and Pairing); 228b (Prayer)

107 II 52b (Eschatology)
III 327b (Material Culture and the Q); 380a (Mercy)
V 485b (Wish and Desire)

108 I 186a (Astray)
III 452b (Muḥammad); 577b (Opposition to Muḥammad)
IV 1b (Pairs and Pairing); 238b (Pre-1800 Preoccupations of Q Studies)
V 82b (Soul)

108-109 III 40a (Jihād)

109 I 516a (Decision)
II 321a (God and his Attributes)
III 64b (Judgment); 452b (Muḥammad)
IV 294b (Prophets and Prophethood)

Sūrat Hūd (11)

I 492a (Curse)
III 200b (Literary Structures of the Q); 211b (Literature and the Q); 472b (Mysterious Letters); 520b (Narratives)
V 308a (Torah); 422b (Verse)

1 I 70b, 71b (Ambiguous)
II 323a (God and his Attributes)
III 394a (Miracles)
V 422b (Verse)

1-24 II 143b (Exhortations)
III 520b (Narratives)

2 II 341b (Good News)
IV 3b (Pairs and Pairing)

3 I 500a (Day, Times of); 523a (Destiny)
II 245a (Forgiveness); 269a (Freedom and Predestination)
III 60a (Joy and Misery)
IV 426b (Repentance and Penance)
V 289a (Time)

4 I 401b (Consecration of Animals)

5 II 550b (Intention)

6 I 95b (Animal Life); 235a (Birth Control); 243a (Book); 523a (Destiny)
II 544b (Instruments)
III 124b (Language and Style of the Q); 327b (Material Culture and the Q)
IV 560a (Scripture and the Q)

7 I 318b (Chronology and the Q); 442a, 443b (Cosmology); 473b, 476a (Creation)
II 326a (God and his Attributes); 410b (Heaven and Sky); 433a (History and the Q)
III 246a, 247a (Magic); 450a (Muḥammad); 530a (Nature as Signs)
IV 4a (Pairs and Pairing); 82b (Philosophy and the Q); 311b (Provocation); 511a (Sabbath)
V 133b (Suffering); 265a, 266a (Theology and the Q); 279b, 287a (Time); 462a (Water)

7-8 IV 311a (Provocation)

8 I 371b (Community and Society in the Q)
II 497b (Illiteracy)
III 400b (Mockery)
IV 310a (Provocation)
V 241b (Textual Criticism of the Q)

9 I 221a (Belief and Unbelief); 521a (Despair)

9-10 V 204b (Teaching)

10 I 241b (Boast)
III 61b (Joy and Misery)

11 II 70b (Ethics and the Q); 245a (Forgiveness)

12 III 39b (Jihād); 450a (Muḥammad)
IV 296a (Prophets and Prophethood); 311b (Provocation)

12-13 III 398b (Miracles)

13 II 527a, 529b (Inimitability)
III 116a (Language and Style of the Q); 199a (Literary Structures of the Q); 451b (Muḥammad); 468a (Muʿtazila); 553a (Numbers and Enumeration)
IV 22b (Parody of the Q); 311b, 312b (Provocation); 443a (Revelation and Inspiration)
V 167a (Sūra)

13-14 I 115a (Apologetics)
V 494a (Witnessing and Testifying)

15-16 II 98b (Evil Deeds)
V 313a (Trade and Commerce)

16 II 161b (Failure)

17 II 439a (History and the Q); 502b (Imām)
III 424b (Moses)
IV 3b (Pairs and Pairing); 300b (Prophets and Prophethood)
V 203a (Teaching); 301a (Torah); 492b (Witnessing and Testifying)

18 I 235b (Blasphemy)
III 140b (Last Judgment); 181a (Lie)
V 494a (Witnessing and Testifying)

19-20 IV 458b (Reward and Punishment)

20 II 273b (Friends and Friendship)
IV 6b (Pairs and Pairing)
V 446a (Vision and Blindness)

21 II 99a (Evil Deeds)

24 II 1b (Ears); 405b, 406b (Hearing and Deafness)
III 209b (Literature and the Q)
IV 2a (Pairs and Pairing); 10a (Parable); 574a (Seeing and Hearing)
V 15b (Simile)

25-49	III	486a (Myths and Legends in the Q); 520b (Narratives)
	IV	321a (Punishment Stories)
25-99	IV	320a (Punishment Stories)
25-100	III	520b (Narratives)
25-123	III	381b (Messenger)
26	I	500a (Day, Times of)
	IV	160a (Polytheism and Atheism)
27	III	449b (Muḥammad)
28	IV	574b (Seeing and Hearing)
29	II	488a (Ignorance)
31	III	452a (Muḥammad)
	IV	216b (Prayer); 311b (Provocation)
32	I	513a (Debate and Disputation)
34	II	59a (Ethics and the Q)
35	III	450a (Muḥammad)
	V	19a (Sin, Major and Minor)
36	I	521b (Despair)
36-48	IV	604a (Ships)
36-49	V	373a (Trips and Voyages)
37	I	450a (Cosmology); 553b (Drowning)
	II	323b, 324b (God and his Attributes)
	IV	574a (Seeing and Hearing)
38	II	355b (Grammar and the Q)
	III	400b (Mockery)
	V	204a (Teaching)
39	IV	453b (Reward and Punishment)
40	II	219a (Food and Drink); 229a (Foreign Vocabulary); 362b (Grammar and the Q)
	III	393a (Miracles); 541a (Noah); 550b (Numbers and Enumeration)
	IV	6b (Pairs and Pairing); 581a (Sex and Sexuality)
	V	126a (Springs and Fountains); 545a (Word of God)
41	I	208b (Basmala); 236b (Blessing)
	II	318a (God and his Attributes)
	IV	495b (Ritual and the Q)
42	V	464b (Water)
43	I	553b (Drowning)
	III	379a (Mercy); 541a (Noah)
	IV	307b (Protection)
	V	464b (Water)

44 I 146b (Ararat); 491b (Curse)
II 437a (History and the Q)
III 68a (Jūdī); 362a (Medicine and the Q); 541a (Noah)
IV 604b (Ships)
V 126a (Springs and Fountains); 543a (Word of God)

45 I 516a (Decision)
II 174a (Family); 321a (God and his Attributes)
III 64b (Judgment); 229b (Lord)
IV 133b (Politics and the Q)
V 102b (Sovereignty)

45-46 IV 21a (Parents)

45-47 II 510b (Indifference)
V 373b (Trips and Voyages)

46 II 174a (Family); 488b (Ignorance)
III 541b (Noah)
V 109b (Speech)

47 II 245a (Forgiveness)
III 379a, 379b (Mercy)
IV 308a (Protection)
V 25a (Sin, Major and Minor)

48 III 487a (Myths and Legends in the Q)

49 II 423b (Hidden and the Hidden)
III 441b (Muḥammad); 536b, 537a (News)
IV 294b, 302b (Prophets and Prophethood); 438b (Revelation and Inspiration)
V 271a (Theology and the Q)

50 I 21b (ʿĀd); 261b (Brother and Brotherhood)

50-55 IV 160a (Polytheism and Atheism)

50-60 II 462a (Hūd); 558a (Invitation)
III 520b (Narratives)
IV 586b (Sheba)

51 V 313b (Trade and Commerce)

52 I 21b (ʿĀd)
II 245a (Forgiveness); 462b (Hūd)

53 II 462b (Hūd)

53-54 I 21b (ʿĀd)

54 II 336a (Good and Evil)
V 492a (Witnessing and Testifying)

55 II 462b (Hūd)

56 I 96a (Animal Life)
II 96a (Everyday Life, Q In); 462a (House, Domestic and Divine)

	III	327b (Material Culture and the Q)
	IV	234a (Prayer Formulas)
57	I	243a (Book); 277a (Caliph)
	II	327b (God and his Attributes); 462b (Hūd)
	IV	307a, 307b (Protection)
58	I	21b (ʿĀd); 519a (Deliverance)
	III	379a (Mercy)
	IV	523b (Salvation)
58-59	II	462b (Hūd)
59	IV	128b (Politics and the Q); 301a (Prophets and Prophethood)
	V	6a (Signs)
59-60	I	536b (Disobedience)
60	I	491b (Curse)
61	I	235a (Birth Control); 261b (Brother and Brotherhood); 472a, 479a (Creation)
	II	245a (Forgiveness); 321a (God and his Attributes)
	IV	5b (Pairs and Pairing); 521a (Ṣāliḥ)
	V	253a (Thamūd)
61-62	IV	160a (Polytheism and Atheism)
61-68	I	149b (Archaeology and the Q)
	II	308a (Geography); 340b (Good Deeds); 558a (Invitation)
	III	520b (Narratives)
	IV	521a (Ṣāliḥ)
62	IV	521a (Ṣāliḥ)
	V	253a (Thamūd)
63	I	538a (Disobedience)
	IV	574b (Seeing and Hearing)
64	II	335b (Good and Evil)
	III	393a (Miracles)
	IV	296b (Prophets and Prophethood); 453a (Reward and Punishment); 521b (Ṣāliḥ)
	V	3b (Signs); 253a (Thamūd)
64-65	III	219a (Literature and the Q)
64-68	I	287a (Camel)
65	III	551a (Numbers and Enumeration)
	IV	296b (Prophets and Prophethood); 521b (Ṣāliḥ)
	V	253a (Thamūd); 280a (Time)
66	I	519a (Deliverance)
	II	92a (Everyday Life, Q In); 320a, 322a (God and his Attributes)
	III	379a (Mercy)
	IV	5b (Pairs and Pairing); 522a (Ṣāliḥ); 523b (Salvation)
	V	253a (Thamūd)

67 I 504a (Day, Times of)
II 178a (Famine); 212a (Fire)
III 418a (Morning)
IV 454a (Reward and Punishment); 521b (Ṣāliḥ)
V 545a (Word of God)

68 I 491b (Curse)

69 I 97a (Animal Life); 237a (Blessing); 513a (Debate and Disputation)
II 218b, 219a (Food and Drink)
IV 225a (Prayer)
V 132a (Strangers and Foreigners)

69-73 III 393b (Miracles)

69-74 II 341a (Good News)

69-76 I 6a (Abraham); 330a (Chronology and the Q)

69-81 IV 290a (Prophets and Prophethood)

69-83 I 500b (Day, Times of)
III 231b (Lot); 520b (Narratives)
IV 319b (Punishment Stories)

69-104 I 193a (Āzar)

70 I 6a (Abraham)
II 196b (Fear)
V 393a (Turkish Literature and the Q)

70-83 III 233a (Lot)

71 I 6b, 7b (Abraham)
II 561b (Isaac)
III 1a (Jacob); 146b, 148a (Laughter)
IV 37a (People of the Book)

71-73 IV 31b (Patriarchy)
V 545b (Word of God)

71-74 III 148a (Laughter)

72 I 194a, 194b (Baal)
II 360b (Grammar and the Q)
III 287a (Marvels)
IV 49b (People of the House)
V 570b (Youth and Old Age)

73 I 237a (Blessing)
II 174a (Family); 186a (Fate); 315b (Glory)
III 287a (Marvels); 437a (Mosque)
IV 5b (Pairs and Pairing); 37a (People of the Book); 48b, 49a, 49b, 53a (People of the House); 213a (Praise)

74 I 513a (Debate and Disputation)

74-76	I	6a (Abraham)
75	I	5b (Abraham)
	III	401b (Moderation)
	IV	429b (Repentance and Penance)
77	I	500b (Day, Times of)
77-79	IV	584b (Sex and Sexuality)
78	I	343b (Cleanliness and Ablution)
	II	361a (Grammar and the Q)
	IV	506a (Ritual Purity)
	V	132b (Strangers and Foreigners)
80	I	533b (Dialogues)
81	I	501a, 504a (Day, Times of)
	II	174a (Family)
	III	393b (Miracles); 417a, 418a (Morning)
	V	281a (Time)
82	I	339b, 340a (Clay)
	II	411a (Heaven and Sky)
	III	383b (Metals and Minerals)
	V	129a (Stone); 470b (Weather)
82-83	II	212b (Fire)
	V	130a (Stoning)
84	I	149b (Archaeology and the Q); 261b (Brother and Brotherhood); 500a (Day, Times of)
	II	46b (Eschatology); 308a (Geography); 545a (Instruments)
	III	334a, 335b (Measurement); 390b (Midian); 393b (Miracles)
	IV	605a (Shuʿayb)
84-85	I	491a (Cups and Vessels)
	II	5b, 8b (Economics)
	III	334b (Measurement)
	IV	605a (Shuʿayb)
	V	313a (Trade and Commerce)
84-87	II	5b (Economics)
84-95	II	558a (Invitation)
	III	390b (Midian); 520b (Narratives)
	IV	605a (Shuʿayb); 115b (Polemic and Polemical Language)
85	I	300b (Cheating)
	II	7b (Economics); 545a (Instruments)
	III	276a (Markets); 334a, 335b, 336a (Measurement)
	IV	288a (Property)
	V	312b (Trade and Commerce)
86	IV	425b (Remnant)

87	III	401b (Moderation)
	IV	218a (Prayer)
	V	468a (Wealth)
88	II	31a (Epigraphy); 96a (Everyday Life, Q In); 462a (House, Domestic and Divine)
	IV	429b (Repentance and Penance); 605a (Shuʿayb)
	V	179a (Sustenance)
89	II	64a (Ethics and the Q)
	III	486a (Myths and Legends in the Q)
	IV	605b (Shuʿayb)
	V	204a (Teaching)
90	II	245a (Forgiveness); 322a (God and his Attributes)
	III	233b (Love and Affection); 378a (Mercy)
	IV	5b (Pairs and Pairing)
91	II	174a (Family)
	III	580b (Oppressed on Earth)
	IV	605b (Shuʿayb)
	V	130b (Stoning)
94	I	504a (Day, Times of); 519a (Deliverance)
	III	379a (Mercy); 393b (Miracles)
	IV	454a (Reward and Punishment); 523b (Salvation); 605b (Shuʿayb)
95	I	491b (Curse)
	III	390b (Midian)
96	I	189a (Authority)
	III	421b (Moses)
	IV	286b (Proof)
	V	8a (Signs)
96-97	IV	106a (Plagues)
96-98	III	520b (Narratives)
97	III	421b (Moses)
98	III	425a (Moses)
	IV	67b (Pharaoh)
100	II	435b (History and the Q)
	III	441a (Muḥammad); 517b (Narratives); 536b (News)
	IV	302b (Prophets and Prophethood)
101	I	523a (Destiny)
101-117	III	520b (Narratives)
102-103	V	4a, 5a (Signs)
103	V	291b (Tolerance and Coercion)
103-111	II	143b (Exhortations)

105	II	354b (Grammar and the Q)
	III	63a (Joy and Misery)
	V	110b (Speech)
105-106	III	63a (Joy and Misery)
105-108	IV	2b (Pairs and Pairing)
106	II	50a (Eschatology); 416b (Hell and Hellfire)
	III	63a (Joy and Misery)
	V	133a (Suffering)
107	II	418b (Hell and Hellfire)
107-108	II	55a (Eternity)
108	II	313a (Gift-Giving); 553b (Intercession)
	III	63a (Joy and Misery); 204a (Literary Structures of the Q)
109-123	II	262a (Form and Structure of the Q)
110	III	424b (Moses)
	IV	36b (People of the Book)
	V	289b (Time); 301a, 302a (Torah); 547b (Word of God)
111	II	361b (Grammar and the Q)
	III	379a (Mercy)
	V	244b (Textual Criticism of the Q)
112	IV	427a (Repentance and Penance)
113	II	357a, 357b (Grammar and the Q)
114	I	35b (Afternoon); 328a (Chronology and the Q); 502b, 503a (Day, Times of)
	II	79b (Evening); 340a (Good Deeds)
	IV	222a, 223a (Prayer)
	V	22a (Sin, Major and Minor); 282b (Time); 431a (Vigil)
114-115	I	328a (Chronology and the Q)
115	I	406a (Consolation)
116	I	32a (African Literature)
	II	293a (Generations); 434a (History and the Q)
	III	70b (Justice and Injustice)
	IV	425b (Remnant)
117	III	71a, 72a (Justice and Injustice)
117-118	I	538b (Dissension)
118	I	523a (Destiny)
	II	72a (Ethics and the Q)
	IV	238b (Pre-1800 Preoccupations of Q Studies); 337a (Races)
118-119	I	472a (Creation)
	III	379a (Mercy)

119 II 50b (Eschatology)
III 46b, 47b (Jinn)
V 547b (Word of God)

120 II 142b (Exhortations); 435b (History and the Q)
III 441a, 453a (Muḥammad); 517b (Narratives); 536b (News)
IV 302b (Prophets and Prophethood); 321a (Punishment Stories); 422b (Remembrance)
V 109b (Speech); 204a (Teaching)

121-122 III 40a (Jihād)

123 IV 4a (Pairs and Pairing)
V 308a (Torah)

Sūrat Yūsuf (12)

I 226b (Benjamin); 290a (Caravan); 490a, 490b (Cups and Vessels); 532b, 534a (Dialogues); 547a, 548b (Dreams and Sleep)
II 10a (Egypt); 241b (Foretelling in the Q); 243b (Forgery); 261a (Form and Structure of the Q); 436a, 441a (History and the Q); 514b (Informants); 545b, 547a (Instruments); 556a (Intoxicants)
III 211a, 211b, 222b, 224b (Literature and the Q); 229b, 230a (Lord); 234a (Love and Affection); 336a (Measurement); 408b (Money); 472b (Mysterious Letters); 518b, 525b (Narratives)
IV 67a (Pharaoh); 246a (Pre-1800 Preoccupations of Q Studies); 288a (Property); 380a (Recitation of the Q); 450b (Revision and Alteration); 495b (Ritual and the Q)
V 61b (Sleep); 104b (Spatial Relations); 167b (Sūra); 363a (Trial); 375a (Trips and Voyages); 530b (Women and the Q)

1 I 243a (Book)
II 263b (Form and Structure of the Q); 497b (Illiteracy)
III 56a (Joseph); 124b (Language and Style of the Q); 512b (Names of the Q); 592a (Orality and Writing in Arabia)
V 6b (Signs); 172a (Sūra); 436a (Virtue)

1-3 II 262a (Form and Structure of the Q)

2 I 132a (Arabic Language)
II 226b (Foreign Vocabulary); 497b (Illiteracy)
III 113b (Language and Style of the Q); 193b (Literary Structures of the Q); 451a (Muḥammad); 507a (Names of the Q); 528b (Nature as Signs); 544b (Nomads); 585a (Orality)
IV 280b (Profane and Sacred); 298a, 299b (Prophets and Prophethood); 443b (Revelation and Inspiration); 566a (Scripture and the Q)
V 203b (Teaching); 340b (Translations of the Q)

3 I 548b (Dreams and Sleep)
II 488b (Ignorance)
III 55b (Joseph); 441b (Muḥammad); 512a (Names of the Q); 517b (Narratives)

	IV	62a (Persian Literature and the Q)
	V	109b (Speech); 392a (Turkish Literature and the Q)
4	I	255a (Bowing and Prostration); 534a (Dialogues)
	III	415a (Moon); 524a (Narratives); 553a (Numbers and Enumeration)
	IV	108b (Planets and Stars)
4-5	II	241b (Foretelling in the Q)
4-6	I	533a (Dialogues)
	V	444a (Vision)
4-7	III	56a (Joseph)
5	I	526a (Devil); 546b, 548b (Dreams and Sleep)
	II	23b, 24a (Enemies); 66a (Ethics and the Q)
6	II	11b, 12a (Election); 561b (Isaac)
	III	517b (Narratives)
	IV	179a (Popular and Talismanic Uses of the Q); 291b (Prophets and Prophethood); 537b (Scholar)
	V	200b (Teaching); 444a (Vision)
7	III	55b (Joseph); 528b (Nature as Signs)
	V	5b (Signs)
8	I	227a, 227b (Benjamin)
	II	25a (Envy); 43b (Error)
	III	234b (Love and Affection)
8-9	II	365b (Grammar and the Q)
8-10	I	532a, 533a (Dialogues)
10	I	290a (Caravan)
	II	360a, 365b (Grammar and the Q)
	V	463a (Water)
11	II	354b, 357b (Grammar and the Q)
11-12	IV	308b (Protection)
11-14	I	533a (Dialogues)
12	V	281a (Time)
13-17	I	99a (Animal Life)
14	II	161b (Failure)
15	III	537a (News)
	IV	217a (Prayer)
	V	271a (Theology and the Q); 463a (Water); 546a (Word of God)
16	I	503a (Day, Times of)
	V	281b (Time); 472b (Weeping)
16-18	I	533a (Dialogues)
	V	134a (Suffering)

17 III 60b (Joy and Misery); 181b (Lie)
V 239b (Textual Criticism of the Q)

18 I 80b (Anatomy); 237b (Blood and Blood Clot); 346b, 347a (Clothing)
III 219a (Literature and the Q)
V 38a (Sīra and the Q); 82b (Soul)

19 I 290a (Caravan); 490b (Cups and Vessels); 533a (Dialogues)
II 341a (Good News); 356b, 360b (Grammar and the Q)

19-20 I 289b (Captives)

20 II 545b (Instruments)
III 335a (Measurement); 408b (Money)
V 313a (Trade and Commerce); 474a (Weights and Measures)

21 II 10a (Egypt); 241b (Foretelling in the Q)
III 305b (Material Culture and the Q)
IV 179a (Popular and Talismanic Uses of the Q); 210b (Power and Impotence); 538b (Scholar)
V 200b (Teaching); 430b (Victory)

22 III 331b (Maturity)
IV 3b (Pairs and Pairing); 452b (Reward and Punishment); 538a (Scholar)

22-32 V 152b (Ṣūfism and the Q)

22-34 I 299b (Chastity)

22-35 IV 584b (Sex and Sexuality)

23 I 163a (Art and Architecture and the Q); 530b (Dialects); 533a (Dialogues)
II 105a (Exegesis of the Q: Classical and Medieval); 162a (Failure); 444b (Homosexuality)
III 211b (Literature and the Q); 229b (Lord)
IV 288b (Property); 308a (Protection); 523a (Salvation)

23-28 III 181b (Lie)

23-31 III 56b (Joseph)

24 I 28a (Adultery and Fornication); 124a (Apparition)
II 336a (Good and Evil); 506b (Impeccability); 550a (Intention)
III 56b (Joseph); 230a (Lord); 234b (Love and Affection); 492a (Myths and Legends in the Q)
IV 286b (Proof); 580b, 585a (Sex and Sexuality)
V 19a, 25a (Sin, Major and Minor)

25 I 299b (Chastity)
II 175b (Family); 335b (Good and Evil); 353a (Grammar and the Q)
IV 276b, 277b (Prisoners)

25-28 I 346b (Clothing)

25-29 I 533a (Dialogues)

26 V 492a, 492b (Witnessing and Testifying)

26-28 V 497b (Witnessing and Testifying)

28 I 347a (Clothing)
V 531a, 531b (Women and the Q)

29 I 536b (Disobedience)
III 482b (Myths and Legends in the Q)
V 19a (Sin, Major and Minor); 174a (Sūra); 428a (Verse)

30 I 255b (Bread); 533a (Dialogues)
II 10b (Egypt); 43b (Error); 447a (Honor)
III 234b (Love and Affection); 367b (Medina)

30-32 V 531a (Women and the Q)

31 II 547a (Instruments)

31-33 I 533a (Dialogues)

32 I 19b (Abstinence)

33 V 531b (Women and the Q)

33-34 III 234b (Love and Affection)

33-35 V 531a (Women and the Q)

34 V 531b (Women and the Q)

35-42 I 549a (Dreams and Sleep)

36 I 99a (Animal Life); 256a (Bread)
II 100a (Exegesis of the Q: Classical and Medieval); 218a (Food and Drink); 360b (Grammar and the Q); 556a (Intoxicants)
V 482a (Wine)

36-37 III 537a (News)
V 200b (Teaching)

36-42 I 533a (Dialogues)

37 IV 401a (Religious Pluralism and the Q)

38 I 6a, 8a (Abraham)
II 563b (Ishmael)
III 1a (Jacob)
IV 401a (Religious Pluralism and the Q)

39 I 147b (Arbitration)
II 320b, 330a (God and his Attributes)
III 229b (Lord)
IV 142b (Politics and the Q)

40 I 148a (Arbitration)
II 30a (Epigraphy)
III 557a (Numismatics)
IV 313a (Provocation); 482b (Rhymed Prose); 538b (Scholar)
V 2a (Ṣiffīn, Battle of); 102b (Sovereignty)

41	I	99a (Animal Life); 255b (Bread); 487b, 488a (Crucifixion); 549a (Dreams and Sleep)
	II	185b (Fate); 269a (Freedom and Predestination); 556a (Intoxicants)
	III	230a (Lord)
	V	482a (Wine); 543a (Word of God)
42	I	526a (Devil)
	III	230a (Lord)
	V	285b (Time)
43	I	362b (Colors); 546b (Dreams and Sleep)
	II	218a, 218b (Food and Drink); 360b (Grammar and the Q)
	III	92a (Kings and Rulers)
	IV	128a (Politics and the Q)
	V	103b (Sovereignty)
43-44	I	533a (Dialogues)
43-48	II	178a (Famine)
	III	552a (Numbers and Enumeration)
43-49	III	56a (Joseph)
44	I	41b (Agriculture and Vegetation); 546b, 548b, 552a (Dreams and Sleep)
	II	241b (Foretelling in the Q)
	IV	178b (Popular and Talismanic Uses of the Q); 537b (Scholar)
	V	546a (Word of God)
45	I	371b (Community and Society in the Q)
	II	497b (Illiteracy)
	III	537a (News)
	IV	523b (Salvation)
	V	241b (Textual Criticism of the Q)
46	I	65a (Almsgiving); 362b (Colors)
	II	218a (Food and Drink)
	III	554b (Numerology)
46-49	I	533a (Dialogues)
47	I	40b (Agriculture and Vegetation)
	II	218a (Food and Drink); 433a (History and the Q)
	III	554b (Numerology)
	V	318a (Tradition and Custom)
47-49	I	548b (Dreams and Sleep)
	V	285b (Time)
48	II	178a (Famine)
49	II	178a (Famine)
	V	560b (Year)
50	III	92a (Kings and Rulers); 230a (Lord); 382b (Messenger)
	V	103b (Sovereignty); 531b (Women and the Q)

50-53	I	299b (Chastity)
51	I	255b (Bread); 533a (Dialogues)
	II	336a (Good and Evil)
	V	288b (Time); 531a (Women and the Q)
52	II	162a (Failure)
	V	531b (Women and the Q)
53	II	336a (Good and Evil)
	III	224a (Literature and the Q); 379a (Mercy)
	V	22a (Sin, Major and Minor); 82b (Soul); 96b (South Asian Literatures and the Q); 138b (Ṣūfism and the Q); 204b (Teaching); 531a, 532a (Women and the Q)
54	III	92a (Kings and Rulers)
	V	103b (Sovereignty)
54-55	I	533a (Dialogues)
54-56	V	549a (Work)
55	IV	537b (Scholar)
56	II	10b (Egypt)
	IV	452b (Reward and Punishment)
56-57	III	55b (Joseph)
58-61	I	533a (Dialogues)
59	I	227a, 227b (Benjamin)
	II	5b (Economics)
	III	336a (Measurement)
59-60	III	334a (Measurement)
60	I	521b (Despair)
62	I	533a (Dialogues)
	III	58b (Journey)
	IV	288a (Property)
63	I	227a (Benjamin)
	III	334a (Measurement)
	IV	308b (Protection)
63-67	I	533a (Dialogues)
64	I	227a, 227b (Benjamin)
	II	37b (Epigraphy)
	III	378a (Mercy)
65	I	286b (Camel); 398b (Conquest)
	II	360b (Grammar and the Q)
	III	60b (Joy and Misery); 334a (Measurement)
	IV	288a (Property); 308b (Protection)
	V	411b (Vehicles); 473b (Weights and Measures)
66	I	227a (Benjamin); 465a (Covenant)

67	II	30a (Epigraphy); 96a (Everyday Life, Q In)
	III	1a (Jacob); 557a (Numismatics)
	V	2a (Ṣiffīn, Battle of)
68	IV	538b (Scholar)
	V	200b (Teaching)
69	I	227a, 227b (Benjamin)
70	I	227a, 227b (Benjamin); 290a (Caravan); 491a (Cups and Vessels)
	III	58b (Journey); 208b (Literature and the Q)
	V	255b (Theft)
70-79	I	533a (Dialogues)
72	I	286b (Camel); 491a (Cups and Vessels)
	II	219a (Food and Drink)
	III	92a (Kings and Rulers); 227b (Load or Burden); 334a (Measurement)
	V	103b (Sovereignty); 411b (Vehicles); 473b (Weights and Measures)
73	III	562a (Oaths)
	V	256a (Theft)
75	II	64b (Ethics and the Q)
	III	58b (Journey); 70b (Justice and Injustice)
76	I	227a, 227b (Benjamin)
	III	92a (Kings and Rulers); 102a (Knowledge and Learning)
	IV	538b (Scholar)
	V	103b (Sovereignty); 270a (Theology and the Q)
77	I	227a (Benjamin); 533a (Dialogues)
78	I	227a, 227b (Benjamin); 255b (Bread)
	II	10a (Egypt)
79	I	227a (Benjamin)
	III	60b (Joy and Misery)
	IV	308a (Protection)
80	I	227b (Benjamin); 465a (Covenant); 516a (Decision); 521b (Despair)
	II	10b (Egypt); 321a (God and his Attributes)
	III	64b (Judgment)
80-82	I	532b, 533a (Dialogues)
81	I	227a (Benjamin)
	V	492a (Witnessing and Testifying)
82	I	290a (Caravan); 532b (Dialogues)
83	I	227a (Benjamin)
	IV	537b (Scholar)
83-87	I	533a (Dialogues)
84	I	364a (Colors)
	II	153b (Eyes)

	III	1a (Jacob)
	V	63a (Smell); 134a (Suffering); 363a (Trial)
85	I	271b (Cain and Abel)
87	I	227a, 227b (Benjamin); 521b (Despair)
	V	63b (Smell); 161b (Suicide); 393a (Turkish Literature and the Q)
88	I	68a (Almsgiving); 255b (Bread)
	II	5b (Economics); 10a (Egypt); 253a (Form and Structure of the Q)
	III	334a, 336a (Measurement)
	V	198a (Taxation)
88-93	I	533a (Dialogues)
89	I	227b (Benjamin)
	II	488b (Ignorance)
90	I	227b (Benjamin)
92	I	449b (Cosmology)
93	I	346b, 347a (Clothing)
	II	174a (Family)
	III	1a (Jacob)
	V	63b (Smell)
93-96	V	63a (Smell)
94	I	52a (Air and Wind); 290a (Caravan); 347a (Clothing)
	III	573a (Odors and Smells)
	V	62a, 63a, 63b (Smell)
94-95	I	533a (Dialogues)
95	II	43b (Error)
	V	63a (Smell)
96	II	341a (Good News)
	III	1a (Jacob); 223a (Literature and the Q)
	V	63a (Smell); 134a (Suffering); 363a (Trial); 444b (Vision)
96-98	I	533a (Dialogues)
97	V	19a (Sin, Major and Minor)
98	V	570b (Youth and Old Age)
99	II	10a (Egypt)
99-100	III	99b (Kinship)
100	I	255a (Bowing and Prostration); 546b, 548b, 549b (Dreams and Sleep)
	III	56b (Joseph)
	IV	33a (Patriarchy); 537b (Scholar)
	V	277a (Throne of God)
101	I	472a (Creation); 506a (Death and the Dead)
	II	100a (Exegesis of the Q: Classical and Medieval)

III 93a (Kings and Rulers); 103a (Knowledge and Learning); 143a (Last Judgment)
IV 4a (Pairs and Pairing); 128a (Politics and the Q)
V 103b (Sovereignty); 106a (Spatial Relations); 200b (Teaching)

101-102 IV 179a (Popular and Talismanic Uses of the Q)

102 III 441b (Muḥammad); 537a (News)
IV 302b (Prophets and Prophethood); 438b (Revelation and Inspiration)
V 271a (Theology and the Q); 532a (Women and the Q)

103 V 291b (Tolerance and Coercion)

105 II 352b (Grammar and the Q)

107 I 501a (Day, Times of)
II 128b (Exegesis of the Q: Early Modern and Contemporary)
III 137a, 138a (Last Judgment)
V 287b (Time)

108 I 237a (Blessing); 437a (Conversion)
III 443a (Muḥammad)
IV 29a (Path or Way); 220a (Prayer)
V 221b (Teaching and Preaching the Q)

109 III 58a (Journey); 451b (Muḥammad)
IV 49a (People of the House); 296a (Prophets and Prophethood); 320b (Punishment Stories); 425a (Remnant); 438b (Revelation and Inspiration)
V 546b (Word of God)

110 I 521b (Despair)
II 354a (Grammar and the Q)
III 453a (Muḥammad)
IV 295b (Prophets and Prophethood)
V 178a (Suspicion)

110-111 III 451a (Muḥammad)

111 II 435b, 441a (History and the Q)
III 362a (Medicine and the Q); 506b (Names of the Q)
IV 439a (Revelation and Inspiration)
V 2b (Signs); 532a (Women and the Q)

Sūrat al-Raʿd (13)

I 322a (Chronology and the Q)
III 472b (Mysterious Letters); 585a (Orality)

1 I 224b (Belief and Unbelief)
II 262a, 263b (Form and Structure of the Q)
III 592a (Orality and Writing in Arabia)
V 6b (Signs); 172a (Sūra)

2 I 163b (Art and Architecture and the Q); 442b, 443b (Cosmology)
II 268a (Freedom and Predestination); 325b, 327b (God and his Attributes); 410b, 411a (Heaven and Sky); 460b (House, Domestic and Divine)

	III	202a (Literary Structures of the Q)
	IV	4b (Pairs and Pairing); 73b (Philosophy and the Q); 127a (Politics and the Q)
	V	163a (Sun); 289b (Time); 544a, 545a (Word of God)
2-3	V	3b, 7b (Signs)
2-4	I	473b (Creation)
	IV	438a (Revelation and Inspiration)
3	II	2b, 3a (Earth)
	III	550b (Numbers and Enumeration)
	IV	4b, 6a (Pairs and Pairing); 183b (Portents); 581a (Sex and Sexuality)
	V	463a (Water); 544a (Word of God)
3-4	I	443a (Cosmology)
4	I	41a (Agriculture and Vegetation); 476b (Creation)
	II	3a, 3b (Earth); 305a (Geography)
	V	462b (Water)
5	I	479a, 479b (Creation)
	II	4b (Earth)
	III	399a (Miracles)
	IV	311a (Provocation)
6	I	530a (Dialects)
	II	354b (Grammar and the Q)
	III	380a (Mercy)
	IV	453a, 453b (Reward and Punishment)
7	III	382a (Messenger); 399a (Miracles); 450a (Muḥammad)
	IV	311b (Provocation)
8	II	289b (Gender)
	III	334b (Measurement)
	IV	85b (Philosophy and the Q)
	V	522a, 522b (Womb)
9	I	158b (Arrogance)
	II	82b (Everyday Life, Q In); 320b (God and his Attributes); 353a (Grammar and the Q)
	IV	4a, 5b (Pairs and Pairing); 478b (Rhymed Prose); 537b (Scholar)
10	I	502a (Day, Times of)
	III	190a (Literacy)
10-11	V	118b (Spiritual Beings)
11	II	187a (Fate); 335b (Good and Evil); 431a (History and the Q)
	III	231b (Lord)
	IV	307b (Protection)
	V	118b, 118b (Spiritual Beings); 493a (Witnessing and Testifying)
12	I	479a (Creation)

12-13 I 512a (Debate and Disputation)
V 471a (Weather)

12-15 V 7b (Signs)

13 I 27a (Adoration)
II 82a (Everyday Life, Q In); 196b (Fear); 37b (Epigraphy); 314b (Glorification of God)
IV 115b (Polemic and Polemical Language); 214b (Praise)

14 II 43b (Error); 401a (Hand)
III 204b (Literary Structures of the Q)
IV 10a (Parable); 228b, 229a (Prayer)
V 15a (Simile); 182a (Symbolic Imagery); 386b (Truth)

15 I 254b (Bowing and Prostration); 502b, 504a (Day, Times of)
II 80a, 80b (Evening)
III 417a, 418b (Morning)
IV 4b (Pairs and Pairing); 221a (Prayer); 378a (Recitation of the Q)
V 281b (Time); 393a (Turkish Literature and the Q)

16 I 103b (Anthropomorphism); 472a, 472b (Creation); 493b (Darkness); 555a (Druzes)
II 317a, 327b, 330a (God and his Attributes)
III 186a (Light)
IV 4a, 6a (Pairs and Pairing); 184a (Possession and Possessions); 280b (Profane and Sacred); 288a (Property)
V 447b (Vision and Blindness)

16-17 I 329b (Chronology and the Q)

17 III 334a (Measurement)
IV 10a (Parable)
V 17a (Simile); 126b (Springs and Fountains); 463a (Water)

18 II 418a (Hell and Hellfire)
IV 2a (Pairs and Pairing); 15a (Paradise); 103b, 104a (Pit)

18-25 II 335b (Good and Evil)

19-23 I 257b (Breaking Trusts and Contracts)

20 I 257b (Breaking Trusts and Contracts); 464b (Covenant)

20-23 I 219b (Belief and Unbelief)
IV 17a (Paradise)

20-24 II 460b (House, Domestic and Divine)

21-22 I 257b (Breaking Trusts and Contracts)

22 I 257b (Breaking Trusts and Contracts)
II 53a (Eschatology); 69b (Ethics and the Q); 160a (Face of God); 323b (God and his Attributes); 450a (Hospitality and Courtesy)
IV 221a (Prayer); 309b (Provocation)
V 264a (Theology and the Q)

23 I 89b (Angel); 220b (Belief and Unbelief); 385a (Community and Society in the Q)
II 282b, 284a (Garden)
IV 13b (Paradise); 21b (Parents)
V 393a, 393b (Turkish Literature and the Q)

24 I 385a (Community and Society in the Q)
II 91b (Everyday Life, Q In)
IV 225a (Prayer)

25 I 464b (Covenant)
II 7b (Economics)
IV 129a (Politics and the Q)

26 II 69b (Ethics and the Q); 186b (Fate)
III 59b, 61a (Joy and Misery)
IV 2a (Pairs and Pairing)
V 179a (Sustenance)

27 I 435b, 437a (Conversion); 523a (Destiny)
II 270a (Freedom and Predestination); 321a (God and his Attributes); 59a (Ethics and the Q)
III 450a, 452a (Muḥammad)
IV 311b, 312a (Provocation); 427b (Repentance and Penance); 432a (Responsibility)

28 I 82a (Anatomy)
II 163a (Faith); 370b (Gratitude and Ingratitude); 408a (Heart)
IV 230a, 230b (Prayer); 420a, 422a (Remembrance)

29 I 406a (Consolation)
II 284b (Garden)
IV 15a (Paradise)
V 361b (Tree)

30 II 96a (Everyday Life, Q In)
III 441b, 443a (Muḥammad)
IV 132b (Politics and the Q); 438a (Revelation and Inspiration)
V 393b (Turkish Literature and the Q); 501a (Witnessing and Testifying)

31 I 113a (Apocalypse); 435b (Conversion)
II 59b (Ethics and the Q)
III 456a (Muḥammad)

32 III 401a (Mockery); 453a (Muḥammad)
IV 309b, 310b (Provocation)

33 I 213a (Beauty); 225b (Belief and Unbelief)

34 II 56b (Ethics and the Q)
IV 307b (Protection); 457a (Reward and Punishment)
V 553a (World)

35 II 54b (Eternity); 283b (Garden)
V 125a (Springs and Fountains)

36 III 61a (Joy and Misery)
V 301a (Torah)

37 I 132a (Arabic Language); 145a (Arabs); 516b (Decision)
II 226b (Foreign Vocabulary); 274b (Friends and Friendship)
III 65a (Judgment); 113b (Language and Style of the Q); 544b (Nomads); 567b (Obedience)
IV 298a (Prophets and Prophethood); 307b (Protection)
V 340b (Translations of the Q)

38 I 11b (Abrogation); 235a (Birth Control); 244b (Book)
II 497b (Illiteracy)
III 398a (Miracles)
IV 296a (Prophets and Prophethood)
V 3b (Signs); 289a (Time)

38-43 I 523a (Destiny)

39 I 247b (Book)
II 189a (Fātiḥa)
IV 81a (Philosophy and the Q); 261b, 262b, 263a (Preserved Tablet); 449a (Revision and Alteration); 560b (Scripture and the Q)

40 III 40a (Jihād); 66b (Judgment); 18b (Jesus)

41 I 516a (Decision)
II 321a, 321b (God and his Attributes)
V 103a (Sovereignty)

42 III 18a (Jesus)
V 480a (Whisper)

43 I 247a (Book)
III 451a (Muḥammad); 577b (Opposition to Muḥammad)
V 493a (Witnessing and Testifying)

Sūrat Ibrāhīm (14)

III 472b (Mysterious Letters)
IV 247a (Pre-1800 Preoccupations of Q Studies)

1 I 245a (Book)
III 186a (Light); 508a (Names of the Q)
IV 5a, 6a (Pairs and Pairing); 29a (Path or Way)
V 374b (Trips and Voyages)

1-4 II 262a (Form and Structure of the Q)

1-21 III 519a (Narratives)

2 IV 4a (Pairs and Pairing)

3 V 138a (Ṣūfism and the Q)

4	I	83a (Anatomy); 132a (Arabic Language); 186a (Astray)
	II	187b (Fate); 227a (Foreign Vocabulary); 330b (God and his Attributes)
	III	108b, 109a (Language, Concept of); 112a, 113b, 114b (Language and Style of the Q); 380b, 382a (Messenger); 443a (Muḥammad); 507a (Names of the Q)
	IV	2a (Pairs and Pairing); 299b (Prophets and Prophethood); 329b (Quraysh); 337b (Races); 444a (Revelation and Inspiration)
	V	203b (Teaching); 341a (Translations of the Q)
5	I	505a (Days of God)
	III	186a (Light); 421b (Moses)
	IV	5a (Pairs and Pairing); 106a (Plagues)
	V	182a (Symbolic Imagery); 203a (Teaching); 279b (Time); 382b, 383b (Trust and Patience)
5-6	III	422b (Moses)
5-8	II	372b (Gratitude and Ingratitude)
5-14	IV	320a (Punishment Stories)
6	I	302a (Children); 304b (Children of Israel); 518b (Deliverance)
	II	335b (Good and Evil); 542a (Insolence and Obstinacy)
	III	422b (Moses)
	IV	67a (Pharaoh); 517a (Sacrifice)
7	II	372a (Gratitude and Ingratitude); 510a (Indifference)
	IV	2a (Pairs and Pairing)
	V	393b (Turkish Literature and the Q)
8	IV	6a (Pairs and Pairing)
9	I	21b (ʿĀd)
	II	350b (Grammar and the Q); 436b (History and the Q)
	III	486a (Myths and Legends in the Q); 518a, 524a (Narratives); 537a (News); 540b (Noah)
	V	379b (Trust and Patience)
10	I	472a (Creation)
	II	439b (History and the Q)
	IV	4a (Pairs and Pairing); 301a (Prophets and Prophethood)
	V	289a (Time)
10-11	III	452a (Muḥammad)
11	I	189a (Authority)
	II	164b (Faith)
	III	43b (Jinn)
	IV	296a (Prophets and Prophethood)
	V	379a, 379b (Trust and Patience)
12	IV	29a (Path or Way)
	V	134a (Suffering); 382a (Trust and Patience)

13 III 449a (Muḥammad)
IV 301a (Prophets and Prophethood); 438b (Revelation and Inspiration)
V 546a (Word of God)

14 I 277a (Caliph)
II 196b (Fear)
IV 432a (Responsibility)

15 I 398b (Conquest)
II 162a (Failure)

16 II 211a (Fire); 416a (Hell and Hellfire)

16-17 II 50b (Eschatology)
III 63b (Joy and Misery); 203b (Literary Structures of the Q)

17 II 416a, 416b (Hell and Hellfire)
V 324b (Traditional Disciplines of Q Studies)

18 I 52a, 54b (Air and Wind); 184b (Ashes); 500a (Day, Times of)
IV 431b (Responsibility)
V 15a (Simile); 182a (Symbolic Imagery); 470b (Weather)

19 IV 4a (Pairs and Pairing)
V 544b (Word of God)

19-20 I 474b (Creation)

21 II 552a (Intercession)
III 580b, 582a (Oppressed on Earth); 583a (Oppression)
V 468b (Wealth)

22 I 190a (Authority); 526a (Devil)
II 356b (Grammar and the Q); 417a (Hell and Hellfire); 558b (Invitation)
V 487a (Wish and Desire); 543a (Word of God)

23 I 88b (Angel); 237a (Blessing)
II 91b (Everyday Life, Q In)

24 V 361b (Tree); 571a (Zaqqūm)

24-26 V 16a, 16b (Simile)

24-27 II 260a (Form and Structure of the Q)
IV 10a (Parable)

25 IV 58b (Persian Literature and the Q)

26 III 533a (Nature as Signs)
V 361b (Tree)

27 I 480b (Creeds); 523a (Destiny)
IV 432a (Responsibility); 460a (Reward and Punishment)
V 547a (Word of God)

28 I 236b (Blessing)

30	II	418a (Hell and Hellfire); 476b (Idolatry and Idolaters)
	III	41b (Jihād)
	IV	29a (Path or Way)
	V	287a (Time)
31	I	500a (Day, Times of)
	III	137b (Last Judgment)
32	II	3a (Earth); 304b (Geography)
	IV	4a (Pairs and Pairing)
	V	412a (Vehicles); 463a, 464a (Water)
32-33	III	304a (Material Culture and the Q)
32-34	I	472a, 473a (Creation)
	II	58a (Ethics and the Q); 259a (Form and Structure of the Q)
	III	379a (Mercy)
33	I	442b (Cosmology); 501a (Day, Times of)
	III	415a (Moon)
	IV	107b (Planets and Stars)
	V	163a (Sun); 280b (Time); 545a (Word of God)
34	I	221a (Belief and Unbelief)
	II	166a (Faith)
	V	393a (Turkish Literature and the Q)
35	II	3a (Earth); 481a (Idols and Images)
	IV	482b (Rhymed Prose)
	V	373b (Trips and Voyages)
35-37	I	7a (Abraham)
	IV	32b (Patriarchy); 516a (Sacred Precincts)
35-38	V	258a (Theology and the Q)
35-39	III	339b (Mecca)
36	I	536b (Disobedience)
37	I	40b (Agriculture and Vegetation)
	II	3b (Earth); 304b (Geography); 564b (Ishmael)
	III	337b (Mecca)
	IV	223b (Prayer); 282a (Profane and Sacred); 329b (Quraysh); 514b (Sacred Precincts); 519a (Ṣafā and Marwa); 589b (Shekhinah)
37-39	II	561b (Isaac)
38	IV	4a (Pairs and Pairing)
39	II	1b (Ears); 564b (Ishmael)
	IV	229a (Prayer); 575a (Seeing and Hearing)
39-40	IV	229a (Prayer)
40	IV	223b, 229b (Prayer)

41 I 7a (Abraham)
III 66b (Judgment); 137a (Last Judgment)
IV 21a (Parents); 33a (Patriarchy)

43 I 51b (Air and Wind); 81b (Anatomy)

44 III 442b (Muḥammad)
IV 430a (Repentance and Penance)

45 IV 425a (Remnant)

47 III 18b (Jesus)
IV 301b (Prophets and Prophethood); 310a (Provocation); 453b (Reward and Punishment)
V 416a (Vengeance)

48 I 91b (Angel)
II 330a (God and his Attributes); 395b (Ḥadīth and the Q)
III 66b (Judgment); 184b (Life); 531b (Nature as Signs)
IV 6a (Pairs and Pairing)

49 II 416b (Hell and Hellfire); 546b (Instruments)

50 II 50b (Eschatology); 210b (Fire); 416a (Hell and Hellfire)

51 III 379a (Mercy)

52 II 329b (God and his Attributes)
III 512b (Names of the Q)
V 500a (Witnessing and Testifying)

Sūrat al-Ḥijr (15)

I 451b, 453a (Cosmology)
II 260a, 263a (Form and Structure of the Q)
III 472b (Mysterious Letters)
IV 54a (People of the Thicket); 247a (Pre-1800 Preoccupations of Q Studies); 496a (Ritual and the Q)
V 172a (Sūra); 425a (Verse)

1 II 497b (Illiteracy)
III 124b, 125a (Language and Style of the Q); 528a (Nature as Signs); 591b (Orality and Writing in Arabia)

1-3 II 261b (Form and Structure of the Q)

3 II 448b (Hope)
III 40a (Jihād); 453b (Muḥammad)
IV 538b (Scholar)

4 I 244a (Book); 523a (Destiny)

4-5 II 45a (Eschatology)
III 185a (Life); 380a (Mercy)

5 V 289a (Time)

6	I	447a (Cosmology)
	II	540a (Insanity)
	III	44a (Jinn)
	IV	112a (Poetry and Poets); 311b (Provocation)
6-7	II	261b (Form and Structure of the Q)
	IV	442b (Revelation and Inspiration)
9	I	361a (Collection of the Q)
	IV	307b (Protection)
10	II	434a (History and the Q)
	IV	403b (Religious Pluralism and the Q); 592a (Shīʿa)
11	III	382a (Messenger); 400a (Mockery)
	IV	301a (Prophets and Prophethood)
13	II	434a (History and the Q)
	V	164a (Sunna)
14	I	398b (Conquest)
	III	46a (Jinn)
15-18	I	544b (Divination)
16	I	213a (Beauty); 442b (Cosmology)
	II	327b (God and his Attributes); 411a (Heaven and Sky)
	IV	107a, 108a (Planets and Stars); 550a (Science and the Q)
	V	283b (Time)
16-17	I	442b (Cosmology)
	IV	550a (Science and the Q)
	V	130a (Stoning)
16-18	III	249b (Magic)
16-25	II	259a (Form and Structure of the Q)
17	I	524b (Devil)
	II	411a (Heaven and Sky)
	IV	307b (Protection)
	V	130a (Stoning)
17-18	IV	108a (Planets and Stars)
18	I	442b (Cosmology)
	III	46a (Jinn)
	IV	107a (Planets and Stars)
19	I	443a (Cosmology)
	II	2b, 3b (Earth); 358a (Grammar and the Q)
	III	531b (Nature as Signs)
21	III	334b (Measurement)
21-22	I	462b, 463a (Court)

22	I	42a (Agriculture and Vegetation); 53b (Air and Wind)
	III	530a (Nature as Signs)
	V	463a (Water)
23	II	320b (God and his Attributes)
25	IV	5b (Pairs and Pairing); 537b (Scholar)
26	I	240a (Bloodshed); 339b (Clay); 446a, 451b (Cosmology); 476a (Creation)
	II	172b (Fall of Man)
	III	383b (Metals and Minerals)
26-27	I	24a (Adam and Eve); 451b (Cosmology)
26-33	II	4b (Earth)
	IV	220a (Prayer)
26-39	III	184a (Life)
26-48	I	448a (Cosmology)
	III	519b (Narratives)
27	I	446b, 447a (Cosmology); 476a (Creation)
	II	433b (History and the Q)
	III	48b (Jinn)
	IV	336b (Races)
	V	120a (Spiritual Beings)
28	I	22b (Adam and Eve); 240a (Bloodshed); 339b (Clay); 476a (Creation)
	II	328a, 330a (God and his Attributes)
	III	383b (Metals and Minerals); 532a (Nature as Signs)
	V	109a (Speech)
28-38	I	447a (Cosmology)
28-40	V	267b (Theology and the Q)
29	I	24b (Adam and Eve); 52a (Air and Wind); 508a (Death and the Dead)
	II	186b (Fate); 327b (God and his Attributes); 442a (Holy Spirit)
	III	14a (Jesus); 293b (Mary)
	V	81b (Soul); 109a (Speech); 114b (Spirit)
29-33	I	24a (Adam and Eve); 255a (Bowing and Prostration)
30	I	447a (Cosmology)
30-33	I	511a (Debate and Disputation)
31	I	447a (Cosmology); 525a (Devil)
	II	172b (Fall of Man)
	III	45a (Jinn)
31-43	II	417b (Hell and Hellfire)
32	III	45a (Jinn)
32-42	V	109a (Speech)

33	I	240a (Bloodshed); 339b (Clay); 476a (Creation); 525a (Devil)
	II	543a (Insolence and Obstinacy)
	III	383b (Metals and Minerals); 490b (Myths and Legends in the Q); 532a (Nature as Signs)
34	I	525a (Devil)
34-40	V	267b (Theology and the Q)
35	III	136b (Last Judgment)
38	I	500a (Day, Times of)
	V	288a (Time)
39	I	506a (Death and the Dead)
	II	172b (Fall of Man); 336a (Good and Evil)
39-40	I	525a (Devil)
40	I	452a, 453a (Cosmology)
	II	550a (Intention)
41	III	491a (Myths and Legends in the Q)
43	II	543a (Insolence and Obstinacy)
43-44	II	50a (Eschatology)
44	II	355b (Grammar and the Q); 415a (Hell and Hellfire)
	III	552a (Numbers and Enumeration); 554b (Numerology)
	V	334a (Traditional Disciplines of Q Studies)
45	II	283b (Garden)
	V	121b, 123a (Springs and Fountains); 464b (Water); 467a (Water of Paradise)
46	II	91b (Everyday Life, Q In); 461b (House, Domestic and Divine)
47	I	263a (Brother and Brotherhood)
	II	159a (Face); 276a (Furniture and Furnishings); 283b (Garden)
	IV	18a (Paradise)
48	II	283b (Garden)
49	I	452a (Cosmology)
	II	330a (God and his Attributes)
	III	519b (Narratives); 536b (News)
49-50	III	380a (Mercy)
49-51	II	435b (History and the Q)
49-60	III	519b (Narratives)
49-77	II	260a (Form and Structure of the Q)
50	V	133a (Suffering)
51	II	254b (Form and Structure of the Q)
	III	519b (Narratives); 536b (News)
	IV	473b (Rhetoric and the Q)
	V	132a (Strangers and Foreigners)

51-55 II 341a, 341b (Good News)
51-56 III 393b (Miracles)
51-59 I 6a (Abraham)
51-60 I 330a (Chronology and the Q)
51-84 IV 320a (Punishment Stories)
52 II 198a (Fear)
53 I 7b (Abraham); 330b (Chronology and the Q)
II 198a (Fear); 357b (Grammar and the Q); 561b (Isaac)
55 I 521b (Despair)
II 341b (Good News)
56 I 521b (Despair)
III 380a (Mercy)
V 161b (Suicide)
57 III 382b (Messenger)
57-76 III 233a (Lot)
57-77 III 231b (Lot)
58 I 375b (Community and Society in the Q)
59 II 174a (Family)
61 II 174a (Family)
61-75 III 519b (Narratives)
62 II 489a (Ignorance)
65 I 501a (Day, Times of)
II 174a (Family)
66 I 504a (Day, Times of)
III 418a (Morning)
IV 425a (Remnant)
67 III 62a (Joy and Misery); 367b (Medina)
IV 37a (People of the Book)
67-71 IV 584b (Sex and Sexuality)
68 V 132b (Strangers and Foreigners)
71 II 360b (Grammar and the Q)
72 V 393b (Turkish Literature and the Q)
73 I 149a (Archaeology and the Q); 503b (Day, Times of)
II 212b (Fire)
III 417b, 418a (Morning)
V 282b (Time); 545a (Word of God)
74 I 339b, 340a (Clay)
II 212b (Fire)

	III	383b (Metals and Minerals)
	V	129a (Stone); 130a (Stoning); 470b (Weather)
76	I	149a (Archaeology and the Q)
	IV	425b (Remnant)
76-79	III	519b (Narratives)
77	III	232b (Lot)
	V	5a (Signs)
78	I	41b (Agriculture and Vegetation)
	II	353b (Grammar and the Q)
	IV	53b (People of the Thicket); 605b (Shuʿayb)
78-79	III	390b (Midian)
79	I	244a (Book)
	IV	425b (Remnant); 453b (Reward and Punishment)
80	II	427a (Ḥijr); 438a (History and the Q)
	III	418a (Morning)
80-83	II	212a (Fire)
80-84	II	427a (Ḥijr)
	III	519b (Narratives)
81	V	5b (Signs)
83	I	504a (Day, Times of)
	III	393b (Miracles); 417a (Morning)
	IV	454a (Reward and Punishment)
84	V	468a (Wealth)
85	I	501a (Day, Times of)
	II	244b (Forgiveness)
	III	40a (Jihād); 137a (Last Judgment)
	IV	4a (Pairs and Pairing)
	V	287b (Time); 291a (Tolerance and Coercion)
85-86	I	473a (Creation)
85-99	II	143a (Exhortations)
86	IV	6a (Pairs and Pairing); 280b (Profane and Sacred)
87	I	210b (Basmala)
	II	189a, 190b, 191a (Fātiḥa); 260a (Form and Structure of the Q)
	III	446b (Muḥammad); 575a, 576a (Oft-Repeated)
	V	242b, 243a (Textual Criticism of the Q); 424b, 425b (Verse)
88	III	452b (Muḥammad)
89-99	III	577b (Opposition to Muḥammad)
90-91	III	24b (Jews and Judaism)

90-92 IV 280b (Profane and Sacred)
91 III 507a (Names of the Q)
92 IV 431a (Responsibility)
94 III 453a (Muḥammad)
94-95 II 209a (Fighting)
III 40a (Jihād)
95 III 401a (Mockery); 454b (Muḥammad)
IV 332a (Quraysh)
96 IV 538b (Scholar)
97 III 452b (Muḥammad)
98 I 27a (Adoration)
IV 214a (Praise); 220b (Prayer)
V 425b (Verse)
99 V 404a (Uncertainty)

Sūrat al-Naḥl (16)

I 93b (Animal Life)
III 534a (Nature as Signs)
IV 496a (Ritual and the Q)
1 IV 220b (Prayer)
V 266a, 266b (Theology and the Q)
2 I 87a (Angel); 329b (Chronology and the Q); 463a (Court)
II 278b (Gabriel); 330a (God and his Attributes); 443b (Holy Spirit)
III 293b (Mary); 537b (Night of Power)
IV 293a (Prophets and Prophethood)
V 81a (Soul); 115b (Spirit); 488b (Witness to Faith); 500b (Witnessing and Testifying)
2-8 III 379a (Mercy)
3 III 70a (Justice and Injustice)
3-8 V 7b (Signs)
4 I 435a (Conversion); 476a, 476b (Creation)
II 303b (Geography)
5 I 95b (Animal Life); 215b (Bedouin); 443a (Cosmology)
II 455b (Hot and Cold)
5-6 I 213a (Beauty)
5-7 III 544a (Nomads)
5-8 I 96a (Animal Life); 473a (Creation)
II 303b (Geography)

	III	534a (Nature as Signs)
	V	373b (Trips and Voyages)
5-18	V	5b (Signs)
6	I	96a (Animal Life); 215b (Bedouin)
	III	417b, 418b (Morning)
	IV	210b (Power and Impotence)
7	III	227b (Load or Burden)
	IV	5b (Pairs and Pairing)
	V	411b (Vehicles)
8	I	96a (Animal Life)
	V	374a (Trips and Voyages); 411a (Vehicles)
9	V	374a (Trips and Voyages)
10	V	358b (Tree)
10-11	II	3a, 3b (Earth)
	V	462b (Water)
10-13	IV	422b (Remembrance)
10-16	IV	438a (Revelation and Inspiration)
10-18	I	473a, 473b (Creation)
11	I	41a, 46b (Agriculture and Vegetation); 494b (Date Palm)
	II	3b, 4a (Earth); 304b (Geography)
11-13	I	246a (Book)
12	I	501a (Day, Times of)
	IV	4b (Pairs and Pairing); 107b (Planets and Stars)
	V	163a (Sun)
13	I	361b (Colors)
	II	363b (Grammar and the Q)
14	I	97a (Animal Life); 443a (Cosmology)
	II	218b (Food and Drink); 467b (Hunting and Fishing)
	IV	604a (Ships)
	V	4a (Signs); 412a (Vehicles); 464a (Water)
15	I	271b (Cain and Abel)
	II	2b, 3a (Earth)
	IV	29a (Path or Way)
	V	463a (Water)
15-16	I	443a (Cosmology)
	V	372b (Trips and Voyages)
16	II	528a (Inimitability)
	IV	107a, 108a (Planets and Stars)
16-80	III	544a (Nomads)

17	I	472b (Creation)
19	IV	4a (Pairs and Pairing)
	V	479b (Whisper)
20	I	371b (Community and Society in the Q); 472b (Creation)
	IV	228b (Prayer)
20-21	I	507a (Death and the Dead)
	IV	313a (Provocation)
21	IV	435b (Resurrection)
	V	288b (Time)
22	I	160b (Arrogance)
	II	329b (God and his Attributes)
23	IV	4a (Pairs and Pairing); 264a (Pride)
24	II	430a (History and the Q)
	III	518a (Narratives)
	IV	302b (Prophets and Prophethood)
26	II	459b (House, Domestic and Divine)
	III	539b (Nimrod)
27	I	247b (Book)
	II	336a (Good and Evil)
	IV	453b (Reward and Punishment); 538b (Scholar)
	V	203b (Teaching)
28	II	336a (Good and Evil)
29	I	160b (Arrogance)
	IV	103b (Pit)
30	V	552a, 552b (World)
30-31	IV	14b (Paradise)
	IV	456b (Reward and Punishment)
31	II	282b, 283b (Garden)
	IV	13b (Paradise)
	V	393a, 393b (Turkish Literature and the Q)
32	IV	225a (Prayer)
34	III	400b (Mockery)
	IV	310a (Provocation)
35	III	125a (Language and Style of the Q); 174b (Lawful and Unlawful); 380a (Mercy)
	IV	300b (Prophets and Prophethood)
	V	291b (Tolerance and Coercion)
35-40	I	523a (Destiny)
36	I	435b (Conversion)
	II	474a (Iconoclasm); 482a (Idols and Images); 497a, 497b (Illiteracy)

	III	380b, 382a (Messenger)
	IV	299b (Prophets and Prophethood); 425a (Remnant)
37	V	291b (Tolerance and Coercion)
38	I	329b (Chronology and the Q)
	II	317a (God and his Attributes)
	IV	538b (Scholar)
39	III	181a (Lie)
40	I	319a (Chronology and the Q); 470b (Createdness of the Q); 475a, 475b (Creation)
	II	327b (God and his Attributes)
	IV	33b (Patriarchy); 82a, 86a (Philosophy and the Q)
	V	109a (Speech); 287a (Time); 485b (Wish and Desire); 542b, 543a, 547a (Word of God); 553b (World)
41	III	38b (Jihād); 579a (Opposition to Muḥammad)
	IV	456b (Reward and Punishment)
42	II	70b (Ethics and the Q)
	V	382a, 382b (Trust and Patience)
43	III	22b (Jews and Judaism); 372b (Memory); 381b (Messenger)
	IV	129b (Politics and the Q); 230a (Prayer); 296a, 302a (Prophets and Prophethood)
	V	546b (Word of God)
43-44	V	301b, 303b (Torah)
43-45	IV	570b (Scrolls)
44	III	441b (Muḥammad)
	IV	302a (Prophets and Prophethood)
47	IV	5b (Pairs and Pairing)
48	II	363b (Grammar and the Q); 401b (Hand)
48-49	I	160b (Arrogance); 254b (Bowing and Prostration)
	IV	221a (Prayer)
48-50	I	435a (Conversion)
49	I	99b (Animal Life); 254b (Bowing and Prostration)
	IV	4b (Pairs and Pairing); 219b (Prayer); 264a (Pride)
	V	393a (Turkish Literature and the Q)
49-50	IV	378a (Recitation of the Q)
51	II	329b (God and his Attributes)
	III	550b (Numbers and Enumeration)
	V	369a (Trinity); 500a (Witnessing and Testifying)
52	I	472a (Creation)
	IV	4a (Pairs and Pairing)
55	I	220b (Belief and Unbelief); 236b (Blessing)

56 I 236a (Blasphemy)

57 I 221b (Belief and Unbelief); 236a (Blasphemy); 330a (Chronology and the Q)
II 317b (God and his Attributes)
III 48a (Jinn)
V 369a (Trinity)

57-58 II 511a (Infanticide)

57-59 I 301b, 302b (Children)
II 329b (God and his Attributes)
IV 255b (Pre-Islamic Arabia and the Q)
V 318a (Tradition and Custom)

58 I 364b (Colors)

58-59 I 38b (Age of Ignorance); 153b (Archaeology and the Q); 221b (Belief and Unbelief)
II 64a (Ethics and the Q); 341a (Good News)
V 524b (Women and the Q)

61 I 98a (Animal Life); 501a (Day, Times of)
II 45a (Eschatology)
III 185a (Life); 335b (Measurement); 378b (Mercy)
V 288a, 289a (Time)

62 I 83a (Anatomy)
IV 15a (Paradise)

63 II 274a (Friends and Friendship)
III 561a (Oaths)
IV 217a (Prayer); 301b (Prophets and Prophethood)

64 III 40a (Jihād); 442b (Muḥammad)

65 II 3a (Earth); 302b (Geography)
V 3b (Signs); 463a (Water); 545a (Word of God)

65-69 I 473b (Creation)

66 I 96a (Animal Life); 237b (Blood and Blood Clot)
II 218a (Food and Drink)
III 391a (Milk)

66-69 III 169a (Law and the Q)
V 482a (Wine)

66-83 I 236b (Blessing)

67 I 495a (Date Palm)
II 221b (Food and Drink); 304b, 305b (Geography); 556a (Intoxicants)
III 152a (Law and the Q)
IV 183a (Portents)
V 179a (Sustenance)

68	II	305a (Geography)
	IV	217a (Prayer); 293b (Prophets and Prophethood); 439b (Revelation and Inspiration)
	V	544a (Word of God)
68-69	I	96b, 100b (Animal Life)
	III	309a (Material Culture and the Q)
69	I	96a (Animal Life); 361b (Colors)
	II	38a (Epigraphy); 445b, 446b, 447a (Honey)
	III	349b (Medicine and the Q)
	IV	29a (Path or Way)
70	I	345b (Clients and Clientage); 479a (Creation)
	IV	6a (Pairs and Pairing)
71	IV	186b (Possession and Possessions); 288a (Property); 579a (Servants)
	V	57a (Slaves and Slavery); 179b (Sustenance); 269b (Theology and the Q); 550b (Work)
72	I	235a (Birth Control); 302b (Children)
	II	328b (God and his Attributes); 510a (Indifference)
	III	277b (Marriage and Divorce)
73	I	472b (Creation)
	IV	4a (Pairs and Pairing)
	V	179a (Sustenance)
75	IV	10a (Parable); 185a (Possession and Possessions); 538b (Scholar); 576b (Servants)
	V	58b (Slaves and Slavery)
76	I	344b (Clients and Clientage)
	II	5b (Economics); 70a (Ethics and the Q)
	III	228a (Load or Burden); 231a (Lord)
	IV	7a (Pairs and Pairing); 10a (Parable)
	V	57a (Slaves and Slavery)
77	I	501a (Day, Times of)
	III	137a, 138a (Last Judgment)
	IV	4a (Pairs and Pairing)
	V	287b, 288a (Time)
78	I	81a, 83b (Anatomy)
	IV	20a (Parents)
	V	570a (Youth and Old Age)
78-81	IV	438a (Revelation and Inspiration)
79	I	51b (Air and Wind); 98a (Animal Life); 473b (Creation)
	IV	183b (Portents)
80	I	96a (Animal Life); 215b (Bedouin)
	II	426a, 426b (Hides and Fleece)

	III	544a (Nomads)
	V	7b (Signs); 12a (Silk); 235b (Tents and Tent Pegs); 374a (Trips and Voyages)
80-81	I	472a, 473a (Creation)
80-83	II	275b (Furniture and Furnishings); 459a, 459b (House, Domestic and Divine)
81	I	346b (Clothing)
	II	455a (Hot and Cold)
	IV	307b (Protection)
	V	12a (Silk)
82	III	40a (Jihād); 125a (Language and Style of the Q)
	V	291b (Tolerance and Coercion)
83	I	220b (Belief and Unbelief)
	II	489a (Ignorance)
84	II	497a (Illiteracy)
	III	382a (Messenger); 447a (Muḥammad)
	IV	300b (Prophets and Prophethood)
	V	493b (Witnessing and Testifying)
86	II	477a, 477b (Idolatry and Idolaters)
	V	494a (Witnessing and Testifying)
87	I	236a (Blasphemy)
	II	99a (Evil Deeds)
88	II	62b (Ethics and the Q)
	IV	458b (Reward and Punishment)
89	II	341a, 341b (Good News); 497a (Illiteracy)
	III	19b (Jesus); 124b (Language and Style of the Q); 382a (Messenger); 442b, 447a (Muḥammad); 506b, 511a (Names of the Q)
	IV	300b (Prophets and Prophethood); 542b (Science and the Q)
	V	319a, 322b, 323a (Traditional Disciplines of Q Studies); 493b (Witnessing and Testifying)
90	I	64b (Almsgiving)
	II	61b, 70a (Ethics and the Q); 176a (Family)
	III	70a, 70b, 71b (Justice and Injustice)
	IV	1b (Pairs and Pairing); 84a (Philosophy and the Q); 580b, 583b (Sex and Sexuality)
	V	438a (Virtues and Vices, Commanding and Forbidding)
91	I	256b (Breaking Trusts and Contracts); 379b (Community and Society in the Q); 431a (Contracts and Alliances); 465b (Covenant)
	II	8b (Economics)
91-92	III	564b (Oaths)
91-93	IV	136b (Politics and the Q)
92	II	431b (History and the Q)
	V	535a (Women and the Q)

93 I 523a (Destiny)
II 72a (Ethics and the Q); 270a (Freedom and Predestination); 320b, 330b (God and his Attributes)
IV 2a (Pairs and Pairing); 337a (Races); 431a (Responsibility)

94 II 199a (Feet); 335b (Good and Evil)
III 564b, 565a (Oaths)

95 III 276a (Markets)

96 IV 5a (Pairs and Pairing)
V 340a (Transitoriness)

97 III 492b (Myths and Legends in the Q)
V 134a (Suffering); 524a (Women and the Q)

98 II 92a (Everyday Life, Q In)
IV 221b (Prayer); 308a (Protection)
V 130a (Stoning)

101 I 15a, 17a (Abrogation); 321a (Chronology and the Q)
III 160b (Law and the Q)
IV 538b (Scholar)
V 6b (Signs)

102 I 87a (Angel)
II 341a, 341b (Good News); 442a, 443a (Holy Spirit)
III 13b (Jesus); 293b (Mary); 442a (Muḥammad); 510b (Names of the Q)
IV 216b (Prayer); 282b (Profane and Sacred); 293a (Prophets and Prophethood)
V 81a (Soul); 115b (Spirit); 120a (Spiritual Beings); 371b (Trinity)

103 I 132a (Arabic Language); 145a (Arabs)
II 226b, 227a (Foreign Vocabulary); 420b (Heresy); 512b, 513a, 513b, 516b, 517a (Informants)
III 103b (Knowledge and Learning); 109a (Language, Concept of); 110a, 113b, 114a, 114b, 117a, 124b (Language and Style of the Q); 450a, 451a, 456a (Muḥammad); 473a (Mysterious Letters); 507a (Names of the Q)
IV 116b (Polemic and Polemical Language); 331a (Quraysh); 337b (Races); 439b, 443b, 444a (Revelation and Inspiration); 473b (Rhetoric and the Q); 566a (Scripture and the Q)
V 132a (Strangers and Foreigners); 202b (Teaching); 301b (Torah); 547a (Word of God)

104 I 523a (Destiny)
II 270a (Freedom and Predestination)

106 I 93a (Anger); 119a, 120b (Apostasy); 224b (Belief and Unbelief); 540a, 541a (Dissimulation)
II 171b (Faith); 408a (Heart)
III 378b (Mercy)
IV 310a (Provocation); 456a (Reward and Punishment); 573a (Secrets)

107 I 368b (Community and Society in the Q)

108 I 82a (Anatomy); 225b (Belief and Unbelief)
II 489a (Ignorance)

110 II 70b (Ethics and the Q)
III 37a (Jihād); 579a (Opposition to Muḥammad)

111 I 512a, 513b (Debate and Disputation)
III 68a (Judgment)
IV 457b (Reward and Punishment)

112 I 346b (Clothing)
III 524b (Narratives)
IV 10a (Parable); 332a (Quraysh)

113 IV 453a (Reward and Punishment)

114 I 236b (Blessing)

115 I 96b, 97a (Animal Life); 237b (Blood and Blood Clot); 291b, 292a (Carrion)
III 174a (Lawful and Unlawful); 378b (Mercy)
IV 517b (Sacrifice)
V 55a (Slaughter)

116 I 83a (Anatomy); 236a (Blasphemy)
III 173a, 174b (Lawful and Unlawful)

117 III 60a (Joy and Misery)

118 III 25a (Jews and Judaism); 173a, 174b (Lawful and Unlawful); 517b (Narratives)

119 II 335b (Good and Evil); 488b (Ignorance)
III 378b (Mercy)
IV 427a (Repentance and Penance)

120 I 5b (Abraham); 373a (Community and Society in the Q)
II 402b (Ḥanīf); 497b (Illiteracy)
IV 35a (Peace); 223a (Prayer)
V 268b, 271a (Theology and the Q)

120-121 II 372b (Gratitude and Ingratitude)

121 I 236b (Blessing)
II 11b (Election)
IV 291b (Prophets and Prophethood)

122-123 V 271a (Theology and the Q)

122-124 I 220b (Belief and Unbelief)

123 I 5b, 6a (Abraham); 330b (Chronology and the Q); 373a (Community and Society in the Q)
II 402b (Ḥanīf)
III 445b (Muḥammad)
IV 299b (Prophets and Prophethood)

124 I 500b (Day, Times of)
II 321a (God and his Attributes)

IV 132b (Politics and the Q); 510b (Sabbath)
V 285b (Time)

125 I 115b (Apologetics); 437a (Conversion); 511b, 513b (Debate and Disputation)
II 142b (Exhortations); 209a (Fighting); 452b (Hospitality and Courtesy); 557b (Invitation)
III 40a (Jihād); 453b (Muḥammad)
IV 71a (Philosophy and the Q); 309b (Provocation)
V 203b (Teaching); 207b, 221b (Teaching and Preaching the Q)

125-128 III 577b (Opposition to Muḥammad)

126 I 450a (Cosmology)
III 40a, 40b (Jihād)
V 417a (Vengeance)

127 I 406a (Consolation)
II 149a (Expeditions and Battles)
III 452b (Muḥammad); 577b (Opposition to Muḥammad)
V 134a (Suffering)

Sūrat al-Isrāʾ (17)

I 176b (Ascension)
II 310b (Geography); 390b (Ḥadīth and the Q)
III 521b (Narratives)
IV 597b (Shīʿism and the Q)
V 172b (Sūra); 376a (Trips and Voyages)

1 I 88a, 89a (Angel); 111a (Antichrist); 125a, 126b (Aqṣā Mosque); 156a (Archaeology and the Q); 163b, 164a (Art and Architecture and the Q); 177a, 177b (Ascension); 320b (Chronology and the Q); 501b (Day, Times of)
II 154a (Eyes); 215b (Flying); 253a (Form and Structure of the Q); 299a, 299b, 309a, 309b (Geography); 314b (Glorification of God); 320b, 324b, 325b (God and his Attributes); 392b (Ḥadīth and the Q)
III 3a (Jerusalem); 77b (Kaʿba); 222a (Literature and the Q); 327a (Material Culture and the Q); 340a (Mecca); 388b (Michael); 427a (Mosque); 440b, 452a (Muḥammad); 482b, 488b, 491b, 496a (Myths and Legends in the Q)
IV 5b (Pairs and Pairing); 64a (Persian Literature and the Q); 179a (Popular and Talismanic Uses of the Q); 216b, 220b (Prayer); 450a (Revision and Alteration); 514a, 515a (Sacred Precincts); 577a (Servants)
V 107a, 107b (Spatial Relations); 138b, 157b (Ṣūfism and the Q); 185a (Syria); 376a (Trips and Voyages); 393a (Turkish Literature and the Q)

1-6 I 126b (Aqṣā Mosque)

2 I 245a (Book)
II 309b (Geography)
III 424b, 425a (Moses)
V 301a, 302a (Torah); 380b (Trust and Patience)

2-8	I	303a (Children of Israel)
	II	260b (Form and Structure of the Q)
3	II	372b (Gratitude and Ingratitude)
	III	486b (Myths and Legends in the Q)
3-4	II	269b (Freedom and Predestination)
4	II	185b (Fate); 562b (Isaiah)
4-8	II	146a, 146b, 147a, 152a (Expeditions and Battles)
	V	456a (War)
5	I	163b (Art and Architecture and the Q)
	IV	577a (Servants)
6	I	302b (Children)
	II	6b (Economics)
	IV	3b (Pairs and Pairing)
	V	468a (Wealth)
7	I	163b (Art and Architecture and the Q)
	II	299b (Geography)
	V	184b (Syria)
8	II	146b, 150b (Expeditions and Battles)
	IV	277b (Prisoners)
9	II	341a, 341b (Good News)
9-10	II	341b (Good News)
10	II	341b (Good News)
11	II	56b (Ethics and the Q)
	IV	229a (Prayer)
	V	203b, 204b (Teaching)
12	I	272b (Calendar); 442b, 443a (Cosmology); 473a, 473b (Creation); 498a (Day and Night); 502a (Day, Times of)
	II	433a (History and the Q)
	III	535a (Nature as Signs)
	IV	4b (Pairs and Pairing)
	V	280b, 284a (Time)
13	I	90b (Angel)
	II	48a (Eschatology); 412b (Heavenly Book)
	III	140b (Last Judgment)
	V	493b (Witnessing and Testifying)
13-14	I	522b, 523b (Destiny)
	V	493a (Witnessing and Testifying)
14	I	298a (Chastisement and Punishment)
	V	493b (Witnessing and Testifying)

15	I	225b (Belief and Unbelief); 297b (Chastisement and Punishment)
	III	228a (Load or Burden); 379b (Mercy); 382a (Messenger)
	IV	1b (Pairs and Pairing); 301b (Prophets and Prophethood); 432a (Responsibility)
	V	22a (Sin, Major and Minor)
16	II	348a (Grammar and the Q)
	V	547b (Word of God)
16-17	V	22a (Sin, Major and Minor)
17	II	293a (Generations)
	IV	320a (Punishment Stories)
18	II	418a (Hell and Hellfire)
19	II	372b (Gratitude and Ingratitude)
20	II	313a (Gift-Giving)
22	I	501a (Day, Times of)
	III	443a (Muḥammad)
22-39	I	366b, 367a (Commandments)
	III	210a (Literature and the Q)
23	II	61b, 75b (Ethics and the Q); 386a (Ḥadīth and the Q); 453a (Hospitality and Courtesy)
	III	252a (Maintenance and Upkeep)
	IV	21a (Parents)
	V	27a (Sin, Major and Minor)
23-24	III	378a (Mercy)
	IV	20b (Parents)
	V	204b (Teaching); 570b (Youth and Old Age)
23-38	V	20b, 27a (Sin, Major and Minor)
23-39	II	71a (Ethics and the Q)
24	I	237a (Blessing); 302b (Children)
	II	175b (Family)
	III	277b (Marriage and Divorce); 379b (Mercy); 385a (Metaphor)
	IV	20b (Parents)
25	IV	428a (Repentance and Penance)
	V	82a (Soul)
26	II	448a (Honor)
	III	252a (Maintenance and Upkeep)
	IV	63b (Persian Literature and the Q)
	V	434a (Virtue)
26-27	IV	186a (Possession and Possessions)
26-29	I	181a (Asceticism)
27	I	220b (Belief and Unbelief); 262b (Brother and Brotherhood)
	III	44b, 46b (Jinn)
	V	434a (Virtue)

28 I 503b (Day, Times of)

29 I 38a (Age of Ignorance)
II 7b (Economics)
V 434b (Virtue)

31 I 2b (Abortion); 233a (Birth); 234b (Birth Control); 301b (Children); 450b (Cosmology)
II 75a (Ethics and the Q); 511a (Infanticide)
III 182a, 183a (Life)
V 19a, 21a (Sin, Major and Minor)

32 I 28a (Adultery and Fornication); 38b (Age of Ignorance); 299b (Chastity)
II 7a (Economics); 63a (Ethics and the Q)
IV 580b (Sex and Sexuality)
V 19a, 21a (Sin, Major and Minor); 528a (Women and the Q); 19a (Sin, Major and Minor)

33 I 38a (Age of Ignorance); 190a (Authority); 239a (Blood Money); 450b (Cosmology)
III 157a (Law and the Q); 182a, 183b (Life); 401a (Moderation); 458b (Murder)
V 83a (Soul); 162a (Suicide); 2a (Ṣiffīn, Battle of); 417a (Vengeance)

34 I 431a, 431b (Contracts and Alliances); 464b (Covenant)
II 8b (Economics); 373b (Guardianship)
III 330a (Maturity); 603b (Orphans)

35 II 8b (Economics); 231b (Foreign Vocabulary); 545b (Instruments)
III 66a (Judgment); 276a (Markets); 334a, 334b, 336a (Measurement)

36 IV 573a (Secrets)

37 III 333a (Measurement)
V 393b (Turkish Literature and the Q)

38 V 21a (Sin, Major and Minor)

39 III 443a (Muḥammad); 512a (Names of the Q)
IV 294b (Prophets and Prophethood)
V 483a (Wisdom); 546a (Word of God)

41 III 212a (Literature and the Q)

42 II 325b (God and his Attributes)
V 277a (Throne of God)

44 II 82a (Everyday Life, Q In); 315a (Glorification of God)
III 552a (Numbers and Enumeration)
IV 5b (Pairs and Pairing); 107b (Planets and Stars); 214b (Praise)

45 V 412b (Veil)
I 203b (Barrier)

45-46 II 510b (Indifference)

46 I 80a (Anatomy); 226a (Belief and Unbelief)
II 370b (Gratitude and Ingratitude)

	IV	118a (Polemic and Polemical Language)
	V	447a (Vision and Blindness); 474a (Weights and Measures)
47	III	44a (Jinn)
	V	479b (Whisper)
49	II	4b (Earth)
	III	448b (Muḥammad)
	IV	435a (Resurrection)
49-51	I	479a, 479b (Creation)
	IV	311a (Provocation)
49-52	IV	311a (Provocation)
50	III	383b (Metals and Minerals)
	V	129b (Stone)
51	IV	119a (Polemic and Polemical Language)
52	II	558b (Invitation)
53	I	453b (Cosmology); 526a (Devil)
	II	23b, 24a (Enemies); 452b (Hospitality and Courtesy)
	III	44b (Jinn)
	IV	309b (Provocation)
54	I	225b (Belief and Unbelief)
	III	40a (Jihād); 452b (Muḥammad)
	IV	2a (Pairs and Pairing)
55	I	235b (Blasphemy); 496a (David)
	III	381b (Messenger); 487a (Myths and Legends in the Q)
	IV	4a (Pairs and Pairing); 36b (People of the Book); 292a, 297b (Prophets and Prophethood); 315a (Psalms)
57	II	448b (Hope)
	III	380a (Mercy)
	IV	163b (Popular and Talismanic Uses of the Q)
58	I	244a (Book); 523a (Destiny)
	III	518a (Narratives)
	IV	457a (Reward and Punishment)
	V	558a (Writing and Writing Materials)
59	I	235b (Blasphemy); 287a (Camel)
	III	219a (Literature and the Q)
	IV	296b (Prophets and Prophethood); 521b (Ṣāliḥ)
60	I	546b, 551b (Dreams and Sleep)
	II	241b (Foretelling in the Q); 305a (Geography)
	III	4a, 5b (Jerusalem); 533a (Nature as Signs)
	IV	179a (Popular and Talismanic Uses of the Q); 295a (Prophets and Prophethood)
	V	359b (Tree); 444a (Vision); 446a (Vision and Blindness); 571a, 571b (Zaqqūm)

61	I	24a (Adam and Eve); 255a (Bowing and Prostration); 339b (Clay); 447a (Cosmology); 476a (Creation); 511a (Debate and Disputation); 525a (Devil)
	II	4a, 4b (Earth); 172b (Fall of Man)
	III	45a (Jinn); 532a (Nature as Signs)
	IV	220a (Prayer)
	V	109a (Speech)
61-65	I	448a, 453b (Cosmology)
	III	521b (Narratives)
	V	109a (Speech)
62	I	453b (Cosmology)
	II	172b (Fall of Man)
62-63	II	417b (Hell and Hellfire)
63	II	172b (Fall of Man)
64	I	98b (Animal Life)
	II	75a (Ethics and the Q); 198b (Feet); 336a (Good and Evil)
	V	468a (Wealth)
65	I	453b (Cosmology)
66	I	52a (Air and Wind)
	III	379a (Mercy)
	V	373a (Trips and Voyages); 412a (Vehicles); 464a (Water)
66-70	I	54a (Air and Wind)
67	I	519a (Deliverance)
	V	464a (Water)
68	IV	530b (Sand)
69	I	52b (Air and Wind); 554a (Drowning)
	V	470b (Weather)
70	I	53b (Air and Wind); 96b (Animal Life)
	II	3a (Earth); 328b (God and his Attributes); 447b (Honor)
	IV	4b (Pairs and Pairing)
	V	373a (Trips and Voyages); 411a (Vehicles)
71	I	243b, 244a (Book)
	II	269b (Freedom and Predestination); 503a (Imām); 558b (Invitation)
	III	177a (Left Hand and Right Hand)
	IV	16a (Paradise); 34b (Peace); 560a (Scripture and the Q)
	V	493a, 493b (Witnessing and Testifying)
71-72	I	522b (Destiny)
73	III	578b (Opposition to Muḥammad)
	IV	532b (Satanic Verses)
73-74	III	41b (Jihād)
73-75	III	454a (Muḥammad)

74	II	508b (Impotence)
75	IV	6b (Pairs and Pairing)
76	III	449a, 454b (Muḥammad)
	V	458b (War)
76-77	IV	301b (Prophets and Prophethood)
77	V	164a (Sunna)
78	I	499a, 502b, 503a, 504b (Day, Times of)
	II	28b (Epigraphy); 79b (Evening); 82a (Everyday Life, Q In); 272b (Friday Prayer)
	III	417a, 419a (Morning); 586a (Orality)
	IV	221b, 222a, 222b (Prayer); 281a (Profane and Sacred)
	V	163a (Sun); 281a, 282b (Time)
78-79	I	327b (Chronology and the Q); 502b (Day, Times of)
	II	340a (Good Deeds)
	III	305a (Material Culture and the Q); 437a (Mosque)
	V	556b (Worship)
78-80	I	502b (Day, Times of)
79	I	182a, 182b (Asceticism); 328a (Chronology and the Q); 503a (Day, Times of)
	II	29a (Epigraphy); 326a (God and his Attributes); 552b (Intercession)
	III	446b (Muḥammad)
	IV	222a (Prayer)
	V	430b (Vigil)
79-80	IV	231b (Prayer Formulas)
80	IV	282b (Profane and Sacred)
81	III	558b (Numismatics)
82	I	77b (Amulets)
	II	446b (Honey)
	III	362a (Medicine and the Q); 512a (Names of the Q)
	IV	166b, 168b, 171b (Popular and Talismanic Uses of the Q)
82-111	II	143a (Exhortations)
83	I	521a (Despair)
	II	56b (Ethics and the Q)
85	I	87b (Angel)
	II	442a, 443b (Holy Spirit)
	III	579b (Opposition to Muḥammad)
	V	81b (Soul); 115b (Spirit); 266a, 266b, 272a (Theology and the Q)
86-87	III	379a (Mercy); 442b (Muḥammad); 512a (Names of the Q)
88	I	115a (Apologetics)
	II	527a, 529b (Inimitability)
	III	46b (Jinn); 116a (Language and Style of the Q); 199a (Literary Structures of the Q); 398b (Miracles); 468a (Muʿtazila); 601a (Ornamentation and Illumination)

IV 22b (Parody of the Q); 211a (Power and Impotence); 280b (Profane and Sacred); 312b (Provocation); 443a (Revelation and Inspiration)

90 I 42a (Agriculture and Vegetation)
IV 296a (Prophets and Prophethood)
V 121b (Springs and Fountains); 463b (Water)

90-91 V 127b (Springs and Fountains)

90-93 I 177a, 177b (Ascension); 222a (Belief and Unbelief)
III 397b (Miracles); 450a, 456a (Muḥammad)
IV 119a (Polemic and Polemical Language); 311b (Provocation); 331a (Quraysh)
V 37b, 41a (Sīra and the Q); 271b (Theology and the Q)

91 I 41a (Agriculture and Vegetation)
II 217b (Food and Drink); 283a (Garden); 304a (Geography)
V 463b (Water)

92 IV 311b (Provocation)

93 I 163a (Art and Architecture and the Q); 250a (Book)
III 452a (Muḥammad); 591b (Orality and Writing in Arabia)
IV 220a (Prayer); 311b (Provocation); 354b (Readings of the Q); 569b (Scrolls)

94 III 449b (Muḥammad)
IV 301a (Prophets and Prophethood)

95 IV 290a (Prophets and Prophethood)

97 II 273b (Friends and Friendship); 406b (Hearing and Deafness)
III 140b (Last Judgment)
IV 103b (Pit)

98 I 479b (Creation)
II 4b (Earth)
III 448b (Muḥammad)

98-99 I 479a (Creation)
II 44b (Eschatology); 166a (Faith)

99 I 479b (Creation)

101 I 365b, 366a (Commandments)
II 542b (Insolence and Obstinacy)
III 394a (Miracles); 421b, 422a (Moses); 552b (Numbers and Enumeration)
IV 67b (Pharaoh); 106a (Plagues); 286a (Proof); 296b (Prophets and Prophethood)
V 8a (Signs)

101-102 IV 287a (Proof)

101-103 IV 320a (Punishment Stories)

101-104 III 521b (Narratives)

102 II 489a (Ignorance)
IV 184a (Possession and Possessions); 288a (Property)

103	I	553b (Drowning)
	II	213a (Fire)
	III	423a (Moses)
	IV	67a (Pharaoh)
104	III	488a (Myths and Legends in the Q)
	IV	589b (Shekhinah)
	V	110b (Speech)
105	II	341b (Good News)
	IV	3b (Pairs and Pairing); 148b (Politics and the Q)
	V	307b (Torah)
106	I	250b (Book)
	III	440b, 442a (Muḥammad); 510b, 514b (Names of the Q)
	IV	343a, 344a, 346a (Ramaḍān); 444a, 446a (Revelation and Inspiration)
107	I	247b (Book); 254b (Bowing and Prostration)
	II	158b (Face)
	III	190a (Literacy)
	IV	221b (Prayer); 378a (Recitation of the Q); 538b, 539a (Scholar)
	V	203b (Teaching); 393a (Turkish Literature and the Q)
107-109	III	23b (Jews and Judaism)
	IV	369a (Recitation of the Q); 494a (Ritual and the Q)
108	IV	220b (Prayer)
109	I	183b (Asceticism)
	II	158b (Face)
	IV	494a (Ritual and the Q)
	V	471b (Weeping)
110	I	327b (Chronology and the Q)
	II	317b, 319b (God and his Attributes); 387b (Ḥadīth and the Q)
	III	378b (Mercy); 401b (Moderation)
	IV	185a (Possession and Possessions); 222a, 229b (Prayer); 380a (Recitation of the Q)
	V	501a (Witnessing and Testifying)
111	I	170b (Art and Architecture and the Q)
	II	273b (Friends and Friendship); 329a, 329b (God and his Attributes)
	III	92b (Kings and Rulers); 299b (Material Culture and the Q)
	IV	128a (Politics and the Q); 213b (Praise); 220b (Prayer)
	V	308a (Torah); 369a (Trinity)

Sūrat al-Kahf (18)

I 292b (Cave); 511b (Debate and Disputation)

II 94a (Everyday Life, Q In); 261a (Form and Structure of the Q); 385a, 393b (Ḥadīth and the Q); 436a (History and the Q)

III 283b (Martyrs); 320b, 327b (Material Culture and the Q); 374b (Men of the Cave); 494a (Myths and Legends in the Q); 508b (Names of the Q); 520a (Narratives); 533b, 535b (Nature as Signs)
IV 238a, 244a (Pre-1800 Preoccupations of Q Studies); 351b (Raqīm); 380a (Recitation of the Q); 495b (Ritual and the Q)
V 61b (Sleep); 98b (Southeast Asian Q Literature); 251a (Textual Criticism of the Q)

1 III 317b (Material Culture and the Q); 513a (Names of the Q)
IV 213b (Praise); 297a (Prophets and Prophethood); 577a (Servants)

1-6 II 143a (Exhortations)

1-8 III 520a (Narratives)

1-25 II 37b (Epigraphy)

2 II 341a, 341b (Good News)
III 513a (Names of the Q)

2-3 II 54b (Eternity)

5 II 365b (Grammar and the Q)

6 II 510b (Indifference)
III 452b (Muḥammad)
V 134a (Suffering)

7 I 213a (Beauty); 473b (Creation)
II 3b (Earth)
III 535b (Nature as Signs)
V 133b (Suffering)

7-8 II 3b (Earth)

8 I 478a (Creation)

9 I 292b (Cave)
III 287a (Marvels); 375a (Men of the Cave); 396a (Miracles)
IV 351a (Raqīm)
V 185a (Syria); 251a (Textual Criticism of the Q)

9-10 III 374a (Men of the Cave)

9-12 I 292b (Cave)

9-25 IV 435a (Resurrection)

9-26 I 314b (Christians and Christianity); 545b (Dog)
III 219a (Literature and the Q); 520a (Narratives)
V 375b (Trips and Voyages)

9-27 I 151b (Archaeology and the Q)

9-98 III 520a (Narratives)

10 I 292b (Cave)

11 I 292b (Cave)
II 1a (Ears); 433b (History and the Q)
V 61b (Sleep); 285b (Time)

11-17	III	374a (Men of the Cave)
12	III	335a (Measurement)
	V	61b (Sleep); 241b (Textual Criticism of the Q); 288b (Time); 475a (Weights and Measures)
13	III	441a (Muḥammad); 517b (Narratives); 537a (News)
	IV	302b (Prophets and Prophethood)
14	IV	4a (Pairs and Pairing); 184a (Possession and Possessions); 288a (Property)
15	I	236a (Blasphemy)
	III	181a (Lie)
16	I	292b (Cave)
	III	523b (Narratives)
17	I	292b (Cave); 503b (Day, Times of); 523a (Destiny)
	II	273b (Friends and Friendship); 401b (Hand)
	III	396a (Miracles)
	IV	107a (Planets and Stars)
	V	163a (Sun); 282b (Time)
18	I	98a, 99a (Animal Life); 546a (Dog)
	II	198a (Fear); 401b (Hand)
	IV	351b, 352a (Raqīm)
	V	61b (Sleep); 251b (Textual Criticism of the Q)
18-21	III	374b (Men of the Cave)
19	II	365b (Grammar and the Q); 433b (History and the Q)
	III	408b (Money)
	V	61b (Sleep); 179a (Sustenance)
20	V	130b (Stoning)
21	I	164a (Art and Architecture and the Q); 501a (Day, Times of)
	III	137a (Last Judgment); 427a (Mosque)
	V	287b (Time); 386b (Truth)
22	I	99a (Animal Life); 546a (Dog)
	II	364a (Grammar and the Q)
	III	550a, 552b (Numbers and Enumeration)
	IV	351b (Raqīm)
22-26	III	374b (Men of the Cave)
23	II	354a (Grammar and the Q)
	III	524a (Narratives)
	V	281a (Time)
23-24	IV	63a (Persian Literature and the Q)
	V	484b (Wish and Desire)
24	III	373b (Memory)
	IV	230b (Prayer); 487b (Ritual and the Q)
	V	138b (Ṣūfism and the Q)

25	I	147b (Arbitration); 292b (Cave)
	II	364a (Grammar and the Q); 433b (History and the Q)
	III	549b (Numbers and Enumeration)
	V	285b (Time)
26	II	273a (Friends and Friendship)
	IV	4a (Pairs and Pairing); 574a (Seeing and Hearing)
	V	103a (Sovereignty)
27	I	245b (Book)
	III	190a (Literacy); 441a, 441b (Muḥammad)
	IV	297a (Prophets and Prophethood)
	V	203a (Teaching); 548a (Word of God)
27-28	I	389b (Companions of the Prophet)
27-31	III	520a (Narratives)
28	I	328a (Chronology and the Q); 503a, 503b (Day, Times of)
	II	80a (Evening); 323b (God and his Attributes); 364b (Grammar and the Q); 489a (Ignorance)
	III	417a, 418b (Morning); 453a (Muḥammad); 567b (Obedience)
	IV	222a, 223a (Prayer); 432a (Responsibility)
	V	281b (Time); 486b (Wish and Desire)
29	I	74a (Ambiguous); 186a (Astray); 225b (Belief and Unbelief)
	II	59b (Ethics and the Q); 210b, 211a (Fire); 270a (Freedom and Predestination); 416a (Hell and Hellfire)
	III	203b (Literary Structures of the Q); 383b (Metals and Minerals)
	IV	238b (Pre-1800 Preoccupations of Q Studies)
	V	15a (Simile); 133a (Suffering); 236a (Tents and Tent Pegs); 465a (Water); 486a (Wish and Desire)
29-31	I	522b (Destiny)
30	II	362b (Grammar and the Q)
30-44	V	486a (Wish and Desire)
31	I	220b (Belief and Unbelief); 362b (Colors)
	II	228b, 231b (Foreign Vocabulary); 276a (Furniture and Furnishings); 282b (Garden); 333b (Gold); 353b, 365b (Grammar and the Q)
	III	204a (Literary Structures of the Q); 383b (Metals and Minerals); 534a (Nature as Signs)
	IV	13b, 18a (Paradise)
	V	11b, 12b (Silk); 106b (Spatial Relations); 393b (Turkish Literature and the Q)
32	I	41a (Agriculture and Vegetation)
	II	3b (Earth); 260a (Form and Structure of the Q); 305b (Geography)
	III	524b (Narratives)
32-35	II	283a (Garden)
32-43	IV	320a (Punishment Stories)

32-44 III 520a (Narratives); 533b (Nature as Signs)
IV 7a (Pairs and Pairing); 10a, 10b (Parable)

32-45 V 14a (Simile)

32-46 V 127b (Springs and Fountains)

33 III 524a (Narratives)

34 V 468a (Wealth)

35 III 71a (Justice and Injustice)

36 I 501a (Day, Times of)
III 137a (Last Judgment)
V 287b (Time)

37 I 477a (Creation)
II 290b (Gender); 328a (God and his Attributes)
III 354b (Medicine and the Q)
V 267a (Theology and the Q); 324b (Traditional Disciplines of Q Studies)

38 II 96a (Everyday Life, Q In); 352b (Grammar and the Q)

39 II 36a (Epigraphy); 367a (Grammar and the Q)
III 586b (Orality)
V 468a (Wealth)

40 I 504a (Day, Times of)
II 3b (Earth)

41 I 42a (Agriculture and Vegetation); 504a (Day, Times of)

42 I 166a (Art and Architecture and the Q); 504a (Day, Times of)
II 401a (Hand)
III 533b (Nature as Signs)

44 IV 307b (Protection)

45 I 40b, 41b (Agriculture and Vegetation); 52a, 54b (Air and Wind); 504a (Day, Times of)
II 3a, 3b (Earth); 260a (Form and Structure of the Q); 320b (God and his Attributes); 369b (Grasses)
III 530b (Nature as Signs)
IV 10a (Parable)
V 339b (Transitoriness); 462b (Water)

45-50 III 520a (Narratives)

46 I 302b (Children)
II 6b (Economics); 448b (Hope)
III 530b (Nature as Signs)
IV 3b (Pairs and Pairing); 10b (Parable); 288b (Property)
V 468a (Wealth)

48 III 140b (Last Judgment)
IV 349b (Ranks and Orders); 435a (Resurrection)

49	I	243b (Book)
	II	412b (Heavenly Book)
	III	147b (Laughter)
	V	19a (Sin, Major and Minor); 493a, 493b (Witnessing and Testifying)
50	I	24a (Adam and Eve); 255a (Bowing and Prostration); 447a (Cosmology); 525a, 526b, 527a (Devil)
	II	23b (Enemies); 172b (Fall of Man); 274a (Friends and Friendship)
	III	44b, 45a (Jinn); 523b (Narratives)
	IV	220a (Prayer); 336b (Races)
	V	109a (Speech)
51	V	82a (Soul)
52	II	64a (Ethics and the Q); 477a (Idolatry and Idolaters)
53	II	64a (Ethics and the Q); 119a (Exegesis of the Q: Classical and Medieval); 416a (Hell and Hellfire)
54	I	512a, 512b, 513b (Debate and Disputation)
	III	398b (Miracles); 579b (Opposition to Muḥammad)
	V	16a (Simile)
55	II	434a (History and the Q)
	IV	332b (Quraysh)
	V	164a (Sunna)
55-59	IV	320b (Punishment Stories)
56	I	512a (Debate and Disputation)
	II	341b (Good News)
	III	382a (Messenger); 400a (Mockery)
	IV	3b (Pairs and Pairing); 300a (Prophets and Prophethood)
	V	5b (Signs); 460b (Warner)
57	I	226a (Belief and Unbelief); 437a (Conversion)
	II	64b (Ethics and the Q); 330b (God and his Attributes)
	IV	309b (Provocation); 422b (Remembrance); 432a (Responsibility)
	V	5b (Signs); 474a (Weights and Measures)
57-58	III	380a (Mercy)
58	II	322a (God and his Attributes)
	IV	5b (Pairs and Pairing)
60	III	426a (Moses); 523b (Narratives)
60-64	II	465a (Humor)
	V	122b (Springs and Fountains)
60-65	V	464a (Water)
60-82	I	61a (Alexander); 189a (Authority)
	III	81b (Khaḍir/Khiḍr); 184b (Life); 249b (Magic); 425b (Moses); 520a (Narratives)
	V	108a (Spatial Relations); 203b (Teaching); 375b (Trips and Voyages)
61	III	426a (Moses)

61-63	I	99a (Animal Life)
62	I	504a (Day, Times of)
	III	58a (Journey); 417b (Morning)
62-82	III	395a (Miracles)
63	I	526a (Devil)
	II	218b (Food and Drink)
	III	287a (Marvels); 394b (Miracles)
64	III	83b (Khaḍir/Khiḍr)
64-65	III	426a (Moses)
65	III	82b (Khaḍir/Khiḍr); 224b (Literature and the Q); 330b (Maturity); 379a (Mercy)
	IV	577a (Servants); 604b (Ships)
	V	200b (Teaching); 381b (Trust and Patience)
65-82	II	465a (Humor)
	IV	61b (Persian Literature and the Q)
	V	381b (Trust and Patience)
66	V	200b (Teaching); 375b (Trips and Voyages)
66-70	III	426a (Moses)
66-82	V	136a (Suffering)
68	III	537a (News)
	V	381b (Trust and Patience)
69	I	537a (Disobedience)
70	V	381b (Trust and Patience)
71	I	158a (Ark)
	IV	604b (Ships)
	V	375b (Trips and Voyages); 381b (Trust and Patience)
71-82	III	225a (Literature and the Q); 426a (Moses)
72	V	381b (Trust and Patience)
73	I	289a (Captives)
74	I	302a (Children)
	II	489a (Ignorance)
	IV	21b (Parents); 505a (Ritual Purity)
	V	83a (Soul); 381b (Trust and Patience)
75	V	381b (Trust and Patience)
76	I	387b (Companions of the Prophet)
	II	359a (Grammar and the Q)
77	I	338a (City)
	II	354a (Grammar and the Q)
	III	603b (Orphans)

	IV	49a (People of the House)
	V	381b (Trust and Patience)
78	III	537a (News)
	V	381b (Trust and Patience)
79	III	92a (Kings and Rulers)
	IV	604b (Ships)
	V	548b (Work)
80	I	302a (Children)
	IV	21b (Parents)
	V	204b (Teaching)
80-81	II	175a (Family)
82	I	338a (City)
	III	603b (Orphans)
83	I	61a, 62a (Alexander)
	II	332a (Gog and Magog)
	III	190a (Literacy); 441b (Muḥammad); 579b (Opposition to Muḥammad)
	IV	61b (Persian Literature and the Q); 302a (Prophets and Prophethood)
83-98	I	189a (Authority)
	III	520a (Narratives)
	V	37a (Sīra and the Q)
83-101	V	375b (Trips and Voyages)
84	IV	210b (Power and Impotence)
84-85	III	46a (Jinn)
86	I	61a (Alexander)
	II	212a (Fire)
	IV	107a (Planets and Stars)
	V	163a (Sun)
86-87	I	295b (Chastisement and Punishment)
89	III	46a (Jinn)
90	IV	107b (Planets and Stars)
	V	163a (Sun)
91	III	537a (News)
92	III	46a (Jinn)
93-99	I	61a (Alexander)
94	I	61a (Alexander); 111a (Antichrist); 112b (Apocalypse)
	II	331b (Gog and Magog)
	V	375b (Trips and Voyages)
94-98	II	332a (Gog and Magog)
95	II	354b (Grammar and the Q)

96 III 383a (Metals and Minerals)

99 II 362a (Grammar and the Q); 547a (Instruments)
III 185a (Life)
IV 435a (Resurrection)

99-110 III 520a (Narratives)

101 I 400a (Conquest)
IV 420a (Remembrance)

102 II 273b (Friends and Friendship)

102-108 II 98b (Evil Deeds)

103 III 536b (News)

103-104 II 337b (Good and Evil)

103-105 II 259b (Form and Structure of the Q)

103-106 III 33a (Jews and Judaism)

105 III 334b (Measurement)
IV 431b (Responsibility)

106 II 418a (Hell and Hellfire)
III 400a (Mockery)
V 6a (Signs)

107 II 51a (Eschatology); 60a (Ethics and the Q); 229a (Foreign Vocabulary); 283a (Garden)
IV 13a (Paradise); 431b (Responsibility)

109 II 545a (Instruments)
III 191b (Literacy); 531a (Nature as Signs)
V 273a (Theology and the Q); 465b (Water); 548a (Word of God); 558a (Writing and Writing Materials)

109-110 II 143a (Exhortations)

110 II 329b (God and his Attributes); 449a (Hope)
III 451b (Muḥammad)
IV 300a (Prophets and Prophethood); 311b, 312a (Provocation); 440a (Revelation and Inspiration)
V 489b (Witness to Faith); 500a (Witnessing and Testifying)

Sūrat Maryam (19)

I 320a (Chronology and the Q); 477a, 477b (Creation)
II 291a (Gender)
III 7b, 13a, 13b, 14b, 17b (Jesus); 179a (Left Hand and Right Hand); 294b (Mary); 313a (Material Culture and the Q); 472b (Mysterious Letters); 508b (Names of the Q); 519b (Narratives)
IV 241a, 244a (Pre-1800 Preoccupations of Q Studies)
V 533b (Women and the Q); 575a (Zechariah)

1 III 270b (Manuscripts of the Q)

1-7 IV 177b (Popular and Talismanic Uses of the Q)

1-22 I 313a (Christians and Christianity)

2 IV 474a (Rhetoric and the Q)
V 574b (Zechariah)

2-7 IV 31b (Patriarchy)

2-15 III 289a (Mary)
V 574a, 575a (Zechariah)

2-33 V 363b (Trial)

2-40 III 519b (Narratives)

2-58 V 574b (Zechariah)

2-63 III 519b (Narratives)

2-74 III 519b (Narratives)

3 II 465a (Humor)

3-6 I 328a (Chronology and the Q)
IV 224a, 229a (Prayer)
V 574a (Zechariah)

3-8 I 233a (Birth)

4 II 91b (Everyday Life, Q In)
III 156b (Law and the Q); 204b (Literary Structures of the Q)
V 570b (Youth and Old Age)

5 I 344b (Clients and Clientage)
III 231a (Lord)

6 III 524a (Narratives)

7 II 309a (Geography); 341a (Good News)
III 51b (John the Baptist); 395b (Miracles)
V 574b (Zechariah)

7-9 V 545b (Word of God)

8 IV 211a (Power and Impotence)
V 574b (Zechariah)

9 I 476a, 477a (Creation)
V 553b (World); 574b (Zechariah)

10 I 499b (Day, Times of)
V 574b (Zechariah)

11 I 149a (Archaeology and the Q); 165a (Art and Architecture and the Q); 503a, 503b (Day, Times of)
II 80a (Evening); 299b (Geography)
III 416b (Morning)

	IV	223a, 227b (Prayer); 293b (Prophets and Prophethood); 439b (Revelation and Inspiration); 516b (Sacred Precincts)
	V	281a (Time); 546a (Word of God)
12	III	8a (Jesus); 51b (John the Baptist)
	V	570b (Youth and Old Age)
12-15	III	289a (Mary)
	V	574b (Zechariah)
13	III	234a (Love and Affection)
14	I	537a (Disobedience)
	II	60b (Ethics and the Q); 98a (Evil Deeds); 447b (Honor)
	III	233b, 234a (Love and Affection)
	V	204b (Teaching)
15	II	91b (Everyday Life, Q In)
	III	17b (Jesus)
	IV	435b (Resurrection)
16	II	260b (Form and Structure of the Q)
	III	8a (Jesus); 441b (Muḥammad); 524b (Narratives)
	IV	302b (Prophets and Prophethood); 470a (Rhetoric and the Q)
	V	173b (Sūra)
16-21	II	19a (Emigration)
	III	13a (Jesus)
	IV	411a (Religious Pluralism and the Q)
16-33	III	292b (Mary)
	III	11b (Jesus)
	V	115a (Spirit); 574b (Zechariah)
16-34	V	533b (Women and the Q)
16-35	III	289a (Mary)
16-40	III	7b, 8a (Jesus)
17	I	52b (Air and Wind); 87a (Angel); 203a (Barrier)
	II	278b (Gabriel); 443b (Holy Spirit)
	III	8a, 14a (Jesus); 293a, 293b (Mary)
	V	81b (Soul); 115a (Spirit); 371a (Trinity); 412b (Veil); 445b (Vision and Blindness)
17-21	III	293a (Mary); 395b (Miracles)
17-22	I	233b (Birth)
18	II	92b (Everyday Life, Q In)
	IV	308a (Protection)
18-19	III	315b (Material Culture and the Q)
19	IV	290b (Prophets and Prophethood); 356a, 356b (Readings of the Q); 505a (Ritual Purity)
19-20	I	298b (Chastity)

20	I	233b (Birth); 299a (Chastity)
	III	294a (Mary)
	IV	585a (Sex and Sexuality)
	V	533b (Women and the Q)
21	I	233b (Birth)
	II	185b (Fate)
	III	16a (Jesus)
	V	574b (Zechariah)
22-23	III	13a (Jesus)
22-26	III	8a (Jesus)
22-33	III	293a (Mary)
23	I	494b (Date Palm); 530a (Dialects)
	II	305b (Geography); 358a (Grammar and the Q)
	V	133b (Suffering)
23-25	I	495a (Date Palm)
23-26	V	533b (Women and the Q)
24	II	234a (Foreign Vocabulary)
	V	127b (Springs and Fountains)
24-25	III	395b (Miracles)
24-26	III	13a, 14a (Jesus)
25	I	494b (Date Palm)
	II	305b (Geography)
26	II	180b (Fasting)
	III	14a (Jesus); 562b (Oaths)
	V	449b (Vow)
27	I	299b (Chastity)
27-28	I	59a (ʿĀʾisha bint Abī Bakr)
27-33	III	13a (Jesus)
28	I	1b (Aaron); 261b (Brother and Brotherhood); 299a (Chastity)
	II	509a (ʿImrān)
	III	519b (Narratives)
	IV	585a (Sex and Sexuality)
	V	54a (Sister)
29	I	149a (Archaeology and the Q); 570b (Youth and Old Age)
29-30	III	395b (Miracles)
30	I	245a (Book)
	III	8a, 16a (Jesus); 508a (Names of the Q)
	IV	579a (Servants); 585a (Sex and Sexuality)

30-31	I	328a (Chronology and the Q)
	IV	224a (Prayer)
30-32	I	161a (Arrogance)
30-33	III	289a (Mary)
30-35	III	295a (Mary)
31	I	66b (Almsgiving); 102b (Anointing); 236b (Blessing)
	III	12b, 16a (Jesus)
	V	197a (Taxation)
32	II	60b (Ethics and the Q); 447b (Honor)
	III	233b (Love and Affection)
33	II	91b (Everyday Life, Q In)
	III	17b (Jesus); 143a (Last Judgment)
	IV	435b (Resurrection)
33-36	I	170b (Art and Architecture and the Q)
34	III	8a, 14b, 15a (Jesus)
	V	533b (Women and the Q); 544b (Word of God)
34-35	I	117a (Apologetics)
	IV	33a (Patriarchy)
	V	369a (Trinity)
34-36	III	300a (Material Culture and the Q)
34-40	III	8a (Jesus)
35	I	319a (Chronology and the Q); 475a, 475b (Creation); 516b (Decision)
	II	185b (Fate); 269a (Freedom and Predestination); 327b, 329b (God and his Attributes)
	IV	33b (Patriarchy)
	V	287a (Time); 542b (Word of God)
36	II	96a (Everyday Life, Q In)
	III	229b, 230a (Lord)
37-39	III	17b (Jesus)
39	I	500a (Day, Times of)
	II	395b (Ḥadīth and the Q)
	III	137a (Last Judgment); 442b (Muḥammad)
	IV	430b (Repentance and Penance)
	V	543a, 545a (Word of God)
41	I	5b (Abraham); 330a (Chronology and the Q)
	II	71a (Ethics and the Q); 260b (Form and Structure of the Q)
	III	441b (Muḥammad); 524b (Narratives)
	IV	291b, 302b (Prophets and Prophethood)
	V	258a (Theology and the Q); 570a (Youth and Old Age)
41-47	IV	33a (Patriarchy)

41-48	IV	21a (Parents)
41-50	I	6b (Abraham); 330a (Chronology and the Q)
	III	494a, 494b (Myths and Legends in the Q); 519b (Narratives)
	V	574b (Zechariah)
42-45	III	212b (Literature and the Q)
42-49	I	193a (Āzar)
43	IV	29a (Path or Way)
44	I	536b (Disobedience)
	II	98a (Evil Deeds)
	III	44b (Jinn)
	V	120b (Spiritual Beings)
45	II	274a (Friends and Friendship)
46	I	7a (Abraham)
	V	130b (Stoning)
47	I	7a (Abraham)
	IV	225a (Prayer)
48	III	63b (Joy and Misery)
	IV	228b, 229a (Prayer)
48-49	I	6a (Abraham)
	III	494b (Myths and Legends in the Q)
49	I	7b (Abraham)
	II	561a, 561b, 562a (Isaac); 563b (Ishmael)
	III	1a (Jacob)
50	I	83a (Anatomy)
	V	574b (Zechariah)
51	II	260b (Form and Structure of the Q)
	III	424b (Moses)
	III	524b (Narratives)
	IV	290a, 292a (Prophets and Prophethood)
51-58	III	519b (Narratives)
52	II	308b (Geography)
	IV	292a (Prophets and Prophethood); 513b (Sacred Precincts)
	V	29a (Sinai); 110a (Speech)
53	I	1a (Aaron); 260a, 260b (Brother and Brotherhood)
	V	574b (Zechariah)
54	II	260b (Form and Structure of the Q); 564a (Ishmael)
	III	524b (Narratives)
	IV	290a, 291b (Prophets and Prophethood)
54-55	I	8a (Abraham)

55	II	358a (Grammar and the Q)
	IV	223b (Prayer)
56	II	71a (Ethics and the Q); 260b (Form and Structure of the Q)
	III	524b (Narratives)
	IV	291b (Prophets and Prophethood)
56-57	II	484a (Idrīs)
	V	249b (Textual Criticism of the Q)
57	V	41b (Sīra and the Q); 249b (Textual Criticism of the Q)
58	I	183b (Asceticism); 236b (Blessing); 254b (Bowing and Prostration)
	II	11b (Election); 571a (Israel)
	III	2a (Jacob); 190a (Literacy); 486b (Myths and Legends in the Q)
	IV	221b, 223b (Prayer); 291a (Prophets and Prophethood); 368b, 378a (Recitation of the Q)
	V	393a (Turkish Literature and the Q); 471b (Weeping); 574a (Zechariah)
60	IV	426b (Repentance and Penance)
61	V	393b (Turkish Literature and the Q)
62	I	503a, 503b (Day, Times of)
	II	80a, 80b (Evening); 91b (Everyday Life, Q In)
	III	109b (Language and Style of the Q); 416b (Morning)
	IV	482b (Rhymed Prose)
	V	281a (Time)
63	II	282b (Garden)
64	IV	293a (Prophets and Prophethood); 310b (Provocation)
65	I	458b (Courage)
	II	322b (God and his Attributes)
	IV	184a (Possession and Possessions); 288a (Property)
66	I	506b (Death and the Dead)
	II	358a (Grammar and the Q)
	III	17b (Jesus)
66-67	I	477a, 479a (Creation)
67	II	57b (Ethics and the Q)
	IV	421a (Remembrance)
68	III	63b (Joy and Misery)
69	IV	592b (Shīʿa)
71	II	240a (Foretelling in the Q)
71-72	II	417b (Hell and Hellfire)
73	III	190a (Literacy)
	V	7a (Signs); 36b (Sīra and the Q)
74	II	293a (Generations); 353b, 355b (Grammar and the Q)
	IV	320a (Punishment Stories)

75	I	501a (Day, Times of)
	III	137a (Last Judgment)
	IV	432a (Responsibility); 538b (Scholar)
	V	287b (Time)
75-76	IV	12a (Paradise)
75-98	III	519b (Narratives)
76	I	435b (Conversion)
77	I	302b (Children)
	IV	31b (Patriarchy)
	V	468a (Wealth)
77-80	I	221b (Belief and Unbelief)
78	I	465b (Covenant)
	II	293a (Generations)
79	I	243b (Book)
	V	493a (Witnessing and Testifying)
83	IV	295a (Prophets and Prophethood)
84	III	40a (Jihād); 550a (Numbers and Enumeration)
85	IV	435a (Resurrection)
87	I	465b (Covenant)
	II	49b (Eschatology); 551a, 552b (Intercession)
	III	379b (Mercy)
88-92	I	236a (Blasphemy)
88-93	IV	33a (Patriarchy)
88-95	III	7b (Jesus)
93	IV	187a (Possession and Possessions); 576b (Servants)
94	III	550a (Numbers and Enumeration)
96	III	233b (Love and Affection)
97	I	132a (Arabic Language)
	II	341a, 341b (Good News)
	III	108b (Language, Concept of); 113b (Language and Style of the Q); 443a (Muḥammad)
97-98	II	143a (Exhortations)
98	II	405b (Hearing and Deafness)
	IV	425a (Remnant)
	V	479b (Whisper)

Sūrat Ṭā Hā (20)

I 320a (Chronology and the Q); 453b (Cosmology)
III 472b (Mysterious Letters); 490b (Myths and Legends in the Q); 503b (Names of the Prophet); 519a (Narratives)
IV 587b (Sheets)
V 324a (Traditional Disciplines of Q Studies); 395b, 395b (Ṭuwā)

1 III 197a (Literary Structures of the Q)

1-8 III 519a (Narratives)

1-77 IV 105b, 106a (Plagues)

1-113 III 519a (Narratives)

2 III 63b (Joy and Misery); 440b, 452b (Muḥammad)

2-3 V 395b (Ṭuwā)

3 II 142b (Exhortations)
IV 230a (Prayer)

4 I 472b (Creation)
IV 292b (Prophets and Prophethood); 446a (Revelation and Inspiration)
V 393b (Turkish Literature and the Q)

5 I 103b, 105b (Anthropomorphism); 443b (Cosmology)
II 325b (God and his Attributes)

5-8 V 500b (Witnessing and Testifying)

6 II 4a (Earth)
V 393a (Turkish Literature and the Q)

7-8 V 137b (Ṣūfism and the Q)

8 II 319b (God and his Attributes)
IV 185a (Possession and Possessions)
V 501a (Witnessing and Testifying)

9 I 532b (Dialogues)
II 254b (Form and Structure of the Q); 435b (History and the Q)
III 524a (Narratives)

9-14 II 211b, 213b (Fire)

9-44 II 558a (Invitation)

9-99 III 519a (Narratives)
IV 320a (Punishment Stories)

10 II 174a (Family)
IV 574b (Seeing and Hearing)
V 95b (South Asian Literatures and the Q)

10-12 III 529b (Nature as Signs)

10-48 I 468b (Createdness of the Q)

11	V	110b (Speech)
11-17	III	421a (Moses)
12	I	329b (Chronology and the Q); 346b (Clothing)
	II	173a (Fall of Man); 348b (Grammar and the Q)
	III	495b (Myths and Legends in the Q); 529b (Nature as Signs)
	IV	282b (Profane and Sacred); 513a (Sacred Precincts)
	V	248a (Textual Criticism of the Q); 393b (Turkish Literature and the Q); 395b (Ṭuwā)
12-14	I	329b (Chronology and the Q)
	II	330a (God and his Attributes)
13	II	11b (Election)
	III	495b (Myths and Legends in the Q)
	IV	217a (Prayer); 291b (Prophets and Prophethood)
14	I	329b (Chronology and the Q)
	II	330a (God and his Attributes)
	III	495b (Myths and Legends in the Q)
	IV	224a, 229b (Prayer); 420a, 423b (Remembrance)
	V	500b (Witnessing and Testifying); 555b (Worship)
14-16	III	143a (Last Judgment)
15	I	501a (Day, Times of)
	II	148b (Expeditions and Battles); 423b (Hidden and the Hidden)
	III	137a (Last Judgment)
	V	287b (Time); 395b (Ṭuwā)
16	V	396b (Ṭuwā); 486b (Wish and Desire)
17-21	II	464b (Humor)
	IV	508b (Rod)
17-23	III	421b (Moses)
	IV	296b (Prophets and Prophethood)
18	II	356b (Grammar and the Q); 465a (Humor); 546a (Instruments)
20	I	99a (Animal Life)
21	V	29b (Sīra and the Q); 393a (Turkish Literature and the Q)
22	I	364a (Colors)
	II	335b (Good and Evil)
24	IV	67b (Pharaoh)
25	III	495b (Myths and Legends in the Q)
25-34	IV	224a (Prayer)
25-35	I	328a (Chronology and the Q)
27	III	113a (Language and Style of the Q)
27-28	III	108b (Language, Concept of)

29	II	174a (Family)
29-30	I	260a (Brother and Brotherhood)
29-36	I	1a (Aaron)
32	I	260b (Brother and Brotherhood)
37-40	III	420b (Moses)
37-41	III	393b (Miracles)
38	IV	439b (Revelation and Inspiration)
38-40	IV	20a (Parents)
39	I	103b (Anthropomorphism); 158a (Ark); 345b (Clients and Clientage)
	II	10b (Egypt); 23b (Enemies); 323b, 324b (God and his Attributes)
	III	202a (Literary Structures of the Q); 233b (Love and Affection)
	V	126b (Springs and Fountains); 375a (Trips and Voyages); 463b (Water)
39-43	I	345b (Clients and Clientage)
40	I	260b (Brother and Brotherhood); 302b (Children); 405a (Consolation); 518b (Deliverance)
	III	390b (Midian)
	IV	37a (People of the Book); 49a (People of the House); 523b (Salvation); 606a (Shuʿayb)
	V	285b (Time)
41	I	345b (Clients and Clientage)
	IV	291b (Prophets and Prophethood)
42	I	260a (Brother and Brotherhood)
	II	308a (Geography)
43	IV	106a (Plagues)
	IV	67b (Pharaoh)
44	IV	35a (Peace)
	V	221b (Teaching and Preaching the Q)
46	I	83b (Anatomy)
	II	196b (Fear)
	IV	574b (Seeing and Hearing)
47	I	260a (Brother and Brotherhood)
	II	399a (Hāmān)
	IV	35a (Peace); 225a (Prayer)
48	IV	440a (Revelation and Inspiration)
51-55	I	523a (Destiny)
52	II	269b (Freedom and Predestination)
53	II	2b, 3a (Earth)
	IV	336a (Races)
	V	132a (Strangers and Foreigners); 462b (Water)

53-54 I 473b (Creation)

54 I 96b (Animal Life)

54-55 I 473a (Creation)

55 I 230b (Biology as the Creation and Stages of Life); 264b (Burial); 476a, 479a (Creation); 556a (Druzes)
IV 6b (Pairs and Pairing)

56 V 6a (Signs)

56-70 III 249b (Magic)

57 III 246a (Magic)

58 III 246a (Magic)

59 I 500b, 504a (Day, Times of)
III 416b (Morning)
V 281b (Time)

61 II 162a (Failure)
III 174a (Lawful and Unlawful)

62 V 479b (Whisper)

63 I 530b (Dialects)
II 359a, 359b (Grammar and the Q)
III 246a (Magic)
V 239b (Textual Criticism of the Q)

64 IV 348b (Ranks and Orders)

65 I 518b (Deliverance)

65-73 III 211b (Literature and the Q)

65-76 III 393b (Miracles)

66 II 546b (Instruments)
III 246a (Magic)
IV 509a (Rod)
V 393b (Turkish Literature and the Q)

67 III 398a (Miracles)

69 IV 523a (Salvation)

70 I 1a (Aaron); 255a (Bowing and Prostration)
III 229b (Lord)
IV 483a (Rhymed Prose)

71 I 295b (Chastisement and Punishment); 487b, 488a (Crucifixion); 494b (Date Palm)
II 305b (Geography)
III 44a (Jinn); 246a (Magic)
IV 67b (Pharaoh)
V 201b (Teaching)

71-73	II	355a (Grammar and the Q)
72	I	516b (Decision)
	III	65a (Judgment)
72-73	IV	286b (Proof)
73	III	246a (Magic); 378b (Mercy)
74	I	385a (Community and Society in the Q)
	II	416b (Hell and Hellfire)
74-76	IV	2b (Pairs and Pairing)
75	III	127b (Language and Style of the Q)
	IV	14a (Paradise)
76	IV	505b (Ritual Purity)
	V	393a, 393b (Turkish Literature and the Q)
77	III	488a (Myths and Legends in the Q)
	IV	35a (Peace); 440a (Revelation and Inspiration)
	V	375a (Trips and Voyages); 464b (Water); 546a (Word of God)
77-78	II	213a (Fire)
	III	394a (Miracles); 423b (Moses)
78	II	10b (Egypt); 184a (Fasting)
	IV	67a (Pharaoh)
	V	126b (Springs and Fountains); 377a (Troops); 463b (Water)
79	III	425a (Moses); 583b (Oppression)
80	I	98a (Animal Life); 518b (Deliverance)
	II	23b (Enemies); 215b (Flying); 308b (Geography)
	III	394a (Miracles)
	IV	443b (Revelation and Inspiration); 513b (Sacred Precincts); 523b (Salvation)
	V	29a (Sinai)
81	I	93a (Anger)
81-82	IV	428b (Repentance and Penance)
82	I	225b (Belief and Unbelief)
	II	321a (God and his Attributes)
	III	379b (Mercy)
	IV	431b (Responsibility)
83-98	I	1b (Aaron); 274a (Calf of Gold)
85	I	274a (Calf of Gold)
	II	358b (Grammar and the Q)
85-91	III	424b (Moses)
85-94	V	155b (Ṣūfism and the Q)
85-95	IV	405a (Religious Pluralism and the Q); 524b (Samaritans)

86 I 93a, 93b (Anger)
III 172b (Lawful and Unlawful); 217b (Literature and the Q); 424b (Moses)

86-89 I 465b (Covenant)

87 I 213a (Beauty); 274a, 276a (Calf of Gold)
II 358b (Grammar and the Q)
III 496a (Myths and Legends in the Q)

87-88 III 394b (Miracles)

88 I 99a (Animal Life); 274b (Calf of Gold)

89 IV 5a (Pairs and Pairing)

90 III 567b (Obedience)

90-94 I 274a (Calf of Gold)

92-93 I 537a (Disobedience)

94 I 276a (Calf of Gold)
II 352b (Grammar and the Q)
IV 20a (Parents); 403b (Religious Pluralism and the Q)
V 524b (Women and the Q)

95 II 358b (Grammar and the Q)

95-97 I 274a (Calf of Gold)

96 I 274b, 275b (Calf of Gold)
III 394b (Miracles)
IV 290b (Prophets and Prophethood)
V 82b (Soul); 474b (Weights and Measures)

97 I 274a, 274b, 275a (Calf of Gold)
II 10b (Egypt); 348a, 358a, 358b (Grammar and the Q)
IV 524b (Samaritans)
V 126b (Springs and Fountains); 463b (Water)

98 V 501a (Witnessing and Testifying)

99 II 435b (History and the Q)
III 420a (Moses); 441a (Muḥammad); 517b (Narratives); 537a (News)
IV 302b (Prophets and Prophethood)

100 V 474a (Weights and Measures)

100-113 III 519a (Narratives)

101 V 474a (Weights and Measures)

102 I 363a, 363b (Colors)
II 439b (History and the Q); 547a (Instruments)
IV 435a (Resurrection); 599b (Shīʿism and the Q)

103 V 479a, 479b (Whisper)

108 V 479a (Whisper)

109	I	463a (Court)
	II	552b (Intercession)
	III	141a (Last Judgment)
	IV	163b (Popular and Talismanic Uses of the Q)
110	IV	4b (Pairs and Pairing)
110-114	I	247b (Book)
111	II	162a (Failure)
	III	182b (Life)
	IV	172b (Popular and Talismanic Uses of the Q)
112	III	70b (Justice and Injustice)
113	II	226b (Foreign Vocabulary); 497b (Illiteracy)
	III	113b (Language and Style of the Q); 193b (Literary Structures of the Q); 585a (Orality)
	IV	280b (Profane and Sacred); 443b (Revelation and Inspiration); 566a (Scripture and the Q)
	V	340b (Translations of the Q)
114	II	321b (God and his Attributes)
	III	91b (Kings and Rulers); 441b (Muḥammad); 519a (Narratives)
	IV	128a (Politics and the Q); 294a (Prophets and Prophethood); 538a (Scholar)
115	I	25a, 25b (Adam and Eve); 465a (Covenant)
	V	334a (Traditional Disciplines of Q Studies)
115-117	I	448a (Cosmology)
115-123	I	448a (Cosmology)
	V	530a (Women and the Q)
115-128	III	519a (Narratives)
115-135	III	519a (Narratives)
116	I	24a (Adam and Eve); 255a (Bowing and Prostration); 447a (Cosmology); 525a (Devil)
	II	172b (Fall of Man)
	III	45a (Jinn)
	IV	220a (Prayer)
116-123	I	525b (Devil)
117	I	447b, 454a, 455a (Cosmology)
	II	172b (Fall of Man)
	III	490a (Myths and Legends in the Q)
118	I	454a (Cosmology)
	I	84a (Anatomy)
118-119	II	172b (Fall of Man)
	III	209b (Literature and the Q)
119	V	281b (Time)

120 I 25a (Adam and Eve); 447a, 447b, 454a (Cosmology); 526a (Devil)
II 54a (Eternity); 172b (Fall of Man); 219b (Food and Drink); 335b (Good and Evil)
III 92b (Kings and Rulers)
IV 295a (Prophets and Prophethood)
V 82b (Soul); 360a (Tree); 479a (Whisper); 530a (Women and the Q); 571a (Zaqqūm)

120-123 I 525a (Devil)

121 I 25a (Adam and Eve); 41b (Agriculture and Vegetation); 84a (Anatomy); 346b (Clothing); 435a (Conversion); 447b (Cosmology); 536a, 536b, 538a (Disobedience)
II 66a (Ethics and the Q); 506b (Impeccability)
IV 581a, 584a (Sex and Sexuality)
V 25a (Sin, Major and Minor)

121-122 III 379a (Mercy)

122 I 25b, 26a (Adam and Eve); 436b (Conversion); 455a (Cosmology)
II 11b (Election)
IV 291b (Prophets and Prophethood); 429a (Repentance and Penance)

122-123 I 436a (Conversion)
II 173a (Fall of Man)

123 I 25a (Adam and Eve)
II 23b, 24a (Enemies); 173a, 173a (Fall of Man)
III 63b (Joy and Misery)
V 109b (Speech)

126 I 454a (Cosmology)

128 II 434a (History and the Q)
IV 425a (Remnant)

129 II 45a (Eschatology)
III 185a (Life)
V 289b (Time); 547b (Word of God)

130 I 14a (Abrogation); 27a (Adoration); 327b (Chronology and the Q); 498a (Day and Night); 503b (Day, Times of)
II 82a (Everyday Life, Q In); 315a (Glorification of God); 340a (Good Deeds)
III 40a (Jihād); 446b, 452b (Muḥammad)
IV 107a (Planets and Stars); 220b, 222a, 222b, 223a, 223b (Prayer)
V 134a (Suffering); 163a (Sun); 282b (Time)

130-135 II 143a (Exhortations)

131 III 453a (Muḥammad)
V 178b, 179a (Sustenance)

132 I 327b (Chronology and the Q)
IV 222a (Prayer)

133 I 245b (Book)
II 434a (History and the Q); 545a (Instruments)
III 425b (Moses); 452a (Muḥammad)
IV 569b, 570b (Scrolls)
V 8a (Signs); 301a (Torah)

134 IV 453b (Reward and Punishment)

135 IV 29a (Path or Way)

Sūrat al-Anbiyāʾ (21)

III 516b, 521a (Narratives)
IV 495b, 496a (Ritual and the Q)

1 II 148b (Expeditions and Battles)
III 138a (Last Judgment)

2 I 222a (Belief and Unbelief)
IV 423b (Remembrance)

2-3 III 247a (Magic)

3 II 361b (Grammar and the Q)
III 246a (Magic); 449b (Muḥammad)
V 479b (Whisper)

3-4 IV 311a (Provocation)

4 II 1b (Ears)
IV 4a (Pairs and Pairing)

5 I 41b (Agriculture and Vegetation); 542b (Divination); 546b, 552a (Dreams and Sleep)
II 241b (Foretelling in the Q)
III 116b (Language and Style of the Q); 219b (Literature and the Q); 450a (Muḥammad)
IV 112a, 112b (Poetry and Poets); 178b (Popular and Talismanic Uses of the Q); 296a, 301a (Prophets and Prophethood); 311b (Provocation); 442b (Revelation and Inspiration); 477a (Rhymed Prose)
V 546a (Word of God)

5-6 III 453a (Muḥammad)

6-15 IV 320b (Punishment Stories)

7 III 372b (Memory)
IV 49a (People of the House); 217a, 230a (Prayer); 302a (Prophets and Prophethood)
V 301b, 303b (Torah)

8 I 80a (Anatomy)
II 217a (Food and Drink)

9 V 258a (Theology and the Q)

11 I 479a (Creation)

16 I 442a (Cosmology)
II 410b (Heaven and Sky)
IV 4a (Pairs and Pairing)

16-17 I 473a (Creation)
V 279b (Time)

18 V 544b (Word of God)

19 I 160b (Arrogance)
IV 264a (Pride)

19-20 I 435a (Conversion)

20 I 501a (Day, Times of)
IV 220a (Prayer)

22 I 236a (Blasphemy)
II 325b (God and his Attributes)
IV 78a, 80b (Philosophy and the Q); 119a (Polemic and Polemical Language); 161b (Polytheism and Atheism); 215a (Praise); 220a, 220b (Prayer); 287a (Proof)
V 393a (Turkish Literature and the Q)

23 IV 431a (Responsibility)
V 136a (Suffering); 393b (Turkish Literature and the Q)

24 IV 286b (Proof); 312b (Provocation); 538b (Scholar)

25 I 329b (Chronology and the Q)
II 330a (God and his Attributes); 557b (Invitation)
IV 300a (Prophets and Prophethood)
V 500b (Witnessing and Testifying)

28 II 197b (Fear)
III 141a (Last Judgment)
IV 4b (Pairs and Pairing); 163b (Popular and Talismanic Uses of the Q)

29 II 418a (Hell and Hellfire)

30 I 95b (Animal Life); 442a (Cosmology); 477b (Creation)
II 327b (God and his Attributes); 410b (Heaven and Sky)
III 530b (Nature as Signs)
IV 554a (Science and the Q)
V 126a (Springs and Fountains); 393b (Turkish Literature and the Q); 462b (Water); 544a (Word of God)

30-33 II 259a (Form and Structure of the Q)

31 II 2b, 3a (Earth)
IV 554a (Science and the Q)

32 I 45a (Agriculture and Vegetation)
II 411a (Heaven and Sky); 460b (House, Domestic and Divine)
IV 307b (Protection)
V 5b (Signs)

33	I	27a (Adoration); 442b, 445b (Cosmology); 501a (Day, Times of)
	II	315a (Glorification of God); 327b (God and his Attributes)
	IV	4b (Pairs and Pairing); 107a, 107b (Planets and Stars); 552b (Science and the Q)
	V	163a (Sun)
34	II	54a (Eternity)
35	II	28b (Epigraphy)
	IV	486a (Ritual and the Q)
	V	83a (Soul); 133b (Suffering); 363a (Trial)
36	III	400a (Mockery); 448b (Muḥammad)
37	II	56b (Ethics and the Q)
	V	204b (Teaching)
38	III	448b (Muḥammad)
39	I	222a (Belief and Unbelief)
	II	210b (Fire); 415a (Hell and Hellfire)
40	V	181a (Symbolic Imagery)
41	III	400a, 400b (Mockery); 453a (Muḥammad)
43	I	387b (Companions of the Prophet)
	IV	307b (Protection)
	V	82a (Soul); 430a (Victory)
45	I	83b (Anatomy)
	III	442b (Muḥammad)
	IV	312a (Provocation)
47	I	522b (Destiny)
	II	70b (Ethics and the Q); 217b (Food and Drink); 305a, 305b (Geography); 545b (Instruments)
	III	140b (Last Judgment); 275b (Markets); 334b (Measurement); 409a (Money)
	IV	457b (Reward and Punishment)
	V	313b (Trade and Commerce); 473b (Weights and Measures); 493a (Witnessing and Testifying)
48	I	486b (Criterion)
	III	186b (Light); 424b (Moses); 507b (Names of the Q); 524a (Narratives)
	IV	343a (Ramaḍān)
	V	300b, 301b (Torah)
48-49	I	1a (Aaron)
48-73	III	521a (Narratives)
49	I	501a (Day, Times of)
	II	196b, 197b (Fear)
	III	137a (Last Judgment)
	V	287b (Time)
50	III	510a, 513a (Names of the Q)
	IV	230a (Prayer)

51	III	524a (Narratives)
	IV	537b (Scholar)
	V	258a (Theology and the Q)
51-70	III	340b (Mecca)
	IV	21a (Parents)
51-71	I	193a (Āzar)
51-73	I	6b (Abraham); 330a (Chronology and the Q)
	III	494a (Myths and Legends in the Q)
52	I	162b (Art and Architecture and the Q)
	II	474a (Iconoclasm); 476b (Idolatry and Idolaters); 481b (Idols and Images)
	IV	160a (Polytheism and Atheism)
52-54	II	474a (Iconoclasm)
53	V	317a (Tradition and Custom)
54	II	43b (Error)
56	I	472a (Creation)
57	II	474a (Iconoclasm); 481a, 481b (Idols and Images)
	III	561b (Oaths)
57-58	I	7a (Abraham)
	III	494b (Myths and Legends in the Q)
58	II	474b (Iconoclasm)
59	II	481b (Idols and Images)
61	I	501b (Day, Times of)
	V	497a (Witnessing and Testifying)
62-67	I	533b (Dialogues)
63	III	210b (Literature and the Q)
66	IV	5a (Pairs and Pairing)
67	IV	21a (Parents)
67-69	III	539a (Nimrod)
68-69	I	7a (Abraham)
	II	211b (Fire)
	III	224b (Literature and the Q); 494b (Myths and Legends in the Q); 529b (Nature as Signs)
68-71	III	219a (Literature and the Q)
	V	574b (Zechariah)
69	II	211b (Fire); 455b (Hot and Cold)
	III	393a (Miracles)
	V	95b (South Asian Literatures and the Q); 109a (Speech); 545a (Word of God)
71	I	6a (Abraham); 519a (Deliverance)
	II	309a (Geography)

	III	494b (Myths and Legends in the Q)
	IV	513b (Sacred Precincts)
	V	107a (Spatial Relations)
72	I	7b (Abraham)
	II	562a (Isaac); 563b (Ishmael)
	III	1a (Jacob); 520a (Narratives)
72-73	IV	439b (Revelation and Inspiration)
73	I	66b (Almsgiving)
	II	358b (Grammar and the Q); 503a (Imām)
	III	95a (Kings and Rulers)
	IV	223b (Prayer); 294b, 300b (Prophets and Prophethood)
	V	197a (Taxation)
74	I	519a (Deliverance)
	II	63a (Ethics and the Q)
	III	524a (Narratives)
	IV	3b (Pairs and Pairing); 538a (Scholar)
	V	21b (Sin, Major and Minor); 574b (Zechariah)
74-91	III	522a (Narratives)
76	I	519a (Deliverance)
	III	63b (Joy and Misery)
76-77	V	430a (Victory); 574b (Zechariah)
77	I	553b (Drowning)
78	I	99a (Animal Life)
	II	394b (Ḥadīth and the Q)
	IV	315b (Psalms)
78-79	I	148a (Arbitration)
	III	226a (Literature and the Q)
	V	77a (Solomon)
78-82	V	77a (Solomon)
79	I	496a (David)
	II	315a (Glorification of God)
	III	524a (Narratives)
	IV	3b (Pairs and Pairing); 315b (Psalms); 538a (Scholar)
80	I	155b (Archaeology and the Q); 346b (Clothing); 496a (David)
	II	145b (Expeditions and Battles)
	III	249a (Magic); 253b (Manual Labor); 487b (Myths and Legends in the Q)
	V	200b (Teaching)
81	I	52a, 52b, 53b (Air and Wind)
	III	487a (Myths and Legends in the Q)
	IV	513b (Sacred Precincts); 537b (Scholar)
	V	77b (Solomon); 412a (Vehicles); 470b (Weather)

81-82	IV	164b (Popular and Talismanic Uses of the Q)
82	I	526b (Devil)
	II	467b (Hunting and Fishing)
	III	44b (Jinn); 253b (Manual Labor); 487a (Myths and Legends in the Q)
	IV	307b (Protection)
	V	77a (Solomon); 120b (Spiritual Beings)
83	III	378a (Mercy)
	V	134a (Suffering); 381a (Trust and Patience)
83-84	III	50a, 50b (Job)
	V	574b (Zechariah)
83-85	V	380b (Trust and Patience)
84	V	134a (Suffering)
85	I	8a (Abraham); 527b, 528a (Dhū l-Kifl)
	II	484a (Idrīs); 564a (Ishmael)
	V	381a (Trust and Patience)
85-86	V	246a, 249b (Textual Criticism of the Q)
87	I	494a (Darkness)
	III	54a, 54b (Jonah); 305b (Material Culture and the Q)
	IV	223b (Prayer); 429b (Repentance and Penance)
	V	488b (Witness to Faith); 500b (Witnessing and Testifying)
87-88	I	93b (Anger); 99a (Animal Life)
	III	53a (Jonah)
	V	574b (Zechariah)
88	IV	430a (Repentance and Penance)
89-90	III	210b (Literature and the Q); 289a (Mary)
	V	574b (Zechariah)
90	III	51b (John the Baptist)
	IV	142b (Politics and the Q)
91	I	52b (Air and Wind); 87a (Angel); 298b (Chastity)
	II	278b (Gabriel); 442a, 443b (Holy Spirit)
	III	14a (Jesus); 289a, 293a, 293b (Mary)
	IV	581a, 583b (Sex and Sexuality)
	V	4a (Signs); 81b (Soul); 114b (Spirit); 371a (Trinity)
91-93	III	7b, 14a (Jesus)
92	I	372a (Community and Society in the Q)
	II	330a (God and his Attributes)
92-93	II	497a (Illiteracy)
93-94	V	387a (Truth)
94	I	243b, 243b (Book)

95	III	173a (Lawful and Unlawful)
96	I	111a (Antichrist); 112b (Apocalypse); 398b (Conquest)
	III	143b (Last Judgment)
	IV	434b (Resurrection)
96-97	I	61a (Alexander)
	II	331b (Gog and Magog)
97	II	361a (Grammar and the Q); 489a, 489a (Ignorance)
	V	387a (Truth)
97-103	IV	34b (Peace)
98	II	415a (Hell and Hellfire)
	V	241b (Textual Criticism of the Q)
101-107	III	436b (Mosque)
102	V	478b (Whisper)
103	II	47b (Eschatology); 198a (Fear)
104	I	479a (Creation)
	II	395b (Ḥadīth and the Q); 411b (Heaven and Sky); 439b (History and the Q); 545a (Instruments)
	III	140a (Last Judgment)
	IV	6b (Pairs and Pairing); 34b (Peace); 435a (Resurrection)
	V	242a (Textual Criticism of the Q)
105	I	244b (Book)
	II	152a (Expeditions and Battles); 340b (Good Deeds)
	III	4a, 6a (Jerusalem); 305b (Material Culture and the Q)
	IV	315a, 316a (Psalms)
105-112	II	143a (Exhortations); 261b (Form and Structure of the Q)
107	III	382b (Messenger); 442b, 443b (Muḥammad)
	IV	299b (Prophets and Prophethood)
	V	393a, 393b (Turkish Literature and the Q)
108	II	329b (God and his Attributes)
	IV	294a (Prophets and Prophethood)
	V	500a (Witnessing and Testifying)
109	III	305b (Material Culture and the Q)
110	IV	4a (Pairs and Pairing)
	V	479b (Whisper)
111	V	288b (Time)
112	III	305b (Material Culture and the Q)

Sūrat al-Ḥajj (22)

I 230b (Biology as the Creation and Stages of Life)
II 264a (Form and Structure of the Q)
IV 250b (Pre-1800 Preoccupations of Q Studies); 496b (Ritual and the Q)
V 174b (Sūra)

1 I 501a (Day, Times of)
II 148b (Expeditions and Battles); 264a (Form and Structure of the Q)
III 137a (Last Judgment)
V 174b (Sūra); 287b (Time)

2 II 556a (Intoxicants)
III 106a (Lactation); 227b (Load or Burden)
V 476b (Wet-Nursing)

3 I 512b (Debate and Disputation); 524b (Devil)
III 579b (Opposition to Muḥammad)

4 I 244b (Book)

5 I 3b (Abortion); 81a (Anatomy); 213a (Beauty); 230b, 231a (Biology as the Creation and Stages of Life); 238a (Blood and Blood Clot); 364b (Colors); 477a, 479a (Creation)
II 3a, 3b (Earth); 28b (Epigraphy); 303a (Geography); 328a (God and his Attributes); 507b (Impotence)
III 304a (Material Culture and the Q); 332a (Maturity)
IV 435b (Resurrection)
V 133b (Suffering); 267a (Theology and the Q); 289a (Time); 522a (Womb); 569b (Youth and Old Age)

5-6 I 479b (Creation)

6 I 213a (Beauty)
II 321b (God and his Attributes)

7 I 232b (Biology as the Creation and Stages of Life); 501a (Day, Times of)
II 29b (Epigraphy); 148b (Expeditions and Battles)
III 137a (Last Judgment)
V 287b (Time)

8 I 512b (Debate and Disputation)
III 579b (Opposition to Muḥammad)

9 II 210b (Fire)
III 58a (Journey)
IV 457a (Reward and Punishment)

11 V 244b (Textual Criticism of the Q)

12 IV 5a (Pairs and Pairing); 228b (Prayer)

13 I 344b (Clients and Clientage)

14 II 340b (Good Deeds)

15	I	93b (Anger)
15-44	I	151b (Archaeology and the Q)
16	II	497b (Illiteracy)
17	I	222b (Belief and Unbelief); 378a (Community and Society in the Q); 516b (Decision)
	III	22a (Jews and Judaism); 244a, 244b (Magians); 246b (Magic)
	IV	403a, 404b, 405a, 407b, 408a (Religious Pluralism and the Q); 511b (Sabians); 586a (Sheba)
18	I	99b (Animal Life); 254b (Bowing and Prostration); 480b (Creeds)
	III	415a (Moon)
	IV	4b (Pairs and Pairing); 221a (Prayer); 378a (Recitation of the Q)
	V	121b (Springs and Fountains); 163a (Sun); 359a (Tree); 393a (Turkish Literature and the Q)
19	I	81b (Anatomy); 222a (Belief and Unbelief); 347a (Clothing); 513b (Debate and Disputation)
	II	210b (Fire); 400a (Ḥamza b. ʿAbd al-Muṭṭalib); 416a (Hell and Hellfire)
19-20	II	211a (Fire); 416a (Hell and Hellfire)
19-21	II	50b (Eschatology)
	V	133a (Suffering)
20	II	426a (Hides and Fleece)
21	II	546a (Instruments)
	III	383a (Metals and Minerals)
22	II	210b (Fire)
	III	63b (Joy and Misery)
23	I	96a (Animal Life); 220b (Belief and Unbelief)
	II	284a (Garden); 333b (Gold)
	III	383b, 384a (Metals and Minerals)
	IV	18a (Paradise)
	V	11b, 12a (Silk)
24	III	583b (Oppression)
25	I	215a (Bedouin)
	II	299a (Geography); 420b (Heresy)
	III	77b (Kaʿba); 340b (Mecca)
	IV	332a (Quraysh); 515a (Sacred Precincts)
26	I	254a (Bowing and Prostration)
	II	56b (Ethics and the Q); 84b (Everyday Life, Q In); 460a (House, Domestic and Divine)
	III	76b (Kaʿba)
	IV	52b (People of the House); 219b (Prayer); 505b (Ritual Purity); 514b (Sacred Precincts)
	V	140b (Ṣūfism and the Q)

26-27 I 7b (Abraham)

26-28 III 340b (Mecca)

26-29 I 330b (Chronology and the Q)

26-33 II 340a (Good Deeds)

27 I 96a (Animal Life)
II 198b (Feet); 462a (House, Domestic and Divine)
IV 91b (Pilgrimage); 104b (Place of Abraham)
V 175a (Sūra); 375a (Trips and Voyages)

27-29 III 340b (Mecca)

27-37 IV 517b (Sacrifice)

28 I 101a (Animal Life)
II 7a (Economics); 216b, 218b (Food and Drink); 450b (Hospitality and Courtesy)
IV 208b (Poverty and the Poor); 420b (Remembrance)
V 179b (Sustenance); 280a (Time)

29 III 77a (Kaʿba); 338b, 340b (Mecca)
IV 52b (People of the House); 93b (Pilgrimage); 514b (Sacred Precincts)

30 I 411b (Contamination)
II 474b (Iconoclasm); 481a, 481b (Idols and Images)
III 172b (Lawful and Unlawful); 190a (Literacy)
IV 282a (Profane and Sacred); 503b (Ritual Purity)
V 21a (Sin, Major and Minor)

31 I 52a, 54b (Air and Wind); 100a (Animal Life); 330b (Chronology and the Q)
II 216a (Flying); 402b (Ḥanīf)
V 470b (Weather)

32 II 408a (Heart); 550a (Intention)

33 III 77a (Kaʿba); 339a, 340b (Mecca)
IV 52b (People of the House); 514b (Sacred Precincts)

34 I 96b (Animal Life)
II 205b (Festivals and Commemorative Days); 329b (God and his Attributes); 341a (Good News); 355b (Grammar and the Q); 432a (History and the Q)
III 583b (Oppression)
IV 420b (Remembrance)

35 II 187b (Fate); 198a (Fear); 450a (Hospitality and Courtesy)
III 372a, 373a (Memory)
V 133b (Suffering)

36 I 97a (Animal Life)
II 205b (Festivals and Commemorative Days)
III 372a (Memory)
IV 420b (Remembrance)
V 3a (Signs)

36-37	II	218b (Food and Drink)
37	I	80b (Anatomy)
	II	82b (Everyday Life, Q In); 341a (Good News)
	IV	517b (Sacrifice)
38	I	220b, 221a (Belief and Unbelief)
39	I	505b (Days of God)
	III	558b (Numismatics); 579a (Opposition to Muḥammad)
	IV	35a (Peace)
	V	437a (Virtues and Vices, Commanding and Forbidding); 456b (War)
39-40	II	209a (Fighting)
	III	40a, 40b, 41b (Jihād); 568a (Obedience)
39-41	III	422b (Moses)
39-49	IV	320b (Punishment Stories)
40	I	164a (Art and Architecture and the Q); 314a (Christians and Christianity); 335b (Church)
	II	92a (Everyday Life, Q In); 228a (Foreign Vocabulary); 322a (God and his Attributes)
	III	23a (Jews and Judaism); 230a (Lord)
	IV	5b (Pairs and Pairing); 230b (Prayer); 404a (Religious Pluralism and the Q); 420b (Remembrance); 516b (Sacred Precincts)
	V	457a, 458b (War)
41	IV	490a (Ritual and the Q)
	V	437a, 437b, 438a (Virtues and Vices, Commanding and Forbidding)
42	I	21b (ʿĀd)
	II	439a (History and the Q)
	III	486b (Myths and Legends in the Q); 540a, 540b (Noah)
	IV	301a (Prophets and Prophethood); 309b (Provocation); 586b (Sheba)
42-45	III	522a (Narratives)
42-49	IV	320b (Punishment Stories)
43	II	308a (Geography)
44	II	489a (Ignorance)
	III	390b (Midian)
45	I	166a (Art and Architecture and the Q)
	II	352b (Grammar and the Q)
	IV	357b (Readings of the Q)
	V	22a (Sin, Major and Minor); 463a (Water)
46	I	81b, 83b (Anatomy); 449b (Cosmology)
	II	370b (Gratitude and Ingratitude)
	II	510b (Indifference)
	IV	574a, 575b (Seeing and Hearing)
	V	447a, 447b (Vision and Blindness)

47	II	410b (Heaven and Sky); 433a (History and the Q)
	V	286a (Time); 560a (Year)
48	III	378b (Mercy)
	IV	310b (Provocation)
	V	22a (Sin, Major and Minor); 287a (Time)
50	II	245a (Forgiveness)
	V	179a (Sustenance)
50-51	II	527a (Inimitability)
	IV	1b (Pairs and Pairing)
52	I	15a (Abrogation)
	II	365a (Grammar and the Q); 392a (Ḥadīth and the Q); 474b (Iconoclasm)
	III	381a, 382a (Messenger); 454a (Muḥammad)
	IV	289b, 295a (Prophets and Prophethood); 532b (Satanic Verses); 537b (Scholar)
	V	25a, 25b (Sin, Major and Minor); 243a (Textual Criticism of the Q); 363a (Trial); 487a (Wish and Desire)
52-53	I	321a (Chronology and the Q)
52-54	IV	532b (Satanic Verses)
53	II	407a, 407b (Heart)
	V	363b (Trial)
53-54	II	469a (Hypocrites and Hypocrisy)
54	I	247b (Book)
	II	320b (God and his Attributes)
	IV	538b (Scholar)
	V	203b (Teaching)
55	I	500a, 501a (Day, Times of)
	III	137a, 138a (Last Judgment)
	V	287b (Time)
55-57	V	103a (Sovereignty)
56	II	282b (Garden); 321a (God and his Attributes)
	III	62b (Joy and Misery); 92b (Kings and Rulers)
	IV	128a (Politics and the Q)
	V	573b (Zealotry)
56-57	IV	2b (Pairs and Pairing)
58	III	38b (Jihād)
	IV	30b (Path or Way)
	V	178b (Sustenance); 457a (War)
58-59	II	45b (Eschatology)
	III	41a (Jihād)
59	IV	6a (Pairs and Pairing); 537b (Scholar)
60	IV	5b (Pairs and Pairing)
	V	456b (War)

61	IV	4b (Pairs and Pairing)
62	I	158b (Arrogance)
	II	82b (Everyday Life, Q In); 99a (Evil Deeds); 320a, 321b (God and his Attributes)
	III	304a (Material Culture and the Q)
	IV	5b (Pairs and Pairing); 228b (Prayer); 263b (Pride)
63	I	362b (Colors)
	II	3a (Earth); 28b (Epigraphy); 303a (Geography)
64	IV	6a (Pairs and Pairing)
65	I	96a (Animal Life); 443a (Cosmology); 473a (Creation)
	II	411a (Heaven and Sky)
	III	379a (Mercy)
	IV	5b (Pairs and Pairing); 186a (Possession and Possessions)
	V	412a (Vehicles); 464a (Water)
66	IV	435b (Resurrection)
67	I	372a (Community and Society in the Q)
	II	432a (History and the Q)
	IV	132b (Politics and the Q)
67-68	I	513b (Debate and Disputation)
67-72	I	523b (Destiny)
68	I	511b, 513b (Debate and Disputation)
	III	40a (Jihād)
	IV	309b (Provocation)
68-69	III	453b (Muḥammad)
	IV	133b (Politics and the Q)
69	II	321a (God and his Attributes)
	V	573b (Zealotry)
70	I	243a (Book); 523a (Destiny)
	II	544b (Instruments)
72	II	435b (History and the Q)
	III	190a (Literacy); 536b (News)
	IV	286b (Proof)
	V	438a (Virtues and Vices, Commanding and Forbidding)
73	I	99b (Animal Life); 472b (Creation)
	II	508a (Impotence)
	IV	79b (Philosophy and the Q)
74	II	92a (Everyday Life, Q In)
	IV	5b (Pairs and Pairing)
75	II	11b, 12a (Election)
	III	446a (Muḥammad)
	IV	5b (Pairs and Pairing); 291a (Prophets and Prophethood)
76	IV	4b (Pairs and Pairing)

77 I 254a (Bowing and Prostration)
IV 219b, 220a (Prayer)

77-78 III 303a (Material Culture and the Q)

78 I 6a, 7b (Abraham); 330b (Chronology and the Q); 461a (Courage); 465a (Covenant)
II 11b (Election); 340a (Good Deeds)
III 38a (Jihād); 231a (Lord); 447a (Muḥammad)
IV 5b (Pairs and Pairing)
V 196b (Taxation); 493b (Witnessing and Testifying)

SŪRAT AL-MUʾMINŪN (23)

I 230b (Biology as the Creation and Stages of Life)
III 11b, 14a (Jesus); 305a (Material Culture and the Q)
IV 478b (Rhymed Prose); 496a (Ritual and the Q)

1 I 220b (Belief and Unbelief)
II 361b (Grammar and the Q)

1-5 I 84a (Anatomy)

1-6 I 219b (Belief and Unbelief)
II 29a (Epigraphy)

1-9 IV 455a (Reward and Punishment)

1-11 I 257b (Breaking Trusts and Contracts)
III 210a (Literature and the Q)

2 I 257b (Breaking Trusts and Contracts)
III 210a (Literature and the Q)

3 I 257b (Breaking Trusts and Contracts)
III 109b (Language and Style of the Q)

4 I 257b (Breaking Trusts and Contracts)

5 I 298b (Chastity)
IV 584a (Sex and Sexuality)

5-6 I 396b (Concubines)
V 58a (Slaves and Slavery); 527b (Women and the Q)

5-7 I 257b (Breaking Trusts and Contracts); 299a, 299b (Chastity)

6 IV 288a (Property); 582a (Sex and Sexuality)
V 57b (Slaves and Slavery); 527b (Women and the Q)

8 I 257a, 257b (Breaking Trusts and Contracts); 464b (Covenant)
II 8b (Economics)

8-11 I 219b (Belief and Unbelief)

9 I 257b (Breaking Trusts and Contracts)
III 210a (Literature and the Q)
IV 224b (Prayer)

11	II	51a (Eschatology); 229a (Foreign Vocabulary); 283a (Garden)
12	I	231a (Biology as the Creation and Stages of Life); 233b (Birth); 339b, 340a (Clay); 446a (Cosmology); 476a (Creation)
	II	4a (Earth); 328a (God and his Attributes); 340a (Good Deeds)
	V	267a (Theology and the Q)
12-13	I	80a (Anatomy)
	III	354b (Medicine and the Q)
12-14	I	3a (Abortion); 233a (Birth); 238a (Blood and Blood Clot); 340a (Clay); 477a, 477b (Creation)
	II	87a (Everyday Life, Q In); 328a (God and his Attributes)
12-16	III	14a (Jesus); 183b (Life)
13	III	597a (Ornamentation and Illumination)
	V	522b (Womb)
14	I	80a, 81a (Anatomy); 479a (Creation)
	IV	220b (Prayer)
	V	522b (Womb)
16	III	183b (Life)
17	I	442a (Cosmology)
	II	51a (Eschatology)
	IV	107b (Planets and Stars)
17-22	I	473a (Creation)
18	II	3a (Earth)
	III	334a (Measurement)
	V	462b (Water)
18-19	III	531a (Nature as Signs)
18-20	II	3a (Earth)
	V	126b, 127b (Springs and Fountains)
19	I	220b (Belief and Unbelief); 478b (Creation)
	II	217b (Food and Drink); 283b (Garden); 304a (Geography)
	V	126b (Springs and Fountains)
20	I	102b (Anointing); 362a (Colors)
	II	218b (Food and Drink); 305a (Geography)
	IV	482b (Rhymed Prose)
	V	28a (Sinai); 185a (Syria); 362a (Tree)
21	I	96a (Animal Life)
21-22	IV	438a (Revelation and Inspiration)
22	III	227b (Load or Burden)
	V	133a (Suffering); 412a (Vehicles)
23	III	524a (Narratives)
	V	123a (Springs and Fountains)

23-30 III 540b (Noah)
IV 438b (Revelation and Inspiration)

23-49 IV 320a (Punishment Stories)

24 IV 296a (Prophets and Prophethood); 311b (Provocation)

25 II 540a (Insanity)
IV 112a (Poetry and Poets)

27 I 96a (Animal Life); 553b (Drowning)
II 154a (Eyes); 213a (Fire); 219a (Food and Drink); 229a (Foreign Vocabulary); 323b, 324b (God and his Attributes)
III 393a (Miracles); 541a (Noah)
IV 6b (Pairs and Pairing); 217a (Prayer); 293b (Prophets and Prophethood); 439b (Revelation and Inspiration); 581a (Sex and Sexuality)
V 271a (Theology and the Q); 546a (Word of God)

28 I 519a (Deliverance)
IV 213b (Praise)

29 III 488a (Myths and Legends in the Q)

31 I 479a (Creation)
II 293a (Generations)

31-41 IV 319b (Punishment Stories)

33 I 235b (Blasphemy)
II 217a (Food and Drink)

35 II 4b (Earth); 358a (Grammar and the Q)

37 I 506a (Death and the Dead)
II 508a (Impotence)

38 I 236a (Blasphemy)

41 I 491b (Curse)

42 I 479a (Creation)

43 V 289a (Time)

44 I 491b (Curse)
II 435b (History and the Q)
III 382a (Messenger); 453a (Muḥammad); 517b (Narratives)
IV 291a, 301a (Prophets and Prophethood)

45 I 1a (Aaron); 260a, 261a (Brother and Brotherhood)
III 421b (Moses)
IV 106a (Plagues)

45-48 III 423a (Moses)

46 I 160a (Arrogance); 395b (Conceit)
II 542a (Insolence and Obstinacy)
III 421b (Moses)
IV 264a (Pride)

49	I	245a (Book)
	III	424b, 425a (Moses)
	V	301a, 302a (Torah)
50	II	10a, 10b (Egypt)
	III	5b (Jerusalem); 7b, 8a, 11a, 13b (Jesus); 293a (Mary)
	V	121b, 127b (Springs and Fountains); 533b (Women and the Q)
51	I	96b (Animal Life)
	II	467a (Hunting and Fishing)
	IV	295b (Prophets and Prophethood)
52	II	330a (God and his Attributes); 349a (Grammar and the Q)
52-53	II	497a (Illiteracy)
	IV	25a (Parties and Factions)
52-54	I	377b (Community and Society in the Q)
53	II	432a (History and the Q)
	III	24b (Jews and Judaism); 61b (Joy and Misery)
	IV	24b (Parties and Factions); 403b (Religious Pluralism and the Q)
54	III	40a (Jihād)
55	IV	3b (Pairs and Pairing)
55-56	V	468a (Wealth)
56	II	61a (Ethics and the Q)
57	II	197b (Fear)
57-61	I	219b (Belief and Unbelief)
	II	259b (Form and Structure of the Q)
60	II	198a (Fear); 359b (Grammar and the Q)
62	IV	432b (Responsibility)
	V	84a (Soul); 111a (Speech)
63-67	III	379b (Mercy)
64	IV	332a (Quraysh); 453a (Reward and Punishment)
65	II	355a (Grammar and the Q)
66	III	190a (Literacy)
68	IV	394b (Reflection and Deliberation)
70	II	540a (Insanity)
	IV	112a (Poetry and Poets)
71	IV	522b (Salvation)
72	III	190a (Literacy)
	IV	452b (Reward and Punishment)
	V	192b, 196a (Taxation)
72-77	II	143b (Exhortations)

73-75 I 437a (Conversion)

75-77 IV 332a (Quraysh)

77 I 398b (Conquest); 521b (Despair); 524b (Devil)

78 I 479a (Creation)

78-79 I 476a (Creation)

78-80 II 67b (Ethics and the Q)

80 I 501b (Day, Times of)
IV 4b (Pairs and Pairing)
V 280b (Time)

82 II 4b (Earth)

83 II 430a (History and the Q)
III 518a (Narratives)

84 IV 311a (Provocation)

86 II 325b (God and his Attributes); 410b (Heaven and Sky)
III 230a (Lord); 554b (Numerology)
IV 107b (Planets and Stars)

88 I 369b (Community and Society in the Q); 519b (Deliverance)
II 401b (Hand)
III 201b (Literary Structures of the Q)
IV 127b (Politics and the Q); 307b (Protection)

91 III 14a (Jesus)
IV 80b (Philosophy and the Q); 220a, 220b (Prayer)
V 369a (Trinity)

92 IV 4a (Pairs and Pairing); 537b (Scholar)

96 II 452b (Hospitality and Courtesy)
III 40b (Jihād); 65b (Judgment); 453b (Muḥammad)

97 I 526b (Devil)
II 92b (Everyday Life, Q In); 344a (Gossip)

97-98 IV 308a (Protection)

99 IV 430a (Repentance and Penance)

99-101 III 379b (Mercy)

100 I 91a (Angel); 204b, 206a (Barzakh); 232b (Biology as the Creation and Stages of Life)
II 229a (Foreign Vocabulary)

101 II 547a (Instruments)
III 99b (Kinship); 379b (Mercy)

101-105 I 522b (Destiny)

102 III 178a (Left Hand and Right Hand); 334b (Measurement)
IV 523a (Salvation)

102-103 III 70a (Justice and Injustice); 140b (Last Judgment); 334b (Measurement)
IV 2b (Pairs and Pairing)
V 313b (Trade and Commerce)

103 III 178a (Left Hand and Right Hand); 334b (Measurement)

104 I 222a (Belief and Unbelief); 556a (Druzes)
II 416a (Hell and Hellfire)
V 133a (Suffering)

105 III 190a (Literacy)

106 III 63b (Joy and Misery)
V 430b (Victory)

109 III 378a (Mercy)

110 III 146b (Laughter); 401a (Mockery)
IV 309b (Provocation)

111 II 98a (Evil Deeds)
IV 523a (Salvation)
V 134b (Suffering); 430a (Victory)

112 II 439b (History and the Q)
V 286a (Time); 553b (World)

115 I 442a (Cosmology)
II 98a (Evil Deeds); 186b (Fate); 327b (God and his Attributes); 336b (Good and Evil); 340a (Good Deeds)
V 553b (World)

116 II 325b (God and his Attributes)
V 103b (Sovereignty); 277a (Throne of God)

116-118 II 143b (Exhortations)

117 III 14a (Jesus)
IV 286b (Proof); 523a (Salvation)

118 III 378a (Mercy)

Sūrat al-Nūr (24)

I 328a (Chronology and the Q)
II 264a (Form and Structure of the Q)
IV 450a (Revision and Alteration); 496a (Ritual and the Q)
V 174b (Sūra); 538a (Women and the Q)

1 I 246a (Book)
IV 286a, 286b (Proof)
V 6b (Signs); 167a (Sūra)

2 I 17b, 18a (Abrogation); 28a (Adultery and Fornication); 295a (Chastisement and Punishment); 299b (Chastity); 352b (Collection of the Q)
II 214a (Flogging)

III 136b (Last Judgment)
IV 277a (Prisoners); 416a (Religious Pluralism and the Q); 449a, 449b (Revision and Alteration); 453a (Reward and Punishment); 580b, 584a (Sex and Sexuality)
V 254b (Theft); 495a, 497b (Witnessing and Testifying); 528a (Women and the Q)

3 I 299a, 299a (Chastity)
III 277a, 277b (Marriage and Divorce)
IV 285a (Prohibited Degrees); 580b (Sex and Sexuality)

4 I 28b, 29a (Adultery and Fornication)
II 214a (Flogging)
III 552b (Numbers and Enumeration)
IV 583b, 584a (Sex and Sexuality)
V 490a (Witness to Faith); 492b, 496b, 497b (Witnessing and Testifying)

4-5 II 214b (Flogging); 344a (Gossip)
IV 427a (Repentance and Penance)
V 498a (Witnessing and Testifying); 511a (Wives of the Prophet)

4-9 III 73a (Justice and Injustice); 551b (Numbers and Enumeration)

4-26 V 528a, 535a (Women and the Q)

5 II 214b (Flogging)
III 379b (Mercy)

6 V 492b (Witnessing and Testifying)

6-9 I 492a (Curse)
III 280b (Marriage and Divorce)
V 498a (Witnessing and Testifying)

6-10 I 29a (Adultery and Fornication)

8 IV 453a (Reward and Punishment)
V 492b (Witnessing and Testifying)

9 I 93a, 93b (Anger)

10 IV 6a (Pairs and Pairing)

10-18 I 29a (Adultery and Fornication)

11 III 448a (Muḥammad)
IV 426b (Repentance and Penance); 432b (Responsibility)
V 21a (Sin, Major and Minor)

11-15 II 391b (Ḥadīth and the Q)

11-20 I 56b, 57a (ʿĀʾisha bint Abī Bakr)
II 344a (Gossip)
V 178a (Suspicion)

11-24 III 181b (Lie)

11-26 V 510b, 511a (Wives of the Prophet)

12 V 523b (Women and the Q)

13	I	56b (ʿĀʾisha bint Abī Bakr)
14	III	378b (Mercy)
15	I	82b (Anatomy)
16	II	314b (Glorification of God)
18	IV	537b (Scholar)
19	I	29b (Adultery and Fornication)
	III	73b (Justice and Injustice)
	IV	580b (Sex and Sexuality); 591b (Shīʿa)
	V	133a (Suffering)
20	III	378b (Mercy)
21	I	523a (Destiny); 526a (Devil)
	IV	505a (Ritual Purity); 580b (Sex and Sexuality)
	V	438a (Virtues and Vices, Commanding and Forbidding); 487a (Wish and Desire)
22	II	244b (Forgiveness)
	III	58a (Journey); 378a (Mercy)
	IV	209a (Poverty and the Poor)
23	I	492a (Curse)
	II	418a (Hell and Hellfire)
	III	38b (Jihād)
	IV	457a (Reward and Punishment); 583b (Sex and Sexuality)
23-26	II	469a (Hypocrites and Hypocrisy)
24	I	83a (Anatomy)
	II	402a (Hand); 416b (Hell and Hellfire)
	III	141a (Last Judgment)
	V	110b (Speech); 494b (Witnessing and Testifying)
26	I	299a (Chastity); 440a (Corruption)
	II	245a (Forgiveness)
	III	277a, 277b (Marriage and Divorce)
	IV	8a (Pairs and Pairing); 285a (Prohibited Degrees)
27	I	349a (Codices of the Q)
	II	453a (Hospitality and Courtesy)
	IV	225a (Prayer)
27-29	I	163a (Art and Architecture and the Q); 299b (Chastity)
	II	460a (House, Domestic and Divine)
	V	538a (Women and the Q)
28	IV	506a (Ritual Purity)
29	II	275b (Furniture and Furnishings)
30	III	403a (Modesty)
	IV	506a (Ritual Purity); 581a, 584a (Sex and Sexuality)
	V	58a (Slaves and Slavery); 414a (Veil)

30-31 I 299b (Chastity)
II 453a (Hospitality and Courtesy)
III 548a (Nudity)
IV 574a (Seeing and Hearing)
V 53b (Sister); 526a, 538a (Women and the Q)

30-33 V 71b (Social Sciences and the Q)

31 I 56a (ʿĀʾisha bint Abī Bakr); 155b (Archaeology and the Q); 194a, 194b (Baal); 259b (Brother and Brotherhood); 302b (Children); 346b (Clothing); 383b (Community and Society in the Q)
II 76a (Ethics and the Q); 175b, 176a (Family)
III 403a (Modesty)
IV 427a (Repentance and Penance); 581a, 584a (Sex and Sexuality)
V 53b (Sister); 57b (Slaves and Slavery); 414a, 414b (Veil); 510b, 515b (Wives of the Prophet); 570a (Youth and Old Age)

32 I 396a, 396b (Concubines)
III 277a, 278a (Marriage and Divorce)
IV 6a (Pairs and Pairing); 580b, 581b (Sex and Sexuality)
V 58a, 58b (Slaves and Slavery)

33 I 19b (Abstinence); 242b (Book); 299b (Chastity); 396a, 396b (Concubines)
II 6b, 7a (Economics); 544b (Instruments)
III 96a (Kinship); 159b (Law and the Q); 279a (Marriage and Divorce); 378b (Mercy); 590b, 592b (Orality and Writing in Arabia)
IV 186a, 186b (Possession and Possessions); 580b, 583b (Sex and Sexuality); 600b (Shīʿism and the Q)
V 57a, 57b, 58a, 60a (Slaves and Slavery); 183a (Symbolic Imagery); 468a, 469a (Wealth); 527b (Women and the Q); 549a (Work)

34 II 142b (Exhortations); 434b (History and the Q)

35 I 85b (Angel); 102b (Anointing); 171a (Art and Architecture and the Q); 199a (Bahāʾīs); 213b (Beauty); 435b (Conversion); 490a, 491a (Cups and Vessels)
II 32a, 34a (Epigraphy); 96a (Everyday Life, Q In); 218b (Food and Drink); 275b, 276a (Furniture and Furnishings); 305a (Geography); 326a (God and his Attributes); 547a (Instruments)
III 108a (Lamp); 187a (Light); 208b (Literature and the Q); 311b (Material Culture and the Q); 387b (Metaphor); 431b (Mosque); 534b (Nature as Signs)
IV 10a (Parable); 172a (Popular and Talismanic Uses of the Q); 4a (Pairs and Pairing); 380a (Recitation of the Q); 555a (Science and the Q); 64a (Persian Literature and the Q)
V 18a, 18b (Simile); 125a, 125b (Springs and Fountains); 138a, 155a, 120b (Ṣūfism and the Q); 181a, 181b (Symbolic Imagery); 361b (Tree); 393a, 393b (Turkish Literature and the Q); 427b (Verse)

35-36 III 4b (Jerusalem)

35-38 III 437a (Mosque)

36	I	502b, 504a (Day, Times of)
	II	80a (Evening)
	III	4b (Jerusalem); 418b (Morning)
	IV	230b (Prayer); 516a (Sacred Precincts)
	V	281b (Time); 393a, 393b (Turkish Literature and the Q)
36-37	III	304b (Material Culture and the Q)
36-38	III	312a (Material Culture and the Q)
	IV	222b (Prayer)
36-39	I	219b (Belief and Unbelief)
37	IV	222b (Prayer)
	V	444b (Vision)
37-38	IV	405b (Religious Pluralism and the Q)
38	II	31b (Epigraphy); 345a (Grace)
39	I	184b (Ashes); 555b (Druzes)
	IV	10a (Parable)
	V	15a (Simile)
39-40	V	182a (Symbolic Imagery)
40	III	186b (Light)
	IV	10a (Parable)
	V	182a (Symbolic Imagery); 465b (Water)
41	I	99b (Animal Life); 473b (Creation)
	II	82a (Everyday Life, Q In); 363a (Grammar and the Q)
	III	528b (Nature as Signs)
	IV	4b (Pairs and Pairing)
	V	446b (Vision and Blindness)
42	III	92a (Kings and Rulers)
	IV	4a (Pairs and Pairing)
	V	287a (Time)
43	I	42a (Agriculture and Vegetation); 52a (Air and Wind)
	II	455b (Hot and Cold)
	IV	443b (Revelation and Inspiration)
	V	463a (Water); 470b, 471a (Weather)
43-44	I	472b (Creation)
44	I	501a (Day, Times of)
	II	327b (God and his Attributes)
	IV	4b (Pairs and Pairing)
44-45	I	473b, 476b (Creation)
45	I	95b (Animal Life); 443a (Cosmology); 476b (Creation)
	II	327b, 328a (God and his Attributes)
	III	530b (Nature as Signs)
	V	462b (Water)

47 II 406a (Hearing and Deafness)
V 501b, 502a (Witnessing and Testifying)

47-56 III 566b (Obedience)

50 II 407b (Heart)
III 359b (Medicine and the Q)

51 II 406a (Hearing and Deafness)
III 568b (Obedience)
IV 523a (Salvation)
V 393b (Turkish Literature and the Q); 502a (Witnessing and Testifying)

52 II 196b (Fear)
IV 523a (Salvation)
V 430a (Victory)

53 II 65b (Ethics and the Q)
V 438a (Virtues and Vices, Commanding and Forbidding)

54 III 40a (Jihād); 125a (Language and Style of the Q); 228a (Load or Burden)
IV 148b (Politics and the Q)

55 I 119b (Apostasy); 277b (Caliph)
III 559a (Numismatics)
IV 431b (Responsibility)

57 IV 103b (Pit)

58 I 84a (Anatomy); 396b (Concubines); 444a (Cosmology); 503a, 504a (Day, Times of)
II 79b (Evening); 358b (Grammar and the Q)
III 417a, 418b (Morning); 549a (Nudity)
IV 217b, 224a (Prayer); 537b (Scholar)
V 7a (Signs); 57b (Slaves and Slavery); 183a (Symbolic Imagery); 281a, 281b, 282b (Time); 570a (Youth and Old Age)

58-59 I 299b (Chastity); 302b (Children)

59 IV 186b (Possession and Possessions); 537b (Scholar)

60 IV 580b (Sex and Sexuality)

61 I 65a (Almsgiving); 246a (Book)
II 176a (Family); 452b (Hospitality and Courtesy); 460a (House, Domestic and Divine); 501b (Illness and Health)
IV 225a (Prayer); 288a (Property)
V 7a (Signs); 53b (Sister); 133b (Suffering)

62 V 501b (Witnessing and Testifying)

62-63 III 447b (Muḥammad)

64 II 91b (Everyday Life, Q In)
IV 483b (Rhymed Prose)

Sūrat al-Furqān (25)

I 486b (Criterion)
IV 372b (Recitation of the Q)

1 I 117b (Apologetics); 237a (Blessing); 486b (Criterion)
II 499a (Illiteracy)
III 440b, 442a, 443b (Muḥammad); 507b (Names of the Q)
IV 220b (Prayer); 343a (Ramaḍān); 443b (Revelation and Inspiration); 577a (Servants)

1-3 II 474b (Iconoclasm)

1-62 IV 478a (Rhymed Prose)

2 II 34a (Epigraphy); 329a, 329b (God and his Attributes)
III 92b (Kings and Rulers)
IV 128a (Politics and the Q)
V 369a (Trinity)

2-3 I 472b (Creation)
IV 185a (Possession and Possessions)

3 I 472b (Creation)
II 474a (Iconoclasm)

4 II 513a (Informants)
III 70b (Justice and Injustice)

4-5 II 512b, 517a (Informants)

4-6 III 450a (Muḥammad)
IV 281a (Profane and Sacred)

5 I 501b, 503b, 504a (Day, Times of)
II 80a (Evening); 430a (History and the Q); 492b, 493a (Illiteracy); 517b (Informants)
III 188b (Literacy); 416b (Morning); 518a (Narratives); 592b (Orality and Writing in Arabia)
V 281a (Time); 400b (Ummī)

7 II 217a (Food and Drink)
III 275a (Markets)
IV 296a (Prophets and Prophethood)

7-8 III 247a (Magic); 450a, 456a (Muḥammad)
IV 331a (Quraysh)

8 II 304a (Geography)

8-9 IV 9b (Parable)

10 I 165b (Art and Architecture and the Q); 237a (Blessing)
IV 18b (Paradise); 220b (Prayer)

11	I	235b (Blasphemy); 501a (Day, Times of)
	II	39b (Epigraphy)
	III	137a (Last Judgment)
	V	287b (Time)
11-13	IV	480a (Rhymed Prose)
11-14	II	418a (Hell and Hellfire)
12	I	93a (Anger)
	II	50a (Eschatology); 211a (Fire); 417b (Hell and Hellfire)
15	II	54b (Eternity); 282b (Garden)
	IV	14b (Paradise)
	V	287a (Time)
17	IV	576b (Servants)
17-19	V	494a (Witnessing and Testifying)
18	I	530a (Dialects)
	III	47a (Jinn)
20	II	154a (Eyes); 216b (Food and Drink)
	III	275a (Markets); 381b (Messenger)
	IV	296a (Prophets and Prophethood)
20-22	III	397b (Miracles)
21	I	395b (Conceit); 530a (Dialects)
	II	449a (Hope)
	IV	264a (Pride); 311b (Provocation)
22	I	89b (Angel)
	II	341b (Good News)
	III	173b (Lawful and Unlawful)
23	I	184b (Ashes)
25	I	88a, 89b (Angel); 463a (Court)
	II	411b (Heaven and Sky)
25-26	IV	34b (Peace)
26	III	91b (Kings and Rulers)
	IV	128a (Politics and the Q); 184b (Possession and Possessions)
27	III	203b (Literary Structures of the Q)
29	III	46b (Jinn)
30	II	18b (Emigration)
31	II	23b (Enemies); 64a (Ethics and the Q)
	III	453a (Muḥammad); 576b (Opposition to Muḥammad)
	V	494b (Witnessing and Testifying)
32	I	250b (Book)
	II	88a (Everyday Life, Q In)

	III	116a, 116b (Language and Style of the Q); 450b (Muḥammad); 510b (Names of the Q)
	IV	368b (Recitation of the Q); 444a (Revelation and Inspiration)
	V	423a (Verse)
32-33	IV	139a (Politics and the Q); 570b (Scrolls)
33	I	250b (Book)
	II	100a (Exegesis of the Q: Classical and Medieval)
	IV	444a (Revelation and Inspiration)
34	III	140b (Last Judgment)
35	I	1a (Aaron); 245a (Book); 260a (Brother and Brotherhood)
	III	424b (Moses)
	V	301a (Torah)
35-40	IV	320a (Punishment Stories)
37	I	553b, 554a (Drowning)
	IV	126b (Politics and the Q)
	V	5a (Signs)
37-38	III	540a (Noah)
	IV	352b (Rass)
	V	250b (Textual Criticism of the Q)
38	I	151a (Archaeology and the Q)
	III	522a (Narratives)
40	I	149a (Archaeology and the Q)
	II	212b (Fire); 449a (Hope)
	IV	425b (Remnant)
	V	470b (Weather)
41	III	400a (Mockery)
41-42	III	448b (Muḥammad)
42	IV	538b (Scholar)
	V	379a (Trust and Patience)
43	III	40a (Jihād)
	IV	160a (Polytheism and Atheism)
	V	486b (Wish and Desire)
44	V	393b (Turkish Literature and the Q)
45	I	500b, 504a (Day, Times of)
	III	524a (Narratives)
	IV	422b (Remembrance)
	V	3a (Signs); 163a (Sun); 282b, 283b (Time)
45-50	II	259a (Form and Structure of the Q)
46	III	222b (Literature and the Q)

47	I	346b (Clothing); 501b, 502a (Day, Times of)
	IV	4b (Pairs and Pairing); 511a (Sabbath)
	V	60b (Sleep); 280b (Time)
47-48	III	379a (Mercy)
47-50	I	472b (Creation)
48	I	53a (Air and Wind)
	II	341a (Good News)
	IV	491b (Ritual and the Q); 505b (Ritual Purity)
	V	119a (Spiritual Beings); 126b (Springs and Fountains); 471a (Weather)
48-49	I	96b (Animal Life)
	II	3a (Earth)
49	I	95b (Animal Life)
51	I	163a (Art and Architecture and the Q)
52	I	461a (Courage)
	II	74a (Ethics and the Q); 340a (Good Deeds)
	III	36b (Jihād); 454b (Muḥammad); 567b (Obedience)
53	I	203b (Barrier); 204b (Barzakh); 443a, 445b (Cosmology)
	II	212b (Fire); 217b (Food and Drink); 229a (Foreign Vocabulary)
	III	173b (Lawful and Unlawful); 531a (Nature as Signs)
	IV	7a (Pairs and Pairing)
	V	126a, 126b (Springs and Fountains); 393b (Turkish Literature and the Q)
53-54	I	472b (Creation)
	V	464a (Water)
54	I	368b (Community and Society in the Q); 476b (Creation)
	II	174b (Family); 328a, 328b (God and his Attributes)
	III	99b (Kinship); 354b (Medicine and the Q); 530b (Nature as Signs)
	IV	486a (Ritual and the Q)
54-55	II	303b (Geography)
55	IV	5a (Pairs and Pairing)
55-60	II	143b (Exhortations)
56	II	341b (Good News)
	IV	3b (Pairs and Pairing); 127b, 148b (Politics and the Q)
	V	307b (Torah)
57	III	451a (Muḥammad)
58	I	507a (Death and the Dead)
	II	314b (Glorification of God)
	III	182b (Life)
58-59	I	473b (Creation)
59	I	318b (Chronology and the Q); 442a, 443b (Cosmology); 476a (Creation)
	II	325b, 327b (God and his Attributes); 410b (Heaven and Sky)

	III	202a (Literary Structures of the Q)
	IV	4a (Pairs and Pairing)
	V	265a (Theology and the Q); 279b, 287a (Time); 553a, 553b (World)
60	I	254b (Bowing and Prostration)
	II	448a (Honor)
	IV	219b (Prayer)
	V	393a (Turkish Literature and the Q)
61	I	237a (Blessing); 442b (Cosmology); 472b, 473b, 477b (Creation)
	II	275b (Furniture and Furnishings); 411a (Heaven and Sky); 547a (Instruments)
	III	108a (Lamp); 187a (Light)
	IV	79b (Philosophy and the Q); 107a, 108a (Planets and Stars); 220b (Prayer)
	V	163a (Sun); 283b (Time)
61-62	II	259a (Form and Structure of the Q)
61-77	II	143b (Exhortations)
62	I	442b (Cosmology); 472b, 473b (Creation); 501b (Day, Times of)
	IV	4b (Pairs and Pairing)
63	I	161a (Arrogance)
	II	453a (Hospitality and Courtesy); 488a (Ignorance)
	III	40b (Jihād); 403a (Modesty)
63-64	I	376a (Community and Society in the Q)
63-68	I	219b (Belief and Unbelief)
	IV	577a (Servants)
63-72	II	71a (Ethics and the Q)
63-74	IV	455a (Reward and Punishment)
63-76	II	259b (Form and Structure of the Q)
64	I	182b (Asceticism); 254a (Bowing and Prostration); 327b (Chronology and the Q)
	IV	222b (Prayer)
64-65	IV	221a (Prayer)
67	III	252a (Maintenance and Upkeep)
	V	434b (Virtue)
67-68	V	21a (Sin, Major and Minor)
68	I	28a (Adultery and Fornication); 239a (Blood Money)
	IV	580b (Sex and Sexuality)
	V	83a (Soul); 417a (Vengeance)
68-69	IV	456a (Reward and Punishment)
69	IV	6b (Pairs and Pairing); 458b (Reward and Punishment)
70	III	140b (Last Judgment)
	IV	431b (Responsibility)

70-71 IV 426b (Repentance and Penance)
72 V 21a (Sin, Major and Minor); 492a (Witnessing and Testifying)
72-74 I 219b (Belief and Unbelief)
73 II 406b (Hearing and Deafness)
IV 422b (Remembrance)
74 I 235a (Birth Control); 302b (Children)
III 235a (Love and Affection)
IV 20b (Parents); 600b (Shīʿism and the Q)
74-75 I 406a (Consolation)
75 I 165b (Art and Architecture and the Q)
V 134b (Suffering)

Sūrat al-Shuʿarāʾ (26)

I 532a, 534a (Dialogues)
III 200b (Literary Structures of the Q); 272a (Manuscripts of the Q); 381b (Messenger); 472b (Mysterious Letters)
IV 113a (Poetry and Poets); 474b (Rhetoric and the Q)
1 IV 496a (Ritual and the Q)
1-9 II 143a (Exhortations)
III 519b (Narratives)
2 II 497b (Illiteracy)
III 124b (Language and Style of the Q); 592a (Orality and Writing in Arabia)
3 II 510b (Indifference)
III 452b (Muḥammad)
V 134a (Suffering)
4 II 363b (Grammar and the Q)
5 I 222a (Belief and Unbelief)
6 III 400b (Mockery); 536b (News)
7 I 472b (Creation)
II 3a, 3b (Earth)
7-8 I 213a (Beauty)
IV 438a (Revelation and Inspiration)
8 III 524b (Narratives)
8-191 IV 320a (Punishment Stories)
9 IV 6a (Pairs and Pairing)
10 V 110a (Speech)
10-17 I 532b (Dialogues)

10-68	I	304b (Children of Israel)
	III	519b (Narratives)
10-189	III	519b (Narratives)
10-191	III	381b (Messenger)
12-14	I	533b (Dialogues)
13	I	1a (Aaron)
14	I	260b (Brother and Brotherhood)
	II	64a (Ethics and the Q)
15-17	III	488a (Myths and Legends in the Q)
16-27	III	494b (Myths and Legends in the Q)
17	I	532b (Dialogues)
18	I	532b (Dialogues)
	II	433b (History and the Q)
	III	420a (Moses)
	V	285b (Time)
18-19	I	220b (Belief and Unbelief)
	III	518b (Narratives)
	IV	67b (Pharaoh)
19	I	260b (Brother and Brotherhood)
	III	420b (Moses)
20	II	43b (Error)
21	III	420b (Moses)
23-24	V	553a (World)
24	II	31a (Epigraphy)
	III	230a (Lord)
27	I	447a (Cosmology)
	II	540a (Insanity)
	IV	67b (Pharaoh); 112a (Poetry and Poets)
28	III	230a (Lord)
	IV	4b (Pairs and Pairing); 184a (Possession and Possessions)
	V	282b (Time)
29	II	542b (Insolence and Obstinacy)
	IV	67b (Pharaoh); 160a (Polytheism and Atheism); 276b (Prisoners)
30-35	III	422a (Moses)
31	IV	296b (Prophets and Prophethood)
31-34	IV	296b (Prophets and Prophethood)
32	I	99a (Animal Life)
	II	546a (Instruments)
	III	219a (Literature and the Q)

33	I	364a (Colors)
34	V	239b (Textual Criticism of the Q)
35	III	246a (Magic)
37	IV	605b (Shuʿayb)
38	I	500b (Day, Times of)
	V	288b (Time)
38-51	III	393b (Miracles)
40	I	445b (Cosmology)
41	IV	452a (Reward and Punishment)
41-51	III	211b (Literature and the Q)
44	II	546b (Instruments)
	IV	509a (Rod)
	V	393b (Turkish Literature and the Q)
45	II	546a (Instruments)
	III	219a (Literature and the Q)
46	I	255a (Bowing and Prostration)
47-48	II	199a (Feet)
48	I	1a (Aaron)
	III	229b (Lord)
	IV	483a (Rhymed Prose)
49	I	487b, 488a (Crucifixion)
	II	199a (Feet)
	III	246a (Magic)
	IV	67b (Pharaoh)
	V	201b (Teaching)
51	II	448b (Hope)
52	III	423a (Moses)
	IV	440a (Revelation and Inspiration)
52-68	III	423a (Moses)
54	V	377a (Troops)
57	II	283b (Garden)
	V	127b (Springs and Fountains)
57-58	III	488a (Myths and Legends in the Q)
59	III	488a (Myths and Legends in the Q)
60	I	503b (Day, Times of)
	III	417b (Morning)
	V	282b (Time)
60-68	III	394a (Miracles)

63	II	546a (Instruments)
	III	219a (Literature and the Q)
	IV	440a (Revelation and Inspiration); 509a (Rod)
	V	464b (Water)
63-66	II	213a (Fire)
	III	423b (Moses)
65	II	184a (Fasting)
65-67	I	553b (Drowning)
67	III	524b (Narratives)
67-68	III	381b (Messenger)
68	IV	6a (Pairs and Pairing)
69	II	254b (Form and Structure of the Q); 340a (Good Deeds); 435b (History and the Q)
	III	190a (Literacy); 441a (Muḥammad); 518a, 524b (Narratives); 536b (News)
	IV	302b (Prophets and Prophethood)
	V	258a (Theology and the Q)
69-82	I	532a (Dialogues)
	II	558a (Invitation)
69-86	I	6b (Abraham)
	III	494a (Myths and Legends in the Q)
69-89	I	330a (Chronology and the Q)
69-104	III	519b (Narratives)
71	II	474a (Iconoclasm); 481a, 481b (Idols and Images)
72	IV	5a (Pairs and Pairing)
74	V	317a (Tradition and Custom)
76	II	434a (History and the Q)
77	II	23b (Enemies)
77-78	I	472a (Creation)
78-80	III	184a (Life)
79	II	217a (Food and Drink)
80	II	501b (Illness and Health)
	IV	178b (Popular and Talismanic Uses of the Q)
	V	133b (Suffering)
81	III	184a (Life)
82	I	147b (Arbitration)
	II	448b (Hope)
	III	136b (Last Judgment)
83	II	33a (Epigraphy)

83-89	I	328a (Chronology and the Q)
	IV	223b (Prayer)
84	I	83a (Anatomy)
85	II	282b (Garden)
	IV	14b (Paradise)
86	I	7a (Abraham); 193a (Āzar)
	II	43b (Error)
	IV	21a (Parents)
88	IV	3b (Pairs and Pairing)
	V	393b (Turkish Literature and the Q); 468a (Wealth)
89	II	408a (Heart)
94-95	I	525a (Devil)
	II	543a (Insolence and Obstinacy)
95	I	447a (Cosmology)
	III	45a (Jinn)
	V	120b (Spiritual Beings); 377b (Troops)
96-97	I	513b (Debate and Disputation)
96-102	II	416b (Hell and Hellfire)
100-101	II	273b (Friends and Friendship)
101	II	71a (Ethics and the Q)
	III	236a (Love and Affection); 237a (Loyalty)
102	III	203b (Literary Structures of the Q)
	IV	430a (Repentance and Penance)
103	III	524b (Narratives)
	V	5a (Signs)
104	IV	6a (Pairs and Pairing)
104-190	III	212b (Literature and the Q)
105	I	222a (Belief and Unbelief)
	III	524a (Narratives); 540a (Noah)
105-106	I	261b (Brother and Brotherhood)
105-118	I	532a (Dialogues)
105-122	III	486a (Myths and Legends in the Q); 519b (Narratives)
105-191	V	313b (Trade and Commerce)
106	III	486a (Myths and Legends in the Q)
	IV	299b (Prophets and Prophethood)
108	III	567b (Obedience)
	IV	478b (Rhymed Prose)
109	IV	452b (Reward and Punishment)

110	III	567b (Obedience)
	IV	478b (Rhymed Prose)
111	II	358b (Grammar and the Q)
113	III	66b (Judgment)
116	V	130b (Stoning)
118	I	398b (Conquest); 519a (Deliverance)
119-121	I	553b (Drowning)
121	III	524b (Narratives)
	V	5a (Signs)
122	IV	6a (Pairs and Pairing)
123	I	21b (ʿĀd); 222a (Belief and Unbelief)
	III	524a (Narratives)
123-138	I	532a (Dialogues)
123-139	IV	586b (Sheba)
123-140	II	462a (Hūd)
	III	519b (Narratives)
124	I	261b (Brother and Brotherhood)
126	III	567b (Obedience)
	IV	478b (Rhymed Prose)
128	V	3a (Signs)
128-129	I	21b (ʿĀd); 150b (Archaeology and the Q)
	II	338b (Good and Evil)
129	I	163b (Art and Architecture and the Q)
	V	340a (Transitoriness); 549a (Work)
131	III	567b (Obedience)
132-133	I	302b (Children)
133	I	96a (Animal Life)
	IV	3b (Pairs and Pairing)
133-134	V	463b (Water)
134	II	283b (Garden)
	V	127a (Springs and Fountains)
135	I	21b (ʿĀd)
136-138	II	510b (Indifference)
137	II	434a (History and the Q)
139	I	21b (ʿĀd); 222a (Belief and Unbelief)
	III	524b (Narratives)
	V	5a (Signs)

140	IV	6a (Pairs and Pairing)
141	I	222a (Belief and Unbelief)
	III	524a (Narratives)
	IV	521b (Ṣāliḥ)
141-142	V	253a (Thamūd)
141-156	I	532a (Dialogues)
141-158	I	149b (Archaeology and the Q)
141-159	II	340b (Good Deeds); 427a (Ḥijr)
	III	519b (Narratives)
	IV	521a (Ṣāliḥ)
142	I	261b (Brother and Brotherhood)
	IV	521a (Ṣāliḥ)
144	III	567b (Obedience)
147	V	127a (Springs and Fountains)
147-148	V	463b (Water)
148	I	494b (Date Palm)
	II	3b (Earth); 305a (Geography)
149	II	339a (Good and Evil)
	V	253a (Thamūd)
150	III	567b (Obedience)
151-152	I	440a (Corruption)
153	IV	521b (Ṣāliḥ)
154	III	449b (Muḥammad)
	IV	521b (Ṣāliḥ)
	V	253a (Thamūd)
154-155	IV	296b (Prophets and Prophethood)
155	I	500b (Day, Times of)
	IV	521b (Ṣāliḥ)
	V	280a (Time)
155-156	V	253a (Thamūd)
155-157	III	219a (Literature and the Q)
155-158	I	287a (Camel)
156	II	335b (Good and Evil)
	IV	453a (Reward and Punishment)
157	IV	521b (Ṣāliḥ)
	V	253a (Thamūd)
158	III	524b (Narratives)
	IV	453a (Reward and Punishment)
	V	5a (Signs)

159	IV	6a (Pairs and Pairing)
160	III	524a (Narratives)
160-161	I	261b (Brother and Brotherhood)
160-169	I	532a (Dialogues)
160-174	III	232a, 233a (Lot)
160-175	III	519b (Narratives)
161	IV	299b (Prophets and Prophethood)
163	III	567b (Obedience)
165	V	21b (Sin, Major and Minor); 552a (World)
165-166	II	444b (Homosexuality)
166	V	526b (Women and the Q)
167	III	449a (Muḥammad)
169-170	I	519a (Deliverance)
173	II	212b (Fire)
	V	470b (Weather)
174	III	524b (Narratives)
	V	5a (Signs)
175	IV	6a (Pairs and Pairing)
176	I	41b (Agriculture and Vegetation); 149b (Archaeology and the Q)
	II	353b (Grammar and the Q)
	IV	53b, 54a (People of the Thicket); 605b (Shuʿayb)
	V	245a (Textual Criticism of the Q)
176-188	I	532a (Dialogues)
176-189	III	390b (Midian); 519b (Narratives)
176-191	IV	319a (Punishment Stories); 605a (Shuʿayb)
177-189	V	245a (Textual Criticism of the Q)
179	III	567b (Obedience)
181	I	170a (Art and Architecture and the Q)
	II	8b (Economics)
	III	334a, 335b, 337a (Measurement)
181-182	IV	605a (Shuʿayb)
182	II	545b (Instruments)
	III	334b, 336a (Measurement)
183	I	300b (Cheating); 440a (Corruption)
	IV	288a (Property)
	V	312b (Trade and Commerce)

184	I	476a (Creation)
186	III	449b (Muḥammad)
189	IV	320a (Punishment Stories); 453a (Reward and Punishment); 605b (Shuʿayb)
190	III	524b (Narratives)
	V	5a (Signs)
190-227	III	519b (Narratives)
191	IV	6a (Pairs and Pairing)
192	III	510b (Names of the Q)
	IV	292b (Prophets and Prophethood); 446a (Revelation and Inspiration)
192-194	II	443b (Holy Spirit)
	IV	216b (Prayer)
192-195	V	371b (Trinity)
192-197	III	600b (Ornamentation and Illumination)
192-227	II	143a (Exhortations); 262a (Form and Structure of the Q)
193	II	278b (Gabriel)
	III	13b (Jesus); 293b (Mary)
	IV	293a (Prophets and Prophethood)
	V	81a (Soul)
193-194	III	442a (Muḥammad)
194	II	497b (Illiteracy)
195	I	83a (Anatomy); 132a (Arabic Language); 145a (Arabs)
	II	226b (Foreign Vocabulary); 497b (Illiteracy); 512b (Informants)
	III	109a (Language, Concept of); 110a, 113b, 114b, 124b (Language and Style of the Q); 451a (Muḥammad)
	IV	439b (Revelation and Inspiration); 566a (Scripture and the Q)
	V	434a (Virtue); 547a (Word of God)
196	II	434a (History and the Q)
	IV	569b (Scrolls)
	V	301b, 307b (Torah)
197	IV	537b, 539a (Scholar)
198	II	497b (Illiteracy)
	V	132a (Strangers and Foreigners)
198-199	II	226b (Foreign Vocabulary)
	III	451a (Muḥammad)
199	I	132a (Arabic Language)
	II	497b (Illiteracy)
200	III	380a (Mercy)
208	III	382a (Messenger)

210 I 526b (Devil)

213 III 443a (Muḥammad)

214 II 174b (Family)
III 443a, 455b (Muḥammad)
IV 331b (Quraysh)
V 39a (Sīra and the Q); 364a (Tribes and Clans); 460b (Warner)

216 I 537a (Disobedience)
III 453b (Muḥammad)

217 IV 6a (Pairs and Pairing)

218 V 288b (Time)

219 I 254a (Bowing and Prostration)
IV 305a (Prophets and Prophethood)

221 I 442b (Cosmology); 526b (Devil)
III 537a (News)

221-227 IV 113b (Poetry and Poets)

224 IV 113a, 113b (Poetry and Poets); 442b (Revelation and Inspiration)
V 393b (Turkish Literature and the Q)

224-226 III 181b (Lie); 219b (Literature and the Q)
IV 473a (Rhetoric and the Q)
V 43b (Sīra and the Q)

224-227 IV 114a (Poetry and Poets)

225 IV 118a (Polemic and Polemical Language)

225-226 IV 113b (Poetry and Poets)

226 I 32a (African Literature)

227 II 32b (Epigraphy)
IV 113b, 114a (Poetry and Poets); 473a, 473b (Rhetoric and the Q)

Sūrat al-Naml (27)

I 93b (Animal Life)
III 94a (Kings and Rulers); 472b (Mysterious Letters); 520a (Narratives); 534a (Nature as Signs)
IV 478b (Rhymed Prose); 586b (Sheba)
V 253b (Thamūd); 342b (Translations of the Q)

1 I 243a (Book)
II 497b (Illiteracy)
III 124b (Language and Style of the Q); 591b (Orality and Writing in Arabia)

1-2 II 341a, 341b (Good News)

1-6 II 143a (Exhortations)
III 520a (Narratives)

2	IV	3b (Pairs and Pairing)
3	II	362b (Grammar and the Q)
	IV	17a (Paradise)
	V	196b (Taxation); 553a (World)
4	II	362a (Grammar and the Q)
5	II	335b (Good and Evil)
6	IV	5b (Pairs and Pairing); 537b (Scholar)
7	III	518a, 518b, 524a (Narratives); 537a (News)
	V	393b (Turkish Literature and the Q)
7-9	II	211b, 213b (Fire)
7-14	I	304b (Children of Israel)
	III	520a (Narratives)
7-58	IV	320a (Punishment Stories)
8	II	366a (Grammar and the Q)
	IV	220a (Prayer)
	V	110b (Speech)
8-9	I	329b (Chronology and the Q)
9	II	330a (God and his Attributes)
10	II	546a (Instruments)
	III	219a (Literature and the Q)
	IV	295b (Prophets and Prophethood); 508b (Rod); 574b (Seeing and Hearing)
	V	120a (Spiritual Beings); 393a (Turkish Literature and the Q)
10-12	III	382a (Messenger)
	IV	296b (Prophets and Prophethood)
11	II	336a (Good and Evil)
	III	379b (Mercy)
12	I	364a (Colors); 365b (Commandments)
	II	335b (Good and Evil)
	III	394a (Miracles); 422a (Moses); 552b (Numbers and Enumeration)
13	II	542b (Insolence and Obstinacy)
	III	246a (Magic)
	V	5b (Signs)
14	II	361b (Grammar and the Q)
15	I	496a (David)
	III	94b (Kings and Rulers); 103a (Knowledge and Learning); 524a (Narratives)
	IV	213b (Praise)
15-44	III	520a (Narratives)
	V	77a (Solomon)

16	I	100b (Animal Life)
	III	94b (Kings and Rulers); 222b (Literature and the Q); 395a (Miracles); 487a (Myths and Legends in the Q)
	V	200b (Teaching)
16-18	V	77b (Solomon)
17	II	361b (Grammar and the Q)
	III	44b, 46b (Jinn); 250a (Magic)
	V	377a (Troops)
17-20	I	99a (Animal Life)
18	I	99a, 100b (Animal Life)
	II	365b (Grammar and the Q)
18-19	II	372b (Gratitude and Ingratitude)
	III	224a (Literature and the Q); 487a (Myths and Legends in the Q)
19	I	236b (Blessing); 436a (Conversion)
	II	367a (Grammar and the Q)
	III	146b, 149a (Laughter); 379b (Mercy)
20	II	537b (Inquisition)
	III	222b (Literature and the Q)
20-44	I	228b (Bilqīs)
21	II	354a (Grammar and the Q); 416a (Hell and Hellfire)
	IV	517a (Sacrifice)
22	II	308a (Geography)
	III	518a (Narratives); 537a (News)
	IV	586a (Sheba)
	V	373b (Trips and Voyages)
22-26	I	100b (Animal Life)
22-43	II	216a (Flying)
22-44	II	558a (Invitation)
	V	532b (Women and the Q)
23	II	291a (Gender)
	III	92a (Kings and Rulers)
	V	77b (Solomon); 277a (Throne of God)
24	III	47a (Jinn)
	V	162b (Sun)
24-25	I	255a (Bowing and Prostration)
25	IV	4a (Pairs and Pairing)
	V	393a (Turkish Literature and the Q)
26	I	480b (Creeds)
	II	325b (God and his Attributes)

	III	467a (Muʿtazila)
	V	500b (Witnessing and Testifying)
28	II	544b (Instruments)
	III	508a (Names of the Q)
28-29	I	242b (Book)
29	I	369a (Community and Society in the Q)
	II	432b (History and the Q)
	V	552a (World)
29-35	I	532a (Dialogues)
30	I	207b, 209b (Basmala); 329b (Chronology and the Q)
	II	92a (Everyday Life, Q In); 318a (God and his Attributes)
	IV	5a (Pairs and Pairing)
	V	393b (Turkish Literature and the Q); 424a, 424b (Verse)
33	I	458b (Courage)
	IV	128b (Politics and the Q)
34	II	62b (Ethics and the Q)
	III	91b (Kings and Rulers)
	V	140b (Ṣūfism and the Q)
35	III	382b (Messenger)
35-36	II	313b (Gift-Giving)
36	II	314a (Gift-Giving)
	III	61b (Joy and Misery)
37	IV	153b (Poll Tax)
	V	377a (Troops)
37-40	V	373b (Trips and Voyages)
38	II	325b (God and his Attributes)
	V	277a (Throne of God)
38-42	V	77b (Solomon)
39	II	486b (ʿIfrīt)
	III	44b (Jinn)
	V	120b (Spiritual Beings)
39-40	III	48b (Jinn)
40	II	344b (Grace); 362b (Grammar and the Q); 371a (Gratitude and Ingratitude); 462a (House, Domestic and Divine); 486b (ʿIfrīt)
	III	395b (Miracles); 487b (Myths and Legends in the Q)
41	V	277a (Throne of God)
41-42	I	166a (Art and Architecture and the Q)
	II	325b (God and his Attributes)
42	V	277a (Throne of God); 373b (Trips and Voyages)

44	I	149b (Archaeology and the Q); 162a, 162b, 168a, 171b (Art and Architecture and the Q); 347a (Clothing)
	IV	586b (Sheba)
	V	77a (Solomon)
45	I	261b (Brother and Brotherhood); 513b (Debate and Disputation)
	III	524a (Narratives)
	IV	521a (Ṣāliḥ)
	V	253a (Thamūd)
45-52	I	149b (Archaeology and the Q)
	II	459b (House, Domestic and Divine)
45-53	II	340b (Good Deeds)
	III	520a (Narratives)
	IV	521a, 522a (Ṣāliḥ)
46	III	379b (Mercy)
47	II	242a (Foretelling in the Q)
48-51	V	253b (Thamūd)
49	II	365b (Grammar and the Q)
	V	492a (Witnessing and Testifying)
50	III	18a (Jesus)
50-51	IV	310a (Provocation)
52	II	360b (Grammar and the Q)
	IV	425a (Remnant); 538b (Scholar)
	V	5a (Signs)
53	IV	522a (Ṣāliḥ)
	V	253a (Thamūd)
54	IV	580b (Sex and Sexuality)
	V	19a (Sin, Major and Minor); 253b (Thamūd)
54-55	II	63a (Ethics and the Q); 488a (Ignorance)
	IV	584b (Sex and Sexuality)
54-58	III	232a (Lot); 520a (Narratives)
55	II	76a (Ethics and the Q); 444b (Homosexuality)
56	I	343b (Cleanliness and Ablution)
	II	357b (Grammar and the Q)
	III	449a (Muḥammad)
	IV	505b (Ritual Purity)
57	IV	523b (Salvation)
58	II	212b (Fire)
	V	470b (Weather)
59	II	11b (Election)
	IV	474a (Rhetoric and the Q)

59-60	IV	312a (Provocation)
59-61	I	472b (Creation)
59-93	III	520a (Narratives)
60	I	41a (Agriculture and Vegetation)
	II	3a, 3b (Earth); 283a (Garden); 304a (Geography)
	III	71a (Justice and Injustice)
	V	359a (Tree)
60-64	IV	161b (Polytheism and Atheism)
61	I	443a (Cosmology)
	II	2b (Earth)
	IV	7a (Pairs and Pairing); 538b (Scholar)
	V	126a (Springs and Fountains); 463a (Water)
62	I	277a (Caliph)
	II	335b (Good and Evil)
63	I	53a (Air and Wind); 494a (Darkness)
	II	3a (Earth)
	III	379a (Mercy)
	IV	4b (Pairs and Pairing); 108a (Planets and Stars)
	V	119a (Spiritual Beings); 464a (Water); 471a (Weather)
64	I	472b, 479a (Creation)
	IV	4a, 6b (Pairs and Pairing); 286b (Proof); 312a, 312b (Provocation); 435a (Resurrection)
65	II	423a (Hidden and the Hidden)
	IV	312a (Provocation); 572b (Secrets)
	V	288b (Time)
67	II	4b (Earth)
67-72	IV	311a (Provocation)
68	II	430a (History and the Q)
	III	518a (Narratives)
69	II	308a (Geography)
	IV	425a (Remnant)
70	I	405b (Consolation)
	III	452b (Muḥammad)
	V	134a (Suffering)
71-75	I	523b (Destiny)
73	II	371a (Gratitude and Ingratitude)
74	IV	4a (Pairs and Pairing)
75	I	243a (Book); 523a (Destiny)
	II	269b (Freedom and Predestination)
	III	124b (Language and Style of the Q)

76	III	443b (Muḥammad); 517b (Narratives)
	V	111a (Speech)
76-93	II	143a (Exhortations)
77	III	511b, 512a (Names of the Q)
78	I	516a (Decision)
	II	185b (Fate)
	IV	6a (Pairs and Pairing)
79	III	453b (Muḥammad)
80-81	III	452b (Muḥammad)
81	II	43b (Error)
	V	7a (Signs)
82	I	100b (Animal Life); 111a (Antichrist); 112b (Apocalypse)
	II	47a (Eschatology)
	III	138b, 139a, 144a (Last Judgment)
	IV	434b (Resurrection)
83	V	377a (Troops)
84	V	547a (Word of God)
86	I	502a (Day, Times of)
	IV	438a (Revelation and Inspiration); 589b (Shekhinah)
	V	280b (Time)
87	I	112b, 114a (Apocalypse)
	II	198a (Fear)
87-88	III	140a (Last Judgment)
88	I	213a (Beauty)
88-90	IV	34b (Peace)
89	II	198a (Fear)
91	III	339b (Mecca); 443b (Muḥammad)
	IV	282a (Profane and Sacred); 514a (Sacred Precincts)
91-93	IV	137b (Politics and the Q)
92	I	225b (Belief and Unbelief)
	III	40a (Jihād); 190a (Literacy); 440b (Muḥammad)
93	IV	438a (Revelation and Inspiration)

Sūrat al-Qaṣaṣ (28)

III 472b (Mysterious Letters); 517b, 518b (Narratives)
V 29a (Sinai)

1-3	II	262a (Form and Structure of the Q)
2	II	435b (History and the Q); 497b (Illiteracy)
	III	124b (Language and Style of the Q)

2-3 III 441a (Muḥammad)

2-46 III 518b (Narratives)

3 III 190a (Literacy); 441a (Muḥammad); 518a, 524a (Narratives); 537a (News)

3-6 IV 211a (Power and Impotence)

3-43 IV 320a (Punishment Stories)

3-47 I 304b (Children of Israel)

4 I 302a (Children)
II 10b (Egypt); 338a (Good and Evil); 542a (Insolence and Obstinacy)
III 583a, 583b (Oppression)
IV 67b (Pharaoh); 106a (Plagues); 126b (Politics and the Q); 517a (Sacrifice); 592a (Shīʿa)
V 375a (Trips and Voyages)

4-5 II 399a (Hāmān)
III 581a (Oppressed on Earth)

4-6 III 581a (Oppressed on Earth)

5 I 306a (Children of Israel)
II 503a (Imām)
III 95a (Kings and Rulers); 437a (Mosque); 583b (Oppression)

6 II 10b (Egypt); 338a (Good and Evil); 399a (Hāmān)
V 377a (Troops)

7 II 10b (Egypt)
III 106a (Lactation)
IV 439b (Revelation and Inspiration)
V 463b (Water)

7-12 III 106a, 106b (Lactation)

7-13 I 302b (Children)
III 393b (Miracles)
IV 20a (Parents)
V 570a (Youth and Old Age)

7-14 III 420b (Moses)

8 II 23b (Enemies); 338a (Good and Evil)
IV 67b (Pharaoh)
V 377a (Troops)

8-9 II 399a (Hāmān)

9 I 405a (Consolation)
V 375a (Trips and Voyages); 532a (Women and the Q)

10 I 405a (Consolation)

11 V 53b (Sister)

12 II 174a (Family)

	III	106a, 106b (Lactation); 173a (Lawful and Unlawful); 420b (Moses)
	IV	37a (People of the Book); 48b, 49b (People of the House)
	V	476b, 477a (Wet-Nursing)
12-13	V	549a (Work)
13	I	213a (Beauty); 405a (Consolation)
	IV	538b (Scholar)
14	III	331b (Maturity); 420b (Moses)
	IV	3b (Pairs and Pairing); 452b (Reward and Punishment); 538a (Scholar)
15	II	10b (Egypt); 23b, 24a (Enemies)
	III	420b (Moses)
	IV	25b (Parties and Factions); 403b (Religious Pluralism and the Q); 592a (Shīʿa)
15-16	V	25a (Sin, Major and Minor)
15-17	V	23a (Sin, Major and Minor)
16	II	187a (Fate)
	III	420b (Moses)
	IV	482a (Rhymed Prose)
17	I	236b (Blessing)
18	I	163a (Art and Architecture and the Q); 504a (Day, Times of)
	II	10b (Egypt)
	III	418b (Morning)
18-19	V	288b (Time)
19	II	10b (Egypt); 23b (Enemies)
20	I	163a (Art and Architecture and the Q)
	II	10b (Egypt); 355b (Grammar and the Q)
	III	211b (Literature and the Q); 421a (Moses)
21	I	519a (Deliverance)
	II	308a (Geography)
	III	421a (Moses)
22	IV	29a (Path or Way)
22-23	III	390b (Midian)
	IV	606a (Shuʿayb)
22-28	III	421a (Moses)
	V	41b (Sīra and the Q)
23	V	548b (Work); 570b (Youth and Old Age)
23-24	V	465a (Water)
24	II	336a (Good and Evil)
25	I	519a (Deliverance)
	III	403b (Modesty); 517b (Narratives)
	IV	523b (Salvation)

25-26 III 234b (Love and Affection)

25-27 IV 452a (Reward and Punishment)

25-31 V 393a (Turkish Literature and the Q)

26 II 353a (Grammar and the Q)
III 253b (Manual Labor)

27 II 433b (History and the Q)
III 421a (Moses)
IV 580b (Sex and Sexuality)

27-29 V 289a (Time)

29 II 174a (Family)
III 58a (Journey); 421a (Moses); 518a (Narratives); 537a (News)
V 375a (Trips and Voyages); 393b (Turkish Literature and the Q)

29-30 II 211b, 213b (Fire)

29-35 I 532a (Dialogues)

30 II 305a (Geography)
III 421a (Moses)
IV 446b (Revelation and Inspiration); 513b (Sacred Precincts)
V 110b (Speech); 362a (Tree)

31 II 546a (Instruments)
III 219a (Literature and the Q)
V 120a (Spiritual Beings)

31-32 III 421b (Moses)
IV 296b (Prophets and Prophethood)

32 I 364a (Colors); 371b (Community and Society in the Q)
II 335b (Good and Evil)
III 421b (Moses)
IV 106a (Plagues); 286b (Proof); 296b (Prophets and Prophethood)

33 V 83a (Soul)

34 III 112a, 113a (Language and Style of the Q)

34-35 I 1a (Aaron)

35 I 1a (Aaron); 260a (Brother and Brotherhood)
III 421b (Moses)

36 III 246a (Magic); 421b (Moses)
IV 286a, 286b (Proof); 296b (Prophets and Prophethood)

37 I 504a (Day, Times of)
III 425a (Moses)
IV 523a (Salvation)

38 I 162b (Art and Architecture and the Q); 340b (Clay); 478a (Creation)
II 338a (Good and Evil); 399a (Hāmān); 415b (Hell and Hellfire); 542b (Insolence and Obstinacy)

	III	383b (Metals and Minerals); 522a (Narratives); 539b (Nimrod); 583b (Oppression)
	IV	67b, 68a (Pharaoh); 483b (Rhymed Prose)
38-39	I	190a (Authority)
39	I	160a (Arrogance)
	II	91b (Everyday Life, Q In)
40	II	10b (Egypt); 213a (Fire)
	IV	67a (Pharaoh)
	V	463b (Water)
41	II	417b (Hell and Hellfire); 503a (Imām); 558b (Invitation)
43	II	434a (History and the Q)
	III	424b (Moses)
	IV	126b (Politics and the Q); 287a (Proof)
	V	301a (Torah)
44	V	29a (Sinai); 492b (Witnessing and Testifying)
45	I	479a (Creation)
	III	190a (Literacy); 441a (Muḥammad)
	IV	37a (People of the Book); 49a (People of the House); 606a (Shuʿayb)
46	II	308b (Geography)
	III	382b (Messenger); 443a (Muḥammad)
	V	29a (Sinai); 110a (Speech); 460b (Warner)
48	III	246a (Magic); 450b (Muḥammad)
50	I	225b (Belief and Unbelief)
	IV	84a (Philosophy and the Q)
	V	486b (Wish and Desire)
51	V	547a (Word of God)
52	I	222b (Belief and Unbelief)
	V	301a (Torah)
52-54	I	219a, 223b (Belief and Unbelief)
	III	23b, 32a (Jews and Judaism)
53	III	190a (Literacy)
54	III	32b (Jews and Judaism)
	IV	6b (Pairs and Pairing); 309b (Provocation); 458b (Reward and Punishment)
	V	134b (Suffering)
54-55	I	219b (Belief and Unbelief)
55	II	488a (Ignorance)
	III	40b (Jihād)
	IV	309b (Provocation)
	V	291a (Tolerance and Coercion)
56	I	435b (Conversion)
	IV	331a (Quraysh)
	V	291b (Tolerance and Coercion)

57 II 224b (Forbidden)
III 172b (Lawful and Unlawful); 338b, 339b (Mecca); 449b (Muḥammad)
IV 282a (Profane and Sacred); 329b (Quraysh); 515b (Sacred Precincts); 538b (Scholar)

58 I 242a (Boast)
IV 425a (Remnant)

58-59 IV 127a (Politics and the Q)

59 I 338b (City)
II 98b (Evil Deeds); 337a (Good and Evil); 340a (Good Deeds)
III 190a (Literacy); 382a (Messenger)
IV 301b (Prophets and Prophethood)

60 III 59b (Joy and Misery)
IV 5a (Pairs and Pairing)
V 340a (Transitoriness)

62-65 II 558b (Invitation)

62-66 V 494a (Witnessing and Testifying)

63 V 547b (Word of God)

64 II 558b (Invitation)

65 IV 298b (Prophets and Prophethood)

67 IV 426b (Repentance and Penance); 523a (Salvation)

68 II 11b, 12a (Election); 327b (God and his Attributes)
IV 220a (Prayer)

69 IV 4a (Pairs and Pairing)

70 I 329b (Chronology and the Q); 480b (Creeds)
IV 214b (Praise)

70-72 IV 161b (Polytheism and Atheism)

71-72 V 279a (Time); 475a (Weights and Measures)

72 IV 574a (Seeing and Hearing); 589b (Shekhinah)

73 II 372a (Gratitude and Ingratitude)
III 209b (Literature and the Q); 379a (Mercy)

74 II 558b (Invitation)

75 I 236a (Blasphemy)
II 67b (Ethics and the Q)
III 447a (Muḥammad)
IV 286b (Proof); 312a, 312b (Provocation)
V 493b (Witnessing and Testifying)

76 II 353b (Grammar and the Q)
III 61b (Joy and Misery); 104a (Korah); 359a (Medicine and the Q)
V 283b (Time)

76-81 III 394b (Miracles)

76-82 I 190a (Authority)
III 104a (Korah); 518b (Narratives)
IV 320a (Punishment Stories)

77 V 106a (Spatial Relations); 436a (Virtue)

79 III 104b (Korah)

80 IV 538b (Scholar)
V 203b (Teaching)

81 II 338b (Good and Evil); 399b (Hāmān)

82 I 504a (Day, Times of)
II 348a (Grammar and the Q)
IV 523a (Salvation)
V 288b (Time)

83 I 163b (Art and Architecture and the Q)
V 553b (World)

85 III 454a (Muḥammad)
IV 435a (Resurrection)

85-87 IV 34b (Peace)

86 III 442b (Muḥammad)
IV 294b (Prophets and Prophethood)

87 I 437a (Conversion)
III 443a (Muḥammad)

88 I 92a (Angel); 329b (Chronology and the Q); 480b (Creeds); 508b (Death and the Dead)
II 30a (Epigraphy); 47b (Eschatology); 159a (Face); 160b (Face of God); 323b (God and his Attributes); 418b (Hell and Hellfire)
III 223b (Literature and the Q); 389a (Michael); 443a (Muḥammad)
V 151a (Ṣūfism and the Q); 393a, 393b (Turkish Literature and the Q); 487a (Wish and Desire)

SŪRAT AL-ʿANKABŪT (29)

I 93b (Animal Life)
II 116a (Exegesis of the Q: Classical and Medieval)
III 6b (Jerusalem); 472b (Mysterious Letters); 520b (Narratives); 534a (Nature as Signs)
V 113a (Spider)

1 V 393a (Turkish Literature and the Q)

1-10 II 469a (Hypocrites and Hypocrisy)

2 V 502a (Witnessing and Testifying)

3 V 434b (Virtue)

5 II 449a (Hope)
IV 575a (Seeing and Hearing)
V 289a (Time)

6 III 37a (Jihād)
V 467b (Wealth)

7 IV 431b (Responsibility); 452b (Reward and Punishment)
V 19a (Sin, Major and Minor)

8 II 175b (Family)
III 37a (Jihād); 567a (Obedience)
IV 20b (Parents); 159a (Polytheism and Atheism)
V 204b (Teaching)

9 I 436a (Conversion)

10-11 II 470a (Hypocrites and Hypocrisy)
III 37b (Jihād)

11 II 468b (Hypocrites and Hypocrisy)

12 V 22a (Sin, Major and Minor)

12-13 III 228b (Load or Burden)

13 IV 431a (Responsibility)

14 II 433a (History and the Q)
III 486b (Myths and Legends in the Q); 542b (Noah); 549b (Numbers and Enumeration)
V 133a (Suffering); 285b (Time); 560a (Year)

14-15 II 558a (Invitation)
III 520b (Narratives)

14-40 IV 320a (Punishment Stories)

15 V 5b (Signs)

16 V 258a (Theology and the Q)

16-17 V 555b (Worship)

16-27 I 6b (Abraham)
I 330a (Chronology and the Q)
III 494a (Myths and Legends in the Q)

16-35 III 520b (Narratives)

17 II 371b (Gratitude and Ingratitude); 481a (Idols and Images)
III 181a (Lie)
V 179a, 179b (Sustenance)

18 III 125a (Language and Style of the Q)
V 291b (Tolerance and Coercion)

19 I 472b (Creation)
IV 6b (Pairs and Pairing); 435a (Resurrection)

19-20	I	479a (Creation)
20	II	355a (Grammar and the Q)
	IV	6b (Pairs and Pairing); 312a (Provocation)
	V	376a (Trips and Voyages)
21	IV	2a (Pairs and Pairing); 457b (Reward and Punishment)
22	II	273a (Friends and Friendship)
	IV	5b (Pairs and Pairing)
23	I	521b (Despair)
	V	7a (Signs)
24	I	7a (Abraham)
	II	211b (Fire)
	III	494b (Myths and Legends in the Q)
	IV	523b (Salvation)
25	II	481a (Idols and Images)
	IV	103b (Pit)
26	I	6a (Abraham)
	II	14b (Emigrants and Helpers); 18b (Emigration)
	III	494b (Myths and Legends in the Q)
	IV	26b (Parties and Factions)
27	I	7b (Abraham); 233a (Birth)
	II	561b, 562a (Isaac); 563b (Ishmael)
	III	1a (Jacob); 127a (Language and Style of the Q); 520a (Narratives)
	IV	297b (Prophets and Prophethood)
	V	302a (Torah)
28	II	444b (Homosexuality)
	IV	580b (Sex and Sexuality)
28-29	IV	584b (Sex and Sexuality)
29	II	444b (Homosexuality)
	V	36b (Sīra and the Q); 373a (Trips and Voyages); 438a (Virtues and Vices, Commanding and Forbidding)
31	I	6a (Abraham)
	II	6a (Economics); 341a, 341b (Good News); 411b (Heaven and Sky)
	IV	49a (People of the House)
	V	132a (Strangers and Foreigners)
31-32	I	330a (Chronology and the Q)
31-35	III	231b (Lot)
32	I	519a (Deliverance)
	II	174a (Family)
33	I	405a (Consolation)
	II	196b (Fear)
	V	393a (Turkish Literature and the Q)

34 II 174a (Family)
IV 49a (People of the House); 454a (Reward and Punishment); 503a (Ritual Purity)

35 II 308a (Geography)
IV 286a (Proof); 425b (Remnant)
V 5a (Signs)

36 I 261b (Brother and Brotherhood)
II 399b (Hāmān); 449a (Hope)
III 136b (Last Judgment); 393b (Miracles)
IV 605a (Shuʿayb)

36-37 II 558a (Invitation)
III 390b (Midian)
IV 605a (Shuʿayb)

36-40 III 520b (Narratives)

37 I 113a (Apocalypse)
III 417a, 418a (Morning)
V 133a (Suffering)

38 I 21b (ʿĀd); 150b (Archaeology and the Q); 163a (Art and Architecture and the Q)
II 339a (Good and Evil); 399b (Hāmān)
IV 425a (Remnant)

39 I 160a (Arrogance)
II 338a (Good and Evil); 399b (Hāmān); 542b (Insolence and Obstinacy)
III 104b (Korah); 421b (Moses); 518b (Narratives)
IV 68a (Pharaoh); 106a (Plagues); 264a (Pride); 286b (Proof)

39-40 III 423b (Moses)

40 I 553b (Drowning)
II 338a (Good and Evil); 399b (Hāmān)
III 583b (Oppression)
IV 530b (Sand)
V 133a (Suffering)

41 I 100a (Animal Life)
II 273b (Friends and Friendship); 338a (Good and Evil)
III 209a (Literature and the Q)
IV 10a (Parable)
V 15a (Simile); 113a (Spider)

42 III 200a (Literary Structures of the Q)
V 203b (Teaching)

43 IV 10a (Parable); 228b (Prayer); 537b, 538b (Scholar)

44 I 473a, 473b (Creation)
IV 438a (Revelation and Inspiration)

45 I 28a (Adultery and Fornication); 245b (Book)
III 190a (Literacy); 441a, 441b (Muḥammad)

	IV	221b (Prayer); 294a (Prophets and Prophethood); 420a, 424b (Remembrance); 580b (Sex and Sexuality)
	V	269a, 271b (Theology and the Q); 438a (Virtues and Vices, Commanding and Forbidding)
46	I	115b, 118a (Apologetics); 222b (Belief and Unbelief); 511b (Debate and Disputation)
	II	452b (Hospitality and Courtesy)
	III	28a (Jews and Judaism); 40a (Jihād)
	IV	238b (Pre-1800 Preoccupations of Q Studies); 281a (Profane and Sacred); 309b (Provocation)
	V	203b (Teaching); 301a, 303b (Torah)
46-47	IV	41b (People of the Book)
47	I	222b (Belief and Unbelief); 247a (Book)
	II	495a (Illiteracy)
	V	303b, 307b (Torah)
47-48	II	492b (Illiteracy)
	V	400b, 401b, 402a (Ummī)
48	II	430a (History and the Q); 495b (Illiteracy)
	III	188b (Literacy); 451b (Muḥammad); 591b, 592a (Orality and Writing in Arabia)
	IV	217a (Prayer)
	V	301b (Torah); 558a (Writing and Writing Materials)
49	II	497b (Illiteracy)
	IV	538b, 539a (Scholar)
	V	6a, 7a (Signs)
49-50	III	398b (Miracles)
50	III	40a (Jihād)
	IV	312a (Provocation)
	V	3a (Signs)
50-51	IV	119a (Polemic and Polemical Language)
51	III	190a (Literacy); 591b (Orality and Writing in Arabia)
53	V	289b (Time)
53-55	II	418b (Hell and Hellfire)
55	IV	453a (Reward and Punishment)
	V	547a (Word of God)
56	II	366b (Grammar and the Q)
	III	531b (Nature as Signs)
57	V	83a (Soul)
58	I	165b (Art and Architecture and the Q)
	V	382b (Trust and Patience)
59	V	382a, 382b (Trust and Patience)

60 I 95b (Animal Life)
III 327b (Material Culture and the Q)
IV 575a (Seeing and Hearing)

60-63 I 329b (Chronology and the Q)

61 I 472b (Creation)
II 317a (God and his Attributes)
IV 160b (Polytheism and Atheism)
V 163a (Sun)

61-65 II 476b, 478a (Idolatry and Idolaters)

61-68 I 236a (Blasphemy)

62 V 179a (Sustenance)

63 II 3a (Earth)
IV 311a (Provocation)

64 I 94a (Animal Life)
IV 15a (Paradise)
V 552b (World)

65 I 37b (Age of Ignorance); 519a (Deliverance)
II 3a (Earth); 317a (God and his Attributes)
IV 161b (Polytheism and Atheism)

66 I 220b (Belief and Unbelief)
IV 538b (Scholar)

67 II 224b (Forbidden)
III 338b, 339b (Mecca); 449b (Muḥammad)
IV 282a (Profane and Sacred); 329b (Quraysh); 515b (Sacred Precincts)

67-69 II 337b (Good and Evil)

68 III 181a, 181b (Lie)
IV 103b (Pit); 309b (Provocation)

69 III 37a (Jihād)
IV 29a, 30a (Path or Way)

Sūrat al-Rūm (30)

I 230b (Biology as the Creation and Stages of Life); 265b, 269b (Byzantines); 399b (Conquest)
II 116a (Exegesis of the Q: Classical and Medieval)
III 6b (Jerusalem); 472b (Mysterious Letters)
IV 246b (Pre-1800 Preoccupations of Q Studies); 537b (Scholar)
V 10a (Signs)

1 V 393a (Turkish Literature and the Q)

1-2 V 80a (Soothsayer)

1-4	II	280a, 282a (Gambling)
1-5	I	265b, 266b (Byzantines)
	II	146a, 147a, 147b (Expeditions and Battles); 262a (Form and Structure of the Q)
2	I	314b (Christians and Christianity)
	II	144a (Expeditions and Battles)
	IV	410a (Religious Pluralism and the Q)
2-4	V	456a (War)
2-5	I	320a (Chronology and the Q)
	V	430b (Victory)
3	II	144a (Expeditions and Battles)
3-4	II	186a (Fate)
4	I	267b (Byzantines)
	III	61a (Joy and Misery)
	V	286a (Time)
4-5	III	557b (Numismatics)
5	III	61a (Joy and Misery)
	IV	6a (Pairs and Pairing)
6	IV	538b (Scholar)
7	II	489a (Ignorance)
	IV	5a (Pairs and Pairing)
8	I	442a (Cosmology); 473a (Creation)
	II	57b (Ethics and the Q); 269a (Freedom and Predestination); 327b (God and his Attributes)
	IV	4a (Pairs and Pairing); 393b (Reflection and Deliberation)
	V	9b (Signs); 289b (Time); 544b (Word of God)
8-11	II	58b (Ethics and the Q)
9	I	40b (Agriculture and Vegetation)
	II	308a (Geography)
	IV	310a (Provocation); 425a (Remnant)
10	III	401a (Mockery)
	V	6a (Signs)
11	I	479a (Creation)
	IV	6b (Pairs and Pairing)
12	I	501a (Day, Times of); 521b (Despair); 524b (Devil)
	III	137a (Last Judgment)
	V	287b (Time)
13	I	220b (Belief and Unbelief)
	V	117b (Spiritual Beings); 494a (Witnessing and Testifying)

14	I	501a (Day, Times of)
	III	137a (Last Judgment)
	V	287b (Time)
14-16	IV	2b (Pairs and Pairing); 34b (Peace)
15	I	41a (Agriculture and Vegetation)
	II	283a (Garden)
15-16	II	58b (Ethics and the Q)
17	I	504a, 504b (Day, Times of)
	III	417a, 418b (Morning)
	IV	213b (Praise); 220a (Prayer)
	V	281a, 282b (Time)
17-18	I	328b (Chronology and the Q)
	II	340a (Good Deeds)
	III	546a (Noon)
	IV	224a (Prayer)
18	I	444a (Cosmology); 503a, 504a (Day, Times of)
	IV	213b (Praise)
	V	282b (Time)
19	II	45a (Eschatology)
	IV	4b (Pairs and Pairing); 435a (Resurrection)
20	I	231a (Biology as the Creation and Stages of Life); 446a (Cosmology); 476a (Creation)
	V	7b (Signs)
20-21	II	4b (Earth)
20-28	IV	438a (Revelation and Inspiration)
21	I	447b (Cosmology)
	II	175a (Family); 275a (Friends and Friendship); 328b (God and his Attributes)
	III	235a (Love and Affection); 277b, 279a (Marriage and Divorce)
	IV	183b (Portents); 394a (Reflection and Deliberation); 581a (Sex and Sexuality)
	V	9a (Signs); 526b (Women and the Q)
21-24	II	548a (Intellect)
22	I	361b (Colors)
	IV	336a (Races); 537b, 538b (Scholar)
22-23	V	4a (Signs)
22-25	V	9a (Signs)
22-27	V	9a (Signs)
23	I	546b (Dreams and Sleep)
	II	241b (Foretelling in the Q); 406a (Hearing and Deafness)
	IV	179a (Popular and Talismanic Uses of the Q)
	V	61a (Sleep); 280b (Time)

24	I	220b (Belief and Unbelief)
	II	3a (Earth); 448b (Hope)
	IV	183a (Portents)
	V	3b, 9a (Signs)
25	II	558b (Invitation)
	V	545b (Word of God); 553a (World)
26	IV	223a (Prayer)
27	I	472b, 479a (Creation)
	IV	4b, 6b (Pairs and Pairing); 435a (Resurrection)
28	I	396b (Concubines)
	IV	10a (Parable)
29	II	59a (Ethics and the Q)
	III	102b (Knowledge and Learning)
30	I	5b (Abraham); 26a (Adam and Eve); 337a (Circumcision); 435a (Conversion); 466b (Covenant)
	II	323b, 329a (God and his Attributes); 402a (Hand); 402b (Ḥanīf)
	III	446a (Muḥammad); 510b (Names of the Q)
	IV	416a (Religious Pluralism and the Q); 482b (Rhymed Prose); 538b (Scholar)
	V	268b (Theology and the Q)
31	IV	25b (Parties and Factions); 399a (Religious Pluralism and the Q); 427b (Repentance and Penance)
31-32	IV	25a (Parties and Factions); 592a (Shīʿa)
32	I	380a (Community and Society in the Q)
	II	432a (History and the Q)
	III	61b (Joy and Misery)
	IV	25b (Parties and Factions); 403b, 416a (Religious Pluralism and the Q); 592a (Shīʿa)
35	IV	311a (Provocation)
	V	3a (Signs); 111a (Speech)
36	I	521b (Despair)
	III	61a (Joy and Misery)
37	IV	2a (Pairs and Pairing)
	V	4a (Signs)
38	II	53a (Eschatology)
	III	252a (Maintenance and Upkeep)
	IV	63b (Persian Literature and the Q); 523a (Salvation)
38-39	II	160a (Face of God)
	IV	221a (Prayer)
39	I	65b (Almsgiving)
	II	8a (Economics)

	IV	6b (Pairs and Pairing); 208b (Poverty and the Poor)
	V	197b, 199a (Taxation); 406b (Usury); 469b (Wealth)
40	I	472b (Creation)
	IV	220b (Prayer); 435b (Resurrection)
	V	545a (Word of God)
41	II	3a (Earth)
	IV	428a (Repentance and Penance)
42	II	308a (Geography)
	IV	312a (Provocation); 320b (Punishment Stories)
43	II	323b (God and his Attributes)
	IV	416a (Religious Pluralism and the Q); 482b (Rhymed Prose)
43-45	IV	2b (Pairs and Pairing)
46	I	53a (Air and Wind); 213a (Beauty); 246a (Book)
	II	341a (Good News)
	III	379a (Mercy)
	IV	438a (Revelation and Inspiration); 604a (Ships)
	V	4a (Signs); 119a (Spiritual Beings); 412a (Vehicles); 471a (Weather)
47	III	382a (Messenger); 454b (Muḥammad)
	IV	453b (Reward and Punishment)
	V	416a (Vengeance)
48	I	42a (Agriculture and Vegetation); 53b (Air and Wind); 213a (Beauty)
	III	62a (Joy and Misery); 530a (Nature as Signs)
	V	463a (Water); 470a, 470b (Weather)
48-51	V	7b (Signs)
49	I	521a (Despair); 525a (Devil)
	IV	443b (Revelation and Inspiration)
50	III	200b (Literary Structures of the Q); 379a (Mercy)
	V	3a (Signs); 393a (Turkish Literature and the Q)
51	I	53b (Air and Wind); 363a (Colors)
	III	530a (Nature as Signs)
52-53	III	452b (Muḥammad)
	IV	2a (Pairs and Pairing)
53	II	43b (Error)
54	I	232a (Biology as the Creation and Stages of Life); 476a (Creation)
	II	327b (God and his Attributes)
	IV	6a (Pairs and Pairing); 211a (Power and Impotence)
	V	569b (Youth and Old Age)
55	I	501a (Day, Times of)
	II	439b (History and the Q)
	III	137a (Last Judgment); 335b (Measurement)

IV 434b (Resurrection)
V 287b, 288a (Time)

56 I 244b (Book)
III 137a (Last Judgment)
IV 296b (Prophets and Prophethood); 435b (Resurrection); 538a, 538b (Scholar)
V 203b (Teaching)

59 I 82a (Anatomy)

60 I 14a (Abrogation)
III 40a (Jihād)
V 386b (Truth)

SŪRAT LUQMĀN (31)

II 116a (Exegesis of the Q: Classical and Medieval)
III 242a, 242b (Luqmān); 472b (Mysterious Letters); 521b (Narratives)
IV 159a (Polytheism and Atheism); 246a (Pre-1800 Preoccupations of Q Studies); 537b (Scholar)

1 V 393a (Turkish Literature and the Q)

3 III 184a (Life)

4 V 196b (Taxation)

5 IV 523a (Salvation)

6 I 160b (Arrogance)
III 400a (Mockery); 517b (Narratives)

7 III 190a (Literacy)
V 7a (Signs); 421b, 422a (Verse); 474a (Weights and Measures)

10 I 95b (Animal Life); 472b (Creation)
II 2b, 3b (Earth); 411a (Heaven and Sky)

11 I 472b (Creation)

12 II 371b (Gratitude and Ingratitude); 441a (History and the Q)
III 242b (Luqmān); 524a (Narratives)
IV 6a (Pairs and Pairing); 68b (Philosophy and the Q)
V 483a (Wisdom)

12-19 I 532a (Dialogues)
III 242a (Luqmān); 521b (Narratives)

13 II 476a (Idolatry and Idolaters)
III 242b (Luqmān)
IV 159a (Polytheism and Atheism)

13-14 IV 20b (Parents)

13-15 IV 21a (Parents)

13-19	II	71a (Ethics and the Q)
	IV	32b (Patriarchy)
	V	570a (Youth and Old Age)
14	I	233b (Birth); 234b (Birth Control); 302b (Children)
	III	99b (Kinship); 106a, 106b (Lactation)
	IV	7a (Pairs and Pairing); 20b (Parents); 32a (Patriarchy)
	V	285b, 287a (Time); 570a (Youth and Old Age)
14-15	II	75b (Ethics and the Q)
	IV	159a (Polytheism and Atheism)
	V	204b (Teaching)
15	I	387b (Companions of the Prophet); 437a (Conversion)
	II	76b (Ethics and the Q)
	III	567a (Obedience)
	IV	29a (Path or Way); 427b (Repentance and Penance)
	V	110b (Speech)
16	II	305a, 305b (Geography); 545b (Instruments)
	III	334b (Measurement); 409a (Money)
	IV	4a (Pairs and Pairing)
	V	473b (Weights and Measures)
17	V	133b (Suffering); 363a (Trial); 437b, 438a, 440a, 440b, 441a (Virtues and Vices, Commanding and Forbidding)
17-18	I	241b (Boast)
18	I	161a (Arrogance); 395a (Conceit)
	III	402a (Moderation)
	V	393b (Turkish Literature and the Q)
19	I	82b (Anatomy)
	II	211a (Fire); 453a (Hospitality and Courtesy)
	III	242b (Luqmān); 402a (Moderation)
20	I	512a, 512b (Debate and Disputation)
	IV	4a (Pairs and Pairing); 107b (Planets and Stars); 186a (Possession and Possessions)
21	I	526a (Devil)
	II	417b (Hell and Hellfire); 455b (Hot and Cold); 558b (Invitation)
	V	317a (Tradition and Custom)
22	I	465a (Covenant)
	II	323b (God and his Attributes)
	III	303a (Material Culture and the Q)
	V	405a (Uncertainty)
23	I	405b (Consolation)
	II	550b (Intention)
	III	40a (Jihād); 134a (Suffering)
24	I	221b (Belief and Unbelief)

25	I	329b (Chronology and the Q); 472b (Creation)
	II	317a (God and his Attributes)
	IV	538b (Scholar)
26	IV	6a (Pairs and Pairing)
26-27	V	273a (Theology and the Q)
27	II	545a (Instruments)
	III	191b (Literacy); 224b (Literature and the Q); 552a (Numbers and Enumeration); 554b (Numerology)
	V	465b (Water); 541b, 547b (Word of God); 558a (Writing and Writing Materials)
28	I	443a (Cosmology); 479a (Creation)
	II	365a (Grammar and the Q)
	IV	5b (Pairs and Pairing); 435b (Resurrection)
	V	84a (Soul); 183a (Symbolic Imagery)
29	I	501b (Day, Times of)
	II	268a (Freedom and Predestination)
	V	163a (Sun); 280b, 289b (Time); 545a (Word of God)
30	I	158b (Arrogance)
	II	82b (Everyday Life, Q In); 321b (God and his Attributes)
	IV	5b (Pairs and Pairing); 228b (Prayer)
31	II	358b (Grammar and the Q)
	V	382b (Trust and Patience); 412a (Vehicles); 464a (Water)
31-32	II	3a (Earth)
	IV	438b (Revelation and Inspiration)
32	I	221a (Belief and Unbelief); 519a (Deliverance)
	II	317a (God and his Attributes)
	III	402a, 402b (Moderation)
	V	6a (Signs); 464a (Water)
33	II	175a (Family); 510a (Indifference)
	III	242b (Luqmān)
	V	386b (Truth)
34	I	42a (Agriculture and Vegetation); 201b (Barēlwīs); 501a (Day, Times of)
	II	424b (Hidden and the Hidden)
	III	137a, 138a (Last Judgment); 243a (Luqmān)
	IV	5b (Pairs and Pairing); 212b (Power and Impotence); 434b (Resurrection); 443b (Revelation and Inspiration)
	V	181a (Symbolic Imagery); 281a, 288a (Time); 376b (Trips and Voyages); 522a (Womb)

Sūrat al-Sajda (32)

I 230b (Biology as the Creation and Stages of Life)
II 116a (Exegesis of the Q: Classical and Medieval); 388b (Ḥadīth and the Q)
III 472b (Mysterious Letters)

1 V 393a (Turkish Literature and the Q)

1-3 II 262a (Form and Structure of the Q)

2 IV 292b (Prophets and Prophethood); 446a (Revelation and Inspiration)

3 I 372b (Community and Society in the Q); 442a (Cosmology)
III 382b (Messenger); 443a (Muḥammad)
V 460b (Warner)

4 I 443b (Cosmology); 472b, 473b, 476a (Creation)
II 273b (Friends and Friendship); 325b (God and his Attributes); 410b (Heaven and Sky)
III 202a (Literary Structures of the Q)
IV 4a (Pairs and Pairing); 82a (Philosophy and the Q)
V 265a (Theology and the Q); 279b, 287a (Time); 553a (World)

4-5 V 266a (Theology and the Q)

4-9 II 259a (Form and Structure of the Q)
V 7b (Signs)

5 I 463a (Court)
II 410b (Heaven and Sky); 433a (History and the Q)
III 46a (Jinn); 335a, 335a (Measurement)
IV 127a (Politics and the Q)
V 118b (Spiritual Beings); 286a (Time)

5-9 V 266b, 267a (Theology and the Q)

6 IV 4a, 6a (Pairs and Pairing); 537b (Scholar)

7 I 339b (Clay); 446a (Cosmology); 476a (Creation)
II 4a (Earth)

7-9 I 231b (Biology as the Creation and Stages of Life)

8 I 340a (Clay); 477b (Creation)

8-9 I 476b (Creation)

9 I 52a (Air and Wind); 446b (Cosmology); 508a (Death and the Dead)
II 186b (Fate)
III 14a (Jesus); 293b (Mary)
V 81b (Soul); 114b (Spirit)

10 I 479a, 479b (Creation)

11 I 89b (Angel)

12 IV 430a (Repentance and Penance)

12-14	I	523a (Destiny)
13	I	435b (Conversion)
	III	46b, 47b (Jinn)
	IV	7b (Pairs and Pairing); 310b (Provocation)
	V	547b (Word of God)
14	II	52b (Eschatology); 54b (Eternity)
15	I	27a (Adoration); 161a (Arrogance); 254b (Bowing and Prostration)
	II	164a (Faith)
	IV	219b (Prayer); 264a (Pride)
	V	393a (Turkish Literature and the Q)
15-16	IV	455a (Reward and Punishment)
15-17	I	219b (Belief and Unbelief)
	II	258b (Form and Structure of the Q)
16	I	183a (Asceticism)
	II	448b (Hope)
17	I	406a (Consolation)
	II	284b (Garden); 358a (Grammar and the Q)
	III	235a (Love and Affection)
	IV	12b (Paradise)
18-20	IV	1b (Pairs and Pairing)
19	IV	14a (Paradise); 103b (Pit)
20	II	416a (Hell and Hellfire)
	IV	103b (Pit)
21	IV	457a, 460a (Reward and Punishment)
21-22	V	133a (Suffering)
22	IV	422b (Remembrance)
	V	5b (Signs); 416a (Vengeance)
23	III	424b (Moses)
	V	302a (Torah)
24	I	306a (Children of Israel)
	II	503a (Imām)
	III	95a (Kings and Rulers)
26	IV	320b (Punishment Stories); 425b (Remnant); 438b (Revelation and Inspiration)
26-27	II	3a (Earth)
27	I	41a, 42a (Agriculture and Vegetation)
	II	3b (Earth); 304b (Geography)
	IV	438a (Revelation and Inspiration); 574a (Seeing and Hearing)

28 I 399a (Conquest)

29 I 500a (Day, Times of)

30 III 40a (Jihād)

Sūrat al-Aḥzāb (33)

I 353a, 355b (Collection of the Q); 380a (Community and Society in the Q)
II 116a (Exegesis of the Q: Classical and Medieval); 149a, 150a (Expeditions and Battles); 176a (Family of the Prophet); 264a (Form and Structure of the Q); 396b (Ḥadīth and the Q); 407b (Heart)
III 234b (Love and Affection)
IV 594b (Shīʿism and the Q)
V 174b (Sūra)

1 II 468b (Hypocrites and Hypocrisy)
III 567b (Obedience)
IV 537b (Scholar)

1-2 III 453b (Muḥammad)
V 380a (Trust and Patience)

2 IV 294b (Prophets and Prophethood)

3 V 380a (Trust and Patience)

4 I 82a (Anatomy)
II 290a (Gender); 407a (Heart)
III 97b (Kinship); 234b (Love and Affection); 563a (Oaths)
V 393a, 393b (Turkish Literature and the Q); 509b, 510a (Wives of the Prophet); 570a (Youth and Old Age)

4-5 I 302a (Children)
II 75a (Ethics and the Q); 266a (Fosterage); 491b (Illegitimacy)
V 57a (Slaves and Slavery)

5 I 82a (Anatomy); 262a (Brother and Brotherhood); 344b, 345a, 345b (Clients and Clientage)
II 64a (Ethics and the Q)
III 378b (Mercy)
V 59a (Slaves and Slavery)

6 I 56a (ʿĀʾisha bint Abī Bakr); 262a (Brother and Brotherhood)
II 74b (Ethics and the Q); 174b (Family); 264a (Form and Structure of the Q); 518b (Inheritance)
III 232b (Lot); 447b, 448a (Muḥammad); 518a (Narratives)
IV 20b, 22a (Parents); 296b (Prophets and Prophethood)
V 509a, 512b, 512b (Wives of the Prophet); 522a (Womb); 558a (Writing and Writing Materials)

7	I	6a (Abraham); 380a (Community and Society in the Q); 464b (Covenant)
	III	8a, 17a (Jesus); 444b (Muḥammad); 486b (Myths and Legends in the Q)
	IV	128b (Politics and the Q); 292a (Prophets and Prophethood)
	V	533b (Women and the Q)
7-8	III	7b (Jesus)
9	I	54a (Air and Wind); 305b (Children of Israel)
	V	377b (Troops); 471a (Weather)
9-10	III	42b (Jihād)
9-27	III	456b (Muḥammad)
	IV	332b (Quraysh)
10	V	458a (War)
11	I	196b (Badr)
	III	38a (Jihād)
12	I	460a (Courage)
	II	407b (Heart); 468b, 470a (Hypocrites and Hypocrisy)
	IV	119b (Polemic and Polemical Language)
13	II	298b, 299b (Geography)
	III	207b, 208a (Literature and the Q); 337b (Mecca); 367b (Medina); 548b (Nudity)
	IV	37a (People of the Book); 49a (People of the House); 259b (Pre-Islamic Arabia and the Q)
	V	457b (War)
15	I	466a (Covenant)
	III	42b (Jihād)
	V	457b (War)
17	I	432a (Contracts and Alliances)
	II	273a (Friends and Friendship); 335b (Good and Evil)
	III	380a (Mercy)
	IV	5b (Pairs and Pairing)
18	V	457b (War)
19	I	460b (Courage); 506b (Death and the Dead)
	II	153b (Eyes); 161b (Failure)
	IV	118a (Polemic and Polemical Language); 486a (Ritual and the Q)
	V	458a (War)
20	I	215a, 216a (Bedouin)
	II	465a (Humor)
	III	537a (News); 544b (Nomads)
	IV	25a (Parties and Factions)
20-25	III	579a (Opposition to Muḥammad)

21 II 74b (Ethics and the Q); 439a (History and the Q); 449b (Hope)
III 136b (Last Judgment); 162b (Law and the Q); 372a (Memory); 380b (Messenger); 447a (Muḥammad)
V 165b (Sunna)

22 II 70b (Ethics and the Q); 264a (Form and Structure of the Q)
IV 25b (Parties and Factions)
V 174b (Sūra)

23 I 431b (Contracts and Alliances); 460b (Courage)
II 71a (Ethics and the Q)
III 42b (Jihād)
IV 486a (Ritual and the Q)

23-24 III 38a, 41a (Jihād)

24 II 468b (Hypocrites and Hypocrisy)
IV 427a (Repentance and Penance)
V 434b (Virtue)

25 I 93b (Anger)
II 92a (Everyday Life, Q In)
IV 5b (Pairs and Pairing)

25-27 III 42b (Jihād)

26 I 222b (Belief and Unbelief); 289a (Captives)
II 198a (Fear)
III 30a (Jews and Judaism); 580a (Opposition to Muḥammad)
IV 41b (People of the Book); 310a (Provocation); 334b, 335a (Qurayẓa, Banū al-); 406a (Religious Pluralism and the Q)

26-27 III 28b (Jews and Judaism)

27 I 277a (Caliph)
III 30a (Jews and Judaism)
V 469a (Wealth)
V 174a (Sūra)

28 II 291a (Gender)
III 280a (Marriage and Divorce)
V 174b (Sūra)

28-29 IV 5a (Pairs and Pairing)
V 511a, 511b, 512b, 513a, 514b (Wives of the Prophet)

28-34 III 448a (Muḥammad)

29 V 552b (World)

30 I 299b (Chastity)
II 74b (Ethics and the Q)
IV 580b, 584a (Sex and Sexuality)

30-31 I 56b (ʿĀʾisha bint Abī Bakr)
IV 6b (Pairs and Pairing)
V 511b, 512a (Wives of the Prophet)

30-34 V 512b (Wives of the Prophet)

31 IV 458b (Reward and Punishment)
V 179a (Sustenance)

32 I 56a (ʿĀʾisha bint Abī Bakr)
II 291a (Gender); 407b (Heart); 448b (Hope); 470a (Hypocrites and Hypocrisy)
III 359b (Medicine and the Q)
V 509a, 511b, 512a (Wives of the Prophet)

32-33 I 299b (Chastity)

33 I 37b, 38b, 39a (Age of Ignorance); 56b, 58b, 59b (ʿĀʾisha bint Abī Bakr); 347a (Clothing); 390a (Companions of the Prophet)
II 174a (Family); 176b (Family of the Prophet); 193a (Fāṭima); 234a (Foreign Vocabulary)
III 558b (Numismatics); 567a (Obedience)
IV 37a (People of the Book); 48b, 49a, 49b, 50a, 51a, 52b, 53a (People of the House); 225a (Prayer); 503a, 505a (Ritual Purity)
V 286b (Time); 414a (Veil); 510b, 510b, 512a, 512b (Wives of the Prophet); 525a (Women and the Q)

33-34 I 163a (Art and Architecture and the Q)
V 511b, 512a (Wives of the Prophet)

34 III 190a (Literacy)
IV 225a (Prayer)
V 7a (Signs); 317b (Tradition and Custom); 483b (Wisdom); 512a (Wives of the Prophet)

35 I 84a (Anatomy); 183a (Asceticism); 298b (Chastity)
II 75b (Ethics and the Q); 175b (Family); 181a (Fasting); 245a (Forgiveness); 291b (Gender)
IV 225a, 230b (Prayer); 404b (Religious Pluralism and the Q); 455a (Reward and Punishment); 581a, 584a (Sex and Sexuality)
V 134b (Suffering); 523b (Women and the Q)

35-36 I 219b (Belief and Unbelief)

36 I 537b (Disobedience)
II 66a, 74b (Ethics and the Q)
III 567a, 568b (Obedience)
IV 402a (Religious Pluralism and the Q)
V 523b (Women and the Q)

37 I 302a (Children); 320a (Chronology and the Q)
II 439a (History and the Q)

	III	97b (Kinship); 448b (Muḥammad)
	IV	237b, 238b (Pre-1800 Preoccupations of Q Studies)
	V	57a (Slaves and Slavery); 179a (Sustenance); 534b (Women and the Q)
37-38	V	509b, 510a (Wives of the Prophet)
37-39	II	197a (Fear)
37-40	V	272b (Theology and the Q)
38	V	164a (Sunna)
40	I	11b (Abrogation); 51a (Aḥmadiyya); 115a (Apologetics); 198a (Bahāʾīs)
	II	148b (Expeditions and Battles); 407a (Heart); 544b (Instruments)
	III	380b, 382b (Messenger); 440a, 444a, 448a (Muḥammad); 501b, 502a (Names of the Prophet)
	IV	259a (Pre-Islamic Arabia and the Q); 299a (Prophets and Prophethood)
	V	489a (Witness to Faith); 501b (Witnessing and Testifying); 509b, 510a (Wives of the Prophet)
41	I	502b (Day, Times of)
	III	372a, 373b (Memory); 418b (Morning)
	IV	230b (Prayer); 487b (Ritual and the Q)
	V	138b (Ṣūfism and the Q); 393b (Turkish Literature and the Q)
41-42	IV	221a (Prayer)
42	I	503b, 504a (Day, Times of)
	II	80a (Evening); 82a (Everyday Life, Q In)
	III	416b (Morning)
	V	281a (Time)
43	II	551b (Intercession)
	III	186a (Light)
	IV	218a (Prayer)
44	I	198a, 198b (Bahāʾīs); 237a (Blessing)
45	II	33b (Epigraphy); 264a (Form and Structure of the Q); 341b (Good News)
	IV	3b (Pairs and Pairing); 300b (Prophets and Prophethood)
	V	307b (Torah)
45-46	III	440b (Muḥammad)
	IV	148b (Politics and the Q)
46	II	275b (Furniture and Furnishings); 547a (Instruments)
	III	108a (Lamp); 186b (Light); 503b (Names of the Prophet)
48	II	468b (Hypocrites and Hypocrisy)
	III	40a (Jihād); 453b (Muḥammad); 567b (Obedience)
	V	380a (Trust and Patience)
49	II	76a (Ethics and the Q)
	III	280b (Marriage and Divorce)

	IV	488b (Ritual and the Q); 580b (Sex and Sexuality)
	V	181a (Symbolic Imagery); 453b, 454a, 454b (Waiting Period)
50	I	251b (Booty); 258a (Bridewealth); 383b (Community and Society in the Q); 396b (Concubines)
	II	74b (Ethics and the Q)
	III	172b (Lawful and Unlawful); 278a (Marriage and Divorce)
	IV	452a (Reward and Punishment); 580b, 582a (Sex and Sexuality)
	V	57b (Slaves and Slavery); 194a (Taxation); 313b (Trade and Commerce); 507a, 507b, 513a, 513b (Wives of the Prophet); 527b, 534b (Women and the Q)
51	I	82a (Anatomy); 517b (Deferral)
	II	353b (Grammar and the Q)
	III	234b, 235a (Love and Affection)
	IV	6a (Pairs and Pairing); 537b (Scholar)
	V	19a (Sin, Major and Minor); 513a, 513b (Wives of the Prophet)
52	I	384a (Community and Society in the Q)
	III	278a (Marriage and Divorce)
	V	493a (Witnessing and Testifying); 513a, 513b (Wives of the Prophet)
53	I	56a (ʿĀʾisha bint Abī Bakr); 203a (Barrier); 220a (Belief and Unbelief); 299b (Chastity); 343b (Cleanliness and Ablution); 384a (Community and Society in the Q)
	II	74b (Ethics and the Q); 276a (Furniture and Furnishings); 392b (Ḥadīth and the Q)
	III	60b (Joy and Misery); 448a (Muḥammad)
	IV	506a (Ritual Purity); 580b (Sex and Sexuality)
	V	412b, 413b (Veil); 510a, 510b, 512b (Wives of the Prophet); 525b (Women and the Q)
54	IV	4a (Pairs and Pairing)
55	I	259b (Brother and Brotherhood); 396b (Concubines)
	II	176b (Family)
	V	53b (Sister); 413b (Veil); 510a, 510b (Wives of the Prophet)
56	II	32b (Epigraphy); 462a (House, Domestic and Divine); 551b (Intercession)
	III	267b (Manuscripts of the Q); 300a (Material Culture and the Q); 446b (Muḥammad)
	IV	34a (Peace); 218a, 225a (Prayer)
	V	174b (Sūra)
57-58	V	21b (Sin, Major and Minor)
58	IV	432b (Responsibility)
	V	19a, 21a (Sin, Major and Minor); 523b (Women and the Q)

59 I 56a (ʿĀʾisha bint Abī Bakr); 299b (Chastity); 346b (Clothing); 384b (Community and Society in the Q)
II 76a (Ethics and the Q); 291a (Gender)
III 403a (Modesty)
V 413b (Veil); 510b (Wives of the Prophet); 526b (Women and the Q)

59-60 V 510b (Wives of the Prophet)

60 I 338a, 338b (City)
II 298b (Geography); 407b (Heart); 468b, 470a (Hypocrites and Hypocrisy)
III 337b (Mecca); 367b (Medina)
IV 119b (Polemic and Polemical Language)

62 V 164a (Sunna); 317b (Tradition and Custom)

63 I 501a (Day, Times of)
II 46b (Eschatology); 148b (Expeditions and Battles); 439b (History and the Q)
III 137a, 138a (Last Judgment)
IV 434b (Resurrection)
V 203a (Teaching); 288a (Time)

64 I 492a (Curse)
IV 119b (Polemic and Polemical Language)

65 I 432a (Contracts and Alliances)
II 54b (Eternity); 273b (Friends and Friendship)

66 II 158b (Face); 354a (Grammar and the Q); 415a (Hell and Hellfire)

67 II 354a (Grammar and the Q)

68 IV 6b (Pairs and Pairing); 458b (Reward and Punishment)

71 I 220b (Belief and Unbelief)
V 334a (Traditional Disciplines of Q Studies); 501b (Witnessing and Testifying)

72 I 86b (Angel); 258a (Breaking Trusts and Contracts); 457a (Cosmology)
II 56b (Ethics and the Q); 187a (Fate); 197b (Fear); 488a (Ignorance)
IV 127a (Politics and the Q)
V 378b (Trust and Patience)

72-73 V 530b (Women and the Q)

73 I 381a (Community and Society in the Q); 436b (Conversion)
II 468b, 470a (Hypocrites and Hypocrisy)
IV 2b (Pairs and Pairing); 399a (Religious Pluralism and the Q); 427a (Repentance and Penance)
V 523b (Women and the Q)

SŪRAT SABĀʾ (34)

II 116a (Exegesis of the Q: Classical and Medieval)
IV 59a (Persian Literature and the Q); 586a (Sheba)

1 IV 5b (Pairs and Pairing); 213b (Praise)

1-5 I 523b (Destiny)

2 I 209a (Basmala)
III 46a (Jinn)
IV 5b (Pairs and Pairing)
V 118b (Spiritual Beings)

3 I 28b (Adultery and Fornication); 243a (Book); 392b (Computers and the Q); 501a (Day, Times of); 522b (Destiny)
II 545b (Instruments)
III 124b (Language and Style of the Q); 137a (Last Judgment); 334b (Measurement); 409a (Money)
IV 311a (Provocation)
V 287b (Time); 473b (Weights and Measures)

4 I 244a (Book)
II 245a (Forgiveness)

5 II 527a (Inimitability)
IV 454a (Reward and Punishment); 503a (Ritual Purity)
V 422a (Verse)

6 IV 6a (Pairs and Pairing); 29a (Path or Way); 538b, 539a (Scholar)
V 203b (Teaching)

7 I 479a, 479b (Creation)
III 536b (News)

8 II 540a (Insanity)
IV 112a (Poetry and Poets); 311b (Provocation)

9 IV 427b (Repentance and Penance); 438a (Revelation and Inspiration)

10 I 99b (Animal Life); 496a (David)
II 344b (Grace); 359a, 359b (Grammar and the Q); 372b (Gratitude and Ingratitude)
III 253b (Manual Labor); 383a (Metals and Minerals); 487a (Myths and Legends in the Q); 524a (Narratives)
IV 213b, 214b (Praise); 315b (Psalms)

10-11 I 496a (David)
II 145b (Expeditions and Battles)
III 487b (Myths and Legends in the Q)

10-13 III 395a (Miracles)

10-14 V 77a (Solomon)

10-19 III 521a (Narratives)

11 II 546a (Instruments)
III 333a (Measurement)

12 I 52a, 54a (Air and Wind); 162b (Art and Architecture and the Q); 503b, 504a (Day, Times of)
III 44b (Jinn); 383a (Metals and Minerals); 410a (Months); 418b (Morning); 487a, 487b (Myths and Legends in the Q)
IV 555a (Science and the Q); 604a (Ships)
V 77b (Solomon); 121b, 127b (Springs and Fountains); 281b, 285a (Time); 475b, 476a (Weights and Measures); 548b (Work)

12-13 I 166b (Art and Architecture and the Q)
II 372b (Gratitude and Ingratitude)
III 253b (Manual Labor)
IV 164b (Popular and Talismanic Uses of the Q)
V 77a (Solomon)

12-14 III 250a (Magic)

13 I 162b, 165a (Art and Architecture and the Q); 490b (Cups and Vessels)
II 219a (Food and Drink); 345b (Grace); 476b (Idolatry and Idolaters); 481b (Idols and Images)
IV 227b (Prayer); 516b (Sacred Precincts)
V 548b (Work)

14 I 99a, 100b (Animal Life)
II 185b (Fate); 547a (Instruments)
III 43b, 44b (Jinn); 208a (Literature and the Q); 253b (Manual Labor); 534b (Nature as Signs)
IV 509a (Rod)

15 I 43a (Agriculture and Vegetation); 151a (Archaeology and the Q)
II 217a (Food and Drink); 283a (Garden); 437b (History and the Q)

15-16 I 151a (Archaeology and the Q)
II 283a (Garden); 459b (House, Domestic and Divine)
IV 586a (Sheba)

15-17 IV 7a (Pairs and Pairing)

15-19 IV 586a (Sheba)

15-21 IV 320a (Punishment Stories)

16 I 44a (Agriculture and Vegetation); 60b (Al-ʿArim); 151a (Archaeology and the Q)
II 305b (Geography); 437b (History and the Q)
III 532b (Nature as Signs)
IV 257b (Pre-Islamic Arabia and the Q)
V 464a (Water)

18 I 236b (Blessing); 501a (Day, Times of)
II 309a (Geography)
III 58a (Journey); 333a (Measurement); 500a, 500b (Najrān)

	IV	411a (Religious Pluralism and the Q); 513b (Sacred Precincts)
	V	107a (Spatial Relations); 373b (Trips and Voyages)
18-19	III	339a (Mecca)
19	II	435b (History and the Q)
	III	58b (Journey)
	V	5a (Signs); 373b (Trips and Voyages); 382b (Trust and Patience)
20	I	447a (Cosmology)
	III	45a (Jinn)
	IV	586b (Sheba)
20-21	I	525a (Devil)
21	I	243a (Book)
	II	320b (God and his Attributes)
	IV	307a (Protection)
22	II	476a (Idolatry and Idolaters); 545b (Instruments)
	III	334b (Measurement); 409a (Money)
	IV	4b (Pairs and Pairing); 311a (Provocation)
	V	473b (Weights and Measures)
23	I	158b (Arrogance)
	II	82b (Everyday Life, Q In); 552b (Intercession)
	IV	5b (Pairs and Pairing); 163b (Popular and Talismanic Uses of the Q)
24	IV	4a (Pairs and Pairing); 78a (Philosophy and the Q)
25	III	40a (Jihād)
	IV	432a (Responsibility)
26	I	399a (Conquest)
	II	320b (God and his Attributes)
	IV	6a (Pairs and Pairing)
27	IV	312a, 312b (Provocation)
28	II	341b (Good News)
	III	443b (Muḥammad)
	IV	3b (Pairs and Pairing); 337a (Races); 538b (Scholar)
	V	38a (Sīra and the Q); 460a, 461a (Warner)
29	II	70b (Ethics and the Q)
30	I	501a (Day, Times of)
	III	335b (Measurement)
	V	288a (Time)
31-33	I	159a, 161a (Arrogance); 296a (Chastisement and Punishment); 532a (Dialogues)
	III	581a, 582a (Oppressed on Earth); 583a (Oppression)
	IV	264a (Pride)
33	I	222a (Belief and Unbelief)
	II	476b (Idolatry and Idolaters)

	III	18a (Jesus)
	IV	430b (Repentance and Penance)
	V	280b (Time)
34	IV	309b (Provocation)
34-35	V	468b (Wealth)
35	IV	3b (Pairs and Pairing); 31b (Patriarchy)
	V	468a (Wealth)
35-37	I	221b (Belief and Unbelief)
36	IV	538b (Scholar)
	V	179a (Sustenance)
	V	268b (Theology and the Q)
37	I	165b (Art and Architecture and the Q)
	IV	6b (Pairs and Pairing); 289a (Property); 458b (Reward and Punishment)
	V	468a (Wealth)
38	II	527a (Inimitability)
40-41	III	141a (Last Judgment)
41	II	273b (Friends and Friendship)
	III	48a (Jinn)
	V	120b (Spiritual Beings)
42	II	418b (Hell and Hellfire)
43	III	190a (Literacy); 246a (Magic); 450b (Muḥammad)
	V	7a (Signs); 421b (Verse)
43-47	III	247a (Magic)
44	I	246a (Book)
	III	443a (Muḥammad)
	IV	297b (Prophets and Prophethood)
	V	203a (Teaching)
45	I	387b (Companions of the Prophet)
46	I	387b (Companions of the Prophet)
	II	540a (Insanity)
	III	450b (Muḥammad)
	IV	112a (Poetry and Poets); 394a (Reflection and Deliberation)
	V	424b (Verse)
47	III	451a (Muḥammad)
	IV	452b (Reward and Punishment)
48	IV	537b (Scholar)
48-49	V	545a (Word of God)
49	I	472b (Creation)

50 I 225b (Belief and Unbelief)
II 1b (Ears); 74b (Ethics and the Q)
IV 6a (Pairs and Pairing)

51 II 198a (Fear)

54 IV 592a (Shīʿa)

Sūrat Fāṭir (35)

I 548b (Dreams and Sleep)
II 116a (Exegesis of the Q: Classical and Medieval)
IV 244b (Pre-1800 Preoccupations of Q Studies)

1 I 88a (Angel); 472a (Creation)
III 550a (Numbers and Enumeration)
IV 213b (Praise); 290a (Prophets and Prophethood); 336b (Races)
V 393b (Turkish Literature and the Q); 424b (Verse)

1-2 II 259a (Form and Structure of the Q)

2 I 398b (Conquest)
III 327b (Material Culture and the Q)

3 I 472b (Creation)
IV 4a (Pairs and Pairing)
V 500a (Witnessing and Testifying)

4 III 453a (Muḥammad)
IV 309b (Provocation)

5 I 526a (Devil)

6 II 23b (Enemies); 66a (Ethics and the Q); 417b (Hell and Hellfire); 430b (History and the Q); 558b (Invitation)

7 II 245a (Forgiveness)
IV 1b (Pairs and Pairing)

8 I 213a (Beauty)
II 330b (God and his Attributes)
III 452b (Muḥammad)
IV 2a (Pairs and Pairing); 432a (Responsibility)

9 I 53b (Air and Wind)
II 3a (Earth)
IV 434a, 435a (Resurrection)
V 5a (Signs)

9-14 II 259a (Form and Structure of the Q)

10 II 215b (Flying); 452b (Hospitality and Courtesy)
III 19b (Jesus)
IV 309b (Provocation)

11	I	244a (Book); 476a (Creation); 523a (Destiny)
	II	175a (Family); 269b (Freedom and Predestination); 292a (Gender); 328a (God and his Attributes)
	IV	6a (Pairs and Pairing); 560a (Scripture and the Q); 581a (Sex and Sexuality)
	V	289a, 290a (Time); 524a (Women and the Q); 569b (Youth and Old Age)
12	I	96a, 97a (Animal Life); 319a (Chronology and the Q); 438b (Coral); 443a (Cosmology)
	II	212b (Fire); 218b (Food and Drink); 303b (Geography); 467b (Hunting and Fishing)
	III	531a (Nature as Signs)
	IV	7a (Pairs and Pairing); 604a (Ships)
	V	126a (Springs and Fountains); 412a (Vehicles); 464a (Water)
13	I	443a (Cosmology); 472b (Creation); 494b (Date Palm); 501b (Day, Times of)
	II	268a (Freedom and Predestination)
	IV	185a (Possession and Possessions); 228b (Prayer)
	V	163a (Sun); 280b, 289b (Time); 474b (Weights and Measures); 545a (Word of God)
13-14	IV	229a (Prayer)
14	I	220b (Belief and Unbelief); 443a (Cosmology)
	II	476a (Idolatry and Idolaters)
15	IV	209a (Poverty and the Poor)
	V	467b (Wealth)
16-17	I	474b (Creation)
18	II	175a (Family)
	III	228a (Load or Burden); 379b (Mercy)
	V	287a (Time); 472a (Weeping); 474a (Weights and Measures)
19	III	186a (Light)
	IV	2a (Pairs and Pairing)
	V	447b (Vision and Blindness)
19-20	I	493b (Darkness)
	V	445a (Vision)
19-22	II	455a (Hot and Cold)
	III	209b (Literature and the Q)
	IV	10a (Parable)
22	II	45b (Eschatology)
	III	452b (Muḥammad)
23	III	40a (Jihād)
24	II	341b (Good News); 497b (Illiteracy)
	III	382a (Messenger); 451a (Muḥammad)
	IV	3b (Pairs and Pairing)
	V	460b (Warner)

25 I 245a (Book)
IV 35b (People of the Book); 296a, 297a, 301a (Prophets and Prophethood); 309b (Provocation); 570b (Scrolls)
V 300b, 301b, 303b (Torah)

27 I 361b, 363b, 364b (Colors)
II 3a (Earth); 217b (Food and Drink)

27-28 I 362a (Colors)
II 259a (Form and Structure of the Q)
IV 336a (Races)

28 I 361b (Colors)
III 102b (Knowledge and Learning)
IV 6a (Pairs and Pairing); 537b, 538b (Scholar)
V 204b (Teaching)

29 II 449a (Hope); 450a (Hospitality and Courtesy)
III 209a (Literature and the Q); 276a (Markets)
IV 221b (Prayer)
V 373b (Trips and Voyages)

30 II 321a (God and his Attributes); 345a (Grace)
IV 6a (Pairs and Pairing); 213a (Praise)

31 I 245b (Book)
III 303a (Material Culture and the Q); 441b, 445a (Muḥammad)
IV 294a (Prophets and Prophethood); 439a (Revelation and Inspiration)

32 I 245b (Book)
II 65a (Ethics and the Q); 11b (Election)
III 71a (Justice and Injustice); 402a, 402b (Moderation)
IV 297b (Prophets and Prophethood)

33 I 96a (Animal Life); 166a (Art and Architecture and the Q); 213b (Beauty); 220b (Belief and Unbelief)
II 333b (Gold)
III 383b, 384a (Metals and Minerals)
IV 18a (Paradise)
V 11b (Silk); 393a (Turkish Literature and the Q)

34 II 283b (Garden)
IV 6a (Pairs and Pairing); 213b (Praise)

34-35 II 284a (Garden)

35 II 283a, 283b (Garden)
III 254b (Manual Labor)
IV 14b (Paradise)

36 I 170b (Art and Architecture and the Q); 221a (Belief and Unbelief)
II 210a (Fire); 416b, 418b (Hell and Hellfire)

37 III 203b (Literary Structures of the Q)
IV 430a (Repentance and Penance)

38 II 550b (Intention)

39 I 277a (Caliph)
IV 310a (Provocation)

40 I 472b (Creation)
II 476a (Idolatry and Idolaters)
III 509a (Names of the Q)
IV 312a, 312b (Provocation)

41 IV 5b (Pairs and Pairing)

42 I 329b (Chronology and the Q)
II 317a (God and his Attributes)
III 450b (Muḥammad)

43 II 308a (Geography); 434a (History and the Q)
V 19b (Sin, Major and Minor); 164a (Sunna); 317b (Tradition and Custom)

44 II 360a (Grammar and the Q)
IV 4a, 6a (Pairs and Pairing); 211a (Power and Impotence); 320b (Punishment Stories); 425a (Remnant)

45 I 98a (Animal Life)
III 378b (Mercy)
V 22a (Sin, Major and Minor); 289a, 289b (Time)

SŪRAT YĀ SĪN (36)

I 264a, 265a (Burial); 548b (Dreams and Sleep)
II 96a (Everyday Life, Q In); 116a (Exegesis of the Q: Classical and Medieval); 394a (Ḥadīth and the Q)
III 272a (Manuscripts of the Q); 324a (Material Culture and the Q); 472b (Mysterious Letters); 503b (Names of the Prophet); 521a (Narratives)
IV 177b (Popular and Talismanic Uses of the Q); 244b (Pre-1800 Preoccupations of Q Studies); 380a (Recitation of the Q); 478b (Rhymed Prose); 494b, 495b, 496b (Ritual and the Q)
V 308b (Torah)

1 III 197a (Literary Structures of the Q)

1-9 III 197a (Sīra and the Q)

2 II 257b, 263b (Form and Structure of the Q)
IV 468b (Rhetoric and the Q)
V 172a (Sūra); 483a (Wisdom)

2-6 I 372b (Community and Society in the Q)
II 143a (Exhortations)

5	II	447a (Honor)
	IV	6a (Pairs and Pairing); 443b (Revelation and Inspiration)
5-6	III	379a (Mercy)
6	II	497b (Illiteracy)
	III	443a (Muḥammad)
7	IV	432a (Responsibility)
8	I	81b (Anatomy); 226a (Belief and Unbelief)
	II	546a (Instruments)
9	V	39a (Sīra and the Q)
11	II	196b (Fear); 245a (Forgiveness)
12	I	243b, 244a (Book); 522b (Destiny)
	II	401a (Hand); 48a (Eschatology); 503a (Imām)
	III	191a (Literacy); 550a (Numbers and Enumeration)
	V	95a (South Asian Literatures and the Q); 493a (Witnessing and Testifying)
13	I	338a (City)
	III	524b (Narratives)
	IV	210b (Power and Impotence)
13-29	III	521a (Narratives)
	IV	10a, 10b (Parable); 353a (Rass)
13-31	IV	438b (Revelation and Inspiration)
13-32	II	260a (Form and Structure of the Q)
	IV	320a (Punishment Stories)
14	III	118b (Language and Style of the Q); 524a (Narratives)
15	IV	301a (Prophets and Prophethood)
17	III	125a (Language and Style of the Q)
18	II	242a (Foretelling in the Q)
	V	130b (Stoning); 132b (Suffering)
20	I	338a (City)
	II	558b (Invitation)
21	IV	452b (Reward and Punishment)
22	I	472a (Creation)
23	II	551a (Intercession)
	IV	523b (Salvation)
23-24	II	43b (Error)
25	II	2a (Ears)
27	II	447b (Honor)
28	V	377b, 378a (Troops)

29 II 359b (Grammar and the Q)
III 125a (Language and Style of the Q)
IV 454a (Reward and Punishment)
V 545a (Word of God)

30 III 400a (Mockery)

30-31 IV 309b (Provocation)

30-32 IV 11a (Parable)

32 II 361b, 366b (Grammar and the Q)

33 I 291b (Carrion)
II 3a, 3b (Earth)

33-35 I 41a (Agriculture and Vegetation)
V 127a (Springs and Fountains)

33-36 II 3a (Earth)

33-47 II 259a (Form and Structure of the Q)
IV 438a (Revelation and Inspiration)

34 I 478a (Creation)
II 283b (Garden); 304a (Geography)
V 463b (Water)

35 I 476a (Creation)

36 I 476b (Creation)
IV 6a (Pairs and Pairing); 220b (Prayer); 336a (Races)

37 I 443a (Cosmology); 493a (Darkness); 499a (Day, Times of)

38 IV 6a (Pairs and Pairing); 550b (Science and the Q)
V 163a (Sun)

39 I 272b (Calendar); 494b (Date Palm)
III 413a (Months)
IV 107a, 108a (Planets and Stars); 571b (Seasons)
V 14b (Simile); 283b (Time)

40 I 498a (Day and Night); 501b (Day, Times of)
II 315a (Glorification of God); 359b, 365a (Grammar and the Q)
IV 107a, 107b (Planets and Stars)
V 163a, 163b (Sun); 280b, 284a (Time)

42 V 412a (Vehicles)

43 I 519a (Deliverance); 553b (Drowning)
IV 523b (Salvation)

45 II 401a (Hand)

46 V 5b (Signs)

47 V 179b (Sustenance)

49	I	513b (Debate and Disputation)
	II	357b (Grammar and the Q)
	IV	454a (Reward and Punishment)
51	I	112b (Apocalypse)
	II	547a (Instruments)
51-64	I	263b (Burial)
52	II	276a (Furniture and Furnishings)
	IV	300b (Prophets and Prophethood)
53	III	203a (Literary Structures of the Q)
54	I	522b (Destiny)
55	III	63a (Joy and Misery)
	V	548b (Work)
55-58	IV	34b (Peace)
56	IV	18a, 18b (Paradise)
56-57	III	204a (Literary Structures of the Q)
57	IV	18a (Paradise)
58	V	547a (Word of God)
60	I	447a, 448a (Cosmology); 465b (Covenant)
	II	23b, 24a (Enemies); 328b (God and his Attributes)
	III	47b (Jinn)
62	II	67b (Ethics and the Q)
65	II	48b (Eschatology)
	III	141a (Last Judgment)
	V	110b (Speech); 494b (Witnessing and Testifying)
66	I	81a (Anatomy)
	II	49a (Eschatology)
67-88	III	520a (Narratives)
69	I	542b (Divination)
	III	512b (Names of the Q)
	IV	112a (Poetry and Poets); 442b (Revelation and Inspiration)
	V	201a (Teaching); 393a, 393b (Turkish Literature and the Q)
69-70	IV	113a (Poetry and Poets)
69-83	II	143a (Exhortations)
70	I	472a (Creation)
	II	33b (Epigraphy)
71	I	95b (Animal Life); 443a (Cosmology)
71-73	IV	185b (Possession and Possessions)

72 I 96a (Animal Life)
V 411b (Vehicles)

73 I 96a (Animal Life)
V 4a (Signs)

75 V 377b (Troops)

76 I 405b (Consolation)
IV 4a (Pairs and Pairing)
V 134a (Suffering)

76-78 I 479a (Creation)

77 I 476b (Creation)

77-79 I 479a (Creation)
II 508a (Impotence)

77-82 I 479a, 479b (Creation)

78 II 4b (Earth)
IV 9b (Parable); 87a (Philosophy and the Q)

78-79 II 45a (Eschatology)
IV 287a (Proof); 311a (Provocation)

78-80 II 213a (Fire)

79 IV 72a (Philosophy and the Q)

80 I 362b (Colors); 478a (Creation)
II 305a (Geography)
IV 87a (Philosophy and the Q)
V 358b, 359a (Tree)

81 II 320b, 327b (God and his Attributes)
IV 6a (Pairs and Pairing); 280b (Profane and Sacred); 287a (Proof)

81-82 I 475b (Creation)

82 I 319a (Chronology and the Q); 475a (Creation)
II 327b (God and his Attributes)
IV 82a (Philosophy and the Q)
V 109a (Speech); 542b, 543a (Word of God)

83 III 90b (Kings and Rulers); 202a (Literary Structures of the Q)
IV 127b (Politics and the Q); 184b (Possession and Possessions); 220b (Prayer)

Sūrat al-Ṣāffāt (37)

I 533b (Dialogues); 548b (Dreams and Sleep)
III 521a (Narratives)
IV 244a (Pre-1800 Preoccupations of Q Studies); 348b (Ranks and Orders)
V 488b (Witness to Faith)

1	I	442b (Cosmology)
	IV	350a (Ranks and Orders)
1-3	II	256a (Form and Structure of the Q)
	IV	464b (Rhetoric and the Q)
	V	80a (Soothsayer)
1-5	IV	466a (Rhetoric and the Q)
3	II	263b (Form and Structure of the Q)
	III	190a (Literacy)
	IV	466a (Rhetoric and the Q)
	V	172a (Sūra)
4	II	329b (God and his Attributes)
	IV	466b (Rhetoric and the Q)
5	II	31a (Epigraphy); 364a (Grammar and the Q)
	IV	4a (Pairs and Pairing)
	V	282b (Time)
6	I	442b (Cosmology)
	II	327b (God and his Attributes); 411a (Heaven and Sky)
6-7	I	213a (Beauty)
6-8	I	462b (Court)
6-10	I	442b (Cosmology)
	III	249b (Magic)
	IV	108a (Planets and Stars)
7	I	524b (Devil)
	IV	307b (Protection)
8	I	369a (Community and Society in the Q); 462b (Court)
	II	405b (Hearing and Deafness)
	IV	220a (Prayer)
8-10	I	463a (Court)
10	III	46a, 48b (Jinn)
	IV	107a, 108b (Planets and Stars)
11	I	339b (Clay); 446a (Cosmology); 476a (Creation)
	II	4a, 4b (Earth); 328a (God and his Attributes)
12	III	149a (Laughter)
12-14	III	401a (Mockery)
13	II	82a (Everyday Life, Q In)
14	IV	183b (Portents)
14-15	III	247a (Magic)
15	III	246a (Magic)
16	II	4b (Earth)

20	I	480b (Creeds)
	II	47b (Eschatology)
	III	66b (Judgment); 136b (Last Judgment)
20-21	IV	8a (Pairs and Pairing)
21	I	500a (Day, Times of); 516b (Decision)
	III	137a (Last Judgment)
22	V	83b (Soul); 524a (Women and the Q)
22-23	III	141a (Last Judgment)
22-32	V	494a (Witnessing and Testifying)
23	II	415a (Hell and Hellfire)
	IV	29b (Path or Way)
	V	374b (Trips and Voyages)
23-24	II	49a (Eschatology)
24	IV	431a (Responsibility)
26	III	66b (Judgment)
31	V	541a, 547b (Word of God)
35	III	556a (Numismatics)
	IV	309b (Provocation)
	V	393b (Turkish Literature and the Q); 488b (Witness to Faith); 500b, 501a (Witnessing and Testifying)
36	I	447a (Cosmology)
	II	540a (Insanity)
	III	450a (Muḥammad)
	IV	112a, 112b (Poetry and Poets); 311b (Provocation); 442b (Revelation and Inspiration); 455b (Reward and Punishment)
36-37	III	219b (Literature and the Q)
37	I	115a (Apologetics)
	II	33b (Epigraphy)
38-39	V	284a (Time)
40	II	550a (Intention)
	IV	577a (Servants)
41	IV	18b (Paradise)
42	IV	18a (Paradise)
44	IV	18a (Paradise)
45	I	490b (Cups and Vessels)
	IV	18b (Paradise)
	V	121b (Springs and Fountains); 482a (Wine)
45-46	V	125a (Springs and Fountains)

45-47	II	51b (Eschatology); 284a (Garden)
	V	464b (Water)
46	I	363b (Colors)
46-47	V	125a (Springs and Fountains)
47	II	556a (Intoxicants)
	V	120b (Spiritual Beings)
48	V	524a (Women and the Q)
48-49	II	456a (Houris)
	IV	585a (Sex and Sexuality)
	V	14b (Simile)
49	I	363b (Colors)
	II	456b (Houris)
	V	125b (Springs and Fountains)
51	II	353b, 366a (Grammar and the Q)
51-59	II	415b (Hell and Hellfire)
53	II	4b (Earth)
	III	66b (Judgment)
54	II	366a (Grammar and the Q)
55-56	V	524a (Women and the Q)
56	II	361b (Grammar and the Q)
60	IV	522b (Salvation)
61	II	30b (Epigraphy)
	III	300b (Material Culture and the Q)
62	I	42a (Agriculture and Vegetation)
	II	211a (Fire); 305a (Geography)
	V	359a (Tree); 571a (Zaqqūm)
62-65	III	203b (Literary Structures of the Q)
	V	359b (Tree)
62-66	III	533a (Nature as Signs)
62-68	I	222a (Belief and Unbelief)
	II	50a (Eschatology)
63	V	571b (Zaqqūm)
64	II	415b (Hell and Hellfire)
	V	571b (Zaqqūm)
64-65	V	571a (Zaqqūm)
65	II	416b (Hell and Hellfire)
67	II	211a (Fire)

71 II 434a (History and the Q)
IV 320a (Punishment Stories)

71-148 IV 320a, 321a (Punishment Stories)

72-148 III 207a (Literature and the Q)

74 II 550a (Intention)

75-79 III 486a (Myths and Legends in the Q)

75-80 III 521a (Narratives)

75-148 III 381b (Messenger)

76 III 63b (Joy and Misery)

78 V 240b (Textual Criticism of the Q)

78-79 I 237a (Blessing)
V 545b (Word of God)

79-181 IV 34a (Peace)

81-82 V 545b (Word of God)

83 IV 25b (Parties and Factions); 591b, 592a (Shīʿa)
V 258a (Theology and the Q)

83-98 I 6b (Abraham); 330a (Chronology and the Q)
II 558a (Invitation)
III 494a (Myths and Legends in the Q)
IV 21a (Parents)

83-101 I 6a (Abraham)

83-113 III 521a (Narratives)

84 II 408a (Heart)

85-99 I 193a (Āzar)

91-92 I 534a (Dialogues)
II 465a (Humor)

93 I 7a (Abraham)
III 494b (Myths and Legends in the Q)

95 II 507b (Impotence)

95-96 I 472b (Creation)

96 I 476a (Creation)
II 330b (God and his Attributes); 474a (Iconoclasm)
IV 86a (Philosophy and the Q)

97 II 211b, 212a (Fire); 414b (Hell and Hellfire)

97-98 I 7a (Abraham)
III 494b (Myths and Legends in the Q)

99-111	I	6a, 6b (Abraham)
	II	564b (Ishmael)
	III	4b (Jerusalem); 239a (Loyalty)
99-113	II	562a (Isaac)
100-101	II	341a (Good News)
100-107	IV	21a (Parents)
100-111	I	330b (Chronology and the Q)
101	I	7b, 10b (Abraham)
	III	401b (Moderation)
102	I	546b (Dreams and Sleep)
	II	241b (Foretelling in the Q); 251b (Form and Structure of the Q)
	III	494b (Myths and Legends in the Q)
	IV	179a (Popular and Talismanic Uses of the Q); 517b (Sacrifice)
	V	61a (Sleep)
102-103	III	223a (Literature and the Q)
102-105	I	547a, 547b (Dreams and Sleep)
	V	444a (Vision)
102-113	III	494b (Myths and Legends in the Q)
103	II	562a (Isaac)
104-107	V	363a (Trial)
105	I	546b, 548a (Dreams and Sleep)
	II	241b (Foretelling in the Q)
	IV	179a (Popular and Talismanic Uses of the Q); 295a (Prophets and Prophethood)
105-131	IV	452b (Reward and Punishment)
106	I	7a (Abraham)
107	I	404b (Consecration of Animals)
	III	341a (Mecca); 393a (Miracles)
	IV	517b (Sacrifice)
108	V	240b (Textual Criticism of the Q)
108-109	I	237a (Blessing)
112	I	6b, 7b (Abraham)
	II	341a (Good News); 561a (Isaac)
	III	393b (Miracles)
112-113	I	330b (Chronology and the Q)
	II	564b (Ishmael)
113	I	7b (Abraham)
	II	561b (Isaac)
	III	71a (Justice and Injustice)
	V	240b (Textual Criticism of the Q)

114	IV	483a (Rhymed Prose)
114-120	I	1a (Aaron)
114-122	III	521a (Narratives)
115	I	518b (Deliverance)
	III	63b (Joy and Misery)
115-116	III	488a (Myths and Legends in the Q)
117	III	125a (Language and Style of the Q)
	V	301a (Torah)
117-118	III	128b (Language and Style of the Q)
119	V	240b (Textual Criticism of the Q)
119-120	I	237a (Blessing)
120	IV	483a (Rhymed Prose)
123	III	381a (Messenger)
123-130	I	194a (Baal)
	III	521a (Narratives)
123-132	II	12b (Elijah); 558a (Invitation)
125	I	194a (Baal)
	II	13b (Elijah)
128	II	550a (Intention)
129	V	240b (Textual Criticism of the Q)
129-130	I	237a (Blessing)
130	II	13a (Elijah); 364a (Grammar and the Q)
	IV	482b (Rhymed Prose)
	V	28a (Sinai)
132	II	13a (Elijah)
133	IV	482b (Rhymed Prose)
133-138	III	232a (Lot); 521a (Narratives)
134	I	519a (Deliverance)
136	I	149a (Archaeology and the Q)
137	I	149a (Archaeology and the Q); 504a (Day, Times of)
	IV	425b (Remnant)
139	III	381a (Messenger)
139-146	III	395b (Miracles)
139-148	II	293a (Generations)
	III	53a (Jonah); 521a (Narratives)
	IV	319b (Punishment Stories)
	V	373b (Trips and Voyages)

140	I	158a (Ark)
	III	207b (Literature and the Q)
	IV	604b (Ships)
	V	41b (Sīra and the Q)
141	II	280a, 282a (Gambling)
142-145	I	99a (Animal Life)
143	II	315a (Glorification of God)
	III	54b (Jonah)
146	II	217a (Food and Drink); 305a, 305b (Geography)
147	V	361b (Tree)
149	I	330a (Chronology and the Q)
	II	317b (God and his Attributes)
	III	48a (Jinn)
149-159	III	295a (Mary)
149-182	II	143a (Exhortations)
150-152	III	48a (Jinn)
151-152	IV	116b (Polemic and Polemical Language)
153	II	11b (Election)
	III	48a (Jinn)
156	IV	312b (Provocation)
156-157	IV	312a (Provocation)
157	III	508a (Names of the Q)
	IV	312b (Provocation)
158	I	236a (Blasphemy); 330a (Chronology and the Q)
	II	317b (God and his Attributes)
	III	47b (Jinn)
158-159	III	97b (Kinship)
159	II	314b (Glorification of God)
	IV	220b (Prayer)
164	IV	350a (Ranks and Orders)
164-165	IV	350a (Ranks and Orders)
164-166	IV	311a (Provocation)
165	IV	349a, 350a, 350b (Ranks and Orders)
165-167	IV	350a (Ranks and Orders)
167-170	III	450b (Muḥammad)
170	IV	538b (Scholar)
171	IV	292b (Prophets and Prophethood)
	V	289b (Time); 371b (Trinity); 547b (Word of God)

173 v 377b (Troops)

174 III 40a (Jihād)
v 288b (Time)

177 I 504a (Day, Times of)
III 417a, 418a (Morning)
v 281a (Time)

180 IV 220b (Prayer)

Sūrat Ṣād (38)

I 453a (Cosmology); 496b (David); 548b (Dreams and Sleep)
III 472b (Mysterious Letters); 519b (Narratives)
IV 496b (Ritual and the Q)
v 422a (Verse)

1 II 257b, 263b (Form and Structure of the Q)
III 372b (Memory); 510a (Names of the Q)
IV 230a (Prayer); 422a (Remembrance); 468b (Rhetoric and the Q)
v 172a (Sūra)

1-11 III 519b (Narratives)

3 II 293a (Generations); 352b (Grammar and the Q)
III 379b (Mercy)

4 II 540a (Insanity)
III 44a (Jinn); 247a (Magic); 287a (Marvels)
IV 311b (Provocation)

4-5 III 399a (Miracles)

4-7 IV 330b (Quraysh)

4-8 III 456a (Muḥammad)

6 I 369a (Community and Society in the Q)
III 338a (Mecca); 422a (Moses)
v 379a (Trust and Patience)

7 II 234a (Foreign Vocabulary)
III 450b (Muḥammad)

8 III 509b (Names of the Q)

10 III 92b (Kings and Rulers)
IV 4b (Pairs and Pairing)

11 II 365b (Grammar and the Q)
v 377b (Troops)

11-13 I 380a (Community and Society in the Q)
IV 25a (Parties and Factions)

12	I	21b (ʿĀd)
	II	542a (Insolence and Obstinacy)
	III	486a (Myths and Legends in the Q); 522a, 524a (Narratives)
	V	236b (Tents and Tent Pegs)
12-14	III	522a (Narratives)
	IV	586b (Sheba)
12-15	IV	320a (Punishment Stories)
12-16	III	519b (Narratives)
13	I	41b (Agriculture and Vegetation)
	II	353b, 355a (Grammar and the Q)
	III	390b (Midian)
	IV	25a (Parties and Factions); 53b, 54a (People of the Thicket); 605b (Shuʿayb)
14	III	453a (Muḥammad)
15	IV	454a (Reward and Punishment)
16	I	500a (Day, Times of)
	III	137a (Last Judgment)
	IV	434a (Resurrection); 457b (Reward and Punishment)
17	III	372a (Memory); 453a (Muḥammad); 524b (Narratives)
	IV	429b (Repentance and Penance)
17-18	III	373a (Memory)
	IV	316b (Psalms)
17-19	III	487a (Myths and Legends in the Q)
17-22	III	310a (Material Culture and the Q)
17-28	III	519b (Narratives)
18	I	502b, 503a, 503b (Day, Times of)
	II	315a (Glorification of God)
	III	417b, 418b (Morning); 487a (Myths and Legends in the Q)
	IV	315b (Psalms)
	V	281b, 282b (Time)
19	I	99b (Animal Life)
20	I	496a (David)
	III	93b (Kings and Rulers)
	IV	68b (Philosophy and the Q)
	V	483a (Wisdom)
20-24	IV	315b (Psalms)
21	I	149a (Archaeology and the Q); 165a (Art and Architecture and the Q)
	II	254b (Form and Structure of the Q); 299b, 309b (Geography)
	III	518a (Narratives); 537a (News)
	IV	227b (Prayer); 516b (Sacred Precincts)

21-22 I 452b (Cosmology)

21-24 I 532b (Dialogues)
III 395a (Miracles)

21-26 III 487a (Myths and Legends in the Q)

22 I 452b (Cosmology)
II 198a (Fear)
IV 29a (Path or Way); 133b (Politics and the Q)

23 I 452b (Cosmology)
II 361a (Grammar and the Q)
III 553a (Numbers and Enumeration)

23-24 I 99a (Animal Life)

24 I 254a (Bowing and Prostration); 452b (Cosmology); 496a (David)
III 379b (Mercy)
IV 219b (Prayer); 315b, 317a (Psalms); 429b (Repentance and Penance)
V 393a (Turkish Literature and the Q)

24-25 I 496a (David)

25 IV 429b (Repentance and Penance)

26 I 23a (Adam and Eve); 277a (Caliph); 452b, 457a (Cosmology); 496a (David); 500a (Day, Times of)
II 30b (Epigraphy); 321a (God and his Attributes)
III 90b, 94a (Kings and Rulers); 137a (Last Judgment); 487b (Myths and Legends in the Q)
IV 133b (Politics and the Q); 315b (Psalms); 434a (Resurrection); 457b (Reward and Punishment)
V 103a (Sovereignty)

27 I 442a (Cosmology); 473a (Creation)
II 327b (God and his Attributes); 337b (Good and Evil); 489a (Ignorance)
IV 4a (Pairs and Pairing)
V 279b (Time); 553a (World)

29 III 509a, 513a (Names of the Q)
IV 69b (Philosophy and the Q); 297a (Prophets and Prophethood); 394b (Reflection and Deliberation); 562a (Scripture and the Q)
V 203b (Teaching)

29-40 III 520a (Narratives)

30 III 50b (Job)
IV 429b (Repentance and Penance)

30-40 V 77a (Solomon)

31 I 503a (Day, Times of)
V 281b (Time)

32	I	203a (Barrier)
	IV	288b (Property); 429b (Repentance and Penance)
	V	412b (Veil)
33	III	12a (Jesus); 333b (Measurement)
34	II	275b (Furniture and Furnishings); 325b (God and his Attributes)
	III	395a (Miracles)
	IV	429b (Repentance and Penance)
	V	277a (Throne of God)
34-40	III	250a (Magic)
	IV	210b (Power and Impotence)
35	III	93a, 94a (Kings and Rulers); 379b (Mercy)
36	I	52a, 52b, 53b (Air and Wind)
	III	487a (Myths and Legends in the Q)
	V	77b (Solomon); 470b (Weather)
36-39	III	395a (Miracles)
37	II	467b (Hunting and Fishing)
	III	44b (Jinn)
	V	120b (Spiritual Beings)
37-38	V	77a (Solomon)
38	II	546b (Instruments)
39	II	313a (Gift-Giving)
	V	321a (Traditional Disciplines of Q Studies)
41	III	524b (Narratives)
	V	134a (Suffering); 363b (Trial); 381a (Trust and Patience)
41-42	III	50a (Job)
41-44	III	520a (Narratives)
	V	380b (Trust and Patience)
42	II	199a (Feet); 455b (Hot and Cold)
	V	465a (Water)
42-43	V	134a (Suffering)
42-44	III	395b (Miracles)
43	II	174a (Family)
44	I	41b (Agriculture and Vegetation)
	II	369b (Grasses)
	III	50b (Job); 563b (Oaths)
	IV	429b (Repentance and Penance)
	V	381a (Trust and Patience)
45	I	8a (Abraham)
	II	402a (Hand)
	III	1a (Jacob); 524b (Narratives)

45-48 II 561b (Isaac)

45-49 III 520a (Narratives)

47 II 11b (Election)

48 I 8a (Abraham); 527b (Dhū l-Kifl)
II 14a (Elisha); 564a (Ishmael)
III 524b (Narratives)
V 246b (Textual Criticism of the Q)

50 I 398b (Conquest)
II 361b, 363b (Grammar and the Q)
V 393b (Turkish Literature and the Q)

50-66 III 520a (Narratives)

51 IV 18a, 18b (Paradise)

52 II 456a (Houris)
IV 585a (Sex and Sexuality)
V 524a (Women and the Q)

53 I 500a (Day, Times of)
III 137a (Last Judgment)
IV 434a (Resurrection); 457b (Reward and Punishment)

54 V 340a (Transitoriness)

55 IV 104a (Pit)

56 III 63b (Joy and Misery)
IV 104a (Pit)

57 II 211a (Fire); 416a (Hell and Hellfire)
V 464b (Water)

59 II 416b (Hell and Hellfire)

60 I 491b (Curse)

61 IV 6b (Pairs and Pairing); 458b (Reward and Punishment)

63 II 358b (Grammar and the Q)
III 401a (Mockery)

64 I 452b (Cosmology); 513b (Debate and Disputation)
IV 49a (People of the House)

65 V 488b (Witness to Faith)

66 II 31a (Epigraphy); 321a (God and his Attributes)
IV 6a (Pairs and Pairing)

67 III 536b (News)

67-70 II 262a (Form and Structure of the Q)

67-85 I 452b (Cosmology)

67-88 II 143a (Exhortations)
III 519a (Narratives)

69 I 22b (Adam and Eve); 369a (Community and Society in the Q); 452b, 453a (Cosmology); 462b (Court)
II 501a (ʿIlliyyūn)
IV 220a (Prayer)

70 III 40a (Jihād); 442b (Muḥammad)

71 I 22b (Adam and Eve); 339b (Clay); 476a (Creation)
II 4a, 4b (Earth); 330a (God and his Attributes)
V 109a (Speech)

71-72 V 84a (Soul)

71-76 III 532a (Nature as Signs)
IV 220a (Prayer)

71-85 I 448a (Cosmology)
V 267b (Theology and the Q)

72 I 24b (Adam and Eve); 508a (Death and the Dead)
II 186b (Fate); 327b (God and his Attributes)
III 14a (Jesus); 293b (Mary)
V 81b (Soul); 109a (Speech); 114b (Spirit)

72-75 I 255a (Bowing and Prostration)

72-76 I 24a (Adam and Eve)

73-74 III 45a (Jinn)
IV 263b (Pride)

73-76 I 511a (Debate and Disputation)

74 I 160a (Arrogance); 447a, 453a (Cosmology)
II 172a (Fall of Man); 543a (Insolence and Obstinacy)
III 45a (Jinn)

74-75 I 395b (Conceit); 453a (Cosmology); 525a (Devil)

74-76 IV 336b (Races)

75 I 24b (Adam and Eve); 160a (Arrogance); 450a, 453a (Cosmology)
II 323b, 325a, 327b (God and his Attributes)
III 45a (Jinn)

75-76 I 476a (Creation)

75-85 V 109a (Speech)

76 I 339b (Clay); 476a (Creation)
II 4a, 4b (Earth)
III 45a (Jinn)
V 269b (Theology and the Q)

77 I 525a (Devil)
II 543a (Insolence and Obstinacy)

77-85 II 336a (Good and Evil)

78 III 136b (Last Judgment)

81 I 500a (Day, Times of)
V 288a (Time)

82 I 453a (Cosmology)

82-83 IV 577a (Servants)

83 I 453a (Cosmology)
II 550a (Intention)

84 I 452b, 453a (Cosmology)

84-85 V 547a (Word of God)

85 II 417b (Hell and Hellfire)

86 III 451a (Muḥammad)
IV 452a (Reward and Punishment)

87 III 372b (Memory)

88 III 40b (Jihād); 536b (News)

Sūrat al-Zumar (39)

I 548b (Dreams and Sleep)

1 IV 446a (Revelation and Inspiration)

1-2 II 262a (Form and Structure of the Q)

2 II 550a (Intention)
IV 297a (Prophets and Prophethood)

3 I 221a (Belief and Unbelief)
II 273b (Friends and Friendship); 357a (Grammar and the Q); 478b (Idolatry and Idolaters)
III 40b (Jihād)
IV 132b (Politics and the Q); 160a (Polytheism and Atheism); 416a (Religious Pluralism and the Q)
V 449b (Vow)

4 II 11b (Election); 327b, 330a (God and his Attributes)

5 I 473a (Creation); 498a (Day and Night); 501b (Day, Times of)
II 268a (Freedom and Predestination)
IV 6a (Pairs and Pairing)
V 163a (Sun); 280b, 289b (Time)

5-7 II 57b (Ethics and the Q)

6 I 95b (Animal Life); 231b (Biology as the Creation and Stages of Life); 238a (Blood and Blood Clot); 447b (Cosmology); 472a, 476a, 476b, 477a (Creation); 494a (Darkness)
II 175a (Family); 328a, 328b (God and his Attributes)
III 551a (Numbers and Enumeration)

IV 20a (Parents); 184b (Possession and Possessions); 581b (Sex and Sexuality)
V 10b (Signs); 84a (Soul); 393b (Turkish Literature and the Q); 501a (Witnessing and Testifying); 530a (Women and the Q)

7 I 443a (Cosmology)
II 550b (Intention)
III 228a (Load or Burden); 379b (Mercy)
IV 2a (Pairs and Pairing); 432a (Responsibility)

8 I 437a (Conversion)
II 476b (Idolatry and Idolaters)
IV 427b (Repentance and Penance)

9 I 182b (Asceticism); 254b (Bowing and Prostration); 328a (Chronology and the Q)
II 449a (Hope)
III 379b (Mercy)
IV 221a, 222b (Prayer); 538b (Scholar)
V 282b (Time); 377b (Troops)

10 I 188b (Authority)

11 II 550a (Intention)

11-12 III 444a (Muḥammad)

12 II 366a (Grammar and the Q)

13 I 538a (Disobedience)

14 II 550a (Intention)

15 II 161b (Failure); 174a (Family)
III 40a (Jihād)

16 II 415a (Hell and Hellfire)

17 II 474a (Iconoclasm); 482a (Idols and Images)
IV 427b (Repentance and Penance)

17-18 II 341a (Good News)
IV 172a (Popular and Talismanic Uses of the Q)

18 III 73b (Justice and Injustice)
V 547a (Word of God)

19 I 519b (Deliverance)
V 547b (Word of God)

20-21 I 165b (Art and Architecture and the Q)

21 I 361b, 363a (Colors)
II 3a, 3b (Earth); 304b (Geography)
IV 70b (Philosophy and the Q); 422b (Remembrance); 438a (Revelation and Inspiration)
V 121b, 126b, 127a (Springs and Fountains)

22 I 226a (Belief and Unbelief)
II 43b (Error); 326b (God and his Attributes); 363b (Grammar and the Q); 407a (Heart)

	III	187a (Light)
	V	393b (Turkish Literature and the Q)
23	I	70b, 71b (Ambiguous); 213b (Beauty); 225b (Belief and Unbelief)
	II	2a (Ears); 323a (God and his Attributes); 408a (Heart)
	III	509b, 512a (Names of the Q); 574b (Oft-Repeated)
	IV	230a (Prayer); 297a (Prophets and Prophethood); 310a (Provocation); 368b (Recitation of the Q)
	V	242b (Textual Criticism of the Q); 425a (Verse)
24	II	6a (Economics); 158b (Face); 323b (God and his Attributes); 335b (Good and Evil)
25	IV	320b (Punishment Stories)
26	IV	453b, 457a (Reward and Punishment)
27	IV	69b (Philosophy and the Q)
	V	16a (Simile)
28	II	226b (Foreign Vocabulary)
	III	113a, 113b (Language and Style of the Q); 193b (Literary Structures of the Q)
	V	340b (Translations of the Q)
29	II	497b (Illiteracy)
	IV	10a (Parable); 538b (Scholar)
	V	57a (Slaves and Slavery)
31	I	513b (Debate and Disputation)
32	I	235b (Blasphemy)
	III	181a (Lie)
	IV	103b (Pit); 309b (Provocation)
33	I	20a (Abū Bakr)
34	IV	452b (Reward and Punishment)
35	III	379b (Mercy)
	IV	452b (Reward and Punishment)
36	I	225b (Belief and Unbelief)
	III	440b (Muḥammad)
36-37	IV	2a (Pairs and Pairing)
37	I	225b (Belief and Unbelief)
	IV	453b (Reward and Punishment)
	V	416a (Vengeance)
38	I	329b (Chronology and the Q); 472b (Creation)
	II	36a (Epigraphy); 317a (God and his Attributes)
	III	300b, 301a (Material Culture and the Q)
	IV	160a (Polytheism and Atheism); 228b (Prayer); 311a (Provocation)
39	III	327b (Material Culture and the Q)
40	V	377a (Troops)

41	I	225b (Belief and Unbelief)
	II	552a (Intercession)
	IV	1b (Pairs and Pairing)
42	I	318b, 319a (Chronology and the Q); 443b (Cosmology); 523a (Destiny); 546b (Dreams and Sleep)
	II	185b (Fate); 241b (Foretelling in the Q)
	III	18b (Jesus)
	IV	179a (Popular and Talismanic Uses of the Q); 394a (Reflection and Deliberation)
	V	61a (Sleep); 83b (Soul); 289a, 289b (Time)
45	III	62a (Joy and Misery); 299a, 299b (Material Culture and the Q)
46	I	472a (Creation)
	IV	4a (Pairs and Pairing); 537b (Scholar)
47	II	335b (Good and Evil)
49	II	56b (Ethics and the Q)
	III	400b (Mockery)
	IV	538b (Scholar)
53	I	522a (Despair)
	II	322a (God and his Attributes)
	III	224a (Literature and the Q)
	IV	531a (Sand)
	V	22b (Sin, Major and Minor); 393b (Turkish Literature and the Q)
53-54	III	324b (Material Culture and the Q); 379b (Mercy)
54	I	437a, 437b (Conversion)
	III	379b (Mercy)
	IV	427b (Repentance and Penance)
55	III	73b (Justice and Injustice)
56	II	323b, 324b (God and his Attributes); 365b (Grammar and the Q)
	III	401a (Mockery)
56-58	I	222a (Belief and Unbelief)
58	IV	430a (Repentance and Penance)
60	I	160b (Arrogance); 241b (Boast); 364b (Colors); 382a (Community and Society in the Q)
	II	158b (Face); 355b (Grammar and the Q); 416a (Hell and Hellfire)
	IV	103b (Pit)
61	I	220b (Belief and Unbelief); 519b (Deliverance)
	II	335b (Good and Evil)
62	I	472a (Creation)
	IV	280b (Profane and Sacred)
	V	380a (Trust and Patience)

62-66 II 259b (Form and Structure of the Q)

63 II 546b (Instruments)
IV 4a (Pairs and Pairing); 183b (Portents)

64 II 354a, 366b (Grammar and the Q); 488a (Ignorance)
V 247a (Textual Criticism of the Q)

65 II 161b (Failure)
IV 136b (Politics and the Q); 159a (Polytheism and Atheism); 399a (Religious Pluralism and the Q)

66 II 58a (Ethics and the Q)

67 II 323b, 325a (God and his Attributes)
III 179a (Left Hand and Right Hand); 209a (Literature and the Q)
IV 220b (Prayer); 474a (Rhetoric and the Q)
V 287b (Time); 474b (Weights and Measures)

67-69 II 316a (Glory)

67-75 III 139a (Last Judgment)

68 I 89b (Angel); 111b, 112b, 113b, 114a (Apocalypse)
II 547a (Instruments)
III 140a (Last Judgment); 203a (Literary Structures of the Q)

69 II 326b (God and his Attributes)
IV 296b (Prophets and Prophethood); 560a (Scripture and the Q)
V 490b (Witness to Faith); 493a, 493b, 494a (Witnessing and Testifying); 524b (Women and the Q)

69-70 I 522b (Destiny)

70 I 243b, 244a (Book)

71 I 398b (Conquest)
III 190a (Literacy)
IV 298b (Prophets and Prophethood)
V 377a (Troops)

71-74 I 91a (Angel)
IV 2b (Pairs and Pairing)

72 I 160b (Arrogance); 165b (Art and Architecture and the Q)
IV 103b (Pit)

73 I 237a (Blessing); 398b (Conquest)
II 51b (Eschatology); 283b, 286b (Garden)
IV 225a (Prayer)
V 377a (Troops); 393a, 393b (Turkish Literature and the Q)

73-75 III 323b (Material Culture and the Q)

74 IV 185a (Possession and Possessions); 213b (Praise)

75 I 27a (Adoration); 442a (Cosmology)
II 326a (God and his Attributes); 410b (Heaven and Sky)
III 65a (Judgment)
IV 213b, 214b (Praise); 220a, 220b (Prayer)
V 277a (Throne of God)

Sūrat Ghāfir/al-Mu'min (40)

I 230b (Biology as the Creation and Stages of Life)
III 378b (Mercy); 472b (Mysterious Letters)

1-4 II 262a (Form and Structure of the Q)

2 IV 6a (Pairs and Pairing); 446a (Revelation and Inspiration)

3 II 31a (Epigraphy); 244b (Forgiveness)
III 378a, 378b (Mercy)
IV 426a (Repentance and Penance); 453a (Reward and Punishment)
V 287a (Time)

4 I 512b (Debate and Disputation)
V 6b (Signs)

4-5 IV 309b (Provocation)

5 III 524a (Narratives); 576b (Opposition to Muḥammad)
IV 25a (Parties and Factions); 115b (Polemic and Polemical Language)

5-6 IV 320a (Punishment Stories)

6 V 547b (Word of God)

7 I 166a (Art and Architecture and the Q); 442a, 442b (Cosmology); 462b, 463a (Court)
II 322a, 326a (God and his Attributes); 410b (Heaven and Sky); 551b (Intercession)
III 227b (Load or Burden)
IV 29a (Path or Way); 213a (Praise); 427a (Repentance and Penance); 537b (Scholar)
V 277a (Throne of God)

7-8 III 324b (Material Culture and the Q)

7-9 I 462b (Court)

8 II 60a (Ethics and the Q); 284a (Garden)
III 99b (Kinship)
IV 21b (Parents)

9 I 220b (Belief and Unbelief)
IV 522b (Salvation)

10 II 416b (Hell and Hellfire)

11 II 45a (Eschatology)
IV 6b (Pairs and Pairing); 460b (Reward and Punishment)

12 I 158b (Arrogance); 320a (Chronology and the Q)
II 30a (Epigraphy); 82b (Everyday Life, Q In)
IV 5b (Pairs and Pairing); 118b (Polemic and Polemical Language)

13 IV 427b (Repentance and Penance)
V 179a (Sustenance)

15 I 500a (Day, Times of)
II 325b (God and his Attributes); 443b (Holy Spirit)
III 137a (Last Judgment)
IV 294b (Prophets and Prophethood); 478b (Rhymed Prose)
V 81a (Soul); 115b (Spirit); 277a (Throne of God); 461a (Warner)

16 II 36a (Epigraphy); 330a (God and his Attributes)
IV 128a (Politics and the Q)

17 II 64b (Ethics and the Q); 330b (God and his Attributes)
III 73b (Justice and Injustice)

18 I 500a (Day, Times of)
III 137a (Last Judgment); 236a (Love and Affection); 442b (Muḥammad)
V 461a (Warner)

20 II 185b (Fate); 362b (Grammar and the Q)
IV 5b (Pairs and Pairing); 228b (Prayer)

21 IV 307b (Protection); 425a (Remnant)

21-22 IV 126b (Politics and the Q); 320b (Punishment Stories)

22 II 92a (Everyday Life, Q In); 308a (Geography)

23 III 421b (Moses)
IV 106a (Plagues)

23-24 IV 68a (Pharaoh)

23-46 IV 320a (Punishment Stories)

23-56 III 519a (Narratives)

24 II 338a (Good and Evil); 399a (Hāmān); 540a (Insanity); 542b (Insolence and Obstinacy)
III 104b (Korah); 518b (Narratives)

24-25 II 399a (Hāmān)

25 I 302a (Children); 306b (Children of Israel)
II 162a (Failure)

25-26 II 542a (Insolence and Obstinacy)

26 IV 416a (Religious Pluralism and the Q)

27 I 159a (Arrogance); 500a (Day, Times of)
III 66b (Judgment); 137a (Last Judgment)
IV 308a (Protection); 434a (Resurrection); 457b (Reward and Punishment)

28	I	540a (Dissimulation)
	II	31a (Epigraphy); 96a (Everyday Life, Q In); 399b (Hāmān)
	III	230a (Lord)
	V	258a (Theology and the Q)
28-45	I	219a (Belief and Unbelief)
29	III	93a (Kings and Rulers); 583b (Oppression)
30	I	500a (Day, Times of)
	IV	25a (Parties and Factions)
30-33	IV	25a (Parties and Factions)
31	I	21b (ʿĀd)
	V	317b (Tradition and Custom)
32	I	500a (Day, Times of)
	II	558b (Invitation)
	III	137a (Last Judgment)
	IV	478b (Rhymed Prose)
33	IV	307b (Protection)
34	II	436b (History and the Q)
	III	57a (Joseph)
	IV	286b (Proof)
	V	258a (Theology and the Q)
35	I	82a (Anatomy); 160b (Arrogance); 395b (Conceit); 512b (Debate and Disputation)
	II	350b, 365b (Grammar and the Q); 542b (Insolence and Obstinacy)
	IV	264a (Pride); 281a (Profane and Sacred); 310a (Provocation)
	V	6b (Signs)
36	I	162b (Art and Architecture and the Q); 478a (Creation)
	II	338a (Good and Evil); 542b (Insolence and Obstinacy)
36-37	I	190a (Authority)
	II	399a (Hāmān)
	III	46a (Jinn)
	IV	68a (Pharaoh)
37	II	162a (Failure); 335b (Good and Evil)
	IV	483b (Rhymed Prose)
38	IV	29a (Path or Way)
39	II	283a (Garden)
	III	59a (Joy and Misery)
	IV	5a (Pairs and Pairing); 14b (Paradise)
39-40	IV	1b (Pairs and Pairing)
40	IV	18b (Paradise); 82a (Philosophy and the Q)
	V	524a (Women and the Q)
41-42	V	181a (Symbolic Imagery)

41-44	II	558b (Invitation)
42	IV	6a (Pairs and Pairing)
42-43	III	143a (Last Judgment)
43	II	418a (Hell and Hellfire)
45	II	335b (Good and Evil)
	III	18a (Jesus)
	IV	307b (Protection)
45-46	IV	67a (Pharaoh)
46	I	501a, 503a (Day, Times of)
	II	80a, 80b (Evening)
	III	137a (Last Judgment); 417a (Morning)
	V	281b, 287b (Time)
46-49	II	45b (Eschatology)
47	III	580b (Oppressed on Earth); 583a (Oppression)
	IV	130b (Politics and the Q)
47-48	II	416b (Hell and Hellfire)
	III	582a (Oppressed on Earth)
	IV	264a (Pride)
48	IV	133b (Politics and the Q)
49	I	222a (Belief and Unbelief)
49-50	IV	286b (Proof)
51	II	355b (Grammar and the Q)
	IV	295b (Prophets and Prophethood)
	V	492b, 494a (Witnessing and Testifying)
52	II	335b (Good and Evil)
	III	137b (Last Judgment)
53	I	245b (Book)
	IV	36b (People of the Book)
53-54	III	425a (Moses)
	V	301a, 302a (Torah)
54	IV	3b (Pairs and Pairing)
55	I	35b (Afternoon); 503a, 503b (Day, Times of)
	III	40a (Jihād); 416b (Morning); 446b (Muḥammad)
	IV	213b, 214b (Praise); 220b, 223a (Prayer)
	V	281a (Time)
56	I	159a (Arrogance); 512a (Debate and Disputation)
	IV	5b (Pairs and Pairing)
	V	6b (Signs)

57	I	474b (Creation)
	IV	538b (Scholar)
57-85	III	519a (Narratives)
58	III	209b (Literature and the Q)
	IV	2a (Pairs and Pairing)
	V	447b (Vision and Blindness)
59	I	501a (Day, Times of)
	V	287b (Time); 148b (Expeditions and Battles)
60	I	396a (Conceit)
	IV	264a (Pride)
61	I	477b (Creation); 502a (Day, Times of)
	IV	589b (Shekhinah)
	V	280b (Time)
61-64	I	472b (Creation)
61-66	II	259a (Form and Structure of the Q)
62	I	472a (Creation)
	V	501a (Witnessing and Testifying)
63	V	6a (Signs)
64	I	45a (Agriculture and Vegetation); 213a (Beauty); 477b, 478a (Creation)
	II	411a (Heaven and Sky)
	IV	220b (Prayer)
64-65	V	500b, 501a (Witnessing and Testifying)
65	III	182b (Life); 303a, 304b (Material Culture and the Q)
66	IV	228b (Prayer)
66-67	V	569b (Youth and Old Age)
67	I	81a (Anatomy); 446a, 446b (Cosmology); 477a (Creation)
	II	328a (God and his Attributes)
	III	332a (Maturity)
	V	204b (Teaching); 267a (Theology and the Q); 290a (Time)
68	I	319a (Chronology and the Q); 446b (Cosmology); 475a, 475b (Creation); 516b (Decision)
	II	185b (Fate); 269a (Freedom and Predestination); 327b (God and his Attributes)
	III	332a (Maturity)
	IV	4b (Pairs and Pairing); 33b (Patriarchy)
	V	109a (Speech); 287a (Time); 371b (Trinity); 542b, 547a (Word of God)
69	I	319a (Chronology and the Q); 512a (Debate and Disputation)
	IV	115b (Polemic and Polemical Language)
70	I	245a (Book)
	IV	538b (Scholar)
70-72	III	529b (Nature as Signs)

71 II 416a (Hell and Hellfire); 547a (Instruments)
72 I 222a (Belief and Unbelief)
II 211a (Fire)
75 III 61b (Joy and Misery)
76 I 160b (Arrogance)
IV 103b (Pit)
77 I 406a (Consolation)
II 91b (Everyday Life, Q In)
III 18b (Jesus); 40a (Jihād)
78 III 381a, 382a (Messenger); 517b (Narratives)
IV 296a, 302b (Prophets and Prophethood)
V 3b (Signs); 109b (Speech)
79 V 411b (Vehicles)
79-80 I 96a (Animal Life); 215b (Bedouin)
80 III 227b (Load or Burden)
V 412a (Vehicles)
81 II 489a (Ignorance)
V 6a (Signs)
82 II 308a (Geography)
IV 126b (Politics and the Q); 425a (Remnant)
82-84 IV 320b (Punishment Stories)
83 III 61b (Joy and Misery); 400b (Mockery)
IV 286b (Proof)
84 V 502a (Witnessing and Testifying)
84-85 II 542b (Insolence and Obstinacy)
III 379b (Mercy)
V 502a (Witnessing and Testifying)
85 IV 126b (Politics and the Q)
V 164a (Sunna)

Sūrat Fuṣṣilat (41)

I 407b (Consultation); 548b (Dreams and Sleep)
III 472b (Mysterious Letters)
IV 496b (Ritual and the Q)
1-4 II 341b (Good News)
1-5 II 262a (Form and Structure of the Q)
V 39b (Sīra and the Q)
1-8 II 262a (Form and Structure of the Q)

2	I	209a (Basmala)
	II	497b (Illiteracy)
	IV	443b, 446a (Revelation and Inspiration)
2-3	IV	562a (Scripture and the Q)
	V	340b (Translations of the Q)
3	II	226b (Foreign Vocabulary)
	III	113b (Language and Style of the Q); 193b (Literary Structures of the Q); 394a (Miracles); 451a (Muḥammad); 592a (Orality and Writing in Arabia)
	IV	280b (Profane and Sacred); 538b (Scholar)
	V	422b, 423b (Verse)
3-4	III	456a (Muḥammad)
3-5	II	510b (Indifference)
4	I	83b (Anatomy)
	II	341b (Good News)
	III	512a (Names of the Q)
	IV	3b (Pairs and Pairing)
5	I	225b, 226a (Belief and Unbelief)
	II	276a (Furniture and Furnishings); 370b (Gratitude and Ingratitude); 408a (Heart)
	III	448b (Muḥammad)
	IV	331a (Quraysh)
	V	412b (Veil)
6	II	329b (God and his Attributes)
	III	451b (Muḥammad)
	IV	300a (Prophets and Prophethood); 311b (Provocation)
	V	500a (Witnessing and Testifying)
7	V	553a (World)
8-12	I	448a (Cosmology)
9	I	442a (Cosmology); 472b (Creation); 499b (Day, Times of)
	II	410b (Heaven and Sky); 476b (Idolatry and Idolaters)
9-11	I	536a (Difficult Passages)
9-12	II	327a (God and his Attributes)
	IV	7a (Pairs and Pairing)
	V	279b (Time); 544a (Word of God)
10	I	443a (Cosmology)
	II	217a (Food and Drink)
	III	551b (Numbers and Enumeration)
	V	178b (Sustenance)
11	I	442a (Cosmology)
	II	327b (God and his Attributes)

	IV	82b (Philosophy and the Q)
	V	64a (Smoke); 110b (Speech)
11-12	II	410b (Heaven and Sky)
	V	544a (Word of God)
12	I	442a, 442b (Cosmology); 499b (Day, Times of); 544b (Divination)
	II	410b, 411a (Heaven and Sky); 547a (Instruments)
	IV	6a (Pairs and Pairing); 107b (Planets and Stars); 293b (Prophets and Prophethood); 439b (Revelation and Inspiration)
	V	64a, 64b (Smoke); 271a (Theology and the Q)
13	II	212a (Fire)
	IV	321a (Punishment Stories)
	V	253a (Thamūd); 460b (Warner); 471a (Weather)
13-16	III	443a (Muḥammad)
13-18	IV	320a (Punishment Stories)
14	II	512b (Informants)
	IV	300a (Prophets and Prophethood)
15	I	21b (ʿĀd); 160b (Arrogance)
	IV	183b (Portents); 263b (Pride)
15-18	II	542a (Insolence and Obstinacy)
16	I	21b (ʿĀd); 52b, 54b (Air and Wind)
	II	455b (Hot and Cold)
	IV	453b (Reward and Punishment)
	V	280a (Time); 470b (Weather)
16-17	III	249a (Magic)
17	II	212a (Fire); 270a (Freedom and Predestination); 362b (Grammar and the Q)
	V	253a (Thamūd)
18	I	519a (Deliverance)
	V	253a (Thamūd)
19	II	23b (Enemies)
	V	377a (Troops)
20	V	492a (Witnessing and Testifying)
20-22	II	426a (Hides and Fleece)
	V	494b (Witnessing and Testifying)
20-23	II	416b (Hell and Hellfire)
	V	110b (Speech)
21	I	476a (Creation)
	V	110b (Speech)
22	III	141a (Last Judgment)
22-23	II	416b (Hell and Hellfire)
	V	177b (Suspicion)

24	IV	103b (Pit)
	V	379a (Trust and Patience)
25	II	417a (Hell and Hellfire)
	III	46b, 47b (Jinn)
	IV	7b (Pairs and Pairing); 336b (Races); 438a (Revelation and Inspiration)
	V	119b (Spiritual Beings); 494b (Witnessing and Testifying); 547b (Word of God)
26	II	87b (Everyday Life, Q In)
	III	109b (Language and Style of the Q)
	V	6a (Signs); 430b (Victory)
28	II	23b (Enemies); 52b (Eschatology); 54b (Eternity)
	IV	14b (Paradise); 118a (Polemic and Polemical Language)
29	II	199a (Feet)
	III	46b (Jinn)
	IV	7b (Pairs and Pairing)
30	I	406a (Consolation)
	III	223a (Literature and the Q); 324b (Material Culture and the Q)
30-31	III	323b (Material Culture and the Q)
31	I	432b (Contracts and Alliances)
33	V	221b (Teaching and Preaching the Q)
34	I	541a (Dissimulation)
	II	69a (Ethics and the Q); 452b (Hospitality and Courtesy)
	III	40a (Jihād); 236a (Love and Affection)
	IV	309b (Provocation)
36	IV	308a (Protection); 575a (Seeing and Hearing)
37	I	254b (Bowing and Prostration); 474b (Creation)
	III	415b (Moon)
	IV	220a (Prayer); 438a (Revelation and Inspiration); 488a (Ritual and the Q)
	V	162b (Sun); 280b (Time)
37-40	II	259a (Form and Structure of the Q)
38	I	502b (Day, Times of)
38-39	II	303a (Geography)
39	II	3a (Earth); 320b (God and his Attributes)
	III	200b (Literary Structures of the Q)
	IV	435b (Resurrection); 438a (Revelation and Inspiration)
	V	463a (Water)
40	II	420b (Heresy)
	IV	280a (Profane and Sacred)
	V	6b (Signs)
41	III	509b (Names of the Q)
41-54	II	262a (Form and Structure of the Q)

42 II 26b (Epigraphy)
III 513a (Names of the Q); 600b (Ornamentation and Illumination)
IV 6a (Pairs and Pairing); 443b, 446a (Revelation and Inspiration)

43 II 244b (Forgiveness)
III 453a (Muḥammad)
IV 2a (Pairs and Pairing); 301b (Prophets and Prophethood); 453a (Reward and Punishment)

44 I 145a (Arabs); 225b (Belief and Unbelief)
II 37b (Epigraphy); 226b (Foreign Vocabulary); 502a (Illness and Health); 512b (Informants)
III 114a, 117a, 117b (Language and Style of the Q); 451a (Muḥammad)
IV 3b (Pairs and Pairing); 444a (Revelation and Inspiration)
V 132a (Strangers and Foreigners)

45 III 424b (Moses)
IV 36b (People of the Book)
V 289b (Time); 301a (Torah)

46 IV 1b (Pairs and Pairing); 84a (Philosophy and the Q)

47 I 494b (Date Palm); 500a, 501a (Day, Times of)
II 477a (Idolatry and Idolaters)
III 137a, 138a (Last Judgment)
V 288a (Time); 494a (Witnessing and Testifying)

48 II 99a (Evil Deeds)

49 I 521a (Despair)
II 355a (Grammar and the Q)
V 204b (Teaching)

49-51 IV 229a (Prayer)

50 I 501a (Day, Times of)
III 137a (Last Judgment)
V 287b (Time)

51 II 56b (Ethics and the Q)

53 II 548b (Intellect)
III 528b, 534a, 534b (Nature as Signs)
IV 107b (Planets and Stars); 438a (Revelation and Inspiration)
V 9b (Signs)

53-54 III 323b (Material Culture and the Q)

Sūrat al-Shūrā (42)

I 407b, 408a (Consultation)
III 472b, 475b (Mysterious Letters)

1-3 II 262a (Form and Structure of the Q)

3	I	442a (Cosmology)
	V	546b (Word of God)
4	IV	5b (Pairs and Pairing); 184a, 184b (Possession and Possessions)
5	II	357a (Grammar and the Q); 497b (Illiteracy); 551b (Intercession)
	III	379b (Mercy)
	IV	220a (Prayer)
6	II	273b (Friends and Friendship)
	III	40a (Jihād); 452b (Muḥammad)
	IV	307a (Protection)
6-9	IV	404a (Religious Pluralism and the Q)
7	I	338b (City); 372b (Community and Society in the Q); 500a (Day, Times of)
	II	226b (Foreign Vocabulary); 495a (Illiteracy)
	III	113b (Language and Style of the Q); 137a (Last Judgment); 193b (Literary Structures of the Q); 338a (Mecca); 443b (Muḥammad)
	IV	2b (Pairs and Pairing); 280b (Profane and Sacred); 299b (Prophets and Prophethood)
	V	340b (Translations of the Q); 460b, 461a (Warner)
8	I	436a (Conversion)
	II	72a (Ethics and the Q); 330b (God and his Attributes); 497a (Illiteracy)
	IV	5b (Pairs and Pairing); 337a (Races)
8-9	II	65b (Ethics and the Q); 273b (Friends and Friendship)
9	II	273b (Friends and Friendship); 320b (God and his Attributes)
	III	231b (Lord)
10	II	30a, 31a (Epigraphy); 96a (Everyday Life, Q In)
	IV	430a (Repentance and Penance)
11	I	106b (Anthropomorphism); 447b (Cosmology); 472a (Creation)
	II	75b (Ethics and the Q); 175a (Family); 323a (God and his Attributes)
	III	201b (Literary Structures of the Q); 549b (Numbers and Enumeration)
	IV	5b, 6a (Pairs and Pairing); 79a (Philosophy and the Q)
	V	18b (Simile); 266a (Theology and the Q); 500a (Witnessing and Testifying); 526b (Women and the Q)
12	II	546b (Instruments)
	IV	4a (Pairs and Pairing)
	V	179a (Sustenance)
13	I	310b (Christians and Christianity); 380b (Community and Society in the Q); 435b (Conversion)
	II	11b (Election)
	III	8a, 17a (Jesus); 445a (Muḥammad); 486b (Myths and Legends in the Q)
	IV	25b (Parties and Factions); 299a (Prophets and Prophethood); 427b (Repentance and Penance)
	V	334a (Traditional Disciplines of Q Studies)

13-14 III 7b (Jesus)

14 II 430b (History and the Q)
IV 35b (People of the Book)
V 289b (Time)

15 II 5b (Economics)
III 27a (Jews and Judaism); 39a (Jihād); 70a (Justice and Injustice); 453b (Muḥammad)
V 68b (Social Sciences and the Q); 287a (Time); 486b (Wish and Desire); 496b (Witnessing and Testifying)

16 I 93a (Anger)
IV 287a (Proof); 310a (Provocation)

16-17 II 148b (Expeditions and Battles)

17 I 501a (Day, Times of)
II 363a (Grammar and the Q); 545a (Instruments)
III 137a, 138a (Last Judgment); 334b (Measurement)
V 203a (Teaching); 288a (Time)

18 I 501a (Day, Times of)
III 137a (Last Judgment)
V 287b (Time)

19 II 92a (Everyday Life, Q In)
IV 5b (Pairs and Pairing)

20 I 41b (Agriculture and Vegetation)
II 304b (Geography)
IV 5a (Pairs and Pairing)

21 I 516a, 516b (Decision)
V 103a (Sovereignty); 289b (Time)

22 I 41a (Agriculture and Vegetation)
II 283a (Garden)

22-23 II 341b (Good News)

23 II 34b (Epigraphy); 174b (Family); 275a (Friends and Friendship)
III 236a (Love and Affection); 557a, 558b (Numismatics)
IV 6a (Pairs and Pairing)

23-26 I 407b (Consultation)

24 I 82a (Anatomy)
II 407a (Heart); 550b (Intention)
IV 311b (Provocation)
V 447a (Vision and Blindness); 547b (Word of God)

25 II 244b (Forgiveness)
III 379b (Mercy)
IV 426a (Repentance and Penance); 431b (Responsibility)

26-27	I	389b (Companions of the Prophet)
27	I	408a (Consultation)
	III	334b (Measurement)
28	I	42a (Agriculture and Vegetation); 521a (Despair)
	II	28b (Epigraphy); 273b (Friends and Friendship)
	III	304a (Material Culture and the Q); 379a (Mercy)
	IV	307a (Protection); 443b (Revelation and Inspiration)
	V	181a (Symbolic Imagery); 470b (Weather)
28-35	II	259a (Form and Structure of the Q)
29	I	95b, 96a (Animal Life); 473b (Creation)
	III	140a (Last Judgment)
29-34	IV	438a (Revelation and Inspiration)
30	II	245a (Forgiveness); 401b (Hand)
	IV	85a (Philosophy and the Q)
	V	22a (Sin, Major and Minor)
31	I	432b (Contracts and Alliances)
	II	273a (Friends and Friendship)
	IV	5b (Pairs and Pairing)
32	II	528a (Inimitability)
	IV	183a (Portents)
	V	412a (Vehicles)
32-33	I	54a (Air and Wind)
32-34	III	379a (Mercy)
33	I	52a (Air and Wind)
	III	530a (Nature as Signs)
	V	382b (Trust and Patience)
34	II	245a (Forgiveness)
35	I	512a (Debate and Disputation)
	IV	115b (Polemic and Polemical Language)
36	II	6b (Economics)
	III	59b (Joy and Misery)
	V	340a (Transitoriness)
36-43	I	219b (Belief and Unbelief)
	II	259b (Form and Structure of the Q)
37	I	93b (Anger); 217a (Bedouin); 408a, 408b (Consultation)
	II	66b (Ethics and the Q)
	III	65b (Judgment)
	IV	580b (Sex and Sexuality)
	V	19a (Sin, Major and Minor)

37-43	V	456b (War)
38	I	406b, 407a, 408a (Consultation)
	III	567a (Obedience)
39-42	V	456b (War)
40	II	448a (Honor)
	III	65b (Judgment)
41	V	456b (War)
43	III	65b (Judgment); 378a (Mercy)
44	II	59a (Ethics and the Q); 273b (Friends and Friendship)
	IV	430a (Repentance and Penance)
45	II	161b (Failure)
46	I	432b (Contracts and Alliances)
	II	273b (Friends and Friendship)
	IV	432a (Responsibility)
47	II	36a (Epigraphy)
48	I	221a (Belief and Unbelief); 449b (Cosmology)
	III	40a (Jihād); 61a (Joy and Misery)
49	I	474b (Creation)
	II	289b (Gender); 327b (God and his Attributes)
49-50	I	302b (Children)
	IV	211a (Power and Impotence)
	V	524b (Women and the Q)
49-53	V	118a (Spiritual Beings)
50	IV	6a (Pairs and Pairing)
51	II	276a (Furniture and Furnishings); 324a (God and his Attributes)
	III	382b (Messenger); 511a, 511b (Names of the Q)
	IV	6a (Pairs and Pairing); 217a (Prayer); 294a (Prophets and Prophethood); 312a (Provocation); 440b (Revelation and Inspiration)
	V	109b (Speech); 275b (Theophany); 412b, 413a (Veil); 546a, 547b (Word of God)
52	II	365a (Grammar and the Q)
	III	186b (Light); 442a (Muḥammad); 512a (Names of the Q)
	IV	3b (Pairs and Pairing); 217a (Prayer)
	IV	294a, 297b (Prophets and Prophethood)
	V	81a (Soul); 371b (Trinity); 546a (Word of God)
52-53	V	271a (Theology and the Q)
53	IV	29a (Path or Way)
	V	287a (Time)

Sūrat al-Zukhruf (43)

I 407b (Consultation)
III 11b, 17b (Jesus); 472b (Mysterious Letters)

2 II 257b, 263b (Form and Structure of the Q); 497b (Illiteracy)
IV 468b (Rhetoric and the Q)
V 172a (Sūra)

2-3 III 592a (Orality and Writing in Arabia)

3 II 226b (Foreign Vocabulary); 497b (Illiteracy)
III 113b (Language and Style of the Q); 193b (Literary Structures of the Q)
V 18a (Simile); 340b (Translations of the Q)

3-4 IV 280b (Profane and Sacred)

4 I 247b (Book)
II 189a (Fātiḥa); 412a (Heavenly Book)
III 513a (Names of the Q)
IV 81a (Philosophy and the Q); 261b (Preserved Tablet); 297a (Prophets and Prophethood); 560b (Scripture and the Q)

5 IV 422a (Remembrance)

6 II 434a (History and the Q)

7 I 222a (Belief and Unbelief)
III 400a (Mockery)

8 II 434b (History and the Q)

9 I 329b (Chronology and the Q); 472b (Creation)

10 II 2b, 3a (Earth)

11 II 3a (Earth)
III 334a (Measurement)

12 I 95b (Animal Life); 478a (Creation)
IV 6a (Pairs and Pairing)

12-13 I 215b (Bedouin)
V 411b (Vehicles)

13 II 92b, 93a (Everyday Life, Q In)
V 376a (Trips and Voyages)

15 I 220b (Belief and Unbelief); 449b (Cosmology)

16 III 48a (Jinn)

16-17 II 341a (Good News)
IV 118a (Polemic and Polemical Language)

17 I 364b (Colors)

19 I 243b (Book)
IV 577b (Servants)
V 492a (Witnessing and Testifying)

19-20 III 295a (Mary)
20 II 360a (Grammar and the Q)
20-21 II 497b (Illiteracy)
22 I 371b (Community and Society in the Q)
II 199b (Feet); 497a (Illiteracy)
V 317a (Tradition and Custom)
23 I 371b (Community and Society in the Q)
II 497a (Illiteracy)
IV 301a (Prophets and Prophethood)
V 317a (Tradition and Custom)
23-25 IV 320b (Punishment Stories)
25 IV 453b (Reward and Punishment)
26 II 24a (Enemies)
V 258a (Theology and the Q)
26-27 I 6b (Abraham); 472a (Creation)
III 494a (Myths and Legends in the Q)
26-28 I 193a (Āzar); 330a (Chronology and the Q)
28 IV 35a (Peace); 429a (Repentance and Penance)
30 III 246a (Magic)
30-31 III 247a (Magic)
31 I 338b (City)
II 295a (Geography)
III 449b (Muḥammad)
32 II 217a (Food and Drink); 362b (Grammar and the Q)
III 253a, 253b (Manual Labor); 379b (Mercy)
IV 149a (Politics and the Q)
V 191b (Talent); 393a, 393b (Turkish Literature and the Q)
33 I 377a (Community and Society in the Q)
II 497a (Illiteracy)
33-35 II 459a (House, Domestic and Divine)
34 IV 18a (Paradise)
35 III 400a (Mockery)
36 I 524b (Devil)
V 119b (Spiritual Beings); 487b (Wish and Desire); 494b (Witnessing and Testifying)
37-39 V 52b (Sirius)
38 II 364a (Grammar and the Q)
V 282b (Time)
40 II 43b (Error); 406b (Hearing and Deafness)
IV 2a (Pairs and Pairing)

41	IV	453b (Reward and Punishment)
43	III	452b (Muḥammad)
44	III	510a (Names of the Q)
	IV	230a (Prayer)
46	III	421b (Moses)
	IV	106a (Plagues)
46-47	III	421b (Moses)
46-56	I	304b (Children of Israel)
	IV	320a (Punishment Stories)
47	III	146b (Laughter)
	V	8a (Signs)
48	IV	453a (Reward and Punishment)
	V	54a (Sister)
49	I	465b (Covenant)
51	II	10a (Egypt)
	III	93a (Kings and Rulers)
	IV	68a (Pharaoh)
52	V	201a (Teaching)
53	II	333b, 334a (Gold)
	III	383b (Metals and Minerals)
55	III	423a (Moses)
	IV	453b (Reward and Punishment)
55-56	I	554a (Drowning)
56	IV	35a (Peace)
57	III	8a, 11a (Jesus); 567b (Obedience)
	IV	35a (Peace)
	V	3a (Signs); 533b (Women and the Q)
57-58	I	512b (Debate and Disputation)
57-65	III	7b (Jesus)
58	I	513b (Debate and Disputation)
59	III	16a (Jesus)
61	I	111a (Antichrist); 501a (Day, Times of)
	III	17b (Jesus); 137a (Last Judgment)
	V	288a (Time)
62	I	526a (Devil)
	II	23b (Enemies); 66a (Ethics and the Q)
63	III	8a, 16a (Jesus); 568a (Obedience)
	IV	68b (Philosophy and the Q)
	V	483a, 483b (Wisdom)

64 II 96a (Everyday Life, Q In)
III 230a (Lord)

65 I 500a (Day, Times of)

66 I 501a (Day, Times of)
III 137a, 138a (Last Judgment)
V 287b (Time)

68 II 196b (Fear); 360a (Grammar and the Q)

68-72 I 171b (Art and Architecture and the Q)
III 310a (Material Culture and the Q)

69-70 I 385a (Community and Society in the Q)

70 II 175a (Family); 283b (Garden)
V 524a (Women and the Q)

70-73 I 165b (Art and Architecture and the Q)
III 493a (Myths and Legends in the Q)

71 I 490b, 491a (Cups and Vessels)
II 276a (Furniture and Furnishings); 283b, 284a (Garden); 333b, 334a (Gold)
III 383b (Metals and Minerals)
IV 18b (Paradise)
V 12b (Silk); 123a (Springs and Fountains)

73 IV 18a (Paradise)

74 II 52b (Eschatology)

75 I 521b (Despair); 524b (Devil)
V 133a (Suffering)

77 I 89b (Angel)
V 119a (Spiritual Beings)

78 II 166a (Faith)
V 387a (Truth)

80 I 243b (Book)
III 191a (Literacy)
IV 290a (Prophets and Prophethood)
V 118b (Spiritual Beings); 493a (Witnessing and Testifying)

81 I 115a (Apologetics)

81-82 III 7b (Jesus)

82 II 325b (God and his Attributes)
IV 220b (Prayer)
V 277a (Throne of God)

83 III 40a (Jihād); 453b (Muḥammad)
IV 309b (Provocation)
V 387a (Truth)

84 IV 5b (Pairs and Pairing); 161b (Polytheism and Atheism); 537b (Scholar)

84-89 II 143a (Exhortations)

85 I 501a (Day, Times of)
III 137a, 138a (Last Judgment)
IV 220b (Prayer)
V 288a (Time)

86 II 49b (Eschatology)
III 379b (Mercy)
IV 163b (Popular and Talismanic Uses of the Q); 228b (Prayer)

87 I 329b (Chronology and the Q); 472b (Creation)

88-89 II 30a (Epigraphy)

89 III 40a (Jihād); 453a (Muḥammad)
IV 538b (Scholar)
V 291a (Tolerance and Coercion)

Sūrat al-Dukhān (44)

I 407b (Consultation)
III 472b (Mysterious Letters); 521a (Narratives)
IV 495b (Ritual and the Q)
V 64b, 65a (Smoke)

1-4 III 496b (Myths and Legends in the Q)

2 II 257b, 263b (Form and Structure of the Q); 497b (Illiteracy)
III 124b (Language and Style of the Q)
IV 468b (Rhetoric and the Q)
V 172a (Sūra)

2-3 III 442a (Muḥammad)
V 284b (Time)

3 I 326a (Chronology and the Q); 501b (Day, Times of)
II 181b (Fasting)
III 414a (Months); 537b (Night of Power)
IV 262b (Preserved Tablet); 292b, 293a (Prophets and Prophethood); 343b (Ramaḍān)

3-4 II 186a (Fate)

3-6 IV 343a (Ramaḍān)

4 IV 343a (Ramaḍān)

6 II 1b (Ears)
IV 575a (Seeing and Hearing)

7 II 31a (Epigraphy)

8 IV 4b (Pairs and Pairing)

10	I	111a (Antichrist)
	II	411b (Heaven and Sky)
	V	64a, 64b, 65a (Smoke)
10-11	V	133a (Suffering)
10-14	III	379b (Mercy)
10-16	IV	332a (Quraysh); 434b (Resurrection)
11	V	64b (Smoke)
12	V	64b (Smoke)
14	II	540a (Insanity)
	III	103b (Knowledge and Learning); 450a, 450a (Muḥammad)
	IV	112a (Poetry and Poets); 310b, 311b (Provocation); 442b (Revelation and Inspiration)
	V	202b (Teaching)
15	IV	430a (Repentance and Penance)
16	IV	332b (Quraysh); 453b (Reward and Punishment)
	V	64b, 65a (Smoke)
17-33	III	521a (Narratives)
	IV	320a (Punishment Stories)
20	V	130b (Stoning)
23	I	501b (Day, Times of)
	V	246b (Textual Criticism of the Q)
23-24	III	423a (Moses)
	V	246b (Textual Criticism of the Q)
23-31	III	423a (Moses)
24	I	553b (Drowning)
	V	377a (Troops); 464b (Water)
24-25	II	213a (Fire)
25	V	127b (Springs and Fountains)
25-28	III	488a (Myths and Legends in the Q)
26	II	3b (Earth); 447b (Honor)
29	V	472b (Weeping)
30	I	518b (Deliverance)
	II	184a (Fasting)
	V	363a (Trial)
30-33	I	304a (Children of Israel)
31	II	542a (Insolence and Obstinacy)
32	II	11b (Election)
	IV	291b (Prophets and Prophethood)

33	V	5b (Signs); 363a (Trial)
36	II	308a (Geography)
37	I	152a (Archaeology and the Q)
	II	437b (History and the Q)
	III	521b (Narratives)
	V	389a (Tubbaʿ)
38	I	442a (Cosmology); 473a (Creation)
	II	31a (Epigraphy)
	IV	4a (Pairs and Pairing); 82a (Philosophy and the Q); 262b (Preserved Tablet)
	V	279b (Time); 553b (World)
38-39	I	442a (Cosmology)
	II	327b (God and his Attributes)
39	I	473a (Creation)
	IV	538b (Scholar)
40	I	272b (Calendar); 516b (Decision)
	III	136a, 137a (Last Judgment)
	IV	228a (Prayer)
	V	288a (Time)
41	I	345a (Clients and Clientage)
	III	231a (Lord)
41-42	III	379b (Mercy)
42	III	200a (Literary Structures of the Q)
	IV	6a (Pairs and Pairing)
43	I	42a (Agriculture and Vegetation)
	II	211a (Fire); 305a (Geography)
	V	359a (Tree); 571a (Zaqqūm)
43-44	V	359a (Tree)
43-46	III	533a (Nature as Signs)
43-48	I	222a (Belief and Unbelief)
44	V	572a (Zaqqūm)
45	III	383b (Metals and Minerals)
45-46	II	211b (Fire)
	V	572a (Zaqqūm)
46	V	182a (Symbolic Imagery); 464b (Water)
47-48	II	50a (Eschatology); 211a (Fire)
48	II	210b (Fire)
49	II	320b (God and his Attributes)
51	I	165b (Art and Architecture and the Q)
	II	283b (Garden)
	IV	14b (Paradise); 103a (Pit); 307b (Protection)

51-52 V 123a (Springs and Fountains)

51-57 IV 16b (Paradise)

52 V 464b (Water)

53 II 228b (Foreign Vocabulary)
V 11b (Silk)

54 II 52a (Eschatology); 154a (Eyes); 284a (Garden); 348b (Grammar and the Q); 456a, 456b (Houris)
III 130b (Language and Style of the Q); 139b (Last Judgment); 277a (Marriage and Divorce); 493a (Myths and Legends in the Q)
IV 18a (Paradise); 354b, 358a (Readings of the Q); 585a (Sex and Sexuality)
V 106b (Spatial Relations)

55 IV 18a (Paradise)

56 IV 486a (Ritual and the Q)

57 IV 522b (Salvation)

58 I 83a (Anatomy); 132a (Arabic Language)
III 108b (Language, Concept of); 113b (Language and Style of the Q); 443a (Muḥammad)

59 III 40a (Jihād)

Sūrat al-Jāthiya (45)

I 407b (Consultation)
III 472b (Mysterious Letters)

1-6 II 262a (Form and Structure of the Q)
IV 438a (Revelation and Inspiration)

2 IV 446a (Revelation and Inspiration)

2-7 I 247b (Book)

3-5 I 474a (Creation)

4 I 95b (Animal Life)

5 I 52a, 53b (Air and Wind); 501b (Day, Times of)
II 3a (Earth)
III 210a, 212a (Literature and the Q)
IV 4a (Pairs and Pairing)
V 179a (Sustenance); 280b (Time)

6 III 190a (Literacy); 441a (Muḥammad)
V 3a (Signs)

8 I 160b (Arrogance)
III 190a (Literacy)

9	III	400a (Mockery)
	V	6a (Signs)
10	II	273b (Friends and Friendship); 418b (Hell and Hellfire)
11	I	446a (Cosmology)
	IV	454a (Reward and Punishment); 503a (Ritual Purity)
12	V	412a (Vehicles); 464a (Water)
12-13	IV	438a (Revelation and Inspiration)
12-15	II	259a (Form and Structure of the Q)
13	I	96a (Animal Life)
	IV	4a (Pairs and Pairing); 107b (Planets and Stars); 393b (Reflection and Deliberation)
14	I	407b (Consultation); 505a, 505b (Days of God)
	II	362a (Grammar and the Q); 449a (Hope)
	III	40a (Jihād)
	V	279b (Time)
15	IV	1b (Pairs and Pairing)
16	IV	127b (Politics and the Q)
	V	105b (Spatial Relations); 301a (Torah)
16-17	I	304a, 305a (Children of Israel)
17	II	185b (Fate)
	IV	133b (Politics and the Q)
18	III	27a (Jews and Judaism); 201b (Literary Structures of the Q); 453b (Muḥammad)
	IV	402b (Religious Pluralism and the Q)
	V	486b (Wish and Desire)
19	II	273b, 274b (Friends and Friendship)
	III	231b (Lord)
	V	138a (Ṣūfism and the Q)
22	I	473a, 473b (Creation)
	IV	82a (Philosophy and the Q)
	V	544b (Word of God)
23	I	225b, 226a (Belief and Unbelief)
	II	330b (God and his Attributes); 407a (Heart)
	IV	160a (Polytheism and Atheism)
24	I	38a (Age of Ignorance); 318b (Chronology and the Q); 509b (Death and the Dead)
	II	54b (Eternity); 185a (Fate); 268a (Freedom and Predestination); 362b (Grammar and the Q)
	IV	162a, 162b (Polytheism and Atheism); 177b (Suspicion)
	V	287a (Time); 475a (Weights and Measures); 486a (Wish and Desire)
24-37	I	522b (Destiny)
25	III	190a (Literacy)
	V	132b, 177b (Suspicion); 422b (Verse)

26 II 268a (Freedom and Predestination)
IV 4b (Pairs and Pairing); 538b (Scholar)

27 I 501a (Day, Times of)
III 137a (Last Judgment)
V 287b (Time)

28 II 432a (History and the Q); 558b (Invitation)

28-29 I 522b (Destiny)
II 269b (Freedom and Predestination); 412b (Heavenly Book)
V 493a (Witnessing and Testifying)

29 I 14b (Abrogation); 243b, 244a, 244b (Book)
V 111a (Speech)

30 I 436a (Conversion)
IV 18b (Paradise); 522b (Salvation)
V 430a (Victory)

30-31 II 362b (Grammar and the Q)

31 III 190a (Literacy)
V 6a (Signs); 19a (Sin, Major and Minor)

32 I 501a (Day, Times of)
II 362b (Grammar and the Q)
III 137a (Last Judgment)
V 287b (Time)

33 II 417a (Hell and Hellfire)
III 400b (Mockery)

34 IV 103b (Pit)

34-35 IV 309b (Provocation)

35 V 6a (Signs)

36 IV 184a (Possession and Possessions); 213b (Praise)

37 I 158b, 159a (Arrogance)
IV 264b (Pride)

Sūrat al-Aḥqāf (46)

I 407b (Consultation)
III 472b (Mysterious Letters)

1-3 II 262a (Form and Structure of the Q)

2 IV 446a (Revelation and Inspiration)

3 I 472a (Creation)
II 269a (Freedom and Predestination); 439b (History and the Q)
III 181a (Lie)

	IV	4a (Pairs and Pairing); 82a (Philosophy and the Q)
	V	289b (Time)
4	I	472b (Creation)
	II	239b (Foretelling in the Q); 476a (Idolatry and Idolaters)
	IV	312a, 312b (Provocation)
5	II	43b (Error)
	IV	228b (Prayer)
6	I	220b (Belief and Unbelief)
7	III	190a (Literacy); 246a, 247a (Magic)
	V	5b (Signs); 421b (Verse)
7-8	I	115a (Apologetics)
8	III	450a (Muḥammad)
9	I	478b (Creation)
	II	365a (Grammar and the Q); 420b (Heresy)
	III	451b (Muḥammad)
	IV	298a (Prophets and Prophethood)
	V	316b (Tradition and Custom)
10	IV	84a (Philosophy and the Q)
	V	492a, 492b (Witnessing and Testifying)
12	I	83a (Anatomy); 117b (Apologetics); 132a (Arabic Language)
	II	226b (Foreign Vocabulary); 341a, 341b (Good News); 502b (Imām)
	III	113b (Language and Style of the Q); 189b (Literacy); 424b (Moses); 445a (Muḥammad)
	IV	3b (Pairs and Pairing); 36b (People of the Book); 300b (Prophets and Prophethood); 439a (Revelation and Inspiration)
	V	300b, 301a (Torah); 461a (Warner)
13	II	365a (Grammar and the Q)
	III	230a (Lord)
15	I	232a (Biology as the Creation and Stages of Life); 302b (Children)
	II	61b (Ethics and the Q); 372a (Gratitude and Ingratitude); 447b (Honor); 453a (Hospitality and Courtesy)
	III	106a (Lactation); 252a (Maintenance and Upkeep); 332a (Maturity); 410a (Months); 551a (Numbers and Enumeration)
	IV	20b (Parents); 427a (Repentance and Penance)
	V	204b (Teaching); 285b, 286a (Time); 475b (Weights and Measures)
16	III	379b (Mercy)
17	II	365b (Grammar and the Q); 430a (History and the Q)
	III	518a (Narratives)
	IV	21a (Parents)
18	III	46b, 47b (Jinn)
	IV	7b (Pairs and Pairing); 336b (Races); 438a (Revelation and Inspiration)
	V	547b (Word of God)

19	IV	458b (Reward and Punishment)
	V	191b (Talent)
21	I	21b (ʿĀd); 261b (Brother and Brotherhood)
	III	524b (Narratives)
21-25	II	459b (House, Domestic and Divine)
21-26	II	462a (Hūd); 558a (Invitation)
21-27	III	353a (Medicine and the Q)
	IV	320a (Punishment Stories)
22	I	21b (ʿĀd)
22-23	II	488a (Ignorance)
24	I	21b (ʿĀd)
	V	133a (Suffering)
	V	471a (Weather)
24-25	II	462b (Hūd)
25	I	21b (ʿĀd); 150b (Archaeology and the Q); 504a (Day, Times of)
	II	338b (Good and Evil)
	III	418a (Morning)
	IV	425a (Remnant)
	V	545a (Word of God)
26	II	370b (Gratitude and Ingratitude)
	III	400b (Mockery)
	IV	210b (Power and Impotence)
	V	6a (Signs)
27	I	246a (Book)
	II	46a (Eschatology)
	III	212a (Literature and the Q)
	IV	438b (Revelation and Inspiration)
28	IV	517a (Sacrifice)
29	II	365b (Grammar and the Q); 405b (Hearing and Deafness)
	III	591b (Orality and Writing in Arabia)
	IV	337a (Races)
	V	460a (Warner)
29-30	II	87a (Everyday Life, Q In)
29-31	III	443b (Muḥammad)
30	III	445a (Muḥammad); 509a (Names of the Q); 591b (Orality and Writing in Arabia)
	IV	28b, 29a (Path or Way); 299b (Prophets and Prophethood); 439a (Revelation and Inspiration)
	V	300b (Torah); 386b (Truth)

31	I	519b (Deliverance)
	II	245a (Forgiveness)
31-32	IV	307b (Protection)
32	II	273b (Friends and Friendship)
33	I	443b (Cosmology); 474b, 479a, 479b (Creation)
	IV	212a (Power and Impotence)
	V	5a (Signs)
33-34	I	479a (Creation)
35	I	501a (Day, Times of)
	III	40a (Jihād); 54b (Jonah); 335b (Measurement); 362a (Medicine and the Q); 382a (Messenger); 453a (Muḥammad)
	IV	292a (Prophets and Prophethood)
	V	287b (Time); 476b (Weights and Measures)

Sūrat Muḥammad (47)

I	322a (Chronology and the Q)
II	264a (Form and Structure of the Q)
V	174b (Sūra)

1	IV	431b (Responsibility)
1-3	IV	1b (Pairs and Pairing); 117a (Polemic and Polemical Language)
2	II	439a (History and the Q)
	III	440a (Muḥammad); 501b (Names of the Prophet)
	IV	259a (Pre-Islamic Arabia and the Q); 431b (Responsibility)
	V	489a (Witness to Faith); 501b (Witnessing and Testifying)
3	II	99a (Evil Deeds)
	V	386b (Truth)
4	I	224a (Belief and Unbelief); 289a (Captives); 397b (Conquest); 460b (Courage)
	II	144a (Expeditions and Battles); 439a (History and the Q)
	III	37b, 38a, 42a (Jihād); 228a (Load or Burden); 577b (Opposition to Muḥammad)
	IV	30b (Path or Way); 277b (Prisoners); 321b (Punishment Stories); 523b (Salvation)
	V	455a, 456a, 458a, 458b (War)
4-6	II	209b (Fighting)
	III	282b, 283a (Martyrs)
5	IV	460b (Reward and Punishment)
8	I	491b (Curse)
9	II	161b (Failure)
10	IV	320b (Punishment Stories); 425a (Remnant)
11	I	344b (Clients and Clientage)
	III	231a (Lord)
	IV	307b (Protection)

12 I 100a (Animal Life)
IV 103b (Pit)
V 464b (Water)

13 II 299a (Geography)
III 338a (Mecca); 449a (Muḥammad); 579a (Opposition to Muḥammad)
V 458b (War)

14 I 213a (Beauty)
II 308a (Geography); 335b (Good and Evil)

15 I 165b (Art and Architecture and the Q); 343b (Cleanliness and Ablution)
II 51b (Eschatology); 211a (Fire); 218a (Food and Drink); 245a (Forgiveness); 283b (Garden); 445b (Honey); 556a (Intoxicants)
III 204a (Literary Structures of the Q); 391a (Milk); 531a (Nature as Signs)
IV 17b, 18b (Paradise)
V 124b, 125a (Springs and Fountains); 464b (Water); 466a (Water of Paradise); 482a (Wine)

16 I 82a (Anatomy)
IV 538b (Scholar)
V 203b (Teaching)

17 I 435b (Conversion)
II 195a (Fear)

18 I 113b (Apocalypse); 501a (Day, Times of)
II 148b (Expeditions and Battles)
III 137a, 138a (Last Judgment)
IV 183a (Portents)
V 287b (Time)

19 I 163b (Art and Architecture and the Q)
II 49b (Eschatology); 75b (Ethics and the Q)
III 299a, 299b, 300b (Material Culture and the Q); 379b (Mercy); 446b (Muḥammad); 556a (Numismatics)
V 22b, 25a (Sin, Major and Minor); 488b (Witness to Faith); 500b, 501a (Witnessing and Testifying)

20 I 506b (Death and the Dead)
II 407b (Heart); 465a (Humor); 470a (Hypocrites and Hypocrisy)
III 37b (Jihād)
IV 118a (Polemic and Polemical Language)
V 457a, 457b (War)

21 II 65b (Ethics and the Q)

22 II 358a, 367a (Grammar and the Q)
V 522a, 522b (Womb)

23 I 492a (Curse)
II 406b (Hearing and Deafness)

	IV	2a (Pairs and Pairing)
	V	446a (Vision and Blindness)
24	I	226a (Belief and Unbelief)
	II	510b (Indifference); 546a (Instruments)
	IV	118a (Polemic and Polemical Language); 394b (Reflection and Deliberation)
	V	203b (Teaching); 447a (Vision and Blindness)
25	I	80a (Anatomy); 526a (Devil)
	V	82b (Soul); 293b (Tolerance and Coercion)
26	V	458a (War)
27	I	80b (Anatomy)
	IV	486a (Ritual and the Q)
28	I	93a (Anger)
	II	161b (Failure); 321b (God and his Attributes)
29	II	407b (Heart)
30	I	82b (Anatomy)
	III	109b (Language and Style of the Q)
31	I	220b (Belief and Unbelief)
	III	37a, 37b (Jihād); 184b (Life); 518a (Narratives); 537a (News)
	V	133b (Suffering); 362b (Trial); 458a (War)
32	III	454b (Muḥammad)
	IV	455b (Reward and Punishment)
34	I	120b (Apostasy)
	II	245a (Forgiveness)
35	I	461a (Courage); 521b (Despair)
	II	439a (History and the Q)
	III	40a (Jihād)
36	II	209b (Fighting)
36-38	V	469b (Wealth)
38	I	277a (Caliph)
	II	361a (Grammar and the Q)
	IV	30b (Path or Way); 209a (Poverty and the Poor)
	V	468b (Wealth)

Sūrat al-Fatḥ (48)

II 148a, 149b (Expeditions and Battles); 264a (Form and Structure of the Q)
III 272a (Manuscripts of the Q); 324b (Material Culture and the Q); 437a (Mosque); 579a (Opposition to Muḥammad)
IV 172b (Popular and Talismanic Uses of the Q); 246b (Pre-1800 Preoccupations of Q Studies)

v 174b (Sūra); 429b (Victory); 435a (Virtue); 501b (Witnessing and Testifying)

1 I 32a (African Literature); 399a (Conquest)
II 144a, 149b (Expeditions and Battles); 462a (House, Domestic and Divine)
III 454a (Muḥammad)
IV 332b (Quraysh); 590a (Shekhinah)
V 393b (Turkish Literature and the Q)

1-2 IV 177b (Popular and Talismanic Uses of the Q)

1-6 II 32a (Epigraphy)

1-22 III 304b (Material Culture and the Q)

2 II 506a (Impeccability)
III 446b (Muḥammad)
V 25a (Sin, Major and Minor); 458b (War)

2-4 III 315b (Material Culture and the Q)

4 I 220b (Belief and Unbelief); 406a (Consolation); 463b (Court)
IV 4a (Pairs and Pairing); 34a (Peace); 537b (Scholar); 590a (Shekhinah)
V 190b (Table); 377b (Troops); 404b (Uncertainty)

5 IV 17b, 18b (Paradise); 522b (Salvation)

5-6 IV 1b (Pairs and Pairing)
V 523b (Women and the Q)

6 I 93a (Anger); 492a (Curse)
II 468b, 470a (Hypocrites and Hypocrisy)
III 314b (Material Culture and the Q)
IV 119b (Polemic and Polemical Language); 456a (Reward and Punishment)
V 287a (Time)

7 I 463b (Court)
IV 4a (Pairs and Pairing)
V 377b (Troops)

8 II 341b (Good News)
IV 3b (Pairs and Pairing); 300b (Prophets and Prophethood)
V 307b (Torah)

9 I 502b, 503b, 504a (Day, Times of)
III 416b, 418b (Morning)
V 281a (Time)

10 I 103b (Anthropomorphism); 431a (Contracts and Alliances); 466a (Covenant)
II 323b, 325a (God and his Attributes); 401b (Hand)
III 201b (Literary Structures of the Q); 340b (Mecca); 447b (Muḥammad); 562b (Oaths); 568a (Obedience)
IV 63b (Persian Literature and the Q); 125b (Politics and the Q); 493a (Ritual and the Q)
V 434a (Virtue); 449b (Vow)

11	I	83a (Anatomy); 216a (Bedouin)
	III	544b (Nomads); 578a (Opposition to Muḥammad)
	V	375b (Trips and Voyages); 457b (War); 469b (Wealth); 548b, 549a (Work)
11-12	III	315b (Material Culture and the Q)
12	V	457b (War)
13	V	458a (War)
14	II	244b (Forgiveness)
	IV	2a (Pairs and Pairing); 457b (Reward and Punishment)
15	I	251b (Booty)
	II	25a (Envy); 262b (Form and Structure of the Q)
	III	511a (Names of the Q)
	V	111a (Speech); 175b (Sūra); 194a (Taxation); 457b (War); 547b (Word of God)
16	I	216a (Bedouin); 458b (Courage)
	III	41b (Jihād); 462b (Musaylima); 544b (Nomads); 578a (Opposition to Muḥammad)
	IV	2a (Pairs and Pairing); 455a, 456a (Reward and Punishment)
	V	458a (War)
17	I	397b (Conquest)
	II	501b (Illness and Health)
	III	41b (Jihād)
	IV	2a (Pairs and Pairing); 34b (Peace)
	V	19a (Sin, Major and Minor); 133b (Suffering); 457b (War); 464b (Water); 501b (Witnessing and Testifying)
18	I	399a, 400b (Conquest); 406a (Consolation); 466a (Covenant)
	II	144a (Expeditions and Battles); 305a (Geography)
	III	340b (Mecca); 447b (Muḥammad); 568a (Obedience)
	IV	17a (Paradise); 34a, 35a (Peace); 63b (Persian Literature and the Q); 125b (Politics and the Q); 456b (Reward and Punishment); 493a (Ritual and the Q); 590a (Shekhinah)
	V	361b (Tree); 404b (Uncertainty); 435a (Virtue)
19	I	251b (Booty)
	V	194a (Taxation)
20	I	251b (Booty)
	III	577b (Opposition to Muḥammad)
	V	4a (Signs); 194a (Taxation)
20-24	III	42b (Jihād)
22	I	80b (Anatomy)
	II	273b (Friends and Friendship)
	IV	5b (Pairs and Pairing)
	V	458a (War)
23	II	209b (Fighting)
	V	164a (Sunna); 317b (Tradition and Custom)

24 II 149b (Expeditions and Battles); 299b (Geography)
III 337b, 338a, 340b (Mecca)
IV 54a (People of the Thicket); 259a (Pre-Islamic Arabia and the Q)
24-25 III 42a (Jihād)
25 I 436a (Conversion)
II 299a (Geography)
III 77b (Kaʿba); 340b (Mecca)
IV 281b (Profane and Sacred); 332a (Quraysh); 515a (Sacred Precincts)
V 458b, 459a (War); 523b (Women and the Q)
26 I 37a (Age of Ignorance); 406a (Consolation); 459b (Courage)
II 195b (Fear); 488a (Ignorance)
IV 590b (Shekhinah)
V 286b (Time); 404b (Uncertainty); 435a (Virtue)
27 I 81b (Anatomy); 320a (Chronology and the Q); 399a (Conquest); 546b, 547a, 551a, 551b (Dreams and Sleep)
II 144a (Expeditions and Battles); 241b (Foretelling in the Q)
III 77b (Kaʿba); 340a (Mecca); 454a (Muḥammad)
IV 179a (Popular and Talismanic Uses of the Q); 281b (Profane and Sacred); 295a (Prophets and Prophethood); 515a (Sacred Precincts)
V 444b (Vision); 446a (Vision and Blindness); 459a (War)
28 II 299a (Geography)
IV 300a (Prophets and Prophethood)
V 489b (Witness to Faith); 503b (Witnessing and Testifying)
29 I 41b (Agriculture and Vegetation); 93b (Anger); 182a (Asceticism); 213a (Beauty); 219b, 220a (Belief and Unbelief); 254a, 254b (Bowing and Prostration); 480b (Creeds)
II 30a, 30b, 34a, 35a (Epigraphy); 245a (Forgiveness); 439a (History and the Q)
III 224b (Literature and the Q); 265b (Manuscripts of the Q); 299a, 299b (Material Culture and the Q); 378a (Mercy); 382b (Messenger); 440a (Muḥammad); 501b, 502a (Names of the Prophet); 556a, 556b, 559a (Numismatics)
IV 10b (Parable); 176b (Popular and Talismanic Uses of the Q); 219b (Prayer); 259a (Pre-Islamic Arabia and the Q)
V 242a (Textual Criticism of the Q); 300b, 307b (Torah); 489a (Witness to Faith); 501b, 502a (Witnessing and Testifying)

Sūrat al-Ḥujurāt (49)

I 322a (Chronology and the Q)
II 264a (Form and Structure of the Q); 569a (Islam)
IV 380a (Recitation of the Q)
V 174b (Sūra)
1 IV 575a (Seeing and Hearing)
1-5 III 447b (Muḥammad)

2-3	I	82b (Anatomy)
	IV	455b (Reward and Punishment)
2-5	I	220a (Belief and Unbelief)
	II	72b (Ethics and the Q)
3	I	82b (Anatomy)
	II	245a (Forgiveness); 538a (Inquisition)
	III	401b (Moderation)
	V	362b (Trial); 489a (Witness to Faith)
6	II	488b (Ignorance)
	III	537a (News)
7	I	537b (Disobedience)
	II	57a, 66a (Ethics and the Q); 98a (Evil Deeds)
	III	235b (Love and Affection); 447b (Muḥammad); 567b (Obedience)
8	IV	537b (Scholar)
9	I	461a (Courage)
	II	70b, 72b (Ethics and the Q)
	III	70a, 70b, 71b (Justice and Injustice); 85a (Khārijīs)
	IV	35a (Peace); 135b (Politics and the Q); 364b (Rebellion)
	V	456a (War); 486b (Wish and Desire)
9-10	I	220a (Belief and Unbelief)
	IV	63b (Persian Literature and the Q)
10	I	220a (Belief and Unbelief); 262b (Brother and Brotherhood)
	II	72b (Ethics and the Q); 363a (Grammar and the Q)
	III	70a (Justice and Injustice); 99b (Kinship)
	V	365a (Tribes and Clans)
11	II	72b (Ethics and the Q); 367a (Grammar and the Q)
	III	401a (Mockery)
	IV	8b (Pairs and Pairing); 427a (Repentance and Penance)
11-12	II	343b (Gossip)
	III	66a (Judgment)
	V	21a (Sin, Major and Minor)
12	I	80a (Anatomy); 261b (Brother and Brotherhood)
	II	72b (Ethics and the Q)
	IV	5b (Pairs and Pairing); 426b (Repentance and Penance)
	V	19a (Sin, Major and Minor); 178b (Suspicion)
13	I	38a, 38b (Age of Ignorance); 368b (Community and Society in the Q); 476a, 476b (Creation)
	II	72a (Ethics and the Q); 202b (Feminism and the Q); 328b (God and his Attributes); 448a (Honor); 462a (House, Domestic and Divine)
	III	211b (Literature and the Q)
	IV	5b (Pairs and Pairing); 337a (Races); 581a (Sex and Sexuality)
	V	364b (Tribes and Clans); 436b (Virtue); 524a (Women and the Q)

14 I 216b (Bedouin); 218b (Belief and Unbelief); 375b, 382a (Community and Society in the Q)
II 169a (Faith); 568b (Islam)
IV 401b (Religious Pluralism and the Q)
V 502a (Witnessing and Testifying)

14-15 I 375a (Community and Society in the Q)
II 72b (Ethics and the Q)
III 37b (Jihād)

15 I 437b (Conversion)
II 164b (Faith); 362b (Grammar and the Q)
III 38a (Jihād)
IV 30b (Path or Way)
V 178b (Suspicion); 501b (Witnessing and Testifying)

16 V 201b (Teaching)

17 I 438a (Conversion)
II 568b (Islam)
IV 404a (Religious Pluralism and the Q)

Sūrat Qāf (50)

III 472b (Mysterious Letters)
IV 495b (Ritual and the Q)
V 308b (Torah)

1 I 350b (Codices of the Q)
II 257b, 263b (Form and Structure of the Q); 315b (Glory)
IV 63a (Persian Literature and the Q); 468b (Rhetoric and the Q)
V 172a (Sūra)

2 III 399a (Miracles)

2-11 I 479a (Creation)

3 II 4b (Earth)

4 I 243a (Book)

6 I 213a (Beauty); 478a (Creation)
II 411a (Heaven and Sky)

6-8 I 474a (Creation)

6-11 II 259a (Form and Structure of the Q)
IV 438a (Revelation and Inspiration)

7 II 2b, 3a (Earth); 362a (Grammar and the Q)

8 IV 427b (Repentance and Penance)

9 II 3b (Earth); 28a (Epigraphy)
III 304a (Material Culture and the Q)
V 126b (Springs and Fountains)

9-10	V	462b (Water)
9-11	II	3a, 3b (Earth); 303a (Geography)
	III	531a (Nature as Signs)
	V	126b (Springs and Fountains); 190b (Table)
10	I	494b (Date Palm)
	II	305a (Geography)
11	II	3a (Earth)
	IV	435a (Resurrection)
12	II	434a (History and the Q)
	III	486a (Myths and Legends in the Q); 524a (Narratives)
	IV	320a (Punishment Stories); 352b (Rass)
12-14	III	522a (Narratives)
	IV	320a (Punishment Stories)
	V	250b (Textual Criticism of the Q)
13	I	21b (ʿĀd); 261b (Brother and Brotherhood)
	II	308a (Geography)
14	I	41b (Agriculture and Vegetation); 152a (Archaeology and the Q)
	II	353b, 363a (Grammar and the Q); 437b (History and the Q)
	III	390b (Midian)
	IV	53b (People of the Thicket); 320a (Punishment Stories); 605b (Shuʿayb)
	V	389a (Tubbaʿ)
15	I	479a, 479b (Creation)
	IV	6b (Pairs and Pairing)
16	I	175b (Artery and Vein); 362a (Colors); 474b, 476a (Creation); 526a (Devil)
	II	57b (Ethics and the Q); 322b, 324a (God and his Attributes); 546b (Instruments)
	III	225a (Literature and the Q)
	V	82b (Soul); 137b (Ṣūfism and the Q); 266a (Theology and the Q); 493a (Witnessing and Testifying)
16-29	II	99a (Evil Deeds)
17	V	119a (Spiritual Beings)
17-18	III	177b (Left Hand and Right Hand)
	V	493a (Witnessing and Testifying)
18	V	118b (Spiritual Beings)
19	I	506b (Death and the Dead)
20	I	500a (Day, Times of)
	II	547a (Instruments)
	III	137a (Last Judgment)
	IV	61a (Persian Literature and the Q)
	V	393b (Turkish Literature and the Q)
20-29	V	494a (Witnessing and Testifying)

21 V 118b (Spiritual Beings); 493b, 494a (Witnessing and Testifying)
22 I 91a (Angel); 400a (Conquest)
II 99a (Evil Deeds); 489a (Ignorance)
V 444b (Vision)
23 V 119b (Spiritual Beings); 494a (Witnessing and Testifying)
24 I 221a (Belief and Unbelief)
II 357b (Grammar and the Q)
27 V 119b (Spiritual Beings); 494b (Witnessing and Testifying)
28 I 513a (Debate and Disputation)
29 V 38b (Sīra and the Q)
30 II 325a (God and his Attributes); 417b (Hell and Hellfire)
V 110b (Speech)
31-34 IV 34a (Peace)
32 IV 428a (Repentance and Penance)
33 II 408a (Heart)
IV 427b (Repentance and Penance)
34 I 500a (Day, Times of)
II 54b (Eternity); 283b (Garden)
III 137a (Last Judgment)
35 II 284a (Garden); 324a (God and his Attributes)
IV 18b (Paradise)
36 I 458b (Courage)
II 293a (Generations)
IV 320a (Punishment Stories)
37 V 203b (Teaching)
38 I 443b (Cosmology); 473b, 474b, 476a (Creation)
II 326a (God and his Attributes); 410b (Heaven and Sky)
III 552a (Numbers and Enumeration)
IV 4a (Pairs and Pairing); 226a (Prayer); 511a (Sabbath)
V 265a (Theology and the Q); 279b, 287a (Time); 553a (World)
39 I 444a (Cosmology); 503b, 504b (Day, Times of)
III 417b (Morning)
IV 107a (Planets and Stars); 223a (Prayer)
V 163a (Sun); 282b (Time)
39-40 I 27a (Adoration); 328a (Chronology and the Q)
II 315a (Glorification of God)
III 446b (Muḥammad); 546a (Noon)
IV 220b (Prayer)
39-44 I 503b (Day, Times of)

40 I 254a (Bowing and Prostration)

41 I 113b, 114a (Apocalypse)
III 3b (Jerusalem); 142a (Last Judgment)

41-42 I 480b (Creeds)
II 558b (Invitation)
IV 435a (Resurrection)

42 I 319a (Chronology and the Q); 500a (Day, Times of)
III 137a (Last Judgment)
IV 454a (Reward and Punishment)
V 287a (Time)

43 IV 4b (Pairs and Pairing)
V 287a (Time)

44 IV 434a, 435a (Resurrection)

45 III 40a (Jihād); 452b (Muḥammad); 504a (Names of the Prophet)

Sūrat al-Dhāriyāt (51)

II 253a (Form and Structure of the Q)
III 200b (Literary Structures of the Q)
V 168b, 171a, 171b (Sūra)

1 I 55a (Air and Wind)
V 119a (Spiritual Beings)

1-4 II 256a (Form and Structure of the Q)
IV 464b, 466a, 468b (Rhetoric and the Q)
V 80a (Soothsayer)

2 I 55a (Air and Wind)
III 227b (Load or Burden)
V 474a (Weights and Measures)

3 I 55a (Air and Wind)
V 412a (Vehicles)

5-6 I 113b (Apocalypse)

6 III 136b (Last Judgment)

7 II 410a, 411a (Heaven and Sky)

7-9 II 256b (Form and Structure of the Q)
IV 468a (Rhetoric and the Q)

10 I 491b (Curse)

10-14 II 258b (Form and Structure of the Q)
V 106b (Spatial Relations)

12 III 136b (Last Judgment)
V 288b (Time)

15	V	123a (Springs and Fountains); 431a (Vigil)
15-18	I	182b (Asceticism)
15-19	II	258b (Form and Structure of the Q)
	V	106b (Spatial Relations)
17-18	I	327b (Chronology and the Q)
	IV	222b (Prayer)
17-19	IV	455a (Reward and Punishment)
18	I	503b (Day, Times of)
	III	417a, 418b (Morning)
	IV	487a (Ritual and the Q)
	V	281a (Time)
19	IV	209b (Poverty and the Poor)
	V	469a (Wealth)
20	III	531b (Nature as Signs)
	IV	438a (Revelation and Inspiration)
20-21	V	3a (Signs)
22	II	268a (Freedom and Predestination)
23	II	410a (Heaven and Sky)
	III	531b (Nature as Signs)
	IV	184a (Possession and Possessions)
24	II	254b (Form and Structure of the Q); 435b (History and the Q); 447b (Honor)
	III	524a (Narratives)
	V	132a (Strangers and Foreigners)
24-28	I	532b (Dialogues)
	II	341b (Good News)
24-30	I	6a (Abraham)
24-34	I	330a (Chronology and the Q)
	V	259a (Theology and the Q)
24-37	II	259b (Form and Structure of the Q)
	V	171b (Sūra)
24-46	III	521a (Narratives)
25	II	489a (Ignorance)
	IV	225a (Prayer)
25-34	V	257b (Theology and the Q)
26	II	218b (Food and Drink)
28	I	7b (Abraham); 330b (Chronology and the Q)
	II	341a (Good News); 561b (Isaac)
	III	398a (Miracles)
29	I	6b (Abraham); 52b (Air and Wind)

30	IV	5b (Pairs and Pairing); 537b (Scholar)
31	III	382b (Messenger)
33	I	339b, 340a (Clay)
	II	212b (Fire)
	III	383b (Metals and Minerals)
	V	129a (Stone); 130a (Stoning)
33-34	V	129a (Stone)
34-37	II	259b (Form and Structure of the Q)
34-46	V	420a (Verse)
35-36	I	218b (Belief and Unbelief)
37	IV	425b (Remnant)
38-40	I	304b (Children of Israel)
	II	259b (Form and Structure of the Q)
39	II	540a (Insanity)
	IV	112a (Poetry and Poets)
40	II	10b (Egypt); 213a (Fire)
	V	377a (Troops); 463b (Water)
41	I	21b (ʿĀd); 52b, 54b (Air and Wind)
	V	471a (Weather)
41-42	II	259b (Form and Structure of the Q)
41-46	III	540b (Noah)
43	II	308a (Geography)
43-44	II	259b (Form and Structure of the Q)
43-45	II	212a (Fire)
44	V	253a (Thamūd)
46	II	259b (Form and Structure of the Q); 434a (History and the Q)
	III	486a (Myths and Legends in the Q)
47	I	442b (Cosmology); 478a (Creation)
	II	354a, 362a (Grammar and the Q)
48	II	2b (Earth)
49	I	95b (Animal Life); 473b (Creation)
	II	292a (Gender)
	IV	6a (Pairs and Pairing); 581a (Sex and Sexuality)
	V	524a (Women and the Q)
52	II	540a (Insanity)
	IV	112a (Poetry and Poets); 301a (Prophets and Prophethood); 310b (Provocation)
52-54	III	453a (Muḥammad)
54	III	40a (Jihād); 453a (Muḥammad)

54-55 IV 8a (Pairs and Pairing)

55 V 203a (Teaching)

56 I 435a (Conversion); 476a (Creation)
II 82b (Everyday Life, Q In)
III 46b, 47b (Jinn)
IV 82a (Philosophy and the Q); 487a (Ritual and the Q); 576a (Servants)
V 274b (Theology and the Q); 553b (World); 555b (Worship)

56-57 IV 578b (Servants)

57 II 217a (Food and Drink)
V 179a (Sustenance)

58 II 268a (Freedom and Predestination); 320b, 322a (God and his Attributes)

60 IV 470b (Rhetoric and the Q)

Sūrat al-Ṭūr (52)

I 385a (Community and Society in the Q)
II 256b (Form and Structure of the Q); 388b (Ḥadīth and the Q)
III 495b (Myths and Legends in the Q)
IV 467b (Rhetoric and the Q)
V 28b (Sinai); 168b, 171b (Sūra)

1 IV 468b (Rhetoric and the Q)

1-6 II 256b (Form and Structure of the Q)
IV 464b (Rhetoric and the Q)
V 80a (Soothsayer); 107a (Spatial Relations); 464a (Water)

1-10 I 179a (Ascension)

2 III 591a (Orality and Writing in Arabia)
IV 468b (Rhetoric and the Q)
V 123a (Springs and Fountains); 558a (Writing and Writing Materials)

2-3 II 257b (Form and Structure of the Q)
III 140b (Last Judgment); 592b (Orality and Writing in Arabia)

3 II 545a (Instruments)
IV 468b (Rhetoric and the Q)

4 I 179b (Ascension)
II 299a (Geography)
III 76a, 77b (Kaʿba)
IV 52b (People of the House); 468b (Rhetoric and the Q); 514a (Sacred Precincts)

5 V 277b (Throne of God)

6 I 446a (Cosmology)
III 389a (Michael)

7	I	113b (Apocalypse)
	V	464a (Water)
7-8	IV	467b (Rhetoric and the Q)
9	II	411b (Heaven and Sky)
9-10	II	258a (Form and Structure of the Q)
	IV	8a (Pairs and Pairing); 467b, 469b (Rhetoric and the Q)
11	IV	455b (Reward and Punishment)
12	V	523b (Women and the Q)
13	V	523b (Women and the Q)
13-14	III	183b (Life)
15	III	246a (Magic)
17	III	63a (Joy and Misery)
17-28	V	426b (Verse)
18	I	519a (Deliverance)
	II	284a (Garden)
	III	63a (Joy and Misery)
20	I	385a (Community and Society in the Q)
	II	52a (Eschatology); 154a (Eyes); 284a (Garden); 348b (Grammar and the Q); 456a, 456b (Houris)
	III	130b (Language and Style of the Q); 139b (Last Judgment)
	IV	18a (Paradise); 354b (Readings of the Q); 585a (Sex and Sexuality)
	V	524a (Women and the Q)
21	I	385a (Community and Society in the Q)
	II	175a (Family); 454a (Hostages)
	IV	12a (Paradise); 21a (Parents); 109b (Pledge); 457a (Reward and Punishment)
22	I	385a (Community and Society in the Q)
	II	284a (Garden)
	IV	18a (Paradise)
23	I	385a (Community and Society in the Q); 490b (Cups and Vessels)
	IV	18b (Paradise)
23-28	IV	467b (Rhetoric and the Q)
24	II	52a (Eschatology); 284a (Garden); 445a (Homosexuality)
	III	384a (Metals and Minerals)
	IV	18a (Paradise); 585a (Sex and Sexuality)
	V	570a (Youth and Old Age)
25	I	385a (Community and Society in the Q)
26	II	174a (Family)
26-28	II	258b (Form and Structure of the Q)
27	II	210b (Fire); 415a (Hell and Hellfire); 455b (Hot and Cold)

28 II 321b (God and his Attributes)
III 233b (Love and Affection)
IV 5b (Pairs and Pairing)

29 I 148a (Arbitration); 447a (Cosmology); 542b (Divination)
II 540a (Insanity)
III 246b (Magic); 451a (Muḥammad)
IV 112a (Poetry and Poets); 216b (Prayer); 295a (Prophets and Prophethood); 442b (Revelation and Inspiration); 463a (Rhetoric and the Q); 477a (Rhymed Prose)
V 78b (Soothsayer); 420b (Verse)

29-30 II 540a (Insanity)
III 247a (Magic)
IV 259b (Pre-Islamic Arabia and the Q)
V 43b (Sīra and the Q)

29-31 I 115a (Apologetics)
II 528a (Inimitability)
IV 112b (Poetry and Poets)

29-34 I 543b (Divination)

29-44 V 426b (Verse)

30 I 542b (Divination)
II 185a (Fate); 268a (Freedom and Predestination)
IV 112a (Poetry and Poets); 311b (Provocation); 442b (Revelation and Inspiration); 463a (Rhetoric and the Q); 477a (Rhymed Prose)
V 38b (Sīra and the Q); 287a (Time)

30-31 III 219b (Literature and the Q)

30-43 III 212b (Literature and the Q)

31 III 40a (Jihād)

32 V 546a (Word of God)

33 III 116a (Language and Style of the Q)
IV 311b (Provocation); 463a (Rhetoric and the Q)

33-34 II 527a, 529b (Inimitability)
III 116a (Language and Style of the Q); 451b (Muḥammad); 468a (Muʿtazila)
IV 22b (Parody of the Q)

34 IV 312b (Provocation); 443a (Revelation and Inspiration)

35-36 I 472b (Creation)

37 II 348a, 354a (Grammar and the Q)

38 IV 286b (Proof); 311b (Provocation)

39 II 329b (God and his Attributes)
III 48a (Jinn)

42 IV 310a (Provocation)
V 480a (Whisper)

43 IV 220a, 220b (Prayer)
45 III 40a (Jihād)
47 IV 460b (Reward and Punishment); 538b (Scholar)
48 I 103b (Anthropomorphism)
II 323b, 324b (God and his Attributes)
III 40a (Jihād)
IV 213b (Praise); 220b (Prayer); 470b (Rhetoric and the Q); 574a (Seeing and Hearing)
48-49 I 327b (Chronology and the Q); 503b (Day, Times of)
II 143a (Exhortations)
III 452b (Muḥammad)
IV 222a (Prayer)
V 170a (Sūra)
49 I 502b, 503b (Day, Times of)
III 417b (Morning)
V 282b (Time)

Sūrat al-Najm (53)

I 177b, 178a (Ascension)
III 415b (Moon); 535a (Nature as Signs)
IV 178a (Popular and Talismanic Uses of the Q); 477b (Rhymed Prose); 532a (Satanic Verses)
V 51b (Sirius); 168b, 171b (Sūra); 261a, 262a, 262b, 264b (Theology and the Q)
1 I 36a (Afternoon)
III 535a (Nature as Signs); 561b (Oaths)
IV 108b (Planets and Stars); 217a (Prayer)
V 52a, 52b (Sirius); 80a (Soothsayer)
1-8 IV 216b (Prayer)
V 116a (Spirit)
1-11 II 181a (Fasting)
1-12 I 178a (Ascension)
1-18 I 89a (Angel); 177b (Ascension); 320b (Chronology and the Q)
II 278a (Gabriel); 411b (Heaven and Sky)
IV 441a, 445a (Revelation and Inspiration)
V 138b (Ṣūfism and the Q); 80a (Soothsayer); 445b (Vision and Blindness)
1-20 II 392a (Ḥadīth and the Q)
2 I 387b (Companions of the Prophet)
V 421b (Verse)
2-3 III 450b (Muḥammad)
IV 116b (Polemic and Polemical Language)
V 486b (Wish and Desire)

4	III	511a (Names of the Q)
	IV	439b (Revelation and Inspiration)
4-5	IV	294a (Prophets and Prophethood)
	V	421b (Verse)
4-7	IV	442a (Revelation and Inspiration)
4-10	III	442a (Muḥammad)
4-18	V	261a (Theology and the Q)
5	III	191a (Literacy)
	V	201a (Teaching)
5-18	II	324a (God and his Attributes)
6-7	III	495b (Myths and Legends in the Q)
7	IV	107b (Planets and Stars)
8	II	63b (Ethics and the Q)
9	II	546a (Instruments)
	III	333a (Measurement)
	IV	60b (Persian Literature and the Q)
	V	393b (Turkish Literature and the Q); 473a (Weights and Measures)
10	I	180a (Ascension)
	IV	445a (Revelation and Inspiration)
10-11	I	115a (Apologetics)
11	II	324b (God and his Attributes)
	V	445b (Vision and Blindness)
11-18	III	442a (Muḥammad)
12-18	I	177b (Ascension)
13-14	II	324b (God and his Attributes)
13-18	I	177b, 178a (Ascension)
14	I	88a (Angel); 180a (Ascension)
	II	305b (Geography); 500b (ʿIlliyyūn)
	III	285a (Martyrs); 532a (Nature as Signs)
	V	126a (Springs and Fountains); 360b (Tree)
14-15	II	283b (Garden)
14-16	II	51b (Eschatology)
15	II	282b (Garden); 411b (Heaven and Sky)
	III	495b (Myths and Legends in the Q)
	IV	14a (Paradise); 103b (Pit)
16	I	180a (Ascension)
	II	305b (Geography)
	V	360b (Tree)

17	IV	64a (Persian Literature and the Q)
	V	445b (Vision and Blindness)
19	IV	533a, 535a (Satanic Verses); 574b (Seeing and Hearing)
19-20	I	37b (Age of Ignorance); 95a (Animal Life)
	II	329b (God and his Attributes); 474a, 474b (Iconoclasm); 483b (Idols and Images)
	IV	160b (Polytheism and Atheism); 216b (Prayer); 256b, 259a (Pre-Islamic Arabia and the Q); 532a (Satanic Verses)
	V	87a, 88a (South Arabia, Religions in Pre-Islamic); 122b (Springs and Fountains)
19-21	I	330a (Chronology and the Q)
19-22	I	236a (Blasphemy)
	II	317b (God and his Attributes)
19-23	I	194b (Baal); 221b (Belief and Unbelief); 320a, 321a (Chronology and the Q)
	IV	330a (Quraysh)
19-30	V	261a (Theology and the Q)
20	V	25a (Sin, Major and Minor)
21-22	IV	532b (Satanic Verses)
23	II	507b (Impotence)
	III	43b (Jinn)
	V	82b (Soul)
26	I	463a (Court)
	II	49b (Eschatology); 552a (Intercession)
	III	379b (Mercy)
26-27	II	317b (God and his Attributes)
28	II	489a (Ignorance)
	III	102b (Knowledge and Learning)
29	III	40a (Jihād)
31-32	V	19a (Sin, Major and Minor)
32	I	29a (Adultery and Fornication); 233a (Birth); 479a (Creation)
	II	245a (Forgiveness)
	IV	20a (Parents); 580b (Sex and Sexuality)
	V	19a (Sin, Major and Minor)
33	IV	109a (Planets and Stars)
33-34	II	7b (Economics)
33-37	II	259b (Form and Structure of the Q)
33-41	I	522b (Destiny)
33-48	V	261b (Theology and the Q)
33-62	I	523b (Destiny)

36	II	545a (Instruments)
	IV	570a (Scrolls)
36-37	I	5b (Abraham); 245b (Book)
	III	381a (Messenger)
	IV	570a (Scrolls)
	V	301a (Torah)
36-44	III	148b (Laughter)
37	I	5b (Abraham)
	III	239a (Loyalty)
38	III	228a (Load or Burden)
	V	274a (Theology and the Q)
38-39	V	262a (Theology and the Q)
43	III	149a (Laughter)
	IV	4b (Pairs and Pairing)
	V	472a (Weeping)
43-44	III	148b (Laughter)
43-49	II	259a (Form and Structure of the Q)
	IV	470b (Rhetoric and the Q)
44	IV	4b (Pairs and Pairing)
	V	274a (Theology and the Q)
44-54	I	319a (Chronology and the Q)
	V	289b (Time)
45	I	95b (Animal Life)
	II	175a (Family); 292a (Gender)
	IV	6a (Pairs and Pairing); 581a (Sex and Sexuality)
	V	267a (Theology and the Q); 524a (Women and the Q)
45-46	I	476b, 479a (Creation)
47	IV	435a (Resurrection)
48	V	274a (Theology and the Q); 467b (Wealth)
49	IV	109a (Planets and Stars); 184a (Possession and Possessions)
	V	51b, 52b (Sirius)
49-50	V	52b (Sirius)
50	I	21b (ʿĀd)
50-54	III	521b (Narratives)
50-58	V	262a (Theology and the Q)
52	II	434a (History and the Q)
53	II	299b (Geography)
	V	184b (Syria)

53-56 II 309a (Geography)

56 V 461a (Warner)

56-62 I 522b (Destiny)

57 I 113b (Apocalypse)
III 137a (Last Judgment); 519b (Narratives)

57-62 III 147a (Laughter)

58 IV 103b (Pit)

59 II 261a (Form and Structure of the Q)
V 170a, 172a (Sūra)

60 III 146b, 147a, 147b, 148a (Laughter)
V 472b (Weeping)

60-62 III 149a (Laughter)

62 II 142b (Exhortations)
IV 470b (Rhetoric and the Q); 532a (Satanic Verses)
V 170b (Sūra); 555b (Worship)

Sūrat al-Qamar (54)

I 235b (Blasphemy)
III 200b (Literary Structures of the Q); 213a (Literature and the Q); 398a (Miracles); 519a (Narratives); 535a (Nature as Signs)
IV 474b (Rhetoric and the Q); 477b (Rhymed Prose); 591b (Shīʿa)

1 I 501a (Day, Times of)
II 148b (Expeditions and Battles); 392a (Ḥadīth and the Q)
III 137a, 138a (Last Judgment); 519a, 519b (Narratives)
V 288a (Time)

1-2 III 398a (Miracles)

1-8 II 143a (Exhortations)
III 519a (Narratives)

2 III 246a, 247a (Magic); 397b (Miracles)
IV 309b (Provocation); 478b (Rhymed Prose)
V 5b (Signs)

4-5 II 441a (History and the Q)

5 III 512a (Names of the Q)
IV 68b (Philosophy and the Q)

6 III 40a (Jihād)

6-8 II 558b (Invitation)

7 I 100a, 100b (Animal Life)
II 363b (Grammar and the Q)
III 209a (Literature and the Q)

8	I	500a (Day, Times of)
9	II	434a (History and the Q); 540a (Insanity)
	III	524a (Narratives); 542b (Noah)
	IV	112a (Poetry and Poets)
9-17	III	485b (Myths and Legends in the Q); 519a (Narratives)
9-42	III	381b (Messenger); 519a (Narratives)
	IV	320a (Punishment Stories)
11	I	398b (Conquest)
	V	371a (Trinity)
11-12	II	219a (Food and Drink)
	V	126a (Springs and Fountains); 464b (Water)
13	I	157b (Ark); 494b (Date Palm)
	II	544b, 546b (Instruments)
14	I	103b (Anthropomorphism)
	II	323b, 324b (God and his Attributes)
15	II	357b (Grammar and the Q)
	IV	425b (Remnant)
	V	5b (Signs)
17	II	82a (Everyday Life, Q In)
	III	113b (Language and Style of the Q); 510a (Names of the Q); 524b (Narratives)
17-40	III	372b (Memory)
18	III	540b (Noah)
18-22	III	519a (Narratives)
19	I	21b (ʿĀd); 52b, 54b (Air and Wind); 500b (Day, Times of)
	II	455b (Hot and Cold)
	V	280a (Time); 470b (Weather)
19-20	V	15b (Simile)
20	I	494b (Date Palm)
	II	305b (Geography)
	III	209a (Literature and the Q)
	V	16a (Simile)
22	II	82a (Everyday Life, Q In)
	III	113b (Language and Style of the Q); 510a (Names of the Q); 524b (Narratives)
23	III	540b (Noah)
23-31	I	149b (Archaeology and the Q)
	IV	521a (Ṣāliḥ)
23-32	II	308a (Geography)
	III	519a (Narratives)

24	II	43b (Error); 540b (Insanity)
	IV	521b (Ṣāliḥ)
	V	253a (Thamūd)
26	II	358b (Grammar and the Q)
	V	281a (Time)
27	IV	237b (Pre-1800 Preoccupations of Q Studies); 521b (Ṣāliḥ)
27-28	V	253a (Thamūd)
27-29	III	393a (Miracles)
27-31	I	287a (Camel)
28	III	549b (Numbers and Enumeration)
	IV	521b (Ṣāliḥ)
29	IV	521b (Ṣāliḥ)
	V	253a (Thamūd)
31	I	41b (Agriculture and Vegetation)
	II	212a (Fire)
	IV	454a (Reward and Punishment); 521b (Ṣāliḥ)
	V	253a (Thamūd); 545a (Word of God)
32	III	510a (Names of the Q); 524b (Narratives)
33-37	III	232a (Lot)
33-40	III	519a (Narratives)
34	I	52b, 54b (Air and Wind); 503b (Day, Times of)
	II	212b (Fire)
	III	417a, 418a (Morning)
	IV	530b, 531a (Sand)
	V	281a (Time)
34-35	III	379a (Mercy)
35	I	236b (Blessing)
36	V	460b (Warner)
37	II	444b (Homosexuality)
	III	393b (Miracles)
	V	132b (Strangers and Foreigners); 134a (Suffering)
38	I	502a, 503b, 504a (Day, Times of)
	III	416b, 417a, 418a (Morning)
	V	281a (Time)
40	III	113b (Language and Style of the Q); 510a (Names of the Q); 524b (Narratives)
41-42	III	519a (Narratives)
42	II	251b (Form and Structure of the Q)
43	I	465b (Covenant)
	II	504b (Immunity)
	V	458b (War)

43-55 II 143a (Exhortations)
III 519a (Narratives)

46 I 501a (Day, Times of)
III 137a (Last Judgment)
IV 434b (Resurrection)
V 287b (Time)

47 II 540b (Insanity)

48 II 210a (Fire); 414b, 415a (Hell and Hellfire)

49 I 448b (Cosmology)
II 328b (God and his Attributes)
III 334b (Measurement)
IV 85b (Philosophy and the Q)

49-50 I 475a, 475b (Creation)

50 III 138a (Last Judgment)
V 287b, 288a (Time); 545a (Word of God)

51 III 524b (Narratives)
IV 592a (Shīʿa)

51-53 IV 570b (Scrolls)

52 I 243b (Book)

52-53 III 191a (Literacy)
V 19a (Sin, Major and Minor)

53 V 558a (Writing and Writing Materials)

54 V 467a (Water of Paradise)

55 IV 14b (Paradise)

Sūrat al-Raḥmān (55)

I 230b (Biology as the Creation and Stages of Life); 322a (Chronology and the Q); 438b (Coral); 448a, 451b (Cosmology)
II 370b (Gratitude and Ingratitude)
III 199a (Literary Structures of the Q); 213a (Literature and the Q); 334b (Measurement); 523b (Narratives)
IV 3a, 7a, 7b (Pairs and Pairing); 15b (Paradise); 394a (Reflection and Deliberation); 474b (Rhetoric and the Q); 477b, 481a (Rhymed Prose); 495b (Ritual and the Q)
V 11b (Silk); 106b (Spatial Relations); 124b (Springs and Fountains); 168b, 169b (Sūra); 265b (Theology and the Q); 426b (Verse)

1 V 393a (Turkish Literature and the Q)

1-2 III 191a (Literacy)

1-3 IV 470b (Rhetoric and the Q)

1-4	III	103a (Knowledge and Learning); 189b (Literacy)
	IV	479a (Rhymed Prose)
1-7	IV	177b (Popular and Talismanic Uses of the Q)
1-15	I	473b (Creation)
1-27	I	189a (Authority)
2	V	201a (Teaching)
3	I	476a (Creation)
3-4	III	124b (Language and Style of the Q)
4	I	435a (Conversion)
	III	118b, 124b (Language and Style of the Q)
	V	201a (Teaching)
5	I	500b (Day, Times of)
	IV	108a (Planets and Stars)
	V	163a (Sun); 283b (Time)
6	I	254b (Bowing and Prostration)
	II	369b (Grasses)
	IV	72a (Philosophy and the Q); 107a (Planets and Stars)
	V	359a (Tree)
7	II	545a (Instruments)
	III	334b (Measurement)
7-9	III	66a (Judgment); 334b (Measurement)
8	III	334b (Measurement)
9	III	276a (Markets); 334b, 335b (Measurement)
10-13	I	448b (Cosmology)
11	I	494b (Date Palm)
	II	217b (Food and Drink); 305a (Geography)
	IV	18a (Paradise)
11-12	III	573a (Odors and Smells)
12	I	41b, 44a (Agriculture and Vegetation)
	II	3b (Earth); 305b (Geography)
	III	573a (Odors and Smells)
	V	62b (Smell)
13	IV	474b (Rhetoric and the Q)
14	I	231a (Biology as the Creation and Stages of Life); 339b (Clay); 446a, 450a (Cosmology); 476a (Creation)
	II	4a (Earth); 328a (God and his Attributes)
	III	354b (Medicine and the Q); 383b (Metals and Minerals)
	V	14b (Simile)
14-15	I	24a (Adam and Eve); 451b (Cosmology)

15 I 446a, 446b (Cosmology); 476a (Creation); 527a (Devil)
II 328a (God and his Attributes)
III 48b (Jinn)
IV 216b (Prayer); 336b (Races)

17 III 230a (Lord)
IV 4b, 7b (Pairs and Pairing)
V 52b (Sirius); 282b (Time)

19 I 443a, 446a (Cosmology)
IV 7a (Pairs and Pairing)

19-20 I 445b (Cosmology)
V 464a (Water)

19-22 I 438b (Coral)

20 I 203b (Barrier); 204b (Barzakh)
II 229a (Foreign Vocabulary)

22 I 96b (Animal Life); 438b, 439a (Coral)
II 467b (Hunting and Fishing)
III 384a (Metals and Minerals)

24 II 353b (Grammar and the Q); 528a (Inimitability)
V 14b (Simile); 412a (Vehicles); 464a (Water)

26 V 393b (Turkish Literature and the Q)

26-27 I 92a (Angel); 264b (Burial)
II 29b (Epigraphy); 47b (Eschatology); 160a (Face of God); 323b (God and his Attributes)
III 389a (Michael)
IV 83b (Philosophy and the Q)
V 340a (Transitoriness); 554a (World)

27 II 53a (Eschatology); 315b (Glory)
IV 221a (Prayer)
V 265b (Theology and the Q)

29 I 443b (Cosmology)
V 274b (Theology and the Q)

29-38 V 265b (Theology and the Q)

33 I 190a (Authority); 546a (Dog)
II 411b (Heaven and Sky)
III 43b, 46b (Jinn)
V 376a (Trips and Voyages)

34-37 II 456b (Houris)

35 II 546a (Instruments)
III 383a (Metals and Minerals)

37	I	362a (Colors)
	II	411b (Heaven and Sky)
	V	15b (Simile)
39	III	46b, 47b (Jinn)
	IV	3a (Pairs and Pairing); 478b (Rhymed Prose)
	V	120a (Spiritual Beings)
41	II	199a (Feet)
	IV	3a (Pairs and Pairing)
43	IV	3a (Pairs and Pairing)
43-44	II	415a (Hell and Hellfire)
44	II	50a (Eschatology); 211a (Fire)
	IV	3a (Pairs and Pairing)
46	II	51a (Eschatology); 196b (Fear); 283a (Garden)
	IV	3a, 7b (Pairs and Pairing); 15a (Paradise)
	V	123b, 124a (Springs and Fountains)
48	IV	3a (Pairs and Pairing)
50	IV	3a (Pairs and Pairing)
	V	121b, 123a, 124a (Springs and Fountains); 464b (Water)
52	IV	3a, 6a (Pairs and Pairing); 18a (Paradise); 581a (Sex and Sexuality)
54	I	220b (Belief and Unbelief); 494b (Date Palm)
	II	234a (Foreign Vocabulary); 276a (Furniture and Furnishings)
	IV	3a (Pairs and Pairing); 18a (Paradise)
	V	12a (Silk)
56	II	284a (Garden); 456a, 456b (Houris)
	III	46b (Jinn); 131a (Language and Style of the Q)
	IV	3a (Pairs and Pairing); 478b (Rhymed Prose); 585a (Sex and Sexuality)
	V	524a (Women and the Q)
56-58	III	493a (Myths and Legends in the Q)
	V	106b (Spatial Relations)
58	I	96a (Animal Life); 439a (Coral)
	III	384a (Metals and Minerals)
	IV	3a (Pairs and Pairing)
60	II	61b (Ethics and the Q)
	IV	3a (Pairs and Pairing)
62	IV	3a, 7b (Pairs and Pairing); 13b (Paradise)
	V	123b, 124a (Springs and Fountains)
64	I	41b (Agriculture and Vegetation); 362b, 364b (Colors)
	II	283b (Garden)
	IV	3a (Pairs and Pairing)

66 v 123a, 124a (Springs and Fountains)

68 I 44b (Agriculture and Vegetation)
II 217b (Food and Drink); 283b (Garden); 305b (Geography); 364b (Grammar and the Q)
III 360b (Medicine and the Q)
IV 3a (Pairs and Pairing); 18a (Paradise)

70 IV 3a (Pairs and Pairing)

72 I 166a (Art and Architecture and the Q)
II 154a (Eyes); 284a (Garden); 456a, 457a (Houris)
III 139b (Last Judgment)
IV 3a (Pairs and Pairing); 585a (Sex and Sexuality)
V 12a (Silk); 235b (Tents and Tent Pegs); 524a (Women and the Q)

74 III 46b (Jinn)
IV 3a (Pairs and Pairing); 478b (Rhymed Prose)
V 524a (Women and the Q)

76 I 362b (Colors)
II 276a (Furniture and Furnishings); 284a (Garden)
IV 3a (Pairs and Pairing); 18a (Paradise)
V 12b (Silk)

78 I 208b (Basmala)
II 315b (Glory); 321b (God and his Attributes)
IV 220b (Prayer); 470b (Rhetoric and the Q)

Sūrat al-Wāqiʿa (56)

III 66b, 67a (Judgment); 272a (Manuscripts of the Q)
IV 2b (Pairs and Pairing); 15b (Paradise); 172b (Popular and Talismanic Uses of the Q)
V 11b (Silk); 168b (Sūra); 183a (Symbolic Imagery)

1 III 137a (Last Judgment)
IV 103a (Pit)
V 283a (Time)

1-6 II 257b, 258a (Form and Structure of the Q)
IV 468a (Rhetoric and the Q)

1-56 I 112a (Apocalypse)

2 IV 103b (Pit)

4 V 283a (Time)

4-5 I 113a (Apocalypse)

7 II 258a (Form and Structure of the Q)
V 83b (Soul)

7-44 III 207a (Literature and the Q)

8	III	177a, 177b (Left Hand and Right Hand)
	IV	15b (Paradise); 102a, 102b (Pit); 454b (Reward and Punishment)
8-9	II	365b (Grammar and the Q)
	IV	2a (Pairs and Pairing)
	V	183b (Symbolic Imagery)
9	II	355a (Grammar and the Q)
	III	177a, 177b (Left Hand and Right Hand)
	IV	102a, 102b (Pit); 454b (Reward and Punishment)
10	IV	15b (Paradise); 332b (Quraysh)
	V	123b (Springs and Fountains)
10-11	IV	16a (Paradise)
	V	47b (Sīra and the Q)
10-26	IV	16b (Paradise)
	V	190b (Table)
10-38	IV	3a (Pairs and Pairing)
11	III	204a (Literary Structures of the Q)
	IV	15b (Paradise); 220a (Prayer)
11-14	IV	2b (Pairs and Pairing)
12	II	282b (Garden)
	III	533a (Nature as Signs)
12-18	I	213b (Beauty)
15	I	166a (Art and Architecture and the Q)
	II	276a (Furniture and Furnishings); 284a (Garden)
	IV	18a (Paradise)
17	I	301b (Children)
	II	52a (Eschatology); 284a (Garden); 445a (Homosexuality)
	III	139b (Last Judgment)
	IV	18a (Paradise); 585a (Sex and Sexuality)
	V	12a (Silk); 549a (Work)
17-26	III	204a (Literary Structures of the Q)
18	I	490b (Cups and Vessels)
	II	219a (Food and Drink); 276a (Furniture and Furnishings); 284a (Garden)
	IV	18b (Paradise)
	V	121b (Springs and Fountains)
18-19	V	482a (Wine)
19	II	556a, 556b (Intoxicants)
	V	125a (Springs and Fountains)
20	IV	18a (Paradise)
21	I	97a (Animal Life)
	II	218b (Food and Drink)

22 II 154a (Eyes); 284a (Garden); 348b (Grammar and the Q); 456a (Houris)
III 139b (Last Judgment)
IV 18a (Paradise); 585a (Sex and Sexuality)
V 12a (Silk); 123a (Springs and Fountains); 524a (Women and the Q)

22-23 V 14a (Simile)

23 I 96a (Animal Life)
II 456b (Houris)
V 123a, 125b (Springs and Fountains)

25 IV 482b (Rhymed Prose)

25-26 I 32a (African Literature)

26 II 91b (Everyday Life, Q In); 283b (Garden)
IV 17b (Paradise)

27 II 365b (Grammar and the Q)
III 178b (Left Hand and Right Hand)
IV 15b (Paradise); 102a, 102b (Pit); 454b (Reward and Punishment); 469a (Rhetoric and the Q)
V 123b (Springs and Fountains)

27-38 V 183b (Symbolic Imagery)

27-40 III 177b (Left Hand and Right Hand)

27-56 IV 2a (Pairs and Pairing)

28 II 305b (Geography)
III 532a (Nature as Signs)

28-29 III 128b (Language and Style of the Q)
V 360b (Tree)

28-30 II 283b (Garden)

28-38 IV 15b (Paradise)

29 I 41b (Agriculture and Vegetation)
III 532b (Nature as Signs)
V 393a (Turkish Literature and the Q)

30 IV 18b (Paradise)
V 393a, 393b (Turkish Literature and the Q)

32 IV 18a (Paradise)

34 II 276a (Furniture and Furnishings)
IV 18a (Paradise)

34-35 II 284a (Garden)

35-38 II 456b (Houris)

36 I 501b (Day, Times of)
V 524a (Women and the Q)

36-37 IV 18a (Paradise)

37	II	284a (Garden)
	V	570a (Youth and Old Age)
38	III	177b (Left Hand and Right Hand)
	IV	15b (Paradise)
41	III	177a, 177b (Left Hand and Right Hand)
	IV	102a, 102b (Pit)
41-42	II	455b (Hot and Cold)
	IV	469a (Rhetoric and the Q)
41-44	V	65a (Smoke)
41-56	II	558b (Invitation)
	III	177a (Left Hand and Right Hand)
	V	183b (Symbolic Imagery)
42	II	211a (Fire); 415a (Hell and Hellfire)
	V	465a (Water)
42-43	II	50a (Eschatology)
	III	140b (Last Judgment)
42-44	V	133a (Suffering)
43	II	415a (Hell and Hellfire)
	V	65a (Smoke)
43-44	II	211b (Fire)
44	II	455b (Hot and Cold)
45	IV	455b (Reward and Punishment)
45-48	II	258b (Form and Structure of the Q)
46	III	563b (Oaths)
47	II	4b (Earth)
	IV	455b (Reward and Punishment)
47-49	IV	442a (Revelation and Inspiration)
50	I	500a (Day, Times of)
	IV	228a (Prayer)
	V	288a (Time)
51	III	177a (Left Hand and Right Hand)
	IV	455b (Reward and Punishment)
	V	572a (Zaqqūm)
52	I	42a (Agriculture and Vegetation)
	II	211a (Fire); 305a (Geography)
	III	533a (Nature as Signs)
	V	358b, 359a, 359b (Tree); 571a (Zaqqūm)
52-56	I	222a (Belief and Unbelief)
54	II	211a (Fire)

54-55 III 531b (Nature as Signs)

55 I 99b (Animal Life)
II 211a (Fire)

56 III 136b (Last Judgment)

57 I 476a (Creation)

57-62 I 472a, 472b, 473b (Creation)

60 II 268a (Freedom and Predestination)
IV 486a (Ritual and the Q)

60-62 III 184a (Life)

61 I 91b (Angel)

62 II 355a (Grammar and the Q)

63-64 I 40b (Agriculture and Vegetation)

63-65 II 3b (Earth)

65 I 42a (Agriculture and Vegetation)
II 358a (Grammar and the Q); 369b (Grasses)

68-69 II 508a (Impotence)
V 462b (Water)

70 III 530a (Nature as Signs)

70-73 II 211b (Fire)

71 II 305a (Geography)

71-73 II 213a (Fire)

72 I 478b (Creation)
V 359a (Tree)

73 II 142b (Exhortations)
III 60a (Joy and Misery); 529a (Nature as Signs)

74 I 208b (Basmala)
IV 470b (Rhetoric and the Q)

75 II 257b (Form and Structure of the Q)
IV 108b (Planets and Stars); 217a (Prayer)

75-76 III 562a (Oaths)

76-79 IV 225b (Prayer)

76-80 II 276b (Furniture and Furnishings)
III 312a (Material Culture and the Q)

77 II 447b (Honor)
III 267b (Manuscripts of the Q); 506b, 513a (Names of the Q)

77-80 III 189b (Literacy); 266b (Manuscripts of the Q); 600b (Ornamentation and Illumination)
V 422a (Verse)

78 II 412a (Heavenly Book); 423b (Hidden and the Hidden)
IV 261b (Preserved Tablet)

79 I 343b (Cleanliness and Ablution)
III 601a (Ornamentation and Illumination)
IV 492a (Ritual and the Q)

80 IV 443b, 446a (Revelation and Inspiration)
V 105b (Spatial Relations); 422a (Verse)

81-87 II 252b (Form and Structure of the Q)

82 II 268a (Freedom and Predestination)

83 I 506b (Death and the Dead)
II 45b (Eschatology); 258a (Form and Structure of the Q)

84-87 IV 486a (Ritual and the Q)

88-94 II 252b, 258b (Form and Structure of the Q)
V 252a (Textual Criticism of the Q)

89 V 62b (Smell)

90 IV 15b (Paradise)

90-91 III 177b (Left Hand and Right Hand)

90-94 V 183b (Symbolic Imagery)

91 III 178b (Left Hand and Right Hand)
IV 15b (Paradise)

92-94 III 177a (Left Hand and Right Hand)

93 II 211a (Fire)

95 V 387b (Truth)

96 I 208b (Basmala)
III 443a (Muḥammad)
V 170b (Sūra)

SŪRAT AL-ḤADĪD (57)

I 322a (Chronology and the Q)
II 264a (Form and Structure of the Q); 394a (Ḥadīth and the Q)
III 383a (Metals and Minerals)
V 174b (Sūra)

1 IV 4b (Pairs and Pairing)

2 I 170b (Art and Architecture and the Q)
III 299b (Material Culture and the Q)
IV 4b (Pairs and Pairing)

3 II 54a (Eternity); 320b (God and his Attributes); 418b (Hell and Hellfire); 434b (History and the Q)

IV 4b (Pairs and Pairing)
V 554a (World)

4 I 443b (Cosmology); 473b, 476a (Creation)
II 325b (God and his Attributes); 410b (Heaven and Sky); 433a (History and the Q)
III 46a (Jinn); 202a (Literary Structures of the Q)
IV 63b (Persian Literature and the Q); 82a (Philosophy and the Q)
V 265a (Theology and the Q); 279b, 287a (Time)

6 II 550b (Intention)
V 280b (Time)

7 I 480b (Creeds)
II 450a (Hospitality and Courtesy)
IV 186a (Possession and Possessions)

8 I 437a (Conversion); 464b (Covenant)

9 II 497b (Illiteracy)
III 186a (Light)
IV 5a, 5b (Pairs and Pairing); 286a (Proof); 293a (Prophets and Prophethood)

10 I 399a, 400a (Conquest)
II 144a (Expeditions and Battles)
III 37b (Jihād)
IV 30b (Path or Way); 458b (Reward and Punishment)
V 457a (War)

10-11 V 269b (Theology and the Q)

11 III 209a (Literature and the Q)
IV 6b (Pairs and Pairing); 457a (Reward and Punishment)
V 457a (War)

12 II 166b (Faith); 341b (Good News)
III 177a (Left Hand and Right Hand)
IV 18b (Paradise)

13 I 149b (Archaeology and the Q); 556a (Druzes)
II 415b, 418a (Hell and Hellfire); 468b, 470a (Hypocrites and Hypocrisy)
III 5a, 6a (Jerusalem); 142a (Last Judgment)
IV 522b (Salvation)

13-15 II 166b (Faith)

14 I 526a (Devil)

15 I 344b (Clients and Clientage)
IV 103b, 104a (Pit); 523b (Salvation)

16 II 407a, 407b, 408a (Heart)
III 335a (Measurement)
IV 146a (Politics and the Q); 230a (Prayer)
V 241b (Textual Criticism of the Q); 288b (Time); 475a (Weights and Measures)

17	II	3a (Earth); 303a (Geography)
18	I	64b (Almsgiving)
	II	8b (Economics); 351b, 366b (Grammar and the Q)
	IV	6b (Pairs and Pairing); 457a (Reward and Punishment)
	V	457a (War); 524a (Women and the Q)
19	III	282a (Martyrs)
	IV	1b (Pairs and Pairing)
	V	486b (Wish and Desire); 490b, 491a (Witness to Faith)
20	I	42a (Agriculture and Vegetation); 213a (Beauty); 241b (Boast); 363a (Colors)
	II	3b (Earth); 36b (Epigraphy); 245a (Forgiveness); 369b (Grasses)
	III	59b (Joy and Misery); 182a (Life)
	IV	5a (Pairs and Pairing); 10b (Parable)
	V	16a (Simile); 340a (Transitoriness); 468a (Wealth); 470b (Weather)
21	II	283b (Garden); 330b (God and his Attributes)
	III	333b (Measurement); 379b (Mercy)
22	I	244b (Book); 478b (Creation)
	II	269b (Freedom and Predestination)
22-23	I	523a (Destiny)
22-24	I	395a (Conceit)
23	I	521a (Despair)
	III	61a (Joy and Misery)
	V	486b (Wish and Desire)
23-24	V	468b (Wealth)
24	IV	6a (Pairs and Pairing)
25	I	245a (Book)
	II	92a (Everyday Life, Q In); 545a (Instruments)
	III	37b (Jihād); 184b (Life); 334b (Measurement); 383a (Metals and Minerals)
	IV	5b (Pairs and Pairing); 126b, 147a (Politics and the Q); 297a (Prophets and Prophethood)
26	I	7b (Abraham); 245b (Book)
	IV	297b (Prophets and Prophethood)
	V	302a (Torah)
26-27	II	199b (Feet)
	III	7b (Jesus)
27	I	123b (Apostle); 183b (Asceticism); 219a (Belief and Unbelief); 244b (Book); 311b, 314a (Christians and Christianity); 478b (Creation)
	II	342a (Gospel); 408b (Heart); 536b (Innovation)
	III	8a (Jesus); 378a (Mercy); 406a, 406b, 407a (Monasticism and Monks); 502b (Names of the Prophet)
	IV	412b (Religious Pluralism and the Q)
	V	139a (Ṣūfism and the Q); 316b (Tradition and Custom); 533b (Women and the Q)

28 III 379b (Mercy)
IV 6b (Pairs and Pairing); 458b (Reward and Punishment)

29 I 222b (Belief and Unbelief)
II 323b, 325a (God and his Attributes); 345a (Grace)
III 24a (Jews and Judaism)
IV 41b (People of the Book)

Sūrat al-Mujādala (58)

V 174b (Sūra); 535a (Women and the Q)

1 I 511b, 513a (Debate and Disputation)
II 1b (Ears)
IV 5b (Pairs and Pairing); 575a (Seeing and Hearing)
V 272b (Theology and the Q)

2 III 563a (Oaths)
IV 20a (Parents)
V 438a (Virtues and Vices, Commanding and Forbidding)

2-3 III 563a (Oaths)
IV 582a (Sex and Sexuality)

2-4 III 280a (Marriage and Divorce)

3 I 253a (Boundaries and Precepts); 289a (Captives)
III 158b, 159a (Law and the Q)
V 57b (Slaves and Slavery)

3-4 I 187b (Atonement)
II 180b, 184b (Fasting)
III 563a (Oaths)

4 I 253a (Boundaries and Precepts); 354b (Collection of the Q)
II 216b (Food and Drink)
III 158b (Law and the Q)
IV 208b (Poverty and the Poor)
V 285a (Time); 476a (Weights and Measures)

5 III 577a (Opposition to Muḥammad)
IV 309b (Provocation); 453b (Reward and Punishment)
V 4b (Signs)

6 I 480b (Creeds)
IV 435b (Resurrection)
V 490a (Witness to Faith)

7 II 364a (Grammar and the Q)
III 550a (Numbers and Enumeration)
V 137b (Ṣūfism and the Q); 493a (Witnessing and Testifying)

8 I 537b (Disobedience)
II 98a (Evil Deeds)
III 31b (Jews and Judaism)

8-9	I	537b (Disobedience)
	V	19a (Sin, Major and Minor)
9	I	537b (Disobedience)
	II	60b, 63b (Ethics and the Q); 98a (Evil Deeds)
	IV	91a (Piety)
10	II	365a (Grammar and the Q)
	V	379a, 379b (Trust and Patience); 487a (Wish and Desire)
11	IV	538a, 538b, 539a (Scholar)
	V	191b (Talent); 203b (Teaching)
12	I	65b (Almsgiving); 343b (Cleanliness and Ablution)
	II	450a (Hospitality and Courtesy)
	III	378b (Mercy)
	IV	496b (Ritual and the Q)
	V	198a, 198b (Taxation)
12-13	I	220a (Belief and Unbelief)
13	V	197b (Taxation)
14	I	93a (Anger)
16	III	564a (Oaths)
17	I	221b (Belief and Unbelief)
	V	468a (Wealth)
18	I	480b (Creeds)
	III	563b (Oaths)
	IV	435b (Resurrection)
19	I	380a (Community and Society in the Q)
	II	72a (Ethics and the Q); 430b (History and the Q)
	III	47a (Jinn); 225b (Literature and the Q)
	IV	25a (Parties and Factions); 118a (Polemic and Polemical Language)
	V	120b (Spiritual Beings)
21	II	92a (Everyday Life, Q In)
	IV	5b (Pairs and Pairing); 211a (Power and Impotence)
21-22	I	380a (Community and Society in the Q)
22	I	82a (Anatomy); 220b, 224b (Belief and Unbelief); 262b (Brother and Brotherhood); 380a (Community and Society in the Q)
	II	72a (Ethics and the Q); 430b (History and the Q)
	III	99b (Kinship); 136b (Last Judgment); 235b (Love and Affection); 238b (Loyalty); 293b (Mary)
	IV	17a (Paradise); 25a (Parties and Factions); 523a (Salvation)
	V	115b (Spirit); 364a (Tribes and Clans); 445b (Vision and Blindness)

Sūrat al-Ḥashr (59)

I 264a (Burial)
II 264a (Form and Structure of the Q); 394a (Ḥadīth and the Q)
III 29b (Jews and Judaism)
V 174b (Sūra); 426b (Verse)

1 IV 4b (Pairs and Pairing)

1-3 III 456b (Muḥammad)

1-4 III 28b (Jews and Judaism)

1-15 III 580a (Opposition to Muḥammad)

1-24 I 320a (Chronology and the Q)

2 I 163b (Art and Architecture and the Q); 222b (Belief and Unbelief)
II 198a (Fear); 402a (Hand); 441b (History and the Q)
III 499a, 499b (Naḍīr, Banū al-)
IV 41b (People of the Book); 70b (Philosophy and the Q); 120b (Polemic and Polemical Language); 308a (Protection); 335a (Qurayẓa, Banū al-); 393b, 394b (Reflection and Deliberation); 583b (Sex and Sexuality)
V 272b (Theology and the Q); 444b (Vision); 459a (War)

2-4 II 459b (House, Domestic and Divine)

2-5 II 262b (Form and Structure of the Q)
V 175b (Sūra)

2-15 III 499a (Naḍīr, Banū al-)
IV 406a (Religious Pluralism and the Q)

3 I 244b (Book)

4 II 358a (Grammar and the Q)
III 454b (Muḥammad)

5 I 494b (Date Palm)
III 42a (Jihād); 498b (Naḍīr, Banū al-)
IV 457a (Reward and Punishment)

6 I 94b, 98b (Animal Life)
II 149a (Expeditions and Battles)
III 43b (Jinn)
V 194a (Taxation); 374a (Trips and Voyages); 411b (Vehicles)

6-7 I 251b (Booty)

6-8 III 42a (Jihād)

6-10 III 499a (Naḍīr, Banū al-)

7 I 252a (Booty)
II 7b (Economics); 176b (Family of the Prophet)
III 166b (Law and the Q); 447b (Muḥammad); 577a (Opposition to Muḥammad)

	IV	49a (People of the House); 145a (Politics and the Q); 208b (Poverty and the Poor)
	V	194a, 194b, 195a, 196b (Taxation); 436a (Virtue)
7-9	V	195b (Taxation)
8	IV	209a (Poverty and the Poor); 333a (Quraysh)
8-9	V	375b (Trips and Voyages)
9	I	262b (Brother and Brotherhood); 338a (City)
	II	7b (Economics); 15a (Emigrants and Helpers)
	IV	308a (Protection); 523a (Salvation)
	V	82b (Soul)
9-10	V	47b (Sīra and the Q)
10	I	263a (Brother and Brotherhood)
	II	554b (Intercession)
	IV	5b (Pairs and Pairing); 332b (Quraysh)
11	I	222b (Belief and Unbelief)
	II	150b (Expeditions and Battles); 468b (Hypocrites and Hypocrisy)
	III	578a (Opposition to Muḥammad)
	IV	42a (People of the Book)
	V	456a, 458a (War)
11-12	II	469b (Hypocrites and Hypocrisy)
	III	28b (Jews and Judaism)
12	I	80b (Anatomy)
	V	393b (Turkish Literature and the Q)
13	II	197b (Fear)
14	I	458b (Courage)
	III	28b (Jews and Judaism)
	IV	42a (People of the Book); 583b (Sex and Sexuality)
15	IV	324b (Qaynuqāʿ, Banū)
16	I	526a (Devil)
	II	196b (Fear)
18	II	164b (Faith)
	V	281a (Time)
19	IV	432a (Responsibility)
20	IV	117a (Polemic and Polemical Language); 523a (Salvation)
	V	430a (Victory)
21	III	484b (Myths and Legends in the Q)
	IV	171b (Popular and Talismanic Uses of the Q)
21-24	III	305a (Material Culture and the Q)
22	I	209a (Basmala)
	IV	4a (Pairs and Pairing); 537b (Scholar)

v 393b (Turkish Literature and the Q); 445a (Vision and Blindness); 501a (Witnessing and Testifying)

22-24 II 94a (Everyday Life, Q In); 319b (God and his Attributes)
III 306a, 312a (Material Culture and the Q)
IV 380a (Recitation of the Q)

23 I 159b (Arrogance); 218b (Belief and Unbelief)
II 164b, 171a (Faith); 276b (Furniture and Furnishings); 320b, 321b (God and his Attributes)
III 91b (Kings and Rulers); 210b (Literature and the Q)
IV 34a (Peace); 220a, 220b (Prayer); 263b, 264b (Pride); 282b (Profane and Sacred); 307a (Protection)

24 I 472a, 478b (Creation)
II 319b, 320b, 327a, 327b (God and his Attributes); 474a (Iconoclasm)
IV 4b (Pairs and Pairing)

Sūrat al-Mumtaḥana (60)

II 538a (Inquisition)
V 174b (Sūra); 362b (Trial); 457b (War); 535a (Women and the Q)

1 I 224b (Belief and Unbelief)
II 18b (Emigration)
III 36b (Jihād); 235b (Love and Affection); 449a (Muḥammad)
IV 4a (Pairs and Pairing); 29a, 30b (Path or Way)
V 458b (War); 486b (Wish and Desire)

1-2 II 23b (Enemies)

2 II 335b (Good and Evil)
III 579a (Opposition to Muḥammad)
V 456a (War)

3 I 221b (Belief and Unbelief); 516b (Decision)
II 174b, 175a (Family)
IV 21a (Parents)
V 522a, 522b (Womb)

4 I 6b, 7a (Abraham); 193a (Āzar)
II 439a (History and the Q)
III 494a (Myths and Legends in the Q)
IV 21a (Parents); 427b (Repentance and Penance)
V 2b (Signs); 287a (Time)

6 II 439a (History and the Q); 449a, 449b (Hope)
III 136b (Last Judgment)
IV 6a (Pairs and Pairing)

7 II 275a (Friends and Friendship)

7-8 II 74a (Ethics and the Q)
III 236a (Love and Affection)

8 II 60b (Ethics and the Q)
III 579a (Opposition to Muḥammad)
V 458b (War); 486b (Wish and Desire)

8-9 I 202b (Barēlwīs)
III 40a (Jihād); 238b, 239a, 239b, 240a, 241a (Loyalty)

9 III 41b (Jihād); 449b (Muḥammad)

10 I 258a, 258b (Bridewealth); 299a (Chastity)
II 321a (God and his Attributes); 374b (Guardianship); 538a (Inquisition)
III 162b (Law and the Q); 277a, 277b (Marriage and Divorce)
IV 452a (Reward and Punishment); 537b (Scholar)
V 313b (Trade and Commerce); 362b (Trial)

12 I 234b (Birth Control); 301b (Children); 466a (Covenant); 537b (Disobedience)
II 20a (Emigration); 511b (Infanticide); 538a (Inquisition)
III 447b (Muḥammad); 568b (Obedience)
IV 580b (Sex and Sexuality)
V 255b (Theft); 524a (Women and the Q)

13 I 93a (Anger); 521b (Despair)
III 33a (Jews and Judaism); 217b (Literature and the Q)

SŪRAT AL-ṢAFF (61)

I 322a (Chronology and the Q)
II 264a (Form and Structure of the Q); 394a (Ḥadīth and the Q)
IV 59a (Persian Literature and the Q); 246a, 246b (Pre-1800 Preoccupations of Q Studies); 348b (Ranks and Orders)
V 174b (Sūra); 426b (Verse)

1 III 299a (Material Culture and the Q)
IV 4b (Pairs and Pairing)

2-3 II 71a (Ethics and the Q)
V 221b (Teaching and Preaching the Q)

3 III 321b (Material Culture and the Q)

4 I 397b (Conquest); 460a, 461a (Courage)
III 42a (Jihād); 558a (Numismatics); 577b (Opposition to Muḥammad)
IV 30a (Path or Way); 348b, 349a (Ranks and Orders)
V 457a (War)

5 II 59a (Ethics and the Q)
IV 299b (Prophets and Prophethood)

5-6 III 382a (Messenger)

6 I 115a (Apologetics); 223a (Belief and Unbelief); 303a, 306a (Children of Israel)

	II	341a, 341b (Good News); 342a (Gospel); 558a (Invitation)
	III	7b, 8a, 16a, 16b, 17a (Jesus); 25b (Jews and Judaism); 246a (Magic); 265b (Manuscripts of the Q); 445a, 445b (Muḥammad); 501b, 502a (Names of the Prophet)
	IV	259a (Pre-Islamic Arabia and the Q); 286b (Proof); 296a, 299a (Prophets and Prophethood); 413b (Religious Pluralism and the Q); 439a (Revelation and Inspiration)
	V	300b (Torah); 533b (Women and the Q)
7	III	181a (Lie)
	IV	309b (Provocation); 404a (Religious Pluralism and the Q)
8	I	82b (Anatomy)
	II	326b (God and his Attributes)
	III	187a (Light)
9	I	397b (Conquest)
	III	299a, 300a (Material Culture and the Q); 557a, 558a (Numismatics)
	IV	300a (Prophets and Prophethood); 416a (Religious Pluralism and the Q)
	V	458b (War); 489b (Witness to Faith); 503b (Witnessing and Testifying)
10	III	276a (Markets)
	V	457a (War)
10-12	III	307a (Material Culture and the Q)
10-13	III	41a (Jihād)
11	I	437b (Conversion)
	II	340a (Good Deeds)
	III	37a (Jihād)
	IV	30a (Path or Way); 455a (Reward and Punishment)
	V	83a (Soul); 501b (Witnessing and Testifying)
11-12	IV	17a (Paradise)
12	I	165b (Art and Architecture and the Q)
	II	282b (Garden)
	IV	18b (Paradise); 522b (Salvation)
	V	393b (Turkish Literature and the Q)
13	I	399a (Conquest)
	II	37b (Epigraphy); 144a (Expeditions and Battles)
	III	304b, 308a, 322a, 322b, 326b (Material Culture and the Q)
	V	393a, 393b (Turkish Literature and the Q)
13-14	III	313a (Material Culture and the Q)
14	I	123a (Apostle); 311a (Christians and Christianity)
	II	23b (Enemies)
	III	7b, 8a (Jesus); 382b (Messenger)
	IV	26b (Parties and Factions)
	V	430a (Victory); 533b (Women and the Q)

Sūrat al-Jumuʿa (62)

I 322a (Chronology and the Q)
II 264a (Form and Structure of the Q); 394a (Ḥadīth and the Q)
III 304b (Material Culture and the Q)
IV 172b (Popular and Talismanic Uses of the Q)
V 174b (Sūra); 426b (Verse)

1 II 321b (God and his Attributes)
III 91b (Kings and Rulers)
IV 4b (Pairs and Pairing); 282b (Profane and Sacred)
V 308a (Torah)

2 I 245b, 246a (Book); 325a (Chronology and the Q)
II 494b, 498b, 498b, 499b (Illiteracy)
III 190a, 191a (Literacy); 441a, 442b, 443a (Muḥammad)
IV 68b (Philosophy and the Q); 505a (Ritual Purity)
V 201b (Teaching); 399a, 400a (Ummī); 483b (Wisdom)

5 I 100a (Animal Life)
II 544b (Instruments)
III 24b (Jews and Judaism); 227b (Load or Burden)
IV 10b (Parable); 118a (Polemic and Polemical Language)
V 15b, 16a (Simile); 300b, 304b (Torah)

6 III 24a (Jews and Judaism)

8 III 536b (News)
IV 4a (Pairs and Pairing); 537b (Scholar)

9 I 328b (Chronology and the Q); 444a (Cosmology); 500b (Day, Times of)
II 271b, 272b (Friday Prayer); 354b (Grammar and the Q)
III 222a (Literature and the Q)
IV 226a (Prayer); 487a, 497a (Ritual and the Q)
V 175a (Sūra); 279a, 285b (Time)

9-10 I 36b (Afternoon)
II 272a (Friday Prayer)
IV 209a (Poverty and the Poor)

10 III 373b (Memory)

11 II 272b (Friday Prayer)
V 178b (Sustenance)

Sūrat al-Munāfiqūn (63)

I 322a (Chronology and the Q)
II 468b (Hypocrites and Hypocrisy)
III 304b (Material Culture and the Q)
V 174b (Sūra)

1 I 160b (Arrogance)
II 468b (Hypocrites and Hypocrisy)
III 181b (Lie)
IV 487a (Ritual and the Q)
V 502a (Witnessing and Testifying)

1-8 III 578a (Opposition to Muḥammad)

2 III 564a (Oaths)

3 I 82a (Anatomy); 226a (Belief and Unbelief)

3-4 II 66a (Ethics and the Q)

4 I 491b (Curse)
II 23b, 24a (Enemies); 197b (Fear)
V 15a (Simile); 447a (Vision and Blindness)

5 II 552a (Intercession)

5-6 II 245a (Forgiveness)
III 379b (Mercy)

6 II 510b (Indifference); 552a (Intercession)
IV 456a (Reward and Punishment)

7 II 468b (Hypocrites and Hypocrisy)

7-9 I 160b (Arrogance)

8 I 338a, 338b (City)
II 298b (Geography); 468b (Hypocrites and Hypocrisy)
III 367b (Medina)

9 IV 230b (Prayer)
V 468a (Wealth); 570a (Youth and Old Age)

10 IV 430a (Repentance and Penance); 486a (Ritual and the Q)

10-11 I 523a (Destiny)
V 289a, 289b (Time)

11 V 289a (Time)

Sūrat al-Taghābun (64)

I 301a (Cheating); 322a (Chronology and the Q)
II 264a (Form and Structure of the Q); 394a (Ḥadīth and the Q)
IV 246a (Pre-1800 Preoccupations of Q Studies)
V 174b (Sūra); 426b (Verse)

1 I 170b (Art and Architecture and the Q); 435a (Conversion)
III 299b (Material Culture and the Q)
IV 4b (Pairs and Pairing); 184b (Possession and Possessions); 214b (Praise)

2-3 I 472a (Creation)

3	I	446b (Cosmology)
	II	31a (Epigraphy); 323a (God and his Attributes)
	V	287a (Time)
4	II	550b (Intention)
	IV	4a (Pairs and Pairing)
	V	479b (Whisper)
5	III	518a, 524a (Narratives)
5-6	IV	320b (Punishment Stories)
6	IV	6a (Pairs and Pairing); 301a (Prophets and Prophethood)
7	IV	442a (Revelation and Inspiration)
8	II	326b (God and his Attributes)
	III	186b (Light)
	IV	293b (Prophets and Prophethood)
9	I	500a (Day, Times of)
	II	54b (Eternity)
	III	137a (Last Judgment)
	IV	18b (Paradise); 522b (Salvation)
	V	464b (Water); 475a (Weights and Measures)
11	I	435b (Conversion)
	IV	85b (Philosophy and the Q)
12	III	125a (Language and Style of the Q)
	V	379b (Trust and Patience)
13	V	379a, 379b (Trust and Patience)
14	II	23b (Enemies); 175a (Family); 197b (Fear); 244b (Forgiveness)
	III	40a (Jihād); 65b (Judgment); 378a (Mercy)
15	IV	289a (Property)
	V	362b (Trial); 468a (Wealth)
16	I	263a (Brother and Brotherhood)
	III	568b (Obedience)
	IV	308a (Protection); 523a (Salvation)
	V	82b (Soul); 468b (Wealth)
17	II	8b (Economics); 372b (Gratitude and Ingratitude)
	III	379b (Mercy); 549b (Numbers and Enumeration)
	IV	6a, 6b (Pairs and Pairing); 457a (Reward and Punishment)
18	IV	4a (Pairs and Pairing); 537b (Scholar)

Sūrat al-Ṭalāq (65)

III	96a (Kinship)
V	174b (Sūra); 528a (Women and the Q)

1 I 28b (Adultery and Fornication); 253a, 253b (Boundaries and Precepts); 299b (Chastity)
II 187a (Fate); 460a (House, Domestic and Divine); 536b (Innovation)
III 71a, 72a (Justice and Injustice); 280b (Marriage and Divorce)
IV 256a (Pre-Islamic Arabia and the Q); 580b, 581b (Sex and Sexuality)
V 179a (Sustenance); 453b, 454b (Waiting Period)

1-2 IV 32a (Patriarchy)
V 495a, 495b (Witnessing and Testifying)

2 II 76a (Ethics and the Q)
III 71b (Justice and Injustice); 136b (Last Judgment); 280a (Marriage and Divorce)
IV 7a (Pairs and Pairing); 17a (Paradise)
V 289a (Time); 454b (Waiting Period); 495b, 496b (Witnessing and Testifying); 528b (Women and the Q)

2-3 I 235a (Birth Control)

3 II 30b (Epigraphy)
III 322a (Material Culture and the Q); 334b (Measurement)

4 III 191a (Literacy); 280b (Marriage and Divorce)
IV 501b (Ritual Purity)
V 285b, 289a (Time); 453b, 454a, 454b (Waiting Period); 476a (Weights and Measures); 527b (Women and the Q)

6 I 302a (Children)
II 76a (Ethics and the Q); 175b (Family); 460a (House, Domestic and Divine)
III 106a, 107a (Lactation); 227b (Load or Burden); 280b (Marriage and Divorce)
IV 32a (Patriarchy); 452a (Reward and Punishment)
V 204b (Teaching); 454b (Waiting Period); 476b, 477a, 477b, 478a (Wet-Nursing); 528b (Women and the Q); 570a (Youth and Old Age)

6-7 III 252a (Maintenance and Upkeep)
V 477a (Wet-Nursing)

7 III 252b (Maintenance and Upkeep)
IV 432b (Responsibility)
V 393b (Turkish Literature and the Q); 454b (Waiting Period); 477a (Wet-Nursing)

10 V 393b (Turkish Literature and the Q)

10-11 IV 424a (Remembrance)

11 II 54b (Eternity)
III 186a (Light); 190a (Literacy); 441a (Muḥammad)
IV 5a (Pairs and Pairing); 18b (Paradise)
V 464b (Water)

12 I 24b (Adam and Eve); 445b (Cosmology); 478a (Creation)
II 410b (Heaven and Sky)
III 554b (Numerology)
IV 107b (Planets and Stars); 292b (Prophets and Prophethood); 537b (Scholar)

Sūrat al-Taḥrīm (66)

ii 264a (Form and Structure of the q)
v 174b (Sūra)

1 iii 174b (Lawful and Unlawful); 565b, 566a (Oaths)
iv 583b (Sex and Sexuality)
v 573a (Zealotry)

1-5 ii 344a (Gossip)
iii 448a (Muḥammad)
v 513a (Wives of the Prophet)

2 iii 172b (Lawful and Unlawful); 231a (Lord); 566a (Oaths)
iv 537b (Scholar)

3 ii 398a (Ḥafṣa)
iii 537a (News)
iv 5b (Pairs and Pairing)

3-4 iv 427a (Repentance and Penance)

4 ii 278a (Gabriel); 364a (Grammar and the q)
iii 454b (Muḥammad)
iv 217a (Prayer)

5 i 183a (Asceticism); 501b (Day, Times of)
ii 181a (Fasting)
iii 12b (Jesus)
iv 426b (Repentance and Penance)
v 374a (Trips and Voyages); 480a (Widow)

6 i 89b (Angel); 536b (Disobedience)
ii 174a (Family); 210b (Fire); 415a, 417b (Hell and Hellfire)
iii 383b (Metals and Minerals)
v 118a (Spiritual Beings); 129b (Stone)

8 iii 177a (Left Hand and Right Hand); 223b (Literature and the q); 440b (Muḥammad)
iv 426a (Repentance and Penance); 455a (Reward and Punishment)

9 i 461a (Courage)
ii 468b, 470a (Hypocrites and Hypocrisy)
iii 454b (Muḥammad)
iv 103b (Pit); 119b (Polemic and Polemical Language); 456a (Reward and Punishment)

10 i 59b (ʿĀʾisha bint Abī Bakr)
ii 418a (Hell and Hellfire)
iii 219a (Literature and the q); 232b (Lot); 379b (Mercy); 524b (Narratives); 541b (Noah)
v 373b (Trips and Voyages)

10-11 iv 68a (Pharaoh)

10-12 III 7b (Jesus)

11 I 519a (Deliverance)
IV 524a (Salvation)
V 532a (Women and the Q)

11-12 I 59a (ʿĀʾisha bint Abī Bakr)
III 81a (Khadīja); 290b, 293a (Mary)

12 I 1b (Aaron); 87a (Angel); 298b (Chastity)
II 291a (Gender); 439a (History and the Q); 509a (ʿImrān)
III 14a (Jesus); 293a, 293b (Mary); 519b (Narratives)
IV 581a, 583b (Sex and Sexuality)
V 81b (Soul); 114b (Spirit); 371b (Trinity); 533b (Women and the Q); 548a (Word of God)

Sūrat al-Mulk (67)

I 264a (Burial)
II 393b (Ḥadīth and the Q)
III 272a (Manuscripts of the Q); 324b (Material Culture and the Q)
IV 380a (Recitation of the Q); 495b (Ritual and the Q)

1 II 33b (Epigraphy)
III 93b (Kings and Rulers)
IV 184b (Possession and Possessions); 220b (Prayer)

1-2 IV 177b (Popular and Talismanic Uses of the Q)

1-3 IV 211b (Power and Impotence)

1-4 II 259a (Form and Structure of the Q)

2 I 473b (Creation)
III 200a (Literary Structures of the Q)
IV 6a (Pairs and Pairing)
V 133b (Suffering); 362b (Trial)

2-5 I 474a (Creation)

3 I 442a (Cosmology); 478a (Creation)
II 410b (Heaven and Sky)
III 184b (Life)
IV 107b (Planets and Stars)

3-4 V 446b (Vision and Blindness)

3-5 I 213a (Beauty)

5 I 442b (Cosmology); 544b (Divination)
II 276a (Furniture and Furnishings); 411a (Heaven and Sky); 547a (Instruments)
III 249b (Magic)
IV 108a (Planets and Stars)
V 105b (Spatial Relations); 130a (Stoning)

7	II	211a (Fire)
7-8	II	50a (Eschatology); 417b (Hell and Hellfire)
10	II	67b (Ethics and the Q)
10-11	I	298a (Chastisement and Punishment)
11	I	491b (Curse)
	III	379a (Mercy)
	V	19a (Sin, Major and Minor)
12	II	245a (Forgiveness)
13	II	550b (Intention)
	V	479a (Whisper)
14	II	320b (God and his Attributes)
15	I	473a (Creation)
	III	531b (Nature as Signs)
	V	132a (Strangers and Foreigners)
15-16	IV	211b (Power and Impotence)
17	I	54a (Air and Wind)
	IV	530b, 531a (Sand)
18	IV	320b (Punishment Stories)
19	I	98a (Animal Life)
	II	154a (Eyes)
	III	534b (Nature as Signs)
20	II	354b (Grammar and the Q)
21	I	395b (Conceit)
	IV	211b (Power and Impotence)
22	III	249a (Magic)
23	IV	211b (Power and Impotence)
23-29	II	143a (Exhortations)
25-26	IV	442a (Revelation and Inspiration)
26	II	322a (God and his Attributes)
28	I	519b (Deliverance)
	IV	307b (Protection)
28-29	I	370a (Community and Society in the Q)
30	I	42a (Agriculture and Vegetation); 504a (Day, Times of)
	III	417a (Morning); 531a (Nature as Signs)
	V	121b, 127b (Springs and Fountains); 462b, 463b (Water)

Sūrat al-Qalam (68)

III 472b (Mysterious Letters)
V 168b (Sūra)

1 II 186b (Fate); 257b (Form and Structure of the Q); 545a (Instruments)
IV 262a, 262b, 263a (Preserved Tablet); 468b (Rhetoric and the Q)
V 64b (Smoke); 393a (Turkish Literature and the Q); 558a (Writing and Writing Materials)

2 I 115a (Apologetics); 447a (Cosmology)
II 540a (Insanity)
III 451a (Muḥammad); 518a (Narratives)
IV 112a (Poetry and Poets); 216b (Prayer); 442b (Revelation and Inspiration); 463a (Rhetoric and the Q)
V 420b (Verse)

4 II 453b (Hospitality and Courtesy)
III 504a (Names of the Prophet)

6 II 540b (Insanity)

8 III 567b (Obedience)

8-16 II 259b (Form and Structure of the Q)

10 III 563b (Oaths); 567b (Obedience)

11 II 344a (Gossip)

13 II 491a, 491b (Illegitimacy)

15 II 430a (History and the Q)
III 190a (Literacy); 518a (Narratives)
V 6b (Signs)

15-16 IV 310b (Provocation)

16 IV 454b (Reward and Punishment)

17 I 504a (Day, Times of)
IV 11a (Parable)

17-32 III 211b (Literature and the Q)

17-33 I 41b (Agriculture and Vegetation)
II 260a (Form and Structure of the Q)
III 211a (Literature and the Q); 520a (Narratives); 563b (Oaths)

17-34 II 259b (Form and Structure of the Q)
IV 10b, 11a (Parable)
V 171b (Sūra)

18 IV 63a (Persian Literature and the Q)

19 V 448b (Visiting)

20 I 494b (Date Palm); 504a (Day, Times of)

21	I	504a (Day, Times of)
21-22	I	501b (Day, Times of)
21-25	III	418a (Morning)
22	I	504a (Day, Times of)
23	V	479b (Whisper)
25	I	501b, 504a (Day, Times of)
	II	268b (Freedom and Predestination)
26	III	211a (Literature and the Q)
26-33	III	418a (Morning)
27	III	211a (Literature and the Q)
28	III	402a (Moderation)
34	IV	11a (Parable); 90b (Piety)
37	I	246a (Book)
	III	190b (Literacy); 509a (Names of the Q)
	IV	312a, 312b (Provocation)
	V	203a (Teaching)
39	IV	312b (Provocation)
41	IV	312b (Provocation)
	V	494a (Witnessing and Testifying)
42	II	48a (Eschatology); 323b, 324b (God and his Attributes)
42-43	I	254b (Bowing and Prostration)
	IV	219b (Prayer)
43	II	363b (Grammar and the Q)
44	II	322a (God and his Attributes)
	III	40a (Jihād)
46	IV	452a (Reward and Punishment)
48	II	70b (Ethics and the Q)
	III	40a (Jihād); 54a (Jonah)
48-49	I	99a (Animal Life)
48-50	II	143a (Exhortations)
	III	53a (Jonah); 453a (Muḥammad)
50	II	11b (Election)
	IV	291b (Prophets and Prophethood)
51	I	83b (Anatomy); 447a (Cosmology)
	II	153a (Eyes); 540a (Insanity)
	III	356a (Medicine and the Q); 448b (Muḥammad); 510a (Names of the Q)
	IV	62b (Persian Literature and the Q); 112a (Poetry and Poets); 165a (Popular and Talismanic Uses of the Q); 442b (Revelation and Inspiration)

51-52 II 143a (Exhortations)
III 305b (Material Culture and the Q)

52 III 510a (Names of the Q)
IV 230a (Prayer)
V 105b (Spatial Relations)

Sūrat al-Ḥāqqa (69)

V 168b, 171b (Sūra)

1 III 137a (Last Judgment); 197a, 203a (Literary Structures of the Q)

1-3 IV 102a, 102b, 103a (Pit); 469a (Rhetoric and the Q)
V 80a (Soothsayer)

2 III 137a (Last Judgment)

2-3 III 203a (Literary Structures of the Q)

3 III 137a (Last Judgment)
V 203a (Teaching)

4 I 113a (Apocalypse)
III 137a (Last Judgment); 524a (Narratives)

4-12 III 521b (Narratives)

5 II 212a (Fire); 308a (Geography)
IV 103b (Pit)
V 253a (Thamūd); 471a (Weather)

6 I 21b (ʿĀd); 52b, 54b (Air and Wind)
II 455b (Hot and Cold)
V 133a (Suffering); 470b (Weather)

6-7 V 280a (Time)

7 I 21b (ʿĀd); 494b (Date Palm); 499b, 502a (Day, Times of)
II 305b (Geography)
III 209a (Literature and the Q)
V 15b, 16a (Simile)

8 IV 425a (Remnant)

9 II 299b, 308a, 309a (Geography)
V 19a (Sin, Major and Minor); 184b (Syria)

10 I 537a (Disobedience)

11 V 464b (Water)

12 II 142b (Exhortations); 435a (History and the Q)

13 I 89b (Angel); 112b (Apocalypse)
II 362a (Grammar and the Q); 547a (Instruments)
III 203a (Literary Structures of the Q)
V 283a (Time)

13-16	II	47a (Eschatology)
13-18	III	209a (Literature and the Q)
15	II	258a (Form and Structure of the Q)
	III	137a (Last Judgment)
16	II	411b (Heaven and Sky)
17	I	463a (Court)
	II	46b (Eschatology); 326a (God and his Attributes)
	III	227b (Load or Burden)
	IV	220a (Prayer)
	V	277a (Throne of God)
18	III	140b (Last Judgment)
18-32	IV	2b (Pairs and Pairing)
19	I	244a, 245b (Book)
	III	178b (Left Hand and Right Hand); 275b (Markets); 508a (Names of the Q)
	IV	16a (Paradise); 101a (Pit); 454b (Reward and Punishment)
	V	493a, 493b (Witnessing and Testifying)
19-24	II	258b (Form and Structure of the Q)
	III	177b (Left Hand and Right Hand)
	V	106b (Spatial Relations)
19-26	II	26b (Epigraphy)
19-31	II	48a (Eschatology)
19-37	III	140b (Last Judgment)
20	IV	101a (Pit)
22	IV	14a (Paradise)
23	I	41b (Agriculture and Vegetation)
	V	123a (Springs and Fountains); 571a (Zaqqūm)
24	V	280a (Time)
25	I	244a (Book)
	II	258b (Form and Structure of the Q)
	III	177a, 178b (Left Hand and Right Hand); 275b (Markets); 508a (Names of the Q)
	IV	101a (Pit); 454b (Reward and Punishment)
	V	493a, 493b (Witnessing and Testifying)
25-29	I	298a (Chastisement and Punishment)
	III	177a (Left Hand and Right Hand)
25-37	II	258b (Form and Structure of the Q)
26	IV	101a (Pit)
28	IV	101a (Pit); 289a (Property)
	V	468a (Wealth)

29	II	354a (Grammar and the Q)
	IV	101a (Pit)
30-32	II	50b (Eschatology)
	IV	480a (Rhymed Prose)
30-33	III	128b (Language and Style of the Q)
30-37	III	177a (Left Hand and Right Hand)
32	II	547a (Instruments)
	III	333a (Measurement)
	V	473a (Weights and Measures)
33	II	258b (Form and Structure of the Q)
33-34	II	258b (Form and Structure of the Q)
34	II	450a (Hospitality and Courtesy)
	IV	455b (Reward and Punishment)
	V	196b (Taxation)
35	III	237a (Loyalty)
36	II	211a (Fire); 416b (Hell and Hellfire)
38-42	V	78b (Soothsayer)
38-43	III	247a (Magic)
40	I	447a (Cosmology)
	III	446a (Muḥammad)
	IV	290a (Prophets and Prophethood)
40-41	III	219b (Literature and the Q)
	V	420b (Verse)
40-42	III	451a (Muḥammad)
	IV	259b (Pre-Islamic Arabia and the Q)
40-43	I	543b (Divination)
41	I	447a (Cosmology); 542b (Divination)
	II	540a (Insanity)
	IV	112a (Poetry and Poets); 442b (Revelation and Inspiration); 477a (Rhymed Prose)
41-42	II	528a (Inimitability)
	IV	295a (Prophets and Prophethood)
42	I	148a (Arbitration); 542b (Divination)
	IV	112a (Poetry and Poets); 216b (Prayer); 311b (Provocation); 442b (Revelation and Inspiration)
43	IV	443b, 446a (Revelation and Inspiration)
	V	105b (Spatial Relations)
48	II	142b (Exhortations)
	III	510a (Names of the Q)
	IV	230a (Prayer)

51 V 387b (Truth); 404a (Uncertainty)

52 I 208b (Basmala)
II 142b (Exhortations)
III 443a (Muḥammad)
IV 470b (Rhetoric and the Q)

SŪRAT AL-MAʿĀRIJ (70)

I 178b, 179a (Ascension)
II 252b (Form and Structure of the Q)
V 168b (Sūra)

1 II 355a (Grammar and the Q)

1-9 I 178b (Ascension)

4 I 87a (Angel)
II 47b (Eschatology); 278b (Gabriel); 433a (History and the Q); 443b (Holy Spirit)
III 46a (Jinn); 293b (Mary); 335a (Measurement); 552a (Numbers and Enumeration)
V 81a (Soul); 116b (Spirit); 286a (Time)

5 III 40a (Jihād)

6-7 III 138a (Last Judgment)

8 III 383b (Metals and Minerals)
V 283b (Time)

8-9 II 251b (Form and Structure of the Q)
IV 8a (Pairs and Pairing)
V 15b (Simile)

8-15 III 379b (Mercy)

9 III 209a (Literature and the Q)

10 III 236a (Love and Affection)

10-14 V 247a (Textual Criticism of the Q)

11 IV 523b (Salvation)

11-12 IV 21a (Parents)

13 II 174b (Family); 353b (Grammar and the Q)

14 I 519a (Deliverance)

15 II 210a (Fire); 414b (Hell and Hellfire)

15-16 II 210b (Fire)

15-18 V 181a (Symbolic Imagery)

17 II 417b (Hell and Hellfire)

19 I 449b (Cosmology)

19-21 II 56b (Ethics and the Q)

22-23 IV 224b (Prayer); 487a (Ritual and the Q)

22-34 IV 455a (Reward and Punishment)

22-35 I 219b (Belief and Unbelief); 257b (Breaking Trusts and Contracts)
IV 17a (Paradise)

24-25 IV 209b (Poverty and the Poor)
V 469a (Wealth)

26 I 480b (Creeds)
III 136b (Last Judgment)

29 I 84a (Anatomy); 298b (Chastity)
IV 581a, 584a (Sex and Sexuality)

29-30 I 299a (Chastity); 396b (Concubines)
V 58a (Slaves and Slavery)

29-31 I 257b (Breaking Trusts and Contracts)

30 I 396b (Concubines)
IV 582a (Sex and Sexuality)
V 57b (Slaves and Slavery); 527b (Women and the Q)

32 I 257b (Breaking Trusts and Contracts); 464b (Covenant)

33 I 257b (Breaking Trusts and Contracts)

34 I 257b (Breaking Trusts and Contracts)
IV 224b (Prayer)

36 II 261b (Form and Structure of the Q)

37 II 401b (Hand)

38 II 448b (Hope)

38-42 II 268a (Freedom and Predestination)

39 I 476b (Creation)

40 IV 4b (Pairs and Pairing)
V 282b (Time)

42 III 40a (Jihād)

42-44 II 143a (Exhortations)
IV 309b (Provocation)

43 II 482b (Idols and Images); 547a (Instruments)
III 5a (Jerusalem); 185a (Life)

SŪRAT NŪḤ (71)

III 485b (Myths and Legends in the Q); 518b (Narratives); 540b (Noah)
IV 320a (Punishment Stories)
V 262a (Theology and the Q)

1	III	524a (Narratives)
	V	460b, 461a (Warner)
1-20	II	558a (Invitation)
1-26	II	558a (Invitation)
1-28	III	485b (Myths and Legends in the Q)
2	II	558a (Invitation)
3	II	558a (Invitation)
	III	568a (Obedience)
4	II	558a (Invitation)
	V	289a (Time)
5	V	280b (Time); 393b (Turkish Literature and the Q)
7	I	160b (Arrogance); 222a (Belief and Unbelief); 437a (Conversion)
	IV	263b (Pride)
10	II	558a (Invitation)
	III	379b (Mercy)
	IV	35a (Peace)
10-11	II	558a (Invitation)
	IV	218b (Prayer)
11	IV	233a (Prayer Formulas)
12	I	302b (Children)
13	II	449a, 449b (Hope)
13-14	III	128a (Language and Style of the Q)
	IV	481a (Rhymed Prose)
13-20	II	558b (Invitation)
14	I	442a (Cosmology); 476b (Creation)
	V	279b (Time)
14-20	I	473b (Creation)
15	I	478a (Creation)
	II	410b (Heaven and Sky)
	IV	107b (Planets and Stars)
16	I	442b (Cosmology); 499b (Day, Times of)
	II	275b (Furniture and Furnishings); 327b (God and his Attributes); 547a (Instruments)
	III	108a (Lamp); 187a (Light); 412b (Months); 415a (Moon)
	V	163a (Sun); 280b, 284a (Time)
17	I	40b (Agriculture and Vegetation)
	II	328a (God and his Attributes)
19	II	2b (Earth); 276a (Furniture and Furnishings); 460b (House, Domestic and Divine)

20 II 3a (Earth)
21 I 536b (Disobedience)
V 468a (Wealth)
22 III 18a (Jesus)
23 II 317b (God and his Attributes); 474a (Iconoclasm); 483a (Idols and Images)
III 518b (Narratives)
IV 160a (Polytheism and Atheism); 258a, 259a (Pre-Islamic Arabia and the Q)
V 92a (South Arabia, Religions in Pre-Islamic)
24-28 I 492a (Curse)
25 I 553b (Drowning)
II 45b (Eschatology)
IV 35a (Peace)
V 19a (Sin, Major and Minor)
28 III 379b (Mercy)
V 523b (Women and the Q)

Sūrat al-Jinn (72)

1 I 213b (Beauty)
II 2a (Ears); 87a (Everyday Life, Q In)
III 49a (Jinn); 506b (Names of the Q)
IV 216b (Prayer)
1-2 III 443b (Muḥammad)
1-19 I 385a (Community and Society in the Q)
3 II 33b (Epigraphy); 329b (God and his Attributes)
5 III 46b (Jinn)
5-6 IV 7b (Pairs and Pairing)
6 I 330a (Chronology and the Q)
III 46b, 48a (Jinn)
IV 216b (Prayer); 308a (Protection)
V 248b (Textual Criticism of the Q)
7 V 178a (Suspicion)
8 II 411a (Heaven and Sky)
8-9 III 46a, 48b (Jinn); 249b (Magic)
IV 107a, 108a (Planets and Stars)
8-10 I 463a (Court)
9 V 288b (Time)
11 IV 403b (Religious Pluralism and the Q)
12 II 489a (Ignorance); 526b (Inimitability)

13 v 313a (Trade and Commerce)

14-15 III 71b (Justice and Injustice)

15 II 415a (Hell and Hellfire)
V 241b (Textual Criticism of the Q)

16 IV 28b (Path or Way)

17 III 373b (Memory)

18 I 164a (Art and Architecture and the Q)
II 349a (Grammar and the Q)
IV 516a (Sacred Precincts)

18-20 III 325b (Material Culture and the Q)

19 III 440b (Muḥammad)

20-28 II 143a (Exhortations)

22 I 519b (Deliverance)
IV 307b (Protection)

23 I 537b (Disobedience)
II 54b (Eternity); 210a (Fire); 363b (Grammar and the Q)
III 382b (Messenger)

24 IV 538b (Scholar)

25 III 335a (Measurement)
IV 487b (Ritual and the Q)
V 241b (Textual Criticism of the Q); 288b (Time); 475a (Weights and Measures)

25-27 III 452a (Muḥammad)

26 II 423b (Hidden and the Hidden)

26-27 I 202a (Barēlwīs)
IV 291b (Prophets and Prophethood)

27 II 423b (Hidden and the Hidden)

27-28 II 161b (Failure)
IV 295b (Prophets and Prophethood)

Sūrat al-Muzzammil (73)

I 12a (Abrogation); 182b (Asceticism)
II 254a (Form and Structure of the Q)
V 95b (South Asian Literatures and the Q); 168b (Sūra); 404a (Uncertainty)

1 III 440b (Muḥammad)
IV 441b (Revelation and Inspiration)
V 80a (Soothsayer)

1-2 IV 470a (Rhetoric and the Q)

1-3	II	262b (Form and Structure of the Q)
1-4	I	182a (Asceticism)
	V	431a (Vigil)
1-5	I	326a (Chronology and the Q)
1-8	I	327b (Chronology and the Q)
	IV	222a (Prayer)
1-9	II	252b (Form and Structure of the Q)
2	I	502b (Day, Times of)
	IV	222a (Prayer)
2-4	V	169b (Sūra)
2-8	II	82a (Everyday Life, Q In)
4	II	88a (Everyday Life, Q In)
	III	116b (Language and Style of the Q); 440b (Muḥammad)
	IV	368b, 373b (Recitation of the Q); 470a (Rhetoric and the Q)
5	IV	441b (Revelation and Inspiration)
	V	547a (Word of God)
6	I	16a (Abrogation); 356b (Collection of the Q); 503a (Day, Times of)
8	III	443a (Muḥammad)
	IV	230b (Prayer)
9	II	31a (Epigraphy)
	IV	4b (Pairs and Pairing)
	V	282b (Time); 500b (Witnessing and Testifying)
10	I	14a (Abrogation); 405b (Consolation)
	II	310b (Geography)
	III	453a (Muḥammad)
	V	134a (Suffering); 434b (Virtue)
10-11	III	40a (Jihād)
10-18	II	252b (Form and Structure of the Q)
12	II	546a (Instruments)
13	II	211b (Fire); 416b (Hell and Hellfire)
14	I	113a (Apocalypse)
	II	358a (Grammar and the Q)
	IV	530b (Sand)
15	III	444b (Muḥammad); 524a (Narratives)
16	I	537a (Disobedience)
	II	66a (Ethics and the Q)
17	V	570b (Youth and Old Age)
18	II	363a (Grammar and the Q)

19 II 142b (Exhortations); 262a (Form and Structure of the Q)
IV 432a (Responsibility)

20 I 182a, 182b (Asceticism); 498a (Day and Night); 501b (Day, Times of)
II 245a (Forgiveness); 262b (Form and Structure of the Q); 268a (Freedom and Predestination); 327b (God and his Attributes); 366b, 367a (Grammar and the Q); 501b (Illness and Health); 6b (Economics)
III 58a (Journey); 335a (Measurement); 378b (Mercy)
IV 30a (Path or Way); 222a, 224b (Prayer); 281a (Profane and Sacred); 490b (Ritual and the Q)
V 176b (Sūra); 284a (Time); 431a, 431b (Vigil); 457a (War)

Sūrat al-Muddaththir (74)

I 346b (Clothing)
II 254a (Form and Structure of the Q)
V 95b (South Asian Literatures and the Q); 168b (Sūra); 404a (Uncertainty)

1 II 357b (Grammar and the Q)
III 440b (Muḥammad)
IV 441b (Revelation and Inspiration)
V 80a (Soothsayer); 170b (Sūra)

1-2 IV 470a (Rhetoric and the Q)

1-5 II 381b (Ḥadīth and the Q)
III 188b (Literacy)
IV 244a (Pre-1800 Preoccupations of Q Studies)

1-7 I 320b, 326a (Chronology and the Q)

1-10 II 263a (Form and Structure of the Q)

2 II 82b (Everyday Life, Q In)
III 382b (Messenger)
V 170a (Sūra); 460b (Warner)

2-5 I 19b (Abstinence)

3 II 82b (Everyday Life, Q In)
IV 220b (Prayer)

4 I 343b (Cleanliness and Ablution)

4-5 IV 503b (Ritual Purity)

5 II 18b (Emigration)
IV 454a (Reward and Punishment)

6 II 313b (Gift-Giving)

7 I 406a (Consolation)

8 I 112b (Apocalypse)
III 140a (Last Judgment)

8-9	V	283a (Time)
9	I	500a (Day, Times of)
11	III	40a (Jihād)
11-15	V	468b (Wealth)
11-22	V	39b (Sīra and the Q)
11-48	II	263a (Form and Structure of the Q)
13	V	492b (Witnessing and Testifying)
16	II	528a (Inimitability)
	V	6b (Signs)
16-26	II	418a (Hell and Hellfire)
18-25	II	465a (Humor)
19	I	491b (Curse)
	II	52a (Eschatology)
19-20	IV	8a (Pairs and Pairing)
20	I	491b (Curse)
22	III	217b (Literature and the Q)
23	III	217b (Literature and the Q)
24	III	246a (Magic); 397b (Miracles)
24-25	II	528a (Inimitability)
25	III	450a (Muḥammad)
26	II	210a (Fire)
	III	203a (Literary Structures of the Q)
26-27	IV	102a, 102b, 103a (Pit)
	V	80a (Soothsayer)
26-31	II	414b (Hell and Hellfire)
27	II	210a (Fire)
	III	203a (Literary Structures of the Q)
	V	203a (Teaching)
28-29	II	210b (Fire)
30	III	553b (Numbers and Enumeration)
	V	119a (Spiritual Beings)
30-31	II	417b (Hell and Hellfire)
31	I	222b, 225b (Belief and Unbelief)
	II	270a (Freedom and Predestination); 320b (God and his Attributes); 407b (Heart); 469a (Hypocrites and Hypocrisy)
	III	141b (Last Judgment); 359b (Medicine and the Q)
	V	38a (Sīra and the Q)

32	III	415a (Moon)
	IV	217a (Prayer)
32-34	V	282a (Time); 80a (Soothsayer)
33	I	501b, 502a (Day, Times of)
34	I	504a (Day, Times of)
	III	417a, 419a (Morning)
	V	281a (Time)
36	III	443b (Muḥammad)
38	II	454a (Hostages)
	IV	109b (Pledge); 458a (Reward and Punishment)
	V	84a (Soul)
38-39	IV	457a (Reward and Punishment)
39-56	III	177b (Left Hand and Right Hand)
40-47	I	532a (Dialogues)
41	II	551a (Intercession)
42	II	210a (Fire)
42-44	II	7a (Economics)
43	V	170a (Sūra)
43-46	II	258b (Form and Structure of the Q)
	IV	455b (Reward and Punishment)
44	II	216b (Food and Drink); 450a (Hospitality and Courtesy)
46	III	136b (Last Judgment)
47	V	404a (Uncertainty)
48	II	551a (Intercession)
	III	141a (Last Judgment)
49	I	222a (Belief and Unbelief)
	II	142b (Exhortations)
	IV	230a (Prayer)
49-51	V	245b (Textual Criticism of the Q)
49-56	II	263a (Form and Structure of the Q)
50-51	I	100a (Animal Life)
52	I	222a (Belief and Unbelief)
	II	545a (Instruments)
	III	189b (Literacy)
	IV	311b (Provocation); 569b (Scrolls)
	V	421b (Verse)
54	II	142b (Exhortations)

54-55 II 143a (Exhortations); 262a (Form and Structure of the Q)
IV 422a (Remembrance)

56 II 351a (Grammar and the Q)
III 373b (Memory); 378a (Mercy)
IV 49a (People of the House)

Sūrat al-Qiyāma (75)

II 252b (Form and Structure of the Q)
III 141b (Last Judgment)
IV 172b (Popular and Talismanic Uses of the Q)
V 168b (Sūra); 399a (Ummī)

1 V 282a (Time)

1-6 II 252b (Form and Structure of the Q)

1-22 IV 468a (Rhetoric and the Q)

2 V 83a (Soul); 96b (South Asian Literatures and the Q)

3-4 III 136a (Last Judgment)

4 II 349a (Grammar and the Q)

6 V 288b (Time)

7-8 V 283a (Time)

7-15 I 112a (Apocalypse)

8 III 416a (Moon)
IV 107a (Planets and Stars)

13 III 536b (News)
V 84a (Soul)

14 III 141a (Last Judgment)

16 I 83a (Anatomy)
V 203b (Teaching)

16-18 IV 368b (Recitation of the Q); 446a (Revelation and Inspiration)

16-19 III 441b (Muḥammad)

17 III 506a (Names of the Q)

17-18 III 586a (Orality)

18 II 87a (Everyday Life, Q In)
III 441a (Muḥammad); 506a (Names of the Q)

19 III 124b (Language and Style of the Q)

20-21 IV 8a (Pairs and Pairing)

22-23 I 480b (Creeds)
II 53a (Eschatology); 284a (Garden); 324a (God and his Attributes)

	III	204a (Literary Structures of the Q)
	IV	17b (Paradise); 435a (Resurrection); 574b (Seeing and Hearing)
26	II	258a (Form and Structure of the Q)
	IV	478b (Rhymed Prose)
	V	283b (Time)
26-28	III	66b (Judgment)
29	IV	486a (Ritual and the Q)
31	IV	487a (Ritual and the Q)
31-35	II	258b (Form and Structure of the Q)
34-35	IV	8a (Pairs and Pairing)
37-39	I	477a (Creation)
	V	267a (Theology and the Q)
37-40	I	479a, 479b (Creation)
38	I	81a (Anatomy)
38-40	V	5a (Signs)
39	II	175a (Family)
	IV	6a (Pairs and Pairing); 581a (Sex and Sexuality)
40	IV	435a (Resurrection)
	V	393b (Turkish Literature and the Q)

Sūrat al-Insān (76)

II 177a (Family of the Prophet)
III 324b (Material Culture and the Q)
IV 177b (Popular and Talismanic Uses of the Q)

1	I	318b (Chronology and the Q)
	II	185a (Fate); 351b (Grammar and the Q)
	V	287a (Time); 475a (Weights and Measures)
2	I	476b (Creation)
	II	1b (Ears)
	IV	574a (Seeing and Hearing)
	V	133b (Suffering); 444b (Vision)
3	I	435b (Conversion)
	III	511b (Names of the Q)
	IV	2a (Pairs and Pairing); 29a (Path or Way); 537b (Scholar)
4	II	546a, 547a (Instruments)
5	I	288a (Camphor); 490b (Cups and Vessels)
	III	573b (Odors and Smells)
	V	467a (Water of Paradise)
5-6	V	62b (Smell)

5-7	V	449b (Vow)
5-19	V	123b (Springs and Fountains)
6	I	165b (Art and Architecture and the Q); 288a (Camphor)
	V	123a (Springs and Fountains); 464b (Water)
6-16	II	259a (Form and Structure of the Q)
	V	420a (Verse)
7	IV	17a (Paradise); 485b (Ritual and the Q)
7-10	I	219b (Belief and Unbelief)
8	I	65b (Almsgiving); 289a (Captives)
	II	450a (Hospitality and Courtesy)
	IV	17a (Paradise); 208b (Poverty and the Poor)
	V	197a (Taxation); 204b (Teaching)
8-9	II	323b (God and his Attributes)
	III	603a (Orphans)
9	II	53a (Eschatology)
	IV	221a (Prayer)
	V	163b (Sun)
10	I	500a (Day, Times of)
	IV	17a (Paradise)
11	I	519b (Deliverance)
	III	63a (Joy and Misery)
	IV	17b (Paradise)
12	I	165b (Art and Architecture and the Q)
	IV	17a (Paradise)
	V	11b (Silk); 134b (Suffering)
12-18	V	62b (Smell)
13	II	283b, 284a (Garden)
	IV	18a, 18b (Paradise)
	V	163a (Sun)
13-14	II	51b (Eschatology)
14	IV	18b (Paradise)
	V	123a (Springs and Fountains)
15	I	490b, 490b (Cups and Vessels)
	II	219a (Food and Drink); 276a (Furniture and Furnishings)
	III	383b (Metals and Minerals)
	IV	18b (Paradise)
	V	123a (Springs and Fountains)
15-16	I	490b (Cups and Vessels)
	V	12b (Silk)

15-17	I	166a (Art and Architecture and the Q)
16	I	166a (Art and Architecture and the Q)
	II	276a (Furniture and Furnishings)
	III	334a (Measurement); 383b (Metals and Minerals)
17	I	490b (Cups and Vessels)
	II	217b (Food and Drink); 229a (Foreign Vocabulary); 305b (Geography)
	IV	18b (Paradise)
	V	466b (Water of Paradise)
17-18	V	464b (Water)
18	II	283b (Garden)
	V	123a (Springs and Fountains); 466b (Water of Paradise)
19	I	96a (Animal Life)
	II	284a (Garden); 445a (Homosexuality)
	III	139b (Last Judgment); 384a (Metals and Minerals)
	IV	18a (Paradise); 585a (Sex and Sexuality)
	V	12a (Silk); 549a (Work); 570a (Youth and Old Age)
20	III	62b (Joy and Misery); 92b (Kings and Rulers)
21	I	166a (Art and Architecture and the Q); 343b (Cleanliness and Ablution); 362b (Colors)
	II	284a (Garden); 333b (Gold); 373a (Gratitude and Ingratitude)
	III	383b (Metals and Minerals)
	IV	18a, 18b (Paradise); 505b (Ritual Purity)
	V	12b (Silk); 125a (Springs and Fountains)
23	IV	292b, 293a (Prophets and Prophethood); 446a (Revelation and Inspiration)
23-31	II	143a (Exhortations); 262a (Form and Structure of the Q)
24	I	405b (Consolation)
	III	40a (Jihād); 567b (Obedience)
25	I	503b, 504a (Day, Times of)
	III	373a (Memory); 416b (Morning); 443a (Muḥammad)
	IV	223a, 230b (Prayer)
	V	281a (Time); 431a (Vigil)
25-26	I	327b (Chronology and the Q)
	III	546a (Noon)
26	I	182b (Asceticism); 254a (Bowing and Prostration); 502b (Day, Times of)
	IV	220b, 222a (Prayer)
27	I	500a (Day, Times of)
27-31	I	523a (Destiny)
29	II	142b (Exhortations)
29-30	V	485a (Wish and Desire)

29-31 II 270a (Freedom and Predestination)

30 I 74a (Ambiguous)

31 V 170a (Sūra)

Sūrat al-Mursalāt (77)

I 230b (Biology as the Creation and Stages of Life); 293b (Cave); 322a (Chronology and the Q); 381b (Community and Society in the Q); 491b (Curse)
II 388b (Ḥadīth and the Q)
III 199b (Literary Structures of the Q); 530a (Nature as Signs)
IV 178a (Popular and Talismanic Uses of the Q); 474b (Rhetoric and the Q)
V 168b (Sūra); 424a (Verse)

1 I 55a (Air and Wind)
III 382b (Messenger)
V 119a (Spiritual Beings)

1-2 IV 479a (Rhymed Prose)

1-4 II 256a (Form and Structure of the Q)
V 373a (Trips and Voyages)

1-5 III 530a (Nature as Signs)
IV 464b, 468b (Rhetoric and the Q)

1-6 IV 465b (Rhetoric and the Q)
V 80a (Soothsayer)

3 I 55a (Air and Wind)

3-4 V 80a (Soothsayer)

5 III 530a (Nature as Signs)
IV 294b (Prophets and Prophethood); 466a (Rhetoric and the Q)

8-10 III 535b (Nature as Signs)

8-13 V 283a (Time)

8-19 V 80a (Soothsayer)

11 V 288a (Time)

13 I 516b (Decision)
III 137a (Last Judgment); 203a (Literary Structures of the Q)

13-14 IV 102b (Pit)

14 I 516b (Decision)
III 137a (Last Judgment); 203a (Literary Structures of the Q)
V 203a (Teaching)

15 V 424a (Verse)

19 V 424a (Verse)

20 V 462b (Water)

20-22	I	476b (Creation)
20-23	II	268b (Freedom and Predestination)
	V	267a (Theology and the Q)
22	III	335a (Measurement)
24	IV	470a (Rhetoric and the Q)
	V	424a (Verse)
25-26	II	3b (Earth)
25-27	II	259a (Form and Structure of the Q)
	V	420a (Verse)
27	II	2b (Earth)
	III	531b (Nature as Signs)
29-31	III	140b (Last Judgment)
30	III	550b (Numbers and Enumeration)
30-31	II	415a (Hell and Hellfire)
31	II	414b (Hell and Hellfire)
32	II	210b (Fire); 415a (Hell and Hellfire)
32-33	I	99b (Animal Life)
33	I	363a (Colors)
	II	210b (Fire)
34-36	V	110b (Speech)
38	I	516b (Decision)
	III	137a (Last Judgment)
39	IV	309b (Provocation)
41	II	283b (Garden)
	IV	18b (Paradise)
	V	123a (Springs and Fountains)
41-43	V	464b (Water)
42	IV	18a (Paradise)
44	IV	452b (Reward and Punishment)
46	I	221b (Belief and Unbelief)
48	I	254a (Bowing and Prostration)
	II	366b (Grammar and the Q)
	V	170b (Sūra)
48-49	III	160a (Law and the Q)
48-50	V	170a (Sūra)

Sūrat al-Nabāʾ (78)

III 272a (Manuscripts of the Q); 320b (Material Culture and the Q)
IV 246b (Pre-1800 Preoccupations of Q Studies); 495b (Ritual and the Q)
V 168b (Sūra)

2 III 536b (News)

4 IV 538b (Scholar)

4-5 IV 8a (Pairs and Pairing)

5 IV 538b (Scholar)

6 II 2b (Earth); 259a (Form and Structure of the Q)
V 236b (Tents and Tent Pegs)

6-11 I 448a, 448b (Cosmology)

6-13 I 473a (Creation)

6-14 IV 79b (Philosophy and the Q)

6-16 II 302b (Geography)
III 531b (Nature as Signs)

8 II 175a (Family)
IV 6a (Pairs and Pairing)
V 524a (Women and the Q)

8-10 I 449a (Cosmology)

9 I 443b (Cosmology); 501b (Day, Times of)
IV 511a (Sabbath)

9-11 V 60b (Sleep)

10 I 346b (Clothing)
V 282b (Time)

11 I 449a (Cosmology); 502a (Day, Times of)

12 I 442a (Cosmology); 478a (Creation)
III 554b (Numerology)
IV 107b (Planets and Stars)

12-13 III 107b (Lamp)

13 I 442b (Cosmology)
II 327b (God and his Attributes); 547a (Instruments)
III 187a (Light)
V 163a (Sun)

14-16 II 3a (Earth)

15 II 3b (Earth)

16 I 41b (Agriculture and Vegetation)

17 I 272b (Calendar); 516b (Decision)
III 137a (Last Judgment)
IV 228a (Prayer)

18 I 112b (Apocalypse)
II 547a (Instruments)
V 283b (Time)

19 I 398b (Conquest)

21-23 V 554b (World)

21-36 IV 3a (Pairs and Pairing)

22 IV 104a (Pit)

23 II 52b (Eschatology); 439b (History and the Q)

24 II 455b (Hot and Cold)

24-25 II 211a (Fire)

25 II 211a (Fire)

27 II 449a (Hope)

27-30 II 258b (Form and Structure of the Q)

28 II 358b (Grammar and the Q)

29 I 243b (Book)

31-36 I 406a (Consolation)

32 II 305b (Geography)

33 IV 18a (Paradise)
V 524a (Women and the Q); 570a (Youth and Old Age)

34 I 490b (Cups and Vessels)
IV 18b (Paradise)

35 IV 482b (Rhymed Prose)

36 II 313a (Gift-Giving)

37 I 463b (Court)

38 I 463a (Court)
II 443b (Holy Spirit)
III 140b (Last Judgment); 293b (Mary)
IV 349b (Ranks and Orders)
V 81a (Soul); 110b (Speech)

40 I 113b (Apocalypse); 298a (Chastisement and Punishment)
V 393a, 393b (Turkish Literature and the Q); 461a (Warner)

SŪRAT AL-NĀZIʿĀT (79)

II 252b (Form and Structure of the Q)
V 168b, 171a (Sūra); 395b, 396a, 396b (Ṭuwā)

1-5 I 90a (Angel)
II 256a (Form and Structure of the Q)

	IV	464b (Rhetoric and the Q)
	V	80a (Soothsayer)
3	I	27a (Adoration)
	II	315a (Glorification of God)
5	V	118a (Spiritual Beings)
6	I	113a (Apocalypse)
	IV	103b (Pit)
	V	253a (Thamūd)
6-7	II	258a (Form and Structure of the Q)
	V	282a (Time)
6-14	II	256a (Form and Structure of the Q)
8	II	258a (Form and Structure of the Q)
10-11	III	136a (Last Judgment)
11	II	4b (Earth)
14	III	5a, 6a (Jerusalem)
15	III	524a (Narratives)
15-19	II	558a (Invitation)
15-26	II	259b (Form and Structure of the Q); 435b (History and the Q)
	V	171b (Sūra); 420a (Verse)
15-29	I	304b (Children of Israel)
16	II	348b (Grammar and the Q)
	III	340a (Mecca); 421a (Moses); 495b (Myths and Legends in the Q)
	IV	282b (Profane and Sacred); 513a (Sacred Precincts)
	V	110a (Speech)
17	III	583b (Oppression)
17-19	III	421b (Moses)
21	I	537a (Disobedience)
24	I	329a, 329b (Chronology and the Q)
	II	319a (God and his Attributes); 338a (Good and Evil)
	IV	68a (Pharaoh)
25	IV	454a (Reward and Punishment)
26	V	171a (Sūra)
27	I	478a (Creation)
27-30	I	474b (Creation); 536a (Difficult Passages)
27-32	II	259a (Form and Structure of the Q)
	V	420a (Verse)
27-33	II	259a (Form and Structure of the Q); 303a (Geography); 326b (God and his Attributes)

28	I	442b (Cosmology)
	II	460b (House, Domestic and Divine)
28-31	V	462a (Water)
29	I	504a (Day, Times of)
	III	416b, 418a (Morning)
	V	281b (Time)
30	II	2b (Earth)
31	I	41a (Agriculture and Vegetation)
32-33	I	473a (Creation)
33	III	60a (Joy and Misery)
34	I	113a (Apocalypse)
	III	137a (Last Judgment)
	IV	103a (Pit)
34-35	I	91a (Angel)
	V	283b (Time)
34-36	II	258a (Form and Structure of the Q)
35-41	IV	12a (Paradise)
37	IV	432a (Responsibility)
37-38	IV	455b (Reward and Punishment)
39	IV	103b (Pit)
40-41	V	83a (Soul)
41	IV	103b (Pit)
42	I	111a (Antichrist); 501a (Day, Times of)
	III	137a (Last Judgment)
	V	288b (Time)
42-44	III	138a (Last Judgment)
42-45	III	442b (Muḥammad)
42-46	II	439b (History and the Q)
43	I	113b (Apocalypse)
46	I	503a, 504a (Day, Times of)
	III	416b, 418a (Morning)
	V	281b (Time); 476a (Weights and Measures)

SŪRAT ʿABASA (80)

V 166b, 168b (Sūra)

1-6	V	447a (Vision and Blindness)
1-10	V	436a (Virtue)

1-16	I	38b (Age of Ignorance)
3	V	203a (Teaching)
10-16	V	421b (Verse)
11	II	142b (Exhortations)
11-16	V	421b (Verse)
12-17	IV	570a (Scrolls)
13	II	545a (Instruments)
	IV	570a (Scrolls)
13-14	III	513a (Names of the Q)
	IV	491a (Ritual and the Q); 505b (Ritual Purity)
13-15	III	189b (Literacy)
14	I	343b (Cleanliness and Ablution)
15-16	I	247b (Book)
	II	387b (Ḥadīth and the Q)
	IV	444a (Revelation and Inspiration)
17	I	449b (Cosmology); 491b (Curse)
	II	261b (Form and Structure of the Q)
	V	172a (Sūra)
17-42	II	326b (God and his Attributes)
18-19	I	476b (Creation)
18-22	I	263b (Burial)
	II	268b (Freedom and Predestination)
	V	569b (Youth and Old Age)
19-22	II	328b (God and his Attributes)
20	I	231b (Biology as the Creation and Stages of Life)
	IV	28b (Path or Way)
24-32	I	42a (Agriculture and Vegetation)
	II	3a (Earth); 259a (Form and Structure of the Q)
	IV	79b (Philosophy and the Q)
25	III	531a (Nature as Signs)
	V	462b (Water)
25-32	II	303a (Geography)
26	II	3a (Earth); 358a (Grammar and the Q)
27	II	3b (Earth)
27-31	V	242a (Textual Criticism of the Q)
28	I	41b (Agriculture and Vegetation)
	II	4a (Earth); 217b (Food and Drink); 305b (Geography)
28-29	I	46b (Agriculture and Vegetation)

29 I 494b (Date Palm)
II 4a (Earth)

30 I 41a (Agriculture and Vegetation)
II 283a (Garden); 304a (Geography)

31 II 4a (Earth)
IV 18a (Paradise)
V 242a (Textual Criticism of the Q); 404b (Uncertainty)

32 III 60a (Joy and Misery)

33 I 113a (Apocalypse)
III 137a (Last Judgment); 203a (Literary Structures of the Q)

33-37 III 99b (Kinship)

33-42 I 112a (Apocalypse)

34 V 283b (Time)

34-35 IV 21a (Parents)

37 II 509b (Indifference)

38-39 II 258b (Form and Structure of the Q)
III 217b (Literature and the Q)

38-41 IV 2b (Pairs and Pairing)

39 III 62a (Joy and Misery); 146b (Laughter)

40-42 II 258b (Form and Structure of the Q)

Sūrat al-Takwīr (81)

I 112a (Apocalypse)
III 324a (Material Culture and the Q)
IV 172b (Popular and Talismanic Uses of the Q)
V 168b (Sūra)

1 V 163b (Sun); 393a, 393b (Turkish Literature and the Q)

1-4 II 47a (Eschatology)

1-13 II 257b (Form and Structure of the Q)
IV 469b (Rhetoric and the Q)

1-14 I 112a (Apocalypse)
III 138b (Last Judgment); 202b (Literary Structures of the Q); 535b (Nature as Signs)
IV 479a (Rhymed Prose)
V 80a (Soothsayer); 283a (Time)

4 I 98a (Animal Life); 113a (Apocalypse); 287a (Camel)

5 III 140a (Last Judgment)

6 V 464b (Water)

7	V	83b (Soul)
8	II	353b (Grammar and the Q)
8-9	I	2b (Abortion); 153b (Archaeology and the Q); 234b (Birth Control); 301b (Children)
	II	511a (Infanticide)
	IV	255b (Pre-Islamic Arabia and the Q)
	V	318a (Tradition and Custom); 524b (Women and the Q); 570a (Youth and Old Age)
9	I	450b (Cosmology)
	II	64a (Ethics and the Q)
10	III	140b (Last Judgment)
	IV	570a (Scrolls)
14	II	511a (Infanticide)
15	II	257b (Form and Structure of the Q)
15-16	IV	8a (Pairs and Pairing); 109a (Planets and Stars)
15-18	V	80a (Soothsayer)
15-19	IV	468a (Rhetoric and the Q)
15-29	I	320b (Chronology and the Q)
17	I	502a (Day, Times of)
17-18	I	502a (Day, Times of)
	IV	8a (Pairs and Pairing)
	V	282a (Time)
18	I	52b, 54b (Air and Wind); 504a (Day, Times of)
	III	204b (Literary Structures of the Q); 385b (Metaphor); 417a, 419a (Morning)
	V	281a (Time)
19	IV	290a (Prophets and Prophethood)
	V	116a (Spirit)
19-21	I	87b (Angel)
19-24	V	116a (Spirit)
19-25	II	324a (God and his Attributes)
	IV	216b (Prayer)
20	II	325b (God and his Attributes)
20-21	III	442a (Muḥammad)
22	I	387b (Companions of the Prophet); 447a (Cosmology)
	II	540a (Insanity)
	III	450b (Muḥammad)
	IV	112a (Poetry and Poets); 295a (Prophets and Prophethood); 442b (Revelation and Inspiration)
	V	420b (Verse)

22-25 I 543b (Divination)

23 II 181a (Fasting)
III 442a (Muḥammad)
IV 107b (Planets and Stars)

23-24 IV 442a (Revelation and Inspiration)

24 II 354a (Grammar and the Q)

25 I 447a (Cosmology); 524b (Devil)
V 130a (Stoning)

26-28 II 143a (Exhortations)

27 III 372b (Memory)
V 105b (Spatial Relations)

27-29 I 523a (Destiny)
III 380a (Mercy)
V 485a (Wish and Desire)

28-29 I 186a (Astray)
II 59a (Ethics and the Q)

29 I 235a (Birth Control)
V 105a, 105b (Spatial Relations)

Sūrat al-Infiṭār (82)

I 322b (Chronology and the Q)
III 324a (Material Culture and the Q)
V 168b (Sūra)

1-4 II 257b (Form and Structure of the Q)
III 209a (Literature and the Q)

1-5 III 202b (Literary Structures of the Q); 535b (Nature as Signs)
V 80a (Soothsayer); 283a (Time)

1-15 IV 34b (Peace)

3 I 204a (Barrier)
V 464b (Water)

5 III 535b (Nature as Signs)
V 84a (Soul)

6-7 I 435a (Conversion)
III 72b (Justice and Injustice)

6-8 II 259a (Form and Structure of the Q)

7 I 446b (Cosmology)

7-8 II 328a (God and his Attributes)

8 I 167b (Art and Architecture and the Q)
II 323a (God and his Attributes)

9 I 235b (Blasphemy)
III 136b (Last Judgment)

10 IV 307b (Protection)
V 118b (Spiritual Beings); 493a (Witnessing and Testifying)

10-11 I 243b (Book)

11 I 243b (Book)
V 118b (Spiritual Beings)

13 III 62b (Joy and Misery)
IV 90b (Piety)

13-14 IV 481b (Rhymed Prose)

14-18 V 80a (Soothsayer)

14-19 IV 102a (Pit)

15 III 136b (Last Judgment)

17 III 136b (Last Judgment)
V 203a (Teaching)

17-18 IV 8a (Pairs and Pairing); 102b (Pit)

18 III 136b (Last Judgment)
V 203a (Teaching)

19 III 137b (Last Judgment)
IV 454b (Reward and Punishment)

Sūrat al-Muṭaffifīn (83)

I 300a (Cheating); 322a (Chronology and the Q)
V 168b (Sūra)

1-3 III 66a (Judgment); 276a (Markets)
IV 455b (Reward and Punishment); 470a (Rhetoric and the Q)

2 III 334a (Measurement)

3 III 334a (Measurement)

6 V 105a, 105b (Spatial Relations)

7 IV 2b (Pairs and Pairing)
V 493a (Witnessing and Testifying)

7-8 IV 102a, 102b (Pit)
V 80a (Soothsayer)

7-9 IV 102b (Pit); 469a (Rhetoric and the Q)

7-24 I 522b (Destiny)

8 IV 103a (Pit)
V 203a (Teaching)

9 III 591a (Orality and Writing in Arabia)
V 558a (Writing and Writing Materials)

10 V 424a (Verse)

11 III 136b (Last Judgment)

12 IV 309b (Provocation)

13 II 430a (History and the Q)
III 190a (Literacy); 518a (Narratives)
IV 463a (Rhetoric and the Q)
V 6b (Signs); 420a, 422a (Verse)

14 I 226a (Belief and Unbelief)
II 355a (Grammar and the Q); 370b (Gratitude and Ingratitude); 510b (Indifference)
IV 310a (Provocation); 432a (Responsibility)
V 447a (Vision and Blindness)

14-15 I 298a (Chastisement and Punishment)

15 I 203b (Barrier)
IV 17b (Paradise)

18 II 353a (Grammar and the Q); 500a (ʿIlliyyūn)
V 493a (Witnessing and Testifying)

18-19 IV 102a, 102b (Pit)
V 80a (Soothsayer)

18-20 IV 102b (Pit); 469a (Rhetoric and the Q)

18-21 IV 14a (Paradise)

19 II 500a, 500b (ʿIlliyyūn)
IV 103a (Pit)
V 203a (Teaching)

20 II 500b (ʿIlliyyūn)
III 591a (Orality and Writing in Arabia)
V 558a (Writing and Writing Materials)

21 IV 220a (Prayer)
V 492b (Witnessing and Testifying)

22 III 62b (Joy and Misery)

23 II 284a (Garden)

24 III 62b (Joy and Misery)

25 II 218a (Food and Drink); 229a (Foreign Vocabulary); 556a (Intoxicants)
V 482a (Wine)

25-26 III 573b (Odors and Smells)

25-27 II 284a (Garden)

25-28 V 62b (Smell); 123b (Springs and Fountains)

26 III 266b (Manuscripts of the Q)
V 393b (Turkish Literature and the Q)

27 II 283b (Garden)

27-28 V 464b (Water)

28 IV 220a (Prayer)

29 III 146b (Laughter)
IV 309b (Provocation)
V 19a (Sin, Major and Minor); 420a (Verse)

29-32 I 222a, 224b (Belief and Unbelief)
II 258b (Form and Structure of the Q)

29-33 II 258b (Form and Structure of the Q)

33 IV 308b (Protection)

34 III 147a (Laughter)

34-35 II 415b (Hell and Hellfire)

36 IV 452b (Reward and Punishment)

Sūrat al-Inshiqāq (84)

III 324a (Material Culture and the Q)
V 168b (Sūra)

1 III 546b (Noon)
V 283a (Time)

1-5 II 257b (Form and Structure of the Q)

1-15 V 80a (Soothsayer)

5-6 V 393b (Turkish Literature and the Q)

6 III 184a (Life)

7 I 244a (Book)
III 178a (Left Hand and Right Hand)
IV 16a (Paradise)
V 493a, 493b (Witnessing and Testifying)

7-8 III 275b (Markets)

7-9 III 177a (Left Hand and Right Hand)
IV 457b (Reward and Punishment)

7-10 III 178a (Left Hand and Right Hand)

7-12 II 412b (Heavenly Book)
IV 2b (Pairs and Pairing)

9 III 62b (Joy and Misery)

10 I 244a (Book)
III 177b (Left Hand and Right Hand); 275b (Markets)
V 493a, 493b (Witnessing and Testifying)

10-11 III 140b (Last Judgment)

10-12 IV 454b (Reward and Punishment)

10-13 III 62b (Joy and Misery)

10-25 III 177a (Left Hand and Right Hand)

13-15 II 258b (Form and Structure of the Q)

16 I 503a (Day, Times of)
II 79b (Evening); 257b (Form and Structure of the Q)
IV 217a (Prayer)
V 281b (Time)

16-17 V 282a (Time)

16-18 V 80a (Soothsayer)

18 IV 108b (Planets and Stars)

19 III 184b (Life)

20 IV 117a (Polemic and Polemical Language)

20-21 IV 221b (Prayer)

21 I 254b (Bowing and Prostration)

24 IV 470b (Rhetoric and the Q)

25 IV 454b (Reward and Punishment)

Sūrat al-Burūj (85)

III 521b (Narratives); 535a (Nature as Signs)
IV 85b (Philosophy and the Q); 172b (Popular and Talismanic Uses of the Q)
V 168b (Sūra); 398a (Ukhdūd)

1 I 442b (Cosmology)
II 410a (Heaven and Sky)
IV 107a, 108b (Planets and Stars); 217a (Prayer)
V 283b (Time)

1-2 V 282a (Time)

1-3 II 256b (Form and Structure of the Q)
IV 464b (Rhetoric and the Q)
V 80a (Soothsayer)

1-7 III 521b (Narratives)
IV 468a (Rhetoric and the Q)

2 I 500a (Day, Times of)
III 137a (Last Judgment)

4 I 491b (Curse)
IV 257b (Pre-Islamic Arabia and the Q); 353a (Rass)
V 397a (Ukhdūd)

4-7 IV 43b (People of the Ditch)

4-8 II 211b (Fire)

4-9 I 154a (Archaeology and the Q)
II 146a, 147b (Expeditions and Battles)
III 500b (Najrān)
IV 411a (Religious Pluralism and the Q)
V 397a (Ukhdūd)

8 IV 6a (Pairs and Pairing); 453b (Reward and Punishment)

8-9 IV 43b (People of the Ditch)

9 IV 128a (Politics and the Q)
V 490a (Witness to Faith)

10 II 210b (Fire); 418a (Hell and Hellfire)
III 500a, 500b (Najrān)
IV 411a (Religious Pluralism and the Q); 426b (Repentance and Penance); 455b (Reward and Punishment)
V 523b (Women and the Q)

11 IV 18b (Paradise); 454b (Reward and Punishment); 522b (Salvation)
V 430a (Victory)

12 IV 85b (Philosophy and the Q)

13 I 472a (Creation)
IV 6b (Pairs and Pairing)

13-16 IV 470b (Rhetoric and the Q)

14 II 321a, 322a (God and his Attributes)
III 233b (Love and Affection)
IV 5b (Pairs and Pairing)

15 II 315b (Glory); 320a, 325b (God and his Attributes)

17 III 524a (Narratives)

17-18 V 377a (Troops)

17-20 III 521b (Narratives)

21 II 315b (Glory)
III 506b, 513a (Names of the Q)
IV 63a (Persian Literature and the Q); 297a (Prophets and Prophethood)

21-22 II 143a (Exhortations); 262a (Form and Structure of the Q)
III 189b (Literacy); 538a (Night of Power)

22 I 87b (Angel); 247b (Book)
II 186b (Fate); 412a (Heavenly Book); 544b (Instruments)
III 189b (Literacy)
IV 81a, 85b (Philosophy and the Q); 261b, 263a (Preserved Tablet); 297a (Prophets and Prophethood); 307b (Protection); 444a, 445b (Revelation and Inspiration)
V 157b (Ṣūfism and the Q); 422a (Verse)

Sūrat al-Ṭāriq (86)

I 230b (Biology as the Creation and Stages of Life)
V 168b (Sūra)

1 II 410a (Heaven and Sky)
IV 108b (Planets and Stars); 464b (Rhetoric and the Q)
V 80a (Soothsayer); 282a (Time)

1-2 IV 102a, 102b (Pit)
V 80a (Soothsayer)

1-3 II 256b (Form and Structure of the Q)
IV 102b (Pit)

1-17 IV 468a (Rhetoric and the Q)

2 V 203a (Teaching)

3 IV 108b (Planets and Stars)

4 II 359a, 361b (Grammar and the Q)
IV 307b (Protection)
V 118b (Spiritual Beings)

5-7 I 476b (Creation)
V 267a (Theology and the Q)

5-8 I 479a, 479b (Creation)
IV 435a (Resurrection)

5-12 IV 211b (Power and Impotence)

6 III 363a (Medicine and the Q)
V 462b (Water)

11 II 257b (Form and Structure of the Q); 410a (Heaven and Sky)

11-12 II 256b (Form and Structure of the Q)
IV 4b, 8a (Pairs and Pairing); 464b (Rhetoric and the Q); 478b (Rhymed Prose)

13 I 516b (Decision)
III 513a (Names of the Q); 528a (Nature as Signs)

13-14 IV 8a (Pairs and Pairing)

15-17 II 143a (Exhortations)
IV 470b (Rhetoric and the Q)

16 V 480a (Whisper)

17 II 143a (Exhortations)

Sūrat al-Aʿlā (87)

I 355a (Collection of the Q)
IV 172b (Popular and Talismanic Uses of the Q)
V 168b (Sūra)

1	I	208b (Basmala); 329a (Chronology and the Q)
	II	319a (God and his Attributes)
	III	443a (Muḥammad); 546b (Noon)
	IV	470a (Rhetoric and the Q)
	V	169b (Sūra); 264b (Theology and the Q); 393b (Turkish Literature and the Q); 426a (Verse)
1-4	I	472a (Creation)
	V	265a (Theology and the Q)
1-5	II	259a (Form and Structure of the Q)
	IV	470b (Rhetoric and the Q)
2	I	451a (Cosmology)
2-3	II	328b (God and his Attributes)
4	I	41a (Agriculture and Vegetation)
5	I	364b (Colors)
6	III	441a (Muḥammad)
	V	203b (Teaching)
6-7	I	15a, 16a (Abrogation); 353a (Collection of the Q)
	IV	449a (Revision and Alteration)
7	IV	4a (Pairs and Pairing)
8	III	179b (Left Hand and Right Hand)
9	IV	422b (Remembrance)
11	III	63b (Joy and Misery)
	V	251b (Textual Criticism of the Q)
14	IV	490b (Ritual and the Q); 505b (Ritual Purity); 523a (Salvation)
14-15	IV	420a (Remembrance); 454b (Reward and Punishment)
14-17	III	425b (Moses)
15	IV	229b (Prayer); 490b (Ritual and the Q)
16-17	IV	8a (Pairs and Pairing)
	V	340a (Transitoriness); 486a (Wish and Desire)
16-19	IV	570a, 570b (Scrolls)
17	III	425b (Moses)
18	I	245b (Book)
	II	434a (History and the Q); 545a (Instruments)
	V	301a (Torah)
18-19	I	5b (Abraham); 330a (Chronology and the Q)
	II	143a (Exhortations); 262a (Form and Structure of the Q)
	III	189b (Literacy); 425b (Moses); 592b (Orality and Writing in Arabia)

19 I 245b (Book)
II 545a (Instruments)
III 381a (Messenger)
IV 296b (Prophets and Prophethood)
V 301a (Torah)

Sūrat al-Ghāshiya (88)

IV 86b (Philosophy and the Q)
V 123b (Springs and Fountains); 168b (Sūra)

1 III 137a (Last Judgment); 524a (Narratives)
IV 103a (Pit)

2-5 IV 86b (Philosophy and the Q)

2-12 V 123b (Springs and Fountains)

4 II 455b (Hot and Cold)

5 II 211a (Fire); 455b (Hot and Cold)
V 126b (Springs and Fountains); 465a (Water)

6 I 41b (Agriculture and Vegetation)
II 305b (Geography)

6-7 II 211a (Fire); 416b (Hell and Hellfire)

8-10 II 284a (Garden)

8-16 I 406a (Consolation)
IV 86b (Philosophy and the Q)

9-12 II 358a (Grammar and the Q)

10 IV 14a (Paradise)

11 II 283b (Garden)
IV 103a (Pit); 482b (Rhymed Prose)

12 V 123a (Springs and Fountains)

12-16 IV 469a (Rhetoric and the Q)

13 II 276a (Furniture and Furnishings); 284a (Garden)
IV 18a (Paradise)

13-14 III 128b (Language and Style of the Q)
IV 481b (Rhymed Prose)

13-16 V 12a (Silk)

14 I 490b (Cups and Vessels)
II 276a (Furniture and Furnishings)

15 II 229a (Foreign Vocabulary); 276a (Furniture and Furnishings)

15-16 III 128b (Language and Style of the Q)
IV 481b (Rhymed Prose)

16 II 276a (Furniture and Furnishings)
17 I 98a (Animal Life); 287a (Camel)
II 259a (Form and Structure of the Q)
IV 70b (Philosophy and the Q)
17-20 I 473b (Creation)
II 259a (Form and Structure of the Q)
21 III 440b (Muḥammad)
IV 470a (Rhetoric and the Q)
22 II 348a, 354a (Grammar and the Q)
III 40a (Jihād)
23 IV 432a (Responsibility)
25-26 IV 481b (Rhymed Prose)

Sūrat al-Fajr (89)

I 322a, 322b (Chronology and the Q); 499a (Day, Times of)
II 465a (Humor)
III 324a (Material Culture and the Q); 416b (Morning); 535a (Nature as Signs)
IV 172b (Popular and Talismanic Uses of the Q)
V 168b, 171b (Sūra); 420b (Verse)
1 I 36a (Afternoon); 444a (Cosmology)
III 417a, 419a (Morning); 535a (Nature as Signs)
IV 217a (Prayer)
V 281a (Time)
1-2 I 444a (Cosmology)
1-4 II 256b (Form and Structure of the Q)
IV 464b (Rhetoric and the Q)
V 80a (Soothsayer); 282a (Time)
1-5 IV 478b (Rhymed Prose)
1-30 IV 468a (Rhetoric and the Q)
2 I 445a (Cosmology); 499b (Day, Times of)
IV 342b (Ramaḍān)
3 III 549b (Numbers and Enumeration)
4 V 282b (Time)
I 502a, 503a (Day, Times of)
III 417b (Morning)
5 III 173b (Lawful and Unlawful)
6-7 I 21b (ʿĀd)
II 559a (Iram)
6-12 V 549a (Work)

6-13	II	338b (Good and Evil)
6-14	III	518b (Narratives)
7	I	152a (Archaeology and the Q)
	II	10b (Egypt); 308a (Geography); 338b (Good and Evil); 438a (History and the Q)
	V	185a (Syria)
8	II	308a (Geography)
9	I	150b (Archaeology and the Q)
	II	339a (Good and Evil)
10	II	542a (Insolence and Obstinacy)
	III	522a (Narratives)
	V	236b (Tents and Tent Pegs)
13	III	489b (Myths and Legends in the Q)
15	II	57b (Ethics and the Q); 354b (Grammar and the Q); 447b (Honor)
15-16	II	268a (Freedom and Predestination)
16	II	186b (Fate); 354b (Grammar and the Q)
	V	133b (Suffering); 362b, 363a (Trial)
17	II	75b (Ethics and the Q)
	III	603a (Orphans)
	IV	455b (Reward and Punishment)
	V	204b (Teaching)
17-18	II	75b (Ethics and the Q)
	IV	8a (Pairs and Pairing)
17-20	III	533b (Nature as Signs); 578b (Opposition to Muḥammad)
	V	196b (Taxation)
18	II	216b (Food and Drink); 450a (Hospitality and Courtesy)
19-20	IV	8a (Pairs and Pairing)
20	III	235a (Love and Affection)
21-22	IV	8a (Pairs and Pairing)
21-30	I	112a (Apocalypse)
22	I	442b (Cosmology); 463a (Court)
	II	325b (God and his Attributes)
	IV	220a (Prayer); 349b (Ranks and Orders)
25-26	IV	8a (Pairs and Pairing)
27	V	83a (Soul); 96b (South Asian Literatures and the Q); 138b (Ṣūfism and the Q)
27-28	V	393a (Turkish Literature and the Q)
28-29	III	230a (Lord)

Sūrat al-Balad (90)

I 322b (Chronology and the Q)
II 256b (Form and Structure of the Q); 306a (Geography)
IV 177b, 178a (Popular and Talismanic Uses of the Q)
V 168b (Sūra); 183a (Symbolic Imagery)

1 III 491a (Myths and Legends in the Q)
IV 468b (Rhetoric and the Q)

1-2 III 443b (Muḥammad)
V 107a (Spatial Relations)

1-3 II 256b (Form and Structure of the Q)
IV 464b, 467b (Rhetoric and the Q)
V 80a (Soothsayer)

1-4 II 252b (Form and Structure of the Q)

1-11 IV 468a (Rhetoric and the Q)

2 IV 468b (Rhetoric and the Q)

4 I 449b (Cosmology)
V 371a (Trinity)

4-6 V 468b (Wealth)

6 II 307a (Geography)

7 I 449b (Cosmology)

8 I 81a (Anatomy)

8-9 I 82b, 83a (Anatomy)

8-10 II 252b, 259a (Form and Structure of the Q)
IV 2a (Pairs and Pairing)

11 V 182b (Symbolic Imagery)

11-12 IV 102a (Pit)
V 80a (Soothsayer)

11-13 IV 469a (Rhetoric and the Q)

12 IV 102b (Pit)
V 203a (Teaching)

12-18 III 177a (Left Hand and Right Hand)
V 57b (Slaves and Slavery)

12-20 V 183a (Symbolic Imagery)

13 I 289a (Captives)

13-17 IV 454b (Reward and Punishment)

13-18 IV 208b (Poverty and the Poor)

13-20 V 196b (Taxation)

14 I 500b (Day, Times of)
II 177b (Famine)

14-15 III 603a (Orphans)

14-16 II 450a (Hospitality and Courtesy)

15 II 174b (Family)

15-16 V 204b (Teaching)

16 III 63a (Joy and Misery)

17 III 378a (Mercy)

17-19 IV 2a (Pairs and Pairing)

18 III 177b (Left Hand and Right Hand)

19-20 III 177a (Left Hand and Right Hand)
IV 455b (Reward and Punishment)

20 II 415a (Hell and Hellfire)

Sūrat al-Shams (91)

I 322b (Chronology and the Q)
III 535a (Nature as Signs)
V 168b (Sūra); 420b (Verse)

1 I 36a (Afternoon); 444a (Cosmology); 504a (Day, Times of)
III 416b, 419a (Morning)
IV 108b (Planets and Stars); 217a, 219a (Prayer)
V 163a (Sun); 281b (Time)

1-2 III 535a (Nature as Signs)

1-3 IV 469b (Rhetoric and the Q)

1-4 V 282a (Time)

1-6 IV 5a (Pairs and Pairing)

1-7 II 256b (Form and Structure of the Q)
IV 464b (Rhetoric and the Q)
V 80a (Soothsayer)

1-15 IV 468a (Rhetoric and the Q)

4 I 501b (Day, Times of)

5 I 478a (Creation)

5-6 I 472a (Creation)

7 V 84a (Soul)

7-10 II 98a (Evil Deeds); 187a (Fate); 336b (Good and Evil); 339b (Good Deeds)

8 II 336b (Good and Evil)
IV 294b (Prophets and Prophethood)

9 II 162a (Failure)
IV 490b (Ritual and the Q); 505b (Ritual Purity)
9-10 IV 8a (Pairs and Pairing)
10 II 162a (Failure)
IV 490b (Ritual and the Q)
11 II 308a (Geography)
III 524a (Narratives)
11-14 I 287a (Camel)
11-15 II 259b (Form and Structure of the Q)
III 393a (Miracles)
IV 521a (Ṣāliḥ)
V 171b (Sūra)
12 V 251b (Textual Criticism of the Q)
13 IV 237b (Pre-1800 Preoccupations of Q Studies); 521b (Ṣāliḥ)
13-14 III 219a (Literature and the Q)
14 III 489b (Myths and Legends in the Q)
IV 521b (Ṣāliḥ)
V 253a (Thamūd)

Sūrat al-Layl (92)

I 322a, 322b (Chronology and the Q); 499a (Day, Times of)
IV 172b, 177b (Popular and Talismanic Uses of the Q)
V 168b (Sūra)
1 I 36a (Afternoon); 501b, 502a (Day, Times of)
IV 217a (Prayer)
V 393a (Turkish Literature and the Q)
1-2 IV 5a (Pairs and Pairing)
V 282a (Time)
1-3 II 256b (Form and Structure of the Q)
IV 464b (Rhetoric and the Q)
V 80a (Soothsayer)
1-13 II 263a (Form and Structure of the Q)
1-21 IV 468a (Rhetoric and the Q)
3 V 524a (Women and the Q)
4 IV 432a (Responsibility)
5-6 IV 454b (Reward and Punishment)
5-7 II 7a (Economics)
5-10 I 186a (Astray)

5-11 I 191a (Avarice)
IV 1b (Pairs and Pairing)

8 IV 455b (Reward and Punishment)
V 468b (Wealth)

10 III 179b (Left Hand and Right Hand)

11 V 468a (Wealth)

12-13 III 425b (Moses)

14 II 414b (Hell and Hellfire)
V 461a (Warner)

14-21 II 263a (Form and Structure of the Q)

15-17 IV 457b (Reward and Punishment)

18 IV 505b (Ritual Purity)
V 196b (Taxation)

18-19 V 469a (Wealth)

18-21 II 159b (Face); 160a (Face of God)

20 II 53a (Eschatology)
IV 221a (Prayer)
V 264a, 264b (Theology and the Q); 487a (Wish and Desire)

Sūrat al-Ḍuḥā (93)

I 322b (Chronology and the Q); 499a (Day, Times of)
III 197b (Literary Structures of the Q); 300a, 324a (Material Culture and the Q); 416b (Morning)
IV 172b (Popular and Talismanic Uses of the Q)
V 36b, 39b (Sīra and the Q); 168b, 169b (Sūra); 436a (Virtue)

1 I 36a (Afternoon); 444a (Cosmology); 502a, 504a (Day, Times of)
III 416b, 419a (Morning)
IV 217a (Prayer)
V 281b (Time); 393a (Turkish Literature and the Q)

1-2 II 256b (Form and Structure of the Q)
IV 464b (Rhetoric and the Q)
V 80a (Soothsayer); 282a (Time)

1-3 IV 244a (Pre-1800 Preoccupations of Q Studies); 480b (Rhymed Prose)

1-8 II 252b (Form and Structure of the Q)

2 I 501b (Day, Times of)
V 36b (Sīra and the Q); 393a, 393b (Turkish Literature and the Q)

3 II 178b (Farewell Pilgrimage); 219a (Food and Drink)
III 446a, 455b (Muḥammad)
V 36b (Sīra and the Q)

3-5 I 405b (Consolation)
II 552b (Intercession)
4 V 552b (World)
6 III 446b (Muḥammad); 603a (Orphans)
6-8 I 302b (Children); 405b (Consolation)
IV 238b (Pre-1800 Preoccupations of Q Studies)
7 III 446b (Muḥammad)
V 25b (Sin, Major and Minor); 374b (Trips and Voyages)
8 III 80b (Khadīja); 446b (Muḥammad)
IV 209a (Poverty and the Poor)
9 II 373b (Guardianship)
III 584a (Oppression); 603a (Orphans)
IV 455b (Reward and Punishment)
9-10 I 450a (Cosmology)
IV 479b (Rhymed Prose)
9-11 II 362b (Grammar and the Q)
11 IV 470b (Rhetoric and the Q)
V 39a (Sīra and the Q); 170b (Sūra)

Sūrat al-Sharḥ (94)

I 322b (Chronology and the Q)
II 263a (Form and Structure of the Q)
III 324a, 327b (Material Culture and the Q)
V 168b (Sūra)
1 I 91b (Angel); 179b (Ascension)
III 496a (Myths and Legends in the Q)
1-3 III 446b (Muḥammad)
1-8 I 405b (Consolation)
2-3 III 228a (Load or Burden)
4 III 19b (Jesus); 446b (Muḥammad)
5 I 289a (Captives)
5-6 IV 8a (Pairs and Pairing); 469a (Rhetoric and the Q)
6 I 289a (Captives)
7-8 II 143a (Exhortations); 252a (Form and Structure of the Q)
IV 470b (Rhetoric and the Q)

Sūrat al-Tīn (95)

I 322a, 322b (Chronology and the Q)
II 256b, 263a (Form and Structure of the Q)
III 324a (Material Culture and the Q); 495b (Myths and Legends in the Q)
IV 58a (Persian Literature and the Q)
V 168b (Sūra)

1 II 217b (Food and Drink); 305b (Geography)
III 4b (Jerusalem)
IV 5a (Pairs and Pairing); 468b (Rhetoric and the Q)
V 184b (Syria)

1-3 II 256b (Form and Structure of the Q)
IV 464b, 466b (Rhetoric and the Q)
V 80a (Soothsayer); 107a (Spatial Relations)

2 II 308b (Geography)
IV 482b (Rhymed Prose)
V 28a, 28b (Sinai)

2-3 IV 468b (Rhetoric and the Q)

3 I 163a (Art and Architecture and the Q)
III 339b (Mecca); 491a (Myths and Legends in the Q)
IV 103a (Pit); 482b (Rhymed Prose); 515b (Sacred Precincts)
V 373b (Trips and Voyages)

4 I 213a (Beauty)
II 328a (God and his Attributes)
IV 467a (Rhetoric and the Q)
V 393a, 393b (Turkish Literature and the Q)

4-5 I 450a (Cosmology)
IV 8a (Pairs and Pairing)

6 I 406a (Consolation)
IV 454b (Reward and Punishment); 466b (Rhetoric and the Q)

7 III 136b (Last Judgment)

8 I 516a (Decision)
II 321a (God and his Attributes)
III 64b (Judgment)
V 102b (Sovereignty)

Sūrat al-ʿAlaq (96)

I 238a (Blood and Blood Clot)
II 381a (Ḥadīth and the Q)
III 130b (Language and Style of the Q); 584b (Orality)
IV 368a (Recitation of the Q)
V 168b (Sūra); 201a (Teaching)

1	I	208b (Basmala); 329a (Chronology and the Q)
	II	319a, 326b (God and his Attributes)
	III	443a (Muḥammad)
	IV	217b (Prayer); 470a (Rhetoric and the Q)
	V	169b (Sūra)
1-2	I	451a (Cosmology)
	II	81b (Everyday Life, Q In)
	IV	8a (Pairs and Pairing)
1-3	III	190b (Literacy)
1-5	I	293b (Cave); 320b, 326a (Chronology and the Q)
	II	181a (Fasting); 259a (Form and Structure of the Q)
	III	188b (Literacy); 455b (Muḥammad)
	IV	244a (Pre-1800 Preoccupations of Q Studies); 470b (Rhetoric and the Q)
	V	403b (Uncertainty)
2	I	81a (Anatomy); 238a (Blood and Blood Clot); 240a (Bloodshed); 476b (Creation)
	II	328a (God and his Attributes)
	V	267a (Theology and the Q)
4	I	392b (Computers and the Q)
	II	26a (Epigraphy); 545a (Instruments)
	IV	262b (Preserved Tablet)
	V	201a, 201b (Teaching); 558a (Writing and Writing Materials)
4-5	III	103a (Knowledge and Learning); 189a (Literacy)
5	V	201a (Teaching)
6	I	449b (Cosmology)
6-7	V	204b (Teaching)
6-8	V	446b (Vision and Blindness)
7	I	241b (Boast)
8	II	91b (Everyday Life, Q In)
9	II	261a (Form and Structure of the Q)
	IV	574b (Seeing and Hearing)
9-10	IV	455b (Reward and Punishment)
	V	170a (Sūra)
9-19	III	454b (Muḥammad)
	IV	331b (Quraysh)
10	IV	487a (Ritual and the Q); 577a (Servants)
14	IV	574b (Seeing and Hearing)
17	V	36b (Sīra and the Q)
18	II	348a, 352b (Grammar and the Q); 417b (Hell and Hellfire)
	V	119a (Spiritual Beings)

19 I 254a (Bowing and Prostration)
II 142b (Exhortations)
III 567b (Obedience)
IV 470b (Rhetoric and the Q)
V 169b (Sūra); 393b (Turkish Literature and the Q)

Sūrat al-Qadr (97)

I 178b (Ascension); 322a (Chronology and the Q)
II 183a (Fasting)
III 328a (Material Culture and the Q)
IV 342b (Ramaḍān)
V 116a, 117a (Spirit); 168b (Sūra); 272a (Theology and the Q)

1 II 181b (Fasting)
III 414a (Months); 442a (Muḥammad); 537b (Night of Power)
IV 292b, 293a (Prophets and Prophethood); 343b, 344a (Ramaḍān)
V 284b (Time)

1-2 IV 102a, 102b (Pit)
V 80a (Soothsayer)

1-3 I 326a (Chronology and the Q); 501b (Day, Times of)
II 268b (Freedom and Predestination); 381b (Ḥadīth and the Q)

1-5 I 178a (Ascension)
IV 34a (Peace); 343a, 346b (Ramaḍān)
V 431b (Vigil)

2 V 203a (Teaching)

3 II 84a (Everyday Life, Q In)
III 222a (Literature and the Q); 410a, 413b (Months)
V 116b (Spirit); 475b (Weights and Measures)

3-5 II 204b (Festivals and Commemorative Days)

4 I 87a, 87b (Angel); 178a (Ascension)
II 278b (Gabriel); 443b (Holy Spirit)
III 293b (Mary)
IV 343a (Ramaḍān)
V 81a (Soul); 115b, 116a, 116b (Spirit); 266a, 272a (Theology and the Q)

4-5 II 84a (Everyday Life, Q In)
V 240b (Textual Criticism of the Q)

5 I 503b (Day, Times of)
III 417a, 417b (Morning)
IV 107a (Planets and Stars)
V 282b (Time)

Sūrat al-Bayyina (98)

I 223b (Belief and Unbelief); 322a (Chronology and the Q)
III 324a (Material Culture and the Q)
IV 86b (Philosophy and the Q)

1 I 222b (Belief and Unbelief)
IV 36b (People of the Book); 120b (Polemic and Polemical Language); 286a (Proof); 409b (Religious Pluralism and the Q)

1-2 IV 569b (Scrolls)

1-4 IV 570a (Scrolls)

2 I 343b (Cleanliness and Ablution)
II 545a (Instruments)
III 190a (Literacy)
IV 505b (Ritual Purity); 570a (Scrolls)

2-3 III 189b (Literacy); 441a (Muḥammad)

3 III 508a, 509a (Names of the Q)

4 I 222b (Belief and Unbelief)
IV 120b (Polemic and Polemical Language); 286a (Proof)

5 I 66b (Almsgiving)
II 366a (Grammar and the Q); 402b (Ḥanīf)
IV 416a (Religious Pluralism and the Q); 482b (Rhymed Prose)

6 I 222b (Belief and Unbelief)
II 54b (Eternity); 210a (Fire)
V 340a (Transitoriness)

6-7 I 224a (Belief and Unbelief); 478b (Creation)

7 IV 431b (Responsibility)

7-8 I 406a (Consolation)

8 II 54b (Eternity); 196b (Fear)
V 340a (Transitoriness); 464b (Water)

Sūrat al-Zalzala (99)

I 322a, 322b (Chronology and the Q)
II 178a (Famine)
IV 86b (Philosophy and the Q)
V 80a (Soothsayer); 117a (Spirit); 168b (Sūra); 183b (Symbolic Imagery); 274a (Theology and the Q); 420b (Verse)

1-2 V 283b (Time)

1-3 II 257b (Form and Structure of the Q)

1-5 II 252b (Form and Structure of the Q)

1-8 I 522b (Destiny)
III 531b (Nature as Signs)
IV 435a (Resurrection)

2 I 114b (Apocalypse)
III 228a (Load or Burden)

4 II 258a (Form and Structure of the Q); 435b (History and the Q)
III 518a (Narratives)

4-5 IV 293b (Prophets and Prophethood)

4-7 V 274a (Theology and the Q)

5 IV 217a (Prayer); 439b (Revelation and Inspiration)

6 II 258a (Form and Structure of the Q)

6-8 III 379a (Mercy)

7 II 77a (Ethics and the Q); 545b (Instruments)
III 409a (Money)

7-8 I 99b (Animal Life)
II 330b (God and his Attributes)
III 334b (Measurement)
IV 458a (Reward and Punishment)
V 473b (Weights and Measures)

8 II 545b (Instruments)
III 409a (Money)

Sūrat al-ʿĀdiyāt (100)

I 322a, 322b (Chronology and the Q)
II 263a (Form and Structure of the Q)
IV 86b (Philosophy and the Q); 465b (Rhetoric and the Q); 478b (Rhymed Prose)
V 168b (Sūra); 420b (Verse)

1 IV 465a (Rhetoric and the Q)

1-3 IV 479b (Rhymed Prose)

1-4 V 282a (Time)

1-5 II 256a (Form and Structure of the Q)
IV 464b (Rhetoric and the Q)
V 80a (Soothsayer)

1-11 IV 480b (Rhymed Prose)

3 I 504a (Day, Times of)
II 144a (Expeditions and Battles)
III 417a (Morning)
IV 465a (Rhetoric and the Q)
V 281a (Time)

Sūrat al-Qāriʿa (101)

5 I 346b (Clothing)
III 138b (Last Judgment); 209a (Literature and the Q)

5-8 V 119a (Spiritual Beings)

6 II 545b (Instruments)
III 178a (Left Hand and Right Hand); 334b (Measurement)

6-7 II 258a (Form and Structure of the Q)
III 70a (Justice and Injustice); 275b (Markets)
IV 100a (Pit); 454b (Reward and Punishment)

6-9 III 140b (Last Judgment)
IV 2b, 8b (Pairs and Pairing); 101b (Pit)
V 313b (Trade and Commerce)

6-11 II 48b (Eschatology)
IV 100a (Pit)
V 251b (Textual Criticism of the Q); 425b (Verse)

8 III 178a (Left Hand and Right Hand); 334b (Measurement)
IV 454b (Reward and Punishment)

8-9 II 258a (Form and Structure of the Q)

8-11 IV 100b (Pit)

9 II 414b (Hell and Hellfire)
IV 101a, 101b (Pit)
V 252a (Textual Criticism of the Q)

9-11 IV 102a (Pit); 469a (Rhetoric and the Q)

11 II 414b (Hell and Hellfire); 455b (Hot and Cold)
IV 103a (Pit)

Sūrat al-Takāthur (102)

I 241b (Boast); 322a, 322b (Chronology and the Q)
IV 86b (Philosophy and the Q)
V 168b (Sūra)

1-3 I 241b (Boast)

2 V 448a (Visiting)

3-4 IV 8a (Pairs and Pairing)

5 V 404a (Uncertainty)

6 I 241b (Boast)

7 V 404a (Uncertainty)
II 416a (Hell and Hellfire)

8 I 241b (Boast)
III 62b (Joy and Misery)

Sūrat al-ʿAṣr (103)

I 197b (Bahāʾīs); 322b (Chronology and the Q); 499a (Day, Times of)
II 268a (Freedom and Predestination)
III 194a (Literary Structures of the Q)
IV 246b (Pre-1800 Preoccupations of Q Studies)

1 I 36a, 36b (Afternoon); 444a (Cosmology); 504a (Day, Times of)
IV 219a (Prayer)
V 80a (Soothsayer); 281b, 282a (Time)

2 II 161b (Failure); 173b (Fall of Man)

2-3 IV 457a (Reward and Punishment)

Sūrat al-Humaza (104)

I 322b (Chronology and the Q)
II 418a (Hell and Hellfire)
V 80a (Soothsayer)

1 II 261b (Form and Structure of the Q); 344a (Gossip)
IV 496a (Ritual and the Q)

1-2 II 259b, 261b (Form and Structure of the Q); 351a (Grammar and the Q)
IV 470a (Rhetoric and the Q)

1-3 III 578b (Opposition to Muḥammad)

2 IV 455b (Reward and Punishment)

3 V 340a (Transitoriness)

3-4 IV 117a (Polemic and Polemical Language)

4 II 210b (Fire); 414b (Hell and Hellfire)
III 203a (Literary Structures of the Q)

4-5 I 526a (Devil)
IV 102a, 102b, 103b (Pit)
V 80a (Soothsayer)

4-6 IV 102b (Pit); 469a (Rhetoric and the Q)

5 II 210b (Fire)
III 203b (Literary Structures of the Q)
V 203a (Teaching)

5-6 II 210b (Fire)

5-9 II 211a (Fire); 414b (Hell and Hellfire)

8-9 II 210b (Fire)

Sūrat al-Fīl (105)

I 4a, 4b (Abraha); 93b, 98b (Animal Life); 322b (Chronology and the Q)
II 129b (Exegesis of the Q: Early Modern and Contemporary); 259b (Form and Structure of the Q); 490b (Ilāf)
III 58b (Journey); 518a, 518b (Narratives); 534a (Nature as Signs)
IV 44b, 45b, 46a (People of the Elephant); 177b (Popular and Talismanic Uses of the Q)
V 168b, 171b (Sūra); 374a (Trips and Voyages)

1 II 307b (Geography)
III 524a (Narratives)
IV 257b (Pre-Islamic Arabia and the Q)

1-2 III 128b (Language and Style of the Q)

1-5 II 146a, 148a (Expeditions and Battles); 212b (Fire)

2 II 162a (Failure)
IV 103a (Pit); 482b (Rhymed Prose)

3 I 101a (Animal Life)
II 348a (Grammar and the Q)

3-4 I 98b (Animal Life); 340a (Clay)

4 II 411a (Heaven and Sky)
III 383b (Metals and Minerals)
V 129a, 130a (Stone); 258a (Theology and the Q)

5 V 16a, 18b (Simile)

Sūrat Quraysh (106)

I 290a (Caravan); 322b (Chronology and the Q)
III 338a, 338b, 339b (Mecca)
IV 45b (People of the Elephant); 495b (Ritual and the Q); 572a (Seasons)
V 168b (Sūra); 373b (Trips and Voyages)

1 I 444a (Cosmology)
III 338a (Mecca)
IV 259a (Pre-Islamic Arabia and the Q); 329a (Quraysh)

1-2 II 307b (Geography); 489b (Ilāf)
IV 8a (Pairs and Pairing)

1-5 IV 34b (Peace)

2 I 290a (Caravan)
III 58b (Journey)
IV 572a (Seasons)

3 I 329a (Chronology and the Q)
II 319a (God and his Attributes)
III 77b, 79a (Kaʿba)

IV 46a (People of the Elephant); 52b (People of the House); 288a (Property); 470a (Rhetoric and the Q)

3-4 I 218b (Belief and Unbelief)
II 143a (Exhortations); 490a (Ilāf)
IV 46a (People of the Elephant); 515b (Sacred Precincts)

Sūrat al-Māʿūn (107)

I 322a (Chronology and the Q)
V 168b (Sūra); 436a (Virtue)

1 III 136b (Last Judgment)
IV 470a (Rhetoric and the Q)

1-7 II 450a (Hospitality and Courtesy)

2 III 603a (Orphans)
IV 455b (Reward and Punishment)

2-3 II 261b (Form and Structure of the Q)

2-7 V 172a (Sūra)

3 II 216b (Food and Drink)
V 196b (Taxation)

4 II 261b (Form and Structure of the Q)
IV 218a (Prayer)

4-5 IV 224b (Prayer)
V 170a (Sūra)

4-7 I 327b (Chronology and the Q)
II 68b (Ethics and the Q)
IV 470a (Rhetoric and the Q)

5-7 II 261b (Form and Structure of the Q)

Sūrat al-Kawthar (108)

I 197b (Bahāʾīs); 209b (Basmala); 322b (Chronology and the Q)
III 130b (Language and Style of the Q); 194a (Literary Structures of the Q); 339b (Mecca)
IV 23b (Parody of the Q); 32a (Patriarchy); 61a (Persian Literature and the Q); 178a (Popular and Talismanic Uses of the Q); 601b (Shīʿism and the Q)
V 36b (Sīra and the Q); 168b (Sūra)

1 I 88b (Angel)
II 283b (Garden); 395a (Ḥadīth and the Q)
III 141a (Last Judgment); 446b (Muḥammad)
IV 23b (Parody of the Q)
V 36b (Sīra and the Q); 125a (Springs and Fountains)

2 I 327b (Chronology and the Q)
II 143a (Exhortations)
III 339a (Mecca)
IV 216b, 218a (Prayer); 487a (Ritual and the Q)
V 170b (Sūra)

3 I 115a (Apologetics)
II 362b (Grammar and the Q)
III 32a (Jews and Judaism)

Sūrat al-Kāfirūn (109)

I 373b, 375b, 381b (Community and Society in the Q)
IV 8b (Pairs and Pairing)
V 290b (Tolerance and Coercion)

1-4 IV 238b (Pre-1800 Preoccupations of Q Studies)

4 IV 578b (Servants)

6 I 224a (Belief and Unbelief); 373b (Community and Society in the Q)
II 151a (Expeditions and Battles)
III 39a (Jihād); 228b (Load or Burden)
IV 238b (Pre-1800 Preoccupations of Q Studies); 400b, 415a, 415b (Religious Pluralism and the Q); 478b (Rhymed Prose)
V 291a, 291b, 293a, 294a (Tolerance and Coercion); 573b (Zealotry)

Sūrat al-Naṣr (110)

II 180a (Farewell Pilgrimage); 385a (Ḥadīth and the Q)
III 194a (Literary Structures of the Q); 457a (Muḥammad); 579a (Opposition to Muḥammad)

1 I 399a, 400a (Conquest)
IV 176a (Popular and Talismanic Uses of the Q)

1-3 IV 332b (Quraysh)

2 I 436a (Conversion)
III 457a (Muḥammad)

3 II 245a (Forgiveness)
III 378b (Mercy)
IV 426b (Repentance and Penance)

Sūrat al-Masad (111)

II 176b (Family of the Prophet); 263a (Form and Structure of the Q); 418a (Hell and Hellfire)
IV 309a (Provocation); 330a (Quraysh); 478a (Rhymed Prose)
V 80a (Soothsayer); 168b (Sūra)

1 I 20a (Abū Lahab); 491b (Curse)
II 261b (Form and Structure of the Q); 401b (Hand); 439a (History and the Q)
III 217b (Literature and the Q)
IV 216b (Prayer); 259a (Pre-Islamic Arabia and the Q); 470a (Rhetoric and the Q); 478a (Rhymed Prose)
V 172a (Sūra)

1-2 V 467b (Wealth)

1-5 III 577a (Opposition to Muḥammad)

2 III 217b (Literature and the Q)

4 II 439a (History and the Q)
V 241b (Textual Criticism of the Q); 393a (Turkish Literature and the Q)

5 I 494b (Date Palm)
II 546b (Instruments)

Sūrat al-Ikhlāṣ (112)

I 115a (Apologetics); 170b (Art and Architecture and the Q); 264b, 265a (Burial); 285b (Calligraphy); 322a (Chronology and the Q)
II 29a, 34b, 36a, 37b, 39a (Epigraphy); 87b, 96a (Everyday Life, Q In); 393b (Ḥadīth and the Q); 461b (House, Domestic and Divine)
III 31b (Jews and Judaism); 99a (Kinship); 197a (Literary Structures of the Q); 299a, 300b, 322b (Material Culture and the Q); 467a (Muʿtazila)
IV 33b (Patriarchy); 78b (Philosophy and the Q); 159a (Polytheism and Atheism); 174b (Popular and Talismanic Uses of the Q); 369b (Recitation of the Q); 387a (Reciters of the Q); 493b (Ritual and the Q)
V 151a (Ṣūfism and the Q); 334b (Traditional Disciplines of Q Studies); 503b (Witnessing and Testifying)

1 II 361a (Grammar and the Q); 465a (Humor)
V 141a (Ṣūfism and the Q); 500a (Witnessing and Testifying)

1-2 II 359b (Grammar and the Q)

1-3 III 299b (Material Culture and the Q)
V 264a (Theology and the Q)

1-4 II 38b (Epigraphy); 329b (God and his Attributes)
III 556b, 559a (Numismatics)
IV 79a (Philosophy and the Q)

2 II 54a (Eternity); 321b (God and his Attributes)
IV 238a (Pre-1800 Preoccupations of Q Studies); 482b (Rhymed Prose)

3 II 54a (Eternity); 217a (Food and Drink)
V 369a (Trinity)

3-4 IV 480a (Rhymed Prose)

Sūrat al-Falaq (113)

i 264a (Burial); 322a (Chronology and the q); 499a (Day, Times of)
ii 87b, 92b (Everyday Life, q In); 189a (Fātiḥa); 393b (Ḥadīth and the q)
iii 247b, 248a, 248b (Magic); 416b (Morning); 535a (Nature as Signs)
iv 165a, 173b (Popular and Talismanic Uses of the q); 233b (Prayer Formulas); 244a (Pre-1800 Preoccupations of q Studies); 369b (Recitation of the q); 478a (Rhymed Prose); 493b, 495a, 495b (Ritual and the q)
v 80a (Soothsayer)

1 i 502a, 503b (Day, Times of)
iii 417a, 418a (Morning)
iv 184a (Possession and Possessions)
v 281a, 282b (Time)

1-2 iv 308a (Protection)

1-5 iv 221b (Prayer)

3 iii 535a (Nature as Signs)

4 iv 486b, 488a (Ritual and the q)

5 ii 25a (Envy); 154b (Eyes)

Sūrat al-Nās (114)

i 264a (Burial); 322a (Chronology and the q)
ii 87b, 92b (Everyday Life, q In); 189a (Fātiḥa); 393b (Ḥadīth and the q)
iii 247b, 248a, 248b (Magic); 300a (Material Culture and the q)
iv 165a, 173b (Popular and Talismanic Uses of the q); 233b (Prayer Formulas); 244a (Pre-1800 Preoccupations of q Studies); 369b (Recitation of the q); 493b, 495a (Ritual and the q)
v 80a (Soothsayer)

1 i 329a (Chronology and the q)
iv 184a (Possession and Possessions)
v 172a (Sūra)

1-4 iv 308a (Protection)

1-6 iv 216b (Prayer); 481a (Rhymed Prose)

2 iii 91b (Kings and Rulers)

3 i 329a (Chronology and the q)

4 i 526a (Devil)

4-5 v 479a (Whisper)

4-6 iv 480a (Rhymed Prose)

6 iii 46b (Jinn)
iv 7b (Pairs and Pairing)